Fodor's Road Guide USA

Alabama

Arkansas

Louisiana

Mississippi

Tennessee

First Edition

Fodor's Travel Publications
New York Toronto London Sydney Auckland
www.fodors.com

Fodor's Road Guide USA: Alabama, Arkansas, Louisiana, Mississippi, Tennessee

Fodor's Travel Publications
President: Bonnie Ammer
Publisher: Kris Kliemann
Executive Managing Editor: Denise DeGennaro
Editorial Director: Karen Cure
Director of Marketing Development: Jeanne Kramer
Associate Managing Editor: Linda Schmidt
Senior Editor: Constance Jones
Director of Production and Manufacturing: Chuck Bloodgood
Creative Director: Fabrizio La Rocca

Contributors
Editor: Constance Jones
Editorial Production: Tom Holton
Additional Editing: Michael de Zayas (Mississippi), JoAnn Milivojevic (Alabama), and Sarah Scheffel (Tennessee), with Kathy Astor, Carol Barkin, Melissa Bogen, Victoria Caldwell, Angela Casey, William Dyckes, Jobie Fagans, Karen Fein, Shannon Kelly, Claudia La Rocca, Denise Mortensen, Candy Moulton, Kathleen Paton, and Virginia Rainey
Writing: Lynn Grisard Fullman (Alabama), Tomika Hall (Mississippi restaurants and lodgings), Heather Heilman (Tennessee), Alan Huffman (Mississippi), Michelle Roberts (Alabama restaurants, lodgings and driving tours), Marcia Schnedler (Arkansas), and Connie Snow (Louisiana), with Michele Bloom, Richard Eastman, William Fox, Keisha Hutchins, Chintamani Kansas, Joe Kovacs, Alia Levine, Kate Lorenz, Melanie Mize, Eric Reymond, Amanda Robinson, Alan Ryan, Marcia Schnedler, Michael Schiller, and Brendan Walsh
Research: Kim Bacon, Alex Bajoris, Niladri Basu, Ephen Colter, Joshua Greenwald, Eric Joseph, Helen Kasimis, Brandon Leong, Tenisha Light, Jordana Roseberg, and Rupa Shah
Black-and-White Maps: Rebecca Baer, Robert Blake, David Lindroth, Todd Pasini
Production/Manufacturing: Bob Shields
Cover: Terry Donnelly/Stone (background photo), Bart Nagel (photo, illustration)
Interior Photos: Alabama Bureau of Tourism and Travel/Karim Shamsi Basha (Alabama), Arkansas Department of Parks and Tourism/A.C. Haralson (Arkansas), Corbis (Louisiana), Photodisc (Tennessee), Natchez Convention and Visitors Bureau (Mississippi)

Special Sales
Fodor's Travel Publications are available at special discounts for bulk purchases for sales promotions or premiums. Special editions, including personalized covers, excerpts of existing guides, and corporate imprints, can be created in large quantities for special needs. For more information, contact your local bookseller or write to Special Markets, Fodor's Travel Publications, 280 Park Ave., New York, NY 10017. Inquiries from Canada should be directed to your local Canadian bookseller or sent to Random House of Canada, Ltd., Marketing Department, 2775 Matheson Boulevard East, Mississauga, Ontario L4W 4P7. Inquiries from the United Kingdom should be sent to Fodor's Travel Publications, 20 Vauxhall Bridge Road, London SW1V 2SA, England.

PRINTED IN THE UNITED STATES OF AMERICA
10 9 8 7 6 5 4 3 2 1

CONTENTS

Great Road Trips

Of all the things that went wrong with Clark Griswold's vacation, one stands out: The theme park he had driven across the country to visit was closed when he got there. Clark, the suburban bumbler played by Chevy Chase in 1983's hilarious *National Lampoon's Vacation*, is fictional, of course. But his story is poignantly true. Although most Americans get only two precious weeks of vacation a year, many set off on their journeys with surprisingly little guidance. Many travelers find out about their destination from friends and family or wait to get travel information until they arrive in their hotel, where racks of brochures dispense the "facts," along with free city magazines. But it's hard to distinguish the truth from hype in these sources. And it makes no sense to spend priceless vacation time in a hotel room reading about a place when you could be out seeing it up close and personal.

Congratulate yourself on picking up this guide. Studying it—before you leave home—is the best possible first step toward making sure your vacation fulfills your every dream.

Inside you'll find all the tools you need to plan a perfect road trip. In the hundreds of towns we describe, you'll find thousands of places to explore. So you'll always know what's around the next bend. And with the practical information we provide, you can easily call to confirm the details that matter and study up on what you'll want to see and do, before you leave home.

By all means, when you plan your trip, allow yourself time to make a few detours. Because as wonderful as it is to visit sights you've read about, it's the serendipitous experiences that often prove the most memorable: the hole-in-the-wall diner that serves a transcendent tomato soup, the historical society gallery stuffed with dusty local curiosities of days gone by. As you whiz down the highway, use the book to find out more about the towns announced by roadside signs. Consider turning off at the next exit. And always remember: In this great country of ours, there's an adventure around every corner.

HOW TO USE THIS BOOK

Alphabetical organization should make it a snap to navigate through this book. Still, in putting it together, we've made certain decisions and used certain terms you need to know about.

LOCATIONS AND CATEGORIZATIONS

Color map coordinates are given for every town in the guide.

Attractions, restaurants, and lodging places are listed under the nearest town covered in the guide.

Parks and forests are sometimes listed under the main access point.

Exact street addresses are provided whenever possible; when they were not available or applicable, directions and/or cross-streets are indicated.

CITIES

For state capitals and larger cities, attractions are alphabetized by category. Shopping sections focus on good shopping areas where you'll find a concentration of interesting shops. We include malls only if they're unusual in some way and individual stores only when they're community institutions. Restaurants and hotels are grouped by price category then arranged alphabetically.

RESTAURANTS

All are air-conditioned unless otherwise noted, and all permit smoking unless they're identified as "no-smoking."

Dress: Assume that no jackets or ties are required for men unless otherwise noted.

Family-style service: Restaurants characterized this way serve food communally, out of serving dishes as you might at home.

Meals and hours: Assume that restaurants are open for lunch and dinner unless otherwise noted. We always specify days closed and meals not available.

Prices: The price ranges listed are for dinner entrées (or lunch entrées if no dinner is served).

Reservations: They are always a good idea. We don't mention them unless they're essential or are not accepted.

Fodor's Choice: Stars denote restaurants that are Fodor's Choices—our editors' picks of the state's very best in a given price category.

LODGINGS

All are air-conditioned unless otherwise noted, and all permit smoking unless they're identified as "no-smoking."

AP: This designation means that a hostelry operates on the American Plan (AP)—that is, rates include all meals. AP may be an option or it may be the only meal plan available; be sure to find out.

Baths: You'll find private bathrooms with bathtubs unless noted otherwise.

Business services: If we tell you they're there, you can expect a variety on the premises.

Exercising: We note if there's "exercise equipment" even when there's no designated area; if you want a dedicated facility, look for "gym."

Facilities: We list what's available but don't note charges to use them. When pricing accommodations, always ask what's included.

Hot tub: This term denotes hot tubs, Jacuzzis, and whirlpools.

MAP: Rates at these properties include two meals.

No smoking: Properties with this designation prohibit smoking.

Opening and closing: Assume that hostelries are open year-round unless otherwise noted.

Pets: We note whether or not they're welcome and whether there's a charge.

Pools: Assume they're outdoors with fresh water; indoor pools are noted.

Prices: The price ranges listed are for a high-season double room for two, excluding tax and service charge.

Telephone and TV: Assume that you'll find them unless otherwise noted.

Fodor's Choice: Stars denote hostelries that are Fodor's Choices—our editors' picks of the state's very best in a given price category.

NATIONAL PARKS

National parks protect and preserve the treasures of America's heritage, and they're always worth visiting whenever you're in the area. Many are worth a long detour. If you will travel to many national parks, consider purchasing the National Parks Pass ($50), which gets you and your companions free admission to all parks for one year. (Camping and parking are extra.) A percentage of the proceeds from sales of the pass helps to fund important projects in the parks. Both the Golden Age Passport ($10), for those 62 and older, and the Golden Access Passport (free), for travelers with disabilities, entitle holders to free entry to all national parks, plus 50% off fees for the use of many park facilities and services. You must show proof of age and of U.S. citizenship or permanent residency (such as a U.S. passport, driver's license, or birth certificate) and, if requesting Golden Access, proof of your disability. You must get your Golden Access or Golden Age passport in person; the former is available at all federal recreation areas, the latter at federal recreation areas that charge fees. You may purchase the National Parks Pass by mail or through the Internet. For information, contact the National Park Service (Department of the Interior, 1849 C St. NW, Washington, DC 20240-0001, 202/208—4747, *www.nps.gov*). To buy the National Parks Pass, write to 27540 Ave. Mentry, Valencia, CA 91355, call 888/GO—PARKS, or visit www.national-parks.org.

IMPORTANT TIP

Although all prices, opening times, and other details in this book are based on information supplied to us at press time, changes occur all the time in the travel world, and Fodor's cannot accept responsibility for facts that become outdated or for inadvertent errors or omissions. So always confirm information when it matters, especially if you're making a detour to visit a specific place.

Let Us Hear from You

Keeping a travel guide fresh and up-to-date is a big job, and we welcome any and all comments. We'd love to have your thoughts on places we've listed, and we're interested in hearing about your own special finds, even the ones in your own back yard. Our guides are thoroughly updated for each new edition, and we're always adding new information, so your feedback is vital. Contact us via e-mail in care of roadnotes@fodors.com (specifying the name of the book on the subject line) or via snail mail in care of Road Guides at Fodor's, 280 Park Avenue, New York, NY 10017. We look forward to hearing from you. And in the meantime, have a wonderful road trip.

THE EDITORS

Important Numbers and On-Line Info

LODGINGS

Adam's Mark	800/444—2326	www.adamsmark.com
Baymont Inns	800/428—3438	www.baymontinns.com
Best Western	800/528—1234	www.bestwestern.com
	TDD 800/528—2222	
Budget Host	800/283—4678	www.budgethost.com
Clarion	800/252—7466	www.clarioninn.com
Comfort	800/228—5150	www.comfortinn.com
Courtyard by Marriott	800/321—2211	www.courtyard.com
Days Inn	800/325—2525	www.daysinn.com
Doubletree	800/222—8733	www.doubletreehotels.com
Drury Inns	800/325—8300	www.druryinn.com
Econo Lodge	800/555—2666	www.hotelchoice.com
Embassy Suites	800/362—2779	www.embassysuites.com
Exel Inns of America	800/356—8013	www.exelinns.com
Fairfield Inn by Marriott	800/228—2800	www.fairfieldinn.com
Fairmont Hotels	800/527—4727	www.fairmont.com
Forte	800/225—5843	www.forte-hotels.com
Four Seasons	800/332—3442	www.fourseasons.com
Friendship Inns	800/453—4511	www.hotelchoice.com
Hampton Inn	800/426—7866	www.hampton-inn.com
Hilton	800/445—8667	www.hilton.com
	TDD 800/368—1133	
Holiday Inn	800/465—4329	www.holiday-inn.com
	TDD 800/238—5544	
Howard Johnson	800/446—4656	www.hojo.com
	TDD 800/654—8442	
Hyatt & Resorts	800/233—1234	www.hyatt.com
Inns of America	800/826—0778	www.innsofamerica.com
Inter-Continental	800/327—0200	www.interconti.com
La Quinta	800/531—5900	www.laquinta.com
	TDD 800/426—3101	
Loews	800/235—6397	www.loewshotels.com
Marriott	800/228—9290	www.marriott.com
Master Hosts Inns	800/251—1962	www.reservahost.com
Le Meridien	800/225—5843	www.lemeridien.com
Motel 6	800/466—8356	www.motel6.com
Omni	800/843—6664	www.omnihotels.com
Quality Inn	800/228—5151	www.qualityinn.com
Radisson	800/333—3333	www.radisson.com
Ramada	800/228—2828	www.ramada.com
	TDD 800/533—6634	
Red Carpet/Scottish Inns	800/251—1962	www.reservahost.com
Red Lion	800/547—8010	www.redlion.com
Red Roof Inn	800/843—7663	www.redroof.com
Renaissance	800/468—3571	www.renaissancehotels.com
Residence Inn by Marriott	800/331—3131	www.residenceinn.com
Ritz-Carlton	800/241—3333	www.ritzcarlton.com
Rodeway	800/228—2000	www.rodeway.com

Sheraton	800/325—3535	www.sheraton.com
Shilo Inn	800/222—2244	www.shiloinns.com
Signature Inns	800/822—5252	www.signature-inns.com
Sleep Inn	800/221—2222	www.sleepinn.com
Super 8	800/848—8888	www.super8.com
Susse Chalet	800/258—1980	www.sussechalet.com
Travelodge/Viscount	800/255—3050	www.travelodge.com
Vagabond	800/522—1555	www.vagabondinns.com
Westin Hotels & Resorts	800/937—8461	www.westin.com
Wyndham Hotels & Resorts	800/996—3426	www.wyndham.com

AIRLINES

Air Canada	888/247—2262	www.aircanada.ca
Alaska	800/426—0333	www.alaska-air.com
American	800/433—7300	www.aa.com
America West	800/235—9292	www.americawest.com
British Airways	800/247—9297	www.british-airways.com
Canadian	800/426—7000	www.cdnair.ca
Continental Airlines	800/525—0280	www.continental.com
Delta	800/221—1212	www.delta.com
Midway Airlines	800/446—4392	www.midwayair.com
Northwest	800/225—2525	www.nwa.com
SkyWest	800/453—9417	www.delta.com
Southwest	800/435—9792	www.southwest.com
TWA	800/221—2000	www.twa.com
United	800/241—6522	www.ual.com
USAir	800/428—4322	www.usair.com

BUSES AND TRAINS

Amtrak	800/872—7245	www.amtrak.com
Greyhound	800/231—2222	www.greyhound.com
Trailways	800/343—9999	www.trailways.com

CAR RENTALS

Advantage	800/777—5500	www.arac.com
Alamo	800/327—9633	www.goalamo.com
Allstate	800/634—6186	www.bnm.com/as.htm
Avis	800/331—1212	www.avis.com
Budget	800/527—0700	www.budget.com
Dollar	800/800—4000	www.dollar.com
Enterprise	800/325—8007	www.pickenterprise.com
Hertz	800/654—3131	www.hertz.com
National	800/328—4567	www.nationalcar.com
Payless	800/237—2804	www.paylesscarrental.com
Rent-A-Wreck	800/535—1391	www.rent-a-wreck.com
Thrifty	800/367—2277	www.thrifty.com

Note: Area codes are changing all over the United States as this book goes to press. For the latest updates, check www.areacode-info.com.

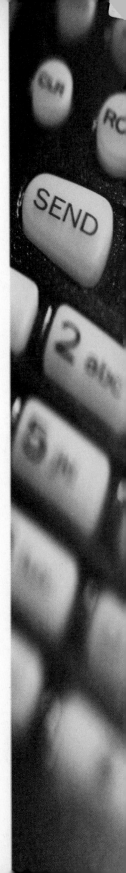

Fodor's Road Guide USA

Alabama
Arkansas
Louisiana
Mississippi
Tennessee

Alabama

Alabama once promoted itself as "the state of surprises" with good reason. Known for cotton fields, steelmaking, and its role in the Civil War and Civil Rights struggles, Alabama is a deep-South state rich in culture, tradition, and natural beauty.

There are rocky wooded hills and vast caves to the north, expansive lakes and broad rivers in the interior, and white beaches along the Gulf Coast. Scattered north to south are cascading waterfalls and wildflowers, archaeological excavation sites, and colonial forts. Alabama has a humid subtropical climate. In winter it rarely dips below 55°F, and the need for a heavy coat is rare.

Many sections of the state have preserved the elegant antebellum homes typical of the 19th century, yet the cities have an eye on the future. The Saturn rocket was designed in Huntsville and the state's largest city, Birmingham, has become a major medical center. The new and progressive blend with the old and historic—Montgomery's modern state government buildings stand just one block from the First White House of the Confederacy.

Alabama has had a difficult time shaking an image projected in the 1960s when key events in the Civil Rights struggle were staged in Birmingham, Montgomery, and Selma. The state has moved ahead to become an appealing place to live and to play, and race relations have improved steadily and continue to do so each decade.

Dining varies somewhat according to where you are in the state. Along the coast, there's plenty of fresh seafood, and inland you'll find more traditional southern dishes. Farm-raised catfish is typically served with a hearty helping of hush puppies. Long-standing favorites include barbecue and grits (and everyone has an opinion on who has the best barbecue in town), but you can also find top chefs working their culinary magic at some of the best restaurants in the South.

CAPITAL: MONTGOMERY	POPULATION: 4,319,000	AREA: 51,705 SQUARE MI
BORDERS: TN, GA, GULF OF MEXICO, FL, MS	TIME ZONE: CENTRAL	POSTAL ABBREVIATION: AL
WEB SITE: WWW.TOURALABAMA.ORG		

Scenic vistas line the interstates and the well-maintained U.S. and state highways lead to charming towns and communities. Throughout the state there are areas for hiking, camping, and simply taking in the view.

In Alabama, you can sleep in bed-and-breakfasts in the mountainous north or along the coastline, sample homemade biscuits and grits, or tee off at one of the state's eight golf courses which make up the renowned Robert Trent Jones Golf Trail. There's also bargain hunting at outlet shopping centers in Boaz and Foley, old fort tours, and frolicking on sandy beaches.

History

Alabama was inhabited as early as 10,000 BC. Moundville, in the western part of the state, and other sites along the Black Warrior River suggest there was a highly advanced civilization that traded up and down the complex riverways.

When the first Europeans arrived in the middle of the 16th century, the region was heavily populated by native Americans including the Creek, Choctaw, Chickasaw, and Cherokee nations. In 1540, Spanish explorers, led by Hernando de Soto, waged a bloody attack against them and for several decades controlled the area. The French also entered the region and in 1702 established the first permanent European settlement near present-day Mobile.

Conflicts between Europeans and Native Americans continued throughout much of the 18th century and the region changed from French to English and finally to American control in 1813. Native American tribes were systematically divested of their lands and were eventually removed from the area. Many also died from European diseases against which they had no immunity.

Alabama achieved statehood in 1819, and until the mid-1860s cotton production was the major industry. Slaves were used in the labor-intensive operation. In January 1861, Alabama ceded from the Union and in May of the same year Jefferson Davis was elected president of the Confederate States of America. The Civil War reached Alabama in 1862 and raged until General Richard Taylor surrendered at Citronelle (north of Mobile) in 1865. Slavery was outlawed and dismantled, but much of Alabama's large black population simply shifted from slavery to tenant-farmer status and segregation took root.

After World War I, Alabama's commerce and industry grew. Ships were built in Mobile, and farmers stepped up production of cotton and food. During World War II, Alabama's agricultural and industrial production expanded once again. The state was thrust into the national spotlight in the late 1950s when a team of German rocket scientists, working at the Army's Redstone Arsenal in Huntsville, developed America's first rocket. Their work put the nation at the forefront of the world's space race.

Alabama was center stage for many pivotal Civil Rights movements including voter's rights and school desegregation. Key Civil Rights events included: the Montgomery Bus Boycott spurred on by Rosa Parks in 1955, the Freedom Rides of 1961, and the Selma to Montgomery march led by Dr. Martin Luther King, Jr. which led the nation to rally against racial inequality.

AL Timeline

10,000 B.C.	1519	1540	1702
Moundbuilder cultures inhabit the areas near present-day Moundville and around the Black Warrior River.	Alonso Alvarez de Pineda of Spain likely sailed into Mobile Bay.	In search of gold, Hernando de Soto explores much of what is now Alabama.	French Canadians establish Fort Louis on the Mobile River.

Regions

INTRODUCTION
HISTORY
REGIONS
WHEN TO VISIT
STATE'S GREATS
RULES OF THE ROAD
DRIVING TOURS

1. NORTH ALABAMA AND BIRMINGHAM

Rolling hills, recreational playgrounds, natural beauty, and history are synonymous with the area from the Tennessee border south to Birmingham and Tuscaloosa. The rocky and mountainous land in the northern section is filled with lakes and hideaways, small sleepy towns, and cities like Huntsville where inventions at the Redstone Arsenal put the first man on the moon.

Several covered bridges remain, and many state parks have recreational facilities and noteworthy sights. East of the Rockies near Haleyville is the longest natural bridge; in DeSoto State Park, there's the 110-ft DeSoto Falls in Little River Canyon; and in Russell Cave National Park you can see the remains of Native American tribes dating back 10,000 years.

Farther south, set in a valley amid rolling hills, is Birmingham, the state's largest city and in the 1920s and '30s the South's major industrial area. Atop Red Mountain on the city's south side is the towering statue of Vulcan, a symbol of the iron and steel industry on which the city's wealth was founded. Steel is no longer the major employer, but the industry is honored at Sloss Furnaces, now a tourist attraction and an outdoor venue for concerts. Today the city is one of the country's leading centers of medical care and study. The Birmingham Museum of Art specializes in Asian and French art, hosts traveling exhibitions from national galleries, and contains a scholarly library. In mid-1998, the city unveiled two major attractions: VisionLand Theme Park, an amusement park, and McWane Center, a hands-on science learning center intended for kids but also embraced by adults.

Towns listed: Anniston, Athens, Birmingham, Boaz, Cullman, Decatur, Florence, Fort Payne, Gadsden, Guntersville, Huntsville, Mentone, Oneonta, Scottsboro, Sheffield, Tuscumbia.

2. CENTRAL BLACK BELT

Often called the Black Belt because of its rich black soil, the midsection of Alabama stretches from the Mississippi border on the west to Montgomery. The land produced King Cotton and until the Civil War, supported immensely rich plantations. It is flat, gentle land, wooded with oak, hickory, sweet gum, beech, magnolias, sycamores, semitropical bay trees, and palmettos. Most of the large land holdings have become cattle farms.

Tuskegee lies on the eastern edge of the central region. In 1881 Booker T. Washington founded a university for blacks (the Tuskegee Institute) and it remains a predominantly black town. The university provides an intellectual and educational haven and carries on the research begun by George Washington Carver, whose work with peanuts and sweet potatoes helped change the life of southern farmers.

1763	1783	1813	1817	1819
France gives the Alabama region to Great Britain.	Great Britain gives the United States much of what is now Alabama and gives the Mobile region to Spain.	The United States captures Mobile Bay from Spain.	The Alabama Territory is created.	Alabama becomes the 22nd state on December 14.

The Black Belt includes quaint towns such as Selma and Demopolis, full of ante-bellum houses and cemeteries canopied with moss-draped trees. Many of the homes are so well preserved you expect Scarlett O'Hara to stroll through the white columns on the wraparound porches. During spring festivals and other special events, some homes are open to the public.

Towns listed: Alexander City, Auburn, Bessemer, Childersburg, Clanton, Demopolis, Dothan, Eufaula, Montgomery, Opelika, Selma, Sylacauga, Talladega, Troy, Tuscaloosa, Tuskegee, Union Springs.

3. GULF COAST DELTA

The southwestern part of Alabama, the Gulf Coast Delta, is dominated by water—by the rivers and streams of the delta draining into Mobile Bay and by the Gulf of Mexico which is lined with glistening white-sand beaches. Throughout much of the region, you'll see large trees curtained with Spanish moss that hangs down 10 ft or more in irregular clusters.

With an active shipping industry, Mobile is Alabama's only important port. The French settled the city in the early 1700s, and you'll see the French influence. In the early spring, stretches of brilliant azaleas turn the town into a fairyland.

Strung along the eastern shore of Mobile Bay are small towns such as Point Clear and Fairhope. Point Clear is best known for the 140-year-old Grand Hotel with half-moon dining rooms overlooking the bay and sweeping lawns so meticulously mani-cured you might hesitate to walk on them.

Towns listed: Atmore, Dauphin Island, Fairhope, Gulf Shores/Orange Beach, Mobile, Monroeville, Point Clear, Theodore.

When to Visit

With a mild year-round climate, Alabama is a suitable destination any month. Choos-ing when to visit depends on your interests. Spring arrives in late February or early March when temperatures warm to the 60s and the azaleas bloom, creating one of the most picturesque times of year. Summer days average in the low 80s, with periods of 90°F and above, making it an ideal time to visit the white-sand beaches or do a little deep-sea fishing.

Fall is summerlike along the coast where temperatures remain pleasant until November. Evenings are cooler, but warm sunny days are ideal for strolling beaches. Although not severe, winters can grow cold, but normally the temperatures moder-ate quickly. Along the coast, sweaters or jackets typically are enough; farther north, however, you'll need warmer jackets.

If it does get cold, it doesn't last long. Snow is rare except in the higher altitudes of northern Alabama. When it does snow, the state can virtually stand still because

1861	1868	1880	1901	1933
Alabama secedes from the Union on January 11 and becomes the Repub-lic of Alabama until February 8, when it joins the Confeder-acy.	Alabama is readmit-ted to the Union on June 25.	The state's first blast furnace begins operating in Bir-mingham.	The present state constitution is adopted.	The federal govern-ment creates the Tennessee Valley Authority.

there is little, if any, snow-removal equipment and most drivers aren't used to driving on snow and ice. Huntsville annually receives 4.1 inches of snow; Birmingham, 1.4 inches, and Montgomery 0.3 inches. Florence holds the record for the most snowfall in a single storm: it was blanketed with 21 inches in January 1964.

The hottest day on record was September 5, 1925, in Centreville, where it reached 112°F. The coldest day recorded was in North Alabama's New Market when the mercury plunged to -27°F on January 30, 1966. Annually, the state receives some 56 inches of rain.

INTRODUCTION
HISTORY
REGIONS
WHEN TO VISIT
STATE'S GREATS
RULES OF THE ROAD
DRIVING TOURS

CLIMATE CHART
Average High/Low Temperature (°F) and Monthly Precipitation (in inches)

	JAN.	FEB.	MAR.	APR.	MAY	JUNE
BIRMINGHAM	52/31	57/35	66/42	75/49	81/58	87/65
	5.1	4.7	6.2	5.0	4.9	3.7
	JULY	AUG.	SEPT.	OCT.	NOV.	DEC.
	90/70	89/69	84/63	75/50	65/42	56/35
	5.3	3.6	3.9	2.8	4.3	5.0

	JAN.	FEB.	MAR.	APR.	MAY	JUNE
HUNTSVILLE	48/29	54/33	63/41	73/49	79/57	87/65
	5.2	4.9	6.6	4.9	5.1	4.1
	JULY	AUG.	SEPT.	OCT.	NOV.	DEC.
	89/69	89/68	83/62	73/49	62/41	53/33
	4.9	3.5	4.1	3.3	4.9	5.9

	JAN.	FEB.	MAR.	APR.	MAY	JUNE
MOBILE	60/40	64/43	71/50	76/57	83/64	89/71
	4.8	5.5	6.4	4.5	5.7	5.0
	JULY	AUG.	SEPT.	OCT.	NOV.	DEC.
	91/73	90/73	87/69	80/57	69/49	60/43
	6.8	7.0	5.9	2.9	4.1	5.3

	JAN.	FEB.	MAR.	APR.	MAY	JUNE
MONTGOMERY	56/36	61/39	69/46	76/53	83/61	90/68
	4.7	5.5	6.3	4.5	3.9	3.9
	JULY	AUG.	SEPT.	OCT.	NOV.	DEC.
	91/72	90/71	87/66	78/53	69/45	60/39
	5.2	3.7	4.1	2.5	4.1	5.2

1940s
The Redstone Arsenal at Huntsville becomes a center of rocket and spacecraft research.

1955–56
Rosa Parks' arrest for refusing to give up her bus seat to a white man sparks the Montgomery Bus Boycott, which catapults Martin Luther King, Jr., pastor of the Dexter Avenue Baptist

Church, to leadership in the Civil Rights movement.

1956
A federal court orders Montgomery to desegregate its public bus system.

1960
The George C. Marshall Space Flight Center is established in Huntsville.

FESTIVALS AND SEASONAL EVENTS

WINTER

Dec.: **Candlelight at Oakleigh** is among Mobile's most popular year-end events. The museum house is decorated in 1800s style | 334/432–1281.

Decorated boats glide along the Black Warrior River during Tuscaloosa's **Christmas Afloat** | 205/391–9200.

During **Christmas on the Tombigbee River** in Demopolis, head to the bluffs to see floats, lighted moving boats, and fireworks | 334/289–0270.

Jan.: In Mobile, some of the country's best college football senior citizens compete in the **Senior Bowl Football Game** | 334/635–0011.

Feb.: Mobile hosts the state's longest and largest party, a **Mardi Gras** celebration, with parades, gala Mystic Krewe balls, and pre-Lenten family entertainment | 334/432–3324.

Gulf Shores hosts an island-style **Mardi Gras** celebration with parades and floats gliding down area streets | 334/968–6904.

SPRING

Mar.: With azaleas in full bloom, Mobile hosts **Historic Home Tours** | 334/433–0259. and an **Azalea Trail Festival** | 334/473–7223. with motorists taking self-guided street tours.

In Selma, **Bridge Crossing Jubilee** | 334/418–0800. commemorates the anniversary of Bloody Sunday and the Selma-to-Montgomery march.

Apr.: **Birmingham International Festival** | 205/252–7652. salutes world cultures in the country's oldest and most comprehensive arts festival, with events held throughout the city.

Some 2,000 reenactors take part in encampments and firing exhibitions during the **Reenactment of the Battle of Selma** | 334/875–7241 or 800/457–3562.

May: Held Memorial Day weekend, **Alabama Jubilee Hot Air Balloon Classic,** with balloon races, Saturday-night balloon glow, arts, crafts, and car shows, is one of Decatur's biggest events | 256/350–2028.

Held in Big Springs Park, **Panoply of the Arts Festival** | 256/564–8100. is one of Huntsville's biggest events, with performing and visual artists, and a children's Discovery Area.

1963	**1963**	**1963**	**1963**	**1965**
Governor George C. Wallace begins the first of four terms.	In Birmingham, Civil Rights–related bombings include that of the 16th Street Baptist Church, where four little girls are killed.	Governor Wallace's "stand in the schoolhouse door" at the University of Alabama protests federally mandated racial integration.	First African-American students (Vivian Malone and James Hood) enroll at the University of Alabama.	Led by Martin Luther King, Jr., the Selma-to-Montgomery March focuses attention on the need for national voting rights legislation.

INTRODUCTION
HISTORY
REGIONS
WHEN TO VISIT
STATE'S GREATS
RULES OF THE ROAD
DRIVING TOURS

South of Selma, **Old Cahawba Festival** | 334/875–7241 or 800/457–3562. celebrates the revival of Alabama's first permanent state capital, with music, arts, crafts, living history, storytelling, and food.

SUMMER

June: On Father's Day weekend, Birmingham hosts major musical talent at **City Stages** | 205/251–1272.

Tuscumbia salutes America's "First Lady of Courage" with the **Helen Keller Festival,** three days of arts, crafts, entertainment, and concerts. An outdoor drama, The Miracle Worker, is held at Ms. Keller's home, Ivy Green, on weekends, mid-June to mid-July | 256/383–4066.

Aug.: The "Father of the Blues" is the focus of the weeklong music **W. C. Handy Music Festival** held in northwest Alabama's Shoals area | 256/740–4141.

Competitors gather from far and wide for the **Selma Rodeo** | 334/875–5417. held at the Agricultural Arena.

AUTUMN

Sept.: DeSoto Caverns Park in Childersburg | 256/378–7252 or 800/933–2283. holds an **Indian Fest,** with bluegrass, gospel, and country music.

The **Trail of Tears Commemoration** | 256/740–4141. with Native American dancing, powwows, arts, crafts, and entertainment takes place outside Florence in Waterloo.

Oct.: Held in Birmingham, the **Alabama State Fair** | 205/786–8100. brings nationally known performers, farm animals, and a midway with rides, games, and food.

Southern Wildlife Festival | 256/350–2028. is held in Decatur, with artists selling original works of wildlife in natural settings.

From late October to early November, Dothan hosts the **National Peanut Festival** with an array of events | 334/793–4323.

Florence pays homage to its Italian namesake with the **Alabama Renaissance Faire** | 256/740–4141.

Gulf Shores is the setting for the **National Shrimp Festival** | 334/968–6904. known as the year's biggest beach party.

1967	**1972**	**1981**	**1986**	**1993–94**
Lurleen Wallace, wife of George C. Wallace, is inaugurated as state's first woman governor. (She dies in 1968.)	Governor George C. Wallace is shot in Laurel, Maryland while campaigning for the Democratic presidential nomination.	Country music group Alabama is selected "Vocal Group of the Year" by the Academy of Country Music.	Guy Hunt becomes the first Republican governor of Alabama since the Reconstruction era.	Robert Trent Jones Golf Trail is unveiled.

Moundville Archaeological Park | 205/371–2572 or 205/371–2234. hosts the **Moundville Native American Festival,** four days with artisans demonstrating native crafts and dances.

Costumed soldiers stage a mock battle outside Fort Morgan, during the **Reenactment of the Battle of Mobile** | 334/540–7125.

State's Greats

In Alabama, you can hike mountain trails, romp sandy beaches, play on world-class golf courses, and explore historical sites. Alabama's lure includes a mild year-round climate, diverse terrain, southern hospitality, and an abundance of museums like hands-on children's museums and those showcasing sports heroes, airplanes, and music legends.

You can paddle down lazy rivers, or fish in either fresh or salt waters. Alabama also has a Shakespeare Festival in Montgomery, outdoor dramas (in Monroeville and Tuscaloosa) and riverboats (in Gadsden and Theodore).

State parks, with chalets, cabins, and lodges, are affordable with recreation options like golf, tennis, lakes and beaches. These places fill up fast, you should call months in advance to secure lodging.

In springtime, much of the state blooms in azaleas and dogwoods, and it's when several towns polish their silver, manicure their lawns, and host tours of historic homes that include access to many private residences not otherwise open to the public. Pilgrimages grant admission into mansions, plantations, churches, gardens, and even cemeteries. Candlelight tours add a special touch.

Beaches, Forests, and Parks

With the Appalachian Mountains stretching into the center of the state, Alabama has two very different types of terrain. The northern half is quite mountainous, and the southern portion tumbles into the sea, with bayous, marshes, pine forests, and pristine beaches popular with sun-worshipers.

In the north, parks are plentiful, with favorite places such as **DeSoto State Park** and **Little River Canyon,** with spectacular views, trails, and natural wonders. The dramatic waterfall and trails at **Noccalula Falls Park** are a favorite with families, and the park includes kid-friendly activities like a playground and minitrain. Just east of Birmingham, **Ruffner Mountain Nature Center** is an oasis of nature with a view of a thriving city. South of Birmingham, **Oak Mountain State Park** is the state's largest park, popular with boaters, golfers, hikers, and anglers. **Tuskegee National Forest** has lots of hiking trails. Lakes, such as **Lake Martin** at Alexander City, are popular with campers, fishermen, and boaters.

1993	**1995**	**1996**	**1998**
Governor Guy Hunt, in his second term, is convicted of misuse of public funds and removed from office.	Alabama's Heather Whitestone, who is deaf, serves as first "Miss America" with a physical challenge.	Near Tuscaloosa, Mercedes-Benz opens its first plant on American soil.	George C. Wallace dies, becoming first Alabama governor to lie in state in the Capitol since Lurleen Wallace.

INTRODUCTION
HISTORY
REGIONS
WHEN TO VISIT
STATE'S GREATS
RULES OF THE ROAD
DRIVING TOURS

Not finding the climate suitable for vines or olives, most of the settlers moved to the more tropical Mobile or New Orleans, though a few families remained. The area was well suited for growing cotton so many plantations operated there. While most of the city's beautiful historic homes are privately owned, two antebellum mansions are open to the public. Allow about two hours to tour them.

Just off U.S. 80, **Gaineswood,** built between 1843 and 1861, is a fine example of Greek Revival architecture. Built by owner-architect General Nathan Bryan Whitfield, the home features ornate plasterwork and has most of the original furnishings. Like any authentic southern mansion, Gaineswood has its own ghost, the general's sister-in-law. Listen for her soft footsteps and singing coming from the basement.

Follow the signs across town to **Bluff Hall,** a historic house museum on North Commissioners Avenue that overlooks the Tombigbee River. Bluff Hall was built in 1832 in the Federal town-house style, but in 1850 the owner added columns and painted it white to transform it into the then-fashionable Greek Revival style of architecture.

In the heart of town, Demopolis Public Square is one of the oldest public squares in Alabama. Relax on a bench in the shade and take note of the restored cast-iron fountain, pavilion, and a Confederate statue.

❷ From Demopolis, follow U.S. 80 east toward Selma. Twelve miles from Selma on Route 22 south, visit **Cahawba,** a ghost town that served as Alabama's first capital. You can learn more about the town in the welcome center, then follow hiking trails among the ruins.

❸ Once you reach **Selma,** cross the **Edmund Pettus Bridge** over the Alabama River in memory of the voting-rights march from Selma to Montgomery in 1965. Near the foot of the bridge, the **National Voting Rights Museum and Institute** documents the struggles that led to the passage of the National Voting Rights Act. Available at the **Selma–Dallas County Chamber of Commerce,** the self-guided **Martin Luther King, Jr., Street Walking Tour** will lead you to other important sites such as **Brown Chapel A.M.E. Church—** the first African Methodist Episcopal church in the state that also served as headquarters for Civil Rights workers.

Stroll along the **Historic Water Avenue District,** where former riverside cotton and ammunition warehouses have been transformed into eateries and shops. The **St. James Hotel** is a luxurious place to stay. At the end of the street, the **Old Depot Museum** is an interpretive history museum located in a former railroad depot. The museum showcases Selma history from 1820 to the present.

The antebellum **Joseph T. Smitherman Historic Building** houses Civil War memorabilia, much of which was manufactured in Selma. Tour **Sturdivant Hall** to see one of the South's finest examples of Greek Revival architecture.

❹ After Selma, continue east on U.S. 80 about 45 mi to **Montgomery,** the state capital, which is also known among politicians as "Goat Hill." The Greek Revival **State Capitol,** built in 1951, has been restored to its Civil War–era appearance. The building features a rotunda whose dome is decorated with murals depicting dramatic scenes from the state's history, and a stained-glass skylight. On the tour of the capitol building, you'll see the Senate Chamber where Jefferson Davis was elected the first and only president of the Confederate States, whose capital was also Montgomery.

Davis's home, the **First White House of the Confederacy** is an 1835 Italianate mansion furnished with antiques from the 1850s and is open for tours.

One block west of the capitol, **Dexter Avenue King Memorial Baptist Church** is the small redbrick building where Dr. Martin Luther King preached. A block behind the church, the **Civil Rights Memorial** is a circle of granite designed by Maya Lin, the same architect of the Vietnam Memorial in Washington, D.C. The memorial commemorates those who died in the Civil Rights movement with a thin veil of water that flows over their names and a favorite biblical inscription of Dr. King's: "Until justice rolls down like waters and righteousness like a mighty stream."

Three blocks north of the memorial, the **Montgomery Visitor Center** is in a restored antebellum home where you can get maps and visitor information.

One block north of the visitor center, **Old Alabama Town** is an authentic reconstruction of a 19th-century central Alabama village featuring 30 buildings in a three-block area.

On the east side of Montgomery (Interstate 85, exit 6, to East Boulevard), don't miss the acclaimed **Alabama Shakespeare Festival** at **Wynton Blount Cultural Park.** The fifth-largest Shakespeare theater in the world, ASF houses a 750-seat festival stage and 225-seat Octagon theater where plays (some Shakespearean, some not) are performed year-round. If you can't see a play, take a behind-the-scenes tour. Located on manicured grounds with a lake, the park also includes the **Shakespeare's Gardens and Amphitheater** and the **Montgomery Museum of Fine Arts,** home to the largest collection of artwork by Zelda Sayre Fitzgerald, a Montgomery native who married F. Scott Fitzgerald. The **F. Scott and Zelda Fitzgerald Museum,** located in the home where they lived in 1931, honors the couple's literary legacy with displays of their letters, original manuscripts, photos, and other memorabilia.

After you tour the museum, which is located in the historic and trendy Cloverdale area, dine at one of the restaurants such as the upscale **Vintage Year,** then perhaps spend the night at a bed-and-breakfast inn.

❺ A worthwhile detour just 12 mi north of Montgomery on Route 152 and U.S. 231 is **Jasmine Hill Gardens and Outdoor Museum,** where you'll see reproductions of famous Greek statues surrounded by beautiful gardens, pools, and fountains.

❻ From Montgomery, continue east along U.S. 80 to **Tuskegee,** where two great African-American educators are honored; Booker T Washington and George Washington Carver, who were both born into slavery. Booker T. Washington founded the Tuskegee Institute, now known as Tuskegee University, in 1881 at **Butler Chapel A.M.E. Zion Church,** where church services are still held in the original building.

In 1896, Washington hired George Washington Carver, a renowned scientist, to lead the Institute's new agriculture college. Carver lived and worked on the campus for 47 years. In 1938, the institute established the **George Washington Carver Museum** where visitors can see his laboratory equipment, samples of his peanut and sweet-potato products, and some of his paintings and needlework. The Carver Museum is part of the Tuskegee Institute National Historic Site which became part of the National Park Service in 1974.

Some of the historic buildings on Tuskegee University's campus were built by the school's first students with bricks made in the nearby brickyard. One such building is Booker T. Washington's own home, **The Oaks,** which is open for hourly tours.

Also worth seeing on the campus is the **Tuskegee University Cemetery,** where both Booker T. Washington and George Washington Carver are buried, and the **Booker T. Washington Monument,** which shows Washington lifting the veil of ignorance from his fellow man. About 1½ mi away is the city's 150-year-old downtown historic district with the Macon County Courthouse, whose tower can be seen from a mile away.

As you leave Tuskegee, take Route 81 south about 6 mi to Interstate 85—it's a faster route back to Montgomery, where Interstate 85 meets Interstate 65.

Alabama Gulf Coast Driving Tour

FROM DAUPHIN ISLAND TO GULF SHORES

Distance: 75 mi   Time: 3 days

Breaks: Stay overnight in Mobile, Fairhope/Point Clear, and Gulf Shores/Orange Beach

Centered on historic Mobile Bay, the charming and diverse cities along Alabama's Gulf Coast—from European-influenced Mobile to tourist-friendly Gulf Shores—are easily accessible. Explore leisurely or do a quick tour, but do take note of hurricane season, which is from June through November: the entire region can suddenly go on alert as tropical storms develop in the warm Gulf of Mexico waters.

❶ Sleepy **Dauphin Island,** the easternmost barrier island between the Mississippi Sound and the Gulf of Mexico, is a good place to start your Alabama's Gulf Coast visit. The dramatic view from the bridge over Mobile Bay, the only route onto the island, is south of Mobile on Route 193. The western end of Dauphin Island is mostly residential, but the eastern end has some interesting areas to explore like **Fort Gaines,** the site of the Civil War's Battle of Mobile Bay (in which Admiral David Farragut issued his famous "Damn the torpedoes, full speed ahead!" command). Check out Dauphin Island Sea Lab's **Estuarium,** which has a boardwalk along the dunes where you can see native birds like seagulls, brown pelicans, and great blue herons. Inside the Estuarium are aquariums and exhibits where you can learn about the four habitats of coastal Alabama: the delta, Mobile Bay, the barrier islands, and the northern Gulf of Mexico.

The **Mobile Bay Ferry** departs from a dock near the Estuarium and leaves you off on the other side of Mobile Bay in Fort Morgan. Use the ferry for a day trip to Fort Morgan and then return, or you can ferry your car or RV across the bay. The advantage to taking your vehicle is that you cut more than an hour off your trip (but bypass Mobile).

❷ If you're continuing by car from Dauphin Island toward Mobile, take a popular and well-worth-it detour to **Theodore** and **Bellingrath Gardens and Home.** Follow the signs from Route 193 north, left onto Route 188, then right on Bellingrath Gardens Road. The riverfront property, on 65 sprawling acres, was developed by Coca-Cola Bottling Company owner Walter Bellingrath and his flower-loving wife, Bessie. Their 15-room home, now a museum that was featured on A&E's "America's Castles" program, was completed in 1935. Bellingrath is open year-round and has beautifully manicured gardens, walking paths, and plenty of blooms. Tour the museum home to see family antiques, and the world's largest public collection of Boehm porcelain. During the warmer months, a sightseeing cruise along Fowl River aboard the *Southern Belle* is a wonderful way to appreciate the area's beauty from the water. It's easy to spend at least half a day touring Bellingrath Gardens and Home.

From the gardens, follow Bellingrath Gardens Road to U.S. 90 east toward Mobile, the state's second-largest and oldest city that celebrates its 300th birthday in 2002. With its location on the Mobile River and Mobile Bay, Mobile's nickname is "the Port City," but it's also known for its gorgeous display of azaleas in early spring, earning Mobile the distinction of being "the Azalea City" as well. Starting in late February, the city is abloom with dazzling displays of azaleas and other flowers, making springtime a wonderful season to visit.

❸ Continue along U.S. 90—which eventually becomes oak-canopied **Government Street,** one of Mobile's most beautiful thoroughfares—until you reach downtown **Mobile.** Eat dinner at one of the many restaurants located in the revitalized downtown entertainment district on and around **Dauphin Street.** For a true taste of Mobile history, spend the night at the antebellum **Malaga Inn,** where the rooms are centered around a romantic brick courtyard. Most downtown attractions are within walking distance of the inn. Start with a visit to the **Fort Condé Mobile Visitor Welcome Center.** Volunteers can answer questions about the area and provide you with brochures. While there, tour the re-created Fort Condé, a partially restored 18th-century fort. Tours are led by guides in French period uniforms.

Drive west from Fort Condé on Church Street back to Government Street for a visit to the 1872 Italianate town house that houses the **Museum of Mobile,** which showcases the city's almost-300-year history under French, British, and Spanish rule. Mobilians love telling visitors that Mardi Gras, the annual pre-Lenten celebration, actually originated in Mobile and then caught on in New Orleans. Mardi Gras still plays a major role in Mobile culture, as evidenced by the museum's Queens' Gallery, which displays the elaborate gowns worn by each queen of Mobile's Mardi Gras, including

INTRODUCTION
HISTORY
REGIONS
WHEN TO VISIT
STATE'S GREATS
RULES OF THE ROAD
DRIVING TOURS

the gown that belonged to young Alexis Herman, a Mobile native and past queen who went on to become the U.S. Secretary of Labor. Another free city museum located nearby is the **Phoenix Fire Museum.** Built in 1859 to house the Phoenix Volunteer Fire Company, the museum now traces the history of the city's volunteer firefighters from 1819.

Continue west on Government Street past Broad Street to the Oakleigh Historic Garden District, a neighborhood of restored historic homes. Turn left onto George Street and follow the signs to the **Oakleigh Period House Museum,** one of Mobile's best examples of Greek Revival architecture. Take a guided tour of the 1833 mansion, which is rumored to have a playful ghost who enjoys turning the lights on and off.

Go back to Broad Street and turn north, then go two blocks to **Dauphin Street,** which stretches east toward the Mobile River. During the day, you can visit an art gallery or relax in Cathedral Square Park, opposite the stately Cathedral of the Immaculate Conception which was built in 1835, or Bienville Square, an oak-shaded oasis in the heart of downtown Mobile.

The **Gulf Coast Exploreum Museum of Science** is at Government and Water streets. (Parking is limited, call ahead for advice on where to park.) The kid-friendly children's museum houses traveling exhibits as well as Hands-on Hall, a permanent exhibit that explains many scientific theories in simple terms. Relax at the locally owned coffee shop while the kids play and learn. There is also an IMAX Dome Theater which shows dazzling, larger-than-life films.

Directly across Water Street from the Exploreum is **Cooper Riverside Park,** where you can learn about Mobile's waterfront. The *Cotton Blossom* riverboat is docked at the adjacent Mobile Convention Center and offers daily, one-hour excursions along the river.

❹ Leaving downtown Mobile via Government Street, you'll enter the Bankhead Tunnel, which takes you under Mobile River and onto the Battleship Parkway, also known as the Causeway, that crosses Mobile Bay. (If you take the Wallace Tunnel from Interstate 10, you'll emerge on the bridge known to locals as the Bayway, which also crosses the bay. Take exit 27 onto Battleship Parkway.) Follow the signs to **Battleship Memorial Park,** where you can tour the World War II battleship USS *Alabama* and the submarine USS *Drum*.

❺ Continue on Interstate 10 east to the Daphne exit and follow U.S. 98 south to U.S. 98 Scenic to **Fairhope.** This charming city's streets overflow with flowers year-round. Take a right off Section Street (U.S. 98 Scenic) onto Fairhope Avenue, park the car anywhere, and check out Fairhope's many shops and restaurants. At the foot of the hill, the **Fairhope Municipal Pier** and adjacent bayfront park is perfect for sunsets. Walk out onto the pier to see what the fishermen are catching. For children, the nearby park area has swings and seesaws on a sand beach and a duck pond. The sidewalk that extends along the bluff overlooks the bay and is a good place to stroll among oak trees laden with Spanish moss. Spend the second night in one of Fairhope's quaint bed-and-breakfast inns.

❻ The next morning, return to U.S. 98 and follow the signs past Magnolia Springs (mail is still delivered by boat to residents who live along Fish River) to **Foley,** and turn south on U.S. 59. Just a couple of miles south of "uptown Foley," as the locals call it, is **Riviera Centre,** a shopper's paradise of more than 120 factory-outlet stores located in **Fairhope.** It's easy to spend the day here.

❼ Also on the way to the beach are several places enticing to children, including the **Waterville USA** water park, the **Track Family Recreation Center,** and **Zooland Animal Park.**

❽ After you cross the intercoastal canal, you've reached Pleasure Island. Route 59 will end at **Gulf Shores,** where the main drag along the beach is Route 182. Drive east on Route

182 and, in addition to countless hotels and condominiums, there are also several well-marked public beaches where families can spend a day sunbathing on sugar-white sand and swimming in the gulf. Beware of occasionally strong currents and in summer-time there can be stinging nettles or jellyfish in the water. Driving east on Route 182 through **Orange Beach,** you'll eventually cross the Alabama Point Bridge, where there is a wonderful panoramic view, and eventually you'll reach the Florida border at the **Flora-Bama Lounge,** which crosses the state line and is famous for its annual Inter-state Mullet Toss. It's easy to spend a day or many more relaxing on the beaches in Gulf Shores and Orange Beach. There are several championship golf courses nearby, deep-sea fishing charters, wave-runner rentals, and other diversions that make the Gulf Coast a wonderful vacation spot for the whole family. From Gulf Shores, follow Route 59 north through the towns of Foley, Robertsdale, and Loxley to Interstate 10 west, which leads back across Mobile Bay to Mobile, where Interstate 10 and Interstate 65 north converge.

ALEXANDER CITY

MAP 3, D4

(Nearby towns also listed: Auburn, Opelika, Sylacauga)

"Elec City," as locals call it, has roots in Indian wars and the Industrial Revolution. Captain James Welch, an English trader, marked a trail through the county in 1698 where the English quickly established trading stations. This is where Andrew Jackson rose to national fame when he defeated the Red Stick Creek Indians at the Battle of Horseshoe Bend near Alexander City in 1814.

Today, Alexander City is among the nation's top retirement communities, and retirees enjoy the moderate year-round climate and Lake Martin with its 760 mi of shoreline. Fishing, boating, and access to Wind Creek State Park are major draws.

Information: Alexander City–Lake Martin Chamber of Commerce | 120 Tallapoosa St. (Box 926), Alexander City 35011-0926 | 256/234–3461 | fax 256/234–0094 | coc@web-shoppe.net.

Attractions

Horseshoe Bend National Military Park. The bloodiest battle of the Creek War, fought on March 27, 1814, is remembered at a bend in the Tallapoosa River. It was here that Andrew Jackson rose to national fame when he defeated the Red Stick Creek Indians and forever broke the power of their nation. Operated by the National Park Service, the park includes the entire battlefield of the historic encounter and a diorama of the battle and Creek life. A 3-mi tour road, hiking trails, and outdoor exhibits and markers interpret battlefield sites. Living history programs are presented on the last Saturday of the month, and the battle's anniversary is celebrated the last weekend in March. There's also a museum with exhibits, slide presentation, and an electric map. | 11288 Horseshoe Bend Rd., Daviston | 256/234–7111 | fax 256/329–9905 | hobe_administration@nps.gov | www.nps.gov/hobe | Free | Daily 8–4:40; museum daily 8–4:40.

Lake Martin. Lake Martin is located about 5 mi east of Alexander City. A sparkling 44,000-acre freshwater lake with over 76 mi of wooded shoreline, the lake has a number of attractions: various islands to explore, an amphitheater used for outdoor performances, Wind Creek State Park, boating, camping, fishing, skiing, and swimming. In addition, Children's Harbor, a nonprofit organization, provides free and confidential counseling and support services to children with long-term serious illnesses as well as to their families. Contact the chamber of commerce for directions, as there are many different entrances depending on what you wish to do at the lake. | Alexander Chamber of Commerce 120 Tallapoosa St. (Box 926), Alexander City | 256/234–3461 | fax 256/234–0094 | www.lake-martin.com | Free.

Wind Creek State Park. Southeast of Alexander City, the park sits on 44,000-acre Lake Martin and includes a fully equipped modern campground; campsites have picnic tables, water, and electricity. Park facilities include a camp store, marina, play areas, hiking trails, heated rest rooms, showers, picnic pavilions, and a 210-ft fishing pier. Sites are available for both nightly and monthly rentals. | 4325 Rte. 128 | 256/329–0845 | fax 256/234–4870 | www.vten.com | $1 | Daily.

ON THE CALENDAR

JUNE: *Jazzfest.* The second weekend of the month marks Alexander City's most festive weekend—two days of live jazz and zydeco. Friday's festivities are downtown. Broad Street is completely closed to traffic. Saturday night's entertainment is at Kowaliga Point on Lake Martin. | 256/234–3461.

Dining

Cecil's Public House. Southern. This casually elegant restaurant serves terrific food in a restored turn-of-the-20th-century house filled with Victorian antiques. The menu includes a seafood salad appetizer, sandwiches, fried shrimp, catfish, and Marion's fillet, the chef's signature steak entrée named in honor of his mother. Kids's menu. There's also a pub with an Old German setting. | 243 Green St. | 256/329–0732 | $11–$25 | AE, MC, V | Closed Sun. No lunch Sat.

Sho'nuff BBQ. Barbecue. Eight-foot styrofoam pigs adorn the walls of the self-styled "best little smokehouse in town." The restaurant is known for its down-home southern cookin'— particularly the barbecued pork. The house speciality is pork-stuffed baked potato, and there's also a pork platter piled with a variety of barbecued pork pieces and all the usual fixin's. The homemade peach and blueberry cobbler is popular. | 651 Dadeville Rd. | 256/234–7675 | $8 | No credit cards | Closed Sun.

Lodging

Holiday Inn Express. Just 2 mi from town, this standard two-story hotel is on a hill overlooking Alexander City. Complimentary Continental breakfast. In-room data ports, microwave, refrigerators, some in-room hot tubs, cable TV. Pool. Laundry facilities. | 2945 Hwy. 280 | 256/234–5900 | fax 256/234–5918 | 42 rooms | $55–$95 | AE, D, DC, MC, V.

Horseshoe Bend Inn. This two-story building built in 1968 is just 1 mi south of downtown Alexander City. Many attractions are nearby, including: Horseshoe Bend National Military Park, Lake Martin, golf courses, and Wind Creek State Park. There is a store and deli on premises, and bass-boat hookups. Children 12 and under stay free. Bar, complimentary Continental breakfast. Cable TV. Pool. Free parking. | 3146 Hwy. 280 | 256/234–6311 | fax 256/234–6314 | 64 rooms | $50–$70 | AE, D, DC, MC, V.

Jameson Inn. Built in an old colonial style, this two-story standard brick motel is close to main highways in a business district and just five minutes from Lake Martin. Complimentary Continental breakfast. Cable TV. Pool. Gym. | 4335 U.S. 280 | 256/234–7099 or 800/541–3268 | fax 256/234–9807 | 60 rooms | $60 | AE, D, DC, MC, V.

Mistletoe Bough Bed & Breakfast. Less than 10 minutes away from Lake Martin and within walking distance of downtown, this restored 1890 Queen Anne Victorian is filled with antiques. The landscaping is lush and well groomed; verandas, a screened porch, and a sunporch surround the elegant home. For breakfast, innkeeper Jean Payne prepares dishes using fresh herbs from her garden; she also makes her own jellies. Complimentary breakfast. Cable TV. | 497 Hillabee St. | 256/329–3717 | bbonline.com/al/mistletoe | 5 rooms | $85–$125 | No credit cards.

Super 8. Two miles from downtown, this three-story standard motel is convenient to U.S. 280, the main thoroughfare through town. Complimentary Continental breakfast. Cable TV. Business services. | 4000 U.S. 280 Bypass | 256/329–8858 | fax 256/329–8858 | 44 rooms | $47 | AE, D, MC, V.

ANNISTON

MAP 3, E3

(Nearby towns also listed: Gadsden, Talladega)

To help rebuild the South after the devastation of the Civil War, textile mills and blast furnaces were established in the mid- to late 1800s. The industrialist owners commissioned architects to design a company town, which today is often called "the Model City."

Fort McClellan, a now closed Army base, dates back to 1912. It was used as a World War II training center, and until 1999, it was home to the Army Chemical Corps and the Women's Army Corps.

Anniston has old homes and churches dating back to 1888, including the Victoria Inn (now a bed-and-breakfast) and the Church of St. Michael and All Angels. Major attractions are the Anniston Museum of Natural History and the Berman Museum. Nestled in foothills, the area touts itself as the Gateway to the Appalachian Mountains. Nearby is Cheaha State Park, the state's highest point.

Information: **Anniston/Calhoun County Convention and Visitors Bureau** | 1330 Quintard Ave. (Box 1087), Anniston 36202 | 256/237–3536 or 800/489–1087 | fax 256/237–4338 | carolm@calhounchamber.org | www.calhounchamber.org.

City of Anniston | 1128 Gurenee Ave., 36201 | 256/236–3422 | fax 256/236–3421 | cityhall@internettport.net | www.anniston-alabama.org.

Attractions

Anniston Museum of Natural History. The museum began as a private collection and evolved into an impressive municipal institution. It contains dinosaur and fossil displays, mammals in open dioramas, a 400-species bird collection, two Egyptian mummies, a walk-through replica of an Alabama cave, and a children's discovery room. Outside are nature trails and picnic areas. | 800 Museum Dr., Lagarde Park | 256/237–6766 | fax 256/237–6776 | www.annistonmuseum.org | $3.50 | Mon.–Sat. 10–5, Sun. 1–5; Children's Discovery Room Wed.–Sun. 1–4.

Berman Museum. Included in this collection are personal items that once belonged to Adolph Hitler and Thomas Jefferson, suits of armor, beheading swords, a chastity belt, and tiny guns that look like cigarette lighters. One of the most valuable pieces is a sparkling, Persian scimitar (a saber with a curved blade) dating to the 16th century. The handle is embedded with 1,295 diamonds, 60 carats of rubies, and a 40-carat emerald. Bronze sculptures by Frederic Remington, medieval arms and armor, and antiquities are also on display. | 840 Museum Dr. | 256/237–6261 | fax 256/238–9055 | $3.50 | June–Aug., Mon.–Sat. 10–5, Sun. 1–5; closed Mon. Sept.–May.

Cheaha State Park. Twenty-five miles south of the Clay Cleburne county line at the state's highest point, the 2,719-acre mountaintop retreat has a 30-unit lodge, a restaurant, 15 chalets and stone cabins, a modern campground with 73 sites, picnic areas, and pavilions. Mountain scenery is the backdrop for hiking, bicycling on the bike trails, and children's play areas. Lake activities include pedal boating, fishing, and swimming. The park is a favorite spot for viewing fall foliage colors. | 19644 Rte. 281, 2141 Bunker Loop, Delta | 256/488–5111 or 800/846–2654 | fax 256/488–5649 | $1 | Daily.

Church of St. Michael and all Angels. Completed in 1890, the church is an outstanding example of Norman architecture. It is noted for its hand-carved angels and crosses, stained-glass windows, and a 95-ft bell tower. The organ has nearly 3,000 pipes. The church has an active congregation. | 1000 W. 18th St. | 256/237–4011 | fax 256/237–4014 | www.brasenhill.com/stmike-saa | Free | Daily 9–4.

Coldwater Covered Bridge. Built in 1850 by a former slave, this is one of Alabama's oldest remaining covered bridges. It has been restored and moved from Coldwater Creek to its current home at the Oxford Lake and Walking Trail. | 401 McCullah Ave. | 256/831–2660 | fax 256/835–6136 | Free | Daily.

ON THE CALENDAR

OCT.: *Lobsterfest.* Held on the second Saturday of the month, this is the biggest event in town, organized by the Grace Episcopal Church as a fund-raiser for Habitat for Humanity (an organization that builds houses for families in need). The church ships in live Maine lobsters and for $15 you can pre-order a lobster plate: 2 pounds of lobster complete with corn on the cob, coleslaw, potatoes, and other trimmings. There's live jazz, folk, and rock music; pony rides; and booths selling local arts and crafts and other foods (for those who aren't partial to lobster). An all-day family event. | 256/236–4457.

Dining

Betty's Bar-B-Q. Barbecue. A favorite locals hang out with good home-cooked southern specialities including, of course, barbecue. Old photos of local residents hang on the wall with other memorabilia. Kids' menu. | 401 S. Quintard Ave. | 256/237–1411 | $7–$10 | AE, D, MC, V | Closed Sun.

Lil Cajun Cookery. Cajun. You'll easily spot this place by the crawfish hanging in the huge bay windows. This 1870 New Orleans–style brick building is on the oldest corner in Anniston. The interior has three floors and a New Orleans bayou motif complete with alligator heads and other animals mounted on the walls. There's live music on the second Thursday of the month, otherwise it's Cajun music playing in the background. Outdoor dining is on the third-floor balcony. The most popular dishes are the blackened prime rib, grilled shrimp over fresh pasta, and of course, the jambalaya, a traditional Cajun dish with chicken, sausage, peppers, onions, celery, and "a whole mess of spices." Also in constant demand is the New Orleans bread pudding. Kids' menu. | 11 W. 10th St. | 256/235–3888 | $12–$20 | AE, MC, V | Closed Sun.

Top O' the River. Seafood. Though not actually on a river, you'll feel like you're on a fishing trip as you eat meals served on tin plates. Favorites include seafood platters, fried catfish fillets, and chicken fingers with sides of coleslaw and corn bread. The decor has a nautical theme with rustic high-back booths. | 3220 McClellan Blvd. | 256/238–0097 | $12–$19 | AE, D, DC, MC, V | No lunch Mon.–Sat.

The Victoria. Contemporary. Located in the downtown historic district, this 1888 Victorian inn offers fine dining in a casual atmosphere. The chef, a Culinary Institute of America graduate, has an ever-changing menu and is especially known for her lump crab cakes. A pianist entertains on Friday and Saturday. Kids' menu. No smoking. | 1604 Quintard Ave. | 256/236–0503 | $16–$34 | AE, D, DC, MC, V | Closed Sun. No lunch.

Lodging

Best Western Riverside Inn. Within easy access of the interstate, this beautifully landscaped two-story property is on Lake Logan Martin. It has a small pier and nearby marina. Restaurant. Cable TV. Pool, lake, wading pool. Boating, fishing. Laundry facilities. Some pets allowed. | 11900 U.S. 78, Riverside | 205/338–3381 | fax 205/338–3183 | 70 rooms | $79 | AE, D, DC, MC, V.

Hampton Inn. This two-story white stucco exterior hotel has a homey southern atmosphere and is just off Interstate 20 on Route 21. Nearby are museums, a raceway, and antiques malls. Complimentary Continental breakfast. In-room data ports, cable TV. Pool. Laundry service. Business services. | 1600 Rte. 21 South, Oxford | 256/835–1492 | fax 256/835–0636 | www.hamptoninn.com | 129 rooms in 3 buildings | $69–$74 | AE, D, DC, MC, V.

Holiday Inn. This inn is just across from the Quintard Mall and about 20 minutes from the Talladega Superspeedway. It has two stories in four buildings with a hunter-green and cranberry interior. Restaurant, bar, picnic area, room service. In-room data ports, cable TV. Pool. Hot tub. Playground. Laundry facilities. Business services. | U.S. 78 and 21 South, Oxford | 256/831–3410 | fax 256/831–9560 | 194 rooms | $59 | AE, D, DC, MC, V.

Jameson Inn, Oxford. Five miles from downtown Anniston, this white-columned, colonial-style building has views of Cheaha Mountain, and offers one- and two-bedroom suites. Complimentary breakfast. In-room data ports. Pool. Gym. Laundry service. Free parking. Children under 18 are free. | 161 Colonial Dr. | 256/835–2170 or 800/541–3268 | fax 256/835–2133 | www.jamesoninns.com | 40 rooms | $63–$159 | AE, D, DC, V.

Lenlock Inn. Five miles from downtown, this brick-and-wood inn is just outside Fort McClellan. Refrigerators, in-room hot tubs in suites, cable TV, in-room VCRs. Pool. Sauna. Laundry facilities. Some pets allowed. | 6210 McClellan Blvd. | 256/820–1515 or 800/234–5059 | fax 256/820–1516 | 44 rooms, 4 suites | $36, $109 suites | A, D, DC, MC, V.

The Victoria. Plenty of trees surround this three-story, four-building inn located in the historic district. Walkways and gazebos lead from the hotel rooms to the main focal point, the 1888 Victorian home. The fine dining restaurant inside the house has a pianist on Friday and Saturday nights. Restaurant, bar, complimentary breakfast, room service. In-room data ports, no-smoking rooms. Cable TV. Pool. Business services. | 1604 Quintard Ave. | 256/236–0503 or 800/260–8781 | fax 256/236–1138 | victoria@thevictoria.com | www.thevictoria.com | 60 rooms | $79 | AE, D, DC, MC, V.

Wingate Inn of Oxford. This inn borders Oxford and Anniston. A sprawling four-story building, the rooms have views of either the Appalachian foothills or the outdoor garden pool. Complimentary snacks and beverages are available every afternoon. Three antiques malls are within walking distance and downtown Anniston is 5 mi away. Complimentary Continental breakfast. In-room data ports, cable TV. Pool. Gym. Video games. Laundry services. Business services. Free parking. | 143 Colonial Dr., Oxford | 256/831–1921 or 800/993–7232 | fax 256/831–1921 | 10014@hotel.cendant.com | www.wingateinns.com | 81 rooms | $84–$100 | AE, D, DC, MC, V.

ATHENS

MAP 3, C1

(Nearby towns also listed: Decatur, Huntsville)

Founded in 1818, Athens became a center for pre–Civil War planters. The town today is noted for the picturesque Athens State College, the state's oldest institution of higher learning. Founders Hall, built in 1843 as Athens Female College, is an excellent example of Greek Revival architecture. Limestone county is dry, no alcohol is served or sold.

Information: **Athens–Limestone Chamber of Commerce** | 101 S. Beaty St. (Box 150), Athens 35611 | 256/232–2600 | fax 256/232–2609 | alcc@companet.net | www.companet.net/cc/athenscc.html.

Attractions

Athens State College. The state's oldest institute of higher learning, Athens State College is known for its 1840s Greek Revival Founders Hall and the Altar of the New Testament, with its elegant wood carvings detailing Jesus and the New Testament story. The life-size carvings, made in tulip wood, took 12 years to complete. Annually on the first Friday and Saturday of October, the campus is the setting for the southern fiddlers' convention, which has sparked a renewed interest in authentic old-time music. | 300 N. Beaty St. | 256/233–8100 | fax 256/233–2565 | www.athens.edu | Free | Daily.

Big Springs Park. At Beaty and Market streets, this is the site of the original Athens settlement. Facilities include three newly renovated tennis courts, one pavilion, playground equipment, and a duck feeding pond. | 101 S. Beaty St. | Free.

Houston Memorial Library and Museum. The house-museum was once home of George Houston, attorney and member of the U.S. Senate and twice governor of Alabama. | 101 N. Houston St. | 256/233–8770 | Free | Weekdays 10–5, Sat. 9–noon.

ON THE CALENDAR

APR.: *Athens-Limestone Dogwood Festival.* This weeklong festival celebrates the beauty of spring in Athens and Limestone County. Events include a kids' day, bike/trike parade, fishing derby, games in the park, concert, fashion show and luncheon, seminar, dinner theater, and a dance. Call for events and locations, as they are many and varied. | Big Spring Park and other locations in Athens | 256/233–8728.
MAY: *Homespun.* This arts-and-crafts fair showcases pioneer-era skills, including blacksmithing, chair caning, quilting, and glass blowing. | 507 S. Hoffman St. | Free | 256/232–3525.
OCT.: *Tennessee Valley Old Time Fiddlers Convention.* Outdoor competition, buck-dancing sessions and harmonica, banjo, fiddle, mandolin, dulcimer, and guitar playing. | Athens State University | 256/232–2600.

Dining

H and H Barbecue Ranch. Barbecue. Situated in the suburbs of Athens, H and H is 3 mi from the town center; the building was a chicken house before it became a restaurant. It is the oldest family-owned restaurant in Alabama, serving barbecue since 1956. The interior is decorated with deer heads, antiques, and old photos. Popular dishes include BBQ, fried-chicken platter, and rib-eye steak, and especially loved are the homemade onion rings. You might want to order dessert with your entrée: the homemade chocolate coconut pie sells out fast. | 23021 Nick Davis Rd. | 256/232–9856 | $7–15 | AE, MC, V | Closed Mon.–Wed.

Hungry Fisherman. Seafood. A brightly painted building off Interstate 65, offering over 20 different kinds of seafood. The walls of the restaurant are covered in fish pictures. The menu includes seafood gumbo, homemade clam chowder, broiled steak and crab-leg platter, chicken, shrimp and scallop fettuccine, and grilled red snapper. Popular desserts are apple walnut pie, and key lime pie. Kids' menu. | 1124 Hwy. 72 east | 256/233–4433 | $7–$14 | DC, MC, V.

Mexico Lindo. Mexican. Mariachi music, along with traditional fajitas and enchilada fare in a colorful, traditional Mexican setting. Chorizo, rice and beans, salsa fresca, and such Mexican standards as flan and fried ice cream for dessert. | 1202 N. Jefferson St. | 256/216–0403 | $6–$12 | AE, D, DC, V.

Lodging

Best Western. This two-story stucco hotel is 3 mi from downtown at Interstate 65 and U.S. 72. Picnic area, Complimentary Continental breakfast. In-room data ports, refrigerators, cable TV. Pool. Laundry facilities. Some pets allowed (fee). | 1329 U.S. 72 east | 256/233–4030 | fax 256/233–4554 | 83 rooms | $54–$64 | AE, D, DC, MC, V.

Comfort Inn. Standard chain motel conveniently just 2 mi from Interstate 65, with restaurants nearby. Complimentary Continental breakfast. In-room data ports, no-smoking rooms. Pool. | 1218 Kelli Dr. | 256/232–2704 or 800/725–4056 | fax 256/230–3783 | 63 rooms | $49–$55 | AE, D, DC, MC, V.

Hampton Inn. Located right off Interstate 65 in a small suburban town, this white stucco hotel is close to state parks and is about a half-hour drive from the Huntsville Space and Rocket Center. Complimentary Continental breakfast. In-room data ports, microwaves, refrigerators, some in-room hot tubs, cable TV, in-room VCRs. Pool. Business services. | 1488

Thrasher Blvd. | 256/232–0030 | fax 256/233–7006 | www.hamptoninn.com | 57 rooms | $62–$77 | AE, D, DC, MC, V.

Mark Motel. This small family-run motel is a one-story brick building, on 4 acres, with some gardens. It is 2 mi from downtown Athens. Microwaves, refrigerators, cable TV. Free parking. Some pets allowed. | 210 U.S. Hwy. 31 south | 256/232–6200 | 21 rooms | $35 | AE, D, MC.

Town & Country Motel. This small and privately run motel has limited facilities and is 5 mi from Athens town center. Microwaves, refrigerators, cable TV. Pool. Free parking. | 2414 Hwy. 31 south | 256/232–2700 | fax 256/230–3771 | 40 rooms | $40 | AE, D, MC, V.

Travelodge. This standard motel provides clean, comfortable accommodations for interstate travelers. In-room data ports, some microwaves, some refrigerators, cable TV. Laundry facilities. Business services. | 1325 U.S. 72 east | 256/233–1446 or 800/578–7878 | fax 256/233–1454 | www.travelodge.com | 59 rooms | $37–$75 | AE, D, DC, MC, V.

ATMORE

MAP 3, C8

(Nearby town also listed: Mobile)

Founded in 1866 as a supply stop along the Mobile and Great Northern railroads, the city was a thriving sawmill town that was first named Williams Station. It was renamed Atmore in 1897 in honor of Charles Pawson Atmore, the general ticket agent for the Louisville–Nashville railroad. The city retains a small-town, rural style of living. Area highlights include the Poarch Creek Indian Reservation and the Claude D. Kelley State Park.

Information: Atmore Area Chamber of Commerce | 501 S. Pensacola Ave., Atmore 36502 | 334/368–3305 | fax 334/368–0800 | commerce@frontiernet.net | www.frontiernet.net/~commerce.

Attractions

Claude D. Kelley State Park. This state park has a large lake for fishing and swimming, camp sites, picnic and play areas, vacation cottages, and hiking trails. It has two family cottages and a group pavilion popular for family reunions. | 580 H. Kyle Rd. | 334/862–2511 | fax 334/862–2511 | $1 | Daily 7–dark.

Creek Bingo Palace. The Poarch Creek Native Americans are part of the original Creek Nation, and have lived together for nearly 150 years. The Poarch Creek Tribe is the only federally recognized tribe in the state of Alabama. The Palace is a high-stakes bingo casino. Also within the complex are the Creek Smoke Shop and Palace Printing. | 120 Poarch Rd. | 800/826–9121 or 334/368–8007 | cbingo@frontiernet.net | $5 | Weekends 1–10:30, Mon. 5–10:30.

ON THE CALENDAR

OCT.: *Williams Station Day.* A regional festival, with fine arts and crafts, entertainment, logging demonstrations, food, and train displays, celebrates Atmore's railroad and sawmill heritage. | 334/368–3305.

Dining

Gerlach's. Cajun. Built in 1930, this downtown Atmore restaurant is one of the fancier places in town. Inside the two-story building are huge bay windows, exposed brick walls, tiled floors, bouquets of fresh flowers, and linen tablecloths. Try the "citified" green tomatoes over smoked gouda grits with shrimp sauce, Gerlach's Crab Cakes with piquant sauce, or the fillet catfish pecan with Creole butter sauce. The most popular desserts are chocolate sin cake, a chocolate mousse with espresso cream, and the homemade cheesecake with raspberry frosting. | 122 S. Main St. | 334/368–2433 | $11–$16 | AE, D, DC, MC, V.

Lodging

Comfort Inn. This standard two-story hotel is convenient to Interstate 65 and near several restaurants, including a 24-hour eatery next door. Some microwaves, some refrigerators, cable TV. Pool. Business services. Some pets allowed (fee). | 198 Ted Bates Rd., Evergreen | 334/578–4701 | fax 334/578–3180 | 60 rooms | $60–$80 | AE, D, DC, MC, V.

Days Inn. Just off Interstate 65, this standard motel is within walking distance of several fast-food restaurants. Complimentary Continental breakfast. Cable TV. No-smoking rooms. Some pets allowed (fee). | Rte. 2 (Box 389), Evergreen | 334/578–2100 | fax 334/578–2100 | 40 rooms, 4 suites | $49, $59 suites | AE, D, DC, MC, V.

Royal Oaks Bed & Breakfast. This is an old French country home with a wraparound porch, surrounded by cotton and soybean fields, vast lawns, an English garden, fruit trees, free-roaming peacocks, guineas, ducks, geese, and chickens. Inside are cathedral ceilings, king-size beds, private or shared baths, and an eclectic mix of antiques and artwork from the area and the owners' frequent trips to England. It's located 5 mi north of Atmore and 6 mi from the Florida state line. A lavish full southern breakfast of bacon, eggs, grits, and fruit is included. The B&B is always open. Complimentary breakfast. Pool. | 5415 Hwy. 21 north | 334/368–8722 | mamalula@frontiernet.net | www.royal-oaks.homepage.com | 2 rooms | $75 | No credit cards.

AUBURN

MAP 3, E5

(Nearby towns also listed: Opelika, Tuskegee)

Many fine examples of period architecture line the streets of this trading and university town in the southeastern corner of the Piedmont plateau. Best known as the home of Auburn University, Auburn got its nickname "the Plains" from the Oliver Goldsmith poem, "The Deserted Village," which includes the line, "Sweet Auburn, loveliest village on the plain."

The Auburn University campus has several interesting buildings, and nearby are Surfside Water Park and Chewacla State Park. Auburn/Opelika has two 18-hole courses and an 18-hole par three course, all links in the state's Robert Trent Jones Golf Trail of public courses.

Information: Auburn–Opelika Convention and Visitors Bureau | 714 E. Glenn Ave., Auburn 36830 | 334/887–8747 or 800/321–8880. | fax 334/821–5500 | maria@auburn-opelika.com | www.auburn-opelika.com.

Attractions

Auburn University. Chartered in 1856, the university is noted for its programs in engineering, agriculture, veterinary medicine, architecture, pharmacy, and business. Since World War II, the university's multimillion-dollar physical complex in Auburn has grown to 215 buildings on some 2,000 acres, plus its Montgomery campus. As Alabama's land-grant university, it is the state's largest public university, with more than 21,500 students. | College St. | 334/844–9999 | fax 334/844–9981 | www.auburn.edu | Free | Daily.

Chewacla State Park. Built during the 1930s under the Civilian Conservation Corps program, the park remains an example of superior craftsmanship and ability. One of 24 state parks in Alabama, it has a lake, unique rock formations, and a variety of trees, flowers, and wildlife. There are also picnic pavilions, a playground, a lakefront beach, trailer and tent camp sites, and five rustic cabins. You can rent rowboats, canoes, and paddleboats. | 124 Shell Toomer Pkwy. | 334/887–5621 | fax 334/821–2439 | $1 | Daily 8–dark.

Surfside Water Park. This outdoor aquatic park has a wave pool, lazy river, children's area, volleyball, four body flumes, and two speed slides. | 2780 S. College St. | 334/821–7873 | $15 | Memorial Day–Labor Day, daily 10–7.

OCT.: *Syrup Soppin' Day/Historical Fair.* Held mid- to late October each year. Museum exhibits, blacksmith shop, country cooking in black pots, weaving, spinning, gristmill demonstration, sweet potato biscuits and fritters, music, and clogging. Cane syrup is made on site using mule-drawn presses to grind the cane. | 1109 E. Glenn Ave. | 334/887–5560.

Dining

Auburn Grille. Southern. A tradition since 1936, the walls of this diner are covered with photos celebrating Auburn's football history. It's within walking distance of the university and you'll often see students studying and otherwise hanging out in the cozy booths and tables. Typical fare includes omelets, waffles, burgers, country-fried steak, pork chops, and pizza. Kids' menu. Beer and wine only. No smoking. | 104 N. College St. | 334/821–6626 | $10–$15 | AE, D, MC, V | Breakfast also available; no dinner Sun.

Noodles Italian Eatery. Italian. Known for authentic Italian food, from pasta dishes to filet mignon, the casual, relaxed atmosphere is reminiscent of an Italian trattoria. Try the Mediterranean salad and the veal rolls à la Romana. The open-air patio seats 50 and overlooks the street. Kids' menu. No smoking. | 103 N. College St. | 334/821–0349 | Reservations not accepted | $10–$15 | AE, D, DC, MC, V | Closed Sun. No lunch.

Terra Cotta Cafe. Contemporary. Serene hand-painted murals of English gardens adorn the walls of this renovated 1920s cottage. On the menu are fresh seafood dishes and nouvelle southern cuisine specialties like fried green tomatoes with chipotle sauce. Check out their martini lounge: it's clad in animal prints. There's open-air dining and live music Wednesday–Saturday. | 415 E. Magnolia Ave. | 334/821–3656 | $15–$30 | D, MC, V | Closed Sun.

Lodging

Auburn University Hotel and Conference Center. Auburn's only full-service six-story hotel is right on the university campus, just 3 mi from downtown. The redbrick, modern Georgian architecture blends right in with the campus; the light-filled lobby has hardwood floors and southern-style columns. Restaurant, bar. In-room data ports, microwaves in suites, refrigerators in suites, cable TV, in-room VCRS in suites. Pool. Gym. Business services. Some pets allowed. | 241 S. College St. | 334/821–8200 or 800/228–2876 | fax 334/826–8755 | auhotel@mail.auburn.edu | www.auhcc.com | 248 rooms, 3 suites | $49, $149 suites | AE, D, DC, MC, V.

Crenshaw Guest House. Listed on the National Register of Historic Places, this 1890 bed-and-breakfast has two buildings and is just three blocks from the Auburn University campus. Guest rooms are furnished with period antiques. Picnic area, complimentary Continental breakfast. In-room data ports, some kitchenettes, some microwaves, some refrigerators, cable TV, in-room VCRs. No smoking. | 371 N. College St. | 334/821–1131 or 800/950–1131 | fax 334/826–8123 | crenshaw-gh@mindspring.com | www.auburnalabama.com | 5 rooms, 2 suites | $65–$85 | AE, MC, V.

Hampton Inn. Located at Interstate 85 exit 51, this hotel is across the street from Chewacla State Park and the Auburn Links Golf Course. In-room data ports, cable TV. Pool. Business services. | 2430 S. College St. | 334/821–4111 | fax 334/821–2146 | www.hamptoninn.com | 104 rooms | $67–$72 | AE, D, DC, MC, V.

Heart of Auburn. A tan, stucco two-story building across from Auburn University. Restaurant, bar. Kitchenettes, some in-room hot tubs, cable TV. Pool. Pets allowed. | 333 S. College St. | 334/887–3462 or 800/843–5634 | fax 334/887–5564 | 100 rooms | $45 | AE, D, V.

Jameson Inn. The inn is next door to the Village Mall in the business district of Auburn, set off the main road. It's a white-columned, colonial-style building with views of the woods in the back, and has one- and two-bedroom suites. Callaway Gardens is 45 minutes away; Still Waters Resort is an hour away. Complimentary breakfast. In-room data ports. Pool. Gym. Laundry service. Free parking. | 1212 Mall Pkwy. | 334/502–5020 or 800/541–3268 | fax 334/502–5021 | www.jamesoninns.com | 40 rooms | $63–$159 | AE, D, DC, V.

Quality Inn University Center. A standard brick motel between Interstate 85 and downtown Auburn. Restaurant, bar, complimentary Continental breakfast. In-room data ports, microwaves and refrigerators in suites, cable TV. Pool. Business services. Some pets allowed. | 1577 S. College St. | 334/821–7001 | fax 334/821–7001 | 122 rooms | $64 | AE, D, DC, MC, V.

Super 8 Motel. This small stucco motel is in the heart of downtown Auburn, near campus. Restaurant, bar. Refrigerators, cable TV. Business services. | 129 N. College St. | 334/821–4632 | fax 334/826–3394 | www.super8.com | 21 rooms | $50–$55 | AE, D, DC, MC, V.

BESSEMER

(Nearby towns also listed: Birmingham, Tuscaloosa)

Just west of Birmingham, Bessemer owes its growth to the manufacturing and steel industries. By the 1930s, such diverse product lines as cast-iron pipe and fertilizer became the mainstay. Today the town is still industrial and also has a medical center.

The town celebrates its industrial roots with two attractions: the steel-themed VisionLand Theme Park, one of the area's most popular diversions, and the Tannehill Ironworks Historical State Park, where Birmingham's iron industry originated. Get a glimpse into pre-industrial days by visiting the Bessemer Hall of History, housed in a restored depot, and several plantation homes on the town's outskirts which date back to the 1830s.

Information: **Bessemer Area Chamber of Commerce** | 321 N. 18th St., Bessemer 35020 | 205/425–3253 or 888/423–7736 | fax 205/425–4979 | www.bessemerchamber.com.

Attractions

Bessemer Hall of History Museum. This renovated Southern Railway Terminal is now a museum with documents, photographs, 1800s furnishings and farm implements, an antique telephone display, Adolf Hitler's typewriter, and Civil War items related to the 28th Alabama Regiment. There also is a library. | Southern Railway Depot, 1905 Alabama Ave. | 205/426–1633 | Free | Tues.–Sat. 9–noon and 1–4.

Plantation Homes. Within a few miles of each other are three plantation homes, once owned by members of the same family, they include: the 1840s McAdory Plantation, which was the center of a plantation covering more than 2,000 acres; the Owen Home, dating to the 1830s; and the Sadler Plantation, which is said to be the state's finest examples of plantation architecture. | Eastern Valley Rd. (1859 Edgehill Rd., Hueytown) | 205/491–5543 | $5 | By appointment only.

Tannehill Ironworks Historical State Park. Built around reconstructed ironworks and blast furnaces that produced munitions for the Confederacy, the park has a museum, crafts demonstrations, a pioneer farm, working gristmill, country store, restaurant, and pioneer cabins. There are also walking trails, a minitrain, and the Iron and Steel Museum of Alabama. | 12632 Confederate Pkwy., McCalla | 205/477–5711 | fax 205/477–9400 | www.tannehillironworks.org | $2 | Daily 7–sunset.

VisionLand Theme Park. Opened in 1998, the complex includes a water park, children's area, dinosaur park, and thrill rides in four themed areas. Included in the 300 acres of rolling terrain is Rampage, a 3,500-ft wooden roller coaster that reaches a top speed of 56 mph through 18 crossovers and 12 turns. Steel Waters (included with park admission) is a 13-acre water park with tube slide, free-flowing waterway, interactive water structure, and children's area with slides, waterfalls, and geysers. | 5051 Prince St. | 205/481–4750 | fax 205/481–4758 | www.visionlandpark.com | $23 | Memorial Day–Labor Day, daily 10–10; Apr.–May and Sept.–Nov., weekends 10–10.

ON THE CALENDAR

JULY: *Fourth of July.* Held in Roosevelt Park in downtown Bessemer, the evening's events and entertainment include a fireworks display, games for kids, concession booths, and tables set up by local clubs offering homemade baked goods. There is also live music. The celebration starts at 5 PM. | Hwy. 150 | 888/423–7736 | Free.

Dining

Bob Sykes Bar-B-Que. Barbecue. Come as you are for some of the region's best barbecue, available for dining in, carrying out, or to go from the popular drive-through. This restaurant stays busy with customers who can't get enough of the tasty 'cue, the smoky-sweet sauce, and homemade side dishes. Known for open-pit barbecued chicken and ribs, smoked ham and turkey. | 1724 9th Ave. north | 205/426–1400 | $7–$9 | AE, D, DC, MC, V | Closed Sun.

Bright Star. Contemporary. Reputed to be the oldest restaurant in Alabama, the same Greek family has run this casual place since it was founded in 1907. Murals in the main dining room were painted in 1915 and depict the European countryside. Specials include marinated Greek beef tenderloin and fried snapper. Kids' menu. | 304 19th St. north | 205/424–9444 | $20–$25 | AE, D, DC, MC, V.

Tippi's Bakery. Café. Built in the 1920s, this bakery/café is in the downtown Bessemer historical district. The small, family-owned business is the only place in the area serving deli-style lunches, and it's always busy. The most popular item on the menu is the chicken salad sandwich, and the macadamia nut cookies are a close runner-up. Decorated to resemble an old ice-cream parlor, it's brightly colored with yellow Formica tables, red-cherry patterned curtains, and an old-style soda fountain chair. There's also outdoor sidewalk seating. | 417 19th St. north | 205/428–7437 | $5–$10 | AE, MC, V | Closed weekends.

Lodging

Ramada Inn. Just a mile away from VisionLand Amusement Park, this standard inn is also close to an outlet mall, and about 10 minutes from Legion Field. Restaurant, bar with entertainment. Cable TV. Pool, wading pool. Laundry facilities. Business services. | 1121 9th Ave. southwest | 205/424–9780 | fax 205/426–4100 | 78 rooms | $51–$125 | AE, D, DC, MC, V.

Sleep Inn. Perched on the outskirts of Bessemer, this is another standard in the chain-hotel industry. A three-story hotel, with brightly decorated rooms, facing the highway, and backing onto a wooded area. Galleria Mall, Tannehill Historical Park, Bent Brook, and golf courses are close by. Downtown is about 10 mi away. Complimentary Continental breakfast. Restaurant. In-room data ports. In-room VCRs (and movies), cable TV. Pool. Free parking. | 1259 Greenmore Dr. southeast | 205/424–0000 or 800/627–5337 | fax 205/424–1971 | 73 rooms | $49–$150 | AE, DC, MC, V.

Travelodge. This standard motel is located just half a mile from VisionLand Amusement Park at the intersection of Interstate 20 and Interstate 59. Restaurant, bar. Some refrigerators, cable TV. Pool. Laundry facilities. Business services. | 1098 9th St. | 205/424–0880 | fax 205/426–2345 | www.travelodge.com | 90 rooms in 2 buildings | $42–$60 | AE, D, MC, V.

BIRMINGHAM

(Nearby towns also listed: Bessemer, Cullman)

Founded after the Civil War in 1871, Alabama's largest city evolved from open farm-land into a steel-manufacturing center, and finally into a renowned medical center. Today, Birmingham is a leader in scientific research and medical treatment. The University of Alabama at Birmingham is the city's largest employer, and the medical center here attracts patients from around the world.

Birmingham was pivotal during the 1960s Civil Rights movement. A particularly horrid event includes a 1963 bombing that killed four little girls. That and other events are memorialized at the Birmingham Civil Rights Institute, one of the city's most visited attractions. Kelly Ingram Park, where protesters once gathered for marches and rallies, contains several poignant statues, most remembering the fire hoses and dog confrontations associated with Birmingham in the 1960s.

In sharp contrast to those days are the current lovely sites such as the Birmingham Botanical Gardens and Oak Mountain State Park, and a large and diverse public park system. A host of museums featuring everything from art and music to steel and motor sports can be found within the city limits. The city's most visible symbol is a towering statue of the mythical god of the forge, Vulcan, that stands atop Red Mountain and overlooks Birmingham in the valley below.

Birmingham is a city reborn, grown up out of the ashes of the steel industry and the scars of racial inequality. Today, the smoke stacks and blast furnaces are gone along with the air-pollution they fostered, and racial tensions have largely subsided. Birmingham is a thriving metropolis that has appealing historic areas, a number of museums, numerous parks and outdoor areas, and plenty of cultural activities.

BIRMINGHAM

INTRO
ATTRACTIONS
DINING
LODGING

Information: **Greater Birmingham Convention and Visitors Bureau** | 2200 9th Ave. north, Birmingham 35203 | 205/458–8000 or 800/458–8085 | fax 205/458–8086 | info@birminghamal.org | www.birminghamal.org.

Attractions

Alabama Jazz Hall of Fame Museum. The museum pays tribute to jazz greats with ties to the state such as Lionel Hampton, Erskine Hawkins, and Sun Ra and His Intergalactic Space Arkestray. Exhibits tell the story of jazz, from its beginnings to today. | 1631 4th Ave. north | 205/254–2731 | fax 205/254–2785 | www.jazzhall.com/jazz | Free | Tues.–Sat. 10–5, Sun. 1–5.

★ **Alabama Sports Hall of Fame Museum.** Dedicated to Alabama's greatest sports legends, this downtown museum holds original memorabilia from more than 180 members, including Coach Paul "Bear" Bryant and boxer Joe Louis. Among the exhibits are Heisman trophies, World Series trophies, awards, bowl rings, touch-screen videos, and a studio where visitors can try sportscasting. | 2150 Civic Center Blvd. and 22nd St. north | 205/323–6665 | fax 205/252–2212 | www.angelfire.com/al/sporthall | $5 | Mon.–Sat. 9–5, Sun. 1–5.

Arlington Antebellum Home and Gardens. Built in the mid-1850s, this house-museum showcases 19th-century furniture, textiles, silver, and paintings. The site is where Union troops made plans to burn the University of Alabama, some 45 mi west in Tuscaloosa. Surrounding gardens are often used for weddings, and a tearoom hosts meetings, receptions, and summer lunches. | 331 Cotton Ave. southwest | 205/780–5656 | fax 205/788–0585 | $3 | Tues.–Sat. 10–4, Sun. 1–4.

Barber Vintage Motorsports Museum. With more than 350 machines dating from 1904 to present, the collection has been called the country's largest motorcycle museum. Included are many limited-edition and one-of-a-kind sports and racing motorcycles. | 2721 5th Ave. south | 205/252–8377 | fax 205/252–8079 | $5 | Wed.–Fri. 9–3.

Birmingham Botanical Gardens. Nestled against the lower slope of Red Mountain and less than 2 mi from the city center, this 68-acre garden showcases regional plants and landscape design. The Garden Center Building and Conservatory has the largest ClearSpan greenhouse in the Southeast. There are more than a dozen gardens of differing character and plant concentrations organized as a series of "rooms" under a master landscape plan. The Japanese Garden includes an arched red bridge, and is a popular backdrop for weddings and photographs. | 2612 Lane Park Rd. | 205/879–1227 | fax 205/879–3751 | www.bbgardens.org | Free | Daily dawn–dusk.

★ **Birmingham Civil Rights Institute.** This facility chronicles the Civil Rights struggle by showcasing people and events from post–World War I racial segregation to the present-day struggle for continued racial equality. Across the street is the 16th Street Baptist Church, where four little girls died in a racially motived 1963 bombing. | 520 16th St. north | 205/328–9696 | fax 205/323–5042 | www.home.scott.net/~bcri | $5 | Tues.–Sat. 10–5, Sun. 1–5.

Birmingham–Jefferson Convention Complex. Anchoring the north end of Birmingham's city center, the complex occupies four city blocks, with a 19,000-seat coliseum, 3,000-seat concert hall, 1,000-seat theater, and a 110,000 square-ft exhibition hall. The coliseum hosts college and professional basketball, the circus, major concerts, truck pulls, ice shows, and other spectacles. The concert hall is home to the Alabama Symphony Orchestra and the occasional host of ballet, opera, Broadway musicals, and other special events. | 1 Civic Center Plaza | 205/458–8400 | fax 205/458–8437 | www.bjcc.org | Free | Daily.

Birmingham Museum of Art. The largest municipal museum in the Southeast, the downtown museum has a permanent collection of 18,000 objects dating from ancient to modern times and representing various cultures. An extraordinary multilevel outdoor sculpture garden enables art to be seen indoors and outdoors in a continuous flow. Highlights are the Asian, European, and American collections, outdoor sculpture garden, and Wedgwood collection. | 2000 8th Ave. north | 205/254–2565 | fax 205/254–2714 | www.artsbma.org | Free (except for some special exhibits) | Tues.–Sat. 10–5, Sun. noon–5.

Birmingham–Southern College. This small four-year liberal arts institution founded in 1856 is set on 188 wooded acres. The major fields of study are business administration, biology, accounting, psychology, and English. It is one of only two colleges in Alabama with a Phi Beta Kappa chapter. | 900 Arkadelphia Rd. | 205/226–4600 or 800/523–5793 | fax 205/226–4913 | www.bsc.edu | Free | Daily.

★ **Birmingham Zoo.** More than 900 rare and exotic animals, including elephants, rhinos, tigers, and cobras, make their home at the zoo. The creatures live in natural outdoor settings and indoor exhibits. At Christmastime, the zoo hosts a light display dubbed ZooLights Safari. | 2630 Cahaba Rd. | 205/879–0409 | fax 205/879–9426 | www.birminghamzoo.com | $5 | May–Aug., daily 9–7; Sept.–Apr., daily 9–5.

Kelly Ingram Park. This one-block park was the gathering site for many historic Civil Rights marches in 1963. Today, a collection of dramatic sculptures let you feel what it was like to be assaulted by police dogs and fire hoses. | 16th and 17th Sts. at 5th and 6th Aves. north | 205/328–9696 | fax 205/323–5042 | Free | Daily.

McWane Center. The center, in a restored former department store downtown, lets you take a hands-on journey into science and technology with exhibits such as Just Mice Size and ScienceQuest. An IMAX Dome theater offers dramatic cinematic action on a giant screen. | 200 19th St. north | 205/714–8300 | fax 205/714–8400 | www.mcwane.org | $11 | Weekdays 9–5, Sat. 9–6, Sun. noon–5.

Miles College. Founded in 1905, the college is a Christian Methodist Episcopal Church, historically African American. This four-year liberal arts institution is the fastest growing United Negro College Fund–affiliated school. It offers bachelor degree programs with a variety of majors like accounting, Asian Studies, business administration, chemistry, English, mathematics education, political science, and social work. Current enrollment is 1,330. | 5500 Myron Massey Blvd., Fairfield | 205/929–1000 | fax 205/929–1453 | www.miles.edu | Free | Daily.

Way Ahead

- ❏ Devise a trip budget.
- ❏ Write down the five things you want most from this trip. Keep this list handy before and during your trip.
- ❏ Book lodging and transportation.
- ❏ Arrange for pet care.
- ❏ Photocopy any important documentation (passport, driver's license, vehicle registration, and so on) you'll carry with you on your trip. Store the copies in a safe place at home.
- ❏ Review health and home-owners insurance policies to find out what they cover when you're away from home.

A Month Before

- ❏ Make restaurant reservations and buy theater and concert tickets. Visit fodors.com for links to local events and news.
- ❏ Familiarize yourself with the local language or lingo.
- ❏ Schedule a tune-up for your car.

Two Weeks Before

- ❏ Create your itinerary.
- ❏ Enjoy a book or movie set in your destination to get you in the mood.
- ❏ Prepare a packing list.
- ❏ Shop for missing essentials.
- ❏ Repair, launder, or dry-clean the clothes you will take with you.
- ❏ Replenish your supply of prescription drugs and contact lenses if necessary.

A Week Before

- ❏ Stop newspaper and mail deliveries.
- ❏ Pay bills.
- ❏ Stock up on film and batteries.
- ❏ Label your luggage.
- ❏ Finalize your packing list—always take less than you think you need.
- ❏ Pack a toiletries kit filled with travel-size essentials.
- ❏ Check tire treads.
- ❏ Write down your insurance agent's number and any other emergency numbers and take them with you.
- ❏ Get lots of sleep. You want to be well-rested and healthy for your impending trip.

A Day Before

- ❏ Collect passport, driver's license, insurance card, vehicle registration, and other documents.
- ❏ Check travel documents.
- ❏ Give a copy of your itinerary to a family member or friend.
- ❏ Check your car's fluids, lights, tire inflation, and wiper blades.
- ❏ Get packing!

During Your Trip

- ❏ Keep a journal/scrapbook as a personal souvenir.
- ❏ Spend time with locals.
- ❏ Take time to explore. Don't plan too much. Let yourself get lost and use your Fodor's guide to get back on track.

Oak Mountain State Park. With landscape features ranging from valleys to rocky ridges, the 9,940-acre park includes modern and primitive campsites, family cottages, a lake with marina, a picnic area, and tennis courts. Adding to the attractions are an 18-hole golf course, demonstration farm, horseback riding stable, swimming, campsites, cabins, picnic shelters, fishing, and biking and hiking trails. | 200 Terrace Dr., Pelham | 205/620–2524 or 800/252–7275 | fax 205/620–2531 | $2 | Summer, daily 7–8; winter, daily 7 AM–6 PM.

Rickwood Caverns State Park. Alabama's only caving state park has an underground "miracle mile" with passages and lighted rooms, accented with thousands of sparkling white limestone formations. The caverns were water-formed more than 260 million years ago. The park has campsites, swimming pool, picnic areas, carpet golf, miniature train ride, game machines, snack bar, hiking trails, and a playground. | 370 Rickwood Park Rd., Warrior | 205/647–9692 | fax 205/647–9692 | www.bham.net/rickwood/index.html | Park $1, cave $7.50, pool $2.50 | Cave, Memorial Day–Labor Day, daily dawn–dusk; Labor Day–Oct., weekends dawn–dusk. Park, daily dawn–dusk.

Ruffner Mountain Nature Center. See a unique view of Birmingham's skyline from this 1,000-acre nature preserve. Just 8 mi from downtown, it features native plants and animals, geological formations, free-flowing springs, and it spotlights the area's ore-mining heritage. A visitor center has educational exhibits on the mountain's natural and human history. More than 7 mi of hiking trails, ranging from $\frac{1}{2}$ to 5 mi, lead through the southern foothills of the Appalachians and have strategically placed benches for resting. | 1214 81st St. south | 205/833–8264 | fax 205/836–3960 | www.bham.net/ruffner | Free | Tues.–Sat. 9–5, Mon. 1–5.

Samford University. Originally Howard College, the university was founded by Baptists in 1841 in Perry County and moved to its current site in 1957. About 6 mi from downtown Birmingham, the 200-acre campus has 50 Georgian Colonial–style buildings. This Christian university enrolls more than 4,500 men and women and offers 24 degree programs and more than 80 majors. | 800 Lakeshore Dr. | 205/870–2807 or 800/888–7218 | fax 205/870–2654 | www.samford.edu | Free | Daily.

16th Street Baptist Church. The church was the site of a 1963 bombing that killed four little girls attending Sunday school. The event attracted international attention to the South's Civil Rights movement. | 6th Ave. north and 16th St. north | 205/251–9402 | Free | Tues.–Fri. 10–4, Sat. by appointment.

Sloss Furnaces National Historic Landmark. Once a place of fire, smoke, and steam, the landmark now stands as a serene but potent symbol of Birmingham's industrial history. For almost 90 years, the giant furnaces of the Sloss-Sheffield Steel and Iron Company produced pig iron that fed the city's foundries and steel mills. When the furnaces closed in 1971, a band of residents joined forces to save the web of pipes and tall smokestacks. Today, the 32-acre city-operated museum is open for self-guided tours and is a center for the creation and exhibit of metal art. On special occasions, former workers guide tours. Exhibits are held regularly in the museum's visitor center. | 20 32nd St. north | 205/324–1911 | fax 205/324–6578 | Free | Tues.–Sat. 10–4, Sun. noon–4.

Southern Museum of Flight. This museum holds aviation artifacts including the first Delta Airlines plane, World War II training planes, and restored aircraft. | 4343 73rd St. north | 205/833–8226 | fax 205/836–2439 | $3 | Tues.–Sat. 9:30–4:30, Sun 1–4:30.

University of Alabama at Birmingham. UAB is a 30-year-old comprehensive, urban university and medical center encompassing 75 city blocks and has a student enrollment approaching 16,000. It is the only Alabama university to earn top ranking in the Carnegie Foundation's classification of American colleges and universities—placing it in the "Research I" grouping with Duke, Harvard, and Johns Hopkins. The school is among the largest employers in the state (just behind governmental agencies) with approximately 16,000 employees and an annual budget of almost $1.2 billion. | 619 19th St. S | 205/934–4011 | fax 205/975–6339 | www.uab.edu | Free | Weekdays.

Vulcan Park. This park atop Red Mountain, provides a panoramic view of Birmingham and a close-up encounter with the 55-ft-tall statue of Vulcan, the Roman god of fire and the forge. The statue was created for the 1904 World's Fair in St. Louis to represent the city's ties to iron making. The base of this now-rusting monument, which is the world's tallest cast-iron statue, is an enclosed observation deck. There's also a circular stairway inside for the hardy, as well as an elevator. Bring a lunch to enjoy at picnic tables afterward. | Valley Ave. at U.S. 31S | 205/328–6198 | $1 | Daily 8 AM–10:30 PM.

ON THE CALENDAR
APR.: *Birmingham International Festival.* The country's oldest and most comprehensive arts festival is a tribute to world cultures. | Various venues and Linn Park | 205/252–7652.
JUNE: *City Stages.* This major downtown music and heritage festival features local and national musicians on multiple stages; kids' activities. | Linn Park | 205/251–1272.
OCT.: *Alabama State Fair.* The fair attracts nationally known performers, and features farm animals, midway with rides, games, and food. | 205/786–8100.
NOV.: *National Veterans Day Parade.* The nation's oldest Veterans Day parade winds through downtown Birmingham. | 205/254–2456.
DEC.: *Christmas in Arlington.* Individuals in Victorian dress lead tours of antebellum homes. | 205/780–5656.

Dining
★ **Arman's at Park Lane.** Italian. You'd never guess that this spacious restaurant with crisp white tablecloths and gleaming hardwood floors was once a grocery store. Thoroughly transformed with a hand-carved antique bar (flown in from Chicago), Arman's is reputed to be among the most romantic restaurants in Birmingham. The French-influenced Italian entrées include grilled swordfish, steaks, beef tenderloin, and pastas, as well as seasonal specialties such as buffalo. Open-air dining. Live jazz Wednesday and Friday nights. | 2117 Cahaba Rd., Mountain Brook | 205/871–5551 | Reservations essential Fri., Sat. | $23–$49 | AE, DC, MC, V | Closed Sun. No lunch.

Azalea. Eclectic. The inventive menu at this casual upscale restaurant includes such creative combinations as pond-raised, grain-fed catfish stuffed with ginger and lightly fried in rice flour, served with black bean chile soy sauce and wasabi, and, for extra flair, it's prepared right at your table. The cigar bar is a great gathering spot for aficionados and the only place where smoking is allowed. Sit indoors at booths or tables in the dimly lit dining room or enjoy your meal in the open-air courtyard. | 1218 20th St. south | 205/933–8600 | $25–$35 | AE, MC, V | No lunch weekends.

Bombay Café. Seafood. Housed in a former theater built in 1920, this unique restaurant boasts 30-ft ceilings, an original marble fireplace, and dramatic art by local artist Arthur Price. The creative menu changes daily and includes seafood, steak, veal, and chicken. Popular dishes include soft-shell crab appetizer, grilled yellowfin tuna with butter pecan sauce, and rack of lamb with crispy onion rings. The Canteen is open for lunch and dinner and offers cigars and martinis as well as a menu of sandwiches, salads, and pizzas. | 2839 7th Ave. south | 205/322–1930 | $27–$40 | AE, DC, MC, V | Closed Sun. No lunch.

Bottega. Mediterranean. Birmingham's celebrated chef Frank Stitt's second restaurant is housed in a beautiful Palladian limestone building with high ceilings and a dramatic mezzanine that overlooks the main dining room. This formal restaurant is open for dinner only. Signature dishes include risotto, chicken scaloppine, Parmesan souffle, seafood, game, and homemade pasta. Open-air dining on a patio surrounded by greenery. | 2240 Highland Ave. | 205/939–1000 | Reservations essential | Jacket required | $27–$45 | AE, MC, V | Closed Sun. No lunch.

Café Bottega. Mediterranean. This casual restaurant features wonderful Mediterranean dishes, many cooked in a wood-burning oven. The casual room has high ceilings and the walls are adorned with lively art. Known for creative salads, sandwiches, and pasta dishes.

Open-air dining. | 2240 Highland Ave. | 205/939–1000 | Reservations not accepted | $13–$28 | AE, MC, V | Closed Sun.

Chez Lulu and Continental Bakery. French. This place is a funky, kitschy offspring of the French bakery next door and features mismatched furniture, twinkling lights, and tables made by a local artist. Lulu's includes vegetarian cuisine among its simple, French country fare and meals are served with freshly baked breads. Try the peasant garlic soup and flaky homemade tarts. Open-air dining on street. Sunday brunch. Wine and beer only. No smoking. | 1909 Cahaba Rd. | 205/870–7011 | $11–$24 | MC, V | No dinner Mon.

Cobb Lane. French. By day, this quaint restaurant hasn't changed much since it was established as a tearoom in 1948; its chicken divan, chicken supreme, and chicken salad plate are still major crowd pleasers. At night, the cuisine becomes more sophisticated with selections like bay scallop gratin, and the setting more romantic, with a candlelit cobblestone patio and two fountains providing soothing sounds. Open-air dining. Live music Saturday nights. | 1 Cobb La. | 205/933–0462 | $20–$30 | AE, D, MC, V | Closed Sun. No dinner Mon.

Connie Kanakis' Café. Mediterranean. Named for its owner, longtime Greek restaurateur Connie Kanakis, this elegant yet relaxed restaurant is a great place to linger over dinner. Comfortable chairs, soothing colors, and excellent service (from the tuxedo-clad waitstaff) are conducive to leisurely dining. Try snapper parmigiana, a snapper fillet broiled in lemon-butter sauce and topped with Italian dressing, scallions, and Parmesan cheese. Kids' menu. | 3423 Colonnade Pkwy. | 205/967–5775 | $23–$46 | AE, D, DC, MC, V | Closed Sun. No lunch Sat.

Formosa. Chinese. Enjoy Chinese specialties from a window seat overlooking a lovely garden and sparkling fountain. Known for hot and sour soup, Mongolian beef, sesame chicken. | 2109 Lorna Ridge La., Hoover | 205/979–6684 | $11–$17 | AE, D, MC, V.

★ **Highlands Bar and Grill.** Contemporary. James Beard Foundation Award–winning Chef Frank Stitt prides himself on uniting southern ingredients with French techniques and a Provençal influence. The result is creative, rustic, French-influenced southern cuisine that makes his bistro-style restaurant one of the most celebrated in the region. Although the menu changes frequently, the baked grits is Highlands' signature dish. The waiting list can be up to a month long. Smoking allowed only in bar. | 2011 11th Ave. south | 205/939–1400 | Reservations essential | Jacket required | $32–$41 | AE, MC, V | Closed Sun., Mon. No lunch.

Hot and Hot Fish Club. Eclectic. Chef Christopher Hastings named his restaurant in honor of the epicurean gentleman's club his great-great-grandfather belonged to in South Carolina—a place where sitting down together to eat a meal was truly a celebration. In that spirit, the chef has created a menu of eclectic cuisine based on regional ingredients. Try the Hot and Hot shrimp and grits with Parma ham and thyme. There is a small patio with four tables for open-air dining (April–November). Live jazz Wednesday at 8:30 PM. | 2180 11th Ct. south | 205/933–5474 | $22–$41 | AE, D, DC, MC, V | Closed Sun., Mon. No lunch.

Irondale Café Inc., The Original Whistle Stop. Southern. *Fried Green Tomatoes* fans—and anyone who loves down-home, southern cooking—must try the café that inspired Fannie Flagg to write her book, which became the award-winning movie. Check out the memorabilia from the filming of the movie and photos from the early days of the Irondale Cafe, which was operated by Flagg's great aunt, Bess Fortenberry, from 1932 to 1972. You can also purchase coffee mugs, T-shirts, cookbooks, and more at the souvenir bar. Try the fried green tomatoes and the skinless fried chicken. À la carte, cafeteria service. | 1906 1st Ave. north, Irondale | 205/956–5258 | $5–$8 | D, MC, V | Closed Sat. No dinner.

La Paree. Greek. Though its name may hint at a French menu, this landmark restaurant, opened in 1944, actually features a tasty combination of Greek and American dishes. Served to a mostly professional downtown lunch crowd, it's also a great place for a quick breakfast. Try the Greek chicken, broiled with a special combination of spices and served with Greek potatoes and two vegetables. Kids' menu. | 2013 5th Ave. north | 205/251–5936 | $4–$8 | MC, V | Breakfast also available; closed weekends; no dinner.

Nabeel's. Mediterranean. This cozy neighborhood eatery and adjacent market is run by a husband-and-wife team. This Greek and Italian couple serve delicious and affordable food. Try the spanakopita (spinach pie), with spinach and feta cheese baked inside flaky phyllo dough. Kids' menu. Beer and wine only. | 1706 Oxmoor Rd., Homewood | 205/879–9292 | $5–$22 | AE, MC, V | Breakfast also available; closed Sun.

Tavern on the Summit. American. Warm wood paneling, gas lights, and intimate booths create a comfortable atmosphere at this Summit Mall restaurant that is known for steaks, seafood, and salad. All salad dressings and sauces are homemade on the premises. Try the spinach-and-artichoke dip served in fresh boule bread. Open-air dining under a large canopy. Live music Monday–Saturday. | 225 Summit Blvd. | 205/298–1222 | Reservations not accepted | $19–$34 | AE, D, MC, V.

The Veranda. Southern. Owner-chef Darryl Borden describes his cuisine as "southern Continental with Creole overtones," for example, buttermilk fried chicken with white cheddar grits and red-basil biscuits. There are eight elegant dining rooms in this renovated 1909 home. Check out the interesting limestone bar designed by local artist Arthur Price. | 2220 Highland Ave. | 205/933–1200 | $17–$40 | AE, DC, MC, V | Closed Sun.

Winston's. Continental. In the beautiful Wynfrey Hotel, Winston's is an elegant, traditional restaurant with a reputation for impeccable service. Try the grilled rainbow trout, topped with crabmeat, mushrooms, and an herb-butter sauce. | 1000 Riverchase Galleria | 205/987–1600 | Reservations essential | $26–$45 | AE, D, DC, MC, V | Closed Sun. No lunch.

BIRMINGHAM

INTRO
ATTRACTIONS
DINING
LODGING

Lodging

AmeriSuites Birmingham Inverness. This hotel is in the center of the Inverness Business District, a suburb 15 mi from downtown Birmingham. You can walk to a number of restaurants, but the main attractions nearby are the Birmingham Zoo and Botanical Gardens (6 mi), and VisionLand Theme Park (16 mi). The Birmingham International Airport is 14 mi away. Complimentary Continental breakfast. In-room data ports, cable TV with VCR. Kitchenette with microwave, refrigerator. Pool. Exercise equipment. Video games. Laundry service. Business services. Free parking. Pets allowed. | 4686 Hwy. 280 east | 205/995–9242 or 800/833–1516 | fax 205/995–2226 | www.amerisuites.com | 128 rooms | $59–$195 | AE, D, DC, MC.

AmeriSuites Birmingham Riverchase. This all-suites six-story building in Riverchase is 15 mi from downtown Birmingham, 16 mi from the airport, and just two blocks from Riverchase Galleria Mall (the largest mall in the Southeast). Complimentary Continental breakfast. In-room data ports, kitchenettes, microwaves, refrigerators, cable TV with VCR. Pool. Exercise equipment. Video games. Laundry service. Business services. Free parking. Pets allowed. | 2980 Hwy. 150 | 205/988–8444 or 800/833–1516 | fax 205/988–8407 | 128 rooms | $59–$195 | AE, D, DC, MC, V.

Baymont Inn and Suites. About 16 mi southeast of downtown Birmingham, this standard motel is near Riverchase Galleria and Brookwood Mall. Complimentary Continental breakfast. In-room data ports, microwaves and refrigerators in suites, cable TV. | 513 Cahaba Park Circle, Inverness | 205/995–9990 | fax 205/995–0563 | www.baymontinns.com | 102 rooms | $54 | AE, D, DC, MC, V.

Candlewood Suites Birmingham. On a hill overlooking the town about 10 mi from downtown Birmingham, the hotel is surrounded by lawns and sits between another hotel and a retirement village. There are no restaurants within walking distance, but the rooms are equipped for long-term stays, as well as just for weekends. There is a convenience store on property. Kitchenettes. In-room data ports. Exercise equipment. Laundry facilities. | 600 Corporate Ridge Dr. | 205/991–0272 or 888/226–3539 | fax 205/991–1549 | www.candlewoodsuites.com | 98 rooms | $75 | AE, D, DC, MC, V.

Clarion Hotel-Airport. This hotel is conveniently located about three minutes from Birmingham International Airport. Restaurant, bar, room service. In-room data ports, cable

TV. Pool. Gym. Laundry service. Business services, airport shuttle. | 5216 Airport Hwy. | 205/591–7900 | fax 205/592–6476 | 195 rooms | $79 | AE, D, DC, MC, V.

Comfort Inn. This standard motel is located a half block from Interstate 65 in Homewood. Complimentary Continental breakfast. In-room data ports, some microwaves, some refrigerators, cable TV. Pool. Gym. Business services. | 195 Oxmoor Rd., Homewood | 205/941–0990 | fax 205/941–1527 | 155 rooms | $69–$99 | AE, D, DC, MC, V.

Courtyard by Marriott. Centrally located hotel across from Brookwood Mall and close to Samford University, the zoo, and downtown. Restaurant, bar. In-room data ports, microwaves and refrigerators in suites, cable TV. Pool. Hot tub. Gym. Laundry facilities. Business services. | 500 Shades Creek Pkwy., Homewood | 205/879–0400 | fax 205/879–6324 | www.marriott.com | 140 rooms, 14 suites in 3 buildings | $59–$109, $85–$109 suites | AE, D, DC, MC, V.

Days Inn. You'll find this standard motel just 1 mi south of Birmingham International Airport on Airport Boulevard. Complimentary Continental breakfast. Cable TV. Pool. Gym. Playground. Business services, airport shuttle. Some pets allowed. | 5101 Airport Blvd. | 205/592–6110 | fax 205/591–5623 | 138 rooms | $62 | AE, D, DC, MC, V.

Embassy Suites. Each room in this hotel has a separate living-room area and either two queen-size or one king-size bed. The hotel is at the intersection of U.S. 31 and U.S. 280, near the Vulcan statue, the Birmingham Botanical Gardens, and the zoo, and just minutes from Brookwood Mall. Restaurant, bar, complimentary breakfast. In-room data ports, microwaves, refrigerators, cable TV. Pool. Hot tub, sauna. Business services, airport shuttle. | 2300 Woodcrest Pl. | 205/879–7400 | fax 205/870–4523 | www.embassy-suites.com | 242 rooms | $109–$300 | AE, D, DC, MC, V.

Fairfield Inn by Marriott. Conveniently located near Interstate 65, this standard inn is about 5 mi from Brookwood Mall, Samford University, and the University of Alabama at Birmingham. Complimentary Continental breakfast. In-room data ports, cable TV. Laundry service. Business services. | 155 Vulcan Rd., Homewood | 205/945–9600 | fax 205/945–9600 | 132 rooms | $55 | AE, D, DC, MC, V.

Hampton Inn Birmingham East. This standard inn is about 2 mi from Interstate 20 and approximately 3 mi from Interstates 59/459, it's also near several restaurants. Complimentary Continental breakfast. In-room data ports, cable TV. Pool. Laundry service. Business services. | 3910 Kilgore Memorial Dr. | 205/956–4100 | fax 205/956–0906 | www.hamptoninn.com | 57 rooms | $74 | AE, D, DC, MC, V.

Hampton Inn Birmingham–Mountain Brook. In the business district, this standard inn is just minutes from three malls. Complimentary Continental breakfast. In-room data ports, cable TV. Pool. Laundry service. Business services. | 2731 U.S. 280, Mountain Brook | 205/870–7822 | fax 205/871–7610 | www.hamptoninn.com | 30 rooms | $82 | AE, D, DC, MC, V.

Hampton Inn–Colonnade. Most rooms in this inn just a half mile from the Summit mall have a good view of the landscaped grounds. It's also close to specialty shops and walking distance from fine restaurants. Complimentary Continental breakfast. In-room data ports, cable TV. Pool. Laundry service. Business services. | 3400 Colonnade Pkwy. | 205/967–0002 | fax 205/969–0901 | www.hamptoninn.com | 133 rooms | $84 | AE, D, DC, MC, V.

Hawthorn Suites. Located on 17½ peaceful acres, this lushly landscaped property is only a 10-minute drive from the airport. Restaurant, bar, complimentary buffet breakfast, room service. In-room data ports, kitchenettes, cable TV. Pool. Gym. Laundry facilities, laundry service. Business services, airport shuttle. Some pets allowed (fee). | 5320 Beacon Dr., Irondale | 205/951–1200 or 800/579–5464 | fax 205/951–1692 | 134 suites in 10 buildings | $65–$85 | AE, D, DC, MC, V.

Historic Redmont Hotel. Built in the 1920s, Birmingham's oldest-operating hotel reflects its Jazz Age heritage. A few years back, the building underwent a multimillion-dollar renovation. Restaurant, bar, room service. In-room data ports, refrigerators, cable TV. Laundry service. Business services, airport shuttle. Some pets allowed. | 2101 5th Ave. north | 205/324–2101 | fax 205/324–0610 | 112 rooms | $79 | AE, D, DC, MC, V.

Hojo Inn. This inn is in a two-story building set off the road about 6 mi downtown. There are a number of restaurants within walking distance, and also nearby are a comedy club, the Botanical Gardens, Birmingham Zoo, a mall, and Samford University. Complimentary Continental breakfast. Cable TV. Pool. Exercise equipment. Laundry services. Pets allowed. | 275 Oxmoor Rd. | 205/942–0919 or 800/406–1411 | fax 205/942–1679 | www.hojo.com | 100 rooms | $39–$69 | AE, D, DC, MC, V.

Holiday Inn Airport. This recently renovated hotel is conveniently located just ³/₄ mi from Birmingham International Airport. Restaurant, bar, room service. In-room data ports, cable TV. Pool. Gym. Laundry service. Business services, airport shuttle. Some pets allowed (deposit). | 5000 10th Ave. north | 205/591–6900 | fax 205/591–2093 | 226 rooms | $98 | AE, D, DC, MC, V.

Holiday Inn–Galleria South on the Lake. This three-story brick hotel is about 3 mi from the Galleria Mall. There is peaceful lake on the property where you are welcome to relax and fish. Restaurant, bar, picnic area, room service. In-room data ports, cable TV. Pool. Hot tub. Gym, volleyball. Laundry facilities. Business services. Some pets allowed (deposit). | 1548 Montgomery Hwy. | 205/822–4350 | fax 205/822–0350 | www.basshotels.com | 166 rooms in 2 buildings | $79 | AE, D, DC, MC, V.

La Quinta Motor Inn. This standard inn is about 4 mi west of downtown Birmingham, just a mile from Legion Field. Complimentary Continental breakfast. In-room data ports, some microwaves, some refrigerators, cable TV. Pool. Laundry facilities. Business services. Some pets allowed. | 905 11th Ct. west | 205/324–4510 | fax 205/252–7972 | 106 rooms | $62 | AE, D, DC, MC, V.

Motel Birmingham. Just off Interstate 20, this motel is five minutes from the Birmingham International Airport, 2 mi from the Birmingham Race Course, and 6 mi from the Civil Rights District. Complimentary Continental breakfast. Some kitchenettes, cable TV. Pool. Playground. Laundry service. Business services, airport shuttle. Some pets allowed. | 7905 Crestwood Blvd. | 205/956–4440 or 800/338–9275 | fax 205/956–3011 | 242 rooms, 12 suites in 4 buildings | $61, $137 suites | AE, D, DC, MC, V.

Mountain Brook Inn. This comfortable, spacious inn is located in the exclusive Mountain Brook residential area, close to Brookwood Village Mall and a variety of shops and restaurants. Rooms range from bi-level suites to patio-level, poolside accommodations. Restaurant, bar (with entertainment). In-room data ports, no-smoking rooms and floors, cable TV. Pool. Laundry service. Business services, airport shuttle. Some pets allowed. | 2800 U.S. 280 south, Mountain Brook | 205/870–3100 or 800/523–7771 | fax 205/414–2128 | www.mountainbrookinn.com | 162 rooms, 12 suites | $115 | AE, D, DC, MC, V.

Pickwick Hotel and Conference Center. This hotel with Art Deco furnishings is centrally located in the heart of the medical district and the historic Five Points South area. Complimentary Continental breakfast. In-room data ports, kitchenettes in suites, cable TV. Beauty salon. Business services, airport shuttle. Some pets allowed (fee). | 1023 20th St. south | 205/933–9555 or 800/255–7304 | fax 205/933–6918 | 63 rooms, 28 suites | $99, $139 suites | AE, DC, MC, V.

Radisson. This downtown-area hotel is in the Five Points South Historic District, and within walking distance from restaurants and pubs. Restaurant, bar, room service. In-room data ports, cable TV. Pool. Beauty salon, sauna. Gym. Laundry service. Business services, airport shuttle. | 808 S. 20th St. | 205/933–9000 | fax 205/933–0920 | www.radisson.com | 298 rooms, 3 suites | $95–$110 | AE, D, DC, MC, V.

Red Roof Inn. This sprawling three-story building is fronted by trees and built on top of a hill overlooking the town. Within a 10-mi radius are golf courses, downtown, Birmingham International Airport, Birmingham Zoo, Galleria Mall, and the Alabama State Fairgrounds. VisionLand Theme Park is about 19 mi away. There's complimentary morning coffee and

newspaper. Cable TV. Video games. Free parking. Pets allowed. | 151 Vulcan Rd. | 205/942–9414 or 800/843–7663 | fax 205/942–9499 | www.redroof.com | 96 rooms | $45–$50 | AE, D, DC, MC, V.

Residence Inn by Marriott. This extended-stay hotel offers all the comforts of home and is located 2 mi from the Summit Mall. Complimentary Continental breakfast. In-room data ports, kitchenettes, cable TV. Pool. Hot tub. Basketball, gym, volleyball. Laundry facilities. Business services. Some pets allowed (fee). | 3 Greenhill Pkwy., Inverness | 205/991–8686 | fax 205/991–8729 | www.marriott.com | 128 suites in 16 buildings | $85 | AE, D, DC, MC, V.

Rime Garden Suites. The hotel complex consists of 16 buildings on landscaped grounds. Each room has a balcony or patio. Adjacent to the property are an outdoor track, playground, and tennis court. It's about 10 mi from the city center and 2 mi from Birmingham International Airport. There are three malls nearby. Restaurant, bar, complimentary Continental breakfast. Kitchenettes, cable TV. Pool. Laundry service. Airport shuttle, free parking. | 5320 Beacon Dr. | 205/951–1200 or 800/772–7463 | fax 205/951–1692 | www.bestwestern.com | 128 rooms | $99 | AE, D, DC, MC, V.

Sheraton Birmingham. Located in the heart of downtown, this 17-story hotel is connected to the Birmingham-Jefferson Convention Complex (which includes the Civic Center, arena, and concert hall) and is within walking distance from the Birmingham Museum of Art. 2 restaurants, bar, room service. In-room data ports, cable TV. Pool. Hot tub, sauna, steam room. Laundry service. Business services, airport shuttle. | 2101 Civic Center Blvd. | 205/324–5000 | fax 205/307–3045 | www.sheraton.com/birmingham | 770 rooms | $115–$170 | AE, D, DC, MC, V.

Sheraton-Perimeter Park South, Birmingham. In the dynamic Perimeter Park area in southern Birmingham, this hotel is next to the Summit and the Colonnade malls, which offer abundant shopping, dining, and entertainment options. Restaurant, bar, room service. In-room data ports, microwaves in suites, refrigerators in suites, cable TV. Pool. Gym. Laundry service. Business services, airport shuttle. | 8 Perimeter Dr. | 205/967–2700 | fax 205/972–8603 | www.sheraton.com | 205 rooms | $79–$175 | AE, D, DC, MC, V.

★ **The Tutwiler.** One of downtown's finest hotels, the historic Tutwiler was the site of actress Tallulah Bankhead's post-wedding party in the 1920s. In the heart of Birmingham, the hotel is next to the Birmingham Museum of Art and Linn Park. Restaurant, bar, room service. In-room data ports, cable TV. Laundry service. Business services, airport shuttle. | 2021 Park Pl. | 205/322–2100 | fax 205/325–1183 | www.wyndham.com/tutwiler | 147 rooms, 52 suites | $134–$174, $144–$260 suites | AE, D, DC, MC, V.

Twin Pines Resort and Conference Center. A 200-acre retreat nestled among trees and mountains, 30 mi southeast of Birmingham, the resort is on the edge of a 46-acre private lake. Each room has a private outdoor deck with rocking chairs and a view of the lake. Log house suites come with complete kitchen, sitting area, and double beds. Activities include fishing, hiking, tennis, volleyball, canoeing, and shuffleboard. There is also a 45-seat thatched-roof pontoon boat available for hire. Restaurant. Lake. Tennis. Free parking. | 1200 Twin Pines Rd. | 205/672–7575 | fax 205/672–7575 | www.twinpinesresort.com | 48 rooms | $110 | AE, D, MC, V.

Wynfrey at Riverchase Galleria. The grand Italian marble lobby sets the tone for this award-winning luxury hotel that prides itself on southern hospitality. The Wynfrey is attached to the Riverchase Galleria, a mall with 250 stores, 20 restaurants, and 10 movie theaters. 3 restaurants (see Winston's, *above*), bar with entertainment, room service. In-room data ports, no-smoking rooms and floors, cable TV. Pool. Gym. Business services, airport shuttle. | 1000 Riverchase Galleria | 205/987–1600 or 800/476–7006 | fax 205/988–4597 | www.wynfrey.com | 329 rooms, 12 suites | $120, $219 suites | AE, D, DC, MC, V.

BOAZ

(Nearby town also listed: Gadsden)

In late 1878, rich soil, abundant timber, and wild game lured a few dozen people from Butts County, Georgia, to the area on the Sand Mountain Plateau. The transplants pitched their tents and began building homes in the area known now as Boaz. In 1896, the town was incorporated and named for the Biblical character in the Book of Ruth. Today, the rural area surrounding Boaz is densely populated, and the town is home to one of the nation's largest collections of shopping outlet stores.

Information: Boaz Chamber of Commerce | 306 W. Main Ave, Box 563, Boaz 35957 | 256/593–8154 or 800/746–7262 | fax 256/593–1233 | boazchamber@ccconnection.com | www.boazalabama.com. **Marshall County Convention and Visitors Bureau** | Box 711, Guntersville 35976 | 256/582–7015 or 800/582–6282 | fax 256/582–3682 | mccvb@mind-spring.com | www.marshallcountycvb.com.

Attractions

Snead State Community College. The campus has been a major cornerstone in Boaz since 1898. Set on 18 rural acres, many of the buildings on campus were built in the early 1900s and are interspersed among the wooded groves on the property. The school originated in 1898 when the Boaz Seminary was authorized by the Methodist Episcopal Church. There is a museum on campus, as well as a Gospel Music gallery. | 220 N. Walnut St. | 256/593–5120 | www.snead.cc.al.us | Free.

ON THE CALENDAR

OCT.: *Annual Boaz Harvest Festival and Native American Pow Wow.* This festival began in 1964, and is the town's largest annual event. There are plenty of arts and crafts for sale and on display, antique car shows, entertainment, shopping, dance performances, live music, and a Miss Harvest Festival Pageant. One of the highlights is the Native American Pow Wow. There are indigenous crafts, performance, story-telling and foods. The main events are held in the Boaz Downtown Mall. | 256/593–8154 | Free.

Dining

Carl's. American. Set a mile out of town, this restaurant can be seen from a long way away because Carl's celebrates Christmas all year round. Both inside and out are bedecked in Christmas trimmings. There are some 50,000 baubles hanging from the ceiling. The country-style fare includes such standards as chicken with corn bread and gravy, and country fried steak. The homemade pies include chocolate coconut, and lemon. | 345 Gold Kist St. | 256/840–5003 | $5–$16 | MC, V | Closed Mon.

Station House Grill. Cajun. In downtown Boaz, this converted cotton warehouse was originally built for the railroad in the late 1800s. The dimly lit interior is furnished with marble tables and the walls are covered with memorabilia: there's the Transportation Wall, the Boaz history wall, a wall of famous men, and a women's wall. Specialties of the house are alligator sauce piquant, jambalaya, and crawfish étouffée. Prime rib is served every Friday and Saturday night. | 101 E. Mann Ave. | 256/593–6567 | $10–$17 | AE, D, MC, V | Closed Sun.

Lodging

Albertville Jameson Inn. In Albertville, about 4 mi from Boaz, this inn is a white-columned, colonial-style, 2 story building with one- and two-bedroom suites. The inn is near Lake Guntersville and Boaz shopping, and 18 mi from the Mountain Top Flea Market. Complimentary breakfast. In-room data ports. Pool. Exercise equipment. Laundry service. Free parking. | 161 Colonial Dr. | 256/891–2600 or 800/541–3268 | fax 256/835–2133 | www.jamesoninns.com | 42 rooms | $63–$159 | AE, D, DC, V.

Boaz Bed and Breakfast Whitman-Hunt House. It's a quiet country setting for this B&B listed on the National Register of Historic Places. Designed in 1924 by architect W. L. Welton, the home has Art Deco details, a 75-ft wraparound porch, and six fireplaces. Complimentary breakfast. No TV, TV in common area. | 200 Thomas Ave. | 256/593–8031 | 6 rooms, 2 with shared bath | $45–$65 | AE.

Days Inn. This two-story standard motel is half a mile from the Boaz Outlet Center and is within walking distance of several restaurants. Bar, complimentary Continental breakfast. Cable TV. Laundry service. Business services. | 12960 U.S. 431 south | 256/593–0000 | fax 256/593–0673 | 60 rooms | $53 | AE, D, DC, MC, V.

Key West Inn. This standard motel is downtown, just across the street from the Boaz Outlet Center. Complimentary Continental breakfast. Some microwaves and refrigerators, cable TV. Business services. Some pets allowed (fee). | 10535 Rte. 168, | 256/593–0800 | fax 256/593–9100 | www.keywestinn.net | 41 rooms | $54–$59 | AE, D, DC, MC, V.

Thunderbird Inn. An ex–Best Western, this is now a privately run two-story motel in the middle of town. There are not many amenities: this is a standard "drive up" motel. Complimentary Continental breakfast. Pool. Cable TV. Pets allowed. | 751 Hwy. 431 south | 256/593–8410 | fax 256/593–8410 | 116 rooms | $43–$60 | AE, D, DC, MC, V.

CHILDERSBURG

MAP 3, D4

(Nearby towns also listed: Anniston, Birmingham, Sylacauga)

Forty miles southeast of Birmingham is Childersburg. In 1540, Spanish explorer Hernando de Soto and his men were the first Europeans to stake a claim on the area. Centuries later during World War II, a gunpowder plant turned Childersburg into a boom-town. Soon after, lumber and farming became part of its economic base. Today, however, the major industry is a paper manufacturing company: its plants are along the Coosa River on the town's western edge. The main attraction is DeSoto Caverns Park with its vast cave and outdoor activities.

Information: Childersburg Chamber of Commerce | 506 3rd St. southwest, Childersburg 35044 | 256/378–5482 | fax 256/378–5811 | wooeagle@aol.com.

Attractions

Kymulga Grist Mill Park. A gristmill is a mill used to grind corn. One of Alabama's oldest water-powered gristmills, Kymulga was built in 1864 and is still in operation and open for guided tours. Opposite the mill is a covered bridge built in the 1860s. You can hike and bike on the trails and camp in the park. | 7346 Grist Mill Rd. | 256/378–7436 | $2 | Mar.–Oct., daily 9–5.

★ **DeSoto Caverns Park.** The grounds are the site of a 2,000-year-old Native American burial ground. The vast onyx caverns were discovered in 1540 by Hernando de Soto. The cave is the setting for a spectacular laser light and sound show. Cave tours are guided. RV camping, a gift shop, shaded picnic grove with pavilions, and nine outside attractions—including a wall climb, cave crawl box, and maze—provide diversions. | 5181 DeSoto Caverns Pkwy., Childersburg | 256/378–7252 or 800/933–2283 | fax 256/378–3678 | www.cavern.com/desoto | Cave $9.99, FunPac ticket (includes tour, maze, and gem-stone mining) $13.99 | Apr.–Oct., Mon.–Sat. 9–5:30, Sun. 1–5:30; Nov.–Mar., Mon.–Sat. 9–4:30, Sun. 1–4:30.

ON THE CALENDAR

APR.: *Indian Dance Festival.* Features Native American dance, arts, crafts, and story-telling. | DeSoto Caverns Park | 256/378–7252 or 800/933–2283.
SEPT.: *Indian Fest.* Includes bluegrass, gospel, and country music performances. | DeSoto Caverns Park | 256/378–7252 or 800/933–2283.

OCT.: _Halloween Festival._ There are said to be ghosts at the mill, and this festival is one of the biggest events of the year. The Kymulga Grist Mill Park is decorated "to scare." You can go on a hayride loop around the property and over the covered bridge, as well as take a ride through the "haunted mill." There are old horror movies playing, ghost stories throughout the evening, and plenty of food available. The events start at 7 PM. | 7346 Grist Mill Rd. | 256/378–7436 | $7.

Dining
Riverside Diner. Seafood. In an old brick house, on 8 acres of land along the Coosa River, this restaurant serves southern-style fare and is especially known for its all-you-can-eat seafood buffet. Crab legs, raw oysters, stuffed shrimp, Cajun catfish, country fried steak, and desserts like banana pudding, peach and blackberry cobbler, and chocolate and lemon pies are all on the buffet. There's a model of an old schooner on display, and pictures of old sea captains all over the place. While not as popular, there is also a regular à la carte menu. | 31870 U.S. Hwy. 280 | 256/378–3489 | $7–$16 | AE, D, DC, MC, V.

Lodging
Childersburg-Days Inn. This three-story brick hotel hotel is 5 mi from downtown Childersburg. There is a steak house next door. Nearby are Desoto Caverns, the Coosa River, and the Kymulga Grist Mill. Bar, complimentary Continental breakfast. In-room data ports, microwaves, refrigerators, cable TV. Pool. Laundry service. Free parking. Pets allowed. | 33669 U.S. Hwy. 280 | 256/378–6007 | fax 256/378–3575 | 40 rooms | $39–$60 | AE, D, DC, V.

CLANTON

MAP 3, C4

(Nearby towns also listed: Birmingham, Montgomery)

Clanton, midway between Montgomery and Birmingham, calls itself the "Peach Capital of World" and you can't miss that claim. A peach-shaped water tower beckons you to the town, and billboards announce when peaches, most picked that same day, are ready. Although primarily a peach- and truck-farming community, Clanton is also a favorite stop for fishermen bound for the Coosa River and its tributaries. Area attractions include Confederate Memorial Park in nearby Mountain Creek and Old Soldiers Home, a small village that housed penniless Confederate veterans after the war, just south of town on U.S. 31.

Information: Chilton County Chamber of Commerce | 500 5th Ave. north (Box 66), Chilton 35046 | 205/755–2400 or 800/553–0493 | fax 205/755–8444 | cccoc@scott.net | www.chilton.al.us.

Attractions
Confederate Memorial Park. Site of Alabama's only home for Confederate veterans, the grounds hold two cemeteries with 313 graves, and a museum houses Civil War uniforms, weapons, and personal relics from soldiers' homes. The park has walking and driving tours, a nature trail, and picnic areas. | 437 Rte. 63, Mountain Creek | 205/755–1990 | fax 205/755–8982 | Free | Daily 9–5.

Peach Park. Right off Highway 31 south, just 4 mi south of Clanton, is this enormous outdoor fruit market. In addition to produce there is fresh-fruit ice cream, cobblers, pies and cakes, a barbecue, and a gift shop. In June there is a peach festival, with events such as a Miss Peach contest. | Hwy. 31 south | 205/755–2065 | Free | Apr.–Nov., daily 9–7.

JUNE: *Peach Festival.* Chilton County salutes its peach crop with beauty pageants, parade, and a peach auction. | 205/755–6740.

Dining

Helen's Place. American. Just three blocks from downtown Clanton, this popular restaurant is in a big, rambling clapboard house, built in 1907. All of the original woodwork has been preserved; there are pocket doors, leaded glass, a wraparound porch, and a gazebo. There are two dining rooms, an enclosed porch, outdoor eating on the deck, and a covered gazebo. The cuisine includes grilled chicken, baked fish, roasted red potatoes, and macaroni and cheese, and for dessert you can indulge in chocolate or coconut butter pies, strawberry or blueberry shortcake, banana pudding, or a selection of fruit cobblers. | 407 2nd Ave. south | 205/755–9130 | $5–$6 | No credit cards | Closed Tues., Thurs., weekends.

Lodging

Days Inn. About 3 mi from the heart of Clanton, this standard inn is near Peach Park, the Alabama Power Water Course, and fishing and recreational areas. Restaurant, bar. In-room data ports, cable TV. Pool, wading pool. Laundry service. Business services. Some pets allowed. | 2000 Holiday Inn Dr. | 205/755–0510 | fax 205/755–0510 ext. 316 | 100 rooms | $49–$60 | AE, D, DC, MC, V.

Key West Inn. This inn is just ¼ mi from the interstate, across the street from the Alabama Power Museum and Peach Park and a fruit market with gardens. Complimentary Continental breakfast. In-room data ports, some microwaves and refrigerators, cable TV. Laundry facilities. Business services. Some pets allowed (fee). | 2045 7th St. south | 205/755–8500 or 800/833–0555 | fax 205/280–0044 | www.keywestinn.net | 43 rooms | $48–$55 | AE, D, DC, MC, V.

Shoney's Inn. This hotel is 5 mi away from the center of town. It is a two-story, L-shape hotel, built around a swimming pool. Shoney's steak-house restaurant is across the street, available for breakfast, lunch, and dinner. In-room data ports. Cable TV. Pool. Free parking. Pets allowed. | 946 Lake Mitchell Rd. | 205/280–0306 or 800/222–2222 | fax 205/755–8113 | 74 rooms | $57 | AE, D, DC, MC, V.

CULLMAN

MAP 3, C2

(Nearby towns also listed: Birmingham, Decatur)

Founded by a German refugee in 1872, Cullman retains some German roots, many of which are showcased at the Cullman County Museum. Timber and coal were early industries that later gave way to the production of electrical equipment and poultry processing.

Major attractions in the area include the Ave Maria Grotto, a shrine of 125 small stone and cement miniatures and figurines that depict biblical events and religious sites. Smith Lake, with 500 mi of shoreline and 21,000 acres of clear waters, is perfect for fishing, skiing, and boating.

Information: Cullman Area Chamber of Commerce | 211 2nd Ave. northeast (Box 1104), Cullman 35056-1104 | 256/734–0454 | fax 256/737–7443 | cullman@corrcomm.net | www.cullmanchamber.org.

Attractions

Ave Maria Grotto. At Alabama's only Benedictine monastery, a quiet, Bavarian monk built a shrine that holds miniatures of well-known structures from around the world. All are made from discarded materials. His works are displayed in a 3-acre grotto. | St. Bernard Abbey, 1600 St. Bernard Dr. southeast | 256/734–4110 | fax 256/734–2925 | www.sbabbeyprep.org | $4.50 | Daily 7–5.

Clarkson Covered Bridge. Alabama's largest covered truss bridge is the site of the 1863 Battle of Hog Mountain. The 1904 bridge spans Cullman County canyon and is the centerpiece of a public park with hiking trails and picnic grounds. It's part of the National Register of Historic Places. | 305 4th Ave. northeast | 256/734–3369 | fax 256/736–2898 | www.forcullman.com | Free | Daily 8–dusk.

Cullman County Museum. The building replicates the home of the city's founder. Inside are thousands of items dating to the early 1800s. Displays include an archaeological room with Native American artifacts, a primitive room showing turn-of-the-20th-century tools used to build Cullman, a clothing store complete with garments, a Main Street exhibit, and a photo gallery detailing the city's history. | 211 2nd Ave. northeast | 256/739–1258 | fax 256/737–8782 | $2 | Mon.–Wed., Fri. 9–noon and 1–4, Thurs. 9–noon, Sun. 1:30–4:30.

Double Springs. During the Civil War era, residents here questioned the value of seceding from the Union over the slavery issue. They also considered seceding from the state of Alabama. Although they never did secede from the state, the area was nicknamed the Free State of Winston. Today, Double Springs, a small town 40 miles from Cullman is known for its statue of a rebel soldier holding both Union and Confederate flags, commemorating the area's dual allegiances during the Civil War, and for an outdoor drama that reenacts that era. Alabama Mountain Lakes Tourist Association | 25062 North St., Double Springs, | 256/350–3500 or 800/648–5381 | fax 256/350–3519 | info@almtlakes.org | www.almtlakes.org.

Hurricane Creek Park. This rustic park has a swinging bridge over a waterfall and a natural spiral staircase. Several miles of nature trails are accented with interesting stones sculptured by Mother Nature. | 22600 U.S. 31, Vinemont | 256/734–2125 | $2.50 | Daily 10–sunset.

Looney's Tavern Amphitheater. The modern structure is the setting for an outdoor musical drama detailing Winston County's struggle during the Civil War. The drama reveals the role that the tavern played in the attempted 1861 secession of the "Free State of Winston" from Alabama. Surrounding the amphitheater is miniature golf (with a Civil War theme), a large gift shop with regional finds, and a restaurant known for its southern buffet. The *Free State Lady*, a replica riverboat, docks about a mile from the amphitheater and journeys down Smith Lake with narrated, two-hour trips. Summer concerts also are held here, and dinner theater is hosted off-season. Reservations suggested. | 22400 U.S. 278 | 205/489–5000 or 800/566–6397 | fax 205/489–3500 | www.bham.net/looneys | $12.

Natural Bridge of Alabama. In the heart of southern woodlands some 200 million years ago, streams and springs carved sandstone into a natural bridge. Erosion wore much of it away but what remains today is still quite impressive—two towering arches, the larger of which is 148 ft long, 60 ft high, and 33 ft wide. The site, 50 mi outside of Cullman, is nearly twice as long as the Natural Bridge of Virginia and was a gathering place during the Civil War for Union sympathizers wanting to join northern forces. | U.S. 278 and I–65 | 205/486–5330 | info@almtlakes.org | www.almtlakes.org | $2.50 | Daily 8–dusk.

Smith Lake. This park has 500 mi of shoreline and 21,000 acres of clear waters perfect for fishing, skiing, and boating. | 416 County Rd. | 205/739–2916 | Free | May–Sept., daily dawn–dusk.

Sportsman Lake Park. Within Cullman city limits, you can partake in plenty of activities like picnicking, fishing, camping, carpet golf, paddleboat rentals, a playground, a minitrain, hiking trails, carousel, and a Ferris wheel. It is also a popular spot for feeding the abundant ducks, geese, and fish. | 1536 Sportsman Lake Rd. northeast | 256/734–3052 | fax 256/736–2898 | Free | Daily 7–dusk.

William B. Bankhead National Forest. With 180,000 acres, this is Alabama's largest national forest and site of the state's first National Wilderness Area. The forest 40 mi from Cullman, is home of the state's only nationally designated Wild and Scenic River. Straddling Lawrence, Cullman, and Winston counties, the forest's bluffs, canyons, waterfalls, and lakes are part of the Alabama "Natural Wonders Trail." The site consists of several areas:

Brushy Lake, Clear Creek, Corinth, Houston, and Sipsey River. | Hwy. 33 North, Double Springs | 205/489–5111 | Free | Daily.

ON THE CALENDAR

APR., NOV.: *Bluegrass Superjam.* Festival featuring Grand Ole Opry–style music. | 256/747–1650.

APR.: *Bloomin' Festival.* Entertainment and crafts festival welcomes spring. | 800/722–0999.

JUNE: *Indian Festival.* Native American arts and crafts, food, dancing, drums, and demonstrations. | 256/737–9163.

SEPT.: *County Fair.* You can enjoy rides, games, food, and entertainment at this old-fashioned county fair. | 256/734–9454.

OCT.: *Oktoberfest.* A salute to Cullman's German heritage with food, entertainment, and song. Don't expect any beer gardens—Cullman is a dry county. | 256/734–0454 or 256/739–5254.

DEC.: *Parade of Homes.* Showcase of many historic homes in the area. | 256/739–4914.

Dining

All Steak. Steak. In downtown Cullman, this popular restaurant has been a tradition for more than 65 years. Choose from an intimate, quiet dining room or a more bustling area filled with booths and tables. Thursday, Friday, and Saturday nights, the special is prime rib. Also popular is the snapper Destin, a red snapper fillet topped with crab and shrimp. Sunday buffet. No smoking. | 314 2nd Ave. southwest | 205/734–4322 | $16–$36 | MC, V | Breakfast also available; no dinner Sun.

Provence Market. French. In an old brick warehouse in downtown Cullman, this bistro is delightfully set with linen tablecloths, fresh flowers, and plants. The furnishings are all antiques, but from a variety of different eras. Classical music plays throughout lunch, which is a variety of salads, pastas, grilled sandwiches, and house specialties. The sweetbreads are popular, as are the white bean chile, the crab cakes, and the hamburger with Swiss cheese and mushrooms served on a croissant. Tempting desserts include brownies with chantilly sauce, and baked cheesecake with a white chocolate caramel. Outdoor sidewalk dining is available. | 105 4th Ave. northeast | 256/734–8002 | $6–$15 | AE, D, MC, V.

Lodging

Best Western Fairwinds Inn. This standard inn is located at Interstate 65, 4 mi from the Cullman Museum, antiques shops, and a golf course, and about 6 mi from Ave Maria Grotto. Complimentary Continental breakfast. In-room data ports, some microwaves, refrigerators, cable TV. Pool. Gym. Laundry facilities. Business services. Some pets allowed. | 1917 Commerce Ave. | 256/737–5009 or 888/559–0549 | fax 256/737–5009 | 50 rooms | $49–$69 | AE, D, DC, MC, V.

Comfort Inn Cullman. Standard two-story motel, 5 mi to downtown Cullman. Many chain restaurants are nearby. Complimentary Continental breakfast. In-room data ports, some microwaves, some refrigerators, cable TV. Pool. Gym. Business services. Some pets allowed. | 5917 SR 157 northwest | 256/734–1240 or 800/228–5150 | fax 256/734–3318 | 50 rooms | $55–$67 | AE, D, DC, V.

Days Inn. This standard inn is minutes away from Smith Lake, a popular fishing spot, and only 4 mi from Ave Maria Grotto. Restaurant, picnic area. In-room data ports, some microwaves, some refrigerators, cable TV. Pool. Business services. Some pets allowed (fee). | 1841 4th St. southwest | 256/739–3800 | fax 256/739–3800 | www.daysinn.com | 119 rooms | $40–$75 | AE, D, DC, MC, V.

Mainstreet Inn Bed and Breakfast. This two-story Victorian house with a wraparound porch was built in 1890. Each of the four bedrooms has a different theme: the Rose Room is pink and floral, with a wooden four-poster bed and a whirlpool tub, and Granny's Room comes equipped with a wrought-iron bed and lace curtains. All the furnishings are Victorian, or reproductions of Victorian antiques. The parlor has a huge fireplace. The Heritage Park is less than a mile away, and there are many antiques shops within walking distance. It is fine to bring children if you mention it at the time of booking. Complimentary breakfast. Cable TV. | 201 Main Ave. northwest | 888/412–3043 | 4 rooms | $69–$99 | AE, D, MC, V.

Ramada Inn. Just off Interstate 65, this standard inn is about 8 mi from Wallace State College and a mile from Heritage Park. Restaurant, room service. In-room data ports, cable TV. Pool. Laundry facilities. Business services. Some pets allowed. | 1600 Rte. 437 | 256/734–8484 | fax 256/739–4126 | 126 rooms | $60 | AE, D, DC, MC, V.

DAUPHIN ISLAND

MAP 3, A9

(Nearby town also listed: Mobile)

Three miles off the coast of Mobile County's mainland, Dauphin Island is a cigar-shape, 15-mi-long island that is 2 mi across at its widest point. The island has no traffic lights, four churches, several fish markets, a handful of shops, and locals accustomed to buying shrimp and flounder fresh directly from fishing boats. You can reach the island by ferry at Fort Morgan Peninsula every half hour from 8 AM to 5 PM.

The first European settlement in the Louisiana Territory was established on Dauphin Island by the French in the 1700s. The settlers called it "Massacre" for the large number of skeletons they found here.

Fort Gaines, which is on Dauphin Island, and its across-bay sister, Fort Morgan, were seized by Alabama troops at the start of the Civil War and became Confederate strongholds. The Mobile Bay Ferry connects Dauphin Island and Fort Morgan. A $4 million Estuarium at the Dauphin Island Sea Lab opened in 1998, spotlighting the unique local ecosystems of the Mobile Bay estuary.

Information: Town of Dauphin Island Town Hall | Bienville Blvd. (Box 610), Dauphin Island 36528 | 334/861–5525 | dialgovmt@aol.com | www.gulfinfo.com.

Attractions

Estuarium. At the Dauphin Island Sea Lab, the Estuarium spotlights the unique local ecosystems of the Mobile Bay estuary. A Living Marsh Boardwalk includes interpretive signs explaining the natural history of the state's marshes, geography, and evolution of the barrier islands. There are displays, interactive exhibits, a 9,000-gallon aquarium simulating the brackish underwater environment of Mobile Bay, a 16,000-gallon tank with sea life from the Gulf of Mexico, and exhibits explaining the fragile environment of the coast's barrier islands. Twenty small aquariums focus on individual species. | 101 Bienville Blvd. | 334/861–7500 | fax 334/861–4646 | www.disl.org | $6 | June–Dec. 15, weekdays 9–6, weekends noon–6.

Fort Gaines. The pre–Civil War fort was the setting for the famous Battle of Mobile Bay when the Union's Admiral Farragut, who would not be deterred, bellowed, "Damn the torpedoes, full speed ahead" and defeated the Confederacy. You can touch cannons used in battle, explore tunnels and bastions, and visit a blacksmith shop, kitchen, and bakery. Living-history events are staged on selected weekends. | 51 Bienville Blvd. | 334/861–6992 | $3 | Daily 9–6.

Mobile Bay Ferry. The ferry, which accommodates cars, RVs, and sightseers, shuttles daily between Fort Morgan and Dauphin Island. | 334/540–7787 | $25 round-trip for cars, $10 one-way for cars, $3 | Call for hrs.

ON THE CALENDAR

MAY: *Spring Festival.* Activities include family events, pier fishing rodeo, beach run, tennis and volleyball tournaments, and a family carnival. | Dauphin Island | 334/861–5524.

JULY: *Deep Sea Fishing Rodeo.* Some 3,000 fishermen take part in the Gulf waters fishing competition, and vie for thousands of dollars in cash and prizes. | Dauphin Island | 334/471–0025.

OCT.: *Fall Bird Festival.* Dauphin Island is a stopping point for tropical birds during the fall migration to the Yucatan. During the season there are over 200 varieties of birds staying on this tiny island. The ornithological association on the island brings in specialists to talk about this phenomena, and there are field trips on Saturday and Sunday. | 334/861–2120 | $15.

Dining

Pelican Pub & Raw Bar/Blue Heron Room. Cajun/Creole. This restaurant and bar in Aloe Bay was built and raised on pilings. The original building is the Pelican Pub, and below it, in the space among the pilings, is the Blue Heron Room Restaurant. There are murals of shrimp buoys and pelicans, and the original pilings, which cut through the restaurant, are also painted. Dine outdoors either up or downstairs: both locations look out onto the bay. The restaurant serves mainly seafood and New Orleans–style étouffée, po'boys, and rib-eye steak. The decadent desserts include chocolate chimichangas, deep fried and topped with ice cream and syrup, and sliced banana in vanilla and honey, served with ice cream. | 1102 Desoto Ave. | 334/861–4376 | $8–$18 | MC, V | Closed Sun. from Memorial Day to Labor Day.

Lodging

Bayside Motel. This small, simple motel in Indian Bay is predominantly used by fishing enthusiasts. The building is surrounded by fishing docks and boat slips. The motel coffee shop only serves lunch. There are no phones in the rooms. The one luxury it offers is a view of Indian Bay from every window. The closest swimming beach is 3 mi away. Restaurant. Some microwaves, some refrigerators, cable TV. | 510 Lemoyne Dr. | 334/861–4994 | 20 rooms | $54 | AE, D, MC, V.

Gulf Breeze Motel. This family-owned motel has spacious rooms and two-bedroom efficiencies with fully equipped kitchens. It's located near the public beach and a boat launch on the bay side of the island. Refrigerators, cable TV. Some pets allowed (fee). | 1512 Cadillac Ave. | 334/861–7344 or 800/286–0296 | www.gulfinfo.com/gulfbreezemotel | 31 rooms, 6 apartments | $49–$59, $69 apartments | AE, D, MC, V.

Harbor Lights Inn. This small island inn is within walking distance from the public beach and offers two-bedroom suites and a view of Mobile Bay. Kitchenettes, cable TV. Dock. Fishing. | 1506 Cadillac Ave. | 334/861–5534 or 800/743–7132 | harborlightsinn@juno.com | www.gulfinfo.com/harborlightsinn | 6 suites | $67 | D, MC, V.

DECATUR

MAP 3, C2

(Nearby towns also listed: Athens, Cullman, Huntsville)

All but leveled by the Civil War and an 1888 yellow-fever epidemic, Decatur has survived and prospered with the influx of chemical companies and other industrial interests. The Tennessee River, bordering Decatur on the north, has molded the city, spurring both industrial growth and recreational opportunities. The Old Decatur District, between the river and Lee Street, is a living scrapbook of early history. Although small, Decatur has major attractions, including a science museum, and Point Mallard Park—with a swimming pool, wave pool, water slide, campgrounds, golf course, miniature golf, and hiking and biking trail. Wheeler Wildlife Refuge, a safe haven for more than 300 species of waterfowl and other birds, is a great place to see thousands of ducks and geese descending upon the water.

Information: Decatur Convention and Visitors Bureau | 719 6th Ave. southeast (Box 2349), Decatur 35602 | 256/350–2028 or 800/524–6181 | fax 256/350–2054 | info@decatur-cvb.org | www.decaturcvb.org.

Attractions

Cook's Natural Science Museum. A local pest-control company president turned an employee education center into one of the South's best public museums of its kind. It features an extensive collection of exotic insects, mounted birds, displays of animal habitats, birds, fish, rocks, minerals, and seashells, all in touch-and-feel exhibits. | 412 13th St. southeast | 256/350–9347 | Free | Mon.–Sat. 9–5, Sun. 2–5.

Old Decatur and Albany Historic Districts. Self-guided tours are the best way to see these districts which have the state's largest concentration of historic Victorian homes. The 116 acres are a wonderland during year-end holidays. | 719 6th Ave. southeast | 256/350–2028 | Free | Daily.

Point Mallard Park. The municipally owned, 750-acre park features year-round family recreation. From Memorial Day through Labor Day, the aquatic center is open and boasts America's first wave pool, an Olympic-size swimming pool, one of the South's largest diving towers, a sand beach, a "Duck Pond" kiddie pool, picnic areas, and one of the state's largest three-flume water slides. Other park facilities include a rustic 175-site campground, an 18-hole golf course, an 18-hole miniature golf course, tennis courts, an outdoor stage, hiking trails, ball fields, and a recreation center. | 1800 Point Mallard Dr. southeast | 256/350–3000 or 800/669–9283 | Park free; aquatic center $10 | Daily 10–6.

Pond Springs. This was the home of General Joe Wheeler, the only officer of the Civil War to be let back into the Union army. The three houses on the property include a "dogtrot" or double log cabin from around 1818, the two-story Federal-style house built in 1830s, and the main wing constructed around 1872. The house is in its original condition, and is being prepared to become a working plantation again. You can explore the grounds as well as the museum. There is a family cemetery on the property, and slave burial grounds. | 12289 Alabama Hwy. 20 | 256/637–8513 | www.wheelerplantation.org | $4 | Thurs.–Sat. 9–4, Sun. 1–5.

Princess Theatre. Built in 1887 as an elegant stable for the Casa Grande Hotel, the theater was used as a vaudeville house and movie theater. The City of Decatur bought the site in 1978 and restored it for concerts, ballets, Shakespearean plays, and old movies. | 112 2nd Ave. northeast | 256/350–1745 | fax 256/350–1712 | Box office, weekdays 9–5.

Town of Mooresville. The picturesque 1818 village, located between Huntsville and Decatur (about 2 mi from Decatur), refused to let the railroad into its city and thus never grew beyond its original nucleus. The oldest incorporated town in Alabama, it has a post office with original call boxes built prior to the Civil War. Also here are a community church (circa 1838) and a stagecoach inn (circa 1828). | Hwy. 31, exit 2 off I-565 | Decatur Convention and Visitors Bureau | 256/350–2028 | www.touralabama.org/locations | Free | Daily.

★ **Wheeler National Wildlife Refuge.** Established in 1938 as a wintering area for ducks, geese, and other migratory birds, the vast refuge includes a great diversity of habitat types and attracts thousands of wintering waterfowl. It hosts 115 species of fish, 74 species of reptiles and amphibians, 47 species of mammals, and 285 different species of songbirds. Start at the visitor center to learn the importance of waterfowl and other area animals. There are two short walking trails, an observation building, and an observation platform. The best wildlife viewing is in the late evenings, December through February. | Rte. 67 east (2700 Refuge Headquarters Rd.) | 256/350–6699 | Free | Mar.–Oct., Wed.–Sun. 10–5; Nov.–Feb., daily 10–5.

ON THE CALENDAR

MAY: *Alabama Jubilee Hot Air Balloon Classic.* The Jubilee features balloon races, Saturday-night balloon glow, arts, crafts, and car shows. | Point Mallard Park | Memorial Day weekend | 256/350–2028.

JULY: *Spirit of America Festival.* Family games, live stage entertainment, arts-and-crafts exhibits, demonstrations of pioneer American skills, sports tournaments, the crowning of Miss Point Mallard, and a fireworks display are highlights of this patriotic festival. | Point Mallard Park | 256/350–2028.

SEPT.: *Civil War Reenactment/September Skirmish.* Horses, cannons, muskets, candlelight tours of campsites, and educational displays bring the Civil War era to life on Labor Day. | Point Mallard | 256/350–2028.

SEPT.: *Racking Horse World Celebration.* This tribute to Alabama's official horse, the Racking (similar to a walking horse but with a four-beat, single-foot gait), showcases world-class champions and the Racking Horse World Grand Champion. | Celebration Arena | 256/353–7225.

OCT.: *Southern Wildlife Festival.* Artists exhibit and sell original paintings, carvings, photographs, books, and merchandise depicting wildlife in natural settings at this popular festival. | Calhoun Community College | 256/350–2028.

DEC.: *Christmas Tour of Homes.* Decatur has the most Victorian houses in the state. On the second weekend of December these private homes are open to the public for tours. | $10 | 256/350–2028 or 800/524–6181.

Dining

★ **Big Bob Gibson's Barbecue.** Barbecue. In 1999 Big Bob's was judged Best Barbecue Restaurant in Alabama, and declared winner of the World Championship Barbecue Cooking Contest. The food is southern, such as smoked hindquarter with white sauce, pork platters, grilled chicken and potato salad, and desserts like homemade chocolate, coconut, and lemon pies. | 1715 Hwy. 31 south | 256/350–6969 | fax 256/353–5411 | $7–$10 | AE, D, MC, V.

Curry's. American. In the basement of a large building in the downtown business district of Decatur, the walls are lined with vintage portrait photographs. The lunch menu includes meat loaf, pot roast, and chicken enchiladas. Dinners, however, are more extravagant. The most popular items are filet mignon and the rib-eye steak. Desserts include cream-cheese brownies, chocolate cheesecake, and key lime pie. There's a screened-in porch for outdoor dining. | 115 Johnston St. | 256/350–6715 | $6–$10 | AE, DC, MC, V | Closed Sun.

★ **Simp McGhee's.** Seafood. Named for an infamous riverboat captain from Decatur and housed in a structure with wooden floors and a tin ceiling, Simp McGhee's has a turn-of-the-20th-century feel. The downstairs area centers around a massive bar and has a rollicking, publike atmosphere; the upstairs dining area is a bit more sedate. Known for fresh fish, Cajun-style seafood, and steak. | 725 Bank St. | 256/353–6284 | $23–$41 | AE, D, DC, MC, V | Closed Sun. No lunch Sat.

Lodging

Country Inn and Suites. Featuring kitchen suites, this hotel is located in Decatur's historic district, 4 mi from Interstate 65 and near the Tennessee River. Bar, complimentary Continental breakfast, room service. In-room data ports, kitchenettes, microwaves, refrigerators, cable TV. Pool. Hot tub. Gym. Laundry facilities. Business services, airport shuttle. | 807 Bank St. northeast | 256/355–6800 or 800/456–4000 | fax 256/350–0965 | www.countryinns.com | 110 suites | $70–$90 | AE, D, DC, MC, V.

Dancy-Polk House. In the downtown area of Decatur, this bed-and-breakfast was built in 1829 by town pioneer Colonel Frank Dancy. This three-story antebellum, Palladian-style home is entirely furnished with 1850s antiques. It was once known as the Polk Hotel and was frequented by railroad travelers. Complimentary breakfast, sitting room. | 901 Railroad St. northeast | 256/353–3579 | fax 256/351–6296 | 2 rooms | $79 | No credit cards.

Hampton Inn. This standard motel is next door to Applebee's restaurant and within walking distance from the Colonial Mall. Complimentary Continental breakfast. In-room data ports, some microwaves, some refrigerators, cable TV. Pool. Gym. Business services. | 2041 Beltline Rd. | 256/355–5888 | fax 256/355–8434 | www.hamptoninn.com | 90 rooms | $64–$69 | AE, D, DC, MC, V.

Holiday Inn Hotel & Suites. This hotel is in the center of town with a park across the road. Restaurant, bar, complimentary breakfast. Pool. Gym. Video games. Free parking. | 1101 6th Ave. northeast | 256/355–3150 or 800/553–3150 | dcualsales@cooperhotels.com | www.holiday-inn.com | 207 rooms | $69–$95 | AE, D, DC, MC, V.

DEMOPOLIS

(Nearby towns also listed: Selma, Tuscaloosa)

Forty miles west of Selma, Demopolis clings to its southern heritage, evidenced by antebellum homes and 18th-century buildings in the historic downtown area. Gaineswood, whose construction began in 1843, has been called one of the finest Greek Revival mansions in the South.

French exiles reached Demopolis in 1817 and attempted, unsuccessfully, to grow vineyards and olive trees. All that remains of their presence is the town's name, which means "city of the people." American planters followed in the 1820s and began the production of cotton in the area. Dairy farms, cattle ranches, and soybean fields have since added to the area's economic base.

Information: Demopolis Area Chamber of Commerce and Tenn-Tom Tourism Association | 102 E. Washington St. (Box 667), Demopolis 36732 | 334/289–0270 | fax 334/289–1382 | dacc@westal.net | www.chamber.demopolis.al.us.

Attractions

Bluff Hall. Built by slaves, Bluff Hall was named for the high chalk bluff where it stands overlooking the Tombigbee River. During the Civil War, Bluff Hall received many Confederate officers as guests, and in late 1863, Confederate President Jefferson Davis was entertained at the house. Furnishings are Empire and early Victorian. Owned by the Marengo County Historical Society, the house has an adjacent crafts shop. | 405 N. Commissioners St. | 334/289–9644 | $5 | Tues.–Sat. 10–5, Sun 2–5 | Closed Mon.

Demopolis Lock and Dam. The construction of this dam created a 10,000-acre lake. Built in the 1950s, the spillway has 1,500 ft of water flowing over it, controlled by locks that raise and lower the water level to let boats down the Tombigbee River. You can come right down to the locks and watch the boats flock in. | 2000 Lock and Dam Rd. | 334/289–0645 | Free | Daily.

Gaineswood. Originally a simple log house, Gaineswood was transformed between 1842 and 1860 into an elegant villa. With domed ceilings, ornate plasterwork, columned and galleried rooms, and period furnishings, it is considered the state's most unusual antebellum mansion. The 30-ft–by–20-ft ballroom is a showplace of Corinthian columns. The house is owned and operated by the Alabama Historical Commission. | 805 S. Cedar Ave. | 334/289–4846 | fax 334/289–4846 | $5 | Mon.–Sat. 9–5, Sun. 1–5.

Magnolia Grove. On 15 acres, this Greek Revival antebellum mansion was the birthplace of Spanish-American War hero Rear Admiral Richmond Pearson Hobson. The state of Alabama operates the eight-room house as a museum, with original furnishings and outbuildings. A trophy room holds a portrait of Hobson, his military uniforms, naval test books, and the nameplate of the ship the *Merrimac*. | 1002 Hobson St., Greensboro | 334/624–8618 | fax 334/624–8618 | $4 | Tues.–Sat. 10–4, Sun. 1–4.

ON THE CALENDAR
JULY: *Freedom on the River.* This fourth of July celebration is a two-day event, held at the City Landing on the Tombigbee River. In addition to fireworks, the weekend also hosts a "best burgers in 'Bama" cookout, duck races, a children's parade, gospel singing, and a "wacky river raft race." | 334/289–0270.

DEC.: *Christmas on the Tombigbee River.* Floats, lighted moving boats, and fireworks decorate the river for the holidays. | Tombigbee River | 334/289–0270.

Dining

Ellis V. Steak. This homey restaurant has an extensive menu and a choice of two dining rooms, one casually furnished with comfortable booths and the other with more formal tables adorned with fresh flowers. Selections include prime rib and marinated steak fingers and bacon-wrapped shrimp, both available as appetizers or entrées. Salad bar. Kids' menu. | 708 U.S. 80 east | 334/289–3446 | $9–$29 | AE, D, DC, MC, V.

Foscue House. American. At the edge of town, the restaurant is housed in an 1840s wooden home. There's a wraparound porch, and four dining rooms inside. The country-style menu includes prime rib and roast tenderloin, with cheescakes, pies, cakes, and puddings for dessert. There is a patio for outside dining. | 21333 U.S. Hwy. 80 | 334/289–2221 | $9–$18 | AE, D, DC, MC, V | Closed Sun., Mon.

Lodging

Best Western–Mint Sunrise. This standard motel is only 2 mi away from fishing and water sports on the Tombigbee and Black Warrior rivers. Complimentary Continental breakfast. In-room data ports, some microwaves, refrigerators, cable TV. Pool. Gym. Business services. | 1034 U.S. 80 east | 334/289–5772 | fax 334/289–5772 | 69 rooms in 3 buildings | $45–$49 | AE, D, DC, MC, V.

Days Inn. This standard inn is on U.S. 80, the main thoroughfare, and near several restaurants. Complimentary Continental breakfast. In-room data ports, microwaves, refrigerators, cable TV. Pool. Gym. Laundry facilities. Business services. | 1005 U.S. 80 east | 334/289–2500 | fax 334/289–2500 | www.daysinn.com | 42 rooms | $51 | AE, D, DC, MC, V.

Holiday Inn Express. Five miles east of Demopolis, this is a standard, minimal-facility hotel on the edge of a main highway. There is a park 2½ mi away. Complimentary Continental breakfast. In-room data ports, cable TV. Pool. Hot tubs. Laundry facilities, laundry service. | 943 Hwy. 80 west | 334/289–9595 | fax 334/289–9750 | 51 rooms | $73 | AE, D, DC, MC, V.

River View Inn. A small independent property, this motel is on a marina and you can see the docked houseboats from every room. The banks of the Tombigbee River are an easy stroll from the motel. In-room data ports, microwaves, refrigerators, cable TV. Pets allowed. | 110 Yacht Basin Dr. | 334/289–0690 | 25 rooms | $45 | AE, DC, MC, V.

Windwood Inn. This standard inn is within walking distance of several restaurants and a 24-hour supermarket and 2 mi from the Demopolis Sportsplex. Complimentary Continental breakfast. In-room data ports, some kitchenettes, microwaves, refrigerators, cable TV. Pool. Business services. | 628 U.S. 80 east | 334/289–1760 or 800/233–0841 | fax 334/289–1768 | 90 rooms | $41 | AE, D, DC, MC, V.

DOTHAN

(Nearby town also listed: Eufaula)

When the railroad reached Dothan in 1889, it was greeted by a rough-and-tumble crowd of lumberjacks and turpentine workers. A strategic location—almost equidistant from Atlanta, Birmingham, Mobile, Jacksonville, and Tallahassee—helped the town grow into a marketing center for local and nonlocal products.

Often called the "Peanut Capital of the World" and known for its warm hospitality, Dothan remembers its past with sprawling murals on the sides of downtown buildings and a living history farmstead at Landmark Park, 3 mi north of downtown.

Places to play include Water World with a wave pool, waterslides, and water bumper boats, and Adventureland, a mini–theme park. A link in the state's trail of public golf courses is here, along with annual events such as Pioneer Peanut Days and the National Peanut Festival.

Information: Dothan Area Convention and Visitors Bureau | 331 Ross Clark Circle northwest (Box 8765), Dothan 36304 | 334/794–6622 or 888/449–0212 | fax 334/712–2731 | dothancvb@mailala.net | www.dothanalcvb.com.

Attractions

Adventureland Theme Park. The family-oriented mini–theme park has two 18-hole minigolf courses, a figure-eight go-cart track, bumper boats, a large arcade, video and novelty games, a laser-tag arena, bungee trampolines, slam dunk, and food. | 3738 W. Main St. | 334/793–9100 | fax 334/794–0594 | Free | Memorial Day–Labor Day, Mon.–Sat. 10–midnight; Labor Day–Memorial, Mon.–Thurs. 2–10, Fri. 2–midnight, Sat. 10–midnight, Sun. noon–10.

Landmark Park. Every corner of the 100-acre park showcases the natural and cultural heritage of southeast Alabama, including an 1890s living-history farmstead with exhibits and demonstrations of tools and implements used by pioneering farmers. There also are wildlife exhibits, an interpretative center, planetarium, picnic area, and nature trails. The park annually hosts several events including Spring Farm Day (third Saturday in March); Pioneer Peanut Days (fourth weekend in October); Fall Folklife Festival (third Saturday in November). | U.S. 431 | 334/794–3452 | fax 334/677–7229 | $2 | Mon.–Sat. 9–5, Sun. noon–6.

Opera House. The turn-of-the-20th-century three-story, neoclassical opera house originally hosted traveling vaudeville and minstrel shows. When the City of Dothan built a civic center across the street, the marble-appointed elegance was restored and the 590-seat auditorium was air-conditioned. Today, it hosts theatrical productions, ballets, and symphony performances, and the spacious parlors are used during intermissions. | 115 N. St. Andrews St. | 334/793–0127 | Free | Tours by appointment.

Water World. This popular water park has a wave pool, water slides, and water bumper boats. | 410 Recreation Rd. | 334/793–0297 | $7 | Memorial Day–Labor Day, Mon., Wed., Fri. 10–6, Tues., Thurs. 10–9, Sat. 10–7, Sun. noon–7; Labor Day–Memorial Day, weekends.

Westgate Park. The sporting complex includes a recreation center, softball complex, soccer fields, baseball complex, tennis courts, and swimming pool. | 501 Recreation Rd. | 334/793–0221 | fax 334/712–2514 | Free | Mon.–Thurs. 9–9, Fri. 9–7, Sat. 10–6, Sun. 2–6.

Wiregrass Festival of Murals. Works by nationally and internationally acclaimed muralists on walls of downtown Dothan buildings depict events from the area's history. | 111 N. St. Andrews St. | 334/793–3097 | fax 334/793–0450 | Free | Guided tours by request.

Wiregrass Museum of Art. Near downtown Dothan, the museum has galleries featuring changing exhibits, permanent collections, and African art. A kids' hands-on ARTventures gallery has interactive art and teaches by appealing to the senses. | 126 Museum Ave. | 334/794–3871 | fax 334/671–0380 | Free | Tues.–Sat. 10–5, Sun. 1–5.

ON THE CALENDAR

MAR.–APR.: *Azalea Dogwood Festival.* Spring showcase of gardens and homes. | Downtown Garden District | 334/793–0191.

OCT.: *Pioneer Peanut Days.* Music, arts and crafts, an antique tractor pull, kids' activities, and demonstrations of peanut harvesting are part of the city's salute to its peanut crop. | 334/794–3452.

NOV.: *National Peanut Festival.* The region's top cash crop is feted with elements of a fair—parades, beauty pageants, livestock exhibits, square dancing, recipes, sports event, and car shows are highlights. | Fairgrounds | 334/793–4323.

Dining

August Moon. Chinese. This popular restaurant features a lunch and dinner buffet seven days a week. | 3530 Montgomery Hwy. | 334/677–6035 | $7 | AE, D, MC, V.

Basketcase. Southern. This is the restaurant equivalent of Jekyll and Hyde; by day it's an unprepossessing café, in the business district of downtown Dothan, serving soups, sandwiches, and burgers, in a nondescript environment (just tables and chairs, no artwork). But by night the portable stage is rolled in, and for $19 you can have a dinner-theater night. Food served at night depends on the theme of the show; for example, the Hilarious Hillbilly Massacre had a full southern-style menu. Call for show-time details. | 228 S. Oates St. | 334/671–1117 | $4–$10 | AE, D, DC, MC, V.

Crystal River Seafood. Seafood. This is a full-service seafood restaurant, on the Dothan overpass on the outskirts of town. The interior is decorated in nautical themes, with pictures and fish mounted on the walls. The most popular dishes are fried alligator, steamed Maine lobster, and grilled mahi mahi. For dessert you have a choice of key lime or peanut butter pie. | 3512 Ross Clark Circle | 334/794–4153 | $10–$15 | AE, D, MC, V.

Dakota Coffee Works. Café. This is a roastery, cigar house, and café, right in the middle of downtown Dothan. Special imported coffees are roasted on the premises. The café serves sandwiches, soups, and danishes, as well as coffee and cigars. | 3074 Ross Clark Circle | 334/677–1718 | fax 334/671–1662 | AE, D, DC, MC, V.

Old Mill Restaurant. American. About a mile out of town, this large brick restaurant is fronted by an old mill house. The interior is lodgelike with cathedral ceilings, bay windows, antlers mounted on the walls, and an enormous rock fireplace. Steak and shrimp is the most popular dish; also on the menu are chicken, steak, and seafood. The house dessert, Old Mill Pie, is a 4-inch-thick pie with a cookie crust, French vanilla ice cream, and whipped cream. There is also a wide selection of wines. | 2557 Murphy Mill Rd. | 334/794–8530 | $15 | AE, MC, V | Closed Sun.

Lodging

Admiral Benbow Olympia Spa Golf Resort. About 4 mi south of Ross Clark Circle, this resort has a championship golf course and several affordable golf packages. Restaurant, bar, room service. Cable TV. Pool. Beauty salon, massage. 18-hole golf course. Laundry facilities. Business services. Some pets allowed (fee). | 7410 U.S. 231 south | 334/677–3321 | fax 334/677–3321 | www.admiralbenbow.com | 93 rooms in 2 buildings | $59 | AE, D, DC, MC, V.

Best Western-Dothan Inn. This basic inn is near the Wiregrass Commons Mall and the Northside Mall, and close to several restaurants. Complimentary Continental breakfast. In-room data ports, some kitchenettes, cable TV. Pool. Laundry service. Business services, airport shuttle. | 3285 Montgomery Hwy. | 334/793–4376 or 800/528–1234 | fax 334/793–7720 | 150 rooms, 30 suites | $53, $63–$81 suites | AE, D, DC, MC, V.

Comfort Inn. This award-winning inn, honored by its peers as one of the top five Comfort inns in the nation, is between two malls and within walking distance from fast-food and fine-dining restaurants and from a movie theater. Complimentary Continental breakfast. In-room data ports, some microwaves, no-smoking floors, some refrigerators, cable TV. Pool. Gym. Business services. Some pets allowed. | 3593 Ross Clark Circle northwest | 334/793–9090 | fax 334/793–4367 | www.comfortinn.com | 122 rooms | $70 | AE, D, DC, MC, V.

Holiday Inn–South. A convenient stopping point for travelers en route to Florida via U.S. 231 south, this inn is located 2 mi from the historic downtown area and 7 mi from a Robert Trent Jones golf course. Restaurant, bar, complimentary breakfast, room service. In-room data ports, some microwaves, some refrigerators, cable TV. Pool. Gym. Laundry service. Business services. Some pets allowed. | 2195 Ross Clark Circle southeast | 334/794–8711 | fax 334/671–3781 | 144 rooms, 14 suites | $61, $71 suites | AE, D, DC, MC, V.

Holiday Inn–West. This standard inn is on the city's busy bypass, less than 2 mi from the Wiregrass Commons Mall and close to several restaurants. Restaurant, bar, room service. In-room data ports, microwaves in suites, refrigerators in suites, cable TV. Pool, wading pool. Laundry service. Business services. Some pets allowed. | 3053 Ross Clark Circle | 334/794–6601 | fax 334/794–9032 | 102 rooms, 44 suites in 3 buildings | $65, $99 suites | AE, D, DC, MC, V.

Motel 6. This standard motel is just minutes from Wiregrass Commons Mall and Northside Mall, and it's also close to Water World and Landmark Park. In-room data ports, cable TV. Pool. Some pets allowed. | 2907 Ross Clark Circle southeast | 334/793–6013 | fax 334/793–2377 | 101 rooms | $40 | AE, D, DC, MC, V.

Ramada Inn. This standard inn is on Dothan's bypass, close to several restaurants, a Robert Trent Jones golf course, and Water World. Restaurant, bar with entertainment, complimentary breakfast, room service. In-room data ports, cable TV. Pool, wading pool. Laundry service. Business services, airport shuttle. Some pets allowed. | 3011 Ross Clark Circle southeast | 334/792–0031 | fax 334/794–3134 | 114 rooms in 4 buildings | $62–$68 | AE, D, DC, MC, V.

Shoney's Inn. This is a standard two-story inn on the edge of Dothan, approximately 5 mi from the center of town. There are a number of restaurants within walking distance. Complimentary Continental breakfast. In-room data ports, microwaves, refrigerators, some in-room hot tubs, cable TV. Pool. Free parking. | 1075 Ross Clark Circle | 334/793–2525 | fax 334/791–7190 | 40 rooms | $50–$55 | AE, D, DC, MC, V.

Travelodge, Dothan. A three-floor stone building, about 1½ mi outside of downtown Dothan, this Travelodge is distinguished by its "Sleepy Bear Den," a guest room designed for families with children. The rooms come with children's videos, toys, and "sleepy bear" decorations. Other than that, this is a standard chain motel. In-room data ports, microwaves, refrigerators, cable TV. Pool. Laundry service. Pets allowed. | 2901 Ross Clark Circle . | 334/793–5200 or 877/353–3311 | 99 rooms | $35–$45 | AE, D, DC, MC, V.

Walker's Deluxe Motel. A privately run motel on the outskirts of Dothan, the name is somewhat misleading as there is nothing deluxe about the motel. The rooms are simple, inexpensive, and clean. Cable TV, room phones. Free parking. | 3214 E. Main St. | 334/792–4177 | 37 rooms | $25 | AE, D, DC, MC.

EUFAULA

(Nearby towns also listed: Dothan, Union Springs)

Rich in southern tradition and antebellum homes, Eufaula's historic district is filled with hundreds of historic and architecturally significant structures. It is said to have the state's most complete collection of intact mid- to late-19th-century small-town commercial buildings.

Seven miles north of Eufaula, Lakepoint Resort State Park overlooks Lake Eufaula, one of the best bass lakes in the country, where you can hike, play tennis, swim, and picnic. Eufaula National Wildlife Refuge is a federal preserve that protects waterfowl and wild game.

Information: **Eufaula/Barbour County Chamber of Commerce** | 102 N. Orange Ave. (Box 697), Eufaula 36027 | 334/687–6664 or 800/524–7529 | fax 334/687–5240 | ebc-tour@hotmail.com.

Attractions

Eufaula National Wildlife Refuge. At the feeding and wintering-over habitat for waterfowl, birds of prey, songbirds, and other migrant birds, you can often see herons, egrets, wood ducks, white-tailed deer, and alligators. It borders the Walter F. George Reservoir on the Chattahoochee River. | 509 Old Rte. 165 | 334/687–4065 | fax 334/687–5906 | www.fws.gov | Free | Daily dawn–dusk.

Hart House. The restored one-story house is noted for its porch with six fluted Doric columns. The house serves as a visitor information center for the Chattahoochee Trace region of Alabama and Georgia. | 211 N. Eufaula Ave. | 334/687–9755 | fax 334/687–6631 | www.hcc-al-ga.org | Free | Weekdays 8–5.

Lakepoint Resort State Park. The resort sprawls across the edge of Lake Eufaula, "Bass Capital of the World." The two-story lodge has large, modern rooms and several suites. There also are two-bedroom cabins, duplexes, and campgrounds. Spring and summer rentals should be made well in advance. Full-service marina, fishing, tennis, golf, picnicking, restaurant, and convention facilities. A park naturalist is available for programs. | 104 Lakepoint Dr. | 334/687–6676 or 334/687–8011 | fax 334/687–6921 | Free | Daily dawn–dusk.

Shorter Mansion. Originally built in 1884 by a wealthy planter, the two-story house, with detailed Corinthian columns, is one of the state's most dramatic house museums. It is furnished with period antiques and displays historic memorabilia, including portraits of six Barbour County natives who served as Alabama governors. | 340 N. Eufaula Ave. | 334/687–3793 | fax 334/687–4536 | www.zebra.net/~pilgrimage/ | $4 | Mon.–Sat. 9–4, Sun. 1–4.

Tom Mann's Fish World. This aquarium houses fish that are native to Lake Eufaula. There is also an indoor stream with waterfalls and a Native American Museum with paintings and relics. Tom Mann, the founder of Fish World, used to fish for largemouth bass and made his living manufacturing and selling fishing lures. On one fishing trip he caught a 1-pound largemouth that was noticeably different from other bass. He put it in his store's aquarium and named it Leroy Brown. When Leroy Brown died in 1984, 800 people attended the funeral. | 1951 N. Eufaula Ave. | 334/687–3655 | $2.50 | Summer, daily 9–5; winter, daily 9–4.

ON THE CALENDAR

APR.: *Pilgrimage.* Alabama's oldest tour of homes, plus antiques show, art show, needlepoint show, and candlelight tours. | 334/687–3793.

OCT.: *Indian Summer Days.* Street fair with arts, crafts, live entertainment, clothesline arts, food, and children's games. | N. Randolph Ave. | 334/687–6664.

DEC.: *Christmas Tour of Homes.* The houses of Eufaula get decorated for Christmas. The homes on tour range from contemporary houses to Greek Revival cottages, Italianate villas, Victorian mansions, and antebellum estates. | $25, $15, $4 depending on how many houses you see. | 334/687–6664 or 888/383–2852.

Dining

Cajun Corner. Cajun. Right in the middle of town, this restaurant is housed in a historic 1885 brick building. Once the town hotel, now the ground floor is occupied by the Cajun Cafe. The interior is decorated à la New Orleans Mardi Gras: everything is purple, green, and gold. The most popular dish is the Northshore Pasta: shrimp, crawfish, andouille sausage, and pasta in a cream sauce with mozzarella cheese. There are also po'boys, and nine different salads. The triple chocolate cheesecake is quite popular. | 114 N. Eufaula Ave. | 334/687–0083 | $7–$16 | AE, D, MC, V | Closed Sun.

Creek Restaurant and Lounge. American. Set on the outskirts of town, this restaurant has three separate dining rooms and a lounge. Native American pictures, maps, and artifacts line the walls. Menu items include steak and seafood. | 3301 S. Eufaula Ave., | 334/687–0083 | $9–$16 | MC, V | Closed Sun.

LA's Barbecue. BBQ. LA's is decorated in the colors of the American flag. You can watch your food as it cooks inside a 30-ft-long BBQ pit. The specialty of the house is the pork rib platter, which comes with baked beans, coleslaw, potato salad, and Brunswick stew. There is a barbecue buffet for lunch at which meats are accompanied by all the southern trimmings like black-eyed peas, baked beans, macaroni and cheese, and candied yams. | 1366 N. Eufaula Ave. | 334/687–7594 | $7–$10 | MC, V | Closed Sun.

Lodging

Best Western Inn. This standard motel is located in downtown Eufaula, just minutes from the lake and near several restaurants. Complimentary Continental breakfast. In-room data ports, some microwaves, some refrigerators, cable TV. Pool. Business services. | 1375 S. Eufaula Ave. | 334/687–3900 | fax 334/687–6870 | 42 rooms | $45–$65 | AE, D, DC, MC, V.

Creektown Inn. On the north end of town, the Creektown is about a mile from Lake Eufaula. This two-story inn has bold white columns which blend in perfectly with the town's architecture. Complimentary Continental breakfast. In-room data ports. Cable TV. Laundry facilities. | 1243 Eufaula Ave. | 334/687–0166 or 888/357–0166 | fax 334/616–0166 | info@creektowninn.com | www.creektowninn.com/ | 46 rooms | $40–$60 | AE, D, DC, MC, V.

Kendall Manor Inn. Innkeepers Tim and Barbara Lubsen give you the opportunity to return to simpler times in their antebellum bed-and-breakfast inn. Relax in a rocking chair on the veranda or on the deck overlooking a garden, play croquet on the lawn, or wander around the 2½ acres of grounds among the magnolia and dogwood trees. Go on the history tour of the Italianate home, which includes a stop at the belvedere tower where you can add your scrawl to the 100-year tradition of inscribing "graffiti" on the walls. The historic district with its many antiques shops is just a short walk away. Complimentary breakfast. In-room data ports, cable TV. Business services. | 534 W. Broad St. | 334/687–8847 | fax 334/616–0678 | kmanorinn@mindspring.com | www.bbonline.com/al/kendallmanor | 6 rooms | $99–$139 | AE, D, MC, V.

Lakepoint State Park Lodge and Conference Center. The lake here is known as "the bass capital of the world" and this state park resort features a full-service marina, boating and fishing opportunities, and a beach and swimming area. Restaurant, bar, picnic area. Some in-room data ports, some kitchenettes, microwaves in suites, refrigerators in suites, cable TV. Pool, lake. Driving range, 18-hole golf, putting green, 8 tennis courts. Dock, water sports, boating, fishing. Playground. Laundry facilities. Business services. | U.S. 431 north (Box 267), | 334/687–8011 or 800/544–5253 | fax 334/687–3273 | 101 rooms, 4 suites, 29 cottages | $55–$80, $118 suites, $79 cottages | AE, MC, V.

Ramada Inn. Located on the Alabama/Georgia border, this inn is situated on beautiful Lake Eufaula. Restaurant, bar, room service. In-room data ports, cable TV. Pool, lake. Laundry service. Business services. Some pets allowed. | Barbour at Riverside Dr. | 334/687–2021 | fax 334/687–2021 | 96 rooms in 2 buildings | $49 | AE, D, DC, MC, V.

FAIRHOPE

MAP 3, B8

(Nearby town also listed: Mobile)

On the eastern side of Mobile Bay, Fairhope revels in the laid-back atmosphere of yesteryear. Live oak trees draped with Spanish moss line streets full of clapboard houses with wide front porches studded with rocking chairs overlooking the inky waters of the bay.

Information: **Eastern Shore Chamber of Commerce** | 327 Fairhope Ave., Fairhope 36532 | 334/928–6387 | fax 334/928–6389 | office@eschamber.com | www.eschamber.com.

Attractions

Riviera Centre. This sprawling shopping paradise of more than 120 factory outlet stores is just a couple of miles south of Fairhope. | 2601 U.S. 59, Foley | 334/943–8888 | Mon.–Sat. 10–9, Sun. 11–6.

ON THE CALENDAR

MAR.: *Fairhope Arts and Crafts Festival.* Held on the third weekend of March, this three-day celebration is the town's largest event of the year. Main streets close down and some 250 arts-and-crafts booths line the streets. For entertainment, there is everything from high school bands to local musicians, gymnasts, and dance performances. Street venders from the local restaurants sell food, and there are also rides and a children's train that circumnavigates the streets. | 334/928–6387 or 334/621–8222.

Dining

Pelican Pointe Grill. Seafood. With views of Mobile Bay and Weeks Bay, this beach house–turned–restaurant provides a Key West atmosphere with open decks, a screened porch, and an inside bar and dining room. The menu features plenty of mostly steamed fresh seafood. Try the steamed Royal Red shrimp, served with potato salad, corn, vegetable relish, and garlic bread. Open-air dining on deck or porch. Live music Sunday afternoons. | 10299 Rte. 1 | 334/928–1747 | Reservations not accepted | $18–$33 | MC, V | Closed Mon. (Nov.–Mar.). No lunch weekdays.

Lodging

Bay Breeze Bed & Breakfast. A winding driveway lined with azaleas and camellias ends at this 1930s stucco home and quaint guest cottage on Mobile Bay. A 462-ft private pier is the perfect spot for an afternoon nap and an unbeatable place to watch the sun set over the bay. Follow a sidewalk that meanders along the bluff overlooking the bay to downtown Fairhope's shops and restaurants. Complimentary breakfast. Cable TV in some rooms. No smoking. | 742 S. Mobile St. | 334/928–8976 | fax 334/928–0360 | www.bbonline.com/al/baybreeze/ | 4 rooms, 1 suite | $100, $120 suite | AE, MC, V.

Church Street Inn. In the center of town, this early 1900s home is listed on the National Register of Historic Places. Three blocks away you will find Mobile Bay and several miles of public beaches, rose gardens, and parks. Restored throughout, this home contains five generations of family antiques and heirlooms. There is a large living room, a front porch lined with highback rockers, and a garden courtyard. There are three guest bedrooms, each with its own private bath, all furnished in period antiques. No children are allowed. Complimentary Continental breakfast. | 51 S. Church St. | 334/928–8976 | 3 rooms | $85 | AE, MC, V.

Holiday Inn Express. This standard inn is conveniently located on U.S. 98, close to Fairhope shops, restaurants, and a golf course, and is 20 minutes from downtown Mobile. Complimentary Continental breakfast. In-room data ports, refrigerators, cable TV. Pool. Laundry facilities. Business services. | 19751 Greeno Rd. | 334/928–9191 | fax 334/990–7874 | 65 rooms | $59–$79 | AE, D, DC, MC, V.

Key West Inn. Conveniently located on U.S. 98 just minutes from downtown Fairhope, this inn's guest rooms feature watercolor paintings by a local artist. Complimentary Continental breakfast. In-room data ports, microwaves in suites, refrigerators in suites, cable TV. Pool. | 231 S. Greeno Rd. | 334/990–7373 or 800/833–0555 | fax 334/990–9671 | www.keywestinn.com | 55 rooms, 9 suites | $52–$69, $85–$99 suites | AE, D, DC, MC, V.

Magnolia Springs Bed & Breakfast. Halfway between Fairhope and Gulf Shores, this 100-year-old house is less than two blocks from Magnolia River, one of the few remaining places in the country where mail is delivered by boat. The restored home features a wide front porch overlooking the property, which is dotted with beautiful live oaks. Inside, the floors, walls, and ceilings are made of heart pine. Complimentary breakfast. In-room data ports, cable TV. No smoking. | 14469 Oak St., Magnolia Springs | 334/965–7321 or 800/965–7321 | fax 334/965–3035 | msbbdw@gulftel.com | www.bbonline.com/al/magnolia/ | 5 rooms | $94 | AE, D, MC, V.

Point of View Guesthouse. Built in the 1900s, this guest house faces the beach and has its own wharf and pier. The rooms are furnished with a combination of beach wicker and antique furniture. The property is on 3 acres of gardens, and is less than 3 mi from the town of Fairhope. Children by negotiation only. Complimentary Continental breakfast. Kitchenettes, cable TV, VCR. Pool. | 19493 Scenic Hwy. 98 | 334/928–1809 | 2 rooms | $95 | AE, MC, V.

FLORENCE

(Nearby town also listed: Tuscumbia)

Florence has operated as a trading center since its founding in the late 1700s. For a small town, Florence enjoys an abundance of attractions, including an Indian Mound and Museum and the log-cabin birthplace of W. C. Handy, "Father of the Blues." The town's most visible attraction is the 300-ft-tall Renaissance Tower that overlooks TVA's Wilson Dam and has a restaurant atop.

Information: Florence/Lauderdale Tourism | 1 Hightower Pl., Florence 35630 | 256/740–4141 or 888/356–8687 | fax 256/740–4142 | dwilson@floweb.com | www.flo-tour.org.

MUSIC IN MUSCLE SHOALS

In the world of pop and rock music, the name Muscle Shoals means state-of-the-art recording studios, top-of-the-heap rock stars, a seemingly endless stream of hit recordings, and a special—and very commercial—background sound produced by some of America's best producers, engineers, and session musicians.

The music business here centers in the town of Muscle Shoals itself and in three nearby small towns: Sheffield, Tuscumbia, and Florence. Easily accessible to southern musicians, from the country kings of Tennessee to the blues masters of Mississippi, Muscle Shoals has been a busy music center since the first recording studio opened in Florence in 1958.

Everyone from Little Richard to Liza Minelli, from Aretha Franklin to Marie Osmond, from Paul Simon to Paul Anka, has recorded songs in Muscle Shoals studios. Other singing visitors have included Cher, Bob Dylan, the Rolling Stones, and Rod Stewart.

Still, it may well be the sound of another man's voice and the songs he recorded in Muscle Shoals that will forever put the place on the map for all of us. In the 1960s, Atlantic Records recorded one of their young singers at the FAME studios. The singer's name was Wilson Pickett, and among the classic tracks he recorded in that building on Avalon Avenue in Muscle Shoals were "Land of 1000 Dances," "Funky Broadway," and "Mustang Sally."

In hindsight, perhaps it all seems inevitable. Florence was the birthplace of Sam Phillips, the quiet visionary whose Sun Records in Memphis first brought Elvis Presley, Roy Orbison, Jerry Lee Lewis, Carl Perkins, Johnny Cash, and country star Charlie Rich into the limelight. Today, the music history of the region and the state is preserved in the Alabama Music Hall of Fame in Tuscumbia.

© Corbis

Attractions

Indian Mound and Museum. The highlight of this riverside attraction is a mound dating back some 10,000 years to the Mississippian-period culture of Native Americans. Visitors may trek to the top of the mound for a view of the Tennessee River. An adjacent museum gives insight into early settlers. | S. Court St. | 256/760–6427 | fax 256/760–6382 | www.flo-tour.org | Mon.–Sat. 10–4.

Wheeler Dam. Thirty miles from Decatur, the dam was completed in 1936 and named for Confederate General Joe Wheeler. Reaching 72 ft high and stretching 6,342 ft across the Tennessee River, the dam creates a 74-mi-long lake where you can fish and boat in the Athens, Decatur, and Huntsville areas. | Rte. 101 | 256/685–3306 | Free | Daily.

Wheeler Lake. The 65,000-acre reservoir on the Tennessee River offers diverse sports fishing with good crappie, white bass, hybrids, bluegill, and catfish angling. Largemouth, smallmouth, and spotted bass are premier game fish. | 1 Hightower Pl | 256/740–4141 | fax 256/740–4142 | www.flo-tour.org | Free | Daily.

Joe Wheeler State Park. Named for the Civil War's famous "Fighting Joe" Wheeler, the park sits on one of the Tennessee Valley Authority's largest dams. The large park has a main lodge 4 mi off U.S. 72 at Rogersville. The park is a water-oriented hideaway created for fishing, swimming, and boating. Open year-round, campgrounds are among the most popular in the state. The park has convention facilities, cabins, an 18-hole golf course, a marina, boat rentals, overnight docking, picnic day-use area, group pavilions, picnic areas with playground equipment, a sandy beach, fishing, hiking, tennis, basketball, and horseshoes. | 201 McLean Dr., Rogersville | 256/247–5461 | fax 256/247–5471 | www.flo-tour.org | $1 | Daily 9–dusk.

Muscle Shoals. This town, south of Florence on Hwy. 72, is the center of a multimillion-dollar music recording business. Muscle Shoals often hosts well-known singers who are recording in area studios. This community, named for the famous rapids that once hindered navigation on the Tennessee River, is now the site of Wilson Dam, a National Historic Landmark completed in 1918. | Hwy. 72 | 256/764–4661 | fax 256/766–9017 | shoals@shoalscc.org | www.shoalscc.org.

Wilson Dam. Begun in 1918 as a part of a World War I munitions project, the engineering feat contains one of the world's highest single lift locks (137 ft. high). Today it is a National Historic Landmark where you can drive through the grounds of the Tennessee Valley Authority. | Rte. 133 south | 256/740–4141 | fax 256/740–4142 | www.flo-tour.org | Free | Daily.

Pope's Tavern. Built by slave labor in about 1830, the 1½-story white-brick building with a long, wide front porch served as a backwoods tavern and stagecoach stop. It later was used as a hospital for wounded Union and Confederate soldiers. The restored structure, which has been named to the National Register of Historic Places, is operated as a house museum by the city of Florence. | 203 Hermitage Dr. | 256/760–6439 | fax 256/760–6382 | www.flo-tour.org | Mon.–Sat. 10–4.

Renaissance Tower. Stretching 300 ft into the air and overlooking Wilson Dam and the heavily wooded Shoals region, the tower is Alabama's tallest attraction. The needle-shape structure, costing $5.5 million, contains 500 tons of steel and 3,500 cubic ft of concrete. Atop the tower is a restaurant and observation deck. On a clear day, visibility is 30 mi. | 1 Hightower Pl | 256/764–5900 | fax 256/766–3296 | www.flo-tour.org | $4 | Mon.–Sat. 10–5, Sun. 11–5.

University of North Alabama. One of the state's top-ranking universities, UNA also offers a popular continuing education program with courses such as computers, communication, and management skills, for adults wishing to further their education. | Wesleyan Ave. | 256/765–4100 or 800/825–5862 | fax 256/765–4872 | www.una.edu | Free | Daily.

W. C. Handy Home, Museum, and Library. The restored log cabin birthplace of the "Father of the Blues" includes displays of Handy's musical scores and instruments, and provides insight into the son of a Baptist minister who chose the blues over his father's desire for him to play organ. When Florence built a housing project on the original site of the house in the 1950s, the city dismantled and stored the log house. Handy advised on its restoration but died in 1958, before it began. Today Handy's trumpet, and the piano on which he wrote his famous "Saint Louis Blues," are on display. A separate log house contains a library. | 620 W. College St. | 256/760–6434 | fax 256/760–6382 | www.flo-tour.org | $2 | Mon.–Sat. 10–4.

Wilson Lake. Anglers choose Wilson Lake for its bass fishing, drop-offs, and well-defined channels. Although most noted for the world's record smallmouth catch in the 1950s, the lake also yields largemouth and crappie. | 1 Hightower Pl | 256/740–4141 | fax 256/740–4142 | ww.flo-tour.org | Free | Daily.

ON THE CALENDAR

MAY: *Tennessee River Fiddlers' Convention.* Plenty of bluegrass music and an old-time fiddlers' convention. | Florence/Lauderdale Coliseum | 256/740–4141.

AUG.: *W. C. Handy Music Festival.* Weeklong event celebrating area music and Florence native W. C. Handy. Includes parades, jam sessions, and a picnic-jazz evening on the banks of the Tennessee River. | Shoals | 256/740–4141.

SEPT.: *Trail of Tears Commemoration and Motorcycle Ride.* Tribute to Native Americans, with powwows, arts, crafts, entertainment, and the South's largest organized motorcycle ride. | Waterloo | 256/740–4141.

OCT.: *Alabama Renaissance Faire.* Medieval/Renaissance atmosphere with authentic costumes, arts and crafts, wandering minstrels, and chamber singers, pays tribute to the city's Italian namesake. A Renaissance dinner is the highlight. | Various venues and Wilson Park | 256/740–4141.

OCT.: *Festival of the Singing River.* Celebrates area's Native American heritage, art, and culture. | Banks of Tennessee River | 256/740–4141.

Dining

Court Street Cafe. American. In the center of town, the café is decorated with a lot of local artwork on the exposed brick walls. On the menu are fried-chicken platters, ribs, steak, or seafood dishes. The black-bean chicken with cheese, chile, tomatoes, scallions, and rice is popular, and the desserts change every week. Recurring favorites are the Pina Colada Cake and Pecan Pie. | 201 N. Seminary St. | 256/767–4300 | $15–$25 | AE, D, DC, MC, V.

★ **Dale's Restaurant.** Steak. This casual steak house was once part of a regional chain; Dale's "Famous" Steak Sauce is still sold in supermarkets. Known for beef tenderloin, prime rib, pork chops, and beef kebabs; fresh seafood is also on the menu. | 1001 Mitchell Blvd. | 256/766–4961 | $26–$32 | AE, DC, M, V | Closed Sun. No lunch.

Renaissance Grille. American. Atop of Renaissance Tower, Alabama's tallest tourist attraction, the restaurant has windows all around, with fabulous views of the Tennessee River. On a clear day, you can see for 40 mi. On the menu: prime rib, steaks, seafood, chicken, pasta, sandwiches, and salads. The most popular meals are chicken cordon bleu, and surf and turf. Leave room for the fudge brownies or the baked cheesecake. | One Hightower Pl. | 256/718–0092 | $7–$15 | AE, D, DC, MC, V.

Lodging

Days Inn. This standard inn is about 2 mi from the Tennessee Valley Authority (TVA) reservation and 5 mi from the University of North Alabama, and across the street from a movie theater. Complimentary Continental breakfast. In-room data ports, cable TV. Pool. Some pets allowed (deposit). | 1915 Florence Blvd. | 256/766–2620 | fax 256/766–2620 | 77 rooms in 5 buildings | $55–$65 | AE, D, DC, MC, V.

Doublehead Resort and Lodge. Named for a Cherokee Indian chief who lived in the area 200 years ago, this rustic resort features 35 cedar-log cottages and a lodge on Wilson Lake, next to a 1,100-acre hunting preserve. | 145 Rte. 314, Town Creek | 256/685–9267 or 800/685–9267 | fax 256/685–0224 | www.doublehead.com | 35 cottages | $150–$275 | AE, D, MC, V.

Homestead Executive Inn. This standard inn is just ¼ mi from a new marina on the Tennessee River, five minutes from Regency Square Mall, and about 10 minutes from the Muscle Shoals Airport. Restaurant, bar, room service. Cable TV. Pool. Laundry facilities. Business services. Some pets allowed (fee). | 504 S. Court St. | 256/766–2331 | fax 256/766–3567 | 120 rooms | $54 | AE, D, DC, MC, V.

Joe Wheeler State Resort Lodge. The modern resort lodge is located on the shores of Wheeler Lake, on the Tennessee River. Restaurant, picnic area. Cable TV. Pool, wading pool. 18-hole golf courses, putting green, 4 tennis courts. Hiking, beach, boating. Playground. Laundry facilities. Business services. | Drawer K, Rogersville | 256/247–5461 or 800/544–5639 | fax 256/247–5471 | www.vten.com | 75 rooms | $62–$125 | AE, MC, V.

Limestone Manor Bed & Breakfast. This 1915 Georgian Revival home is in Florence's historic district. Lovely common areas include a parlor, sunporch, and library. The three guest rooms are named for famous former guests. The Henry Ford Room is furnished with 19th-century antiques. The Thomas Edison Suite is decorated in white wicker and lace. The "Bogart Retreat" has a huge old fireplace. Breakfast includes such country favorites as Angel pie and sourdough pancakes. Complimentary breakfast. Cable TV. VCR. | 601 N. Wood Ave. | 256/765–0314 or 888/709–6700 | info@limestonemanor.com | www.limestonemanor.com | 3 rooms | $72–$105 | AE, MC, V.

Wood Avenue Inn Bed & Breakfast. Twelves miles south of the Natchez Trace Parkway is this 110-year-old custom-built Crossland-Karsner Victorian mansion. There are beautiful wisteria gardens, a courtyard, wraparound porch, and a back porch for outdoor dining. The ceilings rise to 14 ft, and there are 12 fireplaces (two are in bathrooms). Each room has a unique motif, and all are furnished with period antiques. There is also a recreation room with board games and books. Dinner is by special arrangement. Cable TV in common areas only. Complimentary breakfast. Phone. | 658 N. Wood Ave. | 256/766–8441 | woodaveinn@aol.com | www.woodavenueinn.com | 4 rooms | $75–$105 | D, MC, V.

FORT PAYNE

MAP 3, E2

(Nearby town also listed: Gadsden)

Fort Payne, known as the sock capital of the world because of the huge number of socks produced here, has more to showcase than foot coverings. Natural wonders and Native American history are the big draws here.

The area's crowning jewel is DeSoto Falls, a 110-ft waterfall that punctuates the 5,000-acre DeSoto State Resort Park, which has a lake, swimming pool, picnic area, campgrounds, lodge, cabins, chalets, and a restaurant. The town's old depot has been reborn as a museum, with exhibits of early farm equipment, pottery, and Native American items. Fort Payne is home to the country music band Alabama, where band members are known merely as "the boys," even though one of the foursome did not grow up here.

Information: DeKalb County Tourist Association | 1503 Glenn Blvd. southwest, Ft. Payne, 35968 | 256/845–3957 | pattyt@mindspring.com | www.hsv.tis.net/~dekbtour.

Attractions

Alabama Fan Club and Museum. Sounds of award-winning country music waft through the museum, where exhibits range from band members' toddler cowboy outfits to today's gold albums. A gift shop is well stocked with collectibles. | 101 Glenn Blvd. southwest | 256/845–1646 | fax 256/845–5650 | www.thealabamaband.com | $1 | Weekdays 8–6, Sat. 8–8, Sun. noon–5.

DeSoto State Resort Park. In Alabama's northeast corner in DeKalb County, this park sprawls along Little River Canyon and is accented by waterfalls and wildflowers. A 22-mi scenic drive along the edge of the deepest canyon east of the Mississippi River provides views of Little River falls and magnificent rock formations. Here you can hike, picnic, play tennis, swim, boat, and rock climb. The park has a nature center with a naturalist eager to help you identify area finds. Also here are cabins, lodge accommodations, a restaurant, primitive camping, and a modern campground with water and electric hookups. | 13903 Rte. 89 | 256/845–5380 or 800/ALA–PARK | fax 256/845–8286 | www.mentone.com/desoto | Free | Daily dawn–dusk.

Fort Payne Depot Museum. A depot that served as a passenger station from 1891 to 1970 is today a museum with historical displays. The building is of Richardson Romanesque architecture, built of Alabama sandstone. It features Native American artifacts, dioramas, railroad memorabilia, and local history. | 105 5th St. northeast | 256/845–5714 | fax 256/845–5345 | www.hsv.tis.net/~dekbtour | Free | Mon., Wed., Fri. 10–4, Sun. 2–4.

Fort Payne Opera House. This is the state's oldest theater. Since its early days as the scene of operas and musicals, the historic building has served as a temporary college, a movie house (beginning with silent oldies), and a theater for stage shows. Closed in 1935, it served only for private use and storage until its restoration and reopening in 1970. Several times annually plays are performed in the theater which is listed on the National Register. Huge murals inside the theater depict area history. | 510 Gault Ave. north | 256/845–3137 | www.hsv.tis.net/~dekbtour | Free | By appointment.

Little River Canyon National Preserve. Often called the "Grand Canyon of the East," the canyon is one of northern Alabama's most scenic attractions, especially when azaleas, rhododendrons, and mountain laurel bloom in spring. At the canyon's bottom, blue-green waters of Little River rush and tumble along a boulder-strewn course. A road hugs the west rim of the canyon, offering plenty of overlooks. Picnic sites and trails are available. | 2141 Gault Ave. north | 256/845–9605 | fax 256/997–9129 | www.nps.gov/liri | Free | Daily, overlooks close at dark.

Sequoyah Caverns. Named for the Indian who conceived the Cherokee alphabet, the caverns have been called a doorway to the center of the Earth. Inside the cave are formations, fossils, towering stalagmites, and a "looking glass," with waters so still the reflection seems real. | 1438 Rte. 731, Valley Head | 256/635–0024 | fax 256/635–0017 | www.hsv.tis.net/~dekbtour | $7; special rates for groups | Mar.–Nov., daily 8:30–5; Dec.–Feb., weekends 8:30–5.

ON THE CALENDAR

OCT.: *DeKalb County VFW Agricultural Fair.* Named "Best in State" for many years, this fair includes rides, shows, crafts, food, flowers, and livestock judging. | VFW Fairgrounds | 256/845–4752.

OCT.: *Fort Payne Depot Museum Native American Festival.* Held in downtown Fort Payne's Union Park, this two-day festival presents intertribal dancing, flute players, drummers, storytellers, crafts for sale and on display, and indigenous food. On Sunday, there is a Native American Church service. | 256/492–5217.

Dining

Heroes Cafe. American. Originally an old drugstore, this is a 1950s-style café, complete with an old jukebox and booths. There are drawings by a local artist on the walls, as well as black-and-white photos of local heroes (hence the café's name). Diners are welcome to bring black-and-white pictures of their own personal heroes. The menu offers biscuits and gravy, and sandwiches such as roast beef and Swiss cheese, or corned beef and cabbage, and peach, apple, and blackberry cobblers. | 100 First St. southwest | 256/845–1903 | $6 | D, DC, V | Closed weekends.

Little River Cafe. American. This restaurant was built in 1927 by the Fischer family of Hugelheim, Germany. The food and decor has "country style"; the walls are festooned with local memorabilia and antiques such as farming and cooking equipment and old pictures. A lunch favorite is chicken fried steak with gravy, mashed potatoes, green beans, corn, and peach

cobbler. Dinner entrées include smothered beef tips and filet mignon. You can also sit outside on the patio to eat. Kids' menu. Live entertainment on Thursday, Friday, and Saturday nights. | 4608 De Soto Pkwy. | 256/997–0707 | $5–$10 | AE, D, MC, V | Closed Sun.

Lodging

DeSoto State Park Lodge. Known for showcasing the area's vibrant fall and spring colors, this rustic resort built in the 1930s is nestled in the mountains on Little River. Its abundant hiking trails and rushing waterfalls make it a popular vacation spot, especially in May and October. Restaurant, picnic area. Cable TV. Pool. 2 tennis courts. Volleyball. Fishing, bicycles. Playground. Laundry facilities. Business services. | 265 Rte. 951 | 256/845–5380 or 800/568–8840 | fax 256/845–3224 | www.vten.com | 25 rooms, 11 cabins, 11 chalets | $60, $68–$78 cabins, $86 chalets | AE, MC, V.

Fort Payne Travelodge. This standard motel is across from the county fairgrounds, convenient to a movie theater and restaurants, and about 2 mi from the airport. Restaurant. In-room data ports, some microwaves, some refrigerators, cable TV. Pool. Business services. | 1828 Gault Ave. north | 256/845–0481 | fax 256/845–6152 | 68 rooms in 5 buildings | $29–$35 | AE, D, MC, V.

Holiday Inn Express. This three-story stucco building is 4 mi from downtown Fort Payne. Kids under 18 stay free. Complimentary Continental breakfast. In-room data ports, some kitchenettes, cable TV. Pool. Laundry facilities. Free parking. | 112 Airport Rd. | 256/997–1020 or 800/465–4329 | www.hiexpress.com | 60 rooms | $65–$109 | AE, D, DC, MC, V.

Quality Inn. This standard motel is off Interstate 59 near exit 218, next door to a 24-hour restaurant and near others. Some microwaves, some refrigerators, cable TV. Pool. Laundry facilities. Business services. | 1412 Glenn Blvd. southwest | 256/845–4013 | fax 256/845–2344 | 79 rooms | $55 | AE, D, DC, MC, V.

Raven Haven Bed & Breakfast. On Lookout Mountain in Mentone, about 11 mi from Fort Payne, this inn has themed rooms like the Queen Anne, fashioned after an 18th-century boudoir; Casablanca has a tropical island motif; The Nautical has a cannonball bed, port holes, and rope hammock; The Little Room on the Prairie has a cast-iron pot over the stone fireplace. A patio looks over 10 acres of grounds. Complimentary breakfast. No kids under 14. | 651 County Rd. 644 | 256/634–4310 | 4 rooms | $85–$95 | No credit cards.

GADSDEN

MAP 3, E3

(Nearby towns also listed: Anniston, Fort Payne, Guntersville)

The Appalachian foothills, streams, and rivers are the backdrop for Gadsden, one of Alabama's largest industrial areas. Steel, rubber, and electronic devices are among items produced here.

Noccalula Falls Park is a primary attractions. The Center for Cultural Arts and Imagination Place Children's Museum has a place just for kids and a railroad-and-building scale model of early Gadsden. The 450-mi-long Lookout Mountain Parkway Outdoor Sale is held annually on a mid-August weekend.

Information: **Gadsden-Etowah Tourism Board** | 90 Walnut St., Gadsden 35901 | 256/549–0351 | fax 256/549–1854 | getb@cybrtyme.com | www.cybrtyme.com/tourism.

Attractions

Alabama *Princess* Riverboat. On boardwalk in downtown Gadsden, hop aboard the *Princess* for a day cruise along the Coosa River, or check out the nighttime dinner cruises. The boat is a replica of 19th-century excursion boats. | 300 Albert Rains Blvd. | 256/549–1111 | $7.

Center for Cultural Arts and Imagination Place Children's Museum. The triangular-shape center has four galleries featuring a wide range of changing national and local exhibits, a refined eclectic-style restaurant, and a model of Gadsden in the 1940s, with working railroads. Next to the center in the historic Kyle Building is Imagination Place Children's Museum, featuring Science Hall and Kids Town USA, a complete kid-size city with a bank, grocery store, hospital, and other make-believe places. | 501 Broad St. | 256/543–2787 | fax 256/546–7435 | www.culturalarts.com | $3; special rates for children; free Tues. afternoons; senior citizen's program $1.50 | Mon., Wed.–Fri. 9–6, Tues. 9–9, Sat. 10–6, Sun. 1–5. Imagination Place: weekdays 9–5, Sat. 10–5, Sun. 1–5.

Gadsden Museum of Arts. The permanent collection focuses on regional history and local and Alabama artists. American and European paintings, sculpture, and decorative arts enhance the main collections. | 2829 W. Meighan Blvd. | 256/546–7365 | Free | Mon.–Wed., Fri. 10–4, Thurs. 10–8, Sun. 1–5.

Noccalula Falls Park. Legend says the Indian Princess Noccalula jumped to her watery death over a lost love at this site. In reality, it contains a 200-year-old homestead, botanical gardens, miniature golf, zoo, and minitrain rides. A 90-ft waterfall is framed by canyon and nature trails. | Noccalula Rd. | 256/549–4663, 256/543–7412 campground | fax 256/546–5843 | Falls free; village $1.50 | Daily.

ON THE CALENDAR

AUG.: *Lookout Mountain Parkway Outdoor Sale.* The 450-mi sale stretches from Gadsden to Covington, Ohio, and operates typically from dawn to late evening with vendors offering everything imaginable. | 256/845–3957.

Dining

Warehouse. American. In the middle of town, this large wooden building used to be a cotton warehouse. The interior is outfitted with brass and linen tablecloths; an old organ and a huge antique sleigh are on display. Popular dishes are the prime rib and the seafood platter, which includes double crabs, red snapper, shrimp and oysters, and key lime pie for dessert. A local band plays rock 'n' roll every night. | 315 South 2nd St. | 256/547–5548 | $15 | AE, D, DC | Closed Sun.

Lodging

Gadsden Inn & Suites. The only motel in Gadsden with queen-size beds, this downtown inn is locally owned and operated. The property takes up an entire city block and overlooks the Coosa River. There is a deck for sunning and dining also with river views. Gadsden city park is nearby. Restaurant, complimentary breakfast. Some microwaves, some refrigerators, some hot tubs, cable TV, VCR. Laundry facilities. | 200 Albert Rains Blvd. | 256/543–7240 or 800/637–5678 | 83 rooms | $41–$109 | AE, D, DC, MC, V.

Hampton Inn. Standard chain property on the Coosa River, 1 mi from downtown, and across the street from Gadsden Mall. Complimentary Continental breakfast. In-room data ports, cable TV. Pool. Gym. Business services. | 129 River Rd. | 256/546–2337 or 800/HAMPTON | fax 256/547–5124 | www.hamptoninn.com | 100 rooms | $69–$140 | AE, D, DC, MC, V.

Red Roof Inn. This standard motel is on the Coosa River, next door to the popular Top of the River restaurant and within walking distance from other eateries. Picnic area, complimentary Continental breakfast. Cable TV. Pool. Laundry facilities. Business services. Some pets allowed. | 1600 Rainbow Dr. | 256/543–1105 or 800/843–7663 | fax 256/543–7836 | 104 rooms in 3 buildings | $49–$115 | AE, D, DC, MC, V.

GULF SHORES/ORANGE BEACH

MAP 3, B9

(Nearby town also listed: Mobile)

Gulf Shores and Orange Beach are coastal towns—separated from the mainland by the Intracoastal Waterway—with 32 mi of white-sand beaches and plenty of places to play, including amusement parks, golf, minigolf, and sailboat charters that take you into back bays and bayous. On the coast is the 6,000-acre Gulf State Park with a popular fishing pier; bird-watchers marvel at the many feathered inhabitants of the Bon Secour Wildlife Refuge.

Information: **Alabama Gulf Coast Convention and Visitors Bureau** | 3150 Gulf Shores Pkwy., Gulf Shores 36542 | 334/968–7511 or 800/745–7263 | fax 334/968–6095 | info@gulfshores.com. | www.gulfshores.com.

Attractions

Bon Secour National Wildlife Refuge. If nature is your passion, there's plenty to do here: hike among numerous nature trails (some lead to the beachfront); fish in fresh- and salt-water fishing; or paddle a small two-person boat into an alligator-inhabited lake. The area is known for its changing beach dunes, oak forests, and wildlife—keep a look out for bobcats, squirrels, rabbits, opossum, raccoons, and armadillos. | 12295 Rte. 180 west | 334/540–7720 | fax 334/540–7301 | Free | Daily dawn–dusk.

Fort Morgan Historic Site. Built in the early 1800s to guard the entrance to Mobile Bay, Fort Morgan was the scene of fiery action during the Battle of Mobile Bay in 1864: Confederate torpedoes sank the ironclad *Tecumseh,* after Union Admiral David Farragut gave his famous command "Damn the torpedoes! Full speed ahead!" The original outer walls still stand. | 51 Rte. 180 west | 334/540–7125 | fax 334/540–7665 | $3 | Daily 8–6; museum daily 9–5.
The **Fort Morgan Museum** chronicles the fort's history with an emphasis on the Civil War, and also displays artifacts from pre-colonial days through World War II. | 51 Rte. 180 west | 334/540–7125 | fax 334/540–7665 | Admission free with fort admission | Weekdays 8–5, Sat. 9–5.

Gulf State Park. Covering more than 6,000 acres of Pleasure Island, the park stretches along 2½ mi of pure white beaches and glimmering dunes. It has two freshwater lakes where you can canoe and fish, there are also biking, hiking, and jogging trails through pine forests. Near a large beach pavilion, a concrete fishing pier juts some 800 ft into the gulf. There are also a gulf-front resort lodge and convention center, campsites, cottages, tennis, and an 18-hole golf course. | 20115 Rte. 135 | 334/948–7275 or 800/544–4853 (resort) | fax 334/948–7726 | Free | Daily.

Track Family Recreation Center. This popular amusement complex has go-carts, bumper boats, bungee jumping, and video arcades to keep your teens amused while the wee ones enjoy trains, swings, and a Ferris wheel. | 3200 Gulf Shores Pkwy. | 334/968–8111 | www.gulfcoastrooms.com/thetrack | Call for fees | Call for hrs.

Waterville USA. Set on 17 acres, the park has a wave pool that creates 3-ft waves, seven water slides, and a lazy river ride that goes around the park. For younger children there are gentler rides in a play area. Adding to the fun are a 36-hole miniature golf course and a video-game arcade. | 906 Gulf Shores Pkwy. | 334/948–2106 | fax 334/948–7918 | www.watervilleusa.com | $18 | Water park: Memorial Day–Labor Day, daily 10–6. Amusement park: Mar.–Oct., daily 10–midnight.

Zooland Animal Park. Alabama's coastal zoo is the place to explore the natural habitats of more than 250 animals. Elevated decks offer close-up views of everything from alligators to giraffes and lions. | 1204 Gulf Shores Pkwy. | 334/968–5731 | fax 334/967–3358 | www.zooland.org | $8.80 | Daily 9–4:30.

KODAK'S TIPS FOR TAKING GREAT PICTURES

Get Closer
- Fill the frame tightly for maximum impact
- Move closer physically or use a long lens
- Continually check the viewfinder for wasted space

Choosing a Format
- Add variety by mixing horizontal and vertical shots
- Choose the format that gives the subject greatest drama

The Rule of Thirds
- Mentally divide the frame into vertical and horizontal thirds
- Place important subjects at thirds' intersections
- Use thirds' divisions to place the horizon

Lines
- Take time to notice lines
- Let lines lead the eye to a main subject
- Use the shape of lines to establish mood

Taking Pictures Through Frames
- Use foreground frames to draw attention to a subject
- Look for frames that complement the subject
- Expose for the subject, and let the frame go dark

Patterns
- Find patterns in repeated shapes, colors, and lines
- Try close-ups or overviews
- Isolate patterns for maximum impact (use a telephoto lens)

Textures that Touch the Eyes
- Exploit the tangible qualities of subjects
- Use oblique lighting to heighten surface textures
- Compare a variety of textures within a shot

Dramatic Angles
- Try dramatic angles to make ordinary subjects exciting
- Use high angles to help organize chaos and uncover patterns, and low angles to exaggerate height

Silhouettes
- Silhouette bold shapes against bright backgrounds
- Meter and expose for the background illumination
- Don't let conflicting shapes converge

Abstract Composition
- Don't restrict yourself to realistic renderings
- Look for ideas in reflections, shapes, and colors
- Keep designs simple

Establishing Size
- Include objects of known size
- Use people for scale, where possible
- Experiment with false or misleading scale

Color
- Accentuate mood through color
- Highlight subjects or create designs through color contrasts
- Study the effects of weather and lighting

From *Kodak Guide to Shooting Great Travel Pictures* © 2000 by Fodor's Travel Publications

ON THE CALENDAR

FEB.: *Mardi Gras.* Island-style celebration with parades and floats. | Area streets | 334/968–6904.

FEB.: *Pleasure Island Festival of Art.* Artists plus music and food booths. | Lake Shelby picnic area | 334/968–6151.

OCT.: *National Shrimp Festival.* This is the area's biggest beach party of the year showcasing state-harvested shrimp. Also artists, live music, a children's area, skydiving, and sailboat regatta. No pets are allowed. | Public beach | 334/968–6904.

NOV.: *Frank Brown International Songwriters' Festival.* This unique festival started as an end-of-the-year party for local performers and songwriters who played in the Flora-Bama Lounge which straddles the Alabama-Florida border. It has grown into a 11-day event with about 150 songwriters who play blues, country, gospel, and rock music. | 904/492–SONG or 334/981–5678.

Dining

Flora-Bama Lounge. Seafood. Since 1962, this sprawling series of 10 bars and a package store and oyster bar has straddled the Alabama–Florida border, right on the Gulf of Mexico. Open 365 days a year and featuring live bands on three stages, the Flora-Bama epitomizes laid-back life at the beach. Try fresh oysters by the dozen and Royal Red shrimp by the pound; pizza and hot dogs are also on the menu. Rustic, casual setting with open-air dining on deck, live music nightly. | 17401 Perdido Key Dr., Pensacola, FL | 334/980–5118 | fax 850/492–6375 | Call for prices | MC, V.

Gift Horse. Southern. Built as a hunting and fishing lodge in the early 1900s, this downtown Foley building has always been an important part of the community. In the 1940s, it was a USO club; many 50th- and 60th-wedding anniversaries have been celebrated at the Gift Horse, where the couples met during World War II. Known for its southern-style buffet featuring fried and baked chicken, tomato pie, and crawfish bisque. Buffet. Kids' menu. Sunday brunch. No smoking. | 209 W. Laurel Ave., Foley | 334/943–3663 | $9 lunch, $12 dinner | MC, V.

Hazel's. Seafood. In a busy commercial resort area, this comfortable family restaurant is especially popular for its breakfast omelets. There's buffet dining for breakfast, lunch, and dinner. There's also an all-you-can-eat seafood buffet, featuring a variety of fish and shrimp, salads, gumbo, and oysters. Kids' menu. Sunday brunch. | Rte. 182, Orange Beach | 334/981–4628 | $15–$19 | AE, D, DC, MC, V | Breakfast also available.

Kirk Kirkland's Hitchin' Post. American/Casual. This rustic, Western-theme restaurant has red-and-white-checked tablecloths, wooden floors, and a wide front porch with swings and rocking chairs. It attracts families and is known for daily lunch specials that include fried chicken, fried chicken strips, country fried steak, and sweet potatoes. Some seafood is also served: crab claws or shrimp, oysters, or fish fried or broiled. | 3401 Gulf Shores Pkwy. | 334/968–5041 | $10–$20 | AE, D, MC, V.

Mikee's. Seafood. The food at this popular restaurant in the heart of Gulf Shores will be worth the inevitable wait. Meanwhile, enjoy looking around at the mounted fish and photos of the owners' biggest catches, among the other local memorabilia decorating the walls. The special on Tuesday and Friday is all-you-can-eat fried mullet. Also on the menu are pasta dishes, steak, crab legs, and a popular all-you-can-eat fried-shrimp dinner; walk it off at the nearby beach. Kids' menu. | 1st St. north and 2nd Ave. east | 334/948–6452 | $10–$14 | AE, D, DC, MC, V.

★ Original Oyster House. Seafood. Fishing photos and other memorabilia line the walls of this casual restaurant. Enjoy great bayou views while you dine on fresh local catch. Have your shrimp steamed, stuffed, blackened, grilled, or broiled—it's all available. Steak, chicken, and burgers are also on the menu. Salad bar. Kids' menu. | Rte. 59 at Bayou Village | 334/948–2445 | $11–$18 | AE, D, DC, MC, V.

The Outrigger. Seafood. With one of the best locations on the Alabama Gulf Coast, this casual restaurant is at the foot of Alabama Point Bridge. A wall of windows gives you a breathtaking view of the Gulf of Mexico. The menu includes fresh seafood, aged choice steaks, veal, and pasta. The restaurant is well known for its creative sauces. Try the shrimp Perdido, sautéed in a garlicky lemon-butter sauce and served over linguine. Kids' menu. Patio for outdoor dining. Full bar, extensive wine list. | 27500 Perdido Beach Blvd., Orange Beach | 334/981–6700 | $15–$30 | AE, D, DC, MC, V.

Perdido Pass. Seafood. Overlooking busy Perdido Pass Marina and the Gulf of Mexico, you can dine on fresh local seafood, prepared in a wide variety of ways. Kids' menu. Weekend brunch. | 27501 Perdido Beach Blvd., Orange Beach | 334/981–6312 | $18–$24 | AE, D, DC, MC, V.

Sea-N-Suds. Seafood. Fresh seafood is moderately priced at this popular restaurant and oyster bar on the Gulf of Mexico. While you wait for a table, enjoy a frozen drink on the pier and take in the beautiful view. They serve fried fish, oysters, crab claws, and stuffed crabs. No smoking. | 405 E. Beach Blvd. | 334/948–7894 | $6–$12 | AE, MC, V | Closed Sun. and Oct.–May.

Voyagers. Contemporary. Perdido Beach Resort's fine-dining restaurant features the culinary artistry of the renowned Chef Gerhard Brill, who describes his style as Gulf Coast Creole. Specializing in tableside service, Voyagers combines the best in local seafood, meats, and produce with international ingredients. A wall of glass in the elegant dining room gives you an excellent view of the beach. Creative menu choices include the Louisiana-style turtle soup au sherry, fillet of red snapper with roasted pecans, and crepe soufflé praline. | 27200 Perdido Beach Blvd., Orange Beach | 334/981–9811 | Reservations essential | $24–$34 | AE, D, DC, MC, V | No lunch.

Zeke's Landing. Seafood. Large windows overlook Zeke's Landing Marina, where charter fishing boats arrive and depart. This two-story casual restaurant specializes in seafood and also serves prime rib, rib eye, and pasta dishes. Dine outdoors on one of the three decks. The comfortable bar area is a great people-watching spot. Kids' menu. Sunday brunch. | 26649 Perdido Beach Blvd., Orange Beach | 334/981–4001 | fax 334/981–2651 | $17–$25 | AE, D, DC, MC, V.

Lodging

Best Western on the Beach. This motel overlooks the Gulf of Mexico and has a beachside pool with a rock waterfall and a children's wading pool. Some rooms have private balconies, and there's a honeymoon suite with a hot tub. Restaurant. Some kitchenettes, cable TV. 2 pools. 2 hot tubs. Gym. Beach. Laundry facilities. Business services. | 182 E. Beach Blvd. | 334/948–2711 or 800/788–4557 | fax 334/948–7339 | www.bestwestern-onthebeach.com | 104 rooms | $116–$209 | AE, D, DC, MC, V.

Gulf State Park Resort Hotel. This modern beachfront hotel is part of Gulf State Park, which occupies 6,150 acres, including a 2½-mi stretch of white-sand beach. All rooms face the beach, overlooking the Gulf of Mexico. An 825-ft, state-operated fishing pier, the longest on the Gulf, is within easy walking distance. Bar, dining room. In-room data ports, kitchenettes in suites, cable TV. Pool. Driving range, 18-hole golf course, tennis court. Beach. Fishing. Laundry facilities. Business services. No-smoking rooms. | 21250 E. Beach Blvd., Foley | 334/948–4853 or 800/544–GULF | fax 334/948–5998 | www.vten.com | 144 rooms, 18 suites | $107–$113, $214 suites | AE, MC, V.

Hampton Inn. A three-story white stucco building facing the beach, this inn has an open atrium with a large balcony, overlooking the pool. The beach front rooms also have balconies and open onto the beach. Complimentary Continental breakfast. Picnic area. In-room data ports, cable TV. Pool. Beach. Laundry facilities. Free parking. No pets. | 22988 Perdido Beach Blvd. | 334/975–1598 or 888/485–3726 | fax 334/974–1599 | 96 rooms | $55–$159 | AE, D, DC, MC, V.

Hilton Beachfront Garden Inn. On the beach with beautiful gulf views, this lushly landscaped hotel is convenient to golf, charter fishing, and Jet Ski rentals. Each room has a private balcony overlooking the beach. Restaurant, bars. In-room data ports, microwaves, refrigerators, cable TV. Indoor-outdoor pool. Hot tub. Gym, beach. Laundry facilities. Busi-

GULF SHORES/
ORANGE BEACH

INTRO
ATTRACTIONS
DINING
LODGING

ness services. No-smoking rooms. | 334/974–1600 or 888/644–5866 | fax 334/974–1012 | 137 rooms | $154–$184 | AE, D, DC, MC, V.

Holiday Inn Express. This standard inn is across from the Riviera Centre mall, about 10 minutes from Gulf Shores. Complimentary Continental breakfast. Microwaves, refrigerators. Pool. Hot tub. Gym. Laundry facilities. Business services. No-smoking rooms. | 2682 S. McKenzie St., Foley | 334/943–9100 or 800/962–1833 | fax 334/943–9421 | 83 rooms | $69–$89 | AE, D, DC, MC, V.

Island House Hotel. In the center of town, each room in this sleek geometrically shaped hotel has a private balcony with a beautiful view of the pool area, white-sand beach, and the Gulf of Mexico. The hotel has 336 ft of private beach and is across from Zeke's Landing and Marina. Several malls and restaurants are in walking distance, 1 mi from Perdido Key. Bar, room service. In-room safes, cable TV. Pool, wading pool. Beach. Laundry facilities. Business services. No-smoking rooms. | 26650 Perdido Beach Blvd., Orange Beach | 334/981–6100 or 800/264–2642 | fax 334/981–6543 | islndhse@aol.com | www.gulfcoastrooms.com | 161 rooms | $135; 2–night minimum stay in summer | AE, MC, V.

Lighthouse Resort Motel. On 630 ft of private beach, these motel rooms and apartments feature a gulf view. Some kitchenettes, refrigerators, cable TV. 3 pools. Hot tub. Beach. Business services. Some pets allowed (fee). | 455 E. Beach Blvd. | 334/948–6188 | fax 334/948–6100 | www.gulfcoastrooms.com | 219 rooms | $80–$159 | AE, D, DC, MC, V.

Original Romar House Bed & Breakfast Inn. Overlooking the Gulf of Mexico, this is one of the oldest homes in the Gulf Shores area, and Alabama's first seaside bed-and-breakfast. Each bedroom is named after an area festival and is filled with Art Deco furniture. An old Chicago brick walkway leads to the beach. Complimentary breakfast. Cable TV. Hot tub. Beach access. No pets. No kids under 12. | 23500 Perdido Beach Blvd. | 334/974–1625 or 800/487–6627 | fax 334/974–1163 | original@gulftel.com | 6 rooms | $89–$139 | AE, MC, V.

★ **Perdido Beach Resort.** Between Gulf Shores and Perdido Key, Florida, this luxurious, Mediterranean-style, beachfront resort features comfortably furnished rooms with panoramic views of the Gulf. Nearby attractions include six golf courses, several parks, and the first U.S. Naval Air Station and Museum. Children stay free. 3 restaurants, 2 bars (with entertainment). In-room data ports, some refrigerators, cable TV. Indoor-outdoor pool. Hot tub, sauna. 4 tennis courts. Gym. Beach. Children's programs. Business services. No-smoking floors, no-smoking rooms. | 27200 Perdido Beach Blvd., Orange Beach | 334/981–9811 or 800/634–8001 | fax 334/981–5672 | www.perdidobeachresort.com | 345 rooms | $150–$165 | AE, D, DC, MC, V.

Quality Inn Beachside. Directly on the Gulf of Mexico and within walking distance of Gulf Shores restaurants and nightlife, this hotel features a dramatic six-story atrium. All rooms have balconies and living rooms and most rooms face the gulf. Restaurant, 2 bars, room service. Some kitchenettes, cable TV. 2 pools. Beach. Children's programs, playground. Laundry facilities. Business services. No pets. No-smoking rooms. | fax 334/948–5232 | www.qibeachside.com | 158 rooms | $112–$159 rooms, $162–$205 suites | AE, D, DC, MC, V.

Regal Inn and Suites. Just 8 mi from the beach at Gulf Shores, this standard inn is also within a mile of Riviera Centre outlet mall, a 12-cinema movie theater, and numerous restaurants. Complimentary Continental breakfast. Cable TV. Pool. Gym. Business services. No-smoking buildings, no-smoking rooms. | 1517 S. McKenzie St., Foley | 334/943–3297 | fax 334/943–7548 | 90 rooms in 3 buildings | $79–$89 | AE, D, MC, V.

Sleep Inn. This six-story hotel is the third-largest Sleep Inn in the United States. Some rooms overlook the beach; all have balconies. Complimentary Continental breakfast. In-room data ports. Some microwaves, some refrigerators, cable TV. Pool. Beach. Laundry facilities. No pets. | 25400 Perdido Beach Blvd. | 800/430–2738 | 118 rooms | $45–$150 | AE, D, DC, MC, V.

Summerland Bed & Breakfast. This Georgian-style home is surrounded by magnolia, pine, and oak trees. There are a gazebo and a patio and you can fish in the nearby gulf or adjacent Bon Secour and Magnolia rivers. The uniquely themed rooms include tribal art and French Louisiana antiques. No children or pets without prior approval. Complimentary breakfast. Cable TV. Pool. Driving range, golf course. Beach. | 19160 James Rd. | 334/955–6478 | fax 334/955–6479 | summerland@quixnet.net | 4 rooms | $98–$135 | AE, MC, V.

White Sands Resort. In the heart of Gulf Shores, the hotel is convenient to many restaurants, bars, and shops. Room decor is tropical with ceramic tile floors. Each has a private patio or balcony. Restaurant, bar (with entertainment), room service. In-room data ports, cable TV. 2 pools, wading pool. Hot tub. Gym, beach. Laundry facilities. No-smoking rooms. | 365 E. Beach Blvd. | 334/948–6191 | fax 334/948–8240 | www.whitesandsresort.com | 149 rooms | $155–$215 | AE, D, DC, MC, V.

GUNTERSVILLE

(Nearby towns also listed: Gadsden, Huntsville)

Legend has it that in 1540 explorer Hernando De Soto passed through what today is Guntersville as he followed the Tennessee River westward. Cherokee Indians lived in the area until being driven out in the 1830s. Originally named Gunter's Landing for Scotsman John Gunter, the area, along a river port, boomed in the early 1800s with the coming of the steamboat. With the creation of the Tennessee Valley Authority in the 1930s, the area blossomed into a recreational and industrial city.

Today, bass fishing is the prime activity on Lake Guntersville, just 45 minutes south of Huntsville. The area's natural beauty combined with a wealth of outdoor recreational opportunities, such as golf, hiking, camping, and world-class bass fishing, make this a popular vacation destination. Lake Guntersville State Park is one of the state's most popular destinations, with lodge, chalets, cabins, and a restaurant.

Information: Lake Guntersville Chamber of Commerce | 200 Gunter Ave., Guntersville 35976 | 256/582–3612 or 800/869–5253 | fax 256/582–3682 | gcc@lakeguntersville.org | www.lakeguntersville.org. **Marshall County Convention and Visitors Bureau** | Box 711, Guntersville 35976 | 256/582–7015 or 800/582–6282 | fax 256/582–3682 | mccvb@mindspring.com | www.marshallcountycvb.com.

Attractions

Guntersville Dam and Lake. The dam is Alabama's largest impoundment, with 69,000 acres and more than 900 mi of shoreline. Noted nationally as a bass lake, Guntersville also holds abundant bream, crappie, white bass, hybrid bass, and sauger. Miles of milfoil grass line upper reaches, and abundant deep water characterize the lower region. | U.S. 431 | 256/582–7015 | Free | Daily.

Lake Guntersville State Park. Overlooking Guntersville Reservoir, this sprawling park sits on Little Mountain. In addition to the fishing, swimming, and boating offered by the lake, the park has tennis, golf, 12 mi of hiking trails, and winter programs spotlighting the American bald eagles that winter at the park. | 1155 Lodge Dr. Park: 7966 Alabama State Hwy. 227 | 256/571–5444 or 800/548–4553 | fax 256/571–5459 | www.vten.com | Free | Daily.

Lodging

Lake Guntersville Bed and Breakfast. Built in 1910, this inn has 10-ft-wide wraparound porches with incredible views of the surrounding Appalachian Mountain foothills and Lake Guntersville, the state's largest lake—in fact, you can even arrive by boat. Guest rooms have high ceilings, antique furnishings, baths, and private entrances. Downtown is within walking distance and has many restaurants and shops; Boaz outlet stores are just 20 minutes away. Complimentary breakfast. Cable TV. Business services. | 2204 Scott St. | 256/505–0133 | fax 256/505–0133 | www.bbonline.com/al/lakeguntersville | 7 rooms | $59–$115 | AE, D, MC, V.

Lake Guntersville Holiday Inn Resort. Many of the rooms face beautiful Lake Guntersville in this hotel. Boat and water-sports rental facilities are nearby. The renovated lobby and pool area has a screened-in patio overlooking the lake. Restaurant, bar (with entertainment), picnic area, room service. In-room data ports, some kitchenettes, cable TV. Pool. Dock. Laundry facilities, laundry service. Business services. No-smoking rooms. | 2140 Gunter Ave. | 256/582–2220 | fax 256/582–2059 | 100 rooms | $69–$125 | AE, D, DC, MC, V.

Lake Guntersville Lodge. This resort lodge, restaurant, and convention complex are on Little Mountain, overlooking the 66,470-acre Guntersville Reservoir. All rooms have a lake view. Hike the guided trails in Lake Guntersville State Park, which has 5,909 acres of mountaintops and meadows. Dining room. Cable TV. Pool, wading pool. Sauna. 18-hole golf course, putting green, tennis. Hiking, beach, dock, water sports. Playground. Laundry facilities. Business services. | 1155 Lodge Dr. | 256/571–5440 or 800/548–4553 | fax 256/571–5459 | www.vten.com | 100 rooms in lodge, 15 cottages, 20 chalets | $62–$100, $110 cottages, $110 chalets | AE, MC, V.

HUNTSVILLE

MAP 3, D1

(Nearby towns also listed: Athens, Decatur)

Huntsville gained fame when thousands of acres of cotton fields became Redstone Arsenal, which produced chemical weapons and other ammunition during World War II. Following the war, the arsenal's future was uncertain until the army managed to attract Dr. Wernher von Braun and his team of German rocket scientists, who developed America's first rocket. Their work enabled the nation to launch an artificial satellite as early as 1954, only four years after von Braun's arrival. The largest city in northern Alabama, Huntsville retains the influence of those early scientists. The U.S. Army remains the city's largest employer.

Today, the nation's space program—and the men and women who guided it—are showcased at the U.S. Space and Rocket Center, the city's most visited attraction. The state's early years are remembered at another major attraction, Alabama Constitution Village, on the site of Alabama's Constitutional Convention of 1819. Authentic demonstrations of skills such as woodworking, printing, cooking, and weaving are performed by interpreters in period dress. Take a trolley ride into the Historic Huntsville Depot for a look at early 19th-century railroad life.

Information: **Huntsville/Madison County Convention and Visitors Bureau** | 700 Monroe St., Huntsville 35801 | 256/533–5723 or 800/772–2348 | fax 256/551–2324 | info@huntsville.org | www.huntsville.org.

Attractions

★ **Alabama Constitution Village.** The $2 million living-history museum, built on the site where Alabama's first constitution was penned, reenacts 19th-century life in America. Authentically dressed interpreters show what daily life was like in 1800s. They demonstrate candle making, spinning, sheepshearing, wooden printing presses, gardening, and woodworking. | 109 Gates Ave. | 256/535–8100 | fax 256/564–8151 | www.earlyworks.com | $6 | Feb.–Dec. 23, Mon.–Sat. 9–5.

Burritt Museum & Park. The park's centerpiece is an 11-room mountaintop mansion built in the shape of a Maltese cross. Among the unusual exhibits are mineral chunks, Indian pottery fragments, 19th-century surgical instruments, and tiny oil paintings on cobwebs. In fall, the park is the setting for a Fall Sorghum and Harvest Festival. | 3101 Burritt Dr. | 256/536–2882 | fax 256/532–1784 | www.huntsville.org | $5; mansion, grounds, and nature trail free | Buildings: Mar.–mid-Dec., Tues.–Sat. 10–4, Sun. noon–4. Grounds: Apr.–Sept., daily 7–7; Oct.–Mar., daily 7–5.

Huntsville Depot Museum. An 1860s railroad depot has been transformed into a museum named to the National Register of Historic Places. It includes computerized displays, model trains, old steam engines, a roundhouse, and trolley rides. During renovations, builders discovered—and preserved—scrawlings on an upstairs wall, made by Union soldiers stationed at the depot during the Civil War. | 320 Church St. | 256/539–6565 or 800/678–1819 | fax 256/564–8151 | www.earlyworks.com | $5 | Mon.–Sat. 9–5.

Huntsville-Madison County Botanical Garden. In the midst of a dynamic city, the 113-acre site offers serene woodland paths, grass meadows, and colorful blooming plants. There also are a 5-acre Central Corridors gardens and a Center for Biosphere Education and Research. | 4747 Bob Wallace Ave. | 256/830–4447 | fax 256/830–5314 | www.hsvbg.org | $4 | Labor Day–Memorial Day, Mon.–Sat. 9–5, Sun. 1–5. Memorial Day–Labor Day, Mon.–Sat. 8–6:30, Sun. 1–6:30.

Huntsville Museum of Art. This visual arts center focuses on American paintings and art from the 18th century to the present. An art education gallery offers a hands-on experience. Rotating exhibits and educational programs are offered. | 300 Church St. | 256/535–4350 | fax 256/532–1743 | www.hsv.tis.net/hma | Free | Tues.–Wed. and Fri.–Sat. 10–5, Thurs. 10–9, Sun. 1–5.

★ **U.S. Space and Rocket Center.** The largest space museum on Earth includes authentic NASA spacecraft from America's early space pioneer days, thrilling weightlessness simulation rides, exhibits, and demonstrations. A six-story OmniMax Theater shows movies filmed aboard the space shuttle. The Rocket Center is home to the U.S. Space Camp and Space Academy, where you can get a crash course in astronaut training. | 1 Tranquility Base | 256/837–3400 or 800/63–SPACE | fax 256/837–6137 | www.ussrc.com | $14 | Memorial Day–Labor Day, daily 9–6; Labor Day–Memorial Day, daily 9–5.

ON THE CALENDAR

MAY: *Panoply of the Arts Festival.* Visitors enjoy pieces by performing and visual artists, both local talent and guests, and a children's Discovery Area. | Big Springs Park | 256/564–8100.

SEPT.: *Big Springs Jam.* Rock, country, jazz, oldies, and children's acts on outdoor stages. | Big Springs Park | 256/551–2359.

Dining

Fogcutter. Steak. A popular place for special occasions, this restaurant is known for its romantic atmosphere and subdued lighting. Nautical antiques accent the room; in winter, the scene gets cozier when they light up the fireplaces. Try the hand-cut, steer-butt steak. Kids' menu. Sunday brunch. | 3805 University Dr. northwest | 256/539–2121 | $22–$25 | AE, D, DC, MC, V.

Jazz Factory. American/Casual. The interior of this downtown restaurant is reminiscent of the 1930s with mahogany furnishings and intimate lighting. The second-floor martini room and cigar bar is a popular place for the "in crowd." Make reservations early for a wine-tasting dinner held the third Sunday of each month, featuring a gourmet four-course meal paired with compatible wines. Known for organic salads, homemade sauces, pastas, pizza, and seafood. Live music Wednesday–Saturday. Weekend brunch. | 109 North Side Sq | 256/539–1919 | $13–$20 | AE, D, MC, V | No lunch Sat.

Ol' Heidelberg. German. For an authentic German experience, complete with waitstaff dressed in dirndls and lederhosen, Ol' Heidelberg delivers. For almost 30 years, this restaurant has offered Bavarian dishes like schnitzel accompanied by a nice selection of German wines and beers, including Spaten Munich on tap. Outdoor sidewalk dining. | 6125 University Dr. northwest | 256/922–0556 | $18–$25 | AE, D, MC, V.

Victoria's Cafe. American. Dining here is like dining at a friend's house. Cash registers and other restaurant accoutrements are cleverly hidden in sideboards and armoires. Dainty southern casseroles, sandwiches, and salads are served with specialty teas on white table-

cloths. Try the poulet de Normandie, a blend of chicken, mushrooms, and cheese baked en casserole, and the strawberry pretzel salad. | 7540 S. Memorial Pkwy. | 256/881–0403 | $6–$9 | AE, D, DC, MC, V | Closed Sun. No lunch.

Lodging

Baymont Inn and Suites. Completely renovated in 1999, this standard inn is one block from Madison Square Mall and 3 mi from the U.S. Space and Rocket Center. Kids under 18 stay free. Complimentary Continental breakfast. In-room data ports, microwaves in suites, refrigerators in suites, cable TV. Pool. Business services. Some pets allowed. No-smoking rooms. | 4890 University Dr. northwest | 256/830–8999 | fax 205/837–5720 | www.baymontinns.com | 102 rooms | $54–$99 | AE, D, DC, MC, V.

Bibb House Bed and Breakfast. The Bibb is one block from downtown Madison, and just 7 mi from Huntsville. The oldest home in Madison, this Greek Revival plantation home was built in 1867 when the town was just a railroad community. The wide front porch overlooks the 2-acre property, the railway, and Old Madison, and breakfast is served on the back sunporch. The "Beam room" has a king-size bed, beautiful beamed ceiling, full bath, private entrance, and its own porch. Complimentary breakfast. No TV, cable TV in common room. | 11 Allen St., Madison | 256/772–0586 | fax 256/772–7177 | info@bibbhouse.com | www.bbonline.com/al/bibbhouse/index.html | 2 rooms | $85–$100 (weekends require 2–day minimum) | AE, D, MC, V.

Comfort Inn. This standard motel is about 2½ mi from the U.S. Space and Rocket Center, 3 mi from Cummings Research Park, and just minutes from downtown. Complimentary Continental breakfast. Microwaves, refrigerators, cable TV, in-room VCRs. Pool. Laundry service. Business services. | 3788 University Dr. | 256/533–3291 | fax 256/536–7389 | 67 rooms, 8 suites | $52, $60 suites | AE, D, DC, MC, V.

Courtyard by Marriott. This standard hotel was renovated in 2000 and is located about 10 minutes from the U.S. Space and Rocket Center, close to several restaurants and shops. Restaurant, bar. In-room data ports, microwaves in suites, refrigerators in suites, cable TV. Pool. Hot tub. Gym. Laundry facilities. Business services. No-smoking rooms. | 4804 University Dr. | 256/837–1400 | fax 256/837–3582 | 149 rooms, 8 suites | $49–$72, $72–$92 suites | AE, D, DC, MC, V.

Economy Inn. This standard motel is located near Madison Square Mall and many restaurants, and it's minutes from the U.S. Space and Rocket Center. Microwaves in suites, refrigerators in suites, cable TV. Pool. Laundry facilities. No-smoking rooms. | 3772 University Dr. northwest | 256/534–7061 | fax 256/534–7061 | 82 rooms, 3 suites | $30–$40, $45 suites | AE, D, DC, MC, V.

Four Points Hotel. This hotel is located right inside the Huntsville International Airport terminal. You can get off the plane, check into the hotel, and rent a car without stepping outside. The hotel is just five minutes from the U.S. Space and Rocket Center. Restaurant, bar, room service. Cable TV. Pool. Hot tub. 18-hole golf course, 2 tennis courts. Gym. Laundry service. Business services, free parking. No-smoking floors, no-smoking rooms. | 1000 Glen Hearn Blvd. | 256/772–9661 | fax 256/464–9116 | 148 rooms | $109 | AE, D, DC, MC, V.

Guest House Suites. Each room in this conveniently located hotel features a fireplace and a private patio or balcony. Picnic area, complimentary Continental breakfast. In-room data ports, kitchenettes, cable TV. Pool. Hot tub. Tennis. Basketball. Laundry facilities, laundry service. Business services, airport shuttle. Some pets allowed. No-smoking rooms. | 4020 Independence Dr. | 256/837–8907 | fax 256/837–5435 | 112 suites in 12 buildings | $80–$105 | AE, D, DC, MC, V.

Hampton Inn. On the west side of town, this standard inn is convenient to Madison Square Mall and a five-minute drive from the U.S. Space and Rocket Center, restaurants nearby. Complimentary Continental breakfast. In-room data ports, some microwaves, some refrigerators, cable TV. Pool. Hot tub. Laundry service. Business services. No-smoking rooms. | 4815 University Dr. | 256/830–9400 | fax 256/830–0978 | www.hamptoninn.com | 164 rooms | $63–$72 | AE, D, DC, MC, V.

Hilton. This downtown historic district hotel is across the street from the Von Braun Center and near Big Springs Park. Several restaurants and a museum are nearby. Restaurant, bar (with entertainment). In-room data ports, cable TV. Pool. Hot tub. Gym. Business services, airport shuttle. Some pets allowed. No-smoking rooms. | 401 Williams Ave. | 256/533–1400 | fax 256/534–7787 | 277 rooms | $99–$129 | AE, D, DC, MC, V.

Holiday Inn–Huntsville I–565 West. This standard inn is less than 5 mi from the Madison Aquatic Club, Huntsville International Airport, and the U.S. Space and Rocket Center. Restaurant, bar, room service. In-room data ports, cable TV. Pool. Hot tub. Business services, airport shuttle. No-smoking rooms. | 9035 Madison Blvd. west, | 256/772–7170 | fax 256/464–0762 | 172 rooms | $69–$85 | AE, D, DC, MC, V.

Holiday Inn–Research Park. This standard hotel is within walking distance of Madison Square Mall, near several restaurants and major companies. Restaurant, bar (with entertainment), room service. In-room data ports, cable TV. Indoor-outdoor pool. Hot tub. Gym. Laundry facilities. Business services, airport shuttle. No-smoking rooms. | 5903 University Dr. | 256/830–0600 | fax 256/830–9576 | 200 rooms | $79–$85 | AE, D, DC, MC, V.

Holiday Inn–Space Center. Less than 2 mi from the U.S. Space and Rocket Center, this standard hotel is in a busy area near Madison Square Mall. Restaurant, bar, room service. In-room data ports, cable TV. Pool. Gym. Laundry facilities. Business services, airport shuttle. Some pets allowed. No-smoking rooms. | 3810 University Dr. | 256/837–7171 | fax 256/837–9257 | 112 rooms | $75 | AE, D, DC, MC, V.

La Quinta. Just 4 mi from the U.S. Space and Rocket Center, this standard motel is near many restaurants. Complimentary Continental breakfast. In-room data ports, cable TV. Pool. Laundry service. Business services. Some pets allowed. No-smoking rooms. | 3141 University Dr. northwest | 256/533–0756 | fax 256/539–5414 | 130 rooms | $59–$66 | AE, D, DC, MC, V.

Marriott. Just off Interstate 65, this seven-story hotel is a three-minute walk from the U.S. Space and Rocket Center, 5 mi from the Huntsville Botanical Gardens, and 10 minutes from downtown. Restaurants, bar (with entertainment). In-room data ports, some kitchenettes, cable TV. Indoor-outdoor pool. Hot tub. Gym. Business services, airport shuttle. No-smoking rooms. | 5 Tranquility Base | 256/830–2222 | fax 256/895–0904 | 290 rooms | $79–$140 | AE, D, DC, MC, V.

Radisson Suite Hotel. Featuring all suites, this hotel is 20 minutes south of downtown Huntsville. Restaurant, bar. In-room data ports, microwaves, refrigerators, cable TV. Pool. Hot tub. Gym. Laundry facilities, laundry service. Business services, airport shuttle. No-smoking rooms. | 6000 S. Memorial Pkwy. | 256/882–9400 | fax 256/882–9684 | 153 suites | $69–$109 | AE, D, DC, MC, V.

MENTONE

MAP 3, E2

(Nearby town also listed: Fort Payne)

In this mountain retreat you can hike to a waterfall, overlook a canyon created by a river, or browse along the short, quaint streets lined with shops, restaurants, and craft places, many of which are housed in historic buildings.

Early visitors converged on the town to renew themselves in the area's warm spring mineral waters. During the tuberculosis scare, families were lured by the fresh mountain air, and in the late 1800s the area became a health resort. These days, the air is filled with the sounds of fiddles, church chimes, banjos, and harmonizing voices.

Information: Dekalb County Tourist Association | 1503 Glenn Blvd. southwest, Fort Payne 35968 | 256/845–3957 | pattyt@mindspring.com | www.mentone.com/tourist.

Attractions

Cloudmont Ski Resort. North of Fort Payne is Alabama's only snow ski resort, which pumps out snow when temperatures dip to 28°F. The white fluff covers two 1,000-ft slopes with a vertical drop of 150 ft. Ski season is usually from January until March, depending on the temperatures. When the snow melts, there is a golf course. Ski equipment is available for rent. Year-round, you can visit the dude ranch which offers trail rides, cookouts, square dancing, and rental cabins. | 721 Rte. 614 | 256/634–4344 | fax 256/634–4344 | www.cloudmont.com | Rates vary.

Lodging

Cloudmont Ski and Golf Resort. Golfing is both affordable and spectacular at this rustic resort, with the first tee perched atop a towering rock. When temperatures dip to 28°F, snow machines cover two 1,000-ft slopes. You can also hike, fish and swim here. Restaurant. Some kitchenettes (in chalets), no room phones, no TV. 9-hole golf course. Fishing. Downhill skiing. | 721 Rte. 614 | 256/634–4344 | www.cloudmont.com | 6 chalets, 2 motel rooms, log cabin | $65 chalets, $60 motel rooms, $60 log cabin | MC, V.

Shady Grove Dude and Guest Ranch. Just across Little River from Cloudmont Ski and Golf Resort, the state's only dude ranch offers you a place to hike trails, square dance, and ride horses. Choose from breakfast rides, trail rides, or dinner rides on horseback or wagon. Cottages can accommodate up to eight people. Picnic area. Kitchenettes, no room phones. Horseback riding. Fishing. | 721 Rte. 614 | 256/634–4344 | www.cloudmont.com | 2 cottages | $75–$200 | No credit cards.

MOBILE

MAP 3, A8

(Nearby towns also listed: Dauphin Island, Gulf Shores/Orange Beach)

Mobile has been a strategic port and shipping center since its founding in 1702 by Jean Baptiste le Moyne. It is in Mobile that Alabama meets the sea and where Mardi Gras, architecture, and street names are evidence of the city's French and Spanish heritage. Alabama's oldest city is noted for its moss-draped trees, and a lengthy and wartorn history. Museums are abundant, as are Civil War forts, spring-blooming azaleas, and antebellum homes.

The best known of the city's abundant annual events are Mardi Gras, two weeks of pre-Lenten merriment, and the annual Azalea Trail Festival, when thousands of blooming azaleas outline city streets.

Information: Mobile Convention and Visitors Corporation | 1 S. Water St., Mobile 36602 | 334/208–2000 or 800/566–2453 | fax 334/208–2060 | info@mobile.org | www.mobile.org.

Attractions

★ **Battleship Memorial Park, USS *Alabama*.** Public subscription saved the mighty gray USS *Alabama* from being scrapped after her heroic World War II service. A tour of the ship gives a fascinating look into the life of a 2,500-member crew. Anchored next to the battleship is the submarine USS *Drum*, another active battle weapon during World War II. Other exhibits in the 100-acre Battleship Park include a B-52 bomber called *Calamity Jane* and a P-51 Mustang fighter plane. | 2703 Battleship Pkwy. (Hwys. 90/98), just off I-10, exits 27 or 30 | 334/433–2703 or 800/426–4929 | fax 334/433–2777 | www.ussalabama.com | $8 | Daily 8–dusk.

Bragg-Mitchell Mansion. The mansion is one of the Gulf Coast's grandest structures and Mobile's most-photographed building. Built in 1855, the 20-room mansion is framed by 16 slender fluted columns. Mirrors in the double parlors are among the few original furnishings. | 1906 Springhill Ave. | 334/471–6364 | fax 334/471–4686 | $5 | Weekdays 10–4, Sun. 1–4.

Carlen House Museum. An example of a Creole cottage–style farmhouse, it was built by an Irish immigrant family named Carlen. The kitchen and family rooms are furnished with artifacts that portray mid-19th-century farm life in Mobile. | 54 Carlen St. | 334/470–7768 | fax 334/208–7686 | Free | Tues.–Sat. 1–5.

Cathedral of the Immaculate Conception. Built on Spanish burial grounds, the Roman Basilica–designed cathedral stands in the heart of Mobile's Old Town. Construction began in 1835 and was completed in 1850. The cathedral features 14 hand-painted stations of the cross. | 2 S. Claiborne St. | 334/434–1565 | fax 334/434–1588 | Free | Weekdays 8:15–noon and 12:45–3.

Condé-Charlotte Museum House. The house museum is outfitted with period antiques and decorative arts depicting five periods of historic Mobile. Original cannons from French Fort Condé and English Fort Charlotte stand on the grounds. | 104 Theatre St. | 334/432–4722 | $4 | Tues.–Sat. 10–4.

Fort Condé Mobile Visitor Welcome Center. The original Fort Condé has survived, thanks to a $2.2 million restoration. Inside are the city's visitor center, a museum, and several re-created rooms. Costumed guides interpret and enlighten. | 150 S. Royal St. | 334/434–7304 | fax 334/208–7659 | Free | Daily 8–5.

Mobile Greyhound Park. Watch live greyhound racing and partake in pari-mutuel wagering on thoroughbreds and greyhound via closed-circuit simulcast. Clubhouse dining features seafood and steaks. | 7101 Old Pascagoula Rd., Theodore | 334/653–5000 | fax 334/653–9185 | Free grandstand admission | Mon.–Sat. 7:30 PM–11 PM.

Gulf Coast Exploreum Museum of Science. Across from the Mobile Convention Center, the multimillion-dollar facility is a total sensory immersion, hands-on science museum. It is the place to touch, smell, magnify, build, and explore. There also is an OmniMax theater. | 65 Government St. | 334/208–6883 | fax 334/208–6889 | www.exploreum.com | $6.75 | June–Aug., Sun.–Thurs. 9–8, Fri.–Sat. 9–9; Sept.–May, Sun.–Thurs. 9–5, Fri.–Sat. 9–9.

Malbis Greek Orthodox Church. The Malbis Greek Orthodox Church is a replica of a beautiful Byzantine church in Athens, Greece. It was built in the 1960s, at a cost of more than $1 million, as a memorial to the faith of a Greek immigrant and former monk, Jason Malbis, who founded the community but died before his dream for a cathedral could be realized. A master painter was brought from Greece to paint murals on the walls and the 75-ft dome of the rotunda. | 29300 U.S. 27, Daphne | 334/626–3050 | Free | Daily 9–noon and 2–5.

Mobile Museum of Art. The museum has a permanent collection of 5,000 works spanning 2,000 years of cultural history. It offers numerous traveling exhibits from prestigious museums and collections. In the heart of downtown, at 355 Government Street, the museum also operates a gallery with a variety of exhibits, ranging from works by local artists to themed selections from its permanent collection. | Expo Hall, 401 Civic Center Dr. | 334/208–5200 | fax 334/208–5201 | Free | Mon.–Sat. 10–5, Sun. 1–5.

Museum of Mobile. The museum showcases periods of Mobile's history, from colonization, Civil War, and the 19th century to the present. The display of Victorian carriages is a highlight. | 355 Government St. | 334/208–7569 | fax 334/208–7686 | Free | Tues.–Sat. 10–5, Sun. 1–5.

Oakleigh Period House Museum. The imposing Greek Revival mansion has a stairway circling under ancient live oaks to a small portico. The high-ceilinged, half-timber house was built in 1833 and is typical of the most expensive dwellings of its day. Fine period furniture, portraits, silver, jewelry, kitchen implements, toys, and more are displayed. Costumed guides lead tours. | 350 Oakleigh Pl | 334/432–1281 | fax 334/432–8843 | $5 | Mon.–Sat. 10–4; guided tours every ½ hr, last tour 3:30.

Phoenix Fire Museum. Dating from 1855 and once home to the Phoenix Fire Company, the restored firehouse holds steamers and fire engines, dating back to the 19th century. Exhibits showcase the men and equipment that fought the city's early fires. | 203 S. Claiborne St. | 334/208–7554 | fax 334/208–7686 | Free | Tues.–Sat. 10–5, Sun. 1–5.

Richards–DAR House. Built in 1860, the house holds magnificent period furnishings and is one of Mobile's most significant examples of Italianate style. Exterior ironwork is notable. Other highlights are Cornelius chandeliers, Carrara marble mantles, a cantilevered staircase, and a walled-in garden. The Daughters of the American Revolution run the museum,

HANGING AROUND WITH SPANISH MOSS

Swaying palm trees in the tropics. Flat-topped baobab trees in southern Africa. Spiny cactus in the American southwest. Green things such as those have come to represent and instantly identify the areas where they are most common. And in the southern part of the United States, no plant seems more characteristic or atmospheric than Spanish moss.

Of course, there's nothing Spanish about it. Native Americans who lived in the region called it "tree hair." Early French explorers in the area adapted that name but used it as an opportunity to mock their Spanish counterparts in the New World. They called it "Spanish beard." The Spaniards, not to be outdone, also adapted the local name, but they called it "French hair." Over the years, and with a transfer into English, the name comes down to us as Spanish moss.

But it isn't moss either and is completely unrelated to the plant groups that include mosses. In fact, it's a bromeliad and therefore more closely related to the pineapple than any moss. Like tropical orchids, it's also an epiphyte, adhering to a host plant but drawing its own food and water from the air. The seeds of Spanish moss lodge securely in the rough bark of live oaks, set up shop, and start growing, sometimes reaching a length of 25 feet as they hang from a branch. And it only grows on trees, so if you see it on a telephone pole or elsewhere, it only got there courtesy of the wind.

With so much of it around—a large tree can yield as much as a ton of the stuff—human ingenuity has devised a number of uses for it as an element in a caulking compound, as kindling and mulch, and in commercial uses as packing material, saddle blankets, and stuffing for mattresses. It's useful, too, to the bats that love to make a home in it, and to the snakes that love to eat it. But its best use is no doubt in its natural state, lending an air of sleepy mystery and sedate gloom to the trees and forests of the south.

It's a living reminder, also, as the story goes, of a Spanish soldier who fell in love with an Indian maiden. Her father forbade the romance and tied the soldier high in an ancient tree, demanding that he deny his love. The Spanish soldier refused, declaring that his love would grow forever. And indeed, after he died, the Indians noticed that his beard continued to grow, symbolizing his love. Soon the beard covered the tree, and then spread to another, and another, until eventually it covered every tree in the region, a living testament to undying love.

which includes a gift shop. | 256 N. Joachim St. | 334/434–7320 | fax 334/433–3426 | $4 | Tues.–Sat. 10–4, Sun. 1–4.

University of South Alabama. With some 12,000 students at its west Mobile campus, the university is a major center for undergraduate, graduate, and professional study. Also here are a College of Medicine and clinical facilities. The Jaguars boast a top collegiate baseball program with NCAA tournament appearances in nine of the last 10 seasons. | 307 University Blvd. | 334/460–6101 | fax 334/460–7827 | www.southalabama.edu | Free | Daily.

Wildland Expeditions. Led by Captain Gene Burrell aboard his self-designed boat, tours take you into the Mobile-Tensaw Delta, with close-up views of plants and animals. During warm months, it is possible to spot alligators. Captain Burrell's expertise enlivens explorations. | Chickasaw Marina, U.S. 43 | 334/460–8206 | $20 | Feb.–Dec. 14, Tues.–Sat. 8, 10, 2.

ON THE CALENDAR

JAN.: *Senior Bowl Football Game.* The nation's outstanding college football senior citizens compete on teams representing the AFC and NFC for a chance to impress pro scouts. | Ladd Stadium | 334/635–0011.
FEB.: *Mardi Gras.* The state's longest and largest party lasts two weeks and includes parades, gala mystic krewe balls, and pre-Lenten family entertainment. | Various venues | 334/432–3050.
MAR.: *Azalea Trail Festival.* Motorists follow street signs on self-guided tours to streets lined with legendary, blooming azaleas. | City streets | 334/473–7223.
MAR.: *Historic Home Tours.* Self-guided tours of private homes. Several homes with historic architectural merit are showcased. | Downtown Mobile | 334/433–0259.
MAY: *Blessing of the Shrimp Fleet.* Decorated fishing boats receive the church's blessing for full fishing nets. Arts, crafts, and plenty of seafood are available. | Bayou Le Batre | 334/824–2415.
OCT.: *Reenactment of the Battle of Mobile.* Costumed soldiers stage a mock battle outside Fort Morgan. Gun and cannon demonstrations. | Fort Morgan | 334/540–7125.
DEC.: *Candlelight at Oakleigh.* The museum house is decorated in 1800s style with candles in every room and window. | Oakleigh Period House Museum | 334/432–1281.
DEC.: *First Night.* A multimedia, cultural event combining the magic of the arts with the thrill of a nonalcoholic, family celebration. | Downtown | 334/470–7730.

Dining

Brick Pit. Barbecue. It's "the best damn barbecue in the state of Alabama," owner Bill Armbrecht boasts of this Mobile favorite. Chicken, ribs, and pork are smoked for hours over a blend of hickory and pecan to achieve a distinct flavor. Barbecue sauce comes spicy or sweet, with soft white bread for dipping. Be sure to add your name to the graffiti scrawled in red marker all over the walls and ceiling. Try the smoked pulled-pork plate. | 5456 Old Shell Rd. | 334/343–0001 | $7–$12 | MC, V | Closed Sun., Mon.

Dew Drop Inn. Southern. Established in 1924, this is Mobile's oldest restaurant. You may have to wait for a table (it's first come, first served, and there's no waiting list), but you definitely won't go away hungry. The Dew Drop is beloved for its hot dogs, homemade onion rings, and southern-style daily specials, featuring a meat and several vegetables. Try the World Famous Dew Drop Inn Hot Dog, featuring chile, sauerkraut, mustard, and ketchup on a toasted bun. | 1808 Old Shell Rd. | 334/473–7872 | Reservations not accepted | $5–$20 | MC, V | Closed Sun. No dinner Sat.

★ **Justine's Courtyard and Carriageway.** Seafood. Chef/owner Matt Shipp, a Culinary Institute of America graduate and a veteran of New York and New Orleans restaurants, changes his menu frequently to incorporate the freshest seafood, hand-cut prime beef, and—a Justine's specialty—grilled ostrich; vegetarian dishes are also available. His culinary creations include a crawfish and goat-cheese appetizer, baked on a Parmesan crust. Open-air dining in courtyard. Live music Sunday. Sunday champagne brunch. | 80 St. Michael St. | 334/438–4535 | $20–$40 | AE, D, DC, MC, V | Closed Tues. No lunch Mon., Sat.

La Louisiana Ristorante. Italian. This romantic restaurant, in a renovated two-story home in midtown Mobile, has a glassed-in space for dining and dancing, in addition to several existing private dining rooms. On the menu are pasta, fish, and veal. Try the crab Napoleon: lump crabmeat sautéed with shallots, mushrooms, and champagne. | 2400 Airport Blvd. | 334/476–8130 | $11–$16 | AE, D, DC, MC, V | Closed Sun., Mon. No lunch.

The Mariner. Seafood. Enjoy a view of boats traveling the Dog River Bridge and Mobile Bay at rambling waterfront restaurant. On the menu are shrimp, oysters, Alaska king crab legs, snow fish, and meats like rib-eye steak and fried chicken. Try the fried crab claws. Open-air dining on deck. Kids' menu. | 6036 Rock Point Rd. | 334/443–5700 | $9–$29 | AE, D, MC, V | No lunch Mon.–Sat.

Pier 4. Seafood. Just five minutes from downtown on the causeway, large windows overlook Mobile Bay with a view of the Battleship USS *Alabama* and the downtown Mobile skyline. Menu items include seafood, shrimp and crab fettuccine, along with chicken and steak entrées. | 1420 Battleship Pkwy. | 334/626–6710 | $10–$20 | AE, D, DC, MC, V.

The Pillars. Continental. This elegant restaurant has several dining rooms in a restored, two-story historic home. The bar is the enclosed porch. Known for pasta, chicken, steak, and seafood. | 1757 Government St. | 334/478–6341 | $16–$28 | AE, D, DC, MC, V | Closed Sun. No lunch.

Roussos Seafood Restaurant. Seafood. Owned by the same Greek family for more than 40 years, Roussos is a Mobile tradition housed in a renovated warehouse near historic Fort Condé. Memorabilia about the restaurant and Mobile cover the brick and cedar walls in the spacious dining areas. A member of the Roussos family or of the staff will happily escort diners on tours of the restaurant and kitchen. Dishes include Greek-style broiled scampi, rib-eye steak, petite filet mignon, spaghetti and shrimp, and golden fried chicken. Kids' menu. | 166 S. Royal St. | 334/433–3322 | $8–$20 | AE, D, DC, MC, V | Closed Sun.

Ruth's Chris Steak House. Steak. Specializing in steaks, Ruth's Chris features corn-fed, aged beef broiled to juicy perfection. The fine-dining establishment, located in midtown Mobile, also offers a variety of fresh seafood dishes, veal chops, and broiled chicken. | 271 Glenwood St. | 334/476–0516 | $30–$40 | AE, D, DC, MC, V | No lunch.

Lodging

Adam's Mark Hotel. Completely renovated in 1999, this 28-story downtown hotel is connected by a pedestrian bridge across Water Street to the Mobile Convention Center. Guest rooms offer incredible views of Mobile Bay, Mobile River, and historic downtown Mobile. Restaurant, 2 bars (with entertainment), room service. In-room data ports, cable TV. Pool. Hot tub, sauna. Gym. Laundry service. Business services. No-smoking rooms. | 64 S. Water St. | 334/438–4000 or 800/444–2326 | fax 334/415–3060 | 375 rooms | $69–$127 | AE, D, DC, MC, V.

Clarion. This 20-story hotel is in midtown Mobile just east of Interstate 65, near Bel Air Mall and several restaurants. Restaurant, bar. In-room data ports, some microwaves, some refrigerators, cable TV. Pool. Hot tub. Laundry service. Business services, airport shuttle. No-smoking floors, no-smoking rooms. | 3101 Airport Blvd. | 334/476–6400 | fax 334/476–9360 | www.clarion.com | 250 rooms | $59–$99 | AE, D, DC, MC, V.

Days Inn Airport. Renovated in 2000, this standard inn is found at Interstate 65 and Airport Boulevard. It's close to Springdale Mall, Bel Air Mall, and convenient to other shops and many restaurants. In-room data ports, some kitchenettes, cable TV. Pool. Laundry facilities. Business services. Some pets allowed (fee). No-smoking rooms. | 3650 Airport Blvd. | 334/344–3410 | fax 334/344–8790 | 162 rooms | $63 | AE, D, DC, MC, V.

Drury Inn. This inn is conveniently located at Interstate 65 and Airport Boulevard, next to a 24-hour restaurant, and close to Bel Air and Springdale malls. Complimentary Continental breakfast. In-room data ports, cable TV. Pool. Gym. Laundry facilities. Business services. Some pets allowed. No-smoking rooms. | 824 S. Beltline Hwy. | 334/344–7700 or 800/325–8300 | fax 334/344–7700 | 110 rooms | $72 | AE, D, DC, MC, V.

Hampton Inn. With easy access to Interstate 65, this standard inn is centrally located near Airport Boulevard and the Mobile business district. Complimentary Continental breakfast. In-room data ports, cable TV. Pool. Business services. No-smoking rooms. | 930 S. Beltline Hwy. | 334/344–4942 | fax 334/341–4520 | www.hamptoninn.com | 118 rooms | $63 | AE, D, DC, MC, V.

Lafayette Plaza. In the heart of downtown Mobile's business and historic districts, this hotel is within walking distance of the Museum of Mobile, Phoenix Fire Museum, Gulf Coast Exploreum, and more. The rooftop lounge offers breathtaking views of the city and the waterfront. Restaurants, bar. In-room data ports, cable TV. Pool. Beauty salon. Laundry service. Business services. Pets allowed. No-smoking rooms. | 301 Government St. | 334/694–0100 or 800/692–6662 | fax 334/694–0160 | 210 rooms | $59–$89 | AE, D, DC, MC, V.

La Quinta. This standard inn is along Interstate 65 at busy Airport Boulevard, just a mile from Bel Air and Springdale malls and close to many restaurants. Complimentary Continental breakfast. In-room data ports, cable TV. Pool. Laundry service. Business services. Some pets allowed. No-smoking rooms. | 816 S. Beltline Hwy. | 334/343–4051 or 800/531–5900 | fax 334/343–2897 | www.travelweb.com/laquinta.html | 122 rooms | $62–$69 | AE, D, DC, MC, V.

Malaga Inn. In the Church Street East historic district, this inn consists of two 19th-century town houses that wrap around a gas-lighted courtyard centered with a fountain. The rooms are furnished with antiques, have high ceilings and hardwood floors, and each is uniquely decorated. The inn is within walking distance of Mobile Civic Center and downtown attractions. Restaurant, bar, complimentary breakfast, room service. Cable TV. Pool. Business services. | 359 Church St. | 334/438–4701 or 800/235–1586 | 38 rooms | $79–$89 | AE, D, MC, V.

Radisson Admiral Semmes. In the heart of Mobile, walking distance from Cathedral Square Park, Fort Condé, Welcome Center, and the Gulf Coast Exploreum, this hotel has all the modern amenities, while the Art Deco decor, custom furnishings, and designer wall coverings preserve its historic essence. Restaurant, bar (with entertainment), room service. In-room data ports, some refrigerators, cable TV. Pool. Hot tub. Business services. | 251 Government St. | 334/432–8000 | fax 334/405–5942 | 170 rooms | $109–$150 | AE, D, DC, MC, V.

Ramada Plaza Hotel. Convenient to the Airport Boulevard exit off Interstate 65, close to malls and restaurants and home to the popular Cabo Beach Club nightclub, the hotel offers plenty of activities. Restaurant, bar (with entertainment), room service. Some in-room data ports, cable TV, some in-room VCRs. 2 pools, wading pool. Hot tub. Putting green, 2 tennis courts. Gym. Business services, airport shuttle. | 600 S. Beltline Hwy. | 334/344–8030 or 800/752–0398 | fax 334/344–8055 | 236 rooms | $62–$89 | AE, D, DC, MC, V.

Red Roof Inn Mobile–South. In the Tillman's Corner area just off Interstate 10, this standard inn is about 18 mi from Bellingrath Gardens and Home, 10 mi from downtown Mobile, and 30 mi from Dauphin Island. In-room data ports, cable TV. Business services. Some pets allowed. No-smoking rooms. | 5450 Coca-Cola Rd. | 334/666–1044 | fax 334/666–1032 | 108 rooms | $41 | AE, D, DC, MC, V.

Shoney's Inn. This standard inn is along Interstate 10 in the Tillman's Corner area, just 2 mi from Mobile Greyhound Park, 10 mi from downtown Mobile, and 15 mi from Mobile Municipal Airport. Microwaves in suites, refrigerators in suites, cable TV. Pool. Business services. Some pets allowed (fee). No-smoking rooms. | 5472-A Inn Rd. | 334/660–1520 or 800/222–2222 | fax 334/666–4240 | 120 rooms, 15 suites | $54 rooms, $64 suites | AE, D, DC, MC, V.

Towle House. Built in 1874, this lovely bed-and-breakfast is in the Old Dauphinway Historic District, one block from oak tree-lined Government Street and close to downtown Mobile. Rooms are furnished with antiques and have private baths. Breakfast is served in the elegant dining room on china with sterling silver; afternoon tea (or wine and cocktails) is served each day. Complimentary breakfast. Cable TV. | 1104 Montauk Ave. | 334/432–6440 or 800/938–6953 | fax 334/433–4381 | www.towle-house.com | 3 rooms | $80–$95 | AE, D, MC, V.

MONROEVILLE

MAP 3, C7

(Nearby town also listed: Atmore)

The southwest Alabama town of Monroeville hangs its hat on its link to two famous authors—Harper Lee and Truman Capote. Lee set her Pulitzer Prize–winning novel, *To Kill a Mockingbird,* in the sleepy southern town that has changed little since the images she painted in her novel. In his memoir *A Christmas Memory,* Truman Capote recalled the town where he had spent much of his childhood. A marker on South Alabama Avenue notes the site of a house where Capote regularly visited relatives and lived for several years.

Not far from the city square, Riker's Mill, the state's only restored gristmill, stands on its original site and is still operational. It includes a covered bridge and blacksmith shop. Just south of town is the site of the largest massacre in American pioneer history where on August 30, 1813, at Fort Mims, in retaliation for the European invasion and aggression, the Upper Creek Indians, led by Chief Red Eagle, stormed a stockaded settlement near the Alabama River and killed 514 people.

Information: **Monroeville Area Chamber of Commerce** | 32 N. Alabama Ave., Monroeville 36460 | 334/743–2879 | fax 334/575–7934 | monroeco@frontiernet.net. | www.frontiernet.net/~monroeco.

Attractions

Riker's Mill. This is Alabama's only restored gristmill still standing on its original site and operational. There's also a covered bridge and blacksmith shop. | Rte. 265, Beatrice | 334/789–2781 or 334/575–7433 | $3 | Apr.–mid-Dec., Tues.–Sun. 11–dusk.

MONTGOMERY

MAP 3, D5

(Nearby town also listed: Wetumpka)

Montgomery has lured travelers since 1540, when Hernando de Soto staked a Spanish flag on the banks of the Alabama River. Not to be outdone, French settlers made their presence known when they established Fort Toulouse in 1717. The settlements of East Alabama and New Philadelphia sprang up amid this bustling hub of river commerce; they merged together in 1819 to form Montgomery.

Great change swept through the city in the following years as an international audience watched Montgomery's history unfold. In 1846, Montgomery was chosen as the state's capital city. In 1861, the eyes of the nation turned to Montgomery as Jefferson Davis was sworn in as president of the Confederate States of America. On April 11 of that year, the telegram containing the orders to fire on Fort Sumter was sent from the Winter Building on Dexter Avenue, thus beginning the War Between the States.

Nearly a century later, Rosa Parks refused to give up her seat on a Montgomery city bus and ushered in a new era of social change. In 1965, Dr. Martin Luther King, Jr., ended the Selma-to-Montgomery Civil Rights March on the Capitol steps, a block away from the church where he began his career as a minister.

In addition to making history as the birthplace of the Civil War and the Civil Rights Movement, Montgomery has seen many other milestones. The country's first electric streetcar system began operating in Montgomery in 1886. And, in 1910, the Wright Brothers brought their daring aviation deeds to Alabama's capital city, establishing the nation's first school for powered flight.

Today, Montgomery combines the qualities of a leading cultural and recreational center with such assets as world-class theater, museums, history, family activities, and irresistible, down-home southern food.

Montgomery is the epitome of a progressive southern business city. New hotels and restaurants spring up frequently, along with skyscraper office complexes. Alabama's capital city is rich in its past and is striving to become richer in its future.

Information: **Montgomery Convention and Visitors Division** | 300 Water St., Montgomery 36104 | 334/261–1100 or 800/240–9452 | fax 334/261–1111 | tourism@mont-gomerychamber.org | www.montgomery.al.us.

NEIGHBORHOODS

Capitol Heights
Bounded by Upper Wetumpka Road, Federal Drive, Mt. Meigs Road, and Vonora/Lewis streets, Capitol Heights began as a 200-acre plantation owned by the Vickers family. Incorporated in 1908, the town became a part of Montgomery in the mid-1920s. Today, the area maintains its original character as a working-class neighborhood with many of the descendants of original families still living there. A variety of construction materials are evident, but most of the homes have wood siding, brick piers, and porch supports.

Centennial Hill
Developed in the late 1870s, Centennial Hill was the city's first substantially black residential neighborhood. The area is bordered by Jackson, Union, and High streets with Alabama State University at the southern end of Jackson Street. The home at 309 South Jackson Street is where Dr. Martin Luther King, Jr., lived at the time of the bus boycott that spurred the Civil Rights Movement.

Cottage Hill
On a low hill, Cottage Hill overlooks the Alabama River to the north. To the east are the downtown business district and the Capitol center. Listed on the National Register of Historic Places, Cottage Hill is the city's oldest surviving residential area. The district is made up of closely spaced, well-constructed, and unpretentious houses. Built mostly from 1870 to 1910, the homes reflect the taste and lifestyle of the urban middle class. The area is noted for its gingerbread-bedecked cottages, hex-blocked sidewalks, and tree-lined streets.

Garden District
In the hills south of Montgomery, the Garden District is bounded by Noble Avenue, Decatur/Norman Bridge Road, Fairview Avenue, and Court Street. Homes were built here as early as the 1870s, and construction continued until the 1930s, resulting in an eclectic mix of homes in both style and size. Bungalow-style homes dominate the assortment of architectural styles which also include Arts and Crafts, Tudor, Italianate, Colonial, and neoclassical revival. One of the most interesting neoclassical homes is the Alabama Governor's Mansion at 1142 South Perry Street. Most of the area's gardens are tucked behind homes where they are enjoyed by residents and their friends.

Highland Park
With streetcar tracks dissecting a median on Highland Avenue, Highland Park was Montgomery's first streetcar suburb. Bounded by Mt. Meigs Road, Ann Street, the Oak Park/Jackson Hospital complex, and Forest Avenue, the neighborhood is filled today with many second- and third-generation families. The old tracks are obscured by grass and trees. Homes are small, Queen Anne, craftsman bungalows, a style that prompted the nickname, Bungalow City.

Old Cloverdale
One of Montgomery's first suburbs, Old Cloverdale has curving streets, small parks, and lanes tucked off the main thoroughfare. Originally a separate village, it became a part of Montgomery in 1927. Listed on the National Register of Historic Places, the

area is bounded by Hull Street, Carter Hill Road, Fairview Avenue, and Narrow Lane Road. Several architectural styles are evident, including Tudor Revival, bungalow, neoclassical, and Spanish Mission.

Transportation Information

Airport: Montgomery Regional Airport (Dannelly Field) is served by Atlantic Southeast (ASA), Delta, Northwest, and American Eagle (334/281–5040).

Airport transportation: Taxis are readily available and relatively inexpensive at the airport. Many hotels provide transportation from the airport by prior arrangement. Taxis charge $1.75 initially and $1.20 for each additional mile. **Yellow Cab** (334/262–5225).

Amtrak: The nearest Amtrak service is in Birmingham (800/872–7245). Montgomery has a **Thruway Intermodal Transit Terminal** (335 Coosa St.) where you can get bus service to Amtrak terminals in Birmingham and Mobile.

Bus: Greyhound Bus Lines/Capital Trailways, | 950 W. South Blvd. | 334/286–0658 or 800/231–2222.

Driving around Town: Two interstate highways bisect Montgomery; I–65 runs north–south and I–85 east–west. The city is encircled by U.S. 80, U.S. 82, U.S. 231, and Route 152. Rush-hour traffic can be heavy, especially on the encircling bypass—it's busy even during lunch hour. On the other hand, the interstates are primarily busy during the morning commute; they're less crowded in the evenings. Within the city, most downtown streets are one-way, though two- and four-lane thoroughfares crisscross town, easing travel between neighborhoods. Downtown, around the capitol, there is metered parking and a smattering of parking lots and garages. Tickets for expired meters are $4. Speed limits are 25 mph on residential and downtown streets, 45 mph on the wider avenues. **Intra-city transportation: Montgomery buses** (DART Service) runs from 6 AM to 6 PM. One-way fare is $1.50 and round-trip is $3. You must call for pick-up (334/262–7321). **Trolleys** provide transportation downtown during business hours.

Attractions

WALKING TOUR

Begin your walk at the State Capitol. From its steps, beneath the white-columned portico, you have a grand view of Dexter Avenue. Stroll south across the Capitol Grounds and Washington Avenue to the First White House of the Confederacy, a modest two-story house. From here, walk along Washington toward Bainbridge for a block to the white stone Alabama Department of Archives and History. From the archive, walk south on South Bainbridge a block and a half to the Alabama Cattleman's Association Museum where you can learn more of Alabama's agriculture. From the museum walk north, back to Washington Avenue, and turn left. Follow Washington Avenue two blocks until you reach artist Maya Lin's dramatic black-granite Civil Rights Memorial. Walk north on Hull Street one block to Dexter Avenue and turn left. The Alabama Judicial Building will be on your left, its neoclassical facade of columns dominating the south side of the street. Stroll one block toward the capitol, past Hull Street, to see the Dexter Avenue King Memorial Baptist Church. Turn onto Decatur Street and follow it two blocks north to Madison Avenue to find Old Alabama Town. After exploring the many homes and museums in this small restored district, walk west three blocks along Madison Avenue to North Perry Street and St. John's Episcopal Church where Jefferson Davis attended services. Be sure to step inside to see the beautiful plaques that ornament the nave's ceiling. A block and a half west of here, just past where Madison turns into Bibb Street, you'll find Murphy House, a Greek Revival mansion built in 1851. Follow Bibb

Street one block farther southwest, then turn north onto Commerce Street. Here you'll find the Hank Williams Museum. A minor deviation off Montgomery to the corner of Molton Street will bring you to the Rosa Parks Museum (scheduled to open in December 2000). To return to the Capitol Grounds, walk back toward Bibb Street on Commerce and follow Commerce Street until it meets Dexter Avenue. At the fountain, you'll have an unimpeded, dramatic view of the white stone capitol at the end of the six-lane avenue. For a well-worth-it trip to the Montgomery visitor center follow Commerce in the opposite direction, heading toward the river.

ART AND ARCHITECTURE

Alabama Judicial Building. The building is in the home of Alabama's Supreme Court and the Courts of Criminal and Civil Appeals, and the State Law Library. Tours of the public areas include the historical and informational exhibits. | 300 Dexter Ave. | 334/242–4343 | fax 334/242–4484 | www.judicial.state.al.us | Free | Weekdays 8–8, Sat. 9–5.

First White House of the Confederacy. Built in 1840, the house was occupied by Jefferson Davis and his family while the Confederacy was being organized. Today it contains many of their possessions, plus other artifacts of the Civil War period. | 644 Washington Ave. | 334/242–1861 | Free | Weekdays 8–4:30.

Hank Williams Statue. The bronze statue depicts the legendary country music singer holding a guitar, wearing cowboy boots and hat and his trademark suit decorated with musical notes. | Lister Hill Plaza | Free | Daily.

Murphy House. Now home of the Montgomery Waterworks Board, this antebellum mansion housed Union troops during Reconstruction. | 22 Bibb St. | 334/678–0937 | Free | Weekdays 8:15–4:45.

State Capitol. The State Capitol reopened in 1992 after an extensive restoration. It was built in 1850 and for a few months in 1861 served as the first capitol of the Confederate States of America. On the front portico, a bronze star marks the spot where Jefferson Davis took the oath of office as president of the Confederacy. The interior stairway curling up the sides of the circular hallway is freestanding, without visible support. The state's rich history is depicted on colorful murals. Gigantic brick fireplaces are in the large house chamber and smaller senate chamber. | Bainbridge St. at Dexter Ave. | 334/242–3935 | Free | Weekdays 9–5, Sat. 9–4.

BEACHES, PARKS, AND NATURAL SIGHTS

Jasmine Hill Gardens and Outdoor Museum. Atop a wooded hill, 20 acres of beautiful gardens hold replicas of Greek sculptures and of the ruins of the Temple of Hera. The visitor center is a replica of the original facade of the Temple of Hera on Mount Olympus. | 3001 Jasmine Hill Rd., Wetumpka | 334/567–6463 | fax 334/567–6466 | www.jasminehill.org | $5 | Tues.–Sun. 9–5.

CULTURE, EDUCATION, AND HISTORY

Alabama Department of Archives and History. The department houses the first state-funded archives in the United States, plus galleries with artifacts documenting the state's past with an emphasis on 19th-century Alabama. | 624 Washington Ave. | 334/242–4363 | fax 334/240–3433 | www.archives.state.al.us | Free | Weekdays 8–5, Sat. 9–5. Reference Room: Tues.–Sat. 8–5.

Alabama Shakespeare Festival. Shakespearean plays, modern drama, and musicals are performed on two stages at this multimillion-dollar theater. Drama authorities have called it the finest facility of its kind in the world. | 1 Festival Dr. | 334/271–5353 or or 800/841–4ASF | fax 334/271–5348 | www.asf.net | Admission varies | Oct.–Aug.

Alabama State University. Founded as a teachers' college in 1867, the university offers more than 50 courses of study leading to associate, bachelor, masters, or educational special-

ists' degrees. It offers Central Alabama's only Air Force Reserve Officers' Training Corps program. | 915 S. Jackson St. | 334/229–4100 | fax 334/265–0914 | www.alasu.edu | Free | Daily.

Alabama War Memorial. The memorial honors thousands of Alabamians who gave their lives in foreign wars. It includes the Alabama Hall of Honor, a shrine dedicated to servicemen who died in the line of duty and the 27 Alabamians who were awarded the Congressional Medal of Honor. | 120 N. Jackson St. | 334/262–6638 | Free | Daily 8–4.

★ **Civil Rights Memorial.** The black-granite memorial honors those who died during the Civil Rights Movement and serves as a vehicle for education and reflection about the struggle for equality. It was designed by Maya Lin, designer of the Vietnam Veterans Memorial in Washington, D.C. | 400 Washington Ave. | 334/264–0286 | fax 334/264–0629 | www.splcenter.org | Free | Daily.

Hank Williams Memorial Tombstone. Grave site of native son and country-music singer and songwriter Hank Williams, Sr., depicts him, along with sheet music from his most popular songs, including "Your Cheatin' Heart." | 1305 Upper Wetumpka Rd. | 334/264–4938 | Free | Daily.

Huntingdon College. Founded in the mid-19th century and related to the United Methodist Church, the coeducational liberal arts college is accredited by the Southern Association of Colleges and Schools. On a 58-acre campus, it offers a comprehensive college plan and a wide range of educational subjects. Full-time freshmen receive personal computers which they keep upon graduation. | 1500 E. Fairview Ave. | 334/833–4409 | fax 334/833–4486 | Free | Daily.

Maxwell Air Force Base. Home of the prestigious Air University, the base includes the largest military library in the Department of Defense. Passes and information are available at Bell Street Visitor Control Center. Tours are self-guided. Guides are available upon request. | U.S. 85 | 334/953–2014 | fax 334/953–3379 | Free | Weekdays 7:30–4:30.

MUSEUMS

Alabama Cattleman's Association Mooseum. The children's educational center has a unique agriculture theme. Alabama cattle's past, present, and imagined future as they are revealed with a tour led by electronic host, Adam Bainbridge. | 201 S. Bainbridge St. | 334/265–1867 | Free | Weekdays 9–noon and 1–4.

Fort Toulouse/Jackson Park National Historic Landmark. Hernando de Soto visited the site in 1540, and the French established Fort Toulouse in 1717. Fort Jackson was built in 1814 by General Andrew Jackson, marking the end of the Creek Indian War. The 165-acre park includes an arboretum, museum, historic building, Indian mound, boat ramp, pavilion, and campground. Living history reenactments take place monthly. | 2521 W. Fort Toulouse Rd., Wetumpka | 334/567–3002 | fax 334/514–6625 | $2 | Daily dawn–dusk.

F. Scott and Zelda Fitzgerald Museum. The world's only museum to F. Scott Fitzgerald is housed in a brick home he and his wife rented briefly. Zelda Fitzgerald grew up in the area, and some of her art still hangs at Montgomery's Museum of Fine Arts. Her husband, F. Scott, is famous for *The Great Gatsby, Tender is the Night,* and numerous short stories. Included is a brief video on the couple's life in Montgomery. | 919 Felder Ave. | 334/264–4222 | Free | Wed.–Fri. 10–2, weekends 1–5; and by appointment.

Gunter Annex/U.S.A.F. Heritage Hall Museum. The annex is the home of the U.S. Air Force Senior N.C.O. Academy and the Standard Systems Group. The U.S. Air Force Enlisted Heritage Hall Museum showcases the U.S.A.F. and the U.S. Army Aeronautical Division, Air Service, and the Air Corps. Included are artifacts, art collections, pictorial exhibits, written documentation, audiovisuals, and displays of equipment and aircraft parts. | 550 McDonald St. (MAFB–Gunter Annex) | 334/416–3202 | Free | Tues.–Fri. 7–4, Sat. 9–4.

Hank Williams Museum. The museum houses memorabilia of country music great Hank Williams, Sr., including the 1952 blue Cadillac in which he died. A replica of the car is available along with many other items in the museum's gift shop. | 118 Commerce St. | 334/262–3600 | $5 | Mon.–Sat. 9–6, Sun. 1–4.

Hank Williams, Sr., Boyhood Home & Museum. An unpretentious house holds wall-to-wall exhibits detailing the famous singer's birth on a farm in Mount Olive to his death less than three decades later. Records, sheet music, photographs, and other memorabilia reveal Williams' childhood days singing in the church choir and his more famous days performing at Nashville, Tennessee's Grand Ole Opry. Among the treasures are dishes that belonged to Hank and his wife, Audrey, custom-made curtains from their Nashville home, and the church bench where Hank stood as a child to sing. | 127 Rose St., Georgiana | 334/376–2555 | fax 334/376–9850 | $3 | Mon.–Sat. 10–5, Sun. 1–5.

Montgomery Museum of Fine Arts. Alabama's oldest fine-arts museum is housed in an impressive facility within the same park that houses the Alabama Shakespeare Festival Theatre. Among the exhibits are ARTWORKS, a hands-on gallery for children and adults; a permanent gallery exhibiting American Art; and a gift shop, auditorium, print gallery. | 1 Museum Dr. (Wynton Blount Cultural Park) | 334/244–5700 | fax 334/244–5774 | Free | Tues., Wed., Fri.–Sat. 10–5, Thurs. 10–9, Sun. noon–5.

Old Alabama Town. Along tree-shaded streets in the heart of downtown, this village showcases Alabama in the 19th and early 20th centuries. | 301 Columbus St. | 334/240–4500 or 888/240–1850 | fax 334/240–4519 | www.oldalabamatown.com | $4 or $7 | Mon.–Sat. 9–3.

RELIGION AND SPIRITUALITY

Dexter Avenue King Memorial Baptist Church. This church is where Dr. Martin Luther King, Jr., began his career as a minister in 1955. Both the sanctuary and basement are open to visitors. A mural covering one basement wall depicts people and events associated with Dr. King and the Civil Rights movement. | 454 Dexter Ave. | 334/263–3970 | fax 334/263–3910 | www.cr.nps.gov/nr/travel/civilrights/al7.htm | Free | Mon.–Thurs. 10 and 2; Fri. at 10.

St. John's Episcopal Church. Built in 1855, this "church of the angels" features Gothic Revival architecture, a 75-ft-high steeple, and a Tiffany window. A plaque marks the pew of Confederate President Jefferson Davis. | 113 Madison Ave. | 334/262–1937 | Free | Weekdays 8:30–4:30.

SPORTS AND RECREATION

Montgomery Motorsports Park. The park is a NHRA- sanctioned dragway offering year-round drag racing. Annual events feature pro–motor sports, fuel funny cars, and Winston Cup point races on a quarter-mile strip. | 2600 North Belt Dr. | 334/260–9660 | fax 334/260–9320 | $5 Fri., $10 Sat., $5 Sun. | Fri. 6 PM–11 PM, weekends noon–5.

Victoryland Track. Greyhound races are held at the track, where there is racing and pari-mutuel betting every night but Sunday. Matinees are held during the week. | Macon County Greyhound Park, U.S. 40 | 334/727–0540 or 800/688–2946 | fax 334/727–0737 | www.victoryland.com | $1; parking $1; clubhouse $2 | Mon., Wed., Fri. 3 and 7:30; Tues., Thurs. 7:30; Sat. 1 and 7:30.

OTHER POINTS OF INTEREST

Montgomery Zoo. The 40-acre zoo is home to some 800 animals from five continents. Exhibits simulate the animals' natural habitats. A snack bar, gift shop, picnic tables, and minitrain are offered. | 2301 Coliseum Pkwy. | 334/240–4900 | fax 334/240–4916 | $4.50 | Daily 9–5.

Union Station. Montgomery's Romanesque Revival Union Station contains art, art-glass windows, and tile flooring. The adjacent 19th-century Train Shed is one of the few remaining structures of its kind. | 300 Water St. | 334/834–5200 | Free | Daily.

W. A. Gayle Planetarium. Known as one of the major planetariums in the United States, the auditorium theater simulates the natural sky by projecting images of the sun, moon, planets, stars, and other celestial bodies on a 50-ft domed ceiling. | 1010 Forest Ave. | 334/241–4799 or 334/241–4798 | fax 334/240–4309 | www.tsum.edu | $3 | Mon.–Thurs. 7:30–4:30, Fri. 7:30–noon. Shows Mon.–Thurs. 3, Sun. 2; and by appointment.

Dining

INEXPENSIVE

Olive Room. Eclectic. Downtown in a completely renovated 1950s-era building, this restaurant recently won an award from the American Institute of Architects for its design. Taking a cue from its name, the restaurant's decor features shades of green. The menu changes seasonally but always includes noodles and vegetarian dishes. Known for fresh fish and beef. | 121 Montgomery St. | 334/262–2763 | Reservations not accepted | $12–$20 | AE, DC, MC, V | Closed Sun., Mon. No lunch.

Tomatino's. Italian. Regional art decorates the walls at this small, casual Cloverdale eatery, bakery, and coffee shop with outside café tables. Fresh produce and organic flours make the menu as health conscious as it is delicious. Known for pizzas, calzones, focaccia sandwiches, and salads. Beer and wine only. No smoking. Just 10 minutes from downtown Albany. | 1036 E. Fairview Ave. | 334/264–4241 | $12–$20 | AE, DC, MC, V | No lunch Sun.

MODERATE

★ **Sahara.** Continental. A Montgomery tradition, Sahara has kept customers coming back since it first opened nearly a half century ago. The all-male waitstaff is committed to providing excellent service to diners in three separate dining rooms. Known for fresh gulf seafood and Black Angus beef. | 511 E. Edgemont Ave. | 334/262–1215 | $18–$29 | AE, D, DC, MC, V | Closed Sun.

Vintage Year. Eclectic. The unique menu changes seasonally at this elegant but fun restaurant in historic Cloverdale. Original art decorates the walls in the sophisticated main dining room, and the upscale lounge has a spirited New York flair. On the menu are selections like grilled marinated tuna, sesame crusted halibut, mahogany roasted duck, and crab-cake appetizer. After dining, stroll to the historic neighborhood, to see F. Scott Fitzgerald's and the Government Mansion. | 405 Cloverdale Rd. | 334/264–8463 | $22–$40 | AE, MC, V | Closed Sun., Mon. No lunch.

Lodging

INEXPENSIVE

Baymont Inn and Suites. A convenient location for both shopping and sightseeing, this standard inn is located near Eastdale Mall and Montgomery Mall, 6 mi from downtown and the State Capitol. Kids under 18 stay free. Complimentary Continental breakfast. In-room data ports, microwaves in suites, refrigerators in suites, cable TV. Pool. Business services. Some pets allowed. No-smoking rooms. | 5225 Carmichael Rd. | 334/277–6000 | fax 334/279–8207 | 100 rooms, 8 suites | $59 rooms, $89 suites | AE, D, DC, MC, V.

Comfort Suites. This all-suite motel is within 2 mi of the Alabama Shakespeare Festival, 2 mi from Eastdale Mall, and five minutes from Montgomery Motor Sports Park. Complimentary Continental breakfast. In-room data ports, microwaves, refrigerators, cable TV. Pool. Gym. Laundry service. Business services. | 5924 Monticello Dr., | 334/272–1013 | fax 334/260–0425 | 49 suites | $69–$125 | AE, D, DC, MC, V.

Governor's House Hotel and Conference Center. Within walking distance of Montgomery Mall, this hotel is about 4½ mi east of Interstate 65. Restaurant, bar. Some microwaves, some refrigerators, cable TV. Pool. Gym. Business services, airport shuttle. No-smoking rooms. | 2705 E. South Blvd. | 334/288–2800 or 800/334–8459 | fax 334/288–6472 | 200 rooms in 2 buildings | $55 | AE, D, DC, MC, V.

Hampton Inn Montgomery East. Conveniently located near Interstate 85, exit 6, this standard inn is close to the Alabama Shakespeare Festival and a variety of restaurants. Complimentary Continental breakfast. In-room data ports, cable TV. Pool. Laundry service. Business services. No-smoking rooms. | 1401 East Blvd. | 334/277–2400 | fax 334/277–6546 | www.hamptoninn.com | 105 rooms | $69 | AE, D, DC, MC, V.

Holiday Inn South/Airport. This four-story standard hotel is minutes away from Montgomery Mall and Montgomery Airport, near Interstate 65. Restaurant, bar, room service. In-room data ports, cable TV. Pool. Gym. Laundry facilities. Business services, airport shuttle. Some pets allowed. No-smoking rooms. | 1100 W. South Blvd. | 334/281–1660 | fax 334/281–1660 | 150 rooms | $59 | AE, D, DC, MC, V.

La Quinta. Just off Interstate 85, this standard motel is near the Alabama Shakespeare Festival, many restaurants and just 10 minutes from downtown. Complimentary Continental breakfast. In-room data ports, microwaves in suites, refrigerators in suites, cable TV. Pool. Business services. Some pets allowed. No-smoking rooms. | 1280 East Blvd. | 334/271–1620 | fax 334/244–7919 | 130 rooms, 2 suites | $59 rooms, $76–$82 suites | AE, D, DC, MC, V.

Ramada Inn–East. Conveniently located at Interstate Highway 85 and U.S. Highway 231, minutes from the Alabama Shakespeare Festival, Victoryland Greyhound Racing, shopping malls, museums and gardens. Restaurant, bar (with entertainment), complimentary breakfast buffet. In-room data ports, cable TV. Pool. Business services. No-smoking rooms. | 1355 Eastern Bypass | 334/277–2200 | fax 334/270–3338 | www.ramada.com | 154 rooms | $62 | AE, D, DC, MC, V.

Ramada Inn–Statehouse. This standard inn is just a few blocks from the Civil Rights Memorial, State Capitol, and the business district in downtown Montgomery. Restaurant, bar, room service. In-room data ports, cable TV. Pool. No-smoking rooms. | 924 Madison Ave. | 334/265–0741 or 800/552–7099 | fax 334/834–6126 | 161 rooms | $50–$78 | AE, D, DC, MC, V.

MODERATE

Courtyard by Marriott. Near Interstate 85, on the East Boulevard bypass, this hotel is only a block from the Alabama Shakespeare Festival and the Montgomery Museum of Fine Arts. Many shopping centers and restaurants are nearby. Restaurant, bar. In-room data ports, cable TV. Pool. Hot tub. Gym. Laundry facilities. Business services. No-smoking rooms. | 5555 Carmichael Rd. | 334/272–5533 | fax 334/279–0853 | 146 rooms | $92 | AE, D, DC, MC, V.

Holiday Inn–East. This standard hotel is off Interstate 85, near Montgomery Mall, Montgomery Zoo, and the Alabama Shakespeare Festival. Bar, room service. In-room data ports, cable TV. Pool. Hot tub, sauna. Gym. Video games. Laundry facilities, laundry service. Business services. Some pets allowed (fee). No-smoking rooms. | 1185 Eastern Bypass | 334/272–0370 | fax 334/270–0339 | 211 rooms in 3 buildings | $89 | AE, D, DC, MC, V.

Holiday Inn Hotel and Suites. Featuring an atrium lobby and lounge, this centrally located downtown hotel is within walking distance from the Montgomery Civic Center. Restaurant, bar, complimentary breakfast buffet, room service. In-room data ports, microwaves in suites, refrigerators in suites, cable TV. Pool. Gym. Laundry service. Business services. No-smoking rooms. | 120 Madison Ave. | 334/264–2231 | fax 334/263–3179 | www.holidayinn.com | 170 rooms, 19 suites | $79 rooms, $99 suites | AE, D, DC, MC, V.

ONEONTA

MAP 3, D3

(Nearby towns also listed: Birmingham, Gadsden)

Oneonta (pronounced Oh-nee-AHN-tah) is an Indian name meaning "the place we seek," and, indeed, many have sought this mineral rich area of rolling hills. Andrew Jackson and John Coffee battled to clear out Indians. Once they did, many of Jackson's fighters settled in the region. When the railroad arrived, the town quickly grew. Workers mined the land for red and brown iron ore, limestone, dolomite, manganese, shale, and sandstone; timber was another important product. Mountains, flat bottoms, creeks, and lakes are among the natural attractions in this town now noted for its pleasant, measured pace where many retirees and farmers make their homes.

The Oneonta area has three covered bridges on the National Register of Historic Places. Extensively renovated, the still-functional one-lane bridges—Horton, Nectar, and Swann—are the focus of a Covered Bridge Festival on the fourth weekend of October when fall colors are at their peak. Palisades Park is also a popular Oneonta attraction.

Information: **Blount County–Oneonta Chamber of Commerce** | 227 2nd Ave. east, Oneonta 35121 | 205/274–2153 | fax 205/274–2099 | cvbridge@otelco.net | www.coveredbridge.org.

Attractions

Horton Mill Covered Bridge. Built in 1934–35 and rebuilt in 1975, this covered bridge stands 70 ft above the Calvert Prong of the Warrior River. It is the highest covered bridge above water in America and was the state's first to be added to the National Register of Historic Places. The Horton Mill bridge is located 5 mi from Oneonta on State Highway 75. | Blount County–Oneonta Chamber of Commerce, 227 2nd Ave. E | 205/274–2153 | fax 205/274–2099 | Free | Daily.

Palisades Park. There's plenty to do in this popular park: nature trails, picnic areas, a playground, a pioneer building, log cabins, a corn crib, a meditation chapel, a one-room schoolhouse, and a small museum are here to explore. The cliffs are ideal for rappelling, and nearby forks in the Black Warrior River are great for canoeing, kayaking, and white-water rafting. | 1225 Palisades Pkwy., Ebell Mountain | 205/274–0017 | Free | Nov.–Mar., daily 9–5; Apr.–Oct., daily 9–9.

ON THE CALENDAR

OCT.: *Covered Bridge Festival.* Fall celebration of covered bridges on the carefully restored and still operational Horton, Nectar, and Swann bridges. | 205/274–2153.

OPELIKA

MAP 3, E5

(Nearby towns also listed: Auburn, Tuskegee)

In the shadow of nearby Auburn University, Opelika is home to the Museum of East Alabama, which houses thousands of items from the region's early years. Grand National, a link in the state's Robert Trent Jones Golf Trail, is popular. For shoppers, the appeal is the USA Factory Outlet Stores.

Information: **Auburn–Opelika Convention and Visitors Bureau** | 714 E. Glenn Ave., Opelika 36830 | 334/887–8747 or 800/321–8880 | fax 334/821–5500 | maria@auburn-opelika.com | www.auburn-opelika.com.

Attractions

Museum of East Alabama. The Museum of East Alabama is filled with thousands of items from the region's early years. | 121 S. 9th St. | 334/749–2751 | Free | Tues.–Fri. 10–4, Sat. 2–4.

USA Factory Outlet Stores. More than 20 stores offer bargains on popular brand-name items as well as other treasures. | 1220 Fox Run Pkwy. | 334/749–0561 | Free | Mon.–Sat. 9–9, Sun. noon–6.

Dining

Provino's. Italian. Italian music plays in rooms dimly lit by candle and lamplight. Tuxedo-clad waitstaff serve items like boneless chicken sautéed in lemon-butter wine sauce, shrimp scampi, red snapper francese, and cioppino, with steamed clams, shrimp, crab claws, red snapper, and mussels in a spicy garlic-tomato sauce, smothered over linguine. Early-bird supper Sunday–Thursday. Beer and wine only. | 3903-B Pepperell Pkwy. | 334/742–0340 | $13–$26 | AE, D, DC, MC, V | No lunch Mon.–Sat.

Warehouse Bistro. Contemporary. Part of the charm of this dark, intimate, fine-dining restaurant in a renovated warehouse is the fact that it's located "in the middle of nowhere," notes the owner, yet it offers a sophisticated menu of new southern cuisine. The chalkboard-style menu changes daily, and all desserts are homemade. Known for fresh seafood, certified Angus beef, game, rack of lamb, and halibut are also on the menu. | 105 Rocket Ave. | 334/745–6353 | $18–$24 | MC, V | Closed Sun. No lunch.

Lodging

Days Inn. At exit 62 off Interstate 85, this typical motel is less than five minutes from the USA Factory Outlet Stores and about 10 minutes from the Auburn University campus. Complimentary Continental breakfast. Microwaves, refrigerators, cable TV. Pool. Business services. Some pets allowed (fee). No-smoking rooms. | 1014 Anand Ave. | 334/749–5080 | fax 334/749–4701 | 44 rooms | $45–$50 | AE, D, DC, MC, V.

Holiday Inn. This standard inn is along Interstate 85, close to several restaurants and the USA Factory Outlet Stores. Restaurant, bar, room service. In-room data ports, cable TV. Pool. Gym. Laundry service. Business services. No-smoking rooms. | 1102 Columbus Pkwy. | 334/745–6331 | fax 334/749–3933 | 119 rooms in 3 buildings | $59–$104 | AE, D, DC, MC, V.

Travel Lodge. At Interstate 85 and U.S. 280, this standard motel is near several restaurants, the USA Factory Outlet Stores, and just 10 minutes from the Auburn University campus. Bar, complimentary Continental breakfast. In-room data ports, cable TV. Pool. Business services. Some pets allowed (fee). No-smoking rooms. | 1002 Columbus Pkwy. | 334/749–1461 | fax 334/749–1468 | 95 rooms in 3 buildings | $37–$99 | AE, D, DC, MC, V.

POINT CLEAR

INTRO
ATTRACTIONS
DINING
LODGING

POINT CLEAR

MAP 3, B8

(Nearby towns also listed: Fairhope, Mobile)

Affluent Southerners have gathered in Point Clear since the 1830s. In earlier days, this town on the eastern shore of Mobile Bay was a summer retreat. It has been the site of the Grand Hotel, a hospital for Civil War wounded, a World War II training site, and now the Marriott's Grand Hotel Resort and Golf Club.

Information: **Eastern Shore Chamber of Commerce** | 327 Fairhope Ave., Fairhope 36532 | 334/621–8222 | fax 334/928–6389 | www.eschamber.com.

Dining

Wash House. Seafood. This hidden-away, intimate restaurant is housed behind the Punta Clara Kitchen in the rustic building that once served as that Victorian home's kitchen and washhouse. Candlelit tables and a large brick fireplace make it an especially romantic dinner spot. Be sure to consider the nightly specials—there are usually as many specials as regular items offered on the menu. Try "My Favorite Fish"—a broiled flounder fillet topped with tomatoes, crab, cream cheese, blue cheese, and garlic butter. | U.S. 98, Point Clear | 334/928–1500 | $29–$42 | AE, D, DC, MC, V | No lunch.

Lodging

★ **Marriott's Grand Hotel Resort and Golf Club.** This sprawling 558-acre resort fronts Mobile Bay in tony Point Clear, where wealthy families have summer homes. The hotel was originally built some 150 years ago. Most of the resort's rooms have gorgeous bay views. Many of the employees at the Grand Hotel have worked here for years and know guests by name. The central gathering spot is in the heart of the lobby, with huge stone fireplaces, warm wood paneling, and comfortable furniture, where you can enjoy complimentary afternoon tea and cookies. Don't miss the extravagant breakfast buffet in the Grand Dining Room.

5 restaurants, bar, dining room, picnic area, room service. In-room data ports, cable TV. Pool. Beauty salon, hot tub. Two 18-hole golf courses, 8 tennis courts. Gym, horseback riding, beach, boating, fishing, bicycles. Children's programs for ages 5–12, playground. Business services, airport shuttle. No-smoking rooms. | 1 Grand Blvd. | 334/928–9201 or 800/544–9933 | fax 334/928–1149 | www.marriotthotels.com/ptlal/ | 306 rooms, 24 suites | $219 rooms, $350–$950 suites | AE, D, DC, MC, V.

SCOTTSBORO

MAP 3, D1

(Nearby town also listed: Huntsville)

Located in the northeastern corner of the state, with Georgia to the east and Tennessee to the north, the town is set on some of Alabama's most beautiful land. Like many small southern towns, Scottsboro's businesses are arranged around a courthouse.

More than a century ago, when Scottsboro became the county seat, court days attracted crowds who began trading wares, a tradition that continues today on the first Monday of the month. Goose Pond Colony is a popular city-owned resort that offers rustic cottages as well as campsites. The Unclaimed Baggage Center offers a unique shopping experience that attracts thousands of visitors every month.

Information: **Scottsboro-Jackson County Chamber of Commerce** | 407 E. Willow St., Scottsboro 35768 | 256/259–5500 or 800/259–5508 | fax 256/259–4447 | chamber@scottsboro.org | www.sjcchamber.org.

Attractions

Russell Cave National Monument. Seven miles northwest of Bridgeport, Russell Cave National Monument is one of the country's oldest documented shelters of prehistoric man, dating back almost 10,000 years. Archaeologists have uncovered charcoal from fires, animals bones, tools made from bones, spear and arrow points, broken pottery, and graves. Many of these finds are on display in an adjacent museum that depicts the life of cave dwellers. Hiking trails are nearby. | 3729 Country Rd. 98, Bridgeport | 256/495–2672 | fax 256/495–9220 | www.nps.gov/ruca | Free | Daily 8:30–5.

Unclaimed Baggage. This unique store nestled in the foothills of the Appalachian Mountains and bordered by 70,000-acre Lake Guntersville, offers millions of bargain-priced items, most of which come from the unclaimed-baggage areas of airports around the country. The store was founded in 1970 by Doyle and Sue Owens, purchased in 1995 by Bryan Owens, and expanded to fill more than a city block. A concierge desk helps direct visitors to shops and area attractions, and there's a playground for children. | 509 W. Willow St. | 256/259–1525 | www.unclaimedbaggage.com | Free.

ON THE CALENDAR

YEAR-ROUND *First Monday.* A tradition of yard sales, antiques shows, arts and crafts, and more are celebrated at this year-round "First Monday" event, originally the day that the Jackson County Circuit Court was held in the mid-1850s. Today, thousands of shoppers hunt from dawn to dusk. | 256/259–5500 or 800/259–5508 | 1st Mon. and preceding Sat. and Sun. of each month.

Lodging

Days Inn. This standard motel is just off U.S. 72, approximately 10 minutes from Unclaimed Baggage *(see above)*—the famous store where you can shop for treasures retrieved from lost baggage from all over the country. There's a restaurant across the street and a movie theater is a five-minute drive. Complimentary Continental breakfast. In-room data ports, some microwaves, some refrigerators, cable TV. Pool. Business services. Some pets allowed.

No-smoking rooms. | 23945 John T. Reid Pkwy. | 256/574–1212 | fax 256/574–1212 | 84 rooms | $46 | AE, D, DC, MC, V.

Goose Pond Colony. Peace and quiet are the main amenities at this 360-acre city-owned resort which has a lodge and lakefront cottages on Lake Guntersville. Campsites also available. You can golf the 18-hole course, hike and bike among the many scenic trails, partake in water sports, or see what's happening in the 2,000-seat amphitheater. The Alabama Space and Rocket Center and Russell Cave National Monument are about 20 minutes away. The Fourth of July fireworks show is especially popular here. Restaurant, picnic area. Kitchenettes, cable TV. Pool. Golf course. Boating. Playground. | 417 Hembree Dr. | 256/259–2884 or 800/268–2884 | fax 256/259–3127 | gpc@hiwaay.net | www.goosepond.org | 12 cottages, 6 rooms in lodge | $142 cottages, $60 lodge | AE, D, MC, V.

Hampton Inn. This standard inn is near several restaurants and just minutes from Unclaimed Baggage (*see above*) and a golf course. Complimentary Continental breakfast. In-room data ports, microwaves, refrigerators, cable TV. Pool. Business services. | 46 Micah Way | 256/259–4300 | fax 256/259–0919 | www.hamptoninn.com | 50 rooms | $61 | AE, D, DC, MC, V.

SELMA

MAP 3, C5

(Nearby town also listed: Montgomery)

Selma has played major roles in both Civil War and Civil Rights history. With the Confederacy's second-largest arsenal and foundry, Selma was a target of northern aggression and succumbed to Union forces in 1865, marking the end of the era of wealthy plantation owners.

Almost 100 years after that battle, in March 1965, Selma was the setting for "Bloody Sunday," the highly publicized and violent conflict between state troopers and Civil Rights activists who were protesting discriminatory voter-registration practices. Three weeks later, Dr. Martin Luther King, Jr., led another group of demonstrators on a 50-mi march from Selma to Montgomery. The journey sparked the passing of the nation's Voting Rights Act. The span between Montgomery and Selma has been named a National Scenic Byway and an All-American Road, the only U.S. road with the dual designation.

Today, Selma is a marketing, agricultural, and manufacturing center. Farmers raise cattle, pecans, cotton, soybean, and hay, and a number of companies have established corporate headquarters here.

Information: **Selma–Dallas County Chamber of Commerce** | 513 Lauderdale St., Selma 36701 | 334/875–7241 or 800/457–3562 | fax 334/875–7142 | selmacofc@zebra.net | www.selmaalabama.com.

Attractions

Cahawba. From 1820 to 1826, Cahawba was the state capital and a thriving antebellum river town. Shortly after the Civil War, it became a ghost town, and today is an important archaeological and historical site. A visitor center contains artifacts and photographs of early homes and businesses. The site includes an old cemetery, slave quarters, a nature trail, and columns and chimneys of home sites. It's 12 mi south of Selma. | 9518 Cahawba Rd., Orrville | 334/872–8058 | fax 334/875–5168 | www.selmaalabama.com/cahawba/htm | Free | Daily 9–5.

Central Alabama Black Heritage Tour. Outlined in a brochure available from the chamber of commerce, a trail leads from Selma to Montgomery and Tuskegee, highlighting key events in Civil Rights history and prominent African Americans. Selma is noted as a battlefront for the Voter Registration Movement and Bloody Sunday. Montgomery is known as the birthplace of the Civil Rights Movement and where Rosa Parks boldly took a stand against segregation. Tuskegee is linked to remarkable achievements in education, science, and aviation by such outstanding African-Americans as Booker T. Washington and Dr. George Washington Carver. | 513 Lauderdale St. | 334/875–7241 or 800/457–3562 | fax 334/875–7142 | www.selmaalabama.com | Free.

Edmund Pettus Bridge. The bridge was the setting for the 1965 Bloody Sunday attack by law enforcement officials against blacks demonstrating for voting rights. The bridge spans the Alabama River. | Broad St. at Water Ave. | 334/875–7241 or 800/457–3562 | fax 334/875–7142 | www.olcg.com/selma | Free | Daily.

Historic Water Avenue. The area contains the Edmund Pettus Bridge, Bienville Park, antebellum structures, and Civil War and Civil Rights monuments. | Water Ave. | 334/875–7241 or 800/457–3562 | fax 334/875–7142 | www.selmaalabama.com | Free | Daily.

Joseph T. Smitherman Historic Building. The Selma Masonic Order built the structure in the 1840s. Originally, it was a university and later served as a Confederate hospital, a county courthouse, city hospital, and a military school. | 109 Union St. | 334/874–2174 | www.olcg.com/selma/ | $3 | Tues.–Sat. 9–4; and by appointment.

National Voting Rights Museum and Institute. The museum has a pictorial history of the struggle for voting rights in America. It displays an exceptional record of events and participants. The museum is near the foot of the Edmund Pettus Bridge, where voting rights marchers were confronted by the police. | 1012 Water Ave. | 334/418–0800 | fax 334/418–0278 | www.olcg.com/selma/ | $4 | Tues.–Fri. 9–5, Sat. 10–3; and by appointment.

Old Depot Museum. In a renovated 1891 railway depot, the collection includes artifacts from 1841 through the voting rights era. There is a Black Heritage wing, a turn-of-the-20th-century schoolroom, and a military war collection with objects from pre–World War I through the Persian Gulf War. A Victorian firehouse has interesting antique fire-fighting vehicles. | 4 Martin Luther King St. | 334/874–2197 | fax 334/874–1221 | www.olcg.com/selma | $4 | Mon.–Sat. 10–4; and by appointment.

Old Town Historic District. Alabama's largest historic district includes stately, antebellum Sturdivant Hall. The area, with more than 1,250 buildings dating from the 1820s, is best seen on a self-guided driving tour, using brochures available from the chamber of commerce. Among the collection are 116 historic sites. The 9-block–by–14-block district is in the heart of downtown, bordered by Martin Luther King Street, Young Street, Water Avenue, and Jefferson Davis Avenue. | 513 Lauderdale St. | 334/875–7241 or 800/457–3562 | fax 334/875–7142 | www.selmaalabama.com | Free | Daily.

Paul M. Grist State Park. The park is north of Selma and offers improved campsites, a primitive camping area, picnic and play areas, and two hiking trails. You can also boat, fish, or swim in the lake. Boat rentals are available. | 1546 Grist Rd. | 334/872–5846 | $2 | Daily 8–7.

Sturdivant Hall. Circa 1853, the square, two-story stucco brick building is an outstanding example of neoclassical architecture. Six fluted Corinthian columns rise 30 ft to support a portico roof. A cupola crowns the flat, slate roof. The 10-room antebellum home has a detached kitchen (now a gift shop), and formal gardens. | 713 Mabry St. | 334/872–5626 | www.olcg.com/selma | $5 | Tues.–Fri. 9– 4, Sat. 10–4.

ON THE CALENDAR

MAR.: *Bridge Crossing Jubilee.* Commemorating the anniversary of Bloody Sunday and the Selma-to-Montgomery march for voting rights. | Various locations | 334/418–0800.
MAR.: *Historic Selma Pilgrimage.* Showcase of one of the state's best collections of 19th-century buildings. | Water Ave. to Sturdivant Hall | 334/875–7241 or 800/457–3562.
APR.: *Reenactment of the Battle of Selma.* Authentic encampments, nighttime artillery exhibitions, firing exhibitions, and major battles with some 2,000 reenactors, on a Sunday afternoon. | Battlefield Park | 334/875–7241 or 800/457–3562.

MAY: *Old Cahawba Festival.* Celebration of Alabama's first permanent state capital; includes music, arts and crafts, living history, archaeology, storytelling, and a barbecue. | Cahawba Park | 334/875–7241 or 800/457–3562.

AUG.: *Selma Rodeo.* Competitors gather from far and wide at the Agricultural Arena. | 334/875–5417.

OCT.: *African Extravaganza.* Each year an African country is chosen and featured at this festival of foods, native dances, original theater, and displays of native crafts. | Striplin Performing Arts Centre | 334/418–0800.

OCT.: *Riverfront Market Day.* Hundreds of artists and craftsmen, Dixieland music, and square dancers participate in Market Day. | Water Ave. | 334/875–7241 or 800/457–3562.

OCT.: *Tale Tellin' Festival.* Storytellers weave folktales. | New National Guard Armory | 334/875–7241 or 800/457–3562.

DEC.: *Christmas on the River.* About a dozen boats don lights and decorations and glide downriver about 1½ mi from City Marina to the railroad trestle. Edmund Pettus Bridge and the marina are preferred vantage points. | Alabama River | 334/874–2173.

DEC.: *Holiday Festival.* Two-week craft show and bake sale with Santa some afternoons. | Striplin Performing Arts Centre | 334/874–2111.

Dining

Major Grumbles. Southern. Named for Benjamin Grumbles, a self-appointed major in the Civil War, this restaurant is in a renovated 1830s cotton warehouse on the Alabama River. Historic photos and Selma artifacts accent the casual rustic interior. Known for chicken breast marinated for 24 hours, then char-grilled, plus hand-cut steaks. Seafood and ribs are also on the menu. | 1 Grumbles Alley | 334/872–2006 | $25 | AE, DC, MC, V | Closed Sun.

Tally-Ho. Contemporary. Although the entrance to Tally-Ho is through an old log cabin, there's nothing simple about its sophisticated, French-influenced cuisine. The menu includes everything from an escargot appetizer to a center-cut pork chop in Thai sauce. Extra special are the homemade sauces, dressings, and French onion soup. True to its name, the lounge is akin to a British pub with darts and a full-service bar. Kids' menu, early-bird specials. | 507 Mangum Ave. | 334/872–1390 | $19–$27 | AE, D, DC, MC, V | Closed Sun. No lunch.

Lodging

Grace Hall Bed and Breakfast. This pretty mansion in downtown Selma features many original antiques and period wallpapers dating from 1857 when the home was built. Relax on one of two porches furnished with comfortable wicker furniture. Shopping, golf, fishing, and antiques shops are all within 1 mi. This restored antebellum mansion is also on the National Register of Historic Places. Complimentary breakfast. Cable TV, in-room VCRs. Library. Business services. | 506 Lauderdale St. | 334/875–5744 | fax 334/875–9967 | adman@wwisp.com | www.traveldata.com/inns/data/alstbb.html | 6 rooms | $79–$99 | AE, D, MC, V.

Holiday Inn. This standard inn is about 3 mi from downtown Selma, near a variety of restaurants and about 45 minutes from Montgomery. Restaurant, bar, room service. In-room data ports, cable TV. Pool, wading pool. Business services. Some pets allowed. No-smoking rooms. | U.S. 80 west | 334/872–0461 | fax 334/872–0461 | 165 rooms in 3 buildings | $57 | AE, D, DC, MC, V.

St. James Hotel. Jesse James is rumored to have been a guest at this historic 1837 hotel. In addition to standard rooms, the hotel has suites which overlook the Alabama River. The lobby centers around a courtyard with a fountain, and the terrace provides lovely views of the river. Restaurant, bar, room service. Cable TV. Laundry service. Business services, free parking. No-smoking rooms. | 1200 Water Ave. | 334/872–3234 or 888/264–6788 | fax 334/872–0332 | 42 rooms, 4 suites | $75–$95 rooms, $125 suites | AE, D, DC, MC, V.

SHEFFIELD

MAP 3, B1

(Nearby towns also listed: Florence, Tuscumbia)

Although five blast furnaces operated in Sheffield before 1900, the town never grew until the Tennessee Valley Authority prompted growth in industry and population. Alabama's first railroad was chartered in Sheffield in 1830.

Information: **Colbert County Tourism and Convention Bureau** | 719 Hwy. 17 west, Tuscumbia 35674 | 256/383–0783 or 800/344–0783 | fax 256/383–2080 | ins@colbertcountytourism.org | www.colbertcountytourism.org.

Dining

George's Steak Pit. Steak. Owner George Vafinis has run this restaurant since 1957, and his heritage influences the menu which includes Greek salads and meatballs. There are four different dining rooms each dimly lit with candles on the tables. Try George's special rib eye, seasoned with Greek spices and grilled on an open pit over hickory wood. Shrimp, king crab legs, chicken, and grilled pork chops are also available. Kids' menu. | 1206 Jackson Hwy. | 256/381–1531 | $13–$27 | AE, D, DC, MC, V | Closed Sun., Mon. No lunch.

The Southland. Southern. Since 1950, this family restaurant has offered an array of southern dishes, with an emphasis on fresh vegetables. Known for barbecued chicken and pork, catfish. Homemade pies. No smoking. | 1309 Jackson Hwy. | 256/383–8236 | $5–$10 | No credit cards | Closed Mon. No dinner Sun.

Lodging

Holiday Inn. In downtown Sheffield, this standard inn is near the Northwest Alabama Airport and just 2 mi from Florence. Restaurant, bar (with entertainment), room service. In-room data ports, some microwaves, some refrigerators, cable TV. Pool. Hot tub. Gym. Laundry facilities. Business services, airport shuttle. No-smoking rooms. | 4900 Hatch Blvd. | 256/381–4710 | fax 256/381–7313 | 204 rooms | $83 | AE, D, DC, MC, V.

Ramada Inn. This standard inn is less than a mile from McFarland Park on the Tennessee River, which has a boat ramp, dock, and fishing. Restaurant, bar (with entertainment), room service. Microwaves in suites, some refrigerators, some in-room hot tubs, cable TV. Pool. Hot tub. Business services, airport shuttle. Some pets allowed (fee). No-smoking rooms. | 4205 Hatch Blvd. | 256/381–3743 | fax 256/386–7928 | 150 rooms, 3 suites | $55 rooms, $150–$200 suites | AE, D, DC, MC, V.

SYLACAUGA

MAP 3, D4

(Nearby towns also listed: Alexander City, Talladega)

Home to Jim "Gomer Pyle" Nabors, Sylacauga sits on a solid bed of cream-white marble. The bed is more than 24 mi long and more than 1 mi wide. Marble from "Marble City" went into construction of the U.S. Supreme Court Building and the Lincoln Memorial in Washington, D.C. The national headquarters and three large plants of Avondale Mills are in this city, which is a 10-time winner of a national "Keep America Beautiful" Award and five-time recipient of "Cleanest Town in Alabama Under 60,000" (population) award.

Information: **Sylacauga Chamber of Commerce** | 17 W. Fort Williams, Sylacauga 35150 | 256/249–0308 | fax 256/249–0315 | chamber@syclacauga.net | www.sylacauga.net.

Attractions

Isabel Anderson Comer Museum & Arts Center. Sylacauga's white marble serves as a facade for the museum, which spotlights the area's history and pays tribute to native sons Jim "Gomer Pyle" Nabors, James W. Crysel—whose military career spanned 35 years, and U.S. Congressman William Nichols—known as the "Friend of the Serviceman" for his legislative initiatives. The museum holds a permanent art collection, Native American artifacts, and archaeological finds. | 711 N. Broadway Ave. | 256/245–4016 | fax 256/245–4612 | Free | Tues.–Fri. 10–5.

Lodging

Super 8 Motel. Along U.S. 280, this standard motel is midway between Montgomery and Birmingham, about 30 minutes from Talladega Superspeedway. Cable TV. Pool. Laundry facilities. Business services. No-smoking rooms. | 40770 U.S. 280 | 256/249–4321 or 800/800–8000 | fax 256/245–3732 | 44 rooms in 2 buildings | $45–$60 | AE, D, DC, MC, V.

Towne Inn. This locally owned inn is convenient to restaurants and shopping, and the Talladega Superspeedway is only 30 minutes away. Cable TV. Pool. Business services. Some pets allowed. No-smoking rooms. | 40860 U.S. 280 | 256/249–3821 | fax 256/249–4707 | 76 rooms | $42–$50 | AE, D, DC, MC, V.

TALLADEGA

MAP 3, D4

(Nearby towns also listed: Anniston, Birmingham, Sylacauga)

Some of Talladega's early residents earned their fortunes in textiles; their antebellum and Victorian homes are clustered in what now is known as the Silk Stocking Historic District. These days, the wealth comes to those who race at the world's fastest NASCAR track at Talladega Superspeedway. The track hosts the Winston 500 in April and the DieHard 500 in October. Exhibits at the International Motorsports Hall of Fame showcase racing giants and special events.

Founded in 1834 in the foothills of the southernmost extension of the Appalachians, Talladega is today a manufacturing center. The Talladega National Forest, with its 210,000 acres of hardwood trees, lakes, scenic overlooks, waterfalls, and mountain streams, is a popular area attraction.

Information: **Greater Talladega Area Chamber of Commerce** | 210 East St. south, Talladega 35161 | 256/362–9075 | fax 256/362–9093 | chamber@highway.net | www.talladega.com.

Attractions

Silk Stocking Historic District. A collection of antebellum and Victorian homes erected by early residents who earned their fortunes in textiles. Bordered by South, South East, Coffee, Cherry, and Ashbury streets. | 256/362–9075 | Free | Daily.

Talladega National Forest. The 210,000-acre forest has hardwood trees, lakes, scenic overlooks, a waterfall, and mountain streams. Hike short or long trails through diverse topography and scenic beauty. Elevations range from 800 ft to 2,342 ft on Cheaha Mountain. | 1001 N St. | 256/362–2909 | fax 256/362–0823 | Free | Daily.

Talladega Superspeedway. This is a 2.66-mi, high-banked tri-oval that annually hosts two major NASCAR races—the Winston 500 in April and the DieHard 500 in October. Saturday races include ARCA, Busch Series, and IROC events. Crowds in excess of 100,000 are typical for the two Winston events. If you visit the International Motorsports Hall of Fame you can also tour the track unless races are scheduled. The track hosts the Winston 500 in April and the DieHard 500 in October | 3366 Speedway Blvd. | 256/362–2261 | fax 256/761–4777 | Daily; tours 8:30–5.

International Motorsports Hall of Fame. Near the Talladega Superspeedway, the complex preserves the history of motorsports on a worldwide basis and permanently enshrines people responsible for the sport's growth. The facility houses six Halls of Fame with paintings and awards honoring inductees; and a collection of racing vehicles and memorabilia. | 3198 Speedway Blvd. | 256/362–5002 | fax 256/362–5002 | www.motorsportshalloffame.com | $8; museum and bus tour $10 | Daily 8:30–5.

Lodging

Budget Inn. Located just 2 mi from Talladega Superspeedway, this motel is less than 5 mi from Talladega College, the Alabama School for the Deaf, and downtown Talladega. Restaurant, bar (with entertainment). Cable TV. Pool, wading pool. Business services. Some pets allowed. No-smoking rooms. | 65600 Rte. 77 north | 256/362–0900 | fax 256/362–0908 | 100 rooms in 2 buildings | $39–$80 | AE, D, DC, MC, V.

THEODORE

(Nearby town also listed: Mobile)

A rural area flanked by the Fowl River, Theodore might never have made the map had it not been for the vision of Walter and Bessie Bellingrath who so beautified their Theodore fishing retreat that people insisted on being allowed a glimpse. The sleepy town, not far from Mobile, is slow-paced with residents who have sidestepped the bustle of big-city life.

One-hour boat cruises on the Fowl River leave regularly from the dock next to the Bellingrath Home that is filled with antique furniture, Oriental rugs, silver, china, and what today is considered the world's largest public display of Boehm porcelain.

Information: **Bellingrath Gardens and Home** | 12401 Bellingrath Rd., Theodore 36582 | 334/973–2217 or 800/247–8420 | fax 334/973–0540 | bellingrath@juno.com | www.bellingrath.org.

Attractions

★ **Bellingrath Gardens and Home.** One of the South's most popular gardens is some 20 mi south of Mobile in Theodore. Bellingrath Gardens and Home cover 65 magnificently landscaped acres carved out of a semitropical forest, and includes a world-renowned azalea garden, spectacular in spring, and an Oriental-American Garden with teahouses and a bridge. The gardens, which bloom year-round, are a sanctuary to more than 200 species of birds. You can also visit the brick home of the gardens' creators which has among the finest collections of antiques in the Southeast, and the world's largest collection of Boehm porcelain birds. A number of packaged tours are available, including one-hour boat cruises that depart routinely. | 12401 Bellingrath Rd. | 334/973–2217 or 800/247–8420 | fax 334/973–0540 | www.bellingrath.org | $8–$20 | Daily 8–dusk.

Southern Belle. The *Southern Belle* offers sightseeing cruises along the Fowl River. | 334/973–1244.

Lodging

Holiday Inn. Designated the official hotel of Bellingrath Gardens and Home, this inn is about 20 minutes away in Theodore. Ask about their Bellingrath package rates. Restaurant, bar, room service. In-room data ports, cable TV. Pool. Hot tub. Gym. Laundry facilities. Business services, airport shuttle. Some pets allowed. No-smoking rooms. | 5465 U.S. 90 west | 334/666–5600 | fax 334/666–2773 | 159 rooms | $69 | AE, D, DC, MC, V.

TROY

MAP 3, E6

(Nearby town also listed: Montgomery)

Fifty miles south of Montgomery, Troy is home to Troy State University and the Pike Pioneer Museum, a complex with more than 14,000 artifacts from the pioneer period.

Information: **Pike County Chamber of Commerce** | U.S. 231 N., Troy 36081 | 334/566–2294 | fax 334/566–2298 | pikecoc@trojan.troyst.edu | www.pikecounty.com.

Attractions

Pike Pioneer Museum. With more than 14,000 artifacts (including clothing, furniture, and farm implements) from the area's pioneer period, the 30-acre complex includes a turn-of-the-20th-century schoolhouse, working gristmill, vegetable gardens, log house, well-stocked general store, and an 1883 steam-logging locomotive. Spinning and weaving demonstrations are given. Special events, such as fall and spring Pioneer Days, take place throughout the year. Folklife artisans appear the first Saturday of the month, April to December. | 248 U.S. 231 north | 334/566–3597 | fax 334/566–3552 | $3 | Mon.–Sat. 9–5, Sun. 1–5.

Troy State University. Begun by the Alabama Legislature in 1887, Troy State has become a flagship of a multicampus university system, with 17,000 students system-wide and 5,100 in Troy. Troy State offers a wide variety of academic majors and is known for its communications program. Students participate in NCAA Division I athletics and the school has a premiere marching band. | Troy State University, University Ave. | 334/670–3000 | fax 334/670–3274 | www.troyst.edu | Free | Daily.

Dining

Mossy Grove Schoolhouse. Southern. Feel free to ring the bell that still stands outside this schoolhouse built in 1856. Dine casually on large portions of food accompanied by sides like hush puppies, Great Northern beans, fries or baked potatoes, and salad or coleslaw. Known for hand-cut steak and fried, broiled, and grilled seafood. Kids' menu. No smoking. | 1902 Elba Hwy. | 334/566–4921 | $5–$14 | MC, V | Closed Sun., Mon. No lunch.

Lodging

Econo Lodge. Off U.S. 231, this standard motel is convenient to Troy State University, and several restaurants. Complimentary Continental breakfast. Cable TV. Pool. Business services. No-smoking rooms. | 1013 U.S. 231 | 334/566–4960 | fax 334/566–5858 | 66 rooms | $54 | AE, D, DC, MC, V.

Ramada Inn. Located along Interstate 65, this inn is close to several fast-food restaurants and about five minutes from downtown Greenville. Restaurant, bar. In-room data ports, cable TV. Pool. Business services. No-smoking rooms. | 941 Fort Dale Rd., Greenville | 334/382–2651 | fax 334/382–2651 | 96 rooms in 2 buildings | $52 | AE, D, DC, MC, V.

TUSCALOOSA

MAP 3, B4

(Nearby town also listed: Bessemer)

Tuscaloosa, which served as the state capital from 1826 to 1846, comes from the Choctaw word meaning "Black Warrior." Cotton was a major industry here, and, when cotton prices plummeted, the local economy sagged and the capital was moved to Montgomery.

Tuscaloosa is home to the University of Alabama, where football reigns supreme, with ties to legendary coach Paul "Bear" Bryant, who is saluted at a museum bearing his name. University history also includes a time in 1865 when Union troops burned many of the campus's buildings. Most of the action in "T-Town" is related to the university. However, as with many university towns, there are plenty of cultural offerings.

History and architecture buffs favor the Battle-Friedman House, and crafts collectors relish October's Kentuck Festival of the Arts in nearby Northport.

Information: **Tuscaloosa Convention and Visitors Bureau** | 1305 Greensboro Ave., Tuscaloosa 35401 | 205/391–9200 or 800/538–8696 | fax 205/391–2125 | www.tcvb.org.

Attractions

Alabama State Museum of Natural History. Collections represent the state's natural heritage, including dinosaur-age and ice-age fossils displayed in re-created natural habitats. In 1910, state architect Frank Lockwood designed the museum, itself an intriguing wonder with a barrel-vaulted glass roof that illuminates an interior surrounded by a colonnade of Corinthian columns. The Alabama Museum of Natural History is located in historic Smith Hall adjacent to the Quadrangle on the University of Alabama campus. | 6th Ave. and Capstone Dr. | 205/348–7550 | fax 205/348–9292 | www.au.edu/history.htm | Free | Weekdays 8:30–4:30, Sat. 1–4.

Battle-Friedman House. The 1835 Greek Revival mansion was built as a town house by wealthy planter and businessman Alfred Battle. Distinguishing the facade is plastic stucco, scored and painted to look like pink marble. Second owner Bernard Friedman added a two-story brick wing at the rear and imported chandeliers from his Hungarian homeland. Now restored and furnished, it serves as a city cultural center and museum. | 1010 Greensboro Ave. | 205/758–6138 | $3 | Tues.–Sat. 10–noon and 1–4, Sun. 1–4; and by appointment.

Children's Hands-on Museum. Housed in a former department store, CHOM is the place to pretend to be a doctor or nurse, try on clothes in Grandma's attic, run a store, be a bank clerk, and experience a planetarium. An Indian village teaches how Native Americans ground corn and made pottery. | 2213 University Blvd. | 205/349–4235 | fax 205/349–4276 | $5 | Tues.–Fri. 9–5, Sat. 1–5.

Lake Lurleen State Park. Named for Alabama's only female governor, the late Lurleen Wallace, the park is a scenic lakeside retreat. It's a popular fishing spot; the marina accommodates privately owned vessels and also rents boats. The park includes a campground, picnic areas, a beach complex, a country store, and a seasonal nature center/activity program. | 13226 Lake Lurleen Rd., Coker | 205/339–1558 | fax 205/339–8885 | $2 | Daily 7 AM–9 PM.

Mercedes Visitors Center. The first of its kind outside Germany, the museum features historic Mercedes vehicles and offers a multimedia look at the past, present, and future of automotive technology. Museum admission includes a tour of the adjacent factory that produces M-Class All-Activity vehicles which debuted in Steven Spielberg's thriller *The Lost World*. Reservations required for factory tour; no children under 12. | 1 Mercedes Dr., Vance | 205/507–2252 or 888/286–8762 | fax 205/507–2255 | www.mbusi.com | $4 | Weekdays 9–5, Sat. 10–3.

Moundville Archaeological Park. From about AD 1000 to 1500, the site of Moundville Archaeological Park was a thriving settlement and probably the capital of a group of villages that extended from the area of Tuscaloosa to Demopolis. At Moundville, Native Americans held elaborate ceremonies, grew their own foods, and used waterways for transportation and survival. The 317-acre National Historic Landmark contains 20 temple mounds and an archaeological museum which displays artifacts traced back to prehistoric forefathers of local Seminole, Creek, and Cherokee Native Americans. A trail leads to the Black Warrior River, picnic areas, and a campground. Located 14 mi south of Tuscaloosa, on Hwy. 69 south. From Hwy. I–20/59 take exit 71A and proceed 13 mi south. The park entrance will be located on your right on Hwy. 69 | 1 Mound State Pkwy., Moundville | 205/371–2572 or 205/371–2234 | fax 205/371–4180 | www.ua.edu/mndville.htm | $4 | Daily 8–8; museum daily 9–5.

National Headquarters of Gulf States Paper Corporation. The national headquarters' Warner Collection includes several hundred paintings as well as dozens of artifacts and sculptures. The Asian-style, beautifully landscaped headquarters houses a range of art, including numerous works by the Wyeths, Albert Bierstadt, Frederic Remington, Thomas Cole, and George Catlin. | 1400 Jack Warner Pkwy. | 205/553–6200 | fax 205/562–5010 | Free | Tours weekdays 5:30 PM and 6:30 PM, Sat. 10–4, Sun. 1–4.

University of Alabama. Founded in the 1830s as the state's first public university, UA enrolls some 18,500 undergraduate and graduate students. It offers 275 degrees in more than 150 fields. The 180 campus buildings include four original structures that survived the 1865 burning of the university by Union troops. One of those, the observatory where F. A. P. Barnard pioneered the study of astronomy in Alabama, is home of the computer-based Honors Program. | University Blvd. | 205/348–6010 | fax 205/348–7252 | www.ua.edu | Free | Daily.

Gorgas House. Built in 1892 as a hotel or steward's hall, the house was named for Confederate General Josiah Gorgas, who served briefly as president of the university. Now a museum, the house is filled with a wealth of 19th-century furniture and silver. | Capstone Dr. at McCorvey Dr. | 205/348–5906 | www.ua.edu/academic/museums/gorgas/index.html | $2 | Tues.–Sat. 10–4.

Paul W. "Bear" Bryant Museum. The museum follows the University of Alabama's 100-year tradition of football preeminence. It showcases many of legendary coach "Bear" Bryant's personal belongings and spotlights others who helped to lay the foundation for the university's football program. | 300 Paul W. Bryant Dr. | 205/348–4668 | fax 205/348–8883 | www.ua.edu/bryant.htm | $2 | Daily 9–4.

TUSCALOOSA

INTRO
ATTRACTIONS
DINING
LODGING

ON THE CALENDAR

AUG.: *CityFest*. Nationally known musicians perform everything from zydeco to jazz; costume contests, arts and crafts, a children's parade, and regional foods are also featured. | Downtown | 205/553–9009.

OCT.: *Kentuck Festival of the Arts*. Crafts collectors relish this Northport festival. | 205/758–1257.

OCT.: *Moundville Native American Festival*. Four days with artisans demonstrating native crafts, dances, and foods. Native American items are on sale. | Moundville Archaeological Park | 205/371–2572 or 205/371–2234.

DEC.: *Christmas Afloat*. Showcase of decorated boats float down the Black Warrior River. | Black Warrior River | 205/391–9200.

Dining

Henson's Cypress Inn. Seafood. With a beautiful view of the Black Warrior River, this casual restaurant's rustic decor is filled with live plants and flowers and has a large, glassed-in bar area. Try the Shrimp Cypress Inn: shrimp in a lemon-wine-butter sauce served over pasta, topped with broiled cheddar and mozzarella cheeses. The dessert menu includes bread pudding and peanut butter pie. A selection of steaks also available. Open-air dining on deck. Kids' menu. | 501 Rice Mine Rd. north | 205/345–6963 | $10–$19 | AE, D, MC, V | No lunch Sat.

Trey Yuen. Chinese. This restaurant offers an authentic taste of the Orient. The menu includes chicken dishes, fried rice, and lo mein. Buffet (lunch). No smoking. | 4200 McFarland Blvd. east | 205/752–0088 | $5–$12 | AE, D, MC, V.

Lodging

Crimson Inn Bed and Breakfast. This casually elegant, 75-year-old Dutch Colonial home is just blocks away from restaurants, antique malls, and Bryant-Denny Stadium, home of the Crimson Tide. No smoking. Complimentary breakfast. No room phones, no TV. Parking. | 1509 University Blvd. | 205/758–3483 | fax 205/758–9937 | www.bbonline.com/al/crimsoninn | 4 rooms (all with shared baths) | $100 | AE, MC, V.

Days Inn. On U.S. 78, this standard motel is only two blocks from Jasper Mall, and near movie theaters and several restaurants. Complimentary Continental breakfast. Microwaves, refrigerators, cable TV. Pool. Laundry facilities. Business services. No-smoking rooms. | 101 6th Ave. north, Jasper | 205/221–7800 | fax 205/221–7800 | 44 rooms | $50–$55 | AE, D, DC, MC, V.

Four Points Hotel. On the University of Alabama campus, this hotel is convenient to the Paul W. "Bear" Bryant Museum and the Conference Center. Restaurant, bar, room service. In-room data ports, some refrigerators, cable TV. Pool. Gym. Laundry service. Business services, airport shuttle. No-smoking rooms. | 320 Paul Bryant Dr. | 205/752–3200 | fax 205/759–9314 | 150 rooms | $75–$109 | AE, D, DC, MC, V.

Hampton Inn University. This standard inn is just ½ mi from the University of Alabama campus and University Mall, and there are numerous restaurants nearby. Complimentary Continental breakfast. In-room data ports, cable TV. Pool. Laundry service. No-smoking rooms. | 600 Harper Lee Dr. | 205/553–9800 | fax 205/553–0082 | www.hamptoninn.com | 102 rooms | $69–$75 | AE, D, DC, MC, V.

Jasper Inn and Super 8 Motel. The Jasper Motel recently added a four-story Super 8 Motel to its property. The combined establishment is on U.S. 78, about ½ mi from Jasper Mall and close to several restaurants. Restaurant. Cable TV. Pool. Laundry facilities. Business services. No-smoking rooms. | 1301 U.S. 78 W. Bypass, Jasper | 205/221–6430 or 800/554–0238 | fax 205/221–3050 ext. 508 | 55 rooms in Jasper Inn, 99 rooms in Super 8 Motel | $42 | AE, D, MC, V.

Ramada Inn. This standard inn is just ½ mi from McFarland Mall and about five minutes from the University of Alabama campus. Restaurant, bar (with entertainment). Cable TV. Pool. Business services. Some pets allowed. No-smoking rooms. | 631 Skyland Blvd. east | 205/759–4431 | fax 205/758–9655 | 108 rooms in 3 buildings | $53 | AE, D, DC, MC, V.

Sleep Inn. This standard inn is near several museums, two malls, McFarland Mall and the University of Alabama, and 5 mi from the University of Alabama campus. It is approximately 15 mi from the Mercedes plant in Vance. Complimentary Continental breakfast. In-room data ports, cable TV, in-room VCRs. Pool. Gym. Laundry facilities. Business services. No-smoking rooms. | 4300 Skyland Blvd. east | 205/556–5696 | fax 205/556–5696 | 72 rooms, 20 suites | $54 | AE, D, DC, MC, V.

Super 8. In central Tuscaloosa and within walking distance of McFarland Mall, this standard motel is also close to several restaurants. Some microwaves, some refrigerators, cable TV. No-smoking rooms. | 4125 McFarland Blvd. east | 205/758–8878 | fax 205/752–8331 | 62 rooms | $47 | AE, D, DC, MC, V.

Travelodge. Next to Interstates 20/59, this standard motel is across the street from McFarland Mall, about five minutes from the University of Alabama campus. Bar. In-room data ports, cable TV. Pool, wading pool. Business services. No-smoking rooms. | 3920 McFarland Blvd. east | 205/553–1550 | fax 205/553–1550 | 164 rooms in 5 buildings | $55 | AE, D, DC, MC, V.

Travel-Rite Inn. This standard motel is right across the street from the Jasper Mall, several restaurants, and about 1 mi from downtown. Cable TV. Some pets allowed. | 200 Mallway Dr. | 205/221–1161 | fax 205/221–1161 ext. 200 | 60 rooms | $39 | AE, D, DC, MC, V.

Victoria Riverbridge Inn. Filled with Queen Anne furniture, this quaint bed-and-breakfast overlooks Smith Lake. Each room has a king-size bed and antique furniture. The restaurant has a view of the lake and the speciality is Black Angus rib eyes. All rooms have private baths. No smoking. Restaurant, complimentary breakfast. Cable TV. Boating, water sports, fishing. | 323 Old Ferry Rd., Jasper | 205/387–7766 or 800/387–7766 | fax 205/387–9966 | 8 rooms | $100–$150 | AE, MC, V.

TUSCUMBIA

(Nearby town also listed: Florence)

Born in Tuscumbia in 1880, Helen Keller, left deaf and blind at an early age, went on to influence the world. Her birthplace is filled with personal mementos and exhibits from the making of the film *The Miracle Worker*, starring Patty Duke as Helen and Anne Bancroft as Helen's teacher, Annie Sullivan.

Information: **Colbert County Tourism and Convention Bureau** | U.S. 72 west, Tuscumbia 35674 | 256/383–0783 or 800/344–0783 | fax 256/383–2080 | ins@colbertcounty-tourism.org | www.colbertcountytourism.org.

Attractions

★ **Alabama Music Hall of Fame and Museum.** The hall honors Alabama natives who created great rock, rhythm and blues, gospel, and opera. Among the legends are Tammy Wynette, Lionel Ritchie, Emmylou Harris, the group Alabama, the Commodores, Nat "King" Cole, W. C. Handy, and Hank Williams. Memorabilia is displayed, and a recording booth gives you a chance to make your own music. | U.S. 72 west | 256/381–4417 or 800/239–2643 | fax 256/381–1031 | www.alamhof.org | $6 | Mon.–Sat. 9–5, Sun. 1–5.

★ **Ivy Green.** Typically southern in architecture, Helen Keller's childhood home holds many furnishings and personal items. Left deaf and blind from a childhood disease, Keller inspired many by overcoming severe challenges. | 300 N. Commons St. west | 256/383–4066 | fax 256/383–4068 | $3 | Mon.–Sat. 8:30–4, Sun. 1–4.

Key Underwood Coon Dog Memorial Graveyard. This unusual graveyard holds the remains of prized coon dogs. Many headstones have touching epitaphs to these treasured pets. Dog owners gather on Labor Day to swap tales of their "best friends." A small park with picnic facilities is next to the cemetery. | Coon Dog Cemetery Rd., Tuscumbia | 256/383–0783 | Free | Daily.

ON THE CALENDAR

JUNE: *Helen Keller Festival.* Salute to America's "First Lady of Courage" with three days of arts and crafts, entertainment, and concerts. | Various venues | 256/383–4066.
JUNE–JULY: *The Miracle Worker.* Outdoor drama on teacher Annie Sullivan's success in helping the blind and deaf Helen Keller. | Ivy Green | 256/383–4066.

TUSKEGEE

(Nearby towns also listed: Auburn, Montgomery)

Tuskegee was settled by the French and in 1763 it was turned over to the British. In the early 1800s the original French fort became an important stronghold for Andrew Jackson in his war against the Creek Confederacy.

In 1881 educator Booker T. Washington founded Tuskegee University, one of America's first black universities, whose humble beginnings blossomed to garner international recognition and to draw students from around the world. Many of the institute's Victorian buildings were designed and built by students.

The George Washington Carver Museum, which doubles as the campus visitor center, has films explaining the lives of Washington and scientist George Washington Carver.

A former slave, Carver developed hundreds of products using peanuts and sweet potatoes, thus encouraging southern farmers to grow more than just cotton.

Information: **Tuskegee Area Chamber of Commerce** | 121 Main St., Tuskegee 36083 | 334/727–6619 | fax 334/725–1801 | tacc@tuskegee.net.

Attractions

Tuskegee Institute National Historic Site. The campus has 165 buildings, including 27 with historical significance. Self-guided brochures are available at the Carver Museum. At this site is The Oaks, home of Booker T. Washington, first president of Tuskegee Institute. The 1899 house and the bricks to build it were made by students and faculty. It holds original furniture. | 10 Old Montgomery Rd. | 334/727–6390 | fax 334/727–4597 | Free | Daily 9–5.

Booker T. Washington Monument. On the Tuskegee campus, the famed black educator is memorialized with a monument that shows him lifting the veil of ignorance from fellow blacks. A small park is next to the statue. | 1212 Old Montgomery Rd. | 334/727–3200 | fax 334/727–1448 | Free | Daily.

George Washington Carver Museum. Doubling as the campus visitor center, this museum shows films explaining the lives of educator and Tuskegee Institute founder Booker T. Washington and scientist and former slave George Washington Carver. Of special interest are the vegetable samples of Carver's most important crops—peanuts and sweet potatoes—which he used to develop hundreds of other by-products. His work is credited with encouraging southern farmers to grow more than just cotton. | 1212 Old Montgomery Rd. | 334/727–3200 | fax 334/727–1448 | Free | Daily 9–5.

Tuskegee National Forest. The forest provides a place for camping, picnicking, hiking, fishing, and horseback riding. It also has a firing range. The area has a replica of the cabin where famous African-American educator Booker T. Washington was born. The Bartram Trail commemorates naturalist William Bartram, who identified many species of native plants and trees. Bold Destiny/Bedford V. Cash Memorial Trail has horse and hiking trails winding 14 mi through the northern half of the forest. | 125-FS Rd. 949 | 334/727–2652 | fax 334/727–0295 | Free | Daily dawn–dusk.

Lodging

Kellogg Conference Center. Encompassing the historic Dorothy Hall, this modern hotel is on the Tuskegee University campus. Elegant early American decor accents this three-story building, which is conveniently located 8 mi from the Capital City Airport. Several historic attractions are nearby, including the George Washington Carver Museum and the Booker T. Washington Monument. Just minutes away from the university is the Robert Trent Jones–designed Grand National Golf Course. Restaurant, bar, in-room data ports, cable TV. Pool. Hot tub. Gym. Laundry service. Business services. | E. Campus Dr., Tuskegee Institute | 334/727–3000 or 800/949–6161 | fax 334/727–5119 | 165 rooms, 5 suites | $85–$95 rooms, $175–$500 suites | AE, D, DC, MC, V.

UNION SPRINGS

MAP 3, E6

(Nearby town also listed: Troy)

Surrounded by former plantation lands, Union Springs is a small central Alabama town where Victorian and antebellum homes line streets. Within walking distance of the tree-lined residential area is a downtown shopping district with antiques shops, hardware and farm supply stores, and general merchandisers. Known as "The Field Trial Capital of the World," the city hosts annual field dog trials and fox hunts. Hunting clubs and lodges host individuals and groups. Named to the National Register, Bullock

County Courthouse Historic District is a three-block stretch, including Alabama's only Second Empire courthouse. The town hosts an annual pilgrimage and historic home tours on the first Saturday and Sunday of May.

Information: **Union Springs/Bullock County Tourism Council** | 106 E. Conecuh St., Union Springs 36089 | 334/738–8687 | fax 334/738–5068 | www.unionspringsalabama.com.

ON THE CALENDAR
APR.: *Chunnenuggee Fair.* Held in the Prairie Street Business District, the fair includes arts, crafts, games, children's activities, foods, and a cake sale. | 334/738–5399.

Arkansas

Arkansas's billing as "The Natural State" is on target. This relatively small state has more than 17 million acres of public and private forests, 600,000 acres of lakes, and 9,700 mi of rivers and streams. Its Ozark and Ouachita mountains, with their rugged wilderness areas, rival New England's for scenic vistas and fall colors, which can be seen along meandering roadways including eight state and national scenic byways. There's plenty of space for fishing and hunting, float trips, and water sports, plus camping and other outdoor activities. A network of trails provides routes for hikes, mountain bikes, motorcycles, horses, and all-terrain vehicles. Romantic springs bubble up, too—47 at Hot Springs, 63 at Eureka Springs, 7 at Heber Springs, plus the state's largest, Mammoth Spring, from which flow 9 million gallons every hour.

The state's dynamism belies the offensive stereotype of backward "arkies." Two of the nation's major retail chains—Wal-Mart and Dillard's—got their start and are headquartered in Arkansas. Blytheville ranks No. 2 in the nation in steel production. Other major manufacturing firms are in plastics, furniture, prepared foods, boats, chemicals, and pulp and paper products. The state leads the country in the production of rice and commercial broiler chickens, and is No. 2 in catfish farming. It is also a leader in soybeans, cotton, and poultry, and its top three minerals are petroleum, natural gas, and bromine.

Little Rock, the capital, is a city of exciting sophistication. And northwest Arkansas, with the university town of Fayetteville at its core, is one of the fastest-growing U.S. metropolitan areas.

History

The oldest known human burial place in the Americas—more than 10,000 years old— lies in Arkansas, one of some 30,000 registered archaeological sites from all eras.

CAPITAL: LITTLE ROCK	POPULATION: 2,453,000	AREA: 53,187 SQUARE MI
BORDERS: MO, TN, MS, LA, TX	TIME ZONE: CENTRAL	POSTAL ABBREVIATION: AR
WEB SITE ADDRESS: WWW.ARKANSAS.COM		

Spaniards led by Hernando de Soto explored present-day Arkansas in 1541–42. The first permanent European settlement, Arkansas Post, was formed near the mouth of the Arkansas River after 1682, when Robert Cavelier, Sieur de la Salle, claimed the region for France. Real growth began only after the Louisiana Purchase of 1803. Arkansas became a territory in 1819 and a state in 1836.

The WPA Guide to 1930s Arkansas noted that Arkansas is a state in which "contrasting regions meet, and their ways of life sometimes blend." After 1836, Southern planters and their slaves moved primarily into the rich Mississippi Delta and other riverbank areas as well as to the rolling hills in the south and east of the state. Independent-minded southern Appalachian families migrated to the Ozarks in the northwest. The spirit of the frontier reigned along Arkansas's western border, which served as a staging point for wagon trains heading into the Southwest, as well as home bases and hideouts for outlaws like the colorful Belle Starr.

The state joined the Confederacy during the Civil War, and much of the countryside was devastated by Union troops. After the Reconstruction era, political power moved to the Democratic Party, which passed Jim Crow segregation laws as it did in the rest of the South. Also in postbellum years, the extension of railroad lines helped create hundreds of new towns. Thousands of acres were cleared and drained for agriculture, and locally owned lumbering businesses became part of large national companies. Although a few African-Americans became wealthy landowners after the war, the vast majority worked as sharecroppers.

The Great Depression of the 1930s followed droughts, though industry was hit even harder than agriculture during this period. World War II brought social as well as economic change as many Arkansans left the state to serve in the armed forces or work in northern wartime jobs. After the war, the mechanization of agriculture threw landless sharecroppers out of work in the delta. The question of African-American civil rights also loomed. In 1957 Little Rock's Central High School became the focal point in the national struggle to integrate public schools. By the end of the 1960s, the movement toward modernization of the state's infrastructure and economy was under way. The 1992 presidential election of Bill Clinton, an Arkansan, brought further attention to the state.

Regions

1. THE OZARKS

Arkansas is a mosaic of distinct natural regions, each with its own characteristics and economy. Wind and water carved the Ozark Plateau in northwest Arkansas into rugged peaks and hollows that remained remote well into the 1900s. There, the old-time folk arts and crafts, idioms, legends, and music survive, particularly in towns such as Mountain View, and along the Buffalo National River in Jasper.

AR Timeline

ca. 8500 BC		1541–42	1682
Native Americans in the late Pleistocene geologic period, using the Dalton style of toolmaking, bury their dead in the earliest recognized cemetery in the world in northeast Arkansas. They	were precursors of the Quapaw, Caddo, and Osage tribes that were present when the first Europeans arrived.	Spanish explorer Hernando de Soto and his party cross the Mississippi River into Arkansas. After de Soto's death, the party departs down the Mississippi.	Robert Cavalier, Sieur de la Salle, and Henri de Tonti arrive at Quapaw villages near the mouth of the Arkansas River and take formal possession of the region for the King of France. In 1686,

The state's love affair with lake recreation began in the 1940s with the construction of massive U.S. Army Corps of Engineers projects along the upper White River in
the Ozarks, creating Beaver, Bull Shoals, Norfork, and Greers Ferry lakes. Since then, freshwater impoundments have been created elsewhere in the state along the Little Red,
Arkansas, Ouachita, Caddo, Little Missouri, and other rivers. The lakes, combined with
their tailwaters and numerous free-flowing streams, are filled with trout, bass, walleye, catfish, crappie, and other fish, and are used for water and outdoor sports. The
region also has cozy resorts and cabins, Civil War battlefields, numerous scenic drives,
colorful small towns, urban areas chock-full of fine arts and shopping, and a Victorian
spa awash in bed-and-breakfast inns.

Towns listed: Batesville, Bentonville, Berryville, Buffalo National River, Bull Shoals,
Eureka Springs, Fayetteville, Hardy, Harrison, Heber Springs, Jasper, Mountain Home,
Mountain View, Newport, Pocahontas, Searcy, Springdale, Rogers

INTRODUCTION
HISTORY
REGIONS
WHEN TO VISIT
STATE'S GREATS
RULES OF THE ROAD
DRIVING TOURS

2. THE ARKANSAS RIVER VALLEY

From Little Rock to the Oklahoma border, the Arkansas River's
green valley divides the Ozark Plateau and the Ouachita Mountains. The river forms in the Colorado Mountains and enters
Arkansas through Oklahoma. The border town of Fort Smith recalls
its Wild West days and taming down by "Hanging Judge" Isaac C.
Parker. Van Buren, just across the river, shows off a genteel Victorian Main Street with antiques shops and boutiques. Below Mt.
Magazine, the state's highest peak, which is easily visible from the
river, lies a small district where several family-owned and -oper-
ated wineries grow grapes on the rolling hills.

   The river itself was as treacherous as the outlaws Parker
convicted—until the U.S. Army Corps of Engineers transformed it
with locks and dams. In 1968 the river opened as a working waterway that has some
of the state's finest game fishing. Scenic byways and white-water streams lead toward
the river from some of the state's most impressive and unspoiled landscape.

Towns listed: Alma, Altus, Benton, Conway, Fort Smith/Van Buren, Little Rock/North Little
Rock, Morrilton, Paris, Russellville

3. THE OUACHITAS

The Ouachita Mountains of west-central Arkansas, created by the folding and fault-
ing of the earth's surface into east–west ridges, are a treasure chest of natural
wonders—Hot Springs National Park's thermal waters, a diamond crater, and abundant quartz crystals can be found among its forested peaks and valleys. A web of trails
leads through the Ouachita National Forest's backcountry, and float trips are popular on the region's rivers. A scenic byway with awe-inspiring vistas leads west from

1803	1806	1817	
de Tonti establishes a trading post at Arkansas Post.	The Louisiana Purchase gives possession of the territory including Arkansas to the United States.	The District of Arkansas is created by the territorial legislature of Louisiana.	Arkansas's first post office is established at Davidsonville. The Cherokees cede some of their eastern lands in exchange for land in northwestern Arkansas. The Quapaw are forced to	cede most of their land.

Mena across Arkansas's second-tallest peak. You can find everything from primitive camping to luxury resort hotels, and from fishing to fine arts and antiques galleries—as well as the state's only thoroughbred race track.

Towns listed: Arkadelphia, Hot Springs, Mena, Murfreesboro.

4. THE DELTA

The Mississippi Delta of eastern Arkansas is a rich alluvial plain, where fields of rice, cotton, soybeans, and wheat are dotted with restored plantation homes and river towns. The level terrain is interrupted only by Crowley's Ridge, a narrow hill-range with unique geology and plant life that meanders 200 mi through the flatlands.

The delta is as rich in culturally important American sites as it is in fertile farm fields. It is the birthplace of the blues, and the influences of musicians like Bill Broonzy, Howlin' Wolf, and Sonny Boy Williamson carried into the work of country stars like Johnny Cash and Conway Twitty—all Arkansas-born. The region is famous for duck hunting as well as fishing and bird-watching at its cypress-lined lakes, sloughs, and farm reservoirs. Delta museums present prehistoric, pioneer, agricultural, and African-American history, along with Ernest Hemingway's home and studio.

Towns listed: Blytheville, Dumas, Forrest City, Gillett, Helena, Jonesboro, Stuttgart

5. TIMBERLANDS

The timberlands of southeastern Arkansas formed on a gently rolling plain that once lay below the shallow Gulf of Mexico. Teeming with fish and wildlife, the forests attracted pioneers in the early 1800s. In the 1920s, the boom following the discovery of oil around El Dorado drew thousands of speculators along with respectable working people. Today the timber industry is one of the region's most important businesses. Big bass continue to lurk in its rivers and lakes, and the state's best "deer woods" attract thousands of hunters each season.

In Hope, the home where President Bill Clinton lived as an infant and child has been restored and opened to the public. Old Washington, 8 mi away, served as Arkansas's Confederate capital. It began as a bustling community on the Southwestern Trail, and buildings from the 1820s through the 1870s have been preserved to reveal the lives of early pioneers and businessmen.

Towns listed: Ashdown, Camden, El Dorado, Hope, Magnolia, Pine Bluff, Texarkana

When to Visit

Spring begins early in Arkansas compared to the northerly states and is celebrated with wildflower walks, herbal workshops, bird-watching, hikes, walks, runs, river rafting, boating, and camping.

Summertime is filled with fishing tournaments, water carnivals, canoe and cardboard boat races, digging for diamonds, and eating home-grown tomatoes, fresh

---

1819
Congress creates the Arkansas Territory and the first territorial legislature meets at Arkansas Post. William E. Woodruff begins publishing the *Arkansas Gazette*, still in

business as the *Arkansas Democrat-Gazette*.

1820
The first steamboat to navigate the Arkansas River, the *Comet*, arrives at Arkansas Post. Near today's Russellville, construction begins on the Dwight Mission for Cherokees, one of the earliest

mission schools in the west.

1821
Little Rock becomes the new territorial capital.

INTRODUCTION
HISTORY
REGIONS
WHEN TO VISIT
STATE'S GREATS
RULES OF THE ROAD
DRIVING TOURS

peaches, and purple hull peas. On hot days, you can head for the mountains, go out on the water or into the woods, tour a cool cave, browse galleries and boutiques for fine art, antiques, and contemporary crafts, or relax and enjoy the scenery aboard an excursion train or boat.

Autumn brings ripening apples, sorghum-making, and picking grapes. There are blues, bluegrass, jazz, and folk festivals, and juried crafts fairs that draw tens of thousands of visitors, plus homages to the state's pioneer and frontier past. Fall foliage is everywhere—from the cypress that turn rusty brown around the delta's lakes and bayous, to the multiple hues of maple, dogwood, and dozens of other kinds of trees in the Ozark and Ouachita mountains. In November deer-hunting season begins, and there is waterfowl-hunting along the Mississippi Flyway in eastern Arkansas.

Arkansas winters are relatively short and mild. Lights, lights, and more lights illuminate cities and towns across the state in honor of the holiday season. Hundreds of bald eagles arrive from the north, welcomed with boat trips and walks during which they can be viewed. It's a great season to snuggle up in a log cabin or B&B inn in front of a crackling fire, or head to Hot Springs for a relaxing mineral bath and massage.

CLIMATE CHART
Average High/Low Temperatures (°F) and Monthly Precipitation (in inches)

	JAN.	FEB.	MAR.	APR.	MAY	JUNE
FORT SMITH	48/26	54/30	64/39	74/49	81/58	88/66
	1.9	2.6	4.0	4.0	5.2	3.4
	JULY	AUG.	SEPT.	OCT.	NOV.	DEC.
	93/70	92/69	85/62	76/49	63/38	51/29
	3	2.9	3.2	3.7	4	3.0
	JAN.	FEB.	MAR.	APR.	MAY	JUNE
LITTLE ROCK	49/29	54/33	64/42	73/51	81/59	89/67
	3.4	3.6	4.9	5.5	502	3.6
	JULY	AUG.	SEPT.	OCT.	NOV.	DEC.
	92/72	91/70	85/64	75/51	63/42	53/33
	3.6	3.3	4.0	3.8	5.2	4.8

FESTIVALS AND SEASONAL EVENTS
WINTER

Nov., Dec.: **Holiday Lighting Displays.** Millions of holiday lights dress up dozens of Arkansas towns, including Searcy, Bentonville, Blytheville, Hot Springs, Magnolia, Texarkana, Ashdown, Pine Bluff, and Fayetteville. **Arkansas Parks and Tourism** (800/628–8725) has information on these and other holiday festivities.

1828
The Cherokee give up Arkansas lands for those in today's Oklahoma.

1836
Arkansas becomes a state.

1849
The first party of miners leaves Fort Smith for the California Gold Rush.

1861
Arkansas secedes from the United States.

1862
The Confederates lose the battle of Pea Ridge at Elkhorn Tavern in northwest Arkansas.

Jan., Feb.: **Eagle Viewing.** Eagle watches focus on the hundreds of American bald eagles that arrive each winter from the frozen north at dozens of feeding spots on the state's lakes and rivers. Naturalists at various state parks and private companies sponsor lectures, eagle-awareness activities, hikes, and boat trips to observe our national bird. Contact **Bull Shoals** (870/431–5521, or 800/628–8725 for information on other parks), or **Belle of the Ozarks,** on Beaver Lake near Eureka Springs (501/253–6200 or 800/552–3803).

SPRING

Apr.: **Arkansas Folk Festival.** A tradition in Mountain View since 1960 (870/269–8068), this event at the Ozark Folk Center State Park (870/269–3851) draws 30,000 to 40,000 visitors who come for a parade, traditional music, and dancing on the county courthouse square, a craft show and sale, buggy and pony rides, a rodeo, plenty of food, and special music shows at the folk center and other theaters around town.

Apr., May: **Toad Suck Daze.** Visitors pack Conway for toad jumps; live entertainment; puppet and pet shows; arts and crafts; carnival rides; concessions; horseshoe, softball, and volleyball tournaments; and a tug-of-war contest. The event is named for the wild element of boatmen, racehorse owners, gamblers, and liquor drinkers who gathered along the Arkansas River banks "soaking up whiskey like toads," or "having a regular toad suck." (501/327–7788).

SUMMER

June: **The Antique Auto Show and Swap Meet.** This event draws 100,000 aficionados to the Museum of Automobiles atop Petit Jean Mountain (501/727–5427). Antique and classic cars compete for awards, and almost 850 vendors buy, sell, and trade parts. Cars are for sale, as are arts, crafts, and flea market items.

Aug.: **The Hope Watermelon Festival.** The town where President Bill Clinton was born celebrates the region's enormous watermelons with the Watermelon Olympics, seed-spitting and melon-eating contests, arts and crafts booths, food stands, live music, antique car and engine shows, a fiddling contest, a sports card show, a motorcycle show, a 5K run, and a bass tournament (501/777–3640).

1863	1863	1868	1871	1875
The Confederates lose the Battle of Helena.	The Union Army captures Little Rock and the Confederate capital moves to Washington in southwest Arkansas.	Under Reconstruction, Arkansas is readmitted to the United States.	Arkansas Industrial University, today's University of Arkansas, is established by the legislature at Fayetteville.	U.S. District Judge Isaac C. Parker, who became known as the "Hanging Judge," arrives at Fort Smith to bring law and order to western Arkansas and the Indian Territory of today's

Sept.: **Eureka Springs Jazz Festival.** Top-name musicians perform in venues all over this Victorian-era spa town. Eureka Springs has plenty of excellent restaurants, shops, historic buildings, and attractions to round out the fun during the festival (501/253–6258).

Oct.: **War Eagle Fair.** This nonprofit event draws an estimated 120,000 to the War Eagle Farm at Hindsville, near Rogers, to browse and shop among more than 350 craft artisans from four states. This juried event, one of the most respected of its kind in the country, shows off quilts, baskets, pottery, clothing, leather, books, woodworking, and other crafts. Other handicraft events, most for-profit, take place throughout northwest Arkansas and are timed to coincide with the fair. A second and somewhat smaller War Eagle Fair takes place in early May (501/789–5398).

Oct.: **The King Biscuit Blues Festival.** International, regional, and local blues and gospel singers and groups perform on three acoustic and nonacoustic stages within easy walking distance along the levee and in Helena's historic downtown. The sharecropper farms around this Mississippi River community and across the river in Mississippi gave birth to the blues. A barbecue contest, arts and crafts, arm wrestling, a 5K run, and riverboat cruises are also part of this world famous festival (870/338–8798).

Nov.: **World's Championship Duck Calling Contest and Wings Over the Prairie Festival.** At this Stuttgart event, begun in 1936, you can participate in the duck-calling finals, as well as a duck gumbo cook-off, a sports collectibles show, arts and crafts booths, commercial exhibits, and a 10K race (870/673–1602).

State's Greats

In "The Natural State," the scenery is splendid year-round. Arkansas's mountains, streams, springs, lakes, rivers, and winding roads beg to be explored. The waterways make for great float trips, swimming, sailing, powerboating, scuba diving, and other recreational fun, plus camping with a view.

Arkansas's streams, lakes, bayous, reservoirs, and forests also mean that the fishing is fantastic, from the cold, rushing currents in the mountains to the lazy oxbow lakes of the delta and timberlands. The tailwaters below numerous dams are favorite

	1877	**1891**	**1917**	**1921**
Oklahoma. During his 21 years on the bench, Parker hears more than 13,000 cases and sentences 160 to death by hanging.	President Ulysses S. Grant signs an act creating the Hot Springs Reservation, now Hot Springs National Park, to end battles over who owned the springs.	The governor signs Arkansas's first Jim Crow law, the Separate Coach Bill segregating public transportation.	Arkansas allows women to vote in party primaries.	S. T. Bussey discovers oil near El Dorado, starting the relatively short-lived Arkansas oil boom.

trout destinations, and bass action is supreme on lakes and rivers. Walleye, catfish, crappie, and other panfish provide even more action—including world-record catches. White-tailed deer remains the No. 1 big-game animal, with liberal seasons set for archery, muzzleloaders, and modern firearms. Wild turkey and small game are also abundant, and waterfowl hunting along the Mississippi Flyway of eastern Arkansas is tops.

You can also head for the spiderweb of trails that weaves through the mountains and across the delta—for day hikes and backwoods treks, mountain bikes, horses, motorcycles, all-terrain vehicles, and four-wheel-drive sports utilities and trucks. You can observe and take pictures of the wildlife, including the elk in the Buffalo River valleys, the endangered red-cockaded woodpecker in the state's south, abundant waterfowl in the delta, and bald eagles feeding along rivers and lakes in wintertime. You can sightsee and eat dinner on excursion boats and railroad trips through the countryside, and you can drive or hike the state's scenic byways for vistas brightened by spring wildflowers and fall foliage.

The historic spa towns of Hot Springs and Eureka Springs grew where natural mineral waters bubble up from beneath the Ouachita and Ozark Mountains. Today you can come for romance and relaxation as well as family fun, great attractions, shopping, and festivals. Underground in the Ozarks, spectacular public and privately owned caves are open for tours.

Along with the natural beauty, you can explore museums, prehistoric Native American sites, historic battlefields and homes, storied towns, and cultural attractions.

Parks and Forests

You can find some of the best of the state's natural, historic, cultural, and recreational legacies in Arkansas's 50 state parks. **Petit Jean,** on a mountaintop above the Arkansas River valley; **Devil's Den,** in the Ozarks south of Fayetteville; **Mammoth Spring,** on the Missouri border in the eastern Ozarks; and **Village Creek,** on top of Crowley's Ridge in the delta, are naturally beautiful. **Powhatan Courthouse Museum,** a Victorian structure with a nearby 1873 jail and antebellum log house south of Black Rock; **Old Washington,** a 19th-century town near Hope that served as Arkansas's confederate capital; and **Jacksonport State Park,** a restored 1869 county courthouse near Newport, focus on history. You can learn about the state's cultural heritage at the **Ozark Folk Center,** in Mountain View; and at the **Museum of Natural Resources** in Smackover you can find out about the oil boom of the early 20th century. **Toltec Mounds** at Scott and **Parkin Archeological State Park** explore and interpret Native American sites. **DeGray Lake,** northwest of Arkadelphia, and **Bull Shoals,** in the Ozarks, are two of Arkansas's state parks, with many outdoor activities. **Crater of Diamonds State Park** is the only diamond mine in the world open to the public. If you find any, they are yours to keep.

Giant **Blanchard Springs Caverns** northwest of Mountain View has been called "the cave find of the 20th century." The caves are managed by the U.S. Forest Service. The 47 thermal springs in **Hot Springs National Park** have been federally owned since 1832.

1922	1927	1931	1938	1942
Arkansas's first radio station, WOK, goes on the air in Pine Bluff.	The Mississippi River and its tributaries flood, devastating more than 6,000 square mi. Property losses, including railroad tracks and highways, reach $15 million and 127 lives are lost.	The drought of 1930 triggers a food riot at England in east-central Arkansas.	Wilbur Mills is elected to the U.S. House of Representatives and rises to become the powerful chairman of the House Ways and Means Committee until retirement in 1977.	John L. McClellan is elected to the U.S. Senate, where he served until his death in 1978. With Senator Robert S. Kerr of Oklahoma, he brings about the construction of 17 locks and dams at a

INTRODUCTION
HISTORY
REGIONS
WHEN TO VISIT
STATE'S GREATS
RULES OF THE ROAD
DRIVING TOURS

Arkansas's most famous free-flowing stream is the **Buffalo National River** in the central Ozarks, the first federally preserved waterway in the United States. Native American, pioneer, and outlaw history fill its bluffs and forests; you can experience some of Middle America's finest float trips, fish, stay at campsites, observe wildlife, and take part in many other outdoor activities.

The **Ozark, Ouachita,** and **St. Francis national forests** and the U.S. Army Corps of Engineers land surrounding the state's largest lakes provide campsites, pristine scenery, trails, and historic sites. In addition, there are state and federal wildlife refuges and management areas for you to explore.

Culture, History, and the Arts

The number of restored buildings and districts rises each year in Arkansas. The site of **Arkansas Post,** the first settlement in the lower Mississippi Valley when it was established in 1686, is maintained as a national memorial near the confluence of the Arkansas and Mississippi rivers. The state's early years live on at the **Old State House** in Little Rock, built in 1836, and the nearby **Arkansas Territorial Restoration,** a complex of early buildings with a museum and Arkansas crafts shop. **Old Washington Historic State Park,** west of Hope, preserves more than 40 buildings from the 1820s to the 1870s, including the courthouse that served as Arkansas's Confederate capitol.

The history of the Civil War is remembered at **Pea Ridge National Military Park** and the **Prairie Grove Battlefield State Park** in northwest Arkansas. Antebellum and postwar homes, a battle site, and a Confederate cemetery are in the Mississippi River town of Helena, as is the **Delta Cultural Center,** which focuses on the history, music, and culture of the region.

The traditional music, dance, pioneer crafts, gardens, and folkways of the Ozarks are safeguarded at the **Ozark Folk Center State Park** in Mountain View in a wonderfully entertaining way. One of the oldest craft guilds in the mid-South is in Mountain View, and you can see both traditional and contemporary crafts at its galleries there and in Little Rock, Hot Springs, Eureka Springs, and Fayetteville.

The arts abound in Arkansas, particularly in Little Rock with its symphony orchestra, repertory theater, museums, and other arts organizations. Eureka Springs and Hot Springs have active calendars of music, film, and other arts-oriented festivals. Other stages and galleries at Fayetteville, Helena, Jonesboro, Heber Springs, Fort Smith, Springdale, Texarkana, Rogers, Blytheville, Van Buren, Clarksville, Siloam Springs, Russellville, Pine Bluff, Conway, Camden, and El Dorado light up with local talent, regional symphonies, and national shows.

Rules of the Road

License Requirements: In Arkansas, you may apply for a driver's license if you are 14 and can provide a birth certificate, proof of enrollment in school, and proof of grade point average of at least 2.0; a parent or legal guardian must accompany you to the testing site. (For the location of testing sites, call the Arkansas State Police at 501/618–

cost of $1.2 billion to make the Arkansas River navigable year-round, control floods, and create recreational lakes.

1945 J. William Fulbright is elected to the U.S. Senate, where he served for 30 years and gained a reputation as a world statesman.

1957 Following the U.S. Supreme Court's 1954 invalidation of school segregation in Brown vs. the Board of Education of Topeka, Kansas, Governor Orval Faubus calls out the Arkansas National Guard to prevent integration at Little Rock's Central High School. President Eisenhower sends in U.S. paratroopers to enforce desegregation.

1968 The McClellan-Kerr Arkansas River Navigation system opens the river for shipping from its mouth to Catoosa, Oklahoma.

8251.) When driving, an adult with a valid driver's license must be in the car with you. Valid out-of-state and foreign driver's licenses are good in Arkansas.

Right Turn on Red: A right turn on red at a traffic signal is permitted *after* you come to a full stop and yield to pedestrians and other traffic, unless a "No Turn on Red" or similar sign is posted.

Seat Belt and Helmet Laws: State law requires all passengers to wear seat belts. All children under age five must wear safety restraints while the vehicle is in motion. Children under age four or weighing less than 40 pounds must be secured in an approved safety seat.

Speed Limits: Speed limits on major freeways are from 60 to 70 mph.

Other: Vehicle headlights must be turned on when windshield wipers are being operated.

For More Information: For information about driver's licenses, call 501/682–7059. For information about road conditions, call Arkansas Highway and Transportation Department at 501/569–2374.

Crowley's Ridge National Scenic Byway Drive
FROM HEMINGWAY TO HISTORY AND RECREATIONAL HAVENS

Distance: 198 mi   Time: 4.5 hours to 2 days
Breaks: Jonesboro, Forrest City, Helena

The ancient, crescent-shape Crowley's Ridge rises as a welcome, wooded relief to the flat farm fields of the Mississippi Delta in northeastern Arkansas.

In 1997 the U.S. Department of Transportation named a 198-mi route along the ridge a National Scenic Byway, one of more than 50 throughout the country. These byways, Crowley's Ridge among them, are usually off the beaten path and display some of the most interesting and diverse cultural, historical, and geological features in the United States.

If you need a break from interstate highways, you can drive the meandering rural roads along Crowley's Ridge; lodgings, country-style cafés, and campsites are available if you want to make it a leisurely trip. The route zigzags through the countryside, but signs mark its way.

Along the byway you can see Native American archaeological digs, Civil War battlefields, historic homes and districts, and African-American heritage sites. Old-fashioned country stores, antiques shops, and home-grown fruit and vegetable stands lie along the route, and there are lots of scenic views. If outdoor recreation and camping are what you want, you will find that, too.

1978
William Jefferson "Bill" Clinton is elected governor.

1992
Governor Bill Clinton is elected President of the United States.

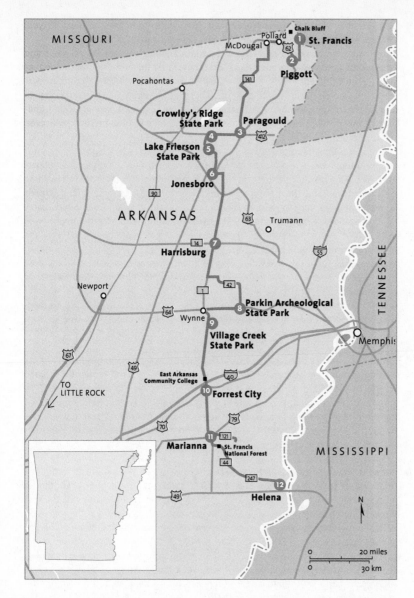

❶ The byway begins in the northeastern corner of Arkansas at the Missouri border on U.S. 62 at the hamlet of **St. Francis.** The first settler here operated a ferry across the St. Francis River. The site lay along a military road called the Buffalo Trail or Old Military Trail blazed in the 1840s from Missouri into Arkansas.

The original river crossing is at **Chalk Bluff** (a spur leading a few miles northwest off U.S. 62). Chalk Bluff was a thriving town before it was bypassed by the railroad, and several skirmishes took place there during the Civil War, the most significant of which was the May 1–2, 1863, action when Confederate General John S. Marmaduke retreated from an unsuccessful raid into Missouri. The battle and the town's history are interpreted through plaques placed along a walking trail.

❷ Head back to St. Francis and proceed south on U.S. 62 for about 5 mi to Piggott. **Piggott,** a railroad town established in 1882, sits on the eastern slopes of Crowley's Ridge. Arkansas State University has restored the **Hemingway–Pfeiffer Museum and Educational Center** at 10th and Cherry Streets. This was the home of Ernest Hemingway's second wife, the wealthy Pauline Pfeiffer, whose family owned 63,000 acres in the county. Hemingway liked to hunt quail here, and he wrote much of *A Farewell to Arms* in the coach house out back. The movie version of this book premiered at Piggott in 1932. The museum also serves as one of four visitors centers along the byway, with maps and general information available. Downtown Piggott has several antiques shops, plus a soda fountain, casual restaurants, and petrified tree trunks on its courthouse square.

Leaving Piggott, proceed west on U.S. 62 for approximately 5 mi to McDougal, then south on Route 141 for about 20 mi to Hooker, where you'll pick up Route 135 and proceed south for another 10 or so miles to Paragould. You'll pass through Pollard, McDougal, Boydsville, and Oak Grove on the way. The roads are clearly marked with Scenic Byway signs, so relax and enjoy the views. There are scenic overlooks on the way to the village of **Pollard,** where there's a small park with picnic tables. Along here in the spring and summer, you can see views of cattle pastures, crop fields, orchards, and roadside wildflowers— blue violets, honeysuckle, trumpet creeper, wild roses, wild phlox, daylily, daffodils, and coneflowers among them. The vistas are also lovely during the fall foliage season, and when covered in snow. Continuing on, the road passes peach orchards and scenic overlooks that contrast the ridge's rolling hills with the flatlands along the Cache River, an outstanding duck-hunting area, and through the towns of McDougal and Boydsville.

❸ Continue south on Route 135, passing the Oak Grove School, built by the Works Progress Administration in 1938. Follow Route 135/U.S. 412 to the center of **Paragould.** Formed in 1882 by competing railroads, it was named for the presidents of the two lines, J. W. Paramore and Jay Gould. Its downtown includes the historic **Pruett Street**; a **mural** that pays tribute to the town's railroad and timber history; the **Collins Theater,** where the 1941 world premiere of *The Man Who Came to Dinner* took place (it starred former usher Richard Travis); and old homes.

❹ From the center of Paragould, return west on U.S. 412, then south on Route 141 for approximately 12 mi to **Crowley's Ridge State Park.** The park marks the location of the homestead of Benjamin F. Crowley, for whom the ridge was named. Crowley was the first known white settler in this part of the ridge in the early 1820s, when the region on either side was a vast swamp for most of the year. A monument marks Crowley's gravesite. A native stone-and-log bathhouse and snack bar, an amphitheater, and other structures in the park were built by the Civilian Conservation Corps in 1930, as was its spring-fed swimming lake with a sandy beach. The park also has a fishing lake and a barrier-free pier, a boat ramp, up-to-date cabins, campsites, hiking trails, an outdoor amphitheater, and interpretive programs by park staff.

❺ From Crowley's Ridge State Park, continue south on Route 141 for about 5 mi to **Lake Frierson State Park.** This is dogwood country in early spring. Built as a soil conservation project, the lake is now a fishing hot spot. The park has camping, boat rentals, a barrier-free fishing pier, a dogwood trail, and interpretive programs by staff.

❻ Leave Lake Frierson State Park heading south on Route 141 and drive for about 10 mi to **Jonesboro.** On the outskirts of Jonesboro, you'll pass a country store near the public 18-hole North Hills Golf Course; its fairways follow the ridge's topography and are filled with spring dogwoods and redbuds and fall foliage. West of the byway on Route 49, you will see the grounds of **Holy Angels Convent.**

In town, follow U.S. 49 B (Johnson Avenue) west to Caraway Road, and turn south to reach the campus of **Arkansas State University.** The museum there shows off the region's prehistory, replicated turn-of-the-century businesses, paintings of the delta and ridge by noted regional artist Carroll Cloar, and more. The museum also is one of the byway's four visitor centers. The **Delta Art Gallery,** a concert hall, and a major athletic complex are also at the university.

Return to U.S. 49 B (Johnson Avenue) and go west, turning south on 49 B/63 B (Main Street) to reach Jonesboro's pleasant historic districts in its downtown and Washington Street neighborhoods. A marker on the lawn of the Art Deco–style county courthouse commemorates a Civil War battle that occurred here. The **Forum** theater, with several galleries nearby, hosts local, regional, and touring performances.

❼ Continue south on Main Street to Route 18 (Highland Drive) and turn east to Route 1 (Stadium Boulevard) to its intersection with Route 163. Head south on Route 163 for about 17 mi to Route 14 and then west for 1 mi to Harrisburg. The site of **Harrisburg** was settled in 1827 by three Harris brothers from Alabama. In 1856 it was laid out to replace Bolivar as the county seat. The neoclassical courthouse went up in 1917.

Return to Route 163 and continue south several miles to **Lake Poinsett State Park,** which surrounds a 640-acre fishing lake atop Crowley's Ridge, with bass, bream, catfish, and crappie. The park has boat launch ramps, boat rentals, picnic pavilions and areas, a playground, a hiking trail, a gift shop, full-hookup campsites and dump station, and accessible showers.

Leaving the park, continue south on Route 163. The border between Poinsett and Cross counties is heavily forested with native hardwoods, creating colorful scenery in the fall and spring. At this point, the byway passes the striking Smith Plantation home, built in 1903 with 16 rooms and 12-ft ceilings by Thomas Benton Smith. It remains in the family and is not open to the public.

❽ At Birdeye, about 5 mi from the cross-county line, you can make a worthwhile side trip 7 mi east on Route 42, then south on Route 75 for about 5 mi to U.S. 64. Go east again a short distance to **Parkin Archeological State Park.** Along the way, you will pass through flat fields of rice, cotton, and soybeans, perhaps spotting birdlife and wildlife.

At Parkin, brass bells, beads, and other 16th-century items shown in the visitors center museum prove that the Spanish expedition led by Hernando de Soto stopped here in 1541. The Spanish called the 17-acre moated village Casqui. Accounts of the expedition describe wood palisades, mounds, probably 400 houses, and 2,000 people. Effigy pots and vessels, tools, and other items are also in the museum. Volunteers are welcome to assist archaeologists in seasonal excavations (reserve ahead).

❾ Leaving Parkin, head west on U.S. 64 to return to the byway and proceed south on Route 284 for about 5 mi toward Village Creek State Park. If a gas-up or meal break is required, continue on U.S. 64 a mile past the byway to Wynne. South along the byway on Route 284 are riding stables and fruit stands filled with juicy peaches. At **Village Creek State Park,** exhibits in the visitors center explain how the formation of Crowley's Ridge began more than 50 million years ago, when the Gulf of Mexico extended over eastern Arkansas. As the water receded, ocean bottom sediments remained. Traveling in vastly different channels than today, the Mississippi and Ohio rivers gradually washed away the sediment rocks, leaving the ridge as a sliver between them.

During the Ice Age, glaciers ground rocks into a fine, powderlike silt called "loess" that was caught by winds and deposited on top of the ridge, where it can be found today. Movement along fault lines lifted the ridge and shifted the rivers away to eventually meet where they do now at Cairo, Illinois. The only land formation similar to Crowley's Ridge is in Siberia.

ARKANSAS | DRIVING TOURS

The easiest place in the park to find the powdery loess and run it through your fingers is the entrance to Big Ben Trail across from the visitor center parking lot. The park also has two lakes, a bathhouse and beach, an auditorium, full-hookup camping, cabins with kitchenettes, picnic pavilions, a golf driving range, and lots of trails and interpretive programs. In one section, you can spot a section of the military road between Memphis and Little Rock completed in 1828.

⑩ From Village Creek State Park continue south on Route 284 toward Forrest City. Along the way, just over the St. Francis County line, a gully across from peach and apple orchards is carved into the loess and covered in kudzu, originally planted to retard erosion. Kudzu becomes prominent along the byway in this region, along with evidence of its aggressive and destructive nature as it chokes off other plants and trees in its path. **Forrest City** was named for Civil War Confederate General Nathan Bedford Forrest, who set up camp here when he came through the area building a railroad. The **St. Francis County Museum,** in a restored home at 603 Front Street, displays a 70-lb fossil saltwater clam shell, shark and mastodon teeth, woolly mammoth bones from nearby Crow Creek, and Native American and pioneer artifacts. It serves as one of the four visitors centers for Crowley's Ridge National Scenic Byway.

⑪ As you continue south from Forrest City on Route 1, the L'Anguille River cuts through the ridge, flattening the landscape. **Marianna** is one of the oldest communities on the ridge. The **Marianna–Lee County Museum** is in the former Elks Club on W. Main Street, with magnificent red gum columns, stairwells, and woodwork. Check out the 1912 McClintock–West home across the street and other National Register mansions. All are privately owned and not open to the public. A statue of Robert E. Lee stands in the town square, where there is also a gazebo and the 1890s Lee County Courthouse.

Return to U.S. 79 and continue south to Route 44, which leads into the **St. Francis National Forest.** It is the nation's smallest national forest, but its beauty is first-rate. More than half of this 21-mi segment of the scenic byway is a meandering gravel road. It follows the backbone of Crowley's Ridge through canopies of dense hardwood trees, across small meadows, and past wildlife food plots and eerie "green ghosts" or "loess puppets"—patches of trees overgrown by kudzu. The byway crosses dams forming two lakes with boat ramps, swimming, fishing piers, and campgrounds.

⑫ The national forest road emerges in West Helena, and the scenic byway continues along U.S. 49 for about 5 mi through commercial districts and neighborhoods into the Mississippi River town of **Helena.** Here you can visit the **Delta Cultural Center,** at the south end of Cherry Street at Missouri Street, and learn about the region's history, culture, and music. If you stroll along Cherry Street you will see the Blues Corner, Bell's Ducks on the Levee restaurant, and S. Elardo Haberdashery. There are lots of antiques and other shops to explore. The **Phillips County Museum** is next to the public library, and you can walk through Civil War battle sites and a cemetery, as well as the Beech Street and Perry Street historic districts. The **Pillow–Thompson House,** a National Register home, is one of several that are open daily for tours.

Crowley's Ridge National Scenic Byway ends beyond a levee with a walking path on top next to the Delta Cultural Center. The path overlooks the powerful Mississippi River, which played a key role in the formation of the ridge.

To return to the Missouri border, go north from Helena on U.S. 49, then take Route 1 to Forrest City, where you can pick up I–40 E to I–55 N. Continue on I–55 N to U.S. 63 to Jonesboro and then take U.S. 49 to Piggott where you'll pick up U.S. 62 to the border.

Scenic 7 Byway Drive

THROUGH THE OUACHITAS AND OZARKS

INTRODUCTION
HISTORY
REGIONS
WHEN TO VISIT
STATE'S GREATS
RULES OF THE ROAD
DRIVING TOURS

Distance: 295 mi   Time: 5 hours to several days
Breaks: Hot Springs, Russellville, Jasper, Harrison

When *Car and Driver* named Arkansas's Scenic 7 Byway (Route 7) one of the country's top 10 driving experiences, the magazine was referring in part to the road's breath-taking vistas.

The route begins at Exit 78 of I-30, about 55 mi southwest of Little Rock, and winds 190 mi north to Harrison, crossing the Arkansas River at its approximate midpoint. The southern portion of Route 7 is a gentle roller-coaster ride across the Ouachita Mountains, whose folds and faults run in a rare east–west pattern rather than the north–south alignment common to most of the world's ranges. North of the Arkansas river town of Russellville, the ride becomes more thrilling thanks to the highway's tortu-ous twists and turns, steep ascents, and low-gear descents, Occasionally, the road rides the tops of mountain ridges for panoramic views before descending to wide valleys and tiny villages.

Although Route 7 passes through the small towns of yesteryear, you'll also be yanked back to the present now and then with a thoroughly modern shopping mall or walled-off retirement community. The byway is famed for its fall foliage. But in early spring, the views across forested ravines and layers of mountainsides are wide open all along the way, not just at occasional pulloffs and clearings. Greening buds on the hardwoods' branches are accented by blooming dogwoods, redbuds, and early wild-flowers announcing that spring is underway. In summer, the landscape is textured by the lush greens of hardwoods and pines interspersed with pastures and farm fields.

You should be aware that hills and curves and occasional fog and snow can make the drive difficult, particularly in the northern portion of the journey.

❶ Heading north from Exit 78 of I-30 (just north of Arkadelphia), **DeGray Lake** soon appears to the west. This 13,800-acre lake was formed by damming the Caddo River. Surrounded by the Ouachita Mountains, its shoreline is dotted with campgrounds, rental cabins, and marinas. At **DeGray Lake Resort State Park,** on the lake's northeast shore, is a 98-room lodge with a restaurant and pool, a championship golf course, a full-service marina, RV and tent campsites, and numerous outdoor activities, plus interpretive programs by park rangers.

❷ From DeGray, Route 7 winds north through the countryside for approximately 25 mi toward Hot Springs. Just south of Hot Springs is the man-made **Lake Hamilton,** which has long been a favorite spot for vacationers, retirees, and residents desiring a water view. The highway passes the docks of the *Belle of Hot Springs,* a 400-passenger excursion boat that sails Lake Hamilton on sightseeing, lunch, dinner, and dance cruises. You'll find shopping malls near the intersection with U.S. 270. Farther toward downtown Hot Springs you will pass the **Oaklawn Racetrack and Jockey Club,** Arkansas's only thoroughbred track.

❸ The thermal springs at **Hot Springs** have drawn visitors since prehistoric days. Bath-house Row—eight turn-of-the-20th-century spa buildings in the heart of town—is the center of **Hot Springs National Park,** where you will find a campground, 30 mi of hiking trails, and picnic areas in mountains and gorges in the surrounding mountains. The visitors center and museum is in the restored Fordyce Bathhouse. Hot Springs has numerous accommodations, restaurants, and additional sightseeing attractions and scenic drives.

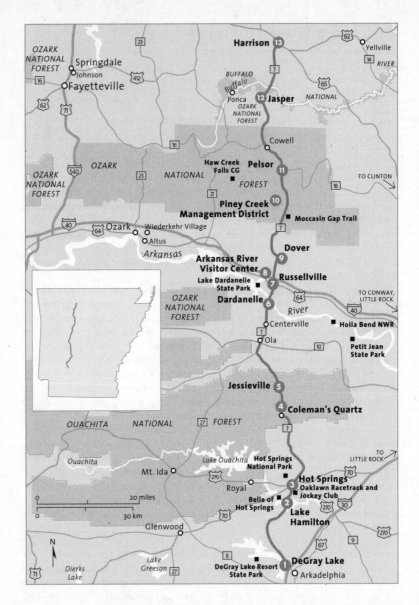

④ From Hot Springs, you'll head north on the byway along U.S. 70 and Route 7 for about 15 mi to Blue Springs. You'll pass Gulfa Gorge, DeSoto Park, the Belvedere Country Club, and, on weekends, the tin-roof stands of Snow Springs Flea Market. Crystal boulders on a weathered, weedy stand mark the edge of Mountain Valley. As you get closer to Blue Springs you'll pass real-estate offices and a full-scale mall across from the gate to the private community of Hot Springs Village. In Blue Springs sits **Coleman's Quartz**, a store in a funky frame building with dozens of tables out back. The tables are covered in hunks of quartz, amethyst, and other rocks, plus a gleaming rainbow of glass slag. Inside the store you can buy or just admire gorgeous agate bookends and other pieces largely from Brazil. Only the clear and white crystals are from Arkansas. Most were dug and polished at Ron Coleman Mining, about a mile and a half west on Little Blakeley Creek Road. Up the road

INTRODUCTION
HISTORY
REGIONS
WHEN TO VISIT
STATE'S GREATS
RULES OF THE ROAD
DRIVING TOURS

at the rust-colored quarry, terraced downhill from a salesroom, you can pay an admission fee to dig for a day and keep all the crystals you find. More and generally finer crystal is for sale here, priced according to clarity and perfection of points. Peering at a $335 crystal ball in a showcase, you may wonder what secrets lurk inside. Several other crystal balls reach the size of portable televisions, and are priced at $10,000 and up.

⑤ Jessieville also lies within Arkansas's crystal-mining region. The town has a handsome native-stone schoolhouse that was established in 1937. Staff at the **Ouachita National Forest Visitors Center,** a mile north of Jessieville, might not know the geological origins of the region's crystals, but there's an excellent video on the subject. And they have plenty of information on the forest's trails, scenic drives, sports-utility-vehicle drives, and outdoor activities.

The next 40 mi through the Ouachita National Forest afford the fine views that earned Route 7 its scenic-byway status. Roadside signs point out picnic tables and trail heads. The route makes ear-popping descents and steep climbs as the Ouachitas loom taller and the valleys narrow. Along the way you'll spot a country store at Hollis and pretty crossings of Fourche LaFave River branches, and you can gaze at long vistas south over Nimrod Lake and north across the Arkansas River valley. Past the village of Ola and the Petit Jean River, the environs of Centerville provide bucolic scenes of cattle and horses grazing in rolling, white-fenced pastures.

⑥ Crossing the flat Arkansas River floodplain, Route 7 enters the old river town of **Dardanelle,** where tall, bare Dardanelle Rock at its northern edge served as a landmark for explorers and pioneers. Among cottages and Victorian homes west of Route 7 on Front Street rises the ancient **Council Oak** (the second old Council Tree toppled a number of years ago). Beneath this imposing white oak, now surrounded by a low iron fence, Chief Black Fox and 100 or more other Cherokees reluctantly agreed to hand over part of their treaty-given lands along the river to white settlers in 1820.

The catfish restaurant **Catfish 'n' Dardanelle** at the base of Dardanelle Rock overlooks Dardanelle Lock and Dam. **Romedio's on the Pier,** a third-generation Italian restaurant on South Front Street, also has a delightful river view.

⑦ Heading north again on Route 7 you will come to **Russellville,** on the north side of the Arkansas River. The town has accommodations, shopping, and sightseeing and is a good place to spend the night. There are also several popular restaurants. The best known is **Stoby's,** whose cheese dip and salsa are marketed in numerous Arkansas grocery stores. You can also find diners, hamburger spots, barbecues, Asian, and other restaurants, plus grocery stores if you want to stock your cooler.

⑧ Just west of Route 7 and Russellville is the **Arkansas River Visitor Center,** in **Lake Dardanelle State Park.** The visitors center is operated by the U.S. Army Corps of Engineers at Old Post Road Park and sits above **Dardanelle Lock and Dam,** whose 54-ft lift makes it the largest on the river as it forms the 35,300-acre, 50-mi-long Lake Dardanelle.

In the park you'll find campsites, picnic shelters, sports fields, and a boat-launching ramp, as well as the visitors center. Not far from the park, Reverend Cephas Washburn established the Dwight Mission in 1821 as the first school for Cherokees west of the Mississippi River. Lake Dardanelle State Park in Russellville has become the state's No. 1 site for bass tournaments, owing to its marina, beach, and campsites.

Jimmy Lile Custom Knives on Route 7, not far north of the river, is worth a stop—even if you don't care anything about hunting implements or combat weapons. Lile has crafted knives for actors Jimmy Stewart and Fess Parker (of TV's *Daniel Boone* fame in the 1950s) and President Richard Nixon. The most dangerous-looking blades were made at Sylvester Stallone's request for the movies *First Blood* and *Rambo.*

⑨ Across I–40 heading north out of Russellville, the Scenic 7 Byway passes the lakeside Shiloh Park as it rolls into the Ozark foothills. Roadside churches, used-car lots, retread tire outlets, homes, and a jerry-built flea market give way to forests and farms. Gradually the hills open into a wide valley where beef cattle graze, and 7 mi from the interstate, a green sign marks the town limits of **Dover,** the Pope County seat before it was moved to Russellville. The McFadden Cemetery lies at the edge of town. A shady park with a playground, a diner, a drugstore, and a gas station are also in the small business district.

Beyond Dover to the north, the landscape returns to pastures and hay barns in a flat valley along Illinois Bayou, which carved cliffs into the limestone layers along its north side. The road runs uphill into mountain terrain, with more cliffs and slopes visible through the leafless trees. The small town of Pleasant Valley is scattered along the highway, with Al and Delores Bowles's old-fashioned gas station and market at its center. A sign warns that the road will be "Crooked and Steep Next 63 Miles" as it snakes uphill through a forest of pine and hardwoods. Vistas reach even greater distances. Road signs mark sharp curves and intersections and are pocked with shotgun holes.

⑩ Scenic 7 enters the Ozark National Forest's **Piney Creek Management District.** Soon there's a turnoff to Long Pool Campground at a scenic spot with a natural pool in Big Piney Creek. The site has hiking trails, fishing, swimming, picnic areas, and a spot to launch canoes. Signs point out rental cabins and a private campground in the area.

In the forest, the road crosses Church Bell Ridge and passes the old Lane Cemetery. Quarried stone, piled by size and color, is for sale next to a house, and you'll spot another reminder sign: "Crooked and Steep Next 53 Miles." The Moccasin Gap horse trail leads west into the trees. The road, still winding uphill, slices through the limestone now and then. The forest floor is strewn with rocks coated with green and gray lichen and moss. You may want to stop and pick up a ham or a wonderfully tacky souvenir in Booger Hollow—"Pop. 7, Countin' One Coon Dog" boasts the town sign. Scenic 7 curves out of Booger Hollow along the top of a ridge, gaining a bit more altitude, and a metal sign arches over the driveway to "God's Little Half Acre." There are more vistas—one of the finest at a turnoff point called Rotary Ann—plus picnic tables, before the next warning: "Crooked and Steep Next 43 Miles."

⑪ Continuing downhill on Scenic 7, the road curves toward the crossroads of **Pelsor,** named for Loretta Pelsor who was appointed postmaster in 1923. At the Pelsor intersection, you can pick up picnic supplies, oak baskets, sandwiches, and other good stuff at the **Hankins Country Store**—"Since 1922"—and after eating your fill, you can try the porch swing outside.

Leaving Pelsor, Scenic 7 soon passes into Newton County. A parking lot sits at an access point to the **Ozark Highlands Trail,** which runs 178 mi between Lake Fort Smith State Park and Tyler Bend Campground on the Buffalo River. The rustic Fairview campground is nearby. Continuing north you'll pass through Lurton, then farms carved into the top of a ridge. Soon you'll enter gift-shop country, where baskets, quilts, dolls, crafts of "hillbilly barnwood," honey, and other items are for sale.

⑫ Closing in on **Jasper,** you'll pass several B&Bs and campgrounds. A sign announces "Very Crooked and Steep Next 3½ Miles," and a brake-check area and two runaway-truck ramps are at the ready as Scenic 7 curves and plummets downhill into the Newton County seat of Jasper. The small town radiates from its weathered stone courthouse. Close by are churches, gifts and crafts shops, a bakery, cafés, and **Arkansas House Bed and Breakfast**; Coco the bear lives out back.

Outfitters for trips along the Buffalo and Little Buffalo rivers are in and around town. With **Ozark Ecotours** you can take one-day and longer excursions led by local residents along the river and throughout the county. Some ecotours involve hiking, canoeing, and spelunking, and others focus on the region's history, culture, and natural history.

The journey from Jasper to Harrison is about 25 mi along Scenic 7. You'll cross the Little Buffalo River, then curve past the Ozark National River Visitor Center, RV parks, cottages, cabins, and shops as the road heads through the forests and bluffs lining the **Buffalo National River.** At the river crossing are an information station, a parking lot, and trail heads. Gravel roads lead to historic homesteads and churches, and it's possible to spot elk, which have been reintroduced to the region. On an uphill curve, a marker commemorates the site where stone was quarried in 1836 for Arkansas's contribution to the Washington Monument in Washington, D.C. Soon Scenic 7 passes the derelict Dogpatch theme park, then Mystic Caverns, beautiful despite heavy damage resulting from centuries of human use.

The terrain flattens as Scenic 7 heads into **Harrison.** RV camps, a smoked meats store, and fast-food spots begin to appear between the farms. A mule trots across a pasture, a white horse hot on its heels. Harrison's population of 12,000 makes it seem a booming metropolis after the small Ozark communities. Restaurants, motels, B&Bs, and shops line its highways and circle its courthouse square.

From Harrison, Route 7 leads northeast through Bergman to Lead Hill and the shores of Bull Shoals Lake. Other highways lead toward Eureka Springs, Mountain Home, Marshall, and Branson, Missouri. All are scenic, but not as breathtaking—or as challenging a drive—as the Scenic 7 Byway.

The best way back to Arkadelphia is to turn around and head the same way you came.

ALMA

MAP 11, A3

(Nearby towns also listed: Altus, Fort Smith/Van Buren, Paris)

Alma bills itself as the "Spinach Capital of the World." Tons of spinach are packed here each year for the Popeye brand. A ferocious-looking 8-ft-tall statue of the cartoon character stands downtown, and a huge spinach can serves as the town's water tower.

Information: Alma Area Chamber of Commerce | Box 2607, 72921-2607 | 501/632–4127.

Attractions

Lake Fort Smith State Park. The 178-mi Ozark Highlands Trail begins in this park. The park has campsites (no sanitary trailer station), picnic sites, a standard pavilion, Olympic-size pool, tennis courts (unlighted), trails, a launch ramp, and 10 fully equipped cabins with kitchens. You can rent canoes, fishing boats, and motors. Look out for the park access sign on U.S. 71, then travel ½ mi east to the northern edge of Mountainburg. | 2714 Lake Fort Smith Rd., Box 4, Mountainburg | 501/369–2469 | lakeftsmith@arkansas.com | Free | Daily.

Sister's 2-TOO Antique Mall. This 12,000-square-ft mall draws local and out-of-state vendors 7 days a week to sell antiques and flea-market collectibles. | 702 U.S. 71N | 501/632–2292 | Free | Daily 9–5:30.

White Rock Mountain Recreation Area. At White Rock, spectacular bluffs encircle mountain rim trails with panoramic views. You also have access to the Ozark Highlands Trail. The easiest way to get there is by interstate 40 on exit 24, then 215 north for 12 mi. Bear left on County Rd. 75 and follow the signs. You're just 7 mi away, 6 of which are dirt roads. | 101 White Rock Rd., Winslow | 501/369–4128 or 501/667–2191 | Free | Daily.

APR.: *Spinach Festival.* A talent show, arts and crafts, entertainment, food, and children's rides celebrate spinach every year during the third weekend of the month. | 501/632–4127.

Dining
J & J's. American. Ham and egg breakfasts are the specialty at this home cooking–style restaurant on the south side of town, but there is also a daily lunch special. It is 2 blocks from I–40. | 7154 Intersection 64 | 501/632–4066 | Mon.–Thurs., 5 AM–7 PM; Fri., 5 AM–9 PM; Sat.–Sun., 5 AM–2 PM | $5.50–$9.25 | MC, V.

Lodging
Alma Meadors Inn. This family-run motel is in front of the Cracker Barrel restaurant and next door to a Burger King. Some microwaves, some refrigerators. Cable TV, room phones. | I–40 at Hwy. 71N | 501/632–2241 or 800/628–6881 | fax 501/632–3240 | 38 rooms | $30–$50 | AE, D, DC MC, V.

Days Inn. This two-floor chain with an interior corridor is 5 mi east of historic Van Buren, right off I–40. Complimentary Continental breakfast. Cable TV. Pool. Business services. | 250 U.S. 71N | 501/632–4595 | fax 501/632–2296 | www.daysinn.com | 48 rooms | $40–$50 | AE, MC, V.

ALTUS
MAP 11, B3

(Nearby towns also listed: Alma, Fort Smith/Van Buren, Paris)

Arkansas's small wine-growing region surrounds this village, a railroad town settled in the 1880s by immigrants from Switzerland and Germany. St. Mary's Church, noted for its paintings and ornate gold-leaf work, overlooks the village, whose one-block-long downtown has cafés and antiques and crafts shops.

Information: **Altus Chamber of Commerce** | Box 404 72821 | 501/468–4684.

Attractions
Altus Heritage House Museum. Housed in the late 1800s German-American State Bank, exhibits here include coal-mining equipment, a winery, and historical memorabilia. There's also a nice city park across the street. | 106 N. Franklin | 501/468–4684 | Free | Tue.–Sat. 10–2.

Mount Bethel Vineyards and Winery. Wine from locally grown fruit is bottled in the original cellar built in the late 1800s, next to its founder's 1888 Ozark Mountain homestead, where the family still lives. The winery is approximately ¼ mi east of town, just off Hwy. 64 and only 3 mi from I–40. | 5014 Mount Bethel Dr. | 501/468–2444 | www.mountbethel-winery.com | Free | Mon.–Sat. 8–8, Sun. noon–5.

Post Familie Vineyards and Winery. Five generations of Posts have cultivated their grapes to make Post Familie wines, the largest wine producers in the state. You can tour the facility and taste the wines, and a gift shop sells wine accessories, stemware, jewelry, and other items. Look for the Altus exit on I–40. | 1700 St. Mary's Mountain Rd. | 501/468–2741 | fax 501/468–2740 | www.postfamilie.com | Free | Mon.–Sat. 8–6, Sun. 12–5.

Wiederkehr Wine Cellars. The Wiederkehr family carries on a wine-making tradition begun more than a century ago. Tours leave from its gift shop and wine-tasting area every 45 min. Its Weinkeller Restaurant serves excellent old-world Swiss-German cuisine. Take I–40 to exit 41, then south to Hwy. 186; the winery is approximately 4½ mi down the road. | 3324 Swiss Family Dr. | 501/468–3611 or 800/622–9463 | fax 501/468–4791 | www.wiederkehrwinecellars1.bizonthe.net | Free | Mon.–Thurs. 8:30–7, Fri., Sat. 8:30–8.

OCT.: *Autumn Fest.* You can celebrate fall in Altus at this festival in City Park, held annually during the second weekend of the month. In addition to food, live music, and arts and crafts booths, there are an Ugly Truck Contest and a Coal Miner's Daughter Contest. | 501/468–4684.

Dining

Fat Tuesday's. Cajun/Creole. Jambalaya, crawfish, and shrimp in a rich étouffée gravy are served up at this establishment in the center of town. The restaurant has a brick front and a saw-brick interior, with a high, exposed ceiling. | 107 N. Main St. | 501/468–2326 | Tues.–Thurs., 4:30–9; Fri.–Sat., 4:30–10; closed Sun. | $13–$20 | AE, D, DC, MC, V.

Kelts Inn. Irish. The tables and chairs at this Celtic pub hail right from Scotland and Ireland. Specials include 8- to 12-oz rib-eye steaks and baked salmon in lemon butter. The inn is at the Altus exit on I–64; if you look for the Welsh and the Scottish flags, the Union Jack, and, of course, the red, white, and blue, you can't miss it. | 119 W. Main St. | 501/468–2413 | Mon.–Sat., 11–10, closed Sun. | $8–$20 | AE, D, MC, V.

Wiederkehr's Weinkeller. Continental. The Swiss roots of Arkansas's premier wine-making family are evident in their restaurant, a converted hand-dug wine cellar from 1888 where you can taste wines made from grapes in the surrounding hillside vineyard. Winery tours are available. The food draws on all of the cultures that border Switzerland, so you can expect a German platter, poulet au vin blanc, and pasta dishes as well as the restaurant's famous Swiss onion soup. For dessert, you might try Grandma Wiederkehr's shortcake or the sorbet in champagne. Kids' menu. Take exit 41 off I–40, then go south on Hwy. 186 about 5 mi. | 3324 Swiss Family Dr. | 501/468–3551 and 800/622–9463 | Mon.–Sat., 11–3, 5–9 dinner; Sun., 11–9 | $10–$25 | AE, D, DC, MC, V.

Lodging

Ozark's Motel. This cut-stone and shingled motel is at the foot of the Ozark Mountains less than 1 mi from the Arkansas River and the River Bridge. It sits amid the wildlife and wooded scenery of west Altus. Restaurant. In-room data ports, some microwaves, some refrigerators. Cable TV, room phones. Some pets allowed. | 1711 W. Commercial St. | 501/667–1500 | fax 501/667–1011 | 35 rooms | $36–$39 | AE, D, MC, V.

St. Mary's Mountain Guest House. This New Orleans–style B&B, with columns and wrought-iron balconies, is nestled on 6 wooded acres with a rustic overlook of the Ozark Mountains. The rooms have queen-size beds and balconies. St. Mary's is within 1 mi of several local wineries; you get a complimentary bottle when you stay there. Complimentary Continental breakfast. Data ports in some rooms. No phones in rooms. | 2121 St. Mary's Mountain Rd. | 501/468–4141 | sheilallama@arkansas.net | 3 rooms | $55–$75 | AE.

ARKADELPHIA

MAP 11, B5

(Nearby towns also listed: Ashdown, Benton, Camden, Hope, Hot Springs, Texarkana)

Arkadelphia, the southern gateway to Scenic Route 7, was established in the early 1800s as a landing on the Ouachita River. It is home to Henderson State University and Ouachita Baptist University. Historical buildings include the 1899 county courthouse, the 1860 Flanagin law office across the street, and the antebellum Steamboat Gothic Barkman house at 406 N. 10th.

Information: **Arkadelphia Area Chamber of Commerce** | Box 38, 71923 | 870/246–5542.

Attractions

Arkadelphia's Historic Homes Tour. You can view some impressive 19th-century buildings in this self-guided, half-hour driving tour. Some of the well-maintained properties date back to the 1840s and are included in the National Register of Historic Places. Brochures are available from the Chamber of Commerce. | 870/246–5542 | fax 870/246–5543 | www.arkadelphia.org.

DeGray Lake. This 13,800-acre man-made lake is a water playground surrounded by the Ouachita Mountains, with cabins, camping, and marinas along its shores. There are 10 Corps of Engineers campsites and day-use areas around this lake. Take exit 78 off I–30, then drive north on Hwy. 7 and turn left at Skyline Drive. The visitors center (543 Skyline Dr.) is on the left, before you cross the dam. | 2027 State Park Entrance Rd., Bismarck | 870/246–5501 | Free | Daily.

DeGray Lake Resort State Park. Along with a championship golf course, full-service marina, RV and tent campsites, horseback riding, tennis, biking, swimming, picnicking, and interpretive activities, the park has a 98-room island lodge, a lakeside swimming pool, meeting and convention services, a restaurant, and a rent-a-yurt (that's a year-round universal recreational tent). On I–30, take exit 78, then go north on Hwy. 7 toward the town of Hot Springs and look for signs. | 2027 State Park Entrance Rd., Bismarck | 501/865–2801 for park information and campsite reservations; 800/737–8355 for lodge reservations | www.degray.com | Free | Daily.

ON THE CALENDAR

APR.: *Festival of Two Rivers.* This event includes canoe races, music, arts and crafts, and other entertainment. The festival takes place on all four sides of the courthouse, in the center of town, near where the Ouachita and the Caddo Rivers meet. Between 500 and 650 children participate in the largest kids' race in the state. | 870/246–5542.

Dining

Bowen's. Southern. This is a casual, cozy family restaurant with nightly theme buffets including Tex-Mex on Tuesday and seafood Friday and Saturday. Bowen's is known for its chicken and dumplings, broasted chicken, and chicken-fried steak. Kids' menu. | 104 Malvern Rd. | 870/246–8661 | Sun.–Thur., 6 AM–8 PM; Fri.–Sat., 6 AM–8:30 PM | $5–$10 | AE, D, MC, V.

The Honeycomb. American. College students and professors congregate at this small, eat-and-go restaurant near Henderson State and Ouachita Baptist Universities. The menu includes homemade breads, desserts, and chicken on Ritz. Needlepoint pieces done by local artists hang on the walls. | 706 Main St. | 870/245–2333 | Mon.–Fri., 7–4 | Reservations not accepted | $5–$7 | No credit cards.

Kreg's Catfish. American. Inexpensive plate lunches and fried catfish fillets by the pound attract hungry crowds to this modest college-town restaurant. It's popular for the catfish and chicken dish, the salad platter topped with fried chicken, and the homemade rolls, among other items. Nonsmokers will appreciate the "no smoking" policy. Kids' menu. | 2805 W. Pine St. | 870/246–5327 | Daily 11–8:30 PM | $6–$9 | AE, D, MC, V.

Lodging

Best Western Continental Inn. This service-oriented hotel, a brick colonial style building, is about 4 mi from downtown, near Hot Springs and two universities, 5 mi from DeGray Lake, and ¼ mi from Caddo River. The inn is at exit 78 off I–30. Complimentary Continental breakfast. Cable TV. Pool. Playground. Laundry facilities. Pets allowed. | 136 Valley Rd. | 870/246–5592 | fax 870/246–3585 | www.bestwestern.com | 58 rooms | $39–$79 | AE, D, DC, MC, V.

Days Inn. Standard accommodations are what you'll find in this two-story motor hotel. DeGray Lake is 5 mi away and the Hot Springs horse track is 30 mi away. The inn is at the second Arkadelphia exit off I–30. Cable TV. Pool. Sauna, hot tub. Business services. Pets allowed.

| 137 Valley St. | 870/246–3031 | fax 870/246–3743 | www.daysinn.com/ctg/cgi-bin/DaysInn | 53 rooms | $45–$59 | AE, D, DC, MC, V.

Degray Lake Resort Lodge. This state-owned lodge, about 6 mi northwest of Arkadelphia, is in Degray Lake Resort State Park. The lodge has a wooden interior and stunning views of DeGray Lake. Restaurant, room service. Some refrigerators. Cable TV. Outdoor pool. Golf course, tennis. Hiking, horseback riding. Beach, boating, fishing, bicycles. Shops. Business services. | 2027 State Park Entrance Rd., Bismarck | 501/865–2851 or 800/605–5675 | fax 501/865–2880 | degray@arkansas.com | www.degray.com/lodge_restaurant.html | 96 rooms | $65–$75 | AE, D, MC, V.

Holiday Inn Express. This two-story hostelry is 4 mi from Lake DeGray. Complimentary Continental breakfast. In-room data ports, in-room safes, some microwaves, some refrigerators. Cable TV, room phones. Outdoor pool. Laundry facilities. Business services. Pets allowed. | 150 Valley St. | 870/230–1506 | fax 870/230–1015 | holiday@ezclick.net | www.holiday-inn.com | 100 rooms | $65–$69 | AE, D, DC, MC, V.

Iron Mountain Lodge and Marina on DeGray Lake. During your stay at DeGray Lake's only lakeside cottages, you can enjoy various activities, including waterskiing, cruises on a party barge, and fishing. There's also a scuba air station. Though fully modern inside, many of the log-sided cottages that make up the lodge have working fireplaces built of stone. The lodge is 5 mi from exit 78 off I–30 and 10 mi from Arkadelphia. Kitchenettes. Boating. | 134 Iron Mountain Marina Dr. | 870/246–4310 | www.iron-mountain.com | 14 2-bedroom cottages | $120–$215 depending on the season | AE, D, DC, MC, V.

Quality Inn. On the interstate and close to restaurants, you can bowl at an alley 3 mi from this simple Quality Inn, and golf is just 7 mi away (but no guest privileges at the course). The inn is on I–30 at exit 78, just outside of town. Some in-room hot tubs. Cable TV. Pool. Laundry facilities. Pets allowed. | 870/246–5855 | fax 870/246–8552 | 63 rooms | $55–$77 | AE, D, DC, MC, V.

ASHDOWN

MAP 11, A6

(Nearby towns also listed: Arkadelphia, Benton, Camden, Hope, Hot Springs, Texarkana)

The courthouse in Ashdown, a small county seat in Arkansas's piney woods, was built in 1907 and is crowned by a copper dome. The town is home to one of the world's largest communication-paper manufacturing complexes and the nation's fourth-largest cement manufacturer.

Information: **Little River Chamber of Commerce** | Box 214, Ashdown, 71822-0214 | 870/898–2758 | www.littleriver.org.

Attractions
Millwood Dam and Lake. This huge man-made lake right off Hwy. 32 is a fishing hot spot known nationwide for largemouth bass, white and hybrid bass, crappie, catfish, and bream, with boat lanes through submerged timber to marshes and oxbow lakes within it. Several marinas and small resorts are on its shores, along with 10 U.S. Army Corps of Engineers sites for camping and day use. | 1528 Hwy. 32E | 870/898–3343 | Free | Daily.

Millwood State Park. This 824-acre park on Millwood Lake has RV and tent camping sites with modern bathhouses, a full-service marina with supplies, a picnic pavilion, hiking trails on which alligators have right of way, interpretive activities, and superb fishing and birding. The park is 9 mi east of town, off Hwy. 71. | 1564 Hwy. 32E | 870/898–2800 | Free | Daily.

ASHDOWN

INTRO
ATTRACTIONS
DINING
LODGING

New Rocky Comfort Museum. This 3-room museum of local memorabilia is in a former jail built in 1902. It's off Hwy. 32 and Hwy. 108, as well as 2 blocks off Hwy. 41, right on the city square. | 3rd Ave. and Schuman St., Foreman | 870/542–7887 | Free | Mon., Wed., Fri. 9–noon and 1–4; also by appointment.

ON THE CALENDAR

MAR., APR.: *Easter Egg Scramble.* Children 12 and under can hunt for eggs containing prizes inside at this event in Millwood State Park. | 1564 Hwy. 32 East | 870/898–2800 | Easter weekend.

MAY: *Memorial Day Fun Fest.* This festival in Millwood State Park has environmental education programs and recreational events for the entire family, including barge trips and guided trail hikes. | 1564 Hwy. 32E | 870/898–2800.

OCT.: *Hometown Festival.* If you come downtown on Saturday night, you can listen to live music at a Jamboree show. Throughout the month, you can take in local arts and crafts, woodwork, handmade linens, dolls, ceramics, antiques (including antique cars), and horse and carriage rides. | 870/898–2758.

NOV., DEC.: *Land O' Lights Christmas Lighting.* In a four-lane town, you can't possibly miss all those white lights—there are millions of them on the courthouse and other buildings, plus Christmas parades, crafts, refreshments, and Kiamichi railroad train rides. Ring in the season county-wide. | Ashdown and Foreman | 870/898–2758.

Dining

Shirley's Corner Kitchen. Southern. Grapevines, leaves, and flowers hang from the walls and ceiling of this eclectic-looking establishment. You can stop by for a quick meal of hamburgers and fried chicken after visiting the antiques stores across the street. | 22 E. Main St. | 870/898–6865 (same number for fax) | Sun.-Fri. | $3–$6 | MC, V.

BATESVILLE

MAP 11, D3

(Nearby towns also listed: Jonesboro, Mountain View, Newport)

Batesville is the home of Lyon College and a riverside park with a white sand beach and picnic tables. Pioneers settled Batesville's site on the White River as early as 1810, and it became a major regional steamboat port and commercial center after the 1830s. The prosperity continued with the arrival of the railroads. Batesville's pioneer cemetery is the oldest preserved burial ground in the state.

Information: **Batesville Area Chamber of Commerce** | 409 Vine St., 72501 | 870/793–2378 | batesville.dina.org.

Attractions

Driving Tour. This audio driving tour takes you past the 1842 Garrott house on Main Street, the oldest surviving home in the city; the Glenn House on Water Street, which was built around an 1849 Methodist school; the home of Governor Elisha Baxter on 8th Street; and dozens of Victorian, Queen Anne, Foursquare, and other styles of buildings. You can get a brochure with a map of the historical downtown and residential districts at the Chamber of Commerce. | Free.

Old Independence Regional Museum. This museum, built in 1936, has historical presentations and exhibits of the 12 counties, which were a part of Independence County in the 1820s Arkansas Territory. In the gift shop you can browse for Arkansas memorabilia from nearly 200 years ago. | 380 S. Ninth St. | 870/793–2121 | www.oirm.org | $3 | Open Tues.–Sat. 9–4:30, Sun. 1:30–4.

APR.: *Arkansas Scottish Festival.* This event, held at Lyon College, includes bagpipes, Scottish music, dance, and sports. | 870/698–4382 | www.lyon.edu/webdata/groups/scotfest.

JULY, AUG.: *Annual White River Water Carnival.* This week-long event has been a Batesville tradition for more than half a century and includes a bass fishing tournament; a Grand Parade; hot air balloon rides; the Miss White River Pageant; live music; recreational contests; volleyball, golf, and basketball tournaments; a firefighter's championship; a motorcycle show; carnival rides; museum exhibits; and a lot of food. The carnival is at Riverside Park. | 870/793–2378 | www.watercarnival.com.

Dining

Elizabeth's Restaurant. American. This three-story, family-owned restaurant on the north side of town has glass tabletops over linen and big windows. Salads, a tropical chicken salad, and a sizeable pineapple boat with grapes, almonds, and other fruits are among the dishes on the menu. | 231 E. Main St. | 870/698–0903 | Lunch Tues.–Sat., 10:30–3; dinner Thur.–Sat. 5–9. Closed Sun. | $11–$14 | AE, DC, MC, V.

The Lockhouse. American. You can sit outdoors at this restaurant on the banks of the White River and dine on Mexican chicken salad, walleye, or shrimp. The restaurant is in the southeast part of town, one block from the White River Bridge. | 50 River Bank Rd. | 870/612–5282 | Lunch Mon.–Sat., 11–2; dinner Mon.–Thur., 4–8 and Fri.–Sat., 4–9. Closed Sun. | $6–$19 | AE, MC, V.

USEFUL EXTRAS YOU MAY WANT TO PACK

- ❏ Adapters, converter
- ❏ Alarm clock
- ❏ Batteries
- ❏ Binoculars
- ❏ Blankets, pillows, sleeping bags
- ❏ Books and magazines
- ❏ Bottled water, soda
- ❏ Calculator
- ❏ Camera, lenses, film
- ❏ Can/bottle opener
- ❏ Cassette tapes, CDs, and players
- ❏ Cell phone
- ❏ Change purse with $10 in quarters, dimes, and nickels for tollbooths and parking meters
- ❏ Citronella candle
- ❏ Compass
- ❏ Earplugs
- ❏ Flashlight
- ❏ Folding chairs
- ❏ Guidebooks
- ❏ Luggage tags and locks
- ❏ Maps
- ❏ Matches
- ❏ Money belt
- ❏ Pens, pencils
- ❏ Plastic trash bags
- ❏ Portable TV
- ❏ Radio
- ❏ Self-seal plastic bags
- ❏ Snack foods
- ❏ Spare set of keys, not carried by driver
- ❏ Travel iron
- ❏ Travel journal
- ❏ Video recorder, blank tapes
- ❏ Water bottle
- ❏ Water-purification tablets

*Excerpted from *Fodor's: How to Pack: Experts Share Their Secrets*
© 1997, by Fodor's Travel Publications

Lodging

Best Western Scenic Motor Inn. This two-story chain hotel near Lyon College has a panoramic view of Batesville and the surrounding Ozark Mountains in all rooms. The inn is on Hwy. 167, $\frac{1}{2}$ mi south of town. Restaurant, picnic area. In-room data ports, refrigerators. Cable TV. Pool. Business services, free parking. | 773 Batesville Blvd. | 870/698–1855 | 40 rooms | $52–$70 | AE, D, DC, MC, V.

Holiday Inn Express. This chain motel is 2 mi from the Independent County Museum on 5th and Vine Streets. You can rent a car at an on-site concierge desk. Complimentary Continental breakfast. In-room data ports, some microwaves, some refrigerators. Cable TV, room phones. Indoor pool. Hot tub, sauna. Gym. Laundry facilities. Business services. No pets. | 1130 White Dr. | 870/698–2700 | fax 870/698–2700 | holidayinn@arkansas.net | www.holiday-inn.com | 38 rooms | $69–$129 | AE, D, DC, MC, V.

Ramada Inn. This chain lodging is 1 mi from White River and 3–4 mi from the airport. The large brick building with a courtyard is right off Hwy. 167N, close to downtown. Restaurant, room service. Some refrigerators. Cable TV. Outdoor pool. Hot tub. Laundry facilities. Pets allowed. | 1325 N. St. Louis St. | 870/698–1800 | 124 rooms | $60–$70 | AE, D, DC, MC, V.

Super 8 Motel. This two-story chain motel near Lyon College is $\frac{1}{2}$ mi outside of town off Hwy. 167. Look for the big yellow and red sign. Cable TV. Free parking. | 1287 N. St. Louis St. | 870/793–5888 | fax 870/793–5888 | 49 rooms | $45–$60 | AE, D, DC, MC, V.

BENTON

MAP 11, C5

(Nearby towns also listed: Arkadelphia, Ashdown, Hot Springs, Little Rock)

Benton is approximately halfway between Little Rock and Hot Springs, and has small-town charm. Benton's industry began with a salt factory and was followed by pottery and brick-making companies. Bauxite was discovered in 1887, and mines here once produced 97% of the nation's needs.

Information: **Benton Chamber of Commerce** | 607 N. Market St., 72015 | 501/315–8272 | bentonchamber.org.

Attractions

Gann Museum. The only known structure in existence built from blocks of bauxite, the primary source of aluminum, the Gann Museum was built in 1893 for a doctor by patients unable to pay for their services. | 218 S. Market St. | 501/778–5513 | Free | Tues., Wed., Thurs., 10–4; and tours by appointment.

Jerry Van Dyke's Soda Shoppe. TV star Jerry Van Dyke bought the entire block. He opened a nostalgic restaurant, with 1940s-style malts, celebrity sandwiches and salads, and a well-known half-pound old-fashioned fox burger, and he restored the Royal Theater next door as an acting and film school, with performances open to the public. Take exit 116 off I–30, then look for it at the second stoplight downtown. | 107 S. Market St. | 501/860–5500 | www.jerryvandyke.net | Free | Theater, call for schedule; shop open daily.

ON THE CALENDAR

APR., MAY: *P.R.C.A. Rodeo.* The Professional Rodeo Cowboy Association holds a nightly rodeo at the Saline County Fairgrounds. You can see team roping, among other specialty acts. | 501/315–8272.

Dining

Brown's. American. All-you-can eat country cooking is served at this freeway restaurant built in the fashion of a general store. There are 5 dining rooms with music, and a 100-ft buffet with 150 choices. Brown's is known for fried catfish and pork ribs. If you finish your homemade cobbler or pie before your friends, you can sit on a bench on the wraparound porch. Smoking is allowed. Kids' menu. To get there, take a right at exit 118 off I–30. | 18718 I–30 | 501/778–5033 | $4–$8 | D, MC, V.

Dizzy's Grill. Eclectic. Chances are good you'll find a dish you like among the Italian, Greek, and Cajun choices on the menu. While you eat, you can take in the antiques, sculptures, paper lanterns, and diverse artwork all around you. | 1217 Ferguson Dr. | 501/776–3004 | Tues.– Thur., 11–8; Fri.–Sat., 11–9. Closed Sun.–Mon. | $7–$12 | AE, D, MC, V.

Lodging

Best Western Inn. This Best Western Inn is near Jerry Van Dyke's soda shop, a movie theater, and the location where the film *Sling Blade* was made. Restaurant. In-room data ports. Business services. Pets allowed. No smoking. | 17036 I–30 | 501/778–9695 | fax 501/ 776–1699 | 65 rooms | $45–$66 | AE, D, DC, MC, V.

Days Inn. A division of the University of Arkansas at Little Rock is near this chain hotel, as are the Jerry Van Dyke soda shop, a movie theater, the *Sling Blade* filming location, and the largest movie theater in the state. You can expect pine trees and the choice of three two-story buildings. The inn is at exit 118 off I–30. Complimentary Continental breakfast. Cable TV. Pool. Laundry facilities. Business services, free parking. No pets. | 17701 I–30 | 501/776– 3200 | fax 501/776–0906 | 117 rooms | $44–$52 | AE, D, DC, MC, V.

Scottish Inn. This inn is 30 mi east of Hot Springs. The cream and green building is off exit 118 on I–30, next to the Bits and Pieces Shopping Center. Microwaves, refrigerators. Cable TV. Outdoor pool. | 17900 I–30 | 501/778–4591 | fax 501/315–9253 | 30 rooms | $32–$42 | AE, D, MC, V.

BENTONVILLE

MAP 11, A2

(Nearby towns also listed: Eureka Springs, Fayetteville, Harrison, Rogers, Springdale)

Bentonville remained a small town from its founding as a county seat in 1837 until Sam Walton arrived in 1950 and opened the five-and-dime store that was the precursor of Wal-Mart, the world's largest retail chain. Today Bentonville's historic downtown, centered on the county courthouse square, retains an old-fashioned aura, as do neighboring residential districts. Wal-Mart's international headquarters, retail stores, and distribution complex are just 1 mi away.

Information: **Bentonville/Bella Vista Chamber of Commerce** | 412 S. Main, 72712-5905 | 501/273–2841 | www.nwanews.com/bbvchamber.

Attractions

Peel Mansion and Historic Gardens. This mansion is the former residence of Colonel Samuel West Peel, attorney, Confederate commander, U.S. Senator, and Indian agent. Its shop is in a circa-1850 log cabin. | 400 S. Walton Blvd. | 501/273–9664 | $3 | Tues.–Sat. 10–4.

Wal-Mart Visitors Center. Sam and Helen Walton and Sam's brother, Bud, opened a dime store here in 1950. Twelve years and 15 stores later, they opened their first Wal-Mart Discount Store. The lively museum downtown on the square chronicles the chain's origins and growth and displays Sam's favorite vehicle, a beat-up red pickup truck, and his modest office at corporate headquarters. | 501/273–2754 | www.walmart.com | Free | Tues.–Sat. 9–5.

ON THE CALENDAR

FEB.: *Incredible Edible Chocolate Fest.* In addition to the chocolate dessert competition among local restaurants, there's an auction of decorated items. | 501/273–2841.

MAY: *Ozark Festival Charity Horse Show.* Every year since 1973, during the first week-end of the month, 83 classes of Tennessee walking horses, racing horses, and Missouri fox-trotting horses give daily performances. The horse show is at the Benton County Fairgrounds or 15 min away at the University of Arkansas. | 501/925–4266.

MAY, SEPT., OCT.: *Arts and Crafts Festival.* Hundreds of crafts artisans display and sell wares at the Ole Applegate Place; entertainment includes cloggers, bluegrass and gospel music, and more; there's also a food courtyard. The festival is in town. | 501/273–7478.

OCT.: *The New Sugar Creek Arts and Crafts Fair.* You can view 200 indoor arts and crafts exhibits, antiques, and collectibles at this fair, held at the Benton County Fair-grounds. | 501/273–3270.

DEC.: *Christmas on the Square and Holiday Trail of Lights.* This event, which began in the early 1900s, includes a parade, the lighting of the downtown square, live Nativity, caroling, and the arrival of Mr. and Mrs. Claus. Performances by local schoolchildren are followed by lighting displays throughout town. | 501/273–2841.

Dining

Fred's Hickory Inn. American. Smoked sirloin, Fred's strip steak, and blackberry cobbler are among the fare that keeps Fred's at near capacity during peak dining hours. The restau-rant, a 30-yr dining tradition in the area, is known for barbecued ribs. Open-air dining is available on the lawn. Kids' menu. To get there, take I–40 north, then exit 93 and south on Walton. The inn sits on a hill on your left. | 1502 N. Walton Blvd. | 501/273–3303 | $8–$30 | AE, D, DC, MC, V | No lunch Sat.

Maude Ethel's Family Restaurant. American. If you're hungry, you can head to Maude Ethel's for such food as chicken-fried steak and catfish. This casual restaurant is filled with old-fashioned pictures of mountains, trees, and waterfalls, and a miniature water fountain. | 927 N. 12th St. | 501/273–1007 | Mon.–Sat., 6 AM–8 PM; Sun., 7 AM–2 PM | $6–$10 | AE, D, MC, V.

Whispering Woods Tea Room. American. For weekday lunches and a Sunday brunch, the homemade bread and casseroles are yummy. The country-style tea room has antique dishes, linen, candles, and local souvenirs. | 911 N.W. 7th St. | 501/464–7531 or 877/237–1128 | Mon.–Fri., 11 AM–2 PM; Fri. by reservation only | $3–$7 | AE, D, DC, MC, V.

Lodging

Best Western. This is a reliable chain option; the notable red-brick building is a short drive from several popular attractions, including the Country Music Show and the Great Eureka Springs Passion Play. The hotel is on Business 71, off Hwy 71 Bypass at exit 65, just 10 mi from the airport. In-room data ports, some refrigerators. Cable TV. Pool. Business ser-vices. Pets allowed. | 2307 S.E. Walton Blvd. | 501/273–9727 | fax 501/273–1763 | www.best-western.com/ | 55 rooms | $50–$58 | AE, D, DC, MC, V.

Comfort Inn. This two-story chain has comfortable accommodations 12 min from the air-port and 20 min from the University of Arkansas. The inn is also near Northwest Arkansas Community College and Beaver Lake, known as the clearest lake in North America. The inn is at exit 85 off I–540 on the edge of town. In-room data ports, microwaves, refrigerators. Cable TV. Indoor pool. Hot tub. Laundry facilities. Business services. | 3609 Moberly Ln. | 501/271–9400 | fax 501/271–7222 | 63 rooms | $65–$80, $160 suites | AE, D, DC, MC, V.

Quality Inn. This chain hotel is on the north side of town, 1½ mi from Wal-Mart headquarters. It has a $3.95 breakfast buffet. Restaurant, room service. In-room data ports, some microwaves, some refrigerators. Cable TV, room phones. Indoor pool. Hot tub, massage. Exer-cise equipment. Business services, airport shuttle. No pets. | 1209 N. Walton Blvd. | 501/273–2451 | fax 501/273–7611 | 150 rooms | $62–$78 | AE, D, DC, MC, V.

Ramada Inn. This quiet Ramada is next to a residential area yet is close to restaurants, shopping, hair salons, and Wal-Mart. The inn is 1 mi from I–540, exit 93. Restaurant. Cable

TV. Indoor pool. Exercise equipment. Business services, airport shuttle. | 1209 N. Walton Blvd. | 501/273–2451 | fax 501/273–7611 | 152 rooms | $57–$65 | AE, D, DC, MC, V.

Super 8 Motel. This bungalow-type motel is 10 mi from the northwest regional Arkansas airport and two blocks from a bus terminal, where there are several popular restaurants and clubs. The motel is off I–540, exit 85. Picnic area, complimentary Continental breakfast. Cable TV. Outdoor pool. Pets allowed (fee). | 2301 S.E. Walton Blvd. | 501/273–1818 | fax 501/273–5529 | 52 rooms | $50–$55 | AE, D, DC, MC, V.

Tudor House at the Oak. This native stone house, listed in the National Register of Historic Places, is surrounded by gardens, fountains, and quiet, wooded areas. You can sleep in a four-poster bed and awake to a three-course gourmet breakfast with specially blended full-bean coffee. The chef shares his culinary skills in hands-on cooking classes. Complimentary breakfast. In-room data ports, some in-room hot tubs. Cable TV, room phones. Laundry facilities. No pets. No smoking. | 806 N.W. "A" St. | 501/273–2200 or 877/777–9990 | lalalong@nwa.quik.com | www.tudorplace.com | 2 rooms | $60–$70 | MC, V.

BERRYVILLE

(Nearby towns also listed: Eureka Springs, Harrison)

The Carroll County seat of Berryville was founded in a fertile Ozark Mountains valley in 1850 and rebuilt after both sides burned the town during the Civil War. In its Pioneer Memorial Park are a 150-yr-old log cabin, the cell from the 1905 county jail, an early newspaper and printing office, and a marker listing the names of early settlers buried there.

Information: **Berryville Chamber of Commerce** | Box 401, 72616-0402 | 870/423–3704 | www.berryvillear.com/.

Attractions

Antiques & Elderly Things. This store sells china, antiques, cookbooks, and Civil War–era books, including biographies of Ulysses S. Grant and Robert E. Lee. | 606 W. Freeman Ave. | 870/423–3775 | gkennett@cswnet.com | www.cswnet.com/~gkennett/ | Daily 10–4.

Carroll County Heritage Center. In the former county courthouse are displayed pioneer items, an antique clock collection, a pioneer funeral parlor and school room, a genealogy department, and more. Follow Hwy. 62 and look for the only three-story redbrick building on the west side of the downtown square. | 870/423–6312 | $2 | Apr.–Oct., weekdays 9–4; Nov.–Mar., Tues.–Fri. 9–4.

Cosmic Cavern. This cavern is the site of a large below-ground lake. There is a 1-hr guided tour through subterranean rooms and across an underground bridge. From whichever direction you come, stay on Hwy. 21 and look for the numerous signs. | 870/749–2298 | $10 | Call for schedule.

Saunders Memorial Museum. An extensive collection of firearms, including antique and unusual pieces, plus knives, Victorian clothing, accessories, textiles, and furniture, is housed here. Go off Hwy. 62 and turn right onto Madison, which is part of the downtown square. Look for the large brick building with four white pillars. | 870/423–2563 | $3 | Apr. 15–Oct., Mon.–Sat. 10:30–5.

ON THE CALENDAR

MAY: *Arkansas State Muzzleloading Championship Shoot.* This black-powder event draws competitors from more than a dozen states. There's another such competition in Berryville each September, begun in 1941, and it's even bigger. The event is off Hwy. 62, in Luther Owens Park. | 870/423–3268.

AUG.: *Summer Toy Run.* The event begins in Eagle Rock, Missouri, and continues to Holiday Island, Eureka Springs, and Berryville, collecting toys for children. Food and beverages are available, and door prizes are awarded. | 870/423–6888.

Dining

Town and Country Lanes and Restaurant. Southern. The waitresses come in early here to prepare the gravy, which you can have over biscuits. Although this restaurant is attached to a 10-lane bowling alley, it's one of the few places in town that isn't a fast food joint. | 702 W. Trimble St. | 870/423–3362 | Mon.–Fri., 6 AM–8 PM; Sat.–Sun., 6 AM–2 PM | $6–$9 | No credit cards.

Lodging

Ruby Motel. This wood-frame motel is at the junction of Hwys. 62 and 21 on the east side of Berryville. Complimentary coffee is available in the morning. Cable TV, room phones. Outdoor pool. | 510 S. Main St. | 870/423–2067 | 18 rooms | $32–$50 | D, MC, V.

Shamrock Inn. Kings River and Osage Creek run through Berryville, and 10 min away *The Great Passion Play* is performed nightly year-round. The Inn has a rough oak exterior and its interior is painted shamrock green. It's next to a major city park and two blocks from a grocery store. Some microwaves, some refrigerators. Cable TV. Pool. | 705 Eureka St. | 870/423–2489 | fax 870/423–5901 | 18 rooms | $35–$40 | AE, D, DC, MC, V.

BLYTHEVILLE

MAP 11, F3

(Nearby town also listed: Jonesboro)

Although it is in the heart of the Mississippi Delta's cotton country, Blytheville is also the nation's No. 2 steel-producing town. Founded in 1880 by H. T. Blythe, a Methodist minister, farmer, and entrepreneur, it promptly turned into a boomtown thanks to railroads and logging. Its Art Deco Ritz Theater now serves as a civic center for visual-arts exhibits, concerts, plays, musicals, variety shows, a summer film festival, and conferences. In the early 1960s the U.S. Army built an airfield on its outskirts that became a Strategic Air Command base until it was closed in 1992.

Big Lake, west of Blytheville, became a national wildlife refuge in 1915. Additional acreage abutting it, plus the man-made Mallard Lake, later became a state wildlife management area. Although waterfowl are protected in the national refuge, the state area is a favorite hunting as well as fishing spot.

Information: Blytheville Area Chamber of Commerce | Box 485, 72316-0483 | 870/762–2012.

Attractions

Blytheville Heritage Museum. Housed in the restored 1938 Kress five-and-dime store—the tallest building in the middle of Main Street—the museum has everything from one of its founder's marriage licenses to exhibits about the cotton industry, military air defense, and downtown as it was in the early 1900s. There is also a John Grisham exhibit. | 210 W. Main St. | 870/763–2525 | Free | Weekdays 9–noon and 1–4; also by appointment.

That Bookstore in Blytheville. That Bookstore has become a mid-American landmark and site of special events such as folk concerts, story hours, jazz and chamber music, or book signings by such authors as John Grisham. Drive downtown and look for the teal green awning on Main Street. | 316 W. Main St. | 870/763–3333 or 800/844–8306 | fax 870/763–1125 | www.tbib.com | Free | Mon.–Sat. 9:30–6, Sun. 1–4:30.

OCT.: *Chickasaw Chili Cook-Off.* Gospel music is a big draw at this chili cook-off, the second-oldest in the state; other attractions are chili tasting, food booths, crafts, antique cars, and live entertainment. The street festival takes up five blocks on Main Street. | 870/763–2525.

NOV., DEC.: *Lights of the Delta.* A holiday open house in the Kress building downtown plus a Parade of Trees is followed by a citywide lighting festival with more than two million lights. The lights are everywhere! | 870/763–2525.

Dining

Big Daddy's. American. Steak and seafood dishes are served in this restaurant in the Holiday Inn. Fillet of jack with a Jack Daniels sauce is one highlight. A dance floor and DJ-spun music Thurs.–Sat., as well as Fri. night karaoke, add to the experience. | 1121 Main St. | 870/763–5800 | Mon.–Sat., 4 PM–1 AM | $13–$19 | AE, D, DC, MC, V.

Grecian Steakhouse. Steak. Pictures of Greece hang on the walls, and gyros with lamb meat are on the menu. But if Greek food is not your thing, you can also order freshly cut T-bone and 16-oz rib-eye Delmonico steaks. | 1600 E. Main St. | 870/763–7550 | Daily, 11 AM–10 PM | $9–$14 | AE, D, MC, V.

Olympia Steakhouse. Italian. This large establishment for steaks, pasta, and seafood seats nearly 350. George's Hawaiian Steak marinated in pineapple and honey is a specialty. Trees, plants, vases, and bottles fill the interior. | 841 E. Main St. | 870/838–1204 | $7–$16 | AE, D, MC, V.

Sharecropper Restaurant. Southern. This restaurant won a 1995 Reader Choice Awards in the *Arkansas Times* for Best Desserts and Best American Cuisine in northeast Arkansas. Its two dining rooms can seat about 150, and chicken-fried steak, barbecued ribs, and catfish are among the choices. Smoking is not allowed. | 211 W. Ash St. | 870/763–5818 | fax 870/763–2624 | Mon.–Fri., 5:30 AM–3 PM; dinner Thur.–Fri., 5–9; Sat., 6 AM–2 PM | $4–$8 | AE, D, MC, V.

Lodging

Best Budget Inn. This two-story, cream-colored inn is 2 mi from I–55. The Kowloon Restaurant serves lunch and dinner. Restaurant. Some microwaves, some refrigerators. Cable TV, room phones. Laundry facilities. | 357 S. Division St. | 870/763–4588 | fax 870/763–4588 | raginigandhi@hotmail.com | 75 rooms | $25–$35 | AE, D, DC, MC, V.

Best Western. These are standard chain accommodations off I–55 and near Mississippi County Community College (MCCC). A movie theater is one exit away. Complimentary Continental breakfast. Some in-room hot tubs. Cable TV. Pool. Laundry facilities. Business services. | 3700 S. Division | 870/762–5200 | fax 870/763–2580 | 40 rooms | $58–$68 | AE, D, DC, MC, V.

Comfort Inn. These are typical chain lodging, but with a newer look. The inn is near Mississippi County Community College (MCCC) and 8 mi from the Mississippi River. Coming from north or south, it's right off I–55 at exit 67. When you see the gazebo, you'll know you're there. Restaurant, complimentary Continental breakfast. Cable TV. Pool. Business services. | Rte. 51E and I–55 | 870/763–7081 | 105 rooms | $48–$54 | AE, D, DC, MC, V.

Days Inn. This typical motor hotel is close to shopping and a casino. Memphis, Tennessee, is 65 mi away, and it's just 4 mi to the Missouri state line. Complimentary Continental breakfast. Cable TV. Pool. Playground. Laundry facilities. Pets allowed (fee). | 200 S. Access Rd. | 870/763–1241 | fax 870/763–6696 | 122 rooms | $51–$62 | AE, D, DC, MC, V.

Drury Inn. This Bavarian-style inn is within walking distance of local restaurants and near the municipal airport, I–55, and the Mississippi River. It's three stories, quaint, and has no elevator. Complimentary Continental breakfast. Some microwaves, some refrigerators. Cable TV. | 201 N. Access Rd. | 870/763–2300 or 800/378–7946 | fax 870/763–2300 | www.drury-inn.com | 51 rooms | $55–$65 | AE, D, DC, MC, V.

Hampton Inn. This standard chain accommodation off I–55 has an exterior stucco finish. The large lobby is warm and denlike, in cherry reds. The inn is next door to the Great Wall of China restaurant and within 2 mi of the industrial park and downtown shopping. You get discounts to the Ultimate Fitness Center less than 1 mi away. Picnic area, complimentary Continental breakfast. Cable TV, room phones. Outdoor pool. Pets allowed (fee). | 301 N. Access Rd. | 870/763–5220 or 800/426–7866 | fax 870/762–1397 | www.hampton-inn.com | 87 rooms | $63–$65 | AE, D, DC, V.

Holiday Inn Holidome. This brick and stucco Holiday Inn is in town, near Walker Park, where you can swim. Walker Park also has a picnic area and the county fair in September. The Holidome is full of plants, and used for parties and gatherings. You can rent a car at an on-site concierge desk. Restaurants, room service. Cable TV. Indoor-outdoor pools. Hot tub, steam room. Laundry facilities. Pets allowed. | 1121 E. Main St. | 870/763–5800 | fax 870/763–1326 | 153 rooms | $65–$68 | AE, D, DC, MC, V.

BUFFALO NATIONAL RIVER

MAP 11, C3

(Nearby towns also listed: Bull Shoals, Harrison, Jasper, Mountain Home, Mountain View)

The Buffalo National River, which cuts west to east through the heart of the Arkansas Ozarks, became the first federally protected waterway in 1972. Imposing limestone bluffs provide a curious, multihued backdrop—created from leaching minerals, lichens, ferns, and other flora. The free-flowing river is popular for float trips, with outfitters near almost every access point and nearby town, as well as anglers, hikers, horseback riders, picnickers, and those attracted by its swimming holes, wildflowers, fall foliage, and shimmering ice and snow in winter. Elk herds have been successfully reintroduced to the area. Along the Buffalo's banks lie historic sites—hollows, caves, and trails used by Native Americans, pioneers, Civil War soldiers, and outlaws; early homesteads and churches; the ghost of a mining boomtown; Civilian Conservation Corps works from the 1930s; and valleys where Ozark farmers still live in harmony with the land. Public and private campsites, plus rental cabins, motels, guest ranches, and commercial stables are scattered along the way.

Information: Buffalo National River | Box 1173, Harrison 72602-1173; it's right off Main Street in Harrison, inside the federal building on Walnut | 870/741–5443.

Attractions

Buffalo Point Ranger Station. You'll find rugged mountain scenery, nature trails to hidden springs and caves, river overlooks, swimming, fishing, naturalist programs in season, picnic pavilions, housekeeping cabins (Apr.–Nov.), river access, and RV and tent camping (electric and water Apr.–Oct.). The station is on Hwy. 14, between Yellville and Marshall. Look for signs. | 2229 Hwy. 268 E, Yellville | 870/449–4311 or 501/741–5443 | Free | Daily; visitors center daily 8–4:30.

Erbie. This unaddressed site includes a nearby cabin and farmstead, as well as a church. There are RV, tent, and equestrian camping (no hookups) as well as hiking and horse trails, picnic sites, swimming, fishing, and river access. It's 3 mi north of Jasper, off Hwy. 7, near the south bank of the Buffalo. Follow signs down a 6 mi gravel road to the site. | 870/446–5373 | Free | Daily.

Lost Valley. A 3-mi round-trip trail up bucolic Boxley Valley brings you to waterfalls and a cave. Historic homesteads, river access, and outfitters are nearby. Tent camping with no hookups is available; drinking water is available Apr.–Oct. Lost Valley is on Hwy. 43, 1 mi south of Ponca. There is no address or township. Look for signs. | 870/446–5373 or 870/741–5443 (headquarters) | Free | Daily.

Rush Historic District. The town of Rush was founded after the discovery of zinc in the 1880s. You can see the remains of homes and the ore smelter that make up the ghost town. Hiking trails and river access are available at all times. For camping, toilets are also always available, but drinking water is available Apr.–Oct. only. Off Hwy. 14 E, take Country Rd. 26, 21 mi south of Yellville, about 10 mi to Rush, then another 7 mi; the road dead ends at the river. | 870/449–4311 | Free | Daily.

Steel Creek Campground. This campground has high, scenic bluffs and a trailhead for wilderness hiking. Amenities include drinking water (Apr.–Oct.), vault toilets, fire grates, river access, equestrian campsites, and a horse trail. Canoeing in the spring, when the river is up, is quite popular. The campground is off Hwy. 74, between Jasper and Ponca. It's a steep dirt road, so you'll need a sturdy vehicle. | 870/741–5446, ext. 130 | Free | Daily.

Tyler Bend Visitor Center. This recreation area has campsites with no hookups (drinking water Apr.–Oct.), hiking trails with river views, several historic homesteads, picnic pavilions, and tables (some have a $50 charge), a nearby horse trail, and ranger-led interpretive programs in summer. The area is handicapped-accessible. After you turn right off Hwy. 65 at Silver Hill, you'll find the center 3 mi down the road on the left. | 870/439–2502 | Free | Visitors center daily 8–4:30.

BUFFALO NATIONAL
RIVER

INTRO
ATTRACTIONS
DINING
LODGING

ON THE CALENDAR

JUNE/JULY: *Buffalo River Elk Festival.* Celebrating the reintroduction of elk to Jasper in the early 1980s, this annual festival is held on a weekend near the Fourth of July. Entertainment includes an arts and crafts show, a Mustang car show, a fish contest, a wildlife exhibit, a Dutch-oven cook-off, a fishing derby, and music. In the past elk have been spotted in a meadow near Little Buffalo River. Call for dates and times. | 870/446–2455.

Lodging

Eagle's Nest Resort. The White River Scenic Railroad weaves through this resort, which is on the Bull Shoals and White rivers, 17 mi from Buffalo River. The 3-story building has an untreated cedar exterior. Camping and antiques shops are nearby. To get there, go south on Hwy. 14E. The resort is ½ mi outside town. Restaurant, complimentary Continental breakfast. Some in-room hot tubs. Cable TV. | Rte. 235, Yellville | 870/449–5050 | fax 870/449–4456 | mburrell@mtnhome.com | www.eagles-nestlodge.com | 20 rooms | $40–$90 | AE, D, DC, MC, V.

Misty Mountain Bed and Breakfast. This down-home country B&B is on scenic Hwy. 21 between Boxley Valley and Kingston. A two-story glass atrium with a panoramic view of Boxley Valley adds to the appeal of these 11 wooded acres. Complimentary Continental breakfast. Hot tub. No kids under 10. | HC 30, Kingston | 870/420–3731 | fax 870/420–3741 | mistymtn@yournet.com | www.mcrush.com/mistymountain | 3 rooms (2 with shared bath) | $55–$75 | D, MC, V.

Red Raven Inn. This is a lovely, restored Queen Anne/Victorian mansion on the river, with high ceilings, antiques, oak woodwork, and an art gallery. From the hotel bluff you can see Crooked Creek, which runs out back. Red Raven Inn is at the intersection of Hwy. 62E and Hwy. 14S. Picnic area, complimentary breakfast. No room phones, no TV in rooms, TV in common area. Library. No kids under 7. No smoking. | 359 E. Valley St., Yellville | 870/449–5168 | 5 rooms | $65–$95 | D, MC, V.

Silver Run Cabins. These traditional, Ozark-style cabins have long front porches, swings, and hardwood floors. Some rooms have fireplaces. The cabins are on Hwy. 14, just 1½ mi from Buffalo National River Park. Keep an eye out for signs. Kitchenettes, microwaves, refrigerators. No room phones. | 14 Silver Run Ln., Yellville | 870/449–6355 or 800/741–2022 (reservations) | 6 cottages (shower only) | $47–$75 | MC, V.

BULL SHOALS

(Nearby towns also listed: Buffalo National River, Harrison, Mountain Home)

Even though the man-made Bull Shoals Lake is almost 50 years old, it still seems off the beaten tourist track compared to the region's other U.S. Army Corps of Engineers lakes. In the namesake town of Bull Shoals and neighboring Lakeview you'll find family resorts, marinas, and campsites; the lake is stocked with lunker bass, crappie, and bream. The White River below the dam and at Cotter and nearby Crooked Creek are home to nationally known fighting rainbow and brown trout. At Bull Shoals Lake you can boat, waterski, swim, and scuba dive, or take advantage of the area's many antiques shops and auctions.

Information: **Bull Shoals Lake-White River Chamber of Commerce** | Box 354, 72619-0354 | 870/445–4443 | www.bullshoals.org.

Attractions

Bull Shoals State Park. Situated below the White River dam forming Bull Shoals Dam, park facilities here include picnic areas, pavilions, playgrounds, and trails; a trout dock with boat, motor, and canoe rentals; supplies, equipment, gifts; RV, tent and "Rent-A-Camp" sites; and rental RV. Take Hwy. 5N about 5 mi; then left (or west) on Hwy. 178; then go through the town of Lakeview and turn left at Powerhouse Road, which leads right on in to the camp grounds. | 129 Bull Shoals Park, Lakeview | 870/431–5521 | Free | Daily.

Mountain Village 1890 and Bull Shoals Caverns. This authentic Ozark village is a community of more than 15 restored buildings that were brought here from the region. Originally built and occupied by pioneers from 1830 to 1890, you can occasionally catch volunteers in period costumes. The caverns, which are 350,000 million years old, were used by prehistoric natives, Civil War soldiers, and others. They contain all the formations found in every other cave in the United States including Rare Boxwork and Cave Pearls. | 1011 CS Woods Blvd. | 870/445–7177 or 800/445–7177 | $9 for one attraction, $13.50 for both | Mar.–mid-May, Wed.– Sun. 10–5; mid-May–Labor Day, daily 9–6; Labor Day–Oct., Thurs.–Mon. 10–5; Nov., Fri.–Sun. 10–4.

White River Scenic Railroad. Restored 1940s passenger cars travel along the famous White River between Flippin and Calico Rock. You can board at Flippin or at Calico Rock from April through November. You can find the Flippin depot at the junction of Hwy. 62 and Hwy. 178, which is the main intersection on the west edge of town. | 800/305–6527 | www.trainfun.com | $24.50 | Round-trip from Flippin Apr.–Nov., Wed., Fri., Sat. 8:45 AM, Sun. 1:30 PM; round-trip from Calico Rock Apr.–Nov., Wed., Fri., Sat. 11 AM.

ON THE CALENDAR

JAN.: *Eagle Awareness Weekend.* Bull Shoals State Park, Gaston's White River Resort, and the Corps of Engineers join to celebrate the bald eagle and other winter wildlife of the Ozarks. There are barge tours to view eagles, as well as waterfowl tours, guided bird walks, guest speakers, owl prowls, and live music. Tours take place on the first weekend in the month. From Hwy. 62 at Flippin, take Hwy. 178 approx. 10 mi north to the park, or drive 6 mi north of Mountain Home on Hwy. 5 and go 8 mi west on Hwy. 178 to the park. Look for signs. | 870/431–5521 | Free.

APR.: *Ozark Springtime Wildflower Weekend.* This is a weekend of guided wildflower walks, lake cruises, and evening slide shows at Bull Shoals State Park. You can learn about medicinal uses of wildflowers while you enjoy their beauty. From Hwy. 62 at Flippin, take Hwy. 178 10 mi north to the park, or drive 6 mi north of Mountain Home on Hwy. 5 and go 8 mi west on Hwy. 178 to the park. Look for signs. | 870/431–5521 | Free.

MAY: *Ozark Birders' Springtime Retreat.* Catch the peak of spring migration in the Ozarks at Bull Shoals State Park. There are activities for beginning to advanced birders:

guided walks, evening slide programs, and basic birding clinics. From Hwy. 62 at Flippin, take Hwy. 178 10 mi north to the park, or drive 6 mi north of Mountain Home on Hwy. 5 and go 8 mi west on Hwy. 178 to the park. Look for signs. | 870/431–5521 | Free.

JUNE: *Troutfest.* World-famous trout fishing on the White River is the focus at Bull Shoals State Park in June; includes fly-tying seminars, trout cooking demonstrations, trout fishing workshops, and a Father's Day trout fishing tournament. From Hwy. 62 at Flippin, take Hwy. 178 10 mi north to the park, or drive 6 mi north of Mountain Home on Hwy. 5 and go 8 mi west on Hwy. 178 to the park. Look for signs. | 870/431–5521 | Free.

JULY: *Fireworks Firepower and Tons of Fun Celebration.* On the evening of the 4th of July, enjoy fireworks and concessions at Bull Shoals, plus prizes and certificates for horseshoe pitching, water balloon toss, and other activities at Bull Shoals State Park. From Hwy. 62 at Flippin, take Hwy. 178 10 mi north to the park, or drive 6 mi north of Mountain Home on Hwy. 5 and go 8 mi west on Hwy. 178 to the park. Look for signs. | 870/445–4424 or 870/431–5521.

SEPT.: *White River Days.* You can celebrate the White River at Bull Shoals State Park with events on ecology, history, and prehistory; or explore the river on guided canoe ($5.50 per person) and johnboat floats ($7.50 per person, plus gas). From Hwy. 62 at Flippin, take Hwy. 178 10 mi north to the park, or drive 6 mi north of Mountain Home on Hwy. 5 and go 8 mi west on Hwy. 178 to the park. Look for signs. | 870/431–5521 | Free except for the river tours.

Dining

Club 178. American. This is a resort-area restaurant featuring a 265-gallon freshwater aquarium. Wildlife photos and fish are mounted on the wall. Known for fresh fish and "refry," in which you can bring in your own fish to be cleaned, cooked, and served at your table. Karaoke night is the last Friday of the month. You can wear casual dress here. Brunch is served on Sundays. Kids' menu. The restaurant has smoking and nonsmoking sections. | 2109 Central Blvd. (Rte. 178) | 870/445–494 | Tue.–Sat., 11–10, Sun., 9:30–8 | $14–$28 | AE, MC, V | Closed Mon.

Connie's Café. American. You can eat home-style steaks, hamburgers, and catfish at this small eatery right across from the boat dock on Bull Shoals Lake. Service can get especially busy in the spring and summer as participants in the local bass-fishing tournaments stop by. Breakfast is served all day. | 1701 Central Blvd. | 870/445–8551 | Tues.–Sat., 6–8; Sun., 6–1; Mon., 6–2 | $6–$12 | No credit cards.

Village Wheel. American. Two dining rooms, including one with a covered wagon, serve a broad menu spanning broasted chicken, fried catfish, and liver and onions. The restaurant is known for homemade bread and pies. There is a salad bar. Kids' menu. It is 1 mi across from Bull Shoals Dam. | 1400 Central Blvd. (Rte. 178) | 870/445–4414 | $5–$25 | MC, V.

Lodging

Bel'arco Bull Shoals Resort. Bel'arco, built in 1955, has cabins and drive-up rooms within sight of Bull Shoals Lake. The rooms are standard, but the restaurant has a particularly nice view of the water. The resort is on Hwy. 178, at the south edge of town. Look for signs. Complimentary Continental breakfast. Some kitchenettes. Cable TV. Pool. Tennis. Basketball, gym. Playground. | 2 Crestline Dr. | 870/423–5253 or 870/445–4242 | fax 870/445–7123 | resort@belarco.com | www.belarco.com | 61 rooms | $45–$195, seasonal | AE, D, DC, MC, V.

Bull Mountain Resort. Rustic stone and log cottages with modern conveniences make up this resort, ¼ mi from Bull Shoals Lake by way of a charming lane. The resort is surrounded by 6 wooded acres and is on Hwy. 178, between Mountain Home and Harrison. Microwaves, refrigerators. Cable TV. Pool. Playground. | 2224 Central Blvd. | 870/445–5971 | fax 870/445–5972 | bullmtn@southshore.com | www.natco.southshore.com | 9 cottages | $45–$70 | AE, MC, V.

Gaston's White River Resort. At this modern, family riverside fishing resort, there's no lack of outdoor activities. The single-story buildings are surrounded by lots of woods and other vegetation. The staff here will show you the hot spots and the kitchen will pack you a box lunch for your outing; or you can enjoy a picnic, a cookout, and the riverside walk. There are two nature trails. To get there, take Hwy. 178 to Bull Shoals dam. The resort is 1½ mi beneath the dam on the river road. Bar, dining room, picnic area. In-room data ports, some kitchenettes, refrigerators. Cable TV. Pool. Tennis. Hiking. Dock, boating, fishing. Playground. Business services, airport shuttle. Pets allowed. | 1777 River Rd., Lakeview | 870/431–5202 | fax 870/431–5216 | 40 rooms, 35 cottages | $76–$120, $169 cottages | MC, V.

Grandview Lodge. You might hear a pin drop in this quiet, secluded area where five wood-frame and shingle-roofed cottages sit on a bluff 450 ft above recreation-friendly Bull Shoals Lake. Kitchenettes, microwaves, refrigerators. Cable TV. Outdoor pool. Dock, water sports, boating, fishing. No pets. | 120 Pinehurst Point | 870/445–4284 or 800/471–6104 | charley@grandviewlodge.net | www.grandviewlodge.net | 5 cottages | $70–$85 | MC, V.

Mar-Mar Resort and Crooked Creek Tackle. This "mosquito-free" hotel in the Ozarks is two blocks from the Bull Shoals boat dock. It's a good place to go if you like to fish, or if you want to visit Bull Shoals State Park. The L-shaped, single-level resort, built in the 1950s, is in the middle of town on Hwy. 178, which becomes Central Blvd. Look for the big white marquee with the fisherman rocking in a boat. Some kitchenettes. Cable TV. Pets allowed. | 1512 Central Blvd. (U.S. 178) | 870/445–4444 | fax 870/445–7173 | www.marmarresort.com/marmar/ | 13 rooms | $39 or $43 | AE, MC, V.

Rocky Hollow Lodge. These six stone and cedar cottages with hardwood floors and full kitchens have provided a Bull Shoals Lake–side experience since the 1950s. Within six blocks of Rocky Hollow there is a large marina with all types of watercraft rentals and a full service scuba shop. Picnic area. Kitchenettes, microwaves, refrigerators. Cable TV. Outdoor pool, lake. Volleyball. Dock, water sports, boating, fishing. Some pets allowed (fee). | 1306 Lake St. | 800/887–6259 or 870/445–4400 | rocky@southshore.com | www.bullshoals.com/rockyhollow | 6 rooms | $65–$90 | MC, V.

Shady Oaks. Guided fishing excursions and many other outdoor activities are available at this resort. Picnic area. Kitchenettes, microwaves, refrigerators. Pool, lake. Dock, water sports, boating, fishing. Video games. Playground. Laundry facilities. Pets allowed. | HC 62, Flippin | 870/453–8420 or 800/467–6257 | fax 870/453–7813 | 11 cottages | $60–$70 cottages | D, MC, V.

Sportsman's Resort. Trout fishing and boating along the White River are the main attractions at this 5½-acre resort. There is a view of the river and the area is rustic and wooded. There are some cabins and some connecting rooms, but no lodge. The resort is 4 mi from town off Hwy. 178. Follow the signs. Restaurant. Boating. | 458 MC 7004, Flippin | 870/453–2424 | dbspt@mtnhome.com | www.whiteriver.net/sportsmans | 22 rooms | $60–$75 | D, MC, V.

CAMDEN

MAP 11, C6

(Nearby towns also listed: Arkadelphia, Ashdown, El Dorado, Hope, Magnolia)

Camden was first settled in 1783 as a French trading post called Ecore Fabre, became a steamboat landing, and grew into one of the leading cotton shipping terminals in the South. It was the site of the Fort Lookout skirmish and the Battle of Poison Spring during the Civil War. Many antebellum and later homes have been restored, and its historic downtown is revitalized. You can fish in the Ouachita River and nearby White Oak Lake.

Information: Camden Area Chamber of Commerce | 314 Adams SW, 71701 | 870/836–6426 | www.camden.dina.org.

Attractions

Graham–Gaughan–Betts Home. This home, listed with the Smithsonian Institution, was built by Joseph Graham and his wife, Mary Washington Graham (the first cousin of George Washington), in 1856–58. The furnishings date back to the 17th century. | 710 Washington St. NW | 870/836–3125 | fax 870/836–2254 | $3–$7 | Advance notice needed to arrange tour.

McCollum–Chidester House and Museum. Built in the mid-19th century, the house was purchased by the well-to-do Colonel John T. Chidester, who operated stage and mail lines through Georgia, Alabama, and Mississippi, and from Arkansas to Fort Yuma, Arizona. During the Civil War, both Union and Confederate generals used it as headquarters. It is now a museum with tours. | 926 Washington St. NW | 870/836–9243 | $3 | Apr.–Oct., Wed.–Sat. 9–4.

Leake–Ingham Building. This former law office on the McCollum–Chidester grounds served as a Freedmen's Bureau after the Civil War and later became Camden's first community library. | 926 Washington St. NW | Included with admission to the McCollum–Chidester House | Apr.–Oct., Wed.–Sat. 9–4.

Oakland Cemetery. A marble obelisk surrounded by Confederate graves dominates Oakland Cemetery, which is rich in local history and culture. More than 200 Confederate soldiers are buried here. This is one of the oldest cemeteries in southern Arkansas, and includes several monuments unique to the period. | N. Adams Ave. and Pearl St. | Free | Daily.

Poison Spring Battleground Historical Monument. A diorama tells the story of the Union Army's unsuccessful Red River Campaign during the Civil War and the battle at Poison Spring. The monument is 14 mi northwest of town, between Camden and Chidester, on Hwy. 76. Look for signs. | 870/836–6426 | Free | Daily.

White Oak Lake State Park. The 725-acre park has tent and RV campsites, picnicking, hiking trails, interpretive programs, and great fishing. From I–30 at Prescott, travel 20 mi east on Hwy. 24 to Bluff City, then take Hwy. 299 approx. 100 yds before turning on Hwy. 387. The park is 2½ mi away. Watch for signs. | 986 Hwy. 387 W (Route 2), Bluff City | 870/685–2748 | Free | Daily.

ON THE CALENDAR

MAR.: *Daffodil Festival.* You can tour local gardens and antebellum homes, including an 8-acre estate with more than 1,000 varieties of daffodils and a Japanese-style garden. You can also find garden-related crafts, food vendors, live music, nature walks, storytellers, stagecoach and hay rides, a petting zoo, an antique car show, and sales of daffodil blooms and bulbs. There are buses for garden tours. The event takes place the second weekend in the month. The street festival is in downtown Camden. | 870/836–6426 or 870/836–0023.

Dining

Woods Place Restaurant. American. This family-owned restaurant serves a mean grilled catfish. One of the largest collections of Grapette soda bottles, dating back to the 1940s, is displayed in the main dining area. | 1173 W. Washington St. | 870/836–0474 | fax 870/836–2947 | $4–$9 | AE, MC, V.

Lodging

Airport Inn. This hostelry in East Camden is right next to Camden Municipal Airport. Restaurant. In-room data ports, some microwaves, some refrigerators. Cable TV, room phones. Outdoor pool. Laundry facilities. No smoking. | 2115 Hwy. 79N | 870/574–0400 | fax 870/574–0400 | 57 rooms | $35–$48 | AE, D, DC, MC, V.

Ramada Inn. In the morning, the sun rises over woods on the east side of this Ramada Inn, which is 5 mi from Camden airport. The inn is at the corner of "business 79" and Hwy. 70, off I–30. Restaurant, bar (with entertainment), complimentary breakfast, room service. Some refrigerators. Cable TV. Indoor pool. Exercise equipment. | 950 S. California Ave. | 870/836–8822 | 112 rooms | $54–$59 | AE, D, DC, MC, V.

Umsted House Bed and Breakfast. A 1923 Mediterranean-style house on the National Register with a landscaped garden. It is on a hill, off Hwy. 79, at the corner of Washington and California, near downtown. Complimentary breakfast. | 404 W. Washington St. | 870/836–9609 | www.umstedhouse.com | fax 870/836–0905 | 4 rooms | $50–$75 | AE.

CONWAY

MAP 11, C4

(Nearby towns also listed: Little Rock/North Little Rock, Morrilton, Searcy)

Conway is a growing community on the edge of the expanding Little Rock–North Little Rock metropolitan area. It was formed after the Civil War as a railroad town, on land deeded to the chief engineer of the Little Rock–Fort Smith Railroad, 5 mi east of Cadron, a late 18th-century French trading post and settlement on the Arkansas River. This Faulkner County seat is the home of Hendrix College, the University of Central Arkansas, and Central Baptist College. Antiques and other shops are nearby and Conway is home base for several large manufacturers and commercial interests.

Information: **Conway Area Chamber of Commerce** | 900 Oak Street, 72032 | 501/327–7788 | www.conwayarkcc.org.

Attractions

Cadron Settlement Park. This park along the Arkansas River has a loop trail that interprets early settlement. The park is on Hwy. 319, off Hwy. 64, 5 mi west of Conway. Watch for signs. | 501/329–2986 | Free | Daily.

Faulkner County Museum. Housed in an 1896 jail, this museum on the county courthouse grounds has exhibits on historical development, a log house, a Native American artifact exhibit, and a great example of the local "dogtrot" architecture. It's off Hwy. 40, at the downtown Conway exit. | 801 Locust St. | 501/329–5918 | Free | Tues.–Thurs. 1–4.

Woolly Hollow State Park. This park is tucked in forested Ozark foothills around Lake Bennett. You can visit a log home, walk a nature trail, participate in summer interpretive programs, camp at RV and tent sites, swim at a beach with lifeguards and a seasonal snack bar, eat at a picnic pavilion, and browse at a gift shop. Off I–40, take Hwy. 65N, go 11 mi to Greenbrier, then go 1 mi north of Greenbrier and turn right on Hwy. 285. Drive 6 mi and take a left into the park entrance. | 82 Woolly Hollow Rd., Greenbrier | 501/679–2098 | Free | Daily.

ON THE CALENDAR

MAR.: *Governor Conway Days.* This event, held on the last weekend of the month, commemorates the first governor of Arkansas, James Sevier Conway. You can attend a beauty pageant or an antiques show and sale; take in arts and crafts, a motorcycle show, or an antique car show; fish at a bass tournament on Lake Erling (the top bass lake in Arkansas); watch a parade or a baton twirling competition; or step out at a dance. The event is in Bradley, in the southwest corner of the state, at the intersection of Hwy. 160 and Hwy. 29. All of downtown Bradley is taken over and converted into a tent city. | 870/894–3554 | Free.

APR.–MAY: *Toad Suck Daze.* You can enjoy arts and crafts, carnival rides, concessions, a 10K run, basketball tournament, entertainment, a softball tournament, puppet shows, a pet show, as well as a "tour de toad" (a bike race), toad jumps, and toad runs at this monthlong festival held downtown (exit 127 off I–40). | 501/327–7788 | Free.

Dining

Amore Italian Restaurant. Italian. This softly lit trattoria serves such favorites as saltimbocca and mostacioli à la carbonara. Fresh flowers on the tables and a fountain in the center of the dining area add to the appeal of what the *Arkansas Times* has called the #1 Italian restaurant in Arkansas. It is 1 mi from I–40, near the University of Central Arkansas. | 505 Donghey Rd. | 501/327–6373 | Mon.–Thur., 11–9; Fri., 11–10; Sat., 5 PM–10 | $8–$23 | AE, D, DC, MC, V.

Fu Lin. Chinese. There's an inexpensive buffet at all meals, along with individually prepared dishes. This casual restaurant has lots of windows and is downtown, right across from the University of Central Arkansas. | 195 Farris Rd. | 501/329–1415 | $4–$9 | AE, D, MC, V | No lunch Sat., no dinner Sun.

Marketplace Grill. American. This warehouse-shape restaurant has a loud, bustling dining area. Among the favorite dishes is the fillet béarnaise. | 600 Skyline Dr. | 501/336–0011 | Sun.–Thur., 11–9:30; Fri.–Sat., 11–10:30 | $5–$17 | AE, D, DC, MC, V.

Yellow Daisy Tea Room and Restaurant. American. Different quiches are made fresh every day except Sunday in this downtown Conway restaurant. They serve breakfast and lunch; bacon, mushroom, ham, and cheddar cheese all find their way in, one way or another. Round-back, cushioned chairs make for comfortable seating. The Conway League of Artists is responsible for most of the portraits and paintings on the wall. | 1113 Oak St. | 501/513–2479 | Mon.–Fri., 10:30 AM–2:30 PM; Sat., 11–3 | $6–$9 | AE, MC, V.

Lodging

Best Western. This is a standard two-story brick building with simple conveniences, 5 mi from the Toadsuck Ferry Lock and Dam. It's on I–40 at exit 127. Restaurant. In-room data ports. Cable TV. Pool. Laundry facilities. Airport shuttle, free parking. Pets allowed. | 816 E. Oak | 501/329–9855 | fax 501/327–6110 | 70 rooms | $59–$69 | AE, D, DC, MC, V.

Comfort Inn. This two-level standard hotel is across from a sports center and atop a sloping rock formation on U.S. 65. From Little Rock, take I–40E, then take a right onto Hwy. 65. The inn is visible from the road. Complimentary Continental breakfast. Cable TV. Pool. Business services. Pets allowed. | 150 U.S. 65N | 501/329–0300 | fax 501/329–8367 | 58 rooms, 2 suites | $56–$59, $109 suites | AE, D, DC, MC, V.

Days Inn. Pink brick, with all outside access, this typical chain hotel is close to many area attractions. Go west on I–40, take a right on exit 127, and look for it from a block away. If coming east, take a left. Complimentary Continental breakfast. In-room data ports. Cable TV. Pool. Business services. Pets allowed (fee). | 1002 E. Oak St. | 501/450–7575 | fax 501/450–7001 | 58 rooms | $47–$55 | AE, D, DC, MC, V.

Howard Johnson Inn. This chain hotel is 30 mi north of Little Rock. Restaurant. In-room data ports, some microwaves, some refrigerators. Cable TV, room phones. Indoor pool. Hot tub. Exercise equipment. Laundry facilities, laundry service. Business services. | 1090 Skyline Dr. | 501/329–2961 or 800/446–4656 | fax 501/329–7131 | www.hojo.com | 105 rooms, 3 suites | $49–$75 | AE, D, DC, MC, V.

Motel 6. This standard 2-story stopover is 6 mi from swimming and other outdoor recreation at Beaver Fork Lake, and 4–5 mi from Lake Conway. It's older but nice. It's off I–40, on Hwy. 65 at exit 125. Pool. | 1105 U.S. 65N | 501/327–6623 | fax 501/327–2749 | 88 rooms | $32–$38 (add $3 for each additional person) | AE, D, DC, MC, V.

Olde Towne Bed & Breakfast. This redbrick 1922 Colonial Revival, listed in the National Register of Historic Places, is adorned with period furniture and original landscape paintings. All rooms have queen-size beds and some have fireplaces. Dining room, complimentary Continental breakfast. In-room data ports, some in-room hot tubs. Cable TV, room phones. Laundry facilities. No pets. No kids under 19. No smoking. | 567 Locust Ave. | 501/329–6989 | oldtown@conwaycorp.net | www.oldetownebb.com | 2 rooms, 2 suites | $75, $95 suites | MC, V.

Ramada Inn. L-shaped, with exterior halls and a circular driveway, this hotel has catfish and trout fishing 2–3 mi away at Lake Conway. You can play tennis, soccer, and baseball in the nearby 5th Avenue Park. You can get there via I–40 to exit 127. Restaurant, room service. In-room data ports, some refrigerators. Cable TV. Pool. Business services. Pets allowed. | 815 E. Oak St. | 501/329–8392 | fax 501/329–0430 | 78 rooms | $50–$59 | AE, D, DC, MC, V.

DUMAS

MAP 11, D6

(Nearby towns also listed: Pine Bluff, Stuttgart)

The country music hit "I'm a Ding Dong Daddy from Dumas" immortalized this Mississippi Delta town. The South's largest cotton warehouse is here, as well as a 1940s soda fountain, and a department store established in 1925. Memorials and monuments at Rowher, 23 mi southeast on Route 1, mark the site of a World War II Japanese internment camp.

Information: Dumas Chamber of Commerce | 165 S. Main St., Box 431, 71639-0431 | 870/ 382–5447.

Attractions
Desha County Museum. Seven restored buildings—including a "shotgun house," an 1840s log house, a plantation commissary, and a bank—recreate life in a typical south Arkansas farming community. The tour takes a good 2 hrs. The museum is three blocks east of Hwy. 165. Look for signs or for the large war memorial in front. | 870/382–4222 or 870/382–6403 | Free | Tues., Thurs., Sun. 2–4; also tours by appointment.

Wilbur D. Mills Park. RV and tent camping with flush toilets, water, hot showers, boat ramp, and dump stations is available here. The park has 21 camp sites, with 30-amp electrical access. There's a charge for overnight camping and for boat launch. The Park is 11 mi north of Dumas on Hwy. 165, and just south of the Arkansas River. | State Hwy. 212 | 870/534–0451 | Free | Mar.–Nov.

White River National Wildlife Refuge. You'll find the largest remaining tract of bottomland hardwoods (160,000 acres) in the state and more than 350 lakes here. You can hunt and fish, or observe birds and wildlife. A number of primitive campsites are available. Call the main office for directions. | 321 West 7th St., Dewitt | 870/946–1468 | www.fws.gov/~r4eao | Free | Daily.

ON THE CALENDAR
JULY: *Ding Dong Daddy Days.* A parade, concessions, volleyball, basketball, dancing, a 5K run, a pancake breakfast, musical entertainment, tennis, kids' games, and water games take place in the city park during the last full weekend of the month. At the park near downtown. Just follow the signs or follow the parade. | 870/382–5447.

Dining
The Diner. American. You can't ask for a better landmark than a '57 Chevy mural painted on the outside wall. Inside, this 1960s-style diner has small Chevrolet and Ford models on shelves near the dining area. The grilled chicken salad goes over well. | 724 Hwy. 65S | 870/ 382–1000 | $6–$7 | No credit cards | Breakfast also available. No supper.

Lodging
Days Inn. You'll find standard accommodations at this stucco, two-story motor hotel. Complimentary Continental breakfast. Some in-room hot tubs. Pool. | 501 U.S. 65S | 870/ 382–4449 | fax 870/382–4449 | 63 rooms | $50–$60 | AE, D, DC, MC, V.

Executive Inn. This family-run, ivory-brick motel is 10 mi from the Mississippi River. Shopping is available next door. Restaurants, room service. Some microwaves, some refrigerators. Cable TV. Pool. | 310 U.S. 65S | 870/382–5115 | fax 870/382–5115 | 57 rooms | $34–$40 | AE, D, DC, MC, V.

Regency Inn. This is your standard motor hotel—two-story, brick, neither new nor old—easily accessed from the highway. Cable TV. Pool. | 722 U.S. 65S | 870/382–2707 | 50 rooms | $32–$38 | AE, D, DC, MC, V.

EL DORADO

MAP 11, C7

(Nearby towns listed: Camden, Magnolia)

In 1843 El Dorado was a rough trading post whose site was chosen as the seat of Union County. In 1902 it was the scene of a dramatic gunfight stemming from a family feud. On January 10, 1921, in a cotton field 1 mi south of town, a gusher of an oil well blew in black gold. Almost overnight, El Dorado's population swelled from 3,000 to 25,000—gamblers and criminals along with hardworking folks. You can still see remnants of oil-boom days by driving through the small towns of Smackover, Standard Umstead, and Norphlet just north of El Dorado.

As El Dorado tamed down, city fathers could afford the fine buildings at the heart of today's busy downtown, as well as in the surrounding neighborhoods with their imposing churches and substantial homes. The main square and streets radiating from it are filled with specialty shops—antiques, crafts, collectibles—and dining spots, including a casual-elegant restaurant, a diner decked out in oil-era memorabilia, and an Italian delicatessen and gourmet grocery. A drugstore has kept its 1920s marble soda fountain.

Information: El Dorado Chamber of Commerce | 201 N. Jackson, 71730 | 870/863–6113 | www.boomtown.org.

EL DORADO

INTRO
ATTRACTIONS
DINING
LODGING

Attractions

Arkansas Museum of Natural Resources. This museum tells the exciting story of the wild boom days after the discovery of oil, with rigs, derricks, a power station, and other oilfield units outside. The museum is on Hwy. 7, approx. 10 mi north of El Dorado. It bypasses the town of Smackover. | 3853 Smackover | 870/725–2877 | Free | Weekdays 8–5, Sat. 9–5, Sun. 1–5.

Moro Bay State Park. This is one of the most popular fishing and water sport areas in south-central Arkansas, with RV and tent campsites, picnic areas, a marina, a store, two playgrounds, two trails, and the Moro Bay Ferry exhibit. Moro Bay is 23 mi north of El Dorado. Turn off Hwy. 63 onto Hwy. 600. | 6071 Hwy. 600, Jersey | 870/463–8555 | Free | Daily.

South Arkansas Arts Center. The South Arkansas Arts Center has a gallery, a theater, performing arts, and workshops. The Arts Center is off Hwy. 7 in the middle of town, one block north of Northwest Ave. | 110 E. 5th | 870/862–5474 | fax 870/862–4921 | Free | Daily 9–5.

ON THE CALENDAR
JUNE–AUG.: *Showdown at Sunset.* Every Saturday evening at 6, downtown at the courthouse, actors reenact a 1902 shoot-out that left three men dead and two seriously wounded. Local legend has it that it all stemmed from a feud involving a love triangle between an affluent family and the city marshall. There's live country music before and after the gunfight. | 870/881–4190 | Free.
JULY: *Juried Competition in Visual Arts.* Artists from around the country show selected works at the South Arkansas Arts Center on the first weekend of the month. The show is off Hwy. 7 in the middle of town, one block north of Northwest Ave. | 870/862–5474 | Free.
DEC.: *Christmas Parade.* This parade, which takes place on the first Thursday of the month on Northwest Ave., the main drag through town, is billed as the largest Christmas parade in Arkansas. It has more than 150 entries, 10 bands, large and small floats, walking groups, cars, trucks, horses, and Santa Claus. Prizes are awarded in all divisions. | 870/863–6113.

Dining

Fay Wrays. American. Along with grilled chicken pasta, crispy noodle–wrapped shrimp, and Maryland crab cakes, there is King Kong memorabilia, including posters, plates, and a miniature statue of the Empire State Building. This one-room eatery, across from the city courthouse, has black-and-white linen tablecloths and napkins; artwork on the walls is for sale. | 110 Elm St. | 870/863–4000 | Tues.–Thur., 5 PM–9; Fri.–Sat., 5–10 | $13–$25 | AE, D, MC, V.

La Bella's Gourmet Delicatessen. Delicatessen. At La Bella's you can order homemade stone-baked pizza and sip one of the 30 different coffees with your dessert. This two-story establishment has a large upstairs banquet hall and a front porch dining area overlooking the city courthouse and the monument of a Confederate soldier marching south. | 101 E. Main St. | 870/862–4335 | Mon.–Thur., 8 AM–9 PM; Fri.–Sat., 8–10 | $4–$7 | AE, D, MC, V.

Lodging

Best Western Kings Inn Conference Center. A big property, the landscape spreads out to hold three brick buildings. This chain hotel is 20 min from Big Sky Airport. There is a recreation facility and pool as well as a full-service restaurant. The hotel, which has a beautiful atrium, is close to golf, Moro Bay State Park, and local museums. The Conference Center is at the intersection of Hwy. "82 business" and Hwy. 167, on the southwest side of town. Restaurant, picnic areas, room service. Refrigerators. Cable TV. Indoor-outdoor pools, wading pool. Hot tub, sauna. Tennis court. Racquetball. Laundry facilities. Business services, airport shuttle, free parking. Pets allowed. | 1920 Junction City Rd. | 870/862–5191 | fax 870/863–7511 | www.bestwestern.com | 131 rooms | $57–$71 | AE, D, DC, MC, V.

Comfort Inn. This is a typical chain hotel 10 min from shopping, movie theaters, and restaurants downtown at "The Square," right off the bypass of "business 82" and Hwy. 167. Complimentary Continental breakfast. In-room data ports. Cable TV. Pool. Hot tub. Laundry facilities. Airport shuttle. Pets allowed. | 2303 Junction City Rd. | 870/863–6677 | fax 870/863–8611 | 70 rooms | $60–$71 | AE, D, DC, MC, V.

Days Inn. Comfortable accommodations in a motor hotel design near the mall and airport, on "business 82." Bar, complimentary Continental breakfast. Pool. Business services. | 301 W. Hillsboro St. | 870/862–6621 | fax 870/862–6621 | 90 rooms | $45–$49 | AE, D, DC, MC, V.

El Dorado Inn Motel. This brick motel is ½ mi from a Super Wal-Mart. Take the first El Dorado exit as you're heading south on Hwy. 167. Some microwaves, refrigerators, some in-room hot tubs. Cable TV, room phones. Laundry facilities. | 3019 N.W. Ave. | 870/862–6676 | fax 870/862–6676 | 44 rooms | $30–$40 | AE, D, MC, V.

Hampton Inn. This three-story, stucco Hampton Inn is at the junction of Hwy. 167 and Hwy. 82B near the industrial loop. Complimentary Continental breakfast. In-room data ports, some kitchenettes, microwaves, refrigerators. Cable TV, room phones. Outdoor pool. Hot tub. Gym. Laundry facilities, laundry service. Business services. No pets. | 2312 Junction City Rd. | 870/862–1800 or 800/426–7866 | fax 870/863–7292 | www.hamptoninn-suites.com | 65 rooms | $66–$77 | AE, D, DC, V.

EUREKA SPRINGS

MAP 11, B2

(Nearby towns also listed: Bentonville, Berryville, Fayetteville, Harrison, Rogers, Springdale)

Eureka Springs has been a tourist town since its earliest days as a Victorian-era spa. Shady streets zigzag up the sides of Ozark hollows, revealing old-fashioned small-town homes, fences of limestone walls, lush gardens, and fern-lined springs.

You can choose from more than 50 B&Bs, 60 motels and hotels, cabins and campsites, and places to eat from down-home barbecue spots to casual-elegant Continental restaurants. The town serves as a backdrop for family holidays, weekend getaways, and romantic weddings and honeymoons. You can take scenic mountain drives, visit colorful caverns, and take part in many outdoor activities. The town's schedule is packed with music, crafts and other shows, festivals, and events, and you can find great shopping in arts, crafts, and antiques galleries, boutiques, and gift shops.

Information: Eureka Springs Chamber of Commerce and Visitor Information Center | 137 W. Van Buren, 72632 | 501/253–8737 | www.eurekasprings.org or www.eurekaspringschamber.com.

Attractions

Eureka Springs Gardens. Thirty-three acres of colorful botanical gardens sprawl up hillsides above a spring that overlooks the White River. The Gardens are on Scenic Hwy., 5½ mi from Hwy. 62 West. | 501/253–9256 | $6.45 | Apr., daily 8–5; May–Nov., daily 8–6.

Eureka Springs Historical Museum. You can view mementos, furnishings, photos, and other artifacts that tell about the colorful past and people of this Victorian village. From Hwy. 62, turn onto Hwy. 23N. The museum is the first three-story stone building on the left. | 95 S. Main St. | 501/253–9417 | $2.50 | Mon.–Sat., 9:30–4 PM; Sun. 12–4 PM; Closed Christmas.

Frog Fantasies. A frogs-only gift shop and 60-yr family collection of the amphibians in all sizes and materials. Guided tours are available. The shop is downtown in the historic district (called the "historic loop"), a block north of the post office. | 151 Spring St. | 501/253–7227 | $1 | 10–5 PM.

The Great Passion Play. This outdoor drama of Christ's final week, billed as one of the biggest draws in the state, is performed from Apr. through Oct. by a cast of hundreds, with animals and state-of-the-art sound delivery. If you have 2 extra hr you can take "The New Holy Land Tour," which includes 40 exhibits and reproductions of biblical scenes. | 935 Passion Play Rd. | 800/882–7529 | www.greatpassionplay.com.

At the **Bible Museum,** on the grounds of the Great Passion Play Road, you can view a collection of rare Bibles and manuscripts. | 800/882–7529 | $2.50 | Year-round, please call for times.

The **Sacred Arts Center** houses religious artwork. | 800/882–7529 | $2.50 | Please call for times.

Also on the grounds of the Great Passion Play Road is the seven-story **Christ of the Ozarks** statue, which is the second-largest statue of Christ in the world. | 800/882–7529 | $17.50 or $15.50 | The last Sat. in April through the last Sat. in Oct.; closed Sun. and Wed.

The **New Holy Land Tour** takes you through 40 biblical scenes, including a life-size reproduction of Moses's Tabernacle in the Wilderness. A tram takes you around 50 acres; there is some walking. The whole tour takes 2 hr. | 800/882–7529 or 501/253–9200 | $8.50 | Apr. 28–Oct. 28, Mon.–Sat. 9–3:30; closed Sun. and Wed.

Hammond Museum of Bells. This is a collection of musical, animal, historical, archaeological, Oriental, temple, religious, ship, and railroad bells. Bells and tuned wind chimes are available in Collectabells Bell Shop. The museum is downtown, across from the post office. | 2 Pine St. | 501/253–7411 | $3 | Apr.–Nov., daily 9:30–5.

Onyx Cave. You can explore the Onyx Cave and take radio-guided tours of the underground formations. There's a gift shop for souvenir hunters. The cave is 5 min from downtown; look for the numerous signs. | 338 Onyx Cave La. | 501/253–9321 | $3.75 | Mar., Apr., daily 8–5; May–Oct., daily 8–6; Nov., daily 8–4; Dec., Jan., Feb., weekends 8–6 PM, weather permitting. Call first.

Thorncrown Chapel. The stunning architecture of this 48-ft-tall glass chapel with 425 windows takes advantage of its setting deep in a woodland. In 2000, the American Institute of Architects voted the chapel one of the top 10 buildings of the 20th century. The chapel is about 3 mi west of downtown. | 12968 Hwy. 62W | 501/253–7401 | www.thorncrown.com | Donations only | Daily. Call for a schedule of services; there are "mini" services for tours during the week.

Turpentine Creek Wildlife Refuge. A shelter and rescue for lions, tigers, and other large cats in distress anywhere in the United States. It's 7 mi outside of town on Hwy. 23. | 239 Turpentine Creek La. | 501/253–5841 | $10 | Every day except Christmas, 9–dusk.

SIGHTSEEING TOURS/TOUR COMPANIES

Belle of the Ozarks. "The best kept secret in Eureka Springs," this excursion boat floats along 12 mi of Beaver Lake shoreline, providing a history of the lake, the Ozarks, and local Native American heritage. The boat also sails around the largest island in the lake, which is a wildlife game preserve. The trip takes 75 min and is a 30-min drive from town. Take Hwy. 62 west to Hwy. 187, then take Hwy. 187 to Mundell Road, which ends at Starkey Park. | Starkey Marina off U.S. 62W | 800/552–3803 or 501/253–6200 | $12 | May–Oct., daily 11, 1, 3, and a 7 PM sunset cruise. Closed on Wed.

Eureka Springs and North Arkansas Railway. Vintage steam locomotives and passenger cars chug into the Ozarks from a historic depot. The railway is on the outskirts of town, on Hwy. 23N. | 299 N. Main St. | 501/253–9623 | $8 | Apr.–Oct., Mon.–Sat. 9–5.

Eureka Springs Trolley. You can ride up and down the steep hills to shopping and attractions on five different routes. Tickets are on sale at the downtown depot, lodgings, and many shops. The trolley is on the edge of town, on Hwy. 62. | 81 Kingsway | 501/253–9572 | $3.50 | May–Dec., Sun.–Fri. 9–5, Sat. 9–8. Please call for more detailed dates and times.

ON THE CALENDAR

JAN.: *Eagle Watch Weekend on Beaver Lake.* On the last weekend of the month, the *Belle of the Ozarks* runs eagle-watch cruises that include guides, lectures, and plenty of bald eagles on this 50-passenger boat. There are three 2-hr cruises a day (10 AM, 12 PM, 3 PM), and they sell out quickly. The trips leave from Rockybranch Marina, just off Hwy. 12, 12 mi east of the town of Rogers on Beaver Lake. | 501/253–6200 or 800/552–3803.

MAR., APR.: *Easter Sunrise Service.* A 7 AM service on Easter Sunday with special speakers and music takes place at the Christ of the Ozarks statue. The service is approx. ¼ mi past the ticket office on the grounds of the Great Passion Play, which is off Hwy. 62 at the end of Passion Play Rd. | 501/253–8559 | Easter.

APR.–OCT.: *The Great Passion Play.* This is an outdoor drama of Christ's final week. An admission fee is charged and package deals for the New Holy Land tour, Sacred Arts Center, Bible Museum, and buffet meal are available. | 800/882–7529 | Last Fri. of Apr.–last Fri. of Oct.

MAY: *Fine Arts Festival.* The month kicks off with the "Art-Rageous" parade, and later includes a gallery tour called "White Street walk," in which local artists open their homes and studios to show their work while providing food and drink (every Fri. and Sat. evening). You'll find plenty of exhibitions, workshops, special arts events, contests, and other activities along the main drag of this suddenly big small town. You can walk, or grab the open air trolley. | 501/253–5366.

JUNE: *Blues Festival.* All along the main drag of this small town, afternoons and into the night, national blues acts perform traditional, acoustic, and electric music at the town's historic ballrooms, clubs, and city auditorium. There is free transportation. Call early for more information and tickets. | 501/253–5366.

JUNE, JULY: *Opera in the Ozarks.* Since 1950, an international cast has presented three major productions "in rep" with orchestra at Inspiration Point. Seating is reserved. | 501/253–8595 or 501/253–8737 | swig@ipa.net | www.opera.org.

AUG.: *Yards and Yards of Yard Sales.* During the second weekend of the month, more than 60 yard sales spring up all over town. | 501/253–7614 or 501/253–8737.

SEPT.: *Jazz Festival.* World-renowned jazz musicians perform at free concerts throughout town; there are some ticketed performances, so you should call in advance if you have particular artists or venues in mind. | 501/253–6258 | www.jazzman.cc.

OCT. *Original Ozark Folk Festival.* Begun in 1966, this street fair includes noted folk performers in concerts given throughout town during the fall season. The Barefoot Ball is worth special note. | 501/253–5366 or 501/253–8737.

KODAK'S TIPS FOR PHOTOGRAPHING LANDSCAPES AND SCENERY

Landscape
- Tell a story
- Isolate the essence of a place
- Exploit mood, weather, and lighting

Panoramas
- Use panoramic cameras for sweeping vistas
- Don't restrict yourself to horizontal shots
- Keep the horizon level

Panorama Assemblage
- Use a wide-angle or normal lens
- Let edges of pictures overlap
- Keep exposure even
- Use a tripod

Placing the Horizon
- Use low horizon placement to accent sky or clouds
- Use high placement to emphasize distance and accent foreground elements
- Try eliminating the horizon

Mountain Scenery: Scale
- Include objects of known size
- Frame distant peaks with nearby objects
- Compress space with long lenses

Mountain Scenery: Lighting
- Shoot early or late; avoid midday
- Watch for dramatic color changes
- Use exposure compensation

Tropical Beaches
- Capture expansive views
- Don't let bright sand fool your meter
- Include people

Rocky Shorelines
- Vary shutter speeds to freeze or blur wave action
- Don't overlook sea life in tidal pools
- Protect your gear from sand and sea

In the Desert
- Look for shapes and textures
- Try visiting during peak bloom periods
- Don't forget safety

Canyons
- Research the natural and social history of a locale
- Focus on a theme or geologic feature
- Budget your shooting time

Rain Forests and the Tropics
- Go for mystique with close-ups and detail shots
- Battle low light with fast films and camera supports
- Protect cameras and film from moisture and humidity

Rivers and Waterfalls
- Use slow film and long shutter speeds to blur water
- When needed, use a neutral-density filter over the lens
- Shoot from water level to heighten drama

Autumn Colors
- Plan trips for peak foliage periods
- Mix wide and close views for visual variety
- Use lighting that accents colors or creates moods

Moonlit Landscapes
- Include the moon or use only its illumination
- Exaggerate the moon's relative size with long telephoto lenses
- Expose landscapes several seconds or longer

Close-Ups
- Look for interesting details
- Use macro lenses or close-up filters
- Minimize camera shake with fast films and high shutter speeds

Caves and Caverns
- Shoot with ISO 1000+ films
- Use existing light in tourist caves
- Paint with flash in wilderness caves

From *Kodak Guide to Shooting Great Travel Pictures* © 2000 by Fodor's Travel Publications

DEC.: *The Candlelight Christmas Tour of Victorian Homes.* You can tour several of the town's historic homes, decked out for the holidays, with costumed guides. The tour has been sponsored by the Eureka Springs Preservation Society since 1982. | 501/253–7525 | william@ipa.net | $10.

Dining

Bavarian Inn Restaurant German. Traditional Chez-German restaurant with an alpine atmosphere inside a Swiss chalet. Specialties include rye bread, smoked bratwurst, and homemade apple strudel. | 325 W. Van Buren | 501/253–8128 | Daily 5–9 PM | $11–$17 | MC, V.

Bubba's. Barbecue. Pork shoulder and ribs are the specialties at this frame cottage converted into a barbecue shack. It has counter and booth seating, whimsical memorabilia, and an acclaimed pit barbecue, along with nachos and special sandwiches. Beer is the only alcoholic beverage, and there is no smoking. | 60 Kings Hwy. | 501/253–7706 | $4–$19 | No credit cards | Sun.

Café Luigi. Italian. This restaurant's salad dressings and breads are homemade. It's next to the Historical Museum and you can eat inside or on the outdoor patio. | 91 S. Main St. | 501/253–6888 | Sun.–Thurs. 11–9; Fri. and Sat. 11–10 | $10–$15 | AE, D, DC, MC, V.

C C Cinnamon American. You can sit on an outdoor deck overlooking downtown Eureka and munch on cinnamon rolls. There is also a baked potato bar and sandwiches for lunch. | 12½ S. Main St. | 501/253–8004 | Daily 9–5 | $3–$6 | No credit cards | Jan. and Feb.

Center Street Restaurant & Bar. Pan-Latin. If you relish fiery food, the 7-salsa platter might be the way to go. Enchiladas and grilled fish are served in this circa 1889 building of original limestone-cut walls. There is a natural spring and grotto behind the bar, strings of chiles hanging from the ceiling, and an upstairs dance floor with live music on Friday and Saturday nights. | 10 Center St. | 501/253–8102 | Fri.–Mon., 6 PM–10 PM | $4–$14 | MC, V.

★ **Chez Charles.** Contemporary. The restaurant, off the lobby of the Grand Central Hotel, serves innovative dishes, such as lump crab cakes with spicy crawfish sauce, pork tenderloin with chutney sauce, duck breast, mushroom torta, and brownie delight. Smoking is not allowed. Chez Charles is downtown, on Hwy. 23N, which turns into Main St. | 37 N. Main St. | 501/253–9509 | Reservations essential | Mon., Thur.–Sat., seatings 6 PM and 9 PM; Sun., seating 7 PM only | $55–$70 | D, MC, V | Closed Tues., Wed. No lunch.

Crest Restaurant. American. This is home to the original "all-you-can-eat catfish" place around Eureka Springs. Pictures of local attractions fill the walls of this restaurant 4 mi west of town. | 14581 Hwy. 62W | 501/253–9113 | Tues.–Sun., 8–8 | $9–$17 | AE, D, MC, V.

DeVito's Restaurant. Italian. You can sit in the elegant dining room or the enclosed glass porch and indulge in Italian food made from scratch using family recipes. Two good choices are the broiled boneless butterfly trout topped with fresh basil sauce and parmesan cheese, and the jumbo shrimp sautéed in lemon butter, fresh pressed garlic, and white wine on a bed of pasta. | 5 Center St. | 501/253–6807 | $15–$16 | AE, D, MC, V | Closed Wed.

Ermilio's Italian Home Cooking. Italian. At Ermilio's you can choose from an assortment of steaks, including filet mignon; chicken and fish; or pasta with any one of 10 sauces. Flowers, drapes, and old family pictures give this restaurant a homey quality. | 26 White St. | 501/253–8806 | Daily, 5 PM–9 PM | $8–$13 | MC, V.

ES & NA Railway. American. That's Eureka Springs and Northern Arkansas, in case you were wondering. This dining car, drawn by a 1926 restored diesel locomotive, offers an unusual lunch or dinner experience over 4½ scenic mi of Ozark valleys and streams. Prime rib and baked chicken are featured meals, with flame-baked Alaska before your "trip" is over. | 299 N. Main St. | 501/253–9623 | Reservations essential | Mon.–Sat., lunch noon–2; dinner 5–8 | $25 | AE, D, MC, V.

Forest Hill Restaurant. American. A wood-fire oven and an open kitchen let you observe the preparation of prime-grade steaks and burgers. Pictures of Arkansas landscapes hang from the walls, and a gift shop lets you take home local art. | 3016 Van Buren St. | 501/253–2422 | Daily, 7 AM–9 PM. | $8–$16 | AE, D, MC.

Gaskins Cabin. American. This restaurant in the historic 1864 home of John Gaskins serves American dishes with a French flair. | Hwy. 23N | 501/253–5466 | Reservations recommended | $8–$13 | MC, V | Sun., Mon. Dinner only.

Gazebo Restaurant. American. At this restaurant you can sit in the sunken, white-rail gazebo in the center of the dining area and eat prime rib and chicken Alfredo, among other dishes. | 101 E. Van Buren St. | 501/253–9551; 800/221–3344 | Mar.–Nov., daily, 7:30 AM–1 PM; dinner, 4:30–8 | $9–$17 | AE, D, DC, MC, V.

Grandma's Beans & Cornbread Southern. This country-style home-cooking restaurant sits next to the Pine Mountain Jamboree. As the name suggests, the highlight of the menu is beans and cornbread, also served with cobblers and soups. | 200 Village Cir. | 501/253–6561 | Daily except Sun., 11–8 | $2–$3 | No credit cards.

The Horizon. Italian. Italian food, seafood, and Continental cuisine are served at this restaurant with views of Beaver Lake. Signature dishes include the salmon grilled and flaked into a caper and cream sauce tossed over linguine; the fresh shrimp sautéed with julienne peppers, mushrooms, and green onion, served with pasta on the side; and the tender veal sautéed with marsala wine with mushrooms. | Mundell Rd. | 501/253–5525 | $10–$15 | MC, V | Sun.

Hungry Hare. American. Breakfast and lunch are served in a garden-like setting. You can choose from soups and salads, burgers and sandwiches, and homemade desserts. | Pine Mountain Village, Hwy. 62E | 501/253–8222 | Daily except Mon., breakfast and lunch only | $6–$7 | AE, D, MC, V.

Hylander Steak and Rib. American. This 1950s-style place has a glass-enclosed dining room where smoked prime rib is served; it is also known for fresh rainbow trout. Kids' menu. | 309 W. Van Buren | 501/253–7360 | Open daily except Tue. Dinner only | $12–$26 | AE, D, MC, V.

Jim & Brent's Bistro. American. This restaurant was built inside an Old Victorian home and still has deck and porch seating. It specializes in filet mignon, roast duck, and pork tenderloin Parmesan. | 173 S. Main St. | 501/253–7457 | Fri.–Wed., 5 PM–1 PM | $15–$26 | AE, D, MC, V.

Mama Serra's Spaghetti. Italian. At Mama Serra's you can sit inside a screened-in porch and choose from such dishes as shrimp scampi, linguine, clams, and manicotti. There is also a family-style "all you can eat" spaghetti dinner with bread, soup, and salad. | 3064 Van Buren St. | 501/253–2345 | Fri.–Sun., noon–8:30 | $4–$9 | D, MC, V.

Mud Street Café. American. The centerpiece of the dining room here is a turn-of-the-century oak bar with beveled mirrors. You will find local art on the walls, oak tables and chairs, Victorian-style carpeting, and a cozy sitting area with magazines and newspapers. House specialties are the chicken marinara, homemade soups, and chicken florentine; you might also want to try the croissant sandwiches and California wrap. | 22 S. Main St. | 501/253–6732 | $4–$8 | AE, D, MC, V | Wed. No dinner.

Myrtie Mae's. American. This place has been around since the 1920s and is known for strip steak, rainbow trout, red snapper, barbecue breast of chicken, and veal cutlet. You can take in a view of the Ozark valley while you eat. | 207 W. Van Buren | 501/253–9768 | $8–$15 | AE, D, MC, V.

The Oasis. Mexican. If you've never heard of Ark-Mex cuisine, you might want to introduce yourself by ordering the Spinach mushroom enchiladas or the deluxe huevos rancheros. Tiny wood stoves get the job done. Local art, drawings, and articles about local people cover the walls in this casual dining environment. | 53C Spring St. | 501/253–0886 | Daily, 10 AM–2:30; dinner Fri.–Sat., 5:30–8:30 | $3–$7 | No credit cards.

Old Town Pub. American. Blues festival posters and Southwestern art enliven this casual spot that dishes up sandwiches, homemade fries, and the occasional surprise, such as fried codfish baskets and a classic grilled Reuben. It is known for half-pound hamburgers. Beer is the only alcoholic beverage. Old Town Pub is in the center of downtown. | 2 N. Main St. | 501/253–7147 | Mon.–Sat., 11:30 AM–3 PM | $6–$10 | No credit cards | Closed Sun. No dinner Sat.

Ozark Village Restaurant. Southern. This restaurant looks like a red barn, but the chickens inside are for eating. Barbecue ribs are also good. Kids' menu. | 104 Huntsville Rd. | 501/253–9339 | Daily, 7 AM–8 PM | $5–$8 | AE, D, MC, V.

Pancake's Family Restaurant. Southern. This restaurant looks like an old Studebaker dealership and is filled with antique toys, airplanes hanging from the ceiling, and pictures of the famous car. Dishes include catfish and ham steak. | Hwy. 62E | 501/253–6015 | May–Oct., 6:30 AM–midnight; Mar.–Apr. and Nov.–Dec., 6:30 AM–2 PM; closed Jan.–Feb. | $4–$9 | D, MC, V.

Plaza. Continental. Elegant dining—beef Wellington and butterflied jumbo shrimp—amid striking original art and a wine-rack wall, with bay-window views of shoppers on busy Main St. The Plaza is on the main drag downtown, across the street from City Hall. Café with outdoor deck upstairs. | 55 S. Main St. | 501/253–8866 | Daily, lunch 11:30–2:30; dinner 5:30–9; no dinner Sun. | $25–$45 | AE, D, DC, MC, V.

Rogue's Manor. Contemporary. This Victorian-style restaurant is filled with oil paintings by local artist Larry Mansker. Specialty dishes are ostrich steaks served with merlot sauce with sautéed portobello mushrooms, and smoked prime rib. Also worth trying are the baked salmon, pan-fried oysters, lobster and pan-fried grouper, and Mediterranean pasta. | 124 Spring St. | 501/253–4911 or 800/250–5827 | $18–$25 | AE, D, MC, V.

Smokehouse Café. American. Crowded license plates from all over the U.S. and photographs of customers make it difficult to tell if this restaurant actually has walls. You can chow down on chopped brisket and baby-back ribs with barbecue sauce. The staff also claims to serve the world's largest biscuits (1 lb). This eatery is on the west side of town, across the street from the Razorback Gift Shop and the observation tower. | 580 W. Van Buren St. | 501/253–9842 | Mar.–Dec., 7–7; closed Wed. | $9–$18 | D, MC, V.

Sparky's Roadhouse Café. American. You can sit outdoors and fill up on gourmet burgers, salmon, grilled chicken, tuna, or seafood enchiladas. | 41 Van Buren | 501/253–6001 | Daily except Sun., 11–10 | $4–$12 | D, MC, V.

Victorian Sampler. Café. You can have a light lunch here (soup, quiche, fruit plates, and the crescent sandwich) and a diet-defying dessert afterward (baked fudge and bread pudding). The Sampler is known for chilled strawberry soup. There is also a gift shop. Smoking is not allowed. Prospect St. is on the "historic loop." Look up and you'll find the place at the top of the hill. | 33 Prospect St. | 501/253–8374 | Mar.–Dec., lunch 11:30–3; dinner 5–8:30 | $8–$10 | D, MC, V | No supper.

Wagon Wheel Tavern. Barbecue. You'll find rustic lodge cabin dining here on the tavern's balcony or in the dining room. You can try the home smoked barbecue, which includes ribs, steaks, NY strip, rib eye, and pork sandwiches. | 85 S. Main | 501/253–9934 | Daily except Sun., 10 PM–2 AM | $10–$16 | No credit cards.

White River Lodge Restaurant. American. Smoked rainbow trout and Southwestern-style crab cakes are served inside an old 1920s lodge adorned with fishing and hunting memorabilia, including old fishing tackle. The restaurant sits on a wooded bluff, overlooking the White River. | 522 County Rd. 109 | 501/253–8596 | Tues.–Sun., dinner only | $11–$18 | D, MC, V.

Lodging

Alpen-Dorf. Alpen-Dorf is a family-owned hotel overlooking a nearby valley. The style is German-Swiss on the outside, contemporary on the inside. The view and the pleasantness of the people who run the place stay with you for a while. Alpen-Dorf is just outside of town, on Hwy. 62, 1 mi east of Passion Play Road. Complimentary Continental breakfast. Some kitchenettes. Cable TV. Pool. Hot tub. Playground. Pets allowed. | 6554 U.S. 62 | 501/253–9475 or 800/771–9876 (reservations) | fax 501/253–2928 | alpdorf@nwaft.com | www.eureka-usa.com | 30 rooms | $24–$125, seasonal | AE, D, MC, V.

Angel at Rose Hall. This B&B is a reproduction of a Victorian house and is filled with many antiques and centuries-old stained-glass windows. Many rooms have fireplaces. The food is delicious—especially the cookies. Angel at Rose Hall is in the historic district, near the Steam Train Depot. Complimentary breakfast. In-room hot tubs. Cable TV, in-room VCRs (and movies). Tennis court. No kids allowed. No smoking. | 56 Hillside | 501/253–5405 or 800/828–4255 (reservations) | rosehall@ipa.net | www.eurekaspringsangel.com | 5 rooms | $140–$165 | AE, D, DC, MC, V.

Arbour Glen Bed & Breakfast. Two restored Victorian homes from the late 19th century offer year-round lodging in a secluded, wooded environment in the historic district. The guest rooms have family-owned antique pieces, and a full breakfast is served on an outdoor veranda. The local trolley route stops here to allow convenient travel through Eureka Springs and you'll have golf, tennis, and swimming privileges at the Holiday Island Country Club 4 mi away. Complimentary breakfast. Refrigerators. Some in-room hot tubs. Cable TV, in-room VCRs (and movies). No pets. No kids. No smoking. | 7 Lema St. | 501/253–9010 or 800/515–4536 | fax 501/253–1264 | arbglen@ipa.net | www.arbourglen.com | 6 rooms, including 5 suites in 2 buildings | $115, $95–$135 suites | AE, D, MC, V.

Arkansas White River Cabins. These six log cabins, perched on a shelf 450 ft above the White River, provide magnificent views of the surrounding wooded area. They are located 5 min by car from Beaver Lake and the botanical gardens. Microwaves, some refrigerators. Cable TV, room phones. No pets. No smoking. | 755 County Rd. 210 | 501/253–7117 | awrc@whiterivercabins.com | www.whiterivercabins.com | 6 cabins | $60–$75 | AE, D, DC, MC, V.

Arsenic and Old Lace. The owner of this inn is an ardent fan of *Arsenic and Old Lace*, the 1940s Broadway hit; she began the tradition of serving the show's notorious elderberry wine. (Her beverage, however, is free of arsenic and free of charge.) Fireplaces, balconies, antiques, and Jacuzzis are in all rooms, as is a video copy of the film version of *Arsenic and Old Lace*, starring Cary Grant. Each balcony has a view of the Ozark hills as well as two gardens. The inn's baked cheese sausage casserole is available year-round. The inn is downtown, between Spring and Garden, which are the main shopping streets. Complimentary breakfast. In-room hot tubs. Cable TV, in-room VCRs (and movies). No kids under 14. No smoking. | 60 Hillside Ave. | 501/253–5454 or 800/243–5223 | fax 501/253–2246 | www.arseniclace.com | 5 rooms | $140–$185 | AE, D, MC, V.

Basin Park. The place is noted in *Ripley's Believe It or Not!* because each of its seven floors is a ground floor. Built in 1905, the Arts and Crafts–style hotel nestles against the side of a mountain, the only seven-story building downtown. Restaurant, bar, complimentary Continental breakfast. Some in-room hot tubs. Cable TV. Pool. Business services, free parking. Pets allowed. | 12 Spring St. | 501/253–7837 or 800/643–4972 | fax 501/253–6985 | www.basinpark.com | 61 rooms, including 3 honeymoon suites | $65–$175 | AE, D, MC, V.

Bavarian Inn Lodge. This Alpine-style villa sits atop a 4-acre mountain 1 mi from downtown, on Hwy. 62W. Restaurant, complimentary Continental breakfast. In-room hot tubs. Pool. | 325 W. Van Buren | 501/253–8128 | fax 501/253–7896 | www.eureka-net.com/bavarian | 14 rooms, 7 suites | $68–$98, $115–$128 suites, seasonal | MC, V | Closed Dec.–Feb.

Beaver Lake Cottages. These glass-front "honeymoon cottages" have high ceilings and a variety of beds, including brass, four-poster, sleigh, and rice beds. The cottages sit on a bluff surrounded by 10 acres of woods. A nature walk winds to nearby Beaver Lake. The style is contemporary. The cottages are 10 mi west of town on the lake, off Hwy. 187, which is off Hwy. 62. Please call for directions. In-room VCRs (and movies). No pets. No kids. No smoking. | 2865 Mundell Rd. | 501/253–8439 | fax 501/253–5057 | www.beaverlakecottages.com | 6 cottages, 2 suites | $95–$205, $55–$115 suites | D, MC, V.

Best Western Inn of the Ozarks. Many of the rooms here have views of the woods. The inn has standard accommodations in a two-story building. It's on Hwy. 62, the Eureka Springs exit, on the west side of town. Restaurant, picnic area. In-room data ports. Cable TV. Pool. Tennis court. Laundry facilities. Business services. Pets allowed. | 207 W. Van Buren | 501/253–9768 or 800/552–3785 | 122 rooms, including 4 suites | $59–$99, $129–$149 suites | AE, D, DC, MC, V.

Bridgeford House. This Victorian hotel has a garden, a fountain, and a goldfish pond, and is well known for its weddings. It was built in 1884 by Captain Bridgeford, a retired Civil War soldier, and the financing of the place has been a question of speculation for years. Some locals believe Bridgeford used stolen Confederate gold that he hid in a cave on the property—the same cave that was later used to keep provisions cool. (It is now boarded up.) The hotel is on the main route downtown. Complimentary breakfast. Refrigerators. Cable TV, no room phones. No smoking. | 263 Spring St. | 501/253–7853 | fax 501/253–5497 | www.bridgefordhouse.com | 7 rooms | $95–$200 | D, MC, V.

Candlestick Cottage Inn Bed & Breakfast. These two late-19th-century houses are on a quiet street, one block from downtown. The wood-frame, Victorian buildings have antique furnishings, hot-tub suites, and outdoor porches for smoking guests. Refrigerators. Cable TV. Hot tubs. No pets. No kids. | 6 Douglas St. | 501/253–6813 or 800/835–5184 | candleci@ipa.net | www.eureka-usa.com/candleci/ | 6 rooms | $65–$120 | AE, D, MC, V.

Cinnamon Valley Resort. This secluded resort's luxury log cabins are on 170 acres in the Cinnamon Valley, near two spring-fed lakes where you can canoe free of charge or catch and release bass and catfish. There are hiking trails and the place has a rustic, romantic flair. The resort is near the local music theater, the Ozark Mountain Hoedown. In-room hot tubs. Cable TV, in-room VCRs, no room phones. No kids. No smoking. | U.S. 62E | 501/253–5354 | www.cinnamon-valley.com | 9 cabins | $140–$180 | D, MC, V.

A Cliff Cottage and The Place Next Door A B&B inn built in 1892 as the home of Eureka's first mayor, it has since been restored and refurbished. There is also an 1890s Victorian cottage (A Secret Cottage) right down the street. It has a living room with fireplace and antique piano, large Laura Ashley bedroom, and a state-of-the-art bath with a big hot tub for two. Complimentary breakfast. Cable TV. Hot tub. | 42 Armstrong St. | 501/253–7409 | cliffctg@aol.com | http://www.eureka-usa.com/cliffctg/ | 4 rooms | $149–$179 | MC, V.

Colonial Mansion Inn. A beautiful front greets you at this inn. Half of the rooms are in a Colonial mansion and half are in an adjacent inn on 6 wooded acres. Some of the rooms are oversized. The town trolley lets you off on Route 23 near the inn, which is also close to a magic show and country-western music. Although the inn is one block from Hwy. 62, it is quiet. Complimentary Continental breakfast. Cable TV. Pool. Business services. Pets allowed. | Rte. 23S | 501/253–7300 or 800/638–2622 | fax 501/253–7304 | 30 rooms, 1 suite | $32–$68, $85–$100 | AE, D, MC, V | Closed Dec. 15–Feb. 12.

Crescent Cottage. Built in 1881, this is the first house in the historic district. A fully restored Queen Anne Victorian (listed in the National Historic Register), some rooms include a fireplace and porch. The views of the Ozarks are great, and you are within walking distance from shops and restaurants. The house is downtown, directly across the street from Crescent Spring, one of 62 various springs around town. Complimentary breakfast. Refrigerators, in-room hot tubs. Cable TV, in-room VCRs (and movies). No kids under 13. No smoking. | 211 Spring St. | 501/253–6022 | fax 501/253–6234 | www.1881crescentcottageinn.com | 3 rooms, 1 suite | $89–$145 | D, MC, V.

Crescent Hotel. Built in 1886, this full-service, four-story Victorian hotel overlooks downtown Eureka Springs. It includes the New Moon Spa, where you'll find hydrotherapy, Vichy water-massage showers, homeopathic healing, and a workout and fitness area. To get there, take Hwy. 62 to the "historic loop," then follow Hwy. 62B to the hotel. 2 restaurants, room service. Cable TV. Pool. Pets allowed. | 75 Prospect Ave. | 501/253–9766 | fax 501/253–5296 | info@crescent-hotel.com | www.crescent-hotel.com | 68 rooms | $89–$145 | AE, D, DC, MC, V.

Dogwood Inn. A family-owned Victorian-style hotel, the place is homey and quiet, and just 1½ mi from downtown. You can take your coffee on a porch that includes a fireplace and overlooks dense woods. The inn is off Hwy. 62 on Hwy. 23S, and about 4 blocks from I-65. Complimentary Continental breakfast. In-room data ports. Cable TV. Pool. Hot tub. Playground. Business services. Pets allowed (fee). | 170 Huntsville Rd. | 501/253–7200 or 800/544–1884 | 33 rooms | $38–$68 | AE, D, MC, V.

1876 Inn. This family-owned hotel sits on the ridge of the Ozarks, with a Bavarian-style exterior of white stucco, split-face timber, and an illuminated six-story tower. The "1876" name commemorates the founding of the state of Colorado, the original home state of the owners. All the rooms have patios or decks with flowering plants or herb gardens, and recorded instrumental music plays throughout the hotel. You'll find the inn at the intersection of Hwy. 62 and Hwy. 23, in the center of town. Restaurant, complimentary Continental breakfast. In-room data ports. Cable TV. Pool. Hot tub. Business services. No pets. | 2023 E. Van Buren St. | 501/253–7183 or 800/643–3030 | inn1876@ipa.net | www.eureka-usa.com/ac/1876.html | 72 rooms | $39–$80 | D, MC, V.

1881 Crescent Cottage Inn. Situated in the heart of the Ozarks, the inn is a classic Queen Anne Victorian "Painted Lady"; its three stories have spindlework front and back porches. A hand-pressed flower chandelier hangs in the living room. All guest rooms and the two back porches (with swings) overlook a series of special English-type gardens and a waterfall. Complimentary breakfast. Cable TV. Refrigerators. Hot tubs. | 211 Spring St. | 501/253–6022 or 800/223–3246 | raphael@ipa.net | www.1881crescentcottageinn.com/ | 4 rooms | $99–$145 | D, MC, V.

Enchanted Forest Resort. This log-cabin getaway is 5 mi west of Eureka Springs and has outdoor porches for barbecueing and viewing the surrounding woodland of the Ozark Mountains. Kitchenettes, microwaves, refrigerators. Cable TV, in-room VCRs (and movies). Hot tub. No pets. No kids under 16. No smoking. | 1858 Ark 23N | 501/253–8639 or 800/293–9586 | fax 501/253–8639 | eforest@arkansas.net | www.eureka-usa.com/enchant | 7 cabins | $115–$208 | AE, D, MC, V.

5 Ojo Inn B and B. A candle-lit, three-course complimentary breakfast is served every morning at 5 Ojo. Why candles? "Mornings we all look better with candles." The English-type garden is natural, not landscaped. Deer come through the yard and armadillos dig up the plants. The majority of the rooms are in two Victorian houses (built around 1900 and 1891, respectively) on a wooded lot downtown. Complimentary breakfast. Refrigerators. Cable TV, no room phones. Hot tub. | 5 Ojo St. | 501/253–6734 | fax 501/253–8831 | www.5ojo.com | 9 rooms, 1 cottage | $89–$130 | AE, D, DC, MC, V.

The Gaslight Inn. Built in 1895, this elegant inn has Victorian antiques along with a dolphin waterfall fish pond. A pavilion is on the property and you are a short walk from downtown. Complimentary breakfast. Cable TV. Hot tub. | 19 Judah St. | 501/253–8887 | bvoiers@aol.com | 5 rooms | $110–$150 | AE, MC, V.

Grand Central Hotel. All of the luxury suites in this 1883 Victorian hotel have access to a balcony on the second floor, which overlooks downtown. The hotel is on Hwy. 23N, which becomes Main St. Restaurant, bar. Refrigerators, in-room hot tubs. Cable TV. Massages, sauna. No small kids allowed. | 37 N. Main St. | 501/253–6756 | fax 501/253–6050 | gcentral@ipa.net | www.eureka-net.com/grandcentral | 14 suites | $95–$135, $155 grand suites | AE, D, DC, MC, V.

Heartstone Inn and Cottages. At this Victorian "pink and white confection," you are near woods and the famous road that loops through town. Built in 1903, the *New York Times* called its breakfast the best in the Ozarks. Heartstone is one block off Hwy. 62W. Complimentary breakfast. Some kitchenettes. Cable TV, in-room VCRs, no room phones. Massage. Golf privileges. No smoking. | 35 Kings Hwy. | 501/253–8916 | fax 501/253–5361 | heartinn@ipa.net | www.heartstoneinn.com | 12 rooms; 2 cottages | $75–$129 | AE, D, MC, V.

Hidden Valley Guest Ranch. These cabins were built on a 650-acre ranch near the Ozark Mountains. They all have vaulted ceilings, stained-glass windows, and verandas. The cab-

ins have different styles, one country, one Victorian. The ranch is 5 mi outside of town, on Hwy. 62, right across from Thorncrown Chapel. Refrigerators, in-room hot tubs. In-room VCRs, no room phones. No smoking. | 777 Hidden Valley Ranch Rd. | 888/443–3368 | fax 501/253–5777 | getaway@hiddenvalleyguestranch.com | www.hiddenvalleyguestranch.com | 5 cabins | $149–$209 | D, MC, V.

Holiday Island Lakeview Lodge and Chalet. There is a breathtaking view of Table Rock Lake and the Ozark Mountains from this family-owned lodge and chalet. The island is 4 mi north of Eureka Springs. To get to the islands from town, go past the Dinner Train Station at the edge of town to Hwy. 23 north, travel 4 mi, then turn left on Holiday Island Dr. You'll come to the information booth. Call the lodge for further directions. Restaurants. Kitchenettes. Cable TV. Spa. Tennis. 18-hole professional golf course; 9-hole executive golf course. | 888/558–4397 | fax 501/253–2474 | www.lakeview-lodge-chalet.com or www.holidayisland.com/lakeview | 4 roomy accommodations: a cabin, a chalet, and a duplex | $125–$175 | D, MC, V | Closed Jan., Feb.

Howard Johnson Express Inn. This chain hotel is on Hwy. 62 on the east side of town; it is approximately 2 mi from the Great Passion Play. Breakfast is in the glassed-in breakfast room. In-room data ports. Cable TV, room phones. Outdoor pool. Spa. Business services. | 4042 E. Van Buren St. | 501/253–6665 or 800/446–4656 | fax 501/253–6973 | www.hojo.com | 35 rooms | $39–$79 | AE, D, DC, MC, V.

Island Motel and Resort. In the heart of the Ozarks on Holiday Island, this resort on the lake offers sports, fishing, and boating. 2 pools. Tennis court. Miniature golf. Playground. Fishing. | 5 Woodsdale Dr., Holiday Island | 501/253–9571 or 800/874–1331 | himotel@ipa.net | www.holidayisland.com/motel/ | 29 | $45–$55 | D, MC, V.

Matterhorn Towers. This is a Bavarian-style motor inn on U.S. 62 with a garden and waterfall, 200 yds from the Queen Anne Mansion tour home. Complimentary Continental breakfast. Some refrigerators, in-room hot tubs. Cable TV. Pool. | 130 W. Van Buren | 501/253–9602 or 800/426–0838 | fax 501/253–7183 | 35 rooms | $69–$74 | AE, MC, V.

Morningstar Retreat. The buildings at Morningstar are round. Built in 1994 and 2000, most are 15-sided with a conical roof, and one is a geodesic dome. The stained-glass windows, wood floors, and ceramic tiles create an old-fashioned aura, but the wood stoves are just for fun. The cottages have outdoor decks and 7-ft windows with views of the Ozark Mountains and the Kings River, which is filled with bass. You can fish, walk the trails, or picnic on the 80 acres. Complimentary afternoon snacks include home-baked brownies and lemon bars. Picnic area. Some kitchenettes, microwaves, refrigerators, some in-room hot tubs. Fishing. No smoking. | 370 Star La. | 501/253–5995 or 800/298–5995 (reservations) | amstar7@aol.com | www.avey.com | 4 suites, 1 cottage | $95–$115 suites, $130 cottage | MC, V.

Motel 6. This motel has a *Gone With the Wind* theme with pictures of Southern mansions, rooms named after the novel's characters, and other furnishings that recall mid-19th-century life. The Victorian-style establishment has steeples, Sheetrock walls, and pastel yellow siding; it is across from the Ozark Mountain Hoedown on the east side of town. Complimentary Continental breakfast. Microwaves, refrigerators, some in-room hot tubs. Cable TV, room phones. Outdoor pool. Pets allowed. | 3169 E. Van Buren St. | 501/253–5600 | fax 501/253–2110 | motel6@arkansas.net | 61 rooms, including 5 suites | $39–$119 | AE, D, MC, V.

New Orleans. The trolley stops at the front door of this downtown Victorian-style hotel. There are balconies on the first and second floors, and local bottled spring water in all the rooms. Restaurant, bar. Refrigerators, in-room hot tubs. Cable TV. Free parking. | 63 Spring St. | 501/253–8630 or 800/243–8630 | fax 501/253–5949 | www.avey.com | 18 suites, 3 rooms | $75–$140 | AE, D, DC, MC, V.

Palace Hotel and Bath House. This small, Victorian-style hotel, built in 1901, has been completely restored. It's furnished with antiques and has large rooms, fine woodwork, and high ceilings. There's a full bath house with massage personnel. The hotel is downtown, near the natural springs that bubble up throughout town. Complimentary Continental breakfast. Refrigerators. Cable TV. | 135 Spring St. | 501/253–7474 | phbh@ipa.net | www.palace-hotelbathhouse.com | 8 rooms | $110–$167 | AE, D, MC, V.

Piedmont House B and B Inn. One of two commercial wooden structures that survived the fires of the early part of the 1900s, this charming place is the oldest continuously operated inn in the state. Built in 1880, it has wraparound porches, rockers, swings, antiques, and panoramic mountain views. On Fridays you can eat a complimentary three-course dinner. The inn is a 2-min walk from downtown. Complimentary breakfast. Cable TV. Free parking. No kids under 12. | 165 Spring St. | 800/253–9258 | 10 rooms | $79–$135 | AE, D, MC, V.

Pond Mountain Lodge. This combination B&B and resort is at Pond Mountain. It has two spring-fed and landscaped ponds at the mountain's top, a 30-mi easterly view, and a southern valley and ridge view. Microwave. Refrigerator. Some in-room hot tubs. | 1218 Highway 23S | 501/253–5877 or 800/583–8043 | fax 501/253–9087 | pondmtn@estc.net | www.eureka-usa.com/pondmtn/ | 7 rooms | $110–$135 | D, MC, V.

Red Bud Manor B and B Inn. There are three rooms reserved for guests in this southern Victorian home (1891) on the "historic loop" downtown. It is shaded by an expanse of woods. The gourmet complimentary breakfast may include strawberry Romanoff, quiche, or soufflé. Complimentary breakfast. Refrigerators, in-room hot tubs. Cable TV. Laundry facilities. Pets allowed. | 7 Kings Hwy. | 501/253–9649 | 3 rooms | $90–$135 | D, MC, V.

Red Bud Valley Resort. This resort is secluded in the Arkansas Mountains, 1½ miles from town in a 180-acre valley. There are log cabins for families or couples, some with wood-burning fireplaces. Picnic area. Furnished kitchenettes, air conditioning, TV, stereo, VCR. No room phones. Hiking, horseback riding. Fishing. Playground. | 369 Rte. 340 | 501/253–9028 | 17 cottages | $79–$135 (2–night minimum) | MC, V.

Roadrunner Inn. This hilltop motel is on a peninsula extending into Beaver Lake. All the rooms have a view of the water. The marina, with boating, swimming, and park recreation, is 1 mi away. The inn is 10 mi west of town, but getting there can be a little tricky, so you may need to call for directions. Picnic area. Kitchenettes, refrigerators. Pets allowed. | 3034 Mundell Rd. | 501/253–8166 or 888/253–8166 (reservations) | 12 rooms | $29–$44 | AE, DC, MC, V | Closed mid-Nov.–mid-Mar.

Rock Cottage Gardens. Inside the rock walls of the romantic cottages designed in the 1930s, you will find a fireplace and in-room hot tub. A three-course gourmet breakfast awaits you when you wake up. A trolley route is on the property and you are four blocks from downtown. Complimentary breakfast. Hot tub. | 10 Eugenia St. | 501/253–8659 or 800/624–6646 | rockbnb@ipa.net | www.eureka-net.com/rockcottage | 5 rooms | $115–$125. | AE, D, MC, V.

Scandia Bed and Breakfast. This 1940s roadside inn faces the highway, but the back has views of woods with 60-ft pines. The property is accessible by trolley. Scandia is in the historic district on Hwy. 62, which becomes Van Buren. Complimentary breakfast. Cable TV, no room phones. Hot tub. Business services. | 227 W. Van Buren St. | 501/253–8922 or 800/523–8922 | scandia@ipa.net | www.scandiainn.com | 6 rooms | $79–$149 | AE, D, MC, V.

Swiss Village. The Eureka trolley stops close to this hotel on U.S. 62; it's also near restaurants and the Opry music hall. The Swiss Village is in town, on the junction of Hwy. 62 and Hwy. 23, next door to the antique mall. Picnic area, complimentary Continental breakfast. Some in-room hot tubs. Cable TV. Outdoor pool. Pets allowed. | 183 E. Van Buren St. | 501/253–9541 or 800/447–6525 | 38 rooms | $49–$69 | AE, D, MC, V.

Tall Pines Motor Inn. Pine log was used to build 6 original cabins and 2 of the suites. This motor inn, listed in the historic register, is hidden from the highway by the region's towering pine trees. The trolley stops nearby. The neighborhood is known as the Tall Pines historic district; it's on the west edge of town, at the corner of Hwy. 62W and Pivot Rock Road. Picnic area. Some refrigerators. Cable TV, some in-room hot tubs. Pool. | 3 Pivot Rock Rd. | 501/253–8096 | 20 accommodations, including cabins, suites, and duplexes | $59–$89 | AE, D, MC, V | Closed Dec., Jan., and weekdays in Feb.

Tradewinds. Some of this motor inn's rooms and cabins were built in the 1960s and some in the 1980s. It's ½ mi from downtown shopping and restaurants and is on Hwy. 62W, next door to the Chamber of Commerce. Picnic area. Some kitchenettes. Cable TV. Pool. Pets allowed. | 77 Kings Hwy. | 501/253–9774 or 800/242–1615 | 17 rooms | $42–$52 | AE, D, MC, V | Closed Jan., Feb.

Travelodge. Outdoor decks at this hostelry look over 2 wooded acres. This Travelodge is on the local trolley line near the junction of Hwy. 62 and Hwy. 23S, and is next to the Ozark Village restaurant. Complimentary Continental breakfast. Some refrigerators, some in-room hot tubs. Cable TV, room phones. Outdoor pool. | 110 Huntsville Dr. | 501/253–8992 | fax 501/253–8993 | 61 rooms | $39–$89 | AE, D, DC, MC, V.

Victoria Inn. Wood-frame paneling, exposed brick, and a dome-ensconced chandelier are among the flourishes at this spacious motor inn. The rooms are Victorian-style and come with vanities. The inn is on the east side, 2½ mi from downtown, across from Passion Play Road. Restaurant, bar. Cable TV. Pool. Hot tub. Video games. Business services. | 4028 E. Van Buren St. | 501/253–6000 or 800/844–6835 | fax 501/253–8654 | victoria@arkansas.net | www.eureka-usa.com/victoria | 90 rooms | $65 | AE, D, MC, V.

FAYETTEVILLE

MAP 11, A3

(Nearby towns also listed: Bentonville, Berryville, Eureka Springs, Harrison, Rogers, Springdale)

Fayetteville is a lively college town, home to the University of Arkansas's beloved Razorbacks. Clubs, restaurants, galleries, museums, and arts centers offer everything from poetry slams to classical music, Broadway hits, jazz concerts, and fine arts events.

Its population of 55,000 is booming, and the metro area boundaries continue to expand. Yet Fayetteville's historical central districts remain well groomed and bustling. The square around a former post office built in 1911 has been transformed into a flower-filled garden spot with restaurants, shops, and a farmers' market Tuesday, Thursday, and Saturday mornings.

Fayetteville's site was chosen as the seat of the new Washington County in 1828. From its earliest days it has been an educational center and the hometown of state and national political and judicial leaders.

Information: **Fayetteville Chamber of Commerce** | Box 4216, 72702-4216 | 501/521–1710 | www.fayettevilleAR.com.

Attractions

Arkansas Air Museum. Vintage aircraft fill this museum. You can see pre–World War II racing planes in flying condition, as well as private, military, and commercial aircraft spanning the history of aviation from its birth. A hands-on flight simulator and a walk-in workshop let you get a feel for the experience of piloting. | 4290 S. School | 501/521–4947 | $2 | Daily 9:30–4:30.

Clinton House. This first home of former President Bill Clinton and Hillary Clinton is also the site of their 1975 wedding. | 930 California Blvd. | Not open to the public.

Devil's Den State Park. The Civilian Conservation Corps (CCC) built this park in an Ozark valley during the 1930s. Rustic wood and stone structures dot the land and a native stone dam creates an 8-acre lake with swimming, canoeing, and paddleboating. You can hike and backpack on trails that lead to caves, crevices, and bluff overlooks. The park has modern cabins with kitchens and fireplaces, RV and tent camping, horse-camp areas, mountain bike trails, and a swimming pool. | 11333 W. Arkansas Hwy. 74, West Fork | 501/761–3325 | Free | Daily 8–5.

Headquarters House. Both Union and Confederate troops used this house as headquarters during the April 18, 1863, Battle of Fayetteville. It was caught in the crossfire, and the hole from a mini-ball is easily visible. | 118 E. Dickson St. | 501/521–2970 | $3 | Mon., Sat. 10–noon, Thurs. 1–4; or by appointment.

Prairie Grove Battlefield State Park. You can visit a museum, battlefields, monuments, historic homes, and a store, and participate in living history programs at this site commemorating an 1862 Civil War battle. | 506 Douglas St., Prairie Grove | 501/846–2990 | Free; museum $2.25 | Daily 8–5; park is open 8–dusk.

Ridge House Museum. Fayetteville's oldest standing home was built with native Ozark logs in 1836. | 230 W. Center St. | 501/521–2970 | wchs@ipa.net | Free | Mon.–Sat. 10–4.

University of Arkansas. The twin towers of Old Main, built in 1874, preside over the campus. You can visit the 1930 Chi Omega Greek Amphitheater and look at the Senior Walk, which is inscribed with the names of every graduating senior since 1876. | 1125 W. Maple St. | 501/575–2000 | fax 501/575–7515 | www.uark.edu | Free | Daily.

　　University Museum. You can view exhibits ranging from a full-scale Triceratops skeleton to a real meteorite and Native American art at this small museum. | Garland Ave. | 501/575–3466 | Free | Jan. 2–Dec. 23, Mon.–Sat. 9–4:30.

Walton Arts Center. This is the home of the North Arkansas Symphony, but you can also take in Broadway touring shows and other theater, galleries, and performing arts. | 495 W. Dickson St. | 501/443–5600 | Call for hours.

ON THE CALENDAR

APR.: *Ozark Mountain Bike Festival.* You can test your biking skills at Devil's Den State Park as you pedal along guided mountain bike rides in the Ozark National Forest, or simply participate in fun events, kids' games, or an evening social. | 501/761–3325.

APR.: *Wildflower Weekend.* If you've always wanted to learn how to identify and find out more about wildflowers, you can do it during guided walks and interpretive programs at Devil's Den State Park. | 501/761–3325.

APR.–OCT.: *Farmers' Market.* You can buy or browse fresh, locally grown produce and plants and handmade Ozark crafts on sale at the historic downtown square. | 501/634–7122.

MAY: *Memorial Day Tribute.* At Prairie Grove Battlefield State Park, you can listen to a musical concert and a patriotic speech, and children can play pioneer games. | 501/846–2990.

MAY: *Ozark Festival Charity Horse Show.* Performances feature 450 entries in 83 classes of Tennessee walking horses, racking horses, and Missouri fox-trotting horses. Proceeds go to local charities. | Dorothy Whitaker Arena, University of Arkansas | 501/925–4266.

SEPT.: *Clothesline Fair.* More than 200 arts and crafts exhibitors are spread over the Civil War battleground. You can hear music, watch the square dancing exhibit or try it out yourself at the competition, participate in living history programs, tour the park's historic houses, and view demonstrations of antique farming equipment. | 501/846–2990.

OCT.: *Haunted Hay Ride.* After a hayride, you can sip a cup of hot cocoa while you roast marshmallows over an open fire and listen to ghost stories. | Devil's Den State Park | 501/761–3325.

OCT.: *Autumnfest.* The festival celebrates fall with food, music, activities, a children's run, and a soccer tournament. | 501/521–1710 or 800/766–4626.

NOV., DEC.: *Lights of the Ozarks Festival.* More than 1.5 million lights bedeck the downtown square, with even more in city neighborhoods. The festival includes the Jingle Bell Job, a parade, caroling, and live performances. | 501/521–1710 or 800/766–4626.

DEC.: *Anniversary of the Battle of Prairie Grove.* More than 1,000 participants set up Civil War camps, conduct drills, and give battle demonstrations. | Prairie Grove Battlefield State Park | 501/846–2990.

Dining

AQ Chicken House. American. "AQ" stands for "Arkansas Quality," and this restaurant has been serving chicken since 1947. The menu, served at 2 locations (including the original in Springdale), has a full range of grilled and pan-fried entrées. Two standouts are the rotisserie chicken and the blue plate lunch specials. | 1925 N. College Ave. | 501/443–7555 | $13–$22 | AE, D, DC, MC, V.

Acropolis. Greek. A refreshing alternative to burgers and barbecue, this busy little eatery near the university serves slow-cooked Mediterranean treats, including moussaka, gyros, and souvlaki. The Mezzeh Sampler entrée is ideal for a first taste. | 1618 N. College Ave. | 501/443–2261 | $10–$17 | AE, D, DC, MC, V | Closed Mon.

Belvedere's Casual Italian. Italian. Hanging baskets create an informal air in a busy restaurant featuring veal, steak, and chicken. The veal piccata and chocolate ganache are two specialties worth trying. Sunday brunch is served. | 3061 N. College | 501/443–7778 | $17–$27 | AE, D, DC, MC, V | Closed Mon.

★ **James at the Mill.** Contemporary. Chef Miles James's heralded Ozark Plateau cookery puts a premium on fresh local ingredients and food worthy of the airy contemporary setting overlooking a churning gristmill. The andouille corn dog, seared beef fillet, and Granny Smith apple tart are especially good. | 3906 Greathouse Spring Rd., Johnson | 501/443–1400 | $30–$40 | AE, D, DC, MC, V.

Jose's Restaurant and Bandito Saloon. Mexican. A sprawling Mexican-style hacienda serves Tex-Mex dishes such as fajitas, nachos, chimichangas, and fried ice cream. Sidewalk tables are available for open-air dining. On Tuesday night you can listen to live music. | 324 W. Dickson | 501/521–0194 | $11–$24 | AE, MC, V.

Ozark Brewing Co. American. The gleaming brass kettles and tubing of a microwbrewery are the backdrop of a bustling college-town mainstay with plenty of bar munchies and sandwiches, as well as more ambitious dinner fare, such as the smoked bacon–wrapped fillet, Bison brew, and crabmeat-artichoke dip. You can dine outdoors on the balcony if you wish. Brunch is served on Sundays. | 430 W. Dickson | 501/521–2739 | $12–$30 | AE, D, DC, MC, V.

Uncle Gaylord's Mountain Café. Eclectic. A book-lined dining room and lounge filled with original art, plush sofas, a chandelier, deep easy chairs, and a mahogany bar grace this all-day restaurant, which pays homage to everyone from Escoffier (eggs) to grandma (meat loaf). Uncle Gaylord's is known for pasta dishes and sandwiches. Open-air dining is available. Sundays you can visit for brunch. Smoking is not allowed. | 315 W. Mountain | 501/444–0605 | $10–$18 | AE, MC, V | No dinner Sun., Mon.

Lodging

Best Western Windsor Suites. This two-story standard chain hotel has many conveniences and is six blocks from the University of Arkansas, 25 mi from Beaver Lake, and 60 mi from Eureka Springs. You can reach the hotel via U.S. Hwy. 71, exit 43; it's near the bypass of Hwy. 62 and 71. Complimentary Continental breakfast. In-room data ports, some refrigerators, some in-room hot tubs. Cable TV. Indoor pool. Hot tub. Exercise equipment. Laundry facilities. Business services. Some pets allowed. | 1122 S. Futrall Dr. | 501/587–1400 | 68 rooms, 37 suites | $60–$70, $130 suites | AE, D, DC, MC, V.

Clarion Inn. The DJ plays music of the 1950s through 1970s every night in the Bobbisox Lounge at this two-story hotel less than ½ mi from the University of Arkansas. Restaurant, room service. In-room data ports, some refrigerators. Cable TV. Indoor pool. Hot tub. Exercise equipment. Laundry facilities. Business services, free parking. | 1255 S. Shiloh Dr. | 501/521–1166 | fax 501/521–1204 | Fayclarion@earthlink.com | 197 rooms | $69–$79 | AE, D, DC, MC, V.

Clarion Inn at the Mill. This inn was originally a grain mill built in 1835 and is on the National Register of Historic Places. Two of the rooms in this two-story inn have interior balconies; six rooms have exterior balconies. The inn is ²/₁₀ mi east of Hwy. 71, exit 69, and 5 mi from the University of Arkansas. Restaurant, complimentary Continental breakfast. Some in-room data ports, some in-room hot tubs. Cable TV. Golf course, tennis. Hiking, horseback riding. Business services. | 3906 Greathouse Springs Rd., Johnson | 501/443–1800 | fax 501/443–3879 | 48 rooms, 8 suites | $104–$109, $140–$160 suites | AE, D, DC, MC, V.

Days Inn. When you stay at this older Days Inn, built around 1963, you can show your hotel key at the Butcher Block restaurant next door and get a discount on all entrées, including the much-loved prime rib. You can shop at the Northwest Arkansas Mall, watch the Razorbacks play football at the University of Arkansas, or visit the Walton Art Center, each just 2 mi away. The inn is 2½ mi from exit 66 on I–540. Complimentary Continental breakfast. Cable TV. Pool. Laundry facilities. Business services. Some pets allowed (fee). | 2402 N. College Ave. | 501/443–4323 | 150 rooms, 6 suites | $50–$70, $100–$125 suites | AE, D, DC, MC, V.

Eton House. Decorated with Victorian antiques, this ranch-style home is a romantic getaway just minutes from downtown Fayetteville and the Walton Arts Center. Indoor details, such as cathedral ceilings and a cozy fireplace, and outdoor elements, such as a screened-in porch overlooking a park, add to this B&B's appeal. Eton House is inappropriate for children and has limited access for the disabled. Complimentary Continental breakfast. | 1485 Eton | 501/443–7517 | 3 rooms | $65–$75 | No credit cards.

Fairfield Inn Fayetteville. Fairfield's bright, clean rooms are made cozy with in-room sitting areas, remote control, cable television, and plenty of desk and closet space to spread out. Children under 17 stay free with parents. Complimentary breakfast. Cable TV. Indoor pool. Sauna, spa. Laundry services. | 720 Millsap Rd. | 501/587–8600 or 800/228–2800 | fax 501/587–8600 | www.fairfieldinn.com/FYVFI | 61 rooms, 8 suites | $49–$62 | AE, D, DC, MC, V.

Hilton. The tallest building downtown, this 15-story hotel has a splendid view of the Ozark Mountains and is only three blocks from Basin Street and the Walton Art Center. The University of Arkansas is ¼ mi away. The hotel is about 5 mi from Hwy. 71 Business. Restaurant, bar. Cable TV. Indoor-outdoor pool. Exercise equipment. Business services, airport shuttle. Some pets allowed. | 70 N. East Ave. | 501/442–5555 | fax 501/442–2105 | 235 rooms | $113–$125 | AE, D, DC, MC, V.

Johnson House Bed and Breakfast. Elegant 1882 country home on the National Register of Historic Places. You can eat a full gourmet breakfast, served in the dining room or on the upstairs veranda. Afterward, you may want to visit the antiques shop, built around an old smokehouse. If you want to continue shopping, Northwest Arkansas Mall is 2 mi away. Johnson House is one block off Hwy. 71 (also called 540), exit 69. Dining room, complimentary breakfast. | 5371 S. 48th St., Johnson | 501/756–1095 | 3 rooms | $105 | AE, MC, V.

Motel 6. This typical chain motel is close to restaurants and shopping at the War Eagle Craft Fair and a 15-min drive from Fort Smith Regional Airport. You are 3 mi from the downtown antiques district and 8 mi from the Fort Smith Historic District. To get to the motel, take I–40 to exit 5. Cable TV. Pool. Some pets allowed. | 2980 N. College Ave. | 501/443–4351 | fax 501/444–8034 | 99 rooms | $35–$52 | AE, D, DC, MC, V.

Park Inn Limited. This low-rise motel is approximately 1 mi from the University of Arkansas. Rooms are modestly furnished and feature satellite television and air-conditioning. Children under 16 stay free with parents. Complimentary breakfast. | 675 N. Shiloh Dr. | 501/575–0777 or 800/437–7275 | 32 rooms, 2 wheelchair accessible | $38–$45 | AE, D, DC, MC, V.

Ramada Inn. All the rooms are reached from outside corridors at this two-story Ramada. The University of Arkansas and the Walton Art Center are both a quick 5-mi drive away. The inn is easy to get to; after you take U.S. 540 to Exit 67 (Hwy. Bus. 71), it's ½ mile away. Restaurant, complimentary breakfast, room service. Cable TV. Pool. Tennis. Playground. Business services, airport shuttle, free parking. Some pets allowed. | 3901 N. College Ave. | 501/443–3431 | fax 501/443–1927 | 120 rooms | $54–$63 | AE, D, DC, MC, V.

Sleep Inn Fayetteville. Renovations in 1999 and daily afternoon tea in the lobby contribute to Sleep Inn's tidy appearance; however, guest rooms are a bit cramped. The small hotel is only 2 mi from the Ozark National Forest visitors center. Children 18 and younger

FAYETTEVILLE

INTRO
ATTRACTIONS
DINING
LODGING

stay free with parents. Complimentary Continental breakfast. | 728 Millsap Rd. | 501/587–8700 or 877/233–9330 | fax 501/587–8700 | www.sleepinn.com | 61 rooms | $43–$79 | AE, D, DC, MC, V.

Super 8 Motel. This three-story chain motel is 1 mi from the University of Arkansas and 3 mi from the Fayetteville airport. You'll find the motel on U.S. 62 (exit 62 off U.S. 540). Complimentary Continental breakfast. Some in-room data ports, some refrigerators. | 1075 S. Shiloh Dr. | 501/521–8866 | 83 rooms | $54–$57 | AE, D, DC, MC, V.

FORREST CITY

MAP 11, E4

(Nearby town also listed: Helena)

Forrest City formed after 1868, when railroads linked Memphis and Little Rock thanks to the work of former Confederate general Nathan Bedford Forrest. The town grew around a commissary Forrest built on Front Street. It sits atop Crowley's Ridge, a narrow north–south highland that runs from southern Missouri to Helena, rising just 300 ft above the flat Mississippi Delta. Along the ridge's rolling terrain north of town are orchards of peach and other fruit trees. Fossils of sea creatures and mastodons have been unearthed within the Forrest City limits.

Information: Forrest City Area Chamber of Commerce | 203 N. Izard St., 72335 | 870/633–1651.

Attractions

Parkin Archaeological State Park. Brass bells, beads, and other 16th-century items shown in the visitors center prove Spanish explorer Hernando de Soto stopped here in 1541. It was then a 17-acre moated village with wood palisades, mounds, probably 400 houses, and 2,000 people. You can also see effigy pots, vessels, and other items and you can assist in seasonal archaeological excavations. | 60 Hwy. 184 N, Parkin | 870/755–2500 | $2.25 for gallery and/or walking tour | Tues.–Sat. 8–5, Sun. noon–5.

St. Francis County Museum. You can view displays of Native American artifacts, the shell of a 70-lb fossil saltwater clam, shark and mastodon teeth, woolly mammoth bones found at nearby Crow Creek, and other exhibits in a restored 1906 home. | 603 Front St. | 870/261–1744 | Free | Weekdays 9–5, Sat. 10–2.

Village Creek State Park. Arkansas's largest state park lies atop Crowley's Ridge and shows off geology unique in North America and forests more like those in the Appalachians. You can stay in housekeeping cabins or at RV and tent campsites; fish in two stocked lakes; visit beaches; or rent a boat. You'll also find picnic pavilions; a grocery and gift shop; interpretive displays and programs; and nature and hiking trails. | 201 CR 754, Wynne | 870/238–9406 | Free | Daily.

ON THE CALENDAR

JUNE: *Explorer and Archeological Day Camps.* Younger kids learn about Spanish explorer Hernando de Soto's expedition and his 1541 stay at Casqui, which is now the site of the state park. Older kids learn the techniques of archaeological excavations. The day camps may not be held every year; call for specifics. | Parkin Archeological State Park | 870/755–2500.

JULY–OCT.: *Arkansas Archeological Survey Excavations.* You can tour the excavations of the Native American village site at Parkin Archeological State Park and, if you like, you can assist archaeologists in the digs. The survey is not held every year; call for specifics. | 870/755–2500.

JULY: *Mightymite Triathlon.* Hundreds of athletes compete in a three-part race consisting of swimming, cycling, and running. The race starts at Village Creek State Park. | Village Creek State Park | 870/238–9406.

SEPT.: *Visions of the Past Living History Fair.* You can watch actors recreate the 1541 expedition of Hernando de Soto, with portrayals of the Native Americans as well as the Spanish explorers. The fair is not held every year; call for specifics. | Parkin Archeological State Park | 870/755–2500.

OCT.: *Arkansas Archeology Week.* During the third or fourth week of the month (call for specifics), you can view special exhibits, listen to talks, and tour excavation sites. | Parkin Archeological State Park | 870/755–2500.

OCT.: *Halloween Hay Rides.* You can begin your evening with a hayride and trick or treating at Village Creek State Park and end it with storytelling, marshmallow roasting, and hot chocolate around the campfire. | Village Creek State Park | 870/238–9406.

NOV.: *Native American Feast.* Held during Thanksgiving weekend, Native wild foods and traditional Native American recipes are here for you to sample, including pemmican, dried fish, Three Sisters Soup, buffalo, alligator, and venison. | Parkin Archeological State Park | 870/755–2500.

DEC.: *Kwanzaa Celebration.* At Parkin Archeological State Park, stories celebrate African-American heritage. | 870/755–2500.

Dining

Pizza Inn. Pizza. Overstuffed pizzas will lure you to Pizza Inn, while the huge buffet of pastas and breadsticks will keep you coming back. | 901 N. Washington St. | 870/633–3440 | $8.95–$12.95 | AE, D, MC, V.

Wilburn's and Jordan Bar-B-Q. Barbecue. No need to be proper at Wilburn's and Jordan. Ribs, pulled pork sandwiches, and other rich, saucy slabs of meat are served with a mound of napkins. | 509 W. Franklin Ave. | 870/633–0380 | $5–$8.50 | No credit cards.

Lodging

Best Western Colony Inn. This standard chain hotel between Little Rock and Memphis is 13 mi from Village Creek State Park and one block from Wal-Mart. Half the rooms are non-smoking. The inn is right off exit 241A (Forrest City) on I–40. Pool. Hot tub. Some pets allowed. | 2333 N. Washington Ave., Forrest City | 870/633–0870 | fax 870/633–3252 | 104 rooms | $62–$76 | AE, D, DC, MC, V.

Best Western–Brinkley. Typical chain accommodations are what you'll find at this hotel off I–40, an hour away from Little Rock and Memphis. The convention center is three blocks away. The hotel is one block south of I–40, exit 216. Restaurant, picnic area, complimentary breakfast. Some in-room hot tubs. Cable TV. Pool. Exercise equipment. Playground. Some pets allowed. | 1306 N. Rte. 17, Brinkley | 870/734–1650 | fax 870/734–1657 | 100 rooms | $59–$69 | AE, D, DC, MC, V.

Days Inn Suites. This motel is 40 mi from Memphis and 90 mi from Little Rock. There is duck hunting and fishing nearby. The inn is 1 mi from Hwy. 1, exit 241. Restaurant, complimentary breakfast. Some microwaves, some refrigerators, some in-room hot tubs. Cable TV. Pool. Business services. | 350 Barrow Hill Rd. | 870/633–0777 | fax 870/633–0770 | 53 rooms, 52 suites | $47–$69, $85–$120 suites | AE, D, DC, MC, V.

Hampton Inn Forrest City. This two-story hotel has an elevator and is ¼ mi from exit 241B on I–40. Complimentary breakfast. Cable TV. Outdoor pool. Hot tub. Gym. Laundry service. | 300 Holiday Dr. | 870/630–9000 or 800/HAMPTON | fax 870/630–0951 | www.hampton-inn.com | 70 rooms | $62–$99 | AE, D, DC, MC, V.

Holiday Inn Forrest City. This hotel has been perched atop Crowley's Ridge since 1965. Renovations in 1996 brought a 24-hr Denny's Restaurant, round-the-clock security, 25-in TVs, and revamped furnishings. Guests receive a $6 breakfast voucher for Denny's, and kids always eat free with parents. Complimentary breakfast, room service. Cable TV. Outdoor pool. Gym.

Laundry service. | 200 Holiday Dr. | 870/633–6300 | fax 870/633–6300 | holiday@arkansas.net | 79 rooms | $55–$67 | AE, D, DC, MC, V.

FORT SMITH/VAN BUREN

MAP 11, A4

(Nearby towns also listed: Alma, Altus, Bentonville, Berryville, Eureka Springs, Fayetteville, Mena, Morrilton, Paris, Rogers, Russellville, Springdale)

Fort Smith was founded in 1817 as a frontier outpost in the American hinterland and rebuilt in 1838. Now it is the state's second-largest city. Its layers of recorded history, which encompass Indian wars, Civil War actions, and an era of frontier justice, remain alive today.

You'll have your choice of excellent restaurants as well as antiques shops and downtown specialty stores. Modern malls are on the outskirts of town.

In neighboring Van Buren, a steamboat port devastated during the Civil War, the Victorian Main Street has been restored to its original condition. You can walk downhill six blocks from the 1901 Frisco train depot, where the Arkansas and Missouri Railroad arrives from Springdale for excursions (*see* Springdale Attractions), past the county courthouse to the Arkansas River. Along the way you can see the turrets, cornices, and herringbone brick sidewalks of 70 National Register buildings. The facades now house classy antiques and art galleries, down-home cafés, and stylish home and fashion boutiques—rounded out by shops awash in funky collectibles and souvenirs.

Information: Fort Smith Convention and Visitors Bureau | 2 N. B St., Fort Smith 72901 | 800/637–1477 | www.fortsmith.org. **Van Buren Chamber of Commerce** | 813 Main St., Van Buren, 72956 | 501/474–2761 | www.vanburen.org.

Attractions

Belle Grove Historic District. This 22-block downtown area consists of restored homes and buildings of varied architecture. You'll find maps and descriptions of the neighborhood structures, including Darby House, Clayton House, and the Patent Model Museum, at Miss Laura's Visitor Center (*see below*).

Darby House. General William O. Darby organized and commanded Darby's Rangers in World War II. Today you can visit his boyhood home in the Belle Grove District. | 311 N. 8th St. | 501/782–3388 | Free | Weekdays 8–1, weekends by appointment.

Clayton House. You can admire the hand-carved woodwork at the Clayton family home. The house was built in the 1850s with extensive additions after 1870. Many of its period furnishings belonged to the Clayton family. | 514 N. 6th St. | 501/783–3000 | $2 | Wed.–Fri. noon–4, Sat. 10–4, Sun. 1–4.

Patent Model Museum. There are 85 working patent models from 1836 to the 1870s housed in this museum, the oldest residence in Fort Smith. | 400 N. 8th St. | 501/782–9014 | Free | Weekdays 9–4:30.

Fort Smith Art Center. The center, housed in a Victorian home, has both changing exhibits and permanent collections. The building is restored in its original colors. | 423 N. 6th St. | 501/782–1156 | $1 | Jan. 2–Dec. 23, Tues.–Sat. 9:30–4:30, Sun. 2–4.

Fort Smith Museum of History. The Fort Smith Museum of History traces the history and culture of the area, covering notable local heroes and outlaws. You can sample a working old-time soda fountain and browse at the gift shop. | 320 Rogers Ave. | 501/783–7841 | $2 | Sept.–May, Tues.–Sat. 10–5, Sun. 1–5; June–Aug., Tues.–Sat. 9–5, Sun. noon–5.

Fort Smith National Historic Site. The remains of two successive frontier forts and a reproduction of "Hanging Judge" Isaac Parker's 1870s gallows are among the things you can see here. The gallows was big enough to hang 12 outlaws at once. From 1875 to 1896, Parker heard more than 13,000 cases and sentenced 160 to "hang by the neck until dead." The basement jail in the former barracks was called "Hell on the Border." | Rogers Ave. and 3rd St. | 501/783–3961 | $2 | Daily.

Fort Smith Trolley Bus. The red-and-yellow rubber-tired bus leaves Miss Laura's Visitor Center for a 30-min interpretive tour of the Belle Grove Historic District and other sites. You can board or get off the trolley at any stop along the route. | 2 N. B St. | 501/783–8888 or 800/637–1477 | $1 | Mon.–Sat., every ½ hr 9:30–4.

Miss Laura's Visitor Center. Built as a hotel just before the turn of the century, the ornate building soon became "Miss Laura's," the town's premier bawdyhouse. After legalized prostitution ended in 1924, the building gradually fell into disrepair until remodeled as a restaurant in the 1980s. In 1992 it became the city's visitors center, and it is reportedly the only former house of prostitution on the National Register of Historic Places. You can pick up maps and descriptions of the Belle Grove Historic District and the city's museums and historic and other sites here, as well as information on dining, lodging, and shopping. The Fort Smith Trolley leaves Miss Laura's every half-hour from 9:30 to 4 (*see above*). | 2 N. B St. | 501/783–8888 or 800/637–1477 | www.fortsmith.org | Tour building by donation | Mon.–Sat. 9–4, Sun. 1–4:30.

ON THE CALENDAR

MAY: *Old Fort Days Rodeo.* Over 65 years old, the Fort Smith rodeo includes bull and bronco riding, team roping, calf roping, clowns, and other contests. | Kay Rodgers Park (Fairgrounds) | 501/783–6176.

MAY: *Old Timers Days Street Dance and Arts and Crafts Festival.* On six blocks of Main St. in Van Buren you'll find more than 250 arts and crafts exhibitors from a seven-state area. There's food, entertainment, and a children's carnival, too. | 501/474–0510.

JUNE: *Old Fort River Festival.* Fort Smith celebrates the visual and performing arts, with a large children's area for games and sporting events. | Harry E. Kelley Park | 501/783–6363.

SEPT., OCT.: *Arkansas–Oklahoma State Fair.* A livestock exposition, a carnival, top-name entertainment, commercial exhibits, and a midway round out the fair, held in Fort Smith. | Kay Rodgers Park (Fairgrounds) | 501/783–6176.

OCT.: *Valley of the Arkansas Gathering.* Native American life, frontier pioneer days, the Civil War, and the era of "Hanging Judge" Isaac Parker are reenacted in Fort Smith. | 501/783–8888.

OCT.: *Fall Festival.* On Main St. in Van Buren, over 300 exhibitors display fine artwork, handcrafted items, antiques, collectibles, and flea market finds; there's a carnival for kids. | 501/474–0510.

Dining

Back Yard Burgers. Fast Food. If you're hankering for a burger but don't want the typical fast food joints, Back Yard Burgers is the place to go. This chain serves several varieties of beef burgers, and also has hot dogs and cheese fries. | 7612 Rogers Ave., Fort Smith | 501/452–6677 | $3–$6 | No credit cards.

Calico County. Southern. Lots of hanging greenery decorates this restaurant where the choices range from morning biscuits to chicken-fried steak with trimmings such as squash casserole and broccoli-rice casserole. The dessert menu includes cherry cobbler, and the restaurant is known for its cinnamon rolls. Beer and wine are served. Kids' menu. | 2401 S. 56th St., Fort Smith | 501/452–3299 | $14–$20 | AE, D, DC, MC, V.

Emmy's German Restaurant. German. An old house, antique beer steins, and pictures of the old country are as authentic as the friendly women who have been dishing up traditional German fare here for nearly 50 years. The rump steak and rouladen or sauerbraten with potato dumplings are not for light eaters. You can also choose chicken, veal, or pork cordon bleu. | 602 N. 16th St., Fort Smith | 501/783–0012 | $16–$29 | AE, D, DC, MC, V.

Folie à Deux. Eclectic. The owners of this bistro call its cuisine "true American" because it is a melting pot of world cuisine—Italian, Asian, French, American. This cozy place in a neighborhood shopping center has booths and mirrors. You can enjoy steak Nicholas (stuffed with a mushroom filling), entrée-size salads (such as spinach with grilled chicken livers), and crêpes. The tart Tatin is a good choice for dessert. Open-air dining is available. | 2909 Old Greenwood Rd., Fort Smith | 501/648–0041 | $16–$37 | AE, D, DC, MC, V.

JazzyBlues. Southern. Uncle Juice, Mamma Rainey, and a whole cast of characters dabble with age-old southern, Caribbean, and Creole recipes to produce some of the best comfort food in town. Succulent crab cakes, spicy jerk chops, and stick-to-your-ribs gumbo make up for the dive's relatively bland atmosphere. | 5708 Towson Ave., Fort Smith | 501/646–9300 | $5–$8 | MC, V | Sun. and Mon.

La Huerta Mexican Restaurant. Mexican. Cornmeal wrapped tamales and chile poblano are memorable choices at La Huerta, the house restaurant for the Ramada Inn. | 5103 Towson Ave., Fort Smith | 501/484–9343 | $6.50–$9.95 | AE, D, MC, V.

The Lighthouse Inn. Seafood. This lighthouse-shaped building never guided craft on the nearby Arkansas River, but it might lure you to a bounteous catch of fresh seafood, served in a nautical-theme dining room. You'll find shrimp in many styles, blackened snapper, king crab legs, and steak, among other choices. Dessert includes homemade carrot and chocolate velvet cakes. Kids' menu. | 6000 Midland, Fort Smith | 501/783–9420 | $16–$47 | AE, D, DC, MC, V | Closed Sun. No lunch Sat.

Tri-Ky Vietnamese and Chinese Restaurant. Pan-Asian. Tri-Ky serves the usual Chinese entrées, such as kung pao chicken, but its spicier Vietnamese dishes are the restaurant's signature. Lemon grass chicken with hot chili sauce is a good one to try, as are any of the daily specials. | 912 Garrison Ave., Fort Smith | 501/782–2173 | $5–$7.50 | MC, V | Sun.

Lodging

Aspen Hotel & Suites. Cherrywood and picklewood accents and grand armoires add a touch of elegance to the rooms and suites at the Aspen. The hotel is ½ mi off exit 8 on I–540. Complimentary breakfast. Cable TV. Outdoor pool. Gym. Airport shuttle. | 2900 South 68th St., Fort Smith | 501/452–9000 or 800/627–9417 | fax 501/484–0551 | www.aspenhotelandsuites.com | 53 rooms, 5 suites | $61–$80 rooms, $120–$175 suites | AE, D, DC, MC, V.

Beland Manor Bed and Breakfast. This old Colonial Revival caters to the businessperson who wants professional conveniences amid period decor. The Fort Smith airport is 2 mi away, and you're only 2½ mi from the national historic district. Beland Manor is 1⅓ mi from I–540, at exit 8A. In-room data ports, some in-room hot tubs. Cable TV, some in-room VCRs. Business services. No smoking. | 1320 S. Albert Pike Ave., Fort Smith | 501/782–3300 | fax 501/782–7674 | belandbnb@ipa.net | www.fort-smith.net | 8 rooms, 1 suite | $75–$110, $150 suite | AE, D, DC, MC, V.

Comfort Inn. This two-story Comfort Inn with inside and outside corridors is about 2 mi from Van Buren. The inn is right off I–540, exit 2A. Complimentary Continental breakfast. In-room data ports. Cable TV. Pool. Laundry facilities. Some pets allowed. | 3131 Cloverleaf St., Van Buren | 501/474–2223 | fax 501/474–9049 | www.comfort.inn | 48 rooms | $65 | AE, D, DC, MC, V.

Days Inn. This chain with outside corridors is 5 mi from the Fort Smith airport, and three blocks from the Fort Smith Museum and downtown. The inn is 3½ mi from I–540, exit 6. Complimentary Continental breakfast. Cable TV. Pool. Airport shuttle. Some pets allowed (fee). | 1021 Garrison Ave., Fort Smith | 501/783–0548 | fax 501/783–0836 | www.daysinn.com | 53 rooms | $39–$49 | AE, D, DC, MC, V.

Fifth Season Inn. The Fifth Season has spacious rooms and a lobby atrium. The inn is adjacent to a shopping center and is a 15-min drive from tennis and golf. Restaurant. Complimentary breakfast. Indoor pool. Hot tub, sauna. Gym. Airport shuttle. | 2219 S. Waldron Rd.,

Fort Smith | 501/452–4880 | fsifs@aol.com | 130 rooms, 8 suites | $69–$80 rooms, $90–$130 suites | AE, D, DC, MC, V.

Four Points by Sheraton. This two-story hotel with outside corridors is two blocks from I–540, exit 8A and is near movie theaters and restaurants. The Central Mall is two blocks away, and you're 1½ mi from the tennis courts at Creekmore Park. Restaurant, complimentary breakfast, room service. In-room data ports, refrigerators. Cable TV. Pool, wading pool. Business services, airport shuttle. Some pets allowed. | 5711 Rogers Ave., Fort Smith | 501/452–4110 | fax 501/452–4891 | 151 rooms | $53, $90 suites | AE, D, DC, MC, V.

Guesthouse Inn. This two-story motel with inside doors is ½ mi from I–540, exit 12. The Guesthouse Inn is in a field and near several restaurants. Downtown Fort Smith is 6 mi away, and the airport is a 5-min drive. Complimentary Continental breakfast. In-room data ports. Cable TV. Pool. | 3600 Grinnell Ave., Fort Smith | 501/646–5100 | fax 501/646–4598 | 63 rooms | $55 | AE, D, DC, MC, V.

Hampton Inn. This 5-yr-old interior corridor hotel is 1 mi from the Fort Smith airport, and near restaurants, shopping, and movie theaters. The historic district is a 10-min drive away. Hampton Inn is 7 mi from I–540, exit 8B. In-room data ports, refrigerators. Cable TV. Pool. Hot tub. Laundry facilities. Business services. | 6201 Rogers Ave., Fort Smith | 501/452–2000 | fax 501/452–6668 | www.hampton-inn.com/hi/ftsmith | 143 rooms | $71–$91 | AE, D, DC, MC, V.

Holiday Inn Civic Center. This Holiday Inn four blocks from the Arkansas River is near downtown, parks, and shopping. You are 10 blocks from Fort Smith's historic district, and four blocks from the Judge Parker Museum and the Fort Smith Historical Museum. The nine-story inn, which has an atrium with a skylight, is 5 mi from I–540, exit 8A. Restaurant (with entertainment). In-room data ports. Cable TV. Indoor pool. Hot tubs. Exercise equipment. Business services. Airport shuttle. Some pets allowed. | 700 Rogers Ave. | 501/783–1000 | fax 501/783–0312 | hi426gm@sagehotel.com | 255 rooms | $79–$89 | AE, D, DC, MC, V.

Ramada Inn Fort Smith. With its freshly painted, ornate facade, the Ramada Inn Fort Smith hasn't the look or the feel of a chain hotel. Rooms are tastefully decorated with wood-framed, king-size or double beds, and suites include a separate sitting area with sofa bed. Many rooms feature courtyard or golf course views. Restaurant. Complimentary breakfast. Some microwaves. Some refrigerators. Cable TV. Outdoor pool. Sauna. Gym. | 5103 Towson Ave., Fort Smith | 501/646–2931 or 800/2–RAMADA | fax 501/648–9085 | www.ramada.com | 156, including 8 suites | $50–$63, $70–$85 suites | AE, D, DC, MC, V.

Super 8. The Fort Smith Airport and the historic district are each 3 mi from this motel. From exit 11 on I–540, the motel is 2½ mi away. Cable TV. Pool. Airport shuttle. | 3810 Towson Ave., Fort Smith | 501/646–3411 | 57 rooms | $40–$45 | AE, D, DC, MC, V.

Super 8 Motel. This two-story Super 8 with outside corridors is 1 mi from the Van Buren area, where you'll find a scenic train ride and antiques stores. The motel is right off exit 5 of I–540. Complimentary Continental breakfast. Cable TV. Pool. Hot tub. Laundry facilities. Some pets allowed (fee). | 106 N. Plaza Ct., Van Buren | 501/471–8888 | 46 rooms | $55–$68 | AE, D, DC, MC, V.

Thomas Quinn Guest House. This B&B is 3 mi from the Fort Smith Airport and 2 mi from Harper Stadium; tennis and golf is nearby. The guest house is 5 mi from I–540, exit 6 (Grand Avenue). Kitchenettes. Cable TV. Hot tub. | 815 N. B St., Fort Smith | 501/782–0499 | 9 suites | $59–$79 | AE, D, DC, MC, V.

GILLETT

MAP 11, D5

(Nearby towns also listed: Dumas, Helena, Pine Bluff, Stuttgart)

This small agriculture-based delta town is best known for its annual Coon Supper, a feast on ring-tailed raccoons (with optional entrées) that for more than 50 years has also served as the state's first, though unofficial, political function of the year. It draws politicians like bees to nectar.

Information: **Dumas Chamber of Commerce** | Box 431, Dumas 71639-0431 | 870/382–5447.

Attractions

Arkansas Post Museum. Authentic structures from the delta, including a child-size playhouse, hanging gallows, and log houses, plus memorabilia from frontier and later days, and a restored prairie, are all here. | Rte. 1 | 870/548–2634 | $2.25 | Mon.–Sat. 8–5, Sun. 1–5.

Arkansas Post National Memorial. This memorial commemorates the site of the first permanent European settlement in the lower Mississippi River valley, established by Henri de Tonti in 1686. The settlement was under Spanish rule from 1765 to 1800 and attacked by the British during the Revolutionary War; it became a bustling frontier town and was captured by Union forces during the Civil War. The visitors center, barrier-free trails, fishing, and picnic areas are some of the attractions here. | Rte. 1 | 870/548–2207 | Free | Daily 8–5.

ON THE CALENDAR

OCT.: *Heritage Celebration.* You can watch demonstrations of such pioneer skills as Dutch oven cooking, blacksmithing, quilting, spinning, and churning at Arkansas Post Museum State Park. Kids can play pioneer games. | 870/548–2634.
OCT.: *Ghosts of the Past.* Ghosts from the state's past come alive in a candlelight tour at Arkansas Post National Memorial. | 870/548–2207.

HARDY

MAP 11, D2

(Nearby towns also listed: Batesville, Bull Shoals, Jonesboro, Mountain Home, Mountain View, Paragould, Pocahontas)

Hardy was officially founded in 1883 as a railroad town and was named for a young subcontractor who saved his boss's life. Hardy's population remained around 50 for its first 10 years; by 1900 the population had grown to around 500. Hardy now has about 600 residents. By 1920, businesses occupied almost two blocks on Main Street. In 1982, after a devastating flood of the Spring River, most businesses moved to higher ground, and crafts shops, antiques shops, and restaurants began to open in those historic buildings on Main Street.

Information: **Spring River Area Chamber of Commerce** | Box 300, 72542-0300 | 870/856–3210.

Attractions

Mammoth Spring State Park. Mammoth Spring flows at an average hourly rate of almost 10 million gallons of 58°F water. The pour-off creates Spring River, popular for canoeing and trout fishing. The 1883 Frisco Depot Museum houses railroad memorabilia. You can also visit picnic sites and a pavilion, hike, take the kids to a playground, and a ballfield, and view remnants of an early mill and hydroelectric plant. The museum is at the junction of Hwy. 9 and Hwy. 63. | Box 36, Mammoth Spring | 870/625–7364 | Free; museum $2.25 | Daily.

Veteran's Military Museum. Thousands of items are on view here, taken from every American conflict from the Revolutionary War to Desert Storm. You'll see photographs, weapons, uniforms, G.I. equipment, and vehicles. | 738 Main St. | 870/856–4133 | $2 | Daily 9–5.

MAY: *Spring River Canoe Race.* The race begins at Dam 3 and Spring River Oaks campground, with takeout at Hardy Beach. | 870/856–2402.

JUNE: *Spring River Car Club Show.* More than 200 cars dating from early 1900 to present time are on show, with more than 150 trophies awarded. You can vote for People's Choice Award, visit concessions, and play games. | 870/856–3566.

AUG.: *Old Soldiers Reunion.* Over 105 years old, this event at Mammoth Spring State Park keeps you entertained with a carnival, bingo, prizes, crafts, food booths by civic organizations, and music. | 870/625–3957.

SEPT.: *Solemn Old Judge Days.* You can listen to an old-fashioned Grand Ole Opry–style musical and watch a bank-robbery reenactment, visit an antique and classic car show, and tap your feet to a fiddle contest at Mammoth Spring State Park. | 870/625–7364.

Dining

Virgil's Hardy Café. American. Known as a place to get a quick bite for breakfast, lunch, or dinner. Many families frequent Virgil's for its catfish suppers. | Main St. | 870/856–3177 or 870/856–2756 | $5.50–$8 | No credit cards.

Lodging

Best Western Village Inn. The Best Western Village Inn is 1½ mi from Hardy on Hwys. 412 and 62W, 15 mi from Cherokee Village. Complimentary Continental breakfast. Refrigerators. Cable TV. Pool. | 3856 Rte. 62/412W | 870/856–2176 | www.bestwestern.com | 42 rooms | $49–$59 | AE, D, DC, MC, V.

Days Inn Hardy. This Days Inn is equipped with the latest amenities, including dual jacks for modems, and has ample facilities for disabled guests. There's golfing at Cherokee Village, about 2 mi from the inn. Complimentary Continental breakfast. Cable TV. Hot tubs. | Junction of 412, 62, and 63 | 870/856–4241 | www.daysinn.com | 43 rooms | $55–$70 rooms, $75–$105 suites | AE, D, MC, V.

Olde Stonehouse B and B. This 1928 B&B is built with Arkansas vernacular rock taken from the Spring River one block away. You are near fishing, canoeing, six restaurants, and Cherokee Village. You can get a discount for the golf course at Cherokee Village. Complimentary breakfast. Some in-room hot tubs. Cable TV. No smoking. | 511 Main St. | 870/856–2983 | fax 870/856–4036 | oldestonehous@centurytel.net | www.bbonline.com/ar/stonehouse | 8 rooms, 3 suites | $69–$85, $125 suites | AE, D, DC, MC, V.

HARRISON

MAP 11, B2

(Nearby towns also listed: Bentonville, Berryville, Buffalo National River, Bull Shoals, Eureka Springs, Fayetteville, Mountain Home, Mountain View, Rogers, Springdale)

Harrison is the northern anchor of Route 7, a State Scenic Byway that winds through the Ozark and Ouachita mountains to Arkadelphia. Harrison lies along Crooked Creek, a cold-water fishing stream particularly noted for its smallmouth bass. You'll find more fishing in the upper section of the Buffalo National River, just 20 mi south of town, plus canoeing, float trips, hiking, and ecotours.

After Harrison's formation in 1870, the surrounding hill country served as a hideout for Frank and Jesse James, Jim and Cole Younger, and other outlaws. A brochure outlines a walking tour of the town's historic buildings, along with cafés, bookstores, and other shops.

Information: **Harrison Chamber of Commerce** | Box 939, 72602-0939 | 870/741–2659.

Attractions

Boone County Heritage Museum. Harrison's past comes alive with this museum's genealogy library, railroad room, Civil War artifacts, and Native American relics. | 110 South Cherry St. | 870/741–3312 | $2 | Mar.–Nov., Mon.–Fri. 10–4; Dec.–Feb., Thurs. only 10–4.

Mystic Caverns. The upper level has enormous formations; the lower level is in pristine state. You may find the climb strenuous. There are a mineral museum and gift shop on the premises. | 870/743–1739 | $8.95 | Mar.–May, Sept.–Dec., Mon.–Sat. 9–4:30, Sun. 1–4:30; June–Aug., Mon.–Sat. 9–5:30, Sun. 1–5:30.

ON THE CALENDAR

JUNE: *North Arkansas Rusty Wheels Old Engine Club Show.* Antique tractors, steam engines, gas engines, and antique cars are on display, and you'll also find sawmill and engine demonstrations, crafts, food, and a tractor pull. | Fairgrounds | 870/743–1511.
SEPT.: *Coca-Cola Airshow of the Ozarks.* Warbird displays, hot air balloons rising into the sky, a concert, fireworks, skydiving, and aerobatic acts of all kinds are what you'll find at this air show. | Boone County Airport | 870/741–2659.
SEPT.: *Northwest Arkansas District Fair.* You'll find agriculture and livestock displays, local arts and crafts, rides, food, games, prizes, and arena events. | Fairgrounds | 870/743–1011.

Dining

Catfish Wharf. American. Deep-fried and grilled catfish are the specialties at this casual family establishment. You'll find speedy service and great hushpuppies. | 1318 Hwy. 62/65N | 870/741–9200 | fax 870/741–9200 | $6.50–$13.95 | D, MC, V | Sunday.

Ol' Rockhouse. Barbecue. An early 1900s home has been converted to a restaurant filled with local memorabilia, including old school photographs and athletic trophies. Hickory-smoked meats (brisket is most popular) are supplemented by Rick's steak and the Rockhouse burger. You can also try Louisiana-style catfish, fried pickles, and bread pudding with rum sauce. There is a deck for outdoors dining. Kids' menu. | 416 S. Pine St. | 870/741–8047 | $12–$22 | MC, V | No dinner Sun.

Lodging

Comfort Inn. You'll find this hotel on Hwy. 65 3 mi from the Boone County Regional Airport and across the street from a golf course, with a free shuttle and discounts on the links. Branson, MO, is 35 mi away, and the White River and Buffalo River in the Ozarks are within a 1-hr drive. Complimentary Continental breakfast. In-room data ports. Cable TV. Pool. Laundry facilities. | 1210 U.S. 62/65 N | 870/741–7676 | fax 870/741–0827 | 93 rooms | $49–$85 | AE, D, DC, MC, V.

The Harrison Inn. This hotel is 2 mi from the Harrison airport and close to a movie theater, shopping, restaurants, and the Boone County Fairgrounds. Restaurant, room service. In-room data ports. Cable TV. Indoor pool. Hot tub. Exercise equipment. Laundry facilities. Business services. | 816 N. Main St. | 870/741–2391 | fax 870/741–1181 | 86 rooms | $38–$53 | AE, D, DC, MC, V.

Holiday Inn Express Hotel & Suites. Harrison's newest property, completed in May 1999, has elegant furnishings, large rooms with queen-size beds, and suites equipped with whirlpool baths. Guests at the hotel get complimentary passes to the full-service TNT Fitness Center across the street. Complimentary Continental breakfast. Some kitchenettes. Cable TV. Indoor pool. Hot tub, sauna. Gym. | 117 Hwy. 43 E. | 870/741–3636 | fax 870/741–8222 | www.basshotels.com/hiexpress | 90 rooms, including 23 suites | $65–$75 rooms, $80–$100 suites | AE, D, MC, V.

Lost Spur Guest Ranch. You can spend 3 days or up to 1 wk riding horses, fishing, and living the cowboy or cowgirl life on the Hunter family's expansive farm. Creekside cedar cabins are decorated with throw rugs, quilts, wreaths, and other country accents. Two cabins are equipped with kitchens. Complimentary meals. Hot tub. Fishing. | 4648 Lost Spur Rd. | 870/743–SPUR or 800/774–2414 | lostspur@aol.com | 4 cabins, 1 cottage allow accommodation for 34 guests | $320–$420 per person for 3 nights, $795 per person for 1 wk | D, MC, V | Nov.–Feb.

Ozark Mountain Inn. The Ozark Mountain Inn is on a hill overlooking the town of Harrison. Lake Harrison is 2 mi away. The large, spacious lobby has plenty of seating. Complimentary Continental breakfast. Cable TV. Pool, wading pool. Playground. Business services. Some pets allowed. | 1222 N. Main St. | 870/743–1949 | fax 870/743–2960 | 100 rooms | $38 | AE, D, DC, MC, V.

Super 8. This motor inn is right behind the Primetime shopping center and near the Catfish Wharf restaurant. Complimentary Continental breakfast. Some in-room hot tubs. Cable TV. Pool. Business services. Some pets allowed. | 1330 U.S. 62/65 N | 870/741–1741 | fax 870/741–8858 | 50 rooms | $48–$63 | AE, D, DC, MC, V.

HEBER SPRINGS

(Nearby towns also listed: Batesville, Conway, Morrilton, Mountain View, Newport, Russellville, Searcy)

Founded around seven sulfur springs as a health spa and watering hole in the late 1800s, Heber Springs is perched on the eastern tip of 40,000-acre Greers Ferry Lake. It anchors an area rich in outstanding angling. The lake is stocked with walleye, large- and smallmouth bass, hybrid striped/white bass, lake trout, crappie, and bream. You can fly fish for four species of trout on the Little Red River below the dam.

You can also find water sports and recreation, hiking, golf, and other outdoor activities, and there are dozens of campsites, family and fishing resorts, B&Bs, dining spots, full-service marinas, and recreational areas. The planned communities of Fairfield Bay and Eden Isle also lie along the lake. You'll find plenty of antiques and other shops, including Panache, the sweet-smelling gallery of the international headquarters of Aromatique bath products and decorative fragrances.

Information: Heber Springs Area Chamber of Commerce | 1001 W. Main St., 72543-2390 | 501/362–2444.

Attractions

Olmstead Museum. This museum used to be the Olmstead Funeral Home, and you can see a horse-drawn hearse, a portable embalming machine, a cosmetic kit, antique coffins and tools, and other artifacts. | 108 S. 4th St. | 501/362–2422 | Free | Weekdays by appointment.

Riddle's Elephant and Wildlife Sanctuary. You can observe elephant behavior and handling at this sanctuary, the only one in the world that will take in any elephant for any reason. If you want, you can bring apples, carrots, or bananas to feed them. | 233 Pumpkin Center Cir., Quitman | 501/589–3291 | Free (donations accepted) | 1st Sat. of month, 11–3 and by appointment.

Spring Park. Open-air stone pavilions built in 1927 protect the capped sulphur springs near a 1933 stone bandshell and a modern amphitheater. One of the town's original hotels, now a B&B, is across the street. | Main St. | 501/362–2444 | Free | Daily.

William Carl Garner Visitor Center. You can visit a museum, exhibition hall, and theater for the Greers Ferry Lake region. The visitors center is home base for tours of the massive dam and hikes on Mossy Bluff and Buckeye trails. There is free weekend entertainment in the summer. | 704 Heber Springs Rd. N | 501/362–9067 | Free | Mar., Nov., weekends 10–4; Apr.–May 15, Sept. 16–Oct., daily 10–5; May 16–Sept. 15, daily 10–6; tours Memorial Day–Labor Day, Tues.–Fri. 10 and 2.

JULY: *World Championship Cardboard Boat Festival.* What you'll find here is youth, adult, and corporate races for boats made completely of cardboard, plus a tug-of-war, regulation volleyball, and a watermelon eating contest. | Sandy Beach | 501/362–2444.

Dining

The Captain's House. Continental. At this early 1900s home with paintings by local artists on the walls, you'll find an alternative to casual resort dining. You can choose from dishes such as fillet Madeira, sautéed tilapia with cilantro pesto, baked orange roughy, and marguerita chicken skewers, and char-broiled steak. There is open-air dining on the veranda. Kids' menu. | 603 W. Quitman | 501/362–3963 | $17–$35 | AE, D, MC, V.

China Delight. Chinese. Casual dining from the buffet or a menu is what you'll find here. The kung pao chicken is one of the dishes worth trying. | 1632 Rte. 25N | 501/362–7054 | $5–$13 | AE, D, MC, V | Closed Mon.

Luigi's Restaurant. Italian. Hearty portions of fresh soups, salads, and pastas are the main attraction at Luigi's. | 2022 Hwy. 25B | 501/362–0669 or 501/362–1689 | fax 501/362–3234 | $7.95–$10 | AE, D, MC, V | Wed.

Mr. B's Catfish. Seafood. You may want to try the fried catfish at this casual restaurant, where lunkers caught in area waters have been stuffed and mounted. Crab, oyster, shrimp, and frogs' legs are also available, along with hamburger steak for landlubbers. Mr. B's is known for choice rib eyes. Kids' menu. | 1120 Rte. 25B N | 501/362–7692 | $7–$14 | No credit cards.

Red Apple Inn. Continental. Native stone, Mediterranean-style wrought iron, fountains, and expansive views of nearby Greers Ferry Lake are all part of the luxury surroundings at this resort restaurant. The operators describe the cooking as Southern gourmet, with such dishes as pine nut–crusted salmon, sesame catfish, prime rib, steak, and traditional accompaniments such as corn pudding and old-fashioned desserts. Black Angus steak is considered one of the specialties of the house. On Friday and Saturday nights you can listen to a music combo, and there is a buffet on Sundays. Kids' menu. Smoking is not allowed. | 1000 Club Rd. | 501/362–3111 | $18–$45 | AE, D, DC, MC, V.

Lodging

Anderson House Inn. Country antiques and handmade quilts decorate guest rooms at this inn. A full breakfast is served in the parlor. There are places to eat dinner in town; fishing packages and boat rentals can be arranged if you ask beforehand. The inn is across from Spring Park. Complimentary breakfast. No kids under 6. No smoking. | 201 E. Main St. | 501/362–5266 or 800/264–5279 | fax 501/363–2326 | innkeepr@cswnet.com | www.yourinn.com | 16 rooms | $67–$84 | AE, D, DC, MC, V.

Azalea Cottage Inn Bed & Breakfast. This turn-of-the-century Colonial Revival home has hardwood floors, antique furnishings, and a wraparound porch with rocker swings. Three rooms come with English gas fireplaces and all accommodations have private baths with whirlpool tubs. Complimentary breakfast. Refrigerators. Cable TV. | 320 W. Sunny Meadow Rd. | 501/362–1665 or 888/233–7931 | www.azaleacottageinn.com | 4 rooms | $89–$110 | MC, V.

Brighton Park Inn. The former Holiday Inn Express changed its name but kept all the amenities, including 25-in TVs, an outdoor pool, and deluxe breakfasts. A majority of the rooms are suites, and all have kitchenettes. Complimentary Continental breakfast. Some kitchenettes. Cable TV. Outdoor pool. Hiking. | 13450 Hwy. 25B N | 501/362–1000 or 866/362–1003 | fax 501/362–8833 | 61 rooms | $68–$125 | AE, D, MC, V.

Budget Inn. Truck parking is available and fishing, boating, and camping are ½ mi away at Greers Ferry Lake. Cable TV. Pool. Some pets allowed. | 616 W. Main St. | 501/362–8111 or 888/297–7955 (reservations) | 25 rooms | $38–$60 | AE, D, DC, MC, V.

Fairfield Bay Resort. This resort is set on 14,000 wooded acres and borders Greers Ferry Lake. 5 restaurants, picnic area. Kitchenettes, microwaves, refrigerators. Cable TV. 4 pools, wading pool. Driving range, 18-hole golf course, miniature golf, putting green. 12 tennis courts. Bowling, horseback riding, water sports, boating. Children's programs (4–16), playground. Laundry facilities. Business services. | Lost Creek Pkwy., Fairfield Bay | 501/884–3333 or 800/643–9790 (reservations) | fax 501/884–3345 (outside AR) or 800/482–9826 (within AR) | 250 apartments | $59–$95 | AE, D, MC, V.

Lake and River Inn. This family-owned inn added a new section in 2000 with Thermo-Masseur thermal bathtubs. Furnishings in the standard rooms are modest. Outdoor pool. | 2322 Hwy. 25B | 501/362–3161 or 800/362–5578 | www.lakeandriverinn.com | 37 rooms | $45–$55 rooms, $65–$75 suites or apt. (sleeps 6) | AE, D, MC, V.

Lakeshore Resort. Lakeshore sits on a lake amid 4 acres of hilly, wooded grounds. Picnic area. Kitchenettes, refrigerators. Cable TV. Dock. Airport shuttle. | 801 Case Ford Rd. | 501/362–2315 | 7 rooms | $54 | AE, D, MC, V.

Oak Tree Inn Bed and Breakfast. This is a Colonial-style building on the edge of the Ozarks, one block from Greers Ferry Lake. Complimentary breakfast. Some kitchenettes, some in-room hot tubs. | Vinegar Hill and Rte. 110W | 501/362–7731 or 800/959–3857 | oaktreeinn@arkansas.net | www.bbonline.com/ar/oaktree | 4 rooms | $85 | AE, D, DC, MC, V.

Red Apple Inn. A student of Frank Lloyd Wright designed this inn, which is on a wooded lot 1 mi from Greers Ferry Lake. Restaurant, bar, room service. In-room data ports, some refrigerators. Cable TV. Pool, wading pool. Driving range, 18-hole golf, tennis court. Playground. Laundry facilities. Business services, airport shuttle. | 1000 Country Club Dr. | 501/362–3111 or 800/733–2775 (reservations) | fax 501/362–8900 | 57 rooms, 2 suites, 20 condos | $115, $125–$135 suites, $120–$150 1–bedroom condos, $140–$175 2–bedroom condos, $160–$195 3–bedroom condos | AE, D, DC, MC, V.

HELENA

MAP 11, E5

(Nearby towns also listed: Dumas, Forrest City, Gillett, Stuttgart)

"Helena occupies one of the prettiest situations on the river," wrote Mark Twain in *Life on the Mississippi*. In this small river town, laid out in 1820 and incorporated in 1833, centuries of history survive in numerous antebellum and post–Civil War homes and in its preserved downtown district. You will find memories of bustling steamboat days, when Helena was an important port, and the seven Confederate generals Helena produced in the Civil War. The most famous, Patrick Cleburne, lies in the Confederate burial ground at Maple Hill Cemetery. Helena became the cradle of the Delta blues, home to great bluesmen such as Sonny Boy Williamson and Robert Jr. Lockwood and a historic radio program devoted to the blues, which continues today.

Information: **Phillips County Chamber of Commerce** | Box 447, 72342-0447 | 870/338–8327.

Attractions

Delta Cultural Center. Photos and artifacts document life and settlement in the Arkansas Delta, music from blues to "rockabilly," and river life, plus changing exhibits. The center is housed in a restored 1921 train station and a nearby building on historic Cherry Street. | 95 Missouri St. and 141 Cherry St. | 870/338–4350 | Free | Mon.–Sat. 10–5, Sun. 1–5.

Marianna–Lee County Museum. The museum contains Native American artifacts, farm implements, an old barn exhibit, and items on local history. | 67 W. Main, Marianna | 870/295–2469 | Free | Wed. 10–noon and 2–4, and by appointment.

HELENA

INTRO
ATTRACTIONS
DINING
LODGING

Phillips County Museum. Varied collections tell the history of this Mississippi River port. The museum has outstanding archives. | 623 Pecan St. | 870/338–7790 | Free | Tues.–Sat. 10–4.

Pillow–Thompson House. This 1896 home is one of the South's finest examples of Queen Anne architecture. | 718 Perry St. | 870/338–8535 | Free | Tues.–Sat. 10–4, Sun. 1–4.

St. Francis National Forest. These 20,000 acres of forest are known for their diversity of plant and animal life; two lakes, camping, picnicking, swimming, and fishing. A scenic byway runs through the forest. | 2675 Hwy. 44, Marianna | 870/295–5278 or 870/295–5279 | Free | Daily.

ON THE CALENDAR

OCT.: *King Biscuit Blues Festival.* Local, regional, and international artists perform blues and gospel. You can also find arts, crafts, a barbecue contest, arm wrestling, a 5K run, and Mississippi riverboat cruises. | 870/338–8798.

SEPT.–MAY: *Warfield Concert Series.* You can listen to classical and popular music and attend dance, children's theater, musical productions, and fine-arts exhibits. | Phillips County Community College | 870/338–8327.

DEC.: *Holiday Open House.* The Pillow–Thompson House invites you to enjoy treats, seasonal music, and period Christmas decorations. | 870/338–8535.

Dining

Bell's Ducks by the River. American. The blue ribbon in Bell's front window declares the restaurant the "best in the county." The eclectic menu relies on Mississippi River bounty, including catfish cooked 12 ways. You'll also find 30-oz Angus steaks, Creole-style pork chops, and creative chicken and vegetarian entrées. | 115 Cherry St. | 870/338–6655 | Reservations essential | $15–$32 | AE, D, MC, V | Sunday.

Pasquale's Tamales. Tex-Mex. It is no wonder that Pasquale's house specialty is the tamale, as the restaurant is attached to the famous tamale factory of the same name. Also sharing the menu at this casual eatery are overstuffed deli-style sandwiches, chili, red beans and rice, muffalettas, and spaghetti and meatballs. Tamales are also available for carry-out. | 211 Missouri St. | 870/338–6722 | $4–$10 | MC, V | Closed Sat. night and Sun.

Casqui. America. Across the street from the Delta Cultural Center, Casqui is an ideal lunch spot, with buffet-style lunches and enormous burgers. | 101 Missouri St. | 870/338–3565 | $3.50–$7.95 | No credit cards.

Lodging

Best Western Inn. This no-frills hotel is a cozy place to hang your hat, especially if you're visiting the nearby Lady Luck casino. Best Western's lobby, with its couches, card tables, and television, does double-duty as a living room. Complimentary Continental breakfast. Microwaves, refrigerators. Outdoor pool. | 1053 Hwy. 49 W, West Helena | 870/572–2592 | fax 870/572–7561 | 64 rooms | $60–$70 | AE, D, DC, MC, V.

Delta Inn. A free shuttle is available from this modern brick building to the Lady Luck casino nearby. Complimentary Continental breakfast. Cable TV. Pool. Business services. Some pets allowed. | 1207 U.S. 49N, West Helena | 870/572–7915 or 800/748–8802 | fax 870/572–3757 | 100 rooms | $45–$89 | AE, D, DC, MC, V.

Edwardian Inn. This 1904 Colonial Revival mansion is listed on the National Register of Historic Places. The inn is set on a rise overlooking a sweeping lawn. You'll find stunning architectural details such as quarter-sewn oak woodwork in the floors, ceilings, staircases, paneling, and columns; and beveled and leaded glass. The inn is 70 mi south of Memphis. Complimentary breakfast. Cable TV. | 317 Biscoe St. | 870/338–9155 or 800/598–4749 | 12 rooms | $65–$75 | AE, DC, MC, V.

SCENIC DRIVES, WILDFLOWERS, BACK-COUNTRY DRIVING TRAILS

"The Natural State" claims thousands of miles of hiking, mountain biking, horse-back, and other trails, plus navigable waterways ideal for everything from a large yacht to a canoe. But its dramatic scenery—some of the finest in Middle America—can also be enjoyed along its major highways and back roads, as well as unpaved routes ideal for increasingly popular four-wheel-drive sport-utility vehicles and trucks.

Many of Arkansas's finest sightseeing itineraries are on curving, two-lane high-ways through the Ozark and Ouachita Mountains. The scenic **Route 23** north to **Route 16** was named the **Pig Trail** because it was once the quickest route for east-ern Arkansans heading to the University of Arkansas at Fayetteville for Razorback games. The **Ozark Highlands** route, **Route 21** north from U.S. 64 through Newton County, follows ridges and hollows through the mountains.

Those traveling east and west might try **U.S. 62** between Rogers and Hardy, or **Route 16** between Clinton and Fayetteville, which borders wilderness areas and travels through country towns. The **Sylamore Scenic Byway, Route 5** between Mountain View and Calico Rock, curves along White River bluffs, and **Scenic Route 14** from Bull Shoals Lake through Yellville and Mountain View to Batesville provides views of massive forests, the Buffalo National River, limestone bluffs, and mountain villages.

In the Ouachita Mountains, **Route 309** between Paris and Havana reaches the top of Mount Magazine, Arkansas's highest point, with panoramic views over the Arkansas River valley. The **Winona Scenic Drive** (Forest Service Rd. 132) has inter-pretive stops. The **Talimena National Scenic Byway, Route 88** from Mena to Tali-hina, Oklahoma, offers historical and recreational sites as well as magnificent views as it stretches across mountain crests. Details of the **Scenic 7 Byway** between Arkadelphia and Harrison and **Crowley's Ridge National Scenic Byway** from Piggott to Helena are featured in the Arkansas driving tours earlier in the chapter.

Although Arkansas is noted for its fall foliage, don't miss its wildflowers. Some 200,000 acres of highway roadsides along some of these and other routes have been beautified with such blossoms as showy evening primrose, purple coneflower, Indian paintbrush, spiderwort, and cardinal flower. Existing wildflower populations have been preserved and new ones established. More than 1,000 mi of wildflower routes are mapped out in the brochure **"Wildflowers of the Arkansas Roadways,"** available through Arkansas Parks and Tourism.

More than 10 million sport-utility vehicles (SUVs) are on U.S. highways, but 90% never leave the pavement. Now is the chance. The **"Arkansas Back Country Driving Trails Guide"** maps out trails for four-wheel-drive vehicles through remote areas of the state to vistas that only a handful of people are lucky enough to see each year. To get a copy of this or the wildflower-route brochure, call 800/NATURAL or look on the Arkansas Web site at www.arkansas.com

Foxglove Bed & Breakfast. Foxglove is a Georgian-style mansion built in the 1900s on a ridge overlooking the town of Helena and ¼ mi from the Mississippi. Complimentary breakfast. Cable TV, some in-room hot tubs. No kids under 12. | 229 Beech St. | 870/338–9391 | www.bbonline.com/ar/foxglove/ | 8 rooms | $79–$109 | AE, MC, V.

Magnolia Hill. This Queen Anne Victorian landmark, situated on the former site of Helena's courthouse in the historic district, is on the National Register of Historic Places. Some of the architectural details you'll find are original broadcloth wallcovering and fireplaces, hand-carved walnut tables, hardwood floors, mantels, and ceramic tile. Period antiques are placed throughout the house. The Lady Luck Rhythm and Blues Casino is 5 min. away and the Tunica, MS, casinos are 30 min. away. Complimentary breakfast. Hot tub. No smoking. | 609 Perry St. | 870/338–6874 | fax 870/338–7938 | 8 rooms, 1 suite | $75–$95 | AE, D, DC, MC, V.

HOPE

MAP 11, B6

(Nearby towns also listed: Arkadelphia, Ashdown, Hot Springs, Magnolia, Mena, Murfreesboro, Texarkana)

Hope is Arkansas's watermelon capital, growing some of the world's largest and tastiest melons. Founded in 1875 as a railroad town, Hope is today an agricultural community as well as a railroad and transportation center. It's also the birthplace of President Bill Clinton, who lived here until he was 6. Old Washington Historic State Park is nearby, in a village established in 1824 on the Southwest Trail; it was the Confederate state capital after Little Rock was captured (1864–65).

Information: Hope/Hempstead Chamber of Commerce | Box 250, 71802-0250 | 870/777–3640.

Attractions

The Clinton Center. The home and gardens where President Bill Clinton lived with his grandparents until age 4 have been restored. | 117 S. Hervey, at 2nd St. | 870/777–4455 | $5. Purchase tickets at house and shop around the corner on 2nd St. | Memorial Day–Labor Day, Tues.–Sat. 10–5, Sun. 1–5; Labor Day–Memorial Day, Mon.–Sat. 10–4:30.

Hope Visitor Center. In this restored 1912 railroad depot, you can learn about the town's history, and get a map showing Clinton sites. | 100 E. Division | 870/722–2580 | Free | Mon.–Sat. 8:30–5, Sun. 1–4.

★ **Old Washington Historic State Park.** Some 40 buildings remain from the 1820s–70s. You can take guided tours of the Confederate Capitol, antebellum homes, a re-created tavern inn, a blacksmith shop, a bladesmithing school, and a weapons museum. To get there, take exit 30 off I-30 and drive 9 mi northwest on Hwy. 4 to Washington. | Hwy. 4, Washington | 870/983–2684 | Free; museum $1.75 | Daily 8–5.

ON THE CALENDAR

FEB.: *Evening of Romance.* You can enjoy a romantic evening of fine food with candlelight and music at the restored Williams Tavern Restaurant in Old Washington Historic State Park. | 870/983–2890.
MAR.: *Jonquil Festival.* Thousands of jonquils, which have been blooming for 150 years, are on view at Old Washington Historic State Park. This also is south Arkansas's premier arts and crafts festival, with more than 200 exhibitors in this restored museum village. | 870/983–2890.
AUG.: *Hope Watermelon Festival.* The festival celebrates the huge watermelons grown in the Hope area. You can wander among 250 arts and crafts booths and concession stands; listen to live music; watch the Watermelon Olympics, a seed-spitting con-

test, a melon-eating contest, a 5K run, and a fiddling contest; and visit an antique car show, an antique engine show, a bass tournament, a motorcycle show, and a sports card show. | Fair Park | 870/777–3640.

OCT.: *Civil War Days.* Cavalry, infantry, and cannons converge on Old Washington Historic State Park, along with actors from across the country portraying scenes from Civil War days; training skirmishes and tactical maneuvers are open to the public. | 870/983–2890.

DEC.: *Christmas and Candlelight.* This holiday event showcases the Old Washington Historic State Park at its loveliest, when it is dressed in 19th-century decorations, with thousands of luminaries lighting the way. | 870/983–2633.

Dining

Cherry's Old Tyme Soda Fountain. Delicatessen. Hope's landmark downtown lunch counter serves creamy milkshakes with chunks of fruit, and sandwiches piled high with roast beef, ham, turkey, or fresh vegetables. | 225 S. Main St. | 870/777–3424 | Reservations not accepted | $3.50–$6 | No credit cards | Weekends.

Little B's Mexican and Steak House. Mexican. You won't go hungry at this casual restaurant, unless you're a vegetarian. Rib eye, porterhouse, and prime rib satisfy a carnivorous craving, and most Mexican entrées come with ground beef, grilled shrimp, fajita-style chicken strips, and mounds of guacamole and sour cream. | 2406 N. Hervey St. (Hwy. 4) | 870/777–3377 | $8–$21 | AE, D, MC, V.

Lodging

Best Western. Standard chain accommodations right off I–30, exit 30. Refrigerators. Cable TV. Pool. Laundry facilities. Some pets allowed. | I—30 and Rte. 278 | 870/777–9222 | fax 870/777–9077 | 75 rooms | $45–$55 | AE, D, DC, MC, V.

Budget Inn Hope. This former Days Inn was renovated and renamed in 1998. Standard rooms feature queen-size beds, a small desk, and a full-size bath. Restaurant. Complimentary Continental breakfast. Cable TV. Outdoor pool. | 1500 N. Hervey St. | 870/722–1904 | fax 870/777–1911 | 57 rooms | $36–$40 | AE, D, MC, V.

Holiday Inn Express. Opened in late 1997, this hotel is right off I–30, exit 30, and less than 1 mi from the Clinton sites. Complimentary Continental breakfast. Some refrigerators. Pool. | 2600 N. Hervey St. | 870/722–6262 | fax 870/722–1922 | 61 rooms | $55–$68 | AE, D, DC, MC, V.

Hope Village Inn. This very basic motel also has spaces for RVs at an extra cost. | 2611 N. Hazel St. | 870/777–4665 | 44 rooms | $28–$35 | AE, D, MC, V.

Super 8. Standard accommodations on landscaped grounds right off exit 30 on I–30 and 2 mi from the Clinton sites. Complimentary Continental breakfast. Some refrigerators. Cable TV. Pool. Tennis. Playground. Laundry facilities. Business services. Some pets allowed. | 2000 Holiday Dr. | 870/777–8601 | fax 870/777–3142 | 100 rooms | $33–$39 | AE, D, DC, MC, V.

HOT SPRINGS

MAP 11, B5

(Nearby towns also listed: Arkadelphia, Ashdown, Benton, Little Rock)

The ancient forests and rivers of the quartz-rich Ouachita (pronounced *Wash*-i-taw) Mountains cradle Hot Springs, nicknamed the "Spa City." The Valley of the Vapors was what Native Americans called today's Hot Springs, whose 47 thermal springs were first encountered by Spanish explorer Hernando de Soto in 1541. In 1832 the U.S. Congress created the first federal reserve around the springs, which in 1921 became a national park. From the 1920s to the early 1960s, Hot Springs was a gambling town famed for its therapeutic bathhouses, some of which are still in business.

In Hot Springs you can find a host of tourist activities and events; it is noted for its art galleries, crafts shops, and antiques stores. The town was the boyhood home of President Bill Clinton, and you can visit many of his old haunts.

If you love water and beautiful scenery, there are five crystal-clear lakes in the region around Hot Springs. You can take white-water trips and go canoeing and fishing on the area's rivers. The Ouachitas are laced with top-notch trail systems and campsites.

Information: **Hot Springs Convention and Visitors Bureau** | Box K 71902 | 800/772–2489 | www.hotsprings.org.

Attractions

Arkansas Alligator Farm and Petting Zoo. You can see more than 300 alligators, some 10 ft long, plus deer, pygmy goats, llamas, lambs, and ostriches, at this small museum. | 847 Whittington Ave. | 501/623–6172 or 800/750–7891 | $3.50 | Labor Day–Apr., daily 9:30–5; May–Labor Day, daily 9–6.

Bath House Show. Songs from the last six decades plus family-style humor are performed during this popular comedy/music show. | 701 Central Ave. | 501/623–1415 | $10.45 | Feb.–Dec., call for hrs.

Coleman's Crystal Mine & Rock Shop. You can dig for crystals and keep what you find, or browse among those already cleaned and polished in this shop, 15 mi north of Hot Springs on Hwy. 7. | 5837 North Hwy. 7, Jessieville | 501/984–5328 | Free; $10 to dig | Daily 8–5.

Hot Springs Mountain Tower. This tower overlooks 140 mi of parkland and mountains. | Fountain St. and Hot Springs Mountain Dr. | 501/623–6035 | $4 | Daily.

Lake Catherine State Park. The Civilian Conservation Corps built the now modernized, fully equipped housekeeping cabins in this park. You'll also find hookups for RV and tent camping, rent-a-camp equipment, swimming, boating, fishing, a store and seasonal restaurant, a playground, picnic areas, and pavilions. | 1200 Catherine Park Rd. | 501/844–4176 | Free | Daily.

Lake Ouachita State Park. The park is on the eastern tip of the state's largest man-made lake. You can swim, ski, go scuba diving, rent a boat, fish, hike trails, and take part in interpretive programs. Fully equipped housekeeping cabins, RV and tent campsites, picnic areas, a marina with boat rentals and supplies, a store, and a snack bar are also available. | 5451 Mountain Pine Rd., Mountain Pine | 501/767–9366 | Free | Daily.

Maxwell Blade's Theater of Magic. This is a 90-min Las Vegas–style production with lavish costumes and lighting, and a story line choreographed with magic and illusion. | 817 Central Ave. | 501/623–6200 | $12 | Feb.–Sept., call for hrs.

Mid-America Science Museum. You can explore science and nature through interactive exhibits at the Mid-America Science Museum. | 500 Mid-America Blvd. | 501/767–3461 or 800/632–0583 | $6 | Tues.–Sun. 10–5.

Ouachita National Forest. The oldest and largest state forest in the United States has 1.6 million acres of woodland dotted with campsites; fishing areas; picnic sites; mountain-bike, ATV, and horseback riding trails; and scenic drives. Hiking trails include the 223-mi-long Ouachita National Recreation Trail, which runs from Talimina, OK, to Pinnacle Mountain State Park near Little Rock. You can canoe and go white-water rafting on the rivers. Call for directions from Hot Springs. | 501/321–5202 | Free | Daily.

SIGHTSEEING TOURS/TOUR COMPANIES

Belle of Hot Springs. You can go sailing on this 400-passenger excursion boat, which sails Lake Hamilton on sightseeing, lunch, dinner, and dance cruises. | 5200 Central Ave. (Rte. 7S) | 501/525–4438 | $9.99 excursion only; dinner cruise $18.99–$25.99 | Feb.–Nov., daily.

President Bill Clinton's boyhood sites. You can get details on this self-guided tour in a brochure and map available from the visitors center. The tour passes two of Clinton's boyhood homes, along with his schools, church, and favorite teenage hangouts. | 629 Central Ave. | 800/772–2489 | Free | Daily.

National Park Duck Tours. You can take a 90-min ride on amphibious ducks through downtown and onto Lake Hamilton. | 418 Central Ave. | 501/321–2911 or 800/682–7044 | $12 | Mar.–mid-Nov., daily, call for hrs; mid-Nov.–Jan., weekends, call for hrs.

ON THE CALENDAR

JAN.–APR.: *Thoroughbred Racing.* Oaklawn Jockey Club, Arkansas's only thoroughbred racing, also has simulcasting days in the off-season. | 2705 Central Ave. | 800/625–5296.

APR.–MAY: *Arkansas Celebration of the Arts.* You can find performances in music, dance, theater, and poetry by celebrity artists. Sculpture exhibitions, painting exhibits, a gallery walk, workshops, lectures, art demonstrations, and artist receptions are also part of the celebration. | 501/321–0234.

MAY–JUNE: *Music Festival.* More than 200 international mentor and apprentice musicians present 24 concerts and nearly 300 open rehearsals of orchestral, chamber, and vocal music. | 501/623–4763.

OCT.: *Arts and Crafts Fair.* More than 350 artisans exhibit quality crafts and fine arts in this juried show. | Garland County Fairgrounds | 501/623–5756.

OCT.: *Documentary Film Festival.* If you're a culture maven, you can feast on U.S. and international films, humanities forums, lectures and question-and-answer periods following the films, visiting Academy Award–winning filmmakers, scholars, and celebrities. | 501/321–4747.

OCT.: *Oktoberfest.* Even if you're not German, you can celebrate German heritage with music, food, beer, dancing, contests, and crafts. | Convention Center | 501/321–1700.

OCT.: *Volksmarsch.* This family walk through Hot Springs National Park is sponsored by the American Volkssport Association. | 501/624–3383, ext. 640.

NOV.–DEC.: *Festival of Lights and Holiday in the Park.* Millions of twinkling lights decorate downtown, with thousands more turned on in Arlington Park in mid-December. In early December, a luminary route glows with more than 35,000 candles. | 501/321–2277.

Dining

Bohemia. Eastern European, German. You can travel all over the European eating map with bratwurst, herring, German pot roast, and sauerbraten, and even venture into the new world for baked Alaska. The Eastern European heritage of the owner-chef is evident in the menu, collector's plates, and original art that adorn one of the city's oldest restaurants. Kids' menu. | 517 Park Ave. | 501/623–9661 | $15–$18 | AE, D, MC, V | Closed Sun. No lunch Mon., Wed., Fri., Sat.

Cajun Boilers. Cajun. At this casual place on the shore of busy Lake Hamilton, dock space is provided along with the food. The Cajun-flavored posters are the tip-off to the food, which includes boiled crawfish, étouffée, fried alligator, and other seafood choices. Beer and wine are the only alcoholic beverages served. Kids' menu. | 2806 Albert Pike Hwy. | 501/767–5695 | $9–$16 | AE, D, DC, MC, V | Closed Sun., Mon. No lunch.

Coy's Steak House. Steak. A clubby, paneled restaurant, Coy's shines with specially seasoned steaks and a couple of seafood items, particularly shrimp cocktail and cold-water lobster. Kids' menu. | 300 Coy St. | 501/321–1414 | $12–$50 | AE, D, DC, MC, V.

Faded Rose. Cajun/Creole. The steaks are cooked New Orleans–style with lemon butter and the seafood is fiery hot at this restaurant, in a hotel building dating back to the 19th century. The soaked salad and fries with buttermilk dressing are meal enough for most people. Open-air dining is available. | 210 Central Ave. | 501/624–3200 | $15–$29 | AE, D, MC, V.

Hamilton House. Continental. This place on the shores of Lake Hamilton comes complete with an underground tunnel to a quick lake getaway. The T-bone and the red snapper are good choices, and you might want to finish with bread pudding and cognac sauce. You can also splurge on a huge lobster if you've had a good day at the races at Oaklawn Park.

Open-air dining is available on the terrace. Kids' menu. | 130 Van Lyell Terr. | 501/525–2727 | $17–$61 | AE, D, DC, MC, V | Closed Sun. No lunch.

Hot Springs Brauhaus. German. This 110-yr-old building wasn't designed with a German beer cellar in mind, but, by happy coincidence, it has a huge selection of imported brews, German fare, lively accordion music, and entertainment on weekends. Kids' menu. | 801 Central Ave. | 501/624–7866 | $15–$17 | AE, D, MC, V | Closed Mon. No lunch.

McClard's Bar-B-Q. Barbecue. Nothing's changed since the 1940s at this sparkling clean stucco building, where you nearly always have to wait for a seat. But the waits are short as veteran waitresses speed orders of smoked meat, hot tamales, shakes, fries, and more to happy diners. Everything, from beans to slaw to fries, is homemade, and the place is known for barbecue ribs. Beer is the only alcoholic beverage served. Kids' menu. | 505 Albert Pike | 501/624–9586 | $10–$15 | No credit cards | Closed Sun., Mon.

Mollie's. Delicatessen, American. It ain't kosher to serve catfish, but this is Arkansas, so you can get both fried catfish along with Jewish-grandma brisket and chicken-in-the-pot at this Hot Springs fixture. You'll also find big sandwiches, including corned beef, and grilled chicken, along with in-house baking. Open-air dining is available. Kids' menu. | 538 W. Grand Ave. | 501/623–6582 | $13–$26 | AE, D, DC, MC, V | Closed Sun.

Mrs. Miller's Chicken and Steak House. American. The white-frame building was out in the country a half-century ago. Now it's part of a busy commercial strip, but the same family is still dishing up the pan-fried chicken, homemade biscuits, and fresh fruit conserve that have made Mrs. Miller's a tradition for 62 years. You might want to try the chicken pot pie. Kids' menu. | 4723 Central Ave. | 501/525–8861 | $13–$24 | D, MC, V | Closed Mon. No lunch.

Ristorante Belle Arti. Italian. Rich woods and an artistic flair contribute to the trendiness of an Italian restaurant where it wouldn't do to choose tap water over San Pellegrino (or at least the local Mountain Valley). Fried calamari and linguine pescatore are two dishes you might want to try. Belle Arti is known for veal dishes and the vanilla crème brûlée. | 719 Central Ave. | 501/624–7474 | $17–$42 | AE, MC, V.

Three Monkeys. Contemporary. A turn-of-the-century building with architectural treasures in every nook has been renovated so carefully that the brass and polished wood and painting appear as if they've been part of the art gallery neighborhood for a century, rather than a few months. There's much you can explore, from a dining room to a billiard room, a cigar room, a disco, a piano bar, and outdoor decks. The food is of the modern American grill genre, with such dishes as crab cakes with portobello mushrooms, sea bass grilled in corn husks, and raspberry strudel. Three Monkeys is known for steaks and seafood. You can hear live music nightly and on Sundays you can visit for brunch. | 707 Central Ave. | 501/321–1682 | $18–$32 | AE, D, MC, V.

Lodging

Arlington Resort Hotel and Spa. If you wish to "take the cure," you can do it in this landmark with views of Hot Springs National Park. 3 restaurants, bar (with entertainment). Cable TV. 2 pools. Barbershop, beauty salon, hot tub, massage. Driving range, putting green, tennis. Exercise equipment. Laundry facilities. Business services. | 239 Central Ave. | 501/623–7771 or 800/643–1502 (reservations, outside AR) | fax 501/623–2243 | 484 rooms | $84–$108 | AE, D, DC, MC, V.

The Austin Hotel and Convention Center. You'll have a hard time missing this hotel, which towers over downtown Hot Springs. The Maxwell Blade Magic Show, music at the Bathhouse Show, and the town's famous mineral water baths are each about two blocks away. Restaurant, bar (with entertainment). Cable TV. Indoor-outdoor pool. Hot tub, spa. Business services. | 305 Malvern Ave. | 501/623–6600 | fax 501/624–7160 | 200 rooms | $79–$89 | AE, D, DC, MC, V.

Avanelle Motor Lodge. The lodge is in the National Park with a view of the Hot Springs Mountains. It's ½ mi from the city, which is accessible by bus. Restaurant, room service. Some kitchenettes. Cable TV. Pool. Some pets allowed. | 1204 Central Ave. | 501/321–1332 or 800/225–1360 | 88 rooms | $42–$56 | AE, D, DC, MC, V.

Best Western. The Oak Lawn racetrack is across the highway from this Best Western, and the Magic Springs theme park is 3 mi away. Restaurant, complimentary Continental breakfast. In-room data ports. Cable TV. Pool. Laundry facilities. | 2520 Central Ave. | 501/624–2531 | fax 501/623–0169 | 120 rooms | $79 | AE, D, DC, MC, V.

Brady Mountain Resort. Built in the 1960s, this quiet resort is surrounded by forest in the Brady Mountain National Park, on the shores of Lake Ouachita. Restaurant, picnic area. Some kitchenettes, refrigerators. Pools. Horseback riding. Dock, water sports, boating, fishing. | 4120 Brady Mountain Rd., Royal | 501/767–3422 | fax 501/767–3801 | bradymtn@hsnp.com | www.hsnp.com/brady/htm | 25 rooms, 7 cabins | $50, $190 cabins | AE, D, MC, V.

Buena Vista Resort. These cottages and hotel units were built in the 1940s and overlook a lake and 10 acres of forest. Picnic area. Kitchenettes, refrigerators. Cable TV. Pool. Miniature golf, tennis court. Fishing. Playground. Laundry facilities. Business services. Some pets allowed. | 201 Aberina St. | 501/525–1321 or 800/255–9030 (reservations, outside AR) | fax 501/525–8293 | 32 rooms, 18 cottages | $50–$74, $82 cottages | MC, V.

Clarion Resort on the Lake. This resort on Lake Hamilton is 4 mi from the airport, and from the Oaklawn Thoroughbred Race Track. When you stay here, you are also 1 mi from the Hot Springs Mall, 7 mi from downtown, and 65 mi from Little Rock National Airport. Restaurant, bar. Some refrigerators. Cable TV. Pool. Tennis. Water sports, boating. Playground, laundry facilities. Business services. Some pets allowed. | 4813 Central Ave. | 501/525–1391 | fax 501/525–0813 | 149 rooms | $99–$149 | AE, D, MC, V.

Downtowner Hotel & Spa. This luxury hotel is one block from Bathhouse Row and 1 mi from the Hot Springs Mountain Tower. Complimentary breakfast. Restaurant. Cable TV. Outdoor pool. Beauty salon, hot tub. Shops. | 135 Central Ave. | 501/624–5521 or 800/251–1962 | downtownhs@aol.com | 139 rooms | $49–$110 | AE, D, DC, MC, V.

Econo Lodge Inn and Suites. The hotel is located downtown near the Hot Springs Mall and several restaurants. Restaurant. Some microwaves, some refrigerators. Cable TV. Pool. Hot tub. Some pets allowed. | 4319 Central Ave. | 501/525–1660 | fax 501/525–7260 | 100 rooms | $55–$64 | AE, D, DC, MC, V.

Gables Inn Bed and Breakfast. This 1905 restored Victorian has hardwood floors, original stained-glass windows, and some original light fixtures. It's in the downtown historic district with its shops, restaurants, and Bathhouse Row. Dining room, complimentary breakfast. No kids under 10. No smoking. | 318 Quapaw Ave. | 800/625–7576 | fax 800/625–7576 | gablesn@ipa.net | www.gablesn.com | 4 rooms | $50–$75 | AE, MC, V.

Hamilton Inn Resort. The resort is in a residential wooded area 100 yards from Lake Hamilton. Lakefront suites are also available. The inn is 1 mi from the Hot Springs Mall. Picnic area. Cable TV, in-room VCRs (and movies). Pool. Hot tub. Playground. | 106 Lookout Point | 501/525–5666 or 800/945–9559 (outside AR) | www.accommodations.com | 52 rooms, 7 suites | $48–$70, $85–$225 suites | AE, D, DC, MC, V.

Hampton Inn. Family suites are available in this hotel in downtown Hot Springs. Complimentary Continental breakfast. In-room data ports, microwaves in suites, refrigerators in suites, some in-room hot tubs. Cable TV. Pool. Laundry facilities. Some pets allowed. | 151 Temperance Hill Rd. | 501/525–7000 | fax 501/525–7626 | 83 rooms, 17 suites | $84–$91, $114–$121 suites | AE, D, DC, MC, V.

Howard Johnson Inn. The accommodations at this chain hotel are modest and inexpensive and near all area attractions. Children under 18 stay free with parents. Complimentary

Continental breakfast. Outdoor pool. | 400 West Grand Ave. | 501/624–4441 or 800/IGO–HOJO | fax 501/623–9449 | ladyofthelake@hsnp.com | 76 rooms | $55–$65 | AE, D, MC, V.

Lake Hamilton Resort. Every room at this resort is a suite with a balcony overlooking Lake Hamilton. Restaurant, bar, picnic area, room service. In-room data ports, refrigerators. Cable TV. indoor-outdoor pools. Hot tub, sauna. Tennis. Exercise equipment. Beach, dock, water sports, boating, fishing. Playground. Laundry facilities. Business services, airport shuttle. Kids under 18 free. Some pets allowed. | 2803 Albert Pike | 501/767–5511 or 800/426–3184 | fax 501/767–8576 | lhresort@direclynx.net | www.cabot-ar.com/hamilton/resort.htm | 104 suites | $79–$94 suites | AE, D, DC, MC, V | Closed Dec.

Quality Inn. The sides and back of this full-service motel overlook the mountains. Downtown Hot Springs is 1 mi away. Restaurant, bar, room service. In-room data ports, some refrigerators. Cable TV. Pool. Hot tub. Playground. Some pets allowed (fee). | 1125 E. Grand Ave. | 501/624–3321 | fax 501/624–5814 | 138 rooms | $59–$64 | AE, D, DC, MC, V.

Ramada Inn Tower. The hot springs are a short walk away, and so are a number of restaurants, including the Faded Rose. A cover band plays in the hotel lounge every weekend. Restaurant, bar (with entertainment). In-room data ports. Cable TV. Pool, wading pool. Business services. Some pets allowed. | 218 Park Ave. | 501/623–3311 | fax 501/623–8871 | 191 rooms | $67–$79 | AE, D, DC, MC, V.

Royale Vista Inn. The balconies on this high-rise hotel overlook the National Park into Gulpha Gorge. A less expensive, two-story motel also sits on the property. Complimentary Continental breakfast. Outdoor pool. Airport shuttle. | 2204 Central Ave. | 501/624–5551 | www.royalevista.com | 207 rooms in 2 buildings | $39.95–$69.95 | AE, MC, V.

Shorecrest Resort. This hotel on Lake Hamilton is just a few miles from downtown Hot Springs, art galleries, music, and shopping. Picnic area. Kitchenettes, refrigerators. Cable TV. Pool. Beach, fishing. Some pets allowed. | 360 Lakeland Dr. | 501/525–8113 or 800/447–9914 | 25 cottages | $52–$60 | D, MC, V.

Spring Street Inn. This B&B is a 3-min walk from the Convention Center and downtown, hiking trails in Hot Springs National Park, and across the street from the Hot Springs Health Spa. Antique furnishings and plush towels and bed linens provide a touch of home. Complimentary breakfast. Cable TV. | 522 Spring St. | 501/624–1901 | springbb@hotsprings.net | 4 rooms | $85–$125 | AE, MC, V.

Stitt House Bed and Breakfast. Captain Stitt, an English entrepreneur, built this 6,000-square-ft pre-Victorian mansion, the oldest home in Hot Springs. Complimentary breakfast. Cable TV. Pool. | 824 Park Ave. | 501/623–2704 | fax 501/623–2704 | stittbb@hspn.com | www.bbonline.com/ar/stitthouse | 4 rooms | $100–$120 | AE, D, DC, MC, V.

Super 8. A block from Lake Hamilton, this hotel is a neighbor of the Clarion Hotel, which hosts several annual conventions, including the famed Hog Rally. Cable TV. Business services. | 4726 Central Ave. | 501/525–0188 | fax 501/525–7449 | 63 rooms | $48–$64 | AE, D, DC, MC, V.

Wildwood 1884 Bed & Breakfast. This Queen Anne–style home is approximately six blocks from downtown. Comfortable rooms are decorated with period pieces and are named after the proprietors' children. Complimentary breakfast. | 808 Park Ave. | 501/624–4267 | www.wildwood1884.com | 5 rooms | $85–$95 | AE, MC, V.

HOT SPRINGS NATIONAL PARK

MAP 11, B5

(Nearby towns also listed: Arkadelphia, Benton, Little Rock)

The national park covers about 5,500 acres in and near the town of Hot Springs. Its heart is Bathhouse Row on Central Avenue—eight turn-of-the-20th-century spa buildings with two open thermal springs behind Maurice Bathhouse. The visitors center in the Fordyce Bathhouse contains exhibits showing the spa town's prehistory and heyday as a health resort. The park also has a campground, scenic drives, 30 mi of hiking trails, a hot-water cascade, and picnic areas in mountains and gorges surrounding the town.

Information: Hot Springs National Park | 369 Central Ave., 71902 | 501/624–3383, ext. 640.

Attractions

Buckstaff Bathhouse. A 1912 National Historic Landmark, Buckstaff is one of only six hotels and spas still providing old-fashioned mineral baths. | 509 Central Ave. | 501/623–2308 | Thermal mineral baths $14; massage $16.50 | Mar.–Nov., Mon.–Sat. 7–11:45 and 1:30–3; Dec.–Feb., weekdays 7–11:45 and 1:30–3, Sat. 7–11:45.

★ **Fordyce Bathhouse.** This restored bathhouse, the most opulent on Bathhouse Row, now serves as the national park's visitors center and a museum; stained-glass windows and an ornate fountain grace the interior along with original facilities. There's also a bookstore and an orientation film. | 369 Central Ave. | 501/624–3383 | Free | Daily 9–5.

National Park Aquarium. Arkansas's largest collections of freshwater and saltwater creatures come together in Hot Springs. Exhibits are built to accommodate and entertain kids. | 209 Central Ave. | 501/624–3474 or 800/735–3074 | fax 501/767–5161 | $3.50 | Summer, daily 9–9; fall/spring, daily 9–5; Closed Dec.–Feb.

HOT SPRINGS
NATIONAL PARK

INTRO
ATTRACTIONS
DINING
LODGING

ON THE CALENDAR

OCT.: *Hot Springs Documentary Film Festival.* Nonfiction filmmakers have come to Hot Springs since 1990 to show their stuff. Documentaries nominated for Academy Awards are often shown here first. | 501/321–4747.

Dining

Yanni's Restaurant in the Park. Eclectic. A variety of American and Greek classics are on the menu for breakfast, lunch, or dinner. Yanni's is just off the lobby of the Park Hotel and opens up onto a veranda in the warmer months. | 211 Fountain St. | 501/338–6655 | $5.50–$11.95 | AE, D, DC, MC, V | Sunday for lunch and dinner.

Lodging

The Park Hotel. This 1930 Art Deco-style, grand hotel is in the heart of Hot Springs National Park and is on the National Register of Historic Places. The Park Hotel is within walking distance of Bathhouse Row and fine shopping. Restaurant. Complimentary breakfast. | 211 Fountain St. | 501/624–5323 or 800/895–7275 | fax 501/623–0052 | www.thehistoricparkhotel.com | 65 rooms | $70–$95 rooms, $110–$135 suites | AE, D, DC, MC, V.

Vintage Comfort Bed and Breakfast. This 1907 restored Queen Anne B&B is a short walk from the downtown historic district, Bathhouse Row, art galleries, and restaurants. Gourmet breakfast is served in the dining room. Dining room, complimentary breakfast. No kids under 6. No smoking. | 303 Quapaw Ave. | 501/623–3258 | fax 501/623–3258 | btberg@ipa.net | www.bbonline.com/ar/vintagecomfort | 4 rooms | $50–$85 | AE, MC, V.

Williams House Bed & Breakfast. The 1890 Williams House was the first B&B in Arkansas, opening its doors to travelers in 1976. The mansion is lavishly furnished with antiques, brass fixtures, and cherry oak accents. Suites and chamber rooms are immaculate. Complimentary breakfast. | 420 Quapaw Ave. | 800/756–4635 | www.1890WilliamsHouse.com | 5 rooms | $95–$145 | AE, D, MC, V.

JASPER

(Nearby towns also listed: Buffalo National River, Harrison)

From the south, Arkansas's Scenic 7 Byway curves and plummets downhill into Jasper, the seat of Newton County, which is so remote that it had no paved highways until the 1960s. The small community radiates from its weathered stone courthouse, with gifts and crafts shops, a bakery, cafés, simple motels, and B&Bs in and near town. It sits on the Little Buffalo River near its confluence with the Buffalo National River, so river-float and fishing outfitters are headquartered here.

Information: Jasper/Newton County Chamber of Commerce, | PO Box 250, Jasper, AR 72641 | 870/446–2455 | www.ozarkmountainvacations.com.

Attractions

Ozark Ecotours. Local residents/guides take small groups on 1-day and overnight trips into the rugged Buffalo River landscape to learn about Native American, pioneer, Civil War, and outlaw history and explore the area's natural history. Some trips involve easygoing hikes; others include canoeing, caving, and horseback riding. | 870/446–5898 | $50 | Apr.–June, Sept.–Nov., call for hrs.

ON THE CALENDAR

APR., MAY: *Spring Fever Days.* You'll find a crafts show, antiques, collectibles, contests, games, barbecue, street dance, live music, and food at this celebration on the town square. A demolition derby at the county fairgrounds is followed by a dance. | 870/446–2455.

Dining

Dairy Diner. American. This is the typical, truck-stop greasy spoon, with a menu full of comfort foods such as hamburgers, meatloaf, and fried chicken. | 217 E. Hwy. 7 | 870/446–5343 | $4.50–$9 | No credit cards.

Ozarks Cliff House Inn. Southern. For homemade biscuits, fried catfish, pinto beans with sugar-cured ham, and just plain good Southern food, you've come to the right place. You may find the circa-1932 boat motor hanging in the dining room a bit odd, but the main distraction will undoubtedly be the stunning view into the Grand Canyon of Arkansas, the state's deepest natural valley. | Hwy. Cty. Rte. 31, Jasper | 870/446–2292 | Daily, 8–3 | $5–$8 | DC, MC, V.

Point of View Family Dining. American. Here you'll find such entrées as chicken-fried steak and catfish with all the trimmings. | 106 W. Hwy. 74 | 870/446–2992 | $6.95–$10.95 | MC, V.

Riverfront Dairy Diner. American. This family-owned diner is part of the Ozarks Arkansas House, a 19th-century–style B&B. Daily specials include apricot chicken and chicken-fried steak. A former owner used to carve stone animals; you can still spy his lizards and fish in the Rock Garden. | Hwy. 7 at Hwy. 74, Box 325, Jasper | 870/446–5179 | $4–$9 | AE, D, MC, V.

Lodging

Arkansas House Bed and Breakfast. The Little Buffalo River flows behind this two-story house made with native cut limestone. In addition to enjoying a complimentary three-course breakfast, you may visit with Coco, a friendly 500-lb bear, who is trotted out once a day to greet the public. Restaurant. Some microwaves, some refrigerators, some hot tubs. Cable TV, in-room VCRs (and movies). Laundry facilities. | 217 E. Hwy. 7, Box 325 | 870/446–5179 | www.mcrush.com/arkansashouse | 2 rooms, 3 suites | $65, $85 suites | AE, D, DC, MC, V.

Brambly Hedge Cottage and Barn. The views are splendid at this secluded, rustic retreat where you can choose to stay in an original Ozarks farmhouse (early 1800s) or its neighboring log cabin. The site is atop Sloan Mountain, 4 mi south of Jasper. No room phones. Laundry facilities. No kids allowed. No smoking. | HCR 31 | 870/446–5849 | BramblyH-COT@aol.com | www.1bbweb.com/brambly | 5 rooms | $100–$125 | No credit cards.

Cliff House Inn and Restaurant. This rustic country inn and restaurant is perched on Mt. Judea above the Arkansas Grand Canyon—it's the largest valley in Arkansas. Restaurant. No phones. No smoking. | HCR 31, Jasper | 870/446–2292 | 5 rooms | $45–$55 | D, MC, V | Closed Oct.–mid-Mar.

Ozarks Crawford's Cabins. Two log cabins with full kitchens, bent-willow furniture, and a back porch swing are in the woods adjoining the Ozark National Forest, 3 mi north of Jasper. The old general store makes deli sandwiches, and you can canoe, fish, and enjoy the water at Buffalo National River less than 2 mi away. Microwaves, refrigerators. Cable TV, in-room VCRs (and movies). Hiking. No pets. No smoking. | Hwy. Cty. Rte. 31, Jasper | 870/446–2478 | fax 870/446–5824 | bmlo-crawford@eritten.net | www.ozarkcabins.com/crawfords | 2 cabins | $65–$90 | AE, D, MC, V.

Parkway Motel. Parkway is a good resting spot if you have plans to visit the Buffalo River, just 5 mi away. The Dairy Diner is across the street. Cable TV. | 210 East Ct., Hwy. 7 | 870/446–2317 | 7 rooms | $27–$32 | No credit cards.

Wolf Creek Hideaway. This vacation rental has the Ozarks as its backdrop and is spacious enough to sleep 10. Rooms have all the amenities, including fresh linens, and hardwood floors open up onto a wraparound deck. If you come here, you must bring your own food. Kitchen. Hot tub. | County Rd. 58, Vendor | 870/365–3097 or 800/435–6188 | fax 870/743–9028 | www.wolfcreekhideaway.com | 5 rooms in 1 cabin | $90 per couple, $12.50 per person extra | No credit cards.

INTRO
ATTRACTIONS
DINING
LODGING

JONESBORO

MAP 11, E3

(Nearby towns also listed: Batesville, Blytheville, Newport, Paragould, Pocahontas, Searcy)

This rapidly growing community is tucked in the rolling, wooded foothills of Crowley's Ridge. It was formed as the Craighead County seat after 1859. After the Civil War, it boomed in the 1880s when three railroad lines came through town. Its historic downtown and residential areas include businesses and homes built during this period. It is the home of the Northeast Arkansas Symphony.

Information: **Greater Jonesboro Chamber of Commerce** | Box 789, 72403-0789 | 870/932–6691.

Attractions

Arkansas State University. Founded in 1909 as an agricultural training school, ASU went on to offer 2- and 4-yr degrees by 1930. Master's degree programs were added in 1955 and doctoral programs starting in 1992. Its colleges include agriculture, arts and sciences, business, communications, education, fine arts, nursing and health professions, and engineering. | Careway Rd. at Aggie Rd. | 870/972–3024 or 800/382–3030 | www.astate.edu | Free | Daily.

Arkansas State University Fine Arts Gallery. You can see changing exhibits of local, regional, and student art at this gallery. | Caraway Rd., ASU campus | 870/972–3050 | Free | Call for hrs.

Arkansas State University Museum. Fossils and prehistoric artifacts found in the region, Native American arts and crafts, a replica of 1886 Main Street, a pioneer home, glassware, and other collections are displayed at this campus museum. | 110 Cooley Dr., ASU campus | 870/972–2074 | Free | Weekdays 9–4, weekends 1–4.

Crowley's Ridge State Park. The state park is on the homestead and burial place of Benjamin F. Crowley, the first known white settler in the region. You can stay in housekeeping cabins or use the RV and tent camping sites. There's also a 30-acre fishing lake, a swimming lake with a pavilion, a snack bar and bathhouse, pedal-boat rental, a playground, picnic pavilions, and hiking trails. The park is on Hwy. 141, 15 mi north of Jonesboro. | 870/573–6751 | Free | Daily.

Forum Theater. This former movie theater has been restored as a performing arts center. | 115 E. Monroe | 870/935–2726 | Call for hrs.

Hemingway–Pfeiffer Museum and Educational Center. The museum, in Piggott, northeast of Jonesboro, includes the family home of author Ernest Hemingway's second wife, Pauline Pfeiffer. Her parents, Paul and Mary, owned more than 60,000 acres of land in northeast Arkansas. During the 1930s, the barn behind the home was converted to a studio to give Hemingway privacy for writing while visiting Piggott. Much of one of his most famous novels, *A Farewell to Arms*, was written in this studio. The buildings have been restored to their 1930s look. Areas of emphasis at the center include the 1930s era, including its literature, politics, agricultural, and family lifestyles, and the development of northeast Arkansas during the Depression and New Deal eras. The center also serves as the visitors center for the northern terminus of Crowley's Ridge National Scenic Byway. | 1021 W. Cherry St., Piggott | 870/598–3487 | hemingway.astate.edu | Free | Weekdays 9–3, Sat. noon–3.

Lake Frierson State Park. If you visit this park in the spring, you will find a blaze of wild dogwoods. Year-round, you can fish on a 350-acre lake with a boat ramp, a barrier-free pier, and rental boats. There are also picnic areas, a playground, campsites, a self-guided trail, and a visitors center. | 7904 Hwy. 141 | 870/932–2615 | Free | Daily.

Lake Poinsett State Park. Anglers find a 640-acre lake atop Crowley's Ridge, with excellent fishing, campsites, picnic areas, a pavilion, a playground, a trail, a launch ramp, and boat rentals. | 5752 State Park La., Harrisburg | 870/578–2064 | Free | Daily.

ON THE CALENDAR

MAY: *Main Street Jonesboro Celebration.* Jonesboro's annual spring celebration features a parade, music, dancing, food, and games for the whole family. | 870/933–0423.
NOV.: *Lit'l Bita Christmas Arts & Crafts Show.* Arts and crafts booths exhibit woodworking, jewelry, and quilts. | Arkansas State University | 870/972–3930.

Dining

Fazoli's. Italian. Standard Italian fare, such as lasagna, fettucine Alfredo, and spaghetti with meatballs, is what you'll find here. | 1730 E. Highland Dr. | 870/931–1300 | fax 870/931–9100 | $5.95–$10 | AE, D, MC, V.

Front Page Café. American. At this casual restaurant, old newspapers and license plates decorate the walls and country vegetables, meats, and desserts decorate the plates. Kids' menu. | 1101 S. Caraway Rd. | 870/932–6343 | $4–$12 | MC, V.

Imperial Chinese Restaurant. Chinese. Lunch and dinner buffets are stocked with white and fried rice, lo mein noodles, and two or three entrées, such as Hunan pork and cashew chicken. If you prefer table service, an extensive menu is also available. | 2512 E. Highland Dr. | 870/933–6700 | $6–$9.50 | AE, MC, V.

Pancho's. Mexican. This family restaurant serves crispy tacos, enchiladas, and hearty south-of-the-border-style casseroles. Alcoholic beverages are not served. | 2240 S. Caraway Rd. | 870/972–6640 | fax 870/930–9952 | $5–$8.95 | MC, V.

Potlickers' Uptown Deli. Delicatessen. The lunchtime casseroles at Potlickers are "so good, you'll want to lick the pot they're made in," according to the owners. Sandwiches and one-dish entrée specials are a good value. | 311-B Main St. | 870/931–4195 | $3.95–$6.95 | AE, MC, V | Sunday.

Lodging

Best Western Inn. Chain accommodations 1 mi from Arkansas State University, 3 mi from the airport, and 90 mi from Memphis. Complimentary Continental breakfast. In-room data ports. Cable TV. Pool. Some pets allowed. | 2901 Phillips Dr. | 870/932–6600 | fax 870/935–1677 | 60 rooms | $50–$57 | AE, D, DC, MC, V.

Comfort Inn Jonesboro. This two-story motel is just one block from Hwy. 63 and ½ mi from Arkansas State University and several restaurants. Complimentary Continental breakfast. | 2904 Phillips Dr. | 870/972–8686 or 800/221–2222 | fax 870/269–2807 | www.comfortinn.com | 50 rooms | AE, D, MC, V.

Days Inn. Standard hotel off Rte. 463, a few blocks from a movie theater and the Regional Medical Center, 3 mi from the airport, and 5 mi from Cricket Forest Park. Complimentary Continental breakfast. Cable TV. Some pets allowed. | 2406 Phillips Dr. | 870/932–9339 or 800/227–9345 (reservations) | fax 870/931–5289 | 46 rooms | $47 | AE, D, MC, V.

Holiday Inn. The hotel is 2 mi from movie theaters, 3 mi from a mall, and 5 min from Cricket Forest Park. Restaurant, bar (with entertainment). Room service. Cable TV. Indoor pool. Hot tub. Exercise equipment. Laundry facilities. Business services. Some pets allowed. | 3006 S. Caraway Rd. | 870/935–2030 | fax 870/935–3440 | 179 rooms | $69 | AE, D, DC, MC, V.

Holiday Inn Express. The Jonesboro Bowling Center and a skating rink are across the bypass; Arkansas State University is 15 min away. Complimentary Continental breakfast. In-room data ports. Cable TV. Laundry facilities. Some pets allowed. | 2407 Phillips Dr. | 870/932–5554 | fax 870/932–2586 | 102 rooms | $65 | AE, D, DC, MC, V.

Motel 6. You're within walking distance of several restaurants; a bowling alley and a movie theater are also nearby. Restaurant. In-room data ports. Cable. Pool. Some pets allowed. | 2300 S. Caraway Rd. | 870/932–1050 | fax 870/935–3421 | 80 rooms | $36–$38 | AE, D, DC, MC, V.

Travelodge. This Travelodge in the Jonesboro business district is 3 mi from Cricket Forest Park. Restaurant. Cable TV. Pool. Laundry facilities. | 1421 S. Caraway Rd. | 870/935–8400 | 135 rooms | $43 | AE, D, DC, MC, V.

Ramada Limited. This two-story motel has both interior and exterior hallways. It is 100 yards from Hwy. 63 and there are restaurants across the street. Downtown is 4 mi to the northwest. Complimentary Continental breakfast. Cable TV. Indoor pool. | 3000 Apache Dr., Hwy. 63 | 870/932–5757 or 800/272–6232 | fax 870/933–8760 | www.the.ramada.com | 61 rooms | $50–$60 | AE, D, DC, MC, V.

West Washington Guest House Bed and Breakfast. This turn-of-the-century, American four square–style house is blocks from downtown Jonesboro. Complimentary snacks in the common area encourage mingling. Complimentary breakfast. Cable TV. Room phones. | 534 W. Washington Ave. | 870/935–9300 | fax 870/802–3299 | kstacks@ssarch.com | 12 rooms | $65–$90 | AE, MC, V.

Wilson Inn. This hotel is on the bypass at the edge of town, across the street from a multiplex theater and beside the Cracker Barrel restaurant. Complimentary Continental breakfast. Some kitchenettes, refrigerators. Cable TV. Business services. Some pets allowed. | 2911 Gilmore Dr. | 870/972–9000 | 108 rooms, 31 suites | $39–$59 | AE, D, DC, MC, V.

LITTLE ROCK AND NORTH LITTLE ROCK

MAP 11, C4

(Nearby towns also listed: Benton, Conway, Hot Springs, Morrilton, Pine Bluff, Stuttgart)

Little Rock is in the center of the state of Arkansas, close to the center of the United States in the Sunbelt. Sitting on the south bank of the Arkansas River, it is the state's

LITTLE ROCK AND
NORTH LITTLE
ROCK

INTRO
ATTRACTIONS
DINING
LODGING

geographical, governmental, and financial center, as well as a major convention hub. A population of 182,274 lives within the Little Rock city limits. More than 513,000 live in the greater Little Rock metropolitan area, including North Little Rock just across the Arkansas River.

Spanish and French explorers passed the site in the 16th and 17th centuries, naming it La Petite Roche because of a small outcrop that marked the transition from the flat Mississippi Delta region to the Ouachita Mountain foothills. A simple translation turned the town into Little Rock when it replaced Arkansas Post as the territorial capital in 1821.

Within an hour of Little Rock's downtown are world-renowned duck hunting in rice-growing regions to the southeast and wild scenic vistas, streams, and trails in forested mountains to the north and west.

Information: Little Rock Convention and Visitors Bureau | Box 3232 Little Rock 72203; Robinson Center, Markham and Broadway | 501/376–4781 or 800/844–4781 | www.littlerock.com.

NEIGHBORHOODS

Quapaw Quarter

All of Little Rock's history—from frontier days to the early years of the 20th century—is encompassed by the Quapaw Quarter, a 9-square-mi area made up of Little Rock's central business district and adjacent residential neighborhoods. "Quapaw Quarter" is a name that since 1961 has been used to identify this oldest and most historic portion of the city. The word "Quapaw" was borrowed from the Quapaw Native Americans, who lived in central Arkansas before the arrival of white settlers in the early 19th century.

The Quapaw Quarter is most closely associated with the neighborhoods surrounding MacArthur Park and the Arkansas Governor's Mansion. It is in these two districts that Little Rock's historic preservation efforts have been concentrated for the past 20 years.

Most of the city's oldest buildings, including some that date from before the Civil War, lie near MacArthur Park, which also includes the Arkansas Arts Center as well as the nearby Decorative Arts Museum, which occupies the antebellum Pike–Fletcher–Terry House. The Villa Marre, an elegant Victorian home built in 1881, is open to the public.

Homes in the Governor's Mansion Historic District generally date from about 1880 to 1920, and they comprise an outstanding collection of Queen Anne, Colonial Revival, and Craftsman architecture. All of the district's restored buildings serve as private homes or businesses. Although they are not open to the public, they can be enjoyed from the street or sidewalk via driving or walking tours.

River Market, Little Rock's newest shopping area, also lies within the Quapaw Quarter on E. Markham Street, within walking distance of the downtown convention center. The River Market itself offers a variety of fresh produce, fresh flowers, unique gifts, groceries, and gourmet foods. Nearby are the Museum of Discovery, the new central library, shops, galleries, and restaurants.

Kavanaugh Boulevard

This street begins off the 3000 block of Markham Street and winds its way uphill through the Hillcrest and Heights neighborhoods. Several shopping areas with a "village" atmosphere lie along the way, with restaurants, boutiques, antiques shops, and galleries interspersed with grocery stores and other practical businesses plus housing areas.

West Little Rock

The area west of I–430 at the I–630 intersection is Little Rock's fastest-growing business and residential area. It includes accommodations and restaurants in all price ranges.

TRANSPORTATION INFORMATION

Airports: Most major airlines, including American/American Eagle, Comair, Continental Express, Delta, Mesa, Northwest, Southwest, TWA, and US Airways Express, fly into **Little Rock National Airport** (501/372–3439), 5 mi east of downtown off I–440.

Airport Transportation: Major Little Rock hotels provide airport shuttles. Cab fare to downtown runs from around $10 to $15. For taxis, call **Black & White/Yellow Cabs** (501/374–0333) or **Capitol Cab** (501/568–0462).

Amtrak: Amtrak's *Texas Eagle* to Little Rock departs from Chicago and Los Angeles, St. Louis, Dallas/Fort Worth, and 38 other cities (800/872–7245).

Buses: The local terminal for **Greyhound Bus lines** is at 118 E. Washington St., North Little Rock. Local telephone number is 501/372–3007 or 800/231–2222 (for fares and reservations)

Intra-city Transit: Central Arkansas Transit (501/375–1163), city-run bus service, covers Little Rock and North Little Rock. Little Rock is easily negotiated by interstate highways and major streets. Plenty of parking facilities and taxis are available.

Attractions

ART AND ARCHITECTURE

Arkansas State Capitol. The neoclassical structure, built between 1899 and 1915 on a hilltop west of downtown, has an imposing rotunda, grand marble staircases and columns, stained-glass skylights, murals, and six intricately crafted, 4-inch-thick bronze doors from Tiffany and Co. | Capitol Ave. and Woodlane St. | 501/682–5080 | Free | Daily 8–5, call to schedule tours.

BEACHES, PARKS, AND NATURAL SITES

Pinnacle Mountain State Park. This mountain, 8 mi west of downtown Little Rock, rises more than 650 ft from the floodplain of Big Maumelle River, which is lined by ancient cypress trees. There are 10 mi of hiking trails on approximately 2,000 acres, an arboretum, picnic areas, a pavilion, and a playground. You'll also find fishing, boating, canoeing trips, exhibits at the visitors center, environmental education, and other events. The park is off Rte. 10 in Roland. | 11901 Pinnacle Valley Rd. | 501/868–5806 | Free | Daily.

Toltec Mounds Archeological State Park. Toltec preserves and interprets Arkansas's tallest Native American mounds in this 182-acre park. The mounds and an earthen embankment are the remains of a large ceremonial and governmental complex inhabited from AD 600 to 1050. Facilities include a visitors center with exhibits, an audiovisual theater, an archaeological research laboratory, a ¾-mi barrier-free trail, and a 1½-mi turf trail. | Off U.S. 165 on Rte. 386 | 501/961–9442 | $2.50 | Tues.–Sat. 8–5, Sun. noon–5.

War Memorial Park. The park contains a public golf course, tennis courts, War Memorial Stadium, the Little Rock home of the University of Arkansas Razorbacks, and the baseball park of the minor-league Arkansas Travelers. It also has a fitness center open to the public. | 501/371–4770 | Free | Daily.

The **Little Rock Zoo** is part of the War Memorial Park and has gorillas, giant anteaters, and 175 other species. | 1 Jonesboro Dr. | 501/663–4733 | $5 | Daily 9–5.

CULTURE, EDUCATION, AND HISTORY

Aerospace Education Center and IMAX Theater. This is a small museum with aviation and aerospace exhibits, artifacts, artwork, and a virtual reality experience, plus a gift shop, as well as the theater and a public library. | 3301 E. Roosevelt Rd. | 501/376–4629 | Free; IMAX $6.75 | Mon.–Thurs. 9–9, Fri.–Sat. 9–10, Sun. 11–6.

Arkansas Repertory Theatre. Arkansas Repertory produces popular classics and modern theatrical fare. | 6th and Main Sts. | 501/378–0405 | www.therep.org | Tickets are from $16 to $26 | Call for hrs.

Arkansas Symphony Orchestra. Classical, pops, chamber, and family concerts. | Robinson Center Music Hall on State House Blvd. | 501/666–1761 | Tickets are from $15 to $50 | Sept.– May., call for hrs.

MUSEUMS

Arkansas Arts Center. The modern center has six galleries, a children's theater, museum school, gift shop, and a restaurant. | 501 E. 9th St. | 501/372–4000 | Free | Mon.–Thurs., Sat. 10–5, Fri. 10–9, Sun. noon–5.

Arkansas Territorial Restoration. Restored and refurnished frontier buildings are visited in living-history tours. Buildings along the tour date from the 1820s to 1840s. The Restoration's museum will open new galleries in the summer of 2001 to exhibit the state's largest collection of Arkansas-made fine and decorative arts. Its shop features the work of Arkansas crafts artists. | 200 E. 3rd St. | 501/324–9351 | www.arkansashistory.com | $2 | Mon.–Sat. 9– 5, Sun. 9–5.

Central High School Museum and Visitor Center. The museum's exhibits and audiovisual presentations mark the school's landmark integration in 1957, when nine black students were enrolled under the protection of federal troops. The school is a National Historic Site. | 2125 W. 14th St. | 501/374–1957 | Free | Mon.–Sat. 10–4, Sun. 1–4.

Decorative Arts Museum. Set in a restored 1840 plantation-style mansion, the museum displays the work of contemporary artists. | 411 E. 7th St. | 501/396–0357 | Free | Mon.–Sat. 10–5, Sun. noon–5.

Museum of Discovery. You can explore science, history, and technology through hands-on exhibits. | 500 E. Markham St. | 501/396–7050 or 800/880–6475 | www.amod.org | $5.50 | Mon.–Sat. 9–5, Sun. 1–6.

★ **Old State House Museum.** The Old State House was built between 1833 and 1842 and was recently restored as a museum devoted to Arkansas history. President Bill Clinton used the building as a backdrop for victory speeches on his two election nights. | 300 W. Markham St. | 501/324–9685 | www.oldstatehouse.com | Free | Mon.–Sat. 9–5, Sun. 1–5.

Plantation Agriculture Museum. Exhibits and programs interpret the history of cotton agriculture from 1836 through World War II, when agricultural practices quickly became mechanized. See how cotton was grown and ginned. Nearby, at the site of a Civil War skirmish, lies the Scott Plantation Settlement, a collection of such restored plantation buildings as a one-room schoolhouse and tenant houses. | 4815 Rte. 161 in Scott, 12 mi east of downtown Little Rock | 501/961–1409 | $2.25 | Tues.–Sat. 8–5, Sun. 1–5.

SHOPPING

River Market. River Market is a lively center of gourmet shops, boutiques, cafés, and ethnic-food stalls in the Market Hall, with an outdoor farmers' market from spring through late fall. It has become the anchor for a revitalized neighborhood of art and home-accessories galleries and restaurants. | 400 E. Markham St. | 501/375–2552 | Free | Daily.

SPORTS AND RECREATION

Alltel Arena. This 18,000-seat multipurpose facility opened in late 1999 in North Little Rock. It is the home court for the University of Arkansas–Little Rock basketball team and the Arkansas RiverBlades minor-league hockey team. Arena football, circuses, ice-skating exhibitions, concerts, and other attractions and entertainment events also take place here. | One Alltel Arena Way, North Little Rock | 501/340–5660 | fax 501/340–5668 | www.alltelarena.com | Box office, daily 9:30–5:30.

Wild River Country. This water theme park with a wave pool, flume rides, inner-tube rapids, and a wading pool for young children is designed for the whole family. | 6820 Crystal Hill Rd., North Little Rock | 501/753–8600 | $15.95 | June–Labor Day, daily; May, weekends, Mon.–Thurs., 9–5.

SIGHTSEEING TOURS/TOUR COMPANIES

Quapaw Quarter Historic Neighborhoods. A series of walking/driving tours lead through several historic areas within the quarter. Brochures are free from the Little Rock Convention and Visitors Bureau. | 501/376–4781 or 800/844–4781 | Free | Daily.

The Governor's Mansion. Completed in 1950, it is a latecomer to its 19th- and early 20th-century neighbors and was home to President Bill Clinton for his 12 years as Arkansas governor. | 1800 Center St. | 501/324–9805 | Free | Tours by appointment.

Villa Marre. This 1881 Italianate-style mansion in the city's Quapaw Quarter is available for guided tours. All rooms have Victorian furnishings. | 1321 Scott St. | 501/371–0075 | $3 | Weekdays 9–1, Sun. 1–5; by appointment only on weekdays.

The Empress of Little Rock. This 1888 Gothic Queen Anne B&B on the National Register of Historic Places offers public tours Mondays through Thursdays. | 2120 S. Louisiana St. | 501/374–7966 | www.theempress.com | $5 | Mon.–Thurs., 11:30 and 3.

LITTLE ROCK AND
NORTH LITTLE
ROCK

INTRO
ATTRACTIONS
DINING
LODGING

OTHER POINTS OF INTEREST

The Old Mill. Built in 1933, this re-creation of an old water-powered gristmill was filmed for the opening scene of *Gone With the Wind*. | Lake Shore Drive and Fairway Ave., North Little Rock | 501/758–1424 | Free | Daily.

ON THE CALENDAR

MAY: *Quapaw Quarter Spring Tour of Homes.* Half-a-dozen historic homes not ordinarily open to the public may be toured in the Little Rock area. | 501/371–0075.

MAY–OCT.: *Farmers' Market.* More than 50 produce, houseplant, and craft vendors gather at Little Rock's Farmers' Market on Tuesdays and Saturdays. | 501/375–2552.

APRIL, MAY: *Arkansas Territorial Restoration Fair.* The Little Rock museum's historic grounds and buildings are filled with 19th-century crafts, music, dance, pioneer demonstrations, and living-history characters. | 501/324–9351.

MAY: *Riverfest.* Six entertainment stages, plus music, art, food, juried handmade art, and children's activities take place in Little Rock's Riverfront Park. | 501/255–3378.

JULY: *Pops on the River Concert.* View fireworks and enjoy an outdoor holiday concert performed by the Arkansas Symphony Orchestra, live in Little Rock's Riverfront Park. | 501/378–3571.

AUG.: *Antiquarian Book Fair.* Arkansas's largest book and paper show draws more than 50 dealers from around the country to Little Rock's Robinson Center. | 501/664–1170.

OCT.: *Arkansas State Fair and Livestock Show.* At the state fairgrounds and Barton Coliseum in Little Rock, the fair features livestock exhibits and shows, a rodeo, carnival and food midways, free live entertainment, arts and crafts, and commercial and educational exhibits. | 501/372–8341.

DEC.: *Arkansas Craft Guild Christmas Showcase.* More than 100 of Arkansas's finest crafts artists display traditional and contemporary crafts among Christmas trees and carolers. | 870/269–3897.

WALKING TOURS

**Downtown Riverfront and MacArthur Park
(approximately 6 hours)**

Little Rock's Quapaw Quarter encompasses the city's historic business and residential downtown areas. The word "Quapaw" was borrowed from the Quapaw Indians, who once lived in the central Arkansas region. A walking tour of the riverfront in the city's central business district and residential neighborhoods leading to MacArthur Park includes a variety of stately homes and buildings.

Begin at the **Old State House,** 300 W. Markham Street, Arkansas's first capitol building constructed from 1833 to 1842 and in use until the early 20th century. It is now a museum. President Bill Clinton announced his candidacy for the presidency and celebrated election-night victories here.

Continue west on Markham to the **Joseph Taylor Robinson Memorial Auditorium,** at Markham and Broadway, built during the Depression. The auditorium is home to the Arkansas Symphony Orchestra, Ballet Arkansas, Broadway plays, and other events.

© Corbis

OZARK MOUNTAIN CRAFTS

From the Ozark Mountains to the Mississippi Delta, Arkansas is noted for its crafts. The roots of this rich legacy reach back into pioneer days. Then both small homesteads and large plantations had to depend on themselves—making their own quilts, candles, baskets, buckets, and building materials. Along with talented native Arkansans, others moved to the state during the counterculture and back-to-the-land movements of the late 1960s and 1970s. They were drawn by a relatively inexpensive cost of living, a mild climate, readily available natural materials, and inspirational settings.

Traditional works along with contemporary American crafts are nurtured today by the Arkansas Craft Guild, the Arkansas Arts Council, Arkansas State Parks, dozens of festivals and special events put on by cities and small towns, privately owned galleries and businesses, and changing exhibitions at such places as Little Rock's Decorative Arts Museum and Territorial Restoration.

Well-known contemporary crafters include Leon Niehues, who uses basketmaking techniques evolved from those used by Native Americans to create striking pieces more like organic sculpture. Joe Bruhin's wood-fired pottery is remarkably energetic. The designs of Sharon Heidingsfelder's quilts are vibrant works of contemporary art, and Irma Gail Hatcher takes historic patterns to new heights. Robyn Horn's wood sculptures have their roots in traditional wood-turning. Particularly good production pottery is produced by David and Becky Dahlstedt. Ed Pennebaker's Red Fern Glass production studio specializes in early American–style tableware, drinking vessels, perfume bottles, and ornaments.

The Arkansas Craft Guild exhibits its members' works in its shops in Mountain View, Little Rock, Hot Springs, Eureka Springs, and Fayetteville and sponsors a Christmas Showcase each December in the Statehouse Convention Center in Little Rock. June's Riverfest in the capital city also features juried craft artists. In mid-October, the nonprofit, juried event at War Eagle Farms, plus shows and festivals in surrounding communities in northwest Arkansas, draw thousands of visitors, as do the somewhat smaller shows each May. Jimmy Lile's Custom Knives, in Russellville, presents knives as beautiful as they are functional, and Ferguson's, south of St. Joe above the Buffalo National River, features oak furniture.

Among cities and towns with particularly good private galleries are Fayetteville, Rogers, Eureka Springs, Little Rock, Hot Springs, and Hardy.

Across the street at 405 W. Markham is the annex of the **Pulaski County Courthouse,** added in 1912–14. Across Broadway at 500 W. Markham is the 1906–08 **Little Rock City Hall.** Go south on Broadway, then east on 2nd Street past the original 1880s Romanesque Revival courthouse.

Continue east across Spring Street to the **Old Federal Building**; take a ride in the state's oldest elevator in continuous use—a brass cage that still requires a human operator. In the next block of 2nd Street are the 1906–07 **Pyramid Place,** Little Rock's first "skyscraper," the 1903 **Sol and Gus Gans Building,** and the late 19th-century **Tripp Building.** Turn north on Louisiana, then east on Markham to the **Capital Hotel** at 111 W. Markham, built in 1873. Note its four-story cast-iron front and go inside to see its restored lobby, off which are a handsome bar and restaurant.

The **Statehouse Convention Center** lies a bit farther west on Markham. Cross Scott and La Harpe Streets and turn north into **Riverfront Park.** Here you will find the site of the "little rock" that gave the city its name, plus exhibits in a pavilion and on markers explaining its history, including Civil War actions.

Continue west through the park to the **River Market** at 400 E. Markham, with an open-air farmers' market Monday–Saturday from spring through late fall. Inside are food stalls, flowers, cafés, delicatessens, and small boutiques. The lively **Museum of Discovery** is at 500 W. Markham, sharing a building with restaurants and shops.

Return east on Markham to Rock Street, go a half-block south, and look in on the award-winning **Central Arkansas Main Library,** at 100 Rock, in a refurbished warehouse. Back on Markham again, go east past restaurants, pubs, and galleries to Cumberland and turn south, then west on 2nd or 3rd Street to the **Arkansas Territorial Restoration** at 200 E. 3rd, an assembly of historic buildings with a museum, a gallery, and a shop.

Go south on Scott Street. The corner building at 120 E. 4th and Scott is the 1941 Y.W.C.A. converted to offices of the **Rose Law Firm,** where Hillary Rodham Clinton once worked. Continue south past the 1911–12 **Woman's City Club,** originally the Elks Lodge. The 1906 building at Scott and Capitol houses the *Arkansas Democrat-Gazette*; across Scott is **Christ Episcopal Church.** Go east on Capitol Street to **Trapnall Hall,** at 423 E. Capitol Avenue, built in 1842 by the attorney Frederic Trapnall. Return west on Capitol to Rock Street, and go south.

Along this stretch are the Italianate **Samuels–Narkinsky** house at 515 Rock and **Kempner** house at No. 521, both built by merchants in 1867; the 1907 **Nash** house at 601 Rock; the circa 1900 Colonial Revival **Riegler** cottage at 610 Rock; and the 1884 **Welch–Cherry** house at 700 Rock.

At the southeast corner of Seventh and Rock stands the Pike–Fletcher–Terry House, built about 1840 by Albert Pike, a flamboyant character in early Arkansas history. After serving as the stylish Arkansas Female College from 1873 to 1889, it became the home of Colonel and Mrs. John Fletcher, whose son, John Gould, became a Pulitzer Prize–winning poet. The home is now the **Decorative Arts Museum,** open daily with free admission. Leave the museum property via the back gate onto 8th Street and go east to Cumberland, north on Cumberland to 9th Street, then east again. Note the homes at 500, 512, and 514 E. 9th, all built by W. D. Holtzman, a contractor, from the 1890s to about 1905.

Across the street lie MacArthur Park and the 1836 **Arsenal** building where General Douglas MacArthur was born in 1880. Immediately west is the **Arkansas Arts Center,** with galleries, a shop, and a restaurant.

Governor's Mansion Historic District
(approximately 6 hours)

The neighborhood around the Arkansas Governor's Mansion is an historic residential area with privately owned houses and churches restored to their late 19th- and early 20th-century elegance. Most were built in the booming period following the Civil War. This can be a driving as well as a walking tour.

Begin the tour at Spring and 14th Streets, going south on Spring past the **Dibrell** house at No. 1400, built as an investment in 1892, and the 1896 **Dunklin** home at 1422

LITTLE ROCK AND
NORTH LITTLE
ROCK

INTRO
ATTRACTIONS
DINING
LODGING

Spring, which combines Queen Anne and Colonial Revival styles. In the next block are the 1890s Queen Anne **Crawford** house at No. 1510, and the first and second **Wait** houses built about 1898 and 1902 at 1515 and 1521 Spring, as well as several charming 1880s cottages. Continue south past the 1884 **Trinity Episcopal Cathedral,** which faces W. 17th Street at No. 310, the 1882 Italianate/Queen Anne **O'Brien** cottage across the street at No. 323, and the 1905 **Remmel Flats** at 1700 Spring, built as a rental property for insurance executive Harmon L. Remmel.

Turn west on 17th to Broadway. On the northeast corner is the 1890s **Reaves** home at 1623 Broadway, originally a school. The ornate 1916 **Kahn–Vestal** house, on the southeast corner at 1701 Broadway, is now the headquarters of the Arkansas Press Association. The 1905 **French–England** house sits on the southwest corner at 1700 Broadway. Continue west on 17th to Arch Street. At this corner, note the 1900 **Neel–Dean** house at 1701 Arch, a rooming house for many years.

Go south on Arch past the 1893 Queen Anne–style **Hemingway** house at No. 1720 (and the carriage house out back), and the 1899 Colonial Revival **Plunkett** house at No. 1719. Next, travel west on 18th, passing the 1899 **Prather** house, surrounded by a granite wall, on the northeast corner of Gaines at 1721 Gaines Street. Go south to see the delightful 1880s–1890s **Stevenson, Robinson,** and **Thompson** cottages at 1726, 1800, and 1806 Gaines. Turn east on Wright, returning to Arch Street. On the southwest corner is the **Kavanaugh** house at 1854 Arch, finished in 1899 for County Judge William M. Kavanaugh. North on Arch, find the imposing **Cornish** and **Gibb** houses across from one another at 1800 and 1801 Arch. The Craftsman-influenced Cornish house was built in 1916 for a banker; the Colonial Revival Gibb house was built about 1906.

Turn east on 18th to see the 1914 **Rogers** house at 400 W. 18th and the 1927 **Methodist parsonage** at No. 401, now a private residence. Cross Spring to the **Caruth–Cochran** house at 320 West 18th, built in 1882 and extensively remodeled about 1905. The **Governor's Mansion** is set back from the street at the corner of 18th and Center, completed in 1950 where the School for the Blind was previously located.

Go north on Center past the 1884–5 **Turner–Back** house at No. 1722, remodeled into the Craftsman style; the 1904 **Lyon** house at No. 1710; the 1881 Pierce house at No. 1704; and the 1904 **Turner–Fulk** house at 1701, built for businesswoman Susan C. Turner. Turning east on 17th, see the **Ledbetter** house on the next corner at 1700 Louisiana Street, which Turner built as an investment. North on Louisiana are the imposing **Hotze** house at 1619 Louisiana, now a B&B, and **Grace United Methodist Church** at No. 1601, built in 1920–26 on property bought from the Hotze family.

Turn west on 16th to Center. The twin **Halliburton** houses stand on the corner facing Center at Nos. 1601 and 1605. Go north on Center to 15th, passing the old 1888 Greek Revival **Winfield Methodist Church** at 1500 Center, now converted to apartments. Traveling one block west on 15th, reach the tour's starting point on Spring Street.

Dining

INEXPENSIVE

Browning's Mexican Food. Tex-Mex. Open since 1946, this dependable Pulaski Heights restaurant serves Tex-Mex food amid walls adorned by serapes and sombreros. The waitresses are pros, always hustling refills of hot chips and salsa and new glasses of punch to wash down the enchiladas and crispy tacos. The discovery here is the country cooking, good fried chicken, and plate lunches with country vegetables. Kids' menu. Beer and wine only are served. | 5805 Kavanaugh Blvd. | 501/663–9956 | $6–$10 | AE, D, MC, V | Closed Sun., Mon.

Bruno's Little Italy. Italian. A member of the Bruno family has been hand-tossing pizzas for over 50 years, and the pies are still a crowd favorite. You can also tuck into copious pasta dishes named for local celebrities, Italian desserts, and more, in an updated suburban restaurant that retains the charm of a neighborhood trattoria. Kids' menu. | 315 N. Bowman Rd. | 501/224–4700 | $7–$15 | AE, D, DC, MC, V | Closed Sun. No lunch.

Buffalo Grill. American. A shaggy buffalo head, worn wood floors, and sturdy furniture are what pass for decor at the Buffalo Grill, but the crowds have been shuffling on down for years, enough to make it the perennial winner of the local best-hamburger title. The hand-cut fries have their fans, too. Salads, cheese dip, and grilled chicken are other options. There is open-air dining on the deck. Kids' menu. Beer and wine only are served, and smoking is not permitted. | 1611 Rebsamen Park Rd. | 501/663–2158 | $4–$14 | AE, MC, V.

Chip's Barbecue. Barbecue. A casual family-owned restaurant where burgers, nachos, and salads offer a break from smoked meats. Known for both barbecue and meringue pies. Kids' menu. | 9801 Markham St. | 501/225–4346 | $9–$11 | AE, D, MC, V | Closed Sun.

Delicious Temptations. American. A western Little Rock shopping center is home to this café, which pioneered healthy cooking in town and still brings folks back for stuffed pita sandwiches, omelettes, fresh fruit, and the occasional dessert that challenges all those good intentions. Kids' menu. Beer and wine only are served; smoking is not permitted. | 11220 N. Rodney Parham Rd. | 501/225–6893 | $7–$9 | AE, D, MC, V | No dinner.

MODERATE

Andre's Hillcrest. Continental. A Craftsman cottage nestled in a lush garden, this restaurant has an interior aglow with floral swag draperies and polished hardwoods. It attracts the business lunch crowd for big salads and sandwiches and a more leisurely crowd at night with a changing menu that can satisfy both the heart-smart and those with a yen for rich sauces and fanciful pastries. The pan-roasted quail and the herbed pork tenderloin are good choices. The pastries are homemade. There is open-air dining on a wooden deck with awnings. Brunch is served on Sundays. | 605 N. Beechwood Rd. | 501/666–9191 | www.andreshillcrest.net | $14–$22 | AE, D, DC, MC, V | Closed Mon. No dinner Sun.

Brave New Restaurant. Contemporary. Fish flown in twice a week, fresh vegetables (many of which Chef Peter Brave grows himself), and light but satisfying and creative lunches and dinners have made this sleekly casual small restaurant a frequent winner of local Best Restaurant awards. You might have to wait for a table on the small deck in back, but most find the likes of grilled fish, pork tenderloin, shrimp with basil, and the unusual sausages and meats on the mixed grill worth the wait. The chocolate crème brûlée is a delicious choice for dessert. Smoking is not permitted. | 3701 Old Cantrell Rd. | 501/663–2677 | Reservations not accepted | $15–$20 | AE, MC, V | Closed Sun.

Faded Rose. Steak. Louisianian Ed David made such a hit with this casual New Orleans–style steak house that it spawned two more in Arkansas. Some of the items on the menu are iceberg lettuce soaked in marinated olives, a habit-forming buttermilk dip for fries, red beans with garlicky sausage, and a bargain hamburger steak. If you like seafood, there are entrées such as boiled and grilled shrimp and trout meunière. Rough-hewn paneling and sturdy wooden furniture stand up to a lively weekend crowd in this downtown eatery. Kids' menu. | 1615 Rebsamen Park Rd. | 501/663–9734 | $10–$18 | AE, D, DC, MC, V.

Graffiti's. Italian. Works of political cartoonist George Fisher and the sleek black-and-white coziness contribute to an urban feel in a bistro known for simple Italian dishes and occasional flights of kitchen fancy. Osso buco and stuffed pork chops are new favorites; tilapia comes in a citrusy finish for lighter eaters. Graffiti's is 5 mi west of downtown. Smoking is not permitted. | 7811 Cantrell Rd. | 501/224–9079 | $10–$19 | AE, D, DC, MC, V | Closed Sun. No lunch.

La Scala. Italian. A Tudor-style building dating from the late 1800s in the leafy Hillcrest area is home to the casual elegance of La Scala and its adjoining Afterthought Lounge, where you can hear jazz nightly. You can prepare for the music with Tuscan rib eye, salmon fillet, or tortellini, but you might want to save room for chocolate Irish crème brûlée. Smoking is not permitted. | 2721 Kavanaugh Blvd. | 501/663–1196 | $12–$20 | AE, D, DC, MC, V | Closed Sun. No lunch Sat.

LITTLE ROCK AND
NORTH LITTLE
ROCK

INTRO
ATTRACTIONS
DINING
LODGING

1620 Restaurant. Continental. Banquettes, subdued lighting, and textured paint set the stage for a menu that pays homage to both French bistro grilling and new American cuisine, with a touch of Chef Evette Brady's country roots tossed in. Silky sauces and crisp fries accompany a variety of grilled meats. | 1620 Market St., West Little Rock | 501/221–1620 | $9.50–$26.50 | AE, D, DC, MC, V | No lunch, no dinner Sun.

Spaule. Contemporary. A sleek Pulaski Heights bistro with a centerpiece floral display and equivalent artistry on the ever-changing menu of new American cooking. Fresh eskolar— a game fish—sautéed with brie and serrano peppers; lamb tenderloin with polenta, and fresh tilapia with raspberry-almond butter were some of the choices on a recent dinner menu. Smoking is not permitted. | 5713 Kavanaugh Blvd. | 501/664–3663 | www.spaule.com | $9.50–$21.50 | AE, MC, V | Closed Sun. No lunch.

Star of India. Indian. Inside this shopping center restaurant decorated with Indian rugs and artifacts all is serene, from the quiet unobtrusive service to food not usually found in Arkansas. The richly satisfying vegetable dishes, based on such ingredients as homemade cheese, spinach, and eggplant, are particularly popular. But spicy curries, lamb stew, and tandoori chicken are also well prepared. The assorted naan is a good side dish. You can also try the lunch buffet. Beer and wine only are served. | 301 N. Shackleford Rd., West Little Rock | 501/227–9900 | Daily | $10–$20 | AE, MC, V.

Trio's. Eclectic. A trellised patio, soft interior lighting, and muted colors provide a comfortably attractive magnet for the smart set from nearby Pulaski Heights and the city's growing western suburbs. This is a restaurant with two faces—meal-sized salads, fine sandwiches, and homemade soups at lunch and more ambitious dinners at night when the chef is always searching for unusual ingredients and unique seasoning. You might try the spinach dip, chicken enchiladas, voodoo pasta, and, if available, lacquered salmon. Open-air dining is available on a brick patio with an overhanging roof. Smoking is not permitted inside. | 8201 Cantrell Rd. | 501/221–3330 | $15–$20 | AE; D, DC, MC, V | Closed Sun.

EXPENSIVE

★ **Alouette's.** French. A native French chef-owner and starchy service in a deluxe mirrored room have helped make this one of the capital city's favorite occasion restaurants, but it is possible to choose carefully and escape with your wallet. Splurge on Arkansas caviar or be equally happy with lobster bisque, sautéed fish, and elegant desserts, led by a Grand Marnier soufflé. Located 10 mi west of downtown. | 11401 N. Rodney Parham | 501/225–4152 | www.alouettes.com | $12–$30 | AE, D, DC, MC, V | Closed Sun. and Mon. No lunch.

Café St. Moritz. Continental. Extravagant draperies, upholstered chairs, and a sophisticated French air make this a special place for a downtown lunch, with fancy salads, sandwiches, and pasta. With the lights low, it's an even more elegant place for dinner, when a well-sauced fillet, pasta with choice seafood, and even a popular vegetarian plate compete for attention. The pastries are delicious. Known for soufflé, seafood, lamb. Kids' menu. You can come here for brunch on weekends. | 225 E. Markham St. | 501/372–0411 | $13–$29 | AE, D, DC, MC, V | Closed Mon. No lunch Sat., no dinner Sun.

Doe's Eat Place. Steak. Don't be put off by the seedy building or the worn linoleum and tattered vinyl tablecloths in this downtown location. This legendary steak house attracts power brokers from the nearby capitol along with everyday lovers of homemade tamales, giant sirloin and T-bone steaks broiled to order, and, at lunch, locally legendary cheeseburgers with crisp fries. The broiled shrimp appetizer is worth a try. A fenced-in patio area is available for open-air dining. | 1023 W. Markham St. | 501/376–1195 | $19–$25 | AE, D, DC, MC, V | Closed Sun. No lunch Sat.

Sir Loin's Inn. Steak. Waiters in Colonial-style knee pants hustle out slabs of prime rib and other hefty fare in the solid comfort of a brick steak house handy to I–40. The shrimp on the salad bar is not to be missed. | 801 W. 29th St., North Little Rock | 501/753–1361 | $15–$30 | AE, D, DC, MC, V | Closed Sun. No lunch.

Lodging

LITTLE ROCK AND
NORTH LITTLE
ROCK

INTRO
ATTRACTIONS
DINING
LODGING

INEXPENSIVE

City Center Plaza. The Plaza is an ideal meeting place for family reunions. Connecting rooms bring the gang together and all of Little Rock's attractions are blocks away. Restaurant, complimentary breakfast. Cable TV. Outdoor pool. Free parking. | Broadway and 6th St. | 501/376–2071 | 274 rooms | $48–$55 | AE, D, MC, V.

Days Inn. Off the interstate, ½ mi from the airport, this hotel is next to a waffle restaurant. Complimentary Continental breakfast. In-room data ports, some kitchenettes, some refrigerators. Cable TV. Outdoor pool. Laundry facilities. Business services. Some pets allowed. | 3200 Bankhead Dr. | 501/490–2010 | fax 501/490–2229 | 108 rooms | $45–$50 | AE, D, DC, MC, V.

Jacksonville Inn. This two-story motel is 3 mi from the club Splash (mix of rock and dance music) and 2 min from Little Rock Air Force base. The inn, which features an outdoor pool surrounded by four separate buildings, is approximately 20 mi north of downtown Little Rock. Cable TV. Pool. Laundry facilities. Business services. Free parking. | 200 U.S. 67N, Jacksonville | 501/982–2183 | fax 501/982–7331 | 98 rooms | $35–$45 | AE, D, DC, MC, V.

Motel 6. City buses stop near this three-story motel 10 mi west of downtown Little Rock. The Red Lobster restaurant is 2 mi away, the Steak Out is across the street, and live bands are at Smitty's one block from the motel. In-room data ports. Cable TV. Pool. Some pets allowed. | 10524 W. Markham St. | 501/225–7366 | fax 501/227–7426 | 146 rooms | $44–$49 | AE, D, DC, MC, V.

Red Roof Inn. The two-story motel is 7 mi from the airport, 3 mi south of downtown, and near the University of Arkansas and the Expo Center. The rooms feature doors that open out into a free parking lot. In-room data ports. Cable TV. Business services. Some pets allowed. | 7900 Scott Hamilton Dr. | 501/562–2694 | fax 501/562–1723 | www.redroofinns.com | 108 rooms | $44–$48 | AE, D, DC, MC, V.

MODERATE

Best Western Inn Towne. This modern style seven-story hotel in downtown Little Rock is 5 mi from the airport. You can have a drink and listen to music in the Coldwater Lounge or walk to several nearby restaurants. Restaurant, bar. Some kitchenettes, some microwaves, some refrigerators. Cable TV, some in-room VCRs (and movies). Pool. Hot tub. Exercise equipment. Laundry facilities. Business services, airport shuttle. | 600 I–30 | 501/375–2100 | fax 501/374–9045 | 134 rooms, 25 suites | $69 for room, $99 for suites | AE, D, DC, MC, V.

Comfort Inn. This hotel is off I–40 on the edge of North Little Rock and Little Rock, with several restaurants nearby. The two-story white brick building has a modern lobby. Refrigerators. Cable TV. Indoor pool. Hot tub. | 3925 McCain Park Dr., North Little Rock | 501/791–3200 | fax 501/791–3200 | 31 rooms, 27 suites | $57–$62, $60–$100 suites | AE, D, DC, MC, V.

Hampton Inn I–30. The University of Arkansas at Little Rock is 5 min from this four-story chain, which is close to several restaurants, a movie theater, and the Park Plaza Mall. The inn, white stucco with teal trim and large windows, is 10 mi south of downtown Little Rock. Complimentary Continental breakfast. In-room data ports. Cable TV. Outdoor pool. Business services. | 6100 Mitchell Dr. | 501/562–6667 | fax 501/568–6832 | 120 rooms | $68 | AE, D, DC, MC, V.

Hilton Inn Riverfront. A two-story, downtown hotel across the street from the Arkansas River, where you can jog or walk through Riverfront Park. Newly renovated. Restaurants, bar, room service. In-room data ports. Cable TV. Pool. Exercise equipment. Business services, airport shuttle. | 2 Riverfront Pl., North Little Rock | 501/371–9000 | www.hilton.com | 220 rooms | $65–$74 | AE, D, DC, MC, V.

La Quinta. This three-story hotel is made of white stucco and teal trim. The drive-through entrance has a Mexican-style shingled red clay roof. The hotel, formerly a Holiday Inn, is 7 mi west of downtown Little Rock, 8 mi from the airport, and close to Ryan's Family Steak House, the Dixie Café, and miniature golfing at Gator Golf. It's 8 mi to the Arkansas Arts Center and 14 mi to the Arkansas State Capitol. Restaurant, bar, complimentary Continental breakfast. In-room data ports. Cable TV. Pool. Laundry facilities. Business services, free parking. Some pets allowed. | 11701 I–30/430 | 501/455–2300 | fax 501/455–5876 | 145 rooms | $65 | AE, D, DC, MC, V.

La Quinta Inn. A modern building with two floors and a fully decorated lobby, this hotel is 5 mi west of downtown, near the Arkansas Repertory Theater and the Alltel Arena. Little Rock International Airport is 13 mi away. The inn is near many of the town's main attractions, including Barton Coliseum (8 mi), the War Memorial Stadium (3 mi), the Arkansas State Capitol (4 mi), and Little Rock Zoo (3 mi). Continental breakfast. Cable TV. Pool. | 200 S. Shackleford Rd. | 501/224–0900 | fax 501/221–7126 | 106 rooms | $59–$69 | AE, D, DC, MC, V.

EXPENSIVE

Amerisuites. This hotel in West Little Rock is 10 minutes from downtown. The hotel has studio apartment-style rooms in two separate buildings. Complimentary Continental breakfast. In-room data ports, kitchenettes, microwaves, refrigerators. Cable TV, in-room VCRs. Pool. Laundry facilities. Business services. | 10920 Financial Center Pkwy. | 501/225–1075 or 800/833–1516 | fax 501/225–2209 | 130 suites | $59–$109 suites | AE, D, DC, MC, V.

Best Western Governors Inn. A New Orleans–style atrium with patio furniture is in the center of this three-story hotel in West Little Rock. Shorty Small's bar is one block away and the Comedy House is five blocks away. Complimentary breakfast. In-room data ports, refrigerators. Cable TV. Pool. Hot tub. Business services. Kids under 12 free. | 1501 Merrill Dr. | 501/224–8051 | 49 suites | $79–$99 suites | AE, D, DC, MC, V.

Courtyard by Marriott. A series of hills partially hide this three-story West Little Rock hotel from the nearby highway. The hotel is 1 mi from the Little Rock Zoo, 2 mi from the Arkansas State Capitol, 8 mi from the Arkansas State Fairgrounds, and 6 mi from the Children's Museum. Restaurant, bar. In-room data ports, microwave in suites, some refrigerators. Cable TV. Pool. Hot tub. Exercise equipment. Laundry facilities. Business services, free parking. | 10900 Financial Center Pkwy. | 501/227–6000 | fax 501/227–6912 | 149 rooms, 12 suites | $59–$92, $119 suites | AE, D, DC, MC, V.

Hilton Inn. This Hilton is 5 min from the university and near two malls and plenty of places to eat. The inn is in the western part of the city only 5 min from downtown and the Statehouse Convention Center. War Memorial Stadium and a golf course are across the freeway from the hotel. Restaurant, bar, room service. In-room data ports. Cable TV. Pool. Exercise equipment. Laundry facilities. Business services, airport shuttle, free parking. | 925 S. University Ave. | 501/664–5020 | fax 501/664–3104 | 263 rooms | $97 | AE, D, DC, MC, V.

Hotze House Bed and Breakfast. A neoclassical mansion (1900) in the downtown Quapaw Quarter district, Hotze is 8 min from the airport. Four rooms have fireplaces. Complimentary breakfast. In-room data ports. Cable TV. | 1619 Louisiana St. | 501/376–6563 | 5 rooms | $90 | AE, D, DC, MC, V.

Premier Suites Little Rock. Premier offers rates for daily, weekly, and month-long stays. Suites have one or two bedrooms, and all suites come with a washer and dryer, plus a fully equipped kitchen. Complimentary Continental breakfast. Cable television, in-room VCRs. Laundry facilities. | 315 North Bowman | 501/221–7378 or 800/735–2955 | fax 501/219–1920 | www.premiersuites.com | 65 rooms | $75–$90 | AE, D, MC, V.

Rosemont Bed & Breakfast. This former Victorian farmhouse is in Little Rock's historic Quapaw Quarter. You can walk from here to the State House or the Repertory Theater, or simply sit a spell on the porch enjoying the breeze. Complimentary breakfast. Library. Business services. | 515 West 15th St. | 501/374–7456 | fax 501/374–2111 | Rosemontbb@aol.com | 5 rooms | $75–$115 | AE, MC, V.

VERY EXPENSIVE

Arkansas Excelsior Hotel. Atop the Statehouse Convention Center on the banks of the Arkansas River, the Excelsior has concierge as well as standard floors. At this modern luxury hotel you can choose among three stylish dining spots. Opened in 1982, the hotel has a 20-story atrium lobby, crowned by a gleaming 40-foot chandelier, and glass elevators. The Excelsior is downtown on the banks of the Arkansas River. Restaurant, bar, 3 dining rooms. In-room data ports. Cable TV. Exercise equipment. Business services, airport shuttle. | 3 Statehouse Plaza | 501/375–5000 or 800/527–1745 | fax 501/375–4721 | www.arkexcelsior.com | 412 rooms, 22 suites | $125–$135, $200–$600 suites | AE, D, DC, MC, V.

The Capital. There's a turn-of-the-century feeling at this historic downtown hotel, built in 1877. Restoration of the four-story building was completed in 2000. Restaurant, bar. In-room data ports, room service. Cable TV. Business services. | 111 W. Markham St. | 501/374–7474 or 800/766–7666 | fax 501/370–7091 | www.thecapitalhotel.com | 125 rooms | $132–$155 | AE, D, DC, MC, V.

Doubletree Hotel. Luxurious accommodations and an elegant lobby are hallmarks of this 14-floor downtown hotel, located 10 min from the airport and near local attractions. Restaurant, room service. Some microwaves, some refrigerators. Cable TV. Pool. Exercise equipment. Business services. No-smoking floors. | 424 W. Markham St. | 501/372–4371 | fax 501/372–0518 | www.doubletree.com | 270 rooms, 17 suites | $94, $154–$304 suites | AE, D, DC, MC, V.

LITTLE ROCK AND
NORTH LITTLE
ROCK

INTRO
ATTRACTIONS
DINING
LODGING

Embassy Suites Little Rock. This all-suites hotel is in West Little Rock, 10–15 min from downtown. The two-room suites have sofa beds and kitchenettes, and there's a gift shop. Child care is available 5–10 PM Friday and Saturday, and there's a reception 5–7 PM nightly. Restaurant, complimentary breakfast. Kitchenettes. Indoor pool. Gym. Business services. | 11301 Financial Centre Pkwy. | 501/312–9000 | fax 501/312–9455 | www.embassy-suites.com | 251 suites | $95–$140 | AE, D, DC, MC, V.

Empress of Little Rock. This three-story Gothic Queen Anne B&B is on the National Register of Historic Places. The rooms are furnished with period pieces from the late 1800s. Complimentary breakfast. In-room data ports. No kids under 10. No smoking. | 2120 S. Louisiana | 501/374–7966 | fax 501/375–4537 | hostess@theempress.com | www.theempress.com | 5 rooms (3 with shower only) | $125–$195 | AE, MC, V.

Holiday Inn Select. This five-story hotel caters to the corporate world in West Little Rock. It's 12 min from downtown and 7 mi from the Little Rock Zoo and War Memorial Stadium. The building is white stucco, with soaring floor-to-ceiling windows, and a drive-through, covered entrance. Restaurant, bar (with entertainment), room service. In-room data ports. Cable TV. Indoor-outdoor pool. Exercise equipment. Laundry facilities. Business services, airport shuttle, free parking. Some pets allowed. | 201 S. Shackelford Rd. | 501/223–3000 | fax 501/223–2833 | 246 rooms, 15 suites | $108, $150–$325 suites | AE, D, DC, MC, V.

Josolyn House Bed & Breakfast. This romantic, turn-of-the-century home is in Little Rock's Hillcrest suburb. Allsopp Park is nearby. Complimentary breakfast. Hot tub. | 501 N. Palm St. | 501/666–5995 or 877/567–6596 | www.josolynhouse.com | 2 rooms and 1 guest cottage | $89–$125 | AE, MC, V.

Marriott Residence Inn Little Rock. One- and two-bedroom suites are like a home away from home if you're staying in Little Rock for an extended period of time. Complimentary breakfast. Kitchenettes. Outdoor pool. Gym. | 1401 S. Shackleford | 501/312–0200 or 800/331–3131 | fax 501/219–2524 | www.residenceinn.com | 96 rooms | $90–$140 | AE, D, MC, V.

Pinnacle Vista Lodge Bed & Breakfast. This ranch-style log lodge sits in the shadow of Pinnacle Mountain. Rooms are decorated with country-style floral linens and come with plush robes for lounging. Complimentary breakfast. | 7510 Hwy. 300 | 501/868–8905 | fax 501/868–8905 | www.pinnaclevista.com | 3 rooms | $89–$115 | MC, V.

MAGNOLIA

MAP 11, B6

(Nearby towns also listed: Ashdown, Camden, El Dorado, Hope, Texarkana)

The town was founded as the seat of newly created Columbia County in 1853 and became an agricultural trading center, with cotton as its chief export. Today it's a busy college town, filled with magnolia trees, and it makes a great shopping stop. Big Boy Toys and Gallery offers art, sculpture, and antler furniture plus train and antique displays, and Lois Gean's high-fashion designer clothes draw customers from Dallas and New York City. You'll also find antiques and decorator shops, clothing stores, cafés, and bakeries among outdoor murals in and around the historic county courthouse square.

Information: **Magnolia-Columbia County Chamber of Commerce** | Box 866, 71754-0866 | 870/234-4352 | www.magnoliachamber.com.

Attractions

Logoly State Park. This environmental education park 6 mi north of Magnolia lies on 368 acres of forested coastal plain with springs, streams, and hillsides. Logoly offers exhibits in the visitors center, an amphitheater, picnic areas, and tent camping. There are 2½ miles of hiking trails with observation stands/photo blinds. | From U.S. 79 at McNeil, go 1 mi on County Rd. 47 (Logoly Rd.) to the park | 870/695-3561 | Free | Daily.

Farm and Home Tours. You can tour southern Arkansas University's 658-acre farm and Magnolia's historic homes. | 420 E. Main St. | 870/234-6122 or 800/237-6122 | magplace@magnolia-net.com | Free | Mid-Mar.–mid-Aug., weekdays, call for hrs; reservations required.

ON THE CALENDAR

MAY: *Magnolia Blossom Festival and World's Championship Steak Cook-Off.* The city's streets are lined with blooming magnolias; and arts, crafts, a juried art show and sale, a 5K run, a fun run, a fishing tournament, and live entertainment take place on the courthouse square and around town. The barbecues sizzle during the steak cook-off. | 870/234-4352.
NOV., DEC.: *Lights Fantastic and Christmas Parade.* The county courthouse and downtown are lighted up for the holiday season with a chili cook-off the first night; the parade is filled with floats, decorated cars, bands, and horses, with cash prizes awarded. | 870/234-4352.

Dining

Little B's Mexican Restaurant. Mexican. When you visit this restaurant 1 mi northwest of downtown on Hwy. 79, you pass through an entryway painted with murals depicting a Mexican courtyard and enter a dining room decorated with Southwestern-style wrought-iron wall hangings, numerous plants, large mirrors, and more murals on the ceiling depicting fruit and twining vines. Popular dishes include the quesadilla and the Mexican turnover, which can be filled with chicken, beef, bacon, shrimp, mushrooms, cheese, or tomatoes. The sopaipillas and apple pie are drizzled from a hot skillet right at your table with hot brandy butter sauce. | 2630 N. Dudney St. | 870/234-2888 | $5–$10 | AE, D, MC, V.

Lodging

Best Western Coachman's Inn. In the heart of town, this two-story brick Colonial style building is next to the First Baptist Church and four blocks from the Greyhound bus terminal. You can enjoy country-style dining nearby at George's Steak House and seafood at the Old Feed House. Restaurant, complimentary Continental breakfast. In-room data ports, refrigerators. Cable TV. Pool. Business services. Some pets allowed. | 420 E. Main St. | 870/234-6122 | fax 870/234-1254 | magplace@magnolia-net.com | www.bestwestern.com | 84 rooms | $53–$69 | AE, D, DC, MC, V.

Magnolia Place. This two-story Craftsman-style home is downtown. It has four-square architecture (1910) and is decorated with antiques, including a grand piano. Complimentary breakfast. Cable TV. No children under 14. No smoking. | 510 E. Main St. | 870/234–6122 or 800/237–6122 | magplace@magnolia-net.com | www.bbonline.com/ar/magnolia | 5 rooms (4 with shower only) | $99 | AE, D, DC, MC, V.

Quality Inn. This two-story hotel is downtown near restaurants, a grocery store, and a church, and next to Beef & Biscuits restaurant. It has outdoor room entrances and is blocks away from Hwy. 79 and 3 mi from Hwy. 82. In-room data ports, refrigerators. Cable TV. Pool. Laundry facilities. Business services. No pets. | 411 E. Main St. | 870/234–3612 | fax 870/234–2862 | 71 rooms | $63–$86 | AE, D, DC, MC, V.

MENA

(Nearby towns also listed: Alma, Altus, Arkadelphia, Benton, Fort Smith, Hope, Hot Springs, Little Rock, Murfreesboro, Paris)

Mena was born as a railroad town in 1896, named for the wife of a Dutch businessman who raised the money necessary for the near-bankrupt Kansas City, Pittsburgh, and Gulf Railroad (now the Kansas City Southern) to complete the line between Kansas City and the Gulf Coast. Mena lies in a wide valley below 2,861-ft Rich Mountain in one of the Ouachita Mountains' most striking scenic regions. Hunting, camping, fishing, water sports, hiking and biking trails, and ATV and equestrian trails lie within easy reach of Mena in the Ouachita National Forest. Many of Mena's early buildings survive and are pictured in a self-guided tour for sale at the Chamber of Commerce in the 1920 railroad depot, restored as a small museum and gallery. Horse and cattle ranching and timbering are the basis for the region's economy.

Information: **Mena/Polk County Area Chamber of Commerce** | 524 Sherwood Ave., 71953 | 501/394–2912.

Attractions

Janssen Park. The centerpiece of this downtown park is the cabin that homesteader William Shelton built in 1851 on the trail from the Butterfield Overland Stage road into the Indian Territory. Ponds, picnic tables, and a playground are also on the grounds. | 7th St. and Port Arthur | 501/394–2912 | Free | Daily.

Queen Wilhelmina State Park. Atop Rich Mountain and 13 mi west of Mena, the first lodge at this location was built by the Kansas City, Pittsburgh, and Gulf Railroad. Today's 460-acre state park has a modern lodge, 10 mi of hiking trails, historic sites, a restaurant, a campground, picnic areas, a miniature railroad, miniature golf, a petting zoo, guided hikes, nature talks, and other interpretive programs. | 3877 Hwy. 88W | 501/394–2863 | Free | Daily.

Talimena Scenic Drive. The 54-mi Talimena Scenic Drive snakes up and down the crests of the Ouachitas' two highest peaks. Along with one breathtaking panorama after another, the road passes scenes of Choctaw and pioneer history, Queen Wilhelmina State Park, an arboretum, lakes, camping and recreation areas, and hiking and mountain-biking trails. The drive leads out of Mena and heads across the state border into Oklahoma. | Highway 88 | 501/394–2382 | Free | Daily.

ON THE CALENDAR

JUNE: *Lum and Abner Days.* A parade plus an arts and crafts fair is named for the nationally syndicated 1930s radio entertainers from Mena. | 501/394–2912.
JULY: *Fun on the Fourth.* Games, programs, and refreshments celebrate July 4th on the mountaintop at Queen Wilhelmina State Park. | 501/394–2863.

Dining

Holland House Restaurant. Southwestern. Several blocks south of the center of town on Hwy. 71, this restaurant specializes in steaks and has a large salad bar. The walls inside are decorated with paintings of Western landscapes and ranches. In addition to the steaks, the vast buffet, with chicken and fish dishes, seafood, and Mexican food, is also a good choice. | Hwy. 71S | 501/394–6200 | $6–$14 | No credit cards | No dinner Sun.

Lodging

Budget Inn. This one-story hotel in the heart of the Ouachita Mountains is on Hwy. 71 in downtown Mena across from Fred's Dollar Store and a Chinese restaurant. Trails for hiking in the Ouachita National Forest are a 20-min drive away. Restaurant. Some refrigerators. Cable TV. No pets. | 1018 Hwy. 71S | 501/394–2400 | 33 rooms | $35 | AE, D, MC, V.

Queen Wilhelmina Lodge. This two-floor modern lodge on Rich Mountain in Queen Wilhelmina State Park is made from native stone. The lobby and restaurant look out onto a view of the mountainside. There is a windmill garden. Dining room, picnic area. No room phones. Miniature golf. Hiking. Children's programs. Airport shuttle. | 3877 Rte. 88W | 501/394–2863 or 800/264–2477 | fax 501/394–0061 | www.arkansasstateparks.com | 38 rooms | $57–$67 | AE, D, MC, V.

MORRILTON

MAP 11, C4

(Nearby towns also listed: Conway, Little Rock, Russellville)

Morrilton was built on the Little Rock and Fort Smith Railroad in the 1870s. Its historic district lies around Church and Broadway Streets and includes the Rialto Theater, Carnegie Library, county courthouse, and handsome churches and homes.

Information: Morrilton Area Chamber of Commerce | Box 589, 72110-0589 | 501/354–2393 | www.morrilton.com.

Attractions

Depot Museum. This museum, housed in the old town depot, showcases the history of Morrilton and the Petit Jean area, and especially how that history was affected by the railroad. You can buy souvenirs at the gift shop. | 101 E. Railroad Rd. | 501/354–8578 or 501/354–4472 | Free | Mon.–Fri. 1–4.

Heifer Ranch. This educational facility, developed by the nonprofit Heifer Project International (HPI), includes a global village showing ways the 55-yr-old organization has helped millions of people in 115 countries become self-sustaining. You can look at exhibits that show how HPI uses animals in projects, including water buffalo, camels, Brahma bulls, and short-haired sheep. Guided tours are available; the gift shop sells international handicrafts. | 55 Heifer Road, Perryville | 501/889–5124 | ranch@heifer.org | Free; lunch $6.50 (reservation required) | Weekdays 9–5; tours weekdays 9–5; gift shop daily; lunch weekdays, reservations required.

Museum of Automobiles. You can take a look at former President Bill Clinton's Mustang convertible—supposedly the only car he ever owned—and dozens more antique and classic cars at this museum 15 mi southwest of downtown Morrilton. | 8 Jones La. | 501/727–5427 | $5 | Daily 10–5.

Petit Jean State Park. This is Arkansas's first state park, set on 3,471 mountaintop acres, approximately 20 mi southwest of downtown Morrilton. It has a 24-room lodge, a restaurant, housekeeping cabins, RV and tent camping, Rent-A-Camp packages, a swimming pool, hiking trails to waterfalls and caves, historic sites, a lake, boat rentals, a visitors center with exhibits, a gift shop, guided hikes, workshops, nature talks, and other interpretive programs. | 1285 Petit Jean Mountain Rd. | 501/727–5441 | Free | Daily.

MAR., APR.: *Great Escape Weekend and Easter Egg Hunt.* Nature walks, a spring scavenger hunt, and an Easter egg hunt make for a lively Easter festival at Petit Jean State Park. | 501/727–5441 | Easter.

JUNE: *National Trails Day.* A weekend is dedicated to the 20 mi of trails on Petit Jean Mountain, with guided hikes, tours, shows, displays, demonstrations, programs, and a drawing for prizes. | 501/727–5441.

JUNE: *Antique Auto Show and Swap Meet.* More than 100,000 visitors come to see 100 antique and classic cars compete for awards in various categories. The show has 845 vendor spaces filled with antique car parts; 500 cars for sale; and 130 vendors with arts, crafts, and flea market items for sale or trade at the Museum of Automobiles on Petit Jean Mountain. | 501/727–5427.

AUG.: *Great Arkansas Pigout.* Popular country and western entertainers come to Morrilton to perform. There are also contests, food, arts and crafts, fireworks, three-on-three basketball, a 5K run, a bike race, volleyball, tennis, and a pig chase. | Morrilton City Park, on Rte. 64E | 501/354–2393.

Dining

W&W Hickory Smoked Barbecue. Barbecue. Ribs, beef brisket, pork, and chicken are smoked on site at this barbecue palace, which also serves the usual beans, cole slaw, and potato wedges for sides. Catfish is also available. | 757 Hwy. 287 | 501/354–2766 | $5–$12 | No credit cards.

Sweeden's Betterburger. Fast food. Fried burgers, chicken, and fish sandwiches go well with the french fries and soda in a paper cup. It's fast food, but the Arkansas-related decor reminds you you're not at home. | 1800 N. Business 9 | 501/354–4253 | fax 501/354–9780 | $4–$6 | No credit cards.

Yesterday's. American. Yesterday's menu veers from pizza to Mexican food to steaks, all prepared and cooked in a comfort food style. | 1502 Hwy. 95 | 501/354–8821 | $12–$20 | AE, MC, V.

Lodging

Cedar Falls Motel. This quiet motel atop Petit Jean Mountain is a scenic 21-mi drive through rolling farmland from downtown Morrilton and is only 1 mi from the visitors center at Petit Jean State Park. The motel's spacious 23-acre grounds are ideal for energetic children and include swings, badminton, volleyball, and horseshoes. The motel is 3 mi away from the beginning of the trail leading to Cedar Falls. The cottage and guesthouse are set back from the motel in a private wooded area and include a kitchenette, and the guesthouse has a fireplace. Some microwaves, some refrigerators. Cable TV. Pool. No pets. | 1627 Petit Jean Mountain Rd. | 501/727–5636 | 16 rooms, 1 cottage, 1 guesthouse | $48, $75 cottage, $120 guesthouse. | AE, D, MC, V.

Mather Lodge. This rustic CCC (Civilian Conservation Corps) log and rock building about 20 mi southwest of Morrilton was built in 1933. Rooms have scenic views overlooking Cedar Creek Canyon. Restaurant. Some kitchenettes. Pool. Tennis. Boating. Playground. | 1069 Petit Jean Mountain Rd. | 501/727–5431 or 800/264–2462 | fax 501/727–5458 | 24 rooms in lodge, 32 cabins | $50–$55, $65–$85 cabins | AE, D, MC, V.

Morrilton Days Inn. This two-story hotel is just off I-40 2 mi from the Arkansas River Wildlife Management area, 16 mi from Petit Jean State Park, and 18 mi from the Antique Auto Museum. There's hunting within 15 mi as well as fishing at Lake Overcup 1 mi away. You can eat at Yesterday's bar and grill across the street. Restaurant. Some in-room dataports, some refrigerators. Cable TV. Pool. Hot tub. Pets allowed (fee). | 1506 N. Hwy. 95 | 501/354–5101 | fax 501/354–8539 | 53 rooms | $52–$58 | AE, D, DC, MC, V.

Petit Jean State Park Cabins. In the midst of this scenic state park are 32 rustic-looking cabins, available for rental year-round. Though they look like something Daniel Boone might have lived in, 20 of the cabins have modern kitchens, all have fireplaces, and a few even have hot tubs. Some kitchenettes, some refrigerators, some in-room hot tubs. Lake. Exercise equipment. Beach, dock. | 1285 Petit Jean Mountain Rd. | 800/264–2462 | 32 cabins | $65–$150 | AE, D, MC, V.

Scottish Inn. This two-story motel is 18 mi from Petit Jean State Park and 1½ mi from downtown. Some microwaves, some refrigerators. Cable TV. Pool. Business services. Some pets allowed. | 356 Rte. 95 and I–40 | 501/354–0181 | fax 501/354–1458 | 55 rooms | $38–$52 | AE, D, DC, MC, V.

Super 8 Motel. A waffle house, shopping, and a movie theater are 1½ miles mi from this two-story motor inn, which is 1 mi north of downtown. Cable TV. Pool. | 1420 Rte. 9 | 501/354–8188 | fax 501/354–6474 | 39 rooms | $47 | AE, D, MC, V.

Tanyard Springs. These historically themed log cabins are nestled into pristine wilderness around a private lake. | 144 Tanyard Springs Rd. | 888/826–9273 | 13 cabins | $150–$175 cabins | AE, D, MC, V.

MOUNTAIN HOME

MAP 11, C2

(Nearby towns also listed: Batesville, Buffalo National River, Bull Shoals, Hardy, Harrison, Heber Springs, Mountain View)

When Baxter County was formed in 1873, Mountain Home became its seat. The town anchors the region between Bull Shoals and Norfork lakes, reaching south to outstanding fly fishing at the historic White River bridge at Cotter, the confluence of the Buffalo and White rivers, and the tailwaters below Norfork Dam. Resorts, ranches, campgrounds, and outdoor activities abound in an area popular with families as well as retirees.

Information: **Mountain Home Area Chamber of Commerce** | Box 488, 72653-0488 | 870/425–5111.

Attractions
Miniature Museum. Over 100,000 miniatures are displayed with 110 pieces of framed art, 50 framed poems, and a host of towns and communities created by miniatures. "Cute" is the overwhelming theme. | 2113 Hwy. 62E | 870/425–4979 or 870/424–3702 | $4 | Mon.–Fri. 10–4.

Norfork Lake and North Fork River. The 550-mi shoreline of Norfork Lake has a variety of resort accommodations, with nonstop action for bass, walleye, stripers, and panfish. Scuba diving and other water sports are popular. The North Fork River, flowing from Norfork Dam, has excellent trout waters for fly fishing. | 324 West 7th St. | 870/425–2700 | www.swl.usace.army.mil | Free | Daily.

Norfork National Fish Hatchery. This hatchery 12 mi south of Mountain Home produces trout for stocking rivers; self-guided tours are available. | 1414 Highway 177S | 870/499–5255 | Free | Daily 7–3:30.

ON THE CALENDAR
SEPT.: *Baxter County Fair.* Live nightly performances by nationally known country, bluegrass, and rock acts are the highlight of this fair. You can also find the usual rides, displays, and contests. | 870/425–5111.

Dining
Chelsea's. Continental. Chelsea's is a downtown restaurant that serves a variety of seafood, steak, and chicken dishes in three elegantly furnished dining rooms. There is also a lounge

and bar area. Kids' menu. | 963 U.S. 62E | 870/425–6001 | www.chelseasfinedining.com | $12–$20 | AE, D, DC, MC, V | Closed Sun. No lunch.

Don Quixote's Gourmet Restaurant. American. Absolutely nothing is fried at Don Quixote's, and all items are prepared from scratch on site. Fresh seafood is served on weekends, and "chalkboard specials" change on a daily basis. The seafood pasta (New Zealand mussels, jumbo shrimp, and scallops in a white saffron sauce) is a fixture on the menu. | 103 Main St., Calico Rock | 888/298–8018 | fax 870/297–3020 | $10–$25 | MC, V | Closed Mon. No dinner Sun.

Fred's Fish House. American. Lake Norfork is at the front door of this restaurant 5 mi east of Mountain Home, so it's no surprise that fried catfish fillets star on the menu, supported by chicken and five-layer pie. You can eat outdoors on the wooden deck. Kids' menu. | U.S. 62E | 870/492–5958 | $8–$18 | AE, D, DC, MC, V | Closed Sun.

Gaston's Restaurant. Continental. This restaurant, which is part of Gaston's Resort, has a polished pine interior with old tools, black and white photographs, and country antiques hanging all over the walls. Steaks, pasta, seafood, and a variety of trout dishes are served with select wines and a variety of cocktails. | 1777 River Rd., Lakeview | 870/431–5203 | fax 870/431–5216 | $10–$20 | MC, V | Limited winter hours.

Lodging

Best Western Carriage Inn. You can stroll around the pond in the landscaped garden at this two-floor hotel, which is near the center of Mountain Home; movie theaters, restaurants, and a shopping mall are within 2 mi. Restaurant, room service. Cable TV. Pool. Some pets allowed. | 963 U.S. 62E | 870/425–6001 | www.bestwesternmtnhome.com | 82 rooms | $49–$69 | AE, D, DC, MC, V.

Comfort Inn. Nestled in the heart of the Arkansas Ozarks, this two-story Comfort Inn is in a quiet area off Route 62 E. Parks, restaurants, and shopping are two blocks away. You can fish in nearby Lake Norfork and Bull Shoals Lake. Complimentary Continental breakfast. Cable TV. Pool. Gym. Laundry facilities. Business services, airport shuttle. | 1031 Highland Cir. | 870/424–9000 | www.comfortinnmtnhome.com | 78 rooms, 2 suites | $70, $125 suites | AE, D, DC, MC, V.

Days Inn. This two-story hotel on Hwy. 62 is ½ mi east of downtown across the street from Twin Lake and 7 mi from an 18-hole golf course. You can walk to five public parks as well as to the Village Mall just down the highway. Rooms on the second floor have scenic views north toward the mountains and Bull Shoals Lake. Complimentary Continental breakfast. In-room data ports, some kitchenettes, some microwaves, some refrigerators. Cable TV. Pool. Spa. No pets. | 1746 Hwy. 62E | 870/425–1010 | fax 870/425–1115 | 53 rooms | $55 | AE, D, DC, MC, V.

Holiday Inn. You can listen to live country-western music in the Red Fox lounge at this two-story hotel in town. A new golf course is ½ mi away. Restaurant, room service. In-room data ports. Cable TV. Pool. Laundry facilities. Business services, airport shuttle. Some pets allowed. | 1350 U.S. 62 SW | 870/425–5101 | fax 870/425–5101 ext. 300 | 100 rooms | $58 | AE, D, DC, MC, V.

Ramada Inn. This comfortable, modern two-story chain hotel is in Mountain Home and 10 mi from the White River, where you can fish for trout. Restaurant, room service. In-room data ports. Cable TV. Indoor pool. Beauty salon. Business services. | 1127 U.S. 62E | 870/425–9191 | fax 870/424–5192 | 78 rooms | $62 | AE, D, DC, MC, V.

Scott Valley Ranch. You can go on guided horseback rides or take a peaceful walk through breathtaking meadows at this rustic ranch, nestled amid more than 600 acres in the Ozarks. The ranch is 7 mi south of Mountain Home. Complimentary meals. No room phones, no TV in rooms, TV in common area. Pool. Hot tub. Tennis. Horseback riding, volleyball. Laundry facilities. Some pets allowed (fee). No smoking. | 223 Scott Valley Tr. | 870/425–5136 or 888/855–7747 | fax 870/424–5800 | www.scottvalley.com | 28 rooms, 1 cottage | $115–$145 | MC, V.

Super 8 Motel. This two-story motel is downtown just off Hwy. 62 next to the Steak House. You can go fishing and boating at nearby Bull Shoals and Norfork lakes. Some in-room data ports, some microwaves, some refrigerators. Cable TV. No pets. | 865 Hwy. 62E | 870/424–5600 | fax 870/424–5600 | 41 rooms | $50–$75 | AM, D, DC, MC, V.

Teal Point. This resort on Lake Norfork's Teal Point and surrounded by the Ozark Mountains dates back to the 1950s and has both new and refurbished cottages. Teal Point is 5 mi east of Mountain Home. Picnic area. Kitchenettes, microwaves. Cable TV, no room phones. Pool. Boating, fishing. Playground. Laundry facilities. Some pets allowed (fee). | 715 Teal Point Rd. | 870/492–5145 | www.norfork.com/tealpoint | 18 cottages | $57–$220 cottages | MC, V.

Town and Country Motor Inn. This inn on Hwy. 62E just 1½ blocks from the center of town is within walking distance of Baxter County Courthouse square, which is ringed with restaurants and shops around a new veteran's memorial. The inn provides picnic tables and barbecue pits for outdoor dining, and you can spend evenings relaxing on the lighted porch in chairs and on swings. Some in-room data ports, microwaves, refrigerators. Cable TV. Some pets allowed. | 145 S. Main St. | 888/224–3323 | 40 rooms | $36 | AE, D, MC, V.

MOUNTAIN VIEW

MAP 11, D3

(Nearby towns also listed: Batesville, Bull Shoals, Hardy, Harrison, Heber Springs, Mountain Home)

Mountain View, the seat of Stone County, calls itself the "Folk Music Capital of the World" for good reason. During spring, summer, and fall, musicians informally gather to play authentic mountain music on banjos, dulcimers, guitars, harmonicas, and other "unplugged" instruments on the shady square around the native-stone county courthouse. Traditional music and dance continues at the Ozark Folk Center Theater and Jimmy Driftwood Barn, and other shows feature country music and comedy.

The historic native-stone and wood buildings surrounding the courthouse square are filled with antiques and crafts galleries, herbs and herbal crafts, a music shop, a soda fountain, cafés, gift shops, and B&Bs. Highways radiating from town provide scenic mountain drives, particularly Route 5 N along the White River to Calico Rock, named for its colorful limestone bluffs.

Information: Mountain View Chamber of Commerce | Box 133, 72560-0133 | 870/269–8068 | www.mountainviewcc.org.

Attractions

Arkansas Craft Gallery. This store sells only the arts and crafts of Arkansas artists. You can choose from hundreds of items ranging from wood sculptures to clothing. | 104 E. Main St. | 870/269–3896 | fax 870/269–3030 | www.arkansascraftguild.org | Free | Mon.–Sat. 9–5, Sun. 12–5.

★ **Blanchard Springs Caverns.** Among the most outstanding caves in North America, these caverns are full of dripstone and flowstone, stalactites, draperies, columns, and other formations. The ½-mi Dripstone Trail Tour goes year-round; the more difficult 1²/₁₀-mi Discovery Trail Tour is only from Memorial Day through Labor Day. The Blanchard Springs Recreation Area next to the caverns has RV and tent camping and hiking trails. The caverns are 15 mi northwest of Mountain View. | Highway 14W | 870/757–2211 | $9 | Nov.–Mar., Wed.–Sun. 9:30–6; Apr.–Oct., daily 9:30–6; Dripstone Trail, Jan.–Dec., Wed.–Sun. 9:30–6; Discovery Trail, Memorial Day–Labor Day, daily.

★ **Ozark Folk Center State Park.** Ozark Folk Center is devoted to the preservation of traditional Ozarks heritage. More than 20 pioneer crafts and skills are demonstrated by Ozark artisans in a collection of workshops and an herb garden. Acoustic music and dance plus gospel concerts take place in a climate-controlled auditorium. The park has a lodge, a gift shop, a restaurant, and conference facilities. It sponsors numerous special events and workshops, including summer programs for kids. The park is 1 mi north of Mountain View. | Rte. 382 | 870/269–3851 or 800/264–3655 (for lodging) | www.ozarkfolkcenter.com | $8 for crafts area; $8 for evening show; $13.50 combination ticket | Crafts area mid-Apr.–Dec., daily 10–5; gift shop mid-Apr.–Oct., daily; auditorium shows mid-Apr.–Oct., daily 7:30; special weekend events throughout the year, call for hours or calendar of events.

ON THE CALENDAR

APR.: *Arkansas Folk Festival.* Around the courthouse square and all over town, there's music—plus a parade, handicrafts, and a rodeo. You can also listen to traditional music and watch pioneer craft demonstrations at the Ozark Folk Center State Park. The park restaurant serves a family buffet. | 870/269–8068.

APR.–AUG.: *Young Pioneers Program.* Three sessions a day at the Ozark Folk Center State Park give kids 7 to 14 years old an understanding of the Ozarks lifestyle of the 18th and 19th centuries. The program is on Saturdays, July through August, and Tuesday through Saturday in April, May, September, and October. | 870/269–3851.

MAY: *Merle Travis Tribute.* Hear the National Guitar Thumbpicking contest and tribute concerts by guest performers in the style of the late Merle Travis, plus jam sessions and seminars at Ozark Folk Center State Park. | 870/269–3851.

MAY, JUNE: *Garden Glory Days.* Garden tours, Friday-afternoon musical herb teas, and special herbal demonstrations celebrate the Heritage Herb Gardens during peak blooming season in this award-winning event at the Ozark Folk Center State Park. | 870/269–3851.

OZARK FOLK CENTER STATE PARK

A vivacious schoolgirl in denim shorts and black hightops bobbed up and down on the auditorium stage at the Ozark Folk Center State Park. Her quick steps were in time to the lively southern Appalachian jig "Sally Ann," played by a trio of folk musicians on guitar, fiddle, and bass.

The Ozark Folk Center is America's only facility dedicated to preserving the region's mountain heritage—and presenting it in a highly entertaining way.

Tap your toes to mountain music. Chat with a blacksmith, potter, quilter, and others at work on 17 other pioneer skills and crafts. Learn to play the dulcimer or autoharp, to jig dance or to grow an organic herb garden. Design your own workshop for the study of the traditional crafts demonstrated here. Children 7 to 14 can sign up for Young Pioneers classes to try their hand at pottery, participate in spelling bees from the *McGuffey Speller,* go on scavenger hunts for items important to everyday pioneer life, make ink from plants, and play fox and geese games with homemade boards and playing pieces on Saturdays in spring and fall or Tuesday through Saturday during summer months.

The folk center's regular season starts the first two weekends in April, then runs daily through October. Workshops, special package weekends, and late fall and holiday events fill out the rest of the year from January through March and November and December.

The folk center has a gift shop, great country cooking at its Iron Skillet Restaurant, and a comfortable lodge. It is just outside Mountain View, the "Folk Music Capital of the World," and near the awesome Blanchard Springs Caverns, trout-filled White River, the Buffalo National Scenic River, and other natural and man-made attractions.

© Corbis

OCT.: *Harvest Festival.* Crafts demonstrations, exhibits, music, shingle and rail splitting, Dutch oven cooking, sorghum molasses making, fall foliage hikes, a quilt show, art exhibits, and special concerts take place during this award-winning festival at Ozark Folk Center State Park. | 870/269–3851.

OCT.: *Herb Harvest Fall Festival.* Some of the events at this festival are lectures given by nationally recognized special guests and seminars on culinary, medicinal, and decorative uses of herbs and herb products. You'll also find guest authors, chefs, and herbalists, crafts demonstrations, and culinary products; and you can buy everlastings, plants, and seeds from vendors throughout the Ozarks. | 870/269–3851.

OCT.: *Bean Fest and Great Arkansas Championship Outhouse Race.* Some 1,500 pounds of pinto beans are cooked and served with corn bread on the courthouse square. Festivities include a crafts show, continuous music, a tall-tale contest, and the Championship Outhouse Race. More concerts and crafts are at the Ozark Folk Center State Park. | 870/269–8068 or 870/269–3851.

NOV.: *National Bluegrass Fiddlers Convention and Championships.* An institution for over 20 years, certified judges award cash prizes and trophies to senior and open division champions from among top competition fiddlers at Ozark Folk Center State Park. You'll also find jam sessions and guest performers. | 870/269–3851.

Dining

Bar None Bar-B-Q and Steakhouse. Barbecue. Solid is the word for this in-town eatery, with its red cedar siding, pine ceiling, and hickory-smoked meats, including brisket and Canadian-style pork loin. The 68-seat open-air dining area includes three separate decks. The service is family-style. Smoking is not permitted. Kids' menu. | 803 W. Main St. | 870/269–2200 | $5–$22 | D, MC, V | Closed Mon., Tues. No dinner Sun.

Crossroads Café. American. Simple country fare is what you'll find at this spot in Anglers White River Resort. The café serves big breakfasts; burgers, sandwiches, and slices of pie for lunch; and barbecue sandwiches and complete dinners in the evening. | Hwy. 5 and Hwy. 9 | 870/585–2226 or 800/794–2226 | fax 870/585–2114 | $5–$9 | MC, V.

Jo Jo's Catfish Wharf. Seafood. Five mi north of Mountain View on Hwy. 5 you'll find this casual spot with a dining room overlooking the White River. Catfish, either blackened, deep fried, or grilled, is the specialty, but those hesitant to feast on the bottom-feeder will find other options as well. | Hwy. 5 | 870/585–2121 | fax 870/585–2123 | $8–$15 | AE, DC, MC, V.

Joshua's Ozark Restaurant. Southern. Whether you line up at Joshua's buffet or order from his menu, you'll choose from down-home cooking items such as fried chicken and okra and a variety of pies, plus the usual burgers, sandwiches, and breakfast items. | Hwy. 9 and Hwy. 14 | 870/269–4136 | $5–$12 | No credit cards | Reduced winter hours.

Lodging

Answered Prayer Bed and Breakfast. A cottage built in the Ozark dogtrot style awaits you at this B&B within walking distance of the town square. All guest rooms have private baths, two have queen-size beds, and one has a full-size bed and two twin beds. Complimentary Continental breakfast. | 420 Clarence | 870/269–5335 or 800/927–8424 | answeredprayerbedandbreakfast@hotmail.com | 3 rooms | $55 | No credit cards.

Best Western Fiddler's Inn. People from miles around bring their violins to play and compete in Mountain View's town square, ½ mi from this typical chain hotel. Cable TV. Pool. Business services. | HC 72, Rte. 59 and 14 N, Mountainview | 870/269–2828 | fax 870/269–2570 | 48 rooms | $60 | AE, D, DC, MC, V.

Country Oaks Bed & Breakfast. Two modern buildings designed in a southern Victorian style, the Carriage House and the Farm House have eight guest rooms with private baths, some with clawfoot tubs. The 69-acre property has a stocked 7-acre lake for fishing, as well as beautiful surroundings to admire. Complimentary breakfast. Cable TV, room phones. Lake. Fishing. | HC 70 | 870/269–2704 or 800/455–2704 | www.countryoaksbb.com | 8 rooms | $70–$90 | AE, MC, V.

Days Inn. This motor inn is at the junction of Routes 5, 9, and 14, at the only stoplight in town. The ground-floor motel is two blocks from the Hoe-Down and local fiddling attractions. Complimentary Continental breakfast. Pool. No smoking rooms. Hot tub. Some pets allowed (fee). | HC 72 | 870/269–3287 | fax 870/269–2807 | 71 rooms | $45–$85 | AE, D, DC, MC, V.

Dogwood. This one-story, newly remodeled Mountainview motel is a 4-min drive from the Ozark Folk Center State Park. A U-shaped building surrounds the motel's outdoor pool. Cable TV. Pool. In-room data ports. | HC 71, Rte. 14E | 870/269–2997 | fax 870/269–3088 | 30 rooms | $48–$54 | D, MC, V.

Dry Creek Lodge. This is a one-story, modern motel in Ozark Folk Center State Park, just outside the northern end of town; it is operated by the Arkansas Department of Parks and Tourism. Restaurant. Cable TV. Pool. | Hwy. 362W to Park Ave. | 870/269–3871 or 800/264–3655 | fax 870/269–2909 | 60 rooms | $52–$57 | AE, D, MC, V.

Inn at Mountain View. A Civil War colonel built this country-style Victorian house in the 1870s. It overlooks the courthouse square in town. The inn has been fully restored, and features antique furniture from the period. Complimentary breakfast. No room phones. No kids under 3. Business services. | 307 W. Washington St. | 870/269–4200 or 800/535–1301 | fax 870/269–9580 | www.inn@mountainview.com | 10 rooms | $68–$98 | D, MC, V.

Miss Ida's Bed and Bath. Five minutes from the town square, this inn in a modern home caters to music lovers—it's fine to stay up till the wee hours listening to music, sleep late, and still enjoy a Continental breakfast in the morning. The owners are performers themselves, and have decorated the three guest rooms in individual styles. All guests have access to a fully equipped kitchen. Dining room, complimentary Continental breakfast. | 204 Maple Heights | 870/563–3762 or 800/543–9430 | 3 rooms | $60 | No credit cards.

Wildflower Bed and Breakfast on the Square. This early 1900s Craftsman-style B&B on the town square downtown is listed on the National Register of Historic Places. Complimentary breakfast. No smoking. | 100 Washington | 870/269–4383 or 800/591–4879 | www.bbonline.com/ar/wildflower/ | 8 rooms | $60–$92 | AE, DC, MC, V.

MURFREESBORO

MAP 11, B5

(Nearby towns also listed: Arkadelphia, Hope, Hot Springs, Magnolia, Mena)

Murfreesboro's central square surrounds its 1931 Art Deco courthouse. The nearby Conway Hotel is now a shop for local arts and crafts. On the other side of the square is a rambling shop that sells antiques, imported fossils, crystals, and other rocks and minerals, Native American artifacts, and some South American pieces.

Two miles away in a volcanic crater formed 95 million years ago, a hog farmer found two raw diamonds lying on the ground in 1906. More than 70,000 diamonds have been discovered since then, most the size of a match head or smaller. The largest, "Uncle Sam," at 40.23 carats, was found in 1924. The crater is now a state park and the world's only public "finders keepers" diamond digs.

Information: **Murfreesboro Chamber of Commerce** | Box 166, 71958 | 870/285–3131.

Attractions
Crater of Diamonds State Park. On these 36 acres of an ancient volcanic crater, you can hunt for diamonds and other precious and semiprecious stones and keep what you find; digging tools are for rent. There are a visitor center with exhibits, campsites, picnic areas, a café, a gift shop, 2½ miles of hiking trails, interpretive programs, and the state's southernmost trout fishing. | 870/285–3113 | www.arkansas.com/state parks | $4.50 | Daily.

The Ka-Do-Ha Indian Village. This privately owned, preserved archaeological site was populated by Moundbuilder Native Americans 1,000 years ago. It includes a small museum with an audio tour, a replica of a wattle-and-daub house, mounds with burial pits, a gift shop, and arrowhead hunting. The village is 2 mi west of the center of Murfreesboro. | Off Rte. 27 | 870/285–3736 | $4 | Memorial Day–Labor Day, daily 9–6; Labor Day–Memorial Day, daily 9–5.

Lake Greeson. A 7,260-acre lake created by the Army Corps of Engineers, Lake Greeson is a great spot for bass, striped bass, and crappie fishing. Several recreation areas border the lake and there are hiking and biking trails, picnic areas, and fishing piers. | Hwy. 27N | 870/285–2151 | Free | Daily.

ON THE CALENDAR

JUNE: *John Huddleston Day.* Crater of Diamonds State Park honors the person who first discovered diamonds here in 1906 with a treasure hunt, a diamond-digging contest, a scavenger hunt, an egg toss, and a three-legged race. | 870/285–3113.

Dining

Pizza Shack. Pizza. Standard and thin crust pizza with all the usual toppings is available at this spot, which also has a lunch buffet as well as a ton of video games. | 112 N. Washington St. | 870/285–2513 | fax 870/285–2690 | $5–$10 | AE, D, MC, V.

Lodging

American Heritage Inn. The American Heritage Inn is a handsome one-story brick building painted white, with a large American flag out front. There is a restaurant across the street. Cable TV. Pool. | 705 N. Washington St. | 870/285–2131 | 20 rooms | $40–$45 | AE, D, DC, MC, V.

Riverside Cabins. A few miles from Murfreesboro on the south end of Lake Greeson just below the Narrows Dam and along the Little Missouri River, this resort has 10 cabins that each sleep four adults, plus a house with a kitchen, dishwasher, and microwave that sleeps up to nine people. Any of the accommodations offer easy access to trout fishing, and all cabins have an outdoor deck. Some microwaves, some refrigerators, no room phones, no TV. Lake. Fishing. | Hwy. 19 | 870/285–2255 or 888/654–6966 | fax 870/285–4125 | www.riversidecabins.com | 10 cabins, 1 house | $65 cabin, $180 house | MC, V.

NEWPORT

MAP 11, D3

(Nearby towns also listed: Batesville, Heber Springs, Jonesboro, Paragould, Pocahontas, Searcy)

Newport, an old White River agricultural town, was developed after the railroad arrived in the 1870s. It became the Jackson County seat in 1891. Sam Walton, founder of Wal-Mart, got his start in retail managing at a Ben Franklin store here. Sightings of the legendary White River Monster—described as being as long as three or four pickup trucks and having gray, peeling skin—have occurred up- and downriver from town.

Information: **Newport Area Chamber of Commerce** | 210 Elm St., 72112-0518 | 870/523–3618 | www.newportchamber.net.

Attractions

Arkansas State University at Newport. A branch campus of Arkansas State University at Beebe, it's primarily a commuter college catering to a wide variety of students attracted by the college's open admission policy. Two plays a year are put on at the school's theater. | 7648 Victory Blvd. | 870/512–7800 | www.asun.arknet.edu | Free | Daily.

Jacksonport State Park. This 165-acre park 3 mi northwest of Newport is the site of an 1869 courthouse and the *Mary Woods II*, a working sternwheeler into the 1960s. Other facilities include riverside campsites, a swimming beach, a pavilion, picnic sites, a playground, a wildflower preserve, and a ½-mile nature trail. Interpretive programs are offered year-round. | 205 Avenue St., Jacksonport | 870/523–2143 | Free | Daily.

ON THE CALENDAR
FEB.: *Miss Three Rivers Pageant*. You can cheer for your favorite beauty queen at this 2-day event, held annually at the end of February. The winner will go on to compete at the state level. | 870/523–3618.

Dining
E&L's Catfish Rainbow. Seafood. Though take-out is the most popular order at this spot, the restaurant area provides comfortable dining in a country atmosphere. The catfish served here is farm-raised in either Arkansas or Mississippi, then deep fried and accompanied by a variety of sauces for individual seasoning. | 1710 Malcolm Ave. | 870/523–9199 | $4–$8 | No credit cards | Closed Sun.

Lodging
Days Inn. Standard two-floor motor hotel in Newport with comfortable accommodations. Truck parking is available. Pool. Some pets allowed. | 101 Olivia Dr. | 870/523–6411 | fax 870/523–3470 | 40 rooms | $40–$65 | AE, D, DC, MC, V.

Lakeside Inn. This hotel has a restaurant on the premises, and friendly staff who are happy to suggest activities and adventures in the Newport area. Cable TV, room phones. No pets. | 203 Malcolm Ave. | 870/523–2787 | 48 rooms | $35–$45 | AE, D, DC, MC, V.

Park Inn International. This two-story motel is near the center of town, and 4 mi away from fishing and hiking in Jacksonport State Park. Restaurant, bar. Some refrigerators. Cable TV. Pool. Laundry facilities. Business services. Some pets allowed. | 901 Rte. 367N | 870/523–5851 | fax 870/523–9890 | 58 rooms | $49–$57 | AE, D, DC, MC, V.

PARAGOULD

MAP 11, E3

(Nearby towns also listed: Batesville, Blytheville, Jonesboro, Newport, Pocahontas)

This Greene County seat was established as a railroad town in 1883, at the site on Crowley's Ridge where two competing railroad lines crossed. The St. Louis and Iron Mountain Railroad (later the Missouri Pacific) was owned by robber-baron financier Jay Gould; J. W. Paramore headed the Texas and St. Louis Railroad (later the Cotton Belt). Residents of the fledgling community combined the names of these two men and called their new town Paragould. (Legend has it that Gould was incensed by his name appearing last.)

In addition to historic buildings, Paragould's downtown district includes cafés, flea markets, antiques shops, banks, and small businesses. A mural depicts the town's railroad and timber history.

Information: Paragould/Greene County Chamber of Commerce | Box 124, 72451-0124 | 870/236–1517.

Attractions
Collins Theater. This restored movie theater hosted the 1941 world premiere of *The Man Who Came to Dinner*, starring former usher Richard Travis. Today, a variety of fine arts performances are held throughout the year. | 2nd and W. Emerson Sts. | 870/236–6252 | Free | Daily.

Crowley's Ridge State Park. This park is on the homestead and burial place of Benjamin F. Crowley, the first known white settler in the region. You can stay overnight in one of the cabins, fish in a 30-acre fishing lake, or swim in a separate lake. There are also a snack bar, a bathhouse, a playground, a pedal-boat rental facility, picnic pavilions, and hiking trails. RV and tent camping are available. The park is 9 mi west of Paragould on U.S. 412, then 2 mi south on Rte. 168. | 870/573–6751 | Free | Daily.

St. Mary's Catholic Church. Before revolutionizing furniture design internationally, a young Charles Eames designed this church during the Great Depression of the 1930s. | 301 W. Highland St. | 870/236–2568 | Free | Daily Tues.–Fri., or by appointment.

ON THE CALENDAR

MAY: *Loose Caboose Festival.* This festival includes live entertainment on 3 stages, arts and crafts, basketball, softball, a carnival, a fish fry, and a 5K run. | 870/236–7684.

Dining

Candlelight Steakhouse. American. You can enjoy juicy steaks or seafood and pasta dishes by romantic candlelight. | 1611 Linwood Dr. | 870/239–8391 | $16–$30 | AE, D, DC, MC, V | Closed Sun.

Guy's Buffet. Southern. You can eat massive buffet lunches and dinners in airy rooms with copper pots, fake ivy, checkered tablecloths, and carpeted floors. The buffets usually include fried chicken, crispy catfish, sliced ham, meatloaf, hush puppies, fried okra, blackeyed peas, and mashed potatoes; there are also big salad and dessert bars. | 403 W. Kings Hwy. | 870/236–2299 | $6 | AE, D, DC, MC, V | Closed Sun.

Lodging

Best Western Rustic Inn. This motel is on U.S. 49, 20 mi from Jonesboro. A stone fireplace graces its rustic lobby, where you can enjoy Belgian waffles in the morning. Complimentary Continental breakfast. In-room data ports, some in-room hot tubs. Cable TV. Pool. | 3009 Linwood Dr. | 870/239–2161 | 41 rooms | $68–$75 | AE, D, DC, MC, V.

Ramada Inn. This motel is on U.S. 412, the major artery that runs through town. Meeting rooms and banquet facilities are available for business travelers. Restaurant, bar (with entertainment), room service. In-room data ports. Cable TV. 2 pools. Hot tub. Golf privileges, tennis courts. Laundry service. Business services. | 2310 W. Kings Hwy. | 870/239–2121 | 81 rooms | $49–$74 | AE, D, DC, MC, V.

PARIS

MAP 11, B4

(Nearby towns also listed: Alma, Altus, Clarksville, Fort Smith/Van Buren, Russellville)

In 1874 the town's site was chosen as the Logan County seat, and when it was incorporated 5 yrs later it was named after Paris, France. In the 1880s, coal was discovered and more than a dozen mines opened in the area. The town is near Arkansas's small wine-growing region and in the middle of a scenic drive from Ozark to Havana, which crosses the state's highest point at Mount Magazine.

Information: **Paris Area Chamber of Commerce** | 301 W. Walnut, 72855 | 501/963–2244 | www.paris-ar.com.

Attractions

Logan County Museum. This small local-history museum is housed in an old jail, built in 1886, where the last hanging in the state took place in 1910. The museum is near the center of town. | 202 N. Vine St. | 501/963–3936 | Free | Mon.–Sat. noon–4.

Mount Magazine State Park. Arkansas's newest state park sits atop the highest peak in the state at 2,753 ft, and has commanding views over the Ouachita Mountains and valleys to the south and the Arkansas River valley and Ozark foothills to the north. You can sightsee, hike 10 mi of trails, and camp at sites in the park. Interpretive programs are also available, and there is a visitor/education center where you can get further information. The 2,200-acre park is 15 mi south of Paris. | Rte. 309 | 501/963–8502 | Free | Daily.

Subiaco Abbey/Academy. The abbey was established in 1878 as a Benedictine monastery. It is now a college preparatory school for boys. The abbey and school are 6 mi east of Paris on Highway 22. | 405 N. Subiaco Ave., Subiaco | 501/934–1034 or 501/934–1001 | Free for tour of abbey | Tours by appointment, 501/934-1290.

ON THE CALENDAR
OCT.: *Mount Magazine Frontier Day.* This event in downtown Paris includes a beauty pageant, arts and crafts, entertainment, food, games, a parade, and log sawing and nail driving competitions. | Courthouse Sq. | 501/963–2244.

Dining
Grapevine Restaurant. American. While the usual fried suspects like hamburgers and breaded chicken sandwiches are available, there's a definite emphasis on lighter, more creative fare at this casual restaurant near the city center. | 105 E. Walnut St. | 501/963–2413 | fax 501/963–8893 | $4–$8 | AE, D, MC, V | Closed Sun.

Lodging
Winery Bed & Breakfast. The single guest accommodation at this B&B has a private entrance, a two-person hot tub, and a balcony. The inn is at the base of Mount Magazine near the Benedictine Abbey of Subiaco, on a working winery. Complimentary breakfast. | 101 N. Carbon City Rd. | 501/963–3990 | cowie@csw.net | 1 room | $75 | No credit cards.

PINE BLUFF

MAP 11, D5

(Nearby towns also listed: Arkadelphia, Benton, Dumas, Gillett, Hot Springs, Little Rock, Stuttgart)

Pine Bluff is the state's fourth-largest city (population 57,140) and is a regional trade, entertainment, recreation, and meetings/conventions center. Pine Bluff's impressive series of murals portrays its colorful local history, from its founding in the early 1800s through boom days in the 1850s when soaring steamboat traffic hauled away ever larger cargoes of cotton. A portion of today's Jefferson County Courthouse went up during that period, as did homes that survived the Civil War and are part of a historic tour of downtown and residential districts.

Railroads first arrived in 1880 and gave the town another boost. Railroad repair and construction shops employed hundreds of residents, and the trains also opened the region to lumbering and related industries. The Pine Bluff Regional Park is the scene of RV campsites, a championship golf course, a softball complex that draws more tournaments each year, and recreational and tournament fishing for largemouth bass and panfish. The town also is the home of Sissy's Log Cabin, a jewelry store noted for its custom designs and antiques shop that has become an Arkansas institution.

Information: Arkansas's Land of Legends Travel Association | Box 8768, 71611 | 870/536–8742 or 888/818–8742 | www.pinebluff.com.

Attractions

Arkansas Entertainers Hall of Fame. An Animatronic Johnny Cash welcomes visitors to exhibits chronicling careers of entertainers with Arkansas roots. | 1 Convention Center Plaza | 870/536–7600 or 800/536–7660 | www.pinebluff.com | Free | Weekdays 9–5; weekends, call for hrs.

Arkansas Railroad Museum. Dozens of historic engines, cars, railroad memorabilia, and model trains are displayed in an old railroad barn, near downtown Pine Bluff. | 1700 Port Rd. | 870/535–8819 | Free | Mon.–Sat. 9–3; call ahead in hot weather because the museum is not air-conditioned.

Arts and Science Center for Southeast Arkansas. Changing exhibits in visual arts and sciences, as well as theater performances, are offered at this downtown location. | 701 Main St. | 870/536–3375 | www.arts-sciencepb.org | Free | Weekdays 10–5, weekends 1–4.

Band Museum. This museum in an 1890 Victorian downtown building is devoted to the history of band instruments, ranging from jazz to high school bands. Hundreds of vintage and antique instruments are on display, dating to the early 1700s; also a 1950s soda fountain is in working order. | 423 Main St. | 870/534–4676 | Free | Weekdays 10–4, weekends by appointment.

Dexter Harding House. Built in 1850, this restored, one-story wooden frame house is now the city tourist information center. | 110 Pine St. | 870/536–7600 | www.pinebluff.com | Free | Weekdays 9–5.

Grant County Museum/Heritage Square. This large, well-organized museum 25 mi west of Pine Bluff displays artifacts from pioneer days and the Battle of Jenkins Ferry during the Civil War through modern times. A dozen restored buildings outside, some dating from the late 1800s, include an early church and a Depression-era café. | 521 Shackleford Rd., Sheridan | 870/942–4496 | Free | Weekdays 9–noon and 1–4:30. Call for weekend hours.

Pine Bluff/Jefferson County Historical Museum. Pioneer tools, cotton farming equipment, Civil War artifacts, antique dolls, and railroad memorabilia are displayed in the restored Union Pacific train depot, which was originally built in 1906. The in-town depot is listed on the National Register of Historical Places. | 201 E. 4th St. | 870/541–5402 | Free | Weekdays 9–4, Sat. 10–2.

ON THE CALENDAR

APR.: *Railroadiana and Model Train Meet.* Find toy trains, railroad memorabilia, miniature train rides, door prizes, an Ark-La-Tex modular layout, and dealers from a wide area at the Arkansas Railroad Museum. | 1700 Port Rd. | 870/535–8819.

NOV., DEC.: *Celebration of Lights.* A 3½-mi driving tour through downtown and into Regional Park passes historic buildings and animated displays decorated with 3.5 million holiday lights. | 800/536–7660.

Dining

Canton Chinese Restaurant. Chinese. In the same brick building for over 20 years, the Canton Chinese Restaurant prides itself on its fresh vegetables, low-fat cooking methods, and emphasis on healthy cuisine. The Diamond Head (shrimp, chicken, pork, and lobster stir-fried with Chinese vegetables) is a specialty. | 6220 Dollarway Rd. | 870/247–4999 | $6–$14 | MC, V | Closed Sun.

The Crowbar. American. A few miles north of downtown Pine Bluff, this sports bar and grill serves up steaks, chicken, burgers, and sandwiches. Entertainment is provided by seven pool tables, darts, a multitude of big-screen TVs, and country and classic rock cover bands on weekend nights. | 6224 Dollarway Rd. | 870/247–0014 | fax 870/247–1453 | $5–$10 | No credit cards | Closed Sun.

Jones Café. American. There really is a Ma Jones. And a trip to her big dining room, within sight of some of the state's richest farmland, is just like heading to the farm for Sunday dinner, except you can do it nearly every day and never tire of the abundant vegetables and low prices. The coconut meringue is worth trying. | 3910 U.S. 65S | 870/534–6678 | $6–$12 | AE, D, DC, MC, V | No dinner Sun.

Southern Cook's Kitchen. Southern. With its emphasis on traditional Southern recipes, Southern vegetables, and Elvis memorabilia, there's no way you'll forget you're in the South at this casual spot. Very popular after church on Sundays. | 3007 S. Olive St. | 870/534–0625 | $5–$10 | AE, D, MC, V | No dinner Sun.

Lodging

Best Western Inn. Regional Park, with its bass fishing, stratton javelin tournaments, and drag boat racing, is just 2 mi away from this standard two-story chain hotel. Restaurant. Cable TV. Pool. Some pets allowed (fee). | 2700 E. Harding Ave. | 870/535–8640 | fax 870/535–2648 | 116 rooms | $57–$61 | AE, D, DC, MC, V.

Comfort Inn. A two-story motel adjacent to the shopping and restaurants of Pines Mall, and about 7 mi from the University of Arkansas at Pine Bluff. Complimentary Continental breakfast. In-room data ports, some microwaves, some refrigerators. Cable TV, room phones. Outdoor pool. | 2809 Pines Mall Dr. | 870/535–5300 | 50 rooms | $55–$100 | AE, DC, D, MC, V.

Days Inn and Suites. This two-story hotel has hair dryers in every room, a microwave in some, and offers all guests a complimentary breakfast. Suites with a small living area are also available. Complimentary Continental breakfast. In-room data ports, some microwaves. Cable TV, room phones. Hot tub. | 406 N. Blake St. | 870/534–1800 | 40 rooms | $48–$83 | AE, D, MC, V.

Hampton Inn. Near the Pines Mall just off Hwy. 65 and about 2 mi southwest of downtown, the Hampton Inn has rooms with either two double beds or one king-size bed. Complimentary Continental breakfast. Cable TV, room phones. | 3103 E. Market St. | 870/850–0444 | 109 rooms | $55–$70 | AE, D, MC, V.

Margland II, III, IV, V. In a residential area two blocks off the expressway and near the center of town, these four separate Victorian houses (1856–1907) are decorated with antiques. Picnic area, complimentary breakfast. Cable TV. Pool. Exercise equipment. Business services. No smoking. | 703 W. 2nd St. | 870/536–6000 or 800/545–5383 | fax 870/536–7941 | 19 rooms | $90–$110 | AE, D, DC, MC, V.

Ramada Inn. This five-floor, downtown hotel is 1 mi from Lake Pine Bluff and Regional Park. Restaurant, bar. In-room data ports, some microwaves, refrigerators. Cable TV. Indoor pool. Beauty salon, hot tub, sauna. Exercise equipment. Business services. Some pets allowed. | 2 Convention Center Plaza | 870/535–3111 | fax 870/534–5083 | 200 rooms, including 84 suites | $60–$100 | AE, D, DC, MC, V.

Regency Inn. This two-story inn is on U.S. 65B 1 mi from the Pines Mall, Broadmor Plaza, and Bad Bob's country-western nightclub. Cable TV. Pool. | 2100 E. Harding St. | 870/535–8300 | fax 870/536–9247 | 70 rooms | $38–$41 | AE, D, DC, MC, V.

Super 7 Inn & Suites. Truck parking is allowed at this two-story hotel, 2 mi from boating, golfing, and fishing at Pine Bluff. Picnic area, complimentary Continental breakfast. Cable TV. Pool. Business services. Some pets allowed. | 210 N. Blake St. | 870/534–7222 | fax 870/534–5705 | 90 rooms | $59 | AE, D, DC, MC, V.

Super 8 Motel. Regional Park is 2 mi away, and the municipal airport is a 5-min drive from this standard two-story motel. Truck parking is available. Cable TV. Laundry facilities. Some pets allowed (fee). | 4101 W. Barraque St. | 870/534–7400 | fax 870/536–1201 | 53 rooms | $45 | AE, D, DC, MC, V.

POCAHONTAS

MAP 11, E2

(Nearby towns also listed: Batesville, Hardy, Jonesboro, Newport, Paragould)

The first town here was established in 1815 on the site of a French trading post on the Black River. It served as a relay point along the country's first overland mail route from Illinois to Louisiana. In 1835 Pocahontas became the seat of Randolph County. It lies at the edge of the flat farmlands of the Mississippi Delta and the rolling Ozark Mountains foothills.

Information: **Randolph County Chamber of Commerce** | Box 466, 72455-0466 | 870/892-3956 | www.randolphchamber.com.

Attractions

Lake Charles State Park. The 645-acre lake 30 mi south of Pocahontas is loaded with bass, crappie, bream, and catfish, with a Game and Fish Management area minutes away for fishing, hunting, and outdoor recreation. RV and tent camping, picnicking, a pavilion, a beach, a playground, a gift shop, and seasonal interpretive programs are available. | 3705 Highway 25, Powhatan | 870/878–6595 | Free | Daily.

Old Davidsonville State Park. The 178-acre park 9 mi south of Pocahontas preserves the site of historic Davidsonville, established in 1815. Bypassed by the Southwest Trail, an overland route from St. Louis to the border with Mexico, the town faded by the 1830s. The park surrounding the old riverport has RV and tent camping, lake and river fishing, boat rental, trails, a pavilion, a playground, and a museum. | 7953 Highway 166S | 870/892-4708 | davidson@cox-internet.com | Free | Daily.

Powhatan Courthouse State Park. From 1869 to 1963, Powhatan was the seat of western Lawrence County. Now the town is virtually gone, but the stately 1888 courthouse is a regional archive with exhibits interpreting the history and culture of north Arkansas. Powhatan is 20 mi southwest of Pocahontas. | 4414 Highway 25S, Powhatan | 870/878–6794 | $2.25; town tour $4 | Tues.–Sat. 8–5, Sun. 1–5.

ON THE CALENDAR

MAY: *Lakefest.* An outdoor sports show, contests, a car show, a bass tournament, music, a kids' fishing derby, and a parade of boats take place at Lake Charles State Park. | 870/886–3232.

Dining

Junction 166 Café. American. Down home cooking is the trademark of this spot, where anyone under 50 is likely to be called "honey." Big breakfasts, hamburgers, and turkey and roast beef dinners are staples. | 3071 W. Hwy. 62 | 870/892-8756 | $4–$8 | No credit cards | No Sun. dinner.

Lodging

Town House Motel. This two-story motel is a block away from the Pocahontas municipal airport (you can see the runway from your room). Truck parking is available. Cable TV. Pool. | 1710 Rte. 67S | 870/892–4531 | 28 rooms | $36 | AE, D, MC, V.

Cottonwood Inn. There is truck parking available at this ground-floor motel, which is near a Wendy's, a movie theater, and the Pocahontas municipal airport. Cable TV. | 2203 U.S. 67S | 870/892–2581 | fax 870/892–7529 | 50 rooms | $46 | AE, D, DC, MC, V.

Scottish Inn Pocahontas. One mi north of downtown near the city park and 7 mi from Old Davidsonville State Park, this hotel offers waterbeds in some rooms. Free coffee, a copy machine, and premium movie channels are also available. Restaurant. In-room data ports. Cable TV, room phones. Business services. | 1501 Hwy. 67N | 870/892–4527 or 800/251–1962 | fax 870/892–4529 | 41 rooms | $33–$42 | AE, D, MC, V.

ROGERS

(Nearby towns also listed: Bentonville, Berryville, Eureka Springs, Fayetteville, Harrison, Springdale)

Rogers got its start as a railroad town in 1881, immediately attracting speculators, tradesmen, and merchants such as J. E. Applegate, whose handsome drugstore—now called Poor Richard's Gift and Confectionery—still sports its original soda fountain, pressed tin ceilings, and delicately tiled floors, along with solid mahogany shelves, drawers, and counters. It lies along a walking tour of the city's downtown historic district, where visitors also find classy fine arts and crafts galleries, antiques shops, restaurants, bookstores, and boutiques. Sam Walton opened his first Wal-Mart at West Walnut and Route 71B in 1962; it is now a 30,000-square-ft antiques and gifts mall.

Information: Rogers/Lowell Area Chamber of Commerce | 317 W. Walnut St., 72756 | 501/636–1240 | rogersareachamberofcommerce.com.

Attractions

Beaver Lake. This huge (31,700 acres) man-made lake has numerous marinas, boat docks, campgrounds, and resorts. You can choose from waterskiing, scuba diving, swimming, picnicking, and other outdoor activities. Fishing is outstanding on the lake and its White River tailwaters. The lake is approximately 4 mi east of Rogers. | 2260 N. Second St. | 501/636–1210 | Free | Daily.

Daisy International Air Gun Museum. The museum has an extensive collection of antique and contemporary air guns and rifles. | 114 S. 1st St. | 501/636–1200 | www.daisymuseum.com | Free | Weekdays 9–5.

House of Webster. This retail store sells the same replica kitchen appliances and jams, jellies, and preserves made from wild fruits that are available otherwise only through House of Webster's mail-order catalog. | 1013 N. 2nd St. | 501/636–4640 | www.houseofwebster.com | Free | Mon.–Fri. 9–5.

Pea Ridge National Military Park. This is the site of the largest Civil War battle west of the Mississippi River. A 7-mi self-guided tour leads visitors around its 4,300 acres. The visitors center includes a museum, an informational film, and a bookstore. Pea Ridge Military Park is 8 mi east of Rogers. | 15930 Hwy. 62W, Garfield | 501/451–8122 | www.nps.gov/peri/index.html | $2 per individual, or $4 per car | Daily.

Rogers Historical Museum. This museum has exhibits on local history, and guided tours of the restored 1895 Hawkins House. You can see period furnishings, and there's a hands-on area for children, as well as a recreation of three turn-of-the-century stores. Located in downtown Rogers. | 322 S. 2nd St. | 501/621–1154 | www.rogersarkansas.com/museum | Free | Tues.–Sat. 10–4.

Shelby Lane Mall. This antiques mall emphasizes regional antiques in its over 300 merchants' booths. Furniture and glassware are particularly well represented. | 719 W. Walnut St. | 501/621–0111 | Free | Daily.

War Eagle Cavern. Guided tours take you past underground formations including onyx, rimstone, and crinoid fossils. War Eagle Cavern is 17 mi east of Rogers, off Hwy. 12E. | 501/789–2909 | Call for fees | Mid-Mar.–Nov. 1, daily 9:30–5.

War Eagle Mill. This reproduction of an 1870s water-powered gristmill has a gift shop and a restaurant. War Eagle Mill is 13 mi east of Rogers, off Hwy. 12E. | 501/789–5343 | Free | Call for hrs.

ON THE CALENDAR

MAY: *War Eagle Fair.* More than 200 crafts artisans from throughout the country draw thousands of visitors to this juried event. | War Eagle Farm, Hindsville | 501/789–5398.

AUG.: *Frisco Festival.* This community street festival in Rogers's downtown historic district includes a chicken barbecue, a chili cook-off, cardboard train races, children's activities, street dance, live entertainment, food, arts, and crafts. | 501/631–4135 or 501/936–5487 | www.friscofestival.com.

OCT.: *Original War Eagle Fair.* This is one of the country's most highly respected juried arts and crafts events, with more than 350 artisans displaying quilts, baskets, pottery, clothing, leather, books, woodworking, and other crafts. | War Eagle Farm, Hindsville | 501/789–5398.

OCT.: *Antique Show.* Quality antiques, collectibles, jewelry, pottery, and glassware are shown by dealers from seven states; you can also find on-site glass and crystal repair. | Rogers Youth Center, 315 W. Olive St. | 501/273–2284.

Dining

Bean Palace. American. A recreated gristmill churns out custom grains, houses a gift shop, and will send you home full of goodies such as beans, made fresh daily and served with smoked ham and turkey; corn bread, biscuits and gravy, and buckwheat waffles. Antique flour sacks decorate the walls. The blackberry cobbler is worth trying. Kids' menu. | 11045 War Eagle Rd. | 501/789–5343 | www.wareaglemill.com | $3–$6 | D, MC, V | No dinner.

Hillbilly Smokehouse. Barbecue. While it's generally a really bad idea to refer to locals as hillbillies, this rustic spot has embraced the derogatory term and turned it on its head. Slow-cooked pork, chicken, ribs, and beef are available for take-out or to eat on the premises. | 1801 S. 8th St. | 501/636–1927 | $5–$10 | MC, V.

Lodging

Beaver Lake Lodge. This one-level, brick motel overlooks Beaver Lake. The Prairie Creek Marina is ½ mi away. The lodge is 4 mi east of Rogers. Picnic area. Kitchenettes, microwaves. Cable TV. Pool. No pets. | 100 Dutchman Dr. | 501/925–2313 | www.beaverlake.com/beaverlakelodge | 23 rooms | $59 | AE, MC, V.

Coppermine Lodge. On the shore of Beaver Lake (and the site of a former copper mine), this lodge 12 mi east of Rogers has rooms with a rustic decor; if you have a boat, there are private dock slips. Kitchenettes, no room phones. Pool. | 18895 Coppermine Lodge Rd. | 501/925–2010 | fax 501/925–2555 | www.coppermineresort.com/coprmine/ | 21 rooms | $60–$70 | D, MC, V | Nov.–Feb.

Days Inn. This single-story, modern structure near the center of Rogers is a place where you can listen to country-western music in the hotel's Nice N' Easy lounge, go antiquing at several nearby shops, or drive 5 mi to Beaver Lake. Restaurant, bar, complimentary Continental breakfast. Pool. Some pets allowed (fee). Airport shuttle. | 2102 S. 8th St. | 501/636–3820 | fax 501/631–8952 | 55 rooms | $42–$100 | AE, D, DC, MC, V.

Park Inn Limited Rogers. A little nicer than your average one-story, drive-up motel, the Park Inn offers a free Continental breakfast and computer hookups in every room. The inn is between Rogers and Bentonville, about 10 min from Beaver Lake. Complimentary Continental breakfast. In-room data ports. Cable TV, room phones. | 3714 W. Walnut St. | 501/631–7000 | 31 rooms | $35–$60 | AE, MC, V.

Ramada Inn. This two-story motel is 25 mi from the Northwest Mall in Rogers, with two movie theaters and a bowling alley, and it's 20 min from the War Eagle Craft Fair. You'll find live entertainment in the motel's lounge. Restaurant, complimentary breakfast. Cable TV. Pool. Business services. Some pets allowed. | 1919 S. 8th St., U.S. 71B | 501/636–5850 | 127 rooms | $60–$85 | AE, D, DC, MC, V.

Super 8 Motel. The rooms in this two-story hotel come with either two full-size or one queen-size bed. Complimentary Continental breakfast. Cable TV, room phones. | 915 S. 8th St. | 501/636–9600 | 82 rooms | $40–$45 | AE, D, MC, V.

RUSSELLVILLE

MAP 11, B4

(Nearby towns also listed: Alma, Altus, Clarksville, Conway, Fort Smith/Van Buren, Little Rock, Morrilton)

Outstanding outdoor recreation and scenic drives lie in all directions from this busy Arkansas River town. It lies on I-40, is the midpoint on the Scenic 7 Byway between Arkadelphia and Harrison, and is a gateway to man-made Lake Dardanelle, 50 river-miles long with 315 mi of shoreline. State parks, national forests, and wildlife management areas are an easy drive away. Russellville has also become Arkansas's No. 1 spot for bass tournaments—now more than 50 competitions a year.

Historically, this was an important crossing on the Arkansas River. It was the site of the first Protestant mission and school west of the Mississippi, founded in 1820 and continuing until 1828, when the Cherokees were relocated to Oklahoma. Sequoya completed development of a Cherokee alphabet at the mission, after which literacy spread rapidly through the Cherokee Nation.

Information: Russellville Area Chamber of Commerce | 708 W. Main St., 72801-3617 | 501/968–2530 | russellville.dina.org.

Attractions

Arkansas River Visitor Center. "Renaissance of the River" exhibits explain the development of the river; tours of Dardanelle Lock and Dam are given in the summer; and RV camping, a boat ramp, tennis courts, a basketball court, a playground, a ball field, a soccer-football field, and pavilions are available. | 1590 Lock and Dam Rd. | 501/968–5008 | www.usac.army.mil | Free | Weekdays 8–4.

Holla Bend National Wildlife Refuge. The 7,055-acre refuge 7 mi south of Russellville is a wildlife-rich area that is also a bird watcher's paradise during the winter; there is seasonal hunting and fishing. | Hwy. 155, Dardanelle | 501/229–4300 | $4.00 | Daily.

Lake Dardanelle. Created by damming the Arkansas River, this 34,000-acre body of water is one of the state's most popular recreational lakes as well as a barge channel. Numerous RV and tent campsites and boat ramps lie along its shoreline, which includes scenic tentacle-like inlets and coves. | 1590 Lock and Dam Rd. | 501/968–5008 | Free | Daily.

Lake Dardanelle State Park. The park has two areas—at Russellville and near Dardanelle. Both have marinas, campsites, picnic areas, and beaches. Interpretive programs are available in Russellville only. The Russellville area park hosts dozens of bass tournaments. | Dardanelle–Highway 22, 10 mi southwest of Russellville; 2428 Marina Rd. | 501/967–5516 | www.cswnet.com/~ldsp/ | Free | Daily.

Lile Handmade Knives. The showroom of "the Arkansas Knifesmith" is filled with knives on display and for sale, including the knives the owner made for Sylvester Stallone for his movies *First Blood* and the *Rambo* series. | 2721 S. Arkansas Ave. | 501/968–2011 | www.lileknives.com | fax 501/968–4640 | Free | Mon.–Sat. 9–4:30.

Mount Nebo State Park. Up a steep, zigzag road not recommended for trailers over 24 ft long, the 3,000-acre Mount Nebo State Park offers spectacular views of the Arkansas River valley. The park has 15 cabins with kitchens, campsites, 14 mi of hiking trails, a swimming pool, tennis courts, picnic areas, playgrounds, pavilions, a small store with bicycle rentals, and a visitors center with exhibits. The park is 12 mi south of Russellville. | 1 State Park Dr., Dardanelle | 501/229–3655 | Free | Daily.

Nimrod Lake. Known for its excellent crappie fishing, this 3,700-acre Army Corps of Engineers lake 30 mi south of Russellville also has waterskiing, camping, picnicking, and swimming, with hiking and hunting in season. | 501/272–4324 | Hwy. 60 | Free | Daily.

Ozark-St. Francis National Forests. At scattered sites among the rugged scenery, you will find numerous campsites, picnic areas, float and canoeing streams, horse and bicycle trails, fishing and swimming spots, five wilderness areas, and access to hiking trails, including the 165-mi-long Ozark Highlands Tr. | 605 W. Main St. | 501/968–2354 | www.fs.fed.us/oonf/ozark | Free | Daily.

Potts Inn Museum. Built in the mid-19th century on 160 acres, this museum in downtown Pottsville is one of the best-preserved stagecoach stations in this part of the country. The museum is near exit 88 of I–40. | Ash St. | 501/968–1877 | $3 | Feb.–Nov., Wed.–Sun. 1–5.

ON THE CALENDAR

SEPT.: *Pope County Fair.* You can get a taste for Arkansas life with a trip to a down-home county fair, featuring livestock judging, a midway with carnival rides, scads of food vendors, and arts and crafts displays, as well as live entertainment. | 501/968–2530. **OCT.:** *Fall Festival.* Downtown bustles with a chili cook-off, a 5K run, a kids' run, a silent auction, games and rides, a petting zoo, a children's costume contest, live entertainment, art center exhibits, crafts, and food. | 501/967–1437 | www.downtownrussellville. com.

Dining

Guido's Deli. Deli. A small dining area gives you the option of eating in, or taking your purchases elsewhere for a picnic. A variety of meats, cheeses, breads, and daily lunch specials is available. | 113 N. El Paso Ave. | 501/967–8781 | fax 501/967–3357 | $4–$8 | No credit cards | No dinner Sat. Closed Sun.

Madame Wu's Hunan Restaurant. Chinese. A plethora of Hunan and Szechuan dishes is available here, including sweet and sour, garlic, lo-mein, and vegetable-based entrees. | 914 S. Arkansas Ave. | 501/968–4569 | $6–$12 | MC, V | No lunch Sat.

Lodging

Best Western Inn. You'll find comfortable accommodations at this two-story Best Western Inn on scenic Highway 7 at I–40. Many parks and scenic areas are nearby and there are restaurants within walking distance. Some microwaves, some refrigerators. Cable TV. Pool. Hot tub. | 2326 N. Arkansas Ave. | 501/967–1000 | fax 501/967–3586 | www.bestwestern.com | 99 rooms | $50 | AE, D, DC, MC, V.

Comfort Inn. This two-story hotel is 3 mi from Dardanelle Lake and 3 mi from Arkansas Technical University. In-room data ports, refrigerators, some in-room hot tubs. Cable TV. Pool. Some pets allowed. | 3019 E. Parkway Dr. | 501/967–7500 | fax 501/967–6314 | 61 rooms | $50 | AE, D, DC, MC, V.

Holiday Inn. This two-story modern hotel is 2 mi south of Russellville and 1½ mi from Arkansas Technical University. Fishing, boating, and camping are available at Dardanelle Lake, only one block away. Restaurant. In-room data ports, room service. Cable TV. Pool. Business services, airport shuttle. Some pets allowed. | 2407 N. Arkansas St. | 501/968–4300 | 149 rooms | $70 | AE, D, DC, MC, V.

Lakeside Knights Inn. All the rooms at this two-story motel face Lake Dardanelle, and there is a boat ramp on the motel's property. It's easily recognizable from afar because of the neon green doors to all the rooms. Cable TV, room phones. | 504 W. Birch St. | 501/968–9715 | 98 rooms | $26–$39 | MC, V.

Russellville Travelodge. All rooms at this hotel near I–40 and Hwy. 7 have a refrigerator, and pets are welcome to stay for an extra $10 a night. Guests can take advantage of the outdoor pool and free Continental breakfast. Complimentary Continental breakfast. In-room data ports, refrigerators. Cable TV, room phones. Outdoor pool. Pets allowed (fee). | 2200 N. Arkansas Ave. | 501/968–4400 | 45 rooms | $89–$179 | AE, DC, D, MC, V.

SEARCY

MAP 11, D4

(Nearby towns also listed: Batesville, Benton, Conway, Heber Springs, Hot Springs, Little Rock, Morrilton, Newport, Russellville)

Searcy lies where the Mississippi Delta meets the Ozark foothills. Duck hunting is minutes away in the rice fields and bottomlands to the east, and trout fishing is great on the nearby Little Red River. The growing community counts on both agribusiness and industry and is the home of Harding University. It's also the headquarters of the Yarnell Ice Cream Co.

The town formed around a sulfur spring in the late 1830s and claimed a population of 700 by the time of the Civil War. Railroads brought prosperity in the following years. The city retains numerous historic buildings, including the 1871 White County Courthouse and the handsome Italianate Benjamin Clayton Black house, built in 1874. You can also see numerous homes built in the Craftsman style and commercial buildings dating from the 1860s to the Art Deco period of the 1940s.

Information: **Searcy Chamber of Commerce** | 2323 S. Main St., 72143 | 501/268–2458 | www.searcy.dina.org.

SEARCY

INTRO
ATTRACTIONS
DINING
LODGING

Attractions

Harding University. This private, Christian, liberal arts college enrolls about 4,500 students in a variety of disciplines. Benson Auditorium plays host to many public events, including lectures from scholars and concerts. | 900 Center St. | 501/279–4316 | www.harding.edu | Free | Daily.

ON THE CALENDAR
NOV., DEC.: *Holiday of Lights.* Millions of lights cover the downtown square and public parks. Events include the lighting ceremony, a parade, pageants, plays, and choral concerts. | 501/279–1010.

Dining

Huckleberry's. American. A popular buffet restaurant despite its rather limited hours, this family spot serves up carved meats, fried chicken, mashed potatoes, vegetables, desserts, and myriad other items that change every day. | 2613 E. Line Rd. | 501/268–0194 | $8–$12 | MC, V | No lunch Mon.–Sat. No dinner Sun.–Wed.

Lodging

Best Western Inn. This two-story hotel is 8 mi from the Locomotion Family Fun Park and close to the Ozark Family Outlet Mall. There is a restaurant next door. In-room data ports. Cable TV. Some pets allowed (fee). | 1394 W. Sunset Ave. | 501/751–3100 | fax 501/756–2490 | 100 rooms | $52 | AE, D, DC, MC, V.

Comfort Inn. This two-story modern red-brick hotel is near the center of Searcy. Complimentary Continental breakfast. Cable TV. Pool. Some pets allowed. | 107 S. Rand St. | 501/279–9100 | 60 rooms | $60 | AE, D, DC, MC, V.

Hampton Inn. This chain hotel is 3 mi from Harding University. Restaurant, complimentary Continental breakfast, room service. Some refrigerators. Cable TV. Indoor-outdoor pool. Hot tub. Exercise equipment. Laundry facilities. Business services. Some pets allowed. | 3204 E. Race St. | 501/268–0654 | fax 501/278–5546 | tn009670@psinet.com | 106 rooms | $64–$69 | AE, D, DC, MC, V.

Lightle House Inn. A red-brick home built in 1923 within walking distance of Harding University, this B&B offers guests rooms with queen- or king-size beds, private baths, a full complimentary breakfast, and a sitting room with a TV and VCR. Dining room, complimentary breakfast. In-room data ports, some in-room hot tubs. Room phones, TV in common area. | 605 E. Race Ave. | 501/279–7190 | fax 501/279–1206 | nkeeper@anaxis.net | 5 rooms | $65–$95 | AE, MC, V.

SPRINGDALE

MAP 11, A2

(Nearby towns also listed: Bentonville, Berryville, Eureka Springs, Fayetteville, Harrison, Rogers)

Springdale is a hardworking community, both industrially and as the international headquarters of Tyson Foods, the world's largest producer of poultry products. It formed after 1840 on land where the Shiloh Museum of Ozark History now stands, and was a stop on the Butterfield Overland mail route from Missouri to San Francisco after 1858. Its new Harvey and Bernice Jones Center for Families, at Emma Avenue and Old Missouri Road, is the envy of much larger cities and towns nationwide. Its lap and leisure swimming pools, multipurpose gymnasium, fitness center, ice-skating arena, indoor and outdoor walking/jogging tracks, game fields, volleyball courts, amphitheater, gardens, and auditorium programs are free to visitors as well as residents.

Visitors also find an outstanding Native American and Western art gallery, a number of antiques and collectibles shops, an outlet mall, and even a shop specializing in chicken-theme gifts, home accessories, and toys.

Information: **Springdale Chamber of Commerce** | Box 166, 72765-0166 | www.springdale.com | 501/872–2222.

Attractions

Arkansas and Missouri Railroad. Take a daylong round-trip through the Boston Mountains from Springdale to Van Buren in restored railway cars, crossing high trestles and chugging through the 1882 Winslow Tunnel; also available are 2-hr excursions from Van Buren. | 306 E. Emms St. | www.arkansasmissouri-rr.com | 501/751–8600 or 800/687–8600 | Call for prices | Call for information.

Arts Center of the Ozarks. Dramas, musicals, comedies, gallery showings, classes, and cultural events take place in this downtown Springdale center. | 214 S. Main | 501/751–5441 | www.nwaonline.net/aco | Free to the gallery. Call for theater prices | Weekdays 8:30–5:30, Sat. 9–3.

★ **Shiloh Museum of Ozark History.** This Springdale museum houses collections from the Ozarks region, including Native American artifacts, pioneer buildings and materials, agricultural tools, and clothing. | 118 W. Johnson Ave. | 501/750–8165 | www.springdaleark.org/shiloh | Free | Mon.–Sat. 10–5.

ON THE CALENDAR
JULY: *Rodeo of the Ozarks.* Thrills and spills at this PRCA/WPRA–sanctioned rodeo, which is part of a nonstop festival with a Western theme. | Parsons Stadium | 501/927–4530.

Dining

A. Q. Chicken House. American. A little roadside café on the north side of Springdale grew up into a sprawling family restaurant and has served happy eaters for five decades. You'll find fluffy rolls, vegetables, and cobbler. The ribs and apple dumplings are well worth trying. Kids' menu. Beer and wine only are served. | 1207 N. Thompson St. | 501/751–4633 | $8–$15 | AE, D, DC, MC, V.

Marketplace Grill. Continental. Adjacent to the Holiday Inn, this upscale casual restaurant serves steaks, chicken, and fish grilled over hardwoods, pastas and soups made from scratch, and wood-fired pizzas. | 1636 W. 48th St. | 501/750–5200 | fax 501/750–3393 | $10–$25 | AE, D, DC, MC, V.

Mary Maestri's. Italian. This two-story wooden frame house has been a family-owned destination for Arkansans since the early 1900s. You can enjoy spaghetti and meatballs or top capellini with 3 seafoods and finish the meal with tiramisu. Kids' menu. Beer and wine only are served. Located 5 mi west of the center of Springdale. | Rte. 412 W, Tontitown | 501/361–2536 | $10–$26 | AE, D, DC, MC, V | No lunch.

Lodging

Comfort Inn. Although hiking trails and Lake Fayetteville offer exercise opportunities less than 5 mi away, you may also visit a local health club for free while staying at this hotel. Rooms are relatively basic, with cable TV and pay-per-view movies. Complimentary Continental breakfast, in-room data ports. Cable TV, room phones. Outdoor pool. Laundry facilities, laundry service. | 4540 W. Sunset Ave. | 501/751–6700 | 60 rooms | $59–$110 | AE, DC, D, MC, V.

Executive Inn. After enjoying a scenic tour of the Ozark Mountain region on the Arkansas Railway Association train, you can relax in the Rendezvous, the motel's lounge. Restaurant, bar. Some microwaves, some refrigerators. Cable TV. Outdoor pool. Laundry facilities. Some pets allowed. | 2005 U.S. 71B S | 501/756–6101 or 800/544–6086 | fax 501/756–6101, ext. 5 | 101 rooms | $49 | AE, D, DC, MC, V.

Hampton Inn. This three-story hotel is 20 min from the Northwest Arkansas Regional Airport and has a fireplace that glows in the lobby all winter long. There are restaurants and a movie theater nearby. Complimentary Continental breakfast. In-room data ports, some kitchenettes. Cable TV. Pool. Business services. Some pets allowed. | 1700 S. 48th St. | 501/756–3500 | fax 501/927–3500 | www.hamptonsuites.com/hisdocs/properties/ | 67 rooms, 35 suites | $69–$85, $106–$116 suites | AE, D, DC, MC, V.

Holiday Inn. This is a seven-story, atrium-style hotel with palm trees, vines, and a five-story waterfall. Some rooms overlook downtown. The inn is near the city's convention center. Restaurant, bar. In-room data ports. Cable TV. Indoor pool. Hot tub. Exercise equipment. Laundry facilities. Business services, airport shuttle. Some pets allowed. | 1500 S. 48th St. | 501/751–8300 | fax 501/751–4640 | 184 rooms, 22 suites | $59–109, $130–$150 suites | AE, D, DC, MC, V.

Magnolia Gardens Inn. This lavishly restored 1800s Victorian mansion is listed on the National Register. The inn has 10 acres of gardens and paths. Banquet, garden wedding, and reception facilities are available. All rooms are distinctly different. Complimentary breakfast. Spa. Business services. No kids allowed. No smoking. | 500 N. Main | 501/756–5744 | fax 501/756–2526 | 10 rooms | $100–$135 | AE, MC, V.

Sunrise Inn. An outdoor pool is open during the summer, but in the off-season you can enjoy in-room movies on cable, or borrow videos from the front desk. A restaurant and cocktail lounge are on site. Restaurant, bar. In-room data ports. Cable TV, some in-room VCRs, room phones. Outdoor pool. Business services. | 2001 S. Thompson Ave. | 501/756–1900 | 84 rooms | $31–$65 | AE, DC, D, MC, V.

STUTTGART

MAP 11, D5

(Nearby towns listed: Benton, Hot Springs, Little Rock, Pine Bluff)

Arkansas is the No. 1 producer of rice in the United States, and Stuttgart is the state's rice-growing capital. Half a dozen agricultural and aquacultural research stations are here. Stuttgart is also an epicenter of duck hunting and hosts the annual World Championship Duck Calling Contests. The town was established by a German Lutheran congregation from Ohio in 1878. Thomas H. Leslie, who gave Stuttgart its real start, moved to the little village from southern Arkansas County in 1887. He organized its first bank, built a railroad to Gillett, lured manufacturing plants to the area, and started a real estate company that established its downtown.

Information: **Stuttgart Chamber of Commerce** | Box 932, 72160-0932 | 870/673–1602 | www.stuttgartarkansas.com.

Attractions

Antiques on Park Ave. This antiques mall has more than 40 booths selling antiques in all price ranges. China, glassware, and linens have a particularly strong presence. | 1703 S. Timber St. | 870/673–1179 | www.antiquesonparkave.com | Free | Mon.–Sat. 9–5.

Stuttgart Agricultural Museum. The displays in this award-winning museum trace the history of agriculture and the pioneers of the Grand Prairie of eastern Arkansas. The in-town museum includes scaled-down reproductions of actual stores; an agricultural aviation display, a recreated duck hunt, plus decoys, Native American effigies, waterfowl memorabilia, a doll collection, and antique farm vehicles and equipment. | 921 E. 4th St. | 870/673–7001 | Free | Tues.–Sat. 10–4, Sun. 1:30–4:30.

White River National Wildlife Refuge. This extensive preserve (160,000 acres) has more than 150 natural lakes and is home to deer, wild turkey, black bear, alligators, and waterfowl. It is 30 mi east of Stuttgart, off Rte 165E. | 321 West 7th St., DeWitt | 870/946–1468 | Free | Refuge daily; fishing Mar.–Oct., daily; hunting, call for hrs.

ON THE CALENDAR

NOV.: *Wings over the Prairie Festival.* The World Championship Duck Calling Contest is the major event in this tribute to the hundreds of thousands of ducks and geese that winter on the Grand Prairie. It takes place downtown. Festivities include a duck gumbo cook-off, arts and crafts, commercial exhibits, a sporting collectibles show, the Great 10K Duck Race, and the Sportsmen's Dinner and Dance. | 870/673–1602.

NOV.: *Queen Mallard Pageant.* Held the first day of the annual World Championship Duck Calling Contest, usually a Saturday in mid-November, the pageant sees the crowning of the Queen Mallard and Junior Queen Mallard who begin their year's service. Held at the Grand Prairie War Memorial Auditorium. | 870/673–1602.

Dining

Country Gossip. American. This country store (imagine a slightly more upscale version of Cracker Barrel) doubles as a café serving light, lunchtime fare. Homemade soups, salads, pastas, and desserts are complemented by a daily special. | 100 S. Main St. | 870/673–6115 | $4–$8 | AE, D, MC, V | Closed weekends. No dinner.

Lodging

Best Western Duck Inn. November 18–January 21 is duck hunting season in Stuttgart. If you come to hunt, you can eat a 4 AM complimentary Continental breakfast at this two-story Best Western, then drive outside the city limits to hide in the rice fields with your rifle. Complimentary Continental breakfast. Some refrigerators. Cable TV, in-room VCRs.

Indoor pool. Some pets allowed. | 704 W. Michigan St. | 870/673–2575 | 72 rooms | $62–$105 | AE, DC, MC, V.

Economy Inn Express. This in-town motor hotel on one floor is at its busiest during duck hunting season. Truck parking is available. In-room data ports, refrigerators. Cable TV. Laundry facilities. | 200 W. Michigan St. | 870/673–7275 | 22 rooms | $35–$55 | AE, D, MC, V.

Holiday Inn Express. The brightly lit, airy rooms at this modern hotel all feature coffee and tea makers, data ports, an alarm clock, and an iron. Fitness equipment is available, as is an outdoor pool. In-room data ports, refrigerators. Cable TV, room phones. Outdoor pool. Exercise equipment. Business services. | 708 W. Michigan St. | 870/673–3616 | fax 870/673–6920 | 40 rooms | $56–$63 | AE, D, DC, MC, V.

TEXARKANA

(Nearby towns also listed: Arkadelphia, Ashdown, Camden, El Dorado, Hope, Magnolia)

Texarkana, which straddles the Arkansas–Texas border, began as a railroad town in 1873. The post office at 500 State Line Avenue and a photographer's island outside 500 State Line Avenue are half in Arkansas, half in Texas. Like many railroad towns, Texarkana's businesses gradually turned their backs on the tracks and moved to the town's highways and interstates.

The Italian Renaissance Perot Theater, opened in 1924 as the Saenger, was restored thanks to a major donation by native son and presidential hopeful H. Ross Perot, and presents a lengthy performing arts calendar. A mural across the street pays tribute to Scott Joplin, the ragtime genius born here in 1868 who was awarded a posthumous Pulitzer Prize for his contributions to American music.

Texarkana is a regional trade center and has an agricultural as well as a commercial economic base.

Information: **Texarkana Chamber of Commerce** | Box 1468, 75504-1468 | 903/792–7191 | www.texarkana.org.

Attractions

Ace of Clubs House. Winnings from a poker game made possible the elaborate 1885 home near the center of town, which was built, fittingly, in the shape of the playing card. | 420 Pine St. | 903/793–4831 | $5 | Tues.–Sat. 10–4 last tour leaves at 3.

Discovery Place. Hands-on exhibits of science and history at this downtown museum are geared to kids. | 215 Pine St. | 903/793–4831 | $4 | Tues.–Sat. 10–4.

Texarkana Historical Museum. In the city's oldest brick building, the museum traces the area's history and prehistory. | 219 State Line Ave. | 903/793–4831 | www.texarkanamuseums.org | $2 | Tues.–Sat. 10–4.

ON THE CALENDAR
MAY: *Strange Family Bluegrass Festival.* Bluegrass bands from throughout the country perform in a natural amphitheater under shade trees where you can sit on lawn chairs you bring from home. The festival also includes livestock shows, crafts, and food vendors. There are 450 RV sites with hookups. The festival is 1 mi north of the center of Texarkana. | Rte. 2 | 903/792–2481.
SEPT.: *Four States Fair and Rodeo.* This fair, more than 50 years old, includes a PRCA rodeo, a concert with a major artist, outdoor stage entertainment, a demolition derby, a carnival, a commercial tent, and fine and home arts. | Fairgrounds, Rte. 245 and 50th St. | 870/773–2941.

NOV., DEC.: *Twice as Bright Festival of Lights.* Millions of lights twinkle on downtown buildings, trees, and seasonal figures. Entertainment is nightly. | 870/774–2120.

Dining

Pena's Mexican Restaurant. Mexican. This relatively small but popular restaurant seats only 70, so expect a wait unless you visit on off-peak hours. Once seated you can order gigantic stuffed burritos, enchiladas, home-made tamales, and a couple of American items as well. | 114 E. Broad St. | 870/772–9586 | $5–$10 | AE, DC, D, MC, V | Closed Sun.

Sterling Crest Restaurant. American. Catering to a predominantly older crowd, this spot serves up a vast array of American and Continental dishes ranging from chicken-fried steak with french fries to filet mignon with grilled asparagus. You might want to try the chicken bordelaise with a red wine and mushroom sauce. | 915 E. Broad St. | 870/779–1732 | $6–$15 | AE, MC, V | No dinner Sun.–Thurs.

Lodging

Baymont Inn. A golf course is 4 mi from this large, comfortable hotel, and Wright Patman Lake is 15 mi away. The four-story structure includes a lobby with a breakfast room, and an outdoor pool and lounge area. Restaurants are within walking distance. Complimentary Continental breakfast. In-room data ports, some microwaves, some refrigerators. Cable TV. Pool. Some pets allowed. | 5102 N. State Line Ave. | 870/773–1000 | www.baymontinns.com | fax 870/773–5000 | 104 rooms | $49–$64 | AE, D, DC, MC, V.

Four Points Hotel–Sheraton. This six-story hotel on the Texas-Arkansas border has a concierge floor with business services. Two restaurants. Indoor pool. Gym. Business services, airport shuttle. | 5301 N. State Line Ave. | 903/792–3222 | www.fourpoints.com | fax 903/793–3930 | 147 rooms | $64–$90 | AE, D, DC, MC, V.

Hampton Inn. This modern, two-story hotel is 3 mi north of the center of Texarkana and is convenient to the interstate as well as downtown. Complimentary Continental breakfast. Pool. | 5300 N. State Line Ave. | 870/774–4444 | fax 870/779–1303 | 60 rooms | $70 | AE, D, DC, MC, V.

House of Wadley Bed & Breakfast. This 1895 Victorian was once the home of one of the 10 wealthiest people in the United States, John Keener Wadley, and shows the elegance one would expect from such a residence. The guest rooms are decorated in rural antiques, while the cottage comes fully equipped with a kitchen, living room, and two bedrooms. A gazebo and front porch are perfect for relaxing. Complimentary breakfast, some kitchenettes. | 618 Pecan St. | 870/773–7019 | www.houseofwadley.com | 4 rooms, 1 cottage | $69–$129 rooms, $150 cottage | MC, V.

Mansion on Main Bed and Breakfast. Truly a mansion, the home is adorned with two-story columns salvaged from the St. Louis World's Fair, all rooms are appointed in antiques, and the public double parlor contains an extensive library. The inn is downtown, near State Line Avenue, museums, the Federal Court House, and restaurants. Complimentary breakfast. In-room data ports, room phones. | 802 Main St. | 903/792–1835 | fax 903/793–0878 | mansiononmain@aol.com | 5 rooms, 1 suite | $65–$79 rooms, $119 suite | AE, MC, V.

Smart Sightseeings

Don't plan your visit in your hotel room. Don't wait until you pull into town to decide how to spend your days. It's inevitable that there will be much more to see and do than you'll have time for: choose sights in advance.

Organize your touring. Note the places that most interest you on a map, and visit places that are near each other during the same morning or afternoon.

Start the day well equipped. Leave your hotel in the morning with everything you need for the day—maps, medicines, extra film, your guidebook, rain gear, and another layer of clothing in case the weather turns cooler.

Tour museums early. If you're there when the doors open you'll have an intimate experience of the collection.

Easy does it. See museums in the mornings, when you're fresh, and visit sit-down attractions later on. Take breaks before you need them.

Strike up a conversation. Only curmudgeons don't respond to a smile and a polite request for information. Most people appreciate your interest in their home town. And your conversations may end up being your most vivid memories.

Get lost. When you do, you never know what you'll find—but you can count on it being memorable. Use your guidebook to help you get back on track. Build wandering-around time into every day.

Quit before you're tired. There's no point in seeing that one extra sight if you're too exhausted to enjoy it.

Take your mother's advice. Go to the bathroom when you have the chance. You never know what lies ahead.

Hotel How-Tos

How to get a deal. After you've chosen a likely candidate or two, phone them directly and price a room for your travel dates. Then call the hotel's toll-free number and ask the same questions. Also try consolidators and hotel-room discounters. You won't hear the same rates twice. On the spot, make a reservation as soon as you are quoted a price you want to pay.

Promises, promises. If you have special requests, make them when you reserve. Get written confirmation of any promises.

Settle in. Upon arriving, make sure everything works—lights and lamps, TV and radio, sink, tub, shower, and anything else that matters. Report any problems immediately. And don't wait until you need extra pillows or blankets or an ironing board to call housekeeping. Also check out the fire emergency instructions. Know where to find the fire exits, and make sure your companions do, too.

If you need to complain. Be polite but firm. Explain the problem to the person in charge. Suggest a course of action. If you aren't satisfied, repeat your requests to the manager. Document everything: Take pictures and keep a written record of who you've spoken with, when, and what was said. Contact your travel agent, if he made the reservations.

Know the score. When you go out, take your hotel's business cards (one for everyone in your party). If you have extras, you can give them out to new acquaintances who want to call you.

Tip up front. For special services, a tip or partial tip in advance can work wonders.

Use all the hotel resources A concierge can make difficult things easy. But a desk clerk, bellhop, or other hotel employee who's friendly, smart, and ambitious can often steer you straight as well. A gratuity is in order if the advice is helpful.

© Artville

Louisiana

Louisiana is shaped like a buccaneer's boot, with the toe nudging Mississippi to the east, Texas hard on its heel to the west, and Arkansas tucked on top. The ragged sole is splashed by the Gulf of Mexico, fringed by grassy marshlands, lagoons, and isolated barrier islands. Along the northern border, piney hills swell to just over 400 feet, then slope down through the central bluffs and prairie to coastal swamps well below sea level. Often visitors are disoriented when they must look up to see rivers or bayous flowing high above surrounding cities and countryside, elevated between ridges built up by centuries of silt deposits. In fact, without the elaborate system of levees and drainage basins, one-third of the state would be inundated whenever the Mississippi tops its banks. As it is, nearly one-twelfth of the total area is water, more than 3,500 square mi, a figure that can increase dramatically during hurricane season.

That's just one of many good reasons to live for today, the closest thing to a prevailing attitude in this haven for independent thinkers and die-hard bons vivants. For generations, visitors have traveled to Louisiana to forget their troubles, diets, doctors' advice, and inhibitions. The food and music are legendary, from the Creole dining palaces and world-class jazz clubs of the French Quarter to the most remote Cajun cafés and zydeco roadhouses. Days may be hot, but the pace remains cool, allowing plenty of time for horse-drawn carriages and electric streetcars, morning coffee and afternoon naps. Here history is not confined to the museums. Wide avenues are lined with thousand-year-old oaks and French colonial landmarks, and residents continue to gossip about their favorite scandals a century after the leading characters have gone to their tombs.

Some 25 million tourists come to Louisiana every year, around 10 million to New Orleans alone. Those who venture beyond the worldly (and otherworldly) pleasures of The Big Easy are rewarded with a self-proclaimed "Sportsman's Paradise." The fish-

CAPITOL: BATON ROUGE	POPULATION: 4,342,334	AREA: 48,114 SQ MI
BORDERS: AR, MS, TX, GULF OF MEXICO TIME ZONE: CENTRAL		POSTAL ABBREVIATION: LA
WEB SITE: WWW.STATE.LA.US		

ing's great on 5,000 mi of waterways and more than 150 natural lakes, with plenty of deep-sea charters chugging out into the Gulf of Mexico. Swamp tours and guided canoe treks explore the murky and mysterious backwaters once controlled by Jean Lafitte and his pirate armada. Bike paths and hiking trails take advantage of the flat terrain and ever-changing landscape. Half of the migrating birds in North America can be spotted along the Great Mississippi Flyway as they stop to feed in the rice fields and tidal marshes. Meanwhile, pigeons flock to the flashy new floating casinos that have sprung up statewide since riverboat gambling was legalized in 1991.

"Laissez les bon temps rouler" (let the good times roll) is a rallying cry statewide, and dozens of festivals scheduled throughout the year showcase everything from wooden boats to Cajun jokes. Food is always cause for celebration, with annual fetes honoring all of the regional delicacies (gumbo, crawfish, crabs, catfish, yams, strawberries), plus such unexpected delights as the Zwolle Tamale Festival and the oddly paired Louisiana Shrimp and Petroleum Festival. The most famous event takes place every winter on Mardi Gras, French for "Fat Tuesday," a wild explosion of feasting and merriment that precedes Ash Wednesday (when Catholics traditionally begin 40 days of prayer and fasting for Lent). People of all faiths join in the final binge as rural communities and big cities celebrate with parades, street dances, and masked balls. The biggest blowout of all is in New Orleans, where parades scheduled throughout Carnival season stop traffic in the city and suburbs for weeks, beginning on Twelfth Night (January 6) and culminating in a day-long bacchanal on Mardi Gras.

But you don't need to plan your trip around a holiday to find a party in New Orleans. Bourbon Street revelers turn every night into New Year's Eve, while bars and music clubs all over town keep it up until dawn. Quieter pursuits are around every corner, from world-class antique shops to contemporary art galleries, from street performers on Jackson Square to classical organ concerts at St. Louis Cathedral. The Crescent City is always a feast for the senses.

Though most closely identified with the French Creoles of New Orleans and the Acadian "Cajuns" of its southwest countryside, Louisiana's melting pot has been liberally spiced by early Native American tribes, as well as later settlers from Spain, England, Africa, Germany, Italy, Ireland, Vietnam, and other cultures. The sultry subtropical atmosphere and freewheeling spirit has also drawn hordes of artistic refugees, such as French Impressionist Edgar Degas; pioneer photographer Ernest James Bellocq; and writers Mark Twain, William Faulkner, and Tennessee Williams. Celebrated natives include writers Truman Capote, Ernest Gaines, Walker Percy, and Anne Rice; Supreme Court Justice Edward Douglas White; singer Mahalia Jackson; and musicians Sidney Bechet, Buddy Bolden, Louis Armstrong, and "Jelly Roll" Morton.

History

A geologist would tell you Louisiana is "new," composed mainly of marine and alluvial sediments deposited long after surrounding states had assumed their final form.

LA Timeline

1400	1551	1682	1714
Major Native American tribes inhabiting the region include the Atakapa, Caddo, Chitimacha, Muskogean, Natchez, and Tunica.	Hernando de Soto claims the region at the mouth of the Mississippi for Spain.	Robert Cavelier, Sieur de LaSalle, claims the vast Louisiana Territory for France and names it for King Louis XIV.	The first permanent European settlement in the Mississippi Valley is established at Fort St. Jean Baptiste, now the city of Natchitoches.

INTRODUCTION
HISTORY
REGIONS
WHEN TO VISIT
STATE'S GREATS
RULES OF THE ROAD
DRIVING TOURS

Even so, by 12,000 BC Paleo-Indians lived here and hunted mastadons, mammoths, and saber-tooth tigers. The big game died out around 4,000 BC, and later residents were forced to dine on smaller animals, supplemented by wild fruits, nuts, and seeds. They built some of the oldest burial mounds discovered in North America, including two dating to 3,000 BC. The most significant mound (circa 1700 BC) is open to the public at Poverty Point, which at that time was at the confluence of the Mississippi and Arkansas rivers. It appears to have been a primary trading center for the entire Mississippi Valley, with remains of goods from as far away as the Great Lakes, Appalachians, and Ozarks.

By AD 1400, major tribes inhabiting the region included the Atakapa, Caddo, Chitimacha, Muskogean, Natchez, and Tunica. Europeans probably arrived on the scene in 1519, when Spanish explorer Alonso Alvarez de Pineda reported his discovery of the mouth of a great river, most likely the Mississippi. Hernando de Soto claimed parts of present-day Louisiana for Spain in 1551, planting the first of 10 flags to fly over the state. In 1682, Frenchman Robert Cavelier, Sieur de La Salle, was the first European to travel down the Mississippi to its mouth, taking possession of the vast Louisiana Territory (now divided amongst several states) and naming it for his king, Louis XIV. In 1762 Louis XV made a secret pact with his cousin, Charles III of Spain, handing over "the island of New Orleans" and all land west of the Mississippi River. A year later the Treaty of Paris confirmed the transfer. The treaty also ended the French and Indian War, assigning some land east of the Mississippi to England. Spain's decline as a world power, plus the trouble and expense of maintaining the distant colony, led to another secret swap in 1800, when the Spanish returned their portion of the territory to French rule via the Treaty of San Ildefonso.

When U.S. president Thomas Jefferson learned of this latest trade, he instructed his foreign minister to negotiate the purchase of New Orleans and surrounding lands. During the two years of bargaining, Napoleon Bonaparte realized he could no longer defend his American holdings and convinced officials to sell the entire Louisiana Territory. The resulting Louisiana Purchase, one of the greatest real estate deals in history, closed on April 30, 1803. In exchange for $15 million, the United States doubled in size and positioned itself as a world power, gaining some 900,000 square mi (nearly 600 million acres) at an average of only four cents per acre. Today the land is divided among Louisiana, Arkansas, Missouri, Iowa, North Dakota, South Dakota, Nebraska, Kansas, Wyoming, Minnesota, Oklahoma, Colorado, and Montana.

Meanwhile, the portions of present-day Louisiana that were known as British West Florida, long occupied by English planters and military, had been captured by Spain during the Revolutionary War. Bernardo de Galvez, Louisiana's Spanish governor and an American ally, had taken British forts at Manchac and Baton Rouge in 1779 to prevent further development of an English stronghold in the Mississippi Valley. The colonists responded with the West Florida Rebellion in 1810, ousting their Spanish oppressors to establish an independent republic. That same year, the republic joined the United

1718	**1751**	**1762**		**1764**
New Orleans is founded and named for Phillippe Duc D'Orleans.	Jesuits begin first successful cultivation of sugar cane.	Louis XV turns Louisiana over to his cousin, Charles III of Spain, ceding "the island of New Orleans" and all land west of the Mississippi River. A year later the Treaty of Paris confirms	the transfer, also assigning some land east of the Mississippi to England.	French Acadian exiles, expelled from Canada by the British, begin the earliest "Cajun" settlements in Louisiana.

States as part of the Louisiana Territory. Louisiana became the 18th state on April 30, 1812.

Though most of the European colonists and early citizens of American Louisiana worked their own farms of 150 to 300 acres, some acquired the huge tracts of land (1,000 acres or more) known as plantations. Unable to find workers willing to perform backbreaking labor for scant wages, these sugar and cotton planters turned to the same traders who supplied African slaves to colonies in the Caribbean and Brazil. The plantation system peaked between 1790 and 1861, when the Civil War disrupted the entire nation. Louisiana followed other southern states that seceded from the Union in 1861 but declared itself an independent republic for six weeks before joining the Confederacy. The strategic port of New Orleans was taken by the Union Navy in April 1862, when forces passed through the Mississippi River gateways of Fort Jackson and Fort St. Philip about 60 mi below the city. They gained complete control of the river in 1863 with the capture of Port Hudson, about 14 mi north of Baton Rouge, after Confederate forces held out for 48 days (the longest siege in American military history). Yankee domination of the country's most important artery effectively cut the Confederacy in two, a major factor in its eventual defeat. In 1865, General Edmund Kirby-Smith surrendered the Trans-Mississippi Department, including Louisiana's Confederate Units, to federal forces. A new state constitution was adopted in 1868 during the tumultuous post-war period known as Reconstruction. It readmitted Louisiana to the Union and granted voting rights to African-Americans. Reconstruction ended in 1877, when President Rutherford B. Hayes withdrew federal troops.

Black gold greased the state's treasury throughout the 20th century, beginning in 1901 with Louisiana's first successful oil well (brought in about 6 mi from the town of Jennings) and a major natural gas field discovered near Monroe in 1916. Another resource was tapped at about the same time, as the distinctive sound known as jazz began traveling from the bordellos of New Orleans to the backstreets of New York, Chicago, and St. Louis. Soon the music would draw visitors as surely as the colorful history, natural beauty, and world-famous cuisine. The construction of the Louisiana Superdome in 1975 and legalization of riverboat gambling in 1991 sealed the deal. Tourism had become one of the state's most important industries.

Regions

1. NEW ORLEANS AND METRO AREA

Like all ports, New Orleans has a multinational personality, along with a distinctive architectural style and a complex culture that has evolved over centuries. This subtropical metropolis was civilized by early European colonists and later waves of immigrants. It is still influenced by visitors from around the world, who are drawn by the living history and graceful atmosphere, plus the serious dedication to food, music, and good times.

1788	1800	1803	1812	1833
The first of three disastrous fires destroys much of New Orleans, which goes up in flames again in 1792 and 1794.	The Treaty of San Ildefonso returns Louisiana from Spanish to French rule.	President Thomas Jefferson authorizes the Louisiana Purchase, and Napoleon I sells the territory to the U.S. for $15 million.	Louisiana joins the Union as the 18th state and adopts its first constitution.	Captain Henry Miller Shreve begins clearing obstructions to commercial navigation on the Red River, leading to the establishment of Shreveport in 1837.

INTRODUCTION
HISTORY
REGIONS
WHEN TO VISIT
STATE'S GREATS
RULES OF THE ROAD
DRIVING TOURS

From fine antiques to Bourbon Street strippers, there is plenty to see in the historic French Quarter, a 100-square-block area that once made up the entire city. Today the limits stretch from Lake Pontchartrain to the Mississippi River, incorporating the stately mansions of the Garden District, the contemporary galleries of the Warehouse/Arts District, the convention hotels and riverfront attractions of the Central Business District, the music clubs of Faubourg Marigny, and the Uptown universities.

The suburban bedroom communities of Metairie, Kenner, and Chalmette still bear traces of their rural past. Across the river, the isolated fishing villages of Jean Lafitte and Barataria are shrouded in swampy landscape and pirate lore. In the piney woods on the north shore of Lake Pontchartrain, town squares and country cottages have been transformed into artsy shops and restaurants in the historic districts of Mandeville, Abita Springs, Covington, Slidell, Ponchatoula, and Hammond.

Towns listed: Covington, Hammond, Jean Lafitte, Kenner, Mandeville, Metairie, New Orleans, Slidell.

2. PLANTATION COUNTRY

If you're searching for the splendor of the Old South, this is the place to begin. Designated by the state as "Plantation Country," the verdant Mississippi River corridor follows the twists and turns of the Big Muddy from the Mississippi state line to New Orleans. America's greatest river once carried enough sugarcane and cotton to finance an impressive collection of antebellum manors, many of which are restored and open to the public. The path leads through Baton Rouge, where tales of outrageous political shenanigans and flamboyant governors add plenty of drama (and comic relief) to guided tours at the Art Deco-style State Capitol and other government sites. To the north, lovely St. Francisville is the heart of English-settled Louisiana, where fine old houses sit on high bluffs, surrounded by historic gardens and woodlands. To the south, huge levees tame the river as it meanders through low delta, past French Creole cottages and oak-shaded mansions.

Towns listed: Baton Rouge, Houma, Jackson, New Roads, St. Francisville, Thibodaux.

3. CAJUN COUNTRY

Southwest Louisiana is famous for the spicy food, good-times music, and distinctive accents of its French Acadian "Cajuns," who were driven from Canada by the British in the 18th century. This colorful region stretches from coastal marshes and swampland through prairie country. At the western edge, the inland port of Lake Charles is surrounded by flat forests of Southern yellow pine. Here the Calcasieu River widens into a lake (with plenty of room for four floating casinos that reel in herds of Texans

1838	1849	1854	1861	1865
The first official Mardi Gras parade takes to the streets in New Orleans.	Baton Rouge becomes the state capital.	The worst in a long series of yellow fever epidemics claims more than 11,000 lives in New Orleans alone.	Louisiana secedes from the Union and becomes an independent republic for six weeks before joining the Confederacy.	General Edmund Kirby-Smith surrenders the Trans-Mississippi Department, including Louisiana's Confederate Units, to Union forces.

from across the Sabine River). Near the center of the territory, Lafayette is the unofficial capital of all things Cajun, with its living museums of Vermilionville and Acadian Village, plus a stellar collection of restaurants and music clubs. Along the southern border, where the huge Atchafalaya Basin drains into the Gulf of Mexico, Morgan City is home port for shrimp boats and swamp excursions, as well as supply and crew vessels for the offshore oil industry. But the tiny prairie town of Eunice is the place to be on Saturday nights, when the historic Liberty Theater presents its weekly Rendez-Vous des Cajuns, a French country jamboree of music and storytelling that is broadcast live throughout the region.

Towns listed: Abbeville, Eunice, Franklin, Jennings, Lafayette, Lake Charles, Morgan City, New Iberia, Opelousas, St. Martinsville.

4. CROSSROADS

The two sides of Louisiana come together in the Crossroads region, which cuts across the middle of the state in a wide swath that stretches from Texas to Mississippi. Southern swamps give way to flat prairies, which eventually roll into small hills. At the western border, the 186,000-acre Toledo Bend Reservoir boasts some of the best fishing in the country. Along the eastern corridor, the tiny town of Ferriday was home to that unholy trinity of musical and preacher cousins: Jerry Lee Lewis, Mickey Gilley, and Jimmy Swaggart. There is an abundance of forest and farmland, as well as a wealth of history. In fact, the oldest settlement in the vast Louisiana Purchase began as a French fort at Natchitoches in 1714. Today this lovely old town maintains a 33-block National Historic Landmark District. The Red River, which gets its name and color from iron oxide sediments, separates Alexandria and Pineville, which are graced by a handful of antebellum buildings that survived the mass destruction by Union troops during the Civil War. The Yankees torched most of the nearby plantations as well, leaving Kent Plantation House (circa 1796) as the oldest remaining structure in central Louisiana.

Towns listed: Alexandria, Many, Natchitoches.

5. SPORTSMAN'S PARADISE

The rolling hills of Northern Louisiana are home to the highest point in the state. Unabashedly known as Driskill Mountain, it soars 535 feet above the swamps and bayous of the south. And the cultural background is equally removed from the European heritage of New Orleans and Cajun Country. This rugged area was The West when second-generation Anglo-Americans from Virginia, Tennessee, and the Carolinas settled here. Sportsman's Paradise is still known for the great hunting that attracted these early pioneers. Deep pine forests teem with deer, duck, wild turkey, and other game. Freshwater lakes and streams offer outstanding fishing and water sports. For bright lights, Shreveport/Bossier City and Monroe/West Monroe have some night life, as well as museums, restaurants, galleries, and family attractions.

1868	1877	1901	1915	1916
A new state constitution is adopted during the tumultuous post-war period of Reconstruction, readmitting Louisiana to the Union and granting voting rights to African-Americans.	Reconstruction ends when President Rutherford B. Hayes withdraws federal troops from the state.	Louisiana's first successful oil well strikes black gold in Jefferson Davis Parish, about 6 mi from the town of Jennings.	The distinctive New Orleans sound, born in the backstreets and bordellos, is first christened "jazz."	A major natural gas field is discovered near Monroe.

INTRODUCTION
HISTORY
REGIONS
WHEN TO VISIT
STATE'S GREATS
RULES OF THE ROAD
DRIVING TOURS

Towns listed: Bastrop, Bossier City, Epps, Minden, Monroe/West Monroe, Ruston, Shreveport.

When to Visit

Though the northern inland areas are slightly cooler and drier than the southern coast, weather patterns are similar throughout Louisiana. Winters are mild and hard freezes are rare, snow even more so. Winter and early spring temperatures are capricious, which makes packing difficult, as you could need short sleeves and a heavy coat in the same week, sometimes the same day. Umbrellas are always advisable. Summer is more predictable, dependably hot and humid with a good chance of afternoon showers, a forecast that extends from May through September. Fall is cool and clear, generally the best time to be outdoors. Though dozens of festivals crowd the state calendar throughout the year, October has the busiest schedule. Hurricane season is another consideration. It runs from June 1 through November 30, with the majority of storms concentrated between August 15 and September 30.

High seasons in New Orleans (with the attendant rate hikes and crowds) peak around the busy convention month of October, the weeks of Carnival leading up to Mardi Gras in February and early March, and Jazz Fest during the last week of April and the first week of May. Prices go down as the temperatures go up, with many downtown hotels and restaurants advertising rock-bottom specials to boost sluggish tourism during July and August. Christmas, New Orleans Style! is a citywide promotion (lodging and dining bargains, free concerts, riverboat races, parades, cooking demonstrations, etc.) from December 1 through 30.

CLIMATE CHART
Average High/Low Temperatures (°F) and Monthly Precipitation (in inches)

	JAN.	FEB.	MAR.	APR.	MAY	JUNE
ALEXANDRIA	57/36	62/40	70/48	78/56	84/63	90/70
	5.2	4.9	5.4	4.1	5.1	4.4
	JULY	AUG.	SEPT.	OCT.	NOV.	DEC.
	93/72	93/72	88/67	80/55	71/50	61/40
	4.5	4.5	4.1	4.3	3.8	6.7
	JAN.	FEB.	MAR.	APR.	MAY	JUNE
LAFAYETTE	60/41	63/44	71/51	79/59	85/65	90/71
	4.9	4.3	4.1	4.0	5.2	5.1
	JULY	AUG.	SEPT.	OCT.	NOV.	DEC.
	91/74	90/73	87/69	80/58	71/50	64/54
	7.0	5.4	5.4	3.8	4.3	5.4

1926
Man-made waterways connect Lake Charles to the Gulf of Mexico, transforming the city into a major port.

1928
"Kingfish" Huey P. Long is elected governor on a populist platform and institutes a network of public assistance programs that will eventually help to inspire the national Social Security Act.

1932
Construction of the new state capitol, the nation's tallest at 27 stories, is completed in Baton Rouge.

1935
Now a U.S. Senator, Huey Long is shot and killed at the state capitol.

1947
The offshore office of Kerr-McGee Corporation, based in Morgan City, drills the first commercially producing oil well that is beyond sight of land.

	JAN.	• FEB.	MAR.	APR.	MAY	JUNE
LAKE CHARLES	60/41	63/44	71/51	78/59	84/66	89/72
	4.5	3.6	3.3	3.3	5.7	5.0
	JULY	AUG.	SEPT.	OCT.	NOV.	DEC.
	91/74	91/73	87/67	80/58	63/44	67/44
	5.2	5.3	5.7	4.0	5.0	4.7
	JAN.	FEB.	MAR.	APR.	MAY	JUNE
MONROE	54/35	59/39	68/46	77/55	84/63	91/70
	4.7	4.7	5.3	4.3	5.6	3.8
	JULY	AUG.	SEPT.	OCT.	NOV.	DEC.
	92/72	92/70	87/65	78/52	71/51	58/37
	3.7	2.7	3.5	3.2	4.4	5.5
	JAN.	FEB.	MAR.	APR.	MAY	JUNE
NEW ORLEANS	60/41.4	63/44	71/51	78/59	84/66	89/72
	.5	3.6	3.3	3.3	5.7	5.0
	JULY	AUG.	SEPT.	OCT.	NOV.	DEC.
	91/74	91/73	87/69	80/59	70/47	64/45
	5.2	5.3	5.7	3.1	5.2	5.8

FESTIVALS AND SEASONAL EVENTS
WINTER

Jan.   **Sugar Bowl College Football Classic,** New Orleans. A local tradition first staged in 1935 at the old Tulane Stadium now
takes place in the Superdome. | 1st week in Jan. | 504/525–
8573, ticket office 504/525–8603, 877/977–8427.

Feb.–Mar.   **Carnival/Mardi Gras,** New Orleans. This New Orleans bash cli-
maxes the Tuesday before Ash Wednesday. Dozens of parades
are scheduled nearly every weekend during Carnival season,
always from Twelfth Night until Ash Wednesday, and nightly
during the final two weeks; Lundi Gras (Fat Monday) is a full
day of free concerts on the downtown riverfront, while Mardi
Gras (Fat Tuesday) itself is chockablock with street parties,
masquerades, and parades throughout the city and suburbs. |
504/566–5009, 504/838–6111, 800/748–8695.

SPRING

Mar.   **Audubon Pilgrimage,** St. Francisville. Tours of landmark
houses and gardens in full spring bloom are given during the
third weekend of the month. The occasion is marked by a chil-

1960	**1975**	**1977**	**1983**	**1991**
Racial integration of public schools begins.	The $163 million Louisiana Super-dome is completed in New Orleans.	New Orleans elects its first African-American mayor, Ernest N. "Dutch" Morial.	Louisiana native Wynton Marsalis becomes the first and only person to win both classical and jazz Grammy Awards in the same year.	Riverboat gambling is legalized on the Mississippi and other state water-ways.

dren's maypole dance, theatrical productions, and gospel concerts at historic churches. | 225/635–6330.

Tennessee Williams/New Orleans Literary Festival, New Orleans. Among the festivities are plays, music, panel discussions, lectures, and special events (such as the annual "Stella!" hollering contest) celebrating the literary heritage of the South in general and New Orleans in particular. It's usually held the third or fourth weekend of the month. | 504/581–1144.

Apr.   **Ascension Pilgrimage,** Baton Rouge. Demonstrations of traditional crafts accompany tours of historic plantation manors and gardens at the height of spring color. | 225/675–6550, 888/775–7990.

French Quarter Festival, New Orleans. Outdoor concerts on stages throughout the French Quarter, dozens of food booths along the riverfront, fireworks, a parade, and children's activities. | 504/522–5730, 800/673–5725.

Festival International de Louisiane, Lafayette. A week of music, dance, art, theater, cinema, and cuisine from South Louisiana and French-speaking nations. | 337/232–8086.

Apr.–May   **New Orleans Jazz and Heritage Festival,** New Orleans. This major local event, held the last weekend in April and the first weekend in May, attracts an international crowd to the New Orleans Fairgrounds near Esplanade Avenue. There are performances by more than 4,000 musicians, authentic Louisiana foods from more than 50 vendors, plus great arts and crafts. Additional evening concerts are scheduled throughout the week, and club schedules are filled with big-name bands. | 504/522–4786.

SUMMER

June   **Bayou Lacombe Crab Festival,** Slidell. Crabs are prepared every way imaginable at this event in Lacombe Park, held the last weekend of the month, and there are arts and crafts, kids' activities, live music, carnival rides, and a beauty pageant. | 504/882–5160.

AUTUMN

Sept.   **Cenlabration,** Alexandria. Live music plays on three stages, interrupted only by a chicken-wing–eating contest, Louisiana food, street dances, art exhibits, carnival rides, and children's activities. Labor Day weekend. | 318/473–1127, 888/772–3652.

Louisiana Shrimp and Petroleum Festival, Morgan City. Cajun music and food sets the stage here every Labor Day weekend; you'll also find a children's village, the blessing of the fleet, a beauty pageant, coronation ball, rodeo, and arts and crafts. | 504/385–0703, 800/256–2931.

Original Southwest Louisiana Zydeco Music Festival, near Opelousas. Every Labor Day weekend, international crowds of music fans travel to the tiny town of Plaisance for Zydeco music (a traditional blend of African and Cajun rhythms),

INTRODUCTION
HISTORY
REGIONS
WHEN TO VISIT
STATE'S GREATS
RULES OF THE ROAD
DRIVING TOURS

Louisiana food and crafts, plus storytelling and cultural talks on the Heritage Stage. | 337/942–2392.

Grand Bois Inter Tribal, Houma. Native Houmas sponsor this pow-wow, which draws other tribes from throughout the United States to Grand Bois Park on the third weekend of September. Native foods, crafts, and dancing mark the occasion. | 504/868–2732, 504/879–2373, 504/594–7410, 800/688–2732.

Festivals Acadiens, Lafayette. These citywide celebrations, held the third weekend in September, include downtown concerts and street dances, the Wetlands Folklife Festival at Girard Park Lake, traditional and progressive Cajun musicians at Festival de Musique Acadienne, authentic Louisiana cuisine at the Bayou Food Festival, the Louisiana Native and Contemporary Crafts Festival, plus "Kids Alive!" children's activities. | 337/232–3808, 800/346–1958.

Madisonville Wooden Boat Festival, Madisonville. This is the largest gathering of wooden boats in Gulf South. Usually more than 100 boats, including many antiques and classics, line the shores of Tchefuncte River during the end of September. Also featured are a marine auction, marine flea market, kids' activities with the Covington Woodworking Guild, food, and music. For the "Quick and Dirty Boat-Building Contest and Race," groups of four must use limited materials to build and operate vessels for a wacky sailing competition. | Last weekend in Sept. | 504/845–9200.

Oct. **Prairie Cajun Folk Art Festival,** Eunice. During the third weekend in October, artisans demonstrate traditional crafts such as tatting, basket weaving, bonnet making, rosary making, and the making of Mardi Gras costumes. Cajun and Zydeco music, a narrative stage with storytelling and cultural talks, and lots of good food are also featured. | 337/457–7389.

Nov. **Celebration of the Giant Omelette,** Abbeville. This town is the only one in America that joins in this traditional French celebration on the first Sunday in November, with 5,000 eggs cooked into a giant omelette shared by the crowd. The festivities also include crafts, music, and dancing in the streets downtown. | 337/893–6517, 337/893–5760, 337/893–2491.

State's Greats

Whether you choose to rock around the clock in New Orleans or lose yourself in a slower world along the backroads and bayous, Louisiana will reset your sense of time. It's too hot to hurry, especially after those languid two-hour lunches. Like the food, most attractions are best enjoyed at a stately pace. Historic houses have wide verandas and secluded courtyards for visitors who prefer solitary daydreams to guided tours. Riverboats and ferries approach old towns as they were meant to be seen—from the water. Parks are filled with moss-draped oaks, winding lagoons, and shady benches instead of speed-walkers and in-line skaters.

For cosmopolitan pleasures, New Orleans can compete with the most celebrated cities of America and Europe. The unique music, architecture, Creole cuisine, and

INTRODUCTION
HISTORY
REGIONS
WHEN TO VISIT
STATE'S GREATS
RULES OF THE ROAD
DRIVING TOURS

subtropical style are recognized around the world. Louisiana's smaller towns, graced by deep-roofed Acadian cottages, plantation manors, artisans' studios, and ancient church-yards, have a charm of their own. Even the names are evocative: St. Francisville, St. Mart-inville, New Iberia, Natchitoches.

The countryside is a patchwork of piney woods, prairie, cypress swamps, and coastal marsh. The dominant force is the mighty Mississippi, which gathers its flow from two-thirds of the continental U.S. on a journey that begins in Minnesota and ends at the Gulf of Mexico, just below New Orleans. The city's opposite boundary is Lake Pontchartrain, really an inland estuary with brackish waters extending for 640 square mi. And Toledo Bend Reservoir near Natchitoches is the nation's fifth-largest manmade lake, spreading out for 70 mi along the Texas border, totalling 186,000 acres and 1,200 mi of shoreline.

Forests and Parks

Louisiana's distinctive natural environment and rural history are showcased by its system of 15 state parks, all on water, and 14 state historic sites, where interpretive programs explore native cultures, colonial life, the Civil War, and other colorful topics. In addi-tion, the **State Arboretum** near Alexandria is designated a State Preservation Area because of its exceptional scenic and ecological value. The **Kisatchie National Forest** sprawls across 600,000 acres in north central Louisiana. Hiking trails follow an old Indian trade route through **Chemin-a-Haut State Park** near Bastrop. **Hodges Gardens** near Many is landscaped with some 4,700 acres of formal plantings. The **American Rose Center** in Shreveport is U.S. headquarters for the national flower, with more than 20,000 bushes in 65 special gardens blooming from April to November. The **Global Wildlife Center** in Folsom is a breeding center for endangered hoofstock, a sanctuary for more than 2,000 exotic animals on 900 acres of rolling pasture and woodland.

Jean Lafitte National Park and Preserve incorporates nine units statewide, includ-ing the unlikely urban neighborhood of the French Quarter in New Orleans. The grass is greener uptown at **Audubon Park,** named for the great naturalist who lived and painted on the riverfront estate that is now home to one of the premier zoos in the country. The 1,500-acre **City Park** is an old southern beauty shaded by more than 30,000 trees, including the largest stand of live oaks in the world.

Culture, History, and the Arts

Jazz is an American original, born around 1900 of ragtime, marching bands, and African work songs. It was nurtured in the dives and dancehalls of New Orleans, where Buddy Bolden, King Oliver, Sidney Bechet, and Louis Armstrong blew their horns. Today the spirit lives on in dozens of local clubs, and the **New Orleans Jazz and Heritage Festival** attracts an international crowd each spring. The music doesn't stop at the city limits, however, as the chank-a-chank of squeezebox and fiddle beckons you to Cajun country for small-town street dances and major annual events, such as **Festi-val de Musique Acadienne** in Lafayette and the **Southwest Louisiana Zydeco Festival** near Opelousas. Live broadcasts every Saturday night from the restored **Liberty Theater** in Eunice are like the Grand Old Opry with a French twist, all songs and jokes en fran-cais. Up north in English-settled Louisiana, country-western tunes enliven the taverns and roadhouses.

At **Vermilionville** and **Acadian Village** in Lafayette, you can travel back in time to Cajun settlements of the 18th and 19th centuries where crafters, cooks, gardeners, and storytellers are all part of the regional history on display. **Poverty Point** near Epps is a National Monument and a State Historic Site, a 3,000-year-old trading center for Native Americans and one of the country's earliest and largest archaeological sites. For *Gone with the Wind* glamour, antebellum manors are around every bend in the rivers and bayous, including such architectural masterpieces as **Madewood** near

Napoleonville and **Rosedown** in St. Francisville. The **Rural Life Museum** in Baton Rouge and **Laura Plantation** near Vacherie present the other side of gracious southern living, exploring the backstairs world from the viewpoint of servants, women, and children. Tours of the Art Deco **State Capitol** in Baton Rouge are spiced with tales of "Kingfish" Huey Long and other roguish governors. Nearby, the turreted **Old State Capitol** building houses interactive displays on Louisiana's colorful political history.

But for a true living museum, you can't beat the 100-square-block **French Quarter** in New Orleans, where more than 7,000 permanent residents live, work, and play. Flanking St. Louis Cathedral on Jackson Square, the graceful colonnaded landmarks known as the **Presbytere** and the **Cabildo** were once headquarters for colonial governments and are now filled with cultural exhibits and early relics. More treasures are on display at the **New Orleans Museum of Art** in City Park, while modern galleries and the massive **Contemporary Arts Center** in the city's revitalized warehouse district have earned the neighborhood a name as the "SoHo of the South." Fans of classic architecture can get an eyeful aboard the St. Charles Avenue streetcar, which rumbles under the oaks past Garden District mansions, grand churches, and universities.

Sports

The nickname "Sportsman's Paradise" is not an idle boast, unless your idea of heaven is downhill skiing or snowmobiling. Even so, you could slalom behind a motorboat or rent a Jet-Ski on the mildest winter days. And ice hockey fans can beat the heat at a couple of indoor arenas, home to the state's most unlikely professional teams, the New Orleans Brass and the Shreveport Mudbugs.

Charter captains take anglers out to the open Gulf or navigate the intricate maze of inland waterways, but anyone with a hook and line can pull in a good catch from the bank of the nearest bayou. Canoeists paddle along forest streams, brave the gator-patrolled swamps, or join ranger-guided treks in the Barataria Unit of **Jean Lafitte National Park and Preserve** on Sunday mornings and full-moon nights.

Boating, fishing, sailing, swimming, hiking, picnicking, and camping are fine in the well-maintained system of 15 state parks, as well as dozens of community recreation areas. The 186,000-acre **Toledo Bend Reservoir** near Natchitoches is stocked with more than 300 pounds of game fish per acre. Bikes or horses can be hired for a cool ride along the **Tammany Trace,** a 31-mi linear park that follows an old railroad bed from Lake Pontchartrain through the tall pines and ozone breezes to Abita Springs. More than 50 public and private golf courses throughout the state are open to visitors, including four within massive City Park in New Orleans. Besides its more notorious indoor sports, The Big Easy also offers plenty of professional sports events and shows in the **Louisiana Superdome.**

Rules of the Road

License Requirements: To drive in Louisiana, you must be at least 15 years old with a learner's permit and 16 years old with a valid driver's license. Residents of Canada and most other countries may drive as long as they have a valid driver's license from their home countries.

Right Turn on Red: Everywhere in the state you may make a right turn at a red light after a full stop, unless a sign is posted prohibiting it.

Seat Belt and Helmet Laws: All drivers and front-seat passengers must wear seat belts. Children under age 13 must wear a seat belt at all times, whether seated in front or back; children under age 4 must ride in a federally approved child safety seat. Motorcyclists may choose to ride without a helmet only if they are at least 21 years of age and carry a medical insurance policy with at least $10,000 in coverage. They are also required to keep their headlights and taillights on at all times.

INTRODUCTION
HISTORY
REGIONS
WHEN TO VISIT
STATE'S GREATS
RULES OF THE ROAD
DRIVING TOURS

Speed Limits: 70 mph on interstate highways, 65 mph on controlled-access highways, 55 mph on state highways, and lower where posted.

For More Information: Contact the Louisiana State Police. | 225/925–6325, 225/754–8510, 800/469–4828 | www.dps.state.la.us./lsp.

Mississippi River Plantations Drive
NEW ORLEANS TO ST. FRANCISVILLE

Distance: 183 mi; 295 kilometers   Time: 3 days

Breaks: Spend the first night in White Castle at the town's namesake, the grand ivory palace known as Nottoway. The 53,000-square-foot mansion is well located for exploring surrounding landmarks, and it's one of the few antebellum plantations to lodge guests in the original bedrooms of the main house. On night two, you can see how the other half slept at Pointe Coupee Bed and Breakfast, an 1835 plantation cottage in the waterfront resort village of New Roads.

In 1850, two-thirds of America's millionaires lived between New Orleans and Natchez along the Mississippi River, a lifeline for the old plantations. Unfortunately, it is also an important transportation artery for the petrochemical plants and other industrial complexes that now share the landscape with the spectacular antebellum manors, but the rewards of this drive outweigh the annoyances, and it's a fascinating view of life along the Mississippi then and now. The historic houses are beautiful at any time of year, but especially when decorated for the Christmas season and in spring when

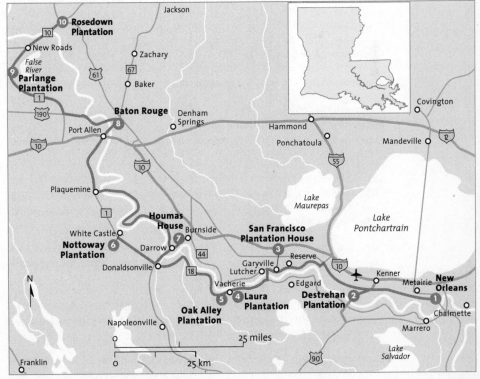

azaleas and magnolia trees are in bloom and gardens are splashed with fresh color. Try to finish the first day's route before late afternoon, as many River Road industries in this area change shifts at 3 PM, causing congestion and impatient driving. Also note that, because of the many twists and turns as the River Road follows the Mississippi, directions such as "east" or "west" are pointless. Locals go with the flow, indicating either "downriver" (towards New Orleans) or "upriver" (towards Baton Rouge and beyond).

❶ The **Great River Road New Orleans,** a vital trade route for more than a century, is actually two roads tracing both sides of the Mississippi River from New Orleans to Baton Rouge. Though many of the historic homes you will pass are private, all of the sites that follow are open for guided tours.

❷ For the first stop at **Destrehan Plantation** in Destrehan, take Exit 6 off I–310 and proceed ¼ mi downriver (back towards New Orleans) on River Road. This French Colonial manor, with hand-hewn cypress timbers and West Indies-style roof, is one of the oldest plantation houses remaining in the Mississippi Valley. It was built in 1787 by planter and legislator Jean Noel Destrehan; a Greek Revival remodeling was completed in 1840. Pirate Jean Lafitte was a frequent visitor, source of persistent rumors that treasure is buried behind the walls.

❸ Continuing for 25 mi upriver from Destrehan on River Road, between Reserve and Lutcher you'll come to Garyville and the **San Francisco Plantation House.** An ornate and colorful Steamboat Gothic extravaganza, the San Francisco is famous for its hand-painted decorative ceilings and faux marbling. Though it would fit right in with the Bay City's "painted ladies," the name of the 1856 mansion was originally "Sans Frusquin," French slang for "without a penny in my pocket," a rueful claim from planter Edmond Bozonier Marmillion, who had spared no expense in the construction of his home.

❹ When you're finished exploring the San Francisco, head about 7 mi upriver from Garyville on River Road, cross Gramercy-Lutcher Bridge, then continue 2 mi upriver on Rte. 18 toward Vacherie. The **Laura Plantation** near Vacherie presents one of the liveliest and best-documented tours in the region, an unusual look at plantation life from the perspective of women, children, and servants. The circa 1805 complex incorporates 12 buildings (two modest manor houses, plus assorted slave quarters and Creole cottages). The folktales of Br'er Rabbit, which originated in West Africa, were first recorded in America on this site in the 1870s.

❺ From the Laura Plantation, drive 4 mi upriver on Rte. 18 to the **Oak Alley Plantation,** one of the most famous sights in the South. Twenty-eight live oaks in two rows create a ¼-mi avenue leading all the way from the river to the Greek Revival manor. The trees, planted by an early settler, were already mature when the house was built in 1839 by planter Jacques Telesphore Roman. One of the original outbuildings has been converted into a casual country café that serves breakfast and lunch daily.

❻ From Oak Alley, follow Rte. 18 upriver to Darrow, then continue on Rte. 1 to Rte. 405 in White Castle. **Nottoway Plantation** in White Castle is the largest surviving antebellum manor in the South, some 53,000 square feet, including a 65-foot Grand White Ballroom. Built in 1859 by planter John Hampden Randolph, the Greek Revival/Italianate house is famous for its intricate plaster friezes, marble fireplaces, and handpainted Dresden doorknobs. It now takes overnight guests, and an atrium restaurant on the grounds serves breakfast, lunch, and dinner daily.

❼ From White Castle, backtrack to Donaldsonville on Rte. 1 and cross the Sunshine Bridge, then head upriver on Rte. 44 to Rte. 942 in Burnside. **Houmas House** once stood on

INTRODUCTION
HISTORY
REGIONS
WHEN TO VISIT
STATE'S GREATS
RULES OF THE ROAD
DRIVING TOURS

the largest sugarcane plantation in the U.S., some 20,000 acres producing up to 20 million pounds of sugar per year. The 1840 Greek Revival mansion, built by planter John Preston Smith, is one of the showplaces of the South, with its three-story spiral staircase and manicured formal gardens. The colonnaded main structure is flanked by two octagonal garconierres, which traditionally housed the young bachelors in wealthy Creole households.

❽ Next stop is **Baton Rouge** and the **LSU Rural Life Museum.** The museum incorporates 20 buidings from 19th-century Louisiana, collected from plantations and farms statewide, including an overseer's house, slave cabins, a blacksmith shop, a grist mill, and a country church with rustic homemade art. A large barn exhibits a wide variety of artifacts, ranging from an African birthing chair to a horse-drawn hearse. **Magnolia Mound Plantation** stands on a ridge facing the Mississippi River. The 1791 French Creole house is furnished with Federal-style antiques from the 19th century. Seasonal cooking demonstrations are presented in the open-hearth kitchen.

❾ From Baton Rouge, take I–90 west to Rte. 1 N to New Roads. **Parlange Plantation** in New Roads is one of the oldest French Colonial manors in Louisiana, and it continues to command a working plantation (sugar, cattle, pecans). The property is still owned and occupied by 7th- and 8th-generation descendants of the Marquis de Trenant, who built the house in 1750. It is open for tours by prior appointment only.

❿ From New Roads, drive east on Rte. 10 for approximately 8 mi to St. Francisville. **Rosedown Plantation** in St. Francisville is one of the country's most distinguished house museums, set on 1,000 acres with 28 acres of historic gardens and 14 restored outbuildings, including the original hothouse, detached kitchen, barn, and doctor's office. The 1835 Greek Revival manor has been painstakingly restored with all of its original furnishings. **Audubon State Historic Site** once attracted naturalist John James Audubon, who painted 32 of his Birds of America while living here at Oakley Plantation House in the 1820s. The 1799 manor is now furnished in the style of the late Federal period, as it would have been when the artist was in residence. Hikers can follow his tracks through 100 acres of nature trails and woodlands. **Butler Greenwood Plantation** is still owned by members of its founding family, who often act as tour guides. The antebellum mansion, circa 1790, furnished in original antiques, features a formal Victorian parlor. **Catalpa Plantation** is also owned and operated by descendants of the original family. Ancient oaks shade 30 acres of gardens and a Victorian manor filled with antique furnishings, silver, and other treasures.

From St. Francisvville, take U.S. 61 south for approximately 20 mi to I–110 S towards Baton Rouge. Exit onto I–10 E and proceed for 75 mi back to New Orleans.

Shreveport to Poverty Point Along I–20

FROM NATIVE AMERICAN BURIAL GROUNDS TO UTOPIAN VILLAGES

Distance: 151 mi; 243 kilometers   Time: 2 days
Breaks: Stop overnight in Monroe or West Monroe to allow plenty of time to explore the historic cotton port and the cafés and shops of Antique Alley.

Louisiana is usually defined by the European heritage and spicy nightlife of its southern regions, but the north was settled by second-generation pioneers from Virginia,

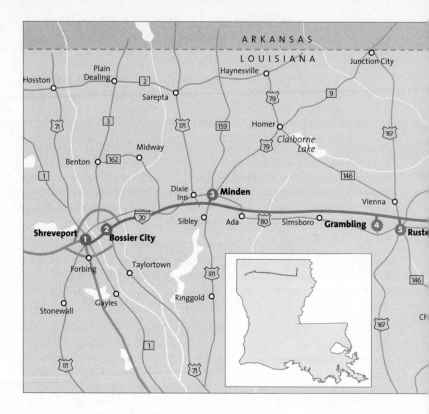

Tennessee, and the Carolinas. Here in the Bible Belt you'll catch a glimpse of several old-time religions, from Native American burial mounds dating back more than 3,000 years at Poverty Point, to the restored 1836 Germantown Colony of Utopian pilgrims, to a 20th-century bible museum in Monroe. The devil gets his due aboard riverboat casinos in Shreveport and Bossier City. Historic gardens and art-filled conservatories are earthly edens, while exhibits dedicated to classic vehicles and modern aircraft show that man really can fly.

❶ Begin your tour along I–20 in **Shreveport. The American Rose Center Gardens** is head-quarters for the American Rose Society. The 118-acre research facility is graced by waterfalls, fountains, and some 20,000 roses in bloom from mid-May through late October. The **Ark-La-Tex Antique and Classic Vehicle Museum** is housed in an original 1920s dealership with 50 vintage automobiles, fire trucks, motorcycles, and other related collectibles on display. The **R.W. Norton Art Gallery** exhibits American and European works spanning four centuries, including silver pieces by Paul Revere and the South's largest collection of Western paintings and sculptures by Frederic Remington and Charles Russell. The **Barnwell Garden and Art Center** is set in a dome-shaped riverfront conservatory with tropical and native plantings, floral displays, a fragrance garden, and a fine arts gallery. **Harrah's Shreveport Casino** offers riverboat gambling.

❷ From Shreveport, take I–20 for approximately 3 mi to **Bossier City.** In Bossier City, the **8th Air Force Museum** showcases more than a dozen aircraft. Dioramas, uniforms, and equipment range from World War I through the present day. **Louisiana Downs** presents thoroughbred racing from June through November. Or you could play riverboat gambler

INTRODUCTION
HISTORY
REGIONS
WHEN TO VISIT
STATE'S GREATS
RULES OF THE ROAD
DRIVING TOURS

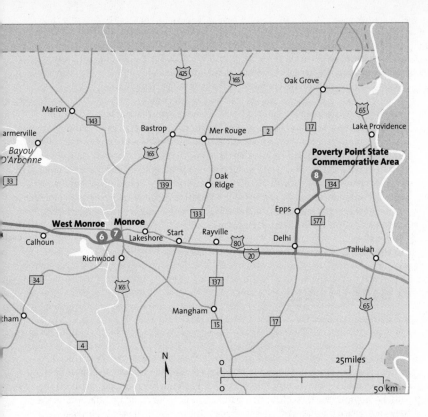

at the three floating casinos, **Casino Magic**, **Horseshoe Casino and Hotel,** or **Isle of Capri Casino.**

❸ Depart Bossier City on I–20 E and proceed for approximately 25 mi toward **Minden.** The **Germantown Colony and Museum** is on the site of a communal village founded in 1836 and operated for 37 years by a group of German refugees, members of the Utopian Movement in search of religious freedom. The collection of restored and replica buildings and hand-hewn cabins is filled with original furnishings, documents, tools, household implements, and other essentials of daily living.

❹ From Minden, continue on I–20 E for approximately 30 mi to exit 81 and Grambling. **Grambling State University** was founded after the Emancipation Proclamation to educate African-Americans "as a community to build the American Dream." It is home to one of the country's premier college football teams, led for decades by legendary coach Eddie Robinson until his 1998 retirement made headlines around the world. The flamboyant Grambling State Marching Band has a national reputation of its own, with flashy moves as famous as its music.

❺ Continue east on I–20 for approximately 10 mi to **Ruston. Odell Pottery** is a fine crafts gallery featuring works by several artists, plus raku firings and wheel demonstrations by three-time U.S. Pottery Olympics champion Bruce Odell.

❻ From Ruston continue east on I–20 for approximately 25 mi to **West Monroe. Antique Alley** has been a top North Louisiana attraction for more than a decade. Three blocks in the historic district are lined with antique shops and malls, specialty stores, cafés, and studios.

❼ **Monroe** is 3 mi east of West Monroe on I–20. The **Emy-Lou Biedenharn Museum and Garden** showcases the grand house of Joseph Biedenharn, first bottler of Coca-Cola. Exhibits in the bible museum explore its impact on Western civilization. The garden and conservatory is graced by flowering plants, fountains, and artworks. The *Twin City Queen* is a triple-deck excursion boat that cruises the Ouachita River.

❽ Leaving Monroe, take I–20 to Exit 153/Delhi onto Rte. 17 north for about 10 mi to Epps. From Epps drive 5 mi east on Rte. 134, then 1 mi north on Rte. 577. **Poverty Point State Historic Site.** is one of the most significant sites in North America, with earthen mounds (in six rows of concentric ridges) dating from 1700 BC to 700 BC. The star attraction is a giant mound, rising 70 feet above the ground, shaped like a bird with outstretched wings. Climb to the top of the bird or an observation tower for panoramic views of the earthworks and surrounding Mississippi flood plain. Museum exhibits and an audio-visual program showcase artifacts found on site. You can take seasonal tram tours or walk on the many surface trails.

The best way home to Shreveport is to simply backtrack the way you came.

ABBEVILLE

MAP 9, D5

(Nearby town also listed: Lafayette)

From mid-October through December, the air is especially sweet in Abbeville, scented by bubbling cauldrons of sugarcane at Steen's Syrup Mill, one of the largest open-kettle operations in the country. This lovely old French town was established in 1843 by Father Antoine Desire Megret, former pastor of the Catholic church in Lafayette, hence the name (which translates as "priest's village"). The tree-shaded Magdalen Square and 19th-century houses of the historic district have attracted quite a few film crews. Other visitors are drawn by legendary oyster bars, professional-quality theater productions from the Abbey Players, and outdoor pursuits in the heart of coastal Cajun country.

Information: Vermilion Parish Tourist Commission. | 1907 Veterans Memorial Dr., Abbeville, LA 70510 | 337/898–6600 | fax 337/893–1807 | vptc@acadian.net | www.vermilion.org | Weekdays 8:30–4:30.

Attractions

Abbeville Cultural and Historical Alliance. In this cooperative of four community organizations, the exhibits include a photographic history of the coastal Cajun community, regional artifacts, and works by local artists. | 108 S. State St. | 337/898–4114 | www.vermilion.org | Free | Weekdays 9–2, weekends by appointment only.

Leland Bowman Lock. Up to 40 million tons of cargo per year passes through Freshwater Bayou, part of the Gulf Intracoastal Waterway network. From a special gazebo room, you can examine this working lock, which adjusts water levels to accommodate passing vessels. Exhibits detail the mechanics of marine lock systems. An elevated pavilion beside the bayou has good views of passing marine traffic and the surrounding marshland. | 25995 Hwy. 333 | 337/893–6790 | fax 337/898–3718 | www.vermilion.org | Free | Weekdays 7–3:30.

ON THE CALENDAR

AUG.: *Delcambre Shrimp Festival and Fair.* This street fair includes Cajun dancing, a shrimp cookoff, and a blessing of the fleet. | Third weekend in Aug. | 337/898–6600, 337/685–2653.

NOV.: *Celebration of the Giant Omelette.* Abbeville is the only American town to join in this traditional French celebration. Featured are 5,000 eggs cooked into a giant omelette, crafts, music, and dancing in the streets. | First Sun. in Nov. | 337/893–6517, 337/893–5760.

Dining
Black's Oyster Bar. Seafood. Fresh "topless salty oysters" and other regional seafood are served in an historic 100-year-old building. Try oysters on the half-shell, seafood, and steaks. | 319 Pere Megret | 337/893–4266 | Closed Sun., Mon. | $15–$20 | AE, DC, MC, V.

Dupuy's Oyster Shop. Seafood. This long-time casual restaurant with a long wooden bar was established in 1869 and can seat about 75 people. Pictures of crawfish and the Bayou decorate the walls, along with neon signs of various beers served. Try oysters on the half shell, softshell crab Dupuy, seafood quesadilla, or the oyster dinner. Sunday buffet. | 108 S. Main St. | 337/893–2336 | Closed Tues. | $9–$16 | AE, MC, V.

Lodging
Local Flavor B and B Inn. This turn-of-the-century Acadian farmhouse in the early Louisiana cypress style is 300 yards from the Vermilion River. It is furnished with antiques and locally made art. All rooms have double beds. The downstairs rooms have claw-foot bathtubs while the two rooms upstairs share a bathroom. From the wraparound porch you can view the native-plant garden, whose 55 rosebushes bloom nearly year-round. Complimentary breakfast. Cable TV. Two swimming and fishing ponds. | 8418 Hwy. 82 | 337/937–4753 | www.thelocalflavor.net | 4 rooms | $75–$95.

Sunbelt Lodge. This modern motel is about 2 mi from the Abbeville historic district and restaurants. Scenic drives are about 20 minutes away by car. Some kitchenettes. Cable TV. Pool. | 1903 Veterans Memorial Dr. | 337/898–1453 | fax 337/898–1463 | 100 rooms | $39–$45 | AE, D, DC, MC, V.

Williams Ducote House. A restored turn-of-the-century residence in the historic district, this arts-and-crafts–style lodging includes antiques, clawfoot tubs, and big wraparound porches. The house is near other historic-district attractions, including restaurants, antiques shops, a coffeehouse, and the Abbey Players Theater. Complimentary breakfast. Cable TV. Laundry service. | 401 N. St. Charles Ave. | 337/898–0048 | fax 337/898–2660 | www.bedand-breakfast.com | 2 rooms | $85–$125 | V.

ALEXANDRIA

MAP 9, D3

(Nearby town also listed: Natchitoches)

Alexandria is a graceful old Southern city surrounded by the hills and bayous of the Red River delta. It is also the commercial hub for area farming communities, whose residents drive into "Alec" to take care of business and do their shopping. Much of the town was burned by retreating Union soldiers after their defeat at Mansfield in 1864, and further damage was inflicted by a disastrous flood in 1866. However, many fine old buildings and outlying plantation manors have survived, and the riverfront historic district is alive with galleries and museums.

Information: **Alexandria/Pineville Area Convention and Visitors Bureau.** | 707 Main St., Alexandria, LA 71301 | 318/442–9546, 800/551–9546 | fax 318/443–1617 | www.apacvb.org | Weekdays 8–5.

Attractions
Alexandria Museum of Art. The spectacular new building opened in 1998, covering an entire block on Alexandria's Riverfront; the original 1898 building is on the National Register of Historic Places. Seven galleries host permanent and changing exhibits. The collection is especially strong in regional contemporary art and North Louisiana folk art. Other attrac-

tions include hands-on displays for children in the Pyramid Gallery, a multimedia theater, art library, garden, and museum store. | 933 Main St. | 318/443–3458 | fax 318/443–3449 | www.themuseum.org | $4; special rate for children | Tues.–Fri. 10–5, Sat. 1–5.

Alexandria National Cemetery. This site, established during the Civil War to bury the thousands of Union and Confederate soldiers killed in the area in 1863 and 1864, now holds the remains of more than 5,000 veterans from every war in which Americans have fought. | 209 E. Shamrock St., Pineville | 601/445–4981, 318/449–1793 | fax 318/449–9327 | Free | Daily.

Bringhurst Park. This community park has playgrounds, a miniature train, and the 22-acre Alexandria Zoo. The Alexandria Aces (of the Texas/Louisiana League) play home games at the baseball stadium, where the season runs from May through September. | 3016 Masonic Dr. | 318/473–1130, 318/449–6586 | www.cityofalex.com | Free | Daily.

Cotile Recreation Area. Boating, swimming, fishing, and waterskiing are the big attractions on 2,000 acres of water and woodland. More than 100 campsites have hookups for RVs or tents. | Hwy. 1200, Hot Wells Rd., Boyce, | 318/793–8995 | $3 per vehicle | Daily.

Kent House. This classic example of French Creole architecture, a raised Creole cottage built circa 1796, is the oldest known standing structure in Central Louisiana. Two deep porches, added to the east and west sides of the original structure in the 1840s, shade the house. Tours also take in several outbuildings, including the kitchen, sugar mill, slave cabins, milk house, carriage house, barn, and blacksmith shop. | 3601 Bayou Rapides Rd. | 318/487–5998 | fax 318/442–4154 | www.kenthouse.org | $5; special rates for senior citizens and children; children under 6 free | Mon.–Sat. 9–5, tours 9–11 and 1–3.

Kisatchie National Forest. The sprawling forest varies from relatively flat prairie to steep, rocky, and rugged terrain. Louisiana's longest trail rambles through miles of pine and hardwood bottoms that are ablaze with wild azaleas and dogwood in spring. There's hiking, picnicking, camping, swimming, horseback riding, fishing, and hunting. *(See* also Natchitoches.)* | Hwy. 6W, Boyce | 318/473–7160, 318/793–9427 | fax 318/473–7117 | www.fs.fed.us | Free | Daily.

Loyd Hall Plantation. This restored antebellum mansion is supposedly haunted by several ghosts, including the original owner, who was hanged from one of his own oak trees by invading Union soldiers during the Civil War. The 640-acre cotton farm has been in continuous operation since 1800, providing a rare opportunity to see an historic manor that is still part of a working plantation. | 292 Loyd Bridge Rd., Cheneyville | 318/776–5641, 800/240–8135 | fax 318/776–5886 | www.louisianatravel.com | $6 | Daily 9–4.

ON THE CALENDAR

SEPT.: *Cenlabration.* The festivities of this Labor Day weekend annual event include live music, chicken wing eating contests, Louisiana cuisine, street dances, art exhibits, carnival rides, and children's activities. | 318/473–1127, 888/772–3652.

Dining

Bentley Room. Continental. Old Southern elegance is seen here in the polished woodwork, grand piano, antique armoires, burgundy linens, and formal service. Specialties include steak Christon (a 6-ounce ribeye with crab-meat stuffing, topped with crispy Tabasco onions), blackberry duckling, and tenderloin bordelaise. Pianist Tues.–Sat. Kids' menu. | 200 DeSoto St. | 318/448–9600 | Breakfast and Sun. brunch also available | $14–$26 | AE, D, DC, MC, V.

Cucos. Mexican. This New Orleans-based chain has a lively cantina style. A foyer with vibrant citrus-colored wall treatments, wooden benches with carved and painted sunflower designs, and an antique cabinet lead to two dining rooms and an atrium that seat 125. Rustic Mexican artifacts and a wagon wheel on the ceiling continue the casual, cheerful look. Popular dishes include vegetarian burritos, enchiladas, and chimichangas. Kids' menu. | 2303 MacArthur Dr. | 318/442–8644 | www.klax-tv.com | $15–$24 | AE, D, DC, MC, V.

Lea's Lunchroom. Southern. The house-made pies from this kitchen are famous statewide, served by the slice or whole for take-out. You can sample Southern country food, such as chicken and baked ham as well as jambalaya, at a cheerful, no-nonsense lunch counter established in 1928. Choose from three lunch specials, which change daily. | U.S. 71 S, Lecompte | 318/776–5178 | www.leaspies.com | Breakfast also available | Closed Mon. Closes at 6 Tues.–Thurs., 7 Fri.–Sun. | $7–$12 | MC, V.

Lodging

Best Western of Alexandria. This up-to-date motel is about 5 mi north of the historic district, museums, and the arts center. Rooms are oversize and decorated in southwest Aztec or garden themes. Bar, picnic area. In-room data ports, microwaves, some refrigerators. Cable TV. Indoor pool, wading pool. Hot tub. Exercise equipment. Business services, airport shuttle, free parking. Some pets allowed. | 2720 W. MacArthur Dr. | 318/445–5530, 800/528–1234, 888/338–2008 | fax 318/445–8496 | www.beswesalex.com | 155 rooms | $67–$127 | AE, D, DC, MC, V.

Days Inn. Exterior-facing rooms let in natural light at this 1-story motel 5 mi from downtown. You can choose a king-sized or a double bed. Complimentary Continental breakfast. Data port, some refrigerators. Cable TV. Pool. | 1146 MacArthur Dr. | 318/443–1841 | fax 318/448–4845 | 66 rooms | $45–$59 | V, MC, AE, D.

Holiday Inn. This motel is on the main highway, which is also known as MacArthur Drive. Downtown, you'll find the arts center, museums, and historic district; it's about 4 mi south of the motel. Restaurant, bar, room service. In-room data ports. Cable TV. Pool. Business services, airport shuttle. | 2716 N. MacArthur Dr. | 318/487–4261, 800/787–8336 | fax 318/445–0891 | www.holidayinn.com | 127 rooms | $54–$74 | AE, D, DC, MC, V.

Holiday Inn Convention Centre. A highrise in the historic district, this hotel is across the street from the Red River and a couple of blocks from the art museum. Restaurant, bar. In-room data ports. Cable TV. Pool. Hot tub. Putting green. Airport shuttle. | 701 4th St. | 318/442–9000, 800/465–4329 | fax 318/442–9007 | www.holidayinn.com | 173 rooms | $64–$79 | AE, D, DC, MC, V.

Loyd Hall Plantation Bed and Breakfast. The original circa-1800 outbuildings of the Fitzgerald family manor on this 640-acre working plantation are now lodgings for guests. Period furnishings and authentic antiques grace the oversized rooms. A house tour is available. Complimentary breakfast. Kitchenettes. Pool. Fishing, bicycles. | 292 Loyd Bridge Rd., Cheneyville | 800/240–8135, 318–776–5641 | fax 318/776–5886 | www.louisianatravel.com/loyd_hall | 6 rooms | $95–$165 | AE, D, DC, MC, V.

Matt's Cabin. A carefully preserved historic setting distinguishes these antebellum accommodations in a secluded grove only 3 mi from town. One room is a converted schoolhouse with 14-foot ceilings and working fireplace. The other is a cabin. Both have Bayou-country charm and modern amenities. Complimentary Continental breakfast. Cable TV, VCR. Pool. Tennis. No pets. No smoking. | 6379 Old Baton Rouge Hwy. | 318/487–8340 | susan@inglewoodplantation.com | 2 rooms | $125–$150 | V, MC.

Radisson Hotel Bentley. A landmark of the historic district, this turn-of-the-century hotel is on the National Register of Historic Places. The oversize rooms are decorated with a French motif. Restaurant, bar (with entertainment). Some refrigerators. Cable TV. Pool. Hot tub. Exercise equipment. Business services. | 200 DeSoto St. | 318/448–9600, 800/333–3333 | fax 318/448–0683. | www.radisson.com | 178 rooms | $69–$99; suites $199–$995 | AE, D, DC, MC, V.

Red Carpet Inn. One mile north of downtown and 1 mi from Interstate 49, this 1-story motel of 1950s, cinder block construction was the third Holiday Inn in the country (it has changed owners several times). Poolside rooms available. Complimentary Continental breakfast. Data port. Cable TV. Pool. Laundry facilities. | 2300 N. MacArthur Dr. | 318/443–7331 | fax 318/445–5581 | | 150 rooms | $42–$66 | V, MC, AE, D, DC.

Rodeway Inn. This motel is 5 mi north of shopping at the Alexandria Mall. Cable TV. Pool, wading pool. Business services. Some pets allowed (deposit). | 742 MacArthur Dr. | 318/448–1611, 800/228–2000 | fax 318/473–2984 | www.hotelchoice.com | 121 rooms | $45–$56 | AE, D, DC, MC, V.

BASTROP

MAP 9, E1

(Nearby towns also listed: Epps, Monroe)

Bastrop, in the northeast corner of the state, is a mill town, supported by two major plants of the International Paper Company, but it's also a convenient base for outdoor pursuits in the surrounding woodlands and campgrounds. Hunters head for the 25,480-acre Georgia Pacific Wildlife Management Area. Anglers land 40-pound catfish and big bass in the freshwater lake at Bussey Brake. Hikers and families follow an ancient Native American trade route into Chemin-a-Haut State Park or visit the observation tower and interpretive displays at Handy Brake National Wildlife Refuge.

Information: **Bastrop-Morehouse Chamber of Commerce** | 512 E. Jefferson St., Bastrop, LA 71220 | 318/281–3794 | erambert@msn.com | www.bastrop-morehouse.com.

Attractions

Handy Brake National Wildlife Refuge. The endangered bald eagle can be seen soaring here, and other wild animals such as waterfowl, wading birds, shorebirds, white-tailed deer, and songbirds can be viewed from the observation tower. Interpretive displays provide background information. The refuge consists mainly of open water and bottomland hardwoods. | Cooper Lake Rd. | 318/726–4400 | fax 318/726–4667 | www.fws.gov | Free | Daylight hours.

Chemin-a-Haut State Park. Chemin-a-Haut is French for "high road." The 503-acre park is on a bluff overlooking Bayou Bartholomew on the Louisiana-Arkansas border. It's ideal for fishing, hiking, or picnicking and was designed with children in mind. Facilities are top-notch, and you can camp or rent comfortable cabins. | 14565 State Park Rd. | 318/283–0812, 888/677–2436 | www.crt.state.la.us | $2 per car | Daily.

Georgia Pacific Wildlife Management Area. These 25,480 acres are managed primarily for timber. The vast area is intersected by the Oauchita River and can be used for hunting. | 368 Century Park Dr., Monroe | 318/343—4044 | www.wlf.stat.la.us | Free | Daily.

Snyder Memorial Museum. This small museum contains restored rooms with antique furniture, memorabila, photographs, and other historical artifacts, including a room called "the old store." An art gallery has changing shows of local and area artists. There are school programs and summer workshops for children and an annual quilt show and demonstration. | 1620 E. Madison Ave. | 318/281–8760 | Free | Tues.–Fri. 9–4.

ON THE CALENDAR

NOV.: *Bastrop Arts and Crafts Festival.* Up to 10,000 people flood the Bastrop Fairgrounds on Marlatt Road on the first Thursday in November for the area's largest crafts festival. Hundreds of vendors sell the work of local artisans. Wood carvings and furniture made of regional cherry oak are the most popular of the festival's treasures, but dolls, quilts, and textiles are also in abundance. The $2 admission fee is well worth it, even if you're there only to browse. Be sure to sample the kettle corn, jambalaya, and corn bread. | 318/281–3794.

Dining

Fara's Restaurant. American. This spacious, bustling restaurant caters to both locals and tourists, with an all you can eat buffet. Turkey with dressing is the Sunday lunch special, and the blackened catfish served Friday and Saturday nights is the house favorite. Children welcome. No alcohol. | 1053 E. Madison Ave. | 318/281–3621 | $7–$12 | V, MC, AE, DC, D.

Lodging

Bastrop Inn. This is a well-equipped privately owned inn. Restaurant, room service. Refrigerators. Cable TV. Pool. Business services. | 1053 E. Madison St. | 318/281–3621, 800/227–8767 | fax 318/283–1501 | 107 rooms | $28–$48 | AE, D, DC, MC, V.

Budget Inn. This 2-story motel in the heart of downtown a block from the Snyder Museum and a couple of blocks from many restaurants and bars. Single and double rooms are available, and one suite has a hot tub. Microwaves, refrigerators. Cable TV, room phones. | 206 S. Franklin Blvd. | 318/281–4352 | fax 318/283–6071 | 32 rooms | $28–$75 | AE, D, MC, V.

Country Inn. This family-run motel allows truck parking and is a block from Granny's family-style restaurant. Refrigerators. Cable TV. Business services. | 1815 E. Madison Ave. | 318/281–8100 | fax 318/281–5895 | 30 rooms | $38–$41 | AE, D, DC, MC, V.

BATON ROUGE

MAP 9, F4

(Suburbs also listed: Hammond, New Roads, St. Francisville)

Baton Rouge is the capital of Louisiana. It is also French for "Red Stick," so christened in 1699 by explorer Pierre LeMoyne, Sieur d'Iberville, when he spied a bloody pole on a bluff high above the Mississippi River. According to legend, the ceremonial marker identified the boundary between two warring Native American tribes, the Houmas of the north and the Bayagoulas of the south. Since then, the city's history has been defined by conflict and contention. The 1763 Treaty of Paris transferred the territory from the French to the British, whose fort was subsequently captured in 1779 by a small army dispatched by the Spanish governor in New Orleans, Bernardo de Galvez. Spanish rule ended in 1810, when local Anglo-Americans reclaimed their fort and established the Republic of South Florida. They surrendered their independence just 74 days later, when American forces from New Orleans travelled upriver and raised the stars and stripes.

W.C.C. Claiborne was appointed the territorial governor by President Thomas Jefferson in 1803. When Louisiana attained statehood in 1812 he was elected state governor. Baton Rouge was first named state capital in 1846. However, after the state seceded in 1861 and Baton Rouge was captured by Union forces in 1862, the capital was moved to New Orleans. The state capital was reestablished at Baton Rouge in 1882.

Today the wheels of government continue to drive this bustling city, which is also fueled by the heavy industrial development that has dominated the landscape since around 1900. The Mississippi River has attracted plenty of factories and petrochemical plants, but in recent years it has also been a draw for tourism, as the downtown waterfront has been revitalized with museums, family attractions, and floating casinos. Louisiana State University also exerts a powerful influence on the local economy and lifestyle, softening the hard business edges with a sporty and youthful exuberance. Lakes, parks, and other green spaces are abundant, and quiet residential areas are cooled by big gardens and plenty of shade trees.

Baton Rouge is at the center of Louisiana's Plantation Country. A wealth of significant antebellum structures and historic gardens are in town or within easy driving distance, especially concentrated along the River Road and in nearby St. Francisville. Students of architecture can also explore the 1850 riverfront castle that houses the Old State Capitol, as well as the current seat of government, an Art Deco skyscraper that (at 34 stories) is the tallest state capitol in the U.S.

NEIGHBORHOODS

Downtown. The downtown area is a cluster of fine old homes and handsome public buildings, such as the Old State Capitol, which resembles a castle, and the Old Governor's Mansion (reopened in 1999). It bustled through the 1940s and 1950s until suburban malls drew people away from the center of town. Today, as people have come to appreciate the beauty and historical significance of old structures, the area is coming back to life and now has several thousand residents. Many old homes are being restored on the oak-lined streets, and new hotels are springing up among older ones.

Spanish Town. Dating to 1805, this is the oldest neighborhood in the city and was the original site of Louisiana State University. This area and neighboring Beauregard were designed with angled streets, all converging on a central spot intended for a church that, alas, never materialized. The area is filled with traditional southern architecture, including Greek Revival, Creole, and bungalow homes.

TRANSPORTATION INFORMATION

Airports: Baton Rouge Metropolitan Airport is a 15-minute drive from downtown Baton Rouge. | 9430 Jackie Cochran Rd. | 225/355-0333 | fax 225/355-2334 | www.ci.baton-rouge.la.us/dept/airport/defaut.htm | Weekdays 8–5.

Intra-City Transit: Capital Transit Corporation provides local bus service. | 225/336-0821.

Driving Around Town: You can approach Baton Rouge from I–10, I–12, and I–110; Florida Street leads into downtown. Expect rush hour around 8 in the morning and again between 4 and 6 in the evening. The downtown area has a number of parking garages; they charge up to $2 per hour and $4 per day. Downtown meters on the street are free in the evenings and on weekends.

For More Information: Baton Rouge Area Convention and Visitors Bureau. | 730 North Blvd., Baton Rouge, LA | 225/383–1825, 800/527–6843 | fax 225/346–1253 | www.bracvb.com | Weekdays 8–5.

Attractions

ART AND ARCHITECTURE

Houmas House. One of the most beautiful antebellum manors on the Mississippi is set in well-tended formal gardens on the River Road. The Greek Revival showplace is flanked by two octagonal wings, shaded by wide verandas and massive old oaks. It was built by Colonel John Preston, once master of a 20,000-acre plantation. Today tours are led by docents costumed in period gowns. | 40136 Hwy. 942, Burnside Darrow | 225/473–7841, 888/323–8314

CAR RENTAL TIPS

- ❏ Review auto insurance policy to find out what it covers when you're away from home.
- ❏ Know the local traffic laws.
- ❏ Jot down make, model, color, and license plate number of rental car and carry the information with you.
- ❏ Locate gas tank—make sure gas cap is on and can be opened.
- ❏ Check trunk for spare and jack.
- ❏ Test the ignition—make sure you know how to remove the key.
- ❏ Test the horn, headlights, blinkers, and windshield wipers.

| fax 225/474–0480 | www.houmashouse.com | $10; special rates for students and children | Daily 10–5.

Magnolia Mound Plantation. This 1791 French Creole manor, set in 16 acres of formal gardens, has been restored as a house museum. The main attraction is a major collection of Louisiana and Federal furnishings. Open-hearth cooking demonstrations are held on Tuesdays and Thursdays from October through May. Self-guided walking tours of the slave cabins and grounds are included in tour admission. If you'd like a special guided tour that focuses on the servants' perspective, call ahead to join one of the "Beyond the Big House" tours, which require advance reservations. | 2161 Nicholson Dr. | 225/343–4955 | fax 225/343–6739 | www.brec.org/museums/magnoliamound | $5; special rates for senior citizens, students, and children; children under 5 free | Tues.–Sat. 10–4, Sun. 1–4, closed Mon.

Nottoway Plantation. The tiny riverfront community of White Castle is named for its most prominent landmark, the largest remaining antebellum mansion in the south. This 53,000-square-foot "white castle" was built in 1859 by sugar planter John Hampden Randolph. The Greek Revival/Italianate beauty still has the original Dresden doorknobs, intricate plasterwork, and marble fireplaces. The white ballroom is a favorite backdrop for weddings. If you stay overnight, you can sleep in a massive four-poster in one of the original bedrooms or in a newer suite on the grounds. The walled rose garden has been converted to a swimming pool for guests, and an upscale atrium restaurant serves lunch and dinner. There are special fees for overnight accommodations. | 30970 U.S. 405, White Castle | 225/545–2730, 225/545–2409 | fax 225/545–8632 | www.nottoway.com | Tours: $10; special rates for children | Daily. Tours 9–5.

Old Governor's Mansion. Built circa 1930 by Governor Huey Long, the Georgian manor is a copy of the White House as originally designed. Long's bedroom and several of the downstairs reception rooms have been preserved. Display spaces feature memorabilia from other Louisiana governors, plus a textile exhibit. The building is listed on the National Register of Historic Places. | 502 North Blvd. | 225/387–2464 | fax 225/343–3989 | www.fhl.org | $4; special rates for senior citizens, students, and children; children under 5 free | Tues.–Fri. 10–4.

St. James Episcopal Church. This structure is a classic example of Gothic revival architecture, Louisiana-style. One of the congregation's founders was President Zachary Taylor's wife. There is a gift shop. | 208 N. 4th St. | 225/387–5141 | Free | Weekdays 8–11:30, 1:30–5 (stop in office for church entry).

St. Joseph's Cathedral. The oldest church in town, this Roman Catholic house of worship was built in 1853. Though the interior has been renovated and modernized, the original Gothic revival exterior remains. | 412 North St. | 225/387–5928 | fax 225/344–9477 | Free | Daily 7–4.

State Capitol. One good thing has come out of Louisiana's colorful political history—tours of the seat of power are anything but dry. You'll hear hair-raising tales of scalawags and antiheroes, including the populist leader who built this edifice and was gunned down on the premises in 1935, the infamous "Kingfish," Governor Huey Long. It's a fitting memorial to a monumental ego, the tallest state capitol building in the U.S. The 34-story Beaux Arts skyscraper was completed in 1932, having used more than 2,500 railroad cars of materials and a wealth of marble and intricate bronzework. Inside you'll see the House and Senate chambers and some of the country's first electronic voting machines, where "legislators pushed the buttons, but Huey pulled the switch." Be sure to visit the 27th-floor observatory for panoramic views of the city. | 333 State Capitol St. | 225/342–7317, 800/527–6843 | fax 225/3461253 | www.batonrougetour.com | Free | Weekdays 8–5, closed weekends.

Capitol Grounds. Moss-draped oaks, magnolia trees, camellias, and azaleas add plenty of Southern grace to 27 acres of landscaped formal gardens. The grave of former Governor Huey Long is directly in front of the Capitol building, marked by a 12-foot-tall bronze statue. | Free | Daily.

Governor's Mansion. Though it could have starred in "Gone With the Wind," this stately house was actually built in 1963. The long row of graceful white pillars is a hallmark of the Greek Revival style. | 1001 Capitol Access Rd. | 225/342–5855 | fax 225/379–2043 | Free | Tours by appointment.

Louisiana State Library. The archives include a massive Louisiana history collection, plus state public documents. The building was constructed in 1958 and extensively remodeled in 1999. | 701 N. 4th St. | 225/342–4913 | fax 225/219–4804 | smt.state.lib.la.us | Free | Weekdays 8–4:30.

Old Arsenal Museum. This former gunpowder storehouse was built in 1838. It was of strategic military value in the Mexican and Civil wars, as well as the settlement of the American Southwest. Today it houses exhibits on Louisiana's military history. It is listed on the National Register of Historic Places. | Eastern grounds of the new state capitol building | 225/342–0401 | $1; special rate for children | Mon.–Sat. 9–4.

Old State Capitol. This turreted castle was completed in 1850, four years after Baton Rouge was named capital of Louisiana. Crowned by a stained-glass dome, it stands on a bluff above the Mississippi, little changed since its 19th-century heyday. However, interior spaces have been renovated to house the Center for Political and Government History, with interactive exhibits and an extensive video archive. | 100 North Blvd. | 225/342–0500, 800/488–2968 | fax 225/342–0316 | www.sec.state.la.us | $4; special rates for senior citizens, veterans, students, and children | Tues.–Sun. 10–4, closed Mon.

The Pentagon Barracks. Built to house U.S. Army personnel serving at the post of Baton Rouge, this former military barracks dates back to 1823. During the Civil War, the facilities were used by Confederate, then Union troops. President Zachary Taylor was among the officers quartered here. Later, the building was the original home of Louisiana State University. Today it houses the gift shop for the Capitol Complex. | 959 N. 3rd St. | 225/342–1866 | www.fhl.org | Free | Weekdays 10–4.

BEACHES, PARKS, AND NATURAL SIGHTS

Laurens Henry Cohn, Sr., Memorial Plant Arboretum. More than 250 varieties of native and site-adapted trees and shrubs are planted on 16 acres of parkland. The specimens are labelled for identification. | 12206 Foster Rd. | 225/775–1006 | fax 225/775–1006 | www.baton-rougetour.com | Free | Daily.

Plaquemine Locks State Historic Site. The 1909 locks allowed passage between the Mississippi River and Bayou Plaquemine. Attractions include the original locks and the lockhouse, plus interpretive exhibits in the visitor's center. The museum is probably the biggest attraction here. | Main St., Plaquemine | 225/687–7158 | fax 225/687–8933 | www.crt.state.la.us | $2 | Daily 9–5.

CULTURE, EDUCATION, AND HISTORY

Louisiana State University and Agricultural and Mechanical College. The first superintendent of this institution, which was founded near Pineville in 1853 as the Louisiana State Seminary of Learning and Military Academy, resigned to assume a Union command in the Civil War. His name was William Tecumseh Sherman. Construction of the present campus began in 1922, and the first classes met in 1926. Today LSU sprawls over 2,000 acres, incorporating more than 250 principal buildings. The original architecture is based on the Renaissance domestic style of northern Italy, with tan stucco walls and red tile roofs. Current enrollment numbers around 30,000 students. | Main gates on Highland Rd. and Nicholson Dr. | 225/388–3202 | fax 225/388–3860 | www.lsu.edu | Free | Daily.

Memorial Tower. The university belltower chimes on the quarter hour. It stands 175 feet tall and was built in 1923 as a memorial to Louisianans who died in World War I. Today it contains a museum with the largest collection of New Orleans-made silver, plus 19th-century lighting devices, early oils and watercolors depicting South Louisiana subjects, and other paintings, prints, and drawings. | Tower Drive | 225/388–4003 | fax 225/334–4016 | Free | Weekdays 10–4, Sat. 10–4, Sun. 1–4.

Geoscience Complex. The most extensive archaeological and geological research collection in Louisiana includes a significant collection of fossils. | Howe-Russel Building on Howard Dr. near Student Union | 225/388–2855 | fax 225/388–3075 | www.museum.lsu.edu | Free | Weekdays 8–4.

Museum of Natural Science. Nine major dioramas depict the flora and fauna of North America, including many representatives of Louisiana animal life, plus one decidedly non-native Bengal tiger, a former LSU mascot that has been stuffed for posterity. | Dalrymple Dr. | 225/388–2855 | fax 225/388–3075 | www.museum.lsu.edu | Free | Weekdays 8–4.

Outdoor Greek Theater. Built in 1925 in a natural amphitheater that fronts a wooded area, this neoclassic structure seats 3500. It is the backdrop for occasional outdoor theatrical productions and musical recitals. | Dalrymple Dr. | 225/388–3386 | fax 225/388–5403 | www.lsu.edu | Daily.

Tiger Cage. Mike V, the fifth in a long line of LSU's Bengal Tiger mascots, lives just outside the Pete Maravich Assembly Center. His home has a grassy yard, tiger-sized wooden scratching post, climbing platform, swimming pool, and indoor area. | N. Stadium Rd. | 225/346–3145 | fax 225/346–5705 | www.lsu.edu | Free | Daily.

Union Art Gallery. A single room in the Union Building displays changing exhibits, primarily student and faculty works. | Union Building | 225/388–5162 | fax 225/388–4329 | www.lsu.edu | Free | Daily 9–6.

Indian Mounds. There's not really much to see except grassy mounds, but these are the oldest known prehistoric burial mounds in the Western Hemisphere, dating back some 5,000 years. | At the intersection of Highland and Dalrymple Rds., 3 mi from LSU visitor's center; follow signs to Indian Mounds | Free | Daily.

LSU Rural Life Museum. A cluster of 19th-century buildings depicts pre-industrial Louisiana life. The compound includes a plantation commissary, schoolhouse, sickhouse, gristmill, overseer's house, blacksmith's shop, open-kettle sugar mill, and church. Typical homes are represented by a dog-trot cabin (with its two wings connected by a covered porch), Victorian cottage, slave quarters, and other residential architecture. Vintage vehicles are housed in a large barn. Classical statuary graces the 25-acre Windrush Gardens. | Essen La. at I–10 S | 225/765–2437 | fax 225/765–2639 | www.rulise1.lsu.edu | $5; special rates for senior citizens and children; children under 5 free | Daily 8:30–5.

Port Hudson State Historic Site. From May 23 to July 9, 1863, 6,800 Confederate soldiers defended this site against a Union force of 30,000. It was the longest siege in U.S. history, also one of the first battles in which freed slaves fought alongside Union troops. The surrender of this vital strategic point cut off the final contact between the Eastern Confederacy and the trans-Mississippi units. Today interpretive displays tell the story as you walk through a portion of the battlefield, viewing towers, trenches, artillery, and a cemetery for more than 3,000 Union soldiers, most unknown. | 756 W. Plains-Port Hudson Rd., Zachary | 225/654–3775, 888/677–3400 | fax 225/654–1048 | www.crt.state.la.us | $2; senior citizens and children under 12 free | Daily 9–5.

Southern University. This is the largest university in the United States whose student body is predominantly African-American. The campus encompasses 512 acres, with an experimental station on an additional 372-acre site 5 mi north of the main campus. The school's population averages about 9,000 students. The Black Heritage Exhibit Series is on display at the University Library. Internationally known artist Frank Hayden designed the Red Stick monument on the campus to symbolize the original site of the place the French called Baton Rouge or "Red Stick." | Harding Blvd. at the Mississippi River | 225/771–4500 | fax 225/771–2495 | Free | Daily.

MUSEUMS

Enchanted Mansion: A Doll Museum. Only several hundred of this museum's collection of more than 2,000 dolls are on display at any given time. You can also see 19th-century antiques, Victorian doll houses, and works by modern artists, such as Marilyn Radzat, Edna Hibel, and Jack Johnson. | 190 Lee Dr., Bldg. 2 | 225/769–0005 | fax 225/766–6822 | $4.50 | Mon., Wed., Thurs., Fri., Sat. 10–5, Sun. 1–4. Closed Tues.

Heritage Museum and Village. A 1906 cottage on the National Register of Historic Places exhibits Victorian-era furnishings and artifacts of rural Louisiana life. Ten outbuildings scattered about the grounds replicate an old country village, including a toy shop, train depot (complete with caboose), bank, general store, and church. | 1606 Main St., Baker; about 5 mi from Baton Rouge | 225/774–1776 | fax 225/775–5635 | www.cityofbakerla.org | Free | Mon.–Sat. 10–4, closed Sun.

Louisiana Arts and Science Center. Egyptian mummies, a five-car train, and a simulated space station are among the eclectic contents of this kid-friendly museum, which is housed in the former railway station of the old Yazoo and Mississippi line. Hands-on exhibits include a simulated mission control center for young astronauts. | 100 S. River Rd. | 225/344–9478 | fax 225/344–9477 | www.lascmuseum.org | $3; special rate for children | Tues.–Fri. 10–3, Sat. 10–4, Sun. 1–4, closed Mon.

Old Bogan Fire Station. This museum was a fire station, and it houses three fire trucks dating from 1919 to 1926, as well as firefighter's uniforms and paraphernalia from that era. The building is also home to the Greater Baton Rouge Arts Council. | 427 Laurel St. | 225/344–8558 | fax 225/344–7777 | Free | weekdays 9–4:30.

West Baton Rouge Museum. Guided tours explore the sugar industry of South Louisiana, detailing the intricate culture "from cane to grain." Structures include a small plantation house (circa 1830), a circa-1850 slave cabin, and a working model of a sugar mill. An "oral history wall" presents recollections of plantation workers. The museum also hosts occasional traveling exhibits and living history displays. The annual SugarFest, always scheduled on the first Sunday in October, features crafts demonstrations, sugar boiling and syrup making, kids' activities, and plenty of sweet foods. | 845 N. Jefferson, Port Allen | 225/336–2422 | fax 225/336–2448 | www.westbatonrougemuseum.com | Free | Tues.–Sat. 10–4:30, Sun. 2–5, closed Mon.

OTHER POINTS OF INTEREST

Downtown Riverfront. The waterfront area around the Old State Capitol has been reborn as a tourist attraction in recent years. You can still watch freighters and tugboats chugging along the Mississippi, but you'll also find a colorful collection of worthwhile family attractions. | 100 North Blvd. | 225/342–0500, 225/389–5502 | Free | Daily.

USS *Kidd*. Volunteer vets staff this World War II destroyer, which has been restored to its VJ Day configuration. Tours of the 369-foot ship include admission to the adjoining nautical museum with a submarine exhibit, ship models, and Veterans' Memorial Wall. Mock air-and-sea battles are staged every year during riverfront Fourth of July celebrations. The ship also hosts overnight groups ranging from Naval reunions to scout troops. | 305 S. River Rd. | 225/342–1942 | fax 225/342–2039 | www.premier.net/uss-kidd/home | $6; special rates for senior citizens, students, and children | Daily 9–5.

Greater Baton Rouge Zoo. More than 1,000 animals live in this landscaped zoological garden. The aquarium exhibits Louisiana fish and reptiles. Other attractions include a train and a KidZoo for smaller children. | 3601 Thomas Rd., Baker | 225/775–3877 | fax 225/775–3931 | $3; special rate for children, children under 2 free | Daily 9:30–5.

ON THE CALENDAR

APR.: *Treasures of the River Road Spring Pilgrimage*. Presented at this event are tours of historic plantation manors and gardens as well as demonstrations of traditional crafts. | 1st weekend in Apr. | 225/675–6550, 888/775–7990 | fax 225/675–6558.

APR.: *Earth Day.* This environmental festival includes hands-on exhibits, food, and music. | 3rd Sun. in Apr. | 225/389–5194, 800/527–6843.

JULY: *Star-Spangled Celebration.* An air show over a World War II Naval destroyer and a mock battle, fireworks, food, and music are the highlights of this event. | July 4 | 225/342–1942, 800/527–6843.

NOV.: *Gathering Under the Son.* Choirs from churches all over Baton Rouge perform from 11–6 on a river levee. Food booths are also available. Call for dates and location. | 225/388–9284, 800/527–6843.

DEC.: *Christmas on the River.* This is a super celebration of Christmas! Features include: Bonfires along the levee, caroling, ice skating, fireworks, candlelight tours of plantation manors, illuminated downtown buildings, theatrical productions, the "Cajun Night Before Christmas" ballet, and other holiday specials. | 225/383–1825, 225/389–5520, 800/527–6843.

WALKING TOUR

Start at the State Capitol at State Capitol Drive and North Street. There's a Visitor Information Center in the lobby with maps and brochures, and the observation deck on the 27th floor has panoramic views of the city and the Mississippi River. From there, go south on 3rd Street to the Pentagon Barracks, built in 1823 and once the home of Louisiana State University; today it's the gift shop of the capitol complex. From 3rd Street, walk east to 5th and then north to State Capitol Drive to the Old Arsenal Museum, an 1839 building that now has hands-on exhibits. To get to the Old Governor's Mansion, go south on 5th Street about nine blocks to North Boulevard. To get to the Old State Capitol, go west on North Boulevard about three blocks to Lafayette Street. The Gothic Revival building from 1849 now houses the Louisiana Center of Political and Government History. Across the street on River Road is a reconstructed 1925 railroad station, home of the Louisiana Arts and Science Center Riverside Museum, which has an Egyptian tomb exhibit, restored trains, and a children's art gallery. The U.S.S. *Kidd* is three blocks south on River Road.

Dining

INEXPENSIVE

The Cabin. Cajun/Creole. This restaurant and the surrounding shops are housed in what once were slave quarters. The dining rooms and grounds are decorated with old domestic artifacts, advertising paraphernalia, and farm implements. Popular dishes include crawfish and red beans with rice. Kids' menu. | Hwys. 44 and 22 | 225/473–3007. | www.the-cajunvillage.com | No supper Mon. Closes at 6 Sun. | $4–$16 | AE, D, MC, V.

MODERATE

Albasha. Middle Eastern. The savory chicken shawarma—thinly sliced marinated chicken served with hummus, salad, and rice—is a favorite in this bustling restaurant. It's popular and far from intimate, with seating for 90 people. The music and the smells of the Mediterranean and the Middle East pervade the room while you dine by the running waters of the indoor fountain. | 5454 Bluebonnet Rd. | 225/292–7988 | $9–$13 | AE, D, MC, V.

Blue Fish Grill. Seafood. The 107,000- gallon aquarium in the center of the dining room is home to four man- eating sharks, among other forms of sea life. Though the daily catch does not come from the tank, it is fresh. Try the grilled yellow fin tuna served over sweet potato mash with wasabi cream and crushed cashews. | 7560 Corporate Blvd. | 225/928–3474 | No breakfast. Closed Mon. | $11–$24 | AE,MC, V.

Don's Seafood and Steak House. Seafood/Steak. This is one of Louisiana's premier seafood restaurants, with outposts across the state. It's a relaxed, comfortable place that welcomes families. Along with the steak and seafood, the menu features such fish as tilapia. Raw bar. Kids' menu. | 6823 Airline Hwy | 225/357–0601 | $8–$20 | AE, D, DC, MC, V.

Mike Anderson's. Seafood. This is a comfortable and casual family restaurant with big seafood platters and a rustic bayou atmosphere. Specialties include broiled Guitreau (grilled fish sauted in white wine and topped with crawfish, mushrooms, and shrimp), shrimp Norman (six jumbo shrimp deep-fried with crabmeat étouffée), and joliet rouge (broiled filet of snapper topped with lump crabmeat and mushrooms). Open-air dining on the side porch. Raw bar. Kids' menu. | 1031 W. Lee Dr. | 225/766–7823 | www.mikeandersonsseafoodbr.com | Reservations not accepted for supper or weekends | $10–$20 | AE, D, DC, MC, V.

EXPENSIVE

Dajonel's. Continental. Gaslights, window boxes filled with flowers, brick walls, and white linens set a pampered mood here. Popular dishes are steak, fish, veal, lamb, and stuffed bell pepper. Try the veal Oscar with crabmeat and asparagus. | 7327 Jefferson Hwy. | 225/924–7537 | $17–$37 | AE, D, DC, MC, V.

Juban's. Creole. The interior courtyard bar, as well as the lace curtains and Provencal print linens, make this place look as if it belongs in the French Quarter. Try Creole duck breast pan-seared with Louisiana fig glaze and fried plantains, or filet Juban (prime beef tenderloin filet with maître d'hôte butter). Kids' menu. | 3739 Perkins Rd. | 225/346–8422. | www.jubans.com | Closed Sun. No lunch Sat. | $16–$34 | AE, D, DC, MC, V.

Randolph Hall. Cajun/Creole. A sunny atrium restaurant built on the grounds of Nottoway Plantation in 1984 echoes the grand manor's style with white pillars, stone floors, and pastel hues. Cajun two-step—two dishes in one, featuring turkey and sausauge with shrimp creole, and jambalaya, a rice dish with lots of meat, spices, and green onions—is a popular dish. Pianist weekends. Kids' menu. | 30970 U.S. 405 | 225/545–2730 | www.nottoway.com | $15–$25 | AE, D, MC, V.

VERY EXPENSIVE

Chalet Brandt. Continental. This semi-formal, Old World restaurant features such dishes as duck breast Travis (cooked pink with a rasberry or cherry sauce), steak Eric (filet mignon grilled and stuffed with seafood such as crawfish or shrimp), and veal. Kids' menu. | 7655 Old Hammond Hwy. | 225/927–6040 | Closed Sun., Mon. and week of July 4. No lunch Sat., Tues. | $20–$38 | AE, DC, MC, V.

The Place. Continental. Cathedral ceilings and a fireplace provide a dramatic look. Try the jumbo lump crabmeat; swamp crab; a fried catfish fillet with mushrooms, onions, and green curry; or steak. Kids' menu. Sun. brunch. | 5255 Florida Blvd. | 225/924–5069 | No supper Sun.–Mon., no lunch Sat. | $20–$40 | AE, D, DC, MC, V.

Ruth's Chris Steak House. Steak. The plush furnishings and formal service are as rich and retro as the prime steaks served in a sizzling pool of butter, though diners tend to dress in business casual attire. Filet mignon, lobster, and lamp chops are among the specialties. | 4836 Constitution Ave. | 225/925–0163. | www.ruthschris.com | Closed Sun. No lunch Sat. | $35–$45 | AE, D, DC, MC, V.

Lodging

INEXPENSIVE

AllRound Suites. Every suite in this 4-story hotel has a queen-sized bed, a kitchen, and a living room. The building has inside entrances and is downtown, three blocks north of the capitol. Cable TV. Pool. | 2045 N. Third St. | 225/344–6000 | fax 225/-387–2878 | 138 rooms | $24.99–$38.99 | AE, D, DC, V.

Bellmont Hotel. This red-brick building with white columns is attached to the Great Hall Convention Center, though they are separate businesses. The 1930s building is two stories tall and 4 mi from the airport. Many of its occupants live there year-round. Cable TV. | 370 Airline Hwy. | 225/357–8612 | fax 225/357–4974 | 245 rooms | $42–$84 | MC, V.

Comfort Inn–University Center. This 4-story, tan stucco hotel is just a 3-minute drive from Louisiana State University and 5 mi from downtown. All rooms, from doubles to executive king suites, have interior entrances. Complimentary Continental breakfast. Cable TV. Pool. | 2445 S. Acadian Thruway | 225/927–5790 | fax 225/925–0084 | www.choicehotels.com | 150 rooms | $47–$100 | AE, D, DC, MC, V.

MODERATE

Baymont Inn. This 3-story stucco hotel is 2 mi from the Blue Bayou Water Park and 11 mi southeast of downtown, alongside Interstate 10 at exit 163. Rooms have either two double or one king-sized bed. Two- and three-room suites are available. Complimentary Continental breakfast. Cable TV. | 10555 Reiger Rd. | 225/291–6600 | fax 225/926–8168 | www.baymontinn.com | 102 rooms | $54–$104 | AE, D, DC, MC, V.

Best Inn. This hotel is right off the interstate and ideal for business travelers. Truck parking is available. Restaurant, bar (with entertainment), room service. Cable TV. Pool. Laundry facilities. | 10920 Mead Frontage Rd. | 225/293–9370 | fax 225/293–8889 | 150 rooms | $69–$79 | AE, D, DC, MC, V.

Hampton Inn. This is an upscale, modern highrise favored by business travelers. LSU is just 3 mi south of the hotel, and the Belle of Baton Rouge Casino and Casino Rouge are a few minutes west on the Mississippi River. There's a wide selection of restaurants within a radius of 2–3 blocks. Complimentary Continental breakfast. In-room data ports. Cable TV. Pool. Business services, free parking. | 4646 Constitution Ave. | 225/926–9990, 800/426–7866 | fax 225/923–3007 | www.hamptoninn-suites.com | 141 rooms, 1 suite | $74–$81, $140 suite | AE, D, DC, MC, V.

La Quinta. This two-story hotel with white exterior, teal trim, and lush landscaping is south of Southern University, east of LSU, and close to many restaurants. T.J. Ribs Restaurant and Lounge is across the street, Lonestar Steakhouse and Outback Steakhouse are ¼ mi south, and a 24-hour Denny's is adjacent to the hotel. The Louisiana Art and Science Center is 3 mi southwest, the New State Capitol is 4 mi northwest, and the U.S.S. *Kidd* and Naval War Museum are 3 mi northwest. Complimentary Continental breakfast. In-room data ports. Cable TV. Pool. Laundry facilities. Business services, airport shuttle, free parking. Some pets allowed. | 2333 S. Acadian Thruway, Exit 157B off I-10 | 225/924–9600, 800/531–5900 | fax 225/924–2609 | www.laquinta.com | 140 rooms, 2 suites | $69–$76, $125 suite | AE, D, DC, MC, V.

Shoney's Inn and Suites. This family-oriented motel is next to Celebration Station Family Entertainment Center and 3 mi from historic plantation homes. There's a Shoney's next door (no relation) and several family-style chain and steak restaurants at the adjacent Cortana Mall. Both standard and oversize rooms are available in this two-story motel. Complimentary Continental breakfast. In-room data ports. Cable TV. Pool. Business services. Some pets allowed. | 9919 Gwenadele Dr. | 225/925–8399, 800/222–2222 | fax 225/927–1731 | www.shoneysinn.com | 196 rooms | $63–$76 | AE, D, DC, MC, V.

EXPENSIVE

Best Western Richmond Suites. This hotel has five brick buildings, all two-story except for the one-story country-style lobby building. It is just off I-10 and about 6 mi south of the state capitol complex. The River Road plantations are 15 mi east. Cortana Mall (more than 70 stores and restaurants) is about 3 mi away. Complimentary breakfast. In-room data ports, some kitchenettes, refrigerators. Cable TV. Pool. Hot tub. Tennis. Exercise equipment. Business services. | 5668 Hilton Ave. | 225/924–6500, 800/528–1234, 800/332–2582 | fax 225/924–3074 | www.bestwestern.com/richmondsuiteshotel | 74 rooms, 71 suites | $84–$104, $129–$149 suites | AE, D, DC, MC, V.

Chase Suite by Woodfin. This modern all-suites hotel near I-10 is about 3 mi from LSU and 6 mi south of the capitol complex, the riverfront, and other downtown attractions. It is a two-story modern brick building with spacious, luxurious suites with fireplaces and VCRs with rental library. The two-bedroom penthouse has a Jacuzzi. Free HBO. Complimentary Continental breakfast, room service. In-room data ports, kitchenettes. Cable TV. Pool. Hot tub. Tennis. Laundry facilities. Business services, free parking. | 5522 Corporate Blvd. | 225/927–5630, 800/966–3346 | fax 225/926–2317 | www.woodfinsuitehotels.com/hotels/baton-rouge.html | 80 suites | $99–$179 suites | AE, D, DC, MC, V.

Embassy Suites. This modern all-suites highrise is built around a spacious garden atrium. Downtown is 4 mi north, LSU 3 mi southwest, and the U.S.S. *Kidd* is 4 mi west. Ruth Chris Steak House is next door, and A-Memphis B-B-Q is in the hotel. Restaurant, bar, complimentary breakfast. In-room data ports, refrigerators. Cable TV. Indoor pool. Hot tub. Exercise equipment. Business services, airport shuttle. | 4914 Constitution Ave. | 225/924–6566, 800/362–2779 | fax 225/923–3712 | www.embassy-suites.com | 223 suites | $99–$169 suites | AE, D, DC, MC, V.

Holiday Inn–South. This is a contemporary highrise hotel with an atrium-style lobby and rooms with a southwestern theme. It's in a suburban area off I–12, about 2½ mi south of Cortana Mall. There are several restaurants within a mile of the hotel and a park 4 mi south. Restaurant, bar, room service. In-room data ports. Cable TV. Indoor pool, wading pool. Exercise equipment. Laundry facilities. Business services. | 9940 Airline Hwy. | 225/924–7021, 800/465–4329 | fax 225/924–7021 | www.holidayinnsouth.com | 333 rooms | $79–$99 | AE, D, DC, MC, V.

Quality Suites. This modern hotel is just off I–10 and a fraction of a mile north of the Mall of Louisiana. The Bluebonnet Swamp's nature trail is about 3 mi south, and the LSU Rural Life Museum is 1 mi west. Oversize rooms are furnished with antique and period pieces. Restaurant, bar, picnic area, complimentary Continental breakfast. In-room data ports, microwaves, refrigerators. Cable TV. Pool. Business services. | 9138 Bluebonnet Centre Blvd. | 225/293–1199, 800/228–5151 | fax 225/296–5014 | www.qualityinn.com | 120 rooms | $99–$109 | AE, D, DC, MC, V.

VERY EXPENSIVE

AmeriSuites. This 6-story, turn-of-the-millenium hotel has one-room suites with a wall partitioning the sleeping and living areas. You can choose one king-size or two double beds. Fifteen miles east of downtown, across from the Mall of Louisiana. Complimentary Continental breakfast. Microwave, refrigerator. Cable TV, VCR. Pool. Exercise equipment. | 6080 Bluebonnet Blvd. | 225/769–4400 | fax 225/769–7444 | www.amerisuites.com | 128 rooms | $129 | AE, D, DC, M, V.

Hilton Baton Rouge. This contemporary highrise hotel is about 4 mi southwest of downtown and the capitol complex. The riverfront is about 5 mi east. Restaurant, bar. In-room data ports. Cable TV. Pool. Exercise equipment. Business services, airport shuttle. | 5500 Hilton Ave. | 225/924–5000, 800/445–8667 | fax 225/925–1330 | www.hilton.com | 300 rooms | $159 | AE, D, DC, MC, V.

Nottoway Plantation. The South's largest surviving plantation home at 53,000 square feet, this structure was spared during the Civil War by a Union gunboat officer who had once been a houseguest. The 1859 Greek Revival/Italianate mansion faces the Mississippi River. Overnight guests may stay in original bedrooms in the main house or in the boys' wing or the overseer's cottage. The Master Bedroom Suite is furnished with original pieces that belonged to John Hampton Randolph, the owner. Antiques and period furnishings give each room an individual non-standardized character. Tours are available. Restaurant, complimentary breakfast. Cable TV. Pool. Library. Business services. | 225/545–2730 | fax 225/545–8632 | www.nottoway.com | 13 rooms, 3 suites | $125–$190, $200–$250 suites | AE, D, MC, V.

Radisson Hotel and Conference Center. This upscale member of the Radisson chain is in the heart of the corporate/LSU and government districts, 2 mi from the Mall of Louisiana. The Plaza level offers a private lounge and concierge service on weekdays with Continental breakfast and evening turndown service with milk and cookies. Restaurant, bar, room service. In-room data ports. Cable TV. Pool. Business services, airport shuttle. | 4728 Constitution Ave. | 225/925–2244, 800/333–3333 | fax 225/930–0140 | www.radisson.com | 294 rooms | $109–$139 | AE, D, DC, MC, V.

BOSSIER CITY

(Nearby towns also listed: Minden, Shreveport)

Just across the Red River from Shreveport, Bossier City is a regional industrial hub and home to Barksdale Air Force Base. It has enjoyed a reputation as a rough-and-ready entertainment center since the earliest days of Louisiana Hayride, the famous country music show that originated here from 1948 to 1960, launching Hank Williams, Elvis Presley, Johnny Cash, and other stars. Today the dockside riverboat casinos and thoroughbred racing at Louisiana Downs draw visitors from the three-state area known as Ark-La-Tex.

Information: Shreveport-Bossier Convention and Tourist Bureau. | 629 Spring St., Shreveport, LA 71101 | 318/222–9391, 800/551–8682. | fax 318/222–0056 | tourism@shreveport-bossier.org | www.shreveport-bossier.org | Weekdays 8–5.

Attractions

Bodcau Wildlife Management Area. The deep forests covering 32,471 acres in Bossier and Webster Parishes are an ideal destination if you like the outdoors, with canoeing, boating, camping, and fishing. | 171 Ben Durden Rd., off Hwy 157, Haughton | 318/371–3050 | www.wlf.state.la.us | Free | Daily dawn to dusk.

Casino Magic. Casino Magic has the latest in interactive, state-of-the-art slots and table games, as well as big-name entertainment. There are also three restaurants ranging in price and free parking. Casino Magic Hotel is next door. | 300 Riverside Dr. | 318/841–2453, 800/562–4425 | www.casinomagic.com | Free | Daily 24 hrs.

Cypress Lake Recreational Area. Cypress Lake has a sand beach and picnic areas for summer relaxing. You can explore the lake by boat, fish in its clear water, or hike on the nature trails. There are rental cabins, campsites, and an RV park. | 135 Cypress Park Dr., Benton | 318/965–0007 | fax 318/965–2099 | www.cypressblackbayou.com | $3 per car up to 3 people, additional person $1 | Daily; hours vary by season.

East Bank Theatre and Gallery. Maintained by the Bossier Arts Council, East Bank features exhibits by local, regional, and national artists. The theater's dramatic productions are very popular among residents. | 630 Barksdale Blvd. | 318/741–8310 | fax 318/741–8312 | Gallery: Free. Ticket prices vary | Weekdays 9–5.

Eighth Air Force Museum. At this museum on Barksdale Air Force Base, you can make a historic journey through World War II. Dioramas, uniforms, and Air Force films shown in a replica World War II briefing room are featured. Aircraft are on display, as well as memorabilia from Desert Storm. | Barksdale Air Force Base, Shreveport Rd., north gate | 318/456–3067 | fax 318/456–5558 | www.8afmuseum.net | Free | Daily 9:30–4.

Horseshoe Casino. Three levels of high-energy gambling keep Horseshoe's riverboat casino buzzing. Several dining options are available, as well as top-notch entertainment and shopping in the casino pavilion and special events in Horseshoe's Riverdome entertainment complex. Horseshoe Hotel is next to the casino. There's free parking. | 711 Horseshoe Blvd. Off I-20, exit 19B Traffic St. | 318/742–0711, 800/895–0711 | fax 318/741–7870 | www.horseshoe.com | Free | Daily 24 hrs.

Isle of Capri Casino. A tropical oasis of slots and table games floats on the Red River. Gift shops and restaurants line the pavilion. Free valet parking is available. | 77 Isle of Capri Blvd. | 318/678–7777, 800/843–4753 | fax 318/425–5450 | www.isleofcapricasino.com | Free | Daily 24 hrs.

Loggy Bayou Wildlife Management Area. Loggy Bayou consists of more than 4,371 acres of alluvial flood plain in south Bossier Parish. This area is good for hunting, fishing, birding, and hiking. There are camping areas and a boat launch. | 2856 Poole Rd., Elm Grove | 318/371–3050 | www.wlf.state.la.us | Free | Daily dawn–dusk.

Louisiana Downs. This throughbred racetrack, one of the state's top atractions, features a four-level glass-enclosed grandstand. The complex also has a variety of restaurants, bars, and seating areas. | 8000 East Texas St., northeast of intersection of I–20 and I–220 | 318/747–7223, 800/551–7223 | www.ladown.com | $3, special rates for senior citizens and children | Mid Jun.–Nov., daily 11 AM–midnight.

Touchstone Wildlife & Art Museum. The permanent exhibit includes dioramas of wildlife in natural habitats with art. It also features collections of war relics and Native American artifacts. | Hwy. 80 E (2 mi east of Louisiana Downs), Haughton | 318/949–2323 | $1, children under 5 free | Tues.–Sat. 9–4.

ON THE CALENDAR

MID-JUNE–MID-NOV.: *Thoroughbred racing.* Enjoy high-stakes racing action at the Downs. The racetrack offers food, drinks, and video poker. | 318/742–5555, 800/551–7223.
JUNE–AUG.: *Rockin' on the Rooftop.* Every Thursday night, Horseshoe Casino hosts this event on the roof of the building. Listen to the sounds of area bands, and enjoy great food and drinks. | 318/742–0711, 800/895–0711.

Dining

Faraday's. Contemporary. This is the most intimate restaurant in the pavilion of the Isle of Capri Casino. The prime rib is popular, but you might want to try the more expensive lobster dishes if lady luck has treated you well at the casino. The dining area is full of antique telephones, suitcases, and souvenirs from around the world. | 711 Isle of Capri Blvd. | 318/678–7720 | No breakfast. No lunch | $14–$58 | AE, D, DC, M, V.

Notini's. Italian. Red-checkered tablecloths and cedar-paneled walls say it all. Spaghetti with marinara or meat sauce are your best bets at this casual *ristorante*. On Mondays and Wednesdays the lasagne special comes with garlic bread and salad. | 2013-A Airline Dr. | 318/742–6660 | No breakfast. Closed Sun. | $7–$10 | AE, D, MC, V.

Presto's Brick Oven Grill. American/Casual. Woodfired brick-oven pizzas, pasta dishes, sandwiches, and salads are the high points of any meal at this dining room in Casino Magic. | 300 Riverside Dr. | 318/746–0711 | www.casinomagic.com | $5–$22 | AE, D, MC, V.

Ralph and Kacoo's. Cajun. At this popular local spot, the mood is festive and the food is spicy. You can sample seafood gumbo, mahi-mahi, or even blackened alligator. Jazz band at Sun. brunch. | 1700 Old Minden Rd. | 318/747–6660 | www.ralphandkacoos.com | $9–$20 | AE, D, DC, MC, V.

Sky Room at the Louisiana Downs. Contemporary. With a fourth-floor view of the racetrack so you won't miss a gallop, this all you can eat buffet is designed for weekend track warriors. Peel-and-eat shrimp, crab salad, and a carving board with roast turkey and beef are just a few of the selections. | 8000 E. Texas St. | 318/742–6660 | Reservations required | Closed weekdays | $17 | AE, D, MC, V.

Lodging

Beauvais House-Cottage Bed and Breakfast. Bossier City's first bed and breakfast is just off I–20 at the Hamilton Rd. exit, less than 2 mi from the casino area and just a mile across the Red River from downtown Shreveport nightlife. Nestled among oak trees, Beauvais House is a comfortable cottage whose rooms are filled with family antiques and collectibles. Complimentary Continental breakfast. | 1289 Delhi St. | 318/221–3735 | beaujo60@aol.com | 4 rooms | $100 | No credit cards.

Best Western Airline Motor Inn. This member of the well-known hotel chain is just a mile from all riverboats, 4 mi from Louisiana Downs, and directly across from Pierre Bossier Mall. Dining room, bar. Cable TV. Pool. | 1984 Airline Dr. | 318/742–6000, 800/635–7639 | fax 318/742–2615 | www.bestwestern.com | 120 rooms | $65–$125 | AE, D, MC, V.

Casino Magic Hotel. Free drinks and live music flow nightly at the on-site casino. In this swanky 6-story hotel each of the 88 suites has a hot tub and a king-sized bed to help you recover from a long night of gambling. Free valet parking, luxurious Frette robes, and in-room coffee makers and Godiva coffee are just a few of the luxuries here. However, there's no pool at this otherwise well-appointed hotel. 3 restaurants, bar with entertainment, room service. In-room data ports. Cable TV. Laundry facilities. Business services. | 300 Riverside Dr. | 318/746–0711 | www.casinomagic.com | 200 rooms | $125–$145 | AE, D, M, V.

Comfort Inn. Casino Magic, the Horseshoe, and other casinos are within a mile of this chain motel. Louisiana Downs is 3 mi east. Complimentary Continental breakfast. Microwaves, some in-room hot tubs. Pool. | 1100 Delhi St. | 318/221–2400 | fax 318/221–2909 | www.comfortinn.com | 77 rooms | $54–$80 | AE, D, MC, V.

Days Inn Bossier. This three-story motel built of tan stucco is 1½ mi from the cluster of riverboat casinos and 2½ mi from Louisiana Downs. The state fair grounds are just 5 mi away from Louisiana Downs and Shreveport-Bossier casinos. | 200 John Wesley Blvd. | 318/742–9200, 800/673–2743 | fax 318/747–5100 | www.daysinn.com | 178 rooms | $44–$62 | AE, D, DC, MC, V.

Holiday Inn. This Holiday Inn is only 1 mi from the local riverboats. Restaurant, bar with entertainment, room service. Cable TV. Pool. Hot tub, steam room. Business services, airport shuttle. | 2015 Old Minden Rd. | 318/742–9700 | fax 318/742–9700, ext. 340 | www.holidayinn.com | 212 rooms | $74–$84 | AE, D, DC, MC, V.

Isle of Capri Casino. This large, modern luxury hotel provides 24-hour free shuttle service to the casino 2 mi away. It also features a "Fantasy Isle Arcade" with the latest video games to keep the older kids occupied and "Eno's Playhouse" childcare for the younger ones. Bars, complimentary Continental breakfast. Cable TV. Pool. Fitness center. Business services, airport shuttle. | 711 Isle of Capri Blvd. | 318/747–2400, 800/221–4095 | fax 318/424–1470 | www.isleofcapricasino.com | 226 rooms | $49–$69 | AE, D, DC, MC, V.

La Quinta. This two-story hotel has the chain's typical look with white exterior and teal trim. The 8th Air Force Museum is 2 mi east, and the Louisiana Downs racetrack is 4 mi in the same direction. All four major casinos are less than 4 mi northwest, the Norton Art Museum 6 mi southwest. Complimentary Continental breakfast. In-room data ports, cable TV. Pool. Business services, airport shuttle. | 309 Preston Blvd. | 318/747–4400 | fax 318/747–1516 | www.laquinta.com | 130 rooms | $79–$85 | AE, D, DC, MC, V.

Le Bossier Hotel. About 4 mi east of the casinos and 3 mi from the Louisiana Downs horse track, this 2-story hotel has suites and doubles, some with a pool view. It features a casino lobby and bar with 35 video poker machines and 24-hour food service. restaurant, complimentary Continental breakfast. Cable TV, phone. Pool. Hot tub. | 4000 Industrial Dr. | 318/747–0711, 800/795–0711 | www.lodginghost.com/lebossier | 196 rooms | $69 | AE, D, DC, M, V.

Red Carpet Inn. This 2-story motel is 2 blocks from the Bossier mall and ½ mi from the casinos. There are outside entrances to all rooms, with a view of the interstate. complimentary Continental breakfast. Cable TV, room phones. Pool. | 1968 Airline Dr. | 318/746–9400, 800/931–3529 | 85 rooms | $49.95 | AE, D, MC, V.

Residence Inn by Marriott. Rooms are oversized and some have fireplaces at this popular member of the Marriott chain. The riverfront in downtown Shreveport is 2 mi west, and the Louisiana Downs racetrack is 3 mi east. Picnic area, complimentary Continental breakfast. In-room data ports, kitchenettes, some refrigerators. Cable TV. Pool. Hot tub. Business services. Some pets allowed (fee). | 1001 Gould Dr. | 318/747–6220 | fax 318/747–3424 | www.marriott.com | 72 rooms | $105–$159 | AE, D, DC, MC, V.

COVINGTON

(Nearby towns also listed: Hammond, Mandeville, New Orleans, Slidell)

The oak-shaded town of Covington has long provided a cool retreat for well-heeled New Orleanians, first as a 19th-century resort braced by ozone breezes and artesian waters, more recently as the suburb of choice for artsy young professionals. Today the high ground between the Bogue Falaya and Tchefuncte Rivers is occupied by a lovely collection of 19th-century houses, parks, and churches. Old commercial buildings and cottages have been transformed into stylish restaurants, galleries, and specialty shops. The historic downtown area is compact and walkable, one of the prettiest in the state.

Information: **New Orleans Northshore St. Tammany Parish Tourist Commission.** | 68099 Rte. 59, Mandeville, LA 70471 | 504/892–0520, 800/634–9443 | mail@neworleansnorthshore.com | www.neworleansnorthshore.com | Weekdays 8:30–4:30.

Attractions

Bogue Falaya Park. Moss-draped oaks and the Bogue Falaya River cool the 13-acre town park. Its spectacular wooden playground is a maze of boardwalks, bridges, and rope ladders leading through turreted castles, treehouses, lookout towers, and pirate boats. It was built by some 2,000 volunteers in 1997 after a year of planning and fundraising. | Park Dr., on Bogue Falaya River | Free | Daily.

Columbia Street Landing. This peaceful greenspace on the banks of the Bogue Falaya River was once a bustling port area crowded with schooners, steamers, and oyster luggers. Throughout the 19th and early 20th centuries, Covington was a center of commerce on the North Shore, exporting lumber products, pine oil, bricks, whiskey, and other regional goods across Lake Pontchartrain to New Orleans. Today the landing is a community gathering spot, site of free evening concerts on the third Friday of the month from March through October. | Columbia St., along Bogue Falaya River | Free | Daily.

Global Wildlife Center. More than 2,500 animals roam free on 900 acres of rolling hills at this non-profit facility dedicated to breeding endangered hoofstock from around the world. Giraffes, zebra, bison, wildebeast, eland, and other exotics approach the guided safari wagons. You can purchase cups of feed ($1) to treat them. Camels, baby animals, and emus sometimes wander around the picnic area near the visitor center, which has a gift shop and snack stand. | 26389 Rte. 40, Folsom | 504/624–9453 | fax 504/796–9487 | www.globalwildlife.com | $10; special rates for senior citizens and children, children under 2 free | Daily 8–5.

St. Tammany Art Association. In the Covington historic district, changing exhibits display works by the many fine artists who have settled in St. Tammany Parish, as well as national and international traveling shows. | 129 N. New Hampshire St. | 504/892–8650 | fax 504/898–0976 | www.sttammanyart.org | Free | Tues.–Fri. 10–4, Sat. 12–4, closed Sun.

ON THE CALENDAR

JUNE: *Northshore Blueberry and Jazz Festival.* Blueberry farmers sell plants and flats of berries. You can also enjoy blueberry dishes from area restaurants, blueberry beer from Abita Brewery, local arts and crafts, a full day of live music, and a children's discovery tent. | 504/892–8650 | First Sat. in June.

SEPT.: *Madisonville Wooden Boat Festival.* Here is the largest gathering of wooden boats in the South, including many antiques and classics. Highlights include a marine auction, marine flea market, kids' activities with Covington Woodworking Guild, food, and music. There is also a "Quick and Dirty Boat-Building Contest and Race." | 504/845–9200 | Last weekend in Sept.

NOV.: *Three Rivers Art Festival.* Artists from all over the southeast U.S. gather for a juried competition. Serious artworks and crafts are for sale, priced from a few dollars to thousands. | 504/892–0520, 800/634–9443 | First Sat. and Sun. in Nov.

DEC.: *Christmas in the Country.* Strolling carolers, tours of historic houses dressed for the season, lighting of oaks, as well as refreshments and holiday decorations in quaint shops and galleries are all part of the fun. | 504/892–1873 | 1st weekend after Thanksgiving and 1st weekend in Dec.

Dining

Abita Brew Pub. Creole. This rustic tavern, housed in Louisiana's oldest former microbrewery, is in a woodsy neighborhood near the trailhead for Tammany Trace. The restaurant is known for fresh beers, crawfish cornbread, seafood, and salads. Open-air dining at umbrella-topped tables. Kids' menu. | 72011 Holly St., Abita Springs | 504/892–5837, 800/737–2311 | www.abita.com | $8–$16 | AE, D, DC, MC, V.

Artesia. French. A restored 19th-century house in the piney woods entices New Orleanians to drive out to the country for John Besh's contemporary spin on rustic French cuisine. Try quail, sweet onion tart with field greens, fresh seasonal produce, or regional seafood. This establishment is owned by Vicky Bayley, who also developed the ultra-chic Mike's on the Avenue in New Orleans. Open-air dining. Kids' menu. Sun. brunch. | 21516 Rte. 36, Abita Springs | 504/892–1662 | www.artesiarestaurant.com | Closed Mon., Tues. No lunch Sat., no supper Sun. | $16–$21 | AE, DC, MC, V.

The Dakota. Contemporary. The heavy wooden doors and stone floors that greet you at the entrance project a rich and clubby atmosphere, and it's continued inside by dark woodwork, white linens, big floral arrangements, and local artwork. The impeccable service is noteworthy. Popular dishes include soft-shell crab, pepper-crusted filet, and tenderloin of pork. | 629 N. U.S. 190 | 504/892–3712 | www.neworleansnorthshore.com | Closed Sun. No lunch Sat. | $17–$24 | AE, DC, MC, V.

Isabella's. Italian. Big front windows overlook the sidewalks of the historic district from this sun-filled cottage. Inside it's light and airy, decorated with plenty of fresh flowers and greenery. Favorites here include Isabella's suprema calzone, stuffed with crawfish, sausage, onions, peppers, marinara sauce, and multiple cheeses, including mozzarella. | 321 N. Columbia St. | 504/875–7620 | $5–$16 | AE, D, DC, MC, V.

Magnolia Grill. American/Casual. Dine on great burgers and baked potatoes in a renovated Victorian cottage with a screened side porch. The restaurant is also known for filet mignon, grilled shrimp, and sandwiches. Another claim to fame—Lee Harvey Oswald once lived here. Kids' menu. | 315 N. Vermont St. | 504/893–0402 | www.neworleansnorthshore.com | Closed Mardi Gras. Closed Sun. | $7–$15 | AE, D, MC, V.

Lodging

Best Western North Park Inn. This 2-story motel with exterior entrances is 3 mi north of downtown, across the street from the Dakota restaurant and bar. Complimentary Continental breakfast. Cable TV. Pool. | 625 N. Hwy. 190 | 504/892–2681 | www.bestwestern.com | 74 rooms | $74 | AE, D, DC, MC, V.

Courtyard by Marriott. This hotel, built in 1997 and the newest in the area, is set back from the highway on a wooded pond with lots of wild birds. In keeping with the setting, its rooms are decorated in a nature theme. It is 2 mi from the downtown historic district and 3 mi from the Lake Pontchartrain Causeway. Restaurant, bar. Some kitchenettes. Cable TV. Indoor pool. Spa. Exercise equipment. Laundry facilities. | 101 Northpark Blvd. | 504/871–0244, 800/321–2211 | fax 504/867–9938 | www.marriott.com | 90 rooms, 3 suites | $65–$102, $85–$129 suites | AE, D, DC, MC, V.

Covington Super 8 Motel. Just off Highway 190 and 5 mi north of downtown, this beige 2-story motel is 1 block or less from several restaurants. Others, along with a number of bars, are about a mile away. Modern rooms have either two queen-sized beds or a king and a sofa bed. Some rooms with microwave or refrigerator. Complimentary Continental breakfast. Cable TV. Pool. | 120 Holiday Blvd. | 504/892–4470 | fax 504/892–0370 | www.super8.com | 61 rooms | $89 | AE, DC, MC, V.

Holiday Inn Holidome. This up-to-date hotel, about 2 mi west of the downtown historic district, is about 45 minutes from downtown New Orleans. Restaurant, bar, room service. Cable TV (in suites). Indoor-outdoor pool. Exercise equipment. Laundry facilities. Business services. | 501 Rte. 190 N | 504/893–3580, 800/465–4329 | fax 504/893–4807 | www.holiday-inn.com, www.neworleansnorthshore.com | 156 rooms, 21 suites | $59–$79, $129–$189 suites | AE, D, DC, MC, V.

Woods Hole Inn. These two rustic one-bedroom cottages with private drives and entrances are set in a wooded estate 7 mi from Covington, near the Global Wildlife Center. The cottages have fireplaces and are furnished with antiques and four-poster beds. They also come with stocked mini-refrigerators and coffeemakers. Complimentary Continental breakfast. Microwaves, refrigerators. Cable TV. Bicycles. No smoking. | 78253 Woods Hole Ln., Folsom | 504/796–9077 | fax 504/796–5444 | www.woodsholeinn.com | 2 cottages | $100–$130 cottages.

EPPS

MAP 9, E2

(Nearby towns also listed: Bastrop, Monroe, West Monroe)

The tiny farming community of Epps is surrounded by thriving fields of cotton, rice, and soybeans. However, this ancient soil along the Boeuf River and Bayou Macon has yielded even greater treasures. About 4 mi east of town, the earthen mounds at Poverty Point State Historic Site mark the main trading and ceremonial center of a 3,000-year-old native culture, one of the earliest and largest such settlements ever discovered in North America.

Information: **Epps Town Hall.** | 120 Maple St., Epps, LA 71237 | 318/926–5224 | fax 318/926–4133 | Weekdays 8:30–4:30.

Attractions

Poverty Point State Historic Site. More than 3,000 years ago, this was the main trading and ceremonial center of a Native American culture. The earthen burial mounds date from about 1700 BC to 700 BC, and they are considered one of the most important historic sites in North America. You can watch a video about the significance of the site, take a guided tour, and explore the museum. There's also hiking and camping. | 6859 Hwy. 577 | 318/926–5492 | fax 318/926–5366 | $2 | Daily 9–5.

Tensas River National Wildlife Refuge. Tensas Refuge's Visitor Center is a large rustic building where you can get a map and look at dioramas and exhibits of the refuge's birds, mammals, and reptiles. In the auditorium, films and slide shows describe the refuge's activities. Tensas is a protected habitat for many kinds of native wildlife, such as the Louisiana black bear. | Quebec Rd. south of Hwy. 80, Tallulah | 318/574–2664 | fax 318/574–1624 | www.franklinla.org | Free | Daily. Visitors' Center weekdays 8–4, Sat. 10–4, Sun. 1–4.

ON THE CALENDAR

SEPT.: *Annual Archeology Week.* Held in the last week of September, this statewide celebration of native American history aims to keep alive the ancient ways of life in the lower Mississippi valley. At Poverty Point State Historic Site, you can hear lectures on archeology and take free workshops in such skills as basket weaving and earth-oven cooking. | 318/926–5492.

Dining

Graham's. Steak/Seafood. It's not just the best restaurant in town, it's the only restaurant in town. The specialties are steak and chicken-fried steak, any way you like them. An inexpensive, extensive menu of fresh oysters, crab, shrimp, and fish offsets the humble interior. | 915 Hwy. 17 | 318/926–5500 | $6 | Cash only.

EUNICE

(Nearby town also listed: Opelousas)

★ Eunice, about 20 mi west of Opelousas in the south-central portion of the state, is best known for its weekly live radio show, Rendez-Vous des Cajuns. To listen to the broadcast of French songs and storytelling from the historic Liberty Theatre, a Cajun version of the Grand Old Opry, tune into NPR's local station KRVS. The old ways are still a part of everyday life in this country town, founded by prairie farmers in 1894. It is surrounded by waterlogged fields that do double duty, used in different seasons for growing rice and for aquaculture of crawfish, two mainstays of the spicy local diet. Area history and customs are on display at the Acadian Cultural Center of Jean Lafitte National Park and Preserve.

Information: The Mayor at City Hall | 200 W. Park Ave., Eunice, LA 70535 | 337/457–7389 | fax 337/457–6506 | www.eunice-la.com | Weekdays 8–5.

KODAK'S TIPS FOR PHOTOGRAPHING PEOPLE

Friends' Faces
- Pose subjects informally to keep the mood relaxed
- Try to work in shady areas to avoid squints
- Let kids pick their own poses

Strangers' Faces
- In crowds, work from a distance with a telephoto lens
- Try posing cooperative subjects
- Stick with gentle lighting—it's most flattering to faces

Group Portraits
- Keep the mood informal
- Use soft, diffuse lighting
- Try using a panoramic camera

People at Work
- Capture destination-specific occupations
- Use tools for props
- Avoid flash if possible

Sports
- Fill the frame with action
- Include identifying background
- Use fast shutter speeds to stop action

Silly Pictures
- Look for or create light-hearted situations
- Don't be inhibited
- Try a funny prop

Parades and Ceremonies
- Stake out a shooting spot early
- Show distinctive costumes
- Isolate crowd reactions
- Be flexible: content first, technique second

From Kodak Guide to Shooting Great Travel Pictures © 2000 by Fodor's Travel Publications

Attractions

Liberty Theater. "Rendez Vous des Cajuns" takes the stage every Saturday night, a foot-stomping revue of songs and storytelling in French that is broadcast live on radio and television to surrounding parishes. The landmark 1924 building, formerly used as a vaudeville hall and movie house, is listed on the National Register of Historic Places. | 200 W. Park Ave. | 337/457–7389, 337/457–6577 | fax 377/457–6506 | www.eunice-la.com | $5; children under 7 free | Sat. 4–7:30.

Prairie Acadian Cultural Center/ Jean Lafitte National Historical Park and Preserve. Permanent and changing exhibits showcase regional culture and early Acadian life. Cajun music, crafts demonstrations, and interpretive programs are presented every Saturday. A video dramatizes the expulsion of French Acadians from Canada. | 250 W. Park Ave. | 337/457–8499 | fax 337/457–0061 | www.eunice-la.com | Free | Daily 8–5.

ON THE CALENDAR

FEB., MAR.: *Mardi Gras*. In rural Mardi Gras tradition, this event features a Saturday night music show at Liberty Theatre, a Sunday *boucherie* (grand butchering) with roast pork and fresh sausages, Monday seminars on Mardi Gras traditions and an evening street dance, and a Tuesday run on horseback with wagons. | Sat.–Tues. before Ash Wednesday | 337/457–7389.

OCT.: *Prairie Cajun Folk Life Festival*. Among the activities at this event are demonstrations of traditional crafts, Cajun and Zydeco music, a narrative stage with storytelling and cultural talks, and lots of good food. | Third weekend in Oct. | 337/457–7389.

Dining

Nick's on 2nd. Cajun/Creole. Garnished with antiques displayed in a fine old bar complete with table linens, this establishment is a favorite with local businesspeople and politicos. Try gumbo, fried shrimp, broiled crawfish, crab, or boudin balls. Kids' menu. | 123 S. 2nd St. | 337/457–4921. | www.nickson2nd.com | Closed Mon. No lunch Sat. | $10–$20 | AE, D, MC, V.

Lodging

Best Western. This motel is in downtown Eunice, about two blocks from the Liberty Theater and the Prairie Acadian Cultural Center. Several restaurants are less than a block away. Some in-room hot tubs. Cable TV. Pool. | 1531 W. Laurel Ave. | 337/457–2800, 800/962–8423 | fax 337/457–2800 | www.bestwestern.com | 35 rooms | $62–$69 | AE, D, DC, MC, V.

Potier's Prarie Cajun Inn. Originally a hospital built in 1927, this 2-story bed and breakfast has a small stage in the back. The suites are done in Cajun motifs with authentic old iron beds and mosquito nets. It's in the heart of historic downtown and next door to the Liberty Theater. Complimentary Continental breakfast. Cable TV. Hot tub. | 110 W. Park Ave. | 337/457–0440 | fax 337/457–1999 | potiers@potiers.net | 9 rooms | $75 | AE, D, DC, MC, V.

FRANKLIN

MAP 9, E5

(Nearby towns also listed: Morgan City, New Iberia, St. martinville)

Founded by English settlers in 1808, Franklin is an oak-shaded beauty with more than 420 properties listed on the National Register of Historic Places, including several plantation manors. Even grander than the official mansion in Baton Rouge, Louisiana Governor Mike Foster's private home, Oaklawn, is open for tours. The tribal center of the Chitimacha Indian Reservation in nearby Charenton also welcomes visitors. During the Civil War, Franklin was the site of the Battle of Irish Bend, significant because it thwarted Union efforts to capture the salt mines on nearby Avery Island and forestalled movement of Yankee troops into Texas. Today it is the seat of St. Mary Parish, whose rich farmland is planted with some 44,000 acres of sugar cane and crisscrossed by a network of natural waterways.

Information: Cajun Coast Visitors and Convention Bureau. | 112 Main St., Patterson, LA 70392 | 504/395–4905, 800/256–2931 | fax 504/395–7041 | ccvcb@petronet.net | www.cajuncoast.com | Weekdays 8:30–5.

Attractions

Arlington Plantation. This Greek Revival–style home on the banks of Bayou Teche is the only antebellum mansion open to visitors between Centerville and Franklin. It still contains many original furnishings. | 56 E. Main St. | 337/828–2644 | By appointment only.

Chitimacha Cultural Center. You can look at artifacts of the Chitimacha tribe such as woven baskets, as well as other exhibits. A video narrates the tribe's culture and history, and there is a walking tour. | 105 Houma Dr., Charenton on the Chitimacha reservation | 337/923–4830, 337/923–4973 | fax 337/923–6848 | www.chitimacha.com | Free | Weekdays 8–4:30.

Cypremort Point State Park. This park is on Vermilion Bay and provides access to the Gulf of Mexico. You can boat, fish, swim, and ski. Cypremort is also one of the finest places for sailing in Louisiana. | 306 Beach Ln. | 337/867–4510, 888/867–4510 | fax 337/867–4240 | $2 per car up to 4 people, each additional person 50 cents | Daily 7–9.

Cypress Bayou Casino. Cypress Bayou has all the qualities of a big-city casino, without the big city. There are almost 1,280 slot machines that cost from a nickel to twenty-five dollars to play, as well as all the hottest table games. There are many restaurants at the casino, and parking is free. | 832 Martin Luther King Rd., Charenton | 337/923–7284, 800/ 284–4386 | fax 337/923–7882 | www.cypressbayou.com | Free | Sun.–Thurs. 10 AM–2 AM, Fri.– Sat. 10 AM–4 AM.

Emery's Antiques. Browse for unusual furniture and other collectibles in these antique stores in the heart of historic Baldwin. | 401 Main St., Baldwin | 337/923–4795 | Free.

Franklin Historic District Tour. This self-guided tour includes sights such as Shadowlawn and Ashbury Methodist Church. Inquire at the Franklin Tourist Center for a map. | Downtown Franklin around Main St. | 337/828–2555, 800/256–2931. | Free.

Grevemberg House. This home, now a museum, has been carefully restored by the St. Mary Landmarks Society. It was built in 1851 for Henry Wilson, a prominent Franklin lawyer. Guides lead you through the rooms to marvel at the distinctive antique furnishings and beautiful architecture. | 407 Sterling Rd./Rte. 322 | 337/828–2092 | fax 337/828–2028 | $4 | Daily 10–4.

Oaklawn Manor Plantation. Home of Louisiana's Governor Mike Foster, elected in 1996, this beautiful antebellum mansion opens its ground floor to visitors. The walls of the house are 20 inches thick. Notable are the elaborate chandeliers and Audubon folios. The gardens are modeled after those at Versailles. | 3 mi W. of Franklin on Irish Bend Rd. | 337/828– 0434 | fax 337/828–4209 | $6, special rates for students and children | Daily 10–4.

St. Mary's Episcopal Church. St. Mary's is an excellent example of Carpenter Gothic-style architecture. Set in the heart of Franklin, this church has served the area since 1871. Inquire at the rectory behind the church to see inside the building. | 805 1st St. | 337/828–0918. | fax 337/413–0700 | Daily 9–3 | Free.

ON THE CALENDAR

FEB.–MAR.: *Franklin Mardi Gras Parades.* Celebrate and indulge on the Tuesday before the beginning of Lent at Franklin's Mardi Gras celebration. Floats make their way down Main St. as festival-goers catch beads and doubloons from Krewe members. | 337/ 352–5867.

APR.: *Festival Sur la Teche.* Along the Bayou Teche, the festival grounds come alive with live music, Cajun food, arts and crafts, and carnival rides. | 337/828–2084, 504/395–2886.
APR.: *Patterson Cypress Sawmill Days.* Many Louisiana college students come to this festival each year to participate in contests in such activities as tennis, softball, horseshoes, gumbo cookoff, and passe patout (tree-cutting using a double-handled saw). Others come for the sawmill exhibit and the arts and crafts. | 1st weekend in April | 504/395–3720, 800/256–2931.
MAY.: *Le Festival du Poisson Arme (Garfish Festival).* A weekend church fair, the Garfish festival has great rides and Cajun cuisine. On Sunday afternoon garfish patties are cooked and the church holds an auction. | 1st weekend in May before Mother's Day | 337/923–7523.

Dining

Charlie's. Seafood. Local folks love this restaurant for its fresh shrimp, crawfish, catfish, and snapper, but you can also enjoy entrees such as rib-eye steak and desserts like the delicious bread pudding. Cedar tables and walls adorned with paintings create a homey environment. | 1416 N.W. Blvd. | 337/828–4169 | No breakfast | $7 | AE, D, DC, MC, V.

Lodging

Best Western Forest Motor Inn. This Best Western is deep in Cajun country and only 6 mi from Cypress Bayou Casino. Fishing is available in many places within 5 mi. Restaurant, room service. Some refrigerators. Cable TV. Pool. Business services. | 1909 W. Main St. | 337/828–1810 | fax 337/828–1810 | www.bestwestern.com | 82 rooms | $68–$85 | AE, D, DC, MC, V.

Hanson House. Built in 1849 by an English ship captain who traded on Bayou Teche, Hanson House is a grand antebellum home in Franklin's Historic District. It is listed on the National Register of Historic Places. As the house is still in the family, many of the furnishings are original antiques and period pieces. | 114 E. Main St./Hwy. 182 | 337/828–3217, 337/828–7675 | fax 337/828–0497 | www.hansonhouse.bigdogz.com | 4 rooms | $125 | AE, D, MC, V.

HAMMOND

MAP 9, F4

(Nearby towns also listed: Baton Rouge, Covington, Mandeville)

Hammond is a pleasant turn-of-the-century town just west of Covington, known for its springtime crop of strawberries and for shady streets lined with Art Deco, Queen Anne, and Renaissance Revival architecture. It is also a convenient base for exploring the 150 manicured acres of Zemurray Gardens in Loranger. Serious collectors have worn a path to nearby Ponchatoula, which bills itself as "America's Antique City" and is home to more than 100 dealers and weekly Saturday night auctions.

Information: Tangipahoa Parish Tourist Commission. | 42271 S. Morrison Blvd., Hammond, LA 70403 | 504/542–7520, 800/542–7520. | fax 504/542–7521 | bstewart@i-55.com | www.tangi-cvb.org | Weekdays 9–5, weekends 10–4.

Attractions

Joyce Wildlife Management Area. Instead of joining a crowded boat tour, get a serene and secluded view on your own. A 1,000-foot boardwalk leads into Manchac Swamp for bird watching, nature study, and photography. Pick up a map and a flyer that details flora and fauna from the Tourist Commission. | Just off exit 22 on I-55. The sign is hard to see, so keep your eyes peeled for the boardwalk | 504/542–7520, 800/542–7520 | fax 504/542–7521 | www.tangi-cvb.org | Free | Daily.

Kliebert's Alligator and Turtle Farm. The main business is supplying meat for restaurants and exporters, but 45-minute tours offer a close-up look at the pens and lots of colorful lore. The gift shop is an old-fashioned roadside attraction, filled with souvenirs. | 41067 W. Yellow Water Rd. | 504/345–3617, 800/854–9164 | fax 504/542–9888 | $6; special rates for senior citizens and children | Mar.–Oct., daily noon–dusk.

ON THE CALENDAR

MAR., APR.: *Azalea Festival.* Historic house tours, a "pooch parade" of costumed pets, storytelling, a cooking contest, and gardening demonstrations are among the activities featured at this event. There's also an open market with food booths, crafts booths, and azalea bushes for sale. | 504/542–7520, 800/542–7520 | Call for exact date.

APR.: *Ponchatoula Strawberry Festival.* Booths selling a wide variety of strawberry dishes, plus other Louisiana foods, cooking contests, live entertainment on three stages, a car show, and midway rides are all part of the festivities. | 504/542–7520, 800/542–7520 | Call for exact date.

Dining

Garrison's Global Cafe. Contemporary. A popular place for breakfast and Sunday brunch, Garrison's daily special has diners coming back for lunch. The chef mixes traditional and contemporary recipes in dishes like black-eyed peas, brown rice, and pork chops. The rolls and sandwich bread come from the on-site bakery. | 222 E. Charles St. | 504/902–8989 | No dinner | $8 | AE, D, MC, V.

Michabelle's Restaurant. French. The three ornately designed rooms at this restaurant in Michabelle's B & B are painted pink, blue, and gold and filled with French antiques and hand-sewn linens. Chef Michel Marcais, who has worked around the globe, prepares classical French cuisine. Popular dishes include the lobster valentine, grilled veal chop, and rabbit terrine. Desserts include Chef Michel's hometown crepes, chocolate souffle, and a Cointreau floating island. | 1106 S. Holly St. | 504/419–0550 | fax 504/542–1746 | $18.50–$24.50 | AE,MC,V.

Trey Yuen. Chinese. You enter this restaurant through a Chinese water garden with pagoda and koi pond. The Wong brothers are nationally known for their innovative Asian dishes based on fresh regional seafood. Specialties include alligator, crawfish, and honey glazed shrimp with a sweet pecan sauce. Alligator is served two different ways–stir-fried with mushrooms and peppers in an oyster-based sauce, and Szechuan. Spicy crawfish is stir-fried in lobster sauce, while tong-cho crawfish is batterfried with a secret sauce containing garlic. | 2100 N. Morrison Blvd. | 504/345–6789. | www.treyyuen.com | No lunch Sat. | $8–$16 | AE, D, DC, MC, V.

Lodging

Holiday Inn Conference Center. This Holidome with an atrium-style lobby is in downtown Hammond, about 1½ mi from the historic district, near the junction of I–55 and I–12. Restaurant, bar, room service. Cable TV. Hot tub. Indoor-outdoor pools. Laundry facilities. | 2000 S. Morrison Blvd. | 504/345–0556, 800/354–9596 | fax 504/345–0557 | www.HI-Hammond.com | 177 rooms | $65–$87 | AE, D, DC, MC, V.

Hospitality Inn. This modern hotel has a large outdoor pool. It is in downtown Hammond, 1½ mi from the historic district, near the jct. of I–55 and I–12. Restaurant, bar, room service. Cable TV. Pool. Laundry facilities. | 42309 S. Morrison Blvd. | 504/542–1000 | fax 504/542–1000 | 111 rooms | $49–$65 | AE, D, DC, MC, V.

Michabelle's Bed and Breakfast. French chef Michel Marcais has turned this 1903 Greek revival house into a B&B;, with a full-service, on-site restaurant that is *magnifique*. Most rooms are furnished with French antiques. There are also thematic rooms, such as the Venetian and the Arabian Nights. Two blocks from downtown. Complimentary breakfast. | 1106 S. Holly St. 70403 | 504/419–0550 | fax 504/542–1746 | www.michabelle.com | 7 rooms | $75–$125 | AE, D, DC, MC, V.

HOUMA

(Nearby towns also listed: Morgan City, Thibodaux)

Houma styles itself "the Venice of America" because of its many waterways, which have attracted their share of industrial development, along with generations of fishermen, hunters, and birdwatchers. Seven bayous (Terrebonne, Grand Caillou, Petit Caillou, Chauvin, Black, du Large, and La Cache) converge in this sporting town that is crisscrossed by more than 50 bridges. Established in 1834, it was named for the Houma (meaning "Red") tribe of Native Americans who have lived in the area since the 18th century.

Information: **Houma Terrebonne Tourist Commission.** | 14 Tourist Dr., Gray, LA 70395 | 504/868–2732, 800/688–2732 | fax 504/868–7170 | info@houmatourism.com | www.houmatourism.com | Weekdays 9–5, weekends 9:30–3:30.

Attractions

Alligator Annie Miller's Swamp and Marsh Tours. Comfortable cushioned seats and experienced guides smooth a 2-hour tour in search of alligators, waterfowl, nutria, turtles, and other wildlife. This colorful excursion has been featured in national and foreign travel documentaries. | 100 Alligator Ln. | 504/879–3934 | www.houmatourism.com | $15; special rate for children | Mar.–Nov., call for hours.

Bayou Terrebonne Waterlife Museum. At this museum you can explore Southeast Louisiana's vital relationship with the seafood industry. Models, photos, videos, and interactive materials explain forms of water transportation, as well as wetland and water-based hunting, gathering, and mining occupations. | 7910 Park Ave. | 504/580–7200 | $3; special rates for children and senior citizens | Mon.–Sat. 10–4.

Southdown Plantation House/Terrebonne Museum. A turreted Victorian mansion is now an historic house museum with original rooms furnished in period antiques, plus changing exhibits on regional history and art. Highlights include more than 130 Boehm and Doughty porcelain birds and the Mardi Gras Room, which is filled with carnival costumes and memorabilia. Twice-yearly craft shows are presented on the Saturday before Easter weekend and the first Saturday in November. | 1208 Museum Dr. | 504/851–0154 | fax 504/868–1476 | www.southdown.org | $5; special rates for senior citizens and children | Tues.–Sat. 10–4.

ON THE CALENDAR

APR.: *Southdown Marketplace.* More than 300 vendors sell handmade arts and crafts at the Southdown Plantation House and Terrebonne Museum on Museum Drive every spring. At the market you can also try the finest in French and Cajun food. | Sat. of the weekend before Easter | 504/851–0154.
Blessing of the Shrimp Fleet. Colorfully decorated boats are blessed by a priest, then paraded along two bayous for this traditional Catholic ceremony. | Third Sun. in Apr. | 504/868–2732, 504/594–5859, 504/563–2325, 800/688–2732.
SEPT.: *Grand Bois Inter Tribal.* Join this national pow-wow sponsored by native Houmas. Native American foods, crafts, and dancing are featured. | Third weekend in Sept. | 504/868–2732, 504/594–7410, 800/688–2732.

Dining

A-Bear's Café. Cajun/Creole. Since 1963, authentic Louisiana cuisine has been served up in this Acadian roadside cabin with a wide porch, rocking chairs, and a tin roof. The café is open for lunch only, except Friday nights, when a Cajun band performs during dinner. Try gumbo, seafood, or plate lunches. Live music Fri. 5:30–9:30. | 809 Bayou Black Dr. | 504/

872–6306 | www.houmatourism.com | Breakfast also available weekdays. Closed Sun. No supper Mon.–Thurs., Sat. | $10–$16 | AE, D, MC, V.

Bayou Delight Restaurant. Cajun. Here's a real Cajun menu with dishes like alligator, crawfish, and plenty of fresh seafood. Pictures of alligators, paintings of swamp scenes, and photos of celebrities who have dined here line the cypress walls of this big eatery. Friday and Saturday nights a Cajun band performs, giving extra flavor to your bayou-side meal. | 4038 Bayou Black Dr. | 504/876–4879 | $5–$16 | AE, V, MC.

Miss Brandi's. Cajun. Lunch specials like pan-fried flounder and catfish are your best bet at this huge, lively restaurant, though rib-eye steak and lemon meringue pie are the local favorites. Come down on a Wednesday night to hear the live band play Cajun, Zydeco, and swamp pop music. | 1257 Grand Caillou Rd. | 504/872–9608 | No breakfast. Closed Sun. No lunch Sat. | $8–$19 | AE, D, DC, MC, V.

Lodging

Allie's B&B. This in-town establishment, built in the 1970s, has three suites, all with queen-sized beds. You can watch alligators in a canal in the back of the property. complimentary Continental breakfast. Cable TV. | 120 Lewald Dr. | 504/868–5543 | 3 suites | $85 | Cash only.

Audrie's Lil Cajun Mansion. Twenty-four columns surround this 1950s colonial house. Rooms are done in pastels and have king-sized beds. Four miles north of the city limit and 1 mi from Lake Houma, near plantations, swamps, and fishing. Complimentary breakfast. Cable TV. Indoor pool. | 815 Funderburk Ave. | 504/879–3285, 800/484–1174x1228 | www2.cajun.net/~abgeorge | 3 rooms | $60 | Cash only.

Fairfield Inn by Marriott. This modern hotel built in 1997 is 3 mi from the downtown historic district. Southdown Plantation is just 2 mi away, Southland Mall is 3 mi. Golf courses are within 5 mi, and several restaurants are 1 block or less from the hotel. Complimentary Continental breakfast. Some microwaves, some refrigerators. Cable TV. Indoor pool. Spa. | 1530 Martin Luther King Blvd. | 504/580–1050, 800/228–2800 | fax 504/580–1050 | www.marriott.com/fairfieldinn | 79 rooms | $66–$76 | AE, D, DC, MC, V.

Holiday Inn–Holidome. Downtown Houma is about 2 mi southeast of this modern hotel. Within a block or two you'll find a steakhouse, a seafood place, and a pizza place, along with several other restaurants. Restaurant, bar. Cable TV. Indoor pool. Hot tub, spa. Miniature golf. Gym. | 210 S. Hollywood Rd. | 504/868–5851, 877/800–9383 | fax 504/879–1953 | www.holiday-inn.com | 198 rooms, 3 suites | $55–$69, $150 suites | AE, D, DC, MC, V.

Plantation Inn. In this contemporary motel with a large indoor pool, the rooms are decorated with bright floral fabrics and Victorian-style furniture; the lounge has stained-glass sporting scenes. The inn is 1 mi from the downtown historic district and about 2 mi from Southland Mall. Restaurants are 1 to 2 blocks away, and golf courses are within 5 mi. Restaurant, bar, room service. Cable TV. Indoor pool. Laundry facilities. | 1381 W. Tunnel Blvd. | 504/868–0500, 800/373–0072 | fax 504/873–8970 | www.bayoucountryinns.com | 104 rooms | $45–$95 | AE, D, DC, MC, V.

JACKSON

MAP 9, E4

(Nearby towns also listed: New Roads, St. Francisville)

Jackson is a gracious old southern town in English Louisiana's plantation country, surrounded by the rolling forested countryside that stretches east of the Mississippi River and north of Baton Rouge. More than 100 buildings here are listed on the National Register of Historic Places, including many fine examples of raised Louisiana cottages, as well as provincial Greek Revival and Victorian architecture. Once known as Bear Corners because of the black bears that gathered along Thompson Creek, the town was formally established in 1815 and named for General Andrew Jackson, who camped here with his troops after their victory in the Battle of New Orleans. Today's well-preserved historic district has quaint bed-and-breakast inns, antique shops, and a regional museum.

Information: **East Feliciana Parish Tourist Commission.** | 3406 College St., Jackson, LA 70748 | 225/634–7155 | fax 225/634–7125 | info@felicianatourism.org | www.feliciana-tourism.org | Mon., Wed. 8–3, Fri. 9–3.

Attractions

Audubon Historic Site. The 1799 West Indies–style Oakley plantation manor where John James Audubon began his "Birds of America" is surrounded by 100 acres of nature. You can tour the house and wander where you like on the grounds. | 10 mi northeast of Jackson, 11788 Louisiana State Hwy. 965, Francisville | 225/635–3739 | fax 225/784–0578 | www.crt.state.la.us | $2, special rates for senior citizens, children, and students | Daily 9–5.

Centenary Historic Site. The College of Louisiana was founded on this site in 1826. Centenary Methodist College of Mississippi took it over in 1846. After 1908 the buildings sat vacant for many years until restoration began in the 1970s. They are now open to the public. | E. College St. | 225/634–7925 | fax 225/635–3739 | $2 | www.crt.state.la.us | Daily 9–5.

Feliciana Cellars Winery. Tour this beautiful Spanish mission-style winery and enjoy a complimentary winetasting. | 1848 Charter St. | 225/634–7982. | fax 225/634–3254 | Free | Weekdays 10–5, Sat. 9–5, Sun. 1–5.

Jackson Historic District. Maps for self-guided tours of this quaint town are available at Feliciana Cellars Winery and The Republic of West Florida Museum. A map of the Historic District is also painted on the outside wall of the Charter Street Market on Charter Street. | 225/634–7155 | www.felicianatourism.org | Free.

Milbank Historic House and Bed and Breakfast. Twelve 30-foot doric columns adorn this antebellum mansion, which was built in 1836 and originally served as a bank and a newspaper office. Guided tours are conducted through the Greek Revival–style house filled with antique furnishings. The gift shop next door sells antiques, books, and gift items. | 3045 Bank St. | 225/634–5901 | fax 225/634–5901 | www.felicianatourism.org | $4 | Daily, call for tour times.

The Republic of West Florida Museum. This museum contains such items as military relics, Model T Fords, and a working 1920s theater pipe organ. Tourist information is available here. | 3406 College St. | 225/634–7155 | fax 225/634–7125 | www.felicianatourism.org | $2, special rates for senior citizens, students, and children | Tues.–Sun. 10–5.

ON THE CALENDAR

MAR.: *Jackson Assembly Antiques Festival and Tour.* From all over the South, 22 dealers come to sell their treasures for three days in downtown Jackson. A renovated antebellum home can be toured during the festival, along with three of Jackson's historic churches. | 225/634–7155.

MAY, JULY, SEPT.: *Pecan Ridge Bluegrass Festival.* Bluegrass lovers flock to this festival of music and food, held three times a year. | 225/629–5852.

NOV.: *Highland Games of Louisiana.* A celebration of Scottish heritage, this festival includes a pipers' competition, sheepdog show, traditional Scottish country dancing, and an informal evening gathering of music and storytelling. | 225/634–7155, 225/924–9208.

Dining

Bobby's Drive-In. American/Casual. Country breakfasts, plate lunches, fish, chicken, hamburgers, and po-boys are the attractions here. You can take out or eat in. | 1427 Charter St. | 225/634–7190 | $6–$10 | No credit cards.

Clubhouse at the Bluffs. Contemporary. This new plantation-style facility houses the Club-house restaurant, which serves the golfers and guests who play and stay at The Bluffs golf club and resort lodge. Specialties include Feliciana chicken (grilled with a white wine mushroom sauce), steak Audubon (diner's choice of rib-eye or filet, topped with jumbo shrimp and a spicy onion, mushroom, and cherry mix), and seafood pasta Louisiana (angel hair pasta with shrimp, crawfish, and a creamy brandy sauce). | U.S. 965 at Freeland Rd. | 225/634–5088 | $14–$23 | Breakfast also available | AE, D, MC, V.

Lodging

Milbank Historic House and Bed and Breakfast. The stately Greek Revival building, furnished with period antiques, is in the Jackson Historic District. There's a library/sitting room. Complimentary breakfast. No room phones, no TV in some rooms. No smoking. | 3045 Bank St. | 225/634–5901 | fax 225/634–5901 | www.felicianatourism.org | 4 rooms (3 share bath) | $90–$125 | Full breakfast | D, MC, V.

Old Centenary Inn. This 1935 brick building has a ballroom and fantasy suites like the Scarlett O'Hara room (opulent, green velvet draperies hang from the windows). All rooms include an oversized tub and a ceiling fan. Fantasy suites have private balconies. The inn is 1/2 block from Feliciana Cellars Winery, also ½ block from the old courthouse, and no more than a ½ mi south of Centenary Historic Site where the Hickory Railroad Steam Engine stops to pick up passengers for a tour of historic Jackson. Complimentary breakfast. Cable TV, some rooms with VCRs. | 1740 Charter St. | 225/634–5050 | 8 rooms | $95–$125 | AE, D, MC, V.

JEAN LAFITTE

(Nearby towns also listed: Metairie, New Orleans)

The pirate Jean Lafitte once controlled the maze of waterways in the fishing village that now bears his name. During the early 19th century his smuggling operation was headquartered here in the swamps of Barataria, employing dozens of ships and more than a thousand men. Many present-day residents proudly claim them as ancestors, though the current economy is based on seafood, either fresh caught for New Orleans–area restaurants or processed for sale out of state. Picturesque but strictly business, shrimpers and crabbers dock their boats right at their own backyards. This is the closest base for exploring the Barataria Unit of Jean Lafitte National Park and Preserve, but the park is an easy 30-minute drive from French Quarter hotels in New Orleans.

Information: Jean Lafitte Tourist Commisssion. | Jean Lafitte Blvd., Jean Lafitte, LA 70067 | 504/689–4754, 800/689–3525 | fax 504/689–7801 | www.jeanlafittetours.com | Weekdays 8:30–4:30.

Attractions

Bayou Barn Fais-Do-Do. A fais-do-do is sort of a Cajun barn dance, a community hoedown recreated weekly at this pleasant tavern on the banks of Bayou des Familles. Cajun bands perform and two-steppers take to the dance floor on Sunday afternoons (band from 2 to 6). Drinks and traditional food (jambalaya, gumbo) are available. You can also rent canoes here daily and paddle right into the Barataria Unit of Jean Lafitte National Historical Park and Preserve. | 313-H Rte. 45, Crown Point | 504/689–2663, 800/862–2968 | fax 504/689–2663, 800/862–2968 | www.bayoubarn.com | $5 ($10 with dinner); children under 12 free | Mar.–mid-Dec., Sun. noon–6; Canoe rentals Wed.–Sun, 10–6.

Jean Lafitte National Historical Park and Preserve/Barataria Preserve Unit. Several miles of marked trails, elevated boardwalks, and canoe routes provide a fascinating glimpse into the swamps, marsh, and hardwood bottomlands of coastal Louisiana. The visitor center has nature exhibits and a short film. Rangers conduct free guided walks and canoe treks, and canoes are available for rent at the Jean Lafitte Inn. | 6588 Barataria Blvd. | 504/589–2330 | fax 504/589–2690 | www.nps.gov/jela | Free | Daily; walks, daily 2 PM, reservations required; canoe treks by appointment.

ON THE CALENDAR

JAN.: *Oyster Food Fest.* On the "hunt of Jean Lafitte," you pick up a map and travel along Bayou Barataria, eating oysters and hunting for "treasures" (samples of Louisiana products from area merchants). Also included are oyster-eating contests, oyster-shucking competitions, and oyster sack races. The celebration ends with a giant barn dance and door prizes. | Third Sun. in Jan. | 504/689–4754, 800/689–4797, 800/689–3525.
AUG.: *Jean Lafitte Seafood Festival.* Food booths with a wide variety of seafood dishes, music, dancing, folklife exhibits, crafts, and carnival rides mark the occasion. | First weekend in Aug. | 504/689–2208.

WHAT'S COOKING?

The first time you pick up a menu in Louisiana, you may feel as if you've stumbled into a foreign country, but proud natives will be more than happy to translate for you—and offer plenty of advice on what they think you should eat for dinner. The seafood is usually great, either perfectly fried or boiled in a peppery mix of pickling spices, lemon, and garlic. Red beans and rice are creamy and satisfying. The ubiquitous French bread has an airy white center and crackly crust, ideal for sandwiches or sweeping up a bit of sauce. (It's even good a day old, baked into a bread pudding soufflé that elevates the nursery classic to haute cuisine.) Here's a basic dictionary to help you through the first meal.

Beignets are pillow-shaped French doughnuts dusted with powdered sugar, usually served with a steaming cup of café au lait. Heaven.

Shrimp or chicken *Creole* is smothered in a Spanish-style tomato sauce seasoned with onion, bell pepper, garlic, and lemon.

Seafood or chicken *étouffée* is smothered in a spicy brown gravy seasoned with onion, bell pepper, garlic, and plenty of pepper.

Grillades are medallions of veal sauteed in a spicy dark tomato sauce, served with grits for breakfast or brunch.

Gumbo is Louisiana's signature dish, a dark and smoky stew that is sometimes thickened with sliced okra. The two most common types are seafood gumbo or chicken and andouille (smoked sausage) gumbo. Some restaurants also serve a traditional gumbo z'herbes, which contains a variety of greens and herbs.

Jambalaya is similar to paella (but without the saffron). This Cajun version of Spanish rice is stocked with any combination of seafood, chicken, sausage, and/or ham.

Po'-boys are long sandwiches on French bread, stuffed with anything from gravy-drenched roast beef to fried oysters. You'll probably be asked if you want it "dressed," which means with mayonnaise, lettuce, tomato, and pickle.

Pralines are crisp pecan patties that are crystallized in a mixture of brown sugar and cream.

Dining

Boutte's. Seafood. This comfortably worn tavern on the bayou is a favorite with locals. Try gumbo, crawfish etouffee, and seafood platters. Wood-paneled walls display nautical pictures and a large ship's wheel. The most impressive feature in the bayou view upstairs from both the dining area and the balcony. These are open for dining only on weekends, but they are always available for enjoying the view. Family-style service. Kids' menu. | Jean Lafitte Blvd. at Boutte St. | 504/689-3889 | Closed Mon. | $4–$16 | AE, D, MC, V.

Restaurant Des Familles. Seafood. The contemporary Acadian-style building with a two-level dining room and spectacular glass wall overlooking the swamp allows close-up views of water birds, alligators, deer, and other bayou wildlife. This restaurant, which is less than 30 minutes from downtown New Orleans, serves fresh Louisiana seafood from surrounding fishing communities and is well worth a special trip. Try softshell crab Foster (sauted with mushrooms and green onions in a butter and wine sauce), crabmeat Remick with bacon, stuffed flounder, huge Gulf shrimp, or "Cajun spaghetti" with shrimp balls in light tomato sauce. Kids' menu. | Hwy. 45, Crown Point | 504/689-7834 | Closed Mon. | $20–$28 | AE, D, MC, V.

Lodging

Victoria Inn. This 9-acre compound contains two West Indies–style houses, an heirloom rose garden, and a Shakespearean herb garden, as well as a private dock on the lake with boats for guests' use. The large and airy rooms are filled with antiques and collectibles, and the double parlor has a fireplace, games, and books. Tours are available. Complimentary breakfast. Some in-room hot tubs. Cable TV. Lake. Boating. Business services. | 4707 Jean Lafitte Blvd. | 504/689-4757, 800/689-4797 | fax 504/689-3399 | www.victoriainn.com | 14 rooms | $89–$149 | AE, D, MC, V.

JENNINGS

INTRO
ATTRACTIONS
DINING
LODGING

JENNINGS

MAP 9, D5

(Nearby town also listed: Lake Charles)

Jennings was just a whistle stop on the Southern Pacific Railroad when it was settled in the 1880s by a New York developer and the Midwestern farmers he recruited, creating a "yankee" outpost on the Cajun prairie. That dual identity still colors this agri-industrial town, set midway between New Orleans and Houston, where the most prosperous fields produce either rice or black gold. In fact, the local petroleum industry has deep roots, as Louisiana's first oil well was drilled at the nearby community of Evangeline in 1901.

Information: **Jeff Davis Parish Tourist Commission.** | 100 Rue de l'Acadie, Jennings, LA 70546 | 337/821-5521, 800/264-5521. | fax 337/821-5536 | jeffdavis@centuryinter.net | www.jeffdavis.org | Weekdays 8:30-5.

Attractions

Louisiana Oil and Gas Park. The park commemorates Louisiana's first producing oil well. The Jeff Davis Visitor Center is in the park, and next door is a live alligator display. An 11-mi walking path circles the lake. | 100 Rue de l'Acadie, exit 64 off I-10 | 337/821-5521 | Free | Visitor Center Mon-Sat 8:30-5, park daily.

W. H. Tupper General Merchandise Store. This authentic country store, opened in 1910, is in the Historic Downtown District. When the store closed its doors in 1949, its complete inventory was carefully stored. In 1971, W. H. Tupper's grandson reopened the store as a museum and put the original merchandise out on display. The relics include such treasures as period clothing, Coushatta Indian baskets, and wind-up Popeye and Olive Oyl toys.

| 311 N. Main St. | 337/821–5532, 800/264–5521 | fax 337/821–5536 | $3, special rates for students | Mon.–Sat. 9:30–5.

Zigler Museum. This museum includes works by Rembrandt, Durer, Van Dyck, Whistler, and many others. One wing is devoted to natural history and wildlife of the area. | 411 Clara St. | 337/824–0114. | fax 337/824–0120 | $2; special rates for students | Tues.–Sat. 9–5, Sun. 1–5, closed Mon.

ON THE CALENDAR

FEB.–MAR.: *Mardi Gras Parade and Festival* Jennings celebrates Fat Tuesday at its annual Mardi Gras parade, and revelers compete to catch beads and doubloons from passing floats. The route runs down Main St. | Sat. before Mardi Gras | 337/821–5500, 800/264–5521.

JULY: *Stars and Stripes Festival.* At this festival local residents enjoy traditional Cajun music and food, as well as a fireworks show. | July 3 | 337/821–5500, 800/264–5521.

OCT.: *Jeff Davis Parish Fair.* This carnival comes through Jennings each year on the first full weekend in October, bringing rides, games, and food to the Jennings fairgrounds. | 337/824–1773, 800/264–5521.

Jennings Alive Arts and Crafts Festival. Stroll through vendors' booths, take a carriage ride, or run the 5K at this Jennings event. Kids have a great time watching clown acts and participating in children's art projects. | Usually 2nd weekend in Oct. | 337/821–5500, 800/264–5521.

DEC.: *Jennings Christmas Festival.* Christmas finds the Louisiana Oil and Gas Park aglow with lights, music, and food. | First Sat. in Dec. | 337/821–5500, 800/284–5521.

Lodging

Creole Rose Manor. Creole Rose Manor is a Queen Anne Gothic Revival midwestern-style two-story house built in 1898 and is listed in the National Register of Historic Places. Antiques and Victorian furnishings combine to give each room its own personality. Complimentary Continental breakfast. No room phones. TV in parlor. No smoking. | 214 W. Plaquemine St. | 337/824–3145 | www.crawfish.net | 4 rooms | $55 | MC, V.

Holiday Inn. This modern hotel is just off I-10, 2 mi south of Jennings Oil and Gas Park and 4 mi south of Zigler Museum. Other attractions include Grand Casino Caushatta (30 mi), Lake Arthur City Park (15 mi), and Lake Charles Beach (35 mi). Restaurant, bar, room service. Cable TV. Pool. Laundry services. Business services. | 603 Holiday Dr., Rte. 26 at I-10 | 337/824–5280, 800/465–4329 | fax 318/824–7941 | www.holiday-inn.com | 131 rooms | $70–$80 | AE, D, DC, MC, V.

KENNER

(Nearby towns also listed: Metairie, New Orleans, Thibodaux)

Kenner is the place many Louisiana tourists see first, since it is home to the New Orleans International Airport. Long before it was pressed into service as a bedroom community for the Big Easy, the fertile land bounded by the Mississippi River and Lake Pontchartrain was filled with small farms. Today it is subdivided into housing developments, commercial offices, and shopping malls. Both residents and visitors try their luck aboard the floating Treasure Chest Casino. For simpler pleasures, the Rivertown historic district is an old town square on the Mississippi, surrounded by small museums and family-oriented entertainments.

Information: **Kenner Convention and Visitors Bureau.** | 2100 Third St., Suite 10, Kenner, LA 70062 | 504/464–9494, 800/231–5282. | fax 504/467–5464 | kennercvb@aol.com | www.kennercvb.com | Weekdays 9–5.

When it Comes to Getting Cash at an ATM,

Same Thing.

Whether you're in Yosemite or Yemen, using your Visa° card or ATM card with the PLUS symbol is the easiest and most convenient way to get cash. Even if your bank is in Minneapolis and you're in Miami, Visa/PLUS ATMs make getting cash so easy, you'll feel right at home. After all, Visa/PLUS ATMs are open 24 hours a day, 7 days a week, rain or shine. And if you need help finding one of Visa's 627,000 ATMs in 127 countries worldwide, visit **visa.com/pd/atm**. We'll make finding an ATM as easy as finding the Eiffel Tower, the Pyramids or even the Grand Canyon.

It's Everywhere You Want To Be.°

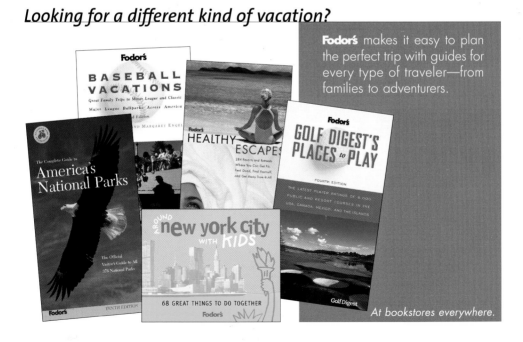

Attractions

Rivertown Welcome Center. Lined up along three blocks at the beginning of Williams Boulevard, between the Mississippi and the railroad tracks, is Kenner's turn-of-the-century historic district. Productions are staged at Rivertown Repertory Theatre (504/468–7221) and the Children's Castle (504/468–7231). However, the main attraction here is a collection of small museums, each devoted to a single theme. | 405 Williams Blvd. | 504/468–7231 | fax 504/471–2159 | www.kenner.la.us | Free | Tue.–Sat. 9–5.

Cannes Brulee Native American Exhibit and Louisiana Wildlife Museum. Over 200 years ago, when French explorer Robert Cavelier de La Salle floated down the Mississippi, he mapped this area as "Cannes Brulee" (Burnt Canes) because he found Native Americans cutting and torching river cane to drive out game. Today their descendents demonstrate their folkways, crafts, singing, and storytelling. They have built traditional huts and other structures on the grounds of this nature museum, which also houses over 700 specimens from the collections of the Louisiana Wildlife and Fisheries Department. Bass, perch, and catfish patrol a 15,000-gallon freshwater aquarium devoted to indigenous species. | 303 Williams Blvd. | 504/468–7274 | fax 504/471–2159 | www.kenner.la.us | $3; special rates for senior citizens and children | Tues.–Sat. 9–5.

Freeport McMoran Daily Living Science Center. This museum looks at science in the skies with a life-sized prototype of a NASA space station and a small (43-seat) planetarium. An observatory is open Friday and Saturday evenings. Other exhibits bring technology to ground level, exploring such everyday wonders as electricity and human digestion. | 409 Williams Blvd. | 504/468–7231 | fax 504/471–2159 | www.kenner.la.us | $3 museum; $5 space station; $1 planetarium; $1 observatory; special rates for senior citizens and children | Museum Tues.–Sat. 9–5; observatory Fri., Sat. 7 PM–10 PM.

Louisiana Toy Train Museum. The collection includes miniature railroad cars, engine, and working models. Preschoolers can climb aboard the half-scale caboose playhouse. Out back, older kids can operate radio-controlled model automobiles on a red-clay racetrack (open in summer only). | 519 Williams Blvd. | 504/468–7231 | fax 504/471–2159 | www.kenner.la.us | $3; special rates for senior citizens and children | Tues.–Sat. 9–5.

Mardi Gras Museum. Kids can dig through trunks to try on Carnival finery while their parents admire wall after wall of antique invitations, ball favors, masks, media clips, and posters for campy Hollywood films like "Holiday for Sinners." And if you're wondering what paradegoers do with all those trinkets tossed from the floats, take a look at the 1976 Gremlin, a car lovingly encrusted with nearly one million plastic beads. | 415 Williams Blvd. | 504/468–7231 | fax 504/471–2159 | www.kenner.la.us | $3; special rates for senior citizens and children | Tues.–Sat. 9–5.

Saints Hall of Fame. You can try your foot at kicking the pigskin or view Tom Dempsey's shoe with which he made the 63-yard field goal of 1970 (still a world record). This lively display of team memorabilia includes interactive exhibits, photographs, videos, and busts of inductees. | 409 Williams Blvd. | 504/468–7231 | fax 504/471–2159 | www.kenner.la.us | $3; special rates for senior citizens and children | Tues.–Sat. 9–5.

Treasure Chest Casino. This glitzy riverboat-style casino cruises Lake Pontchartrain or operates dockside in inclement weather. In addition to a complete range of gambling, services include a dockside buffet restaurant and lounges with live music. | 504/443–8000, 800/298–0711 | fax 504/443–8104 | www.treasurechest.com | Free | Daily 24 hours.

ON THE CALENDAR

DEC.: *Kenner Christmas Village.* A decorated miniature village and train, illuminated figures, and food booths are presented at this holiday event on the Saturday after Thanksgiving. | 504/468–7293.

Dining

Brick Oven Cafe. Italian. Wonderful home-style cooking includes succulent roasted chicken, spaghetti carbonara, veal piccata, and traditional desserts. You may have to wait a half hour or more for a table at peak dinner hours. The three dining rooms are festooned with foodstuffs, tins, jars, and culinary artifacts. | 2805 Williams Blvd. | 504/466–2097 | Reservations not accepted | $18–$26 | AE, D, DC, MC, V.

Jazz Seafood and Steak House. Seafood/Steak. This comfortable family restaurant is 3 blocks from the airport's runway and across the street from several hotels. It's known for Cajun seafood dishes, steaks, and ribs. Family-style service. Kids' menu. | 2722 Williams Blvd. | 504/468–3237 | Closed Mardi Gras | $15–$25 | AE, D, MC, V.

Lodging

Best Western Inn at the Airport. This 4-story hotel, which has interior room entrances, is at the New Orleans International Airport. Restaurant. Data port. Cable TV. Indoor pool. Exercise equipment. | 1021 Airline Dr. | 504/464–1644 | fax 504/469–1193 | www.bestwestern.com | 166 rooms | $139 | AE, CB, D, DC, MC, V.

Holiday Inn Select–New Orleans Airport. This Holiday Inn's proximity to the airport (it's about 2 mi from the terminal) make it popular with business travelers. Restaurant, bar, room service. In-room data ports. Cable TV. Indoor pool. Exercise equipment. Video games. Laundry facilities. Business services, airport shuttle, free parking. | 2929 Williams Blvd. | 504/467–5611, 800/465–4329 | fax 504/469–4915 | www.holiday-inn.com | 303 rooms in 2 buildings | $79–$134 | AE, D, DC, MC, V.

La Quinta. During the week many executives stay at this upscale La Quinta, while vacationing families tend to make reservations on the weekends. It's about 2 mi from the main airport terminal and less than a mile from restaurants. Complimentary Continental breakfast. In-room data ports. Cable TV. Pool. Laundry facilities. Business services, airport shuttle. Free parking. | 2610 Williams Blvd. | 504/466–1401, 800/531–5900 | fax 504/466–0319 | www.laquinta.com | 194 rooms | $89–$99 | AE, D, DC, MC, V.

New Orleans Airport Hilton. This highrise is across from the entrance to New Orleans International Airport. Pontchartrain Center is 4 mi to the north, Treasure Chest Casino is 4.1 mi to the north, and the rivertown historic district is 4 city blocks to the east. It is about 20 minutes from downtown New Orleans. Restaurant, bar. In-room data ports, minibars. Cable TV. Pool. Hot tub. Putting green, tennis. Exercise equipment. Airport shuttle. Business services. | 901 Airline Dr | 504/469–5000, 800/445–8667 | fax 504/466–5473 | www.hilton.com | 317 rooms | $175–$199 | AE, D, DC, MC, V.

Radisson Airport. Located about 20 minutes from downtown New Orleans, this modern highrise is about 2 mi from the airport entrance. Pontchartrain Center, Treasure Chest Casino, and the rivertown historic district are all about 2 mi away. Restaurant, bar, room service. Cable TV. Pool. Business services, airport shuttle, free parking. | 2150 Veterans Blvd. | 504/467–3111, 800/333–3333 | fax 504/469–4634 | www.radisson.com | 244 rooms | $119–$179 | AE, D, DC, MC, V.

Sleep Inn Airport Hotel. This 6-story hotel, built in the late 1990s, has free shuttle service to the airport, which is a 5-minute ride away. Rooms have one king-sized bed or two doubles. Twenty minutes from downtown. Complimentary Continental breakfast. Cable TV. Exercise equipment. | 2830 Loyola Dr. | 504/466–9666 | 120 rooms | $69 | AE, D, DC, MC, V.

LAFAYETTE

MAP 9, E5

(Nearby towns also listed: Abbeville, Opelousas, St. Martinville)

Lafayette is the undisputed capital of Cajun Country. The modern metropolitan hub serves an eight-parish area in the heart of Acadiana, the South Louisiana region settled by Acadian refugees who were expelled from Canada by the English. They put down roots here beginning in 1763, officially incorporating in 1836 as Vermilionville. That is still the name of one major attraction, a colorful museum village that recreates life as it was for those early colonists. In 1884 the act of incorporation was amended to honor the Marquis de Lafayette, who fought in the American Revolution. Today there is plenty of industrial development, primarily from the oil business, but those petrodollars have also helped build a thriving network of upscale restaurants, hotels, and other services. For comfort and convenience, this is the ideal base for exploring the region's legendary bayou towns, swamp gardens, Zydeco dancehalls, and roadside cafés.

Information: **Lafayette Convention and Visitors Commission.** | 1400 NW Evangeline Thrwy., Lafayette, LA 70501 | 337/232–3737, 800/346–1958 | fax 337/232–0161 | www. lafayettetravel.com | Weekdays 8:30–5, weekends 9–5.

Attractions

Acadian Village: A Museum of Acadian Heritage and Culture. Amble through the furnished cottages of a reconstructed 19th-century village, complete with general store and chapel. The complex is peaceful and non-commercial, set in 10 acres of gardens and woodland. Admission to the on-site Mississippi Valley Museum is included. The log building, a replica of a frontier mission, displays Native American artifacts, such as a 400-year-old dugout canoe and prehistoric spear points. | 200 Greenleaf Rd. | 337/981–2364, 800/962–9133 | fax 337/988–4554. | www.acadianvillage.org | $6.50; special rates for senior citizens and students | Daily 10–5.

Alexandre Mouton House/Lafayette Museum. The restored home of Louisiana's first Democratic governor, elected in 1826, is also a repository of regional history and culture. In addition to the original family living areas, furnished in antebellum period antiques, exhibit rooms display Civil War and Reconstruction artifacts and Mardi Gras costumes. The original one-room house was built in 1817, with grander additions in 1826 and 1849. | 1122 Lafayette St. | 337/234–2208 | fax 337/234–2208 | $3; special rates for senior citizens and students | Tues.–Sat. 9–5, Sun 3–5, closed Mon.

Chretien Point. Hypolite Chretien built this graceful French Creole manor in 1831 for his dashing wife Felicite, an early liberated lady who smoked, gambled, and rode astride. The 12-room mansion was once the center of a 10,000-acre cotton plantation. Original architectural features include a European marble fireplace, arched windows modeled on the Palace of Versailles, and a famous staircase that was reproduced for Tara in "Gone With the Wind." Though the house had fallen into disrepair during the mid-20th century, with cows and chickens wandering through the ground floor rooms, it is now beautifully restored and furnished with period antiques. You can stay overnight in one of the original bedrooms. | 665 Chretien Point Rd., Sunset | 337/662–5876, 800/880–7050 | fax 337/662–5876 | www.louisianatravel.com | $6.50; special rate for children | Daily 10–4.

Lafayette Natural History Museum, Planetarium and Nature Station. Natural artifacts include collections of meteorites and marine skeletons. Crafts, textiles, and photographs trace cultural development of Native American, Creole, and Acadian communities. Also on the two-acre site are a Discovery Room for hands-on learning, 58-seat planetarium, and an exhibit hall with changing displays. Planetarium closed until spring, 2002; call for information. | 637 Girard Park Dr. | 337/291–5544 | fax 337/291–5464 | www.lnhm.org | Free | Daily 10–4.

University Art Museum. The permanent collection includes 19th- and 20th-century paintings and drawings, contemporary Louisiana works, Egyptian artifacts, Japanese prints, and collages by American modernist Henry Botkin. Changing exhibits feature regional, national, and international artists. | 207 Joel L. Fletcher Hall, 101 Girard Park Dr. | 337/482–5326 or 337/291–8448 | fax 337/482–5907 | www.usl.edu | Free | Weekdays 9–5, Tue. 9–9, Sat.-Sun. 1–5.

University of Southwestern Louisiana. Established as a trade school in 1901 with fewer than 200 enrollees, the cypress-shaded campus now serves 17,000 students in 115 degree programs. The Dupre Library houses the world's largest collection of French, Spanish, and British Colonial records of Louisiana; the Women in Louisiana collection; more than 1,500 photographs of the sugar industry; and archives of Acadian and Creole life and folklore. Congress chose USL's Research Park as the site of its National Wetlands Research Center. The men's and women's Ragin' Cajun teams compete in 15 sports programs of NCAA's Division 1. | E. University Ave. | 337/482–1000 | www.usl.edu | Free | Daily.

Vermilionville. Take the ferry across Petite Bayou into an authentic recreation of an Acadian village, circa 1765 to 1890. The 23-acre living history museum puts on a vibrant show of folk music, storytellers, cooking demonstrations, furnished period houses, and costumed interpreters. Crafters work at spinning, blacksmithing, quilting, and other frontier skills. Old-fashioned celebrations of Christmas, Mardi Gras, Bastille Day, and other special events are scheduled seasonally. You might even see a real wedding at the tiny church known as La Chapelle. Amenities include a restaurant, bakery, art gallery, and gift shop. The non-profit facility is funded in part by the National Endowment for the Humanities. | 1600 Surrey St. | 337/233–4077, 800/992–2968 | fax 337/233–1694 | www.vermilionville.org | $8; special rates for senior citizens and children, children under 6 free | Daily 10–5.

CAJUN COUNTRY

Local audiences groan every time Hollywood produces yet another movie starring New Orleans characters who talk like Cajuns, which is akin to hanging a Maine accent on a Brooklyn cop. The French Acadians are country people who settled on the prairies and remote swampland of Southwestern Louisiana, but in recent years their spicy cuisine and chank-a-chank music have twirled into the national consciousness, and their culture has spread all over the country. If you'd like to sample the real thing, book a room at a cozy inn or big hotel in Lafayette and spend your days on the nearby backroads and bayous.

Begin at the living museums of Vermilionville and Acadian Village in Lafayette to get a feel for the daily joys and struggles of the earliest pioneers. Take an airboat tour across the swamps or tromp through the subtropical greenery and water bird sanctuary at Jungle Gardens on Avery Island. Ease into the sleepy pace of life on the bayou in St. Martinville and New Iberia, two of the state's prettiest towns. And if you're around on a Saturday night, head for the restored Liberty Theater in Eunice, where musicians and storytellers perform in the regional French dialect for the weekly "Rendez-vous des Cajuns."

Lafayette has its share of big-city restaurants, but authentic Cajun food is country cooking, best had in unpretentious surroundings. At Mulate's or Prejean's, you can two-step to live music every night after you chow down on jambalaya, crawfish pie, and filé gumbo. And be sure to watch for signs on grocery marts and roadside cafés—even gas stations—advertising hot boudin links that are smoked and sold on the premises. The spicy rice-based sausage is a regional specialty and the pride of every amateur chef. You can even pick up a brochure and map tracing "The Boudin Trail" at area tourist information centers.

Related towns: Abbeville, Eunice, Lafayette, New Iberia, Opelousas, St. Martinville.

© Artville

MAR.: *Azalea Trail.* A free brochure, available from the address below, maps a 20-mi drive through city streets lined with azaleas in bloom. | 337/232–3808, 800/346–1958.
APR.: *Festival International de Louisiane.* A week of music, dance, art, theater, cinema, and cuisine from South Louisiana and French-speaking nations is presented. | Third week in Apr. | 337/232–8086.
APR.–SEPT.: *Thoroughbred racing at Evangeline Downs.* "Ils sont partis!" is Louisiana-speak for "They're off!" at this modern racetrack in the heart of Cajun Country. | Thurs., Fri., Sat. and Mon. at 6:45 PM | 337/896–7223.
SEPT.: *Festivals Acadiens.* Celebrations citywide include downtown concerts and street dances, as well as the Wetlands Folklife Festival, traditional and progressive Cajun musicians, authentic Louisiana cuisine at Bayou Food Festival, Louisiana Native and Contemporary Crafts Festival, plus children's activities. | Third weekend in Sept. | 337/232–3808, 800/346–1958.

Dining

Blair House. Seafood. This comfortable family-style restaurant has been a local favorite for more than 40 years. Photos of New Orleans and other nearby places adorn the walls, and tables are dressed in pink over white tablecloths. Specialties include angel hair pasta with seafood, snapper de la maison, and steak de la maison. Kids' menu.Semi-formal dining. | 1316 Surrey St. | 337/234–0357. | No lunch Sat. | $12–$18 | AE, D, DC, MC, V.

Café Vermilionville. Cajun/Creole. Southern elegance and genial service prevail in an early 1800s Acadian inn in a historic plantation home that is on the National Register of Historic Places. As you enter, there's a feeling of being in a private home rather than a business. But once you've walked past the faint blood-stain on the hardwood floor where a soldier was shot long ago, you reach two intimate sunken dining rooms where white linen tablecloths, historic paintings, and photos of the house and its surroundings are enclosed by glass with views of the flower garden and gazebo. You can also dine outside on the patio. Choices range from steak Diane to pecan tilapia to Creole bronze shrimp. Formal dining. | 1304 W. Pinhook Rd. | 337/237–0100 | No lunch Sat. | $25–$35 | AE, D, DC, MC, V.

Charley G's Seafood Grill. Cajun/Creole. The innovative Louisiana cuisine here is characterized by seafood and steak grilled over Southern hardwoods and by crab cakes and duck gumbo. Inventive entrees such as speckled trout filet, pan-sautéed and served with sweet potato, and andouille hash topped with an oyster and mushroom meuniere sauce dominate the menu. Also try veal tournedos, two three-ounce pannseared veal tournedos wrapped in prosciutto, served with mushroom and leek risotto laced with a rosemary and marsala demiglaze. A mixture of ceramic tile and carpeted areas provides interesting contrasts. The upscale bar area offers a wide assortment of specialty liquors, liqueurs, and cigars. Live music Fri.–Sun. Kids' menu. | 3809 Ambassador Caffery Parkway | 337/981–0108 | www.charleygs.com | $15–$25 | AE, DC, MC, V.

I Monelli. 11:30 or 12 Cajun/Creole. Southwest Louisiana cuisine has an Italian accent here. Try the stuffed rainbow trout or the crawfish fettucine. Two candlelit dining areas, each seating 50 persons, feature prints by many European artists. Live music in the rear jazz room Thurs.–Sat. | 4017 Johnston St. | 337/989–9291 | Closed Sun., Mon. and Mardi Gras. No lunch Tues.–Fri., no lunch Sat. | $8–$28 | AE, D, MC, V.

La Fonda. Tex-Mex. Pink adobe walls and carved woodwork set the mood at this comfortable local favorite, which has been serving Tex-Mex food since 1957. Try fandango (chili con queso, chicken taco, and enchilada) or boneless rabbit, fried and served with guacamole salad, beans, and Spanish rice. | 3809 Johnston St. | 337/984–5630 | Closed Sun., Mon. and week of July 4 | $4–$18 | AE, D, DC, MC, V.

Original Don's Seafood and Steak House. Seafood. This is the home base for one of Louisiana's premier seafood chains, established in 1934 and now with outposts statewide. Noted as the first restaurant in Louisiana to serve crawfish dishes, the restaurant provides a comfortable family atmosphere. Exposed brick, an arching entrance, landscape paintings, and white tablecloths are the backdrop for historic photos taken at Don's over the years. Kids' menu. | 301 E. Vermilion St. | 337/235–3551. | Closed Mardi Gras | $13–$19 | AE, D, DC, MC, V.

Original Mulate's. Cajun. Despite its world-famous status, this is the real thing: a Cajun roadhouse with live music nightly during dinner and also during lunch on weekends. Rough-hewn cypress walls are covered with game trophies, international media clippings, and bronzed dancing shoes. Try crawfish dishes, zydeco salad, gumbo, crab-stuffed mush-rooms, or fried seafood. | 325 Mills Ave., Breaux Bridge, | 337/332–4648, 800/422–2586 | $8–$17 | AE, MC, V, DC, D.

Poor Boy's Riverside Inn. Seafood. This large, casual, country-style restaurant overlooking a pond was established in 1934. Lovely cypress woodwork and natural pine decks complement the gardens filled with bamboo, oaks, cypress, and pines. Walk the grounds, gather on the decks, feed the ducks, or just enjoy the setting. Inside are white-covered tables with views of the scenery, the fireplace, and the beautiful pine wood walls. Popular items are the house salad, flounder, and lump crab meat. Kids' menu. | 240 Tubing Rd., Broussard | 337/235–8559 | www.poorboysriversideinn.com | Closed Sun. No lunch Sat. | $20–$30 | AE, D, DC, MC, V.

★ **Prejean's.** Cajun/Creole. Walls lined with culinary awards, game trophies, and bayou arti-facts encourage a festive feeling, along with entertainment provided by a Cajun band and the two-steppers on the dance floor. The excellent service has a fun attitude, exemplified by giant yam cans on the dining tables holding rolls of paper towels. Eggplant, catfish, yellowfin tuna, and seafood are a few of the specialties. Live music nightly. Kids' menu. | 3480 U.S. 167 N | 337/896–3247 | www.prejeans.com | $20–$30 | AE, D, DC, MC, V.

Prudhomme's Cajun Café. Cajun/Creole. This wood-frame country cottage (circa 1890) is filled with antiques and old photographs. It was originally established by Enola Prudhomme (sister of superstar chef Paul Prudhomme) and is now owned and operated by Marty Cos-grove, former corporate chef for Paul Prudhomme. Try a low-fat entree like shrimp fettuccine, or there's always jambalaya, gumbo, or crawfish etouffee. Also try the home-baked breads, such as jalapeno cornbread, sweet potato muffins, banana bread, and biscuits. | 4676 NE Evangeline Thruway, Carencro | 337/734–2120 | Closed Sun. | $30–$35 | AE, D, MC, V.

Randol's Restaurant and Cajun Dance Hall. Cajun/Creole. Cajun live music and Louisiana cooking in a replica of a 19th-century dance hall set a festive mood. Steak, crawfish, shrimp, broiled crab, and chicken are among your choices. Live music nightly. Kids' menu. | 2320 Kaliste Saloom Rd. | 337/981–7080, 800/962–2586 | www.randols.com | No lunch | $20–$30 | MC, V.

Robin's. Cajun/Creole. Pronounced "row-BAN's," this family restaurant offers food by Lionel Robin, one of the premier chefs in the region. Crawfish, seafood platter, frog leg etouffee. Favorites include the frog leg etouffee, which is smothered frog leg with onion and bell pepper gravy served over rice, and crawfish bisque, a crawfish shell stuffed with crawfish meat, cracker crumbs, and other secret incredients in bisque with crawfish tails. Dining is casual despite the white tablecloths, and photos by a local photographer and stuffed ducks (this is a hunting area) hang on the walls. Kids' menu. | 1409 Henderson Hwy., Hen-derson | 337/228–7594. | No supper Sun. | $8–$20 | AE, D, DC, MC, V.

Ruth's Chris Steak House. Steak. Here in Lafayette you'll find the same plush furnishings and formal service that distinguish the Baton Rouge version of this steak house. It's known for prime beef, Maine lobster, and prime steaks sizzling in pools of butter. | 507 W. Pinhook Rd. | 337/237–6123 | www.ruthschrissteakhouse.com | No lunch weekends | $35–$45 | AE, DC, MC, V.

Lodging

★ **Aaah! T' Frere's.** This landmark Acadian-style farmhouse, built in 1880 of red cypress, is owned by retired restaurateurs who serve "ooh-la-la" breakfasts. Complimentary t'juleps (iced tea spiked with peppermint schnapps and Canadian whiskey) and Cajun canapes are served each evening. Rooms are furnished with antiques, and all have private baths.

The farmhouse is in the southeast corner of Lafayette 2 mi west of Vermilionville Bayou, the Acadian Cultural Center, and the airport. Complimentary breakfast. Some in-room hot tubs. Cable TV. | 1905 Verot School Rd. | 337/984–9347, 800/984–9347 | fax 337/984–9347 | www.tfreres.com | 6 rooms | $80–$100 | AE, D, DC, MC, V.

Alida's. This Queen Anne–revival cottage, built in 1902, was reconstructed and moved to this site in 1989. The interior is filled with antiques and family mementos, 3 mi from downtown Lafayette. Complimentary breakfast. In-room data ports. Business services, airport shuttle. No smoking. | 2631 Evangeline Thruway | 337/264–1191, 800/922–5867 | fax 337/264–6915 | www.alidas.com | 4 rooms | $75–$125 | AE, D, MC, V.

Best Western Hotel Acadiana. This modern highrise hotel is 3 mi from Vermilionville, 4 mi from Lafayette Museum, 7 mi from the historical Acadian Village, and 9 mi from Evangeline Downs, The oversized rooms have Victorian-style furnishings. Restaurant, bars (with entertainment). In-room data ports, refrigerators. Cable TV. Pool. Laundry facilities. Business services, airport shuttle. | 1801 W. Pinhook Rd. | 337/233–8120, 800/826–8386 | fax 337/234–9667 | www.bestwestern.com | 295 rooms | $89–$109 | AE, D, DC, MC, V.

Bois Des Chenes. The former Charles Mouton Plantation House, built in 1820, is a raised Creole cottage. It is shaded by 300-year-old oak trees on two acres in the downtown historic district. The rooms are decorated in regional antiques and period furnishings, and several open onto deep porches. A nature guide is on site. Complimentary breakfast. Refrigerators, cable TV. Airport shuttle. | 338 N. Sterling St. | 337/233–7816 | fax 337/233–7816 | www.members.aol.com/boisdchene/bois.html | 5 rooms, 3 suites | $85–$125, $100–$200 suites | AE, MC, V.

Chretien Point. This magnificent French Creole manor, built in 1831, houses grand antiques, old family portraits, and deep verandas with long views across sugar cane fields. The staircase that Scarlett descended in the movie "Gone With the Wind" was inspired by this manor. You will stay in one of the original bedrooms with four-poster beds, lavish drapery, and antique and period furniture. Hors d'oeuvres and mint juleps are served each day, and ancient oaks and a formal garden are on the grounds. In-room hot tubs. Pool. Tennis court. Airport shuttle. | 665 Chretien Point Rd., Sunset | 337/662–5876, 800/880–7050 | fax 337/662–5876 | www.louisianatravel.com | 5 rooms | $95–$225 | AE, D, DC, MC, V.

Cypress Tree Inn. This family-oriented hotel is 1 mi from the airport and within a mile of several fast food restaurants. It is the closest hotel to Vermilionville, less than a mile. Complimentary Continental breakfast. Some refrigerators. Cable TV. Laundry facilities. Business services, airport shuttle. | 2503 SE Evangeline Thruway | 337/234–2000 | fax 337/234–6373 | 102 rooms | $54–$64 | AE, D, DC, MC, V.

Hilton and Towers. The guest rooms and the outdoor pool in this contemporary waterfront highrise overlook Vermilion Bayou, and there is also a river walk. The Oil Center business district is just two blocks away. Across the street are two seafood restaurants, and just a few blocks away are Café Vermilionville and Ruth's Chris Steak House. Acadiana Mall and Vermilionville are both 5 mi from the hotel. Restaurant, bar. In-room data ports, cable TV. Pool. Exercise equipment, dock. Business services. Airport shuttle. | 1521 W. Pinhook Rd. | 337/235–6111, 800/445–8667 | fax 337/261–0311 | www.hilton.com | 327 rooms | $95–$185 | AE, D, DC, MC, V.

La Maison de Campagne. Set on nine rural acres shaded by 250-year-old oak trees, this house is 15 minutes from downtown Lafayette and major restaurants. The rooms in the main house, as well as the cottage built circa 1908, are all furnished with antiques and period pieces. Complimentary breakfast. TV in common area and some rooms. Pool. Business services, airport shuttle. | 825 Kidder Rd., Carencro | 337/896–6529, 800/895–0235 | fax 337/896–1494 | www.cajuncountryhouse.com | 3 rooms; 1 cottage | $110–$145; $120 cottage | AE, DC, MC, V, D.

La Quinta. This modern motel on I–10 offers a good central location for swamp tours and exploring Cajun Country towns and attractions. Acadian Village is 6 mi to the southwest,

Vermilionville is 6 mi southeast. Heymann Convention Center is 4 mi away, and University of South Louisiana is 3 mi to the southwest. Complimentary Continental breakfast. In-room data ports. Cable TV. Pool. Business services. Pets allowed. | 2100 Evangeline Thruway NE | 337/233–5610, 800/687–6667 | fax 337/235–2104 | www.laquinta.com | 140 rooms | $59–$69 | AE, D, DC, MC, V.

Red Roof Inn. The swamps and other delights of Cajun Country can be reached easily from this motel, which is 4 mi northwest of downtown Lafayette. Cajun Dome is just 3 mi away, Pelican Park and Vermilionville are each within 5 mi, and Acadian Village is 12 mi away. Cable TV. Business services, free parking. Pets allowed. | 1718 N. University Ave. | 337/233–3339, 800/843–7663 | fax 337/233–7206 | www.redroof.com | 108 rooms | $63–$87 | AE, D, DC, MC, V.

Travelodge. There are plenty of places to eat and shop near this chain motel. The Acadian Mall, which offers lots of shopping and eating, is about 5 mi to the south, and the Oil Center business district is just 2 blocks away. Complimentary Continental breakfast. In-room data ports. Cable TV. Pool. Free parking. | 1101 W. Pinhook Rd. | 337/234–7402, 800/578–7878 | fax 337/234–7404 | www.travelodge.com | 61 rooms | $60–$65 | AE, D, DC, MC, V.

LAKE CHARLES

MAP 9, C5

(Nearby town also listed: Jennings)

Lake Charles is an industrial hub, a center for petrochemicals and shipping, but it also attracts sporting tourists with its gambling casinos, duck hunting, and more than 50 mi of well-stocked waterways. Deep-sea anglers head just a few miles out into the Gulf for tarpon, marlin, and other large game fish. As late as 1810, these lands were still home to the cannibalistic Atakapas tribe, who were followed by undesirables exiled from Europe. A town was incorporated in 1867 and named for early settler Charles Sallier. The current success began in the 1880s, when railroad tracks were laid from New Orleans to Houston. Today Lake Charles is the largest city in Southwest Louisiana and the state's third-largest port, site of huge cargo terminals that receive shipments from all over the world.

Information: **Southwest Louisiana/Lake Charles Convention and Visitors Bureau.** | 1205 N Lakeshore Dr., Lake Charles, LA 70601 | 337/436–9588, 800/456–7952 | fax 337/494–7952 | swlalc@laol.net | www.visitlakecharles.org | Weekdays 8–5, weekends 8–3.

Attractions

Brimstone Historical Society Museum. The Brimstone Museum showcases local arts and crafts and has a special focus on sulphur mining in the district. | 800 Picard Rd., Frasch Park | 337/527–7142 | Free | Weekdays 9:30–5, Sat. 12–3, closed Sun.

Charpentier Historical District. A 20-block neighborhood of elaborate Victorian homes in the downtown area of Lake Charles. Maps are available at the Southwest Louisiana/Lake Charles Convention and Visitors Bureau. | 337/436–9588, 800/456–7952 | fax 337/494–7952 | www.visitlakecharles.org.

Cottage Shops. Popular with Cajun chefs and also Cajun food lovers, these shops sell gourmet food, cookware, and accessories, as well as Louisiana collector's items. For information and directions, call the Southwest Louisiana/Lake Charles Convention and Visitors Bureau. | Hodges St. | 337/436–9588, 800/456–7952. | fax 337/494–7952 | www.visitlakecharles.org.

Creole Nature Trail Scenic Byway. This route takes you on 180 mi of black-topped roads through the bayous of Southwest Louisiana to the Gulf of Mexico. For information and a map, call the Southwest Louisiana/Lake Charles Convention and Visitors Bureau. | Off I–10 on highway 397 on the eastern outskirts of town | 337/436–9588, 800/456–7952 | fax 337/494–7952 | www.visitlakecharles.org, www.creolenaturetrail.org | Daily.

Delta Downs Racetrack. Enjoy the action and excitement of live thoroughbred and quarter horse racing, and video poker too. | U.S. 3063 in Vinton | 800/737–3358 (reservations), 337/433–3206 (in Lake Charles), 337/589–7441 (in Vinton) | www.deltadowns.com | $1.50 | Jan.-June; Racing times: Thurs.–Sat. 6:15, Sun. 1:15.

Imperial Calcasieu Museum. The museum is on the site of a cabin built by Charles Sallier, the first European settler in the area. Exhibits show you what life was like from 1850–1900. Exhibits include complete rooms and shops, and there is also an art gallery. A live oak tree on the grounds is more than 300 years old. | 204 W. Sallier St. | 337/439–3797 | fax 337/437–6040 | $2 | Tues.–Sat. 10–5.

Players Island Casino. This hotel, casino, and entertainment complex features a buffet for the players. | 507 Lakeshore Dr. | 337/437–1500, 800/977–7529 | fax 337/437–6021 | www.harrahs.com | Free | Daily 24 hours.

Sabine National Wildlife Refuge. This is the largest and most accessible of four federally supervised sanctuaries around the Creole Nature Trail. It includes a 1½-mi Marsh Trail. | Off U.S. 27 S, Hackberry | 337/762–3816 | fax 337/762–3780 | www.fws.gov | Daily dawn to dusk.

Sam Houston Jones State Park. This park offers a variety of hiking trails, along with boat rentals, fishing, picnic areas, cabins, and facilities. | Rte. 378 | 337/855–2665, 888/677–7264 | fax 337/217–3526 | $2 per car | Daily dawn to dusk.

ON THE CALENDAR

FEB.–MAR.: *Lake Charles Mardi Gras.* Smaller than its New Orleans cousin but still very lively, this Mardi Gras celebration takes place on the Tuesday before Ash Wednesday. | 337/436–9588, 800/456–7952.

MAY: *Contraband Days.* During the first two weeks in May, the city returns to the rollicking days of the pirates and buccaneers who once sailed the area's waterways. This twelve-day extravaganza features scores of games, musical perfomances, puppet shows, and even a lighted boat parade. | 337/436–9588, 800/456–7952.

JULY: *Cajun Music and Food Festival.* The Cajun French Music Association hosts a two-day fund-raising festival that features an impressive roster of Cajun musicians, Cajun food, arts and crafts, and accordion and dance contests. | 337/436–9588, 800/456–7952.

SEPT.: *Lake Charles Gatorman Triathlon.* An annual triathlon consisting of a 1K swim, a 33K bicycle ride, and a 6K run. | 337/477–7733.

Dining

Aladdin. Mediterranean. | 2009 Enterprise Blvd. | 337/494–0062 | Closed Sun., Mon. No lunch Sat. | $15–$20 | AE, MC, V.

Cafe du Lac. Creole. The suberb Southern breakfast includes grits, bacon, toast, and eggs made to your liking. This quiet, casual cafe has daily lunch specials like smothered steak and potato salad. It is also a popular dinner spot; try the gumbo. | 1214 N. Lakeshore Dr. | 337/439–1510 | 24 hours on Sat. | $7–$23 | AE, D, DC, MC, V.

Café Margaux. French. Think candlelight, soft pinks, white linens, and tuxedoed waiters. This restaurant is known for lobster bisque, rack of lamb, and homemade pastries. | 765 Bayou Pines E. | 337/433–2902 | dcslyntmw@laol.net | Closed Sun. No lunch Sat. | $19–$28 | AE, D, DC, MC, V.

Cajun Tales Seafood. Cajun. This restaurant has a well-earned reputation for crawfish omelettes, crawfish pie, and other cajun dishes. The large dining room is often crowded, be it breakfast, lunch, or dinner time. Go for the excellent dinner entrees like stuffed catfish and desserts like the chocolate pie. | 501 N. Adams | 337/734–4772 | $9–$16 | AE, D, DC, MC, V.

Hunter's Harlequin. Seafood/Steak. This cozy, family-owned restaurant is set in a single-story brick structure on beautifully landscaped grounds. The kitchen serves hearty steak-house fare, such as a seafood platter and prime rib. Kids' menu. | 1717 Rte. 14 | 337/439–2780 | Closed Sun. No lunch Sat. | $25–$30 | AE, MC, V.

Pat's of Henderson. Seafood. Featuring an elegant candle lit dinner, portraits of Louisiana plantation homes in the area, and wood grain with Nautical brass tables, the dining area lies beyond a wooden floored foyer sitting area and candle shop. An oyster bar is also on premise. Popular dishes include stuffed snapper, crawfish, steak, and stuffed lobster. Kids' menu. | 1500 Siebarth Dr. | 337/439–6618 | www.visitlakecharles.org | 25$–$30 | AE, D, DC, MC, V.

Tony's Pizza. Italian. This small, family-owned restaurant is friendly, casual, and welcoming. Italian pictures decorate the walls, and patrons eat at wooden tables. Besides pizza, you can get deli sandwiches and salads. | 335 E. Prien Lake Rd. | 337/477–1611 | www.visit-lakecharles.org | $10–$20 | AE, D, MC, V.

Lodging

Aunt Ruby's Bed and Breakfast. Set in the heart of downtown Lake Charles's historic district, this home was built in 1911 and features period furnishings that give each room an individual character. Riverboat casinos, downtown nightlife, and a charming boardwalk are all within 5 blocks' walk. Complimentary Continental breakfast. Cable TV. | 504 Pujo St. | 337/430–0603 | fax 337/430–0609 | www.auntrubys.com | 6 rooms | $75–$95 | AE, D, MC, V.

Best Western–Richmond Suites. This large modern hotel is 12 mi from Lake Charles Regional Airport, 3 mi from the convention center, and 4 mi from Lake Charles Beach and the riverboat casinos. Complimentary breakfast and newspaper. In-room data ports, some kitchenettes. Cable TV. Pool. Hot tub. Exercise equipment. Playground. Laundry facilities. Business services, airport shuttle. | Hwy. 171 at I–10 | 318/433–5213, 800/643–2582 | fax 337/439–4243 | www.bestwestern.com | 145 rooms | $74–$119 | AE, D, DC, MC, V.

Days Inn. A family-friendly chain hotel 3 mi west of the riverboat casinos. | 147 rooms. Complimentary Continental breakfast. Pool. Some pets allowed. No smoking. | 1010 N. Martin Luther King/Hwy. 171 | 337/433–1711, 800/544–8313 | fax 337/491–9753 | www.daysinn.com | $45–$55 | AE, D, DC, MC, V.

Fairfield Inn by Marriott. On Sulphur's main commercial strip, this contemporary hotel is just five minutes from downtown Lake Charles. The Creole Nature Trail is ½ mi away and the casinos are within 5 mi. An hour's drive takes you to either Lafayette, Louisiana or Beaumont, Texas. In-room data ports. Cable TV. Pool. Laundry service. | I-10 and Ruth St., Sulphur | 337/528–2629, 800/228–2800 | fax 337/528–2629 | www.fairfieldinn.com | 79 rooms | $57–$67 | AE, D, DC, MC, V.

Players Island Hotel. The Players Island Hotel is next to Players Island Casino, so you can enjoy non-stop gaming action and live entertainment while you stay. Five outstanding restaurants are available throughout the 8-acre Player's Island complex, which features lush greenery, waterfalls, and rockscapes. It's less than a mile north of Imperial Calcasieu Museum and 3 or 4 blocks west of downtown restuarants and shopping. Five restaurants, bar. Pool. Free parking. | 505 N. Lakeshore Dr. | 337/437–1500 or 800/977–PLAY | fax 337/437–1612 | 268 rooms, 8 suites | $89–$119 | AE, D, DC, MC, V.

MANDEVILLE

MAP 9, G4

(Nearby towns also listed: Covington, Hammond, New Orleans, Slidell)

Long before the 24-mi Causeway transformed the journey across Lake Pontchartrain into a half-hour drive, Mandeville was a summer resort for New Orleanians, who arrived on steam paddlewheelers. Lakeshore Drive is still lined with their graceful 19th-century vacation houses, and the surrounding streets of the old waterfront neighborhood are filled with colorful cottage gardens and Victorian gingerbread. Today a strong artistic community supports a casual and stylish collection of restaurants, coffeehouses, and nautical taverns. Sailors tie up at the marina or yacht club. Walkers cruise the oak-shaded park along the seawall. Cyclists and horseback riders can hire a mount and head into the deep green seclusion of Tammany Trace, a former railway corridor converted into a paved trail.

Information: New Orleans Northshore St. Tammany Parish Tourist Commission | 68099 Rte. 59, Mandeville, LA 70471 | 504/892–0520, 800/634–9443 | mail@neworleansnorthshore.com | www.neworleansnorthshore.com.

Attractions

Fontainebleau State Park. Enter through the famed oak alley, past the ruins of a sugar mill built in 1829, a plantation, and a brickyard. Bordered on three sides by water (Lake Pontchartrain, Bayou Castine, and Bayou Cane), the 2,800-acre oasis has a beach, sailboat ramp, swimming pool, marked nature trail, picnic facilities, pavilions, overnight camping, and group camps. | U.S. Hwy. 90, Box 8925, 70470 | 504/624–4443, 888/677–3668 | fax 504/624–4444 | www.crt.state.la.us | $2 per vehicle for up to four, 50¢ for each additional passenger | Daily.

Tammany Trace. A century-old rail corridor linking north shore towns from Covington to Slidell is seeing new life as a linear park for cycling, in-line skating, horseback riding, jogging, and walking. The completed 31-mi segment runs from the hub town of Mandeville north to Abita Springs and east to Lacombe. This oak-shaded corridor is 200 ft wide, with a paved pedestrian/bike trail and parallel equestrian trail. It's a quiet pathway that crosses more than 30 bridges through old towns, wetlands, and woodlands. Trailheads with parking, rest rooms, and other facilities are located in or near each of the towns. Bike rentals and horses are available at the Mandeville trailhead. | 21411 Koop Dr., | 504/867–9490, 800/438–7223 | Free | Daily.

ON THE CALENDAR

APR.: *Great Louisiana BirdFest.* Bird watchers travel from several states to join excursions led by experienced local naturalists on the first weekend in April. Also included are workshops on building bird feeders and bat houses, seminars on regional wildlife and Native American culture, plus food, music, and children's activities. | 504/871–9272, 800/634–9443.

JULY: *Mandeville Seafood Festival.* Highlighted at this event around the 4th of July are lakefront food booths, music, and fireworks. | 504/624–9762.

Dining

La Provence. French. Since 1972, regulars have made the drive from surrounding parishes to dine with Provence-born Chris Keragiorgiou in his romantic replica of a French country inn, complete with garden, imported antiques, and fireplaces. Try duck with garlic or à l'orange or rack of lamb with Provençal herbs. The restaurant is on the north shore of Lake Ponchartrain, 3 mi east of Mandeville past the Fountainebleau State Park, and about 45 mi west of from central New Orleans. Sun. brunch. No smoking. | 25020 U.S. 190 E, Big Branch | 504/626–7662 | Closed Mon., Tues. No lunch, except Sun. brunch | $18–$30 | AE, DC, MC, V.

Nuvolari's. Italian. This restaurant is in a beautifully renovated general store, built in 1937, that has a brick exterior, milled mahogany bar, and strings of twinkling white lights. It's two blocks from the historic lakefront in Old Mandeville and has been a local favorite since 1983. Try cioppino, escargots and crawfish tails appetizer, Mediterranean-style shrimp with penne rigate, linguine frutta di mare, or roast duck with cherries and peppercorns. Kids' menu. | 246 Gerard St. | 504/626–5619 | No lunch | $20–$30 | AE, D, DC, MC, V.

Trey Yuen. Chinese. Enter through an elaborate Chinese garden whose winding koi pond, arched bridge, pomegranate trees, and weeping willows are beautifully illuminated after dark. The Wong brothers are nationally known for innovative Asian cuisine that incorporates Louisiana seafood. The restaurant is on the Causeway in Mandeville a ½ mi from the north end of the "Causeway Approach." Try crawfish in spicy lobster sauce, Szechuan alligator, soft shell crab, or honey pecan shrimp. | 600 N. Causeway Blvd., | 504/626–4476 | www.treyyuen.com | No lunch Mon., Tues., Sat. | $12–$20 | AE, D, DC, MC, V.

Lodging

Cozy Corner Guest House. Five blocks from the lakefront, this 100-yr-old cypress cottage is landscaped with a peaceful garden. One room has a queen-size bed, the other a king; both are furnished with antiques. You can borrow bicycles for free. Complimentary breakfast. Cable TV. | 736 Lafayette St., | 504/626–9189 | 2 rooms | $85–$95 | AE, MC, V.

Mildred Fishe Guest Cabin. An offbeat choice, ideal for nature lovers, this wooden cabin is nestled in the trees of the 12,000-acre Big Branch Marsh National Wildlife Refuge, right on Bayou Lacombe, 1½ mi by water to Lake Pontchartrain and 10 mi east of Mandeville. The well-equipped rustic structure has two bedrooms and one bath, a screened porch, full kitchen with supplies, TV, stereo, CD player, telephone. Outside are a boat house, private dock, and fish-cleaning station. Also provided are fishing poles and a canoe and paddles. Kitchen. Cable TV. Dock. No kids under 10. No smoking. | 26545 Mildred Dr., Lacombe | 800/647–1824 | www.bbonline.com/la/mildredfishe | 1 2-bedroom cabin | $95–$120 cabin | MC, V.

Pollyanna. Two bedrooms with private baths share a common sitting area and private entrance on the second floor of this Victorian cottage, built in 1875. The B&B, which has British owners, is in the historic district near Lake Ponchartrain. Outdoors you will find a white picket fence, a porch with swing and rockers, a small water garden, and a weeping willow tree. The house is only one block from the Old Mandeville lakefront, so you can walk to restaurants, antique shops, parks, the marina, and the North Star Theater. Complimentary breakfast. Cable TV. | 212 Lafitte St., | 504/626–4053 | 2 rooms | $85 | No credit cards.

MANY

MAP 9, C3

(Nearby town also listed: Natchitoches)

Many was founded in 1843, named for Colonel John B. Many, who commanded the troops at nearby Fort Jesup, which is now a National Historic Landmark and State Historic Site. The town is a convenient base for exploring the 12,500-acre Sabine Wildlife Management Area and the 4,700 acres of formal plantings and scenic drives at Hodges Gardens.

Information: Sabine Parish Tourist and Recreation Commission | 920 Fisher Rd., Many, LA 71449 | 318/256–5880, 800/358–7802 | www.lapage.com/parishes/sabin. .

Attractions

Fort Jesup State Historic Site. Ft. Jesup was built in 1822 and commanded by Zachary Taylor, who named it after his good friend Brigadier General Thomas Sidney Jesup. Costumed guides take you through this restored fort where American soldiers were stationed in 1845, waiting to invade Mexico. It is 6 mi. east of Many, off Hwy. 6. There is a museum and picnic area. | 32 Geoghagan Rd., | 318/256–4117, 888/677–5378 | Daily 9–5.

Hodges Gardens. This breathtaking horticultural park covers about 4,700 acres, with 70 acres of amazing gardens filled with every flower imaginable. Over 20 mi of trails for hiking, biking, and horseback riding wind through the park, and a 225-acre lake offers boating and bass fishing. Hodges Gardens holds special holiday events on Easter, Fourth of July, and in December. | U.S. 171 near Florien, | 318/586–3523, 800/354–3523 | www.hodges-park.com | $6.50 Feb.–Aug., $5 Sept.–Jan.; special rates for children | Daily 8–4:30.

Los Adaes State Historic Site. Los Adaes is the 14-acre site of a Spanish outpost built in 1719 that was the capital of the Province of Texas from 1729 to 1772. Exhibits include displays of archaeological findings. It is 13 mi northeast of Many. | Rte. 485, Robeline | 888/677–5378 | Free | Daily 9–5.

Louisiana Long Leaf Lumber Co. This building, which now houses a very nice flea market (antiques and collectibles), was built in 1899 in Fisher's town square. "Silk-stocking row" includes the Fisher Commissary Flea Market and Coffee Shop, the opera house, an office building, a post office, and several homes. Boise Cascade bought the property in 1966 and now maintains it under the eye of the historical society. In May, the Fisher Sawmill Days Festival is held in the square. | Fisher Sq., Fisher | 318/586–0057 | Free | Wed.–Sat. 10–5, closed Sun.–Tues.

Toledo Bend Dam and Reservoir. Said to be the number one bass fishing lake in the state, Toledo Bend is also a prime spot for watersports. The 186,000-acre reservoir is man-made with 1,200 mi. of shoreline. Gamefish population is 300 lbs of fish per acre. The Sabine River Authority Welcome Center, located at the base of the Pendelton Bridge on Rte. 6, provides a free map of the area that points out interesting sights. Camping, Olympic-size pool, picnic areas, playground. | Just outside Zwolle off Rte. 171, Sabine Parish | 318/645–4715, 800/259–LAKE | www.toledo-bend.com | Sabine River Welcome Center: Daily 8–4:30.

ON THE CALENDAR

APR.: *Battle of Pleasant Hill Re-Enactment.* This two-day event includes a Confederate ball and a re-creation of the critical 1864 battle to repel Union forces intent on capturing Shreveport. (Confederate resistance ultimately prevented the Yankees from accomplishing this goal.) Held on weekend closest to the 6th, which is when the battle actually occurred. | 800/358–7802 or 318/796–2777.

MAY: *Fisher Sawmill Days.* Held the 3rd weekend in May, this festival celebrates one of Louisiana's last sawmill towns with music, crafts, horse and wagon rides, and lumberjack skill contests. | Village Square, Fisher | | 800/358–7802, 318/256–6263.

OCT: *Zwolle Tamale Festival.* The Zwolle School grounds play host to a huge local gathering on the second weekend of every October. Learn how to make tamales, watch the parade, and listen to live music. Arm-wrestling and wood-chopping contests are annual events. | 318/645–6988.

NOV.: *Sabine Free State Festival.* This festival commemorates the time (1806–1822) when the area was a Free State located between Spanish land and the United States. Shoot-out skits provide comedy, and there are trail rides, street dances, beauty pageants, a flea market, and food. Regional crafts such as basket-weaving and quilting are also celebrated at this festival held the first weekend of the month. | 318/256–2068.

Dining

Pearl's. Soul. The all-you-can-eat buffet at this modest-size lunch spot changes daily, but you can count on chicken and dumplings, pork chops, collard greens, and black-eyed peas. If you are a fish lover, try the fried catfish with hush puppies. | 642 San Antonio Ave., | 318/256–5508 | Closed Sat. No supper | $6–$14 | AE, D, MC, V.

Lodging

Cypress Bend Golf Course and Resort. Many rooms in this modern luxury three-story hotel overlook the lake, woods, or golf course. Fishing and golf packages available. 2 restaurants. In-room data ports, refrigerators. Cable TV. Indoor-outdoor pool. 18-hole golf course. Conference center. | 2000 Cypress Bend Pkwy. | 877/519–1500, 318/590–1500 | www.cypress-bend.com | 67 | $119–$169 | AE, D, DC, MC, V.

Emerald Hills Motel and Golf Resort. This resort, which is across from Hodges Gardens and near the Toledo Bend Reservoir, is 15 mi south of Many. It features a championship 18-hole golf course, and golf packages are available. You can choose among rooms, suites, or condominiums that have full kitchens and decks overlooking the golf course. The brown wooden buildings are set in the trees of the Kisatchie National Forest. Restaurant, bar. 2 pools. 18-hole golf course, putting green. | 42618 Rte. 171 S, Florien | 800/533–5031 | www.emeraldhillsresort.com | 103 rooms, 7 suites, 6 condominiums | $75 rooms, $110 suites, $165 condos | AE, D, DC, MC, V.

Lakeview Lodge Resort. All of these comfortable cabins are directly on the lake in a rustic setting 9 mi from Many with lots of trees for shade. Professional fishing guides are available, as well as golf packages for play at the Cypress Bend Resort course. One-bedroom cabins sleep up to 4, 2-bedroom cabins up to 8 people. There is a banquet room with catering. Kitchenettes, microwaves, refrigerators. Cable TV. Pool, lake. Boating. Playground. Pets allowed (fee). | 1558 Matthews Lodge Rd. | 318/256–9261, 888/445–9266 | www.lakeviewldg.com | 9 cabins | $65–$100 | MC, V.

Siesta Motel. This 1960s economy motel is on the edge of town, about 25 mi from I–49. Several restaurants are directly across the street, and it's a 20-min drive to Toledo Bend Lake. Cable TV. | 295 Fisher Rd. | 318/256–2005 | 24 rooms | $35 | AE, D, MC, V.

METAIRIE

MAP 9, G5

(Nearby towns also listed: Jean Lafitte, Kenner, New Orleans)

Metairie, which got its name from the French term for "small leased farms," was once a prosperous agricultural district. Today it is a busy suburb of New Orleans and the gateway to more distant bedroom communities, via the 24-mi Causeway that crosses Lake Pontchartrain to Mandeville on the north shore. In addition to modern shopping malls and upscale restaurants, you can still find a corner of scruffy old charm in the lakefront neighborhood known as Bucktown, which is scattered with noisy seafood eateries overlooking a small fishing harbor.

Information: Jefferson Parish Department of Tourism and Community Affairs | 1221 Elmwood Park Blvd., Suite 1006, Jefferson, LA 70123 | 504/736–6417 or 877/572–7474 | info@jptourism.com | www.jptourism.com.

Attractions

Lake Pontchartrain Causeway. The world's longest over-water bridge crosses 610-square-mi Lake Pontchartrain between Metairie and Mandeville, a 24-mi cruise by car. The first span was completed in 1956; the second was added in 1969. During summer months, up to 200,000 purple martins roost under the southbound span on the Metairie side. Every evening at sundown, crowds gather along the observation deck to watch the enormous black cloud of birds swooping under the bridge en masse, an amazing show. | $1.50 per car | Daily.

ON THE CALENDAR

OCT.: *Jeff Fest.* Live music from major national and local bands is presented on three stages, and there are food booths featuring savory Louisiana cuisine, children's activities, and arts and crafts. | 504/888–2900.

Dining

Andrea's. Italian. Pastel walls, gilt-framed paintings, and crystal chandeliers impart a romantic yet formal feeling to this restaurant in a ranch-style low-ceilinged brick home set with other small businesses in a primarily residential neighborhood. It's a local favorite, especially for fresh seafood dishes. Chef Andrea Apuzzo often presents special menus devoted to various Italian provinces, complete with regional wines. Try stuffed eggplant crabmeat cake, swordfish steamed in olive oil, tomato, olives, garlic, and capers, or crabmeat ravioli sautéed in onions, garlic and herbs. Kids' menu. Sun. champagne brunch with live music. | 3100 19th St. | 504/834–8583 | No lunch Sat. | $15–$22 | AE, D, DC, MC, V.

Byblos. Middle Eastern. You will find hummus, baba ghanouj, moussaka, and stuffed grape leaves at this Lebanese restaurant just north of town. The main course kebabs, especially the chicken and beef, are juicy and flavorful. Pleasantly seasoned rice accompanies most entrées, and the custard desserts are very good. | 1501 Metairie Rd. | 504/834–9773 | Closed Sat. | $8–$16 | AE, D, DC, MC, V.

Charley G's Seafood Grill. Cajun/Creole. The crabcakes and chicken-and-sausage gumbo impress even the most critical local connoisseurs. Not only does the menu have some of the best Creole-Cajun food around, but the wine list is also superb. | Heritage Plaza Bldg., 2nd level, 111 Veterans Blvd. | 504/837–6408 | No lunch Sat. | $8.50–$21 | AE, D, DC, MC, V.

Crozier's Restaurant Français. French. Dark woods and gleaming brass transform this modern storefront in a strip shopping mall into a cozy Parisian bistro. You can start with typical French fare such as escargots or duck pâté, and then try coq au vin, veal sweetbreads sautéed in butter, Dover sole meunière, Chauteaubriand for two, or filet mignon topped with a brandy cream mustard sauce. Kids' menu. | 3216 W. Esplanade N | 504/833–8108 | Closed Sun. No lunch Sat. | $16–$29 | AE, D, DC, MC, V.

Impastato's. Italian. Sedate and traditional, this restaurant is very popular with locals. Beneath stained glass windows, you can dine on such Italian classics such as veal parmigiano and homemade pastas with alfredo. Also popular are the prime ribs, ribeye, and lobster specialties. Live entertainment is nightly. Early bird suppers. Kids' menu. | 3400 16th St. | 504/455–1545 | Closed Sun., Mon. No lunch | $25–$40 | AE, MC, V.

CITIES OF THE DEAD

Cemeteries in Southern Louisiana are a graceful solution to deep trouble: How do you bury people 6 ft underground if the mourners are standing below sea level? Soon after any digging began, most graves would be awash. This was yet another strange challenge for early settlers to overcome. After hurricanes and yellow fever epidemics, even death brought no peace. Coffins had to be drilled with holes so they would fill with water as they were pushed below ground with long poles. It was an unpleasant spectacle for the loved ones, especially during the rainy season, when it was not uncommon for late citizens to rise back up through the mud—or even to float down a flooded street.

Raised tombs were the answer, a regional tradition that has produced thousands of utilitarian structures and architectural masterpieces that are crowded along mazes of ancient streets and sidewalks in the state's celebrated "cities of the dead."

The oldest tombs are in the New Orleans complexes that border the French Quarter, known as St. Louis Cemeteries Numbers One and Two. Beyond the Orleans Parish line, Lake Lawn Metairie Cemetery is the most spectacular, an extravaganza of miniature cathedrals, pagodas, pyramids, mosques, and temples that's on the National Register of Historic Places. Other cemeteries are spread throughout the region, from stately oak-shaded parks to remote whitewashed churchyards. The best time to visit is on November 1, All Saint's Day, when custom dictates that survivors meet to scrub and decorate their family tombs.

© Corbis

India Palace. Indian. This restaurant in a contemporary suburban building has comfortable, spacious dining areas brightened by exotic fabrics and Eastern art. Service is genial, and there's a lavish brunch buffet on weekends. Specialties include lamb *moghlai korma* (a mild almond curry), fried shrimp in a mint and cilantro marinade, and tandoori chicken roasted in a traditional clay oven. Weekday lunch buffet. Sat. and Sun. brunch. No smoking. | 3322 N. Turnball Dr. | 504/889–2436 | $12–$20 | AE, D, DC, MC, V.

La Riviera. Italian. This restaurant in a modern suburban building has walls splashed with murals of the Italian Riviera, antique hand-painted chandeliers from Florence, and white over peach table linens. Chef Goffredo Fraccaro makes his own pasta and spikes dishes with herbs from his garden. He's been cooking since 1969, and his cuisine has a devoted local following. His signature dish is crabmeat ravioli; veal, calamari, and red snapper are also popular. The staff speaks Spanish, French, and Italian in additional to English. Kids' menu. Early dinners 5:30–6:30. | 4506 Shores Dr. | 504/888–6238 | www.larivierarestaurant.com | Closed Sun. and Sept. 1–8. No lunch Mon., Sat. | $12–$20 | AE, D, DC, MC, V.

Morning Call. Café. Gleaming dark wood cabinets, paneling, and furniture, mirrors, and bright lights from the historic French Market coffee stand were relocated in 1974 to this suburban shopping strip across from the Lakeside Shopping Center. Famous *beignets* (French doughnuts with powdered sugar) and café au lait made with rich New Orleans chicory coffee are served. | 3325 Severn Ave. | 504/885–4068 | Open 24 hours | $1–$5 | No credit cards.

Lodging

Best Western Landmark. This high-rise on I–10 (Exit 228) is across the street from some restaurants, around the corner from others. It's 2 blocks from the Lakeside Shopping Center and Lake Pontchartrain Causeway, 2 blocks from the Mardi Gras parade route, and 10 minutes by car from downtown New Orleans. Free French Quarter shuttles are available. The hotel, built in the 1970s, has a rooftop bar and cafe. Restaurant, bar (with entertainment). Microwaves (in suites), refrigerators (in suites). Cable TV. Pool. Sauna. Exercise equipment. Laundry service. Business services, airport shuttle, free parking. | 2601 Severn Ave. | 504/888–9500, 800/277–7575 | fax 504/885–8474 | www.bestwestern.com | 331 rooms, 11 suites | $109–$129; suites, $150–$250 | AE, D, DC, MC, V.

Courtyard Inn by Marriott This six-story hotel built in 1999 has several rooms with balconies. It is 6 mi from New Orleans's French Quarter, and 1 mi from restaurants and the Lakeside Mall. Restaurant, bar. Cable TV. Pool. Laundry service. | 2 Galleria Blvd. | 504/838–3800 | 153 rooms | $109–$139 | AE, D, DC, MC, V.

Doubletree-Lakeside. This contemporary high-rise with glass exterior is about ¼ mi from restaurants. The Lake Pontchartrain Causeway and a bike path are directly behind the hotel. It's also only 10 minutes from downtown New Orleans, and there's a complimentary shuttle to the French Quarter. Restaurant, bar, room service. In-room data ports, refrigerators (in suites). Cable TV. Indoor pool. Beauty salon, hot tub, massage, sauna. Tennis. Basketball, gym. Laundry service. Business services, airport shuttle. | 3838 N. Causeway Blvd. | 504/836–5253, 800/222–8733 | fax 504/846–4562 | www.doubletreelakeside.com | 210 rooms, 12 suites | $129–$199, $174–$200 suites | AE, D, DC, MC, V.

Hampton Inn Metairie. This clean, contemporary, five-story hotel is three blocks from the restaurants and bars. It is 7 mi from the airport and 7 mi from New Orleans. Free shuttle service gets you downtown. Complimentary Continental breakfast. Pool. Exercise equipment. Laundry service. | 2730 N. Causeway | 504/831–7676, 800/426–7866 | fax 504/8317478 | www.hamptoninn.com | 110 rooms | $149 | AE, D, DC, MC, V.

Holiday Inn. This four-story hotel in the heart of Metairie's business district was built around 1970. It's just off I–10, about 10 min from downtown New Orleans, and 1 mi from the Lakeside Shopping Center. Restaurants are about 2 mi from the hotel in all directions. Shuttles to the airport, shopping mall, and movies are available. Restaurant, bar, room service. In-room data ports. Cable TV. Pool. Exercise equipment. Laundry service. Business services, airport shuttle, free parking. | 3400 I–10S Service Rd. | 504/833–8201, 800/465–4329 | fax 504/838–6829 | www.holiday-inn.com | 195 rooms | $90–$120 | AE, D, DC, MC, V.

Holiday Inn I–10. At this seven-story hotel with a marble lobby, some rooms have a view of the landscaped courtyard and pool. The hotel is 3 mi from the airport and 15 min from downtown New Orleans. Restaurants and the Esplanade Mall are less than 5 mi west. Restaurant, bar, room service. In-room data ports. Cable TV. Pool. Hot tub. Exercise equipment. Laundry service. Business services, airport shuttle, free parking. | 6401 Veterans Memorial Blvd. | 504/885–5700, 800/465–4329 | fax 504/454–8294 | www.holiday-inn.com | 220 rooms | $89–$129 | AE, D, DC, MC, V.

La Quinta. In-room VCRs at this three-story motel offer Nintendo games. Near I–10's exit 225, the hotel is 5 mi from the airport and several restaurants and 15 min from downtown New Orleans. Esplanade Mall and Treasure Chest Casino are 4 mi east. Complimentary Continental breakfast. In-room data ports. Cable TV. Pool. Laundry service. Business services, airport shuttle, free parking. Some pets allowed. | 5900 Veterans Memorial Blvd. | 504/456–0003, 800/687–6667 | fax 504/885–0863 | www.laquinta.com | 153 rooms | $79–$99 | AE, D, DC, MC, V.

Orleans Courtyard Hotel. This two-story hotel is a 15-min drive from downtown New Orleans and about 4 blocks from the Lakeside Shopping Mall and restaurants. Indoor or outdoor entrances to rooms. Complimentary Continental breakfast. Cable TV. Pool. | 3800 Hessmer Ave. | 504/455–0940 | 52 rooms | $125 | AE, D, MC, V.

Quality Hotel. This contemporary high-rise on I–10 at exit 228 is a 10-min drive from downtown New Orleans (there's also a shuttle to the French Quarter). Restaurants and the Lakeside Shopping Mall are 1/2 mi from hotel, and the Causeway is right next to it. The Jazz Festival and the Fairgrounds are 5 mi southeast. Restaurant, bar, room service. In-room data ports, some microwaves. Cable TV. Pool. Exercise equipment. Laundry facilities. Business services, airport shuttle, free parking. Some pets allowed. | 2261 N. Causeway Blvd. | 504/833–8211, 800/228–5151 | fax 504/833–8213 | www.qualityinn.com | 204 rooms | $79–$129 | AE, D, DC, MC, V.

MINDEN

MAP 9, C1

(Nearby towns also listed: Bossier City, Ruston, Shreveport)

Minden was settled circa 1837 and is still graced by several antebellum houses, mostly private residences not open to the public. However, you can tour the restored historic structures at the nearby Germantown Colony and Museum, founded in 1836 as a communal village by immigrant members of the Utopian Movement who were seeking religious freedom. Minden is also a convenient base for exploring the Caney Lakes region of Kisatchie National Forest.

Information: **Webster Parish Tourist Commission** | 110 Sibley Rd., Box 819, Minden, LA 71058 | 318/377–4240, 800/264–6336 | suegruber@minden.org | www.minden.org.

Attractions

Germantown Colony and Museum. In the early 19th century, a group of German immigrants in search of religious freedom settled 7 mi northeast of Minden and lived there for almost forty years as a commune. Three buildings on one acre of the colony have been preserved from 1835. They include a cabin once occupied by the Countess von Leon, the kitchen-dining hall, and the Goentgen cottage. | Parish Rd. 114 | 318/377–6061 | $3, special rates for children | Wed–Sat. 9–5, Sun. 1–6, closed Mon.–Tues.

Lake Bistineau State Park. This park is in a forest of pine, cypress, and tupelo trees about 18 mi southwest of Minden. It has two boat launches, hiking trails, playgrounds, two pools, a baseball field, largemouth bass fishing, cabins, lodges, and camping and trailer sites. Camp-sites cost $12. The lake is dam-controlled and has a surface area of 27 square mi. | 103 State Park Rd., Doyline | 318/745–3503, 888/677–2478 | $2 | Daily.

Minden Historic District. Take a moment to drive through Minden's historic residential district just north of downtown, which includes 71 properties. Directions to the homes, as well as brief descriptions of the buildings, are available at the Webster Parish Tourist Commission. | 110 Sibley Rd. | 318/377–4240, 800/264–6336 | www.minden.org.

ON THE CALENDAR

MAY–AUG.: *Minden Rodeo.* A 40-yr tradition. Every Friday at 8 PM there's bull and steer riding, barrel racing, breakaway and team roping, and goat throwing/tying. Located 10 mi south of Minden. | 318/377–6787, 800/264–6336.

DEC.: *Candlelight Tour.* The first weekend in December, tours of several homes and churches are given in Minden's Historic District. | 800/264–6336.

Dining

Country Place. American. Come here for great desserts, especially the banana-blueberry pie. Antique clocks and red-checkered tablecloths give the room country charm. The daily buffet has hot-water corn bread, three meats, and eight vegetables. | 1302 Country Club Circle | 318/377–8398 | Closed Sat. and Sun. No dinner Mon.–Wed. | $5.50–$6.50 | Cash only.

Lodging

Best Western Minden Inn. This two-story hotel opened in 1997. It's 2 mi from downtown at the intersection of I–20 and Hwy. 7 (Exit 47). A 24-hr restaurant is across the street. Complimentary Continental breakfast. In-room dataports, some microwaves, some refrigerators. Pool. Hot tub. Exercise equipment. Laundry facilities. Business services. Some pets allowed. | 1411 Sibley Rd. | 318/377–1001 | www.bestwestern.com | 40 rooms | $55–$73 | AE, D, DC, MC, V.

Exacta Inn–Minden. This one-story hotel is near I–20 and 1½ mi from downtown Minden. The Louisiana Downs Racetrack and casinos are about 30 min away. Restaurant, complimentary breakfast. Cable TV. Pool. | 1404 Sibley Rd. | 318/377–3200 | 62 rooms | $48 | AE, D, MC, V.

MONROE/WEST MONROE

MAP 9, D2

(Nearby towns also listed: Bastrop, Epps, Ruston)

Monroe is an attractive college town, home to Northeast Louisiana University and a thriving community of visual and performing artists. You'll find a fine collection of small museums, galleries, historic houses, gardens, and parks. The land along the Ouachita River (variously translated as "silver water," "clear water," or "good hunting") was originally settled by a Native American tribe of the same name. In 1790 Spanish colonists established Fort Miro, which was incorporated as a city in 1819 and named for the *James Monroe,* the first steamboat to ascend the Ouachita River and open trade by water with the cotton markets of New Orleans. The discovery of the Monroe Gas Field in 1919, followed by the growth of the paper industry in the 1920s, made this agricultural center one of the state's industrial leaders as well. Today the "twin cities" of Monroe and West Monroe are the commercial hub of northeast Louisiana.

Information: **Monroe-West Monroe Convention and Visitors Bureau** | 1333 State Farm Dr., Box 6054, Monroe, LA 71211 | 318/387–5691, 800/843–1872 | mwmcvb@centuryinter.net | www.bayou.com/visitors.

Attractions

Antique Alley. Over 20 dealers sell their treasures amid a collection of art galleries and eateries. | 200–300 Trenton St., West Monroe | Tues.–Sat. 10–5, some shops open Sun., Mon.

D'Arbonne National Wildlife Refuge. This 17,400-acre refuge on D'Arbonne Bayou is predominantly bottomland hardwoods which are managed for migratory birds and resident wildlife. The upland habitat is managed for the endangered red-cockaded woodpecker. Opportunities for hunting, fishing, birding, and hiking. | On Rte 143, 7 mi NW of Monroe | 318/726–4222 | Free | Daily 7:30–4:30.

Emy-Lou Biedenharn Foundation. The foundation includes three sites: the Bible Museum, which exhibits rare Bibles and other artifacts; the Elsong Garden and Conservatory; and the Biedenharn family house built in 1914 by the first bottler of Coca-Cola, Joseph Biedenharn. The formal gardens are adorned with fountains linked by winding paths. The house contains 18th-century furnishings and antiques and Coca-Cola memorabilia. | 2006 Riverside Dr., Monroe | 318/387–5281 | Free | Tues.–Fri. 10–4, weekends 2–5, closed Mon.

Kiroli Park. The entrance to 126-acre Kiroli Park, framed by tiers of flower beds, beckons you in to enjoy nature trails, paved jogging paths, and a fishing pond. Facilities include tennis courts, a lodge, playgrounds, an amphitheater, and rest rooms. There's a Christmas lighting and display in December. | 800 Kiroli Rd., W. Monroe | 318/396–4016 | 50¢ | April–Oct., daily 7 AM–9 PM; Nov.–Mar., daily 7 AM–8 PM.

Louisiana Purchase Gardens and Zoo. This zoo, set on 82 acres a few blocks west of Rte. 165S, contains a primate house, reptile house, big cat collection, birds of the world, and more. Ride the Delta swamp on a Bayou Safari to see the rhinos and zebras. You can also visit the gift shop or take part in one of many special events the zoo sponsors. | Bernstein Park Dr., Monroe | 318/329–2400 | www.ci.monroe.la.us/zoo | $3.25; special rates for children and senior citizens | 10–5 daily.

Masur Museum of Art. This gallery is housed in a modified English Tudor–style building and showcases a collection of paintings, graphics, sculpture, and photographs. The permanent collection is primarily contemporary art. Traveling exhibits are displayed throughout the year. Masur Museum also offers art classes. | 1400 S. Grand St., Monroe | 318/329–2237 | www.ci.monroe.la.us/mma | Free | Tues.–Thurs. 9–5, Fri.–Sun. 2–5, closed Mon.

Northeast Louisiana Delta African-American Heritage Museum. This museum contains historical artifacts and documents, as well as an art collection. It's sometimes listed as the Ouachita African Museum. | 503 Plum St. | 318/323–1167 | $2, special rates for children | Tues.–Sat. 9–1, 2–5, closed Sun.–Mon.

University of Lousisana at Monroe. Bayou DeSiard flows through this tree-shaded, 238-acre campus, which was founded in 1931. Annual enrollment is 9,000 undergraduate and 1,000 graduate students. | 700 University Ave., 3601 Desiard St., Monroe | 318/362–4672, 800/372–5127 | www.nlu.edu | Free | Daily.
Bry Hall Art Gallery The gallery presents art exhibits and photographs by international artists and also by students and faculty. | Free | Mon.–Fri. 8–8; closed mid-Aug.–early Sept., mid-Dec.–early Jan.
Museum of Natural History Displays emphasize Native American and South American artifacts. | 3rd floor of Hanna Hall | Free | Mon.–Fri. 8–4:30; closed mid-Aug.–early Sept., mid-Dec.–early Jan.
Museum of Zoology This museum displays technical research collections, specimens, and Native American artifacts. | 1st floor of Garret Hall | By appointment only Mon.–Fri.; closed mid-Aug.–early Sept., mid-Dec.–early Jan.

ON THE CALENDAR

JULY: *Louisiana Watermelon Festival.* You'll find a watermelon auction at this event, as well as eating and seed-spitting contests. There's also a parade, a street dance, a pageant, a treasure hunt, and lots of food and music. | 318/368–0044.

MONROE/WEST
MONROE

INTRO
ATTRACTIONS
DINING
LODGING

SEPT.: *Louisiana Folklife Festival.* A massive celebration of all the cultures that have contributed to the state and how they cook, tell stories, and create crafts and art. In addition, three music stages offer everything from blues to bluegrass, from Celtic to zydeco. | 318/387–5691, 800/843–1872.

SEPT.: *Southern Pickin' & Ginnin' Festival.* Actors in historical costumes stroll the grounds and reenact historical events on three stages. There's live music and more than 200 vendors. | 318/728–4127.

Dining

Chateau. Italian. This large restaurant features three dining rooms, lavishly decorated in Italianate style with lovely chandeliers and romantic candlelight. The kitchen serves a wide array of traditional and modern cuisine, from pasta to po'-boys, steak to swordfish. Italian seafood combinations include fettucine with sautéed crab and baked redfish with marinara sauce, onions, and shrimp. Or try seafood gumbo, red beans and rice, rib eyes, veal Parmesan, or shrimp Creole. Private rooms. Entertainment Fri., Sat. | 2007 Louisville Ave., Monroe | 318/325–0384 | Closed Sun. | $11–$30 | AE, D, MC, V.

Danken Trail Barbecue. Barbecue. This large, no frills barbecue establishment serves up five types of meat. Select from chicken, ribs, beef, sausage, and ham, served as plate dinners with vegetable and potato side items. Near Northeastern Louisiana University. | 7702 DeSiard St. | 318/343–0773 | Reservations not accepted | Closed Sun. | $4–$7 | AE, D, MC, V.

Garden District Cafe. Contemporary. This café on Old Hwy. 80, six blocks east of the Ouachita River Bridge, is in a 75-yr-old house. Three different rooms are used for dining. The lounge features a 100-yr-old Tiger Mahogany bar purchased from a saloon in Oklahoma. Tables are set with white linen, silver, china and votive candles, and fresh flowers at lunch. A dinner favorite is duck, served stuffed with prosciutto, veal, and portobello mushrooms. Other entrées include crab cakes, veal chops, lamb, steaks (Angus tenderloin and prime), and fresh fish. If you like martinis, there are 15 types to choose from and 10 different kinds of olives. For dessert, go for the bread pudding. | 605 Louisville Ave. | 318/387–1414 | No lunch Sat. Closed Sun.–Mon. | $15–$30 | AE, D, MC, V.

Rialto Cafe. American/Casual. This small, New Orleans–style café is in the Antique Alley district across from the Rose Lee Inn. Kids' meals are half-portions and half the price of adult meals. The food follows the locally popular SugarBuster's diet created by a New Orleans physician. This means it is prepared without sugar, and white pastas and breads are replaced with whole wheat products. The health-oriented eating includes sandwiches, soups, salads, pasta, quiche, and quesadillas. Herbal teas and specialty coffee drinks are also served. | 319 Trenton St., W. Monroe | 318/323–5004 | Reservations not accepted | Open 9–3. Closed Sun.–Mon. No dinner | $4–$7 | D, MC, V.

Sixth Street Grille. Continental. The menu varies greatly, and lunch may include London broil, shrimp Lafitte, steak Diane, and sometimes a seafood or country buffet. At night, live jazz music and the bar are the focus. Casual American fare is currently served in the evenings, but there are plans to add a full restaurant for dinner. Antique moldings and colorful murals add spice to the environment. Live music Tues.–Sat. | 1026 N. 6th St. Monroe | 318/323–0010 | $10–$20 | AE, MC, V.

Warehouse No. 1. Seafood. A restored cotton warehouse on the levee overlooking the Ouachita River offers a range of Louisiana seafood such as fried catfish, crawfish étouffée, and blackened fish, as well as steaks, pasta, and chicken dishes. Try their famous hushpuppies (fried cornbread). Open-air dining available on the deck above the river. Kids' menu. | 1 Olive St., Monroe | 318/322–1340 | Closed Sun. No lunch | $8–$30 | AE, D, DC, MC, V.

Waterfront Grill. Seafood. Windows here overlook scenic Bayou DeSiard, and old photographs of the area adorn the walls. The house specialty is catfish DeSiard, served with seasoned breadcrumbs, green onions, Parmesan cheese, mushrooms, and shrimp. You can also get catfish baked, grilled, Cajun-style, or with almonds. Other seafood items include barbecued shrimp, grilled shrimp, and oysters on the half shell. This waterfront spot also serves

Angus steak, pork chops, burgers, po'-boy sandwiches, gumbo, and salads. Kids' menu. | 5201 DeSiard St. | 318/345-0064 | www.waterfrontgrill.com | Closed Sun. | $10–$20 | AE, D, MC, V.

Lodging

Baymont Inn and Suites. Baymont Inns and Suites This three-story inn opened in 1999. Follow exit 114 (Thomas Road) off I–20. It's 3 mi from the Civic Center and 5 mi from Louisiana Purchase Gardens & Zoo and Pecanland Mall. There is no onsite restaurant but there are several restaurant choices within 1/4 mi of the inn. Complimentary Continental breakfast. Some in-room data ports, some microwaves, some refrigerators. Cable TV. Pool. Pets allowed. | 503 Constitution Dr., W. Monroe | 318/387-2711, 800/301-0200 | fax 318/324-1143 | www.baymontinn.com | 68 rooms, 9 suites | $55–$65, $75–$85 suites | AE, D, DC, MC, V.

Best Western Airport Inn. This two-story hotel with a peach-colored exterior and outside entrances is 1 mi from the Monroe airport, 2 mi from Northeastern University, and 1 mi from Pecanland Mall. Restaurants are just across the Interstate. Complimentary Continental breakfast. In-room data ports, microwaves, refrigerators. Cable TV. Pool. Hot tub. Laundry facilities, laundry service. Pets allowed (fee). | 1475 Gerratte Rd., Monroe | 318/345-4000 | fax 318/345-4455 | www.bestwestern.com | 50 rooms | $54–$70 | AE, D, DC, MC, V.

Civic Center Inn. In the heart of Monroe, near antique stores and the Civic Center, this is an older establishment, with two stories and interior entrances. Most major restaurants are located two exits farther along the Interstate. Cable TV. Pool. | 610 Leajoyner Expy., Monroe | 318/323-4451 | fax 318/323-1728 | 92 rooms | $42–$46 | AE, D, DC, MC, V.

Comfort Suites. This hotel, which opened in 2000, is off I–20, exit 118-A, three mi from Antique Alley, 2 mi from Pecanland Mall, and 5 mi from the Monroe Airport. It's a three-story hotel with interior corridors and an elevator. Complimentary Continental breakfast. In-room data ports, microwaves, refrigerators, some in-room hot tubs. Cable TV. Pool. Hot tub. Exercise equipment. Laundry facilities. Business services. | 1401 Martin Luther King Dr., Monroe | 318/410-1005, 800/228-5150 | fax 318/410-0145 | www.comfortinn.com | 72 rooms | $85–$135 | AE, D, DC, MC, V.

Courtyard by Marriott. This three-story hotel got input on its design from frequent business travelers. It opened in January 2000 at the Pecanland Mall, off I–20, exit 120, about 2 mi from the airport and 3 mi from the Civic Center. In-room data ports, some in-room hot tubs. Cable TV. Indoor pool. Exercise equipment. Free parking. Pets allowed. | 4915 Pecanland Mall Dr., Monroe | 318/388-0034, 800/321-2211 | fax 318/388-1450 | www.courtyard.com | 90 rooms | $79–$129 | AE, D, DC, MC, V.

Days Inn. This two-story hotel, off I–20 at Exit 120 and across from the Pecanland Mall, opened in the mid-1980s. Chain restaurants are about 1/4 mi away. Complimentary Continental breakfast. In-room data ports, microwaves, refrigerators. Cable TV. Pool. Business services. Pets allowed. | 5650 Frontage Rd., Monroe | 318/345-2220, 800/544-8313 | fax 318/343-4098 | www.daysinn.com | 58 rooms | $43–$58 | AE, D, DC, MC, V.

Hampton Inn. The Hampton Inn is 2 mi from the University of Louisiana at Monroe, at the junction of I–20 and Hwy. 165S. Opened in 1994, the two-story hotel has exterior corridors. Several restaurants are available within 1 mi. Complimentary Continental breakfast. In-room data ports, microwaves, refrigerators. Cable TV. Pool. Laundry services. Business services. | 1407 Martin Luther King Dr., Monroe | 318/361-9944, 800/426-7866 | fax 318/322-1785 | www.hamptoninn.com | 69 rooms | $58–$70 | AE, D, DC, MC, V.

Holiday Inn Holidome. This upscale hotel that caters to business travelers is at the crossroads of I–20 and Hwy. 165, 2 mi from the downtown Civic Center, 2 mi east of the airport, and 1 mi from the shopping mall. The on-site restaurant serves Cajun cuisine. In-room access to Nintendo games. Restaurant, bars, room service. In-room data ports. Cable TV. 2 pools (1 indoor), wading pool. Hot tub, saunas. Putting green. Exercise equipment. Video games. Laundry facilities, laundry service. Business services, airport shuttle. | 1051 U.S. Hwy. 165 Bypass,

MONROE/WEST
MONROE

INTRO
ATTRACTIONS
DINING
LODGING

Monroe | 318/387–5100, 800/465–4329 | fax 318/329–9126 | www.basshotels.com | 260 rooms | $89–$109 | AE, D, DC, MC, V.

La Quinta Inn and Suites. This two-story inn is 3 mi from the airport and next door to a 24-hr restaurant. Complimentary Continental breakfast. In-room data ports. Cable TV. Pool. Laundry service. Business services, airport shuttle. Pets allowed. | 1035 U.S. 165 Bypass South, Monroe | 318/322–3900 | fax 318/323–5537 | www.laquinta.com | 130 units | $64–$71 | AE, D, DC, MC, V.

Red Roof Inn. This three-story hotel with white exterior is 9 mi from the airport, 3 mi southwest of downtown Monroe, at exit 114 off I–20. Cable TV. Business services. Pets allowed. | 102 Constitution Dr., West Monroe | 318/388–2420, 800/843–7663 | fax 318/388–2499 | 97 rooms | $49–$4 | AE, D, DC, MC, V.

Rose Lee Inn. This B&B is in the Antique Alley area of West Monroe, in the midst of antique stores, gift shops, and restaurants. The owner, Carolyn Chandler, has her own antique shop on the first floor of this hotel, restored in 1895. The five guest rooms, on the second floor, have antique furnishings, and four of them have claw foot tubs. Complimentary breakfast. Refrigerators. Cable TV. No kids under 6. | 318 Trenton St., W Monroe | 318/322–1990, 318/322–5998 | 5 rooms | $80–$95 | AE, D, MC, V.

Stratford House Inn. This quiet family-run inn, about 1 mi from old downtown Monroe, was opened around 1986. The two-story building has exterior entranceways. Off I–20, Exit 118B. Complimentary Continental breakfast. Cable TV. Business services. | 927 U.S. 165S, Monroe | 318/388–8868, 800/338–9893 | fax 318/322–9893 | 40 rooms | $48 | AE, D, DC, MC, V.

Travelodge. This one-story hotel in a park setting 1 mi east of downtown welcomes both business travelers and families. It was built in 1958. There is a large grass courtyard where children can play. From I–20, take the Bastrop Exit for 165 North. Restaurant, bar, complimentary Continental breakfast. Cable TV. Pool. Laundry service. Business services. Pets allowed. | 2102 Louisville Ave., Monroe | 318/398–0129318/325–5851, 888/515–6375 | fax 318/323–3808 | www.travelodge.com | 98 rooms | $40–$48 | AE, D, DC, MC, V.

MORGAN CITY

MAP 9, E5

(Nearby towns also listed: Franklin, Houma, Thibodaux)

Morgan City is a major hub for regional petroleum, fishing, and shipbuilding industries. However, visitors will also find plenty of architectural charm in the downtown historic district and more than 500,000 acres of unspoiled nature in the Atchafalaya Basin to the north, a living delta through which the Atchfalaya River flows. Swamp tours take you where the wild things are. In fact, the first Tarzan movie (starring Elmo Lincoln) was filmed here in 1917.

Information: Cajun Coast Visitors and Convention Bureau | Box 2332, Morgan City, LA 70381 | 504/395–4905, 800/256–2931 | www.cajuncoast.com.

Attractions

Brownell Memorial Park and Carillon Tower. The centerpiece of this non-denominational devotional park, a 106-ft-tall obelisk, houses 61 bronze bells that chime on the half hour. It is surrounded by a 9½-acre nature retreat in preserved swampland next to Lake Palourde. | 3359 Rte. 70 | 504/384–2283 | Free | Daily 9–5.

International Petroleum Museum and Exposition. Walk aboard an offshore drilling rig turned museum to see the inner workings of the petroleum industry in the Gulf of Mexico. Known as "Mr. Charlie," the historic structure was built in 1952 and retired in 1986. It was the first of its kind, a submersible drilling platform that could be transported from site to site. The 220-ft-long self-contained "industrial island" had living quarters for up to 58 employees. It is still used for training new workers. | 111 First St. | 504/384–3744 | fax 504/384–3743 | www.rigmuseum.com | $5; special rates for senior citizens and children, children under 5 free | Mon.–Sat. 10–2, closed Sun.

Lake End Park. This community recreational park on Lake Palourde has a sand beach, walking trails, playgrounds, a boat launch, and 118 full hookups for campsites. | LA Hwy. 70, 1.5 mi north of Morgan City | 504/380–4623 | fax 504/384–7519 | 50¢/person, $2/car, weekends only | Daily.

Swamp Gardens and Wildlife Zoo. Set in 10 acres of preserved natural swampland, paths and footbridges traverse a deep green forest of cypress trees and murky waters. A small zoo houses penned alligators, a Louisiana black bear, and other wildlife indigenous to the Atchafalaya Basin. A museum set in an Acadian cabin has displays on Cajun culture. Guided walks are available. | 725 Myrtle St. | 504/380–4624 | fax 504/380–4624 | $3; special rates for students, children under 5 free | Daily 10–5.

Cajun Jack's. Jack Hebert's friendly tours go into areas where people still live in the swamp, often stopping for chats with working crawfishermen or crabbers. Tours last 2½ hours, and the covered boat (with rest room facilities on board) takes up to 25 passengers. | 112 Main St., Patterson | 504/395–7420 | fax 504/395–7041 | $20; $10 children under 10 | Daily 9, 2:30, call to confirm tour schedule.

Scully's. A small boat, six passengers maximum, travels the narrow bayous on the southern side of the levee where you're more likely to spot alligators. Bob Scully has more than 10 years of experience as a tour guide in the Atchafalaya Basin. Advance reservations are essential, due to limited space. Tour lasts 2 hours. | 3141 Rte. 70 | 504/385–2388 | $20; special rate for children | Mon.–Sat. 12:30 daily, call to confirm tour schedule.

Turn-of-the-Century House. A small community museum in a white-frame 1906 restored Acadian cottage is home to a colorful collection of Mardi Gras costumes and memorabilia. Other regional artifacts include antique toys, bottles, clothing, and more. | 715 Second St. | 504/380–4651 | fax 504/384–3343 | $3; special rate for students and children | Tues.–Sat. 10–5, Sun. 1–5, closed Mon.

Wedell-Williams Memorial Aviation Museum of Louisiana. A unit of the Louisiana State Museum System, this complex of lofty exhibit spaces incorporates a hangar full of vintage aircraft, including Eisenhower's 1956 Presidential Aerocommander, a 1939 Beechcraft Staggerwing, and a 1940 Stearman Crop Duster. During the roaring '20s, this site was a center for design, construction, and racing of early airplanes. At that time, the airfield was owned and operated by two of America's foremost aviators, Harry P. Williams and James R. Wedell, who broke the world speed record in 1933 when he flew over 305 mph. The museum preserves many artifacts of its namesakes' careers, including airworthy replicas of Wedell's winning racers. Their pioneering company, The Wedell-Williams Air Service Corporation, was bought by Eastern Airlines in 1936. | 394 Airport Circle, Patterson | 504/395–7067, 504/568–6968 | fax 504/395–3179 | www.crt.state.la.us/crt/museum/lsmnet3 | $2; children under 12 free | Tues.–Sat. 10–4, closed Sun.–Mon.

ON THE CALENDAR

SEPT.: *Louisiana Shrimp and Petroleum Festival.* Cajun music and food, a children's village, blessing of the fleet, a rodeo, arts and crafts, and other festivities mark the occasion. | Labor Day weekend | 504/385–0703, 800/256–2931.

NOV., DEC.: *Christmas on the Cajun Coast.* Each year, the town of Morgan City celebrates the holiday season with neighboring towns Franklin and Patterson. Historic homes are decorated with seasonal finery. There are a trail of lights, parades (both on land and water), an arts and crafts show, concerts, and more. Call the Cajun Coast Visitors and Convention Bureau for a detailed schedule and location information. | 800/256–2931.

Dining

Dixie Grill. American. This comfortable family restaurant in the Ramada Inn is known for steaks, barbecue, seafood, and breakfast any time. The Dixie platter lets you sample two of four choices: catfish, shrimp, oysters, or crawfish. The barbecue platter includes chicken, ribs, and shredded beef. Buffet lunch weekdays. Kids' menu. | 7420 Rte. 182 | 504/385–1302 | Breakfast also available | $10–$18 | AE, D, MC, V.

Lodging

Best Western Morgan City Inn and Suites. This two-story hotel is behind a Shoney's restaurant and within two blocks of several other restaurants. It opened in 1999 and is 1½ mi from the Civic Center and the same distance from the local swamp tours. Take the Brashear Ave. exit off Hwy. 90. Complimentary Continental breakfast. In-room data ports, refrigerators. Cable TV. Pool. Hot tub. Laundry services. Business services, free parking. | 1011 Brashear Ave., | 504/385–9175 | fax 504/385–9177 | www.bestwestern.com | 61 rooms | $62–$91 | AE, D, DC, MC, V.

Holiday Inn. This motel is 4 or 5 blocks away from Swamp Gardens and 3 mi from the downtown historic district. The 1973 building has exterior corridors. Restaurant, bar, room service. In-room data ports, some microwaves, some refrigerators. Cable TV. Pool. Hot tub. Exercise equipment. Laundry service. Business services. | 520 Roderick St., | 504/385–2200, 800/465–4329 | fax 504/384–3810 | www.basshotels.com | 219 rooms | $61–$69 | AE, D, DC, MC, V.

Ramada Inn. Only 3 mi from the downtown historic district and a few blocks away from Swamp Gardens, this hotel built in 1975 is a two-story building with exterior corridors. Restaurant, bar, room service. Cable TV. Pool. Laundry service. Pets allowed. | 7408 Hwy. 182, | 504/384–5750, 888/298–2054 | fax 504/385–0224. Website: www.ramada-inn.com | 150 rooms, 3 suites | $65–$70, $85–$90 suites | AE, D, DC, MC, V.

NATCHITOCHES

MAP 9, C3

(Nearby towns also listed: Alexandria, Many)

Natchitoches (pronounced Nack-a-tish) is the oldest settlement in Louisiana. It was founded in 1714 on the Red River to promote commerce between local Native Americans, including the Natchitoches tribe, and Spanish colonists in Mexico. Eventually several overland highways, including the Natchez Trace from the east and El Camino Real from Mexico, met at this important trading post, and Natchitoches became a gateway for covered wagons heading to Texas. During the 1830s the Red River jumped its channel and shifted course about 5 mi east of town, leaving the former steamboat port without a direct outlet to the sea. However, this economic catastrophe created a natural beauty. The cut-off stream that remained, now known as Cane River Lake, meanders for 32 mi through the downtown area and surrounding cotton plantations, past a stellar collection of historic houses and antebellum mansions.

Information: Natchitoches Parish Tourist Commission | 781 Front St., Natchitoches, LA 71457 | 318/352–8072, 800/259–1714 | est1714@cp-tel.net | www.natchitoches.net.

Attractions

★ **Bayou Folk Museum.** The museum is in the Kate Chopin House, the home in the 1880s of the author of *The Awakening*. The house is constructed of heart cypress and handmade bricks and put together with wooden pegs. The museum, which is 20 mi south of Natchitoches, contains memorabilia and first editions of Chopin's works. | 243 Hwy. 495, Cloutierville | 318/379–2233 | $5 | Mon.–Sat. 10–5, Sun. 1–5.

Bayou Pierre Gator Park and Show. A great show for kids and adults. Visit Alligator Island where children can feed gators through feeding chutes while learning about the reptiles' lifestyle through demonstrations and displays. Watch as park owner Terry Rogers feeds the park's biggest gators (800–1,000 lbs) in the Marsh area. There is also a gift shop and a snack shop that features "gator" cuisine. | Old Bayou Pierre Rd off Hwy. 1 North | 318/354–0001 | $5.95 adults, $4.50 ages 3–12, under 3 free | Apr. 15–Oct., daily 10–6; Nov.–Apr 14, closed for hibernation season.

Beau Fort Plantation This handsome home was constructed in the 1880s of hand-hewn cypress and insulated with *bousillage* (a mixture of Spanish moss and mud). The rooms are furnished with family heirlooms and other antiques. Notable is the tall gallery lined with French doors. The house today is a B&B. | Rte. 119, Bermuda | 318/352–5340 | $5 | Daily 1–4.

Fort St. Jean Baptiste State Historic Site. This is a reconstruction of the fort that stood here in 1716. The replicated buildings include a church, powder storehouse, warehouse, barracks, guardhouse, and kitchen, all built using 18th-century hardware and hand-forged iron work. | 130 Morrow St. | 318/357–3101 | Daily 9–5.

Kisatchie National Forest. Kisatchie is an Indian word meaning "long cane." The only national forest in Louisiana, Kisatchie was established in 1930. Its 600,000 acres stretch from the bluffs and mesas of the Red Dirt Area through hardwood and pine forests. It offers over 100 mi of trails for hiking, biking, and horseback riding and over 40 developed recreation areas. Located in seven central and northern LA parishes, the forest is not one large unit but 6 geographically separate ranger districts. Ranger stations are located in Pineville, Boyce, Bentley, Natchitoches, Winfield, and Homer. Family campsites and picnic grounds are available (*See* also Alexandria). 10 mi east of town on U.S. I–84 | 318/473–7160 | www.fs.fed.us/r8/kisatchie | Free | Daily.

Magnolia Plantation. The outbuildings on this plantation include a barn with the only cotton press in the U.S. in its original location. The 27 rooms of the mansion contain an extensive collection of Southern Empire and Louisiana antiques. Already designated a National Bicentennial Farm, it will become part of the projected Cane River Creole National Historical Park. | Off Hwy. 1S, Derry | 318/379–2221 | $5 adults, $4 students, $2 children ages 6-12, children under 6 free | Mon.–Sat. 1–4, closed Sun.

Melrose Plantation. This plantation, a National Historic Landmark, has a fascinating history. Building was begun by Marie Therese Coin-Coin, a freed slave who succeeded in freeing her whole family. This was also the home of Clementine Hunter, sometimes called the black Grandma Moses. Her mural can be seen in the interesting African House, an unusual Congo-style structure on the plantation. Another woman who lived here was Miss Cammy Henry, who hosted and encouraged such writers as Erskine Caldwell, William Faulkner, John Steinbeck, and Alexander Woollcott. | About 20 mi south of Natchitoches, Exit 119 off I–49 | Rte. 119, Melrose | 318/379–0055 | $6 adults, $4 ages 13–17, $3 ages 6–12 | Daily 12–4.

National Fish Hatchery & Aquarium. The aquarium displays native fish. | 615 Hwy. 1S, | 318/352–5324 | Free | Daily 8–3.

National Historic Landmark District. The historic district consists of 33 downtown blocks and includes the Prudhomme–Rogier House. Built in 1906, it is one of the few 2-story bousillage houses in the US, made from a mixture of clay, deer hair, and Spanish moss in a cypress framework. The tourist commission distributes a map of the area and has information about guided tours. | Bordered by College Ave. and Texas St. | 318/352–8072, 800/259–1714 | Free | Daily.

Northwestern State University. On Chaplain Lake, this 916-acre campus is just west of the city. Established in 1884, it offers many degrees and has a current enrollment of about 9,000 students. | College Ave. at end of 2nd St. | 318/357–6361 | Free | www.nsula.edu | Daily.

"Steel Magnolias" and Historic Tour. A self-guided tour available from the Tourist Commission downtown will take you to places seen in the movie "Steel Magnolias," filmed here and at other historic sites in 1988. | 781 Front St., | 318/356–8687, 800/259–1714 | Tours by reservation, Sun.–Tues. 11, 1:30, 4, Wed.–Sat. 9:30, 11, 1, 4, 6 | $7.50 adults, $6.50 senior citizens, $4.50 ages 6-12.

ON THE CALENDAR

APR.: *Louisiana State Fiddlers Championship.* This contest, sponsored by the Office of State Parks, is open to all Louisiana residents and features competition in four age categories. Held the first Saturday in April. | 318/472–6255, 800/259–1714.

APR.: *Natchitoches R&B Festival.* More than 20 bands play continuously on three stages in downtown historic Natchitoches on the banks of the Cane River. | 800/259–1714, 800/737–7311.

JUNE: *Melrose Plantation Arts & Crafts Festival.* More than 150 regional artists and their baskets, pottery, sculpture, and paintings are represented in this juried show held the second weekend of June at this National Historic Landmark. | 800/259–1714.

JULY: *Natchitoches–Northwestern Folk Festival.* Every year a different Louisiana theme is celebrated with dozens of master folk artists, Cajun, zydeco, country, and folk bands, storytellers, and foods on the 3rd weekend of July. | 318/357–4332.

Dining

Almost Home. Southern. This place serves up home-cooking at its lunch buffet. The selection varies daily to include items such as fried pork chops, fried catfish, fried chicken, Cajun rice, chicken and dumplings, and smothered ground steak. Choose one meat and three vegetables; meals come with iced tea and bread. Try the all-you-can-eat seafood buffet on Friday evenings. | Hwy. 1 Bypass, | 318/352–2431 | Breakfast also available. No supper Sun.–Thurs. Closed Sat. | $6–$10 | No credit cards.

The Landing. Cajun. This large, noisy bistro is one of the town's most popular restaurants, offering casual dining in the heart of the historic district. The main dining is downstairs in one large room. Upstairs is used for banquets, and the balcony has a view of the Cane River across the street. The extensive menu includes shrimp rémoulade, potato skins, and fried cheese sticks as starters. Pasta, steak, chicken, and seafood entrées are prepared in a variety of ways. Try the spicy country-fried steak, garlic bread, and bread pudding. Kids' menu. Sun. brunch. | 530 Front St. | 318/352–1579 | Closed Mon. | $12–$22 | AE, MC, V.

Lasyone's Meat Pie Kitchen. Cajun. Natchitoches is famed for its succulent meat pies, and the best place to sample them is this ultracasual country-kitchen café. Well known throughout the state, this family-owned and -run establishment was built in 1859. Other offerings include meat, chicken, red beans and rice, and seafood, and Cane River creme pie for

PACKING IDEAS FOR HOT WEATHER

- ❑ Antifungal foot powder
- ❑ Bandanna
- ❑ Cooler
- ❑ Cotton clothing
- ❑ Day pack
- ❑ Film
- ❑ Hiking boots
- ❑ Insect repellent
- ❑ Rain jacket
- ❑ Sport sandals
- ❑ Sun hat
- ❑ Sunblock
- ❑ Synthetic ice
- ❑ Umbrella
- ❑ Water bottle

*Excerpted from *Fodor's: How to Pack: Experts Share Their Secrets*
© 1997, by Fodor's Travel Publications

dessert. | 622 2nd St. | 318/352–3353 | Breakfast also available. Closed Sun. | $5–$10 | No credit cards.

Mariner's. Southern. Sample the regional specialities, such as bayou beef, or try boiled shrimp, fresh oysters, deep-fried fish, or alligator. You can also get standard steaks, chicken, and salads at this nautical-theme restaurant. There are views of the lake from the dining room. Open-air dining on the patio. Salad bar. Kids' menu. Sun. brunch. | 318/357–1220 | No lunch Mon.–Sat. | $12–$30 | AE, D, MC, V.

Papa's Bar and Grill. American/Casual. This pit grill in the heart of the historic district has always been popular with the locals. The prime draws are the burgers and steaks, including rib eye and filet mignon, and there's also a variety of po'-boy sandwiches (chicken, ham and cheese, shrimp, fish, chicken, and oyster). | 604 Front St. | 318/356–5850 | $6–$15 | AE, D, MC, V.

Pioneer Pub. Creole. This upscale pub and restaurant occupies the oldest building in the downtown historic district. Built in 1830 as a bank, it was the stepping-off point to register your land deeds before heading out west. The downstairs dining tables are set with linen tablecloths and napkins, but you don't have to get too dressed up. The upstairs dining on a wraparound porch, overlooking Cane River and the main streets of town, is used for private functions or during the busy season when the downstairs fills up. Freshness is the focus. Gulf seafood is shipped up twice a week, and the chefs cut their own steaks. Entrées include a variety of steaks and seafood, burgers, steamed shrimp, oysters on the half-shell, sushi, gumbo, étouffée, and other Creole dishes. Daily specials include jerk-style baby back ribs and blackened or grilled red fish. Over 20 international draft beers and a selection of wines. Live music Thurs.–Sat. | 812 Washington St. | 318/352–4884 | fax 318/354–1420 | Reservations not accepted | No lunch weekdays | $7–$16 | AE, D, MC, V.

Lodging

Beaufort Plantation. On the banks of the Cane River, 10 mi south of Natchitoches, the home of Ann and Jack Brittain is a 265-acre working cotton and corn plantation. Built in 1790, the house, with its 84-ft gallery, is approached via a long alley of oak trees. Louisiana Empire and European antiques, including stunning tester beds, blend with other heirlooms that include original Audubon and Clementine Hunter paintings and fascinating 19th-century artifacts. Suites, each with a private entrance, are unusually large—the master suite is 28 by 26 ft. There are also large modern tile baths that were originally screened porches. You can see all of this during a complimentary tour of the home. Complimentary breakfast. Some room phones. No children. No smoking. | 4078 Hwy. 494, Box 2300 | 318/352–8352, 318/352–9580 | 3 suites | $125–$145 | AE, MC, V.

Best Western Natchitoches. This is no-frills lodging less than a mile from several restaurants and across town from the movie theater at the intersection of I–49 and Hwy. 6W. The two-story building has exterior entranceways, and a Shoney's restaurant is adjacent. Complimentary Continental breakfast. Cable TV. Pool. Laundry service. | 5135 Hwy. 6, | 318/352–6655, 800/528–1234 | www.bestwestern.com | 41 rooms | $67–$74 | AE, D, DC, MC, V.

Breazeale House Bed and Breakfast. This Victorian mansion was built in 1890 by Congressman Phanor Breazeale, and local legend says it is haunted by his ghost. This majestic three-story home, now a B&B, has 11 fireplaces, many stained-glass windows, 3 balconies, 12-ft ceilings, and almost 6,000 square feet of living space. Complimentary breakfast. No smoking. | 926 Washington St. | 318/352–5630, 800/352–5631 | 4 rooms | $70–$100 | AE, MC, V.

Cloutier Townhouse. This B&B is a turn-of-the-20th-century, 12-room town house, furnished with a collection of antiques dating mostly from the Louisiana Empire and Victorian periods. The purchase of two early 19th-century four-poster beds that had been in the old St. Mary's Convent in Natchitoches inspired the Nun Suite. The master suite has a four-poster queen-size bed, an embroidered bedspread, and wing chairs. In the heart of the historic district, one-half block from the Front Street shops and restaurants. Complimentary breakfast. In-room hot tubs (in master suite). Cable TV and in-room VCR (in master suite). Pets allowed. No children. No smoking. | 416 Jefferson St. | 318/352–5242, 800/351–7666 | www.cloutierbandb.com | 2 suites | $95–$110 | AE, MC, V.

Comfort Inn. This hotel with exterior entranceways is near the intersection of I–49 and Hwy. 6 on the west side of town, about 4 mi from historic sites. Complimentary Continental breakfast. In-room data ports, microwaves, refrigerators. Cable TV. Pool. Business services. Pets allowed. | 5362 Hwy. 6 | 318/352–7500, 800/228–5150 | www.comfortinn.com | 59 rooms | $60–$75 | AE, D, DC, MC, V.

Fleur-de-Lis Bed and Breakfast Inn. Formerly a boardinghouse for college girls, Fleur-de-Lis was the first B&B in Natchitoches. Built in 1903, this Queen Anne Victorian home has beautiful woodwork, a wraparound porch with rockers and a swing, and many antique furnishings. Complimentary breakfast. No room phones, cable TV in sitting room. No smoking. | 336 2nd St. | 318/352–6621, 800/489–6621 | www.virtualcities.com | 5 rooms | $65–$80 | AE, D, MC, V.

Hampton Inn. This Hampton Inn opened in 1999, 3 mi from the downtown historic district, off I–49, exit 138. It is ideal for families with children who don't want to stay at one of the many local B&B establishments. Complimentary Continental breakfast. Microwaves, refrigerators. Cable TV. Pool. Hot tub. Exercise equipment. Laundry services. | 5300 Hwy. 6 W | 318/354–0010, 800/426–7866 | fax 318/354–7771 | www.hamptoninn.com | 74 rooms | $64–$74 | AE, D, DC, MC, V.

Jefferson House. The back veranda of Gay and L. J. Melder's 1960s white-frame house in the historic district affords a mesmerizing view of Cane River lake. Although the house occupies a busy extension of Front St., the weeping willows, herb garden, pier, and rocking chairs on the veranda create a sense of peace. The house is split-level; its lower floor is hidden from the street. It contains a blend of Asian objets d'art and traditional furnishings. The large parlor has a high cypress beam ceiling, a brick fireplace, and doors that open onto the veranda. Complimentary breakfast. TV in common area. No children under age 5. No smoking. | 229 Jefferson St. | 318/352–3957, 318/352–5756 | 4 rooms | $75–$95 | AE, MC, V.

Laureate House. This antiques-filled B&B on the west side of the river is in the heart of the historic district, within a few blocks of downtown. The house is an 1840 National Register home designed by Italian architects in a traditional European style. Enter through double doors into a wide hallway down the middle of the house. The current kitchen and den were added in the 1950s. The two-bedroom suite on one side of the house has a double bed in one room and two twin beds in the second room. There's also a lovely patio and garden. Complimentary Continental breakfast. TV in common area. No kids under 10. No smoking. | 225 Rue Poete | 318/352–8672 | 1 room, 1 suite | $85–$150 | No credit cards.

Levy-East House Bed and Breakfast Inn. This elegant Greek Revival home (circa 1838) on a tree-lined street in the heart of the historic district is furnished with fine antiques that have been in the house for over 100 years. The balcony has Spanish iron work, and the front veranda overlooks Cane River Lake. Tennis courts are within 4 blocks, swimming and golf 1.5 mi away. The inn is just one block from the Front St. shops and restaurants. Complimentary breakfast. In-room hot tubs. Cable TV, in-room VCRs. No kids. No smoking. | 358 Jefferson St. | 800/840–0662 | 4 rooms | $95–$200 | AE, MC, V.

Ryder Inn. Directly on the highway and on the south edge of the airport, this two-story hotel has exterior corridors. It's a 5-minute drive from downtown. Restaurant, bar, room service. Cable TV. Pool. Exercise equipment. Laundry facilities. Business services, airport shuttle. | 7624 Rte. 1 Bypass | 318/357–8281, 888/252–8281 | www.ryderinn.com | 144 rooms | $53–$90 | AE, D, DC, MC, V.

Tante Huppé. Robert "Bobby" DeBlieux (pronounced dub-you), a former mayor of Natchitoches, restored, and now lives in, this 1830 Creole house in the historic district. Most of the furnishings and family heirlooms are original to the house. His library contains the state's oldest collection of 18th-century Creole books. A candlelit breakfast, made from recipes in a 1745 Creole cookbook, is served in the formal dining room. Two suites are in the restored, detached former servants' quarters, each with bedroom, parlor, full kitchen, private entrance, patio, and modern tile bath. A third suite in the main house, a former slave's quarters, has exposed, old brick walls, beamed ceilings, and a bedroom as well as a loft bed. Complimentary breakfast. Some kitchenettes. Cable TV, VCRs. Pets allowed. No children under 13. No smoking. | 424 Jefferson St. | 318/352–5342, 800/482–4276 | www.tantehuppe.com | 3 suites | $95 | AE, MC, V.

NEW IBERIA

(Nearby towns also listed: Franklin, St. Martinville)

Shadows-on-the-Teche is the most famous, but it's just one of the gorgeous old houses set under the oaks along Bayou Teche in New Iberia. The town was settled in 1779 by a group of Spaniards led by Colonel Francisco Bouligny, who named it for Spain's Iberian Peninsula. If you prefer a quaint village atmosphere to the brighter lights of Lafayette, New Iberia makes a pleasant home base in Cajun country, with a central location and a good variety of services.

Information: Iberia Parish Convention and Visitors Bureau | 2704 Hwy. 14, New Iberia, LA 70560 | 337/365–1540, 888/942–3742 | info@iberiaparish.com | www.iberiaparish.com.

Attractions

Acadian Museum. The town of Erath is a quintessential tiny Cajun village. The museum is filled to the rafters with memorabilia donated by local folks—everything from antique radios and butter churns to patchwork quilts and yellowed newspaper clippings. There's even a costume that was worn by Armand Assante in the film *Belizaire The Cajun,* which was filmed in these parts. | 203 S. Broadway, Erath; 18 mi west of town | 337/233–5832, 337/937–5468 | Free, donations welcome | Weekdays 1–4.

★ **Avery Island.** Surrounded by water and marshland, this "island" is actually the tip of a subterranean mountain of salt. The ancient dome is thousands of feet deep. It is best known as the home of Tabasco, the ubiquitous hot sauce brewed here from native capsicum peppers and Avery Island salt. | Hwy. 329, 10 mi southwest of New Iberia .

Jungle Gardens. Tropical flowers and gator ponds share 250 acres with a Buddhist temple and bird sanctuary, home to more than 20,000 waterfowl. Herons and egrets nest here in early spring and summer. The bird sanctuary was founded by naturalist E. A. McIlhenny of Tabasco fame. Wildlife includes alligators, deer, nutria, raccoons, and black bears. Azaleas peak in spring. | Avery Island; Hwy. 14W to Hwy. 329S | 337/369–6243 | fax 337/369–6326 | $5.75 adults, $4 age 6–12, children under 6 free | Daily 8–5.

McIlhenny Company Tabasco Factory. View an 8-min film on the history of Avery Island's world-famous export. Then walk past peppers brewing in ancient oak casks and the Tabasco sauce bottling line, where labels in eight different languages are stuck to bottles bound for more than 100 countries around the globe. A charming shop offers a wide variety of items stamped with the Tabasco logo and other Cajun gifts. | Avery Island, Hwy. 329 | 337/365–8173, 800/634–9599 | fax 337/637–8678 | www.tabasco.com | Free | Daily 9–4.

Conrad Rice Mill and Konriko Company Store. Guided tours present a unique view of the oldest operating rice mill in America, which still uses a belt-drive power system. The 1912 landmark, built of rough cedar planks, is listed on the National Register of Historic Places. The gift shop sells rice products and regional crafts. | 309 Ann St. | 337/364–7242, 800/551–3245 | fax 337/365–5806 | $3.25 adults, $2.75 senior citizens, $1.75 children 11 and under | Mon.–Sat. 9–5, tours 10, 11, 1, 2, 3, closed Sun.

Episcopal Church of the Epiphany. Built in 1856, this is one of the oldest Gothic Revival brick churches in the state and the oldest nonresidential building in New Iberia. It's on the National Register of Historic Places. | 303 W. Main St. | 337/369–9966 | Free | Call for viewing hours.

★ **Rip Van Winkle Gardens.** This 25-acre showplace on Lake Peigneur is an explosion of color, especially when the tulips, hyacinths, and azaleas bloom in spring. Also on the grounds are a Japanese teahouse, lily pond, aviary, and the sunny Café Jefferson. Admission includes a tour of the 1870 manor built by actor Joseph Jefferson, who made his fortune playing Rip van Winkle on stage. | 5505 Rip Van Winkle Rd., Jefferson Island; 6 mi west of New Iberia off Hwy. 14 | 337/365–3332, 800/375–3332 | fax 337/365–3354 | www.ripvanwinkle.com | $9 adults, $8.50 senior citizens, $7 ages 13–18, $5 ages 5–12, under 5 free | Daily 9–5.

Shadows-on-the-Teche. A National Trust Historic House Museum and Gardens, this French Colonial beauty is framed by towering white columns and a gabled slate roof. It was built in Greek revival style between 1831–1834 by a sugarcane planter and used for four generations by the family. In the 1920s, an amazing find of more than 17,000 family letters, photographs, receipts, and other papers stashed away in 40 trunks in the attic led to the house's restoration. It is on the Bayou Teche, surrounded by three acres of azaleas, camellias, and huge live oak trees with hanging Spanish moss. | 317 E. Main St. | 337/369–6446, 877/200–4924 | fax 337/365–5213 | www.shadowsontheteche.org | $6; special rate for children | Daily 9–4:30, tours every 30 min.

ON THE CALENDAR

FEB., MAR.: *Andalusia Mardi Gras Parade.* This is a traditional Mardi Gras parade with marching bands and costumed riders on floats. | 337/365–1540, 888/942–3742.
APR.: Bunk Fest–Bunk Johnson/New Iberia Jazz Arts and Heritage Festival. This three-day festival commemorating the legendary jazz trumpeter Bunk Johnson, includes music, crafts, food, gospel, a second-line parade, a mock funeral, and a memorial mass. | 888/942–3742.
SEPT.: *Louisiana Sugar Cane Festival and Fair.* Among the many festivities here are a Queen's parade, a children's parade, a boat parade down Bayou Teche, a street dance, a livestock show, a flower show, photo displays, carnival rides, and a beauty pageant. | Last weekend in Sept., Thurs.–Sun. | 337/365–1540, 888/942–3742.

Dining

Duffy's. American/Casual. Favorites served at this 1950s diner in the heart of town are po'-boy sandwiches, burgers, hot dogs, seafood dinners, and baby back ribs. | 1106 Center St., | 337/365–2326 | Reservations not accepted | Closed Sun. | $4–$12 | AE, MC, V.

Lagniappe Too Café. Cajun. This is a charming, affordable French restaurant with a Cajun twist, just one block from Shadows-on-the-Teche. Lagniappe is Cajun slang meaning "a little something extra." The co-owner cook, Elaine, also makes the squeezable, stuffed dolls with funny faces that perch here and there throughout the restaurant. Husband Al is the painter of the pieces on the walls. The café, in business since 1986, seats 100 and attracts an international crowd. Menu includes gumbo, bisques, stuffed eggplant, stuffed mirliton squash (a local vegetable), grilled chicken, trout, steaks, and a variety of seafood. | 204 E. Main St. | 337/365–9419 | Closed Sun. No lunch Sat. No dinner Mon.–Thurs. | $11–$19 | AE, D, DC, MC, V.

Little River Inn. Seafood. The casual Acadian dining room, in the Bayou Landing shopping center, adjoins the boardwalk on Bayou Teche. Seafood such as fried shrimp, fried crawfish, and crab dishes is served, as well as sirloin steaks and filet mignon. Kids' menu. | 1000 Parkview Dr. | 337/367–7466 | Closed Sun. No lunch Sat. | $10–$24 | AE, D, DC, MC, V.

Lodging

Bayou Teche Guest Cottage. There could scarcely be a better way to appreciate the Queen City of the Teche than to spend a night in this refurbished 18th-century cottage right on the banks of the legendary bayou, only four blocks from downtown attractions. There are three acres of quiet grounds to explore, or you can sit in the front porch rocking chairs and watch towboats. The two-room cottage, which sleeps up to four, is simply furnished. You can prepare meals in the kitchen. Complimentary Continental breakfast. Kitchenette, refrigerator. Cable TV. No smoking. | 100 Teche St. | 337/364–1933 | 1 cottage | $80–$100 | No credit cards.

Best Western. This contemporary motel is 1 mi from downtown and 1.25 mi south of the historic district. Built circa 1980, the two-story building has both interior and exterior entranceways. Restaurant, bar, complimentary Continental breakfast, room service. In-room data ports. Cable TV. Pool, wading pool. Hot tub. Laundry facilities. Free parking. | 2714 Hwy. 14 | 337/364–3030, 800/528–1234 | fax 337/367–5311 | www.bestwestern.com | 150 rooms | $62–$98 | AE, D, DC, MC, V.

Cook's Cottage at Rip Van Winkle Gardens. Cook's Cottage is on the 25-acre landscaped gardens that sit adjacent to Lake Peigneur. The three-room former cook's dwelling has been transformed into a private guest house. It is furnished with a blend of antique and reproduction early French Louisiana pieces, including a handmade mahogany four-poster bed. The kitchenette includes a wet bar, toaster oven, coffeemaker, and the makings for a do-it-yourself Continental breakfast in the refrigerator. You get unlimited access to the gardens and a complimentary tour of the Jefferson House. There is a restaurant overlooking the Lake, and boat tours are given daily. Restaurant, complimentary Continental breakfast. Kitchenette, microwave, refrigerator, in-room hot tub. Cable TV, in-room VCR (and movies). No smoking. | 5505 Rip Van Winkle Rd. | 337/365–3332, 800/375–3332 | fax 337/365–3354 | www.ripvanwinkle.com | 1 cottage | $145–$175 | AE, D, MC, V.

Holiday Inn. Convenient to the historic district, this motel was built circa 1978 and has two stories with exterior entranceways. Restaurant, bar, room service. In-room data ports. Cable TV. Pool. Exercise equipment. Playground. Laundry facilities. Business services. Pets allowed. | 2915 Hwy. 14 | 337/367–1201, 800/465–4329 | fax 337/367–7877 | www.bassho-tels.com | 177 rooms | $62 | AE, D, DC, MC, V.

Le Rosier Country Inn Bed and Breakfast. This charming cottage is in the heart of the historic district, across the street from Shadows-on-the-Teche. The two-story Acadian-style home has a front porch and veranda, white painted fence, rose gardens, a rear deck and patio, and a gourmet restaurant that seats 50, guests with priority. "Le Rosier" means The Rose Bush, named for the ancient rose that sprang forth during the refurbishing of the 100-yr-old fence. The upper floors are made of old cypress wood, and windows and sashes were salvaged from the original house built in 1870. Restaurant, complimentary breakfast. Refrigerators. No kids under 12. No smoking. | 314 E. Main St. | 337/367–5306, 888/804–7673 | fax 337/365–1216 | www.leRosier.com | 6 rooms | $95–$115 | AE, MC, V.

NEW ORLEANS

MAP 9, G5

(Suburbs listed: Covington, Jean Lafitte, Kenner, Mandeville, Metairie, Slidell)

The Big Easy is known around the world, a name that immediately evokes images of smoky jazz clubs, lacy ironwork balconies, tropical patios, fine old Creole restaurants, riverboats, and Carnival parades. One of the oldest cities in the U.S., New Orleans was founded in 1718 by Jean Baptiste LeMoyne, Sieur de Bienville. It was named for the French Regent, Philippe Duc d'Orleans. In the beginning, it was little more than a remote outpost set in swampland bounded by the Mississippi River and Lake Pontchartrain, a murky backwater plagued by yellow fever, hurricanes, floods, and fires. When it was named capital of the Louisiana territories in 1723, the total population numbered fewer than 500 European colonists and 300 slaves, but a gracious Creole society had already taken root. In 1762, when Louis XV of France ceded "the island of New Orleans" and all of the Louisiana Territory west of the Mississippi River to his cousin, Charles III of Spain, aristocratic Spaniards continued the tradition of civilized life in the wilderness.

The sugar industry was booming, thanks to development of nearby plantations, and the city's already legendary taste for high living was raised to new heights in 1789 when it became a favored refuge for European nobles and royal sympathizers fleeing the French Revolution. France regained the territory briefly after the 1800 Treaty of San Ildefonso, but it was resold to the U.S. by Napoleon I in 1803 for $15 million, a part of a transaction known as The Louisiana Purchase.

Louisiana was admitted to the Union in 1812, and by 1840 New Orleans had become the fourth-largest city in the U.S., with some 100,000 residents. It was also the second-busiest port, with water traffic surpassed only by New York. Travellers arrived by steamboat to join the thriving social life enlivened by opera houses, restaurants, cafés, and bordellos. After Louisiana joined the Confederacy in 1861, New Orleans quickly fell to Union forces in 1862. The onset of the Reconstruction Era in 1865 caused tremendous political upheaval and social unrest. The state was readmitted to the Union in 1868 with a new constitution that granted voting rights to African-American citizens for the first time, but municipal government was not returned to local control until 1872.

By the 1880s, flooding and yellow fever epidemics had been greatly reduced by new drainage systems, and a deeper navigational channel allowed ocean-going freighters to travel up the Mississippi River. Around the turn of the 20th century, syncopated ragtime was evolving into jazz at local clubs, led by Buddy Bolden, Louis Armstrong, and other home-grown musicians. In 1901 the first oil well was drilled upstate, a discovery that would eventually replace many of the great riverfront plantations with petrochemical plants. Louisiana had been dragged into the modern age.

There's still plenty of kicking and screaming, though, as city residents and their guests try to hold onto the romance of the past. Here the world moves slowly, life is meant to be savored, and trendy fads are viewed with suspicion. Waves of immigration have stirred Spanish, English, Irish, German, Italian, and Asian cultural flavors into the French- and African-based melting pot. The French Quarter is still the main attraction, but if you limit yourself to its considerable charms, you'll miss many other rich experiences. Ride the streetcar through the oak canopy of St. Charles Avenue, past the mansions of the Garden District to Audubon Park's world-class zoo. Take a cruise on a paddlewheel steamer, swamp boat, or river ferry. Club-hop through the wee hours to catch a world of new and traditional sounds. Cheer on the Saints at the Louisiana Superdome or play a round at one of City Park's four golf courses. Crack some boiled crabs at one of the seafood restaurants on Lake Pontchartrain. View works by old masters at New Orleans Museum of Art or emerging artists at the galleries along Julia Street. Above all, follow local example and allow plenty of time to relax.

NEIGHBORHOODS

★ The French Quarter

The French Quarter (a.k.a. the Vieux Carré, or "Old Quarter") was once the entire city of New Orleans, 100 square blocks bounded by the Mississippi River, Canal Street, Rampart Street, and Esplanade Avenue. Today it is one of the best-preserved historic districts in the U.S., a living museum of colonial landmarks, courtyards, gaslit streets, and cobblestone alleyways. Despite the name, the architecture is primarily Spanish in style, as most of the earlier French colonial buildings were destroyed by major conflagrations in 1788 and 1794. In the shadow of St. Louis Cathedral, Jackson Square remains the primary public gathering place, surrounded by upscale boutiques, sidewalk cafés, street performers, and the riverfront Woldenberg Park. Young chefs are attracting international attention at newer restaurants such as Bayona, The Bistro, and Peristyle. Still, locals and visitors continue to dine in grand old Creole style at Antoine's, Galatoire's, and Brennan's. Royal Street is lined with world-class antique stores and art galleries. True to its naughty reputation, Bourbon Street is a boozy parade of strip joints, overpriced lounges, and loud-mouthed conventioneers. Lesser-known side streets are crammed with shops, coffeehouses, museums, music clubs, and other diversions, both traditional and new. In other words, there's something to suit just about any taste—and you'll never go to bed hungry.

The Central Business District

The Central Business District (CBD) is the financial heart of the city, a concrete maze of towering banks, law offices, and other commercialbuildings between the French Quarter and the Garden District. Mainline Canal Street is still impressive in scale (more than 170 ft wide), though most of the downtown department stores and historic movie palaces have joined the flight to suburban malls. This once-grand boulevard is now populated by street vendors and budget clothing boutiques but retains its spirit near the riverfront, where you'll find several major convention hotels, the Aquarium of the Americas, Riverwalk Marketplace, and the posh vertical mall known as The Shops at Canal Place.

The Warehouse/Arts District

The Warehouse/Arts District is the site of an ongoing renaissance, as former cotton warehouses and factory lofts are converted into galleries, restaurants, and trendy living quarters. "The SoHo of the South" is tucked in a waterfront corner of the CBD, bounded by the Mississippi River, Lafayette Street, Howard Avenue, and Baronne Street. The unofficial headquarters is the Contemporary Arts Center, a massive 19th-century industrial building that now contains exhibit spaces and theaters. Most of the independent art dealers are concentrated along a few blocks of Julia Street between St. Charles Avenue and Commerce Street, an area known as Gallery Row. Stop by The Preservation Resource Center (604 Julia Street) to pick up a map of the neighborhood's architectural treasures for a self-guided walking tour.

The Garden District

The Garden District was settled after the 1803 Louisiana Purchase by Americans who travelled down the Mississippi River to take advantageof the booming local economy. The insular European colonists who preceded them had built the shuttered town houses and walled patios of the French Quarter, but these later arrivals favored flashy Italianate and Greek Revival architecture with elaborate gardens open to view. Today their homes remain among the showplaces of the city, block after block of grand mansions cooled by moss-draped oaks and banks of tropical blooms. The historic neighborhood is bounded by St. Charles and Louisiana avenues, Magazine and Jackson streets. You can pick up a detailed map for a self-guided walking tour at any visitor information office. If your budget can stand it, reserve a table for brunch in the landmark courtyard at Commander's Palace. And be sure to allow some time to poke through the dusty collectibles and antiques in the Magazine Street shops.

Uptown

Uptown is home to Tulane and Loyola Universities, Audubon Park, and the oak-shaded neighborhoods that have housed the city's elite for generations. It is bounded by the Mississippi River and by Louisiana, Carrollton, and Claiborne avenues. Shops, restaurants, and traditional old taverns cater to a mixed crowd of aristocrats, bohemians, and students. Cool and stately St. Charles Avenue is the main artery, its vintage electric streetcars still a daily means of transportation for residents of all classes. Magazine Street is closer to the river, a funky strip lined with miles of contemporary art galleries, coffeehouses, antiques dealers, bookshops, music clubs, and ethnic cafés.

Mid-City

Mid-City is true to its name, a midtown neighborhood characterized by its mid-19th-century houses, mid-priced restaurants and bars, and the centrally located City Park. Here Canal Street terminates amidst a cluster of 14 historic cemeteries. Architecture fans should walk past the Victorian cottages on the upper blocks of Esplanade Avenue, turning onto Moss Street to view the antebellum structures that remain along Bayou St. John from plantation days.

Faubourg Marigny

Faubourg Marigny was named for the French Creole aristocrat who developed the area's first planned community during the 19th century.When high living and gambling debts decimated his huge fortune, Bernard Philippe de Marigny de Mandeville subdivided one of his family plantations into this "faubourg" (suburb) on the outskirts of the French Quarter, which was then the entire city of New Orleans. It is separated from the Vieux Carre by Esplanade Avenue and bounded by the Mississippi River, Rampart Street, and Elysian Fields Avenue. Today many of the picturesque Creole cottages, crowded along narrow streets, are occupied by artists and musicians, as well as a lively collection of offbeat clubs, cafés, and shops that have been priced out of the Quarter by commercialization and inflated rents.

The Lakefront

The Lakefront offers a breezy and wide-open respite from the densely populated older neighborhoods of the inner city. Once swampy and uninhabitable, the land has been reclaimed by a system of levees and canals for contemporary housing developments, yacht harbors, and a 5-mi linear park along the southern shore of Lake Pontchartrain. The eastern boundary is anchored by the University of New Orleans and the floating Bally's Casino. The commercial area known as West End is a bright scene of waterfront seafood restaurants and clubs, with sand volleyball courts at Mickey Retif Coconut Beach Sports Complex, a public fishing pier and boat launch, plus several marinas.

TRANSPORTATION INFORMATION

Airports: New Orleans International Airport is located in suburban Kenner, about 11 mi west of downtown New Orleans. | Airline Hwy. | 504/464–0831.

Amtrak: Union Terminal serves as the local station for both Amtrak trains (800/872–7245) and Greyhound buses (800/231–2222). | 1001 Loyola Ave.

Intra-City Transportation: The Regional Transit Authority (RTA) provides local bus and streetcar service. In addition to regular single fares, a special VisiTour pass is available for either one day or three consecutive days of unlimited travel on all lines. | 504/248–3900.

For More Information: New Orleans Metropolitan Convention and Visitors Bureau | 1520 Sugar Bowl Dr., New Orleans, LA | 800/672–6124, 504/566–5011 | www.neworleanscvb.com.

Attractions

ART AND ARCHITECTURE

Beauregard–Keyes House and Garden. This French Quarter house museum is named for two of its most famous former residents, Confederate General P.G.T. Beauregard (who is rumored to haunt the premises) and novelist Frances Parkinson Keyes (whose books, penned here in the 1940s, are on sale in the gift shop). The raised Greek Revival mansion was built in 1826 for auctioneer Joseph Le Carpentier. Costumed docents lead tours of the building and formal French garden. | 1113 Chartres St. | 504/523–7257 | $5; special rates for senior citizens, students, and children; children under 6 free | Mon.–Sat. 10–3, closed Sun.

Delaronde Street Houses. Take the free ferry across the river to Algiers, a quiet district filled with interesting buildings. This row of cottages and shotgun doubles includes interesting examples of bevelled glass, brackets, iron fence work, and other period details. | 218, 236, 301, 307, 323-325 and 335-337 Delaronde Street, Algiers.

Destrehan Plantation. The closest plantation manor of note is just 8 mi west of New Orleans International Airport. It was built in 1787 in French Colonial style by Robin de Logny, who passed it on to his son-in-law Jean Noel Destrehan in 1802. It's a lovely example of French Colonial architecture, with its broad verandas and deep West Indies–style roof supported by fat round columns. It was a filming site for the movie "*Interview With the Vam-*

pire," based on the novel by local author Anne Rice. | 13034 River Rd., Destrehan | 504/764–9315 | fax 504/725–1929 | www.destrehanplantation.org | $7; special rates for students and children, children under 5 free | Daily 9–4.

Gallier House Museum. This classic 1857 town house, complete with a vintage carriage parked in the carriageway, benefitted from a meticulously documented restoration conducted by Tulane University. It was built as a home for his own family by one of the city's premier architects, James Gallier, Jr. Today it's open for guided tours and is especially beautiful when decorated for the Christmas holidays in 19th-century style. | 1118–32 Royal St. | 504/525–5661 | fax 504/525–9735 | www.gnofn.org/~hggh | $6; special rates for senior citizens, students, and children, children under 8 free; Combination tickets for both Hermann–Grima and Gallier Houses $10; special rates for senior citizens, students, and children, children under 8 free | Mon.–Sat. 10–4, closed Sun.

★ **Hermann–Grima Historic House.** Built in 1831, this is one of the earliest examples of American architecture in the French Quarter. The house was built for wealthy merchant Samuel Hermann and occupied after 1844 by the family of Judge Felix Grima. It has been restored to represent the gracious life enjoyed by the upper middle classes of that period. Guided tours also visit the courtyard and stables. Open-hearth cooking demonstrations are held in the original kitchen every Thursday from Oct.–May. During Halloween season the house is usually dressed in mourning, with draped mirrors, wreaths, an antique coffin laid out in the parlor, and other accoutrements of a traditional 19th-century funeral. | 820 St. Louis St. | 504/525–5661 | fax 504/525–9735 | $6; special rates for senior citizens, students, and children, children under 8 free; Combination tickets for both Hermann-Grima and Gallier Houses $10; special rates for senior citizens, students, and children, children under 8 free | Mon.–Sat. 10–4, closed Sun.

Lafitte's Blacksmith Shop. It looks like it might fall down around your head, but it won't. One of America's most famous and atmospheric old watering holes is set in a listing brick-and-beam cottage with creaky wood furnishings and a great piano bar. Built in the 1770s, it has long been associated with dark tales of pirate dealings and other intrigues (mostly undocumented). Legend has it the ghost of a pirate hangs out at the bar awaiting his bride. | 941 Bourbon St. | 504/523–0066 | Free | Daily.

Longue Vue House and Gardens. This city estate with sprawling 8-acre grounds is the former home of the late Edgar Bloom Stern (a wealthy cotton broker) and Edith Rosenwald Stern (an heiress to the Sears fortune). Today the lavish grounds and Greek Revival mansion, built in 1942 and listed on the National Register of Historic Places, are open to the public. Tours highlight the original furnishings and antiques, plus changing exhibits in the galleries and gardens. | 7 Bamboo Rd. | 504/488–5488 | fax 504/486–7015 | www.longue-vue.com | $7; special rates for senior citizens and children | Mon.–Sat. 10–4:30, Sun. 1–5.

★ **Old Ursuline Convent.** The only example of true French colonial architecture in the French Quarter (which is primarily Spanish in style) is also believed by many historians to be the oldest remaining structure in the Mississippi Valley. Built in 1745, the three-story masonry building is graced by a steep roof with dormer windows. In addition to holding classes for wealthy Creole children, it was also the first school on American soil to teach children of Native American and African heritage. Guided tours also visit the formal gardens, which include a traditional herb garden. | 1100 Chartres St. | 504/529–3040. | fax 504/529–2001 | www.accesscom.net/ursuline | $5; special rates for senior citizens and students, children under 8 free | Weekdays 10–3, weekends 11:15–2.

Pitot House. The former home of James Pitot, first mayor of the incorporated city, is a few blocks from City Park and the Museum of Art on the Bayou St. John. Pitot bought it in 1820 from the grandmother of French impressionist painter Edgar Degas. It was converted into a convent in 1904 by Mother Frances Xavier Cabrini, the first U.S. citizen to be canonized as a saint by the Catholic Church. Furnishings represent early life of the area. | 1440 Moss St. | 504/482–0312 | fax 504/482–0312 | $5 adults; $4 senior citizens, students; $2 children; children under 5 free | Wed.–Sat. 10–3, closed Sun.–Tues.

San Francisco Plantation. This frilly Steamboat Gothic mansion, built in 1856 by planter Edmond Bozonier Marmillon, is an architectural confection lavished with gingerbread trim and bright pastels. The interior is just as ornate, with lofty rooms and famous ceiling frescoes. In a wry joke about the expense of building it, the house was originally known as "Sans Frusquin," French slang for "without a penny in my pocket." | River Road, Reserve; 34 mi west of New Orleans, between Reserve and Garyville | 504/535–2341 | fax 504/535–5450 | www.sanfranciscoplantation.org | $8; special rates for students and children | Daily 10–4:30.

BEACHES, PARKS, AND NATURAL SIGHTS

Jackson Square. The heart of New Orleans is the busy urban park between St. Louis Cathedral and the river, a formal tropical garden surrounded by a tall iron fence and a flagstone pedestrian mall populated by sidewalk artists, musicians, fortune tellers, and hundreds of tourists. Originally a military training ground, known as Place d'Armes to early French colonists, it was renamed in 1815 to honor General Andrew Jackson, who successfully defended the city against the British in the Battle of New Orleans. (That's him immortalized in bronze, rearing up on his horse, high above all the modern commotion.) | Free | Daily.

Carriage Rides in Jackson Square. In front of Jackson Square, there is a long line of mule-drawn carriages waiting to take you on a tour of the Vieux Carre. The drivers possess extensive knowledge about the Quarter and can usually answer any questions you might have. The carriages, which can hold anywhere from two to twelve passengers, charge varying rates. You can expect to pay around $8 for an adult and $4 for a child, with discounts on bigger groups.

Jean Lafitte National Historical Park and Preserve. Nine distinct sites located throughout the state showcase the natural and cultural diversity of Louisiana. More information on each unit or center may be found in listings for individual cities and towns, but the following three are within the metropolitan New Orleans area. Check under the town of Jean Lafitte for details on the Barataria Unit, which is a 30-min drive from the French Quarter. | Various locations | 504/589–3882 | fax 504/589–3851 | Fees vary | Hours vary.

Chalmette Unit. General Andrew Jackson and his troops defeated the British here at the Battle of New Orleans on Jan. 18, 1815. The victors were a wild assortment of Creole gentlemen, Tennessee sharpshooters—even a band of pirates led by Jean Lafitte. The oak-shaded riverfront field has a marked drive, and there are tours of the small plantation house, plus exhibits and a video in the visitors center. The Chalmette National Cemetery adjoins. | 8606 W. Saint Bernard Hwy, Chalmette; 6 mi east of downtown, along the river | 504/589–4428 | fax 504/589–3851 | Free | Daily.

Isleño Center. This frame cottage on a riverfront country road is staffed by descendants of hardy Canary Islanders (Isleños), who were first brought to the area in the 18th century by Spanish galleons in order to defend coastal Louisiana. The small museum celebrates their unique culture, past and present, as local fishers, hunters, trappers, boat builders, and crafters. | 1357 Bayou Rd/Rte. 46; 14 mi southeast on Rte. 46 | 504/682–0862 | fax 504/589–3851 | Free | Wed.–Sun. 11–4, closed Mon.–Tues.

New Orleans Unit. This unlikely national park is also known as the French Quarter. The entire historic neighborhood has been designated as the New Orleans Unit, with exhibits and other information on display at the Folklife/Visitor Center on North Peters Street. Ranger-led tours are available. | Folklife/Visitor Center, 916 N. Peters | 504/589–2636 | fax 504/589–3851 | Free | Daily.

Lake Pontchartrain. The largest inland estuary in the U.S. sprawls across 610 square mi. It was christened in honor of Jerome Phelypeaux, Count Pontchartrain, who was minister of marine during the reign of Louisiana's namesake, Louis XIV of France. It is spanned by the world's longest over-water bridge, the Lake Pontchartrain Causeway, a 24-mi drive connecting the New Orleans suburb of Metairie with Mandeville on the north shore. | North of downtown | Free.

Mississippi River Levees. Like much of Louisiana, New Orleans is surrounded by a system of levees that protects it from the waters of the Mississippi. The river actually flows above the city, which is situated around 6 ft below sea level on average. These grassy manmade banks are also the venue of choice for dog walkers, lovers, picnickers, and the occasional lone musician. The best places to stroll in good company are Woldenberg Park and the Moonwalk (Gov. Nicholls St. to Canal St.), both in the French Quarter, and the River View area of Audubon Park (Magazine St. between Broadway and Exposition). | Free | Daily dawn to dusk.

St. Bernard State Park. Palmettos and pines shade this 358-acre retreat on the Mississippi River in the tiny suburban community of Poydras. There are more than 50 campsites with electricity and water, plus a swimming pool, picnic tables, and trails. | On Hwy. 39, Poydras | 504/682–2101, 888/677–7823 | fax 504/682–9960 | www.crt.state.la.us | Free | Daily.

Woldenberg Riverfront Park. This linear park follows the Mississippi from Moonwalk in the French Quarter to the Canal Street ferry landing, some 17 acres of sweeping port views and shade trees. A significant collection of outdoor sculpture includes works by Ida Kohlmeyer and John Scott. | Along the Mississippi River between Toulouse and Canal Sts. | Free | Daily.

CULTURE, EDUCATION, AND HISTORY

Blaine Kern's Mardi Gras World. If you're not in town during Carnival season (Jan. 6 to Ash Wednesday), you can get a taste of the wild scene at this unusual attraction in the suburb of Algiers, across the river from the city. A Mardi Gras museum is attached to the riverfront studios of Blaine Kern, who builds the extravagant mechanized floats for most of the New Orleans parades. You can also wander through some of the hangar-sized buildings to view works in progress. Tours include King Cake, a traditional cake served during the Carnival season, and coffee. Afterward, be sure to walk up on the levee out back for a fine view of the New Orleans skyline. | 233 Newton St., | 504/361–7821, 800/362–8213 | fax 504/368–4628 | www.mardigrasworld.com | $11.50; special rates for senior citizens and children, children under 3 free | Daily 9:30–4:30.

Contemporary Arts Center. A 40,000-square-ft drugstore warehouse was converted in 1976 to this award-winning extravaganza that now houses high-tech galleries, theaters, studios, offices, and New Orleans Net Café (a popular meeting spot with high-speed Internet access terminals). The nerve center of the city's Warehouse/Arts District presents more than 20 exhibitions each year, as well as theatrical productions, live music, and other special events. | 900 Camp St., one block from Lee Circle and the St. Charles streetcar line | 504/528–3805 | fax 504/528–3828 | www.cacno.org | Free; Gallery $5, special rates for senior citizens and students, free Thurs.; Prices vary for theater productions and special events | Tues.–Sun. 11–5, closed Mon.

Le Petit Theatre du Vieux Carre. The country's oldest continuing community theater group (established in 1916) is headquartered in a 1922 reproduction of the 1796 home of the last Spanish governor of Louisiana, which once stood here. Patrons gather in the tropical courtyard during intermissions. The season runs from September through June, usually featuring a schedule of six musicals and plays, plus four Children's Corner productions. | 616 St. Peter St., just off Jackson Square | 504/522–2081 | fax 504/524–9027 | Call for a schedule of performances and ticket prices.

Loyola University. Originally established downtown in 1847 as the College of the Immaculate Conception, the doors opened in 1904 at this stately uptown campus, a St. Charles Avenue landmark facing Audubon Park. Today the 20-acre campus serves about 5,500 students. The music school presents first-class concerts by students and visiting performers. Call to find out about drama productions, the excellent speakers' series, and athletic events. | 6363 St. Charles Ave. | 504/865–2011 | www.loyno.edu | Free | Daily.

The Old Absinthe House. Business cards from thousands of international customers are stapled all over walls and ceilings that are also cluttered with sports memorabilia. Today this is a comfortably seedy bar that's usually populated by noisy Bourbon Street tourists, but it has a colorful history. It was built in 1806, and back when New Orleans was the absinthe capital of the New World (and before the narcotic liquor was outlawed), the antique marble fountains attracted such sophisticated company as Mark Twain, William Thackeray, Oscar Wilde, Walt Whitman, and Russia's Grand Duke Alexis. | 240 Bourbon St. | 504/523–3181 | fax 504/523–3181 | Free | Daily from 9:30 AM.

Preservation Hall. Living legends perform traditional jazz every night before standing-room-only audiences. No food or drinks are served and the only seating is on hard wooden benches, but the musty 1920s atmosphere and Jazz Age sounds are the real stuff. No advance tickets are sold, so join the line at least 30 min before doors open at 8 PM if you hope to claim a seat. The musicians play 20-min sets until midnight. No minimum age for entry. | 726 St. Peter St. | 504/522–2841, 504/523–8939 (after 8 PM), 800/785–5772 | fax 504/558–9192 | www.preservationhall.com | $5 | Daily.

Saenger Theatre. Broadway road shows, concerts, and other special events are presented in the Italian Renaissance splendor of this ornate former movie palace. The midnight blue ceiling is alight with twinkling stars. | 143 N. Rampart St.; Just off Canal St. | 504/525–1052 | fax 504/569–1533 | www.saengertheatre.com | Call for a schedule of performances and ticket prices.

Southern Repertory Theatre. The only full-time equity theater in New Orleans lies behind golden doors on the third level of the upscale vertical mall known as The Shops at Canal Place. The repertoire is strictly Southern, featuring works by established and emerging playwrights. An intimate setting with only 150 seats. | 333 Canal St. | 504/861–8163 | fax 504/861–5875 | $10–$17 | Sept.–Mar., Fri.–Sat. 8 PM, Sun. 2 PM.

Tulane University. "The Harvard of the South" is set on an oak-shaded campus facing Audubon Park, with imposing stone buildings that house 11 schools and colleges serving some 12,000 students. Tulane was founded in 1834 as the Medical College of Louisiana and still administers the downtown Tulane Medical Center, one of the country's premier teaching hospitals. It became the University of Louisiana in 1847 and was renamed in 1884 for philanthropist Paul Tulane. The university's Amistad Research Center houses the world's largest archive on U.S. racial relations. Changing exhibits in the Woldenberg Art Center and Newcomb Art Gallery showcase works by nationally known artists, promising students, and faculty. Check for performances by the music and drama departments or special events sponsored by the student union known as TUCP. Football, basketball, baseball, and other athletic teams wear the emerald jerseys of the Tulane Green Wave. | 6823 St. Charles Ave. | 504/865–5000 | www.tulane.edu | Free | Weekdays.

University of New Orleans. The 420-acre lakefront campus, founded in 1958 as part of the LSU system, is the state's second-largest university, serving more than 16,000 students. The Jazz Studies Program has attracted international attention. Entertainments are presented by the school's music, drama, and athletic departments. The UNO Lakefront Arena on Franklin Avenue is a 10,000-seat auditorium that hosts a wide range of professional concerts and sports events. | Elysian Fields Ave. at Lakeshore Dr. | 504/280–6000 | www.uno.edu | Free | Weekdays.

MUSEUMS

Confederate Museum. The 1891 Romanesque building is worth a trip in itself. Beamed 24-ft ceilings and stained glass create an abbey-like space that is lined with polished red cedar and a major display of restored battle flags. Portraits, swords, guns, uniforms, furnishings, and artillery are also included in the world's second-largest collection of Confederate memorabilia. (The largest is in Richmond, Va.) | 929 Camp St. | 504/523–4522 | fax 504/523–8595 | www.confederatemuseum.com | $5; special rate for children | Mon.–Sat. 10–4, closed Sun.

Historic New Orleans Collection. Changing displays in the first-floor Williams Gallery are beautifully mounted, free and open to the public. A small admission is charged for guided tours of the Louisiana History Galleries upstairs. It's all drawn from the truly amazing archives amassed by the late Kemper and Leila Williams, who willed their graceful 1792 town house and thousands of local documents and photos to the city. | 533 Royal St. | 504/523–4662 | fax 504/598–7108 | www.hnoc.org | Free, $4 guided tours | Tues.–Sat. 10–4:30, tours 10–3, closed Sun.–Mon.

Louisiana Children's Museum. Hands-on exhibits include a working kid-size television studio, along with dozens of other high-tech amusements that are fun for parents, too. Use your body to create kinetic paintings on a gigantic video screen or trap your shadow on a phosphorescent wall. The First Adventures Play Space is scaled for toddlers. | 420 Julia St. | 504/523–1357 | fax 504/529–3666 | www.lcm.org | $5; children under 1 free | Tues.–Sat. 9:30–4:30, Sun. 12–4:30, Mon. 9:30–4:30 (summer only).

Louisiana State Museum. The Louisiana State Museum is a system of historic sites and museums that includes several units in New Orleans. You may buy admission to a single building or a combination ticket. If you purchase tickets to two or more buildings, there's a 20% discount. French Quarter properties include the Cabildo, Presbytère, 1850 House, Old U.S. Mint, Madame John's Legacy, the Arsenal, Creole House, and Jackson House. | 751 Chartres (and various historic sites in French Quarter) | 504/568–6968, 800/568–6968 | fax 504/568–4995 | www.crt.state.la.us | $5, special rates for senior citizens and students | Tues.–Sun. 9–5, closed Mon.

The Cabildo. The Cabildo and The Presbytère (*see* below) are nearly identical twins that stand on either side of St. Louis Cathedral. The stately colonnaded buildings with arched windows and mansard roofs now house museums, but both played important roles in the state's history. The Cabildo gets its name from "The Illustrious Cabildo," a Spanish governing council that was stationed here from 1799 to 1803. It hosted ceremonies on November 30, 1803, when the Louisiana territory was returned from Spain to France. Three weeks later, France deeded the property to the U.S. in one of the second floor chambers, a famous transaction now known as The Louisiana Purchase. Today exhibits trace regional history from early exploration through the Civil War. | 701 Chartres St. | 504/568–6968, 800/568–6968 | fax 504/568–4995 | www.crt.state.la.us | $5; children 12 and under free | Tues.–Sun. 9–5, closed Mon.

Madame John's Legacy. Though disagreement continues, many historians claim this raised Creole cottage is the oldest existing building in the Mississippi Valley. (The dispute springs from the fact that the original building, constructed in 1724, was extensively repaired after a 1788 fire.) According to legend, and the eponymous short story by 19th-century writer George Washington Cable, it was willed to a beautiful quadroon by her aristocratic lover, John (hence "Madame John's Legacy"). Today it houses a good collection of Southern regional art and is administered by the Louisiana State Museum. | 632 Dumaine St.,. | 504/568–6968, 800/568–6968 | fax 504/568–4995 | www.crt.state.la.us | $3; children 12 and under free | Tues.–Sun. 9–5, closed Mon.

Old U.S. Mint. This Greek-Revival style building was constructed in 1835 to help finance the development of the western frontier. When Louisiana seceded from the Union, state authorities seized the property and transferred it to the Confederate Army, which minted currency and housed troops there. Today the Mint functions as a museum, with exhibits on everything from history to pottery and jazz. | 400 Esplanade Ave. | 504/568–6968 | fax 504/568–4995 | www.crt.state.la.us.

The Presbytère. The name means "Monastery," as the Cabildo's twin was built in 1799 on the site of a 1720 monastery destroyed by fire. In 1834 it became a courthouse, and in 1911 it became part of the Louisiana State Museum. Today it houses cultural displays, including documentary photos, decorative arts, and maps. | 751 Chartres St., | 504/568–6968, 800/568–6968 | fax 504/568–4995 | www.crt.state.la.us | $5; children 12 and under free | Tues.–Sun. 9–5, closed Mon.

Musée Wax-Conti. This little charmer is an especially cool destination on a hot summer day. Strikingly lifelike figures imported from France are arranged in illuminated tableaux. You'll see local legends as well as famous monsters (Dracula, Wolfman, et al.), all represented in the Chamber of Horrors. | 917 Conti St., | 504/581–1993, 800/233–5405 | fax 504/

566–7636 | $6.75; special rates for children and senior citizens | Mon.–Sat. 10–5:00, Sun. 12–5:00, closed Dec. 20–26.

New Orleans Historic Voodoo Museum. Cramped and creepy, this tiny museum may be a bit too realistic for you if you prefer not to view authentic fetishes, old bones, black magic altars, or dead cats. Practitioners are available in the gift shop for readings or to mix custom ju-ju preparations to cure your problems. Ask about occasional ritual performances and special tours. | 724 Dumaine St. | 504/523–7685 | fax 504/523–8591 | www.voodoomuseum.com | $6; special rates for students and children | Daily 10–8.

New Orleans Museum of Art. The original Neoclassical building (circa 1910) in City Park has been updated and vastly expanded over the years and is now home to some 35,000 works valued at well over $300 million. The 46 galleries are filled with European, American, Asian, African, and Oceanic art. The collection is especially strong in photography, Spanish colonial art of South America, Japanese paintings of the Edo period, pre-Columbian and Native American works, and vibrant paintings by Southern self-taught artists. An impressive collection of European and American decorative arts includes a whole room of Fabergé and one of the largest glass collections in the U.S. Light breakfasts and lunches are served in the Courtyard Café. | 1 Collins Diboll Cir. | 504/488–2631 | fax 504/484–6662 | www.noma.org | $6; special rates for senior citizens and children | Tues.–Sun. 10–5, closed Mon.

New Orleans Pharmacy Museum *(La Pharmacie Française).* Now restored as a museum, this is the original 19th-century shop of pharmacist Louis Dufilho, Jr., who earned one of the first U.S. licenses in 1816. Among the sights are patent medicines, alarming medical contraptions, apothecary supplies, vintage advertising—even voodoo preparations. Gentler attractions include an antique soda fountain and a courtyard planted with medicinal herbs. | 514 Chartres St. | 504/565–8027 | fax 504/565–8028 | www.pharmacymuseum.org | $2; special rate for students | Tues.–Sun. 10–5, closed Mon.

RELIGION AND SPIRITUALITY

St. Louis Cathedral. Originally consecrated in 1794, the cathedral was named for Louis IX of France, known as the Sun King. The present building, completed in 1851, replaces two earlier structures that were demolished by hurricane and fire. It was designated a minor basilica by Pope Paul VI in 1964. | 721 Chartres St. at Jackson Sq. | 504/525–9585 | Free | Daily. Tours Mon.–Sat. 9–5, Sun. 2–5.

Cathedral Garden. Once the preferred meeting place for dueling gentlemen, this lovely garden behind St. Louis Cathedral is much quieter these days. The marble statue honors members of the French navy who died here during yellow fever epidemics. It was erected by order of Napoleon I. | 721 Chartres St. | Free | Daily.

SHOPPING

Adelina Patti's House and Courtyard. Now known as the Old Town Praline Shop, this French Quarter town house was once home to international opera star Adelina Patti, who lived and performed in New Orleans in the early 1860's. The 17-yr-old diva attracted scores of gentlemen admirers, who used to crowd the street in front of her residence where she sometimes sang from the balcony. Photos and mementos line one wall of the shop, which has sold authentic Creole pralines and other goodies since 1935. The crumbly old courtyard is filled with ginger plants and hungry birds, who beg for pecan dust from the kitchen. | 631 Royal St. | 504/525–1413 | Free | Mon.–Sat. 10–5.

French Market. The oldest open-air market in the U.S. rambles along the riverfront from Jackson Square to Esplanade Avenue. During the 18th and early 19th centuries it was the city's central commercial area, with vendors offering everything from parrots and monkeys to outdoor dentistry. Built on the site of an ancient Native American trading post, the series of colonnaded structures dates to 1813. Today they house upscale shops and restaurants near the Jackson Square end. From Ursulines Street to Esplanade Avenue, open stalls still supply local cooks with fresh produce. The daily flea market provides an entertaining rummage for handmade masks, ethnic jewelry, and leather goods. The farmers' market is open 24 hours and sells produce, hot sauces, Cajun/Creole food products, and more. | 1008 N. Peters | 504/522–2621 | fax 504/596–3410 | Free | Daily.

Jackson Brewery/Millhouse. The riverfront brewery that produced Jax Beer from 1891 to 1974 and an adjoining industrial mill were converted to festival malls during the 1980s. Today they're filled with dozens of colorful shops and casual restaurants, live entertainment during holiday seasons, plus great views of the Mississippi from panoramic terraces. | 600 Decatur St. | 504/566–7245 | fax 504/566–7246 | Free | Mon.–Sat. 10–9, Sun. 10–7.

Riverwalk Marketplace. More than 100 shops and restaurants are in this festival mall that stretches for ½ mi along the riverfront. Huge walls of glass frame views of the traffic on the Mississippi, and vendor carts scattered along the walkways create a street-fair atmosphere. Major tenants include Abercrombie and Fitch, Banana Republic, The Sharper Image, and Eddie Bauer. The mall has several entry points, including an elevated walkway from the lobby of the New Orleans Hilton Riverside. | 1 Poydras St. | 504/522–1555 | fax 504/586–8532 | www.riverwalkmarketplace.com | Free | Mon.–Sat. 10–9, Sun. 11–7.

SPORTS AND RECREATION

The Louisiana Superdome. This massive indoor stadium, completed in 1975, sprawls over 52 acres with a total height equivalent to 27 stories. The diameter of the dome is 680 ft. The seating capacity runs from 70,000 to almost 90,000, depending on the event. These are just a few of the statistics you'll hear on one of the daily tours. The Superdome is home to the New Orleans Saints and the annual Sugar Bowl game. | Sugar Bowl Dr. | 504/587–3663, 800/756–7074 | fax 504/587–3848 | www.superdome.com | Prices vary for events | Call for schedule of events; tours weekdays 10:30, 12, 1:30.

NFL (New Orleans Saints). The New Orleans Saints are Louisiana's NFL franchise. Home games are played in the Louisiana Superdome. | Louisiana Superdome, Sugar Bowl Dr. | 504/733–0255 | fax 504/731–1782 | www.neworleanssaints.com | $50, $75 | Call for schedule.

SIGHTSEEING TOURS/TOUR COMPANIES

Gray Line Bus Tours. In addition to general city tours, you may book longer jaunts that take in River Road plantations or swamps and bayous. Some packages add a paddlewheeler cruise on the Mississippi. A good selection of walking tours is offered, including the spooky "Hauntings, Gris-Gris, and Cemeteries." The ticket booth is on the riverfront at Toulouse St., next to Jax Brewery. | 2 Canal St. | 504/569–1401, 800/535–7786 | fax 504/587–0742 | www.graylineneworleans.com | $15–$63 | Daily 7 AM–8 PM.

New Orleans Paddlewheelers. The riverboat *Cajun Queen* and paddlewheeler *Creole Queen* are replicas of 19th-century passenger steamboats. Daily 90-min cruises travel through the harbor to the Chalmette Battlefield, scene of the Battle of New Orleans. Nightly dinner jazz cruises offer a Cajun/Creole buffet and live Dixieland music. | 610 S. Peters | 504/529–4567, 888/311–4109 | fax 504/524–6265 | www.visitnola.com | $10–$49 | Ticket office daily 9–8pm. Tours 10:30–4, 8.

OTHER POINTS OF INTEREST

★ **Aquarium of the Americas.** One of the top U.S. aquariums showcases the aquatic life of the Gulf of Mexico and South America. Exhibits include an offshore rig, Amazon rainforest, underwater tunnel, sharks, penguins, and the world's largest collection of jellyfish. The Entergy IMAX Theatre is part of the complex, presenting nature films (some in 3-D) on a five-story movie screen with 12,000 watts of sound. River cruises connect the downtown aquarium with the uptown Audubon Zoo. Combination tickets are available. | 1 Canal St. | 504/581–4629 | fax 504/565–3865 | www.auduboninstitute.org | Aquarium: $12; discounts for senior citizens and children. IMAX: $7.75; discounts for senior citizens and children. Combination tickets for aquarium and IMAX: $17.25; discounts for senior citizens and children. Combination tickets for aquarium and zoo: $17.50; discounts for senior citizens and children. Combination tickets for aquarium and zoo with connecting cruise: $28.25; discounts for children. Combination tickets for aquarium, IMAX, and zoo with connecting cruise: $34.50; discounts for children | Sun.–Thurs. 9:30–6, Fri.–Sat. 9:30–7.

Audubon Zoological Garden. Set in oak-shaded Audubon Park on the former estate of artist John James Audubon, one of the top five zoos in the U.S. is a lavish tropical garden populated by more than 1,500 animals. Major attractions include the award-winning Louisiana Swamp Exhibit, the art-filled tropical bird house, an exotic walk through "Butterflies in Flight," rides along an African-style savannah aboard the Mombassa Train, two white tigers, monkeys galore, and daily feedings at the vintage 1920s sea lion pool. Meanwhile, humans can chomp down some lunch overlooking the alligators from the deck of the Cypress Knee Café, which serves gumbo, red beans and rice, jambalaya, crawfish pie, and other local specialties. | 6500 Magazine St. | 504/581–4629, 800/774–7394 | fax 504/565–3865 | www.auduboninstitute.org | Zoo: $9.00; discounts for senior citizens and children. Combination tickets for aquarium and zoo: $17.50; discounts for senior citizens and children. Combination tickets for aquarium and zoo with connecting cruise: $28.25; discounts for children. Combination tickets for aquarium, IMAX, and zoo with connecting cruise: $34.50; discounts for children | Daily 9:30–5; Apr.–Aug., weekends 9:30–6.

Canal Street Ferry. The best deal in the city is a 30-min (round-trip) cruise across the Mississippi, free for foot passengers and $1 per car. It's a great way to see one of the world's busiest harbors, where you may pass right beside tugboats guiding strings of barges or huge freighters bound for exotic ports. The view of the city skyline and French Quarter is breathtaking on the return trip from the suburb of Algiers, especially when the buildings are illuminated after dark. | Canal St. at the Mississippi River | 504/364–8114 | Free, cars pay $1 for return trip | Daily.

© Corbis

CARNIVAL

Like many European, Caribbean, and South American cities with a strong Catholic influence, Louisiana celebrates Carnival (Latin for "Farewell to Flesh"), a season of parties and parades that extends from Epiphany (January 6) until Ash Wednesday, when the faithful begin 40 days of fasting and deprivation for Lent. Mardi Gras (French for "Fat Tuesday"), the final day of the celebration, provides one last chance for overindulgence before starting the annual sin-free diet.

Smaller communities may present a single parade or street dance, but larger towns host a full schedule of masquerades and other special events. The most famous bacchanal takes place in New Orleans, where more than 60 parades stop traffic throughout the city and its suburbs for weeks. They're sponsored by private clubs, known as *krewes*, which also produce elaborate masked balls for members and their guests. By early morning on Mardi Gras, sidewalks and balconies are jammed with spectators scrambling for "throws," the trinkets tossed from floats by costumed riders. Rowdy marching groups, like the Jefferson City Buzzards and Pete Fountain's Half-Fast Walking Club, wind through the crowds, trading paper carnations for kisses from the ladies. The entire city shuts down for a full day of picnicking and dancing in the streets.

Meanwhile, out in the country, Cajun Mardi Gras is an entirely different scene, as masked riders gallop on horseback through villages and fields, stopping at farmhouses to beg ingredients (especially live chickens) for a huge community gumbo feast and street dance held later in the day. The most famous of these *courirs* (or "runs") is held in Mamou, but many of South Louisiana's Cajun communities continue the old tradition.

Moonwalk. This lighted boardwalk is a great place to stroll atop the levee for dazzling views of both the river and Jackson Square. You'll usually be serenaded by at least one freelance musician. The aromas of beignets and brewing coffee from the adjoining Café du Monde are hard to resist. | On the river, across from Jackson Square | Free | Daily.

New Orleans Steamboat Company. The Natchez is the city's only authentic sternwheel steamboat, offering daily 2-hr cruises of the New Orleans harbor and nightly dinner cruises, both featuring live jazz and an optional Cajun/Creole buffet. The riverboat John James Audubon shuttles between the Aquarium of the Americas on Canal Street and the Audubon Zoo, which is located upriver in Audubon Park. Ask about special packages that include admission to the aquarium and zoo, with the river cruise in between. | 2 Canal St. | 504/586–8777, 800/233–BOAT | fax 504/587–0708 | www.steamboatnatchez.com | $16–$26 | Call for schedule of cruises.

Riverfront Streetcar Line. The bright red cars are the same 1923 models that once crisscrossed the entire city, a system whose only remaining survivor is the St. Charles Avenue line. This newer track was created in the 1980s to service the main tourist corridor along the riverfront, stopping at several points in the French Quarter, Central Business District, and Warehouse/Arts District. | On the riverfront, from Esplanade Ave. to Julia St. | 504/248–3900 | $1.25 | Daily 24 hrs.

St. Charles Avenue Streetcar. If there is one must-see attraction in New Orleans, this is it. Like the San Francisco trolley, it is a regular mode of transportation for residents, which makes the ride even more fun. The electric cars, installed in 1923, are part of the oldest street railway system in the world, first powered by steam locomotives in 1835. They rumble beneath overarching oak trees through some of the most beautiful neighborhoods in New Orleans. On the 13-mi round trip from mainline Canal Street, you'll clang past the elaborate mansions of the Garden District, Tulane and Loyola Universities, Audubon Park, the stylish shops and restaurants in the Riverbend area, and the Victorian cottages of Carrollton. Allow about 90 min to make the full circuit, if you can resist the mighty temptation to hop off and on every few blocks. | Along St. Charles and Carrollton Aves., from Canal St. to Palmer Park | 504/248–3900 | $1.25 | Daily 24 hrs.

ON THE CALENDAR

JAN.: *Sugar Bowl College Football Classic.* A tradition for local football fans since 1935, this event is set in the ultra-modern Superdome, usually in the first week of January. | 504/525–8573; 504/525–8603 ticket office.

JAN.–MAR.: *Carnival/Mardi Gras.* Dozens of parades are scheduled nearly every weekend during Carnival season and nightly during the final two weeks. Lundi Gras (Monday) is a full day of free concerts on the downtown riverfront, and Mardi Gras is a full day of street parties, masquerades, and parades throughout the city and suburbs. | Jan. 6–Ash Wednesday; Mardi Gras is always the Tues. before Ash Wednesday | 504/566–5009, 800/748–8695.

MAR.: *Spring Fiesta.* Historic private houses and gardens are open for tours at the height of spring color. | 504/581–1367.

MAR.: *Tennessee Williams/New Orleans Literary Festival.* Music, theater, lectures, panel discussions, walking tours, and special events (such as the annual "Stella!" hollering contest) celebrate the literary heritage of the South, New Orleans in particular. Writers, scholars, actors, and fans converge on the city for this 5-day annual festival honoring Tennessee Williams, who wrote "A Streetcar Named Desire" and who lived and worked in New Orleans for a time. | Usually 3rd or 4th weekend of the month | 504/581–1144.

APR.: *French Quarter Festival.* Outdoor concerts throughout the Quarter by more than 500 local musicians, food from more than 40 local restaurants along the riverfront, fireworks, a parade, and children's activities celebrate the French Quarter. | 504/522–5730, 800/673–5725.

APR., MAY: *New Orleans Jazz and Heritage Festival.* This major event attracts an international crowd for two long weekends of performances by more than 4,000 musicians, authentic Louisiana foods, plus quality arts and crafts. This is the second busiest weekend in the city, after Mardi Gras. Twelve different music venues inside the Fairgrounds showcase diverse music types such as gospel, R&B, jazz, Cajun, zydeco, folk, rock, Latin, African, Caribbean, swing, rap, reggae, and more. Additional evening concerts are scheduled throughout the week, and club schedules are filled with big-name bands. | Last weekend in Apr, Fri.–Sun., and first weekend in May, Thurs.–Sun. | 504/522–4786.

NOV.–MAR.: *Horseracing at New Orleans Fairgrounds.* Thoroughbred racing takes place on a historic track in a Mid-City neighborhood of New Orleans just a few blocks from City Park. The 3rd oldest racetrack in the country, it was built in 1852 but a fire in 1993 devastated the original grandstand. View historic photos inside the new grandstand. The Louisiana Derby is held each March. | Thurs.–Mon., from Thanksgiving through Mar. | 504/944–5515, 800/262–7893.

DEC.: *Christmas, New Orleans Style!* Celebrate the holiday during this full month of parades, bonfires, fireworks, riverboat races, cooking demonstrations, concerts, special deals at restaurants and hotels, candlelight house tours, theatrical productions, and other special events. The trees in City Park are illuminated by over 1 million lights. | Throughout Dec. | 504/522–5730, 800/673–5725.

Dining

INEXPENSIVE

Acme Oyster and Seafood Restaurant. Seafood. A rough-edge classic in every way, this no-nonsense eatery at the entrance to the French Quarter is a prime source of cool and salty raw oysters on the half shell; great shrimp, oyster, and hot roast beef po'-boys; and state-of-the-art red beans and rice. There's table service in the front dining room. Expect a rather lengthy queue at the marble-top oyster bar and cafeteria-style sandwich counter during peak hours. Crowds are sparser in the late afternoon. Take out also available. | 724 Iberville St. | 504/522–5973 | fax 504/524–1595 | Reservations not accepted | $5–$14 | AE, D, DC, MC, V.

Café Atchafalaya. Creole. Homespun cooking with a definite Southern accent is the focus inside this ancient, white-clapboard building near the uptown riverfront. Fresh vegetables and hearty fruit pies are specialties, as are the fried green tomatoes, stuffed pork chops, boiled beef brisket with potato, chicken and dumplings, and lemon chess pie. You'll find Southern cheese grits, jalapeño bread, black eyed peas, and lima beans. The modest dining room has bare-top tables, a specials chalkboard, and posters and fish prints. Have a leisurely weekend breakfast or brunch and watch the locals stop in after their morning jogs. | 901 Louisiana Ave. | 504/891–5271 | Closed Mon. | $6–$16 | MC, V.

★ **Café Du Monde.** Café. Savoring chicory coffee and *beignets* (hot French doughnuts) served around the clock at the city's most famous sidewalk café has been a local tradition since the 1860s. Both residents and tourists flock to this café across from Jackson Square near the river. There's open-air seating on the covered patio under ceiling fans. Street musicians perform nearby, and it's a great place for late-night people watching. Early morning hours are the best time to avoid lines, though they generally move quickly. | 813 Decatur St. | 504/525–4544 | www.cafedumonde.com | Open 24 hrs | $2–$6 | No credit cards.

Café Maspero. Cajun/Creole. Big portions and low prices keep the locals lining up at the door for po'-boys and two-fisted hot and cold sandwiches. Arched doors and windows give the vast, noisy brick dining room a little character. Maspero also serves red beans and rice and jambalaya. Very casual. Open late night. | 601 Decatur St. | 504/523–6250 | fax 504/523–6246 | No reservations accepted | $3–$9 | No credit cards.

Café Pontalba. Cajun. A line of French doors opens onto busy Jackson Square from this café, which is popular with tourists. It serves a variety of Cajun dishes, from basics such as red beans and rice, jambalaya, and gumbo to more elaborate preparations such as blackened tuna Orleans and stuffed trout. | 546 St. Peter St. | 504/522–1180 | $6–$19 | D, DC, MC, V.

Camellia Grill. American. Every diner should be as classy as Camellia Grill, a one-of-a-kind eatery near the waterfront just west of Tulane that deserves its loyal following. Late into the night, students, physicians, and other locals pile in for one of the 29 counter stools at the gleaming counter. The hamburger—four oz of beef on a fresh bun with any number of embellishments—is excellent. Other blue-ribbon dishes are the omelets—try with potato, onion, chili, and cheese—and pecan waffles. The pecan pie heated on the grill and served with ice cream is superb. To wash all the food down, try an orange or coffee freeze with ice cream. Everything is made on the premises; you can watch from your counter seat. Wait staff is bow-tied, white-waistcoated, and very polite. Open late night. | 626 S. Carrollton Ave. | 504/866–9573 | No reservations accepted | $5–$9 | No credit cards.

Casamento's. Seafood. Casamento's, which is west of the Garden District, has been serving seafood since 1918. Family members still staff the marble, raw-oyster bar up front and the immaculate kitchen out back; between the two is a small dining room with a similarly small menu. The specialties are oysters lightly poached in seasoned milk, oyster loaf, fried shrimp, tenderloin of trout, spaghetti with meatballs, and *daube* (a Creole roast). Meals are served with fried potatoes, and there's a good selection of domestic beers. | 4330 Magazine St. | 504/895–9761 | Closed early June–late Aug., Mon. | Reservations not accepted | $5–$18 | No credit cards.

Central Grocery. Continental. A Sicilian market open since 1906, the deli stacks imported meats and cheeses on fresh Italian breads. Its famous muffuletta sandwich consists of round Italian bread stuffed with ham, salami, mozzarella cheese, and a homemade green olive spread. The sandwiches are sold in quarters or halves, and the olive spread is sold in jars as well. No tables, this is more of an old-time grocery store, but there are a couple of bar stools. Or you can dine outside on a bench near the Mississippi River. | 923 Decatur St. | 504/523–1620 | Breakfast also available. Closes at 5:30. | $6–$10 | No credit cards.

Clover Grill. American. This small no-nonsense diner, established in 1939, caters to an eclectic late-night crowd and is open around the clock. The jukebox sends out some great New Orleans sounds, and service is outgoing and cheerful. There are 11 red stools at the counter and 4 tables near big windows to watch the scene passing on Bourbon St. The menu adds humor to the food with names like Geaux Girl Waffles with Pecans (you won't need to add butter to this heavenly item). Breakfast is served 24 hrs. Burgers are a house specialty, and other non-breakfast items include sandwiches and chicken-fried steak. | 900 Bourbon St. | 504/598–1010 | www.clovergrill.com | Open 24 hrs | $5–$10 | No credit cards.

Crescent City Brewhouse. Cajun. Sample house beers in sight of giant copper kettles in the working brewery. Outdoor tables on the second-floor balcony have views across busy Decatur Street to the Mississippi River. This is a casual spot very popular with tourists. Monthly exhibits by local artists are on the exposed brick walls. Oysters on the half shell are a specialty (check out the size of the oyster shucker's forearms as you walk in the door). American fare such as nachos, chili, burgers, chicken sandwiches, and beer basted ribs are served, as well as such Louisiana fare as shrimp étouffée, oyster club sandwiches, shrimp po'-boys, crabmeat enchiladas. Live jazz nightly. | 527 Decatur St. | 504/522–0571 | www.crescentcitybrewhouse.com | $10–$19 | AE, D, DC, MC, V.

Croissant D'or. Café. In a quiet section of the French Quarter, locals compete with tourists for a table in this colorful and pristine pastry shop that serves excellent and authentic French croissants, pies, tarts, and custards, as well as an array of soups, salads, and sandwiches. Wash them down with real French breakfast coffee, cappuccino, or espresso. In good weather the courtyard, with its quiet fountain, is the place to sit. A filling lunch can be had for less than $10. | 617 Ursulines St. | 504/524–4663 | Reservations not accepted | Daily 7–5, breakfast also available | $4–$9 | MC, V.

Desire Oyster Bar. Cajun. Opening onto lively Bourbon Street, this casual, noisy bistro in the Royal Sonesta Hotel is named for the Tennessee Williams play. You can watch expert oyster shuckers work while you sample oysters on the half shell, boiled shrimp and crawfish, red beans and rice, shrimp rémoulade, seafood platters, po'-boys, soups, salads, burgers, or steaks. Oyster bar. Kids' menu. | 300 Bourbon St. | 504/586–0300 | www.royalsonestano.com | $9–$25 | AE, D, DC, MC, V.

Dooky Chase. Creole. Authentic Creole soul food is served at this longtime favorite of locals and visiting musicians that's also popular with families after church on Sundays. Artwork by local African-American artists is on display in the warm, elegant dining area. The dining room is pretty with plum colored walls and mauve and burgundy table linens. Recipes for the homestyle dishes date back more than a century, with cooking techniques handed down the generations. The menu includes fried chicken, gumbo, sausage jambalaya, stewed okra, sweet potatoes, bread pudding, and apple pie. Buffet lunch weekdays. | 2301 Orleans Ave. | 504/821–0600 | $10–$15 | AE, DC, MC, V.

Felix's Restaurant. Seafood. This old-time oyster house in the French Quarter piles plates high with crawfish, shrimp po' boys, chicken, or steak. Oyster lovers eat them raw or choose from stews, soups, and omelettes. | 739 Iberville St. | 504/522–4440 | $8–$18 | AE,D,MC,V.

Figaro's Pizzeria. Italian. Even in Creole-Cajun country, pizza holds considerable sway. Doubters can stop in at Figaro's, the favorite uptown spot for New Orleanians who can't shake the craving for American- or Italian-style pizza. In the small interior dining room, or at a table in the connecting tented space, the faithful come for traditional favorites and more exotic pies—such as crawfish étouffée with wild mushrooms and ginger or yellowfin tuna with a salsa of carmelized onions, roasted sweet peppers, and mangoes. Other dishes include veal with linguine, roasted duck or chicken, and a corn-and-crab soup spiked with bourbon. Outdoor dining on two terraces. | 7900 Maple St. | 504/866–0100 | Reservations not accepted | $8–$16 | AE, D, MC, V.

Fiorella's Café. Café. Scouring the booths at the French Quarter's flea market can sharpen any appetite. A few steps away from the hubbub is this very casual eatery specializing in classic po'-boys and New Orleans–style plate lunches. Red beans and rice show up on Monday, meat loaf on Tuesday, Thursday is the day for butter beans, and a hearty breakfast is an everyday feature. The spaces are tight and rather dark, but you can't beat the prices. The café closes at five PM. | 45 French Market Pl. | 504/528–9566 | Closed Sun. No dinner | $5–$12 | AE, D, DC, MC, V.

Five Happiness. Chinese. The three sprawling dining rooms and efficient service here accommodate a thriving local trade. The black and burgundy color scheme is accented with a fish tank and Asian artifacts. Try the shrimp with honey-roasted pecans, asparagus chicken, or baked duck. Takeout and delivery available. | 3605 S. Carrollton Ave. | 504/482–3935 | $11–$19 | AE, D, DC, MC, V.

Franky and Johnny's. Seafood. Seekers of the quintessential New Orleans neighborhood restaurant need look no further. Team pennants, posters, and football jerseys vie for space on the paneled walls of the low-ceiling bar and dining room, while a jukebox blares beneath them. From the kitchen's steaming cauldrons come freshly boiled shrimp, crabs, and crawfish, piled high and ready to be washed down with an ice-cold beer. On the day's po'-boy roster might be fried crawfish tails or oysters, meatballs in tomato sauce, or roast beef with gravy. Table service is rudimentary. Near the waterfront east of Audubon Zoo. | 321 Arabella St. | 504/899–9146 | Reservations not accepted | $11–$16 | AE, D, MC, V.

Irene's Cuisine. Italian. Go very early or prepare to wait at this popular French Quarter spot. The lighting is quite dim and the walls are filled with snapshots, olive jars, garlic braids, and crockery. Try garlicky Italian sausage steeped in roasted peppers; chicken roasted with garlic, olive oil, and rosemary; tubes of manicotti stuffed with ground veal and mozzarella; and fresh shrimp seasoned, grilled and served with linguine and herbed olive oil. For dessert, there's an Italian-style baked Alaska, covered with a blue flame of ignited grappa liqueur. | 539 St. Philip St. | 504/529–8811 | Reservations not accepted | No lunch | $11–$22 | AE, MC, V.

Johnny's Po-boys. Delicatessen. Strangely enough, good po'-boys are hard to find in the French Quarter. But Johnny's has a cornucopia of them, put together in the time-honored New Orleans manner. Inside soft-crust French bread you'll find the classic fillings—lean boiled ham, well-done roast beef in a garlicky gravy, crisply fried oysters or shrimp, and a wide variety of others. Also serves red beans and rice. | 511 St. Louis St. | 504/523–9071 | No reservations accepted | Breakfast also available. Weekdays 7–4:30, weekends 9–4 | No dinner | $6–$10 | No credit cards.

La Crêpe Nanou. French. This welcoming uptown bistro serves French chic for the budget-minded. During peak hours you may have a half-hour wait at the bar. Left Bank Paris is evoked with woven café chairs out on the sidewalk, a velvet curtain inside the door, awnings that resemble Metro-station architecture, and a menu loaded with pâté maison, hearty lentil soup, french fries that are really French, and lavish dessert crêpes. Other popular items include mussels *mariniere* (in wine, cream, and herbs), chicken roasted with herbs and garlic, and the daily whole-grilled fish. Spaces are a little tight in the oddly configured dining areas filled with paintings and greenery. Regulars, mostly young professionals from the nearby frame cottages, give the place a clubby air. | 1410 Robert St. | 504/899–2670 | www.lacrepenanou.com | Reservations not accepted | No lunch | $7–$18 | MC, V.

La Madeleine. French. Authentic French pastries, such as napoleons, éclairs, and croissants, and 15 styles of country breads come fresh from a heartstone wood-fired oven. Wood beams, rustic French antiques, and antique bricks add to the country French theme. The tall French doors open onto Jackson Square. Tomato basil is a signature soup. Other choices include pasta, pizza, soups, quiche, rotisserie chicken, Caesar salad, and sandwiches. Beer and wine only. | 547 St. Ann St. | 504/568–9950 | Breakfast also available | $9–$15 | AE, D, DC, MC, V.

Lemon Grass Café. Vietnamese. Regulars come to the Lemon Grass, relocated to the International House hotel in the Central Business District, for spicy Vietnamese cuisine—specifically that of Saigon, with occasional French influences. Rows of small, abstract watercolors by a local painter hang on gray walls; table linens are lined with butcher paper. Try crisp spring rolls filled with minced chicken, jicama root, wood-ear mushrooms, carrot and onion; soft-shell crab; seared fish; or thin slices of duck breast served with sticky rice. Tiny cubes of roasted sweet potato accompany a delicious pork chop dry-rubbed with chilies. Desserts include chocolate Bavarian creme pie, crème brûlée, and a strawberry napoleon. | 217 Camp St. | 504/523–1200 | No lunch weekends | $9–$20 | AE, D, DC, MC, V.

Mandina's. Seafood. The interior of this pink clapboard corner building is a study in 1940s nostalgia. A functional bar faces a roomful of laminated tables. Regulars sometimes endure a standing wait at the bar or outside. The fried shrimp po'-boys—overstuffed with lots of large Louisiana shrimp and served on soft French bread—are popular, and Mandina's turtle soup is considered one of the best soup in town. Shrimp rémoulade and old-fashioned gumbo are a good beginning. There's a large menu with specials for each day of the week, including chicken, catfish, red beans, seafood platters, étouffée, and more. Try bread pudding for dessert. | 3800 Canal St. | 504/482–9179 | Reservations not accepted | $7–$24 | No credit cards.

Mike Anderson's. Seafood. A bustling Bourbon Street favorite created by the former all-American football player for L.S.U., this restaurant has an easygoing bayou decor and balcony tables overlooking the passing crowds. Signature dishes include trout Norman (topped with crab étouffée) and *guitreau* (grilled fish with sautéed crawfish, shrimp, and mushrooms in white wine butter sauce). Also on the menu are fried and raw oysters, boiled shrimp, crawfish and crabmeat fettucini, choice rib eye, and chicken. Raw bar. | 215 Bourbon St. | 504/524–3884 | www.mikeandersons.com | $11–$28 | AE, D, DC, MC, V.

Mother's. Cajun. Big Southern breakfasts and hot roast beef sandwiches are local traditions at this popular establishment. Or try homestyle biscuits, jambalaya, or chicken gumbo. Service is cafeteria style. | 401 Poydras St. | 504/523–9656 | Breakfast also available | $7–$15 | No credit cards.

Mulate's. Cajun. This Cajun mainstay is lively, crowded, and brimming with seafood and jambalaya. If you like crawfish, you're in for a treat—Mulate's demi et demi, or fried crawfish and crawfish etouffee, is just one of the dishes you'll find on the menu. The Cajun seafood platter, piled high with crab, crawfish, shrimp, catfish, oysters, jambalaya, and fries, is another. | 201 Julia St. | 504/522–1492 | $7–$19 | AE,D,MC,V.

Napoleon House. Cajun/Creole. An ancient bar in a historic building is filled with unvarnished atmosphere and intriguing history. It was once fitted out as a refuge for Napoleon by local sympathizers, who hatched an unsuccessful plot to rescue the emperor from exile. Drinking and dining take place in a small central courtyard and moody interior rooms. A favorite local hangout for writers, artists, and an eclectic crowd, it serves sandwiches, salads, and a warm muffuletta sandwich. Good wine list and homemade desserts. Open-air dining in courtyard. | 500 Chartres St. | 504/524–9752 | Closes at 7 on Sun. | $8–$15 | AE, D, DC, MC, V.

Pascal's Manale. Italian. Few restaurants are identified with one dish as strongly as is Pascal's with barbecued shrimp. The original version, introduced a half century ago, remains: jumbo shrimp, still in the shell, cooked in spiced butter. The rest of the menu is mostly seafood and Italian creations. Turtle soup, fried eggplant, and baked or raw oysters are good starters. Sautéed veal with shrimp, chicken bordelaise, and seafood pasta are popular entrées. The restaurant's popularity with out-of-towners usually means a wait for a table on weekends, even with a reservation. There is a lively bar with lots of old photos to browse through while you wait. | 1828 Napoleon Ave. | 504/895–4877 | Reservations essential | No lunch weekends | $9–$20 | AE, D, DC, MC, V.

Praline Connection. Southern. Speedy service, low prices, a sharp black-and-white decor, and plastic tablecloths provide the setting for no-nonsense Southern home cooking such as smothered pork shops, fried chicken, barbecued ribs, jambalaya, gumbo, red beans and rice, and sweet potato pie. All dinners come with choice of lima beans, peas, mustard, collard, or cabbage greens, and okra and rice. Try the stuffed bell peppers. An adjoining confectionery sells pralines and other house-made candies. Kids' menu. | 542 Frenchmen St. | 504/943–3934 | Reservations not accepted | $11–$20 | AE, D, DC, MC, V.

Red Fish Grill. Seafood. A high energy level and a riotous color scheme put this casual, bouncy place, owned by Ralph Brennan of the city's premier restaurant family, right in tune with Bourbon Street's festive atmosphere. The large, central dining space is edged by banquettes, smaller rooms, and a huge oyster bar. The kitchen's handiwork includes a delicious barbecued shrimp po'-boy, a seafood gumbo with alligator sausage, baked oysters, and a good selection of fresh grilled fish garnished with combinations such as crabmeat and corn. The signature dessert is a variation on the bananas Foster theme, with banana beignets soaking up vanilla ice cream and a brown-sugar sauce. A bar menu is available after 3 PM. Sun. brunch's belt-buster is a three-egg omelet with crabmeat, asparagus, and hollandaise sauce. | 115 Bourbon St. | 504/598–1200 | www.redfishgrill.com | $10–$27 | AE, DC, MC, V.

Rémoulade. Creole. Although operated by the same owners as Arnaud's, Rémoulade is much more laid-back, with minimal frills and easier prices. It offers the same Caesar salad and pecan pie, shrimp Arnaud in rémoulade sauce, oysters stewed in cream, turtle soup, and shrimp bisque. Casual diners will find po'-boys, burgers, pizzas, and many seafood dishes with south Louisiana pedigrees. Dark wood walls, tile floors, mirrors, a pressed tin ceiling, and brass ceiling lights create an environment made for such New Orleans staples as boiled shrimp, crawfish, crabs, red beans and rice with smoked hot sausage, barbecued shrimp, and jambalaya. Sit at the marble-top oyster bar or the mahogany cocktail bar dating to the 1870s. Open until about midnight, it's a good stopping-off point during a late evening round in the French Quarter nightlife. | 309 Bourbon St. | 504/523–0377 | fax 504/581–7908 | Reservations not accepted | $5–$12 | AE, D, DC, MC, V.

Sante Fe. Mexican. Sunny dining rooms sport rattan furnishings and lots of greenery in an old frame cottage near a park. The white walls have mirrors and bright prints. An innovative Mexican cuisine incorporates fresh Gulf seafood. Try tamales with chipotle pork, crawfish fajitas, and enchiladas. Other specialties are margaritas made with fresh-squeezed lime juice and, for dessert, chocolate coconut pecan pie. | 801 Frenchman | 504/944–6854 | Closed Sun., Mon. No lunch | $10–$22 | AE, MC, V.

Shalimar Indian Cuisine. Indian. This former stable near Jackson Square is softly lit and filled with sinuous Indian art, antique tapestries, and ornately carved screens. The small downstairs room has tables and booths and elegant Indian carved panels. Upstairs is more informal with the setup for the lunch buffet. The extensive 11-page menu includes shrimp with peanuts, cashews, and almonds and lamb with tomato and raisin curry, as well as many tandoori items, vegetarian dishes, and curries ranging from mild to fiery hot. | 535 Wilkinson St. | 504/523–0099 | www.shalimarno.com | No lunch Sat. | $11–$20 | AE, MC, V.

Tony Moran's Pasta e Vino. Italian. This quaint restaurant is on the first floor of the historic Old Absinthe House. You can choose from homemade pastas such as fettucine Alfredo, cannelloni, or the daily ravioli or entrées such as chicken parmigiana and veal milanese. Wonderful desserts include tiramisu, spumoni, tortoni, and cheesecake. Open-air dining in two courtyards available. | 240 Bourbon St. | 504/523–3181 | Closed Mon. No lunch | $11–$24 | AE, DC, MC, V.

Uglesich Restaurant and Bar. Seafood. In business since 1924, Uglesich's is in an old neighborhood, still untouched by gentrification. Don't be put off by the weatherbeaten appearance of the restaurant. Go for the food and the character of a real New Orleans joint. The oysters are the big draw, shucked to order at the bar. They come served on the half shell, fried up for po'-boy sandwiches, or barbecue-style, roasted in olive oil with potatoes and heavy garlic. There is no printed menu here. You'll find the daily plate lunch specials on signs behind the bar, and the po'-boy choices on lists on the dining room wall. Fried green tomatoes with shrimp rémoulade is a good appetizer option. Bring your appetite and know that the chefs love cayenne pepper. Most dishes are seafood, but there is usually a roast beef po'-boy available. | 1238 Baronne St. | 504/523–8571 | Reservations not accepted | Closed weekends. No dinner | $7–$10 | No credit cards.

Vaqueros. Mexican. Expect surprises at Vaqueros—chili con carne appears with black beans and venison and grilled fish might show up in a zesty sauce flavored with both chilies and tropical fruit. But there's no scarcity of tacos, fajitas, enchiladas, and the like in the two spacious, busy dining rooms, with stretched-leather chairs and a little tortilla-cooking station. One of the offbeat desserts is the *galleta* taco (a thin, folded cookie enveloping fresh diced fruits with pastry cream). The southwestern-style Sunday brunch buffet, served on the covered patio, is a special treat. | 4938 Prytania St. | 504/891–6441 | Reservations not accepted | No lunch Sat. | $7–$18 | AE, D, DC, MC, V.

MODERATE

Antoine's. French. The oldest restaurant in New Orleans, established in 1840, Antoine's has a maze of 15 dining rooms that are graced by polished woods, potted palms, and antique furnishings. Oysters Rockefeller was created here. The menu's many selections include shrimp, crawfish, crab, lamb, veal, tenderloin, and chateaubriand for two. Cherries jubilee flamed in brandy is served tableside. | 713 St. Louis St. | 504/581–4422 | www.antoines.com | Reservations essential | Jacket required (dinner) | Closed Sun. | $15–$35 | AE, DC, MC, V.

Bangkok Cuisine. Thai. Exotic art and furnishings transform this storefront dining room in a strip shopping center into something out of the ordinary. The cuisine includes pad Thai, coconut soup with chicken, duck, scallops, and whole fish. | 4137 S. Carrollton Ave. | 504/482–3606 | No lunch weekends | $15–$17 | AE, DC, MC, V.

Begue's. Contemporary. Sun-washed dining rooms and floral fabrics echo the huge tropical courtyard that's visible through the wide, arched windows of this restaurant at the Royal Sonesta Hotel. The dinner menu includes contemporary presentations of yellowfin tuna, Maine lobster, duck, rack of lamb, beef tournedos, veal medallions, pork chops, and chicken. Try the tomato and tasso ham bisque or the turtle soup for a starter. Pianist Thurs.–

Fri. Fri. lunch seafood buffet. Sunday jazz brunch. | 300 Bourbon St. | 504/586–0300 | www.royalsonestano.com | Breakfast also available | $16–$32 | AE, D, DC, MC, V.

Café Giovanni. Italian. Archways and mirrors enrich a traditional decor that has lots of warm brown wood and white linens. Though the restaurant is on a busy block of Decatur Street, romantic enclosed courtyard dining is available, as well as occasional serenades by opera-singing waiters. New Orleans native chef Duke LoCicero brings New World Italian fare to the French Quarter, incorporating Asian and Louisiana spices. Try the daily ravioli special or pasta *gambino* (a penne pasta with rock shrimp, sundried tomatoes, and herb peppers in a cream cheese sauce). Other possibilities are chicken stuffed with Italian sausage, veal, beef tenderloin, and nightly seafood specials. Kids' menu. | 117 Decatur St. | 504/529–2154 | Closed Sun. in July, Aug. No lunch | $13–$27 | AE, D, DC, MC, V.

Café Volage. French. An herb garden lines the entryway to this historic cottage built in the late 1800s and now converted into an intimate bistro. A local clientele, bentwood chairs, wood tables, and pastel tablecloths fill the dining room. The open-air dining patio in back is shaded by trees. The menu is French Mediterranean with items such as quail *à la Felix* (a roasted quail in rosemary glaze), escargots, gumbo, smoked Norwegian salmon, steak Diane, lamb chops, and red snapper florentine. The chef's own specialty is buster crab *à la Gregory*, sautéed in a meunière sauce. Earlybird suppers (Mon.–Thurs.). Sun. brunch. | 720 Dublin St. | 504/861–4227 | No supper Sun. | $13–$20 | AE, D, MC, V.

Chez Nous Charcuterie. Creole. Gourmet ready-to-eat takeout such as pâté, salads, spreads, sandwiches, breads, soups, quiche, various hors d' oeuvres, entrées, and desserts. There are a few small indoor tables, or you can bag a picnic and head a few blocks to Audubon Park. Menu changes every day. | 5701 Magazine St. | 504/899–7303 | Closed Sun. Closes at 6:30, 5 on Sat. | $12–$20 | MC, V.

Court of Two Sisters. Creole. This famous restaurant has a brunch buffet offering more than 80 items and the largest courtyard for dining in the French Quarter. Sit under the canopy of wisteria and enjoy the fountains and jazz band. Legend has it the gates were blessed by Queen Isabella in Spain before they were shipped to New Orleans and those who touch the gates will havegood luck. The daily brunch buffet includes traditional breakfast items, southern grits, soup, and seafood. Weekend brunch offers eggs Benedict and an omelette station. More formal dining takes place inside the Royal Court Room, where menu items include fresh fish, soft shell crab, snapper soup, lobster étouffée, and breast of duck. Jazz trio at brunch. Kids' menu. | 613 Royal St. | 504/522–7261 | www.courtoftwosisters | $15–$27 | AE, D, DC, MC, V.

Gabrielle. Contemporary. Lace curtains, windowboxes, and pastel still lifes on the walls accent the French style of this cottage restaurant. Sample the cuisine of a cooking couple, Greg and Mary Sonnier, who are famous for his house-made charcuterie and her desserts. Both trained under chef Paul Prudhomme. The seasonal menu features fresh regional seafood and game, as well as gumbos and étouffées and some produce grown by the chef. Homemade sausages, spicy rabbit, and desserts, especially ice creams, are especially popular. | 3201 Esplanade Ave. | 504/948–6233 | Reservations essential | Closed July–Aug. Closed Sun.–Mon. No lunch June–Sept. | $17–$29 | AE, D, DC, MC, V.

Gamay-Bistro. Contemporary. Dine at the new spinoff from the cooking couple who established a national reputation at their Mid-City restaurant, Gabrielle. Greg and Mary Sonnier present a stylish dining room with mahogany bar, European antiques, original artworks, and white linens. They are known for contemporary Creole cuisine, including duck and gumbo, and creative combinations such as rabbit and tomatillo or smoked salmon and pistachios. Save room for homemade pastries and ice creams. Open-air dining on the stone courtyard patio seats 20. The restaurant is in the Bienville House Hotel. | 320 Decatur St. | 504/299–8800 | www.gamaybistro.com | Closed Sun., Mon. No lunch | $17–$30 | AE, D, DC, MC, V.

Gautreau's. Contemporary. Dark wood cabinetry and historic photos recall the turn-of-the-20th-century pharmacy that once occupied this building in a toney residential neighborhood. No sign for the restaurant exists, but you'll spot the awning and parking valets. The embossed tin ceiling makes for a loud room, though the 2nd floor dining area is quieter. The menu changes about every six weeks. The emphasis is on fresh interpretations of French Creole classics, such as duck confit with truffle oil and dried mission figs or veal T-bone with a marsala thyme butter. No smoking. | 1728 Soniat St. | 504/899–7397 | Reservations essential | No lunch. Closed Sun. | $17–$30 | AE, D, DC, MC, V.

Kelsey's. Creole. The simple and stylish storefront dining room has an antique bar and Louisiana prints. Prudhomme protégé Randy Barlow presents fresh spins on Cajun/Creole classics, often using regional seafood and rabbit. Try eggplant Kelsey (fried and stuffed with shellfish), grilled fish with cream pesto, or pecan-crusted fish with shrimp in mango teriyaki sauce. Appetizers include stuffed poblano peppers and fried oysters, and there's orange–poppy seed cheesecake for dessert. | 3923 Magazine St. | 504/897–6722 | Closed Sun., Mon. No lunch Sat. | $15–$25 | Reservations essential | AE, D, DC, MC, V.

Martinique. Caribbean. The tiny woodframe cottage with window boxes, lace curtains, and a tropical patio evokes a setting in the French West Indies. Chef/owner Hubert Sandot, a native of Martinique, presents a seasonal menu. Try Caribbean-style curries, pork chop with coconut and balsamic vinaigrette, shrimp with sundried mango, or salmon in pineapple-sesame sauce. There's open-air dining on the terrace enclosed by a wooden fence. No smoking. | 5908 Magazine St. | 504/891–8495 | Reservations not accepted | No lunch. Closed Mon. | $15–$28 | MC, V.

Maximo's Italian Grill. Italian. The glossy contemporary decor is warmed by antique light fixtures, regional art, and an open kitchen with a 17-seat grill bar. A variety of pasta dishes are served, such as linguini in clam sauce and penne portobello. Try the *zupetta* (shrimp, scallops, and fish in a saffron tomato broth). Rack of lamb, filet mignon, and pork chops are also on the menu, and more than 50 wines are available by the glass. Open-air dining on balcony. | 1117 Decatur St. | 504/586–8883 | No lunch | $15–$30 | AE, D, DC, MC, V.

Michaul's. Cajun. This cavernous dance hall and eatery attracts tourists by the busload for live music, Cajun food, and free dance lessons. Gumbo, boudin, étouffée, and other Cajun specialties are served. A $5 cover is charged when the band starts. Live Cajun and zydeco music Mon–Fri. nights; dancing lessons Mon.–Sat. Kids' menu. | 840 St. Charles Ave. | 504/522–5517 | www.michauls.com | Closed last 2 weeks in Aug. No lunch | $12–$24 | AE, D, DC, MC, V.

Mosca's. Italian. This dowdy-looking roadhouse is a favorite with generations of locals, who make the 30-min trek from New Orleans for enormous portions of New Orleans–accented Italian food. It's surrounded by marsh and hard to spot, so make sure you get good directions. Popular dishes include shrimp, spaghetti bordelaise, roasted chicken, and oysters Mosca (oysters baked with artichoke in seasoned bread crumbs in a casserole with lots of garlic), as well as homemade pasta. Family-style service. It's always busy, and even with reservations you may have to wait at the bar. | 4137 U.S. 90, Waggaman | 504/436–9942 | Reservations not accepted Fri. or Sat. | Closed Aug. Closed Sun., Mon. No lunch | $14–$22 | No credit cards.

Original French Market Restaurant and Bar. Cajun. A huge pot of seafood simmers in spicy broth at the front window, as exposed brick, wood beams, and gaslights complete the old New Orleans atmosphere. Open-air dining on the balcony overlooks the French Market. This place is known for its excellent crawfish, fresh boiled seafood, and oysters on the half shell. Raw bar. Kids' menu. | 1001 Decatur St. | 504/525–7879 | $15–$20 | AE, D, DC, MC, V.

Palace Café. Creole. This cosmopolitan Parisian-style bistro has bi-level dining linked by a grand staircase. Glass frames the busy kitchen, and the second-floor walls are splashed with murals of local music stars. Imaginative creole dishes include rabbit ravioli, seafood Napoleon, Creole bouillabaisse, Ella's whole roasted gulf fish, and white chocolate bread pudding. Live music during Sat., Sun. brunch. Some outdoor seating at sidewalk tables. | 605 Canal St. | 504/523–1661 | Reservations essential | $16–$25 | AE, DC, MC, V.

Royal Café. Creole. This restaurant occupies the first two floors of the LaBranch House, built in 1832 at the corner of Royal and St. Peter in the French Quarter. Tables on the second-tier balcony are popular and afford an excellent view of the "Main Street." The café is famous for its oyster and artichoke soup. The house specialty dish is trout LaBranche (seared and topped with a crawfish pecan cream sauce). Other items include chicken, duck, pasta, fresh fish, veal chops, barbecued baby back ribs, choice steaks, étouffée, shrimp creole, red beans and rice, and Louisiana crabcakes. Live piano six nights. Brunch on weekends. | 700 Royal St. | 504/528–9086 | www.royalcafe.com | Reservations accepted for parties of 7 or more only | $14–$24 | AE, D, DC, MC, V.

Snug Harbor Jazz Bistro. American. The long, narrow storefront dining room with brick walls and exposed beams shares an entrance with the jazz club, where internationally known musicians perform in the adjoining bi-level concert area. Known for huge char-grilled burgers, the restaurant also serves seafood items such as gumbo, barbecued shrimp, shrimp rémoulade, crawfish étouffée, and blackened fish. Modern jazz nightly. | 626 Frenchmen St. | 504/949–0696 | No lunch | $13–$22 | AE, MC, V.

Tavern on the Park. Contemporary. A historic 19th-century coffee house has been transformed into a dapper bistro with polished marble floors and brass accents overlooking City Park. Try porterhouse, stuffed soft shell crab, trout Martha, veal cutlets, and broiled lobster tails. Open-air dining on patio. Kids' menu. | 900 City Park Ave. | 504/486–3333 | Closed Sun., Mon. No lunch Sat. | $16–$19 | AE, D, DC, MC, V.

Upperline. Creole. A cottage garden blooms in front of this 1877 town house, where three dining rooms are filled with Southern folk art and fresh flowers. Innovative Creole dishes attract a regular local clientele. The menu varies, but examples include fried green tomatoes topped with shrimp rémoulade, soft shell crab with hot sauce buerre blanc, crawfish enchiladas, duck gumbo, oyster stew, turtle soup, duck and sausage étouffée, roast duck with a confit of orange thyme demi glace, rack of lamb with mint Madeira reduction, and filet mignon. | 1413 Upperline St. | 504/891–9822 | www.upperline.com | Closed Mon., Tues. No lunch | $16–$20 | AE, DC, MC, V.

The Veranda. Continental. This atrium garden restaurant in the high-rise Hotel Inter-Continental has a glass-enclosed room that's furnished with tropical plants and lacy garden furniture. The other rooms are done in a formal antebellum style. Try red snapper with lump crabmeat, smoked salmon rémoulade, crabcakes, or beefsteak in pepper sauce. Steaks, lamb, and veal are also served. Buffet brunch with jazz on Sun. and holidays. | 444 St. Charles Ave. | 504/525–5566 | Breakfast also available | $13–$27 | AE, D, DC, MC, V.

EXPENSIVE

Alex Patout's Louisiana Restaurant. Contemporary. A New Iberia native, Alex Patout made his reputation in Cajun country before moving on to this simply decorated pastel space in the French Quarter. Try duck and oyster gumbo, corn and crab bisque, rabbit sauce piquant, Louisiana courtbillion (similar to bouillabaise), Cajun smothered roast duck, seafood pasta, filet mignon, veal chops, or smothered chicken. Kids' menu. | 221 Royal St. | 504/525–7788 | www.patout.com | No lunch | $24–$38 | AE, D, DC, MC, V.

Allegro Bistro and Cocktails. Eclectic. The bistro fare attracts a business lunch crowd and includes Italian pastas, Louisiana-inspired dishes, sandwiches, salads, and daily fish specials. Try the eggplant St. Charles (topped with crabmeat, tomato sauce, and hollandaise) or the salad with fresh tuna and Thai peanut sauce. The bistro, designed with an art deco theme, is in the Energy Center office building and has outdoor patio dining. No food is served in the evenings, but the bar is open nightly. | 1100 Poydras | 504/582–2350 | No dinner, no lunch weekends | $20–$35 | AE, D, DC, MC, V.

Andrew Jaeger's House of Seafood. Seafood. Live blues and jazz can be heard nightly on the first floor of this three-level restaurant with exposed brick walls. The upper floors are more formal, though still casual. Favorites on the menu of everyday Cajun and Creole dishes include turtle soup, jambalaya, crabcakes, duck, and fresh seafood. Open-air dining on second-floor balcony. | 622 Conti St. | 504/522-4964 | No lunch | $20–$25 | AE, DC, MC, V.

★ **Bayona.** Contemporary. Chef Susan Spicer is nationally known for her stylish Mediterranean cuisine, which is served in a 19th-century Creole cottage on a quiet French Quarter street. The elegant main dining room is decorated with photos of historic Italian gardens and another, more intimate dining room with murals of Mediterranean landscapes. The rear patio is is available for outdoor dining. Signature dishes include grilled shrimp in coriander sauce with a black bean cake, duck breast with pepper jelly, and lamb loin in zinfandel sauce with goat cheese. | 430 Dauphine St. | 504/525-4455 | www.bayona.com | Reservations essential | Closed Sun. No lunch Sat. | $20–$30 | AE, DC, MC, V.

Bella Luna. Italian. In this place, voted one of the most romantic restaurants by locals, French-style windows line the dining room and offer grand panoramas of the river, the city skyline, and the French Quarter rooftops. Tables are placed a step up to take full advantage of the views. Penne with roasted eggplant, fettucine, crabcakes, veal chops, pork chops, and quesadillas with smoked shrimp and spicy goat cheese are among the choices. Kids' menu. | 914 N. Peters St. | 504/529-1583 | No lunch | $20–$32 | AE, D, DC, MC, V.

Bistro at Maison De Ville. Contemporary. Polished woodwork, paneling, and red leather banquettes transform this space into a tiny Parisian-style bistro attached to the Maison De Ville hotel. Try duck confit, sautéed foie gras, quail ravioli, grilled salmon with pecan rice, lamb tenderloin, or regional seafood. Open-air dining on the umbrella-shaded patio. | 733 Toulouse St. | 504/528-9206 | Closed Sun. | $21–$34 | Ties suggested | AE, DC, MC, V.

Bon Ton Café. Cajun. The large, brick-walled dining room lined with gaslights and shuttered windows has been a regular haunt of the downtown business crowd since 1953. It's just 3 blocks from the French Quarter and Harrah's casino. Upscale but traditional Cajun favorites such as gumbo, crawfish étouffée, jambalaya, and oyster omelets are popular, and there's delicious warm bread pudding for dessert. Kids' menu. | 401 Magazine St. | 504/524-3386 | Closed weekends | $18–$27 | AE, DC, MC, V.

Brigtsen's. Creole. Nationally known chef Frank Brigtsen creates a contemporary southern Louisiana cuisine in this charming 19th-century cottage with yellow walls, lacy curtains, and quaint murals near a Mississippi River levee in the Garden District. Regulars pack the three small dining rooms, and there are two tables in the enclosed sunroom. Chef Brigtsen spent years as Paul Prudhomme's protégé, and his menu is ever-changing. Try the oysters Rockefeller soup to start. Entrées may include blackened prime rib, gumbos, crawfish, shrimp, oyster dishes, rabbit, and chicken in creative styles. No smoking. Early dinners Tues.–Thurs. | 723 Dante St. | 504/861-7610 | Reservations essential | Closed Sun., Mon. No lunch | $20–$32 | AE, DC, MC, V.

Broussard's. Creole. French furnishings and elaborate wall coverings, chandeliers, porcelain, and polished woods formalize two of the dining rooms at this restaurant that's been open since 1920. Outdoor seating is in a tropical manicured courtyard, which is also visible from the more rustic third dining room set in a former stable. The menu offers turtle soup, gumbo, fresh pompano, braised quail, rack of lamb, duck, veal, and wild game grill. Specialties include veal Broussard with creole mustard and leeks. Pianist Fri., Sat. | 819 Conti St. | 504/581-3866 | www.broussards.com | No lunch | $23–$36 | AE, D, DC, MC, V.

Café Rue Bourbon. Cajun. Here you can dine on an open balcony overlooking noisy Bourbon Street or in the quieter atmosphere of the Blue Napoleon Wine Room. The restaurant's three floors have colorful Provençal decor. The menu offers gumbo, salads, creole dishes, steaks, seafood, duck, veal, and pasta. Try the grilled snapper with crawfish pesto or New York sirloin with béarnaise sauce. Kids' menu, early-bird suppers. | 241 Bourbon St. | 504/524-0114 | www.neworleans.com/rue_bourbon | No lunch | $18–$28 | AE, DC, MC, V.

Christian's. Creole. Original stained-glass windows still illuminate this turn-of-the-20th-century former church. It is now painted bright pink with a wood-paneled bar in the vestibule and a soaring ceiling in the formal dining room. Located in Mid-City and founded by members of the Galatoire family in 1977, Christian's serves some of the family recipes, such as smoked soft shell crab, creole bouillabaise, and fried oysters wrapped in bacon. | 3835 Iberville St. | 504/482–4924 | Reservations essential | Closed Sun. No lunch Mon., Sat. | $18–$30 | AE, D, DC, MC, V.

Clancy's. Contemporary. Its easy charm and classy menu have made this minimally decorated bistro a favorite with professional and business types from nearby uptown neighborhoods. Many of the dishes are imaginative treatments of New Orleans favorites. Some specialties, such as the fresh sautéed fish in cream sauce flavored with crawfish stock and herbs, are exceptional. Other must-tries are the expertly fried oysters matched with warm Brie, the grilled chicken breast in lime butter, and a marvelous peppermint–ice cream pie. Simpler dishes include fettucine Alfredo and filet mignon in Madeira sauce. A few ceiling fans spin above gray walls, bentwood chairs, and white linen cloths. The small bar separating the two rooms is usually filled with regulars. | 6100 Annunciation St. | 504/895–1111 | Closed Sun. No lunch Mon. and Sat. | $22–$31 | AE, MC, V.

Delmonico. Contemporary. Emeril Lagasse bought Delmonico in 1997 and spent several million dollars on renovations. Now, this extravagantly appointed restaurant offers revamped Creole dishes and formal service. The many high-ceilinged dining spaces have upholstered walls and luxe draperies. Past menus have included oysters on the half shell in various sauces, barbecued shrimp, crawfish in puff pastry, and sautéed fish meunière, as well as other fresh fish specials, filet mignon, duck, rabbit, veal, and rack of pork. Desserts are Lagasse variations on the traditional, such as cheesecake with Creole cream cheese. | 1300 St. Charles Ave. | 504/525–4937 | www.emerils.com | Reservations essential | Jackets preferred | No lunch Sat. | $19–$30 | AE, D, DC, MC, V.

Dickie Brennan's. Steak. "Straightforward steaks with a New Orleans touch" is the axiom at this 350-seat steaks-and-chops restaurant, the creation of a younger member of the Commander's Palace clan. In lavish spaces lined with dark-cherry walls and a drugstore-tile floor, diners dig into classic cuts of top-quality beef, veal, and lamb. The standard beefsteak treatment is a light seasoning and a brush of butter. Other options are a garlic rub, deeper charring, or a crust of either black peppercorns or mushroom duxelle, along with five buttery sauces. The menu doesn't lack for typical New Orleans seafoods and desserts, such as shrimp rémoulade, fried oysters, fresh local fish in heartily seasoned sauces, and bread pudding. Headlining the wine list are more than 120 reds. Free valet parking. | 716 Iberville St. | 504/522–2467 | fax 504/523–0088 | www.dbrennanssteakhouse.com | No lunch Sun. | $18–$34 | AE, D, DC, MC, V.

Dominique's. Contemporary. A sunny courtyard and tropical flowers on the tables supply bright accents for this restaurant in the Maison DuPuy Hotel. Mauritius-born chef Dominique Macquet serves a contemporary French cuisine with Louisiana influences. The menu changes seasonally and may include local snapper, fillet of beef, shrimp, sweetbreads, lamb, and whole Maine lobster. Open-air dining in courtyard. Earlybird suppers. Sun. brunch. No smoking. Free valet parking. | 504/522–8800 | www.maisondupuy.com/dominiques | Breakfast also available | No lunch weekends | $22–$28 | AE, D, DC, MC, V.

Emeril's. Contemporary. Chef/author/television star Emeril Lagasse's empire started here, surrounded by the galleries of the Warehouse/Arts District. Lofty dining rooms have ultra-modern furnishings, gleaming wood floors, aluminum lamps, and abstract oil paintings. Request a table at the Chef's Food Bar for a view of the open kitchen and commentary from the cooks. The menu changes seasonally, and this restaurant focuses on the classics with Emeril's creative twist. Possible entrées are ricotta-stuffed quail, double-cut pork chop in chile mole sauce, black pepper filet of beef with bourbon mashed potatoes, pecan-crusted redfish, and barbecued salmon with andouille hash, as well as duck, lamb, and veal. The seven-course menu is offered at $75, but the whole table must participate. | 800 Tchoupitoulas St. | 504/528–9393 | Reservations essential (dinner) | Closed first 2 weeks in July. Closed Sun. No lunch Sat. | $20–$35 | AE, D, DC, MC, V.

Feelings Café. Cajun/Creole. This café is in the former carriage house of the 18th-century D'Aunoy plantation in the Faubourg Marigny neighborhood. Brick-walled dining rooms are furnished with antiques, and a gorgeous antique bar overlooks the water garden in the courtyard. Four- and five-course dinners are available, and the menu includes barbecued shrimp, catfish pecan, red snapper, and steak stuffed with blue cheese. There's open-air dining in the courtyard or at romantic tables for two on the balcony above it. Pianist Fri.–Sat. Sun. brunch. | 2600 Chartres St. | 504/945–2222 | www.feelingscafe.com | No lunch Sat., Mon.–Thurs. | $20–$34 | AE, D, DC, MC, V.

Galatoire's. Creole. This historic French bistro, a family tradition since 1905, is lined with antique mirrors, ceiling fans, and bright lights. Generations of fanatically loyal local customers have waited in line for tables, but now there's a second floor dining room that accepts reservations. Try the crabmeat maison, trout Marguery, or the popular turtle soup. The Creole bouillabaise must be ordered a couple of hours in advance. | 209 Bourbon St. | 504/525–2021 | www.galatoires.com | Jacket required (dinner and Sunday) | Closed Mon. | $22–$40 | AE, D, DC, MC, V.

Gerard's Downtown. Contemporary. This warm, understated restaurant in the Best Western Parc St. Charles has earthy olive walls and a classic, red mahogany bar. The glass walls of the corner location permit views of Lafayette Square's oak trees, the stately columns of Gallier Hall, and passing streetcars. Chef Gerard Maras is an alumnus of Commander's Palace and Mr. B's Bistro. His creations include paper-thin, freshly made ravioli with bits of lobster floating in a saffron broth with leeks and herb-crusted lamb chops with a moist cake of "satin" potatoes, baked and layered with cream and Camembert. Salads consist of greens freshly picked from Maras's own farm. For dessert, try dark-chocolate cake floating in chocolate "soup." | 500 St. Charles Ave. | 504/592–0200 | www.gerardsdowntown.com | Closed Sun.–Mon. No lunch Sat. | $19–$29 | AE, D, DC, MC, V.

Hunt Room Grill. Contemporary. In this restaurant in the Hotel Monteleone, a cosmopolitan and clubby mood is set with dark woods, cushy furnishings, a hushed atmosphere, and formal service. It's known for prime beef, regional seafood, and game. Try gumbo garnished with fried okra, veal tenderloin with eggplant and porcini mushrooms, and peach Bavarois for dessert. | 214 Royal St. | 504/523–3341 | No lunch | $20–$32 | AE, D, DC, MC, V.

★ **K-Paul's Louisiana Kitchen.** Cajun. Godfather and icon of the Cajun craze and initiator of the blackening technique, chef Paul Prudhomme makes his home base in this busy French Quarter restaurant. There's communal seating at long tables downstairs and dining at individual tables upstairs. Both floors feature open-air kitchens. The menu changes daily and is noted for large portions of regional seafood and Cajun dishes. Try one of his inventive gumbos, blackened tuna, rabbit, or fresh fish. No reservations are taken at lunch, so come early or join the line. Open-air dining in courtyard. No smoking. | 416 Chartres St. | 504/524–7394 | www.kpauls.com | Reservations essential for upper level (dinner), not accepted for lunch | Closed Sun. | $23–$33 | AE, DC, MC, V.

Louis XVI. French. Polished brass and gilt accents reflect the Old World atmosphere and cuisine, and ceremonious service adds that extra touch to big occasions at this restaurant in the St. Louis Hotel. The menu leans to seafood dishes, including sea bass, yellowfin tuna, and red snapper, but also offers lamb, duck, and veal. A specialty is flaming desserts and other tableside preparations. Open-air dining in courtyard. Pianist Wed.–Sun. | 730 Bienville St. | 504/581–7000 | www.louisxvi.com | Jacket required | Breakfast also available | No lunch | $19–$37 | AE, DC, MC, V.

Mandich's. Creole. This favorite of locals since 1922 occupies a neat but unremarkable building in a blue-collar neighborhood. Mandich's is a mix of bright yellow paint, captain's chairs, and wood veneer. The food ranges from homestyle dishes to trout and shellfish dishes. Fried oysters come in a butter sauce with garlic and parsley. Shrimp and andouille sausages trade flavors on the grill. The trout Mandich is breaded, broiled, and served with a butter, wine, and Worcestershire sauce. | 3200 St. Claude Ave. | 504/947–9553 | Reservations not accepted | Closed Sun.–Mon. No lunch Sat. No dinner Tues.–Thurs. | $18–$25 | MC, V.

Metro Bistro. Contemporary. At this cushy spot, a block off Canal Street at the Pelham Hotel, traditional French and contemporary New Orleans style meet. Near the mahogany bar, a huge, stylized mural suggests the New Orleans skyline. Golden walls rise to the 15-ft ceiling. Tiny cobalt blue lamps above each table give a soft light. The salade Niçoise holds bits of tuna carpaccio. Double-cut pork chops in a natural sauce, Burgundian beef stew, and a garlicky cassoulet with duck sausage, duck confit, and smoked pork are tailor-made for hefty appetites. Grilled fish sit between Creole stewed corn and a frizzle of sweet potato. Brunch on weekends. | 200 Magazine St. | 504/529–1900 | $20–$25 | AE, D, DC, MC, V.

Midi. French. The chef is a native of Aix-en-Provence, France, and serves Provençal cuisine at this restaurant in Le Meridien hotel, with tall windows overlooking Canal Street. The dining room is decorated with the blues and yellows of Provence, and there is outdoor café seating as well. Try the crawfish bisque, escargots, foie gras, or the bouillabaisse with red ruby trout, snapper, and tilapia. There's also lobster, lamb chops, and veal filet, and the signature dessert is lavender crème brûlée. Sun. brunch. Free parking. | 614 Canal St. | 504/527–6712 | www.midirestaurant.com | $20–$30 | AE, D, DC, MC, V.

Mr. B's Bistro. Contemporary. The cosmopolitan menu, open kitchen, polished brass, and long mahogany bar here appeal to a professional crowd. One of the Brennan family restaurants, this was the first gourmet bistro in New Orleans, and it's known for house-made pastas and meal-sized salads. Try bacon-wrapped oysters, pasta jambalaya, roasted garlic chicken, daily fish selections, steak, chops, or the gumbo ya-ya made with chicken and sausage. Lunch is prix fixe. Piano nightly, jazz Sun. (at brunch). Sun. brunch. | 201 Royal St. | 504/523–2078 | $20–$32 | AE, D, DC, MC, V.

★ **Nola.** Contemporary. Contemporary furnishings and fanciful modern art transform this 19th-century town house into a trendy stage for owner Emeril Lagasse and his crew of chefs, best viewed from counter seating that faces an open kitchen and wood-fired grill. The dining room has two floors, accessible by a glass elevator. An in-house butcher creates custom charcuterie, and the on-premises bakery builds architectural desserts. Try Lafayette boudin (stewed with beer, onions, cane syrup, and Creole mustard) or hickory-roasted duck with a whiskey caramel glaze. The tasting menu at dinner is a great way to try several of Emeril's creations. Service is very attentive. No smoking. | 534 St. Louis St. | 504/522–6652 | www.emerils.com | Reservations essential | No lunch Sun. | $20–$30 | AE, D, DC, MC, V.

Pelican Club. Contemporary. Tucked away on a flagstone alley, three sophisticated dining rooms and a candlelit piano bar are set in a 19th-century town house. Each dining room displays a consignment of art from local galleries. Rooms have marble floors and panels of old doors. New Orleans–born chef/owner Richard Hughes trained in New York and fuses Asian and Louisiana techniques in such dishes as grilled fish in ginger lime sauce and Thai seafood salad. Other menu offerings include filet mignon with cabernet mushroom sauce and a bisque of bourbon, crab, and corn. Piano bar Fri., Sat. nights. | 615 Bienville St. | 504/523–1504 | No lunch | $23–$39 | AE, D, DC, MC, V.

Peristyle. French. Huge paintings of City Park dominate the historic dining rooms and bar, and the classic French country cuisine draws a devoted local clientele. Reserve far in advance, especially for Fri. lunch. Veal and sweetbreads ravioli, grilled seabass with pickled lemon vinaigrette, and mussels steamed in saffron shellfish broth are among the offerings. | 1041 Dumaine St. | 504/593–9535 | Reservations essential (weekends) | Jacket and tie | Closed Sun., Mon. No lunch Tues.–Thurs., Sat. | $22–$24 | DC, MC, V.

Rib Room. Creole. Understated elegance with formal service, fine linens, and tall windows overlooking the sidewalks and antique shops of Royal Street pamper the patrons of this restaurant in the Omni Royal Orleans hotel. Prime beef, seafood, and fowl are prepared on giant rotisseries or the mesquite grill. Also available are rack of lamb, crawfish specialties in season, veal escallop, and crab bisque. Sun. brunch. | 621 St. Louis St. | 504/529–5333 | Breakfast also available | $22–$33 | AE, D, DC, MC, V.

Ruth's Chris Steakhouse. Steak. The original Ruth's Chris was founded in New Orleans in 1965 and is sacred to New Orleans steak lovers. The plush but casual dining rooms of this flagship location are lined in pale wood paneling and landscape paintings. Politicians, both actual and aspiring, are everywhere. The main draw at this Mid-City restaurant is aged U.S. prime beef in he-man portions, charbroiled and served atop a sizzling, seasoned butter sauce. If you're feeling adventurous, order a side of bordelaise sauce to add to the excess. The hefty filet mignon is often taller than it is wide, the New York strip is packed with flavor, and a monstrous porterhouse serves several. Potato dishes are popular side items. Lighter entrées include chicken, veal and seafood. | 711 N. Broad St. | 504/486–0810 | www.ruthchris.com | Reservations essential | $18–$30 | AE, D, DC, MC, V.

VERY EXPENSIVE

Arnaud's. Creole. The turn-of-the-20th-century, high-ceiling rooms are still decorated with antique ceiling fans, chandeliers, oil paintings, palms, and mosaic tile floors. There is a formal dining room and an adjacent, more casual bistro. The menu offers classic Creole and contemporary dishes. A speciality is shrimp Arnaud (shrimp rémoulade with lots of horseradish), and shrimp bisque, oyster soup, and beef Wellington are popular. Live jazz at Sun. brunch. | 813 Bienville St. | 504/523–5433 | Jacket required (for dinner in main dining room) | No lunch Sat. | $29–$47 | AE, D, DC, MC, V.

Bacco. Italian. The chic Tuscan decor is complete with vaulted ceilings, Baroque frescoes, and Venetian silk chandeliers. The Chartres room has large windows and a mural of Bacchus. There's also a Skylight room, a Courtyard room overlooking the pool, and a Wine room with a French ironwork gate to divide it. House specialties include homemade pastas such as crawfish ravioli, fresh grilled fish, and pizzas from the wood oven fired with hickory and pecan logs. Contemporary Italian fare includes polenta, pork tenderloin, osso bucco, and gnocchi. Located next to the W Hotel. Sun. brunch. | 310 Chartres St. | 504/522–2426 | www.bacco.com | Breakfast also available. Closed Mardi Gras | $25–$35 | AE, DC, MC, V.

Brennan's. Creole. This stately old Royal Street mansion was originally built, and appropriately named Casa Faurie, for Spanish merchant Jose Faurie in 1795. In the late 1850s, it was home to international chess champion Paul Morphy, a native of New Orleans. Today you will find tables on a glassed-in balcony and a terrace overlooking one of the city's most famous courtyards. The formal dining rooms and attentive service suit the historic mansion. Brennan's is known for its lavish three-course breakfast, which can include turtle soup and eggs Sardou (with artichoke). Other specialties are oysters Rockefeller, seafood crêpes, the signature blackened redfish, filet mignon, veal, fresh fish and seafood, and bananas Foster for dessert. | 417 Royal St. | 504/525–9711 | Reservations essential | Breakfast also available | $35–$39 | AE, D, DC, MC, V.

★ **Commander's Palace.** Cajun/Creole. A flagship local restaurant set in a turreted turqoise mansion in the Garden District provides open-air dining in its famous courtyard. The upstairs Garden Room has glass walls that provide a wonderful view of the oak trees and outside patio. Other rooms are colorful with bright pastels and wall paintings. The restaurant is known for its Bloody Marys and also its bread pudding. The menu includes roasted quail, poached oysters in cream sauce with caviar, trout with pecans, veal chop, and filet mignon. There's also a tasting menu at $75 for dinner. Dixieland band at Sat. and Sun. brunch. | 1403 Washington Ave. | 504/899–8221 | www.commanderspalace.com | Jacket required (dinner and brunch) | $28–$75 | AE, D, DC, MC, V.

★ **Grill Room.** Contemporary. Elaborately presented cuisine, lavish furnishings, monumental paintings from the Windsor Court Hotel's collection of art, and formal European service help to cushion the sticker shock at this establishment. Get a taste of the same luxury at weekday prix fixe lunches, a relative bargain. The menu changes daily and features exotic ingredients flown in from Europe and the Orient. Selections may include escargots, beluga caviar, New Zealand venison, lamb, Japanese oysters, foie gras, Maine lobster, and crawfish. Sun. jazz brunch. | 300 Gravier St. | 504/522–1992 | www.orient-expresshotels.com | Jacket and tie required (dinner) | Reservations essential | Breakfast also available | $38–$48 | AE, D, DC, MC, V.

Sazerac Bar and Grill. Contemporary. The historic fine dining room of the Fairmont Hotel was completely redesigned in 1999 and is now a clubby and urbane bistro that opens onto the lobby. The atmosphere is enhanced by polished dark woods, white linens, and original 1939 wall murals by Paul Ninas of cityscapes and plantation scenes. The baroque chandeliers remain. The restaurant's namesake, the Sazerac, was America's first cocktail and is a must-try drink at least once. Signature dishes include lobster bisque and creole bouillabaise. Try grilled fresh seafood and meats, pasta, pizzas, specialty salads, and homemade breads and pastries. Buffet (Sun. brunch). | 123 Baronne St. | 504/529–7111 | www.fairmont.com | Breakfast also available | $28–$46 | AE, D, DC, MC, V.

Tujague's. Creole. Pronounced "two jacks" and operating since 1856, this is the second-oldest restaurant in New Orleans. It still has the original ornate French bar imported by the restaurant's founder and an 18th-century mirror brought from Paris in 1856. Formal service is from the daily table d'hote menu, including five set courses with choice of entrée from five daily selections. These might include filet mignon, beef brisket, lamb shank, chicken bonne femme sautéed with lots of garlic (best to order this one ahead), or chicken and andouille gumbo. | 823 Decatur St. | 504/525–8676 | $26–$35 | AE, D, DC, MC, V.

Lodging

INEXPENSIVE

Ambassador Hotel. Exposed brick walls, ceiling fans, and hardwood floors, as well as four-poster iron beds and armoires in the guest rooms, add to the character of this hotel composed of three pre-Civil War renovated warehouses. It's on the border of the Central Business District and the Arts and Warehouse District, three blocks from the Convention Center, Riverwalk, and the French Quarter. Restaurant, bar, room service. In-room data ports. Cable TV. Exercise equipment. Business services, airport shuttle, parking (fee). Some pets allowed (deposit). | 535 Tchoupitoulas St. | 504/527–5271, 888/527–5271 | fax 504/599–2110 | www.neworleans.com/ambassador | 73 rooms | $119–$189 | AE, D, DC, MC, V.

Avenue Plaza Hotel. The spartan lobby of this 12-story St. Charles Avenue accommodation belies the luxurious inner rooms. Public rooms include a romantic lounge with dark wood panels from a French chalet and a small, intimate restaurant. The spacious guest rooms have generous dressing areas and kitchenettes with full-size refrigerators; the decorations are either traditional or art deco. The spa has a Turkish steam bath, Swiss showers, and a Scandinavian sauna, all of which you can use for $5 per day. The pool is in a pleasant courtyard; a sundeck and hot tub are on the roof. Restaurant, bar. Kitchenettes, refrigerators. Pool. Beauty salon, hot tub, massage, sauna, spa, steam room. Health club. Parking (fee). | 2111 St. Charles Ave. | 504/566–1212, 800/535–9575 | fax 504/525–6899 | 256 rooms | $90–$225 | AE, D, DC, MC, V.

B and W Courtyards. B and W Courtyards is in the Faubourg Marigny neighborhood, four blocks from the French Quarter. Three 19th-century cottages are joined by two courtyards filled with sculpted fountains, statuary, and the scent of jasmine. Innkeeper Rob Boyd, trained at the Culinary Institute of America, prepares the complimentary breakfast. His partner Kevin Wu speaks Mandarin Chinese in addition to English. Rooms are furnished with antiques and reproductions, and the terra-cotta floors and beds with mosquito netting attempt to add a Caribbean feel to the accommodations. There are three dogs on the property. Complimentary breakfast. Cable TV. Hot tub. No children under 12. No smoking. | 2425 Chartres St. | 504/945–9418, 800/585–5731 | fax 504/949–3483 | www.bandwcourtyards.com | 4 rooms, 1 suite | $130–$150 rooms, $175–$225 suites | AE, D, MC, V.

Bienville House. This stylish small hotel in an 18th-century building is across Decatur Street from Woldenberg Riverfront Park and Aquarium of the Americas. The renovated lobby resembles that of a French manor house. There are four sundecks and murals on the walls, and the individually decorated rooms overlook French Quarter streets or the courtyard pool. Some have iron balconies and views of the Mississippi River. Gamay-Bistro, operated by nationally known chefs Greg and Mary Sonnier, is in the hotel. Restaurant (see

Gamay-Bistro), bar, complimentary Continental breakfast. Cable TV. Pool. Laundry service. Business services, parking (fee). | 320 Decatur St. | 504/529-2345, 800/535-9603 | fax 504/525-6079 | www.bienvillehouse.com | 83 rooms, 3 suites | $129-$149, $280-$500 suites | AE, D, MC, V.

Bon Maison Guest House. Within the gates of this 1840 town house on the quiet end of Bourbon Street are a lush courtyard and pleasantly furnished rooms. There's no elevator, so be prepared for lots of stair climbing to upper floors. Less than a block from the Clover Grill Restaurant. Kitchenettes (in suites), microwaves, refrigerators. Cable TV. | 835 Bourbon St. | 504/561-8498 | www.bonmaison.com | 3 rooms, 2 suites | $135 | MC, V.

Bourbon Orleans. Queen Anne–style furnishings and marble baths, as well as an elegant lobby with towering white pillars, Oriental rugs, and crystal chandeliers, provide a graceful setting here. Some sections of the hotel were constructed in 1815 as part of the Orleans ballroom. It's a few steps from St. Louis Cathedral and Jackson Square, and some rooms overlook Bourbon Street. Restaurant, bar, room service. In-room data ports, some minibars, some refrigerators. Cable TV. Pool. Laundry service. Business services, parking (fee). | 717 Orleans St. | 504/523-2222, 800/521-5338 | fax 504/525-8166 | www.bourbonorleans.com | 166 rooms, 50 suites | $119-$199, $219-$294 suites | AE, D, DC, MC, V.

Chateau Hotel. This two-story hotel with wrought iron balconies is just two blocks from Jackson Square, and your room will overlook the courtyard or French Quarter streets. Guest rooms vary in size, and furnishings are either antiques or contemporary pieces. A silo in the courtyard contains the stairway to the penthouse suites. Restaurant, bar, complimentary Continental breakfast, room service. Cable TV. Pool. Business services. Free parking. | 1001 Chartres St. | 504/524-9636, 800/828-1822 | fax 504/525-2989 | www.chateauhotel.com | 45 rooms, 5 suites | $79-$134, $149-$184 suites | AE, DC, MC, V.

Chimes. A butterfly garden separates the guest annex from a friendly family home. These lodgings are in a tranquil residential area, two blocks off St. Charles streetcar line and a couple of blocks from shops and the galleries of Magazine Street. Rooms in the main house and carriage house overlook with shaded brick courtyard and have antique furnishings, high ceilings, and hardwood or slate floors, all with private entranceways. English, French, Arabic, and Spanish are spoken in the house. Complimentary Continental breakfast. Cable TV. Pets allowed. No smoking. | 1146 Constantinople St. | 504/488-4640, 800/729-4640 | fax 504/899-9858 | www.historiclodging.com | 5 rooms (2 with shared bath) | $85-$140 | AE, MC, V.

Clarion Grand Boutique Hotel. When Al Copeland (the man behind Popeye's Famous Fried Chicken) first renovated this building to house Straya Restaurant and the Grand Boutique Hotel, local author Anne Rice protested the neon deco facade, claiming it clashed with the genteel ambience of uptown New Orleans. In the end, though, Copeland persevered, and the flashy structure has become just another part of life along St. Charles Avenue. Opened in 1997, the decor of the three-story, all-suites Grand Boutique Hotel, incorporating marble, glass, brass, and wrought iron, is considerably tamer than the downstairs restaurant. Restaurant, bar, room service. In-room data ports, microwaves, refrigerators, some in-room hot tubs. Cable TV. Laundry services. Business services, parking (fee). | 2001 St. Charles Ave. | 504/558-9966, 800/976-1755 | fax 504/522-8044 | www.alcopeland.com/hotelsgb | 44 suites | $119-$279 | AE, D, DC, MC, V.

Columns Hotel. This impressive, white-columned 1883 Victorian-style hotel, listed on the National Register of Historic Places, was the setting for the film *Pretty Baby*. The wide veranda, set with cloth-covered tables for outdoor dining or cocktails, is very inviting, as are the two period-furnished parlors. The dark, intimate lounge with two wood-burning fireplaces is a favorite with locals and has excellent live progressive jazz on Tuesdays and Thursdays. There's also a Sunday jazz brunch. An impressive staircase leads to large, somewhat sparsely furnished rooms. Breakfast is served either in the dining room or on the veranda. Bar with entertainment. Complimentary Continental breakfast. No TV. | 3811 St. Charles Ave. | 504/899-9308, 800/445-9308 | fax 504/899-8170 | 20 rooms | $100-$170 | AE, MC, V.

Crescent on Canal. This contemporary high-rise on Canal Street, about eight blocks from the French Quarter, offers free shuttle service. It is about a block from I-10 and less than a mile north of the Superdome. The five-story hotel was built in the late 1960s. In-room video games. Complimentary Continental breakfast. Some refrigerators. Cable TV. Laundry service. Business services. | 1732 Canal St. | 504/412–4000, 800/236–6119 | fax 504/529–1609 | 370 rooms, 50 suites | $109–$179, $129–$250 suites | AE, D, DC, MC, V.

Degas House. Edgar Degas, the French Impressionist painter, stayed in his uncle's home (his mother and grandmother were New Orleans natives) from 1872 to 1873, during which time he produced 17 works. This historic home, built in 1852, has been carefully restored, following original floor plans and colors, which include pale peach, celadon, and golden mustard. Spacious, second-floor rooms have chandeliers and 14-ft ceilings. One room has a whirlpool bath; another has exclusive use of a balcony that stretches across the front of the house. Third-floor garret rooms are small and have no windows, but are decorated with reproductions of Degas's works. You can enjoy breakfast on a small private rear courtyard, where there is a garden with period flowers. Parlors on the first floor display the artist's prints (more than 60 can be seen in the house) and can be visited by nonguests (call for specific dates and times). Near City Park and managed by the Degas Foundation. Complimentary breakfast (Continental on weekdays). Some in-room hot tubs. Cable TV. No smoking. | 2306 Esplanade Ave. | 504/821–5009, 800/755–6730 | fax 504/821–0870 | www.degashouse.com | 6 rooms, 1 suite | $125–$175 rooms, suite $230 | MC, V.

French Quarter Guest House. Comfortable and intimate, this 1800s building in the residential area of the French Quarter is only one block from Bourbon St. and three blocks from Jackson Square. Some rooms have balconies. All rooms have private baths but some with shower only. Complimentary Continental breakfast. Cable TV. | 623 Ursulines Ave. | 504/529–5489 | fax 504/524–1902 | 19 rooms | $79–$155 | AE, D, DC, MC, V.

The Frenchmen. These two 1850s town houses in Faubourg Marigny were once private homes. The comfortable inn, furnished with some period antiques, opened in 1984 and is just steps from great music clubs and coffeehouses and only one block from the French Quarter. Across the street are the Old U.S. Mint and the French Market. Rooms have high ceilings and ceiling fans. Some have balconies overlooking the courtyard and pool. Complimentary Continental breakfast. Kitchenettes (in suites). Cable TV. Pool. Hot tub. Business services, free parking. | 417 Frenchmen St. | 504/948–2166, 888/365–2877 | fax 504/948–2258 | www.french-quarter.org | 25 rooms, 2 suites | $65–$125, $165–$180 suites | AE, MC, V.

Hampton Inn on St. Charles Avenue. This six-story Hampton Inn opened in 1997 in a wonderful Garden District location, right on St. Charles Ave. It has streetcar access to the French Quarter (about 2 mi east) and the Audubon Park and zoo (about 1 mi northwest). Board the streetcar right in front of the hotel. If you're lounging by the pool, keep in mind that there is a Mexican restaurant next door with cool and refreshing take-out margaritas. Complimentary Continental breakfast. In-room data ports, refrigerators. Cable TV. Pool. Laundry services. Business services, free parking. | 3626 St. Charles Ave. | 504/899–9990, 800/426–7866 | fax 504/899–9908 | www.hamptoninn.com | 100 rooms | $119–$189 | AE, D, DC, MC, V.

Historic French Market Inn. The quiet brick courtyard, where you can enjoy cocktails or breakfast or a swim in the pool, seems a world away from the action just outside on Decatur Street. This inn was originally built in the 1800s for Baron Joseph Xavier de Pontalba. Rooms are furnished with antique-style fourposter beds. Bar, complimentary Continental breakfast. In-room data ports. Cable TV. Pool. Laundry service. Business services. | 501 Decatur St. | 504/539–9000, 800/256–9970 | fax 504/566–0160 | www.nolacollection.com/frenchmarket | 54 rooms | $79–$199 | AE, D, DC, MC, V.

Holiday Inn Downtown–Superdome. This modern high-rise is in the heart of the Central Business District in the neighborhood where the first sounds of jazz were born. A favorite of Saints fans and Superbowl ticket holders, it's less than a mile east of the Superdome and only 4 blocks from Canal Street and the French Quarter. A mural of a clarinet is painted on its 18-story outer wall. There is a rooftop outdoor swimming pool. In-room movies and Nintendo. Restaurant, bar. In-room data ports. Cable TV. Pool. Exercise equipment. Laundry service. Business services, parking (fee). | 330 Loyola Ave. | 504/581–1600, 800/835–7830 | fax 504/586–0833 | www.basshotels.com | 296 rooms, 3 suites | $119–$139 | AE, D, DC, MC, V.

Holiday Inn Express. This two-story motel is just off I-10 at exit 244, less than a mile north of the Louisiana Nature Center and 7 mi from the French Quarter and downtown. It is across town from the airport (22 mi). Complimentary Continental breakfast. In-room data ports, microwaves, refrigerators. Cable TV. Pool. Exercise equipment. Laundry service. Business services. | 10020 I–10 Service Rd. | 504/244–9115, 800/821–4009 | fax 504/244–9150 | www.basshotels.com | 140 rooms, 2 suites | $62–$85, $125 suites | AE, D, DC, MC, V.

Hotel St. Pierre. Exposed brick, old beams, and armoires provide the decor on this complex of renovated slave quarters, arranged around courtyards and two pools. Originally built in the 1700s, it's 5 blocks from Riverwalk shops and Harrah's Casino. Complimentary Continental breakfast. In-room data ports. Cable TV. 2 pools. | 911 Burgundy St. | 504/524–4401, 800/225–4040 | fax 504/524–6800 | www.historicinnsneworleans.com | 74 rooms, 7 suites | $79–$129, $139–$159 suites | AE, D, DC, MC, V.

Hotel Villa Convento. Lela and Warren Campo and their son Larry provide round-the-clock service in their four-story, 1833 Creole town house. It's in a quiet end of the French Quarter, close to the Old Ursuline Convent. Each morning you can enjoy croissants and fresh-brewed coffee on the lush patio. Furnished with reproductions of antiques, rooms vary in price; some have balconies, chandeliers, or ceiling fans. Complimentary Continental breakfast. Cable TV. Parking (fee). No children under 10. | 616 Ursulines St. | 504/522–1793 | fax 504/524–1902 | www.villaconvento.com | 23 rooms, 2 suites | $99–$175 | AE, D, DC, MC, V.

House on Bayou Road. This B&B offers an elegantly renovated old home and cottage on two landscaped acres in a remote setting between the French Quarter and City Park. The French West Indies Creole style house, which is on the National Register of Historic Places, was built in 1798, with wide galleries, French doors, screened porches, a patio, gardens, and a pond. Breakfast is served in the sunny dining room overlooking the gardens. Many of the antiques-filled rooms have four-poster beds. The cottage suite has a skylight, kitchenette, and hot tub. It's about a mile from the New Orleans Museum of Art and City Park and 11 blocks from the French Quarter. Complimentary breakfast. Cable TV. Pool. Hot tub. No kids under 12. Business services, free parking. | 2275 Bayou Rd. | 504/945–0992, 800/882–2968 | fax 504/945–0993 | www.houseonbayouroad.com | 8 rooms (1 with shower only), cottage $320 | $155–$175 rooms, 235–$295 suites, $320 cottage | AE, MC, V.

Hyatt Regency. The tallest atrium in town connects to the Superdome and luxury shopping at New Orleans Centre. Visit the gigantic sports bar in the lobby. This downtown hotel has two towers, 27 floors, and a steakhouse restaurant on the revolving rooftop offering a panoramic view of the city. 2 restaurants, 3 bars, room service. In-room data ports. Cable TV. Pool. Beauty salon, hot tub. Exercise equipment. Laundry service. Business services, airport shuttle. | 500 Poydras Plaza | 504/561–1234, 800/233–1234 | fax 504/587–4141 | www.hyatt.com | 1,184 rooms, 100 suites | $119–$264, $400–$625 suites | AE, D, DC, MC, V.

Josephine Guest House. This 1870 Italianate mansion, one block from St. Charles Ave., provides you with the pleasures of an old New Orleans home. French empire, English, and Gothic period antiques fill the rooms, and Oriental rugs cover hardwood floors. Four rooms and a parlor are in the main house, which has 13-ft ceilings. There are two smaller rooms in the garconnier (where the original owners' sons lived). A complimentary Creole breakfast of fresh-squeezed orange juice, café au lait, and homemade biscuits can be brought to your room (served on Wedgwood china and a silver tray) or taken on the secluded patio. Complimentary Continental breakfast. Cable TV. No smoking. | 1450 Josephine St. | 504/524–6361 | fax 504/523–6484 | 6 rooms | $105–$155 | AE, D, DC, MC, V.

Lafitte Guest House. Period decor and antiques set a historic scene in this house in a quiet residential section of Bourbon St. A four-story, French-style manor house built in 1848, it has been meticulously restored. Beds are furnished with goose down comforters and pillows, and homemade pralines are left on your pillow each night. Grounds include a patio, two communal balconies, and some private balconies. One suite takes up the entire fourth floor. Complimentary Continental breakfast. Some minibars, some refrigerators. Cable TV. Business services, free parking. No smoking. | 1003 Bourbon St. | 504/581–2678, 800/331–7971 (in LA), 800/889–7359 | fax 504/581–2677 | www.lafitteguesthouse.com | 14 rooms, 2 suites | $99–$199 | AE, D, DC, MC, V.

Lamothe House. This 150-yr-old town house with a patio and Victorian antiques sits across Esplanade Ave. from the French Quarter, about 1 block from great music clubs and the coffeehouses of Faubourg Marigny. This restored Greek Revival brick house was originally built in the 1850s as a double town house. Rooms have hand-carved canopied beds and individual decor. The courtyard includes a goldfish pond, and another patio has a pool. Complimentary Continental breakfast. Cable TV. Pool. Hot tub. Business services, free parking. | 621 Esplanade Ave. | 504/947–1161, 800/367–5858 | fax 504/943–6536 | www.new-orleans.org | 20 rooms, 12 suites | $115–$150, $160–$175 suites | AE, MC, V.

Lanaux House. This stately 1879 mansion with three suites sharing a main courtyard, plus one private cottage with its own garden and fountain, is in Faubourg Marigny across Esplanade Avenue from the French Quarter and one block from music clubs. All of the lodgings are furnished with original antiques. There are 14-ft ceilings both upstairs and downstairs. Some of the original mantels, ceiling medallions, and wall coverings are still on display, as well as the original furnished library. Complimentary Continental breakfast. Some in-room data ports, kitchenettes. Cable TV. No smoking. | 547 Esplanade Ave. | 504/488–4640, 800/729–4640 | fax 504/488–4639 | www.historiclodging.com | 3 suites, 1 cottage with 2 suites, 1 room | $110–$190, $262 cottage | No credit cards.

★ **Le Richelieu.** This hotel, a favorite with visiting musicians and other celebrities, is a good base for exploring the trendy hangouts and music clubs of the lower Quarter and Faubourg Marigny. The owner lives on the premises and tries to combine the personal touches of a small hotel with some luxuries of larger establishments. The 2 Greek Revival town houses—one built circa 1845 and the other a former macaroni factory built in 1902—are 4 stories high with European-style furnishings, including oriental rugs, artwork, and ceiling fans. An intimate bar overlooks a courtyard and pool. Restaurant, bar. In-room data ports, some refrigerators. Cable TV. Pool. Business services, free parking. | 1234 Chartres St. | 504/529–2492, 800/535–9653 | fax 504/524–8179 | www.neworleansonline.com/richelieu | 86 rooms, 17 suites | $85–$170, $170–$475 suites | AE, D, DC, MC, V.

Maison Dupuy. This group of 19th-century buildings surrounding a lush courtyard was the site of the first U.S. cotton press. Today it's a quiet oasis in a residential area, just two blocks from Bourbon Street. The rooms and suites are furnished in traditional style with local art and marble baths. Some have balconies overlooking the patio and courtyard. Contemporary tropical fusion cuisine is served in Dominique's Restaurant. Restaurant (*see* Dominique's), bar. In-room data ports, minibars. Cable TV. Pool. Hot tub. Exercise equipment. Business services, parking (fee). | 1001 Toulouse St. | 504/586–8000, 800/535–9177 | fax 504/525–5334. | www.maisondupuy.com | 198 rooms | $99–$209 | AE, D, DC, MC, V.

McKendrick-Breaux House. If you're looking for an alternative to the city's touristy quarters, this three-story, 1865 Greek Revival town house and two-story, 1858 frame cottage in the Magazine Street antiques district are excellent choices. The large rooms, spread throughout the two buildings, are among the best values in the city. Features such as the original plaster arches, medallions, some woodwork, and flooring were preserved. The high-ceilinged rooms are decorated with fresh flowers and work by local artists; many have their own entrances to the garden courtyard. Each room has at least a queen bed, and many can accommodate a third guest. The owners, Lisa and Eddie Breaux, are gracious and helpful. Complimentary Continental breakfast. In-room data ports. Cable TV, some in-room VCRs. Pond. Hot tub. Free parking (limited). No smoking. | 1474 Magazine St. | 504/586–1700, 888/570–1700 | fax 504/522–7138 | www.mckendrick-breaux.com | 9 rooms | $125–$195 | AE, MC, V.

Olivier House Hotel. Owned and operated by the friendly Danner family, this very casual guest house is popular with Europeans and visiting theatrical troupes. It was built as a Creole town house in 1836, and no two rooms are alike: Some have canopy beds and antiques, others have a tropical flavor. Many have balconies and kitchenettes with microwaves, some are split-level. Rooms 107 (a two-bedroom, two-bath suite) and 103 open directly onto the pool area in one of the two plant-filled courtyards. The colorful caged birds in the other courtyard are pretty, but they can be chattering nuisances. Some kitchenettes, some microwaves. Pool. | 828 Toulouse St. | 504/525–8456 | fax 504/529–2006 | 43 rooms, 9 suites | $105–$279$105–$165 rooms, $165–$580 suites | AE, DC, MC, V.

Omni Royal Crescent. This stylish boutique hotel with a rooftop pool and well-equipped fitness center is a renovated office building with high ceilings and spacious rooms. In the downtown financial district, it is well suited to business travelers, only one block from the streetcar. Restaurant, room service. In-room data ports, minibars. Cable TV, in-room VCRs. Pool. Hot tub, saunas. Exercise equipment. Laundry service. Business services, parking (fee). | 535 Gravier St. | 504/527–0006, 800/843–6664 | fax 504/523–0806 | www.omnihotels.com | 98 rooms, 7 suites | $129–$259, $279–$309 suites | AE, D, DC, MC, V.

Parkview Guest House. Adjacent to beautiful Audubon Park, this Victorian guest house has been an uptown landmark since 1884. Rooms on the east side have great views of the park. The general rule seems to be that you get either antiques or a view ("view" rooms have brass beds and ceiling fans). There is a lounge with TV and fireplace and a large bay-window dining room where breakfast is served. Complimentary Continental breakfast. Cable TV. | 7004 St. Charles Ave. | 504/861–7564 | fax 504/861–1225 | www.parkviewguesthouse.com | 23 rooms (7 with shared bath) | $85–$149 | AE, D, MC, V.

Pelham. A renovation of an 1850s building has created this boutique hotel and its stylish restaurant, Metro Bistro. It is located in the downtown financial district (CBD), just one block from the French Quarter, one block from Harrah's casino, and three blocks from the Convention Center. Guest rooms have fine antiques and marble baths. Restaurant (*see* Metro Bistro), bar, room service. In-room data ports. Cable TV. Business services. | 444 Common St. | 504/522–4444 | fax 504/569–0640 | www.decaturhotel.com | 60 rooms, 4 suites | $129–$199, $199–$219 suites | AE, MC, V.

Provincial. This hotel has been owned and operated by the Dupepe family since 1959. The complex of historic buildings surrounds five patios and two pools and has a carriageway entrance. Four of the five interconnected buildings are on the National Historic Register. The guest rooms are furnished with antiques. Stylish food and drink are served at NuNu's Café and Bar. Two blocks from Jackson Square. Restaurant, bar, room service. In-room data ports. Cable TV. 2 pools. Business services, parking (fee). | 1024 Chartres St. | 504/581–4995, 800/535–7922 | fax 504/581–1018 | www.hotelprovincial.com | 105 rooms, 8 suites, 11 apartments | $119–$279, $149–$529 suites/apts | AE, D, DC, MC, V.

Prytania Park. This small, European-style hotel is in a transitional neighborhood undergoing renovations in the lower Garden District. It is only one block to the streetcar, and then a short ride to the French Quarter. The property is a renovated 1850s Greek Revival home with modern additions and is popular with business travelers, families, and leisure travelers. Complimentary Continental breakfast. Microwaves, refrigerators. Cable TV. Business services, free parking. | 1525 Prytania St. | 504/524–0427, 888/498–7591 | fax 504/522–2977 | www.prytaniaparkhotel.com | 62 rooms, 5 suites | $99–$109, $109–$129 suites | AE, D, DC, MC, V.

Quality Inn–Midtown. An economical choice for Superdome events, though rather remote from other attractions, this hotel is in a busy inner-city area, near LSU and Tulane Medical Centers. I–10 Exit 232 to U.S. Hwy. 61 (Tulane Ave.). Restaurant, bar, room service. In-room data ports, some microwaves, some refrigerators. Cable TV. Pool. Hot tub, sauna. Exercise equipment. Laundry facilities, laundry service. Free parking. | 3900 Tulane Ave. | 504/486–5541, 800/228–5151 | fax 504/488–7440 | www.qualityinn.com | 102 rooms | $89–$179 | AE, D, DC, MC, V.

NEW ORLEANS

INTRO
ATTRACTIONS
DINING
LODGING

Queen and Crescent. This boutique hotel, decorated in traditional style, is in a 19th-century building named for the former railway home office. It is in the financial district, three blocks from the French Quarter and one block from the streetcar. Bar, complimentary Continental breakfast. In-room data ports, minibars. Cable TV. Exercise equipment. Laundry service. Business services, parking (fee). | 344 Camp St. | 504/587–9700, 800/975–6652 | fax 504/587–9701 | www.queenandcrescent.com | 196 rooms | $79–$159 | AE, D, DC, MC, V.

Ramada Inn French Quarter Hotel–Chateau Dupré. Convenient to both the Central Business District and the French Quarter, this hotel is a mere one-half block from Canal Street near Aquarium of the Americas, IMAX, Riverwalk marketplace, and the ferry terminal, and just three blocks from Bourbon St. The four-story inn was built in 1813. The lobby has high ceilings and french doors, and rooms are furnished with fourposter beds. Restaurant, bar, room service. Complimentary Continental breakfast. In-room data ports, refrigerators (in suites). Cable TV, some in-room VCRs. Laundry service. Business services, free parking. | 131 Decatur St. | 504/569–0600, 888/211–3447 | fax 504/569–0600 | www.ramada.com | 43 rooms, 11 suites | $129–$220, $250 suites | AE, D, DC, MC, V.

Ramada Inn on Bourbon St. This five-story Ramada Inn, at the intersection of Toulouse and Bourbon, has a courtyard and rooms with balconies. It occupies the former site of the Old French Opera House. The rooms facing the courtyard are quieter, but the 32 rooms with balconies on Bourbon are coveted during Mardi Gras. Restaurant (breakfast only), bar, room service. In-room data ports, minibars. Cable TV. Pool. Exercise equipment. Laundry services. Business services, parking (fee). | 541 Bourbon St. | 504/524–7611, 800/535–7891 | fax 504/568–9427 | www.innonbourbon.com | 186 rooms, 2 suites | $89–$195 | AE, D, DC, MC, V.

Ramada Plaza–St. Charles. This is a modern hotel in the heart of the historic Garden District, right on the streetcar line and 1½ mi from the French Quarter. The hotel is on the main parade route during Mardi Gras. Restaurant, bar. In-room data ports, some refrigerators. Cable TV. Exercise equipment. Laundry service. Business services. | 2203 St. Charles Ave. | 504/566–1200, 800/443–4675 | fax 504/581–1352 | www.ramada.com | 132 rooms | $99–$169 | AE, D, DC, MC, V.

Rathbone Inn. Built in 1850 as a private family mansion, the inn's antebellum decor includes an ornamental cast-iron fence. The two-story front porch is supported by columns. The high-ceilinged rooms vary in size. It's just two blocks from the French Quarter, four blocks from Bourbon St. Complimentary Continental breakfast. Kitchenettes, microwaves, refrigerators. Cable TV. Hot tub. Laundry facilities. Business services. Some pets allowed. | 1227 Esplanade Ave. | 504/947–2100, 800/947–2101 | fax 504/947–7454 | www.rathboneinn.com | 9 rooms, 3 suites | $90–$165, $100–$175 suites | AE, D, DC, MC, V.

Rue Royal Inn. A pot of hot coffee and three Persian cats greet you in the lobby at Rue Royal Inn. Many rooms are pleasantly oversized in this circa 1830 home with exposed brick and high ceilings. Four rooms have balconies overlooking Royal Street and a school playground, two have hot tubs, and each has a coffeemaker and a small refrigerator. The complimentary Continental breakfast comes from the nearby Croissant d'Or. Complimentary Continental breakfast. In-room data ports, refrigerators, some in-room hot tubs. Cable TV. Parking (fee). | 1006 Royal St. | 504/524–3900, 800/776–3901 | fax 504/558–0566 | www.rueroyalinn.com | 17 rooms | $85–$165 | AE, D, DC, MC, V.

St. Charles Inn. The canopied entrance to this small, uptown hotel squeezed between a restaurant and a café is almost hidden from view. Inside are large rooms, each with a dressing area. Rooms in the front with a St. Charles Avenue view are best unless streetcar noise bothers you. Breakfast and a newspaper are brought to your room each morning. The staff is friendly and accommodating. Complimentary Continental breakfast. Cable TV. Free parking. | 3636 St. Charles Ave. | 504/899–8888, 800/489–9908 | fax 504/899–8892 | 40 rooms | $80–$100 | AE, D, DC, MC, V.

Pack an easy way to reach the world.

Wherever you travel, the MCI WorldCom Card℠ is the easiest way to stay in touch. You can use it to call to and from more than 125 countries worldwide. And you can earn bonus miles every time you use your card. So go ahead, travel the world. MCI WorldCom℠ makes it even more rewarding. For additional access codes, visit **www.wcom.com/worldphone**.

MCI WORLDCOM.

EASY TO CALL WORLDWIDE

1. Just dial the WorldPhone® access number of the country you're calling from.
2. Dial or give the operator your MCI WorldCom Card number.
3. Dial or give the number you're calling.

Canada	1-800-888-8000
Mexico	01-800-021-8000
United States	1-800-888-8000

EARN FREQUENT FLIER MILES

6 "I'm thirsty"s, 9 "Are we there yet"s, 3 "I don't feel good"s,
1 car class upgrade.
At least something's going your way.

Hertz rents Fords and other fine cars. ® REG. U.S. PAT. OFF. © HERTZ SYSTEM INC., 2000/005-00

Make your next road trip more comfortable with a free one-class upgrade from Hertz.

Let's face it, a long road trip isn't always sunshine and roses. But with Hertz, you get a free one car class upgrade to make things a little more bearable. You'll also choose from a variety of vehicles with child seats, Optional Protection Plans, 24-Hour Emergency Roadside Assistance, and the convenience of NeverLost, the in-car navigation system that provides visual and audio prompts to give you turn-by-turn guidance to your destination. In a word: it's everything you need for your next road trip. Call your travel agent or Hertz at **1-800-654-2210** and mention PC# **906404** or check us out at **hertz.com** or AOL Keyword: **hertz**. Peace of mind. Another reason nobody does it exactly like Hertz.

Hertz
exactly.®

Saint Louis. A feeling of luxury is provided here by the toney Louis XVI Restaurant, French provincial antiques and period reproductions in the guest rooms, and one of the most sumptuous courtyards in the Quarter. All rooms overlook this space filled with plants, banana trees, and a fountain. Breakfast is served in the courtyard as well. The hotel is in the French Quarter between Bourbon and Royal Streets. Restaurant (see Louis XVI), bar (with entertainment), room service. In-room data ports, minibars (in suites). Cable TV. Laundry service. Business services. | 730 Bienville St. | 504/581–7300, 800/535–9111 | fax 504/524–8925 | www.stlouishotel.com | 40 rooms, 32 suites | $99–$219, $229–$329 suites | AE, DC, MC, V.

St. Peter Guest House. Constructed in 1788 as a private residence, this hotel has a pink exterior and iron balconies. It's just two blocks North of Bourbon St. in the French Quarter. Complimentary Continental breakfast. Cable TV. | 1005 St. Peter | 504/524–9232, 888/604–6300 | fax 504/523–5198 | www.crescent-city.org | 28 rooms, 5 suites | $80–$100, $120–$200 suites | AE, MC, V.

Sully Mansion. More than a century ago, New Orleans architect Thomas Sully built this handsome, rambling Queen Anne–style house. In the foyer, furnished with a grand piano, light filters through pastel, stained-glass windows, which are original to the house. A beautiful carved staircase, 14-ft ceilings, 10-ft cypress wood doors, heart-of-pine floors, and oriental rugs convey a feeling of old New Orleans elegance, enhanced by oil paintings, fireplaces, and tall windows with swagged, floor-length drapes in the public rooms. The upstairs guest rooms have 1950s French provincial furnishings. Downstairs rooms have four-poster beds, damask draperies, and upholstered sofas and chairs. Neighbor to other grand mansions, the house is on a pretty tree-lined street, a block from the streetcar. Cable TV. No children. No smoking. | 2631 Prytania St. | 504/891–0457 | fax 504/899–7237 | www.sullymansion.com | 5 rooms, 2 suites | $129–$249 | AE, D, MC, V.

Travelodge. This two-story motel built in 1971 is in a suburban/industrial area across the Mississippi from New Orleans. Shuttle service to a ferry to the French Quarter and the casino is available, about a 20-min ride. Restaurant, bar, room service. In-room data ports, some microwaves, some refrigerators. Cable TV. 2 pools, wading pool. Laundry facilities, laundry service. Business services, free parking. | 2200 Westbank Expressway, Harvey | 504/366–5311, 800/578–7878 | fax 504/368–2774 | www.travelodge.com | 211 rooms | $55–$125 | AE, D, DC, MC, V.

MODERATE

Chateau Sonesta. This hotel in the French Quarter is an elegant renovation of the historic D. H. Holmes Department Store, with a central courtyard and pool. Guest rooms have 12-ft ceilings, and most have views of Bourbon Street or the interior courtyard. The rear of the building faces Canal Street, convenient for the Central Business District and St. Charles Avenue streetcar. Restaurant, bar (with entertainment), room service. In-room data ports, minibars. Cable TV. Pool. Beauty salon. Exercise equipment. Business services. | 800 Iberville St. | 504/586–0800, 800/766–3782 | fax 504/586–1987 | www.sonesta.com | 250 rooms, 26 suites | $155–$330, $350–$760 suites | AE, D, DC, MC, V.

Claiborne Mansion. Enormous rooms with high ceilings, canopy or four-poster beds, polished hardwood floors, spacious marble baths, and rich fabrics are features of this handsome 1859 mansion in Faubourg Marigny on the fringe of the French Quarter. The house overlooks Washington Square Park and has a lush rear courtyard and pool. Enjoy complimentary evening cocktails and gourmet breakfasts. Vases of fresh flowers accent the contemporary furnishings. Complimentary breakfast. Cable TV. In-room VCRs (and movies). Pool. Business services, free parking. Pets allowed (with advance notice). No smoking. | 2111 Dauphine St. | 504/949–7327 | fax 504/949–0388 | 2 rooms, 4 suites | $150–$185 rooms, $210–$300 suites | AE, D, MC, V.

Dauphine Orleans. Opened in 1969, this hotel occupies several buildings. The lounge is in a former bordello, still known as May Bailey's Place. The suites are in the 1834 former home of a wealthy merchant, who built it with the best country brick and cypress wood available. John James Audubon painted his "Birds of America" portraits while staying in one of the cottages. Old brick and cypress beams also adorn the Dauphine Patio guest rooms, located just across Dauphine St. All rooms are furnished with robes and goose down comforters. The hotel is one block from Bourbon Street, two blocks from antique shops and art galleries on Royal St. Bar, complimentary Continental breakfast. In-room data ports, minibars. Cable TV. Pool. Hot tub. Exercise equipment. Library. Laundry service. Business services, parking (fee). | 415 Dauphine St. | 504/586–1800, 800/508–5554 | fax 504/586–1409 | www.dauphineorleans.com | 111 rooms, 15 suites and cottages | $149–$229, $179–$359 suites | AE, D, DC, MC, V.

French Quarter Courtyard. The rooms in this two-story hotel with balconies overlook a landscaped courtyard with fountains and a pool. Rooms, some with original fireplaces, have four-poster beds and hardwood and brick flooring. It's across Rampart Street from the French Quarter, three blocks from Bourbon Street. Bar, complimentary Continental breakfast. Cable TV. Pool. Laundry service. Business services, parking (fee). Pets allowed. | 1101 N. Rampart | 504/522–7333, 800/290–4233 | fax 504/522–3908 | www.neworleans.com/fqch | 51 rooms, 10 suites | $159–$189, $219 suites | AE, D, DC, MC, V.

Girod House. This three-story Creole house was built in 1833 by the first mayor of New Orleans, Nicholas Girod. All rooms are high-ceilinged suites, each with a living room and kitchen. The two-floor suites also have balconies. Furnishings include fine European and American antique and goose down pillows. The hotel is across Esplanade Ave. from the French Quarter, 2 blocks from great music clubs and the coffeehouses of Faubourg Marigny. Complimentary Continental breakfast. In-room data ports, kitchenettes, refrigerators. Cable TV. Business services, parking (fee). | 835 Esplanade Ave. | 504/522–5214, 800/650–3323 | fax 504/522–7208 | www.girodhouse.com | 6 suites | $175–$250 suites | AE, MC, V.

Hilton Riverside. A huge atrium lobby offers direct access to the Riverwalk marketplace with over 140 shops and the Riverfront Streetcar. In the hotel you'll find outdoor track and indoor tennis at Rivercenter Racquet and Health Club and live jazz at Pete Fountain's Nightclub. Tower rooms and suites have spectacular views of the Mississippi. Opened in the late 1970s, this 29-story hotel is across the street from Harrah's Casino and 2 blocks from the Convention Center, Aquarium of the Americas, and IMAX. 3 restaurants, 3 bars, room service. In-room data ports, minibars. Cable TV. 2 pools. Beauty salon, hot tub, sauna. Putting green, 8 tennis courts. Basketball. Exercise equipment. Laundry service. Business services, parking (fee). | 2 Poydras St. | 504/561–0500, 800/445–8667 | fax 504/568–1721 | www.hilton.com | 1,600 rooms, 70 suites | $179–$289, $700–$1,000 suites | AE, D, DC, MC, V.

Hotel Ste. Hélène. If you can afford one of the enormous suites (note that the one with the whirlpool bath does not have a shower) with a balcony overlooking Emeril Lagasse's restaurant Nola, 14-ft ceilings, fireplaces, and chandeliers, by all means book it. This inn has two buildings, each with a courtyard where a Continental breakfast is served daily. Each evening complimentary champagne is served in the brick courtyard of the main building. Standard rooms are functional and clean but are on the small side and lack charm. However, there are occasional, eclectic surprises—such as marble-topped, lyre-design bedside tables or a four-poster bed—mixed in with run-of-the-mill reproduction antiques and halogen lamps. There's one apartment-style suite with two bedrooms and two baths. Both buildings have three floors and no elevators. Complimentary Continental breakfast. Cable TV. Pool. | 508 Chartres St. | 504/522–5014 | fax 504/523–7140 | www.stehelene.com | 26 rooms, 10 suites | $165–$195 rooms $235–$325 suites | AE, D, DC, MC, V.

International House. This gorgeous renovation of a beaux-arts style building has 23-ft ceilings in the lobby and 12-ft ceilings in the guest rooms. Chic Louisiana decor complete with native plants, linen slipcovers, and ornate columns sets a fashionable mood. Guest rooms in the 12-story boutique hotel have down comforters, fresh Louisiana wildflowers, CD players and jazz CDs, and black and white photos of great local jazz artists. The penthouse suites offer views of the skyline and river. Sample the stylish French/Vietnamese cuisine at the Lemon Grass Café. Just south of the French Quarter. Restaurant, bar, room service. In-room data ports, minibars, some in-room hot tubs. Cable TV. Exercise equipment. Laundry service. Business services, parking (fee). | 221 Camp St. | 504/553–9550, 800/633–5770 | fax 504/553–9560 | www.ihhotel.com | 108 rooms, 11 suites | $149–$269, $259–$399 suites | AE, D, DC, MC, V.

Lafayette. This small brick building was built in 1916 and overlooks shady Lafayette Square, which is on the streetcar line in the Warehouse/Arts District and on the main parade route during Mardi Gras. Spacious guest rooms have four-poster beds, marble baths, and big windows. Some rooms have door-size windows opening onto a balcony. Dining and room service are provided by Mike Ditka's Steakhouse, which adjoins the hotel on the first floor. Restaurant, bar (with entertainment), room service. In-room data ports, minibars. Cable TV. Business services, airport shuttle, parking (fee). | 600 St. Charles Ave. | 504/524–4441, 800/733–4754 | fax 504/523–7327 | www.nolacollection.com/lafayette | 44 rooms, 20 suites | $155–$350, $285–$650 suites | AE, D, DC, MC, V.

Le Pavillon. This eight-story hotel with a rooftop pool was built in 1907 and is on the National Register of Historic Places. The gargantuan lobby is decorated with ornate antiques, crystal chandeliers, marble floors, Italian columns, and original art. Peanut butter and jelly sandwiches and milk are served there nightly. The first basement built in the city is now a nightclub where you can dance to swing bands. Brocades and canopied beds adorn the suites. The hotel is 5 blocks south of the French Quarter. Restaurant, bar, room service. In-room data ports, refrigerators, minibars. Cable TV. Pool. Hot tub. Exercise equipment. Laundry service. Business services, airport shuttle, parking (fee). | 833 Poydras St. | 504/581–3111, 800/535–9095 | fax 504/522–5543 | www.lepavillon.com | 219 rooms, 7 suites | $149–$250, $390–$1,495 suites (each has different price) | AE, D, DC, MC, V.

Monteleone. This is a 16-story Baroque granite landmark with ceiling frescoes, huge chandeliers, antiques, individually decorated guest rooms, and liveried doormen. The French Quarter's oldest hotel, operating since 1886, is run by the 4th generation of the founding family. Famous guests have included William Faulkner, Tennessee Williams, and Truman Capote. The large rooms still have four-poster beds, and you can still enjoy the famous Carousel Bar on the lobby level, a gilded revolving beauty. Sample contemporary Creole cuisine in the Hunt Room Grill. In the upper French Quarter, just one block from the central business district and streetcar. 3 restaurants (see Hunt Room Grill), bar (with entertainment). In-room data ports. Cable TV. Pool. Exercise equipment. Laundry service. Business services. | 214 Royal St. | 504/523–3341, 800/321–6710 | fax 504/528–1019 | www.hotelmonteleone.com | 600 rooms, 28 suites | $150–$250, $330–$600 suites | AE, D, DC, MC, V.

★ **Omni Royal Orleans.** Although this stately hotel was built in 1960, it acquires plenty of Old World elegance from gilt mirrors, Italian marble, and French chandeliers. It was built as a replica of the grand St. Louis Hotel of the 1800s. Offering famous views from the rooftop pool area of the Mississippi and the French Quarter, it is ideally situated at the very center of the French Quarter. Rooms have marble baths and marble top dressers and tables. Some rooms have balconies. Restaurants (see The Rib Room), 3 bars (with entertainment), room service. In-room data ports, minibars, some hot tubs. Cable TV. Pool. Barbershop, beauty salon. Exercise equipment. Business services, parking (fee). | 621 St. Louis St. | 504/529–5333, 800/843–6664 | fax 504/529–7089 | www.omnihotels.com | 346 rooms, 25 suites | $169–$349, $329–$999 suites | AE, D, DC, MC, V.

Pontchartrain. A Garden District landmark that's been in business since 1927, this hotel is traditional and sedate. It is on the streetcar line, 5 min to the French Quarter, and right on the main parade route during Mardi Gras. Rooms vary from basic with shower only to quite lavish. 2 Restaurants, bar (with entertainment), room service. In-room data ports, some refrigerators. Cable TV. Business services, airport shuttle, parking (fee). | 2031 St. Charles Ave. | 504/524–0581, 800/777–6193 | fax 504/529–1165 | www.grandheritage.comm | 104 rooms, 46 suites | $145–$180, $225–$275 suites | AE, D, DC, MC, V.

Radisson. A modern renovation of a landmark on Canal Street, this hotel is on the National Register of Historic Places and features a rooftop pool. Although it's several blocks from the main tourist area, it is only ½ block from the Superdome. Free shuttle service to the

French Quarter is available. Restaurant, bar. In-room data ports, refrigerators (in suites). Cable TV. Pool. Hot tub. Exercise equipment. Laundry facilities, laundry service. Business services, parking (fee). | 1500 Canal St. | 504/522–4500, 800/333–3333 | fax 504/522–3627 | www.radisson.com | 759 rooms, 15 suites | $149–$189, $279–$359 suites | AE, D, DC, MC, V.

Royal Sonesta. This is a grand seven-story hotel with lacy iron balconies, a rich marble lobby, and an enormous courtyard. Rooms on the Bourbon Street side can be noisy but offer the best views of wild nightlife, especially during Mardi Gras and other special events. Most rooms have sound proofing. The third floor has a deck and pool, and there is a bar in the courtyard. 2 restaurants (*see* Begue's *and* Desire Oyster Bar), 2 bars (with entertainment). In-room data ports, minibars. Cable TV. Pool. Exercise equipment. Business services, parking (fee). | 300 Bourbon St. | 504/586–0300, 800/766–3782 | fax 504/586–0335 | www.royalsonestano.com | 500 rooms, 35 suites | $185–$320, $425–$975 suites | AE, D, DC, MC, V.

Saint Ann-Marie Antoinette. This is a small, elegant hotel in a centrally located French Quarter building, one-half block from Bourbon Street and the restaurants and shops of Royal Street. The large rooms have modern furnishings and marble and tile baths. Some balconies overlook the pool. Breakfast is served in the tropical courtyard. Restaurant, bar, room service. Cable TV. Pool. Business services, parking (fee). | 717 Conti St. | 504/581–1881, 888/508–3980 | fax 504/524–8925 | www.stannmarieantoinette.com | 66 rooms, 18 suites | $159–$209, $179–$249 suites | AE, DC, MC, V.

Soniat House. These three meticulously restored town houses on both sides of Chartres St. have secluded tropical courtyards. They were built in 1829 and combine classic Greek Revival detail and Creole style, including a stone carriageway and lacy ironwork. It's one of the city's most luxurious small hotels, with service in grand European style. The rooms have polished hardwood floors and are decorated with hand-carved four-poster beds, fine linens, classic antiques, oriental rugs, and contemporary paintings by local artists. If you opt for the in-house breakfast, you can enjoy it in your room or by the lily pond and fountain in the courtyard. Just two blocks from the French Market and Cafe du Monde. Some in-room hot tubs (in suites). Cable TV. Parking (fee). No kids under 12. | 1133 Chartres St. | 504/522–0570, 800/544–8808 | fax 504/522–7208 | www.soniathouse.com | 20 rooms, 14 suites | $145–$250, $295–$625 suites | AE, MC, V.

W Hotel New Orleans. This contemporary high-rise, formerly the Crowne Plaza, is between the Central Business District and the Warehouse/Arts District. It's about 3 blocks from the Convention Center, 1 block from Riverwalk, and 5 blocks from the St. Charles Ave. streetcar. Guest rooms are very modern in red and black colors. Each has a 27-inch TV with Internet access, VCR and library of movies, radio, and CD player and library of discs. Randy Gerber's fashionable Whiskey Blue Lounge is in the lobby. Restaurant, 3 bars. In-room data ports. Cable TV. Pool. Massage. Health club. Laundry service. Business services, parking (fee). | 333 Poydras St. | 504/525–9444, 800/777–7372 | fax 504/525–3156 | www.whotels.com | 423 rooms, 23 suites | $159–$269, $425–$675 suites | AE, D, DC, MC, V.

Wyndham New Orleans at Canal Place. The lobby and restaurant of this French Quarter hotel are on the 11th floor and guest rooms begin on the 14th floor, sitting atop a high-rise shopping mall and overlooking the river. The hotel is connected to the luxury shops of Canal Place at the south end of Canal Street near the river. The huge marble lobby, furnished with European antiques and a grand piano, has two-story arched windows that overlook the river and French Quarter. You'll find luxurious marble baths, marble foyers, private bars, and other European-style perks in the guest rooms. Restaurant, bar (with entertainment), room service. In-room data ports, minibars. Cable TV. Pool. Exercise equipment. Laundry service. Business services, parking (fee). | 100 Iberville St. | 504/566–7006, 800/996–3426 | fax 504/553–5120 | www.wyndham.com | 437 rooms, 40 suites | $179–$339, $259–$3,000 suites | AE, D, MC, V.

Wyndham Riverfront. Directly across from Riverwalk marketplace, this hotel is 5 blocks south of the French Quarter in an area known as "uptown." It's popular with business travelers. Original masonry buildings from a 19th-century rice mill and a silo have been restored and renovated, with modern additions incorporated around them. A circular drive and splashing fountain are found at the entrance, and the interior has a cool neutral decor. The silo rooms are large with king beds, and the other rooms are smaller but have high ceilings. Restaurant, bar, room service. In-room data ports. Cable TV. Exercise equipment. Laundry service. Business services, parking (fee). | 701 Convention Center Blvd. | 504/524–8200, 800/996–3426 | fax 504/524–0600 | www.wyndham.com | 202 rooms, 2 suites | $159–$298, $245–$330 suites | AE, D, DC, MC, V.

EXPENSIVE

Best Western Parc St. Charles. New in 1998, this upscale property is on one of the Big Easy's best Carnival corners, the intersection of Poydras Street and St. Charles Avenue. The Parc St. Charles is an intimate, business-class hotel; rooms are decorated with contemporary furniture, and large, plate-glass windows provide lots of light and wide views of the bustling business district. Complimentary coffee is served in the lobby, and there's a rooftop pool. In-room video games and Nintendo. Restaurant (*see* Gerard's Downtown *listing*), bar, room service. Some in-room data ports. Minibars. Cable TV. Pool. Exercise equipment. Laundry services. Business services, parking (fee). | 500 St. Charles Ave. | 504/522–9000, 800/521–7551 | fax 504/522–9060 | www.bestwestern.com | 120 rooms, 2 suites | $199–$219 | AE, D, DC, MC, V.

Doubletree. This contemporary high-rise is across Canal street from the French Quarter, near Aquarium of the Americas, IMAX, Riverwalk marketplace, and the ferry terminal. It's 8 blocks from the Convention Center. In-room Nintendo. 2 restaurants, bar, room service. Kitchenettes (in suites), refrigerators (in suites), hot tubs (in suites). Cable TV. Pool. Bas-

JAZZ

Born in the dives and dancehalls of New Orleans around 1900, jazz is an original American art form with roots in ragtime, marching bands, and African work songs. Pioneers Buddy Bolden and King Oliver blew their horns in the syncopated rhythm that came to be known as Dixieland. Louis Armstrong, Sidney Bechet, and Jelly Roll Morton carried the message around the world during the Jazz Age of the 1920s.

A handful of their contemporaries are among the living legends who still perform nightly in the French Quarter at Preservation Hall. In turn, the early giants inspired modern stars who broadcast the New Orleans sound to the TV generation, including clarinetist Pete Fountain, trumpeter Al Hirt, and pianist Ronnie Kole.

Today, aficionados gather at Snug Harbor Jazz Bistro and Palm Court Jazz Café. Visiting performers from around the world sit in on impromptu late-night jam sessions at Fritzel's European Jazz Pub. Young brass bands are the hottest acts in town, drawing enthusiastic fans to Donna's Bar and Grill. Ellis Marsalis (father of Wynton and Branford) schools the artists of the future as director of the Jazz Studies Program at the University of New Orleans. And for 10 days every year, from the last weekend in April through the first weekend in May, the New Orleans Jazz and Heritage Festival presents a citywide feast of music and special events for an international audience that rivals the crowds of Carnival.

© Corbis

ketball, exercise equipment. Laundry service. Business services. | 300 Canal St. | 504/581–1300, 800/222–8733 | fax 504/522–4100 | www.doubletree.com | 363 rooms, 10 suites | $189–$250 rooms, 10 suites $250–$400 | AE, D, DC, MC, V.

Embassy Suites. A modern all-suites high-rise, this hotel is right on gallery row in the Warehouse/Arts District, only two blocks from the Convention Center and Riverwalk marketplace, six blocks from the French quarter, and five blocks from the St. Charles Ave. streetcar line. The huge atrium has French Quarter–style balconies and fanciful Mardi Gras decor. Restaurant, bar. In-room data ports, microwaves, refrigerators. Cable TV. Pool. Hot tub. Exercise equipment. Video games. Laundry service. Business services. | 315 Julia St. | 504/525–1993, 800/362–2779 | fax 504/525–3437 | www.embassy-suites.com | 282 suites | $220–$265 | AE, D, DC, MC, V.

★ **Fairmont.** This historic 1893 landmark offers turn-of-the-20th-century elegance with liveried doormen, crystal chandeliers, gilt mirrors, and an extravagant block-long lobby. The lobby's Christmas decorations of strands of white angel hair attract many viewers. Luxurious rooms and suites have big marble baths, high ceilings, goose down comforters, and Sony Playstations for the kids. You can sample contemporary bistro cuisine in the Sazerac Bar and Grill and enjoy the rooftop pool and tennis courts. It's one block from the French Quarter. Restaurant (*see* Sazerac Bar and Grill), bar, room service. In-room data ports. Cable TV. Pool. Beauty salon. 2 tennis courts. Exercise equipment. Laundry service. Business services, parking (fee). | 123 Baronne St. | 504/529–7111 | fax 504/522–2303 | www.fairmont.com | 700 rooms, 85 suites | $239–$299, $350–$1150 suites | AE, D, DC, MC, V.

Holiday Inn–Chateau Le Moyne. Don't let the chain name throw you. Guest rooms spread from a 5-story hotel 1 block from Bourbon St. through four 19th-century town houses with two tropical courtyards, lacy ironwork, and old masonry. Suites are in a Creole cottage off a courtyard. Restaurant, bar, room service. In-room data ports. Cable TV. Pool. Laundry service. Business services, parking (fee). | 301 Dauphine St. | 504/581–1303, 800/747–3279 | fax 504/523–5709 | www.basshotels.om | 171 rooms, 11 suites | $225–$270, $310–$410 suites | AE, D, DC, MC, V.

Hotel Inter-Continental New Orleans. This stylish marble high-rise with understated contemporary decor, sculpture garden, and atrium restaurant is on the streetcar line, convenient to the Central Business District and the Warehouse/Arts District. This is a major convention hotel. It is on the main parade route, with reviewing stands set up annually during Mardi Gras. Some rooms have balconies overlooking the courtyard. In-room Nintendo video games are available for the kids. 2 Restaurants (*see* Veranda), 2 bars (with entertainment), room service. In-room data ports, minibars, some refrigerators. Cable TV. Pool. Beauty shop, massage. Exercise equipment. Laundry service. Business services, parking (fee). | 444 St. Charles Ave. | 504/525–5566, 800/445–6563 | fax 504/523–7310 | www.neworleans.interconti.com | 482 rooms, 20 suites | $199–$260, $500–$1,500 suites | AE, D, DC, MC, V.

Hotel Maison de Ville. This hotel's main building was constructed circa 1800. There are also four former slave homes across the courtyard that are believed to be about 50 years older, and seven cottages called the Audubon Cottages are on Dauphine Street. Originally a private house, the main building became a boarding house in the 1920's; Tennessee Williams completed "A Streetcar Named Desire" while staying in room 9. The hotel opened in 1986. Guest rooms have classic European decor with antiques, four-poster beds, and marble basins, and the gorgeous courtyard has a fountain, banana trees, and flowering plants. You can savor the contemporary French cuisine and great wine list in The Bistro. The complimentary Continental breakfast arrives on a silver tray with a newspaper and a fresh rose. A secluded patio and pool in the Audubon Cottages complex two blocks away may be used by hotel guests. Restaurant (*see* The Bistro at Maison De Ville), complimentary Continental breakfast, room service. In-room data ports. Cable TV, in-room VCRs. Pool (2 blocks away). No kids under 12. Business services, parking (fee). | 727 Toulouse St. | 504/561–5858, 800/634–1600 | fax 504/528–9939 | www.maisondeville.com | 16 rooms, 7 cottages | $215–$375, $245–$1,005 cottages | AE, D, DC, MC, V.

Landmark French Quarter. This modern motor hotel on the outer fringe of the French Quarter is across from Louis Armstrong Park, three blocks from Bourbon Street, and within 10 blocks of the Saenger Performing Arts Center, Municipal Auditorium, and Mahalia Jackson Theatre of the Performing Arts. There is a complimentary shuttle to Decatur St. in the French Quarter. Rooms are built around a tropical courtyard, fountain, and pool. Restaurant, bar. Cable TV. Pool. Laundry facilities. Business services. | 920 N. Rampart | 504/524–3333, 800/535–7862 | fax 504/522–8044 | 100 rooms, 2 suites | $199–$225, $350 suites | AE, D, DC, MC, V.

Marriott. This modern 41-floor high-rise has two towers connected by an enormous lobby and courtyard pool area, and offers views of the Mississippi from River Tower guest rooms and the rooftop restaurant. The hotel is popular with conventioneers and corporate travelers. The back entrance is in the French Quarter, the front on Canal Street. It's a couple of blocks from the Aquarium of the Americas, IMAX, ferry terminal, Riverwalk marketplace, Harrah's casino, and the St. Charles Avenue streetcar. 3 restaurants, 3 bars (with entertainment), room service. In-room data ports. Cable TV. Pool, wading pool. Sauna. Exercise equipment. Laundry facilities, laundry service. Business services, parking (fee). | 555 Canal St. | 504/581–1000, 800/228–9290 | fax 504/523–6755 | www.marriott.com | 1,290 rooms, 54 suites | $249–$365, $400–$700 suites | AE, D, DC, MC, V.

Melrose Mansion. This exquisite restoration of lodgings built in 1884 has a lavish parlor filled with antiques. Spacious rooms have high ceilings, hardwood floors, and sumptuous baths, and suites have 19th-century antique furnishings. A full Creole breakfast is served poolside, in the dining room, or in your room. The property overlooks oak-lined Esplanade Ave., across the street from the French Quarter. Complimentary breakfast, room service. Some refrigerators, hot tubs (in suites). Cable TV. Pool. Exercise equipment. Library. Business services. | 937 Esplanade Ave. | 504/944–2255, 800/650–3323 | fax 504/945–1794 | www.melrosemansion.com | 4 rooms, 5 suites | $225–$250 rooms, $325–$425 suites | AE, D, DC, MC, V.

Sheraton. This modern skyscraper (49 floors) features an atrium, multi-level lobby, and live jazz nightly. A huge fitness center offers massages, aerobics classes, and other special services. It's on the edge of the French Quarter, and the riverfront is 3 blocks away. 3 Restaurants, bar (with entertainment), room service. In-room data ports. Cable TV. Pool. Hot tub, massage, sauna, steam room. Health club. Laundry service. Business services, parking (fee): | 500 Canal St. | 504/525–2500, 800/253–6156 | fax 504/561–0178 | www.sheraton.com/new orleans | 1,048 rooms, 53 suites | $199–$239, $675–$1,000 suites | AE, D, DC, MC, V.

W Hotel New Orleans–French Quarter. Formerly the Hotel de la Poste, this renovated hotel has luxurious room furnishings, including goose down comforters, 27-inch TVs, VCRs and CD players with tape and disc libraries. Suites are in a separate carriage house. There is a garden courtyard, and some rooms have French doors opening onto a patio or balconies overlooking the courtyard or the Quarter. The adjacent restaurant serves trendy Tuscan food (see Bacco). Restaurant, bar, room service. In-room data ports. Cable TV. Pool. Laundry service. Business services, parking (fee). | 316 Chartres St. | 504/581–1200, 800/448–4927 | fax 504/522–3208 | www.whotels.com | 100 rooms, 13 suites | $199–$269 | AE, D, DC, MC, V.

★ **Windsor Court.** Consistently voted among the world's best by readers of Conde Nast's *Traveler*, Windsor Court features serious service and luxurious traditional accommodations. The collection of 17th- to 20th-century European art and antiques displayed throughout the public areas of the hotel is worth millions. Rooms have Italian marble bathrooms, while suites feature private balconies or bay windows overlooking the Mississippi or the city and have canopied four-poster beds and wet bars. Enjoy afternoon tea or savor grand dining in the Grill Room. The hotel is four blocks from the French Quarter. 2 restaurants (see Grill Room), 2 bars (with entertainment), room service. In-room data ports, minibars. Cable TV. Pool. Hot tub, massage. Health club. Driving range, putting green. Laundry service. Business services, airport shuttle, parking (fee). | 300 Gravier St. | 504/523–6000, 800/262–2662 | fax 504/596–4513 | www.windsorcourthotel.com | 58 rooms, 264 suites | $230–$400, $280–$800 suites | AE, D, DC, MC, V.

VERY EXPENSIVE

Le Meridien. This high-rise opened in 1984 combines sleek French style with a waterfall behind glass and live jazz in the lobby lounge. Guest rooms have contemporary furnishings and neutral hues. Some bi-level suites come with two-story windows. The hotel is across Canal Street from the French Quarter, eight blocks from the Convention Center and Superdome. Restaurant (*see* Midi), bar (with entertainment), room service. In-room data ports, minibars. Cable TV. Pool. Hot tub, massage, sauna. Gym. Shops. Laundry service. Business services, parking (fee). | 614 Canal St. | 504/525–6500, 800/543–4300 | fax 504/525–1128 | www.meridienneworleans.com | 494 rooms and 7 suites | $275–$315, $800–$2,500 suites | AE, D, DC, MC, V.

NEW ROADS

MAP 9, E4

(Nearby towns also listed: Baton Rouge, Jackson, St. Francisville)

For more than a century, vacationers from New Orleans and Baton Rouge have escaped the summer heat in the waterfront resort of New Roads, a cool oasis on the crescent-shape lake known as False River. Though citizens celebrated the town's 100th anniversary in 1994, New Roads really dates back to 1822, when a settlement was established at the terminus of a "new road" linking it with older communities along the Mississippi River. Today, New Roads, which houses a collection of French Creole and Victorian landmarks, is a prime spot for enjoying water sports and historic architecture. The town is part of the Louisana "Main Street Program," which helps restore historic buildings like the Old Poydras High School and the Tourist Museum.

Information: **Pointe Coupee Tourist Commission** | 160 E. Main St., New Roads, 70760 | 225/638–3998.

Attractions

False River. This oxbow lake was once a main channel of the Mississippi. It was created from a bend in the river around 1722, when seasonal flooding finally cut a shorter channel to the east. During the late 19th century, steamboats transported cotton, sugar, and passengers up and down the 22-mi crescent. Today it's a major destination for fishing, sailing, and water skiing. | 225/638–3995 | Free | Daily.

Parlange Plantation. One of the oldest examples of French Colonial architecture in Louisiana, this National Historic Landmark house is surrounded by wide verandas and ancient oaks. Built in 1750 of native materials, it was framed by cypress beams and bricks made on the grounds, then plastered with a traditional mixture of mud, moss, and deer hair. The beautifully maintained manor is set on a working plantation, originally a land grant from the French crown, that is still owned and operated by seventh- and eighth-generation members of the Parlange family. | 8211 False River Rd. | 225/638–8410 | fax 225/638–3453 | $7 | Daily, by appointment.

Pointe Coupee Parish Museum. There's no shortage of grand manors in the heart of plantation country, but here is a rare look at a typical middle-class home. The 1760 cottage is furnished with period antiques appropriate to a family of modest means. Authentically restored in its original location on the banks of False River, this small museum also houses a general information center for visitors. | 8348 False River Rd. | 225/638–7788 | fax 225/638–3915 | Free | Daily 10–3.

FEB., MAR.: *Mardi Gras.* Fat Tuesday has been celebrated here for more than 75 years, on the day before Ash Wednesday. Come join the festivities, which include morning and afternoon parades, costume contests, and a masquerade ball. | 504/838–6111.

DEC.: *Christmas on False River.* Carriage rides, candlelight walking tours of historic houses, a Christmas tree lighting, a parade, fireworks, an arts and crafts fair, and children's activities are highlighted at this event, which takes place the first Sat. in December. | 225/638–3998.

Dining

Satterfield's Riverwalk. Seafood. Choose the dining room that includes a fireplace and a glass wall overlooking False River, or dine on the outdoor deck. The building, a former Ford Motor Company dealership built in 1917, is on the National Register of Historic Places. Memorabilia includes a 1927 Ford Model A in the lobby and vintage photos of the dealership and town. Try catfish Satterfield, seafood angel hair pasta, chicken Florentine, or Satterfield rib-eye. Open-air dining on deck. | 108 E. Main St. | 225/638–5027 | $13–$26 | AE, D, DC, MC, V.

Lodging

Mon Rêve. Joe and Cathi Hinckley opened this B&B called Mon Rêve—"My Dream" in French—in 1992. The three-story French Creole plantation home was originally built by Joe's great-grandfather in 1820. Like many Creole homes of that time, the house is constructed of cypress wood, brick, and bousillage (a mixture of mud, moss, and deer hair). Its full-length gallery affords an excellent view of False River across the street. One bedroom is on the first floor, and three are on the second floor. All are rented with private baths unless a suite is requested, in which case two bedrooms share a connecting bath. Rooms are furnished with period antiques, including armoires, and have hardwood floors. A pier is available for fishing, boating, or swimming in False River. Two mi southwest of New Roads on LA Hwy. 1. Complimentary breakfast. Cable TV. No room phones, phone in kitchen). Dock, fishing. No smoking indoors. | 9825 False River Rd. | 225/638–7848, 800/324–2738 | www.monreve-mydream.com | 4 rooms | $75–$95 rooms, $135–$150 suites | D, MC, V.

Pointe Coupee Bed and Breakfast, the Samson House. This 1835 plantation cottage in the historic district is listed on the National Register of Historic Places. It contains antiques, gardens, courtyards, and an outdoor fireplace. Candlelight suppers are available by reservation. Complimentary breakfast. Cable TV. Library. | 405 Richey St. | 225/638–6254 | fax 225/638–6254 | 2 rooms | $90–$100 | MC, V.

OPELOUSAS

MAP 9, D4

(Nearby towns also listed: Eunice, Lafayette)

Louisiana food and music have strong roots in and around Opelousas. Superstar chef Paul Prudhomme was born and raised on this prairie farmland, where home kitchens and modest restaurants are still warmed by the spicy country cooking that he made famous. The late Clifton Chenier was another local lion, father of the exuberant sound now known worldwide as Zydeco, a traditional blend of African and Cajun rhythms. Established as a trading post to promote commerce between French settlers and Native Americans in 1720, the town was named for a tribe that had previously occupied the area. Today the Opelousas Museum and Interpretive Center offers a flavorful dip into the melting pot of regional culture.

Information: **Opelousas Tourist Information Center** | 828 E. Landry St., Opelousas 70570 | 337/948–6263 or 800/424–5442 | stlandry@iamerica.net | www.sue.edu/acadgate/opelous.htm.

Attractions

Chicot State Park. Louisiana's largest and most-visited state park is an impressive 6,000 rolling acres, complete with a 2,000-acre reservoir filled with trophy bass. Here you'll find a boat house with rentals, launching ramps, two 400-ft fishing piers, an Olympic-size swimming pool, picnic facilities, overnight campsites, cabins, and more. | 3469 Chicot Park Rd., Ville Platte | North Landing Road. (North Landing) | 318/363–2403, 888/677–2442 | fax 318/363–2413 | www.crt.state.la.us | $2 per vehicle | Daily.

Louisiana State Arboretum. Next to the main entrance of Chicot State Park, plantings on rolling woodland represent every Louisiana ecosystem, except coastal marsh and prairie. Highlights include a beech-magnolia climax forest, an interpretive shelter with educational exhibits, and a network of trails and footbridges. | 4213 Chicot Park Rd., Ville Platte | 318/363–6289, 888/677–6100 | fax 318/363–5616 | www.crt.state.la.us | Free | Daily.

Opelousas Museum and Interpretive Center. The home of the Southwest Louisiana Zydeco Festival archives also presents a colorful interpretation of regional history from prehistoric to modern times. Exhibits feature agricultural and domestic artifacts, Cajun music and food, Civil War displays, and more than 400 dolls. | 315 N. Main St. | 337/948–2529, 800/424–5442 | fax 337/948–2534 | Free | Mon.–Sat. 9–5.

ON THE CALENDAR

APR.: *International Cajun Joke Telling Contest.* Tall tales attract a fun crowd. 3rd Sat. in April. | 337/948–6784.

SEPT.: *Original Southwest Louisiana Zydeco Music Festival.* Each Labor Day Weekend, international crowds of music fans travel to Plaisance for Zydeco music. Louisiana food and crafts, storytelling, and cultural talks are also presented. 6 mi northwest of Opelousas on Hwy. 167 | 337/942–2392.

OCT.: *Louisiana Yambilee.* Cajun food and music, cooking contests, a flower show, beauty pageants, agricultural exhibits, and country arts and crafts are all part of the fun on the last weekend in Oct. | 337/948–8848.

Dining

Palace Café. Cajun/Creole. At lunchtime, a lively legal crowd frequents this café, which opened in 1927 across from the courthouse. Try baked eggplant with crab meat dressing, crawfish dishes, fried chicken salad, or fried crawfish salad. Kids' menu. | 135 W. Landry St. | 337/942–2142 | Breakfast also available. No supper Sun. | $10–$15 | AE, D, MC, V.

Steamboat Warehouse. Cajun/Creole. Sample the fare in this building from the early 1800s with great river views. A specialty is steak Annie, an 8-oz filet mignon of certified Angus beef topped with lobster, crab meat, and shrimp stuffing, served with a caramelized onion and mushroom demi-glaze and fresh grilled asparagus. Kids' menu. | 525 N. Main St., Washington | 337/826–7227 | Closed Mon. No supper Sun. No lunch Tues.–Sat. | $10–$30 | AE, D, MC, V.

Lodging

Best Western Opelousas. This motel, built in 1996 on I–49, is convenient for visits to local Cajun prairie towns and the Evangeline Downs racetrack. Complimentary Continental breakfast. Cable TV. Pool. Business services. Pets allowed (fee). | 5791 I–49 Service Road S | 337/942–5540, 888/942–5540 | fax 318/942–5540 | www.bestwestern.com | 46 rooms | $63–$83 | AE, D, DC, MC, V.

Estorge House. Double galleries and eight sets of French doors grace the front of this white-column house on a residential street near the courthouse square. Built in 1827, it is on the National Register of Historic Places and was opened as a B&B in 1997. The high ceilings in the parlor and foyer have trompe l'oeil paintings, an etched-glass chandelier shines over polished hardwood floors in the central hall, and another splendid chandelier hangs over the dining room table. Guest rooms are furnished with 19th-century French and Louisiana antiques. Baths are modern but with original claw-foot tubs. The upstairs bedroom has a handcarved wood bed, the downstairs a half-tester bed. You're greeted with wine or tea served in the parlor or in the outdoor hot tub, and you can eat your large breakfast in the rear room overlooking the garden. Complimentary breakfast. Cable TV. Hot tub. No children under 12. No smoking. | 427 Market St. | 337/942–8151, 888/655–9539 | www.bbonline/la/estorge | 2 rooms | $95–$125 | MC, V.

Quality Inn. Built in 1985, this two-story brick motel has an atrium and botanical gardens and is 7 mi from downtown. Restaurant, bar. In-room data ports, room service. Cable TV. Pool. Hot tub, sauna. Business services. | 4165 I–49S, | 337/948–9500, 800/228–5151 | fax 337/942–5035 | www.qualityinn.com | 67 rooms | $68–$85 | AE, D, DC, MC, V.

RUSTON

(Nearby towns also listed: Minden, Monroe/West Monroe)

Ruston is a convenient base for exploring the historic houses, old general stores, and country antique shops among the peach orchards and piney woods of Lincoln Parish. The town sprang up during construction of the Vicksburg, Shreveport, and Pacific Railroad in 1884. Today, it is best known as the home of Louisiana Tech University, established in 1894. The downtown historic district has many fine examples of Plantation-style houses.

Information: **Ruston-Lincoln Convention and Visitors Bureau** | 400 N Trenton St., Second Floor, Ruston, LA 71270 | 318/255–2358, 800/392–9032.

Attractions

Dixie Jamboree. Every Saturday night, the Dixie Theater is filled with the sounds of country music and dancing feet. | Dixie Theater, 206 North Vienna St. | 318/255–0048 | Sat. 7.

Jackson Bienville Wildlife Management Area. This 32,460-acre area of upland pine woods provides opportunities for hunting, fishing, birding, and hiking 12 mi southwest of Ruston. | LA 147 | 318/371–3050.

Lincoln Parish Museum. The museum has exhibits on the region's past. | 609 N. Vienna St. | 318/251–0018 | Free | Tues.–Fri., 10–4.

Louisiana Tech University. The university, whose wooded, hilly campus is on the west side of Ruston, has 10,000 undergraduate and graduate students and is known for its aviation, engineering, and architecture departments. | 700 W. California Ave. | 318/257–0211, 318/257–4427 | Free | Weekdays.

Idea Place This children's museum features hands-on exhibits. | Woodard Hall, Wisteria Street | 318/257–2794 | Mon.–Sat., 10–3.

Louisiana Tech Art Gallery. Part of the School of Art, this small gallery has six shows a year, three featuring contemporary artists, three with differing themes. | Visual Arts Center, Mayfield Ave. | 318/257–3077 | Free | Mon.–Fri., 9–4.

Louisiana Tech Farm Salesroom. Shoppers can purchase premium dairy products, including milk, cheese, butter, and various flavors of ice cream, all produced by Tech students. | Reese Hall, U.S. 80W | 318/257–3550 | Weekdays 9–5:30.

O'Dell Pottery. The owners of this studio and showroom, Bruce and Tami O'Dell, demonstrate pottery techniques that combine a current artistic approach with ancient pottery traditions. | Cooktown Rd. | 318/251–1707 | Free | Mon.–Sat. 10–6.

Piney Hills Art Gallery. This gallery on the ground floor of the historic Harris Hotel shows original works by some 90 north-central Louisiana artists and craftspeople. The pieces range from fine arts to contemporary crafts and traditional folk arts. | 206 W. Park Ave. | 318/255–7234 | Free | Tues.–Sat., 10–4.

ON THE CALENDAR

YEAR-ROUND: *Bonnie and Clyde Trade Days.* Each weekend before the third Mon. of the month, Louisiana's largest outdoor marketplace fills with acres and acres and acres of vendors, craftspeople, and antique dealers. | 888/835–6112 or 318/263–2437.

JUNE: *Louisiana Peach Festival.* A very popular local affair that includes sporting contests, an antique car show, beauty pageants, a parade, hot-air balloon races, a rodeo, a 5K run, and arts and crafts. Almost everything is free, except for a few activities like the rodeo. Fathers Day weekend. | 318/255–2031.

SEPT.: *Louisiana Chicken Festival.* The eve of this weekend festival features a live band and a street dance. Things really get hopping on Saturday with barbecue chicken dinners, chicken cooking contests, a 5K run, a 1-mi walk, cloggers, arts and crafts, a petting zoo, a male beauty contest, and children's activities. | 318/777–8365.

SEPT., OCT.: *Louisiana Passion Play.* This outdoor event depicts the life of Jesus. | First full weekend in Sept., 2nd full weekend in Oct. | 318/255–6277.

Dining

Log Cabin Smokehouse. Tex-Mex. This casual restaurant is housed in an 1886 dogtrot home (a local style of log cabin). The Smokehouse serves authentic mesquite grill barbecue as well as ribs, steaks, burgers, fajitas, and quesadillas. | 1906 Farmerville Hwy. | 318/255–8023 | $10–$30 | AE, D, MC, V | Closed Sun.

"Ole" Feed House. Cajun/Creole. The all-you-can-eat buffet at this casual, family-oriented restaurant serves such traditional items as fried catfish, frog legs, shrimp, chicken, stuffed crab, and chicken and dumplings to a mix of locals and tourists. Thursday is senior citizens night. | 2780 U.S. 33 | 318/255–6668 | $11–$16 | Closed Sun.–Mon.

Trenton Street Café. American. Modest fare, including salads, burgers, and sandwiches, is served at this Ruston café in a turn-of-the-20th-century house in the historic district. | 201 N. Trenton St. | 318/251–2103 | $7–$15 | AE, D, MC, V.

Lodging

Best Western Kings Inn. This two-story stone building, with a hint of flair in its covered entrance with white columns and floor-to-ceiling windows, was built in 1975. It's a good link in the Best Western chain, in a well-lit, safe neighborhood that is 6–8 blocks from downtown and area restaurants and less than 2 mi from the business district and LA Tech University. Easy off and on access to I–20 and U.S. Hwy. 167. Complimentary Continental breakfast. In-room data ports. Cable TV. Pool. Laundry facilities. Business services. | 1105 N. Trenton, | 318/251–0000 | fax 318/251–1453 | www.bestwestern.com | 52 rooms | $58–$64 | AE, D, DC, MC, V.

Comfort Inn. Louisiana Tech College is two exits away from this brick, two-story building built in 1994 and located in a commercial area. Grambling State University is 6 mi to the south. Complimentary Continental breakfast. In-room data ports. Cable TV. Pool. Business services. | 1801 N. Service Rd. E | 318/251–2360 | 60 rooms | $54–$72 | AE, D, DC, MC, V.

Hampton Inn. This three-story hotel opened in 1997 and is 1 mi North of downtown Ruston, 2 mi from Louisiana Tech University. From I–20, exit 85 to Hwy. 167 to N. Trenton Exit. Complimentary Continental breakfast. Some microwaves, some refrigerators. Cable TV. Pool. Laundry services. | 1315 N. Trenton | 318/251–3090, 800/426–7866 | fax 318/251–3315 | www.hamptoninn.com | 83 rooms | $79 | AE, D, DC, MC, V.

Maxwell's Inn and Conference Center. This one-story, brick hotel with exterior corridors and parking right outside the door was built in 1962. It sits in the heart of the downtown

Ruston area, close to plenty of shopping and fast food restaurants. Restaurant, room service. In-room data ports. Cable TV. 2 pools, wading pool. Playground. Laundry facilities. Free parking. Pets allowed. | 318/255–5901 | fax 318/255–3729 | 140 rooms | $69–$79 | AE, D, DC, MC, V.

Melody Hills Ranch. This one-story white frame, Cape Cod–style house and has a white picket fence out front. It's popular with Louisiana Tech University parents, football game attendees, wedding guests, and long-term business travelers looking for something cozier than a typical hotel. The mini-kitchen has a microwave and refrigerator but no stove. Complimentary Continental breakfast. Microwave, refrigerator. Pool. Exercise equipment. No smoking. | 804 N. Trenton St. | 318/255–7127, 318/255–3023 | 1 suite with 2 bedrooms, 1 bath | $75–$95 | MC, V.

ST. FRANCISVILLE

MAP 9, E4

(Nearby towns also listed: Baton Rouge, Jackson, New Roads)

St. Francisville, about 30 mi north of Baton Rouge in the southeastern part of the state, is one of Louisiana's most beautiful small towns, settled circa 1729 and chartered in 1807. This gorgeous time-warped ensemble of antebellum mansions, formal gardens, and stately commercial buildings has more than 140 structures listed on the National Register of Historic Places. Several houses are open for tours, some presented by proud descendents of the original families. The ruggedly beautiful Tunica Hills are fine for hiking, biking, golfing, and fishing. Modern naturalists follow in the footsteps of John James Audubon, who lived and painted some of his "Birds of America" folio here.

Information: West Feliciana Parish Tourist Commission | 11757 Ferdinand St., St. Francisville 70775 | 225/635–6330, 800/789–4221 | tourism@st-francisville.la.us | www.st-francisville.la.us.

Attractions

Audubon State Historic Site/Oakley House. John James Audubon painted 32 of his Birds of America at Oakley House. A fine example of Colonial architecture with West Indies influences, the house was built in 1799 but is furnished in the style of the 1820s, when the artist lived here. You can also explore the detached plantation and weaving room, formal and kitchen gardens, two slave cabins, a barn, and 100 acres of forested grounds with a nature trail and picnic area. | 11788 Hwy. 965 | 225/635–3739 or 888/677–2838 | fax 225/635–3739 | www.crt.state.la.us | $2 | Daily 9–5.

Butler Greenwood Plantation. Members of the founding family guide tours at this National Register of Historic Placesproperty, a 1790s plantation set in oak-shaded gardens. Rooms in the antebellum manor are furnished with original antiques, and there's a formal Victorian parlor. | 8345 U.S. 61 | 225/635–6312 | fax 225/635–6370 | www.butlergreenwood.com | $5 | Daily 9–5, Sun. 1–5.

Catalpa Plantation. Descendents of the original family still live in this National Register of Historic Places plantation home, set in 30 manicured acres abloom with azaleas, camellias, and hydrangeas. The four-bedroom, raised Victorian cottage was built in the 1890s to replace a plantation-style house that burned down after the Civil War. Furnishings from the original house were saved and can be seen here. The house is filled with opulent antiques, including silver, china, and portraiture. | 9508 U.S. 61 | 225/635–3372 | $6 | Daily.

Rosedown Plantation. An oak alley leads to an 1835 manor set in a 1,000-acre plantation. More than a dozen restored outbuildings include the original hot house, barn, detached kitchen, doctor's office, and milk shed. Some 28 acres of historic gardens are graced by formal parterres, classical landscapes, and fine statuary. Tours are self guided, with audio record-

ST. FRANCISVILLE

INTRO
ATTRACTIONS
DINING
LODGING

ings set up along the way to provide details (eight presentations that total about 1 hr). You can also view a 30-min video. | 12501 Rte. 10 | 225/635–3332 | $10 | Daily 9–5, tours by curator by appointment only, $37.50.

ON THE CALENDAR

MAR.: *Audubon Pilgrimage.* Tours of landmark houses and gardens at the height of spring color, a children's maypole dance, theatrical productions, and gospel concerts at historic churches are some of the activities at this event, held the third weekend in March. | 225/635–6330.

OCT.: *Angola Prison Rodeo.* Held since 1966, this is one of the biggest events in the area. Every Sunday in October, the Louisiana State Penitentiary in Angola opens its gates to the general public and hosts the "Wildest Rodeo in the South." Arts and crafts produced by the inmates are for sale. The prison band provides additional entertainment. It's about 20 mi northwest of St. Francisville. | 225/655–4411.

Dining

Clubhouse at the Bluffs Dining Room. Cajun/Creole. This restaurant serves Louisiana cuisine with a French influence, including fresh seafood dishes such as red snapper with a beurre blanc sauce, seafood pasta, and prime filet and rib eye steaks. It's at The Bluffs on Thompson Creek, 9 mi southeast of St. Francisville, east of the Audubon State Historic Site. | Freeland Rd. at Hwy. 965 | 225/634–5088 | www.thebluffs.com | $12–$31 | AE, D, MC, V.

Steamboat Charley's Sports Bar and Grill. American/Casual. You can't miss the large neon sign out front after sunset. The exterior of this place looks like a house, but the interior is a sports bar and grill, with fans hanging from the A-frame ceiling, a 100-yr-old pine bar, and pool tables and video games in a side room. Outside dining is available. The menu includes real root beer, burgers, rib eye steaks, chicken-fried steak, fried or grilled shrimp, crawfish and oyster plates, po'-boy sandwiches, club sandwiches, buffalo wings, and salads, as well as daily specials. Live music Friday and Saturday. Thursday is karaoke night. On Hwy. 61 across from the Rosedown Plantation. | 7193 Hwy. 61 | 225/635–0203 | Reservations recommended for parties of 10 or more | $6–$14 | AE, MC, V.

Lodging

Barrow House Inn. This historic district home, built in the 1850s, is graced with period antiques and canopy beds in its four rooms: Peach, Rose, and Blue rooms, and King suite. If you stay in a suite at the separate Printer's House, a full kitchen and a collection of 21 first-edition Audubon prints in the sun room are the highlights, as well as the large collection of teddy bears. In the Victorian Suite, a crystal chandelier lights the late 1800s French canopied queen-size bed, and the parlor has 1860s rosewood furniture and a needlepoint carpet. In the Empire suite are an 1870s bed with draped canopy, matching dresser, and lace-covered daybed. The parlor has an 1840s brocade sofa, a large marble-top table, an Empire gaming table, and an Oriental carpet. Dinner is served in Barrow House's dining room by advance reservation. Complimentary Continental breakfast. TV (some with cable). In-room VCRs, some room phones. | 9779 Royal St. | 225/635–4791 | fax 225/635–1863 | www.topteninn.com | 5 rooms, 3 suites | $95–$150, $130–$160 suites | AE, D, MC, V.

Bluffs on Thompson Creek. This luxury, all-suites lodge in a wooded setting includes an Arnold Palmer–designed championship golf course which sits on the high bluffs above Thompson Creek. The guest rooms are filled with antiques, dried flowers, and Audubon prints, and all open onto a wide veranda with rocking chairs and ceiling fans. Restaurant, bar. Refrigerator. Cable TV. Pool. Golf, tennis. | Freeland Rd. and Hwy. 965 | 225/634–3410, 888/634–3410 | fax 225/634–3528 | www.thebluffs.com | 37 suites, 2 two-bedroom suites | $119–$129 suites, $219–$239 2–bedroom suites | AE, D, DC, MC, V.

Butler Greenwood. Shaded by huge oak trees dripping with Spanish moss, writer Anne Butler's two-story frame house with a wraparound veranda was built in the early 1800s and is still the center of a working plantation, 2 mi North of St. Francisville on Hwy. 61. Seven cottages spread over 50 landscaped acres. Each cottage is unique, some with exposed brick walls and beams, fireplaces, claw-foot tubs, and skylights. One cottage has a front porch with rocking chairs, another has a three-level rear deck overlooking the bluffs. All have either a full kitchen or a kitchenette. Guided nature/birdwatching walks are available. Complimentary Continental breakfast. Kitchenettes. Some in-room hot tubs. Cable TV. Pool. Some pets allowed. | 8345 U.S. Hwy. 61 | 225/635–6312 | fax 225/635–6370 | www.butlergreenwood.com | 7 cottages | $110 | AE, MC, V.

Cottage Plantation. Built between 1795 and 1850, Cottage Plantation is one of only a handful of antebellum plantations that retain their original outbuildings. The office, one-room schoolhouse, kitchen, milk house, barns, and other dependencies are still intact. Another is an antique shop. On 400 acres of oaks, dogwood, mimosa, and crape myrtle trees, 5 mi North of St. Francisville, this is St. Francisville's oldest B&B. All rooms have four-poster beds and modern baths. Coffee arrives in the morning at your door, but breakfast is served later in the dining room. The house is furnished with antebellum Louisiana pieces. Restaurant (dinner only). Complimentary breakfast. Cable TV. No room phones but phone available on premises. Pool. No children under 13. No smoking. | 10528 Cottage Ln. | 225/635–3674 | www.virtualcities.com | 5 rooms | $95 | MC, V.

Wolf Schlesinger House–St. Francisville Inn. A Victorian Gothic landmark in the historic district, this house, built in 1880, features moss-draped oaks and a peaceful courtyard. The antique-filled rooms open onto a New Orleans–style courtyard. Dessert, coffee, and cocktails are served, as well as a full buffet breakfast. One room has a hot tub. Restaurant, complimentary breakfast. Cable TV. Pool. Library. Business services. | 5720 Commerce St. | 225/635–6502, 800/488–6502 | fax 225/635–6421 | 10 rooms | $55–$90 | AE, D, DC, MC, V | www.stfrancisvilleinn.com.

ST. MARTINVILLE

MAP 9, E5

(Nearby towns also listed: Franklin, Lafayette, New Iberia)

The town of St. Martinville, in the south-central portion of the state near Lafayette, is the very picture of a Louisiana bayou settlement, with its soft French accents, ancient oaks, and graceful church on the central square. If the local attitude and architecture seem a bit more refined than some Cajun neighborhoods, residents will be quick to point out that their little village once harbored a gang of European aristocrats fleeing the French Revolution, hence the nickname "Le Petit Paris d'Amerique." Today it is

KODAK'S TIPS FOR USING LIGHTING

Daylight
· Use the changing color of daylight to establish mood
· Use light direction to enhance subjects' properties
· Match light quality to specific subjects

Dramatic Lighting
· Anticipate dramatic lighting events
· Explore before and after storms

Sunrise, Sunset, and Afterglow
· Include a simple foreground
· Exclude the sun when setting your exposure
· After sunset, wait for the afterglow to color the sky

From Kodak Guide to Shooting Great Travel Pictures © 2000 by Fodor's Travel Publications

best known as the setting for Henry Wadsworth Longfellow's epic poem "Evangeline," a tragic tale of the hardships endured by local Acadians following their expulsion from Canada. A six-square-block historic district centers around the Church Square, which includes St. Martin de Tours Church, the presbytere, and the Petit Paris Museum.

Information: **St. Martinville Tourist Center** | 127 S. New Market St., St. Martinville 70582 | 337/394–2233.

Attractions

Acadian Memorial. This museum is in the former city hall, a building on the National Register of Historic Places. Exhibits include a 30-ft mural depicting Acadian people in Louisiana by area artist Robert Dafford. There are also a wall of names of Acadian exiles, a genealogy and media center, and live theatrical performances. | 120 N. Market St. | 337/394–2258 | fax 337/394–2260 | www.acadianmemorial.org | Free, donations welcome | Daily 10–4.

Evangeline Oak. Here is the oak tree immortalized in Henry Wadsworth Longfellow's epic poem, "Evangeline," the story of a young woman separated from her lover during the expulsion of French Acadians from Canada by the English from 1764–68. According to the tale, she waited faithfully under these ancient branches for him to find her and finally died of grief. Today it's the signature image and gathering spot for St. Martinville, a much happier scene where local musicians and storytellers entertain visitors daily. | Next to St. Martin de Tours Catholic Church | Free | Daily.

Longfellow-Evangeline State Historic Site. This was the first state park in Louisiana. Established in 1934, it is a shady retreat of 157 well-manicured acres on Bayou Teche. Admission includes a tour of Maison Olivier, a plantation house built in 1815 and now on the National Register of Historic Places. You can also explore the detached kitchen, Acadian-style barn (1818), blacksmith shop, and an 18th-century Acadian cabin. Small gardens are planted with indigo, cotton, and medicinal herbs. | 1200 N. Main St. | 337/394–3754 or 888/677–2900 | fax 337/394–3553 | www.crt.state.la.us/longfellow | $2 | Daily 9–5.

St. Martin de Tours Catholic Church. The "mother church of the Acadians" is one of the oldest in Louisiana. Built in 1844, the graceful masonry structure with three arched doorways is topped by a simple border of crosses. Jean François Mouchet's painting over the altar depicts St. Martin sharing his cloak with a beggar. A replica of the sacred grotto at Lourdes was built in the late 1870s by Paul Martinez. | 133 S. Main St. | 337/394–6021 | fax 337/394–6020 | Free | Daily 8:30–5.

Evangeline Monument. A bronze statue beside St. Martin de Tours Catholic Church honors Emmeline Labiche, the real-life model for the heroine of Longfellow's poem "Evangeline." To further complicate matters, it is actually an image of actress Dolores Del Rio, who starred in the silent film version. The Hollywood cast and crew, who filmed on site in 1929, donated the monument to the town. | Church Sq | Free | Daily.

Petit Paris Museum. This quirky little museum in St. Martin Square is devoted primarily to Mardi Gras memorabilia. The main display is a collection of elaborate costumes from a 1984 carnival ball. | 103 S. Main St. | 337/394–7334 | fax 337/394–7334 | $1 | Daily 9:30–4:30.

·ON THE CALENDAR

FEB., MAR.: *La Grande Boucherie.* "The Great Butchering" recreates the traditional butchering of a hog for a community fete, resulting in roasted pork, fresh sausages, and fried cracklings. Also included are live music and Cajun dancing. The celebration is on the Sun. before Ash Wednesday at Magnolia Park on Main St. | 337/394–2233.

Dining

La Place d'Evangeline. Cajun/Creole. Relax on Bayou Teche near the Evangeline Oak in the Old Castillo B&B;, a 1930s brick home. The dining room has high-backed chairs and stark white walls. Try one of the popular Cajun dishes such as blackened chicken, alligator boullettes (meatballs), or crabmeat au gratin. | 220 Evangeline Blvd. | 318/394–4010, 800/621–

3017 | Reservations not accepted Fri.–Sat. | Breakfast also available. No supper Sun. Closes at 5 Mon.–Tues. | $12–$18 | AE, D, MC, V.

Maison de Ville Restaurant. Cajun. This downtown restaurant is in a landmark building, a restored two-story, late-Victorian home, and looks out over St. Martin Square. Lunch and dinner entrées include Louisiana crabcakes, fried shrimp, grilled salmon, soft shell crabs, catfish, seafood platters, salads, burgers, and po'-boys. Try cornbread dressing as a side item. For dinner, try veal St. Martin (pan-seared veal topped with asparagus, hollandaise sauce, and lump crabmeat). | 100 N. Main St. | 337/394–5700 | Closed Mon. No lunch Sat. | $15–$23 | AE, D, MC, V.

Lodging

Bienvenue House. Built circa 1830, this antebellum home has porches, swings, and gardens. It's just two blocks from the historic town square and several restaurants. Three rooms have queen beds, one has two double beds. Complimentary breakfast. No TV. No room phones, phone in common area. No kids under 15. No smoking. | 421 N. Main St. | 337/394–9100, 888/394–9100 | www.bienvenuehouse.com | 4 rooms | $95–$120 | AE, MC, V.

Old Castillo Bed & Breakfast. Almost beneath the moss-draped branches of the legendary Evangeline Oak, the Greek Revival structure of the Old Castillo B&B rises from the banks of Bayou Teche. The building, listed on the National Register of Historic Places, was acquired and opened as a restaurant and B&B in 1987 by Peggy and Gerald Hulin. There are hardwood floors and four-poster beds, and rooms have views of the bayou or the Evangeline Oak. The Hulins also offer personal tours of the Atchafalaya Basin and fishing in the bayou. Restaurant, complimentary breakfast. No room phones. Golf, tennis. | 220 Evangeline Blvd. | 318/394–4010, 800/621–3017 | fax 318/394–7983 | www.virtualcities.com | 5 rooms | $50–$80 | AE, MC, V.

SHREVEPORT

MAP 9, C2

(Nearby towns also listed: Bossier City, Minden)

Shreveport was founded on the banks of the Red River in 1839. It is named for Captain Henry Miller Shreve, who at one time cleared the waters of a giant log jam. Today this regional hub of transportation and industry attracts sporting tourists from the tri-state area known as Ark-La-Tex. They come for casino gambling, thoroughbred racing at Louisiana Downs, professional hockey, and baseball. Quieter pursuits abound in more than 3,000 acres of landscaped parks, including the riverfront conservatory and fine arts exhibits at R. S. Barnwell Memorial Garden and Art Center. The American Rose Society is headquartered at Shreveport's American Rose Center, 118 acres of waterfalls, fountains, and gazebos.

Information: **Shreveport-Bossier Convention and Tourist Bureau** | 629 Spring St., Shreveport 71101 | 318/222–9391, 800/551–8682 | tourism@shreveport-bossier.org | www.shreveport-bossier.org.

Attractions

American Rose Center. North America's largest rose garden has 118 acres of roses. There are displays of every variety of rose, including antique ones. From Thanksgiving to New Year's they are transformed into "Christmas in Roseland." | 8877 Jefferson-Paige Rd. | 318/938–5402 | $4 | Weekdays, 9–5, weekends, 9–dusk.

Ark-La-Tex Antique and Classic Vehicle Museum. More than 40 models of classic and antique vehicles are housed in this 1927 original Graham Truck/Dodge showroom and assembly area. The exhibits are rotated every six months. | 601 Spring St. | 318/222–0227 | $5 | Tues.–Fri. 9–4:30, Sat. 9–5, Sun. 1–5.

Boothill Speedway. Stock racing on Louisiana's largest dirt track, off I–90. | W. Shreveport | 318/938–5373 | Racing Mar.–Nov., Sat. evenings.

Casa D'Arte. This gallery specializes in contemporary paintings and sculpture by regional artists. | 214 Texas Ave. | 318/424–6415 | Free | Weekdays 10–5, weekends 1–5.

Harrah's Casino. This casino on Shreveport's riverfront has more than 20 table games and is known for the "Loosest Slots in Louisiana." A brand-new, 23-floor hotel has just opened, with 514 rooms. Fiore's restaurant offers fine dining. Hotel, 2 restaurants, 2 cafes. | 315 Clyde Fant Pkwy. | 318/424–7777 | Open 24 hrs.

Louisiana State Exhibit Museum. The museum shows the history of Louisiana with murals, dioramas, and displays. Exhibits of prehistoric Native American relics and Louisiana agriculture and industry are featured. | 3015 Greenwood Rd. | 318/632–2020 | $3 | Weekdays 9–4, weekends 12–4.

Meadows Museum of Art. The permanent collection in this museum, on the campus of Centenary College, includes a series of paintings of Indochina and its peoples by French Academic artist Jean Despujols. Temporary exhibitions from cultures around the world augment the museum's permanent collection of more than 1,000 works in a variety of media. | 2911 Centenary Blvd. | 318/869–5169 | Free | Tues.–Fri. noon–4, weekends 1–4.

R. S. Barnwell Memorial Garden and Art Center. Barnwell is one of the few centers in the South that combines both art exhibits and gardens. The Art Center presents painting, sculpture, and cultural shows, along with a permanent collection. The domed conservatory features tropical plants, as well as seasonal and native plantings. There is information on art and horticulture. | 601 Clyde Fant Pkwy. | 318/673–7703 | Free | Weekdays 9–4:30, weekends 1–5.

R. W. Norton Art Gallery. This beautiful gallery displays American and European art that spans four centuries, including sculptures of the American West by Remington. The gallery is in a 40-acre park and, in spring, the grounds are in full bloom with every color of azalea imaginable. | 4747 Creswell Ave. | 318/865–4201 | Free | Tues.–Fri. 10–5, weekends 1–5.

Sci-Port Discovery Center. Sci-Port is a center for hands-on learning and fun for children and adults. There are over 200 hands-on experiences, eight interactive discovery areas, and an IMAX theater. | 820 Clyde Fant Pkwy. | 877/724–7678 | $8.50 | Memorial Day–Labor Day, Mon.–Sat. 10–6, Sun. 1–6; Labor Day–Memorial Day, Mon.–Sat. 10–5.

Shreveport Captains Baseball. The Captains are an AA affiliate of the San Francisco Giants, and they play at Fairgrounds Field, a perfect spot for a family outing. | Fairgrounds Field, 2901 Pershing Blvd. | 318/636–5555, 800/467–3230 | $2–$15 | Apr.–Aug.; call for game schedule.

Shreveport Historical Downtown Walking Tour. Embark on this self-guided tour through the designated historic downtown area. You'll pass sights such as the Strand Theatre, built in 1925, and Oakland Cemetery, which dates from 1849. A map is provided by the Shreveport-Bossier Convention and Tourist Bureau. | 629 Spring St. | 318/222–9391, 800/551–8682 | www.shreveportbossier.com | Free | Tourist Bureau: weekdays 8:30–5.

Shreveport Mudbugs Hockey. Join die-hard Shreveport hockey fans to watch the Mudbugs tear up the ice in an action-packed game. Of course, there is plenty of stadium food. | Hirsch Coliseum, 2000 Century Tell Center Dr., Bossier City | 318/636–2847 | Call for ticket information; parking $3 | 35-game season begins in October.

Shreveport Parks and Recreation Planetarium. Features free star-gazing every fourth Friday at Worley Astronomical Observatory, Jan.–Nov., and shows at the planetarium. | 2820 Pershing Blvd. | 318/673–7827 | $4 | Shows: First Sat. of every month at 3, 5, 7 pm.

Spring Street Historical Museum. The only remaining example in town of New Orleans–style cast-iron grill work, this downtown museum was built in 1865 and is Shreveport's oldest building. It houses a collection of 19th-century artifacts from northwest Louisiana; Indian artifacts, documents, firearms, furnishings, and other Civil War–era treasures are among the collection. | 525 Spring St. | 318/424–0964, 318/865–0529 | Free | Oct.–June, Tues. 10–1, Fri.–Sun. 1:30–4:30.

Stephens African-American Museum. This museum features local and national memorabilia, including political posters from the civil rights era, historical artifacts, ancient farm equipment, and a collection of paintings and sculptures by African-American artists from Louisiana. | 2810 Linholm St. | 318/635–2147 | $2 | Noon–4 Tues.–Sat.

The Strand Theatre. This ornate 1,600-seat theater built in 1925 is listed in the National Register of Historic Places. Still in use, it hosts a wide variety of entertainment, including plays, musicals, and concerts. | 619 Louisiana Ave. | 318/226–8555, 318/226–1481 | www.thestrandtheatre.com | Call for ticket prices | Call for schedule of events.

Walter B. Jacobs Park. This park is Louisiana bottomland covered with hardwoods and gently rolling hills. There are exhibits, hiking trails, and interpretive programs. | 8012 Blanchard-Furrh Rd. | 318/929–2806 | Free | Wed.–Sat. 8–5, Sun. 1–5.

Water Town USA. Water Town is the place to cool off, whether you want to surf in the wave pool or chute through the black hole. It's a great idea for a fun family afternoon. | 7670 W. 70th St. | 318/938–5475 | $14.95 | May, weekends 10–6; June–late Aug., weekdays 10:30–6 and weekends 10:30–8 | www.watertownusa.com.

ON THE CALENDAR

APR.: *Holiday in Dixie.* Celebrate spring in the south with an air show, balls, parades, a treasure hunt, and a riverfront carnival complete with rides, games, and plenty of food. 3rd Fri.–4th Sun. | 318/865–5555.

APR.–MAY: *Cinco de Mayo.* This Hispanic festival on the weekend closest to May 5 celebrates the popular Mexican holiday with music, food, arts and crafts, and a Chihuahua dog race. | 318/688–5553.

MAY: *Artbreak.* The largest children's festival in the state includes juried exhibits of children's art, art activities, dance, music, theater, food, and a 5K road race. | 318/673–6500.

MAY: *Mudbug Madness.* A Shreveport favorite, Mudbug Madness hails a Louisiana staple–crawfish. There is plenty of Cajun food, as well as Zydeco and other types of local music, at this festival.Thur.–Sun., weekend before Memorial Day | 318/222–7403.

MAY: *Jazz and Gumbo Music Festival.* Pretty much what you'd think—live jazz and spicy gumbo, along with a gumbo-eating contest, craft booths, and music clinics. Mother's Day weekend. | 318/226–4552.

SEPT.–OCT.: *Red River Revel Arts Festival.* Hundreds of top artists, craftsmen, entertainers, and culinary masters from all over the world come together for this annual eight-day celebration of the arts that is North Louisiana's largest outdoor festival. In past years, visitors have seen acrobats from Kenya, a sand painting created over eight days by Tibetan lamas, and Scottish bagpipers playing rock.Starts last weekend in Sept. | 318/424–4000.

OCT.–NOV.: *Louisiana State Fair.* With over 70 rides, this fair has the largest midway in Louisiana. What's more, it hosts one of the finest livestock gatherings in the country. Lots of entertainment and competitions.3rd weekend in Oct.–1st weekend in Nov. | 318/635–1361.

Dining

Amore Italian Restaurant. Italian. Set on Cross Lake, this restaurant is known for spaghetti and broccoli, fettucine Alfredo, and shrimp marinara. You can look out over the lake from the two dining rooms and bar. | 6100 S. Lakeshore Dr. | 318/635–8104 | $25–$30 | AE, MC, V.

Anthony's Steak and Seafood. Steak. Hidden away in an old mall on the south side of town, Anthony's is a laid-back, cozy restaurant with booths and tables, little-known to outsiders. It's got a salad bar with marinated onions, marinated broccoli, and blue cheese. Many locals say Anthony's has the best steaks in town. Try the au gratin potatoes. | 7504 Mansfield Rd. | 318/688–6830 | $10–$25 | AE, D, DC, MC, V.

Earthereal Restaurant and Bakery. Vegetarian. This Line Avenue gem is only open for lunch, but is well worth a visit. Wooden tables crowd together and the shelves overflow with fresh baked breads and sweets. Try the daily special or the popular smoothies, sandwiches, and gazpacho. | 3309 Line Ave. | 318/865–8947 | No supper | $5–$10 | No credit cards.

Herby-K's. Southern. This tiny eatery is a Shreveport legend. There are only a few booths and bar stools, but nobody seems to mind. The walls are covered with LSU pennants and posters, and the shelf above the bar is filled with vintage beer bottles. Paul Newman has eaten at Herby-K's, as proven by a letter displayed on the wall. Known for its Shrimpbuster po'-boy, seafood gumbo, and plate lunches. | 1833 Pierre Ave. | 318/424–2724 | $10–$15 | AE, D, DC, MC, V.

Monsieur Patou. French. Monsieur Patou offers formal dining, Louis XV style. Eat your meal surrounded by gold, candlelight, porcelain, china, and crystal. Must-have's include cream of white asparagus soup with leeks and beluga caviar, delicate puffed pastry filled with crab, bacon, and fava beans, and rack of lamb with artichoke and fennel. | 855 Pierremont Rd. #135 | 318/868–9822 | Closed Sun. No lunch Mon., Sat. | $50 | AE, D, DC, MC, V.

Noble Savage Tavern. American/Casual. This downtown restaurant serves wild game dishes, creative sandwiches, and fresh pizzas prepared by chef Mark Colby. The lights are low, and there's original artwork on the walls. You can shoot darts or play pool or video poker. Live music every night. | 417 Texas St. | 318/221–1781 | Closed Sun. No lunch | $15–$20 | AE, MC, V.

Smith's Cross Lake Inn. Seafood. Many Cross Lake residents come to Smith's for dinner in their boats. This neighborhood restaurant is known for its fried catfish, steaks, and broiled shrimp. Try the lemon pie. | 5301 S. Lakeshore Dr. | 318/631–0919 | Closed Sun. | $20–$25 | AE, DC, MC, V.

Strawn's Eat Shop. American/Casual. Strawn's is across from Centenary College in a row of shops and is the area favorite for breakfast and burgers. This '50s style café has an old-fashioned soda fountain and a collection of diner tables, usually filled with students. Known for delicious homemade pies. | 125 Kings Hwy. | 318/868–0634 | Breakfast also available | $5 | AE, D, MC, V.

Superior Bar and Grill. Mexican. This popular social spot filled with beverage signs and Mexican paraphernalia can get quite crowded in the evenings. The restaurant serves American dishes, fish, and game such as deer and moose, but it is best known for its Mexican food, including sizzling fajitas and frozen margaritas. Open-air dining. Patio, with canopy. | 6123 Line Ave. | 318/869–3243 | $20–$25 | AE, MC, V.

Lodging

Best Western Chateau Suite. Built in 1975, this five-story brick building is in a commercial area 2⅓ mi from downtown. Families tend to pull in on the weekends, then leave the accommodations to business travelers during the week. Restaurant, bar. In-room data ports. Cable TV. Pool. Business services, airport shuttle. | 201 Lake St. | 318/222–7620, 800/845–9334 | www.bestwestern.com | 80 rooms, 40 suites | $89–$179, $129–$199 suites | AE, D, DC, MC, V.

Best Western Richmond Suites. Formerly a Howard Johnsons, this two-story, white stucco building has been around since 1989. It is 1 mi north of Shreveport Regional Airport, off I-20. Complimentary breakfast. In-room data ports. Cable TV. Pool, wading pool. Hot tub, sauna. Exercise equipment. Laundry facilities. Business services, airport shuttle. | 5101 Monkhouse Dr. | 318/635–6431 | fax 318/635–6040 | www.bestwestern.com | 65 rooms, 56 suites | $69–$89, $94–$129 suites | AE, D, DC, MC, V.

Columns on Jordan. Surrounded by magnolia trees, the Columns on Jordan is in the Highland Historical Restoration area. Erected around 1896, it is one of very few homes built at the turn of the 20th century that still stands today. The interior has hardwood floors and 13-foot ceilings and is furnished with antiques. Complimentary breakfast. No smoking.

Pool. Hot tub. | 615 Jordan | 318/222–5912, 800/801–4950 | fax 318/459–1155 | www.bbon-line.com/la/columns | 5 rooms (3 with shared bath) | $85–$125 | AE, D, DC, MC, V.

Courtyard by Marriott. This three-story hotel off I–20, exit 10/Pines Road, was built in 1999. The on-site restaurant is open for breakfast only, but room service is available from local restaurants. Restaurant (breakfast only), bar, room service. In-room data ports, microwaves (in suites), refrigerators (in suites). Cable TV. Indoor pool. Hot tub. Exercise equipment. Laundry facilities, laundry services. Business services, free parking. | 6001 Financial Plaza | 318/686–0880, 800/321–2211 | fax 318/686–0545 | www.courtyard.com | 90 rooms, 4 suites | $89, $139 suites | AE, D, DC, MC, V.

Days Inn. This Days Inn, built in 1974, is a three-story, white stucco building with exterior corridors and windows overlooking the parking lot. Five minutes from downtown. Complimentary Continental breakfast. Cable TV. Pool. Business services. | 4935 W. Monkhouse Dr. | 318/636–0080 | fax 318/635–4517 | 148 rooms | $35–$66 | AE, D, DC, MC, V.

Fairfield Inn by Marriott. This three-story, white stucco building is 4½ mi from Shreveport and 8 min by car from casino boats, movie theaters, and restaurants. Complimentary Continental breakfast. In-room data ports. Cable TV. Pool. Exercise equipment. Business services, free parking. | 6245 Westport Ave. | 318/686–0102 | fax 318/686–8791 | www.fairfieldinn.com | 105 rooms (2 with shower only) | $82 | AE, D, DC, MC, V.

Holiday Inn Downtown. This six-story hotel is in the heart of downtown, two blocks from Harrah's casino and close to the entertainment district. Restaurant, bar. In-room data ports. Cable TV. Pool. Exercise equipment. Laundry service. Business services, airport shuttle. Pets allowed (fee). | 102 Lake St. | 318/222–7717, 800/465–4329 | fax 318/221–5951 | www.basshotels.com | 185 rooms | $69–$94 | AE, D, DC, MC, V.

Holiday Inn–Financial Plaza. This brick, six-story building, built in 1994, is in west Shreveport, close to the industrial park and offices of such firms as GM, GE, Schlumberger, SCAPA, Pennzoil, and GNB. Nestled in a natural pine setting, it has easy access to all major arteries and is 10 mi from Shreveport. There are three casinos in the area, the closest about 15 mi away, as well as several shops and restaurants. Restaurant, bar (with entertainment). Cable TV. Indoor-outdoor pool, wading pool. Hot tub. Exercise equipment. Laundry facilities. Business services, airport shuttle, free parking. | 5555 Financial Plaza | 318/688–3000 | fax 318/687–4462 | www.basshotels.com | 227 rooms | $99 | AE, D, DC, MC, V.

Ramada Inn. This Ramada Inn is made up of two brick buildings, one with two floors, the other with four. It is on I–20 at Exit 13, two blocks from the airport and handy to all areas of the surrounding Art-La-Tex. Landscaped atrium with plants and waterfalls has a sauna, car rentals, and a gift shop. There is also an outdoor garden. Restaurant, bar (with entertainment), room service. Cable TV. Pool. Hot tub. Exercise equipment. Business services, airport shuttle. Pets allowed. | 5116 Monkhouse Dr. | 318/635–7531 | fax 318/635–1600 | 255 rooms | $59–$72 | AE, D, DC, MC, V | www.ramada.com.

Remington Suite. This former pharmaceutical warehouse was renovated and opened as an all-suites hotel in 1986 in the heart of the downtown area. The first two floors house the hotel and floors three through five are offices. Restaurant, complimentary Continental breakfast. Refrigerators, in-room hot tubs. Cable TV. Indoor pool. Steam room. Exercise equipment, racquetball. Laundry services. Airport shuttle, free parking. Pets allowed. | 220 Travis St. | 318/425–5000, 800/444–6750 | 22 suites | $110–$175 | AE, D, DC, MC, V.

Sheraton. Built in 1985, this five-story, tan brick building is 8 mi south of the downtown area and 8 mi from the Shreveport Municipal Airport. Restaurant, bar, room service. Cable TV, in-room data ports, refrigerators. Pool. Hot tub. Exercise equipment. Business services, airport shuttle. | 1419 E. 70th St. | 318/797–9900 | fax 318/798–2923 | 267 rooms | $109–$129 | AE, D, DC, MC, V | www.sheraton.com.

Slattery House. This 1903 Victorian bed and breakfast is on the National Register of Historic Places. It sits in the middle of more than an acre of grounds and gardens in the Old Highland historic district. The three-story home has a large wraparound front porch and a second-floor balcony. The entrance holds a grand stairway, and an 1830 Chickering piano is in the library. Furnished with antiques from the 1800s and the turn of the 20th century. Complimentary breakfast. Cable TV. Pool. Library. No children under 12. No smoking. | 2401 Fairfield Ave. | 318/222–6577 | www.shreveportbedbreakfast.com | 6 rooms | $95–$195 | AE, D, DC, MC, V.

Twenty-Four Thirty-Nine Fairfield. Built at the turn of the 20th century, this small inn is filled with antiques. Landscaped gardens surround the building, which houses a cozy library/sitting room. It's less than a mile south of downtown. Complimentary breakfast. Cable TV, in-room data ports. Business services. No smoking. | 2439 Fairfield Ave. | 318/424–2424 | fax 318/459–1839 | 4 rooms | $135–$200 | AE, D, DC, MC, V.

SLIDELL

MAP 9, G5

(Nearby towns also listed: Covington, Mandeville, New Orleans)

Slidell is an ever-growing suburban community wedged between two substantial bodies of water, Lake Pontchartrain and the Honey Island Swamp, which is one of America's most pristine river estuary environments. Originally settled in the 1850s, Slidell helped to supply the bricks and lumber that built New Orleans. More recently it has been colonized by families escaping the city's congestion, with further growth fueled by the regional aerospace industry. Antique shops and casual eateries in the Olde Towne historic district are fun for an afternoon ramble.

Information: **New Orleans Northshore St. Tammany Parish Tourist Commission** | 68099 Rte. 59, Mandeville, LA 70471 | 504/892–0520, 800/634–9443 | mail@neworleansnorthshore.com | www.neworleansnorthshore.com.

Attractions

Ft. Pike State Historic Site. Named for explorer General Zebulon Montgomery Pike (who also discovered Pike's Peak), this masonry fort was built between 1819 and 1826. To protect coastal Louisiana from invasion, it overlooked a wetlands area known as the Rigolets, a narrow passage between Lake Pontchartrain and the Gulf of Mexico. Museum exhibits are housed in the original Citadel, and you can climb the battlements for views. There are picnic tables, a boat launch, and a pavilion. | Route 6, Box 194; approximately 23 mi east of New Orleans off U.S. 90 | 504/662–5703, 888/662–5703 | fax 504/662–5703 | www.crt.state.la.us | $2 | Daily 9–5.

John C. Stennis Space Center. NASA's lead center for rocket propulsion testing also develops components for the space shuttle and future generations of space vehicles. Tour buses take you around the 13,800-acre facility, where models and interactive displays illustrate the history of space flight and historic NASA missions. Indoor exhibits include a moon rock and the Apollo 4 command module. Outdoor exhibits include a 149-ft solid rocket booster, F-1 rocket, Jupiter C rocket, and a Nomad buoy used to gather weather data at sea. | Rte. 607, Stennis Space Center | 228/688–2370, 800/237–1821 (LA and MS) | fax 228/688–1094 | www.ssc.nasa.gov | Free | Daily.

Slidell Cultural Center. Changing shows in the gallery feature works by local artists, as well as occasional national traveling exhibits. | 444 Erlanger St. | 504/646–4375 | fax 504/646–4231 | www.slidell.la.us | Free | Mon.–Fri. 9–4 plus Thurs. 6–8, Sat. 10–2.

Dr. Wagner's Honey Island Swamp Tours. The primary guide for these 2-hr excursions is Dr. Paul Wagner, a wetland ecologist and environmental consultant who has conducted tours of the area since 1982. Compact boats allow access deep into small bayous and shallow backwaters. Customized trips are available for birding, duck hunting, evening tours, or special occasions. | Crawford Landing at the West Pearl River | 504/641–1769; 504/242–5877 | fax 504/643–3960 | www.honeyislandswamp.com | $20 | Year-round, by reservation.

Gator Swamp Tours. Two-hour tours in compact boats allow access deep into small bayous and shallow backwaters. Overnight accommodations and customized excursions are available. | 504/649–1255, 504/484–6100 (in New Orleans), 800/875–4287 | fax 504/649–1563 | $20 | Year-round, by reservation.

ON THE CALENDAR
APR., OCT.: *Slidell Antique District Street Fair.* Hundreds of vendors from throughout the Southeast U.S. sell antiques and collectibles at this twice-yearly event, the third weekend in Apr. and the last weekend in Oct. Food and music keep things lively. | 504/643–1409.
JUNE: *Bayou Lacombe Crab Festival.* This popular event, held the last weekend in June, features crab prepared every way imaginable, live music, carnival rides, and a beauty pageant. | 504/882–5160.

Dining
Old Town Slidell Soda Shop. Café. This soda shop serves old-fashioned malts, shakes, ice cream sodas, snowballs—you name it. On the food side of the menu, there's a wide variety of choices, including po'-boys, peanut butter and jelly sandwiches (or the Elvis, with bananas added), muffuletta sandwiches, pimento cheese or ham and cheese sandwiches, soup, chili, burgers, hot dogs, and french fries, to name a few. No smoking. | 301 Cousin St. | 504/649–4806 | No reservations accepted | $4–$7 | No credit cards.

Osaka. Japanese. Slidell's first sushi bar opened in 1999. Patrons can dine in the tatami-mat room, at the hibachi grill or the sushi bar, or at tables. You'll find an assortment of sushi dishes on the menu, including the "stoplight" roll, a presentation of red smelt roe, yellow lemon slice, and green roe. If you like your dinner cooked, try shrimp or vegetable tempura or chicken teriyaki. Expect a bustling crowd, especially Friday and Saturday nights. | 792 I–10 Service Rd. | 504/643–9276 | $8–$20 | AE, MC, V.

Sal and Judy's. Italian. A nondescript exterior conceals one of the area's favorite restaurants. Small dining rooms are filled with autographed photos of famous customers, and housemade pasta sauces are sold in upscale groceries statewide. Kids' menu. | U.S. 190 W., Lacombe | 504/882–9443 | Reservations essential | Closed Mon.–Tues. and 1st 2 weeks in Aug. No lunch Wed.–Sat. | $18–$30 | AE, D, DC, MC, V.

Young's. Steak. Young's interior has dim lighting, dark-stained wood paneling, and brass light fixtures. Family-owned and -operated, this spot gets mostly locals in the mood for Midwestern beef—filet mignon, prime rib, rib eye, and strip steak. There are no appetizers or desserts served, and poultry and seafood items are scarce. | 850 S. Robert Blvd. | 504/643–9331 | Closed Sun.–Mon. | $16–$20 | AE, MC, V.

Lodging
Garden Guest House. This 1905 cottage sits on 10 acres of gardens and bayou woodlands with paths. Bromeliads are seen everywhere, and there is an 1800-square-ft greenhouse. The house has two completely private suites with living/dining areas and private baths, glass walls with panoramic views, and decks on both sides. The suites are furnished with antiques and Louisiana memorabilia. Complimentary breakfast. Kitchenettes. Laundry service. No children. No smoking. | 34514 Bayou Liberty Rd. (Rte. 433) | 504/641–0335, 888/255–0335 | bonnie@gardenbb.com | 2 suites | $95–$135 suites | MC, V.

Hampton Inn and Suites. This three-story hotel opened in 1998 off I–10, exit 263. It's 3 mi east of Olde Towne, 4 mi west of the riverfront casinos. Complimentary Continental breakfast. Cable TV. Pool. Hot tub. Exercise equipment. Laundry facilities. | 56460 Frank Pichon Rd. | 504/726–9777, 800/426–7866 | fax 504/726–0141 | www.hamptoninn.com | 60 rooms | $79 | AE, D, DC, MC, V.

La Quinta. Built in 1960, this two-story brick hotel is right off I–10 in a commercial area. It's 10 mi from Honey Island Swamp Tours, 1½ mi from I–12 and I–59, and about 45 min from downtown New Orleans. Bar, complimentary Continental breakfast. In-room data ports. Cable TV. Pool. Laundry facilities. Business services. Pets allowed. | 794 E I–10 Service Rd. | 504/643–9770, 800/531–5900 | fax 504/641–4476 | www.laquinta.com | 172 rooms | $65 | AE, D, DC, MC, V.

Ramada Inn. This modern two-story motel is 10 mi from Honey Island Swamp Tours and near three interstates (I–10, I–12, and I–59). It is about 45 min from downtown New Orleans. Restaurant, bar (with entertainment). In-room data ports. Cable TV. Pool, wading pool. Laundry facilities. Business services. | 798 E I–10 Service Rd. | 504/643–9960 | fax 504/643–3508 | www.ramada.com | 149 rooms | $60–$95 | AE, D, DC, MC, V.

Salmen–Fritchie House. Home of one of Slidell's founding families and former mayor, this house was built in 1895. It sits on 3½ landscaped acres and has hardwood floors, velvet curtains, and half-canopied beds. It is filled with antiques and town memorabilia. Complimentary breakfast. Cable TV. Business services. No kids under 10. No smoking. | 127 Cleveland Ave. | 504/643–1405 | fax 504/643–2251 | www.salmen-fritchie.com | 6 rooms, 3 suites, 1 cottage | $85–$125 | AE, D, MC, V.

Slidell Super 8. Built in 1980, this two-story brick motel is 3 mi from Honey Island Swamp Tours, off I–10 and 2 mi south of I–12 and I–59. New Orleans tours depart from the lobby. It is about 45 min from downtown New Orleans. Cable TV. Pool. Business services. | 1662 Gause Blvd. | 504/641–8800 | fax 504/643–1201 | www.super8.com | 96 rooms | $65–$89 | AE, D, DC, MC, V.

Woodridge Bed and Breakfast. This red-brick B&B with white gables and window frames was built in 1980 and was once a schoolhouse. Though it appears quite rural, the area actually hides two nearby residential subdivisions. The plantation-style residence is surrounded by hundred-yr-old oak trees and twelve wooded acres. All rooms have queen-size beds and private baths. In Pearl River, 4 mi from Slidell. Complimentary breakfast. Cable TV. Free parking. No children under 10. No smoking. | 40149 Crowes Landing Rd., Pearl River | 504/863–9981 | www.woodridgebb.com | 5 rooms | $79–$129 | AE, D, MC, V.

THIBODAUX

MAP 9, F5

(Nearby towns also listed: Houma, Kenner, Morgan City)

Thibodaux is in the heart of sugarcane country. It is a commercial center for area farmers and a bedroom community for surrounding oilfields. It makes a convenient base for exploring the antebellum plantation manors along the River Road and Bayou Lafourche.

Information: Lafourche Parish Tourist Commission | Box 340, 4484 Rte. 1, Raceland, LA 70394 | 504/537–5800 | tourism@lafourche-tourism.org | www.lafourche-tourism.org.

Attractions

Laura Plantation House. Twelve buildings (circa 1805) on the National Register of Historic Places include two manor houses and the slave cabins where the African-born tales of Br'er Rabbit were first recorded in America. Group tours focus on the complicated roles of French Creole plantation women, slaves, and children. The fascinating stories and ongoing restoration of the property have been informed by more than 5,000 pages of documentation, including the diaries of 19th-century owner Laura Locoul. | 2247 Hwy. 18, Vacherie | 225/265–7690 | fax 225/265–7690 | www.lauraplantation.com | $8 | Daily 9:30–5.

Laurel Valley Plantation Village. Restoration of this authentic plantation village is an ongoing project. You can view antique farm implements and household goods in the original general store, two Acadian cottages, the old schoolhouse, antique boats in the boat shed, and ruins of a sugar mill. Dozens of other weathered structures, in various stages of repair, are set within 3,000 acres of sugar cane. The store also sells regional arts and crafts. | 595 Rte. 308 | 504/446–7456 | $3 | Tues.–Sun. 9:30–5.

Madewood Plantation House. This showplace on the banks of Bayou Lafourche is one of the largest and most famous houses in the state. Designed by Irish-American architect Henry Howard, the 21-room mansion was built in 1846 by Colonel Thomas Pugh, a sugar cane planter. The classic facade is framed by stately white columns and tall windows with black shutters. The interior is graced by Waterford chandeliers and English antiques, many collected by current owner Keith Marshall. The National Historic Landmark has been featured in several films, including "A Woman Called Moses" and "Sister, Sister." It is also now a B&B. | 4250 Rte. 308, Napoleonville | 504/369–7151, 800/375–7151 (reservations) | fax 504/369–9848 | www.madewood.com | $6 | Daily 10–4:30.

Oak Alley Plantation. The 1/4-mi alley of 28 oaks is one of the most celebrated sights in Louisiana. The trees were originally planted circa 1700 by an unknown French Creole farmer. A pink manor house, embellished with 28 columns and wide verandas, was added in 1839 by planter Jacques Telesphore Roman. One of the plantation cottages has been converted to a cozy, country-style restaurant that serves breakfast and lunch daily. | 3645 U.S. Hwy 18 | 225/265–2151 | fax 225/265–7035 | www.oakalleyplantation.com | $10 | Daily 9–5.

Wetlands Acadian Cultural Center/Jean Lafitte National Historical Park and Preserve. This facility on the banks of Bayou Lafourche incorporates a modern museum, performing arts theater, video theater, gallery with changing exhibits, waterfront boardwalk, and museum shop with a good assortment of books and recorded music. Permanent displays interpret the history, language, music, and architecture of the coastal Acadian community. A spacious craft room presents occasional demonstrations of boat building, net making, duck carving, and other regional handiwork. | 314 St. Mary St. | 504/448–1375 | fax 504/448–1425 | www.nps.gov | Free | Mon. 9–8, Tues.–Thur. 9–6, Fri.–Sun. 9–5.

ON THE CALENDAR

APR., OCT.: *Laurel Valley Heritage Festival.* A reunion of families whose members have lived and worked on the plantation is one element of this event, held the last Sun. in Apr. and second Sun. in Oct. It also features a Cajun meal served at long communal tables in a restored house, demonstrations of traditional crafts, sales of homemade cakes and candies, and Cajun music and dancing. | 504/446–7456.

Dining

Dansereau House. Cajun/Creole. A restored French Acadian mansion on the National Register of Historic Places presents contemporary interpretations of Cajun/Creole classics, making good use of regional seafood. Try Louisiana bluepoint crabcakes, veal Oscar, or prime 8-oz fillet. Sun. brunch. | 506 St. Philip St. | 504/447–1002 | www.dansereauhouse.com | Closed Mon. No lunch Sat. No supper Sun. | $25–$35 | AE, D, MC, V.

Doug's Restaurant. Cajun. Wooden chairs, ceiling fans, and white over green table cloths decorate Doug's. The chef prepares fresh soup, homemade bread, grilled fish, and certified black Angus steaks. Daily specials may include breaded veal topped with shrimp and hollandaise sauce or grilled tilapia with lump crab served over angel hair pasta with a lemon-butter sauce. At the Howard Johnson's hotel at the intersection of Hwy. 308 and Hwy. 20. | 201 N. Canal Blvd. | 504/447–2461, 504/447–9071 | No lunch | $10–$18 | AE, D, MC, V.

Lodging

Holiday Inn. This two-story, brick motel is right in downtown Thibodaux, a central location for exploring bayou plantations, scenic drives, swamp tours, and antique shops.

Restaurant, bar, room service. Cable TV. Pool. Tennis court. Laundry facilities. | 400 E. First St. | 504/446–0561 | fax 504/446–0559 | www.holidayinn.com | 106 rooms | $55–$65 | AE, D, DC, MC, V.

Howard Johnson. Built in 1972, this motel is in downtown Thibodaux near Civic Center. It's a good location for exploring swamp tours, bayou plantations, scenic drives, and antique shops. Restaurant, bar (with entertainment), room service. Refrigerators. Cable TV. Pool. Tennis. Exercise equipment. Video games. Business services, free parking. Pets allowed (fee). | 201 N. Canal Blvd. | 504/447–9071, 800/952–2968 | fax 504/447–5752 | www.hojo.com | 118 rooms | $65–$100 | AE, D, DC, MC, V.

Madewood Plantation House. The house was built in the 1840s, in Greek revival style of brick and stucco. Cypress used in the house was taken from the plantation. The landscaped grounds are adorned with moss-draped oaks, a formal garden, and an old family grave-yard. Inside in the original bedrooms you will find antiques, feather pillows, and fine linens. A house tour is available. Complimentary breakfast. Business services. No smok-ing. | 4250 Rte. 308, Napoleonville | 504/369–7151, 800/375–7151 | fax 504/369–9848 | www.madewood.com | 8 rooms | $225 | MAP | AE, D, MC, V.

Magnolia Manor Bed and Breakfast. This 1901 Acadian-style house was converted to a B&B by Pam and Ruben Villagram in 1999. It's near downtown, across from the Jean LaFitte National Historical Park, a cultural museum and theatre, a library, and an antique mall. There are two rooms available upstairs. The Magnolia Room is decorated in Cajun/Country style with a full-size, four-poster bed and private bath with a bathtub and separate shower. The Rose Room is decorated in Victorian style, with a reproduction four-poster queen-size rice bed and a private bath with hot tub and shower. Full breakfast is available for an extra charge. Complimentary Continental breakfast. No TV in rooms. No smoking. | 317 St. Mary St. | 504/446–3029 | www.bbonline.com/la/magnolia | 2 rooms | $85–$115 | MC, V.

VACATION COUNTDOWN Your checklist for a perfect journey

Way Ahead

- ❏ Devise a trip budget.
- ❏ Write down the five things you want most from this trip. Keep this list handy before and during your trip.
- ❏ Book lodging and transportation.
- ❏ Arrange for pet care.
- ❏ Photocopy any important documentation (passport, driver's license, vehicle registration, and so on) you'll carry with you on your trip. Store the copies in a safe place at home.
- ❏ Review health and home-owners insurance policies to find out what they cover when you're away from home.

A Month Before

- ❏ Make restaurant reservations and buy theater and concert tickets. Visit fodors.com for links to local events and news.
- ❏ Familiarize yourself with the local language or lingo.
- ❏ Schedule a tune-up for your car.

Two Weeks Before

- ❏ Create your itinerary.
- ❏ Enjoy a book or movie set in your destination to get you in the mood.
- ❏ Prepare a packing list.
- ❏ Shop for missing essentials.
- ❏ Repair, launder, or dry-clean the clothes you will take with you.
- ❏ Replenish your supply of prescription drugs and contact lenses if necessary.

A Week Before

- ❏ Stop newspaper and mail deliveries.
- ❏ Pay bills.
- ❏ Stock up on film and batteries.
- ❏ Label your luggage.
- ❏ Finalize your packing list—always take less than you think you need.
- ❏ Pack a toiletries kit filled with travel-size essentials.
- ❏ Check tire treads.
- ❏ Write down your insurance agent's number and any other emergency numbers and take them with you.
- ❏ Get lots of sleep. You want to be well-rested and healthy for your impending trip.

A Day Before

- ❏ Collect passport, driver's license, insurance card, vehicle registration, and other documents.
- ❏ Check travel documents.
- ❏ Give a copy of your itinerary to a family member or friend.
- ❏ Check your car's fluids, lights, tire inflation, and wiper blades.
- ❏ Get packing!

During Your Trip

- ❏ Keep a journal/scrapbook as a personal souvenir.
- ❏ Spend time with locals.
- ❏ Take time to explore. Don't plan too much. Let yourself get lost and use your Fodor's guide to get back on track.

Mississippi

In the minds of many travelers, Mississippi carries a lot of baggage. From the Civil War to Civil Rights, its history has been as turbulent as any in America. But the broader reality of contemporary Mississippi is complex and interesting. This is a state where hospitality, good manners, and violence have historically shared equal billing; where one of the world's great literary traditions is matched by a high rate of illiteracy; where blues musicians, country music singers, and classical opera stars from poor beginnings have risen to the top of their respective fields; where Bible Belt conservatism and booming casino resorts exist side-by-side. By almost any measure, there's no other place quite like it.

Mississippi is becoming increasingly mainstream. Race relations are markedly improved, industrial parks and suburbs are creeping across the landscape, and even the smaller cities are in many ways nearly indistinguishable from their counterparts elsewhere in the United States. Yet the state still seems somehow apart, and that is part of its attraction. For example, you could spend a morning visiting the shack where Elvis was born and watch an internationally renowned ballet that evening; try your luck at blackjack and then take a midnight swim on a deserted beach; watch the Martin Luther King Day parade and visit Jefferson Davis's boyhood home, all in the same town (Tupelo). Stick to the interstates and you'll miss much of what makes the state interesting. It's along the side roads, in places like Biloxi, Greenville, Holly Springs, Oxford, Vicksburg, and Woodville that the real Mississippi stands out in bold relief.

Mississippi is still mainly a state of small towns and rural countryside. The few large urban areas, such as they are, center around Jackson and the Gulf Coast. There are miles of cotton fields in the Delta region, great expanses of pine forests on the coastal plain, and a mixture of hills and forests almost everywhere else.

If you're looking for the quintessential Deep South, stick close to the Mississippi River. Go to Natchez in particular and to the Delta, which retains its plantation econ-

CAPITAL: JACKSON	POPULATION: 2.57 MILLION	AREA: 47,233 SQUARE MI
BORDERS: LA; AR; TN; AL; THE GULF OF MEXICO		
TIME ZONE: CENTRAL	POSTAL ABBREVIATION: MS	WEB: WWW.MISSISSIPPI.ORG.

omy and blues-music traditions. The most important Civil War sites are around Corinth and Vicksburg. The greatest concentration of antebellum homes is along the river and the coast. The most interesting Native American sites are around Natchez and in Neshoba County, the location of the Choctaw Indian reservation. Civil Rights sites can be found statewide. As for outdoor recreation, you're never far from a national forest or wildlife preserve.

The state is divided into five basic regions: the Delta, a flat alluvial plain of the Mississippi River, to the northwest; the river bluffs to the southwest; the northeast hills, which is the most economically diverse region; the coastal plain, with its large expanses of forest; and the Gulf Coast. You can drive from Memphis, Tennessee, just across the northern border, to Biloxi on the Gulf Coast in about six hours. You can cross the state, driving from Vicksburg to Meridian, in less than three hours.

History

When Spanish explorer Hernando de Soto passed through here in 1541–42, the area was dominated by the Choctaws, Chickasaws, and Natchez. A few smaller tribes lived in the Delta and on the Mississippi River. The first settlers were French, followed by the Spanish, and then the English. When the territory was bought by the United States as part of the Louisiana Purchase, immigrants from eastern states, primarily those of English and Scots-Irish descent, flooded into the area. Soon after, they brought slaves from Africa. In 1817, Mississippi became a state, and by the 1850s—mainly as a result of its rich cotton lands—had one of the highest per capita incomes in the nation. Mississippi withdrew from the Union just before the Civil War, and was readmitted in 1870.

The 20th century brought steady growth in cities, towns, and transportation. In the 1960s, the era of Civil Rights activities marked the end of racial segregation. Today, the state has the highest percentage of African-American elected officials in the country.

Agriculture remains the state's major business, with forest products making up the largest sector. Although there are isolated clusters of heavy industry along the Mississippi River and on the coast, the economy is more closely tied to small manufacturing and distribution.

Regions

1. JACKSON METRO AREA

Located near the center of the state, Jackson is Mississippi's largest urban area. In the early 20th century, nearby Vicksburg (pop. 20,000) was larger, but the capital quickly outpaced the river city after World War II. Today Jackson's population of 400,000 is

MS Timeline

1541–42	1673	1699	1716
Spanish explorer Hernando de Soto heads up the Mississippi River.	French explorers Marquette and Joliet pass through on their way down the Mississippi River.	Pierre LeMoyne Sieur d'Iberville establishes the first French colony in what is now the Biloxi–Ocean Springs area.	The French build Fort Rosalie in present-day Natchez.

INTRODUCTION
HISTORY
REGIONS
WHEN TO VISIT
STATE'S GREATS
RULES OF THE ROAD
DRIVING TOURS

made up largely of people who moved there from other Mississippi cities, and increasingly, from other states.

Jackson offers a broad array of entertainment, ranging from the International Ballet Competition to the Dixie National Rodeo. It's also the site of the state's Museum of Art, Museum of Natural Science, Agriculture and Forestry Museum, and Old Capitol Historical Museum. There are several smaller museums, including one dedicated to African-American history.

In recent years, Jackson has been plagued by crime. Although the statistics are improving, it remains a serious problem. Many of the city's more affluent residents are moving to the suburbs of Madison, Rankin, and western Hinds counties, where construction is booming.

The downtown area is dedicated primarily to government, banking, and law. There are several attractive residential areas, including Belhaven, Woodland Hills, and Eastover. Because the city was burned several times during the Civil War and underwent rapid, unplanned growth in the 1960s, few 19th-century buildings have survived. Notable exceptions include the Old Capitol, City Hall, and the Governor's Mansion. In part because of its erratic growth, the downtown area claims a particularly impressive collection of architecture from different periods.

Towns listed: Jackson, Mendenhall, Vicksburg.

2. CENTRAL MISSISSIPPI

Central Mississippi is surrounded by several very distinct regions but has a flavor all its own. It has many small cities and farming communities, as well as the suburbs of Jackson, Vicksburg, and Meridian. There are several scenic sites along the Mississippi River and the Ross Barnett Reservoir, along with numerous Civil War and Civil Rights historical sites.

Towns listed: Meridian, Philadelphia.

3. THE DELTA

This is probably Mississippi's best-known region, due to its role in the development of blues music and for U.S. 61, which crosses the Delta as it unfolds from Memphis to New Orleans. The Delta is also the state's primary agricultural region, with large plantations that sometimes stretch unbroken to the horizon. Because the land is flood-prone, most of its rivers (including the Mississippi) are lined with earthen levees. Near Memphis, legalized casino gambling is changing the face of the area; the state's tallest building—a casino hotel—towers above nearby cotton fields.

Towns listed: Belzoni, Canton, Clarksdale, Cleveland, Greenville, Greenwood, Grenada, Holly Springs, Indianola, Kosciusko, Robinsonville, Sardis, Yazoo City.

1729	1762	1776	1779	1795
In retaliation for an Indian attack, the French annihilate the Natchez tribe.	The French withdraw, leaving the territory to England.	When the eastern colonies revolt in 1776, British West Florida, which includes the Natchez District, remains loyal to the crown.	Spanish troops take over Natchez.	Spain cedes its holdings to the United States.

4. NORTHEAST MISSISSIPPI

This region includes several historic cities: Columbus, Corinth, Holly Springs, and Oxford. Among the more popular sites are five large man-made lakes, two national forests, several Civil War and Civil Rights sites, and the birthplaces of William Faulkner, Tennessee Williams, and Elvis Presley. Much of the area is made up of small farms and towns, and the landscape ranges from flat river bottoms to rolling hills and rocky outcrops that rise as high as 800 ft—the highest point in the state. There are three universities in the area.

Towns listed: Columbus, Corinth, Iuka, Louisville, Starkville, Tupelo.

5. SOUTHWEST MISSISSIPPI

Once one of the wealthiest regions of the United States, southwest Mississippi is best known today for its antebellum architecture. There are several interesting sites, including two ghost towns on the Mississippi River, another on the Natchez Trace Parkway, and an important Civil War battlefield. Port Gibson and Natchez are two of the most important cities historically (and two of the prettiest) in the state. This area also has the most appealing scenery along the Mississippi, with several overlooks from high bluffs, the most impressive of which is at Natchez.

Towns listed: McComb, Natchez, Port Gibson, Woodville.

6. THE PINEY WOODS

This region is largely forest, with little agriculture and few antebellum homes. The largest city is Hattiesburg, a lumber, manufacturing, and distribution center. Because the landscape has been better protected than in other parts of the state, you'll find many outdoor attractions, including two popular canoe or float streams, one national forest, the state's only federally designated wild and scenic river, and two wilderness areas.

Towns listed: Hattiesburg, Laurel.

7. THE COAST

The Mississippi Gulf Coast extends for just 80 mi between Alabama and Louisiana. The land is sculpted by wind and water, and is continually changing. You can pass serene beachfront houses, neatly set on green and shady lawns, then find yourself in bayous and marshes that are teeming with wildlife. The coast is actually the Mississippi Sound, separated from the Gulf of Mexico by the unspoiled barrier islands. Biloxi, Gulfport, and Ocean Springs are the largest cities.

The coast is culturally distinct from the rest of Mississippi. Its population is more urban, more ethnically diverse, and less conservative. This is in large part due to the fact that it has an international port and a popular resort area. The legalization of gambling led to a dramatic increase in tourism in Hancock and Harrison counties.

1798	1817	1820	1830–32	
After a three-year delay, Spain withdraws and the Mississippi Territory is formed.	Mississippi becomes the 20th state.	Choctaws sign the Treaty of Doak's Stand, ceding 5.5 million acres of land to the government for white settlement.	The remaining Choctaw lands are ceded to the government at the Treaty of Dancing Rabbit Creek. The remaining Chickasaw lands, the last Native American holdings in the	state, are soon lost, too.

Towns listed: Biloxi, Gulf Islands National Seashore, Gulfport, Ocean Springs, Pascagoula, Pass Christian, Picayune, Waveland, Wiggins.

When to Visit

Summer is a fine time to visit Mississippi if you don't mind the heat or if your travel plans include outdoor recreation near the water. It's not as much of an off-season as you might expect, since many travelers pass through on their way to Florida or New Orleans. But it is hot and humid, particularly in the Delta. Temperatures are considerably more moderate in the other seasons. In spring, the landscape is at its most scenic, with pink and red azaleas, flowering dogwoods, and lavender wisteria blossoms.

Spring is also known for intense storms and tornados, but for sheer beauty it's the best time to visit. Fall has the most reliably pleasant weather, with many clear days with highs in the 70s and lows in the 50s. The foliage may not be as spectacular as in New England, but it can be vivid, particularly in the northern counties. The foliage season is a long one, from September to the end of December in some areas. Winters are relatively mild but are the rainiest season, and the weather can turn bitterly cold for brief periods. It is not unusual for a 70°F day in January to end with a sleet storm. Winters on the coast are generally too cold for swimming, but typically last only from January to mid-February. Snow flurries are not uncommon in northern counties but are rare elsewhere. On average, central and northern counties only have snow accumulations every five or six years.

The annual average temperature varies from around 60°F in the north to near 70°F on the coast; the highest recorded temperature in Mississippi was 115°F, at Holly Springs in July 1930. Winter temperatures can vary as much as 30 degrees between the northern and southern counties, and even the coastal counties aren't immune to frost. The record low, -16°F, was set at Batesville in February 1966. Annual mean rainfall is around 50 inches (slightly more in the south), but some areas have received more than 100 inches during unusually wet years. The record rainfall is 8.42 inches in 24 hours in April 1979. The record snowfall was 18 inches, at Mount Pleasant in December 1963. Hurricane Camille, in August 1969, set records for sustained winds (220 mph) and tidal surge (30 ft).

CLIMATE CHART

Average Monthly Temperatures (in °F) and Monthly Precipitation (in inches).

	JAN.	FEB.	MAR.	APR.	MAY	JUNE
JACKSON	56/33	60/36	69/44	77/52	84/60	91/67
	5.2	4.7	5.8	5.6	5.1	3.2

	JULY	AUG.	SEPT.	OCT.	NOV.	DEC.
	92/71	92/70	88/64	79/50	69/42	60/36
	4.5	3.8	3.6	3.3	4.8	5.9.

1848	1861	1863	1870	1890
University of Mississippi founded.	Mississippi secedes from the Union and joins the Confederate States of America.	After a 47-day siege, Vicksburg—the state's largest city and most important fortification on the Mississippi River—falls to the Union Army.	After five years of military occupation Mississippi is readmitted to the Union. Reconstruction begins.	Reconstruction ends and white political dominance returns.

	JAN.	FEB.	MAR.	APR.	MAY	JUNE
MERIDIAN	56/33	61/37	70/44	77/51	84/59	90/66
	5.2	5.4	6.8	5.5	4.4	3.6

	JULY	AUG.	SEPT.	OCT.	NOV.	DEC.
	92/70	92/69	87/64	78/51	69/42	60/37
	5.2	3.6	3.5	3.0	4.5	6.0.

	JAN.	FEB.	MAR.	APR.	MAY	JUNE
TUPELO	49/31	55/34	64/43	74/51	81/60	88/67
	4.9	4.7	6.0	5.3	5.7	3.8

	JULY	AUG.	SEPT.	OCT.	NOV.	DEC.
	91/70	90/69	85/63	75/50	64/42	53/34.
	4.3	3.0	3.6	3.4	4.9	6.2.

FESTIVALS AND SEASONAL EVENTS

WINTER

Dec.: **Christmas at the Old Capitol.** This event in Jackson features a giant Christmas tree with period decorations. A few blocks away, the Manship House also gets done up for a 19th century Christmas. | 601/359–6920.

Jan.–Feb.: **Dixie National Livestock Show and Rodeo.** A number of equestrian events and contests take place during this show in Jackson, which draws participants nationwide. | 601/961–4000.

Feb.: **Mardi Gras.** Biloxi celebrates the weeks preceding Lent with parties and parades. | 228/432–8806.

SPRING

Mar.: **Vicksburg Spring Pilgrimage.** This tour of historic homes takes place during the height of spring foliage. | 601/636–9421 or 800/221–3536.

Apr.–May: **Natchez Opera Festival.** This festival offers everything from operas to Broadway musicals. | 800/862–3259.

May: **Jubilee! Jam.** Many kinds of music, along with food and libations, top the bill in this festival, which lasts all weekend in downtown Jackson. | 601/982–9588.

May: **Canton Flea Market and Arts and Crafts Fair.** This giant flea market draws artisans and craftspeople from across the South to sell their wares in booths around the Courthouse Square. | 800/844–3369.

1927
The Mississippi River overflows its banks, washing away levees and homes, killing hundreds and inundating much of the delta.

1954
The first of several Supreme Court rulings strikes a blow against racial segregation.

1963
Medgar Evers, a Jackson Civil Rights activist, is killed by a sniper.

1964
"Freedom Summer" brings scores of voting-rights activists to the state, registering thousands of black residents. Three are murdered, sparking national outrage.

1969
Hurricane Camille batters the Mississippi coast with 220-mph winds and a 30-ft storm surge; more than 200 die.

July: **Mississippi Deep Sea Fishing Rodeo.** This off-shore fishing competition at the Gulfport waterfront takes place July 4th weekend. | 228/388–2271.

Aug.: **Mississippi Wildlife Extravaganza.** Held in Jackson, this is the largest wildlife show in the state, with hunting and fishing equipment, art, supplies, exhibits, and seminars. | 601/656–4011.

Neshoba County Fair. This annual event has been held at the Neshoba City Fairgrounds, just 8 mi from Philadelphia, since 1889. It features week-long gatherings at rustic cabins, a horse-racing track, political speeches, exhibits, and rides. | 601/656–1742.

FALL

Sept.: **Mississippi Delta Blues and Heritage Festival.** This is the king of the Delta's blues festivals, offering big-name acts in a rural setting near Greenville. | 662/335–3523 or 888/812–5837.

Oct.: **Canton Flea Market and Arts and Crafts Fair.** This giant flea market draws artisans and craftspeople from across the South to sell their wares in booths around the Courthouse Square. | 800/844–3369.

Nov.: **Natchez Pilgrimage Garden Club Annual Antiques Forum.** This important antiques event features lectures by experts, workshops, and tours. | 601/445–2072 or 877/442–9796.

Southern Farm Bureau Classic. This PGA tournament stop features a field of 132 participants competing for a total purse of $2.2 million at the Annandale Golf Course in Madison. | 800/856–9290.

State's Greats

Most travelers come to Mississippi to visit historical sites, to enjoy blues music, to camp, or to gamble, and every region offers opportunities for each. With Memphis, Mobile, and New Orleans just across the state lines, big city attractions are nearby as well.

The premier destinations in Mississippi are Biloxi, with its casinos and beaches; the Delta, with its fabled plantations and blues clubs; Oxford, with its scenic square, tree-lined streets, and the home of William Faulkner; and Natchez, which has one of the largest concentrations of antebellum homes in the United States. Tunica and

1970	1977	1992
Mississippi's public schools are integrated.	Elvis Presley dies.	Casino gambling is legalized along the Mississippi River and on the Coast.

Coahoma counties, just south of Memphis, are also becoming important travel destinations, with a dozen casinos, fine dining, golf, and hunting and fishing packages. Jackson also offers museums, shopping districts, restaurants, and cultural events. Southern
Mississippi offers the greatest range of camping sites and float trips, mostly in the
De Soto National Forest.

Beaches, Forests and Parks

The Gulf Coast has what local promoters say is the longest man-made beach in the
world. It's a good place for wading, jet-skiing, volleyball, or sun bathing, but for surf-
ing you'd do better on the offshore islands. The islands, part of the **Gulf Islands National
Seashore,** are accessible only by boat. You can charter your own or take a passenger
ferry from Gulfport.

Mississippi has six national forests: **De Soto** in the southeast; **Homochitto** in the
southwest; **Bienville** in the central region; **Delta,** in the Delta; and **Holly Springs** and
Tombigbee to the northeast. There are also many national wildlife areas, state hunting and fishing areas, and state and federal natural areas. Most offer camping, hiking
trails, and picnic areas, and some also have cabins you can rent.

All of the public forests have their own allure, but south Mississippi's have the most
attractions as well as many streams that are excellent for swimming, canoeing, or hiking.
Black Creek Wild and Scenic River and Black Creek Wilderness, both in the De Soto National
Forest, are especially good for these sports.

State parks are widely distributed across Mississippi. Among the more popular are
J. P. Coleman, on scenic Pickwick Lake in the northeast corner of the state; **Leroy Percy,**
known for its moss-draped cypress trees, in the Delta; **Percy Quin,** which has cabins
and a new golf course, in southwest Mississippi; and **Buccaneer,** with extensive campgrounds and nature trails, on the coast.

Culture, History and the Arts

The largest number of cultural attractions are in Jackson, but some of the smaller cities
also offer quality sites and events. In Jackson, the most esteemed event is the **International Ballet Competition,** which is held every four years (and on other years in three
European cities). Also in Jackson are the state **Art Museum, Museum of Natural
Science, Agriculture and Forestry,** and **Old Capitol Historical Museum;** as well as
several smaller public and private museums, including **Smith-Robertson,** which is
dedicated to African-American history.

Elsewhere in the state, notable cultural, historic, and artistic offerings include the
Lauren Rogers Museum in Laurel; **Rowan Oak,** Faulkner's Oxford home; the **Delta
Blues Museum** in Clarksdale; **Natchez National Historical Park,** in Natchez; the **Walter
Anderson Museum** and the **George Ohr Museum** on the coast; **Vicksburg National Mili-
tary Park,** in Vicksburg; and the **Natchez Trace Parkway,** which runs across the state
from southwest to northeast.

The **Jackson Symphony** offers classical and alternative musical concerts, and
Natchez hosts an annual Opera Festival.

Sports

Jackson is home to the **Mississippi Sports Hall of Fame,** dedicated to such Mississippi-
born heroes as baseball star Dizzy Dean. Bicycle and running races are held in several
cities, and football, baseball, basketball, and track events are held at various state

universities. Outdoor recreation opportunities, including hunting and fishing, hiking and canoeing, are all available statewide. The coast also has its own hockey league. Sailing and water-skiing are popular on lakes, bays, and the Gulf of Mexico. Soccer is also popular, particularly with students.

Rules of the Road

License Requirements: The legal driving age is 16.

Right Turn on Red: Right turns are permissible on red unless otherwise posted, and left turns are permissible on red when turning from a one-way street onto another one-way street, unless otherwise posted.

Seatbelt and Helmet Laws: Seatbelts are required for front seat passengers/driver, and car seats are required for children under four. Motorcycle helmets are required.

Speed Limits: Unless otherwise posted, speed limits are 70 mph on interstate highways, 65 on non-limited access four-lane highways, 55 on other highways, and 50 on the Natchez Trace Parkway, where commercial trucking and hauling are prohibited.

For more information: Contact the **Mississippi Department of Public Safety** at | 601/987–1212.

Historic River Cities and the Natchez Trace Driving Tour

FROM VICKSBURG TO ROCKY SPRINGS.

Distance: 225 mi   Time: 3 days.

Breaks: Vicksburg and Natchez are the most convenient spots for overnight stays. Both are scenic and offer a range of restaurants, attractions, and lodgings.

This tour follows many kinds of routes, from winding country roads to four-lane highways and the Natchez Trace Parkway. It stretches from Jackson to the historic cities of Vicksburg, Port Gibson, and Natchez. If you begin in Jackson, you'll head west to Vicksburg, travel south on the Great River Road to Natchez, then return to Jackson on the scenic parkway. You'll see some of Mississippi's grandest antebellum homes, one of the nation's most important Civil War battlefields, and several marvelous panoramas of the Mississippi River. The best time to visit is in the spring, when the dogwoods, redbuds, and azaleas are in bloom, and many historic homes are open for tours. Fall is also a good time to visit. Skies are generally clear and temperatures are more moderate than in summer.

❶ The first stop on the tour is **Vicksburg.** High on a bluff overlooking the river, this city is famous for its strategic importance during the Civil War, when it was besieged by the Union Army and Navy for 47 days. Many buildings from the era of the war are still standing, and much of the battlefield is preserved. Both the soldiers and the public suffered heavy casualties during the siege, which ended with the Confederate surrender on July 4, 1863; the memory was so bitter that the city did not officially celebrate Independence Day until 1976—more than a century later.

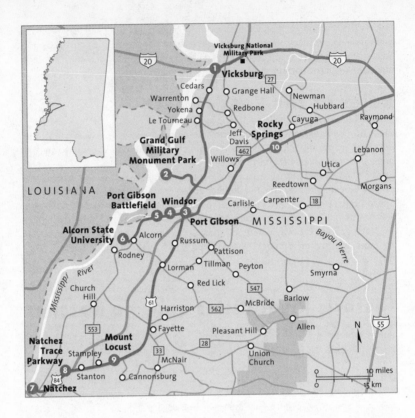

The **Vicksburg National Military Park** offers information, a museum, hiking trails, the U. S. S. *Cairo* gunboat (with its own museum), the picturesque National Cemetery, and a driving tour of the battlefield with several scenic overlooks.

The **Old Court House Museum,** housed in one of Mississippi's grandest and most historic buildings, stands atop a high hill near the old center of town; both Confederate President Jefferson Davis and Gen. U. S. Grant delivered speeches from its balconies. The museum has a refreshingly local feel, is crammed with interesting artifacts and has a friendly, knowledgeable staff.

Nearby **Cedar Grove** is a lavish antebellum home that doubles as a bed-and-breakfast inn; a cannonball lodged in the parlor wall testifies to repeated shelling by Union gunboats during the Civil War. Other tour homes include **Anchuca,** where Jefferson Davis visited after his release from prison; **Balfour House,** site of a Confederate ball interrupted by the Union assault on the city and later the Union Army headquarters; and **McRaven,** built in three stages in distinct architectural styles beginning in the 1830s, with many original furnishings and pretty landscaped grounds. Several other homes are opened for tours during the March Spring Pilgrimage.

Vicksburg also has four casinos: **Ameristar, Isle of Capri, Rainbow,** and **Harrah's.** You can take hydro-boat tours of the Mississippi and Yazoo rivers to get a wide-angle view of the city.

❷ From Vicksburg, the tour proceeds south on U.S. 61 for approximately 24 mi to Grand Fult Road. Several miles west is the **Grand Gulf Military Monument Park.** It occupies the site of a former Mississippi River town where Confederate forces engaged Union gunboats in 1863, and it includes an interesting cemetery, museum, restored buildings, campground, hiking trails, earthworks, observation tower, driving tour, and the best access to the Mississippi River between Vicksburg and Natchez.

INTRODUCTION
HISTORY
REGIONS
WHEN TO VISIT
STATE'S GREATS
RULES OF THE ROAD
DRIVING TOURS

❸ Leave Grand Gulf Military Monument Park and head east on Grand Gulf Road back to U.S. 61S, then approximately 2 mi south to **Port Gibson.** One of the best-preserved towns in Mississippi, Port Gibson was "too beautiful to burn," according to Gen. U. S. Grant, who passed through on his way to Vicksburg. Drive down tree-lined Church Street, with its stately churches and antebellum homes, and you'll see why. **First Presbyterian Church** may well be the most photographed church in the state, owing to the golden hand that points skyward from atop the steeple; inside are chandeliers from the steamboat Robert E. Lee. Interesting nearby churches include **St. Joseph's Catholic Church,** with striking, deep-blue stained-glass windows, and **Temple Gemiluth Chassed,** the oldest synagogue in the state. Port Gibson also has a Spring Pilgrimage, when many of the city's homes are open for tours.

❹ West of Port Gibson is **Windsor,** once Mississippi's most palatial antebellum plantation home. Today only the ruins of this four-story mansion remain: 23 towering columns and a few sections of cast-iron railing. Once a prominent landmark for steamboat pilots on the nearby Mississippi River, it was used as a Union hospital during the Civil War. Having survived the war, it burned during a party in 1890.

❺ Also in the vicinity is the **Port Gibson Battlefield.** Here outmanned Rebels were beaten back by the advancing Union Army. The battlefield is on a scenic, winding road that's little changed since the war, and includes the war-era Shaifer House.

❻ From Port Gibson take U.S. 61S for 10 mi, turn west onto Hwy. 552 at Lorman, then continue 6 mi to **Alcorn State University.** Originally a college for planters' sons and later one of the first land-grant colleges for blacks in the United States, the campus has several historic buildings. The ornate iron steps leading to the university chapel came from nearby Windsor.

❼ From Alcorn State, take Hwy. 552 east to U.S. 61S, and follow the business route approximately 30 mi to **Natchez.** This is Mississippi's most architecturally significant city, with hundreds of historic buildings ranging from the opulent **Melrose** (1841–45), which is the centerpiece of Natchez National Historical Park, to the **Smith-Bontura-Evans House,** built by a free man of color before the Civil War. There are also several Federal-style riverfront taverns in what used to be the rowdiest part of town, Natchez-Under-the-Hill, where the steamboats American Queen, Delta Queen and Mississippi Queen still dock. The Lady Luck casino is also there. Atop the hill is Bluff Park, with gazebos, benches and a sweeping panorama of the Mississippi River.

Natchez has several very interesting buildings. **Longwood** is a rare octagonal mansion. Its construction was interrupted by the Civil War. Not only was it never completed, the tools and paint cans remain where the workers left them when they fled.

Stanton Hall is an imposing Greek Revival home that occupies an entire city block. **Dunleith** is the quintessential "big house," with colonnades on all four sides.

Natchez has the largest and oldest Spring Pilgrimage in the nation, and if you don't mind crowds, it's a good time to tour some of the homes. (There's also a Fall Pilgrimage that's not usually as crowded.) Many of the homes also serve as bed-and-breakfast inns, and the **Eola Hotel** is listed among the Historic Hotels of America.

East of downtown is the **Grand Village of the Natchez Indians,** with large ceremonial mounds, a reconstructed house, and small museum commemorating the tribe for which the city is named.

❽ Approximately 5–10 mi east of Natchez pick up the **Natchez Trace Parkway.** The parkway follows the route of a trail estimated to be 8,000 years old. It was originally trod by buffalo and by Native Americans, and later used by explorers, settlers, bandits, itinerant preachers, and boatmen returning from Natchez to Nashville. There are plenty of opportunities to stop and admire the scenery or explore historic sites.

❾ Continuing north on the Natchez Trace Parkway, you'll come to **Mount Locust.** Dating to 1780, this is one of the few surviving frontier inns, or "stands," that offered lodging and food to early travelers on the Trace.

❿ From Mount Locust, continue north on the Natchez for approximately 45 mi to **Rocky Springs.** The town this park commemorates was destroyed by erosion and yellow fever. The park has a campground, picnic areas, rest rooms, hiking trails, and some pretty streams. Adjacent to the park is **Rocking Springs Methodist Church,** built in 1837. It is the town's only remaining structure, and its cemetery is worth exploring.

From Rocky Springs, proceed north on the parkway to I–20 and return east to Jackson.

Mississippi Gulf Coast Driving Tour
FROM OCEAN SPRINGS TO BAY ST. LOUIS.

Distance: 35 miles   Time: 2 days.
Breaks: The best place to stay overnight is Biloxi, which has many motels and bed-and-breakfast inns.

This tour encompasses everything from stately antebellum homes to casinos and beaches. Most attractions lie along U.S. 90, a live oak– and palm-lined beachfront thoroughfare that's alternately scenic and congested. Beginning in the small town of Ocean Springs, you'll travel west through highly developed Biloxi and Gulfport and pretty Pass Christian to Bay St. Louis, another scenic coastal town. As an optional side trip, you can take a passenger ferry to Ship Island, part of the Gulf Islands National Seashore, about 6 mi from the mainland. The weather can be perfect any time of year, but summers tend to be hot and humid, and the beaches (and adjacent U.S. 90) can get crowded. Hurricane season lasts from August to November, so keep that in mind when you make vacation plans.

❶ **Ocean Springs** is a good place to begin your tour. The city retains its small-town charm despite commercial sprawl along U.S. 90 and its location between Biloxi's casinos and Pascagoula's heavy-industry corridor. The city, which prides itself on its artistic traditions, is primarily residential.

There are many interesting sites along the quiet side streets of Ocean Springs, including **Shearwater Pottery,** set in a scenic wooded area by the Mississippi Sound. You can buy thrown, glazed wares in the style popular in the 1920s. The **Walter Anderson Museum of Art,** next to the Ocean Springs community center, contains the artist's bold, colorful murals from the 1950s and includes a room from his cottage, which is painted with wall-to-wall murals. The headquarters of the **Gulf Islands National Seashore** offers camping, nature trails, nature programs, and a boat launch on Davis Bayou.

❷ From Ocean Springs take U.S. 90 west for 4 mi across the bridge to **Biloxi.** This is the most famous city on the Mississippi coast, and the most diverse: In addition to swimming, boating, and beach-combing, you can tour the home of Confederate President

INTRODUCTION
HISTORY
REGIONS
WHEN TO VISIT
STATE'S GREATS
RULES OF THE ROAD
DRIVING TOURS

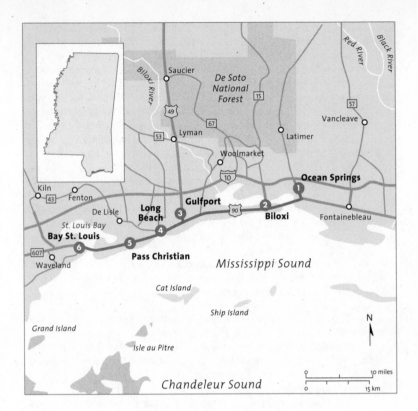

Jefferson Davis or test your luck at a Las Vegas–style casino. Five flags have flown over the city since the founding of the Biloxi Colony in 1699, and its population remains ethnically mixed. The city is an architectural hodgepodge, and within its boundaries are some of the most scenic and the most congested sections of U.S. 90.

Beauvoir, the last home of Confederate President Jefferson Davis, is typical of the large summer homes built along the beach before and after the Civil War. Surrounded by landscaped grounds, it is a peaceful sanctuary between casinos and the sprawling coast coliseum.

Other noteworthy Biloxi homes include the **Old Brick House,** built in the early 1700s and the **Tullis-Toledano Manor,** built by a New Orleans cotton-and-sugar broker circa 1856. There's also a self-guided walking tour of more than 20 structures that range from French Colonial to Greek Revival designs.

If history is not what you're after, you can try your hand at Biloxi's casinos, which range from the upscale **Beau Rivage** to the fanciful **Treasure Bay.** Others include Boomtown, Casino Magic, Biloxi Grand Casino, Biloxi Imperial Palace, Isle of Capri, Palace Casino, and President Casino. Some casinos offer hotels, golf courses, convention facilities, restaurants, and live entertainment.

Opportunities for outdoor activities include public beaches and charter boats for fishing or passage to the **Gulf Islands National Seashore.** Cultural offerings include the **George E. Ohr Arts and Cultural Center,** dedicated to internationally acclaimed works of "the mad potter of Biloxi."

As you head west, notice the **Biloxi Lighthouse,** a 58-ft cast-iron landmark in the U.S. 90 median. It's been a beacon to boaters since 1848.

❸ From Biloxi, continue west on U.S. 90 for approximately 12 mi to **Gulfport.** This is the busiest seaport in Mississippi. Founded in the late 19th century, the city is fairly young by coast standards. It has several attractive residential areas overlooking the Gulf.

If you're traveling with children, you may want to check out the **Marine Life Oceanarium.** It has porpoise and sea lion shows, a giant reef tank, underwater dive shows, bird shows, and a narrated mini-train tour of the Gulfport Small Craft Harbor and docks.

Casinos include the **Copa,** and the **Grand Casino Gulfport**; the latter has a 400-room hotel, several restaurants, and a golf course. Nearby is an antebellum tour home, **Grass Lawn,** built in 1836. You may also want to take a passenger ferry for a day-trip to **Ship Island;** a ferry runs from the Gulfport Small Craft Harbor twice a day. The island is part of the Gulf Islands National Seashore and site of the Civil War–era Fort Massachusetts. Charter boats are available for fishing or sight-seeing.

❹ From Gulfport, continue west on U.S. 90 for approximately 4 mi to **Long Beach.** The draw here is **Friendship Oak,** a giant live oak said to be 500 years old that dominates the University of Southern Mississippi's Gulf Park Campus.

❺ Continue west on U.S. 90 for 6 mi to **Pass Christian.** This is a small city with graceful homes overlooking the Gulf. It's a pleasant place to stroll the beach, and downtown shops offer jewelry, art, and gourmet foods.

❻ From Pass Christian, take U.S. 90 west for 8 mi across the St. Louis Bay bridge into **Bay St. Louis.** This is a small, friendly, and attractive city less than an hour from bustling New Orleans. The city dates from 1818, and there are more than 100 historic buildings in the downtown area. The movie *This Property is Condemned,* based on a Tennessee Williams play, was filmed in the depot district of Bay St. Louis.

Nearby is **Casino Magic,** which has a hotel, RV park, three restaurants, golf course, convention facilities, entertainment, and also activities for those under 21. Or you can take a boat tour of nearby bayous, marshes, the Jordan River, and St. Louis Bay. **St. Augustine Church and Seminary** is the state's oldest seminary that trains black Roman Catholics for the priesthood.

BELZONI

MAP 4, C4

(Nearby towns also listed: Greenville, Greenwood, Indianola, Yazoo City)

Belzoni calls itself "The Catfish Capital of the World" in honor of the thriving farm-raised-catfish business that originated here. The catfish ponds themselves aren't much to see—just vast checkerboards of squares of impounded water stretching across the flat landscape. The town, however, is a good stopping point when touring the Delta, and the Catfish Visitors Center does offer an interesting view of the area's aquatic agriculture. Belzoni is also a regional farm-equipment trade center, which explains the large tractor and farm-machine graveyards that line parts of U.S. 49. Lodging is scarce in town, so look to the nearby towns of Greenwood, Indianola, and Yazoo City.

Information: The Catfish Visitors Center | 111 Magnolia St., Box 145, Belzoni 39038 | 662/247–4838 or 800/408–4838.

Attractions

Wister Gardens. This 14-acre park is filled with horticultural splendor: 120 varieties of trees, thousands of azaleas (best viewing, March and April), hundreds of roses, and a 4-

acre lake that is home to local ducks and imported black and white swans. | 500 Henry Rd. | 662/247–3025 | Free | Daily 9–5.

ON THE CALENDAR
APR.: *World Catfish Festival.* This one-day event (a Saturday in April) offers entertainment, arts and crafts, a catfish-eating contest, the crowning of the World Catfish Queen, and free tours of Wister Gardens. | 662/247–4838 or 800/408–4838.

Dining

Peter Bo's. Southern. This popular family restaurant, about 8 mi north of Belzoni, is surrounded by cotton fields. It serves the best fried catfish, crispy and sweet, in the county. The country breakfast of eggs, biscuits, grits, ham, and sausage costs $4.50. Sun. brunch. | 320 U.S. 49, Isola | 662/962–7281 | fax 662/962–7281 | $6–$13 | D, MC, V.

BILOXI

MAP 4, E8

(Nearby towns also listed: Gulf Shores National Seashore, Gulfport, Ocean Springs, Pascagoula, Pass Christian, Picayune, Waveland, Wiggins)

BILOXI

INTRO
ATTRACTIONS
DINING
LODGING

An odd amalgam of the old and new, Biloxi has a look and feel unlike any other city on the Gulf Coast. Here you'll find a sometimes bewildering mix of attractions: grand mansions in groves of moss-draped oaks, glitzy Las Vegas–style casinos, and tacky T-shirt shops, all vying for space along what the locals claim is the longest man-made beach in the world.

Since the founding of the Biloxi Colony by the French in 1699, five flags have flown over the city: French, Spanish, English, American, and Confederate. The population is diverse, with many residents of French, Italian, Scots-Irish, Slavic, and, more recently, Vietnamese descent.

Biloxi has had a long run as a beach resort—more than 150 years—and during that time it has weathered economic booms and busts. The city's economy is anchored primarily by the seafood industry and tourism. Many lavish summer homes line the beach, some built before the Civil War by Delta planters and wealthy families from New Orleans. Huge casino complexes now crowd the waterfront. Most of the city's attractions lie along or near Beach Boulevard, a thoroughfare lined with live oak and palm trees that can become congested during the summer tourist season. The Gulf Islands National Seashore lies a few miles offshore, offering pristine, sugar-white beaches in a wilderness setting. It is accessible only by boat.

Countless hurricanes have blown into Biloxi from the gulf. The most notorious of these was Camille, which struck the city with 220-mph winds and a 30-ft storm surge in 1969. Biloxi residents have not been forced to evacuate in many years, but it's always a good idea to keep track of developing storms during summer and fall.

Information: **The Biloxi Visitors Center** | 710 Beach Blvd., Biloxi 39530 | 228/374–3105 or 800/245–6943. **Harrison County Tourism Commission.** | Box 6128, Gulfport 39506 | 228/896–6699 or 800/237–9493. **Mississippi Gulf Coast Convention and Visitors Bureau.** | Box 6128, Gulfport 39506-6128 | 228/377–2254 or 800/237–9493 | www.gulfcoast.org/mgccvb.

Attractions

Beauvoir, the Jefferson Davis Shrine. A National History Shrine, this is the last home and the presidential library of the President of the Confederacy, Jefferson Davis. | 2244 Beach Blvd. | 228/388–1313 | $7.50 | Mar.–Oct., daily 9–5; Nov.–Feb., daily 9–4.

Biloxi Lighthouse. This cast-iron landmark has been a beacon to boaters since 1848. It remained dark throughout the Civil War, and went electric in the 1920s. The tower and an exhibit are open to the public one hour each day. | U.S. 90 and Porter Ave. | 228/435–6293 | $2 | Mon.–Sat. 10 AM–11 AM.

Biloxi Mardi Gras Museum. This museum in the Magnolia Hotel displays glittering krewe costumes and other Mardi Gras memorabilia. | 119 Rue Magnolia | 228/435–6245 | fax 228/435–6246 | biloxi.ms.us.com | $2 | Mon.–Sat. 11–4.

Casinos. Most casinos listed here are inside hotels. All are open daily, 24 hours. There are no admission fees but you need to be 21 years old or over to enter the gaming areas. **Beau Rivage Casino** (875 Beach Blvd. | 888/750–7111) is in the deluxe, grand Beau Rivage Hotel overlooking beach and bay. **Boomtown Biloxi Casino** (676 Bayview Ave. | 800/627–0777). **Casino Magic** (195 Beach Blvd. | 800/562–4425). **Grand Casino Biloxi** (265 Beach Blvd. | 800/WIN–2WIN). **Imperial Palace Casino** (850 Bayview Ave. | 228/436–3000 or 800/634–6441) **Isle of Capri Casino Crowne Plaza Resort** (151 Beach Blvd. | 800/THE–ISLE) The **Palace Casino** (158 Howard Ave. | 800/725–2239) is a floating palace of glass that offers table games, slots, and electronic games. **President Casino** (2110 Beach Blvd. | 800/THE–PRES). **Treasure Bay Casino** (1980 Beach Blvd. | 800/PIRATE–9 | www.treasurebay.com) has an elaborate re-creation of a pirate ship, part of the complex's buccaneer theme.

Church of the Redeemer. Only the 1894 bell tower remains of the original historic church, which was rebuilt after devastating Hurricane Camille. | 610 Water St. | 228/436–3123 | Free | Weekdays 9–3:30.

George E. Ohr Arts and Cultural Center. Dedicated to "the mad potter of Biloxi," the center also displays the work of local artists and hosts traveling exhibitions. | 136 George E. Ohr St. | 228/374–5547 | $3 | Mon.–Sat. 9–5.

Gulf Coast Research Lab/J. L. Scott Marine Education Center and Aquarium. A must for budding Jacques Cousteaus, this world-renowned education center contains more than 60 aquariums, including a 42,000-gallon miniature Gulf of Mexico. Additional highlights include hands-on exhibits, murals, seashell collections, continuous videos, and a gift shop. | 115 Beach Blvd. | 228/374–5550 or 228/872–4200 | fax 228/374–5559 | $4 | Mon.–Sat. 9–4.

Maritime and Seafood Industry Museum. The museum contains historic photographs, exhibits, and artifacts relating to the Gulf Coast seafood industry, and has a replica of a Biloxi schooner. | 115 1st St. | 228/435–6320 | fax 228/374–6309 | www.maritimemuseum.org | Mon.–Sat. 9–4:30.

Old Brick House. This restored 1850s house, which serves as a community meeting center, combines American and French architectural elements. | 622 Bayview Dr. | 228/435–6121 | fax 228/435–6246 | $2 | Mon.–Sat. 11–4.

Shrimp Boat Trip. This 70-minute living marine adventure cruise gives you a taste of what shrimping is really like. Tours are available from March to November at the Small Craft Harbor. | 228/385–1182 | www.gcww.com/sailfish | $7–$11.

Tullis-Toledano Manor. Built by a New Orleans cotton and sugar broker in 1856, this Greek Revival antebellum house is now a historic museum. | 360 Beach Blvd. | 228/435–6293 | $2 | Mon.–Sat. 11–4.

Vieux Marché Walking Tour. This hour-long self-guided stroll through the heart of Old Biloxi is a virtual history lesson in Southern architecture, from a turn-of-the-century house to the neoclassical City Hall. For a map and other tours, contact the Visitor Center. | 710 Beach Blvd. | 228/374–3105 or 800/245–6943 | www.biloxi.ms.us | Free.

ON THE CALENDAR

FEB. OR MAR.: *Mardi Gras.* Biloxi has a notable Mardi Gras celebration in the weeks preceding Lent, with parties and three parades. | 228/432–8806.

FEB.: *Martin Luther King Day Parade.* This parade in downtown Biloxi honors the great Civil Rights leader. | 800/237–9493.

MAR.: *Oyster Festival.* This festival in honor of the succulent shellfish is celebrated with food and entertainment at Point Cadet Plaza. | 228/374–2330.

MAR.: *Saint Patrick's Parade and Irish Heritage Celebration.* The coast's Irish heritage is celebrated with a parade and party. | 228/875–9414.

MAR.: *Spring Pilgrimage at Beauvoir.* Jefferson Davis's last home is dressed up and opened for special tours. | 228/388–9074.

APR.: *Confederate Memorial Day.* This event honors the city's Confederate ancestors at Jefferson Davis's last home. | 2244 Beach Blvd. | 228/388–9074 or 228/388–1313.

MAY: *Blessing of the Fleet.* Fishing, shrimp, and pleasure boats are blessed at this popular event in Small Craft Harbor. | 228/377–2254 or 800/237–9493.

JUNE: *Mississippi Coast Coliseum Fair and Expo.* This fair features amusement rides, petting zoo, fireworks, and music. | 228/388–8010 or 800/726–2781.

SEPT.: *Biloxi Seafood Festival.* Every imaginable type of Gulf Coast seafood is celebrated at this festival in Point Cadet Plaza. | 228/374–2717.

SEPT.: *Mississippi Gulf Coast Blues Festival.* The blues festival draws both big-name and regional acts. | 228/497–5493.

SEPT.: *Sun-Herald Sand Sculpture Contest.* Beach artists compete for prizes in this competition on the beach opposite the Edgewater Mall, on Edgewater Drive. | 228/896–2434 or 800/332–4853.

OCT.: *Beauvoir Fall Muster.* This re-creation of a Confederate boot camp is held on the grounds of Jefferson Davis's last home. | 228/388–1313.

OCT.: *George E. Ohr Extravaganza.* The city celebrates Ohr's pottery work with the Mad Potter's Ball, an arts and crafts festival featuring pottery-making exhibits. | 228/374–5547.

DEC.: *Christmas on the Water.* This event off Beach Boulevard features a parade of lighted boats. | 228/374–3611 or 800/245–6943.

Dining

Cuco's. Mexican. This attractive, casual restaurant two blocks north of the beach has Mexican art on its walls. The large open dining room is brought to life by margaritas, and beef and chicken fajitas. | 1851 Beach Blvd. | 228/388–1982 | $8–11 | AE, D, DC, MC, V.

The French Connection. Continental. This restaurant, not far from Gulfport casino action, is known for its tar babies (boneless chicken wrapped with bacon in an herb-and-pecan sauce). Four kinds of steak, plus smoked oysters, are also popular. It has three intimate dining areas—including one in an open courtyard with a fountain—with lace curtains, candlelight, and recorded piano music. | 1891 Pass Christian Rd. | 228/388–6367 | $16–$30 | AE, D, DC, MC, V | Closed Sun.–Mon.

Hook, Line, and Sinker. Seafood. This veteran eatery is known for broiled stuffed flounder and its seafood platter. The walls are decorated with nautical items, and there is a view of the gulf. | 2018 Beach Blvd. | 228/388–3757 | $7–$28 | AE, D, DC, MC, V | Closed Mon. and Dec. 17–27.

Mary Mahoney's Old French House. Continental. This restaurant, housed in a 1736 building, is known for lobster Georgo (chunks of lobster in a brandy cream sauce), the St. Patrick (a shrimp and crab dish), and the jumbo shrimp sautéed with spinach in a soy butter sauce. You can dine outside to enjoy the sea breeze. | Rue Magnolia and U.S. 90 | 228/374–0163 | www.marymahoneys.com | $20–$42 | AE, D, DC, MC, V | Closed Sun.

McElroy's Harbor House Restaurant. Seafood. Fishing boats unload their catch just outside McElroy's, a place where both locals and visitors eat hearty meals. This is a bright casual family restaurant known for its po'boys, oysters on the half shell, stuffed flounder, and stuffed crabs. | 695 Beach Blvd. | 228/435–5001 | fax 228/435–8003 | Reservations not accepted | $7–$19 | AE, D, DC, MC, V.

O'Charley's. American. This restaurant is becoming one of the South's most notable. Pasta, seafood, and chicken are the most-popular dishes, but there is also a broad choice of steaks and regional specialities. The outdoor dining area is covered and overlooks the beach. Weekend brunch. Kid's menu. | 2590 Beach Blvd. | 228/388–7883 | $6–$16 | AE, D, DC, MC, V.

Ole Biloxi Schooner. Seafood. Coast residents flock to this small restaurant run by the Lancon family, a few blocks from the beach in Biloxi's back bay. You can get gumbo and po'boys, which come "dressed" and wrapped in paper. | 159 E. Howard Ave. | 228/374–8071 | Reservations not accepted | Breakfast also available | $6–$15 | No credit cards | Closed Sun.

Lodging

Beau Rivage Resort & Casino. This 32-story resort and casino has an oak-canopied entrance, lush gardens, and panoramic views of the gulf. All rooms have custom furnishings and marble baths. You can arrange fishing excursions and sunset cruises at Beau Rivage's marina. 12 restaurants, 8 bars (2 with entertainment). In-room data ports, some kitchenettes, some microwaves, some refrigerators, cable TV. Pool. Beauty salon, hot tub, spa. Beach, dock, water sports, boating, fishing. Laundry services. Golf privileges. Business services. | 875 Beach Blvd. | 228/386–7111 or 888/750–7111 | fax 228/386–7446 | www.beaurivage.com | 1,714 rooms, 66 suites | $89–$299, $199–$325 suites | AE, D, DC, MC, V.

Breakers Inn. This inn, 3 mi from downtown and opposite a sandy beach, offers two-story condo-style rooms with kitchens. There is free shuttle service to casinos. | 47 rooms. In-room data ports, kitchenettes, microwaves, refrigerators, in-room laundry facilities. Cable TV. Pool, wading pool. Tennis. Playground. Business services. Some pets allowed. | 2506 Beach Blvd. | 228/388–6320 or 800/624–5031 | fax 228/388–7185 | $99–$150 | AE, D, DC, MC, V.

Comfort Inn. This comfortable two-story hotel is across from the beach and just a few miles from malls, casinos, and restaurants. Downtown is 3 mi west. | 68 rooms. Complimentary Continental breakfast. Cable TV. Pool, hot tub. Business services. | 1648 Beach Blvd. | 228/432–1993 or 800/228–5150 | fax 228/432–2297 | www.comfortinn.com | $69–$115 | AE, D, DC, MC, V.

Days Inn. This three-story building has some rooms overlooking a tropical courtyard from private balconies. The motel is directly across from beach, near casinos 3 mi east of downtown. | 165 rooms. Complimentary Continental breakfast. Some kitchenettes, cable TV. Pool. Tennis. Laundry facilities. | 2046 Beach Blvd. | 228/385–1155 | fax 228/385–2532 | www.daysinnbiloxi.com | $59–$85 rooms; $139 suites | AE, D, DC, MC, V.

Edgewater Inn. This three-story inn has two- and three-bedroom cottages with full kitchens, as well as regular rooms with ocean views and kitchen facilities. The property is steps from the beach and the casino strip, 3 mi west of downtown. | 43 rooms, 19 suites. Restaurant. In-room data ports, kitchenettes, microwaves, refrigerators, cable TV. Pool. Exercise equipment. | 1936 Beach Blvd. | 228/388–1100 or 800/323–9676 | fax 228/385–2406 | www.gcww.com/edgewaterinn | $59–$250 | AE, D, DC, MC, V.

Father Ryan House. This 1841 inn across from the gulf is listed on the National Register of Historic Places. All rooms have views of the ocean, gardens, or the courtyard and pool. Rooms are furnished with handcrafted beds and early 19th-century antiques. Rooms have access to an upstairs terrace. The house is named for Father Abram Ryan, Poet Laureate of the Confederacy. Complimentary breakfast. In-room data ports, some in-room hot tubs, cable TV. Pool. | 1196 Beach Blvd. | 228/435–1189 or 800/295–1189 | fax 228/436–3063 | www.frryan.com | 10 rooms, 5 suites | $100–$135, $165–$175 suites | AE, D, DC, MC, V.

Holiday Inn. This motel ½ mile from downtown is made up of five low-rise buildings set around a flowered courtyard in the center of the property. | 268 rooms. Restaurant, bar. In-room data ports, room service, cable TV. Pool. Laundry facilities. Business services, airport shuttle. | 2400 Beach Blvd. | 228/388–3551 or 800/465–4329 | fax 228/385–2032 | www.holiday-inn.com | $69–$169 | AE, D, DC, MC, V.

Grand Casino Biloxi. The complex consists of two 12-story hotels, the Island View and the Bay View, which are across the street from each other. The hotels are 1 mi west of downtown. | 985 rooms, 79 suites. 9 restaurants, 6 bars. In-room data ports, some kitchenettes, some microwaves, some refrigerators, cable TV. Pool. Beauty salon, hot tub. Exercise equipment, children's programs (ages 1–12). Business services, airport shuttle. | 265 Beach Blvd. | 228/432–2500 or 800/946–2946 | fax 228/435–8901 | www.parkplace.com | $79–$179 | AE, D, DC, MC, V.

Green Oaks Bed and Breakfast. Mississippi's oldest antebellum mansion, built in the 1820s, occupies 2 acres and a private beach. The three-story house is listed on the National Register of Historic Places, and is furnished with hardwood floors and fine antiques, including Oriental rugs and four-poster beds. A gourmet breakfast and afternoon tea are offered. | 5 rooms. Restaurant, bar, complimentary breakfast. In-room data ports, room service, cable TV. Business services. | 580 Beach Blvd. | 228/436–6257 or 888/436–6257 | fax 228/436–6225 | www.gcww.com/greenoaks | $135 | AE, D, DC, MC, V.

Isle Of Capri Casino Crowne Plaza Resort. This beachfront, 12-story hotel was the first gaming resort on the Gulf Coast. Many of the spacious rooms come with balconies overlooking the gulf. The casino can be reached from the mezzanine level. The resort is ½ mile from downtown. | 370 rooms. 3 restaurants, 3 bars, room service. In-room data ports, cable TV. Exercise equipment. Pool, hot tub. Business services. | 151 Beach Blvd. | 228/435–5400 or 800/843–4753 | fax 228/436–7834 | www.casinoamerica.com | $119–$139 | AE, D, DC, MC, V.

The Old Santini House Bed & Breakfast. This 1837 cottage, across the street from the beach, is on the National Register of Historic Places. Innkeepers James and Patricia Dunay serve wine and cheese afternoons in the garden. You can spend evenings in front of the fireplace, surrounded by Louis XIV furnishings. Complimentary breakfast. In-room data ports, hot tub, cable TV. Beach, bicycles. | 964 Beach Blvd. | 228/436–4078 or 800/686–1146 | fax 228/432–9193 | www.santinibnb.com | 3 rooms, 1 cottage | $70–$115, $150 cottage | AE, D, MC, V.

Quality Inn Emerald Beach. This older two-story motel, 5 mi west of downtown, sits on its own sandy gulf beach. | 72 rooms. Complimentary Continental Breakfast. In-room data ports, microwaves, refrigerators, cable TV. Pool. Business services. | 1865 Beach Blvd. | 228/388–3212 or 800/342–7519 | fax 228/388–6541 | www.qualityinn.com | $59–$149 | AE, D, DC, MC, V.

President Casino Broadwater Resort. This 1970s resort 5 mi west of downtown offers many recreational options: it faces white-sand beaches, has an 18-hole golf course, and runs deep-sea fishing excursions from its marina. A free shuttle to the President Casino departs every 10 minutes. The complex includes an eight-story building, two- and three-bedroom cottages, and motel-style buildings. | 491 rooms, 9 cottages. 4 restaurants, 2 bars. In-room data ports, some kitchenettes, some microwaves, some refrigerators, cable TV. 3 pools, 18-hole golf course, 10 tennis courts. Basketball, gym, volleyball, boating. Playground. | 2110 Beach Blvd. | 228/388–2211 or 800/647–3964 | fax 228/385–1801 | www.president-broadwater.com | $59–$79, $110–$220 cottages | AE, D, DC, MC, V.

Treasure Bay Casino Resort. This nine-story resort hotel, formerly called the Royal D'Iberville, has a casino built to resemble a fort, and a 400-foot replica of an 18th-century pirate ship. The beach is across the street. Some rooms have views of the casino, the pirate ship, and the gulf. The hotel garden has a two-tier swimming pool with waterfalls. Legend has it that buccaneers roamed the area in the 1700s. 4 restaurants, bar (with entertainment). In-room data ports, some kitchenettes, some microwaves, some refrigerators, some in-room hot tubs, cable TV. 2 pools, wading pool. Golf privileges. Beach, video games. Business services. | 1980 W. Beach Blvd. | 228/385–6000 | fax 228/385–6067 | www.treasurebay.com | 252 rooms, 6 suites | $89–$119 | AE, D, MC, V.

CANTON

MAP 4, D5

(Nearby towns also listed: Jackson, Kosciusko, Natchez Trace Parkway, Yazoo City)

Canton's primary allure is its attractive downtown square, which was used in the filming of the movie *A Time to Kill*. The impressive 1857 Madison County Courthouse is the star of the square, but the city has many other well-preserved buildings, including several that have connections to African-American history. Canton is less than 30 minutes from Jackson on I–55. It is near the Ross Barnett Reservoir, a popular place for sailing, water-skiing, sightseeing, and other outdoor activities.

Information: Canton Convention and Visitors Bureau | Box 53, Canton 39046 | 601/859–1307 or 800/844–3369. **Canton Welcome Center** | 141 N. Union St., Canton 39046 | 601/859–0347. .

Attractions

Casey Jones Railroad Museum. This museum 14 mi north of Canton commemorates the folklore legend whose steam engine wrecked nearby. | 10901 Vaughan Rd., Vaughan | 662/673–9864 | $1 | Mon.–Tues., Thurs.–Fri. 8–4; Wed., Sat. 8–noon.

Freedom House. This circa 1940 home served as a headquarters for local and national civil rights advocates. Freedom House was often visited by Dr. Martin Luther King, Jr. You can catch a roadside glimpse of the house, but it is not open to the public. | 818 George Washington Ave. | 601/859–1307 or 800/844–3369.

Howcott Monument. This monument was erected in the 1890s "to the memory of the good and loyal servants who followed the fortunes of the Harvey Scouts during the Civil War." | E. Academy St. | 601/859–0347 | Free | Daily.

Ross Barnett Reservoir. This 33,000-acre lake was created by the damming of the Pearl River. You can go boating, swimming, enjoy scenic drives, and even visit nightclubs. The reservoir is 15 mi north of Canton. | 115 Madison Landing Cir., Richland | 601/354–3448 | Free.

Tilda Bogue. This restored, circa-1830 log house with an open hallway, or "dogtrot," through the center, is listed on the National Register of Historic Places. It can be visited by arrangement with the Canton Visitors Bureau. | 731 Davis Crossing Rd. | 601/859–1307 or 800/844–3369 | $5.

ON THE CALENDAR

MAY, OCT.: *Canton Flea Market.* Artisans and crafts people from across the South ply their wares around the town's central square at this giant flea market held the second Thursday in May and October. | 800/844–3369.

JULY: *Mississippi Championship Hot Air Balloon Fest.* As many as 75 colorful balloons fill the sky during this annual event. | 800/844–3369.

Dining

Two Rivers Restaurant. American. This popular spot for steaks and seafood is just minutes from Pearl River and Big Black River, at the intersection of I–55 and Highway 22. There is a full-service cocktail lounge with a New Orleans atmosphere. | 111 Soldier Colony Rd. | 601/859–9999 | $10–$22 | AE, D, MC, V | Closed Sun. No lunch.

Lodging

Best Western Canton Inn. This two–story motel, opened in 2000, is off I–55 at exit 119. There are fast food restaurants next door. In-room data ports, microwaves, refrigerators, cable TV. Pool. Laundry services. Business services. | 137 Soldier Colony Rd. | 601/859–8600 or 800/528–1234 | fax 601/859–4455 | www.bestwestern.com | 50 rooms | $45–$75 | AE, D, DC, MC, V.

CLARKSDALE: DEEP IN THE DELTA BLUES

For more than half a century, and well into his most golden decades, the name of John Lee Hooker has meant the blues . . . the real blues, dark, deep, painful, plaintive, sometimes bemused, but always the genuine article, untouched by fad or fame, the real Mississippi Delta blues.

John Lee Hooker was born in Clarksdale, Mississippi. That alone is reason enough to make a pilgrimage to this sunbaked little town deep in the Delta, 75 miles south of Memphis. But there are plenty of other reasons too.

Back in the days when cotton was king in the South, much of the South's cotton passed through Clarksdale and its railroad station, heading north. And with it came many of the men who picked the cotton and many who just followed the railroad tracks. And many of them made music—honest, heartfelt music that would continue on its own path while, at the same time, giving birth in later years to rhythm and blues and rock 'n' roll. But it started—and, to a large extent, remains—right here in Clarksdale.

Among the legendary blues masters who were born in or near Clarksdale, or whose music is closely tied to Clarksdale roots, are Charley Patton, Son House, Robert Jordan, "Big Boy" Crudup, Elmore James, "Pinetop" Perkins, and Sonny Boy Williamson. Ike Turner is from Clarksdale. So was the sweet-voiced Sam Cooke. Back in the 1930s, the musicians playing guitars in the Delta style and singing the blues on the street corners included two men whose names would later be known to all fans of America's most genuine homegrown music: Muddy Waters and Howlin' Wolf.

W. C. Handy himself lived in Clarksdale for three years and later wrote about "the blind singers and footloose bards that were forever coming and going." Clarksdale was a place, he said, of "rich traditions and inspirational fertility."

After World War II, after the turn of the century, after cotton production was reduced in the South, those same trains from Clarksdale began to carry increasing numbers of people northward, looking for jobs, a better opportunity, a new life. Most of them just rode the train straight on through to Chicago. Many, of course, were bluesmen. Muddy Waters, for example, settled in Chicago and spread the music outward from there. Bo Diddley, another Mississippian, played with Waters in Chicago before going off on his own and inventing a sound that would be the basis of rock 'n' roll.

Stackhouse Records is in Clarksdale, and so is the Delta Blues Museum, and seven miles northwest of town is the Stovall Plantation where Muddy Waters grew up in a tiny cabin. But after you've loaded up on CDs and videos and "Highway 61" T-shirts at the Ground Zero Blues Store at the museum, the thing to do is to listen to some live music in the bars and clubs and on the street corners of Clarksdale. The spiritual sons and grandsons of giants are playing there right now.

CLARKSDALE

MAP 4, C2

(Nearby towns also listed: Cleveland, Oxford, Robinsonville, Sardis)

This otherwise unremarkable town in the Mississippi Delta is internationally known as the cradle of the blues. A number of blues greats grew up in the city or on nearby plantations, including W. C. Handy, Robert Johnson, Muddy Waters, and Howlin' Wolf. Johnson, more than any other musician, put Delta blues on the map with his mournful song "Crossroads," which gave its name to a movie about the blues. The legend says, if you go to the crossroads at midnight, the devil will tune your guitar. Then you'll be able to play anything, but you've made a contract with him and sold your soul. The location of this particular crossroads has been the subject of much debate, but most agree it was near the present junction of U.S. 49 and U.S. 61. However, the legend has spread, and the South has many crossroads.

Clarksdale's musical roster also includes country singer Conway Twitty, Ike Turner (of Ike and Tina fame), and Sam Cooke, but the town is ground zero for true blues buffs. You can hear live blues at a number of locations. It's best to seek reliable local advice, since schedules are subject to change (right up to the last minute) and some clubs are in potentially dangerous parts of town. The best source for what's playing where is the Delta Blues Museum (662/627–6820).

Clarksdale hosts an annual Tennessee Williams Festival. The Mississippi playwright spent part of his life here, and many of the area's sites, including Moon Lake and the Cutrer Mansion, are believed to be models for settings in Williams' plays.

Information: Clarksdale-Coahoma County Chamber and Industrial Foundation and Tourism Commission | 1540 Desoto Ave., Clarksdale 38614 | 662/627–7337 or 800/626–3764.

Attractions

Delta Blues Museum. Exhibits and programs trace the history of the blues and the impact of the blues on rock, jazz, and pop music. The museum recently moved into the old Clarksdale Depot. | 1 Blues Alley | 662/627–6820 | Free | Mon.–Sat. 9–5.

Great River Road. This less traveled road follows the Mississippi River levee. U.S. 61 runs along the east side of the river and U.S. 65 on the west. Both routes run from the gulf all the way to Canada.

Lady Luck Rhythm and Blues Casino. This casino in the Isle of Capri hotel boasts two 112-foot neon guitars on its roof. It is 35 mi north of Clarksdale. | 777 Isle of Capri Pkwy., Lula | 800/789–5825 | Free | Daily 24 hours.

ON THE CALENDAR

JUNE: *Delta Jubilee.* This three-day event features a barbecue championship, sports tournaments, and live music. | 662/627–7337 or 800/626–3764.
AUG.: *Sunflower River Blues and Gospel Festival.* This blues event draws top-notch gospel and blues groups. It includes music workshops. | 662/627–2209.
OCT.: *Tennessee Williams Festival.* The festival includes lectures, plays, music, and tours of historical sites relating to the authors life and work. | 662/627–7337 or 800/626–3764.

Dining

Rest Haven. Middle Eastern. The Delta's large Lebanese community has made the country's cuisine locally popular. Rest Haven opened in the late 1980s. Specialities are *kibbe* (seasoned ground lamb with cracked wheat), cabbage rolls, meat pies, and red beans and sausage over rice. There are daily lunch plate specials. | 419 State St. | 662/624–8601 | $5–$13 | No credit cards | Closed Sun.

Lodging

Comfort Inn. This two-story hotel on U.S. 61 opened in 1998 with rooms including coffeemakers, wet bars, and recliners. Complimentary Continental breakfast. In-room data ports, microwaves, refrigerators, cable TV. Pool. Health club. Business services. | 818 S. State St. | 662/627–5122 or 800/228–5150 | fax 662/627–1668 | www.comfortinn.com | 74 rooms | $75 | AE, D, DC, MC, V.

Hampton Inn. This two-story motel right off U.S. 61 offers rooms with balconies 2½ miles east of downtown. | 93 rooms. Complimentary Continental breakfast. In-room data ports, some refrigerators, cable TV. Pool. Exercise equipment. Laundry facilities. Business services. | 710 S. State St. | 662/627–9292 or 800/426–7866 | fax 662/624–4763 ext. 650 | www.hamptoninn.com | $55–$62 | AE, D, DC, MC, V.

The Isle of Capri. This hotel 35 mi north of Clarksdale on the Mississippi River is associated with two Lady Luck casinos near U.S. 49. It has a large swimming pool, two movie theaters, and offers headliner entertainment. | 487 rooms. Restaurant, bar (with entertainment). Refrigerators, cable TV. Pool. Exercise equipment. Laundry facilities. Business services. | 777 Lady Luck Pkwy., Lula | 662/363–4600 or 800/789–5825 | fax 662/363–4590 | www.isleofcapri.com | $89–169 | AE, D, DC, MC, V.

CLEVELAND

MAP 4, C3

(Nearby towns also listed: Clarksdale, Greenville, Greenwood, Indianola)

Cleveland is a handy stop for those touring U.S. 61, the legendary artery that stretches from New Orleans to Chicago. Cleveland's Delta State University has a number of attractions. And take a few minutes to see Memorial Drive, lined with stately pin oaks planted in 1923 in honor of local men who died in World War I.

Information: Cleveland Chamber of Commerce/Tourism | 600 3rd St., Cleveland 38732 | 662/843–2712 or 800/295–7473 | fax 662/843–2718 | www.ci.cleveland.ms.us.

Attractions

Delta State University. Most of the town's cultural institutions are found on this university campus. In addition to the sites below, the Roy E. Wiley Planetarium and a small museum of natural history are here. | Hwy. 8W | 662/846–3000 | www.deltast.edu | Free | Daily.

Bologna Performing Arts Center. This state-of-the-art 1,200-seat theater presents a diverse program of opera, dance, and music. | 662/846–4626 | www.deltast.edu/perf-arts.

Charles W. Capps, Jr., Archives and Museum. This new building holds the Delta State archives of Mississippi history. The gallery hosts local and traveling exhibitions. | 662/846–4780 | www.lib.deltast.edu | Free | Mon.–Thurs. 8–5, Fri. 8–4.

Fielding Wright Art Center. The museum has changing exhibitions of painting and sculpture, including faculty and student shows. | 662/846–4721 | Free | Mon.–Thurs. 8–8:30, Fri. 8–4:30.

Great River Road State Park. This state park is 18 mi west of Cleveland. You can camp, fish, hike along nature trails, and use the boat launch. | Hwy. 1, River Road State Park exit, Rosedale | 662/759–6762 | $2 per vehicle | Daily 6 AM to 10 PM.

Mound Bayou. This town 9 mi north of Cleveland was founded in 1886 by Isaiah Thornton Montgomery, a former slave. Both Isaiah and his father, Benjamin Montgomery, were encouraged in their education by Joseph E. Davis, the brother of Jefferson Davis. After the

Civil War, Isaiah purchased some 4,000 acres of the Davis estate, Brierfield Plantation, and laid out the town. A brochure about the history of the town is available at Mound Bayou City Hall. City Hall also has a photo, artifact, and outdoor sculpture exhibit that illustrates the lives of the founding families. | City Hall, 106 W. Green St. | 662/741–2193 or 800/353–4392 | Free | Daily.

ON THE CALENDAR

MAR.: *Southern Home Ideas Expo.* This interior decorating and building ideas show takes place at the Bolivar County Expo Building off Hwy. 61 N. | 662/843–2712.

APR.: *Annual Crosstie Arts Festival.* This is a juried art contest and festival on the Bolivar County Courthouse lawn. | 662/846–4087.

OCT.: *Cleveland's Octoberfest.* A barbecue contest, arts and crafts, children's activities, and entertainment are part of this fest on Cotton Row. | 662/843–2712.

Dining

KC's Restaurant. Eclectic. This restaurant is a hidden treasure in the heart of the Delta. It has a Spanish mission–style exterior, brightly colored walls, and a 28-ft-high cathedral ceiling. Fare ranges from French to Asian to Southwestern. Popular dishes include grilled rack of lamb with roasted garlic, and seared diver sea scallops served with sweet corn and applewood-smoked bacon. | U.S. 61 at 1st St. | 662/843–5301 | www.kcrestaurant.com | $16–$38 | AE, MC, V | Closed Sun.

Lodging

Cleveland Inn. This two-story motel is undergoing major renovations to modernize its facilities. The pleasant lounge is open from 4 to midnight. The motel is on the west side of U.S. 61, just south of downtown. | 119 rooms. Restaurant, bar, room service. In-room data ports, cable TV. Pool. Business services. Some pets allowed. | U.S. 61 | 662/846–1411 | fax 662/843–1713 | $50–$79 | AE, D, DC, MC, V.

Comfort Inn of Cleveland. This comfortable chain motel is 1 mi north of Hwy. 8, off U.S. 61. Complimentary Continental breakfast. In-room data ports, microwaves, refrigerators. Pool. Business services. | 721 N. Davis Ave. | 662/843–4060 or 800/228–5150 | fax 662/843–2444 | www.comfortinn.com | 80 rooms | $57 | AE, D, DC, MC, V.

Molly's. This B&B a few blocks from downtown is in a restored two-story frame house built in the early 1900s. The Melon Room, the Cowboy Room, the Victorian Room, and the Oasis Room have wood floors and are decorated with images and colors to match their name themes. Molly's husband is a sculptor whose work is displayed throughout the house. | 214 S. Bolivar Ave. | 662/843–9913 | www.deltaland.net/~shamscbb | 4 rooms | $65–$75 | MC, V.

COLUMBUS

MAP 4, F4

(Nearby towns also listed: Starkville, Tupelo)

Blanche Dubois of *A Streetcar Named Desire* would feel right at home in Columbus. Although her Belle Reve Plantation was fictional, any number of antebellum homes in the area resemble it. That's probably because Columbus was the birthplace of playwright Tennessee Williams, author of *Streetcar* and the dean of Southern drama.

Columbus was founded in 1821 as a cotton port on the Tombigbee River. Because the town was never invaded during the Civil War, many of the original mansions survive. But beneath this impressive veneer is a city emerging as a manufacturing and commercial center. The Tennessee-Tombigbee Waterway, a man-made barge canal, stretches from Tennessee to the port of Mobile by way of Columbus. By far the best time to visit—despite the crowds—is during the Columbus Spring Pilgrimage, when a dozen or more homes are decked out in their finest and opened for tours. Riverboat rides and driving and walking tours are available.

The nearby city of Aberdeen also offers tours of stately homes. Some are open year-round; others operate as bed-and-breakfasts. More than 50 are included in a self-guided driving tour.

Information: Columbus Convention and Visitors Bureau | Box 789, Columbus 39703 | 662/329–1191 or 800/327–2686 | www.columbus-ms.org. **Mississippi Welcome Center** | 300 Main St., Columbus 39703 | 662/328–0222. **Aberdeen Visitors Bureau and Historic Aberdeen Association** | Box 288, Aberdeen 39730 | 662/369–9440 or 800/634–3538.

Attractions

Aberdeen Historic Homes. The Historic Aberdeen Association promotes self-guided driving tours of more than 50 area homes. Brochures are left outside the office at all hours. | 300 Main St., Aberdeen | 662/369–9440 | Weekdays 8–5.

Amzi Love Home. Built in 1848, this villa has been occupied by the same family for eight generations. It is now a bed-and-breakfast. | 305 7th St. S | 662/328–5413 | $5 | Tues., Thurs. by appointment.

Blewett-Harrison-Lee Museum. The restored 1847 home of Confederate general Stephen D. Lee contains Lee's possessions and a collection of antebellum gowns. | 316 7th St. N | 662/327–8888 | $5 | Fri. 10–4.

Tennessee-Tombigbee Waterway Attractions. This waterway connects the Tennessee River to the Tombigbee River. There are three areas that offer cabins, boat launching facilities, and nature trails. | 662/328–3286.

Columbus Lock and Dam. You can walk onto portions of the dam and locks at this site along the west bank of the waterway. | 4873 W. Plymouth Rd., Columbus | 662/328–7075 | Free | Dawn–dusk.

DeWayne Hayes Campground. You need to bring your own tent or RV if you want camp at this site. You can bike on the trails and there is a playground for children. | 7934 Barton Ferry Rd., Columbus | 662/434–6939 | Free | Dawn–dusk.

Waverly Recreation Area. Picnic tables and pavillions are scattered throughout this recreational area which is 20 mi west of Columbus. | Waverly Rd., West Point | 662/494–0039 | Free | Dawn–dusk.

Friendship Cemetery. Memorial Day traces its roots to this cemetery. In 1866, local women came here to honor the Confederate dead. However, they placed flowers at the grave of every soldier, noting that the Union dead were also somebody's sons. | 4th St. S | fax 662/328–2565 | Free.

Lake Lowndes State Park. This park offers camping, swimming, fishing, boating, nature trails, lodging, softball, and tennis. | 3319 Lake Lowndes Rd. | 662/328–2110 or 662/328–9182 | $2 per vehicle | Daily 6–10.

Lenoir Plantation. This circa 1847 working plantation, about 20 mi northwest of Columbus, is still owned by descendants of its original builder. Many of the original furnishings are on display. | 10032 Lenoir Loop, Prarie | 662/369–9440 | $5 | By appointment.

Mississippi University for Women. Founded in 1847 as the Columbus Female Institute, this university was the nation's first state-supported college for women. It has been co-ed since 1982. Some of the buildings on the picturesque campus date from the 1860s. | 1100 College St. | 662/329–4750 | www.muw.edu | Free.

Temple Heights. This bed-and-breakfast boasts the best view in town. The four-story, colonnaded mansion was built on this hilltop in 1837. The owners, a local historian and an educator, are good area resources. | 515 9th St. N | 662/328–0599 | Free.

Tennessee Williams Birthplace. This Victorian house, where the playwright was born in 1911, is now the Mississippi Welcome Center. You can tour the house—though none of Williams possessions remain. | 300 Main St. | 662/329–3533 or 662/328–0222 | Free | Daily 8:30–5:30.

Waverley Plantation. This mid-19th century plantation home, 12 mi west of Columbus, has an unusual octagonal shape. | Waverly Ferry Rd. (off Hwy. 50 W), West Point | 662/494–1399 | $7.50 | Daily 9–5.

Williams-Gass House ("The Haven"). This house was built in 1843 by brothers Thomas and Isaac Williams in the antebellum Greek Revival style. Both were free men of color; one was a slave trader. It is not open to the public. | 315 2nd Ave. N | 662/329–1191 or 800/327–2686.

ON THE CALENDAR

FEB.: *Battle of West Point and Prairie.* This battle reenactment commemorates Civil War battles in the countryside around Columbus. | 662/329–1191 or 800/327–2686.

APR.: *Columbus Spring Pilgrimage.* Local historic mansions are decorated and open for walking tours at the height of the spring foliage season. | 662/329–1191 or 800/327–2686.

MAY: *Golden Triangle Powerboat Regatta Festival.* This boating event takes place on the Tenn-Tom Waterway. | 662/327–4631.

OCT.: *Decorative Arts Forum, Antique Show and Sale.* Organized by the Columbus Historic Society, the Forum features lectures, a symposium, and tours of nearby antebellum homes. These events are held in conjunction with the Antique Show and Sale at the James M. Trotter Convention Center. | 662/329–1191 or 800/327–2686.

APR., OCT.: *Trash to Treasures.* Hundreds of vendors gather at the Columbus fairgrounds for this huge flea market. | 662/329–1191.

Dining

Harvey's. American. This is a mid-sized café housed in a restored tannery a few miles from the Mississippi University for Women. The most popular dishes are Cajun chicken pasta and prime rib. Kid's menu. | 200 Main St. | 662/327–1639 | $9–$17 | AE, D, MC, V | Closed Sun.

Old Hickory Steak House. Steak House. Local residents come to this restaurant for steak dinners served with a baked potato, salad, and bread. The specialty is a 32-ounce steak for two. | 1301 U.S. 45 | 662/328–9793 | $7–$15 | MC, V | Closed Sun. No lunch.

Peppers Deli & Market. Delicatessen. Neon peppers illuminate this bustling U.S. 45 deli, which serves New York–style steamed sandwiches, salads, and the "biggest potatoes in town." | 2017 Jackson Sq. | 662/328–6889 | fax 662/328–9772 | $7–$9 | AE, D, MC, V.

Lodging

Amzi Love/Lincoln Home B & B. The Amzi Love House is an Italianate villa built in 1848 and has been maintained by eight generations of Amzi Love's decendants. The Lincoln Home is a Greek Revival structure built in 1833. These two adjacent properties in the historic district are run by the Caradine family. You can tour the two homes, and arrange a cruise of the nearby Tenn-Tom Waterway on their 42-ft Chris-Craft. Complimentary breakfast. In-room data ports, cable TV. | 305 7th St. S | 662/328–5413 | fax 662/328–5413 | 5 rooms, 2 suites | $85–$125 | AE, MC, V.

Backstrom's Country Bed and Breakfast. This two-story house built in 1980 is in a quiet wooded area ½ mile outside town. The large bedrooms have private baths. The house is decorated with stained glass, paintings, and sculptures. | 3 rooms. Complimentary breakfast. Cable TV, no room phones. | 4567 U.S. 182 | 662/328–7213 | $75 | MC, V.

Comfort Inn. This two-story motel is 1 mi southeast of downtown, next to the Lee Mall. Golden Triangle Regional Airport is 10 mi away. | 106 rooms. Complimentary Continental breakfast. In-room data ports, cable TV. Business services. | 1210 U.S. 45 | 662/329–2422 or 800/228–5150 | fax 662/327–0311 | www.comfortinn.com | $49–$79 | AE, D, DC, MC, V.

Gilmer Inn. This three-story motel built in 1965 is in the center of the Columbus historic district. A nearby tunnel, now caved in, leads to the river and was used for transferring slaves and wounded Civil War soldiers. The Gilmer Inn is home to Lydia's Southern Cafe. Restaurant. Pool. Free parking. | 321 Main St. | 662/328–0070 or 800/328–0722 | fax 662/328–1700 | 64 rooms | $45 | AE, D, MC, V.

Ramada Inn. This clean two-story motel is ¼ mi west of downtown. | 98 rooms. Restaurant, bar, room service. Cable TV. Pool. Business services. | 506 U.S. 45 | 662/328–5202 or 800/228–2828 | fax 662/241–4979 | www.ramada.com | $55–$79 | AE, D, DC, MC, V.

Landmark Hotel. This four-story, full-service hotel three blocks from downtown has an atrium lobby, where you'll find the Atrium Café and Atrium Lobby Bar. There's nightly entertainment in the Southern Nights Lounge. | 119 rooms. Restaurant, 2 bars. Complimentary breakfast. In-room data ports, cable TV. Laundry service. Business services. | 1200 U.S. 45 | 662/327–7077 or 800/472–5964 | fax 662/327–2807 | www.landmarkhotelms.com | $49–$69 | AE, D, DC, MC, V.

CORINTH

(Nearby towns also listed: Holly Springs, Iuka, Tupelo)

Corinth is known primarily for its Civil War history. Union and Confederate forces swept across the area numerous times, and at one point there was hand-to-hand combat in the city's streets. The city saw more action than any other city in the Confederate west, though ultimately eclipsed by Vicksburg's romantic fame. Corinth was so hotly contested because it lay at the intersection of two railroads and was essential to lines of supply.

Unlike most Mississippi cities, Corinth has always been an industrial center. In fact, the Corinth Machinery Building is the state's oldest industrial building. Many Civil War–era buildings and homes survive, and the town is steeped in Civil War sites. Corinth is also a short drive from one of the nation's most storied battlefields—Shiloh National Military Park—which is just across the Tennessee line. After that battle, Confederates retreated to Corinth and made it their medical center.

Information: **Tourism Promotion Council** | 810 Tate St., Corinth 38834 | 662/287–5269 or 800/748–9048 | www.corinth.net.

Attractions

Battery Robinette. This park and cemetery, also called Fort Robinette, saw the heaviest fighting in the two-day Battle of Corinth. Two thousand Confederate soldiers killed in that battle are buried here. | W. Linden St. | 662/287–5269 or 800/748–9048 | Free.

Borroum's Drug Store. This quaint drugstore still has a functioning soda fountain. It could pass for a museum if it were not for the constant flow of customers. | 604 Waldron St. | 662/286–3361 | Mon.–Sat. 8–5:30.

Corinth Civil War Interpretive Center. The center offers a video and self-guided walking and driving tours of the Siege and Battle of Corinth National Landmark sites. | 301 Childs St. | 662/287–9501 | www.corinth.org | Free | May–Sept., weekdays 9–5, Sun. 1–5; Oct.–Apr., weekdays 9–4, Sun. 1–4.

Corinth Hiking and Biking Trail. This trail links various historic sites around the city. It begins at Trail Head Park on Cruise Street. | 662/287–5269 or 800/748–9048.

Curlee House. Built in the mid-19th century, this mansion was used by both the Confederate and Union commands. It is now owned by the city. | 705 Jackson St. | 662/287–9501 | $2.50 | May–Sept., weekdays 9–5, Sun. 1–5; Oct.–Apr. weekdays 9–4, Sun. 1–4.

Jacinto Courthouse. This Federal-style courthouse built in 1854 has a re-created period court-room. Other pre-1870s buildings in the neighborhood of the courthouse are being restored. Jacinto, a town on the National Register of Historic Places, is 15 mi southwest of Corinth on Hwy. 45. | Washington and 4th Sts., Jacinto | 662/286–8662 or 662/287–4296 | Free | Tues.–Fri., Sun. 1–5; Sat. 10–5.

National Cemetery. More than 6,000 Union soldiers are buried here. | Horton and Cemetery Sts. | 662/286–5782 | Free.

Northeast Mississippi Museum. One of the more endearing museums in the state holds a collection that ranges from fossils to war relics. It also serves as a local clearinghouse for historical anecdotes, thanks to its knowledgeable (and loquacious) curators. Civil War and Chickasaw Indian artifacts and folk art are displayed in three rooms. A research library contains genealogical records, local letters, and diaries. | 204 E. 4th St. | 662/287–3120 | Free | Mon.–Sat. 10–5, Sun. 2–5.

ON THE CALENDAR
OCT.: *The Battle of Corinth Reenactment.* This annual reenactment commemorates the October 1862 battle with thousands of participants, wagons, horses, and observers. | 800/748–9048.
OCT.: *Hog Wild in Corinth Barbecue Festival.* This barbecue cook-off also features live music. | 662/287–5269 or 800/748–9048.

Dining
Martha's Menu. Southern. This homey, bustling eatery downtown is where residents go for cornbread, meats, taters, and beans. Old pictures of the town hang on the walls. Breakfast costs less than $3, and lunch and dinner include meat, three vegetables, and corn bread. Choices include fish, steak, frogs' legs, and turnip greens. There's also a salad bar. | 702 Cruise St. | 662/287–2590 | $3–$13 | No credit cards.

Lodging
Comfort Inn. This chain motel is a little over a mile west of downtown. Guests get access to a nearby YMCA. | 98 Rooms. In-room data ports, some kitchenettes, some microwaves, some refrigerators, some in-room hot tubs, cable TV. Outdoor pool. | 2101 U.S. 72 | 662/287–4421 or 800/228–5150 | www.comfortinn.com | $49–$89 | AE, D, DC, MC, V.

Executive Inn. This three-story building 2 mi west of downtown has clean and attractive rooms. | 70 rooms. Restaurant. Some kitchenettes, cable TV. Pool. | 2104 U.S. 72, at U.S. 45 | 662/286–6071 or 800/354–3932 | fax 662/286–9608 | $45–$65 | AE, D, DC, MC, V.

The General's Quarters. This B&B occupies a restored Victorian home originally built in 1872 as a church. It has landscaped grounds that include a pond and gardens and is within walking distance of museums, antiques shops, restaurants, and shopping. Innkeepers Charlotte and Luke Doehner can arrange home-cooked lunches or dinners. Complimentary breakfast. In-room data ports, cable TV, in-room VCRs. Outdoor hot tub. Library. | 924 Fillmore St. | 662/286–3325 | fax 662/287–8188 | www.thegeneralsquarters.com | 6 rooms, 4 suites | $75–$85, $90–$120 suites | D, MC, V.

GREENVILLE

MAP 4, C4

(Nearby towns also listed: Belzoni, Cleveland, Greenwood, Indianola, Vicksburg, Yazoo City)

As the largest city in the sparsely populated Delta, Greenville is the de facto capital of the area and a logical stop on any tour of the region. But Greenville is a haphazard jumble of shopping centers, plantations, barge docks, blues clubs, and casinos that can seem confusing. Stick it out and you're likely to find it as appealing as any city in the region. A good place to start is the River Road Queen Welcome Center, a replica of a paddle wheeler that looks oddly marooned at the intersection of U.S. 82 and Reed Road. The Delta is arguably the state's most controversial and intriguing region. Flat, prone to floods, incredibly fertile, and characterized by extremes of wealth and poverty, the Delta has earned the dubious title, "The Most Southern Place on Earth." Travel the entire South and you're unlikely to find a place that suggests so strongly the best and the worst of the Southern stereotypes. The river that created the Delta is now hidden behind massive earthworks. The devastating flood of 1927 was a defining moment in Greenville's history, when a break in the old levee released torrents of water that inundated the city.

Originally established as a cotton port in the mid-19th century, Greenville has grown into a regional center of agriculture, commerce, industry, and inland shipping. Although it lacks the genteel good looks of other Deep South river towns, its musical and literary traditions are vibrant, and a dizzying number of festivals are celebrated throughout the year. Life in Greenville is still comparatively slow-paced, and despite universal air-conditioning, anyone who visits during the sweltering summer months will understand why.

In other ways, however, the city defies the sleepy-Southern-town stereotype. It has nurtured nationally famous authors like Civil War historian Shelby Foote and novelist Walker Percy. And a long-time atmosphere of racial tolerance has set Greenville apart from other cities in the region. With sizeable Italian, Lebanese, and Chinese populations, there is more cultural diversity here than you might expect. Note that Greenville has some streets that should be cautiously navigated at night,., including parts of Nelson Street where many of the best blues clubs are found.

Information: **River Road Queen Welcome Center** | Hwy. 82 W and Reed Rd., Greenville 38704 | 662/332–2378. **Washington County Convention and Visitors Bureau.** | 410 Washington Ave., Greenville 38701 | 662/334–2711 or 800/467–3582 | www.thedelta.org.

GREENVILLE

MISSISSIPPI MUSIC

Few states can claim as many varied contributions to American music as Mississippi. Among the natives who've reached the pantheon of their musical genres are rocker Elvis Presley; opera diva Leontyne Price; blues greats Muddy Waters, Robert Johnson, B. B. King, and W. C. Handy; and country stars Jimmie Rodgers, Tammy Wynette, Charlie Pride, and Faith Hill.

The rich musical tradition is even more remarkable considering that there is no real musical center in the state. Music has sprung from cotton fields, shotgun shacks, trailer parks, and concert halls. The delta was the cradle of the blues, and that music remains popular there today. Country tends to dominate the hills of eastern Mississippi, where Rodgers, known as the father of country music, was born. Opera and classical music can be heard in Jackson and Natchez. The state has more than its share of popular music festivals and live-music clubs. In addition, there are numerous music-history sites scattered across the state, so you can take the Elvis pilgrimage tour, visit the home of rock great Jerry Lee Lewis, browse the Jimmie Rodgers museum. Or you can just listen to the real thing, just about anywhere you happen to be.

© Corbis

Attractions

Birthplace of the Frog Exhibit. This Jim Henson mini-museum, in the Leland Chamber of Commerce building 15 mi east of Greenville, commemorates the native son who created Kermit the Frog and the rest of his Muppet cronies. Several of the original Muppets are on display. | U.S. 82 at S. Deer Creek Dr. E, Leland | 662/686–2687 | Free | Mon.–Sat. 10–4.

Casinos. Both Greenville casinos are open 24 hours; admission is free. **Bayou Caddy's Jubilee Casino** (211 S. Lakefront Rd. | 800/WIN–MORE) in a large, fixed riverboat; a hotel is being built on the site. The **Light House Point Casino** (308 Washington Ave. | 800/878–1777) is in the Marriot Fairfield Inn.

Greenville Writers' Exhibit. The Greenville Memorial Public Library pays tribute to the rich local literary tradition, showcasing the works of local authors Foote, Percy, Hodding Carter (II and III), David L. Cohn, Ellen Douglas, Beverly Lowry, and Clifton Taulbert. | 341 Main St. | 662/378–3141 | Free | Weekdays 9–5, Sat. 9–noon.

Lake Washington. See plantation homes along the Lake Washington scenic route on Hwy. 1 South, near Chatham. You can get a map from the Convention and Visitors Bureau. | 662/334–2711 or 800/467–3582.

Leroy Percy State Park. You can camp and fish in cypress-filled bayous at this state park 19 mi south of Greenville on Hwy. 12. | Hwy. 12 | 662/827–5436 | fax 662/827–5181 | leroyp@tech-info.com | $2 per vehicle | Daily 8–5.

Weatherbee House. This Victorian cottage built circa 1873 contains an art gallery with local, regional, and national exhibits. | 509 Washington Ave. | 662/332–2246 | Free | Weekdays 10–4, and by appointment.

Winterville Mounds State Park. This is one of the most important complexes of Native American mounds in the South, constructed between the years 400 and 1000. Park rangers give tours, and there is a museum and gift shop. | 2415 Hwy. 1 N | 662/334–4684 | $1 | Grounds daily 8–8. Office Mon.–Sat. 8–5, Sun. 1–5.

ON THE CALENDAR

MAY: *Delta Democrat Times Grand Prix Catfish Race.* Yes, this is just what it sounds like: a fish race, held in a long water tank. | 662/335–1155 or 800/844–1618.

MAY: *Mainstream Arts and Crafts Festival.* This event showcases the skills of local artisans. | 662/378–3141.

JULY: *Greenville Celebrates America.* Greenville's week-long Fourth of July celebration includes music, fireworks, and music at the waterfront on Lake Ferguson. | 662/378–8663.

JULY: *Farm Fest.* This major national agriculture trade show, held each year at the Greenville Municipal Airport, features exhibits and demonstration crops on 250 acres. | 662/334–2711 or 800/467–3582.

JULY: *International Food Festival.* This event showcases different national cuisines, starring those of Greenville's ethnically diverse population. | 662/378–8663.

SEPT.: *Mississippi Delta Blues and Heritage Festival.* This is the king of the Delta's blues festivals, featuring big-name acts. | 662/335–3523 or 800/467–3582.

OCT.: *Delta Wildlife Expo.* This event at the Washington County Convention Center showcases hunting and fishing exhibits, art, and equipment. Highlights include a 42-ft-long fish tank. | 662/334–2711.

OCT.: *Mississippi International Balloon Classic and Air Show.* This event at the Greenville Municipal Airport includes ground displays and air shows featuring hot-air balloons. | 662/334–2711 or 800/467–3582.

Dining

Doe's. American. The decor is bright and tables are Formica, but the food is worth the trip. Doe's is a family-style restaurant known for enormous steaks, hot tamales, and a special salad dressing. | 502 Nelson St. | 662/334–3315 | $7–$18 | MC, V | No lunch.

Sherman's. American. This casual eatery was a family-owned grocery store before becoming a restaurant in 1947. The most popular items are the 28-ounce prime rib steak with lemon ice-box pie for dessert. | 1400 S. Main St. | 662/332–6924 | $15–$20 | AE, D, DC, MC, V | Closed Sun.

Lodging

Comfort Inn. There are two casinos within 2 mi of this two-floor motel. A restaurant is across the street. In-room data ports, microwaves, refrigerators. Pool. Laundry facilities. | 3080 U.S. 82 | 662/378–4976 or 800/228–5150 | fax 662/378–4980 | www.comfortinn.com | 77 rooms | $59–$69 | AE, D, DC, MC, V.

Hampton Inn. There are restaurants near this two-story hotel 3 mi east of downtown. | 120 units. Complimentary Continental breakfast. In-room data ports, cable TV. Outdoor pool. Business services. | 2701 U.S. 82 | 662/334–1818 or 800/426–7866 | fax 662/332–1761 | www.hamptoninn.com | $59–$73 | AE, D, DC, MC, V.

Holiday Inn Express. There is a casino 3 mi from this pleasant two-floor motel, and a restaurant across the street. Downtown is 2 mi west. | 104 rooms, 13 suites. Complimentary Continental breakfast. In-room data ports, refrigerators, cable TV. Pool, wading pool. Hot tub. Business services. | 2428 U.S. 82 | 662/334–6900 or 800/465–4329 | fax 662/332–5862 | www.holiday-inn.com. $59–$80 | AE, D, DC, MC, V.

Ramada Inn. This two-story motel is 3 mi west of downtown. The Weatherbee House is 3½ mi away. | 121 rooms. Restaurant, bar, complimentary breakfast (weekdays), room service. In-room data ports, some refrigerators, cable TV. Pool. Playground. Business services, airport shuttle. | 2700 Hwy. 82 | 662/332–4411 or 800/228–2828 | fax 662/332–4411 | www.ramada.com | $69–$129 | AE, D, DC, MC, V.

GREENWOOD

MAP 4, D4

(Nearby towns also listed: Belzoni, Cleveland, Greenville, Grenada, Indianola, Yazoo City)

More than any other city in the Delta, Greenwood seems caught in a time warp. Straddling the banks of the languorous Yazoo River, its leafy streets lined with graceful mansions and stark shotgun shacks, Greenwood still projects an aura of the old South. This is partly because the city still revolves around the crop that ushered it into being: King Cotton. The surrounding countryside includes some of the best cotton-producing land in the world, and the city claims the second-busiest cotton exchange in the United States (after Memphis). Greenwood's historic district is still occupied by cotton buyers and sellers. Not surprisingly, the city was named for a cotton planter, Greenwood Leflore, who was half French and the last chief of the Choctaw nation.

Greenwood is also the shopping and cultural center for this part of the Delta, with plenty of events and sights—cotton and non-cotton—to keep you entertained. And, if nothing else, it is a pleasant, picturesque city.

Information: **Greenwood Convention and Visitors Bureau** | 1902 Leflore Ave., Greenwood 38930 | 662/453–9197 or 800/748–9064.

Attractions

Cottonlandia Museum. This museum tells the story of Delta cotton through photographs, artifacts, and agricultural tools. One room holds treasures from Malmaison, the former home of Greenwood Leflore, which burned in 1942. There are also Civil War relics and early Indian objects. | 1608 U.S. 82 | 662/453–0925 | www.gevb.com | $2.50 | Weekdays 9–5, weekends 2–5.

Florewood River Plantation State Park. Florewood is a living-history museum. In addition to the planter's mansion, there is a church, school, smokehouse, blacksmith's shop, grist and shingle mills, out buildings, and orchards and vegetable gardens. The gift shop sells local crafts. At the entrance to the plantation is the Cotton Museum, which has a video/audio presentation about the impact of cotton on the South. You can take guided tours. | Fort Loring Rd. off U.S. 82 | 662/455–3821 | www.gevb.com | $3.50 per vehicle. Museum free | Mon.– Sat. 9–4, Sun. 1–5.

Greenwood Cemetery. This cemetery contains 40 graves of Confederate soldiers killed in the nearby Battle of Fort Pemberton. | Strong Ave. | 662/453–9197 or 800/748–9064 | Free.

Mississippi Valley State University. This university 9 mi west of Greenwood in nearby Itta Bena was established in 1946 to train teachers for schools in rural areas. Today it is a full-service university. | 1400 U.S. 82, Itta Bena | 662/254–9041 | www.mvsu.edu.

National Wildlife Refuges. You can hike, hunt, and fish at three wildlife refuges within driving distance of Greenwood. The Matthews Brake, Morgan Brake, and Hillside refuges are 10, 25, and 40 miles south of town, respectively, along Hwy. 49. A public use permit—valid for 1 year—can be obtained at the visitor center. | 1562 Providence Rd., Cruger | 662/839–2638 or 662/235–4989 | $12 permit.

Robert Johnson Memorial. This monument to the blues great is in the cemetery of Mt. Zion Missionary Church, 16 mi south of Greenwood. Though the location of his actual grave is disputed, fans leave tokens of appreciation at the site. | Mt. Zion Missionary Church, Morgan City | 662/453–9197 or 800/748–9064 | Free.

ON THE CALENDAR
SEPT.: *300 Oak Race.* There are 5-K and 10-K races along the city's tree-lined streets. | 662/453–9197 or 800/748–9064.

Dining

Belinda's Cotton Patch Restaurant. American/Casual. This small restaurant is 5 mi from downtown and serves a little bit of everything, including a noon buffet, short orders, subs, plate lunches, baskets, and steaks. Should you have a late-night weekend craving, the restaurant is open 24 hours Thursday through Saturday. | 801 U.S. 82 Bypass | 662/453–4155 | $5–$9 | AE, D, MC, V | No dinner Sun.

Crystal Grill, Inc. American. Southern hospitality is served here along with each meal. Known for veal cutlets and steak. This restaurant also has a few Greek dishes like baklava and a platter with grape leaves, olives, and feta. It's near U.S. 82 in the center of town. Kid's menu. | 423 Carrollton Ave. | 662/453–6530 | $8–$18 | AE, D, MC, V | Closed Mon.

Lodging

Bridgewater Inn. This Greek Revival home was built in 1910 and opened as a B&B in 1997. The two king bedrooms have a view of the Yazoo River and open onto a columned porch. The inn, which is within walking distance of downtown, has antique bathrooms, porch swings, and rocking chairs. Complimentary breakfast. In-room data ports, cable TV, in-room VCRs. | 501 River Rd. | 662/453–9265 | fax 662/453–4248 | www.microsped.com/bridgewater | 7 rooms | $70–$90 | AE, MC, V.

Comfort Inn. This two-story motel built in 1989 is across the street from a park with picnic grounds. Some rooms have park views. The motel is 3 mi east of downtown. | 40 rooms, 20 suites. Complimentary Continental breakfast. In-room data ports, cable TV. Pool. Business services. | 401 U.S. 82 | 662/453–5974 or 800/228–5150 | fax 662/455–6401 | www.comfortinn.com | $59–$79 | AE, D, DC, MC, V.

Hampton Inn Greenwood. This big motel has clean, comfortable rooms, good amenities, and is less than 1 mi south of downtown. | 100 rooms. Restaurant, complimentary Continental breakfast, room service. In-room data ports, refrigerators, cable TV. Pool, wading pool. Tennis. Exercise equipment. Laundry facilities. Business services. | 635 U.S. 82 | 662/455–5777 or 800/426–7866 | fax 662/455–4239 | www.hamptoninn.com | $70 | AE, D, DC, MC, V.

GRENADA

MAP 4, D3

(Nearby towns also listed: Greenwood, Oxford)

At first glance, Grenada seems to offer few reasons to linger. If you approach from the main exit off I–55, the city appears to be a case of classic American commercial sprawl at its worst. Shopping centers, fast-food restaurants, and gas stations compete for space. To make matters worse, the development has been carved from stark, eroded red-clay hills. But before you get back on the highway, you'd do well to take a look at the largely forgotten downtown area. There are many fine examples of local architecture and several landmarks from the Civil Rights era. And immediately to the northeast is blue Grenada Lake, which is dotted with sailboats on warm, sunny days.

Information: Grenada Chamber of Commerce | 1321 Sunset Dr., Suite FF, Grenada 38901 | 662/226–2571. **Grenada Tourism Commission** | Box 1824, Grenada 38902 | 662/226–2571 or 800/373–2571.

GRENADA

INTRO
ATTRACTIONS
DINING
LODGING

Attractions

Belle Flower Missionary Baptist Church. A landmark of the Civil Rights movement, where Dr. Martin Luther King Jr. spoke on several occasions. After his last visit, the church was partially burned, but has since been rebuilt. | 388 Lake St. | 601/483–2458 | Free | By appointment.

Confederate Cemetery. This cemetery contains 180 graves of unknown soldiers. Tours can be arranged by the Grenada Tourism Commission. | Cemetery St. | 662/226–2571 or 800/373–2571 | Free.

Grenada Lake. The lake has a 54-mi shoreline, boat launches, and fishing and swimming facilities. | Scenic Loop Hwy. 333, off Hwy. 8 | 662/226–5911 | Free | Daily.

Grenada Confederate Forts. In the vicinity of Grenada Lake, this series of earthworks was built to protect the city from Union assault. | Scenic Loop Hwy. 333 | 662/226–5911 | Free | Daily.

Grenada Lake Visitors Center Museum. You'll find displays of native animals, Native American and Civil War artifacts, an observation deck, and a bookstore at this visitors center. | 2151 Scenic Loop Hwy. 333 | 662/226–1679 | Free | Daily 9–noon and 1:30–5.

Hugh White State Park. This park on the lake's south shore has high bluffs, deep ravines, and a beach. You can camp in cabins, a lodge, or at primitive sites. | Scenic Loop Hwy. 333 | 662/226–4934 | $2 per vehicle | Daily 6AM–10PM.

Historic Grenada Walking and Motor Tour. For a brochure detailing the tour of historic homes and other landmarks, visit the chamber of commerce. | 662/226–2571 or 800/373–2571.

ON THE CALENDAR

JUNE: *Grenada "Thunder on Water" Lake Safe Boating Festival.* This festival offers music, a 10K run, tennis and softball tournaments, a car show, arts and crafts, and a children's fishing rodeo. | 662/226–2851.

JUNE: *Dizzy Dean World Series.* Contact the Grenada Tourism Commission for specifics on this youth baseball tournament. | 662/226–2571 or 800/373–2571.

OCT.: *The Annual National Fox Hunt.* In this event, riders in traditional dress chase foxes or faux foxes across the countryside. | 662/226–2571 or 800/373–2571.

Dining

Jake & Rip's. Southern. Deer trophies hang on the walls of this spot where locals come for barbecue, steaks, and catfish. You can eat in the dining room or have your food packed to go. | 1525 Sunset Dr. | 662/227–9955 | $7–$16 | AE, D, MC, V.

Lodging

Best Western Motor Inn. This two-story motel has rooms with balconies. It's west of downtown, off I–55 at exit 206. | 61 rooms. Restaurant, complimentary breakfast, room service. In-room data ports, cable TV. Pool. Business services. Some pets allowed. | 1750 Sunset Dr. | 662/226–7816 or 800/528–1234 | fax 662/226–5623 | www.bestwestern.com | $55–$79 | AE, D, DC, MC, V.

Comfort Inn. This two-story motel has rooms with balconies, a pool, a lounge, and restaurant. It's west of downtown, off I–55 at exit 206. | 66 rooms. Complimentary Continental breakfast. Refrigerators, cable TV. Pool. Hot tub. Business services. | 1552 Sunset Dr. | 662/226–1683 or 800/228–5150 | fax 662/226–9484 | www.comfortinn.com/ | $60–$90 | AE, D, DC, MC, V.

Days Inn. This two-story motel built in 1987 is near Hugh White State Park, west of downtown off I–55 at exit 206. | 52 rooms. In-room data ports, cable TV. Pool. Hot tub. Business services. | 1632 Sunset Dr. | 662/226–8888 | fax 662/227–9592 | $49–69 | AE, D, DC, MC, V.

Hampton Inn. This two-story motel has contemporary rooms with coffeemakers. Some 35 items are available at the complimentary breakfast, and snacks are served in the evening. The motel is off I–55 at exit 206. In-room data ports, some microwaves, some refrigerators, cable TV. Pool. Exercise equipment. | 1622 Sunset Dr. | 662/226–5555 or 800/426–7866 | fax 662/226–5581 | www.hamptoninn.com | 62 rooms | $66 | AE, D, DC, MC, V.

Holiday Inn. This hotel, at the intersection of Hwy. 8 and I–55, is made up of two two-story buildings. | 128 rooms. Restaurant, complimentary Continental breakfast, room service. In-room data ports, cable TV. Indoor pool, wading pool. Laundry facilities. Business services. | 1796 Sunset Dr. | 662/226–2851 or 800/465–4329 | fax 662/226–5058 | www.holiday-inn.com | $68–$75 | AE, D, DC, MC, V.

GULF ISLANDS NATIONAL SEASHORE

MAP 4, F9

(Nearby towns also listed: Biloxi, Gulfport, Ocean Springs, Pascagoula)

Pristine Gulf Islands National Seashore is one of the hidden treasures of the Gulf Coast. The Mississippi portion (the park boundary extends to Florida) consists of four islands about 9 mi off the coast and a small enclave of bayous on the mainland. The shores are almost wholly undisturbed by development. Indeed, the two larger islands, Horn and Petit Bois, are federally designated wilderness areas. The surf pounds hard on the island beaches—unlike those on the mainland, where waves seldom exceed a foot or two—because the islands are separated from the mainland by the shallow Mississippi Sound.

Reaching the islands can be a challenge. Passenger ferries run from Gulfport to West Ship Island, but the other islands are accessible only by private boat. The islands can also be inhospitable. There are hordes of mosquitoes and biting "no-see-ums," and there is little or no shelter from storms or the relentless summer sun. Finally, there is always a chance of encountering sharks or alligators.

For privacy and natural solitude, however, the islands can't be beat. Except for sunny weekends in summer and fall, it's possible to walk half a day here without encountering another human being. You can share an afternoon swim with none but a family of curious porpoises. The sand is sugar white, dunes rise as high as 30 ft, and the water is clear with a blue-green tint. Wildlife—particularly bird life—is abundant.

The islands can be pleasant in any season, but the best time to visit is in spring and fall, when temperatures are generally moderate. Storms are common any time of year, but particularly during hurricane season, which lasts from August to November. With the exception of West Ship, visitors must pack their own food and water, and the only available lodging is primitive camping.

Information: **Gulf Islands National Seashore** | 3500 Park Rd., Ocean Springs 39564 | 228/875–9057.

Attractions

Davis Bayou Area. On the mainland near Ocean Springs, this part of the Gulf Islands National Seashore consists of 400 acres of salt marsh, bayous, and maritime forests. You can camp, fish, picnic, and hike scenic trails. You'll find a tent area, picnic shelters, a boat launch, and self-guided nature trails. There is no beach access. | Park Rd., off U.S. 90 | 228/875–9057 | Free | Daily.

The Gulf Shore Islands. West Ship is the only one of these beautiful islands accessible by passenger ferry. The others can be reached by charter or private boat.

East Ship Island was severed from West Ship Island when Hurricane Camille passed through in 1969. It is uninhabited and undeveloped, although there is a bathhouse; you can swim, fish, and camp.

Thirteen miles long and about ¾ mi at its widest point, **Horn Island** is the largest and probably the most scenic of the Gulf islands. It has natural beaches, tall sand dunes, subtropical forests, and inland lagoons. There are ranger stations on Horn Island (though these are not always manned), and primitive camping is allowed. Painter Walter Anderson of Ocean Springs once tied himself to a pine tree on the island in order to experience the full force of a hurricane.

Petit Bois Island, about 7 mi long, is the easternmost of the islands. It is the most remote and has the least vegetation—and the fewest visitors. Primitive camping is allowed.

West Ship Island has the only real facilities—some concessions and showers—and is the only island where most visitors simply come for a day on the beach. Its beach was ranked

GULF ISLANDS
NATIONAL
SEASHORE

INTRO
ATTRACTIONS
DINING
LODGING

KODAK'S TIPS FOR PHOTOGRAPHING WEATHER

Rainbows
· Find rainbows by facing away from the sun after a storm
· Use your auto-exposure mode
· With an SLR, use a polarizing filter to deepen colors

Fog and Mist
· Use bold shapes as focal points
· Add extra exposure manually or use exposure compensation
· Choose long lenses to heighten fog and mist effects

In the Rain
· Look for abstract designs in puddles and wet pavement
· Control rain-streaking with shutter speed
· Protect cameras with plastic bags or waterproof housings

Lightning
· Photograph from a safe location
· In daylight, expose for existing light
· At night, leave the shutter open during several flashes

From *Kodak Guide to Shooting Great Travel Pictures* © 2000 by Fodor's Travel Publications

among the nation's top ten by *USA Today*. Camping is not allowed. The Civil War–era Fort Massachusetts is on West Ship, and can be toured. It is an impressive brick structure that was used by the U.S. Navy as a base of operations for the coastal blockade during the Civil War.

Gulf Islands National Seashore Visitors Center. At Davis Bayou in Ocean Springs, the center offers exhibits, nature trails, campgrounds, ranger programs, showers, a boat launch, and picnic areas. The bayou and surrounding woodlands are one of the last unspoiled areas on the coast. | 3500 Park Rd., Ocean Springs | 228/875–9057 | Free | Daily 8:30–5.

Ship Island Ferry. You catch the ferry to West Ship here at the Gulfport Small Craft Harbor, which is at the end of Hwy. 49 S. Should you not have time for a stroll on the island, you can can take a turnaround cruise as well. | Hwy. 49 S, Gulfport | 228/864–1014 or 800/388–3290 | $16 round-trip | Departures Mar.–mid-May and Sept.–Oct., weekdays 9, weekends 9 and noon; mid-May–Aug., daily 9 and noon.

Transportation by charter. Boat charters are available at marinas in Biloxi, Gulfport, and Ocean Springs. This is the only way to reach East Ship, Horn, and Petit Bois Islands. Fees are usually about $50 each way. | Biloxi Visitors Center, 800/245–6943; Point Cadet Marina, 228/864–3797; Mississippi Gulf Coast Chamber of Commerce, 228/863–2933; Gulf Islands National Seashore Visitor Center, 228/875–9057.

ON THE CALENDAR

APR.: *Earth Day*. Exhibits fill the National Park Service's William M. Colmer Visitor Center in Ocean Springs one Saturday during the month. | 228/875–9057 | www.nps.gov/guis.

Lodging

Gulf Islands National Seashore Visitors Center. This campsite offers RV facilities for $18 per night. The site has showers, hookups, a dump station, and electricity. Three islands, which can be reached by boat charter, offer primitive camping. Be sure to bring about a gallon of water per person for every day you'll be camping. | 3500 Park Rd., Ocean Springs 39564 | 228/875–0821 or 228/875–9057 | www.nps.gov/guis | 51 campsites | $18 | MC, V.

GULFPORT

MAP 4, E8

(Nearby towns also listed: Biloxi, Gulf Islands National Seashore, Ocean Springs, Pascagoula, Pass Christian, Picayune, Wiggins)

As Mississippi's largest seaport, Gulfport is more working town than tourist resort. But as a coastal city—particularly one less than an hour from rowdy New Orleans— it's a place where people know how to enjoy life.

Gulfport is a fairly young city by Gulf Coast standards, since most of its early growth came during the railroad boom in the late 19th century. But owing to its location and massive investments, it quickly surpassed every other port between New Orleans and Mobile. It is still growing by leaps and bounds, thanks to increasing shipping, booming casino development, and frenzied construction in the I–10/U.S. 49 interchange area. Not surprisingly, there are growing pains: traffic in particular has become a problem. But once you reach Beach Boulevard (U.S. 90), you'll be treated to a panorama view of the Gulf of Mexico, And some of the most beautiful homes on the coast are concentrated along the city's eastern beaches.

There are also several nearby nature areas, including the Gulf Islands National Seashore, the De Soto National Forest, and scenic Wolf River.

Information: Mississippi Gulf Coast Convention and Visitors Bureau | 942 Beach Blvd., Gulfport 39502 | 228/896–6699 or 800/237–9493 | www.gulfcoast.org/mgccvb.

Attractions

Casinos. All casinos have free admission and are open 24 hours. **Copa Casino** | 39501 Copa Blvd. | 800/946–2672) offers separate activities for those under 21. **Grand Casino Gulfport** (3215 W. Beach Blvd. | 800/946–7777) is in the Oasis Resort and Spa.

CEC/Seabee Museum. This museum is dedicated to the U.S. Navy's Civilian Engineer Corps (CEC). You can learn the history of the CEC and the Seabees through exhibited photographs and documents. | 5200 2nd St. | 228/871–3164 | Free | Weekdays 9–5 and Sat. 9–3.

De Soto National Forest. The 500,487 acres of this national forest cover the southeast corner of the state, south from Laurel to the Gulf of Mexico, a few miles inland from Gulfport. The area includes Airey Lake, Big Biloxi Recreation Area, Big Foot Horse Trail, and the Tuxachanie National Recreation Trail. You can hunt, canoe, hike, and camp on the grounds. | 654 W. Frontage Rd., Wiggins | 601/928–4422 | Free | Daily.

Grass Lawn. This stately beachfront mansion was built in 1836 with wooden-peg construction and pine and cypress from nearby forests. The upper and lower galleries face the sea. | 720 E. Beach Blvd. | 228/868–5907 | Free | Weekdays 7:30–4:30.

Gulf Coast Winery. The winery offers guided tours and tastings. | 1306 29th Ave. | 228/863–0790 or 800/401–9463 | Free | Tasting hours daily 10–6.

Gulf Islands National Seashore. *See* Gulf Islands National Seashore, *above.*

John C. Stennis Space Center. (*See* Picayune.)

Port of Gulfport. More bananas pass though Gulfport than any other port in North America. It also does big business shipping cotton, seafood, and lumber. | 30th Ave. | 228/865–4300 | Free.

Small Craft Harbor. The Small Craft Harbor offers boat tours to West Ship Island. You can also charter boats. | U.S. 49 and U.S. 90 | 228/868–5173 or 228/864–1014. .

Marine Life Oceanarium. This aquarium features porpoise and sea lion shows, a giant reef tank, underwater dive shows, bird shows, and a narrated mini-train tour of the Gulfport Small Craft Harbor and docks. | Jones Memorial Park, at the Gulf Port Small Craft Harbor at the end of Hwy. 49 S | 228/863–0651 | $13.75 | Daily 9–4.

Mid-South Sailing and Charters. This company offers sailboat cruises at the Gulfport Small Craft Harbor | 228/863–6969 | $35 | Daily 10–5.

Wolf River Canoes, Inc. This outfitter rents canoes and provides shuttle services for trips on the scenic Wolf River. Full-day tours commence at 9 and 10 in the morning; half-day tours start at noon in winter, and at 2 in summer. | 21652 Tucker Rd. | 228/452–7666 | $33 per boat.

ON THE CALENDAR

MAR.: *Annual Gulf Coast Spring Pilgrimage.* This spring tour covers some of the coast's finer homes. | 228/863–0550.

JUNE: *Gem and Mineral Society Annual "Rock" Show.* Rockhounds gather in Gulfport to compare, trade, buy, and sell minerals and stones. | 228/863–6312.

JULY: *Mississippi Deep Sea Fishing Rodeo.* This July 4th weekend off-shore fishing competition began in 1948 as a way to promote Gulf Coast fishing. It offers cash prizes to the winners. | 228/388–2271.

OCT.: *Biloxi Highlands and Islands Scottish Games and Celtic Festival.* This festival honors the coast's Scottish and Irish heritage with games, food, and entertainment. | 228/392–0360.

Dining

Chappy's. Creole. This local favorite just outside Gulfport has an exterior made of cypress. It is surrounded by oak trees and has a view of the gulf. Chef Chappy prepares such spe-

cialities as Cajun-style redfish, barbecued shrimp, and flaming desserts like Bananas Foster. | 624 E. Beach Blvd., Long Beach | 228/865–9755 | fax 228/864–4061 | www.chappys.net | $9–$24 | AE, D, DC, MC, V.

Vrazel's. Continental. The restaurant is surrounded by attractive, landscaped grounds. Choose from red snapper, gulf trout, and shrimp cooked a dozen ways. Eggplant la rosa (baby shrimp and fresh crabmeat blended with eggplant, spices, and cheese in a casserole) is a top pick. | 3206 W. Beach Blvd. | 228/863–2229 | fax 228/863–2240 | www.gcww.com/vrazels | $15–$25 | AE, D, DC, MC, V | Closed Sun. No lunch Sat.

Lodging

Best Western Beach View Inn. This motel is across from the Grand Casino and the Copa Casino, two blocks from the Marine Life Oceanarium, and 2 mi southwest of downtown. | 150 rooms. Complimentary Continental breakfast. Cable TV. Pool. Laundry facilities. | 2922 W. Beach Blvd. | 228/864–4650 or 800/528–1234 | fax 228/863–6867 | www.bestwestern.com | $59–$99 | AE, D, DC, MC, V.

Gulfport Grand Casino. This complex covers two seven-story hotel buildings in the center of Gulfport's Casino Row on Beach Boulevard: the Gulfport Grand Casino, built in 1995, and the Oasis, built in 1999. The two have great views of the Gulf coast. The casino offers unlimited gaming activities and Las Vegas-style shows and live entertainment. | 600 rooms. 7 restaurants, 4 bars. In-room data ports, some refrigerators, cable TV. Indoor pool, wading pool. Beauty salon, hot tub. Exercise equipment. Children's programs (ages 1–12). Business services, airport shuttle. | 3215 W. Beach Blvd. | 228/870–7200 or 800/946–7777 | fax 228/870–7220 | www.grandcasinos.com | $69–$179 | AE, D, DC, MC, V.

Holiday Inn Beachfront. This complex of low-rise beachfront buildings was built in 1979. | 229 rooms. Restaurant, bar, room service. In-room data ports, cable TV. Pool, wading pool. Laundry facilities. | 1600 E. Beach Blvd. | 228/864–4310 or 800/465–4329 | fax 228/865–0525 | www.holiday-inn.com | $73–$129 | AE, D, DC, MC, V.

Red Creek. This three-story B&B was built in 1899 in a raised French cottage style, with a 64-ft front porch. The 11½-acre grounds are filled with fragrant magnolias and ancient live oak trees. There is also a vineyard and a racing stable (but no riding). Rooms are individually named and decorated in different period styles. Red Creek, 4 mi west of Gulfport, was the first B&B on the Gulf Coast. | 5 rooms. Complimentary Continental breakfast. No room phones, no smoking. Business services. | 7416 Red Creek Rd., Long Beach | 228/452–3080 or 800/729–9670 | www.redcreekinn.com | $65–$137 | No credit cards.

HATTIESBURG

MAP 4, E7

(Nearby towns also listed: Laurel, McComb, Mendenhall, Wiggins)

Hattiesburg isn't the sort of city most travelers expect to find in southern Mississippi. There isn't a cottonfield for miles around, there are no antebellum homes, and the local history is peaceful compared to some parts of the state. Perhaps because of this it seems oriented toward travelers looking for a quiet place to spend the night, grab a meal, or gas up the car. That said, the city does have its charms, not least of which is proximity to some of the best outdoor recreation sites in the state.

Hattiesburg was first and foremost a lumber town, located in an area known as the Piney Woods. What most visitors first notice is the forested setting—pines groves, magnolias, dogwoods, and azaleas that put on a flowery spectacle in spring. In the late 19th and early 20th century, the town benefitted from the wholesale harvesting of the area's virgin forests. That lumber boom brought railroads and then highways to what had been a remote place.

Today, city boosters brag that modern Hattiesburg is a "livable" city, with good schools, a thriving economy, and one of the largest historic districts in the region. The University of Southern Mississippi is home to a variety of cultural programs. Outdoor activities are abundant in the area, with scores of parks, hiking trails, scenic streams, and nature areas in the nearby De Soto National Forest.

Information: **Hattiesburg Convention and Visitors Bureau** | 1 Convention Center Plaza, Hattiesburg 39401 | 601/268–3220 or 800/638–6877.

Attractions

Ashe Lake. Around the lake, you can fish, camp, or follow nature trails. | 654 W. Frontage Rd., Wiggins | 601/928–4422 | Free | Daily.

Camp Shelby Armed Forces Museum. The museum contains artifacts and displays related to armed forces history, including the Civil War and Gulf War. | Building 350, S. Gate Rd. | 601/558–2757 | Free | Weekdays 9–4, Sat. noon–4.

International Checker Hall of Fame. This museum, 5 mi southwest of Hattiesburg, hosts international checkers tournaments and displays books, paintings, and trophies. | 220 Lynn Ray Rd., Petal | 601/582–7090 | Free | By appointment only.

Isaac Carter Cabin. This restored 1846 cabin, 5 mi southwest of Hattiesburg, displays photos of Isaac Carter, his family, and a Native American scout. Carter inherited much of the area's land during pioneer days. | 1701 Old Richton Rd., Petal | 601/268–3220 or 800/638–3249 | Free | By appointment only.

Paul B. Johnson State Park. Just outside the De Soto National Forest, this park offers camping, hiking trails, and other outdoor recreation. | 319 Greiger Lake Rd. | 601/582–7721 | $2 per vehicle | Daily 6AM–10PM.

University of Southern Mississippi Museum of Art. The museum has three galleries: the Lok Exhibition Gallery, Gallery II, and the C. W. Woods Art Gallery. This last contains notable bronzes by Richmond Barthe. The museum hosts shows by major modern artists and sponsors exhibitions from around the world. | Fine Arts Building, 2700 Hardy St. | 601/266–4491 or 601/266–4972 | www.arts.msu.edu/museum | Free | Tues.–Fri. 10–5, Sat. 10–4.

ON THE CALENDAR

MAY: *Hub City Triathlon.* The name of this grueling three-sport contest (a run, swim, and bike race) alludes to Hattiesburg's moniker, Hub City. | 601/268–5010.
OCT.: *Hubfest.* This festival features food and crafts throughout the downtown area, as well as tennis and golf tournaments, and a 5K run. | 601/268–3220 or 800/638–6877.
OCT.: *Living Legend Bluegrass Reunion.* This mountain music festival features veteran as well as younger musicians. | 601/268–3220 or 800/638–6877.

Dining

Chesterfield's. American. This is part of a popular Mississippi chain of restaurants. The decor is colorful. One of the most popular dishes here is the chicken 49er, chicken marinated in Italian seasonings and then grilled with Monterey Jack and mushrooms. | 2507 Hardy St. | 601/582–2778 | fax 601/544–0006 | $6–$18 | AE, D, DC, MC, V.

Crescent City Grill. Creole. This restaurant is known for its pasta margarita, a dish of seafood and bell peppers in a cream sauce over pasta, and for its fried eggplant with shrimp and crawfish served over rice. | 3810 Hardy St. | 601/264–0656 | fax 601/264–0128 | www.nsrg.com | $8–$16 | AE, D, MC, V.

Lodging

Baymont Inn & Suites. This four-story hotel opened in 1999 in the center of town. All rooms and suites have coffee makers, and guests may use a nearby fitness center. Complimentary breakfast. Some in-room data ports, some microwaves, some refrigerators, cable TV.

Pool. Pets allowed. | 123 Plaza Dr. | 601/264–8380 or 800/789–4103 | fax 601/264–6381 | www.baymontinns.com | 74 rooms, 12 suites | $65, $80–$110 suites | AE, D, DC, MC, V.

Cabot Lodge. This two-story lodge was built in the late 1980s. It's at the intersection of U.S. 49 and I–59, near shopping and dining, and 3 mi from the University of Southern Mississippi. | 160 rooms | 6541 U.S. 49 | 601/264–1881 or 800/225–9429 | fax 601/268–3226 | www.cabotlodge.com | $61–$74 | AE, D, DC, MC, V.

Comfort Inn. This pleasant two-story chain hotel built in the 1970s, is less than a mile from the University of Southern Mississippi. | 119 rooms. Restaurant, bar (with entertainment), complimentary breakfast, room service. Cable TV. Pool. Laundry facilities. Business services. Some pets allowed. | 6595 U.S. 49 | 601/268–2170 | fax 601/268–1820 | www.comfortinn.com | $55–$89 | AE, D, DC, MC, V.

Hampton Inn. You'll find simple, attractive rooms with comfortable beds in this two-story chain motel. It's near U.S. 49, minutes from the University of Southern Mississippi. | 155 rooms. Complimentary Continental breakfast, room service. In-room data ports, cable TV. Pool. Business services. | 4301 Hardy St. | 601/264–8080 or 800/426–7866 | fax 601/268–9916 | $59–$79 | AE, D, DC, MC, V.

Holiday Inn. Four two-story buildings with balconies make up this motel complex, on U.S. 49, 2 mi north of downtown. | 128 rooms. Restaurant, bar (with entertainment), room service. Some refrigerators, cable TV. Pool. Hot tub. Business services. | 6563 U.S. 49 | 601/268–2850 or 800/465–4329 | fax 601/268–2823 | www.holiday-inn.com | $67–$89 | AE, D, DC, MC, V.

HOLLY SPRINGS

MAP 4, E2

(Nearby towns also listed: Corinth, Memphis, TN, Oxford, Robinsonville, Sardis)

Holly Springs lies just west of the sprawling Holly Springs National Forest, and 30 minutes south (though a world apart) from metropolitan Memphis. Holly Springs retains the look and feel of a town of the old South, even though it changed hands more than 50 times during the Civil War. According to local lore, Holly Springs remained intact only because Union General Grierson disobeyed Grant's order to burn it. The best time to see the many lovely antebellum homes is during the spring Pilgrimage, when they are open to the public. Walking and driving tours are available year-round.

Holly Springs, halfway between Elvis Presley's birthplace in Tupelo and his home in Memphis, offers one of the most unusual stops on the unofficial Elvis tour. Graceland Too is an archives of Elvis memorabilia collected by a father and son over the course of four decades.

Information: Holly Springs Chamber of Commerce | 154 S. Memphis St., Holly Springs 38635 | 662/252–2943.

Attractions

Hill Crest Cemetery. This is the final resting place of 13 Confederate generals. It is known for its elaborate iron fence and for the statues of six nuns who died while tending to Yellow Fever victims in the early 19th century. | Elder Ave. at Center St. | 662/252–2943 | Free.

Holly Springs Historic Path System. This self-guided walking and driving tour takes in 90 historic homes, churches, and other buildings in town, and to the south. | Hwy. 215, near Abbeville | 662/252–2943.

Holly Springs National Forest. You can camp, picnic, hunt, and fish in the 15,000 acres of this forest immediately east of the city at the intersection of Hwy. 4 and Hwy. 7. | 662/236–6550 | www.gorp.com | Free.

Kate Freeman Clark Art Gallery. This gallery is dedicated to a Mississippi artist who painted more than 1,000 works and refused to sell a single one. | 300 College Ave. | 662/252–4211 or 662/252–2511 | Free | By appointment only.

Marshall County Historical Museum. The museum has a collection of Native American artifacts and personal mementos and relics from the period of the War of 1812 to the Korean War. | 220 E. College Ave. | 662/252–4074 | Free | Jan.–mid-Dec., weekdays 10–5.

Montrose. This 1858 Greek Revival mansion is home to the Holly Springs Garden Club. There are period antiques displayed in every room. | Salem Ave. | 662/252–2045 | $5 | By appointment only.

Rust University. This university was established in 1866 for the education of freed slaves. | 150 E. Rust Ave. | 662/252–6107 | By appointment only.

Wall Doxey State Park. At this park between Holly Springs and Oxford, you can camp, stay in cabins, use the boat ramp, fish, and swim. | Hwy. 7 S | 662/252–4231 | $2 per vehicle | Daily 6AM–10PM.

ON THE CALENDAR

APR.: *Holly Springs Pilgrimage.* As many as seven homes open their doors to visitors during this event, which includes the crowning of a pilgrimage queen. | 109 E. Gholson Ave. | 662/252–2943.

MAY: *White Oaks Classic Walking Horse Show.* This interesting horse show features the Tennessee Walkers, a group named for the distinct gait of the horses. | 662/838–2796.

JULY: *Kudzu Festival.* This festival, named after the smothering vine that grows abundantly in the southeast, features a barbecue contest, arts and crafts show, and entertainment. | 662/252–2943.

Dining

City Café. American. This popular eatery in the town square serves breakfast and lunch specials with three side orders. Choices include homemade soups, roast beef, and fried chicken livers. | 135 E. Van Dorn Ave. | 662/252–9895 | $4–$5 | No credit cards | Closed Sun. No dinner.

Lodging

Heritage Inn. Rooms at this motel have either a king-size or two double beds, and home-style southern cooking fills the restaurant's lunch buffet. The motel is less than 1 mi south of town on U.S. 78 where it meets Hwys. 7 and 4. Restaurant, bar. In-room data ports, cable TV. Outdoor pool. Pets allowed. | 120 Heritage Dr. | 662/252–1120 | 48 rooms | $45–$50 | AE, D, DC, MC, V.

INDIANOLA

MAP 4, C4

(Nearby towns also listed: Belzoni, Cleveland, Greenville, Greenwood, Yazoo City)

Indianola is best known as the birthplace of blues great B. B. King. He began his career playing in juke joints here, and he returns each year for an open-air show hosted by Club Ebony, a blues legend in its own right. The city is also the birthplace of celebrated chef and food critic Craig Claiborne, who credited his mother's kitchen with launching his career. Although Claiborne wrote in his autobiography that his mother never served catfish because she considered it too common, the fish farms of Indianola have made it a major catfish-producing center and home of the largest catfish-processing plant in the world.

Information: **Indianola Chamber of Commerce** | 315 Main St., Indianola 38751 | 662/887–4454.

Attractions
Indianola Pecan House. The Pecan House taps the local orchards and offers fresh pecans, gift packs, and a gourmet food line. They ship nationwide. | 1013 U.S. 82, Indianola | 662/887–5420 | Free | Mon.–Sat. 8–5.

ON THE CALENDAR
MAY: *Indian Bayou Festival and B. B. King Homecoming.* This is the major event in Indianola, with King himself topping the roster of blues acts. | 662/887–4454.

Dining
The Crown Restaurant. Eclectic. European cuisine with a southern twist has been a tradition at this restaurant since 1976. Its known for a dish called catfish Allison, a poached fillet grilled with a parmesan, green onion, and butter sauce. The antique tables and chairs are for sale, along with other antiques and packaged food goods like catfish pâté and Mississippi mousse, in the attached shop. | 110 Front St. | 662/887–4522 or 800/833–7731 | fax 662/887–4522 | $5–$9 | AE, D, MC, V | Closed Sun.–Mon. No dinner.

Lodging
Holiday Inn Express. Local residents often put up visiting friends at this new motel, less than 1 mi west of town. In-room data ports, cable TV. Pool. | 601 U.S. 82 | 662/887–7477 or 800/465–4329 | fax 662/887–2032 | www.holiday-inn.com | 58 rooms | $64 | AE, D, DC, MC, V.

IUKA

MAP 4, F2

(Nearby towns also listed: Corinth, Natchez Trace Parkway, Tupelo)

Iuka is in the northeast corner of the state, where Mississippi, Alabama, and Tennessee meet in the foothills of the Appalachians.

The main reason to visit this relatively remote corner of the state is the scenic countryside, particularly in spring, when dogwoods, redbuds, and wild azaleas are in bloom, and in fall, when its hardwood forests put on spectacular foliage shows. Not far away is Pickwick Lake, Tishomingo State Park, and the Tennessee-Tombigbee Waterway, a series of lakes and canals stretching from the Tennessee River to the port of Mobile, Alabama. Iuka makes a good starting point for tours of the region.

Information: **Tishomingo County Tourism Council** | 203 E. Quitman St., Iuka 38852 | 601/432–0051 or 800/386–4373.

Attractions
J. P. Coleman State Park. Coleman State Park, on Pickwick Lake, offers a boat launch, cabins, camping, fishing, swimming, and other outdoor recreation opportunities. | 613 Hwy. 321 | 662/423–6515 | $2 per vehicle | Daily 6AM–10PM.

Old Tishomingo County Courthouse. The courthouse, built circa 1870, houses a museum that focuses on the area's history. | Quitman St. | 601/432–0051 or 800/386–4373.

Tishomingo State Park. This park 15 mi south of Iuka is known for its steep ravines and waterfalls. It offers rustic cabins, hiking trails, camping, and canoeing along Bear Creek. | Hwy. 25 and Natchez Trace Parkway, Tishomingo | 662/438–6914 | $2 per vehicle | Daily 6AM–10PM.

OCT. OR NOV.: *Fall Foliage Cruise.* The Tishomingo County Tourism Council sponsors cruises of the Tennessee River for one weekend in late October or early November. Boats board at J. P. Coleman State Park, and you will see foliage in Mississippi, Alabama, and Tennessee. An all-day dinner cruise is available. | 800/FUN–HERE | www.tishomingo.org.

Dining

Country Squire. Southern. Opened by the Norman family in 1975, is the oldest family restaurant in the county. It's known for hushpuppies, fried catfish, and rib-eye steaks prepared over an open charcoal pit. | Old Hwy. 72 W | 662/423–9984 | $7–$16 | AE, D, MC, V | Closed Mon. No lunch.

Lodging

Victorian Inn. This two-story motel 2 mi east of town is a collection of blue Victorian buildings with outdoor corridors that look like balconies. Complimentary Continental breakfast. In-room data ports, some microwaves, some refrigerators, some in-room hot tubs, cable TV, in-room VCRs. Pool. | 199 Hwy. 180 | 662/423–9221 or 800/839–1662 | fax 662/423–9221 | 46 rooms, 14 suites | 45–$63 | AE, D, DC, MC, V.

JACKSON

MAP 4, C5

JACKSON

INTRO
ATTRACTIONS
DINING
LODGING

(Nearby towns also listed: Canton, Mendenhall, Natchez Trace Parkway, Vicksburg, Yazoo City)

Mississippians once joked that the state's three largest cities were Memphis, Mobile, and New Orleans, but since the 1940s Jackson has grown from a small government town to a metropolis with a population of 400,000. The Jackson metro area represents the state's greatest concentration of wealth, and construction is booming in surrounding suburbs.

There are a surprisingly large number of cultural attractions for a city this size, ranging from Civil War reenactments to the International Ballet Competition (Jackson is the only U.S. city to host this event). In addition to the expected Confederate shrines, there are African-American and Jewish historic sites and a wide array of high-quality museums and stores, restaurants and bars. The city also has one of the state's most beautiful parks, LeFleur's Bluff. Although Jackson is a friendly town, you should be aware that Jackson ranks high nationally in crime statistics.

Originally named LeFleur's Bluff after a French trading post on the Pearl River, Jackson was incorporated as the capital in 1821; it was burned several times during the Civil War (local residents called it "Chimneyville" because of the many chimneys left standing), and most of the surviving antebellum homes were torn down in the 1960s. Noteworthy architectural survivors include the Governor's Mansion, City Hall, the Old Capitol and two pre–Civil War tour homes. There are also several fine examples of 20th-century architecture and some exceptionally pretty residential areas. Among the historic sites are several from the Civil Rights era, when Jackson was at the vanguard of divisive social change.

Jackson has its requisite commercial strips, the most popular being County Line Road on the northern rim. Downtown is pretty much given over to banking, law offices, and government, and they roll the sidewalks up at night. Entertainment venues are scattered throughout the city, from basement blues clubs to country-and-western bars and everything in between. The Ross Barnett Reservoir, northeast of Jackson, is the city's playground, with fishing, sailing, and water-skiing the most popular activities. There are also a higher-than-average number of golf courses in the surrounding area. The city's economy is driven by government, health care, retail sales, technology development, distribution services, and a scattering of manufacturing industries.

Jackson has long had a reputation as a racially polarized town; the image is somewhat dated now, since the city's restaurants, schools, businesses, and many of its neighborhoods are thoroughly integrated.

Information: **Metro Jackson Convention and Visitors Bureau** | 921 N. President St., Jackson 39202 | 601/960–1891 or 800/354–7695 | www.visitjackson.com. **Jackson Tourist Information Center (Agriculture and Forestry Museum)** | 1150 Lakeland Dr., Jackson 39216 | 601/354–6113.

TRANSPORTATION INFORMATION

Airports: Jackson International Airport. East of the city off I–20, this airport (actually "international" only for cargo flights) is served by American, Continental Express, Delta, Northwest Airlines, Southwest Airlines, and US Airways. | 601/939–5631.

Airport Transportation: There is no public transportation to the airport, but taxis, rental cars, and hotel shuttles are available. | 601/939–5631.

Amtrak: The Amtrak rail depot | 300 W. Capitol St. | 601/355–6350. offers passenger service to New Orleans, Chicago, and points between.

Bus Lines: Greyhound buses arrive at and depart from | 201 S. Jefferson St. | 601/353–6342.

Driving around Town: The major interstates that lead into Jackson include I–20, which leads to Atlanta, Dallas, and points beyond; I–55, leading to New Orleans, Memphis, and beyond; and U.S. 49, which runs from the Gulf Coast to Arkansas and beyond. Most downtown attractions are within walking distance of each other, so you can usually park your car and leave it. There is metered parking and many garages, so you'll pay less than 50 cents an hour. Some attractions have lots where you can park at no charge, and you may also be able to find free parking on the street. When you do drive, it's worth remembering that most downtown streets are one-way. Rush hour runs between the hours of 7:30 and 8:30 in the morning and 4:30 to 5:30 in the evening; delays are usually no more than ten minutes.

Intra-city Transit: JATRAN in-city buses run until 7 PM. | 601/948–3840.

Attractions

ART AND ARCHITECTURE

The Oaks House Museum. Also known as the Boyd House, this 1840s Greek Revival cottage with period furnishings is the oldest house in Jackson. It was built by three-term mayor James Hervey Boyd. | 823 N. Jefferson St. | 601/353–9339 | $3 | Tues.–Sat. 10–3.

Governor's Mansion. The official residence of the first family since 1842, it is the second-oldest continuously occupied governor's residence in the U.S. General Sherman used it as headquarters in 1863. It is a National Historic Landmark. | 300 E. Capitol St. | 601/359–6421 | fax 601/359–6473 | Free | Tours Tues.–Fri. 9:30–11.

Jackson City Hall. This stately Greek Revival structure was built in 1847. During the Civil War, it was used as a hospital by both Union and Confederate armies. Renovations, including a formal garden plaza with a statue of Andrew Jackson, were made in the 1960s. | 219 S. President St. | 601/960–1084 | Free | Weekdays 8–5.

New Capitol. Built in 1903, the New Capitol was modeled after the nation's capitol building. It recently underwent a three-year restoration. There are six daily tours, and you can attend sessions of the legislature. | 400 High St. | 601/359–3114 | Free | Weekdays 8–5.

Manship House. The 1857 Gothic Revival house is known as the home of Jackson's Civil War–era mayor Charles Henry Manship, who surrendered the town to Gen. Sherman in 1863.

He was also a decorative painter and grainer, and his work is one of the highlights of the house. It has been restored to its mid-19th century state. | 420 E. Fortification St. | 601/961–4724 | fax 601/354–6043 | Free | Tues.–Fri. 9–4, Sat. 10–4.

BEACHES, PARKS, AND NATURAL SITES

Coal Bluff Park. You can swim, fish, and camp at this park on the scenic Pearl River. It is 35 mi northeast of Jackson. | 1319 Coal Bluff Rd., Lena | 601/654–7726 | Free.

LeFleur's Bluff State Park. LeFleur's Bluff State Park embraces both the scenic cypress swamps of Mayes Lake and the adjacent river bluffs. There is also a public golf course, swimming pool, tennis, nature trail, boat rentals, and camping, fishing, and picnic areas. | 2140 Riverside Dr. | 601/987–3923 or 601–987–3985 | $2 per vehicle | Daily 6AM–10PM.

Mississippi Petrified Forest. The petrified forest 20 mi north of Jackson off I–55 contains the fossilized remains of ancient trees. You can see them along a short nature trail and in a museum. There are also displays of mining techniques and local wildlife, a picnic area, and a campground. | Forest Park Rd., Flora | 601/879–8189 | www.mspetrifiedforest.com | Trail $5 | Daily 9–5. .

Mynelle Gardens. This "botanical wonderland" was the work of Jackson native Mynelle Westbrook Hayward, renowned in the 1920s and 1930s for gardening and flower arranging. It's also a wildlife sanctuary and songbird haven, popular for meetings, picnics, and photography. | 4736 Clinton Blvd. | 601/960–1894 | www.instar.com/mynelle | $2 | Mar.–Oct., daily 9–5; Nov.–Feb., Mon.–Sat. 8–4:15, Sun. noon–4:15.

Ross R. Barnett Reservoir. At this 33,000-acre lake, you can rent boats, water-ski, and fish for bass. There are restaurants here as well. The reservoir is about 8 mi north of Jackson off the Natchez Trace Parkway, at exit 103. | 115 Madison Landing Cir., Ridgeland | 601/354–3448 | Free.

CULTURE, EDUCATION, AND HISTORY

Farish Street Historical District. The district covers 125 acres, with 700 elements listed in the National Register of Historic Places. Once the commercial and residential center of the city's black community, it contains examples of many styles of Southern architecture, including antebellum, bungalow, Creole, Queen Anne, and shotgun cottages. The district runs from Amite to Fortification streets and Mill to Lamar streets. | 601/960–1891 or 800/354–7695 | www.farishstreet.com.

Greenwood Cemetery. Six of the Confederacy's brigadier generals, more than 100 Confederate soldiers, and several of the city's leaders are buried here. A walking tour of the cemetery is available. | Lamar Ave. and West St. | 601/960–1891 or 800/354–7695 | Free | Tours only.

Jackson State University. This small but respected state school traces its origins to a church school founded in 1877. Campus highlights include the Art Gallery and the F. D. Hall Music Center. | 1400 Lynch St. | 601/968–2272 or 601/968–2040 (art gallery) | www.jsums.edu | Free | Museum weekdays 8–5.

MUSEUMS

Chimneyville Crafts Gallery. This gallery at the Mississippi Agriculture and Forestry Museum is the primary sales center for local artists and members of the Craftsmen's Guild of Mississippi. The shop's unique merchandise includes traditional and contemporary works. On Saturdays in warmer months, members of the guild offer craft demonstrations. | 1150 Lakeland Dr. | 602/981–2499 | Free | Memorial Day–Labor Day, Mon.–Sat. 9–5, Sun. 1–5; Labor Day–Memorial Day, Mon.–Sat. 9–5. .

Margaret Walker Alexander National African-American Research Center. This gallery on the Jackson State University campus focuses on life during the period of segregation and the Civil Rights era. Topics include education, business, rural life, churches, and music at which African-Americans have excelled. Dr. Margaret Walker Alexander established and

directed the institute that now bears her name. (The center will eventually be moved to Ayer Hall.) | 1400 Lynch St. | 601/968–2040 | Free | Weekdays 8–5.

Mississippi Agriculture and Forestry Museum. Mississippi's two most important industries, farming and lumbering, are the focus of this 40,000-square-ft center. Two restorations of life in the 1920s, the Fortenberry-Parkman Farm and the crossroads town, are among the highlights. There are 90-minute tours. | 1150 Lakeland Dr. | 601/354–6113 or 800/844–8687 | $4 | Memorial Day–Labor Day, Mon.–Sat. 9–5, Sun. 1–5; Labor Day–Memorial Day, Mon.–Sat. 9–5.

Mississippi Museum of Art. This museum established in 1978 houses a permanent collection of more than 5,000 works. Highlights include works by Picasso, Georgia O'Keeffe, Japanese prints, 19th- and 20th-century American landscape paintings, and a number of Mississippi and other Southern artists. | 201 E. Pascagoula St. | 601/960–1515 | fax 601/960–1505 | www.msmuseumart.org | $5 | Mon.–Sat. 10–5, Sun. noon–5.

Mississippi Museum of Natural Science. This newly expanded museum has been relocated to a spot on the banks of the Pearl River in LeFleur Bluff State Park. It includes exhibits, dioramas, and aquariums depicting the ecological history of the state. The aquarium system represents state aquatic habitats, with specimens of 200 species of native fishes, reptiles, and amphibians. There is a huge greenhouse called "The Swamp," outdoor walking trails, an auditorium, a library, and a gift shop. | 2148 Riverside Dr. | 601/354–7303 | $4 | Weekdays 8–5, Sat. 9–5, Sun. 1–5.

Mississippi Music Hall of Fame. Many native-born Mississippi musicians are honored here, including Leontyne Price, Elvis Presley, Jimmie Rodgers, Jimmy Buffett, B. B. King, and Tammy Wynette. | 1150 Lakeland Dr. | 601/354–6113 or 800/844–8687 | fax 601/982–4292 | www.msmusic.org | $4 | Memorial Day–Labor Day, Mon.–Sat. 9–5, Sun. 1–5; Labor Day–Memorial Day, Mon.–Sat. 9–5.

Mississippi Sports Hall of Fame and Museum. The Sports Hall of Fame lets you play with interactive golf, soccer, football, and baseball exhibits. Local athletes profiled include Dizzy Dean, Archie Manning, and Walter Payton. | 1152 Lakeland Dr. | 601/982–8264 or 800/280–FAME | fax 601/982–4702 | www.msfame.com | $5 | Mon.–Sat. 10–4.

Municipal Art Gallery. This gallery dedicated to local artists is housed in one of the oldest antebellum homes in Jackson. The gallery launches a new show with a public reception the first Sunday of each month. | 839 N. State St. | 601/960–1582 | Free | Tues.–Sat. 9–5, Sun. 2–5.

Museum of the Southern Jewish Experience. This museum 25 mi south of Jackson exhibits religious artifacts, and photographs of the rural South by Bill Arron. | 3863 Old Morrison Rd., Utica | 601/362–6357 (Sept.–May) and 601/885–6042 (June–Aug.) | www.msje.org | $5 | By appointment only.

Old Capitol State Historical Museum. Built around 1833, this structure served as the state capitol from 1839 to 1903. Its simple columns and elegant proportions make it a notable example of Greek Revival architecture. In 1959 it was restored to house the State Historical Museum. Exhibits include the Vandorn Map, which is a blueprint of the city's original layout, and excellent displays on civil rights. | 100 N. State St. | 601/359–6920 | Free | Daily 9–5.

Archives and History Building. Government records, private documents, photographs, maps, and Mississippiana are available to the public in the Search Room of the Mississippi Department of Archives and History. | 100 N. State St. | 601/359–6876 | Free | By appointment only.

Smith-Robertson Museum and Cultural Center. One of the finest African-American museums in the nation, the Smith-Robertson focuses on the story of black Mississippians from the first importation of slaves in 1719 through the Civil Rights era. It is housed in what was once Jackson's first public school for African-American children, in the heart of the historic Black community. | 528 Bloom St. | 601/960–1457 | fax 601/960–2070 | $1 | Weekdays 9–5, Sat. 9–noon, Sun. 2–5.

RELIGION AND SPIRITUALITY
Old Mt. Helm Baptist Church. This church, which is part of the Farish Street Historical District, has long been a religious center for the city's black community. | 300 Church St. | 601/353–3981 | Free | Daily 9:30–5.

OTHER POINTS OF INTEREST
Russell C. Davis Planetarium. You can watch daily laser light shows in a domed theater at the planetarium. | 201 E. Pascagoula St. | 601/960–1550 | $5 | Daily.

Jackson Zoological Park. This 1919 zoo has added a Discovery Zoo for children. | 2918 W. Capitol St. | 601/352–2580 | $4 | Jun.–Aug., daily 9–6; Sept.–May, daily 9–5.

ON THE CALENDAR
JAN., FEB.: *Dixie National Livestock Show and Rodeo.* You can watch a variety of equestrian events and animal contests at this show at the Mississippi State Fairgrounds. | 601/961–4000.

MAR., OCT.: *Bagwell Antique Show and Sale.* This show, held twice a year at the Mississippi State Fairgrounds, gathers about 75 dealers. | 662/844–3095.

MAR.: *Chevy Eastern National Cutting Horse Show.* This equestrian event at the Mississippi State Fairgrounds Expo Center showcases the skills of horses and riders. | 601/961–4000.

MAR.: *Mal's St. Paddy's Day Parade.* The city rolls out the green carpet for this downtown party and parade, which features food and music. | 601/355–7685.

MAY.: *Trustmark Tour Le Fleur.* This U.S. Cycling Federation–sanctioned Olympic trial bicycle race features professional and amateur cyclists in seven events. | 601/984–5273.

APR.: *Zoo Blues.* Hear live blues music at this festival at the Jackson Zoo. | 601/352–2582.

MAY: *Jubilee! Jam.* You can eat, drink, and hear live music at this downtown festival. | 601/960–2008.

JUNE: *Hog Wild.* This is an annual barbecue contest held at the Agriculture and Forestry Museum. | 1150 Lakeland Dr. | 601/354–6113.

JULY: *Deposit Guaranty Golf Classic.* This PGA golf tournament draws professional players to the Annandale Golf Course. | 601/856–0886.

AUG.: *Mississippi Wildlife Extravaganza.* The largest wildlife equipment show in the state features exhibits and seminars at the Trade Mart Building in the Mississippi State Fairgrounds. | 601/420–2100.

SEPT.: *Farish Street Festival.* This event commemorates the city's African-American heritage with food and entertainment in the downtown Farish Street Historical District. | 601/960–2384.

OCT.: *Mississippi State Fair.* This is the biggest fair in the state. It features a midway lined with rides, concessions, and exhibits at the Mississippi State Fairgrounds. | 601/961–4000.

NOV.: *Mistletoe Marketplace.* Christmas decorations and a broad range of gifts are on sale at this pre-holiday at the Trade Mart Building at the Mississippi State Fairgrounds. | 601/948–2357.

DEC.: *Christmas at the Old Capitol.* A giant Christmas tree with period decorations is the centerpiece for holiday festivities at the Old Capitol historic site. | 601/359–6920.

DEC.: *The Singing Christmas Tree.* The Belhaven College Choir stands atop a Christmas tree–shaped scaffold and sing carols at the Belhaven College soccer field on Peach Street. | 601/968–8707.

Dining

INEXPENSIVE

Broad Street Baking Co. & Café. You can enjoy breakfast, lunch, or dinner here, where some dozen different breads are baked fresh daily using European and old family recipes. Specialties include pizzas, sandwiches, pastries, and croissants. | 101 Banner Hall, I–55 at Northside Dr. | 601/362–2900 | $6–$8 | MC, V | Closed Sun. at 3.

Ding How. Chinese. The finest Chinese buffet in the area offers plenty of hot, well prepared items. It's in a mid-size building, with traditional Chinese decoration. The staff is friendly. It's known for its duck and the buffet and salad bar. | 5350 I–55 N | 601/956–1717 | $6–$16 | AE, DC, MC, V.

Palette. Eclectic. This restaurant in a gallery of the Mississippi Museum of Art is one of the most pleasing lunch spots in the state: the space is large and light, there's art on the walls, and the food on the changing menu is carefully prepared and beautifully presented. If it's offered, try the wine country pie: layers of meats, cheeses, and vegetables in a flaky crust. | 201 E. Pascagoula St. | 601/960–1515 | $6–$16 | AE, D, MC, V | No dinner. Closed weekends.

MODERATE

★ **Bravo!.** Italian. Rated Jackson's 1999 Restaurant of the Year by the Metro Jackson Convention and Visitors Bureau, this restaurant has also received the *Wine Spectator* award of excellence. Specialties are traditional Italian dishes, such as wood-fired pizza, zesty pastas, and grilled meats topped with imaginative sauces. It's also known for grills, homemade breads, and desserts. | 244 Highland Village | 601/982–8111 | fax 601/981–1463 | www.bravobuzz.com | $8–$22 | AE, D, DC, MC, V | No lunch Sat.

Cock of the Walk. Seafood. This casual restaurant offers nightly live music, a dance floor, and a fully stocked bar. The specialty of the house is Mississippi pond-raised catfish. | 141 Madison Landing Cir., Ross Barnett Reservoir, Ridgeland | 601/856–5500 | www.cockofthewalk.com | $18–$27 | AE, D, MC, V.

Copeland's. Cajun/Creole. This new restaurant, part of a Louisiana-based chain, is in north Jackson, but you can detect the spicy aroma of the Cajun cooking from a mile away. Try the traditional, rich gumbo. It's also known for steaks and seafood. | 6390 Ridgewood Rd. | 601/899–0100 | $10–$19 | AE, D, DC, MC, V.

Dennery's. Seafood. The circular dining room of this eatery is decorated with Greek style columns and a fountain in the center. Try the charbroiled chicken with scallops over pasta or the Snapper Anna, a broiled filet of snapper served with hollandaise sauce. | 330 Greymont Ave. | 601/354–2527 | $11–$18 | AE, D, DC, MC, V | Closed Sun. No lunch Sat.

Fernando's. Mexican. Fernando's serves a variety of sizzling Mexican dishes. Even though lunchtime tends to be very busy, service is prompt. Try the fajitas with rice. | 880 Lake Harbour Dr., Ridgeland | 601/957–1882 | $9–$16 | AE, DC, MC, V.

EXPENSIVE

Bonsai Japanese Steakhouse. Japanese. Come here for the total Japanese steakhouse experience, with chefs who prepare Teppanyaki meals at your table with much style. The steaks and seafood are great. | 1925 Lakeland Dr. | 601/981–0606 | $15–$28 | AE, D, DC, MC, V | Closed Sun. No lunch Fri.–Sat.

Poets. Continental. Tiffany-style lamps and tin ceilings lend a European flair to this restaurant, where you can also dine outdoors in a courtyard patio. It's known for scrumptious seafood: try the scampi or the redfish Kathryn. The wine list is extensive and there's entertainment every night except Monday, with live bands and dancing. | 1855 Lakeland Dr. | 601/982–9711 | $9–$25 | AE, D, DC, MC, V | No lunch. Closed Sun.

Primos Restaurant. Continental. This north Jackson restaurant with country French decor features an array of excellent homestyle dishes and a fine wine list. Try the tender steaks or the interesting salads. There's live piano music on weekend evenings. There's also a separate deli, and a Kid's menu. | 4330 N. State St. | 601/982–2064 | www.primos-northgate.com | $8–$19 | AE, MC, V | Closed Sun.

Schimmel's. Schimmel's specializes in prime meat and fresh Gulf seafood. Signature dishes include the veal chop, breadless crab cake, fried lobster tails, and the Asiago-crusted flounder, which nestles tender flounder under a layer of Italian cheese. | 2615 N. State St. | 609/981–7077 | $16–$27 | AE, MC, V | Closed Sun.

Tico's Steakhouse. Steaks. A fireplace at this restaurant lends a cozy touch. Try the Maine lobster or one of a number of sizzling steaks. The restaurant is near Ridgeland's Northpark Mall. | 1536 E. County Line Rd., Ridgeland | 601/956–1030 | $16–$26 | AE, D, DC, MC, V | Closed Sun. No lunch.

VERY EXPENSIVE

Huntington's Grille. Continental. This new hot spot, beside the Hilton Jackson Convention Center, has an eclectic menu of wild game, steaks, fresh seafood, as well as extensive wine list. | 1001 E. Countyline Rd. | 601/957–1515 | $25–$40 | AE, D, DC, MC, V | No lunch Sat. Closed Sun.

Nick's. Continental. One of Jackson's best restaurants offers casually elegant dining with exquisite cuisine and excellent service. Try the grilled blackfish with crabmeat at lunch, and at dinner, don't miss the white-chocolate mousse with raspberry sauce dessert. It's expensive, but worth it. Known for seafood, beef, veal. Kid's menu. Extensive wine list. | 1501 Lakeland Dr. | 601/981–8017 | fax 601/982–9640 | $16–$25 | AE, D, DC, MC, V | No lunch Sat. Closed Sun.

Lodging

MODERATE

Best Western Metro. This motel, 3 mi west of town, has a heated pool and hot tub in the center of an atrium. A 24-hour restaurant is next door. Complimentary Continental breakfast. In-room data ports, cable TV. Pool. Hot tub. | 1520 Ellis Ave. | 601/355–7483 or 800/528–1234 | fax 601/353–8869 | www.bestwestern.com | 133 rooms | $59 | AE, D, DC, MC, V.

Cabot Lodge Millsaps. This six-story hotel is convenient to Millsaps and Belhaven colleges, and 1 mi from the capitol. Built in the 1970s, it has a minimalist-modern exterior with rustic decor inside. A spacious lobby features a large stone fireplace and antler chandeliers. | 205 rooms. Bar, complimentary Continental breakfast. In-room data ports, cable TV. Pool. Laundry facilities. Business services. | 2375 N. State St. | 601/948–8650 or 800/874–4737 | fax 601/948–8650 | www.cabotlodge.com | $49–$88 | AE, D, DC, MC, V.

Econo Lodge. Near Jackson State University, a mall, and major restaurants, this is a good budget choice. It's 4 mi southwest of the capitol. | 40 rooms. Complimentary Continental breakfast. Cable TV. Laundry services. Business services. | 2450 U.S. 80 | 601/353–0340 or 800/553–2666 | fax 601/353–0340 | www.econolodge.com | $45–$89 | AE, D, DC, MC, V.

Edison Walthall. Marble floors, gleaming brass, and paneled rooms make this largely new building look like a 19th-century restoration. In the heart of busy Capitol Street, it's well-appointed, with good service and a good restaurant. Rooms are on the small side, but are decorated with mahogany furniture. Nearby are historic sites and cultural and performance centers. | 165 rooms, 23 suites. Restaurant, bar (with entertainment). In-room data ports, some refrigerators, some microwaves, cable TV. Pool. Hot tub. Exercise equipment. Business services, airport shuttle. | 225 E. Capitol St. | 601/948–6161 or 800/932–6161 | fax 601/948–0088 | www.edisonwalthallhotel.com | $70–$89, $100–$195 suites | AE, D, DC, MC, V.

La Quinta North. The white and teal exterior is characteristic of the attractive motels in this chain. The motel is just east of Hwy. 51, 10 minutes from downtown and 20 minutes from the airport. | 145 rooms. Complimentary Continental breakfast. In-room data ports, cable TV. Pool. Laundry services. Business services. Some pets allowed. | 616 Briarwood Dr. | 601/957–1741 or 800/687–6667 | fax 601/956–5764 | www.laquinta.com | $54–$79 | AE, D, MC, V.

Hampton Inn & Suites. This four-story hotel is 13 mi from the Jackson International Airport, 1 mi from the capitol, and 2 mi from Millsaps College. Complimentary Continental breakfast. In-room data ports, some kitchenettes, cable TV, in-room VCRs. Pool. Exercise equipment. Laundry facilities. | 320 Greymont Ave. | 601/352–1700 or 800/426–7866 | fax 601/362–9988 | www.hamptoninn.com | 111 rooms | $72 | AE, D, DC, MC, V.

Holiday Inn Express. This five-story motel is five minutes from downtown and convenient to the fairgrounds. Rooms are basic, with basic amenities. Kid's suites are available. | 87 rooms, 12 suites. Complimentary Continental breakfast. In-room data ports, refrigerators, cable TV. Exercise equipment. Business services. | 310 Greymont Ave. | 601/948–4466 or 800/333–9457 | fax 601/352–9368 | www.holiday-inn.com | $65–$75, $85–$99 suites | AE, D, DC, MC, V.

Poindexter Park Inn Bed & Breakfast. This inn in one of Jackson's oldest neighborhoods, was the property of Mississippi's second goovernor, George Poindexter. The home, built around 1907, has received the Heritage Award of Merit for Residential Architecture. Some rooms have footed baths, and all have old tube radios. Owner Marcia Weaver has designed self-guided tours of Jackson's historic blues sites. Complimentary Continental breakfast. TV in common area. | 803 Deer Park St. | 601/944–1392 | ppinn@yahoo.com | 5 rooms | $59–$60 | AE, D, MC, V.

TownePlace Suites by Marriott. This three-story town house–style complex, opened in 1999, was designed for extended stays, with studios and one- and two-bedroom units. The hotel is near the capitol, and the zoo. In-room data ports, kitchenettes, cable TV. Pool. Health club. Business services. | 572 Beasley Rd. | 601/206–5757 | fax 601/206–5747 | www.marriott.com | 68 stuidos, 26 suites | $75, $85–$95 suites | AE, D, DC, MC, V.

EXPENSIVE

Crowne Plaza. In the heart of downtown, the largest hotel in Jackson provides top amenities, including a skywalk to a small shopping mall. In addition to the oversize guest rooms, there is a relaxed and warm atmosphere and a friendly hotel staff. | 354 rooms. Restaurant, bar. In-room data ports, some microwaves, some refrigerators, cable TV. Outdoor pool. Fitness center. Laundry services, business services. Some pets allowed. | 200 E. Amite St. | 601/969–5100 or 800/465–4329 | fax 601/969–9665 | www.crowneplaza.com | $100–$130 | AE, D, DC, MC, V.

★ **Millsaps-Buie House.** Housed in one of the few surviving Victorian mansions in the downtown area, this lavish bed-and-breakfast is the best in the city. Built in the 1880s (and restored in the 1980s), its rooms are filled with period antiques. The large guest rooms all have private baths, telephones, and cable TV. It is a peaceful oasis in the heart of the city. | 11 units. Picnic area, complimentary breakfast, complimentary afternoon refreshments. In-room data ports, some refrigerators, cable TV. Business services. No kids under 12. | 628 N. State St. | 601/352–0221 or 800/784–0221 | fax 601/352–0221 or 800/784–0221 | www.millsaps-buiehouse.com | $105–$175 | AE, D, DC, MC, V.

Old Capitol Inn. Southern hospitality and pleasantly furnished rooms at this large, new B&B make for a pleasant stay. The inn is in a historic building near the Old Capitol. Richly appointed rooms are done in a variety of decorative styles. | 24 suites. Complimentary Continental breakfast. In-room data ports, cable TV. Pool. | 226 N. State St. | 601/359–9000 or 888/359–9001 | www.visitjackson.com | $99–$169 | AE, MC, V.

Residence Inn by Marriott. This two-story hotel 1 mi from downtown is an excellent choice for an extended stay. One- and two-bedroom suites have full kitchens and daily housekeeping service. Some rooms have fireplaces. | 120 suites. Complimentary buffet breakfast, room service. In-room data ports, kitchenettes, microwaves, refrigerators, cable TV. Pool. Hot tub. Tennis. Playground. Laundry facilities. Business services. Some pets allowed. | 881 E. River Pl. | 601/355–3599 or 800/331–3131 | fax 601/355–5127 | www.residenceinn.com | $89–$129 | AE, D, DC, MC, V.

VERY EXPENSIVE

Fairview. This B&B is in a stately Colonial Revival mansion built in 1908 and listed in the National Register of Historic Places. Public rooms display period antiques, and guest rooms are decked out in Laura Ashley style. It is near major attractions 1 mi north of downtown. | 2 rooms, 6 suites. Restaurant, complimentary breakfast. In-room data ports, cable TV, in-room VCRs. Some in-room hot tubs. Library. | 734 Fairview St. | 601/948–3429 or 888/948–1908 | fax 601/948–1203 | www.fairviewinn.com | $115, $165 suites | AE, D, MC, V.

Hilton. After a recent renovation, this hotel is once again the premier lodging for northeast Jackson, and one of the South's finest hotels. Convenient to I–55 and the busy County Line Road shopping district, it has ample meeting facilities and numerous restaurants in the hotel and nearby. | 278 rooms, 22 suites. Restaurants, bar (with entertainment). In-room data ports, some kitchenettes, refrigerators, some in-room hot tubs, cable TV. Pool. Business services, airport shuttle. | 1001 E. County Line Rd. | 601/957–2800 or 800/445–8667 | fax 601/957–3191 | www.hilton.com | $105–$155, $135–$255 suites | AE, D, DC, MC, V.

KOSCIUSKO

MAP 4, E4

KOSCIUSKO

INTRO
ATTRACTIONS
DINING
LODGING

(Nearby towns also listed: Canton, Louisville, Natchez Trace Parkway, Philadelphia, Starkville, Yazoo City)

The town is named for a Polish general who fought in America's Revolutionary War. Today, however, the big name in town is Oprah. Kosciusko was the birthplace of TV talk show host, actress, and media maven Oprah Winfrey, although there are few sites here actually relevant to her upbringing. For travelers, the city is primarily a way station for exploring the historic sites along the Natchez Trace Parkway, paralleling the Yockanookany River on the town's eastern edge. Kosciusko is a pleasant place, with a scenic square that bustles with small-town life. Numerous historic homes line the pretty, tree-shaded streets, and the Koscuisko Museum offers changing exhibits that highlight the town's history. But it's best to treat the city and surrounding area as a single package.

Information: **Kosciusko Chamber of Commerce** | 301 E. Jefferson Ave., Box 696, Kosciusko 39090 | 662/289–2981. **Kosciusko Museum and Information Center** | Natchez Trace Pkwy., Kosciusko 39090 | 662/289–2981.

Attractions

Holmes County State Park. The park offers camping, nature trails, and archery fields. There are two lakes in this 450-acre park where you can swim, fish, and rent boats. | Hwy. 1, Durant | 662/653–3351 | $2 per vehicle | Daily 6–10.

Kosciusko City Cemetery. The city cemetery includes a melancholy statue erected by a man to memorialize his young wife; he was able to view the statue from the window of his nearby Victorian mansion. | S. Huntington St. | 662/289–2981 | Free.

Kosciusko Museum and Information Center This museum documents Kosciusko—the man and the town. You can also pick up brochures and information about Mississippi attractions. | Natchez Trace Pkwy. at Hwy. 35 | 662/289–2981 | Free | Mon.–Sat. 9–4, Sun. 1–4.

Oprah Winfrey Road. This road, north of Hwy. 12, will take you past Oprah Winfrey's first church, her family cemetery, and her birthplace. | Oprah Winfrey Rd. | 662/289–2981.

ON THE CALENDAR

MAR.: *His Last Days Passion Play.* This production is held the last three nights before Easter at the First Union Methodist Church, on East Washington Avenue. | 662/289–1412.

APR.: *Natchez Trace Festival.* This event at Courthouse Square downtown features a 10K run, activities for kids, food, and entertainment. | 662/289–2981.

AUG.: *Central Mississippi Fair.* This quintessential small town fair offers rides, food, and exhibits at the Kosciusko Fairgrounds on Hwy. 12. | 662/289–2981.

DEC.: *Candlelight Tour of Homes.* Several of the city's most beautiful homes, decorated for Christmas, are open for evening tours. | 662/289–2981.

Dining

Gaf's. American/Casual. This local favorite is convenient to the Natchez Trace Parkway and serves breakfast specials, sandwiches, steaks, and seafood. | 1048 Veterans Memorial Dr. | 662/289–9990 | $6–$15 | AE, D, MC, V | No dinner Sun.

Lodging

Best Western Parkway Inn. This one-story motel is just off the Natchez Trace Parkway. Microwaves, refrigerators, cable TV. Pool. | 1052 Veterans Memorial Dr. | 662/289–6252 | fax 662/289–4007 | www.bestwestern.com | 51 | $50–$60 | AE, D, DC, MC, V.

LAUREL

MAP 4, E6

(Nearby towns also listed: Hattiesburg, Mendenhall, Meridian)

Laurel is a staging ground for lumber, petroleum, and poultry operations, and as such has a rough-and-tumble look. Laurel's biggest contribution to the world of commerce was the invention of Masonite, a type of particle board made from lumber waste. The Masonite Corporation, located in Laurel and started by native William Mason, is today the world's largest hardboard manufacturer. Laurel has a small but pretty historic district and an interesting history—during the Civil War the city seceded from *both* the North and the South, and was known as "The Free State of Jones." (It's in Jones County.) Because of the city's commercial atmosphere, it may come as a surprise to find the Lauren Rogers Art Museum, one of the South's finer small museums. This collection alone makes a visit to Laurel worthwhile. The city also gave the world one of its greatest opera singers, Leontyne Price.

Children will love Trapper's Gator Farm, Sam Lindsey's Model Train Collection, and Landrum's Country Homestead and Village. The nearby De Soto National Forest offers horse trails, hiking, fishing, swimming, and camping.

Information: Jones County Chamber of Commerce | 153 Base Dr., Suite 3; Box 527, Laurel 39440 | 601/428–0574 or 800/392–9629 | fax 601/428–2047 | www.edajones.com.

Attractions

De Soto National Forest. The De Soto National Forest, a huge expanse of pine and hardwood forest, includes the Longleaf Horse Trail and the Turkey Fork Recreation Area. (*See* Hattiesburg and Wiggins.) | Off U.S. 49 | 601/428–0594 | Parking $3, camping $13 | Daily 6AM–10PM.

Lake Bogue Homa. This 1,200-acre lake, operated by the Mississippi Department of Wildlife, Fisheries, and Parks, offers a full range of outdoor activities and camping. The lake is on Hwy. 8, 7 mi east of Laurel. | 601/425–2148 | Free | Daily dawn–dusk.

Lauren Rogers Museum of Art. This was the first art museum built in Mississippi, and it remains one of the best small museums in the South. It houses an excellent collection of paintings, 18th-century English silver, and Native American baskets. There are rotating exhibits, a gift shop, and a reference library. | 565 N. 5th St. | 601/649–6374 | fax 601/649–6379 | www.lrma.org | $3 (suggested donation) | Tues.–Sat. 10–4:45, Sun. 1–4.

Sam Lindsey's Model Train Collection. This collection is every model train buff's dream, with more than 50 trains and 400 ft of track set up in the Hobby Corner store. | 1535 N. 1st Ave. | 601/649–4501 | Free | Tues.–Sat. 9–5.

Trapper's Gator Farm. This farm, about 9 mi from Laurel on Hwy. 15, is home to alligators, as well as deer, snakes, birds, foxes, and bobcats. There is a petting zoo with smaller animals. | 6 Gator Farm Rd., Landrum | 601/428–4967 | By appointment only.

Landrum's Homestead. Landrum's Country Homestead is a re-creation of an 1800s settlement. There is a blacksmith shop, water mill, jail, general store, chapel, and an 1860 log house. | 1356 Hwy. 15 | 601/649–2546 | $4 | Mon.–Sat. 9–5.

Old Order German Baptist Community. Residents of this anachronistic community get around in horse-drawn buggies, on foot, or by bicycle, and dress in simple, Amish-like attire. This is a great place for gift-buying: there's handmade furniture and quilts, homemade soap, and hand-churned butter. Nearby are two similar attractions, a group of old-fashioned stores at Hot Coffee and Mitchell Farm, and a number of old buildings. The communtiy is rather far out of town—between Mt. Olive and Collins along Hwy 532. | Salem School Rd., Mt. Olive | 601/765–6012 | Free | Daily.

ON THE CALENDAR

APR.: *Landrum's Homestead Pinefest Celebration.* You can go on walking tours of working period buildings at this re-created late 19th-century settlement. | 601/649–2546.

MAY: *Day in the Park.* This Laurel Arts League–sponsored event features food, entertainment, and work by local artisans the first Saturday in May at Mason Park. | 601/649–8856 or 601/649–1206.

YOUR FIRST-AID TRAVEL KIT

- ❑ Allergy medication
- ❑ Antacid tablets
- ❑ Antibacterial soap
- ❑ Antiseptic cream
- ❑ Aspirin or acetaminophen
- ❑ Assorted adhesive bandages
- ❑ Athletic or elastic bandages for sprains
- ❑ Bug repellent
- ❑ Face cloth
- ❑ First-aid book
- ❑ Gauze pads and tape
- ❑ Needle and tweezers for splinters or removing ticks
- ❑ Petroleum jelly
- ❑ Prescription drugs
- ❑ Suntan lotion with an SPF rating of at least 15
- ❑ Thermometer

*Excerpted from *Fodor's: How to Pack: Experts Share Their Secrets*
© 1997, by Fodor's Travel Publications

JUNE: *Lonesome Pines Bluegrass Festival.* You can take in three days of pure bluegrass music at this charity music festival just outside Laurel. Many choose to stay in Lonesome Pine Bluegrass Park, which has about 200 RV sites. | 601/426–9071.

OCT.: *South Mississippi Fair.* This traditional fair, at the South Mississippi Fairgrounds, has rides, concessions, and exhibits. | 601/649–3535 or 601/649–9010.

Dining

Parker House. Continental. This family-owned restaurant is known for steaks and seafood, as well as its upscale, candle-lit dining room. Be sure to try the Catfish Mable, a house specialy of fried catfish with shrimp, crabmeat, crawfish, and gravy. | 3115 Audubon Dr. | 601/649–0261 | $11–$23 | AE, D, DC, MC, V | No lunch. Closed Sun.–Mon.

The Secret Garden Tea Room. Continental. This whimsical bistro in the heart of downtown features a small weekday lunch menu. There is always at least one pasta dish, as well as bread pudding, the house specialty, for dessert. English-style teas such as Earl Grey and mint are served from 4 to 6 on the second Thursday of every month. | 408 Short 7th Ave. | 601/428–4448 | fax 601/425–5563 | $5–$7 | MC, V | Closed weekends. No dinner.

Lodging

The Laurel Inn. This two-story, 1917 B&B in the historic district overlooks Gardiner Park. All rooms have king-size beds, a sitting area, and a private bath. The common area has a large-screen TV, as well as fax and Internet access, and there is a playroom for children. Innkeepers Kevin and Peggy O'Connell can help map out a walking tour of the area. Complimentary breakfast. TV in common area. | 803 N. 2nd Ave. | 601/428–8773 or 800/290–5474 | fax 601/428–8773 | www.laurelinn.com | 3 rooms | $85 | AE, MC, V.

Sawmill Ramada. This full-service hotel downtown has with an on-site restaurant and bar, and a sparkling pool. | 207 rooms, 6 suites. Restaurant, bar (with entertainment), room service. Cable TV. Pool. Laundry services. Business services. | 1105 Sawmill Rd. | 601/649–9100 or 800/272–6232 | fax 601/649–6045 | www.ramada.com | $60–$75, $75–$150 suites | AE, D, DC, MC, V.

LOUISVILLE

MAP 4, E4

(Nearby towns also listed: Ackerman, Kosciusko, Philadelphia, Starkville)

The landscape around Louisville—mostly red-clay hills covered in kudzu and mixed pine and hardwood forests—is more akin to the Piedmont region of Georgia than to most of Mississippi. The Tombigbee National Forest is nearby, and the city itself is a pleasant mix of quiet streets and old storefronts with the ubiquitous Confederate monument standing guard downtown.

Information: **Louisville Chamber of Commerce** | 311 E. Park St., Box 551, Louisville 39339 | 662/773–3921.

Attractions

American Heritage "Big Red" Fire Museum. The "Big Red" is a private collection of early fire-fighting equipment. | 332 N. Church Ave. | 662/773–3421 | Free | By appointment only.

Legion State Park. This park was an outgrowth of the Civilian Conservation Corps, one of the New Deal programs of the Great Depression. It has rustic period cabins, a Gothic-style lodge, a lake, and ponds. | 635 Legion State Park Rd. | 662/773–8323 | $2 per vehicle | Daily 6AM–10PM.

Nanih Waiya State Park. You can picnic and hike along nature trails at this park. | 4496 Hwy. 393 | 662/773–7988 | $2 per vehicle | Daily 6AM–10PM.

Tombigbee National Forest. A few miles north of Louisville, the 66,000-acre Tombigbee National Forest provides miles of scenic woodland roads for exploring. There are campsites, fishing lakes, hunting, hiking, and mountain bike trails. | Route 1, Box 98A, Ackerman, | 662/285–3264 or 601/965–4391 | www.fs.fed.us | Mar.–mid-Nov., daily dawn–dusk.

On the Calendar
MAY: *Red Hills Festival.* This event includes a car show, quilt show, arts and crafts, entertainment, and food. | 662/773–3921.

OCT.: *East Mississippi Classic Walking and Racing Horse Show.* This equestrian show, at the Louisville Coliseum on Ivy Avenue, features Tennessee walking horses competing in various events. | 662/773–8524.

Dining
Brandi's Family Restaurant. American/Casual. This popular restaurant is adjacent to the Best Western Red Hills Inn. The menu includes burgers, catfish, and steaks. | 193 Hwy. 15 | 662/773–4644 | $5–$18 | AE, D, MC, V | No dinner Sun.

Lodging
Best Western Red Hills Inn. This two-story motel west of town opened in 1996, surrounded by pasture lands and wooded hillsides. In-room data ports, some in-room hot tubs, cable TV. Pool. Business services. | 201 Hwy. 15 | 662/773–9090 | fax 662/773–9330 | www.bestwestern.com | 52 rooms | $49–$79 | AE, D, DC, MC, V.

Lake Tiak O'Khata. This otherwise unremarkable motel has a wonderful wooded setting (Tiak O'Khata means "Lake of the Pines" in Choctaw). The first cabins were built in 1957; a restaurant was added in 1960. RV parking is available. | 77 rooms, 5 duplex cabins. Restaurant, picnic area, snack bar. Cable TV. Tennis. Business services. Beach, boating. | 213 Smyth Lake Rd. | 662/773–7853 or 888/845–6151 | fax 662/773–4555 | www.ltok.com | $50–$55 | AE, D, DC, MC, V.

MCCOMB

MAP 4, C7

(Nearby towns also listed: Hattiesburg, Natchez, Woodville)

McComb is an old railroad town known for ornamental azaleas that add vivid splashes of pink, white, red, and lavender to even the plainest homes each spring. Beyond that, the best reasons to visit are nearby parks: Bogue Chitto, Holmes, and Percy Quin. The nearby town of Brookhaven (north via I–55) has many fine homes from the railroad era.

Information: Pike County Chamber of Commerce | 617 Delaware Ave., Box 83, McComb 39648 | 601/684–2291 or 800/399–4404 | fax 601/684–4899.

Attractions
Atwood Water Park. On the Pearl River near Monticello, Atwood Water Park has a boat ramp, campground, and picnic areas, and offers fishing and other outdoor activities. | U.S. 84, Monticello | 601/587–2711 | Free | Daily 24 hours.

Bogue Chitto Water Park. This park, 12 mi east of McComb on U.S. 198, offers a full range of outdoor activities—camping, fishing, swimming, tubing, birdwatching, and hiking— on the Bogue Chitto River. There are also cabins for rent. | 1068 Dogwood Tr | 601/684–9568 | $2 per vehicle | Daily 8 AM–10 PM.

Percy Quin State Park. This park 6 mi south of town, in the Homochitto National Forest, is one of the most developed in the state. It includes a large lake, many recreational and camping facilities, and a new golf course. | 1156 Camp Beaver Dr. | 601/684–3938 | $2 | Daily 8AM–10PM.

ON THE CALENDAR

APR.: *Brookhaven Tour of Homes.* This pilgrimage-style event allows peeks into Brookhaven's finest homes. Brookhaven is 25 mi north of McComb on I-55. | 601/833–1411 or 800/613–4667.

JULY: *Iron Horse Festival.* This Main Street event pays tribute to the area's railroad heritage with music, food, and entertainment. | 601/249–0116.

SEPT.: *Summit Fall Fest.* There are arts and crafts displays in this autumn festival in downtown Summit, which is 15 mi south of Brookhaven on Hwy 51. The festival also includes a chili cook-off, an antique cards display, carnival rides, family activities, and live blues music. | 601/276–7518.

OCT.: *Ole Brook Festival.* This festival at the Brookhaven Sports Complex offers a hot-air balloon race, talent show, and sporting events. | 601/833–1411 or 800/613–4667.

Dining

Dinner Bell. Southern. At this fun, home-style restaurant, you sit with other diners around a large, circular table with a Lazy Susan in the center; turn it to bring a dish around to your side. Fried chicken, chicken and dumplings, and corn bread are among the specialties. | 229 5th Ave. | 601/684–4883 | $10–$15 | No credit cards | Closed Mon. No lunch Apr.–Sept.

Lodging

Days Inn of McComb. This two-story motel is 4 mi from Percy Quinn State Park and 16 mi from the Boque Chitto River. Restaurant, bar, complimentary Continental breakfast. In-room data ports, some refrigerators, some microwaves, cable TV. Pool. | 2298 Delaware Ave. | 601/684–5566 | fax 601/684–0641 | www.daysinn.com | 151 rooms | $59 | AE, D, DC, MC, V.

Ramada Inn. Nicely landscaped grounds and a friendly staff greet you at this two-story motel 3½ mi from downtown. | 141 rooms, 2 suites. Restaurant, bar, room service. In-room data ports, cable TV. Pool. Laundry facilities. Business services. Some pets allowed. | 1900 Delaware Ave. | 601/684–6211 or 800/228–2828 | fax 601/684–0408 | www.ramada.com | $59–$79, $125 suites | AE, D, DC, MC, V.

MENDENHALL

MAP 4, D6

(Nearby towns also listed: Jackson, Hattiesburg, Laurel, Vicksburg)

"Come on in" reads a billboard on U.S. 49. This small town with a pleasant downtown area that is best known for Revolving Tables restaurant (*see below*). The downtown area ascends a long hill and is lined with the kinds of local stores that have vanished from many other small towns. At the top is the imposing Simpson County courthouse.

Another attraction is the nearby Strong River. Don't be deceived by the ugly stretch you pass over on U.S. 49; elsewhere the river is swift and rocky, with great shade trees forming a canopy overhead. The best place to stop is at the park in nearby D'Lo. (Some say the name alludes to an early-settlers' complaint that the site was "too damn low." Others attribute it to a corruption of French.)

Information: Mendenhall Chamber of Commerce | 619 Pittman Dr., Mendenhall 39114 | 601/847–1725.

Attractions

Bienville National Forest. Bienville National Forest, 50 mi northeast of Mendenhall, and east of Jackson, covers 178,000 acres. There are four campsites, and horseback and hiking trails. | 3473 Hwy. 35, Forest | 601/469–3811 | fax 601/469–2513 | www.gorp.com/dow/southern/bien.htm.

Shongelo Lake. Within the forest, this five-acre lake offers fishing, a bathhouse, swimming, picnic shelters, and a nature trail. | Hwy. 35 | 601/469–3811 | Free | Apr. 15–Oct. 15, daily.

Marathon Lake. The Marathon Recreation Area was built in the 1950s on the site of a former logging camp. The 50-plus-acre lake has a boat ramp, bathhouse, swimming, water-skiing, and other outdoor activities. | 601/469–3811 | www.gorp.com/dow/southern/biencmp.htm | Free | Daily.

D'Lo Water Park. This water park along a river 2 mi north of Mendenhall on U.S. 49 offers picnic areas, swimming, and boating. | U.S. 49, D'Lo | 601/847–4310 | Free; camping $7–$10 | Daily.

Simpson County Legion Lake. This lake has a boat ramp, camping, fishing, a nature trail, and water-skiing. | Legion Lake Rd. | 601/849–4886 | $5 | Daily dawn–dusk.

ON THE CALENDAR

JULY: *Mize Watermelon Festival.* This festival in downtown Mize, which is 10 mi south of Mendenhall, has food, crafts, and entertainment, and is highlighted by watermelon-eating and seed-spitting contests. | 601/733–2227.

SEPT.: *Crazy Day.* This wild (and crazy) mix of events in nearby Magee, 10 mi southwest of Mendenhall, includes an arts and crafts fair, barbecue, gospel music, a 5K run/biathlon, and golf tournament. | 601/849–2517.

Dining

Revolving Tables. Southern. This family-style restaurant in the old railroad hotel in the center of town has been in the Morgan family since 1915. Food is served on lazy Susans, which are constantly replenished with seven entrées, including southern fried chicken and stuffed bell peppers; there are also a dozen vegetables, salads, corn bread, and biscuits. The house special is a dark custard pie. | 100 William Gerald Morgan Memorial Dr., Mendenhall, | 601/847–3113 | $9.35 | No credit cards | Closed Mon. No dinner.

Lodging

Comfort Inn of Magee. This two-story motel with indoor corridors is 7 mi south of town on U.S. 49. Basic rooms come with coffeemakers. In-room data ports, some microwaves, some refrigerators, in-room VCRs. Pool. | 5441 Simpson Hwy. | 601/849–2300 or 800/228–5150 | fax 601/849–2300 | www.comfortinn.com | 50 rooms | $63–$70 | AE, D, DC, MC, V.

MERIDIAN

MAP 4, F5

(Nearby towns listed: Laurel, Philadelphia)

Meridian was once the largest city in Mississippi. The railroad town was torched during the Civil War by General Sherman, who later boasted that "Meridian no longer exists."

The town was rebuilt—although with no apparent plan. It now has a haphazard look, magnified by commercial growth along I–20 and I–59. There are some attractive residential areas—downtown architecture is particularly interesting—and the city has a large number of important civil rights sites.

Meridian's chief claim to fame is that it is the birthplace of "singing brakeman" Jimmie Rodgers, known as the father of country music. The city is also home to a Naval Air Station employing 2,000. Not far away is Bienville National Forest (*see* Mendenhall), west of Meridian on I–20.

Important civil rights sites include the circa 1910 Beale's Café, once a gathering place for the city's black community; Con Sheehan Block, site of the Meridian Riot Trials in

1871, which marked the end of the Reconstruction Era; the E. F. Young Jr. Hotel, with its vintage 1940s beauty salon and barbershop; the James Chaney Memorial, which commemorates the Meridian native slain in Neshoba County in 1964 with two other civil rights workers; and several churches.

Information: **Meridian Chamber of Commerce** | 1915 Front St., Meridian 39301 | 601/693–1306 or 800/748–9970. **Lauderdale County Tourism Bureau** | 212 21st St., Meridian 39302 | 601/482–8001 or 888/868–7720 | fax 601/486–4988 | www.visitmeridian.com.

Attractions

Dentzel Carousel. This small, unique carousel is one of the oldest in the nation, and a National Historic Landmark. It was created around 1892 by a German immigrant named Gustav Dentzel, and is noteworthy for its beautifully carved figures and ornate artwork. | Highland Park, 39th Ave. | 601/485–1987 | 25 | June–Aug., daily 1–6; Sept.–May, weekends 1–5.

Dunn's Falls Water Park. Along a scenic stretch of the Chunky River, 10 mi west of Meridian, Dunn's Falls Water Park has camping, canoeing, picnic areas, and nature trails. | 6890 Dunn's Falls Rd., Enterprise | 601/655–8550 | $1 | May–Sept., daily 11–7; Oct.–Apr., Wed.–Sun. 9–5.

First Union Baptist Church. The First Union Baptist Church, where Martin Luther King Jr. spoke, was a staging ground for civil rights efforts. | 610 38th St. | 601/483–8932 | Free | By appointment only.

Grand Opera House of Mississippi. Both Sarah Bernhardt and Helen Hayes performed in this 1890 hall. | 2206 5th St. | 601/693–5239 | Free | Tours by appointment only.

Hamasa Shrine Temple Theatre. The 1928 Hamasa Shrine Temple Theatre is now a multipurpose theater featuring gospel, country, and other concerts. | 2320 8th St. | 601/693–1361 | Free | Weekdays 8:30–4:30, by appointment only.

Jimmie Rodgers Museum. This museum commemorates the "Father of Country Music," native son Jimmie Rodgers. Exhibits include personal items, guitars, concert clothing, and documents of this hometown legend. | Highland Park, 19th St. and 41st Ave. | 601/485–1808 | $2 | Mon.–Sat. 10–4, Sun. 1–5.

Key Brothers Aviation Pictorial Exhibit. In 1935, two local brothers set an aviation endurance record, staying aloft more than 650 hours. Exhibits here document their exploit. | 2811 U.S. 11 | 601/482–0364 | Free | Daily 6 AM–9 PM.

Meridian Museum of Art. Housed in the historic Carnegie Library, the Meridian Museum of Art has four galleries of rotating exhibitions. The museum hosts the Bi-State (Mississippi and Alabama) Art Competition and several other special events. | 628 25th Ave. | 601/693–1501 | Free | Tues.–Sun. 1–5.

Merrehope. This 20-room Greek Revival home was built in 1858, and served as the headquarters of Confederate General Joseph E. Johnston. | 905 Martin Luther King Jr. Memorial Dr. | 601/483–8439 | $3 | Mid-Oct.–mid-Mar., Mon.–Sat. 9–4; mid-Mar.–mid-Oct., Mon.–Sat. 9–5.
Frank W. Williams House. This elaborate Victorian home, directly beside the Merrehope, is filled with period furniture. The home was built in 1885 by Frank Williams for his bride. | 905 Martin Luther King Jr. Memorial Dr. | 601/483–8439 | $3 | Mid-Oct.–mid-Mar., Mon.–Sat. 9–4; mid-Mar.–mid-Oct., Mon.–Sat. 9–5.

Okatibbee Dam and Reservoir. The Okatibbee Lake features a marina, restaurant, and motel. Fishing tournaments and water events are held here. | Pine Springs Rd. | Free | 601/626–8431.

Peavey Visitors Center. You can't play Delta blues without an instrument, and that's just what the family-owned Peavey Electronics Corporation has been providing for two generations—amps, keyboards, and guitars, all of which are displayed in an exhibit tracing the history of the company. | Montgomery Industrial Park, 711 A St. | 601/483–5365 | Free | Weekdays 10–4, weekends 1–4.

Rose Hill Cemetery. The city's founders are buried in this cemetery, as are Gypsy royalty Emil and Kelly Mitchell. | 40th Ave., between 7th and 8th Sts. | 601/483–4225 | Free | Weekdays 8–5.

ON THE CALENDAR

MAY: *Jimmie Rodgers Memorial Festival.* This week-long festival pays tribute to the father of country music with entertainment, fishing, and a golf tournament. Events take place at Hamasa Shrine Temple Theatre and Highland Park. | 601/483–5763.

MAY: *Sandy Ridge Bluegrass Festival.* This three-day musical event on Clarkdale School Rd. 12 mi south of Meridian offers bluegrass music and food. You can camp at the festival for a small fee. | 601/693–2996 or 888/868–7720.

JUNE: *State Games of Mississippi.* These Olympic-style games feature more than 4,500 amateur athletes from across the state competing in different sports. | 800/482–0205 | www.stategamesofms.org.

OCT.: *Mississippi/Alabama State Fair.* This regional fair offers rides, food, exhibits, and entertainment at the Meridian Fairgrounds. | 601/693–3294.

OCT.: *Union Station Railfest.* Railroad memorabilia, a flea market, and entertainment are among the highlights of this fest on Front Street. | 601/485–1802.

DEC.: *Trees of Christmas.* The Merrehope and F. W. Williams houses are decorated with Christmas trees from around the world in this holiday tradition. | 601/483–8439.

MERIDIAN

INTRO
ATTRACTIONS
DINING
LODGING

Dining

A. Rodgers Bar-B-Que. Barbecue. You can order barbecued ribs or shredded pork sandwiches at this informal restaurant, which claims the "best ribs in town." It's about five minutes from downtown. | 818 18th Ave. S | 601/693–0423 | $6–$17 | No credit cards | Closed Sun.

D.T. Grinders. American. This restaurant is in a renovated Victorian home built around 1909 in the mid-town historic district. The home is listed on the National Register of Historic Places. Local residents come for the extensive beer list, steaks, seafood, and weekend night entertainment in the pub. | 1600 24th Ave. | 601/693–1988 | fax 601/693–1930 | $5–$23 | AE, D, MC, V | Closed Sun.–Mon.

The Hungry Heifer. Eclectic. This local favorite specializes in unusual menu options, like emu burgers and cow patty brownies. The daily specials include made-from-scratch seafood dishes, and on Tuesday you can have oysters on the half shell for 20¢ apiece. | 1310 14th St. | 601/483–2509 | $10–$25 | AE, D, MC, V | Closed Sun. No lunch.

Weidmann's. Southern. Here you'll find fine, sophisticated Southern cuisine served by a pleasant staff. Weidmann's has been in business since 1870, and is known for its seafood dishes. | 210 22nd Ave. | 601/693–1751 | Breakfast also served | $18–$31 | AE, D, DC, MC, V | No dinner Sun.–Mon.

Lodging

Baymont Inn & Suites. This three-story hotel built in the 1980s is in a safe area near major restaurants, about 2½ mi from downtown. It's a good budget choice. | 102 rooms, 9 suites. In-room data ports, cable TV. Outdoor pool. Business services. Pet allowed. | 1400 Roebuck Dr. | 601/693–2300 or 800/301–0200 | fax 601/485–2534 | www.baymontinns.com | $54, suites $64–$74 | AE, D, DC, MC, V.

Best Western. This standard two-story mid-sized hotel was built in 1965. It is convenient to the interstate and is ½ mi from downtown. The building is brick, with gable roofs, on 4 acres of landscaped grounds. | 120 rooms. Restaurant, bar with entertainment Wed.–Sat. Cable TV. Pool. Basketball court. Laundry services. | 2219 S. Frontage Rd. | 601/693–3210 or 800/528–1234 | www.bestwestern.com | $45–$69 | AE, D, DC, MC, V.

Comfort Inn. This hotel is less than a mile from the historic district, Bonita Lakes Mall, and Bonita Lakes and their jogging paths. Breakfast includes homemade waffles. Complimentary Continental breakfast. Some microwaves, some refrigerators, some in-room hot tubs. Pool. Health club. Business services. | 701 Bonita Lakes Dr. | 601/693–1200 or 800/228–5150 | fax 601/485–3138 | www.comfortinn.com | 52 rooms | $73 | AE, D, DC, MC, V.

Holiday Inn Express. This basic chain motel is about 1 mi from downtown, off I–59 at exit 153. The Spanish-style building was built in the 1960s. It is set back from the road amid trees, giving it a country feeling. | 110 rooms. Complimentary Continental breakfast. In-room data ports, cable TV. Pool. Laundry facilities. Business services. Some pets allowed. | 1401 Roebuck Dr. | 601/693–4521 or 800/465–4329 | fax 601/693–4521 | www.holiday-inn.com | $60–$70 | AE, D, DC, MC, V.

Howard Johnson. This downtown hotel offers good, basic rooms and an indoor pool. | 136 rooms. Restaurant, bar (with entertainment). In-room data ports, cable TV. Indoor pool. Hot tub. Laundry facilities. Business services. | 110 U.S. 11/80 | 601/483–8281 or 800/446–4656 | fax 601/485–1411 | www.hojo.com | $48–$99 | AE, D, DC, MC, V.

Jameson Inn. This white-columned, colonial-style hotel opened in 1999 and offers king-size beds. It is adjacent to the Bonita Lakes Mall. Complimentary Continental breakfast. In-room data ports, some in-room hot tubs, cable TV. Pool. Health club. | 524 Bonita Lakes Dr. | 601/483–3315 or 800/JAMESON | fax 601/483–2675 | www.jamesoninns.com/meridian-ms | 60 rooms | $59 | AE, D, DC, MC, V.

Ramada Limited. This standard hotel about 2 mi from downtown has a brick exterior. | 45 rooms, 5 suites. Restaurant. Complimentary Continental breakfast. Some refrigerators, some microwaves, cable TV. Pool. Hot tub. Exercise equipment. Business services. | 2915 St. Paul St. | 601/485–2722 or 800/272–6232 | fax 601/485–3960 | www.ramada.com | $50–$70, $75–$95 suites | AE, D, DC, MC, V.

NATCHEZ

MAP 4, B7

(Nearby towns also listed: McComb, Natchez Trace Parkway, Port Gibson, Vicksburg, Woodville)

For many, Natchez is the most important travel destination in Mississippi. The city is known for having one of the largest and finest collections of antebellum architecture anywhere in the South. It also has some of the most important Native American sites in the country, and is near a number of parks, wildlife preserves, and other outdoor attractions. Add to that some of the most striking scenery in the Mississippi valley, numerous cultural offerings, and the lure of riverboat gambling, and it's easy to see why so many are drawn here.

Situated atop 200-ft bluffs that overlook the Mississippi River, Natchez is the oldest settlement along the lower river. Started by the French in 1716, it was later ruled by Britain, Spain, and finally the United States (with a hiatus during the Confederacy). Natchez's heyday was the antebellum period, when cotton turned many area planters into millionaires almost overnight, resulting in a mansion-building boom that was without precedent. Early in the Civil War, city fathers capitulated to the Union, sparing residents the destruction that Union armies wreaked upon many resisting cities. Visiting today, you can be grateful for that action, although for many years other cities in the South showed great enmity toward "preserved" Natchez. Today the downtown core is amazingly intact, and it seems as if no patch of ground is without some significance. You'd do well to set aside several days to explore the town.

Many of the homes are open for tours, especially during spring and fall pilgrimages, and many have beautiful gardens. Even if you can't go inside, they offer a visual treat from the street. Other historic sites include: several homes built by free men of color before the Civil War; the once rowdy and now slightly touristy Natchez-Under-the-Hill district; the Grand Village of the Natchez Indians; and the Natchez Trace Parkway, which follows the route of an ancient trail from Natchez to Nashville.

Information: Natchez Convention and Visitors Bureau | 640 S. Canal St., Natchez 39121 | www.natchez.ms.us | 601/446–6345 or 800/647–6724.

Attractions

Antebellum homes. In addition to those listed below and others in the Historical Park, antebellum homes built between 1780 and the Civil War include Auburn (1812); The Briars (1812), now an inn; The Burn (1836), which served as a Union hospital during the Battle of Vicksburg; D'Evereux (1840); Governor Holmes House (1794); Landsdowne Plantation (1853); Linden (1800); and Stanton Hall (1857), a palatial house that is shaded by ancient live oaks and occupies an entire city block. These may be visited during pilgrimage weeks. There are daily tous of all the homes that follow. Call the Visitor Center for hours and info. | 800/647–6724 | www.natchezpilgrimage.com | $6 per house.

Cedar Grove Plantation. Built in 1838, this plantation was the family home of noted U.S. Senator John Sharp Williams, who resigned in protest when Congress voted not to join the League of Nations. There is a B&B here today (*see below*). | 617 Kingston Rd. | 662/746–1815 or 800/381–0662 | Free.

Dunleith. Now an 11-room B&B, Dunleith was built in 1856. This National Historic Landmark Building is an archetypal "big house," with Tuscan columns on four sides. The house contains furnishings from 1850 and earlier, and has French Zuber wallpaper. The 40-acre former plantation has a lovely garden (note the magnificent the flowering magnolia tree). | 84 Homochitto St. | 601/446–8500 or 800/433–2445 | www.natchez-dunleith.com | $6 | Mon.–Sat. 9–4:30, Sun. 1–4:30.

The House on Ellicott's Hill. Built by Andrew Ellicott in 1798, this house is now a National Historic Landmark. | N. Canal St. | 601/442–2011 | www.natchezpilgrimage.com | $6 | Daily 9–4:30.

Longwood. The architectural equivalent of an unfinished symphony, Longwood was an octagonal brick mansion under construction when the Civil War broke out. It was never completed, and its owner, Dr. Haller Nutt, died in 1864, before the war was over. Longwood was to have 32 rooms, each opening onto a center rotunda topped by a dome—designed to offer perfect air circulation during hot southern summers. | 140 Lower Woodville Rd. | 601/442–5193 | www.natchezpilgrimage.com | $6 | Daily 9–4:30.

Magnolia Hall. This Greek Revival mansion from 1858 has been restored to its original brownstone color. It contains 18th- and 19th-century antiques, and the Natchez Costume Museum is housed on the second floor. | 2155 Pearl St. | 601/442–6672 | www.natchezpilgrimage.com | $6 | Daily 9–4:30.

The Monmouth. Built circa 1818, the Monmouth was the home of General John A. Quitman, an early Mississippi governor. It is now a luxury hotel, and is also open for daily tours. | 36 Melrose Ave. | 601/442–5852 or 800/828–4531 | www.natchezpilgrimage.com | $6 | Daily 9:30–4.

Ravenna. Listed on the National Register of Historic Places, Ravenna was built in 1835 by William Harris, a cotton broker, for his wife, Caroline Harrison, niece of President William Henry Harrison. This elegant building is noted for its lovely garden and a three-story elliptical stairway. It's now a bed-and-breakfast. | 8 Ravenna La. | 601/442–8516 | www.natchezpilgrimage.com | $6 | Sept.–June, daily 9–4.

Rosalie. Built in the early 1820s, Rosalie has been called the "quintessential Southern Plantation house." The mansion was constructed of redbrick with a Greek Revival portico. The cautious owner buried the house's antique mirrors in the yard just before the Union Army turned the house into its headquarters. Now restored—both the house and the mirrors—Rosalie's interior furnishings are among the grandest in Natchez. It's a National Historic Landmark. | 100 Orleans St. | 601/445–4555 | www.natchezpilgrimage.com | $6 | Daily 9–4:30.

Stanton Hall. A National Historic Landmark completed in 1857, Stanton Hall was constructed with the finest materials available, including gas-burning chandeliers, marble mantels, and silver doorknobs. Briefly a girls' school, Stanton Hall now belongs to the Pilgrimage Garden Club. | 401 High St. | 601/442–6282 | www.natchezpilgrimage.com | $6 | Daily 9–4:30.

Church Hill. One of the state's best-preserved antebellum plantation communities, Church Hill has several palatial homes (including Springfield Plantation, below) and an exquisite Gothic church for which the community was named. The community is about 20 minutes north of Natchez on Hwy. 553. | 601/786–3802 | Free | Mon.–Sat. 9:30–sunset, Sun. 10:30–sunset.

Historic Springfield Plantation. This has been a working plantation for over 200 years. The house, begun in 1789, reflects the architectural style of the time; the furnishings are from a somewhat later era. Andrew Jackson was married in this house. | Hwy. 553, Fayette | 601/786–3802 | $7 | Daily 9:30–5.

Grand Village of the Natchez Indians. The Natchez lived in the southwest Mississippi area from around AD 700 to 1730. Toward the end of that period, Grand Village was their main ceremonial center. The present village is a reconstruction. You will also find exhibits of the life of the Natchez, ceremonial mounds, a typical house, and a small museum. | 400 Jefferson Davis Blvd. | 601/446–6502 | fax 601/446–6503 | www.mdah.state.ms.us/hprop/gvni.html | Free | Mon.–Sat. 9–5, Sun. 1:30–5.

Holy Family Catholic Church. This is the home of the oldest black Catholic congregation in the state. Holy Family's present building dates from 1894 and is still in its original state. | 16 Orange Ave. | 601/445–5700 | Free | By appointment only.

Homochitto National Forest. Thirty mi north of Natchez, this vast public forest includes Clear Springs Recreation Area—where you can hike, camp, fish, and swim—and Pipe's Lake—where you can fish and hike along nature trails. The numerous clear streams here are rare in Mississippi. | Hwy. 1, Meadville | 601/384–5876 | fax 601/384–2172 | www.fs.fed.us | Free.

Jefferson College. Jefferson College, 5 mi north of Natchez in nearby Washington, is a restored complex of circa 1802 buildings. This was the first college in territorial Mississippi. Today it's a museum and historic site, often used as a setting for films. An unlikely legend has it that America's third vice president, Aaron Burr, was arraigned for treason here under a pair of large live oaks. | U.S. 61, Washington. | 601/442–2901 | fax 601/442–2902 | Free | Mon.–Sat. 8–5, Sun. noon–5.

Isle of Capri Casino and Hotel. This is a reproduction of a river boat with the usual range of table and video gambling games, and restauraunts. | 70 Silver St. | 601/445–0605 or 800/722–5825 | www.isleofcapricasino.com | Free | 24 hours.

Mostly African Market. Housed in the 1850s Angelety House, the market displays art exhibits and sells regional arts and crafts. | 125 St. Catherine St. | 601/442–5448 or 800/647–6724 | Free | Sept.–May, Wed.–Sat. 1–5.

Natchez City Cemetery. Perhaps the city's most serene historic district, the Natchez City Cemetery has graves dating to the 18th century. | 2 Cemetery Rd. | 601/445–5051 | Free.

Natchez in Historic Photographs. This permanent exhibit of more than 300 photos includes some of the best documentation of the great paddle-wheel boats. | 408 N. Pearl St. | 601/442–4741 | $3 (suggested donation) | Mon.–Sat. 10–5, Sun. 1–5.

Natchez National Historical Park. The Natchez National Historical Park includes three sites. **Melrose,** one of the finest Greek Revival mansions in the country, retains its original furnishings, outbuildings, and park-like estate. The antebellum **William Johnson House,** built by a free man of color, is being restored. **Fort Rosalie,** built by French colonists in 1716, is not open to the public. | 1 Melrose-Montabello Pkwy. | 601/442–7047 | Melrose House $6; grounds, free | Grounds 8:30–5, tours 9–4.

Natchez State Park. This park is a large wooded area with trails, cabins, campgrounds, and a lake. | U.S. 61 | 601/442–2658 | $2 per vehicle | Park open daily dawn–dusk; office weekdays 8–5.

Natchez Under-the-Hill. The city's original waterfront, Natchez-Under-the-Hill was once a notorious draw for pirates, riverboat gamblers, and outlaws. Dwindling use of riverboats brought an end to its infamy. These days, Natchez-Under-the-Hill attracts tourists with its restaurants, bars, gift shops, inns, and the Isle of Capri casino. Three passenger paddle-wheelers dock here: the *Mississippi Queen,* the *Delta Queen,* and the *American Queen.* | Silver St. | 800/647–6724 or 800/99–NATCHEZ.

Natchez Pilgrimage Tours. Natchez Pilgrimage Tours offers carriage and bus tours of the downtown area. | 601/446–6631 or 800/647–6742 | www.natchezpilgrimage.com.

St. Catherine Creek National Wildlife Refuge. This wooded expanse in the Mississippi River lowlands offers fishing, hiking trails, and wildlife watching. | York Rd. off Hwy. 31 | 601/442–6696 | Day pass $5, one year user permit $12.50 | Daily dawn–dusk.

St. Mary's Cathedral. A 200-ft Gothic Revival spire towers over 12 lesser spires in this 1842 cathedral. The adjacent cemetery contains graves from the Spanish colonial era. | 107 S. Union St. | 601/445–5616 | Free | Daily dawn–dusk.

Zion Chapel African Methodist Church. Built in 1858, the Zion Chapel was the second Presbyterian church to serve a rural black congregation. Hiram Revels, the nation's first black congressman, was one of its pastors. (Revels was appointed to fill the unexpired term of Jefferson Davis.) | 228 N. Martin Luther King Jr. Rd. | 601/442–1396 | Free | By appointment only.

ON THE CALENDAR

JAN.: *Eleventh Moon Storytelling Festival.* This two-hour event features yarns by local and regional story-tellers. | 400 Jefferson Davis Blvd. | 601/446–6345 or 800/647–6724.
FEB.: *Mystic Krewe of Alpheus Mardi Gras Parade and Ball.* This downtown event is the first of the city's big pre-Lenten carnival fetes. | 601/446–6345 or 800/647–6724.
FEB.: *Annual River City Classic.* The route of this 5-K run wends through several of the city's scenic historic districts. | 601/446–6345 or 800/647–6724.
MAR.: *Krewe of Phoenix Mardi Gras Parade and Ball.* This is the second in the city's series of Mardi Gras parades. | 601/446–6345 or 800/647–6724.
MAR.: *Annual Natchez Pow Wow at Grand Village of the Natchez Indians.* This event celebrates the region's Native American heritage. | 601/446–6502.
MAR.: *Krewe of Killarney St. Patrick's Day Parade.* This downtown parade celebrates the city's Irish heritage. | 601/446–6345 or 800/647–6724.
MAR., OCT.: *Natchez Pilgrimage.* This event, held in spring and fall, includes tours of homes and gardens, the Confederate Pageant, and the play *Southern Exposure.* | 601/446–6631 or 800/647–6742 | $18–$24.
MAR., APR.: *Southern Road to Freedom.* Held during Spring Pilgrimage, this is a gospel musical festival illustrating African American history from the colonial era to the present. | 601/446–6631 or 800/647–6742.
APR.: *Andrew Jackson Day, War of 1812 Re-enactment.* This event, held at Jefferson College in nearby Washington, is one of the few to commemorate the War of 1812. | 601/442–2901.
APR., MAY: *Natchez Opera Festival.* This festival features operas, Broadway musicals, and recitals. | 601/446–6345 or 800/647–6724.
MAY: *Natchez Literary Celebration.* This event includes scholarly lectures and entertainment at various sites. | 601/446–1208 or 800/862–3259.
JUNE: *Natchez Bicycle Race.* This downtown competition features races for pros and amateurs. as well as crafts, music, petting zoos, and other entertainment. | 601/446–6345 or 800/647–6724.

JUNE: *Steamboat Jubilee and Floozie Day.* This party coincides with the arrival of the steamboats *Mississippi Queen* and *Delta Queen* during their "race" to St. Louis. | 601/446–6345 or 800/647–6724.

OCT.: *Great Mississippi River Balloon Race.* This event features dozens of hot-air balloons, parties, and sundry activities. | 601/446–6345 or 800/647–6724.

OCT.: *Mississippi Medicine Show.* This is an old-style stage show on Linton Avenue with audience interaction. | 601/446–6345 or 800/647–6724.

OCT.: *Natchez Fall Flea Market.* Arts and crafts from throughout the region are on sale at this market. | 601/445–8201.

NOV.: *Natchez Pilgrimage Garden Club Annual Antiques Forum.* This event includes workshops and programs by antiques experts and tours of local homes. | 601/446–6345 or 800/647–6724.

DEC.: *Christmas in Natchez.* Tours of historic homes in Christmas livery, entertainment, and living history displays, highlight this holiday event | 601/446–6345 or 800/647–6724.

Dining

Biscuits and Blues. Creole. Formerly called Scrooge's, this restaurant serves a New Orleans–style menu. House specialties are the crawfish and mushroom beignet appetizer, smoked chicken and ribs, grilled or fried catfish, and J. P.'s famous gumbo. For lunch, try one of the shrimp, catfish, or beef po'boys. | 315 Main St. | 601/446–9922 | $12–$26 | AE, DC, MC, V.

Carriage House Restaurant. Southern. This restaurant, with its charming Victorian ambience, is located on the grounds of landmark Stanton Hall. Delicious traditional meals include the miniature biscuits. The restaurant is also known for its southern-fried chicken and gumbo. | 401 High St. | 601/445–6108 | $9–$18 | AE, MC, V | No dinner.

Cock of the Walk. Southern. Set in an old train depot that overlooks the Mississippi River, this is the original restaurant of a regional chain. Specialities are fried or blackened catfish, fried dill pickles, mustard greens, and grilled chicken. There is a fully stocked bar with nightly entertainment. | 200 N. Broadway | 601/446–8920 | $16–$32 | AE, D, DC, MC, V.

King's Tavern. Continental. The first written history of this Natchez Trace meeting place dates back to 1620—voyagers would meet at the tavern and form traveling parties to combat the dangers of the Trace. It's now a restaurant paneled in wood from ships that once sat in the harbor, and is known for its prime rib, stuffed flounder, and rotating pasta dishes. All desserts are homemade. | 619 Jefferson St. | 601/446–8845 | $11–$18 | AE, D, MC, V | No lunch.

Magnolia Grill. Cajun. You can get your catfish grilled, amandine, or served with crawfish etouffé at this casual restaurant "under the hill." The Magnolia shrimp, prepared with green onions, mushrooms, garlic, and served over rice or angel hair pasta keeps locals coming back for more. | 49 Silver St. | 601/446–7670 | $7–$21 | AE, MC, V.

Monmouth Plantation. Contemporary. A five-course candlelight dinner from the prix-fixe-only menu is served at this antebellum home. Dinner begins at 7:30; hors d'oeuvres are at 6:30 in the courtyard. Entrees include seared tuna wrapped in bacon with molasses sauce and stuffed quail with crab-cake dressing. | 36 Melrose Ave. | 601/442–5852 | Reservations essential | $37 | AE, D, DC, MC, V.

Pearl Street Pasta. Eclectic. Creative pastas are the main choice on the menu of this intimate place. Try the Cajun shrimp pasta, the Italian chicken salad pasta, or the pasta jambalaya. The restaurant has two rooms, one lighter and more traditional, the other darker, with exposed-brick walls. | 105 S. Pearl St. | 601/442–9284 | www.members.nbci.com/pearlsp | $10–$19 | AE, MC, V | No lunch Sun.

Lodging

The Briars. This opulent antebellum home, built in 1818, is on a bluff with one of the city's finest views of the Mississippi River. The 19 acres of landscaped grounds invite strolling.

The mansion, 1 mi south of town, was the site of the wedding of Jefferson Davis and Varina Howell. | 15 rooms. Complimentary breakfast. Cable TV. Pool. Business services. No kids under 12. | 31 Irving La. | 601/446–9654 or 800/634–1818 | fax 601/445–6037 | www.the-briarsinn.com | $150–$240 | AE, MC, V.

The Burn. This lovely 1834 Greek Revival building has antique furnishings and 2 acres of gardens that grow 100 varieties of camellia. The prominent feature of the interior is a free-standing semi-spiral staircase. All rooms are individually decorated. The inn is 1 mi north-east of the city. | 8 rooms. Complimentary breakfast. No room phones, cable TV. Pool. Business services. No pets. No kids under 12. | 712 N. Union St. | 601/442–1344 or 800/654–8859 | fax 601/445–0606 | $122–$200 | AE, D, MC, V.

Cedar Grove Plantation. This archetypal Greek Revival plantation house was built in 1838 by U.S. Senator John Sharp Williams. Set in 150 acres of forest and farmland, and surrounded by moss-draped trees and landscaped grounds, the plantation enjoys one of the most roman-tic settings in the state. It is about 20 minutes north of Natchez. | 7 rooms. Complimen-tary breakfast. TV in common area. Pool. Ponds. Library. No smoking. | 617 Kingston Rd. | 601/445–0585 or 877/508–6800 | fax 601/446–5650 | www.cedargroveplantation.com | $80–$170 | MC, V.

Dunleith. Although it stands in the heart of Natchez, this magnificent Greek Revival man-sion is surrounded by 40 acres of landscaped grounds. Because of its classic Southern look and riverside setting, it has appeared in *Showboat* and a number of other epic films. The 11 rooms in the courtyard wing and the eight rooms in the main house have elegant period furnishings. | 19 rooms. Complimentary breakfast. Some in-room hot tubs, cable TV. No kids under 14. | 84 Homochitto St. | 601/446–8500 or 800/433–2445 | www.natchez-dunleith.com | $110–$225 | AE, D, MC, V.

Executive Inn. This two-story stucco hotel has a reasonably priced restaurant inside. Built in the 1970s and in a commercial zone, it's about 1 mi from the center of the city. | 131 rooms. Restaurant, room service. In-room data ports, cable TV. Pool. Business services. | 45 Sergeant Prentiss Dr. | 601/442–1691 | fax 601/445–5895 | $69–$99 | AE, D, DC, MC, V.

The Guest House Historic Inn. Built in 1840, this is a cozy inn on Antique Row in the heart of the city. Decorated with antiques and reproduction antiques, the place has the feel of a small European hotel. | 17 rooms. Restaurant, bar, complimentary Continental breakfast. Refrigerators, cable TV. | 201 N. Pearl St. | 601/442–1054 | fax 601/442–1374 | www.mem-bers.aol.com/gsthous/gsthous.htm | $104–$114 | AE, D, DC, MC, V.

Highpoint. This Victorian country manor is on the grounds of the Clifton Plantation in a quiet neighborhood of tree-lined streets. Rooms have hardwood floors, braided rag rugs, and grand four poster beds. Complimentary breakfast. No room phones, no TV. No kids under 12. | 215 Linton Ave. | 601/442–6963 or 800/283–4099 | www.travelbase.com/destina-tions/natchez/highpoint | 3 rooms | $90–$125 | MC, V.

Linden. In a city filled with exquisite antebellum homes, Linden is impressive enough to have been depicted in one of Hollywood's greatest moments: the front door was copied for Tara in the movie *Gone With The Wind*. The mansion (built around 1800) is furnished with fine Federal furniture. Each bedroom is furnished with antiques and a canopied bed. | 7 rooms. Complimentary breakfast. No room phones. Business services. No pets. No kids under 10. | 1 Linden Pl. | 601/445–5472 or 800/254–6336 | fax 601/442–7548 | $90–$120 | No credit cards.

Magnolia Hill Plantation Bed and Breakfast. This Greek Revival planter's cottage sits on a plot that includes 30 acres of old growth forest. You can hike, mountain bike, or ride horse-back on the many trails, or fish for largemouth bass, bluegill, or catfish at one of the two ponds on the property. You can also attend the innkeepers' daily wine and cheese gath-ering, enlivened by their 500 bottle wine cellar. Complimentary breakfast. Some microwaves, some refrigerators, no TV in some rooms, TV in common area. Ponds, golf privileges, 9-hole golf course. Hiking, horseback riding. Fishing. Laundry service. Pets allowed. | 16 Wild

Turkey Rd. | 601/445–2392 or 877/642–2392 | www.magnoliaplantation.com | 6 rooms | $125–$150 | AE, D, MC, V.

Monmouth. Staying in this early 19th-century Greek Revival mansion is an unforgettable experience. The Monmouth has 26 acres of grounds with broad, landscaped vistas. Its splendid rooms have period furniture and private baths. Some rooms have fireplaces and Jacuzzis. A five-course dinner is served by candlelight. | 15 rooms, 16 suites. Complimentary Continental breakfast. Cable TV. Business services. No kids under 14. | 36 Melrose Ave. | 601/442–5852 or 800/828–4531 | fax 601/446–7762 | www.monmouthplantation.com | $145–$200, $175–$375 suites | AE, D, MC, V.

Oak Wood Plantation. This Mississippi planter's cottage has been in the family since it was built in 1836; it still has its original furnishings. The home can only be rented in its entirety. There is a full kitchen, huge porch, living room, dining room, breakfast bar, and two bedrooms—all on 300 acres of land, with ponds, a lake, and plenty of walking trails. Complimentary breakfast. Lake, pond. Hiking. Laundry facilities. No kids under 12. | 1 Oakwood Plantation Rd. | 800/699–4755 or 800/936–4424 | fax 334/636–7118 | www.bestinns.net/usa/ms/oakwood | 2 rooms | $150 | No credit cards.

Radisson Natchez Eola Hotel. An expertly restored early 20th-century hotel, the Natchez Eola is now grander than it was in its heyday. It's in the heart of the city's historic downtown area, only three blocks from the mighty Mississippi. Most rooms are small but some have spectacular views of the city and river. Julep's and Café Lasalle restaurant are featured here. The hotel is listed in the National Register of Historic Places. | 132 rooms. 3 restaurants, bar. Some refrigerators. Cable TV. Room service. Exercise equipment. Business services. Some pets allowed. | 110 N. Pearl St. | 601/445–6000 or 800/888–9140 | fax 601/446–5310 | www.radisson.com | $70–$150 | AE, D, DC, MC, V.

Ramada Inn Hilltop. This two-story brick hotel built in the 1970s is 1 mi south of town. It is on a bluff that offers spectacular views the Mississippi River, and is surrounded by 30 beautiful acres. | 172 rooms and 6 suites. Restaurant, bar (with entertainment). In-room data ports, some refrigerators, room service, cable TV. Pool, wading pool. Laundry facilities. Business services, airport shuttle. | 130 John R. Junkin Dr. | 601/446–6311 or 800/228–2828 | fax 601/446–6321 | www.ramada.com | $66–$79; $140 suites | AE, D, DC, MC, V.

NATCHEZ TRACE PARKWAY

MAP 4, D5

(Nearby towns also listed: Canton, Iuka, Jackson, Kosciusko, Natchez, Port Gibson, Starkville, Tupelo)

The Natchez Trace, a parkway running almost 450 mi from Nashville to Natchez, follows the route of Mississippi's oldest road—a trail created by buffalo more than 8,000 years ago. Native Americans followed it, as did explorers, flatboat men, outlaws, itinerant preachers, post riders, soldiers, and settlers. The Trace offers an opportunity to see Mississippi's rural landscape at its best. It's particularly beautiful in spring, when dogwoods, redbud trees, and wild azaleas are in bloom, and in fall, when the hardwood trees turn yellow and red. But it is lovely all year-round. Lush and green in summer and striking in winter, when the pines, magnolias, and hollies stand out against the bare limbs of the hardwood trees. Wildlife is abundant—so much so that drivers should be especially vigilant for herds of deer at night.

Almost all of the parkway is in Mississippi, with shorter segments in Alabama and Tennessee. Meticulously manicured, devoid of busy intersections, advertising, or commercial traffic, and with a strictly enforced speed limit of 50 mph, the Trace offers the most peaceful route through the state with a large number of historic or nature sites along the way.

The northern end of the Trace in Mississippi is near Iuka; from there the parkway cuts a diagonal swath to the southwest. It passes to the west of Tupelo and after passing Kosciusko reaches the Ross Barnett Reservoir, a large man-made lake. The Trace then barely skirts Jackson before continuing to its terminus at Natchez.

Be aware that there is only one gas station located directly on the Trace (at Jeff Busby State Park) 10 mi west of Ackerman at mile marker 193.1. Most of the stops are unmanned, in relatively remote locations, and without phones. Also note that continued construction near Jackson may mean that you must exit onto I–55 and pick up the parkway west of the city, on I–20.

Information: Natchez Trace Parkway Visitors Center | 2680 Natchez Trace Pkwy., MM 266, Tupelo 38804 | 662/680–4025 or 800/305–7417.

Attractions

Chickasaw Village. This former fortified village 7 mi south of Tupelo has interpretive markers and an exhibit shelter explaining the history of the Chickasaw. | Natchez Trace Pkwy. MM 261.8 | 662/680–4025 or 800/305–7417 | Free | Daily dawn–dusk.

Cypress Swamp. A circular nature trail with boardwalks over the water gives you a chance to explore a swamp of water-tupelo and bald-cypress trees. You'll probably see a few turtles and maybe even an alligator. The walk takes about 20 minutes. | Natchez Trace Pkwy., milepost 122, south of Kosciusko | No phone | Free.

Emerald Mound. This rectangular mound of earth was probably used for religious rituals. It's 35 ft high and covers 8 acres. It was built over several centuries by the Mississippians, who lived here between 1250 and 1600. Excavation of this Native American site has been going on since 1838, and the fragments of pottery, bones, and tools offer clues to life along the Mississippi 500 years ago. The site has been run by the National Park Service since the 1950s. | Natchez Trace Pkwy., milepost 10.3, north of Natchez | 601/842–1572 | www.cr.nps.gov/aad/feature/emerald.htm | Free | Daily dawn–dusk.

French Camp. In 1812, a French-Canadian trader set up an inn here, serving travelers on the Trace. The village that grew up around the inn was called French Camp in honor of the trader. It features the 1840 Huffman log cabin, a blacksmith shop, and re-creations of other 19th-century buildings. Molasses-making demonstrations are given here in October. Profits from the shops and demonstrations support French Camp Academy, a school for children from troubled homes. | Natchez Trace Pkwy., milepost 180.7 | No phone | Free | Daily dawn–dusk.

Jeff Busby State Park. If you need a break from the road, you can camp, hike, or picnic at this park with a scenic overlook atop Little Mountain. | Natchez Trace Pkwy., milepost 193.1 | 601/289–3671 | $2 per vehicle | Daily dawn–dusk.

Mount Locust. Built in 1779, this home was used as an inn in the mid-1800s and has been restored to its original state with pioneer furnishings. The inn and grounds are open to the public. | Natchez Trace Pkwy., milepost 15.5 | 662/680–4025 or 800/305–7417 | Free | Inn Feb.–Nov. daily 8:30–5; grounds year-round 8:30–5.

The Mississippi Crafts Center. You can purchase quality crafts from Native Americans and other local craftspeople at this center modeled after a dogtrot log cabin. Saturdays March through October, some of the craftsmen demonstrate their crafts on site. | Natchez Trace Pkwy., milepost 102.4, Ridgeland | 800/305–7417 or 601/856–7546 | www.mscraftsmensguild.org | Free | Daily 9–5.

Rocky Springs. The Rocky Springs Methodist Church, built in 1837, is all that remains of this town that fell prey to yellow fever and soil erosion. The adjacent park has a ranger station, scenic streams, picnic areas, nature trails, and a campground. | Natchez Trace Pkwy., milepost 54.8 | 601/535–7142 | Free.

Ross Barnett Reservoir. This section of the Natchez Trace Parkway skirts the 45-mi-long lake for almost 10 miles, making it one of the more scenic parts of the parkway. You can fish and go boating here. You'll see the lake shortly after you leave Jackson and pass through Ridgeland. The reservoir was named for the 52nd governor of Mississippi. | Natchez Trace Pkwy., MM 105.6 | Free.

ON THE CALENDAR

APR.: *Mid-South Star Gaze.* The Rainwater Observatory, in French Camp, is host to over 170 amateur astronomers who meet to share ideas, listen to speakers, and look at stars. The Observatory has over 70 meteor specimens and 16 telescopes, one of which is 32 inches–a star gazing dream come true. | 662/547–6865.

Lodging

French Camp Bed and Breakfast Inn. Two century-old log cabins with wide front porches make up this bed and breakfast halfway between Jackson and Tupelo, just two blocks off of the Trace on the campus of the French Camp Academy. The innkeepers display their collection of quilts and antique books. Complimentary breakfast. Some in-room VCRs, no room phones, no TV in some rooms, TV in common area. Laundry facilities. | 190 Robinson Rd. | 662/547–6835 | www.bbhost.com/frenchcamp | 5 rooms | $60–$75 | No credit cards.

OCEAN SPRINGS

MAP 4, F8

(Nearby towns also listed: Biloxi, Gulf Islands National Seashore, Gulfport and Pascagoula, Pass Christian, Waveland, Wiggins)

Don't be misled by the four-lane commercial sprawl along U.S. 90—Ocean Springs is, along with Bay St. Louis, the closest you'll come to the quaint villages once common along the Mississippi Coast. A small enclave of tree-shaded streets, many with views of the Mississippi Sound, the town has a local feel that's all the more remarkable given the comparatively touristy areas further west and the heavily industrial areas to the east.

The town's main claim to fame is Shearwater Pottery, a family artists' compound that nurtured the eccentric and gifted Walter Anderson, whose works can be seen in the nearby Community Center and in the museum of art that bears his name. Ocean Springs is also home to the headquarters of the Gulf Islands National Seashore Visitor Center. And just north of the city, along I–10, is the Mississippi Sandhill Crane National Wildlife Refuge.

Information: Ocean Springs Chamber of Commerce | 1000 Washington Ave., Ocean Springs 39564 | 228/875–4424.

Attractions

Mississippi Sandhill Crane National Wildlife Refuge. This refuge is a safe haven for approximately 120 of the tall endangered cranes. Tours to view the cranes are offered in January and February. There are ten species of carnivorous plants in the refuge, and a ³/₄ mi nature trail through savannah and bayou areas. The refuge is 5 mi northeast of Ocean Springs. (*See* also Pascagoula.) | 7200 Crane La., Gautier | 228/497–6322 | www.gorp.com/gorp/resource/us_nwr/ms_missm.htm | Free | Weekdays 8–3.

Shearwater Pottery. Set in a scenic wooded area by the Mississippi Sound, Shearwater Pottery offers thrown, glazed wares in a style popular in the 1920s. It's still operated by the founding family, who nurtured artist Walter Anderson. This was also the original site of Anderson's cottage, since moved to the museum of art, below. Prints made from Anderson's fanciful block prints are for sale here (some tinted with watercolor by family members), as are books about Anderson. | 102 Shearwater Dr. | 228/875–7320 | Free | Mon.–Sat. 9–5:30 and Sun. 1–5:30.

Walter Anderson Museum of Art. This museum, next to the Ocean Springs Community Center, contains the artist's bold, colorful murals from the 1950s depicting area wildlife and plants. Anderson often spent weeks at a time on the offshore islands, painting and communing with nature, and created hundreds of paintings and scores of journals. The museum includes his private cottage, one room of which is painted wall-to-wall-to-ceiling with intricately detailed murals. There are also several school-room murals he painted in the 1930s. | 510 Washington Ave. | 228/875–4494 | $5 | Mon.–Sat. 10–5, Sun. 1–5.

ON THE CALENDAR

FEB.: *Elks Mardi Gras Parade.* This parade along Washington Avenue is part of the city's pre-Lenten carnival celebrations. | 228/875–7046.

APR.: *Fort Maurepas Living History Weekend.* Actors in period clothes portray everyday life in the French colonial era at this replica of a French fort on Front Beach. The fort is normally open only to groups. | 228/875–7979.

MAR.: *Ocean Springs Pilgrimage.* This event features tours of the city's beautiful, older homes. | 228/875–4424.

APR.: *Re-enactment of the Landing of D'Iberville.* This event commemorates the arrival of the French explorer who founded the first colony on the coast in 1699. | 228/875–4424.

SEPT.: *Art Walk.* Local art galleries sponsor this downtown event, which includes demonstrations by artists. | 228/875–4424.

OCT.: *Great Oaks Storytelling Festival.* Cajun, African-American, Appalachian, Native American, and Good Ol' Boy story-tellers gather under oak trees downtown to tell their tales. | 228/875–4424.

NOV.: *Peter Anderson Arts and Crafts Festival.* Named in honor of the late artist, one of the three famous Anderson brothers, this festival showcases artists and craftsmen from across the South. | 228/875–4424.

Dining

Fisherman's Wharf. Seafood. This colorful building is near the wharf, with a view of oyster-shuckers working on the pier. You can feast on soft-shell crab, gumbo, oyster po'boys, or the broiled catch of the day. The dessert specialty is "mystery pie." The family-owned restaurant was established in 1974. | 1409 Bienville Blvd. | 228/872–6111 | www.thefishermanswharf.com | $6–$17 | AE, D, DC, MC, V | Closed Mon.

Germaine's. Creole. The little house surrounded by live oaks has a New Orleans ambience, with its antique clocks, local art, plain wooden floors, and superb food. Try broiled trout, sautéed veal in a creamy port-wine sauce, and sautéed crabmeat. | 1203 Bienville Blvd. | 228/875–4426 | $21–$32 | AE, D, DC, MC, V | Closed Mon.

★ **Jocelyn's.** French. The hot pink exterior isn't the only thing that makes this renovated 1890s cottage stand out. The coast seafood is the best in Mississippi, and dining here is an experience you won't soon forget. Specialties are fresh crabmeat cooked several ways, trout, flounder, and red snapper subtly seasoned and served with delightful garnishes. For dessert, try the peanut-butter pie. | 2105 School St. | 228/875–1925 | Reservations not accepted | $25–$32 | No credit cards | No lunch. Closed Sun.

Lodging

Ocean Springs Days Inn. Several local casinos run shuttles right to the door of this budget motel, which is a 10-minute drive to the Gulf of Mexico. In-room data ports, some microwaves, some refrigerators, some in-room hot tubs. Outdoor pool. Pets allowed. | 7305 Washington Ave. | 228/872–8255 | fax 228/872–8210 | www.daysinn.com | 58 rooms | $60–$170 | AE, D, DC, MC, V.

Ocean Springs Super 8 Motel This two-story budget chain motel is close to casinos, restaurants, golf, the beaches, and fishing. | 60 rooms. Complimentary Continental breakfast. In-room data ports, cable TV. Pool. Laundry facilities. Business services. | 500 Bienville Rd. | 228/872–1888 or 800/800–8000 | fax 228/875–8750 | $49–$89 | AE, D, DC, MC, V.

OXFORD

MAP 4, E2

(Nearby towns also listed: Clarksdale, Grenada, Holly Springs, Robinsonville, Sardis and Tupelo)

Oxford has garnered its share of international fame, both as the setting for William Faulkner's novels and as the site of violent confrontations during the Civil Rights era. Today the city has a peaceful, old-fashioned look that belies booming growth—both in town and at the adjacent University of Mississippi (or, as it's better known, "Ole Miss"). Even the most jaded travelers often fall for Oxford's charm as they stroll around its square or along its quiet, tree-lined streets. The town still looks and feels like a Faulkner novel, in spite of the outlying shopping malls and suburban growth of recent years. Much has changed, however, since September 1962, when die-hard segregationists battled with federal marshals over the admission of the university's first black student. It resulted in a riot that left three dead and 160 injured. Today the university is racially mixed, and it's not unusual to see integrated groups in restaurants or stores.

Oxford's long and colorful history has been entwined with Ole Miss since 1848. At one time, many residents grudgingly tolerated the hordes of students, but today most recognize the cultural richness—and economic boon—that proximity to Ole Miss brings. For a town its size (pop. 12,000), Oxford has a remarkable array of nightclubs, ethnic restaurants, and sporting events. The area is also rich in historic sites, and nearby Holly Springs National Forest and Sardis Lake offer lovely scenery and opportunities for hunting, fishing, and other outdoor activities. Partly because of the mixture of small-town charm and big city offerings, Oxford's retirement community is also growing.

Information: Oxford Tourism Council | 115 S. Lamar Blvd., Oxford 38655 | 662/234–4680 | www.touroxfordms.com.

Attractions

College Hill Presbyterian Church. William Faulkner was married at this little church. | College Hill Rd. | 662/234–5020 | Free | Daily dawn–dusk.

Courthouse Square. This square features National Historic Landmarks including the Lafayette County Courthouse, which was partly burned during the Civil War. Its classic appearance has led to its use in several movies. It is also one of the best people-watching spots in Mississippi. | Between Jackson Ave. and Van Buren Ave.

Holly Springs National Forest. Oxford is at the south end of Holly Springs National Forest, an expanse of wooded hills and valleys, including pretty Puskus Lake, with camping, fishing, a boat ramp, and sailing. | 1000 Front St. | 662/236–6550 | fax 662/234–8318 | Free | Daily 6AM–10PM; closed Dec. 1–Apr. 1.

Lamar Boulevard. Among the most scenic residential streets in the state, Lamar Boulevard boasts an eclectic array of architecture and stately old trees.

★ **Rowan Oak.** Rowan Oak was the home of Nobel- and Pulitzer Prize–winning author William Faulkner. He not only wrote many of his novels here, he outlined one of them on the wall. The house has been preserved as it was the day he died in July 1962. The 1848 building, now a National Historic Landmark, is owned by the University of Mississippi. | Old Taylor Rd. | 662/234–3284 | Free | Tues.–Fri. 10–12 and 2–4, Sat. 10–4, Sun. noon–4.

St. Peter's Cemetery. Faulkner and other notable local figures are buried at this cemetery. | 113 S. 9th St. | 662/234–1269 | Free | Daily dawn–dusk.

St. Peter's Episcopal Church. St. Peter's is the oldest religious structure in town. Note the stained-glass windows. | 113 S. 9th St. | 662/234–1269 | Free | Sanctuary daily; office weekdays 9–5.

Southside Gallery. This gallery dedicated to Southern artists hosts about 10 shows a year. | 150 Courthouse Sq. | 662/234–9090 | www.southsideoxford.com | Free | Mon.–Thurs. 10–5:30, Fri.–Sat. 10–9:30.

Square Books. This down-home local bookstore has an unrivaled selection of local and regional titles. You can read your selections in the coffee shop. | 160 Courthouse Sq. | 662/236–2262 or 800/648–4001 | www.squarebooks.com | Free | Mon.–Thurs. 9–9, Fri.–Sat. 9–10, Sun. 10–6.

University of Mississippi. The legendary Ole Miss campus includes the scenic Grove, where alumni and students hold parties before and after football games. A brochure is available at the Lyceum on University Avenue. | University Ave. | 662/232–7282 | www.olemiss.edu | Free.

Center for the Study of Southern Culture. Housed in the Barnard Observatory at Ole Miss, the center has archives and exhibits on folklore, literature, photography, and music. It's also home to the largest blues archives in the world. | Farley Hall | 662/915–5993 | www.olemiss.edu | Weekdays 8–5.

LITERARY MISSISSIPPI

Literary lights have long wondered how a sparsely populated, comparatively unsophisticated state like Mississippi has so consistently produced great writers, from Nobel Prize–winning novelist William Faulkner to playwright Tennessee Williams and best-selling author John Grisham. Still, it is a surprisingly bookish state. Just about every town has a book store, and some of those stores, like Square Books in Oxford and Lemuria in Jackson, are exceptional.

Another answer lies in the colorful people of the cities and villages of Mississippi, who clearly supply much of the raw material and inspiration. In southwestern Mississippi you can pick up the trail of Eudora Welty. From Columbus to Clarksdale you'll see antebellum homes and landscapes that Tennessee Williams used in his plays. (And if you watch movies like *Cat on a Hot Tin Roof,* you may even see the original sites.) In Oxford you may encounter characters like those who populate Faulkner's novels, and you can even visit his home. Oxford is also the home of novelists Grisham, Barry Hannah, and Larry Brown. Welty and novelists Richard Ford and Richard Wright grew up in Jackson; Yazoo City was the birthplace of Willie Morris; and Greenville lays claim to authors Shelby Foote, William Alexander Percy, Hodding Carter, Clifton Taulbert, Walker Percy, and Beverly Lowry.

© Corbis

John Davis Williams Library. The Mississippi Room of the library has a permanent exhibit on Faulkner, his Nobel Prize, and first editions of his works. It also displays works by other Mississippi authors. | University Ave. | 662/915–7091 | www.olemiss.edu | Free | Call for hours.
University Museums. Housed here are five permanent collections endowed to the museum by the Skipwith family; they include Greek antiquities, African, Southern, and South American art, and Civil War artifacts. | University Ave. | 662/232–7073 | www.olemiss.edu | Free | Tues.–Sat. 10–4:30, Sun. 1–4.

ON THE CALENDAR
JULY: *Faulkner and Yoknapatawpha Conference.* Each year, this scholastic event on the University of Mississippi campus considers a different contemporary theme in the context of Faulkner's work. | University Ave. | 662/232–5993 | www.olemiss.edu.
JULY: *Oxford July 4th Celebration.* This three-day festival includes a community band concert, parade, street dance, a fun run, and fireworks. | 662/234–4680 or 800/880–6967.

Dining
Bottletree Bakery. Café. This is the closest to crusty European-style bread that you'll find in Mississippi, and perhaps in all of the South. If that isn't reason enough to stop in to this spot right off the Square, check out the saucer-size cinnamon rolls or butter croissants. Breads include nine grain and rosemary garlic. Sandwiches range from vegetarian to roast beef, and all are served on freshly baked bread. | 923 Van Buren St. | 662/236–5000 | Breakfast also available | $3–$8 | AE, D, MC, V | No dinner.

★ **City Grocery.** Creole. Once a livery stable, the building now houses a bistro with appealing hardwood floors and exposed brick walls. The Courthouse Square restaurant is downstairs; a bar is on the second floor. The Grocery's innovative cooking is reminiscent of New Orleans style. Specialties include shrimp & grits, Creole-style dishes, and an outstanding flourless Grand Marnier chocolate espresso soufflé cake. | 152 Courthouse Sq. | 662/232–8080 | www.citygroceryoxford.com | $17–$23 | AE, D, DC, MC, V | Closed Sun.

Downtown Grill. Seafood. This restaurant on Courthouse Square has incomparable style and taste, and serves mouthwatering dishes such as catfish Lafitte and a wonderful array of rich desserts. You can people-watch from the bar's second-floor balcony, which overlooks the square, or eat in the downstairs dining room. There's live entertainment Thursday through Saturday. | 110 Courthouse Sq. | 662/234–2659 | $25–$34 | AE, D, MC, V | Closed Sun.

Smitty's Blues Café. Southern. Look for home-style red-eye gravy and grits, biscuits with blackberry preserves, fried catfish, chicken and dumplings, corn bread, and black-eyed peas at this spot two blocks off Courthouse Square. The oak paneled walls are covered with pictures of old Oxford. | 208 S. Lamar Blvd. | 662/234–9111 | Breakfast also available | $4–$9 | MC, V | No dinner Sun.–Tues.

Lodging
Alumni Center Hotel. This hotel, which is part of the university, is open all year. East wing rooms are a bit larger than west wing rooms and, you can get free passes to use the Ole Miss gymnasium. Complimentary Continental breakfast, in-room data ports, some refrigerators. Outdoor pool. | Alumni Dr. | 662/234–2331 or 888/486–7666 | fax 662/234–0437 | www.olemiss.edu | 96 rooms | $63–$69 | MC, V.

Days Inn Oxford. This friendly, basic two-story motel is about a mile from Courthouse Square. | 90 rooms. Restaurant, bar, room service. Cable TV. Pool. Laundry services. Business services. | 1101 Frontage Rd. | 662/234–9500 or 800/329–7466 | fax 662/234–9500 | www.daysinn.com | $59–$99 | AE, D, DC, MC, V.

Downtown Inn. This 1963 inn is a bit on the old side, but has a convenient location two blocks north of Courthouse Square. | 123 rooms. Restaurant, bar, room service. In-room data ports, cable TV. Outdoor pool. Laundry facilities. Business services, airport shuttle. Pets allowed. | 400 N. Lamar Blvd. | 662/234–3031 | fax 662/234–2834 | $60–$70 | AE, D, DC, MC, V.

Oliver-Britt House. This B&B is in a restored 1905 manor house. Rooms are small but comfortable. The house is conveniently located between the university and Courthouse Square. | 5 rooms. Complimentary breakfast. Cable TV, no room phones. Business services. Some pets allowed. | 512 Van Buren Ave. | 662/234–8043 | fax 662/281–8065 | $75–$150 | AE, D, MC, V.

Park Place Inn. This two-story inn has pillars out front and a winding staircase in the lobby. It is near the interstate and the Ole Miss campus, less than 2 mi west of downtown. | 116 rooms. Cable TV. Pool. Business services. | 2201 Jackson Ave. W | 662/234–7013 | fax 662/236–4378 | $69–$99 | AE, D, DC, MC, V.

Puddin Place. This 1892 Victorian house near the Ole Miss campus includes a back porch with swings and rockers. The two suites—each with sitting room, separate bedrooms, and private baths—are furnished with antiques and collectibles. The downstairs suite has its own washer and dryer as well as two working fireplaces. The upstairs suite has two bedrooms and four working fireplaces—including one in the bathroom. Complimentary breakfast. Some refrigerators, no room phones. Laundry facilities. | 1008 University Ave. | 662/234–1250 | fax 662/236–4285 | turnbow@dixie-net.com | 2 suites | $99–$150 | No credit cards.

PASCAGOULA

MAP 4, F8

(Nearby towns also listed: Biloxi; Gulf Islands National Seashore; Gulfport; Mobile, AL; Ocean Springs; Pass Christian; Waveland; and Wiggins)

Pascagoula is primarily a center for heavy industry and ship-building, and it looks the part. Giant cranes line the waterfront, and refineries and fish-rendering plants tower above the outlying marshes. The water is murky, of course, so you won't be inclined to swim.

THE GULF COAST

Mississippi's coast is an almost unbroken string of cities and towns, each with its own character. It is a place of contrasts, where quiet seaside villages nestle between industrial corridors and sprawling casino resorts; where congested highways wind past beautiful wilderness areas; where construction booms in the oldest of cities.

The range of attractions is broad: casino resorts that offer gambling, golf, white beaches, and live entertainment; historic homes, including the last home of Jefferson Davis; deep-sea fishing and sunset cruises on the Gulf of Mexico.

Because the weather is more moderate here than in inland Mississippi, the coast may be crowded at any time of year. Spring and fall are the best times to visit, but vacation plans may be subject to change during hurricane season, which lasts from August to November. Or Spring Break, which can produce similar effects.

Related towns: Biloxi, Gulfport, Ocean Springs, Pascagoula, Pass Christian, Waveland.

© Corbis

Pascagoula, on the gulf in the southeastern corner of the state, has been a significant port since the early 1800s, when the river was dredged. The volume of cotton and lumber production upriver led the city to deepen and widen the channel again in the 1870s. More changes took place after the Jackson County Port Authority was established in 1956.

Now, only the shrimp boats and a few old homes hint at Pascagoula's former life as a quiet coastal town. But you don't have to pass up Pascagoula. Of interest are three nature areas, two museums, and several scenic neighborhoods along the waterfront. Ingalls Shipbuilding, south of the Pascagoula River bridge on U.S. 90, is impressive, too. And then there is the river itself, which sometimes emits an unusual high-pitched buzz.

Information: **Jackson County Area Chamber of Commerce** | 720 Krebs Ave., Pascagoula 39568-0480 | 228/762–3391 | www.jcchamber.com.

Attractions

Gulf Coast Gator Ranch. On the Gator Ranch, you can walk along boardwalks above alligators basking in the sun, or take a tour and a boat ride. Beavers and other animals can also be seen. | 10300 U.S. 90, Pascagoula | 228/475–6026 | $4–$12 | Mon.–Sat. 9–5, Sun. 1–5.

Longfellow House. The Longfellow House, built in 1850, is so called because it is believed to have been visited by American poet Henry Wadsworth Longfellow (1807–1882). He mentioned "Pascagoula's sunny bay" in his poem "The Building of the Ship." The house is not open to the public. | E. Beach Blvd. | 228/762–1122.

Old Spanish Fort Museum. This is not really a fort—it's a house—and it's not really Spanish—it's French. The La Pointe-Krebs House, as it's sometimes called, *is* the oldest private building in the Mississippi Valley. The house was built in 1718 with cypress and juniper, and chinked with a mix of clay, moss, and a plaster made of ground oyster shells. The adjacent museum displays 18th-century objects and Native American artifacts. It also has a hands-on exhibit for kids. | 4602 Fort St. | 228/769–1505 | fax 228/769–1432 | www.pascagoula.com/spanishfort | $3 | Mon.–Sat. 9:30–4:30, Sun. noon–4:30.

Pascagoula River Wildlife Management Area. This remote labyrinth of freshwater swamps offers hunting, fishing, and primitive camping. It is one of the last remaining stands of old-growth forest in the region, and quite spectacular. The Pascagoula River Wildlife Management Area, which lies to the east of town, includes some of the only surviving old-growth swamp forests on the gulf coast. | 816 Wade-Vancleave Rd., Moss Point | 228/588–3878 | fax 228/588–6248 | Free.

Scranton Nature Center and Museum. Housed in part on a 70-ft-long retired shrimp boat, this museum has exhibits covering fossils, rocks, plants, and animals. The boat has a preserved deck, galley, bunkroom, and wheelhouse, and on its lower level, a wetlands diorama and three large aquariums. The center, off U.S. 90 west of town near the drawbridge, also has a playground. | I. G. Levy Park North | 228/938–6612 | fax 228/938–6795 | Free | Tues.–Sat. 10–4, Sun. 1–4.

Shepard State Park. You can sail, camp, bike, and hike along nature trails at this park west of town off U.S. 90. | 1034 Graveline Rd., Gautier | 228/497–2244 | fax 228/497–3468 | $2 per vehicle | Daily 6 AM–10 PM.

ON THE CALENDAR

OCT.: *Jackson County Fair.* This free agricultural and industrial fair includes rides, livestock, arts and crafts, and food. | 228/475–8418 and 228/762–6043.

OCT.: *Zonta's Arts and Crafts Festival.* This one-day arts and crafts show at the Downtown Plaza has food and live entertainment. | 228/475–2366 and 228/762–7018.

Dining

Fillets Family Restaurant. American. Lage, tasty po'boys, catfish, and onion rings are among the top sellers at this laid-back diner. | 1911 Denny Ave. | 228/769–0280 | $7–$15 | AE, D, DC, MC, V.

Tiki Restaurant, Lounge, and Marina. Seafood. A variety of seafood dishes and steaks—including a 10-oz blackened prime rib and red snapper cones—can be enjoyed inside or on two decks over the water at this restaurant on the bayou. There's karaoke all week and a band performs weekends. The restaurant is 3 mi west of Pascagoula. | 3212 Mary Walker Dr., Gautier | 228/497–1591 | fax 228/497–1575 | $8–$23 | AE, D, DC, MC, V.

Lodging

Days Inn Moss Point. This three-story motel is 8 mi from the Gulf of Mexico and 6 mi from downtown. The '90s stucco building is near several excellent restaurants. | 54 rooms. Complimentary Continental breakfast. Refrigerators, microwaves, cable TV. Pool. | 6700 Hwy. 63, Moss Point | 228/475–0077 and 800/544–8313 | fax 228/475–3783 | www.daysinn.com | $35–$80 | AE, D, DC, MC, V.

La Font Inn Resort. This 1963 two-story brick hotel 5 mi from downtown has a distinctive glass and metal pyramid. It is set on 9 acres of landscaped grounds, a few minutes from casinos, beaches, fishing, and golf courses. | 192 rooms. Restaurant, bar, room service. In-room data ports, some kitchenettes, refrigerators, cable TV. Pool, wading pool. Sauna, hot tub. Tennis courts. Exercise equipment. Playground. Laundry facilities. Business services. Some pets allowed. | 2703 Denny Ave., Pascagoula | 228/762–7111 or 800/647–6077 (800/821–3668 within MS) | fax 228/934–4324 | www.lafont.com | $53–$79 | AE, D, DC, MC, V.

PASS CHRISTIAN

INTRO
ATTRACTIONS
DINING
LODGING

PASS CHRISTIAN

MAP 4, E8

(Nearby towns also listed: Biloxi; Gulfport; New Orleans, LA; Ocean Springs; Pascagoula; Picayune; Waveland; and Wiggins)

With sailboats plying the gulf, and waterfront mansions framed by magnificent live oak trees, Pass Christian comes as close to the idealized vision of a Gulf Coast city as any in Mississippi. Free of the sprawl of casinos, fast-food restaurants, and T-shirt shops, it is largely residential and, as a result, noticeably more quiet and sedate. Still, it's just a short drive (relatively—it's 65 mi) to New Orleans, the casinos of Bay St. Louis, and the tourist areas of Gulfport and Biloxi. Pass Christian's unusual name comes from the fact that it is located near the pass (a narrow waterway) that leads into the Bay of St. Louis.

Along Scenic Drive (U.S. 90) you can see pre–Civil War homes that were built by wealthy families from New Orleans who used them as summer getaways. However, the only time you can go inside these elegant homes is during the pilgrimage tour. There's a quiet beach for strolling and wading (the water is shallow, with little surf under normal conditions). The small downtown area has inviting specialty shops and gourmet food markets, and the harbor is picturesque. Also worth seeing are some particularly impressive live oak trees, including the Friendship Oak in nearby Long Beach on the University of Southern Mississippi's Gulf Park Campus, which is believed to be 500 years old.

Information: Mississippi Gulf Coast Convention and Visitors Bureau | Box 6128, Gulfport 39506 | 800/237–9493 and 888/467–4853 | www.gulfcoast.org.

Attractions

Buccaneer State Park. You can picnic, camp, play tennis, or fish from the seawall at this park 15 mi west of town. The park has no affiliation with nearby Buccaneer Bay water park.

| 1150 S. Beach Blvd., Waveland | 228/467–3822 | www.mdwfp.com | $2 per vehicle | Daily 6 AM–10 PM.

The Friendship Oak. Legend has it that if you walk with someone in the shade of the huge 500-year-old Friendship Oak on the Gulf Coast campus of the University of Southern Mississippi, you will remain friends forever. | 730 E. Beach Blvd., Long Beach | 228/865–4573 | fax 228/865–4596 | www.usm.edu | Free.

ON THE CALENDAR
MAY: *Annual Tour of Homes.* A small number of the town's charming homes are open for public inspection during this tour. | 228/452–0063 and 228/452–2242.
MAY: *Blessing of the Fleet.* All manner of craft, from jet skis to shrimp boats, are ceremonially blessed by the Bishop of the Biloxi diocese at the church of St. Michael the Archangel, the Maritime and Seafood Industry Museum, and the Biloxi Community Center and Beachfront. A shrimp festival and parade are held in conjunction with the blessing, which takes place the first full weekend in May. | 228/435–6339 or 800/245–6943.

Dining
Annie's. American/Casual. You can eat your meal sitting in copper booths at this Southern cottage overlooking the Gulf of Mexico. It has a glass-roofed patio decorated with flowers, plantation bells, iron pots, a fireplace used in winter, and a fountain that gushes in summer. Kids go for chicken fingers, adults enjoy broiled flounder and fried chicken plates. | 120 W. Bayview St. | 228/452–2062 | $10–$20 | AE, D, MC, V | Closed Mon.–Tues., and Dec.

Lodging
Casino Magic Inn. This four-story gulf-front hotel features a golf course designed by Arnold Palmer, four restaurants, a marina, and an RV Park. Across the street is the Magic Casino. | 201 rooms. 4 restaurants, bar, complimentary breakfast. Some refrigerators, cable TV. Heated pool. Outdoor hot tub. Laundry facilities. | 711 Casino Magic Dr., Bay St. Louis | 228/466–0891 or 800/562–4425 | fax 228/466–0870 | www.casinomagic.com | $59–$119 | AE, D, DC, MC, V.

PHILADELPHIA

MAP 4, E5

(Nearby towns also listed: Kosciusko, Louisville, and Meridian)

For a small city in a predominately rural area, Philadelphia offers unusually diverse attractions. There is a wealth of Native American historic sites, one of the largest casino resorts in the state, and many cultural events.

It is also the home of the Neshoba County Fair, a week-long gathering of families and friends of primarily Scots-Irish and English descent. It takes place at a rural complex of wooden cabins, and is known for its food, politics, sing-alongs, and horse-racing. Despite its homespun character, this fair is billed as "Mississippi's Giant House Party."

Philadelphia is near the legendary birthplace of the Choctaw Nation, Nanih Waiya, and the reservation of the Mississippi Band of Choctaws. That group was able to remain behind when most of the nation was forced to move to Oklahoma. Lately, they have begun to establish themselves as an economic force through industrial development and the sprawling Silver Star Resort and Casino. Each year, the Choctaws put on a cultural festival, the Choctaw Indian Fair, that celebrates their heritage.

In 1964, three civil rights workers who came to investigate the burning of a church were murdered. Those deaths divided the community, provoked national outrage, and led to the first successful federal prosecution of a civil rights case in Mississippi.

Information: **Choctaw Tourism Commission** | Box 6010, Philadelphia 39350 | 601/656–5251 or 601/650–3684. **Philadelphia–Neshoba County Chamber of Commerce** | 410 Poplar Ave., Philadelphia 39350 | 601/656–1742.

Attractions

Choctaw Museum of the Southern Indian. When European explorers arrived, there were three major Indian tribes in what is now Mississippi: the Chickasaw, the Natchez, and the Choctaw. This museum, which tells their story, is on the Choctaw Reservation. | 101 Industrial Rd. | 601/656–1537 and 601/656–5251 | fax 601/656–6696 | www.choctaw.org | Free | Weekdays 8–4:30, Sat. 9–4.

Florence Mars House. Florence Mars, a local white outraged some townspeople by speaking out against the murders of three visiting Civil Rights workers. Mars wrote a book about the experience, *Witness in Philadelphia*. The house is not open to the public. | 518 Poplar Ave.

Golden Memorial State Park. This park has picnic tables, grills, shelters, nature trails, and a 15-acre, spring-fed lake stocked with bass and bream. | Hwy. 1, Walnut Grove | 601/253–2237 | Free | Wed.–Sun. 8–5.

Indian Mission Site, Holy Rosary Catholic Church. This Indian mission and school was founded by Dutch missionary priests in 1884. It's just a few miles south of town. | 10131 Holy Rosary Rd., Tucker | 601/656–2880 | Free | By appointment only.

Nanih Waiya State Historic Site. This group of sacred mounds, over 2,000 years old, mark the geographical origin of the Choctaw Nation. The site, often referred to as the "mother mound," also includes a hiking trail and a picnic area. | Rte. 3, Box 251-A, Louisville | 662/773–7988 or 800/GO–PARKS | www.mdwfp.com | Free | Wed.–Sat. 8–5.

Neshoba County–Philadelphia Historical Museum. This museum building was built around 1860 on land that had belonged to the Choctaw Indian Tribe before they were forcibly relocated to Oklahoma. The museum documents the exile and has a collection of Choctaw and Civil War artifacts. | 303 Water Ave. | 601/656–1284 | www.phillypages.com | Free | Weekdays 9–4:30.

Philadelphia Historic District Driving Tour. The chamber of commerce can tell you about good routes to view the city's turn-of-the-century architecture. | 410 Poplar Ave. | 601/656–1742 | Free.

Silver Star Resort and Casino. This casino on the Choctaw Indian Reservation has a full range of table and video games, a 500-room hotel, six restaurants, convention facilities, and golf course. | Hwy. 16 W | 601/650–1234 or 800/922–9988 | fax 601/650–1334 | www.silverstarresort.com | Free | Open 24 hours.

ON THE CALENDAR

JULY: *Choctaw Indian Fair.* This Choctaw Indian Reservation mid-month event showcases Native American heritage with dances, exhibits, food, stickball, and art. | 601/656–1742.

JULY, AUG.: *Neshoba County Fair.* Locals take their fair seriously—more than 600 cabins are set up in order for locals to be able to live on-site for the week. A race track, show barns, a grandstand, and a dance pavilion are among the venues spread across the 150-acre fairgrounds, which has been the main location since 1889. | 601/656–1742.

PHILADELPHIA

INTRO
ATTRACTIONS
DINING
LODGING

PICAYUNE

MAP 4, D8

(Nearby towns also listed: Biloxi; Gulfport; New Orleans, LA; Pass Christian; Waveland; and Wiggins)

Picayune is a good place to regroup before moving on to busy New Orleans. The city offers a few nearby diversions of its own, including the Stennis Space Center, the Crosby Arboretum Old River Wildlife Management Area, a hunting and fishing preserve on the Pearl River; and further downstream from Old River, Walkiah Bluff, a scenic spot for picnics, near the site of a landmark ecological restoration project designed to return water flows to the main channel of the river. The city also has a Mississippi Welcome Center on I–59.

Information: Picayune Chamber of Commerce | Box 448, 201 Hwy. 11 N, Picayune 39466 | 601/798–3122.

Attractions

Crosby Arboretum. A visitors center here welcomes you to explore the surrounding wetlands, woodlands, and Piney Woods Lake. Special events include a hummingbird walk in August and a scarecrow contest in October. | 370 Ridge Rd. | 601/799–2311 | fax 601/799–2372 | www.ext.msstate.edu | $4 | Wed.–Sun. 9–4:30.

John C. Stennis Space Center/NASA Test Facility. This NASA lab and research center re-opened in spring 2000 with a museum of space artifacts. Interactive exhibits, including simulations of space sensations, a gift shop, and a restaurant are open to the public; you can watch rockets being tested from a protected area within a 13,500-acre wooded buffer zone. | Stennis Space Center, Stennis | 228/688–2370 or 800/237–1821 | fax 228/688–7528 | www.ssc.nasa.gov | Free | Daily 9:30–5.

Walkiah Bluff. At this scenic bend of the Pearl River, you can use the boat ramp, swim, fish, and camp. | 662/781–3019 | Free | Daily.

KODAK'S TIPS FOR NIGHT PHOTOGRAPHY

Lights at Night
· Move in close on neon signs
· Capture lights from unusual vantage points

Fireworks
· Shoot individual bursts using a handheld camera
· Capture several explosions with a time exposure
· Include an interesting foreground

Fill-In Flash
· Set the fill-in light a stop darker than the ambient light

Around the Campfire
· Keep flames out of the frame when reading the meter
· For portraits, take spot readings of faces
· Use a tripod, or rest your camera on something solid

Using Flash
· Stay within the recommended distance range
· Buy a flash with the red-eye reduction mode

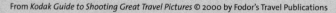

From *Kodak Guide to Shooting Great Travel Pictures* © 2000 by Fodor's Travel Publications

PORT GIBSON

(Nearby towns also listed: Natchez, Natchez Trace Parkway, Vicksburg)

This is one of the prettiest towns in the South. For support, local residents point to General Grant's statement in 1863 that the town was "too beautiful to burn." Church Street, the main thoroughfare lined with live oaks and splendid antebellum homes, appears little changed since the general passed through on his way to Vicksburg. There are also several interesting churches worth a visit. Several homes are open for tours—more during the spring pilgrimage—and the downtown area has some fine examples of 19th-century architecture.

After you've seen Port Gibson, make time for the scenic and historic countryside. Many of the old wagon roads are worn deep into the earth under a canopy of moss-draped trees. The Grand Gulf Military Monument offers the only easily accessible Mississippi River vista between Vicksburg and Natchez, along with the ruins of an old river town and its Confederate forts. Nearby is the Natchez Trace Parkway, with several historic sites, and Rodney, a Mississippi River "ghost town" (although the few residents may take exception to the term). But you might most remember a visit to the ruins of Windsor, which was once Mississippi's most palatial antebellum home.

Information: Port Gibson/Claiborne County Chamber of Commerce | 1601 Church St. (Box 491), Port Gibson 39150 | 601/437–4351.

Attractions

Alcorn University. Alcorn University, founded in 1871, was the nation's first land grant college for blacks. Some of its buildings once belonged to Oakland College, a school for planters' sons closed at the beginning of the Civil War. Several of its buildings are of architectural note. | 1000 ASU Dr. | 601/877–6147 | fax 601/877–6347 | www.alcorn.edu | Free.

First Presbyterian Church. Built in 1859, this is probably the most photographed church in the state because of the unique golden hand atop its steeple. Inside are chandeliers from the steamboat *Robert E. Lee.* | Church St. | 601/437–4351 | Free | Daily 8–5.

Grand Gulf Military Monument. This park overlooking the Mississippi River commemorates a major Civil War naval battle at what was then the town of Grand Gulf. You can visit Fort Cobun, Fort Wade, log houses, a church, and, in the visitors center, a museum. The park also has picnic grounds, hiking trails, and campsites. | 12996 Grand Gulf Rd. | 601/437–5911 | www.grandgulfpark.state.ms.us | $3 | Daily 8–5.

Port Gibson Battlefield. One Union soldier called this location "romantic in the extreme." The battlefield area includes Shaifer House, a Civil War–era structure. | Old Bruinsburg Rd. | 601/437–4351 | Free | Daily 8–5.

Oak Square. An 1850 Greek Revival plantation, mansion, and former slave quarters now serve as a luxurious B&B. The house is notable for its spacious veranda and second-story porches, massive, divided staircase, ornate millwork, chandeliers in public rooms, and courtyard fountain. | 1207 Church St. | 601/437–4350 or 800/729–0240 | fax 601/437 5768 | $5 | By appointment only.

Old Rodney Presbyterian Church. Scarred by a cannonball lodged in its front wall, the Rodney Presbyterian Church stands in the nearly abandoned town of Rodney, 10 mi south of Port Gibson. | Hwy. 61 S, Alcorn exit | www.southpoint.com/rodney.html.

Rosswood Plantation. The history of Rosswood Plantation echoes much of the state's history: it has been a thousand-acre cotton plantation, a Civil War battle site and hospital, and a sharecropper tenant house. Today the house, 10 mi south of Port Gibson on Rte. 552, is a fully restored B&B listed on the National Register of Historic Places. Amid the period antiques is the diary of the original owner, Dr. Walter Wade, relating life in the mid-1800s. | Hwy. 552, Lorman | 800/533–5889 | www.rosswood.net | $7.50 | Mon.–Sat. 9–5, Sun. 12:30–5.

The Ruins of Windsor. Completed in 1861, this palatial house had four floors surmounted by a cupola. The roof was used by the Confederates as an observation deck during the Civil War, and it was a landmark that Mississippi River steamboat pilots used for navigation. Although it survived the war, Windsor was destroyed by fire in 1890. All that remains today are 22 Corinthian columns, a few sections of balcony railing, one ancient live oak, and a dangerously tilted tenant house. The ruins appeared in the 1950s movie *Raintree County.* | Old Rodney Rd. | 601/437–4351 | Free | 8–6.

St. Joseph's Catholic Church. This 1849 Gothic Revival structure is the oldest church in Port Gibson. Its almost-psychedelic blue windows and remarkably accomplished altar were carved by a 17-year-old artisan. | Church St. | 601/437–5790 | Free | Daily 9–6.

Temple Gemiluth Chassed. Across the street from St. Joseph's, this 1891 Moorish–Byzantine Revival synagogue is the oldest Jewish place of worship in Mississippi. | 708 Church St. | 601/437–4350 or 800/729–0240 | $4 | By appointment only.

Wintergreen Cemetery. One of the state's most beautiful and interesting graveyards, the 1807 cemetery has elaborate tombstones and fence work under towering magnolia and cedar trees. Wintergreen was the original family cemetery of the Gibson family, founders of the city. | Greenwood St. | 601/437–5776 | Free | Daily 7–5.

ON THE CALENDAR

MAR.: *Main Street Heritage Festival.* This event celebrates the city's history with entertainment and food on Main Street the last Saturday in March. | 601/437–4234 or 601/437–4500.

MAR.: *Port Gibson Spring Pilgrimage.* This event opens some of the city's finest homes for tours. | 601/437–4351.

Dining

Old Depot. Southern. This cozy restaurant, not far from the Natchez Trace Parkway, is known for its red beans and rice, steak, seafood, and railroad memorabilia. There's a menu for kids. | 1202 Market St. | 601/437–4711 | $15–$25 | AE, D, MC, V | Closed Sun.

Lodging

Canemount Plantation. This rural home built in 1855 is on the grounds of a 6,000-acre working plantation. You can stay in guest rooms in the plantation house, the barn, or the servant quarters. Evening cocktails and a gourmet dinner are included in the price. You can also take Jeep tours of a 10,000-acre natural game preserve. The plantation, listed on the National Register of Historic Places, is midway between Natchez and Vicksburg, 3 mi from Alcorn State University, 18 mi south of Port Gibson. | 6 suites, 2 cottages. Complimentary breakfast, complimentary dinner. No room phones. Pool. Business services. No kids under 12. No smoking. | Hwy. 2, Lorman | 601/877–3784 or 800/423–0684 (outside MS) | fax 601/877–2010 | www.canemount.com | $195–$225 | AE, MC, V.

Oak Square Country Inn. This breathtaking two-story 1850 Greek Revival mansion is in a lovely residential area in the center of Port Gibson. The exterior is graced by six fluted Corinthian columns over 20 ft tall. Rooms have an Old South theme, and many have canopy beds. | 10 rooms. Complimentary breakfast. Cable TV. | 1207 Church St. | 601/437–4350 or 800/729–0240 | fax 601/437–5768 | www.oaksquare.com | $95–$125 | AE, D, MC, V.

Rosswood Plantation. This 1857 Greek Revival B&B is set on plantation grounds 10 mi south of Port Gibson that include former slave quarters, and a battlefield. Rooms have 14-ft ceilings, fireplaces, and antiques. | 14 rooms. Complimentary breakfast. Cable TV. Pool. Hot tub. Business services. | Hwy. 1, Lorman | 601/437–4215 or 800/533–5889 | fax 601/437–6888 | www.rosswood.net | $115–$135 | AE, D, MC, V.

ROBINSONVILLE

(Nearby towns also listed: Clarksdale, Holly Springs; Memphis, TN; Oxford; and Sardis)

Much as Las Vegas grew from dusty desert origins, so the casinos of Tunica County emerged from a landscape of seemingly endless cotton fields. Before casinos, the area was rural and comparatively remote—unless you count nearby Tunica—the poorest town in America a decade ago—or Robinsonville, then little more than a plantation crossroads. Neon-lit gambling halls and high-rise hotels glitter on the horizon at night. The Gold Strike Casino is the tallest building in Mississippi.

Some of the casinos are adding facilities in an effort to make Tunica County a resort destination, but for most travelers gambling is the one and only reason to visit. With nearly a dozen full-fledged casinos, and more on the way, Robinsonville appears destined to become one of the nation's gambling meccas. A quirk in state law allows gambling boats to float in man-made lagoons linked with the river by long ditches. If you're game, you can hop from one casino to the next, though to see them all you'll need a car or shuttle.

Information: **Tunica County Convention and Visitors Bureau** | 13625 Hwy. 61 N; Box 2739, Tunica 38676 | 662/363–3800 or 888/488–6422 | fax 662/363–1493 | www.tunicamiss.org. **Desoto County Chamber of Commerce** | 295 Lobster St., Hernando 38632 | 662/429–9055.

ROBINSONVILLE

INTRO
ATTRACTIONS
DINING
LODGING

THE GREAT RIVER ROAD

The Great River Road runs beside the Mississippi River, through the heart and soul of the state. Between Memphis and the Louisiana line, it passes plantations that were immortalized by playwright Tennessee Williams, juke joints that serve up down-home blues, Vicksburg's famed Civil War battlefield, and the antebellum homes of Natchez. Gamblers, history buffs, blues fans, and lovers of gardens and architecture will find plenty to keep them entertained.

Just south of Memphis are more than a dozen casinos and a hotel that's the tallest building in Mississippi. Elsewhere in the delta the landscape is decidedly rural—fields of cotton stretching to the horizon interspersed with cypress swamps and occasional access points to the river, which is hidden from view behind massive flood-control levees.

From Vicksburg south, the landscape is hilly and more forested; attractions include Civil War battlefields, Native American sites, the boyhood home of Confederate President Jefferson Davis, and columned mansions that overlook the river. For a change of pace there are also several nature preserves, one with waterfalls as high as 30 ft.

Related towns: Robinsonville, Clarksdale, Cleveland, Greenville, Vicksburg, Port Gibson, Natchez, Woodville.

© Corbis

Attractions

Arkabutla Lake. This man-made reservoir offers a range of outdoor activities, including camping facilities. | 3905 Arkabutla Dam Rd., Coldwater | 662/562–6261 | fax 662/562–8972 | Free | Daily 6 AM–10 PM.

Desoto County Courthouse. Hernando, 22 mi east of Tunica, was named after the explorer Hernando de Soto. His exploits are depicted on a wall mural on this 1836 courthouse. | 2535 U.S. 51, Hernando | 662/429–5011 | fax 662/429–1311 | Free | Daily 8–5.

Casinos. The casinos listed here have free admission and are open 24 hours. **Fitzgerald's Casino** (711 Lucky La., | 800/766–5825). **Grand Casino** (13615 Old Hwy. | 800/946–4946). **Harrah's Casino** (1600 Harrah's Dr. | 800/HARRAHS). **Harrah's Tunica Mardi Gras Casino** (1100 Casino Strip Blvd. | 888/789–7900). **Hollywood Casino** (1150 Casino Strip Blvd. | 800/871–0711). **Horseshoe Casino** (1021 Casino Center Dr. | 800/303–7463). **Sheraton Casino** (1107 Casino Center Dr. | 800/391–3777).

Hernando de Soto Memorial Trail. With a map provided by the Desoto County Chamber of Commerce, you can embark on a self-guided quest to find the spot where (it is believed) de Soto first saw the Mississippi River, 25 mi east of Tunica. | 295 Lobster St., Hernando | 662/429–9055 | Free | Weekdays 8–5.

Jerry Lee Lewis Ranch. You can tour the rock 'n' roll legend's home. | 1595 Malone Rd., Nesbit | 662/429–1290 | fax 662/429–9830 | www.jerryleelewis.com | $15 | Weekdays 10–4 by appointment.

SARDIS

MAP 4, D2

(Nearby towns also listed: Clarksdale; Holly Springs; Memphis, TN.; Oxford; and Robinsonville)

The best reason to visit Sardis is to use the recreation facilities at nearby Sardis Lake, a Tallahatchie River reservoir. The town itself has some interesting old buildings, including many late 19th- and early 20th-century homes, some of which were designed by a noted local architect Andrew "Swede" Johnson.

Information: Sardis Chamber of Commerce | 114 Lee St. Box 377, Sardis 38666 | 662/487–3451. .

Attractions

Cobb's Sorghum Mill. This mill sells syrup made the old-fashioned way, from sorghum. Outside of fall, call ahead for visits. | 944 River Rd. | 662/487–1088 | Free | Sept.–Oct. 8–4.

George Payne Cossar State Park. On a peninsula-like arm jutting into Enid Reservoir, the park has cabins, campsites, a swimming pool, a nature trail, and miniature golf. The restaurant here is known for its catfish. | 165 Hwy. 170 | 662/623–7356 | fax 662/623–0113 | www.mdwfp.com | $2 per vehicle | Daily 8–5.

Sardis Lake. This 98,500-acre lake is one of the largest in Mississippi. The novelist William Faulkner liked to sail here. You can also camp, fish, water-ski, hike along nature trails, and take in scenic vistas. | Hwy. 315, | 662/563–4531 | fax 662/563–4433 | www.mvk.usace.army.mil | Free | Daily 7–3:30.

John W. Kyle State Park. The 740-acre park on the lake has a swimming pool, tennis courts, cabins, a campground, and swimming and nature trails on Sardis Lower Lake. | 4235 State Park Rd. | 662/487–1345 | fax 662/487–0409 | $2 per vehicle | 24 hours.

OCT.: *Antique Engine and Tractor Show/Tractor Pull.* See antique tractor displays, demonstrations, a flea market, and tractor and mule pulls at this event on Sardis Industrial Park Rd. | 662/487–3451.

Lodging
Knights Inn. This two-story brick motel built in 1965 is near the interstate, John W. Kyle State Park, and downtown. | 79 rooms. Restaurant, bar, room service. Cable TV, in-room VCRs (and movies). Pool, wading pool. Business services. | 598 E. Lee St. | 662/487–3431 or 888/488–3748 | fax 662/487–2424 | www.bestwestern.com | $45–$75 | AE, D, DC, MC, V.

STARKVILLE

MAP 4, E4

(Nearby towns also listed: Columbus, Kosciusko, Louisville, Natchez Trace Parkway, Tupelo)

Mississippi State University, a center for agricultural and industrial research, was founded in Starkville in 1878. The city has a typical college town look, with block after block of fast-food restaurants, chain motels, and retail outlets. The older sections have more charm. The city dates to 1835, although most of its early buildings were destroyed by the Union army in the Civil War. There are several museums and nearby natural areas, but not surprisingly, the most popular local events are college sports.

Information: Starkville Convention and Visitors Bureau | 322 University Dr., Starkville 39759 | 662/323–3322 or 800/649–TOUR.

Attractions
Carpenter Place. This 1835 home, open for tours, is one of the oldest homes in the area. | 120 Oakridge St. | 662/323–4669 | $5 | By appointment only.

Mississippi State University. Mississippi State is a university well regarded in agriculture, sciences, and engineering. The National Science Foundation has honored the school for its research institutes, including the Raspet Flight Research Laboratory, the Magnetic Resonance Facility, the High Voltage Laboratory, and College of Veterinary Medicine. | University Dr. | 662/325–2323 | fax 662/325–1846 | www.msstate.edu | Free | Daily.

Mississippi Entomological Museum. Part of the Department of Entomology and Plant Pathology at Mississippi State, the collection includes 850,000 specimens in insect displays and live exhibits. | 103 Clay-Lyle Bldg., MSU | 662/325–2085 | fax 662/325–8837. | Free | Weekdays 8–5.

National Wildlife Refuge. The National Wildlife Refuge, 18 mi south of Starkville, offers canoeing, hunting, fishing, bird-watching, and hiking in a picturesque setting. | Hwy. 1, Brooksville | 662/323–5548 | fax 662/323–5806 | www.noxubee.sws.gov | Free | Daily 8–4:30.

OCT.: *Blackhills Festival.* There's blues and gospel music, arts and crafts, a local talent show, and a tennis tournament at this festival at Westside Park. | 662/323–5321 or 800/649–TOUR.

Dining
Harvey's. American. This family-oriented local chain has wooden floors and walls, and brass railings. The menu offers ribs, steak, and chicken. | 406 Hwy. 12 | 662/323–1639 | fax 662/323–2897 | $10–$15 | AE, D, MC, V | Closed Sun.

Lodging

Ramada Inn. This two-story building three blocks from downtown was built in the 1960s, and recently renovated. | 142 rooms. Restaurant, bar, room service. Cable TV. Outdoor pool. Business services. Some pets allowed (fee). | 403 Hwy. 12 | 662/323–6161 or or 800/228–2828 | fax 662/323–8073 | $69–$99 | AE, D, DC, MC, V.

The Cedars. This spacious 1836 antebellum plantation home is an architectural blend of late Colonial and Greek Revival. Each room has its own theme and character. The 183-acre site, complete with lovely gardens, is in a residential area 8 minutes from downtown and the university. | 9 rooms | 2173 Oktoc Rd. | 662/324–7569 | $129–$199 | MC, V.

TUPELO

MAP 4, E2

(Nearby towns also listed: Columbus, Corinth, Holly Springs, Iuka, Natchez Trace Parkway, Oxford, and Starkville)

The shack in Tupelo where Elvis Presley was born, and the Memphis mansion where he died, are bookends of the rock icon's remarkable life story. Presley grew up dirt poor, and his family's Tupelo house was repossessed. That tiny shotgun shack is, naturally enough, the biggest Tupelo draw. Fans would also do well to consult the town's festival calendar before planning a visit. Other attractions include two small Civil War battlefields, two small museums, and an art gallery. Tupelo (named after the gum tree) is noteworthy for its recent, rapid growth as a regional furniture manufacturing and shopping center.

Information: Tupelo Convention and Visitors Bureau | 399 E. Main St. Tupelo 38801 | 662/841–6521 | www.tupelo.net.

Attractions

Brices Cross Roads National Battlefield. This battlefield in north Tupelo remains much as it was in June 1864 when Union forces met a vastly outgunned and outmanned Confederate cavalry under General Nathan Bedford Forrest. Confederates succeeded in interrupting General Sherman's supply line, though soon after Sherman pressed on toward Atlanta. | 607 Grisham St. | 662/365–3969 or 800/305–7417 | www.nps.gov/natr | Free | Tue.–Sat. 9–5; Sun 12:30–5.

Elvis Presley Birthplace Center. The royal birthplace includes a park, chapel, museum, gift shop, and Presley mementos. But don't expect anything regal—this is a small, two-room shotgun house. Period furnishings within date from the 1930s. | 306 Elvis Presley Dr. | 662/841–1245 | $5 | Mon.–Sat. 9–5, Sun. 1–5.

Lyric Theatre. This turn-of-the-century performance venue is still popular for plays. | N. Broadway St. | 662/844–1935 | fax 662/844–0221 | $10 | By appointment.

Oren Dunn Museum of Tupelo. The Tupelo City Museum, as it's also called, has an eclectic collection of artifacts that includes an American flag planted on the moon, 65-million-year-old dinosaur fossils, and, of course, Elvis memorabilia—all housed in a former dairy barn. | Hwy. 6 at Ballard Park | 662/841–6438 | fax 662/841–6458 | $1 | Weekdays 8–4. May 15–Sept. 15, also open weekends.

John Allen Birthplace. You can make an appointment to tour the circa-1850 birthplace of the former Mississippi congressman and distinguished orator, who served the Confederacy as a 15-year-old scout. | 105 Elizabeth St. | 662/842–2935 | Free.

Private John Allen National Fish Hatchery. The U.S. Fish and Wildlife Service hatches millions of fish here each year for its restocking programs. The beautifully maintained grounds

TUPELO: WHERE A KING WAS BORN

In recent years, it's sometimes seemed that more people have seen Elvis Presley since his death than saw him in concert when he was alive. And they've been seeing him in some pretty strange places.

But if there's any chance at all of seeing Elvis again, the place to look for him—or, at least, the place where you're most likely to feel close to him—is Tupelo, Mississippi.

In the dark days of the Depression, a young husband named Vernon Presley borrowed $180 for wood and nails and hammered together a two-room "shotgun shack" (so named because a bullet would pass through both front and back doors) on a blue-collar street at the edge of town. Vernon's wife Gladys gave birth to Elvis here on January 8, 1935, and no one could have imagined then that the humble street outside would one day be called Elvis Presley Drive.

You can visit the house, now grandly called the Birthplace and Museum, and see some memorabilia, including a jumpsuit Elvis wore in a Las Vegas act. More telling, though, is the fact that none of the original contents or furnishings survive. Who would keep such poor things?

Elvis grew up in Tupelo. His parents brought him to church for the first time at the First Assembly of God Church (now Victory Holiness Church, 909 Berry St.). He attended Lawhon Grammar School (on Lake St.) and Milam Junior High School (on Jefferson St.). When he was 10, he sang "Old Shep" in a talent contest at the fairgrounds (on Mulberry Alley, off W. Main St.) and won five dollars for second place. (Eleven years later, in 1956, he played that fairground again but, this time, the National Guard had to be called out to hold back his fans.) When he was 11, his mother bought him his first guitar at the general store, the Tupelo Hardware Co. (114 W. Main St.). And when he was 13, the Presleys fled Tupelo in the middle of the night to escape creditors. Those experiences shaped his life.

So it hardly seems surprising that later, when he was a teenager in Tennessee, his idea of a Saturday night date was to drive in his pickup out to a black church in the fields, join the congregation at the service, and listen all night to the rocking spirituals and the passionate hymns. Elvis was shaped for life by little Tupelo, with its world of music and homemade fun, loving parents, poverty, and spirituality.

After you stroll the streets here and take a thoughtful look at the grammar school, the fairgrounds, the general store, and that old church, the glittery jumpsuit back at the house seems very much out of place. Memphis, Las Vegas, and Hollywood may have captured Elvis later in life, but Tupelo, somewhere deep in his heart, was always his home.

So if you think there's a chance of seeing Elvis anywhere, it's most likely going to be here.

are popular with local picnickers. | 111 Elizabeth St. | 662/842–1341 | fax 662/842–1341 | www.fws.gov | Free | Weekdays 7–3:30.

Tombigbee State Park. This park has camping, some cabin units, nature trails, a tennis court, a visitor center, and a lake. | 264 Cabin Dr. | 662/842–7669 | fax 662/840–5594 | $2 per vehicle | Daily 6 AM–10 PM.

Trace State Park. This 2,500-acre park in Pontotoc County, 10 mi west of Tupelo on Hwy. 6, has campsites, cabins, fishing, hiking trails, water-skiing, boat rentals, and a launch ramp. | 2139 Faulkner Rd., Belden | 662/489–2958 | fax 662/489–6917 | $2 per vehicle | Daily 6 AM–10 PM.

Tupelo Artist Guild Gallery. This public arts gallery, housed in a former bank, exhibits local, regional, and national artists. | 211 W. Main St. | 662/844–ARTS | fax 662/844–9751 | Free | Tues.–Thurs. 10–4, Fri. 1–4.

Tupelo National Battlefield. This small park off the Natchez Trace Parkway is on the site of the July 1864 Battle of Tupelo. | 2680 Natchez Trace Pkwy. | 662/680–4025 or 800/305–7417 | www.nps.gov | Free.

ON THE CALENDAR

MAR.–JULY, SEPT.–JAN.: *Tupelo Gigantic Flea Market and Craft Show.* This event at the Tupelo Furniture Market is, held every weekend except in February and August, is one of the largest of its kind in the South, offering furniture, clothes, and collectibles. | 662/842–4442.

MAY: *Gum Tree Festival.* This festival began as a juried fine arts show and grew into a two-day community party. Food, dances, literary competitions, and other entertainment round it out. The 10K race is one of the state's most popular. | 662/844–2787.

AUG.: *Elvis Presley Festival.* This three-day event, licensed by Elvis Presley Enterprises, celebrates the singer's life from its earliest days in Tupelo. There are tours of local sights, music ranging from vintage rock to gospel, a motorcycle rally, a parade of 1950s cars, street dances, and a 5K run. | 662/841–6598 or 888/273–7798.

SEPT.: *Tri-State Sportsmen's Bonanza.* This mid-month event showcases hunting and other outdoor equipment. | 662/842–4442.

SEPT.: *Tupelo Marathon.* Marathon and half-marathon races are complimented by food and entertainment. | 662/842–2039.

OCT.: *Mississippi Invitational Marching Band Festival.* As many as 30 northeast Mississippi marching bands compete in this festival. | 662/841–8975.

Dining

Jefferson Place. American/Casual. This restaurant, in a 19th-century house, is decorated with colorful tablecloths and bric-a-brac. It's popular with the college crowd and families alike, and known for its seafood and hand-trimmed beef. | 823 Jefferson St. | 662/844–8696 | fax 662/842–6026 | $9–$22 | AE, DC, MC, V | Closed Sun.

Malone's Fish and Steak House. American. This cozy restaurant near the interstate has a large menu of smoked, grilled, and fried fish, and steaks smothered in onions. There's also a salad bar and a menu for kids. | 1349 Hwy. 41 | 662/842–2747 | $11–$17 | MC, V | Closed Sun.–Mon., mid-late Dec.

Vanelli's. Greek. This popular place in the heart of Tupelo is adorned with family pictures, scenes of Greece and Italy, and checkered tablecloths. It's known for Papa Vis grilled chicken salad, pizza, the pasta buffet, and ethnic specialities. | 1302 N. Gloster St. | 662/844–4410 | fax 662/680–4746 | $15–$25 | AE, D, DC, MC, V.

Lodging

Comfort Inn. This two-story hotel built in 1987 is 1½ mi from the Tupelo National Battlefield in the downtown area. | 83 rooms. Complimentary Continental breakfast. In-room data ports, cable TV. Business services. | 1190 N. Gloster St. | 662/842–5100 or 800/221–2222 | fax 662/844–0554 | www.comfortinn.com | $50–$69 | AE, D, DC, MC, V.

Executive Inn. This five-story, brick hotel built in 1982 is 4 mi from downtown. | 118 rooms. Restaurant, bar, room service. In-room data ports, cable TV. Indoor pool. Hot tub, sauna, exercise equipment. Business services. | 1011 N. Gloster St. | 662/841–2222 or 800/533–3220 | fax 662/844–7836 | $60–$70, $125–$250 suites | AE, D, DC, MC, V.

Holiday Inn Express. This two-story, stucco hotel built in 1956 is near the Natchez Trace Parkway. There is complimentary access to a local gym. | 124 rooms. Complimentary Continental breakfast. Cable TV. Pool. Laundry facilities. Business services. | 923 N. Gloster St. | 662/842–8811 or 800/465–4329 | fax 662/844–6884 | www.holiday-inn | $55–$79 | AE, D, DC, MC, V.

Mockingbird Inn. This two-story brick B&B was built in 1925. Each room is decorated with a theme of a different country; some have fireplaces, and one has a whirlpool tub. There's a shady porch and gazebo for lounging on hot summer days. | 7 rooms. Complimentary breakfast, complimentary afternoon snacks. Some in-room hot tubs, cable TV. Business services. No kids under 13. | 305 N. Gloster St. | 662/841–0286 | fax 662/840–4158 | www.bbonline.com/ms/mockingbird | $79–$129 | AE, D, MC, V.

Ramada Inn. This two- and three-story motel, built in 1972, is near the Elvis Presley Birthplace Center. | 230 rooms. Restaurant. In-room data ports, cable TV. Pool. Gym. Laundry service. | 854 N. Gloster St. | 662/844–4111 or 800/228–2828 | fax 662/840–7960 | www.ramada.com | $49–$65 | AE, D, DC, MC, V.

Red Roof Inn. This two-story chain hotel 3 mi from downtown has standard facilities and rooms. | 100 rooms. In-room data ports, cable TV. Pool. Laundry facilities. Pets allowed. Business services. | 1500 McCullough Blvd. | 662/844–1904 or 800/733–7663 | fax 662/844–0139 | www.redroofinn.com | $39–$99 | AE, D, DC, MC, V.

VICKSBURG

MAP 4, C5

(Nearby towns also listed: Port Gibson, Greenville, Jackson, Mendenhall, Natchez, and Yazoo City)

Few cities are more closely identified with the Civil War than Vicksburg. Its downfall, which gave the Union control of the Mississippi River, played a major role in General Grant's election as president. The fact that Grant succeeded was remarkable. First, Vicksburg stands atop steep bluffs that command the Mississippi—the city was known as the "Gibraltar of the Confederacy." Second, the terrain north of the city is riddled with swamps, while steep hills and deep valleys to the south and east act as natural defenses. Grant, after failing in assaults from the south and east, marched his troops down the Louisiana bank, entering enemy territory cut off from supply lines. This gamble went down in history as a stroke of military genius.

After fighting his way into the interior, Grant and fellow general Sherman attacked Vicksburg from the rear. The siege lasted for 47 days, during which many civilians were killed. The city surrendered on July 4, 1863, and Vicksburg did not celebrate Independence Day again for more than 100 years.

Vicksburg's primary allure is as a Civil War site. But don't expect a time capsule of pretty antebellum mansions. Vicksburg is a working town, characterized by an architectural hodgepodge. There is also a cultural mix of people of African, Chinese, English, Lebanese, Irish, and Italian descent.

Vicksburg is also a good base of operations for exploring the nearby river towns and the legendary delta, one of the richest agricultural regions in the world.

Information: Vicksburg Convention and Visitors Bureau | 1221 Washington St., Vicksburg 39183 | 601/636–9421 or 800/221–3536 | www.vicksburg.cvb.org. **Tourist Information Center** | 3300 Clay St., Vicksburg 39183 | 601/636–9421 or 800/221–3536.

Attractions

African-American Historical Sites. Vicksburg has several points of significance in African-American history, including **Bethel A.M.E. Church,** founded in 1864, where the state's first black Masonic Lodge was organized. The **Holly Grove Baptist Church,** established midway through the Civil War; **Pleasant Green Baptist Church** which was built around 1898, a church where Martin Luther King Jr. spoke in 1964; and **Wesley United Methodist Church,** which was given to slaves by a white congregation. Call the Convention and Visitors Bureau for more information. | 601/636–9421 or 800/221–3536.

Antebellum homes. A number of homes survived the war, and many now serve as bed-and-breakfasts.

Anchuca. This Greek Revival home, built around 1830, was visited by Confederate President Jefferson Davis after his release from prison. It has been magnificently restored to its original elegance. | 1010 1st East St. | 888/686–0111 | $5 | Wed.–Sat. 11–3.

Balfour House. A Christmas ball in this grand Greek Revival house was interrupted by the Union assault on the city. It later served as Union headquarters. This home belonged to Emma Balfour, whose diary of the siege of Vicksburg can be viewed in the Mississippi Department of Archives. The house has a rare three-story elliptical staircase. | 1002 Crawford St. | 601/638–7113 or 800/294–7113 | www.balfourhouse.com | $5 | Mon.–Sat. 10–5; no tours Jan.–Feb.

Martha Vick House. This mini-mansion was built in the mid-19th century for an unmarried daughter of the city's founder, Newitt Vick. The house has been carefully restored, and is notable for its elegant furnishings and collection of French paintings. | 1300 Grove St. | 601/638–7036 | $5 | Mon.–Sat. 9–5, Sun. 1–5.

McRaven. McRaven began as a frontier house around 1797, became a two-story brick Empire-style house 30 years later, and subsequently underwent a Greek Revival renovation. There is visible Civil War cannon damage inside and out. Among its impressive antiques are collections of porcelain and needlepoint. | 1445 Harrison St. | 601/636–1663 | www.mcraven.com | $5 | Mar.–Nov., Mon.–Sat. 9–5, Sun. 10–5.

Biedenharn Coca Cola Museum. Although it was invented in Atlanta in 1886, the famous soft drink was first bottled in this plant in Vicksburg in 1894. The company had previously sold Coca-Cola syrup and bottled soda water to soda fountains. One day it occurred to Joseph Biedenharn, a local candy merchant, to do the bottling himself—and history was made. The museum features a 1900 soda fountain and a 1890 candy store with Cokes, candy, and ice cream. | 1107 Washington St. | 601/638–6514 | fax 601/636–5010 | $2.25 | Mon.–Sat. 9–5, Sun. 1:30–4:30.

Casinos. These casinos are open 24 hours a day, and entrance is free. **Ameristar** (4116 Washington St. | 800/700–7770), **Harrah's Vicksburg** (1310 Mulberry St. | 800/843–2343). **Isle of Capri** (3990 Washington St. | 800/946–4753), and **Rainbow Casino** (1380 Warrenton Rd. | 800/503–3777).

City Front. This is the local name for the downtown waterfront, the landing site for the river boats *Mississippi Queen* and *Delta Queen.* | 1221 Washington St. | 601/636–9421 or 800/221–3536 | Free.

Delta National Forest. This is the only bottomland hardwood national forest—a wetlands forest rich in wildlife species—in the country. About 15 mi north of Vicksburg, it offers opportunities for hunting, fishing, and wildlife watching. The Green Ash, Overcup Oak, and Sweet Gum Research Natural Areas, and the Cypress Bayou Botanical Area are of particular interest. | 402 U.S. 61, North Rolling Fork | 662/873–6256 | fax 662/873–2770 | $3 | Daily.

Gray and Blue Naval Museum. At this museum, see Civil War gunboats, paintings, and a 250-square-ft diorama of the 1863 Vicksburg battlefield. | 1102 Washington St. | 601/638–6500 | fax 601/638–8746 | www.vicksburgcvb.org/museums.htm | $2.50 | Mon.–Sat. 9–5.

Jacqueline House. This museum details the history of African-Americans from the Civil War to the present through paintings, photographs, artifacts, and memorabilia. | 1325 Main St. | 601/636–0941 | www.vicksburgcvb.org/museums.htm | $1.50 | Sat. 10–5.

Mississippi River Adventure. March through November you can take three-hour hydro-jet boat tours of the Mississippi and Yazoo rivers. | Clay St. | 601/638–5443 or 800/521–4363 | fax 601/634–0808 | www.vicksburgcvb.org | $20 | Sun. and Mon.

Old Court House Museum. This Greek Revival building, constructed by slaves in 1858, is Vicksburg's most historical site. A fascinating museum documents the speeches delivered by Jefferson Davis and U.S. Grant from the balcony of this building. | 1008 Cherry St. | 601/636–0741 | $3 | Mon.–Sat. 8:30–4:30, Sun. 1:30–4:30.

Onward Store. The Onward Store is close to the spot where President Teddy Roosevelt, while bear hunting, refused to kill a tethered cub, sparking the creation of a Teddy Bear displayed in the window. It offers some memorabilia, lots of local color, and lunches to go. Rolling-fork is located 25 mi north of Vicksburg. | Hwy. 61 and Rte. 2, Rollingfork U.S. 61 | 662/873–6804 | fax 662/873–9734 | Free | Sun.–Thurs. 7–7, Fri.–Sat. 7 AM–8 PM.

Pemberton's Headquarters. This mansion, built around 1835, was used by General Pemberton of the Confederacy during the siege. It was here that he made the decision to surrender the city. | 1018 Crawford St., Vicksburg | 601/636–9581 or 877/636–9581 | Adults $5; special rates for children | Mon.–Sat. 9–5, Sun. 1–5.

The Vanishing Glory. A 30-minute wide-screen film at the Old Strand Theater tells the story of the siege of Vicksburg through the diaries and letters of its townspeople. | 717 Clay St. | 601/634–1863 | $5 | Mon.–Sat. 9–5, Sun. 1–5.

Vicksburg National Military Park and Cemetery. You can ride in a van with a guide, or conduct your own tour of the 1,325 historic monuments and markers along the park's 16-mi driving tour. Along the way, you will see trenches and earthworks, rifle pits, 144 cannons, and the graves of 17,000 Union soldiers. | 3201 Clay St. | 601/636–0583 | fax 601/636–9497 | www.nps.gov/vick | $4 per vehicle, guides $20–$30 | Daily 8–5.

U.S.S. Cairo Museum. Alongside the military park is a museum that showcases a Union ironclad gunboat with the dubious distinction of being the first ship ever sunk by an electrically detonated torpedo. | 3201 Clay St. | 601/636–2199 | fax 601/638–7329 | www.nps.gov/vick/cairo | Free | Nov.–Mar., daily 8:30–5; Apr.–Oct., daily 9:30–6.

ON THE CALENDAR

MAR., OCT.: *Vicksburg Spring and Fall Pilgrimage.* Take a morning or afternoon tour of antebellum and Victorian homes. | 601/636–9421 or 800/221–3536.

APR.: *Riverfest.* This Friday and Saturday event on Washington St. in downtown Vicksburg features music, dancing, children's activities, and food. | 601/631–0376.

MAY: *Assault on Vicksburg.* This re-enactment of the Battle and Siege of Vicksburg includes Confederate and Union camps, tours of the McRaven home, and demonstrations of period fashions. | 601/636–1663.

JULY: *Gold in the Hills.* This vaudeville-style production at Parkside Playhouse is a nod to the days of can-can dancers and dastardly villains—the audience is encouraged to cheer and boo. | 601/636–0471 or 800/221–3536.

SEPT.: *Over the River Run.* This 5-mi race takes place on the old Mississippi River bridge. | 601/631–2131 or 800/221–3536.

OCT.: *Old Court House Flea Market.* This is a small but interesting flea market on the historic Old Court House lawn. | 601/638–1195.

DEC.: *Balfour Ball.* This event at Balfour House commemorates the 1862 Christmas ball that was interrupted by the Union assault on Vicksburg. It features period food, music, and dance, and tour of the house. | 601/638–7113 or 800/294–7113.

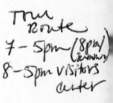

Dining

★ **Cedar Grove Inn.** Southern. This split-level dining room is in a stylish restored mansion built in 1840. The restaurant has a cozy, romantic atmosphere, with chandeliers, and brick walls. You can eat inside or outside on the veranda. Among Chef Andre's signature dishes are New Orleans catfish and an herb grilled chicken Andre. | 2200 Oak St. | 601/636–1000 or 800/862–1300 | fax 601/634–6126 | www.cedargroveinn.com/dining.htm | Reservations essential | $26–$32 | AE, D, MC, V | No lunch. Closed Mon.

Eddie Monsour's. American. This restaurant offers a variety of Lebanese and American dishes, each with an imaginative touch. Popular dishes include grilled redfish and filet mignon. There is a view of a golf course. | 127 Country Club Dr. | 601/638–1571 | $9–$25 | AE, MC, V | No lunch Sat. No dinner Sun.

Farradays' Steakhouse. Steak. The restaurant is inside the Isle of Capri casino, with river views, a romantic atmosphere, and decorations from around the world. Good dishes include the shrimp and crawfish pasta and the fisherman special. There's also an all-you-can-eat buffet. The brass kitchen can be seen from the dining room. | 3990 Washington St. | 601/630–4451 | fax 601/630–4312 | $18–$59 | AE, D, DC, MC, V.

Jacques' Cafe. Cajun. This is a popular spot with a casually elegant dining atmosphere for breakfast and dinner. Its known for its Mississippi catfish dishes and excellent steaks cooked by French chef Jacques Parmegiani. | 4137 N. Frontage Rd. | 601/638–5811 and 800/359–9363 | fax 601/638–9249 | Breakfast also served | $5–$16 | AE, D, DC, MC, V | No lunch.

Maxwell's. American. This creatively decorated restaurant in the heart of Vicksburg has a casual atmosphere. Signature dishes include the prime rib and the whitened redfish. There is a lunch buffet and a kid's menu. | 4207 Clay St. | 601/636–1344 and 800/418–7379 | Reservations essential | $8–$24 | AE, D, DC, MC, V | Closed Sun.

Walnut Hills Round Tables. Southern. This restaurant feels like the Old South, with original wood floors, and paintings and antiques displayed throughout. Top dishes include the fried chicken and fried catfish. | 1214 Adams St. | 601/638–4910 | $13–$17 | AE, D, DC, MC, V | Closed Sat. No dinner Sun.

Lodging

Ameristar Casino Hotel. This eight-story brick hotel is across from the Riverboat Casino and the Mississippi/Louisiana State Bridge, 1 mi from downtown. The western-themed rooms come with amazing river views. | 149 rooms. Restaurant, bar. In-room data ports, some in-room hot-tubs, cable TV. Pool. Hot tub. Business facilities, airport shuttle. | 4155 Washington St. | 601/638–1000 or 800/700–7770 | fax 601/630–4657 | www.ameristarcasinos.com | $59–$189 | AE, D, DC, MC, V.

Anchuca. This magnificently restored 1830 B&B is listed on the National Register of Historic Places. The Greek Revival–style home features period furnishings including early 1800 Victorian, Empire, Sheraton, and Hepplewhite pieces. Jefferson Davis spoke on the balcony after the Civil War. | 7 rooms. Complimentary breakfast. Cable TV. Pool. Hot tub. Business services. No kids under 15. | 1010 1st East St. | 601/661–0111 or 888/686–0111 | fax 601/630–4121 | www.vicksburgcvb.org/bedbreak.htm | $80–$140 | MC, V.

Annabelle Bed-and-Breakfast. This two-story, circa-1868 mansion is lavishly appointed, and has a courtyard shaded by pecan and magnolia trees. Rooms are in the main house and in the 1882 guest house. The inn is in the heart of the historic district, six blocks from downtown. | 7 rooms. Picnic area, complimentary breakfast. Pool. No smoking. | 501 Speed St. | 601/638–2000 or 800/791–2000 | fax 601/636–5054 | www.annabellebnb.com | $80–$125 | AE, D, DC, MC, V.

Battlefield Inn. This Southern-style two-story motel, built in 1973, is next to Vicksburg National Military Park and Cemetery. You'll be greeted at the inn by talking parrots, as well as the human staff. | 117 rooms. Restaurant, bar (with entertainment), complimentary breakfast. In-room data ports, some refrigerators, room service, cable TV. Pool. Business services, airport shuttle. Pets allowed. | 4137 N. Frontage Rd. | 601/638–5811 and 800/359–9363 | fax 601/638–9249 | www.battlefieldinn.org | $55–$99 | AE, D, DC, MC, V.

Belle of the Bends. Built in 1876, this three-story Italianate brick house is decorated with antiques, Oriental rugs, and memorabilia from the steamboats that traveled the Mississippi in the late 19th century. A traditional plantation-style breakfast and an afternoon tea are served. There is free casino shuttle service. | 4 rooms. Complimentary breakfast. In-room VCRs (and movies), Cable TV. | 508 Klein St. | 601/634–0737 or 800/844–2308 | fax 601/638–0544 | www.belleofthebends.com | $95–$150 | AE, D, MC, V.

★ **Cedar Grove Inn.** This beautifully restored Greek Revival mansion has one of the largest collections of antiques in the South. A Union cannonball is lodged in its parlor wall. Gazebos, fountains, and statues pepper 4 acres of lush landscaping. The inn is in a residential area of Vicksburg 1 mi from the downtown area. | 30 rooms. Restaurant, complimentary breakfast. Cable TV. Pool. Tennis. Exercise equipment. Business services. | 2200 Oak St. | 601/636–1000 or 800/862–1300 (800/448–2820 within MS) | fax 601/634–6126 | www.cedargroveinn.com | $85–$165 | AE, D, DC, MC, V.

Days Inn. This three-story motel is 2 1/2 mi from downtown, and surrounded by restaurants and shopping malls. | 83 units, 20 suites. Complimentary Continental breakfast. In-room data-ports, microwaves, refrigerators, cable TV. Pool. | 2 Pemberton Blvd. | 601/634–1622 | fax 601/638–4337 | $69–$129 | AE, D, DC, MC, V.

★ **Duff Green Mansion.** One of Mississippi's oldest mansions, this B&B offers fireplaces in every room, antiques, Oriental rugs, and overstuffed furniture. This three-story brick mansion built in 1856 is an excellent example of Palladian architecture. The National Historic Landmark is in the historic district, eight blocks from downtown. | 7 rooms. Complimentary breakfast. Cable TV. Pool. Hot tub. Business services. Some pets allowed. | 1114 1st East St. | 601/638–6662 or 800/992–0037 | fax 601/661–0079 | www.duffgreenmansion.com | $95–$125 | AE, D, MC, V.

Harrah's Casino Hotel. This luxurious eight-story brick Victorian hotel is in downtown Vicksburg next to the Mississippi River. The hotel is part of the fabulous Riverboat Casino and only one block from the new Vicksburg Convention Center. | 117 rooms. Restaurant, bar. Cable TV. Business facilities, airport shuttle. | 1310 Mulberry St. | 601/636–3423 or 800/843–2343 | www.harrahs.com | $45–$149 | AE, D, DC, MC, V.

Holiday Inn. This hotel is across from Vicksburg National Military Park and Cemetery. | 173 rooms. Restaurant, bar, complimentary breakfast. In-room data ports, room service, cable TV. Indoor pool. Video games. Laundry facilities. Business services. Some pets allowed. | 3330 Clay St. | 601/636–4551 or 800/847–0372 | fax 601/636–4552 | www.holiday-inn.com | $56–$99 | AE, D, DC, MC, V.

Quality Inn. This two-story stucco motel is in a commercial area near the Vicksburg Military Park and Cemtery. | 70 rooms. Complimentary Continental breakfast. Refrigerators, cable TV. Pool. Hot tub, sauna. Business services. Free parking. | 2390 S. Frontage Rd. | 601/634–8607 | fax 601/634–6053 | $55–$99 | AE, D, DC, MC, V.

Super 8. This two-story stucco motel was built in 1988. It's next to the National Military Park and Cemetery. | 58 rooms. In-room data ports, some microwaves, some refrigerators, cable TV. Pool. Hot tub. | 4127 N. Frontage Rd. | 601/638–5077 | fax 601/638–5077 | $40–$60 | AE, D, DC, MC, V.

WAVELAND

(Nearby towns also listed: Biloxi, Gulf Island National Seashore; Gulfport; New Orleans, LA; Ocean Springs; Pascagoula; Pass Christian; Picayune; and Wiggins)

Waveland and neighboring Bay St. Louis share a nearly indistinguishable border. Although they are essentially part of the greater New Orleans area, they have somehow managed to retain their small town coastal charm. Both are popular weekend destinations for city dwellers, and nearby Buccaneer State Park can get crowded during the summer months.

Waveland, incorporated in 1888, is a young coastal town. It suffered major damage during Hurricane Camille in 1969, and there are still many vacant lots where houses were washed or blown away. Its main thoroughfare, busy U.S. 90, can become choked with traffic. It's full of fast food chains and major discount stores.

Bay St. Louis, which dates to 1818, is surrounded by the Mississippi Sound and St. Louis Bay. It is the more attractive of the bordering towns. More than 100 buildings here are listed in the National Register of Historic Places, and the movie *This Property is Condemned,* based on a Tennessee Williams play, was filmed in the depot district downtown. The area north of the city is predominately rural, aside from the upscale residential development called Diamondhead, which is just off I–10, and NASA's Stennis Space Center, which is the largest employer in the county.

Information: **Hancock County Tourism Development Bureau** | 408A U.S. 90, Bay St. Louis 39520 | 800/466–9048 | fax 228/463–9227 | www.hancockcountyms.org.

Attractions

Buccaneer State Park and Water Park. The park has a seasonal wavepool, water slide, tennis courts, an outdoor amphitheater, swimming, nature trails, and more than 400 campsites. | 1150 S. Beach Blvd. | 228/467–3822 | $2 per vehicle | Daily 11–6:45.

Casino Magic. The casino is in the Casino Magic Inn, and offers all the usual table and video games. | 711 Casino Magic Dr., Bay St. Louis | 800/562–4424 | Free | Daily 24 hours.

Cookie's Bayou Tour. This company offers daily 90-minute tours with narration of scenic bayous, marshes, and the Jordan River. | 10774 Hwy. 603, Bay St. Louis | 228/466–4824 | cookies@ametro.net | $15.

Historic Downtown Walking Tour of Old Bay St. Louis. This tour of town includes numerous antique shops and historic buildings. | 228/467–6252.

R. Barthe Sculpture. The Hancock Public Library displays work by native sculptor Richmond Barthe, whose internationally acclaimed *Woman's Head* was the subject of an exhibition at the Smithsonian Institution's Anacostia Museum in 1993. | 312 U.S. 90, Bay St. Louis | 228/467–5282 | fax 228/467–5503 | www.hancock.lib.ms.us | Free | Mon.–Thur. 9:30–6, Fri. 9:30–5.

St. Augustine Seminary and Grotto. This is the state's oldest seminary for the training of African American Roman Catholics for the priesthood. | 119 Seminary Dr., Bay St. Louis | 228/467–6414 | fax 228/466–4393 | Free | By appointment.

ON THE CALENDAR

JULY: *Fourth of July Crab Festival.* In addition to traditional July 4th activities, this festival spotlights the area's favorite shellfish. | 228/467–6509.

SEPT.: *Diamondhead Arts and Creative Crafts Show.* This juried crafts show features over 150 participants the last weekend in the month at the Diamondhead Country Club. | 228/255–2697 or 800/466–9048.

OCT.: *Hancock County Historical Society Cemetery Tour.* This Halloween tour high-lights historic and colorful graves, with actors portraying the lives of those citizens of earlier ages. Meet at the Cedar Rest Cemetery in Bay St. Louis. | 228/467–4090.

OCT.: *International Food Festival.* This event at Our Lady of the Gulf Church includes a wide selection of international foods, music, and arts and crafts. | 228/467–7048.

WIGGINS

(Nearby towns also listed: Biloxi, Gulfport, Hattiesburg, Ocean Springs, Pascagoula, Pass Christian, Picayune, Waveland)

Wiggins is known as the home of baseball great Dizzy Dean, and as a base for explor-ing some of the finest remaining natural areas in the Deep South. Within a short distance in almost any direction from Wiggins are broad expanses of botanically diverse forests, including hilly lands crossed by clear streams, and wild, almost impenetrable swamps. The area's history is tied to the timber industry and the landscape around the town remains largely wooded. Wildlife is abundant and the rivers and streams are almost pristine. There are two federally designated wilderness areas, and numerous state wildlife management areas with plenty of opportunities for hunting, fishing, and wildlife-watch-ing.

Information: Stone County Economic Development Foundation | 311 Court St.; Box 569, Wiggins 39577 | 601/928–5418 | www.stonecounty.com.

Attractions

Ashe Lake. You can hike on nature trails, camp, and fish—no swimming, though—at this lake north of Wiggins via U.S. 49. From Brooklyn take Ashe Nursery Road to Hwy. 308 | Hwy. 308, Brooklyn | 601/928–4422 | Free | Daily.

Batson's Log Home and Fish Farm. The farm offers camping on Red Creek, fishing in clear, spring-fed ponds, and log-cabin and nature-trail tours. | 1802 Hwy. 26 | 601/928–5271 (fish-ing) or 601/928–2310 (tours) | $5 | By appointment.

Black Creek. This is a federally designated Wild and Scenic River in the De Soto National Forest, 10 mi north of Wiggins. You can take scenic float and canoe trips, swim, camp, and hike up to 40 mi alongside Black Creek. | Hwy. 29 | 601/928–4422 | www.bpbasecamp.com/ wilderness. For information on boating, contact **Black Creek Canoe Rental** | Hwy. 29 | www.blackcreekcanoe.com | $25 | Daily Mar.–Oct. **De Soto National Forest Trails.** *(See also Hattiesburg and Laurel.)* For more than 30 mi, the **Big Foot Horse Trail System** has a rider's camp, parking, and camping, but no potable water. **Tuxachanie Trail** has almost 20 mi for hiking. **Bethel ATV Trail** is for those who like to do their exploring on motorized vehicles; there's also camping. **Black Creek Trail** has 40 mi of very challenging hiking, 10 mi in the Black Creek Wilderness. | 601/928–4422 | Free | Daily.

Red Creek. This lazy creek flows through terrain that ranges from hilly pine forests to cypress swamps. The name is accurate: the water has a reddish-brown hue that comes from tan-nic acid in decaying leaves. Canoe rentals are available. There is a privately run RV park and camp ground called Perk Beach. The creek is 5 mi north of Wiggins. | U.S. 49, Perkin-ston | 601/928–4422 or 601/928–9111 (Perk Beach) | Free.

De Soto National Forest. This is the largest national forest in the state, covering half a mil-lion acres. The primarily piney woods forest includes Black Creek Wilderness—a 5,025-acre area along the banks of Black Creek known for its lush foliage and typically southern Mis-sissippi topography. You can take a Black Creek float trip, or one of Mississippi's most chal-lenging hikes, the Black Creek Trail. | 654 W. Frontage Rd., Wiggins | 601/928–4422 | Free | Daily.

Flint Creek Water Park. Just north of town, this park offers camping, cabins, fishing, swimming, and nature trails. | 1216 Parkway Dr. | 601/928–3051 | www.waterparkin.com | $1 | Daily 7 AM–8 PM.

ON THE CALENDAR

JUNE AND OCT.: *Magnolia State Bluegrass Festival.* National bluegrass recording artists take the stage at this festival, one of the oldest in the state. There's food and other entertainment offered, as well as some camping, at Stone Country Music Park in Wiggins the first week in June and October. | 601/928–3831 or 800/228–8779.

WOODVILLE

MAP 4, B7

(Nearby towns also listed: Baton Rouge, LA; McComb; Natchez; and St. Francisville, LA)

Local promoters often quote an old Harvard University study that described Woodville as "the town most typical of the antebellum South . . . least changed in appearance and tradition." Indeed, few southern cities more clearly reflect the large-mansions-and-little-shacks stereotype; and numerous historical markers make clear that change comes to this town languorously. Woodville claims the state's oldest newspaper, oldest railroad building, and three churches that are the oldest of their denominations in the state. On top of that, it was the boyhood home of Confederate President Jefferson Davis. After a while, you may wonder if the snow-cone stand you just passed is a venerable institution as well. (And it may very well be.) Among the other worthy sites are the downtown square, several antebellum town houses and rural plantation homes, the Clark Creek Natural Area, and Fort Adams.

Part of the town's antique quality is no doubt due to its relative isolation, wedged as it is in a corner of southwest Mississippi between two towns that are closely identified with Old South traditions—Natchez to the north and St. Francisville, Louisiana, to the south. Still, change has come in more subtle ways. Businesses have moved to the U.S. 61 Bypass, the African-American majority is now represented by many African-American elected officials, and residents celebrate both Confederate Memorial Day and Martin Luther King Jr. Day.

Information: **Wilkinson County Museum** | Bank St.; Box 1055, Woodville 39669 | 601/888–3998.

Attractions

Clark Creek Natural Area. Clark Creek, 13 mi southwest of town, is a lush enclave of steep ravines, magnolia forests, and waterfalls up to 50 ft tall. | 182 Fort Adams-Pond Rd. | 601/888–3998 | Free.

Fort Adams. Fort Adams was the site of a treason trial that inspired the short story "The Man Without a Country." The fort is still here, along with a country store and grocery store, but most come for views of the water. | Main St., Fort Adams | 601/888–3998 | Free | Daily. **Pond Store.** This country store was built in 1881 and is still open for business, thanks in large part to those who visit the nearby Clark Creek Natural Area. | 182 Pond Rd., Fort Adams | 601/888–4426 | Free | Daily 7–7.

St. Paul's Episcopal Church. St. Paul's, built in 1824, is believed to be the oldest Episcopal church west of the Alleghenies. | Church at S. 1st Sts. | 601/888–3418 | Free.

Wilkinson County Museum. Housed in the West Feliciana Railroad building, constructed in 1838, this museum offers regional exhibits. | Bank St. | 601/888–3998 | Weekdays 10–noon and 2–4, Sat. 10–noon.

Woodville United Methodist Church. This church, built in 1824, is the oldest Methodist church in the state. | Main at Sligo St. | 601/888–3343 | By appointment.

ON THE CALENDAR
OCT.: *Woodville Craft Fair.* This fair features local and regional art displays, crafts, and food the first Sunday in the month at the Wilkinson County Museum on Courthouse Square. | 601/888–3211.

Lodging
Desert Plantation. This wooden Federal-style B&B, still part of a 1,000-acre working plantation, was built 1808–12. The home has period furnishings and antiques, including canopy beds. It's in a residential area 20 mi north of Woodville. | 4 rooms. Complimentary country breakfast. Pool. Some pets allowed. | 411 Desert La., St. Fancisville | 601/888–6889 | fax 601/888–7231 | www.desertplantation.com | $99–$125 | V.

YAZOO CITY

MAP X, C5

YAZOO CITY

INTRO
ATTRACTIONS
DINING
LODGING

(Nearby towns also listed: Belzoni, Canton, Greenville, Greenwood, Indianola, Jackson, Kosciusko, and Vicksburg)

Yazoo City straddles two distinct landscapes. There are the wind-blown loess bluffs, where topsoil deposited by ancient dust storms runs as deep as 50 ft, and the flat alluvial plain of the Mississippi delta, where eons of flooding have produced some of North America's most fertile land. Not surprisingly, the city has farming in its blood, and its largest industry—Mississippi Chemical Corporation—manufactures chemicals used for row-crop cultivation.

The city was named for the nearby Yazoo River, which was diverted from the Mississippi years ago by the U.S. Army Corps of Engineers. Most of the once-legendary "big woods" of the delta have long since been cleared, but there's enough left for Yazoo County to claim some of the best hunting in the South.

Travel around Yazoo City and it becomes apparent that the city has distinct economic lines as well. Juke joints and lower-income houses generally occupy the swampy terrain and steep ravines, while whitewashed mansions sit atop the bluffs. The city is simultaneously funky and genteel. The downtown area is a tour de force of turn-of-the-20th-century commercial architecture. A few antebellum homes survive, all with stories that local historians are happy to relate. And this is a town of story-tellers: one of its most famous native sons was the writer and *Harper's* magazine editor Willie Morris.

Information: **Yazoo County Convention and Visitors Bureau** | 1509 N. Jerry Clower Blvd., Yazoo City 39194 | 662/746–1815 or 800/381–0662 | fax 662/746–1816 | www.yazoo.org.

Attractions
Bell Road. Bell Road, in use since the 1820s, is a scenic "trace" road—its bed was worn deep into the earth years ago by the hooves of horses and wheels of wagons and carriages. | 1509 N. Jerry Clower Blvd. | 662/746–1815 or 800/381–0662 | fax 662/746–1816 | www.yazoo.org | Free.

Bethel A.M.E. Church. This 1890 church was founded by freed slaves in 1868. | 214 S. Monroe St. | 662/746–7932 | Free | By appointment only.

Oakes African-American Cultural Center. This museum, which honors the achievements of local black residents, is housed in the former home of A. J. Oakes, a successful businessman who freed his wife from slavery and helped educate his neighbors. | 312 S. Monroe St. | 662/746–5038 | Free | Weekdays 9–noon and 1–3.

Panther Swamp National Wildlife Refuge. This is a large expanse of flood-prone forest with opportunities for hunting, fishing, and hiking. Nearby Lake George is also a hunting and fishing site. | 728 Refuge Rd., Hollandale | 662/746–5060 | Free | www.fws.gov/r4eao | Daily.

Wolf Lake. An oxbow in the delta, Wolf Lake has campgrounds, trails, a boat ramp, and areas for swimming and water-skiing. | Wolf Lake Rd. | 662/746–1815 | Free | Daily.

Yazoo County Agricultural Tours. These tours spotlight cotton, catfish, and rice farming, with a side trip to sample southern foods at a country store. | 1509 N. Jerry Clower Blvd. | 662/746–1815 or 800/381–0662 | fax 662/746–1816 | www.yazoo.org | By appointment.

Yazoo City Historic Driving Tour. This self-guided tour showcases mostly 19th-century architecture in the business and residential districts. Brochures are available from the Yazoo County Convention and Visitors Bureau. | 1509 N. Jerry Clower Blvd. | 662/746–1815 or 800/381–0662 | fax 662/746–1816 | www.yazoo.org | By appointment.

Yazoo Historical Museum. Exhibits at this museum deal with local history and the Civil War. | 332 N. Main St. | 662/746–2273 or 800/381–0662 | Free | By appointment.

ON THE CALENDAR

SEPT.: *Yazoo County Fair.* This traditional small town fair has rides, food, exhibits, and entertainment. | 662/746–3211 or 800/381–0662.

KODAK'S TIPS FOR TAKING GREAT PICTURES

Get Closer
- Fill the frame tightly for maximum impact
- Move closer physically or use a long lens
- Continually check the viewfinder for wasted space

Choosing a Format
- Add variety by mixing horizontal and vertical shots
- Choose the format that gives the subject greatest drama

The Rule of Thirds
- Mentally divide the frame into vertical and horizontal thirds
- Place important subjects at thirds' intersections
- Use thirds' divisions to place the horizon

Lines
- Take time to notice lines
- Let lines lead the eye to a main subject
- Use the shape of lines to establish mood

Taking Pictures Through Frames
- Use foreground frames to draw attention to a subject
- Look for frames that complement the subject
- Expose for the subject, and let the frame go dark

Patterns
- Find patterns in repeated shapes, colors, and lines
- Try close-ups or overviews
- Isolate patterns for maximum impact (use a telephoto lens)

Textures that Touch the Eyes
- Exploit the tangible qualities of subjects
- Use oblique lighting to heighten surface textures
- Compare a variety of textures within a shot

Dramatic Angles
- Try dramatic angles to make ordinary subjects exciting
- Use high angles to help organize chaos and uncover patterns, and low angles to exaggerate height

Silhouettes
- Silhouette bold shapes against bright backgrounds
- Meter and expose for the background illumination
- Don't let conflicting shapes converge

Abstract Composition
- Don't restrict yourself to realistic renderings
- Look for ideas in reflections, shapes, and colors
- Keep designs simple

Establishing Size
- Include objects of known size
- Use people for scale, where possible
- Experiment with false or misleading scale

Color
- Accentuate mood through color
- Highlight subjects or create designs through color contrasts
- Study the effects of weather and lighting

From Kodak Guide to Shooting Great Travel Pictures © 2000 by Fodor's Travel Publications

Tennessee

The first thing people think of when Tennessee comes to mind is music. In fact Tennessee is associated with the most important forms of American music—country music in Nashville, blues in the west around Memphis, and bluegrass in the east. Elvis Presley, who changed the face of popular music forever, recorded most of his classics in Memphis. The blues, with its roots in the sad conditions of slavery, came into being on Memphis's Beale Street under W. C. Handy and B. B. King. And Nashville, home of the Grand Ole Opry, has become the center of the country music industry. This rich musical heritage attracts visitors from around the world.

Tennessee is also a state of great natural beauty. The Great Smoky Mountains National Park, which straddles the Tennessee—North Carolina border to the northeast, is an Eden for hikers, canoers, fisherman, and bird-watchers, among others. It is one of the most visited of all the national parks, drawing over 10 million nature-lovers each year. Middle Tennessee's many placid lakes and rivers offer milder charms, and the rolling hills and plains south of Nashville are the birthplace of the Tennessee Walking Horse. Along the state's western border, the flat, fertile floodplains of the Mississippi River are dotted with restored antebellum homes and plantations, offering visitors a glimpse of what life was like in the Old South.

Part of the original American frontier, Tennessee was home to such explorers as Davy Crockett and Daniel Boone and U.S. presidents Andrew Jackson, Andrew Johnson, and James K. Polk. Sites celebrating these figures abound. The Civil War is also remembered at historic sites throughout the state. The largest and best known is Shiloh National Military Park, setting of one of the grimmest and bloodiest battles of the Civil War. More recent events are recounted at the Oak Ridge National Historic Site, where the world's first graphite reactor was built, and at the National Civil Rights Museum, which is housed in the motel where Dr. Martin Luther King, Jr. was killed.

CAPITAL: NASHVILLE	POPULATION: 5,320,000	AREA: 42,143 SQ MI
BORDERS: MO, KY, VA, NC, GA, AL, MS, AR	TIME ZONES: EASTERN, CENTRAL	POSTAL ABBREVIATION: TN
WEB SITE: WWW.TENNESSEETOURIST.COM		

Although the state's capital is much more than Music City, USA, millions of people are drawn to Opryland USA and the Country Music Hall of Fame each year. Nashville is also a leading center for gospel and bluegrass music. You can check out the young hopefuls at the now-legendary Bluebird Café, or get an earful of old-time bluegrass at the Station Inn. In Memphis, take a pilgrimage to Graceland, Elvis's palatial home and the city's biggest attraction. Every August visitors come from as far away as Europe and Japan to commemorate the anniversary of the singer's death with a candlelight vigil, Elvis impersonator contests, and more. Memphis's Beale Street, the first urban home of the blues, is once again a lively entertainment district, lined with bars and clubs that feature live music.

Tennessee feels like a large state, although its size is actually rather modest—no more than 115 mi from its northern to its southern border, and about 500 mi from east to west. Its three regions are so geographically distinct that the state flag symbolizes them with three stars, connected by an unbroken circle.

History

When Hernando DeSoto, the first European to set foot in the region, led his ill-fated expedition into Tennessee, the eastern half of the territory was held by the Cherokees, while the lands in the west were inhabited by the Chickasaw. After he died near the present site of Memphis, his dispirited retinue headed home without leaving behind a settlement. In later centuries the land's original inhabitants were not to be so lucky. In the 1600s, both the British and the French laid claim to the region, and this contest eventually erupted into the French and Indian War in 1754. The French fought and defeated the Chickasaw near the present site of Memphis in 1739. In 1763 the Treaty of Paris ceded all North American land east of the Mississippi to England. But it was not until the Treaty of Sycamore Shoals, when the Transylvania Company purchased 20 million acres from the Cherokee in 1775, that the land west of the Appalachians was opened to settlers.

On the heels of the American Revolution, settlers poured into the Tennessee territory and continued to push west. The territory was still a part of the state of North Carolina, but in 1784, dissatisfied settlers formed the short-lived state of Franklin. Many soon returned to North Carolina, and it was not until 1796 that Tennessee was established as the nation's 16th state. As its first U.S. representative to Washington, the new state chose a young Nashville lawyer named Andrew Jackson—in 1828 he became the first elected president to come from outside the original 13 colonies.

Up until 1830 the Cherokee Nation had held on to their Tennessee land in some form, though they had been pushed into the southeastern corner of the state. The Indian Removal Act brought the nation to a final end—in 1838, 13,000 Cherokee from Georgia and Tennessee were marched out of the state to a reservation in Okla-

TN Timeline

ca. 500 BC	ca. AD 1000	1540	
The Woodland Indians build ceremonial mounds in the area.	The Early Mississippians, also mound builders, inhabit the area.	Hernando DeSoto's expedition arrives at the Mississippi River near the future site of Memphis. What is now western Tennessee is inhabited by the Chickasaw; the Cherokee inhabit	the eastern part of the region.

homa. On this forced migration, known as the Trail of Tears, thousands died of star-
vation or disease.

Its geographical diversity and frontier philosophy has meant that Tennessee developed differently both from its new neighbors in the Deep South and the older states
on the East Coast. Tennessee was largely an area of small farms, although slavery was
a significant factor, especially along the Mississippi. Jackson and frontiersmen like Davy
Crockett personified the region's populist philosophy.

The Civil War bitterly divided the state, which was the last to secede from the Union.
The small farmers of East Tennessee remained pro-Union, at one point attempting to
secede and form a new Union-loyal state. As a border state between the Union and
the Deep South, Tennessee, after Virginia, became the fiercest battleground of the Civil
War. Some 454 battles and skirmishes were fought on its land, and the end of the war
left Tennessee devastated.

Tennessee was the first state to return to the Union after the war ended at Appo-
mattox in 1865. In 1867 the Tennessee General Assembly endorsed black suffrage—
two years before Congress passed the 15th Amendment. However, Tennessee's first
post-war governor, Radical Republican William Brownlow, created such a punitive
climate that bitterness lingered long after, and in 1865, the Ku Klux Klan, which became
a powerful weapon against reconstruction, was born in Pulaski, Tennessee.

Recovery was slow, but Tennessee led the way in the campaign to build a "New
South" by reducing dependency on a farm economy and replacing it with one based
on industry, skilled labor, and outside capital. Progress was made in education, and the
urban population grew: Knoxville and Chattanooga became shipping centers, and
Nashville also prospered. However, despite continued industrialization, it was not
until 1933 when the Tennessee Valley Authority (TVA) was created that real economic
benefits began to reach the state's rural areas. Inexpensive and abundant electrical
power not only attracted large industries to Tennessee but brought jobs and rural elec-
trification. World War II brought further benefits to the state with the Manhattan Project at Oak Ridge and war contracts for the state's industries.

Today, although much of the state remains agrarian, most of the population lives
in the cities, and the state has a varied manufacturing base, an important role in the
music industry, and a growing tourism trade. The second half of the 20th century has
seen major societal changes as well. The long-term trend of Tennessean emigration
has been turned around, and youthful vigor and a population with a more varied ethnic
background has helped to break up the timeworn dichotomy of black and white.
Tennessee is no longer isolated, and, as a result, some feel that the state's regional flavor
has begun to disappear. Yet certain things remain—the drawl of a Southern accent,
stretches of wild land, homemade biscuits and barbecue, blues and bluegrass, country music, dramatic mountains, and the Tennesse River.

1673	1739	1754	1756	1760
French explorers Louis Jolliet and Father Jacques Mar-quette arrive by canoe at the present site of Memphis. British explorers James Needham and Gabriel Arthur explore East Ten-nessee.	The Chickasaw Indi-ans are defeated by the French near the present-day site of Memphis.	The French and Indian War breaks out.	Construction begins on Fort Loudon, on the Little Tennessee River, then the west-ernmost English fort in America.	The Cherokee attack and defeat Fort Loudoun. Daniel Boone explores Northeastern Ten-nessee.

Regions

1. WEST TENNESSEE

The western end of Tennessee fronts the Mississippi River and is composed of flat, rich farmland where cotton and soybeans are grown. Dotting the region are friendly little towns like Henning, where author Alex Haley was raised, and larger but still friendly towns like Savannah. In the northwest corner of this region is Reelfoot Lake, a large, shallow lake formed by a series of massive earthquakes in 1811–12. Adjacent to the lake is Reelfoot National Wildlife Refuge, one of several national wildlife refuges in the region.

Nestled in the southwestern corner of the state is Memphis, the largest city in Tennessee and the commercial and cultural center of West Tennessee, north Mississippi, and eastern Arkansas. Situated on high bluffs overlooking the Mississippi River, it is both a sleepy Southern river town and a focal point of modern industry, where traditional businesses such as cotton and hardwood trading flourish alongside relative newcomers such as the regional office of Federal Express. The birthplace of the blues and a mecca for music lovers, Memphis is home to one of the state's biggest tourist attraction, Elvis Presley's mansion Graceland.

Towns listed: Bolivar, Covington, Dyersburg, Henning, Jackson, Memphis, Paris, Savannah, Tiptonville, Union City, Wildersville.

2. MIDDLE TENNESSEE

The midsection of Tennessee is known for gently rolling hills, bluegrass meadows, and historic towns like Franklin, site of a significant Civil War battle; Lynchburg, the home of the Jack Daniel's distillery; and Chattanooga, where blues singer Bessie Smith was born.

In the heart of Middle Tennessee is Nashville, the state capital and one of the South's most prosperous and fast-growing cities. Not only is Nashville Music City, USA, home of the popular Grand Ole Opry, it is also known as the "Athens of the South" because of its 16 colleges and universities, including the prestigious Vanderbilt University. The city has preserved many historical sites, including the Hermitage, home of President Andrew Jackson.

Towns listed: Celina, Chattanooga, Clarksville, Cleveland, Columbia, Cookeville, Dayton, Dickson, Fayetteville, Franklin, Gallatin, Hendersonville, Hohenwald, Hurricane Mills, Lawrenceburg, Lebanon, Lewisburg, Lynchburg, Manchester, McMinnville, Monteagle, Murfreesboro, Nashville, Pulaski, Shelbyville, Wartburg.

3. EAST TENNESSEE

With its forested mountains and white-water rivers, the eastern region is the wildest section of Tennessee. Natural landmarks include the Applachian Mountains, the

1761	1763	1775	1779	1780
Col. James Grant destroys Lower Cherokee towns in retaliation for the defeat of Fort Loudon.	The Treaty of Paris is signed, making all of North America east of the Mississippi the possession of Great Britain.	In the Treaty of Sycamore Shoals, Great Britain buys the Cumberland Valley of East Tennessee from the Cherokee; the region is opened to British settlement.	Nashville is founded by a pioneer group led by James Robertson.	Tennessee frontiersmen and local farmers defeat the British in the Battle of King's Mountain in South Carolina, a pivotal conflict of the American Revolution.

INTRODUCTION
HISTORY
REGIONS
WHEN TO VISIT
STATE'S GREATS
RULES OF THE ROAD
DRIVING TOURS

Cumberland Plateau, the Great Valley, and the mighty Tennessee River. Great Smoky Mountains National Park, where the Appalachians reach their highest point, is accessed through the tourist town of Gatlinburg.

Two East Tennessee cities are of particular interest to travelers. The third-largest city in the state, Knoxville was once the state capital and today is the headquarters of the Tennessee Valley Authority (TVA) and home of the University of Tennessee's main campus. About 100 mi south of Knoxville is Chattanooga, an up-and-coming small city and home of the Tennessee Aquarium, the world's largest-such freshwater facility. Nearby are the popular, and unabashedly hokey tourist attractions, Rock City and Ruby Falls.

Towns listed: Athens, Bristol, Caryville, Crossville, Elizabethton, Gatlinburg, Great Smoky Mountains National Park, Greeneville, Harrogate, Jamestown, Jellico, Johnson City, Jonesborough, Kingsport, Knoxville, Lenoir City, Maryville, Morristown, Norris, Oak Ridge, Pigeon Forge, Rogersville, Sevierville, Sweetwater, Townsend, Tusculum, Walland.

When to Visit

The weather varies across Tennessee—summers are pleasant in mountainous eastern Tennessee but miserably hot and humid in the western end of the state. Winters tend to be brief and mild in the west; snow is a relatively rare occurrence, but the cold winter rains can create some dreary days. Winters grow increasingly severe as you move east. In the mountains, accumulated snow can make winding mountain roads even more treacherous than normal. West Tennessee is most beautiful in the spring, which arrives early with a riot of flowers and blooming trees and bushes. Autumn in Middle and East Tennessee is spectacular. The fall foliage rivals that of New England, and it peaks later. Festivals and special events across the state tend to be scheduled in the spring or fall.

CLIMATE CHART
Average High/Low Temperatures (°F) and Monthly Precipitation (in inches)

	JAN.	FEB.	MAR.	APR.	MAY	JUNE
MEMPHIS	48/31	53/35	63/43	73/52	81/61	89/69
	4.6	4.5	5.3	5.6	5.0	3.9
	JULY	AUG.	SEPT.	OCT.	NOV.	DEC.
	92/73	91/71	84/64	74/52	62/43	52/35
	4.0	3.4	3.3	2.9	4.9	5.3
	JAN.	FEB.	MAR.	APR.	MAY	JUNE
NASHVILLE	47/29	51/31	60/39	71/48	79/57	87/65
	4.2	4.0	5.0	4.1	4.6	3.9
	JULY	AUG.	SEPT.	OCT.	NOV.	DEC.
	90/70	89/68	83/61	72/48	60/38	50/32
	3.9	3.4	3.5	2.6	4.0	4.4

1784
The state of Franklin is founded when North Carolina cedes its western lands to the federal government.

1791
Knoxville is founded, the state's first capital.

1796
The state of Tennessee is established.

1819
The city of Memphis is founded on the Mississippi.

1826
Nashville becomes the permanent capital of Tennessee.

	JAN.	FEB.	MAR.	APR.	MAY	JUNE
KNOXVILLE	46/29	50/32	61/40	71/48	77/57	84/64
	4.9	4.5	4.6	3.8	3.6	4.0

	JULY	AUG.	SEPT.	OCT.	NOV.	DEC.
	87/68	86/68	81/62	70/49	60/41	50/33
	4.0	3.4	3.2	2.8	3.6	4.5

	JAN.	FEB.	MAR.	APR.	MAY	JUNE
CHATTANOOGA	47/28	52/31	62/39	71/47	78/55	86/64
	5.2	5.1	6.0	4.3	4.0	3.7

	JULY	AUG.	SEPT.	OCT.	NOV.	DEC.
	89/68	88/68	82/63	72/49	61/40	51/31
	4.8	3.5	4.1	3.2	4.5	5.1

FESTIVALS AND SEASONAL EVENTS

WINTER

Dec. **The Liberty Bowl Football Classic.** Top college teams compete in this post-season game in Memphis. | 901/795–7700.

Jan. **Elvis Presley's Birthday Celebration.** A variety of events, including contests, concerts, and a candlelight ceremony, are held at Graceland, Elvis's Memphis mansion. | 800/238–2000.

Feb. **Kroger St. Jude Tennis Championships.** A professional tennis tournament in Memphis. | 901/765–4400.

National Field Trial Championships. Hunting dog fanciers come from all over to watch bird dogs at work at Ames Plantation in Grand Junction, near Bolivar. | 901/878–1067.

Mar. **Tennessee Old-Time Fiddler's Championship.** Musicians compete in 14 categories at this Clarksville event. | 931/648–0001.

SPRING

May **Spring Music and Crafts Festival.** Held in Historic Rugby, near Jamestown, the event features English and Appalachian folk music. | 423/628–2430.

The Iroquois Steeplechase. This horse race is a Nashville tradition. | 615/322–7284.

Memphis in May International Festival. The month-long festival includes a Sunset Symphony, the Beale Street Music Festival, and a barbecue contest. | 901/525–4611.

Tennessee Crafts Fair. The state's largest market of local crafts takes place in Nashville. | 615/665–0502.

1828	**1838**	**1839**	**1848**	**1860**
Tennessean Andrew Jackson is elected president.	The Cherokee are forceably removed to Oklahoma: the infamous Trail of Tears.	Chattanooga is established; it experiences growth after the arrival of the railroad in 1850.	Outbreak of the Mexican War. The eagerness of Tennesseans to fight earns the state the nickname of "The Volunteer State," a designation that Tennessee at once embraced.	Tennessee secedes from the Union.

INTRODUCTION
HISTORY
REGIONS
WHEN TO VISIT
STATE'S GREATS
RULES OF THE ROAD
DRIVING TOURS

SUMMER

June

International Country Music Fan Fair. Country stars perform and meet their fans at this popular Nashville event. | 615/889–7503.

Riverbend Festival. Chattanooga's nine-day music festival. | 423/265–4112.

Aug.

Elvis Presley International Tribute Week. The anniversary of Presley's death is marked with events at Graceland, and elsewhere in Memphis. | 800/238–2000.

Aug. and Sept.

International Grand Championship Walking Horse Show. The major walking horse event takes place in Murfreesboro. | 615/890–9120.

Aug. and Sept.

Tennessee Walking Horse National Celebration. The largest show of the breed, the 10-day event draws more than 200,000 people to Shelbyville. | 931/684–5915.

AUTUMN

Sept.

Tennessee Valley Fair. Knoxville is home to this old-fashioned fair, which features music, rides, and agricultural and livestock contests. | 865/637–5840.

Fall Folk Arts Festival. The regional arts and crafts fair is held on the grounds of the Exchange Place in Kingsport. | 423/288–6071.

Tennessee State Fair. The traditional agricultural fair takes place in Nashville. | 615/862–8980.

Sept., Oct.

Mid-South Fair. There are concerts, rides, rodeo events, and agricultural and commercial exhibits at this Memphis fair. | 901/274–8800.

Oct.

National Storytelling Festival. Three days of stories, tall tales, and other oral traditions in Jonesborough. Performances fill up fast. | 423/753–2171 or 800/525–4514.

Tennessee Fall Homecoming. At the Museum of Appalachia in Norris. | 865/494–7680.

Fall Color Cruise and Folk Festival. Chattanooga's seasonal celebration features music, dance, entertainment, and food. | 423/892–0223 or 800/322–3344 | www.chattanooga.com.

1862–63	1865	1866	1867	1873
Grant makes a name for himself at the Battle of Shiloh. Battles of Franklin, Nashville, Chicamauga, and Chattanooga take place on Tennessee soil.	The Klu Klux Klan is founded in Pulaski, Tennessee.	Fisk University, one of the first African-American universities, is founded in Nashville. Tennessee is accepted back into the Union.	Tennessee legislature endorses black suffrage.	Vanderbilt University is founded in Nashville. Nashville becomes known as "the Athens of the South."

State's Greats

For the nature–lover and outdoor enthusiast, Tennessee offers great hiking, canoeing, rafting, camping, hunting, and fishing—not to mention some breathtaking scenery. The state's landscape also presents travelers with many chances to encounter history— to look out over the Great Smoky Mountains and see what the Cherokee saw, or to stand on ground once soaked with the blood of Civil War soldiers. The rich musical heritage of Tennessee is its living history, one that visitors can experience at the Grand Ole Opry and at festivals, fairs, juke joints, church services, and country dances across the state.

Beaches, Forests, and Parks

With six federal parks and 52 state parks, there is no shortage of natural beauty to explore in Tennessee. The most popular sight is **Great Smoky Mountains National Park** in East Tennessee, accessed via the town of Gatlinburg. This park boasts 800 mi of maintained trails, including part of the Appalachian Trail, which also passes through the adjacent **Cherokee National Forest,** which you can enter through Greeneville. **Roan Mountain** (6,285 feet) is one of the highest peaks in the eastern United States. Atop the mountain, which is in Roan Mountain State Park near Elizabethton, is a 600-acre rhododendron garden that blooms in early summer.

Moving to West Tennessee, **Pickwick Landing** outside Savannah is a popular site for fishing, boating, and swimming. At **Reelfoot Lake State Park,** in the northwest corner of the state near Tiptonville, park naturalists offer guided tours to see the American Bald Eagles that winter there.

Culture, History, and the Arts

It would be almost impossible to explore Tennessee without finding yourself face to face with the state's history. **The Museum of Appalachia** in Norris offers a look at life during the earliest part of the state's history, featuring a farm/village complex of 30 log cabins and 250,000 artifacts. At the **Andrew Johnson National Historic Site** in Greeneville, visitors can see the tailor shop, home, and burial place of the 17th president. **The Hermitage,** in Nashville, was the home of another president from Tennessee, Andrew Jackson. Thanks to a major restoration, the mansion once again looks as it did from the end of Jackson's term in 1837 until his death in 1845. The **Ancestral Home of James K. Polk,** the third U.S. president from Tennessee, is preserved in Columbia.

The sites of many Civil War battles across the state have been preserved. The most well-known among them is **Shiloh National Military Park** in West Tennessee, near Savannah. Others include the **Fort Donelson National Battlefield and Cemetery** near Clarkesville; the **Chickamauga and Chattanooga National Military Park** near Chattanooga; and the **Stones River National Battlefield** near Murfreesboro, home of the oldest Civil War monument still intact.

1878	1900	1909	1920	1925
Memphis is decimated by yellow fever epidemic.	The state's population tops 2 million.	W. C. Handy, "Father of the Blues," writes "The Memphis Blues," the first blues song to be written down.	Tennessee casts the deciding vote that ratifies the 19th Amendment, giving women the right to vote.	The "Scopes monkey trial," begun as a test case against the state's law forbidding the teaching of the theory of evolution in public schools, draws nationwide attention to Tennessee.

Other historic sites include, in tiny Henning, the **Alex Haley House Museum,** boyhood home and burial place of the Pulitzer Prize–winner author of *Roots,* which has become an increasingly popular attraction. The **National Civil Rights Museum** is in the old Lorraine Motel in Memphis, where Dr. Martin Luther King, Jr., was assassinated in 1968. The museum documents the American Civil Rights Movement through interpretive exhibits and audiovisual displays. A crucial episode in modern history is preserved in the town of **Oak Ridge,** the site of the Manhattan Project. Today, the town is home to the **American Museum of Science and Energy,** which offers hands-on demonstrations of the **Historic Graphite Reactor,** once a secret technology.

Sports

East Tennessee begs to be hiked. There are more trails in the mountains than could be walked in a lifetime, but the portion of the **Appalachian Trail** that passes through the **Cherokee National Forest** and **Great Smoky Mountains National Park** is a must for serious hikers. Rock climbers will find **Lookout Mountain** near Chattanooga a challenge. Southeastern Tennessee is also the hang-gliding capital of the eastern United States, with events and facilities centered around **Lookout Mountain** and the **Sequatchie Valley.**

Some of the most popular lakes for fishing and boating are **Kentucky Lake,** near Paris, the second largest man-made lake in the world, which was created by Tennessee Valley Authority, and **Dale Hollow Lake,** near Celina, known for its clear water and scenic shoreline. The **Ocoee River** was the site of the white-water events in the 1996 Olympics, and the **Nolichucky River,** near Johnson City, is another favorite with white-water rafters.

There are dozens of public golf courses throughout the state. One of the best is the **Hermitage Golf Course** in Nashville, which each year hosts the Ladies' Professional Golf Association (LPGA) Sara Lee Classic.

For those who prefer to enjoy their sports sitting down, Tennessee has two professional teams, both based in Nashville: the National Football League's Tennessee Titans and the National Hockey League's Nashville Predators.

Other Points of Interest

Thousands of visitors come to Tennessee every year on a musical pilgrimage to **Graceland,** the Memphis mansion of Elvis Presley and one of the biggest attractions in the state. Music fans should not miss **Sun Studio,** a modest Memphis building where the careers of Elvis Presley, Jerry Lee Lewis, Ike Turner, Howling Wolf, Roy Orbison, Johnny Cash, and Carl Perkins were launched.

In Nashville, the **Grand Ole Opry** is now broadcast from **Opryland, U.S.A.,** a huge hotel, conference, and entertainment complex. The original home of the Opry, the **Ryman Auditorium** downtown, is still open for tours and concerts. It's near **Music Row,** the center of the city's recording industry and site of the **Country Music Hall of Fame and Museum.**

1927	1933	1934	1945–46
The Grand Ole Opry begins.	The country music recording business begins in a makeshift studio in Bristol with the voices of Jimmy Rogers and the Carter family.	Creation of the Tennessee Valley Authority (TVA).	The Great Smoky Mountains National Park is created.	Oak Ridge, Tennessee, is the site of the Manhattan Project. The world's first graphite reactor here produces plutonium that is used in the atomic bombs dropped on Japan.

f Middle Tennessee's famous whiskey distilleries are open for tours: **George** and Co. in Tullahoma and, nearby, the nation's oldest registered distillery, the iel Distillery in Lynchburg. They are the world's only producers of Tennessee sh whiskey.

highly acclaimed **Tennessee Aquarium** in Chattanooga is the world's largest ater aquarium. You can view the inhabitants of a spectacular 60-foot under-canyon with two living forests and 22 tanks.

Rules of the Road

License Requirements: You must be 16 years of age to get a driver's license in Tennessee. Persons with valid driver's licenses issued in other U.S. states or foreign countries are permitted to drive in Tennessee.

Right Turn on Red: Unless otherwise posted, you are permitted to make right turns on red in the state of Tennessee.

Seatbelt and Helmet Laws: All front-seat passengers are required to wear safety belts. Children under 4 must travel in a child restraint device that meets Federal Motor Vehicle Safety Standards. Motorcyclists must wear helmets.

Speed Limits: The speed limit on rural Tennessee interstates is 70 mph; speed limits on metro-area interstates are regulated by the specific metro area—watch for signs. The speed limit on major highways is 55 mph, unless otherwise indicated on highway signs.

Other: Headlights must be used during foggy or otherwise inclement weather.

For More Information: For Road Conditions: 800/342–3258. For license information: 615/251-5119.

A Driving Tour Along the Edge of the Great Smoky Mountains

FROM JONESBOROUGH TO DAYTON

Distance: 220 mi   Time: 2 days
Breaks: Knoxville is a good overnight stopping point with a variety of accommodations.

Beginning in the starkly beautiful mountain country east of the Cherokee National Forest, this tour takes you to the eastern edge of the Cumberland Plateau and down into Tennessee's Great Valley. It offers travelers the chance to explore rural East

1954	1968	1980–82	1992	1996
Elvis Presley records his first song.	Civil rights leader Dr. Martin Luther King, Jr. is assassinated at the Lorraine Motel in Memphis.	Nissan and GM pick Tennessee for new plants. Graceland opens. Knoxville hosts the World Fair.	Native son Albert Gore, Jr. is chosen as Vice-President.	The state's bicentennial. Olympic Games whitewater rafting event is held on the Ocoee River. Tennessee celebrates four Olympic gold medalists and a Nobel Prize winner.

Tennessee and to learn more about the early history and culture of the region. Take this trip in the fall, when the leaves turn gorgeous shades of orange and red. This is not a drive to attempt in the winter, when the roads can turn treacherous.

❶ Laid out in 1780, **Jonesborough** is the oldest incorporated town in Tennessee and was the site of the protracted struggle over the State of Franklin, which would have been the 14th state. Downtown is well preserved; you can get a tour or maps from the **Jonesborough Visitors Center and History Museum,** which also features year-round exhibits and special shows and displays that offer a glimpse of everyday life in Tennessee's oldest town. The **Chester Inn,** near the Visitors Center, is the oldest frame structure in Jonesborough and the site of the National Storytelling Festival. Jacob Howard printed the nation's first abolitionist newspapers in the **May-Ledbetter House**; it's now a bed-and-breakfast inn.

❷ Head southwest of Jonesborough on U.S. 11E for approximately 15 mi to **Davy Crockett Birthplace State Park,** on the Nolichucky River. Crockett was born here in 1786. The spot is marked by a plaque and a reconstructed cabin.

❸ From Davy Crockett State Park, drive south on U.S. 11E/321 for approximately 3 mi to **Tusculum.** Here, the **Andrew Johnson Library** houses the 17th president's papers and manuscripts, as well as a good collection of Civil War–era newspapers.

❹ Leaving Tusculum, proceed west for approximately 10 mi on U.S. 11E to **Greeneville,** site of the **Andrew Johnson National Historic Site.** Two homes of the 17th president, his

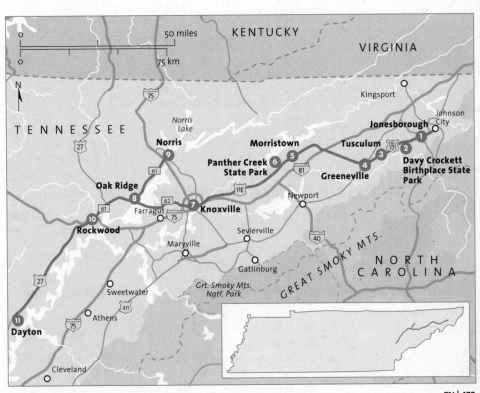

tailor shop, and his gravesite are here. The **Nathaniel Green Museum of Greene County** offers exhibits on Johnson's impeachment and aspects of Greene County history.

⑤ Approximately 20 mi west of Greeneville on U.S. 11E, you'll come to **Morristown,** the boyhood home of Davy Crockett. The **David Crockett Tavern and Pioneer Museum** is a reconstruction of the tavern run by Crockett's parents.

⑥ Continue west for about 5 mi on U.S. 11E to **Panther Creek State Park** is on a portion of Cherokee Lake used by the Tennessee Valley Authority for flood control purposes. The park is a good for camping and viewing deer, waterfowl, and other wildlife.

⑦ **Knoxville** is approximately 40–45 mi west of Panther Creek on U.S. 11E. This is a good place to spend the night, with a wide variety of dining and hotel options. You might add a day to your tour to see some of the city's attractions. Don't miss the **Blount Museum,** the first frame house west of the Appalachians, or the **Knoxville Museum of Art,** the state's newest and largest art museum.

⑧ Take Route 62 west from Knoxville for approximately 25 mi to **Oak Ridge,** site of the Manhattan Project. The **American Museum of Science and Energy** includes exhibits on the area's atomic history. The **University of Tennessee Arboretum** features 250 acres and excellent nature trails.

⑨ Take Rte. 95/61 fifteen miles northeast of Oak Ridge to **Norris** to visit the **Museum of Appalachia,** which has re-creations of period cabins, displays of Cherokee baskets, and even old jail cells. While in Norris, don't miss the **Lenoir Museum,** which features early Americana, including an 18th-century grist mill next to the museum.

⑩ Take Route 61 south for about 25 mi to U.S. 27 and **Rockwood,** which sits on the southeastern edge of the Cumberland Plateau and offers a terrific view of the Great Valley to the south.

⑪ From Rockwood, continue south on U.S. 27 for about 30–35 mi to **Dayton.** Visit the **Rhea County Courthouse,** which has a museum featuring items from the 1925 Scopes Monkey Trial, including the original benches and jury seats.

From Dayton, you may wish to continue south on U.S. 27 to Chattanooga. Or, return to Jonesborough via U.S. 27 north to I–75 east to I–40 north to Route 34 east.

Driving Tour from Franklin to Memphis
THE NATCHEZ TRACE, SHILOH, AND BARBECUE

Distance: 230 mi   Time: 2 days
Breaks: The tour can be completed in one day, but for a leisurely drive with plenty of time to explore Franklin, Savannah, and Shiloh, plan on spending the night in Savannah or camping out at Pickwick Landing State Park.

This tour begins in Franklin, follows part of the Natchez Trace Parkway, and continues through the southwest portion of the state, with stops in historic Savannah and Shiloh National Military Park, then on to Memphis. It offers a scenic and leisurely alternate route between two of the state's two largest cities—Nashville and Memphis.

INTRODUCTION
HISTORY
REGIONS
WHEN TO VISIT
STATE'S GREATS
RULES OF THE ROAD
DRIVING TOURS

❶ Take I–65 south from Nashville to Exit 65 and go west on Rte. 96 to **Franklin.** Now a rapidly growing suburb of Nashville, Franklin has a charming downtown historic district and much to recommend it in its own right. The town was the site of a Civil War battle, and two surviving antebellum mansions, **Carter House** and the **Historic Carnton Plantation,** were caught in the middle of the action.

❷ From Franklin, take Route 96 west for approximately 11 mi to the entrance to the **Natchez Trace Parkway.** You will travel about 65 mi on the parkway, from Franklin to U.S. 64. Some points of interest along the way are: the **Tennessee Valley Divide** which was the boundary between the United States to the north and the Chickasaw Nation to the south when Tennessee joined the Union in 1796; the **Gordon House and Ferry Site,** an 1818 house from which the Gordon family ran a ferry across the Duck River; and the **Meriwether Lewis Park, Grave, and Monument,** which includes the gravesite of the famous explorer, as well as a picnic area and campsite.

❸ Get off the Natchez Trace Parkway at U.S. 64 and head west for approximately 45 mi to **Savannah.** A city rich in Civil War history, Savannah is also situated along the path of the Trail of Tears. Be sure to stroll along the **Savannah Historic Trail,** a 2-mi stretch off Main Street that's lined with impressive residences built between 1860 and 1930. You can get a map for a self-guided tour at the **Hardin County Tourism Board.** The **Tennessee River Museum** features exhibits on paleontology, archaeology, steamboats, and the Civil War. Savannah is a good place to spend the night, at the **White Elephant Bed and Breakfast Inn** or at any of several motels in town.

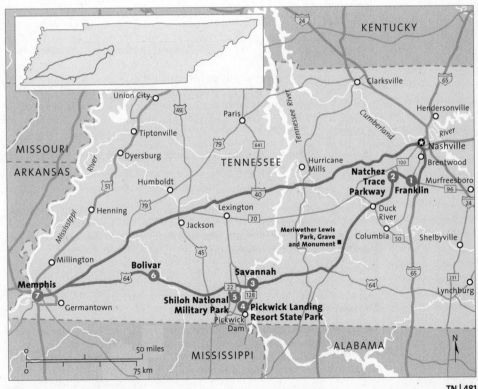

❹ About 15 mi south of Savannah on Route 128 is **Pickwick Landing Resort State Park.** This spot on the shores of Pickwick Reservoir has campsites and offers swimming, boating, and hiking.

❺ From Pickwick Landing, return north on Route 128 to U.S. 64 west, proceed for about 4 mi to Route 22 then south on Route 22 for 7 mi into **Shiloh National Military Park.** This was the site of one of the Civil War's bloodiest and most important battles, where combined casualties reached a total of 23,746. A self-guided auto tour leads past markers explaining monuments and battle sites. More than 3,000 Union soldiers are buried here in the **National Cemetery.**

❻ From Shiloh, return north on Route 22 to U.S. 64 west and proceed west on U.S. 64 for a little over 40 mi to **Bolivar,** a town that was occupied by the Union army during the Civil War. One hundred of its buildings are on the National Historic Register.

❼ Continue west on U.S. 64 for approximately 55 mi to **Memphis.** There's enough to see and do in the city to keep you occupied for several days. Some of the most interesting historic attractions in town are: **A. Schwab's Dry Goods Store** on Historic Beale Street; farther down Beale, the **Hunt-Phelan Home,** a handsome antebellum home rich in Civil War history; the **Mallory-Neely House,** a 25-room Victorian mansion; and the **National Civil Rights Museum.** The **Beale Street Historic District** features four blocks of nightclubs, shops, and restaurants.

Spend the night in Memphis—there are lodging places for all budgets here—before taking I–40 (the direct route) back to Nashville, 210 mi away.

ATHENS

MAP 12, H3

(Nearby towns also listed: Chattanooga, Cleveland, Dayton, Lenoir City, Sweetwater)

Athens, a pleasant town in the southeastern part of the state, was laid out in 1822 and became the county seat a year later. Today the town's economy centers on dairy farming and a variety of industry, but in the 1940s it was home to the manufacturer of the popular Swift Aircraft, an all-metal two-seater you can view today at the Swift Museum Foundation.

Information: Athens Area Chamber of Commerce | 13 N. Jackson St., Athens 37303 | 423/745–0334 | www.athenschamber.org.

Attractions

McMinn County Living Heritage Museum. Thirty permanent exhibits depict life in Southeast Tennessee from the time of the Cherokee Indians and early pioneer settlers through the beginning of World War II. | 522 W. Madison Ave. | 423/745–0329 | www.usit.com/livher/index.html | $3 | Weekdays 10–5; Sat. 10–4.

Mayfield Visitors Center. Tours of the 75-year-old dairy give you a look at milk bottling and ice-cream production. For a price, you can sample a range of goods at the visitor center's shop and fountain. | 806 E. Madison Ave. | 423/745–2151 | fax 423/744–9403 | www.mayfielddairy.com | Free | Mon., Tue., Thurs., Fri. 9–3.

Swift Museum Foundation. This is the international headquarters, museum, and parts department for Swift Aircraft, a classic polished-aluminum two-person plane built in the 1940s that is still sought after today. | 4 McMinn County Airport | 423/745–9547 | www.napanet.net/ārbeau/swift | Free | Weekdays 9–5.

APR.–MAY: *Spring Quilt Show.* This spring event at the McMinn County Living Heritage Museum is one of the largest exhibits of antique and contemporary quilts in the South. | 423/745–0329.

Dining
Jackson Street Restaurant. American/Casual. This popular restaurant near Route 30 is surrounded by trees. It has all the American standards, including buffalo burgers, blackened everything, daily specials, and homemade peanut-butter pie. Relax on the enclosed deck or warm up near stone fireplaces. Kids' menu. | 411 S. Jackson St. | 423/746–0204 | $6–$13 | AE, D, MC, V | No lunch Sun.

Lodging
Hampton Inn. This three-story motel at Exit 49 off I–75 is 5 mi west of downtown. Complimentary Continental breakfast. Some microwaves, some refrigerators, cable TV. Pool. Exercise equipment. Laundry service. Business services. | 1821 Holiday Dr. | 423/745–2345 | fax 423/745–1172 | www.hampton-inn.com | 64 rooms, 6 suites | $69–$77, $75–$129 suites | AE, D, DC, MC, V.

BOLIVAR

MAP 12, C3

(Nearby towns also listed: Covington, Jackson, Memphis, Savannah)

Bolivar began as a trading post on land bought from the Cherokee in 1818. In 1823 it became the seat of Hardeman County, which today produces more hardwood lumber than any other county in Tennessee. Although occupied by Union forces that set fire to Courthouse Square when they left town in 1863, Bolivar has managed to preserve a large number of its historic buildings. These can be visited via chamber of commerce tours.

Information: Bolivar/Hardeman County Chamber of Commerce, Hardeman County Chamber of Commerce | 500 W. Market St., Bolivar 38008 | 901/658–6554 | www.bolivar.com.

Attractions
Bills-McNeal District. Bolivar boasts more than 100 buildings and homes on the National Historic Register. Many of these private residences are in the Bills-McNeal District. | Bounded by N. Union, McNeal, Union, and Bills Sts. | 901/658–6554 | Free | Daily.

The Little Courthouse. The original 1824 log structure is the oldest original courthouse in western Tennessee. In 1827, the building was moved to its present site; in 1849 it was converted into a Federal-style home, thus escaping the fate of the new courthouse, which was burned during the Civil War. It now serves as the county museum. | 116 E. Market St. | 901/658–3390 | oeh@aeneas.net | $3 | By appointment only.

National Bird Dog Museum. Photos, paintings, and sculptures at this one-of-a-kind museum celebrate the 36 breeds of pointers, setters, spaniels, and retrievers. In the town of Grand Junction, 18 mi southwest of Bolivar, where national bird dog championships have taken place off and on since the turn of the century. | 505 Rte. 57, Grand Junction | 901/764–2058 | www.fielddog.com/foundation/museum.html | Free | Tues.–Fri. 10–2, Sat. 10–4, Sun. 1–4.

The Pillars. Built around 1826 (originally with the eight columns installed upside down), the Pillar's was the town's first brick home. The first owner, John Houston Bills, was one of the original settlers of West Tennessee, and here he entertained famous guests such as Ulysses S. Grant, Davy Crockett, and James K. Polk. | Bills and Washington Sts. | 901/658–6554 | $3 | By appointment only.

Walking Tours of Bolivar's Historic Districts. The Bolivar Chamber of Commerce provides maps and brochures to help you tour the town's four historic districts, including public buildings and private homes on the National Historic Register. | 500 W. Market St. | 901/658–6554 | Free | Daily.

ON THE CALENDAR

FEB.: *National Field Trial Championships.* Bird dogs compete against each other for 10 days starting on February 14. Although the dogs are looking for quail, the "hunters" they're assisting shoot blanks. May the best man's best friend win. Takes place annually at the Ames Plantation in nearby Grand Junction, 18 mi southwest of town. | 901/878–1067.

Dining

Dossie's Grill. American. This comfy, local restaurant is two blocks from the chamber of commerce/tourist information center downtown. It offers country ham, red-eye gravy, homemade biscuits, and the only Angus beef rib-eye in town. | 701 W. Market St. | 901/658–5400 | Breakfast also available | $4–$10 | AE, D, MC, V.

Lodging

Super 8 Motel. Off U.S. 64 west, right downtown, this motel is typical of the chain. Complimentary Continental breakfast. Microwaves, refrigerators, cable TV. Pool. Pets allowed (fee). | 916 W. Market St. | 901/658–7888 | fax 901/658–2794 | www.super8.com | 28 rooms | $50–60 | AE, D, DC, MC, V.

BRISTOL

MAP 12, H5

(Nearby towns also listed: Elizabethton, Johnson City, Kingsport)

Bristol, positioned on the state line between Tennessee and Virginia, is along a route between the southeast and northeastern United States that was popular in Colonial times. Around 1771 an enormous fort, now in ruins, was built here for trade and the protection of settlers. Today Bristol is best known as the home of the Bristol Motor Speedway, one of the nation's premier venues for NASCAR action.

Information: **Bristol Convention and Visitor's Bureau** | 20 Volunteer Pkwy., Bristol 37620 | 423/989–4850 | www.bristolchamber.org.

Attractions

Bristol Caverns. Among the most spectacular caverns in the state, the 200-million-year-old caves were used by Cherokees in hide-and-seek skirmishes with unsuspecting settlers. Tours begin every 20 minutes. | 1157 Bristol Caverns Hwy. | 423/878–2011 | $8 | Weekdays 9–5, Sun. 12:30–5.

Bristol Motor Speedway. The "World's Fastest Half-Mile Track" and the largest sports arena in Tennessee hosts a Winston Cup Series race and two Grand National events that are among the most well-attended stock car races in the country. | 151 Speedway Blvd. | 423/764–1161 | fax 423/764–1646 | www.bristolmotorspeedway.com | Prices vary | Call ahead for schedule.

ON THE CALENDAR

MAR.: *NASCAR Winston Cup Series Food City 500.* One of 34 national stock car races is held at Bristol Motor Speedway during the third week of March. | 423/764–1161.

AUG.: *Goracing.com 500 NASCAR Race.* This popular stock car event held at Bristol Motor Speedway is sponsored by a stock car Web site. | 423/764–1161.

Dining
Troutdale Dining Room. Contemporary. This charming restaurant 1 mi south of downtown has candlelight, fireplaces, and an open-air dining room. Specialties include basil pesto pizza, stuffed filet mignon, and a boneless breast of duck with an orange-port wine sauce. | 412 6th St. | 423/968–9099 | Closed Sun. No lunch | $18–$26 | AE, D, MC, V.

Lodging
New Hope Bed & Breakfast. This Victorian home with a Queen Anne influence was built in 1892 and is just 1 mi west of downtown. Each room has a private bath and there are some antiques. Common space includes a parlor and billiard room, and "Murder Mystery Weekends" are offered. Complimentary breakfast. | 822 Georgia Ave. | 423/989–3343 or 888/989–3343 | www.newhopebandb.com or www.bbonline.com/tn/newhope/ | 4 rooms | $95–$155 | AE, MC, V.

CARYVILLE

(Nearby towns also listed: Harrogate, Jellico, Knoxville, Norris)

This small town on the eastern edge of the Cumberland Mountains in northeast Tennessee was settled in 1806. Along the town's western boundary is Cove Lake State Park, a popular recreational area established in the 1930s by the Tennessee Valley Authority.

Information: **Campbell County Tourism Council** | 551 Main St., Jacksboro 37757 | 423/566–0329.

Attractions
Cove Lake State Park. This 667-acre park offers 97 full-amenity campsites, year-round fishing, and recreation equipment that can be borrowed or rented at the camper check-in station. The lake's quiet inlets and the park's marshes, and fields are the wintertime home of some 400 Canada geese. | 110 Cove Lake La. | 423/566–9701 | Free | Daily.

Dining
Cove Lake State Park Restaurant. American. This park-side spot is open year-round, except when there's a heavy snow. It serves steaks, chicken, hamburgers, and prime rib. The indoor dining room has a view of the lake, and there is an outdoor patio in season. | 110 Cove Lake La. | 423/566–6676 | No dinner Sun. | $5–$15 | MC, V.

Scottie's Restaurant. American. This Main Street diner has greasy spoon dishes like burgers with french fries, sandwiches with chips, and fried chicken. | 159 Main St. | 423/562–2976 | $5–$10 | No credit cards.

Lodging
Budget Host Inn. This one-story, drive-up motel is across the highway from Cove Lake. Prices are among the most reasonable in the area. Cable TV. Laundry service. Some pets allowed. | 115 Woods Ave. | 423/562–9595 | fax 423/566–0515 | members.nbci.com/bhinn | 22 rooms | $25–$37 | AE, D, MC, V.

Days Inn–Lake City. A representative of the reliable motel chain, this Days Inn is conveniently off I–75, 6 mi south of Caryville in Lake City. Its rooms (on three stories) have outside entrances. Complimentary Continental breakfast. Cable TV. Pool. Playground. | 221 Colonial La., Lake City | 865/426–2816 | fax 865/426–4626 | 60 rooms | $61 | AE, D, DC, MC, V.

Hampton Inn Caryville. This hotel, in the business district off I–75 and 1 mi southeast of downtown, has rooms with fireplaces, as well as rooms with balcony views of the Cumberland Mountains. Complimentary Continental breakfast. Some microwaves, some refrigerators, some in-room hot tubs, cable TV. Outdoor pool. Laundry facilities. | 4459 Veterans Memorial Hwy. | 423/562–9888 or 800/426–7866 | www.hampton-inn.com | 62 rooms | $69–$94 | AE, D, MC, V.

Lakeview Inn. Cove Lake State Park is just ¼ mi south of this homey, privately owned motel. It consists of two brick buildings with outside entrances. Professional bluegrass musicians perform every Monday night in the lounge. No cover charge. Some refrigerators, cable TV. Pool. Beauty shop. Laundry facilities. Business services. | 276 John McGhee Blvd. | 423/562–9456 or 800/431–6887 | 92 rooms | $33.60 | AE, D, DC, MC, V.

Shanghai Resort. This complex 15 mi east of Caryville, on Norris Lake in La Follette, has cabins, campsites, and motel rooms. There is a two-night minimum for cabin rentals. Guests and nonguests can rent boats, dine at the lake-side restaurant, or fish from the pier. Restaurant. Some kitchenettes, no room phones. Boating, fishing. | 1042 Shanghai Rd., La Follette | 423/562–7651 or 800/245–7651 | fax 423/562–8650 | www.shanghairesort.com | 10 rooms, 2 cabins, 28 campsites | $45, $150–$250 cabins, $15 campsites | AE, MC, V.

CELINA

MAP 12, G1

(Nearby towns also listed: Cookeville, Jamestown)

Settled in 1848 and incorporated in 1870, Celina is the seat of Clay County; it is on the east side of the Cumberland River near the Kentucky state line. A destination for people who are serious about fishing, the town is adjacent to Dale Hollow Lake, which offers a variety of sport fish and the Dale Hollow National Fish Hatchery, where trout are bred to stock federal waters.

Information: **Dale Hollow/Clay County Chamber of Commerce** | 100 Courthouse Sq., Celina 38551 | 931/243–3338 | claygov@twlakes.net.

YOUR CAR'S FIRST-AID KIT

- ❏ Bungee cords or rope to tie down trunk if necessary
- ❏ Club soda to remove stains from upholstery
- ❏ Cooler with bottled water
- ❏ Extra coolant
- ❏ Extra windshield-washer fluid
- ❏ Flares and/or reflectors
- ❏ Flashlight and extra batteries
- ❏ Hand wipes to clean hands after roadside repair
- ❏ Hose tape

- ❏ Jack and fully inflated spare
- ❏ Jumper cables
- ❏ Lug wrench
- ❏ Owner's manual
- ❏ Plastic poncho—in case you need to do roadside repairs in the rain
- ❏ Quart of oil and quart of transmission fluid
- ❏ Spare fan belts
- ❏ Spare fuses
- ❏ Tire-pressure gauge

*Excerpted from *Fodor's: How to Pack: Experts Share Their Secrets*
© 1997, by Fodor's Travel Publications

Attractions

Dale Hollow Lake. This large lake east of town is the place for all manner of water sports, including swimming, waterskiing, boating, and deep-water skin diving. Its spectacularly clear, cold-water can yield good fishing results; the world record for the biggest small-mouth bass catch (11 lbs., 13 oz.) was set here. (Because the lake crosses the Tennessee border, it's best to call ahead for fishing regulations.) | 5050 Dale Hollow Dam Rd. | 931/243–3136 | www.dalehollow-lake.net | Free | Daily.

Dale Hollow National Fish Hatchery. The primary purpose of this facility, 2 mi north of downtown on U.S. 53 is to provide rainbow trout, along with some brown and lake trout, to federal waters in Tennessee, although its annual production of some 300,000 pounds of fish allows it to distribute some rainbow trout to federal waters in Alabama and Georgia as well. In addition to the hatch house, there is a visitors center and an aquarium. | 50 Fish Hatchery Rd. | 931/243–2443 | fax 931/243–3962 | Free | Daily 7–4.

Standing Stone State Park. This 11,000-acre park is named for an 8-ft-tall rock that once served as a boundary between Indian nations. In addition to cabins, camping sites, hiking trails, and bass fishing, the area, 10 mi south of Celina, boasts spectacular spring wildflowers and excellent fossil hunting. | 1674 Standing Stone Park Hwy. | 931/823–6347 | fax 931/823–3984. | www.wwns.com/clay/tourism/sspark/sspark.html | Free | Daily.

ON THE CALENDAR

AUG.: *Home Coming Days.* Craft booths featuring pottery, rustic willow furniture, activities, and music dot downtown's Courthouse Square during this annual event in the first weekend of August. Includes a carnival. | 931/243–3338.

Dining

The Crow's Nest. American. Locals flock to this popular restaurant with a candlelit dining room. Meals, including prime rib and fried catfish, are served with homemade breads. There is a seafood buffet on weekends, and a kids' menu is available. | 820 E. Lake Ave. | 931/243–3333 | $6–$13 | MC, V.

Lodging

Cedar Hill. Approximately 4 mi north of Celina, this wooded resort overlooks Dale Hollow Lake, offering great opportunities for fishing and other water-related activities. Boats rentals are available, and there's a grocery store within walking distance. Restaurant. Some kitchenettes, some cable TV, no room phones. Pool. Water sports, boating, fishing. Some pets allowed. | 2371 Cedar Hill Rd. | 931/243–3201 or 800/872–8393 | 14 rooms, 37 cottages | $52; $107 cottages | MC, V.

Valley View Motel. This single-story motel 1 mi north of downtown doesn't actually overlook a valley, but it offers basic accommodations at a price that can't be beat. It's 3 mi from the lake and there is a restaurant across the street. Cable TV. | 815 E. Lake Ave. | 931/243–2641 | 13 rooms | $27.50–$29.90 | AE, D, MC, V.

CHATTANOOGA

MAP 12, G4

(Nearby towns also listed: Athens, Cleveland, Dayton, Monteagle)

Founded in 1838, Chattanooga got its name from the Cherokee name for Lookout Mountain, the geographical feature that dominates the city skyline. Located in the southeastern corner of the state along the Tennessee River, it was a vital railroad junction and a strategic site during the Civil War. The pivotal battles of Chickamauga and Lookout Mountain took place nearby.

Today Chattanooga is one of the South's up-and-coming small cities. Until recently it was ravaged by pollution, the result of years of exploiting natural resources, and its downtown was decaying. Since the mid-1980s, however, the city has worked to clean up its outmoded industries, turning to tourism and the service industry over the manufacturing that was once its bread and butter. Civic pride plus an $8 million downtown revitalization effort have transformed it into a clean and prosperous place.

Information: **Chattanooga Area Convention and Visitors Bureau** | 2 Broad St., Chattanooga 37402 | 423/756–8687 or 800/322–3344.

Attractions

CULTURE, EDUCATION, AND HISTORY

Chattanooga Choo-Choo Hotel. The 1909 train station made famous by the Glenn Miller song with the same name is now a Holiday Inn. Some guest rooms are restored Victorian train cars. Even if you don't stay overnight, stop by to see the lobby under an 85-ft free-standing dome—it looks much as it did in the years before the terminal was shuttered in 1970. A variety of shops, restaurants, and gardens are on the premises. | Terminal Station, 1400 Market St. | 423/266–5000 or 800/872–2529 | fax 423/265–4635 | www.choo-choo.com | $2 | Daily 10–6.

Chattanooga Theatre Centre. Founded in 1923 as the Little Theatre of Chattanooga, this is now one of the largest and oldest community theaters in the country. More than 18 volunteer-supported productions are staged each year in this $8.5-million, 40,000-square-ft facility on the banks of the Tennessee River. | 400 River St. | 423/267–8534 | fax 423/267–8617 | www.theatrecentre.com | Prices vary | Call for schedule.

Chattanooga VA National Cemetery. Union soldiers were reinterred here from the many battle sites in the Chattanooga area. | 1200 Bailey Ave. | 423/855–6590 | Daily 8–4:30.

Cravens House. The oldest building on Lookout Mountain served as headquarters to both Union and Confederate forces during the 1863 Battle Above the Clouds. Destroyed by the Union army after the fighting, the house was rebuilt shortly thereafter by the owner, Robert Cravens. It has been restored and decorated with period furnishings. | 110 Point Park Rd. | 423/821–7786 | $2 | Apr.–Oct., daily 8–dusk.

Horsin' Around Carving School. This is America's only school of carousel art. Visitors can view the wooden animals made at the school, which are copies of figures that date back to the 1860s, the heyday of this craft. Call ahead for tour arrangements. | 302 Walmart Dr. | 423/332–1111 | $1 | Mon.–Sat. 9–6.

Tennessee Valley Railroad. Restored steam and diesel locomotives pull trains over historic railroad tracks and through a pre–Civil War tunnel. It's the South's largest operating historic railroad. | 4119 Cromwell Rd. | 423/894–8028 | www.tvrail.com | $9.50 | June–Labor Day, daily 10–1:30; Apr.–May and Sept.–mid-Nov., Sat. 10–5, Sun. noon–5.

Tivoli Theatre and Memorial Auditorium. The Tivoli has been known as the "Jewel of the South" since it was built in 1924 in the Beaux Art style popular at the time. Named to the National Register of Historic Places, the theater underwent a multimillion dollar restoration/renovation in the 1980s. Memorial Auditorim, while not as ornate, was one of the largest public auditoriums in the state. It has been the site of boxing matches, roller derbys, ice shows, religious revivals, tennis tournaments, circuses, and even the occasional aquacade. Now these two historic downtown theaters host concerts, touring Broadway shows, and the Chattanooga Symphony. | 399 McCallie Ave. | 423/757–5042 | www.chattanooga.gov/showplaces/index.htm | Ticket prices vary | Box office open weekdays 10–4:30, Sat. 10–2.

University of Tennessee at Chattanooga. UTC had been a private institution for 83 years when it joined the University of Tennessee's system of statewide campuses. UTC retains the best aspects of that private tradition, yet offers all the resources of a modern public university. Located downtown in the historic district. | 615 McCallie Ave. | 423/755–4662 | www.utc.edu | Free for visitors | Daily.

MUSEUMS

Battles for Chattanooga Museum. The battles of Chickamauga and Chattanooga are re-created in a three-dimensional electronic map with 5,000 miniature soldiers, hundreds of lights, and a computerized soundtrack and sound system. | 1110 E. Brow Rd. | 423/821–2812 | $6 | Daily 10–5.

Chattanooga African-American Museum. Located in Bessie Smith Hall, the museum focuses on the local and national contributions and accomplishments of African-Americans, including blues singer Bessie Smith, who was born in Chattanooga. | 200 E. Martin Luther King Blvd. | 423/266–8658 | $5 | Weekdays 10–5, Sat. noon–4.

Chattanooga Regional History Museum. Housed in a 1910 school building two blocks from the Tennessee River, the museum preserves and interprets the history of the region's everyday life. It also has outstanding collections of artifacts relating to prehistoric Chattanooga, the Civil War, 19th- and early-20th-century business and industry, and the history of tourism in the region. | 400 Chestnut St. | 423/265–3247 | fax 423/266–9280 | www.chattanooga.net/history | $4 | Weekdays 10–4:30, weekends 11–4:30.

Creative Discovery Museum. Multiple, creative hands-on activities and displays for kids situated in four exhibit areas including an artist's studio, a musician's workshop, an inventor's lab, and a field scientist's stations. Activities at this riverfront district museum include digging for replicas of dinosaur bones and recording music. | 321 Chestnut St. | 423/756–2738 | www.cdmfun.org | Adults $7.95, children 2–12 $4.95, under 2 free | Memorial Day–Labor Day, daily 10–6; Labor Day–Memorial Day, Tues.–Sat. 10–5, Sun. noon–5.

Houston Museum of Decorative Arts. This collection of 18th-, 19th-, and early 20th-century decorative arts, including glass, ceramics, furniture, and textiles is in the Bluff View Art District. | 201 High St. | 423/267–7176 | $5 | Apr.–Oct., Mon.–Sat. 9:30–4; Sun. noon–4.

Hunter Museum of American Art. In a historic mansion with a sleek contemporary wing in Chattanooga's Bluff View Art District—which overlooks the Tennessee River—this is one of the most significant collections of American art in the Southeast. It includes works from the colonial period to the present day, with paintings, works on paper, sculpture, furniture, and glass pieces covering a diverse range of periods and movements. Some of the artists represented include Winslow Homer, Mary Cassatt, Robert Henri, Thomas Hart Benton, Helen Frankenthaler, Louise Nevelson, Duane Hanson, and Robert Rauschenberg. | 10 Bluff View | 423/267–0968 | fax 423/267–9844 | www.huntermuseum.org | $5 | Tues.–Sat. 10–4:30; Sun. 1–4:30.

International Towing and Recovery Hall of Fame and Museum. In 1916, Ernest Holmes came to the aid of a friend whose car lay overturned in a creek after an accident. He bolted a tripod of poles on the frame of his 1913 Cadillac, attached a pulley and ran a chain from the back, creating the world's first tow truck. This unique museum is a celebration of that moment—and all the towing and recovery equipment and efforts that have occurred since then. | 401 Broad St. | 423/267–3132 | www.internationaltowingmuseum.org | $3.50 | weekdays 10–4:30, weekends 11–5.

National Medal of Honor Museum of Military History. The museum chronicles the history of the medal of honor, an award established by the U.S. Army in 1862. Four of the first recipients of the medal are buried at the National Cemetery at Chickamauga National Battlefield. The city also has one of the nation's longest running Armed Forces Day celebrations. | 400 Georgia Ave. | 423/267–1737 | www.smoky.com/medalofhonor | $3.50 | Tues.–Sat. 10–4.

PARKS, NATURAL AREAS, AND OUTDOOR RECREATION

Audubon Acres. The nature and cultural history center in the East Brainderd neighborhood of Chattanooga includes easy walking trails and a reconstructed Cherokee cabin. | 900 N. Sanctuary Rd. | 423/892–1499 | $2 | Mon.–Sat. 9–dusk, Sun. 1–dusk.

Booker T. Washington State Park. Named for the African-American educator, this 353-acre park is on the shores of Chickamauga Reservoir. There are lodging and camping accommodations for small and large groups. | 6801 Champion Rd. | 423/894–4955 | fax 423/855–9879 | www.state.tn.us/environment/parks/bookert | Free | Mar.–Oct., daily 7–sundown.

Chester Frost Park. This popular park in Hixon, north of Chattanooga, has 200 RV and tent campsites, picnic areas, playgrounds, lake swimming with sand beaches, tennis and volleyball courts, as well as walk/jog and bicycle paths. | 2318 N. Gold Point Cir., Hixon | 423/842–0177 | Free | Daily.

Chickamauga and Chattanooga National Military Park. Established in 1890, this is the nation's first and largest military park, covering 8,200 acres that span the Georgia-Tennessee border, spreading into Lookout Mountain to the north. The two-day 1863 battle at Chickamauga was amongst the bloodiest of the Civil War. In 1864, General Sherman would start from Chattanooga on his march to Atlanta and the sea. In addition to the hiking and driving trails past monuments and beautiful scenery, you can explore a gun museum, watch a multimedia presentation about the battles, or witness a musket/cannon firing demonstration in the summer (June–Aug.). No lodging or camping. | off U.S. 24, Exit 180B; 3370 Lafayette Rd., Oglethorpe, GA | 706/866–9241 | www.nps.gov/chch | Free | Memorial Day–Labor Day, daily 8–5:45; Labor Day–Memorial Day, daily 8–4:45.

Harrison Bay State Park. The 1,200-acre park offers swimming, fishing, boating, and hiking. In addition, it boasts the Bear Trace, a golf course designed by Jack Nicklaus; seven of its 18 holes skirt along the Chickamauga Reservoir. | 8411 Harrison Bay Rd. | 423/344–6214 or 423/344–2272 | www.state.tn.us/environment/parks/harrison/index2.html | free | Daily 8 AM–10 PM.

Lookout Mountain. Dominating Chattanooga's skyline is this 2,215-ft mountain, which offers views of Tennessee, Georgia, Alabama, North Carolina, and South Carolina from its spine. Clustered on and around the mountain are a variety of tourist attractions. South of downtown, accessible via Rte. 148 | 423/756–8687 or 800/322–3344 | Free | Daily.

Point Park. The windswept, wooded promontory on the far northern end of the ridge offers panoramic views of the area. Markers relate tales of the Union soldiers who struggled up the craggy mountainside in order to escape the relentless showers of Confederate bullets during the Battle Above the Clouds in 1863. Park rangers give tours and talks June through August; inquire at the visitors center. | 110 Point Park Rd. | 423/821–7786 | Free | Daily 8–4:45.

Rock City Gardens. The 200-million-year-old rock formations on Lookout Mountain have been made famous by seven decades of SEE ROCK CITY barn-roof advertisements from Florida to the Canadian border. The unusual, even Disney-esque, wind-carved stone behemoths have been given names like "Lover's Leap," "Mushroom Rock," and "Fat Man's Squeeze." There are also extensive gardens with more than 400 species of plants. | 1400 Patten Rd. | 706/820–2531 | www.seerockcity.com | $10.95 | June–Labor Day, daily 8:30–8, Labor Day–Memorial Day, daily 8:30–6.

Ruby Falls/Lookout Mountain Caverns. Caverns lead to the spectacular 145-ft waterfall inside Lookout Mountain, named after the wife of the man who discovered it. The caves were used as campsites by both Confederate and Union troops, and as hideouts by Native Americans. An elevator takes you to the cave, then guided tours lead you through the cave and to the waterfall. | 1720 S. Lookout Mountain Scenic Hwy. | 423/821–2544 | www.rubyfalls.com | $9.50 | Daily 8 AM–9 PM.

Tennessee Wildlife Center. Formerly the Chattanooga Nature Center, this comprehensive education facility located at the base of Lookout Mountain features wildlife exhibits, a children's Discovery Room, a 1,700-ft-long wetland walkway, and a wildlife rehabilitation clinic. There is also a 3-mi scenic driving tour. | 400 Garden Rd. | 423/821–1160 | www.tnwildlife-center.org | $6 | Mon.–Sat. 9–5, Sun. 1–5.

Nickajack Dam and Lake. The 512-acre dam was the work of the Tennessee Valley Authority; the lake stretches over 10,000 acres. Both are located on top of Raccoon Mountain, 20 mi west of Chattanooga. Opportunities for fishing, boating, and other entertainments line its shores. | 3490 TVA Rd., Jasper | 423/942–1633 | Free | Daily.

Raccoon Mountain Caverns and Campground. The full-facility campground offers tours of local caverns. You can either take the easy walking tour of "Crystal Palace" with its stalactites, stalagmites, rimstone pools, and fossils, or do the "Wild Cave Tour" where you're outfitted with a helmet—complete with miner's lamp—and pads for your knee's and elbows. You'll walk, crawl, climb, and squeeze your way through a large network of chambers, canyons, tunnels, small streams, and large waterfalls beneath the mountain. | 319 West Hills Dr. | 423/821–9403 or 800/823–CAMP | www.raccoonmountain.com | Free | Daily.

Raccoon Mountain Pumped-Storage Plant. Take a 1,100-ft elevator ride through solid rock to visit the mountaintop Nickajack Dam—the largest of its kind. On top, you'll find a visitors center, overlooks, and picnic areas, all with amazing views of the Tennessee River Gorge. You can also visit the powerhouse chamber located inside Racoon Mountain, which has four of the largest reversible pump-turbines in the world. The fisherman's facilities at the base of the mountain are open around the clock. | U.S. 41 off I–24 (Exit 174) | 423/825–3100 | Free | Daily.

Signal Point. The Cherokee used this high-elevation spot for conveying signals to each other. During the Civil War Confederate soldiers followed suit from this point and other lookouts on Signal Mountain, transmitting messages to Edwards Point, also on Signal Mountain, and all the way to Bridgeport, Alabama. | U.S. 27 N off I–27 | Free | Daily.

OTHER POINTS OF INTEREST

IMAX 3D Theater. Don't worry, that shark just looks like it's swimming directly at you. You've probably never seen fish on film look as lifelike as this. | 201 Chestnut St. | 423/265–0695 or 800/262–0695 | $6.95 | Call ahead for schedule.

★ **Tennessee Aquarium.** The world's largest freshwater aquarium is one of the most popular attractions in the city. It features a 60-ft canyon, two living forests, and more than 9,000 fish, mammals, birds, reptiles, and amphibians in natural habitats—all found in the city's redeveloped riverfront district. | 1 Broad St. | 423/265–0695 or 800/262–0695 | www.tennis.org | $11.95 | Weekdays 10–6, weekends 9–8.

Lookout Mountain Incline Railway. This National Historic Site is the world's steepest passenger railway, with a 72.7° grade. Passengers sit in glass-topped cars and enjoy spectacular views as the train goes straight up Lookout Mountain. The boarding station is located at the base of the mountain, 2 mi south of downtown. | 3917 St. Elmo Ave. | 423/821–4224 | www.lookoutmountain.com | $9 | Labor Day–Memorial Day, daily 8:30 AM–9 PM.

SIGHTSEEING TOURS

Southern Belle Riverboat. Board the riverboat for sightseeing breakfast, lunch, or dinner cruises on the Tennessee River, some with live entertainment. | 201 Riverfront Pkwy., Pier 2 | 423/266–4488 or 800/766–2784 | fax 423/265–9447 | www.chattanoogariverboat.com | $10–$40 (includes meal) | Apr.–Dec., daily noon–7.

ON THE CALENDAR

MAY: *River Roast.* The festivities downtown, along the Tennessee River, include a barbecue cooking competition, a volleyball tournament, and a rowing regatta. | Ross's Landing | 423/265–4397.

JUNE: *Riverbend Festival.* This nine-day music festival takes place on the waterfront. | Ross's Landing | 423/265–4112.

OCT.: *Fall Color Cruise and Folk Festival.* Music, dance, entertainment and food are all part of the fun at this folk event in the town of Jasper, 31 mi west of Chattanooga. | 423/892–0223 or 800/322–3344.

Dining

INEXPENSIVE

Country Place. Southern. A very popular family place with booths, handmade crafts, and a country theme. Try hand-breaded chicken tenders, chicken and dressing, and homemade salmon patties. Kids' menu. | 7320 Shallowford Rd. | 423/855–1392 | $5–$8 | AE, D, MC, V | Breakfast also available.

Rembrandt's Coffee House. Café. Salvaged architectural treasures from now-demolished area homes have been worked into the interior decorating of this eatery in the Bluff View neighborhood. Coffee, handmade chocolates, pastries, and sandwiches can be eaten inside or on the garden terrace in season. | 204 E. High St. | 423/265–5033, ext. 3 | $5–$10 | AE, MC, V.

Vine Street Market. Café. A bakery in a converted 1930s cottage, with a cozy café tucked inside, the small but bustling Vine Street Market is known for robust soups, sandwiches made on homemade bread, daily specials like quiches, pasta, and smoked turkey maple salad—and a wide selection of fresh-baked pastries and other desserts. Although it is now in the Riverview neighborhood rather than its original location on Vine Street, this beloved place retains a loyal following. Kids' menu. | 1313 Hanover St. | 423/266–8463 | $6–$8 | AE, MC, V | Closed Sun.

MODERATE

Bea's. Southern. This authentic home-style restaurant 3 mi south of downtown serves the classic "meat and three." You can choose one meat and three vegetables, including Jell-O and macaroni and cheese; drink refills are unlimited. | 4500 Dodds Ave. | 423/867–3618 | $8 | No credit cards | Closed Mon.–Tue.

El Meson Restaurante Mexicano. Mexican. Authentic enchiladas, burritos, taco salads, and vegetarian fajitas are available at this eatery 10 mi north of downtown. | 2204 Hamilton Place Blvd. | 423/894–8726 | $6–$12 | AE, D, MC, V.

India Mahal Restaurant. Indian. Order from the menu or belly-up to the lunch or dinner buffet at this small spot 5 mi south of town. Chicken vindaloo is a specialty. | 5970 E. Brainerd Rd. | 423/510–9651 | $8–$12 | D, MC, V.

Provino's Italian Restaurant. Italian. Waiters set down garlic rolls and a giant bowl of salad before you're even given a chance to order your pasta at this smoky, dimly lit spot 7 mi southwest of downtown. | 5084 South Terr. | 423/899–2559 | Reservations not accepted | $7–$15 | AE, D, MC, V | No lunch.

Riverside Catfish House. Seafood. This restaurant, 15 mi west of downtown, has a view of the Tennessee River from both the indoor dining room, which is decorated like a fisherman's wharf, and the outdoor patio. Burgers are available in addition to catfish and other types of seafood. | 18039 U.S. 41 | 423/821–9214 | $8–$12 | No credit cards.

EXPENSIVE

Back Inn Café. Continental. This upscale bistro is in the Bluff View Inn's Martin House. Entrees include Tuscan beef stew for lunch, and for dinner, try seafood paella with mussels, shrimp and lobster. Crème brûlée and tiramisu are popular desserts; an extensive wine list is also featured. The outdoor terrace is open during warm weather. | 412 E. 2nd St. | 423/265–5033, ext. 1 | $10–$25 | AE, D, MC, V.

Tony's Pasta Shop and Trattoria. Italian. The homemade pastas and sauces served at this downtown restaurant are complemented by rustic, European-style breads. | 212-B High St. | 423/265–5033, ext. 6 | $10–$20 | AE, D, MC, V.

Southside Grill. Southern. The swank grill serves upscale Southern cooking in a chic setting, including stately columns, soft lighting, linens, and an outside patio. Specialties include fried green tomatoes, grilled quail breast, and filet mignon. The menu changes every six weeks. Kids' menu. | 1400 Coward St. | 423/266–6511 | $14–$35 | AE, MC, V | No lunch Sun.

★ **212 Market.** Continental. This stylish downtown restaurant has an upstairs balcony, wine cages in front and back, hardwood floors, and a lightwood bar. Known for fresh seafood, steak, and rack of lamb. Special dishes include grilled salmon in rosemary dill sauce, filet mignon with shitake mushrooms, and seafood bisque. Kids' menu. Sun. brunch. | 212 Market St. | 423/265–1212 | $11–$25 | AE, D, DC, MC, V.

Lodging

INEXPENSIVE

Chanticleer Inn. This stone B&B is set in a secluded mountainous area a half-block from Rock City. Picnic area, complimentary Continental breakfast. Cable TV. Pool. | 1300 Mockingbird La., Lookout Mountain | 706/820–2015 | fax 706/820–1060 | 16 rooms | $48 | AE, D, MC, V.

Days Inn–Airport. These conveniently located accommodations are just 2 mi south of Hamilton Place Mall, 5 mi south of the airport, and 15 mi east of downtown. Complimentary Continental breakfast. Cable TV. Indoor pool. Hot tub. Some pets allowed (fee). | 7725 Lee Hwy. | 423/899–2288 | www.daysinn.com | 80 rooms | $45 | AE, D, MC, V.

Econo Lodge East Ridge. This drive-up, two-story motel is in an older brick building 5 mi east of downtown. Complimentary Continental breakfast. Cable TV. Pool. | 1417 St. Thomas St. | 423/894–1417 | 38 rooms | $30–$60 | AE, DC, D, MC, V.

King's Lodge. Rooms with balconies are available at this reasonably priced hotel. It's about 4 mi west of the incline chair lift up Lookout Mountain, about 5 mi west of Hamilton Place Mall, and many restaurants are within 2 mi radius. Restaurant, bar. Refrigerators, room service, cable TV. Pool. Business services. Some pets allowed. | 2400 West Side Dr. | 423/698–8944 or 800/251–7702 | fax 423/698–8949 | 180 rooms, 20 suites | $45; $75 suites | AE, D, DC, MC, V.

MODERATE

Best Inn. This property is conveniently located 3 mi from the Hamilton Place Mall—the largest shopping mall in Tennessee, with about 100 stores, 135 restaurants, and four movies theaters. Just 10 miles west of downtown. Complimentary Continental breakfast. Cable TV. Pool. Some pets allowed (fee). | 7717 Lee Hwy. | 423/894–5454 | fax 423/499–9597 | 64 rooms | $59 | AE, D, DC, MC, V.

Budget Host Inn. These standard chain accommodations off I–24 are in a small town 24 mi west of Chattanooga. Several restaurants and small shops are within walking distance. Complimentary Continental breakfast. In-room data ports, some microwaves, some refrigerators, cable TV. Pool. Laundry facilities. Business services. | 395 Main St., Kimball | 423/837–7185 | 65 rooms | $53 | AE, D, DC, MC, V.

Days Inn Rivergate–Aquarium. The Tennessee Aquarium is 7 blocks from this downtown hotel, and restaurants and shopping are within easy walking distance. Complimentary Continental breakfast. Cable TV. Pool. Business services. Free parking. | 901 Carter St. | 423/266–7331 | fax 423/266–9357 | www.daysinn.com | 138 rooms, 1 suite | $75 | AE, D, DC, MC, V.

Fairfield Inn Chattanooga. This hotel is situated at the foot of both Signal and Lookout Mountains, 5 mi south of the airport. Rooms with king beds have a work space and lounge chair; rooms with two double beds include a desk and 25-inch television. Complimentary Continental breakfast. In-room data ports, cable TV. Business services. | 2350 Shallowford Village Dr. | 423/499–3800 | 105 rooms | $59–$65 | AE, DC, D, MC, V.

Inn at Lookout Mountain. This two-story property is about 5 minutes west of Lookout Mountain and 3 mi south of Chattanooga. Restaurant, bar with entertainment, picnic area. Room service, cable TV. Pool. Exercise equipment, basketball, volleyball. Video games. | 3800 Cummings Hwy., Tiftonia | 423/821–3531 | fax 423/821–8403 | 162 rooms | $69 | AE, D, DC, MC, V.

La Quinta. This stucco-clad hotel is about 15 minutes northeast of downtown, just ½ mi east of a mall and 4 mi north of the airport. Complimentary Continental breakfast. Some refrigerators, cable TV. Pool. Some pets allowed. | 7015 Shallowford Rd. | 423/855–0011 | fax 423/855–0011, ext. 72 | 132 rooms, 4 suites | $68; $92 suites | AE, D, DC, MC, V.

Red Roof Inn–Chattanooga Airport. Restaurants and shopping are within walking distance of this standard chain motel. The airport is 4 mi northwest and downtown is 11 mi west of the inn. Cable TV. Some pets allowed. | 7014 Shallowford Rd. | 423/899–0143 | fax 423/899–8384 | 112 rooms | $56 | AE, D, DC, MC, V.

Super 8. This standard member of the Super 8 chain is about 2 mi west of Ruby Falls and Rock City tourist attractions. Restaurants are within a 4 mi radius. Picnic area. Cable TV. Laundry facilities. Some pets allowed. | 20 Birmingham Hwy. | 423/821–8880 | 73 rooms | $70 | AE, D, DC, MC, V.

EXPENSIVE

Clarion. Conveniently located in the downtown area, this hotel is within walking distance of the Tennessee aquarium (about five blocks away), the Discovery Museum (about three blocks), and theaters (six blocks), as well as to various shops and restaurants. Restaurant, bar. Cable TV. Pool. Exercise equipment. Business services. Parking (fee). | 407 Chestnut St. | 423/756–5150 | fax 423/265–8708 | 201 rooms | $89 | AE, D, DC, MC, V.

Comfort Suites–Hampton Place. This hotel is conveniently located near the Hamilton Place Mall—the largest shopping mall in Tennessee, which has more than 200 stores, 30 restaurants, and 17 movie theaters. Complimentary Continental breakfast. Refrigerators, microwaves, cable TV. Indoor pool. Hot tub. Exercise equipment. Laundry facilities. Business services. Free parking. | 7324 Shallowford Rd. | 423/892–1500 | fax 423/892–0111 | 62 rooms | $90 | AE, D, DC, MC, V.

Hampton Inn. This dependable chain hotel is in the northern part of Chattanooga, convenient to the airport, restaurants, and Hamilton Place Mall. Complimentary Continental breakfast. Cable TV. Pool. Exercise equipment. | 7013 Shallowford Rd. | 423/855–0095 | fax 423/874–7600 | 168 rooms | $79 | AE, D, DC, MC, V.

VERY EXPENSIVE

Adams Hillborne. Sixteen-foot-high coffered ceilings are a feature of this former mayor's mansion, a 3-story stone Victorian built in 1889. Rooms with fireplaces are available. Five minutes west of the aquarium. Restaurant, room service, complimentary breakfast. In-room data ports, cable TV, in-room VCRs and movies. Exercise equipment. Business services. Free parking. | 801 Vine St. | 423/265–5000 | fax 423/265–5555 | innjoy@worldnet.att.net | 11 rooms; 4 suites | $175; $295 suites | AE, DC, MC, V.

Bluff View. This upscale B&B comprises three buildings: a three-story English Tudor house, a two-story Colonial Revival, and a two-story wood structure, built in 1890, 1928, and 1908 respectively. Located in the Bluff View Art District convenient to the Hunter Museum of Art. Dining room, complimentary breakfast. Cable TV. | 412 E. 2nd St. | 423/265–5033 | fax 423/757–0120 | www.bluffviewinn.com | 13 rooms, 3 suites | $185; $250 suites | AE, D, MC, V.

Country Suites Chattanooga. Just off I–75 near the Hamilton Place Mall, this hotel has both indoor and outdoor swimming pools. Kids stay free in the oversized rooms. Complimentary Continental breakfast. In-room data ports, cable TV. Indoor-outdoor pool. Exercise equipment. Laundry service. Airport shuttle. | 7051 McCutcheon Rd. | 423/899–2300 | 67 suites | $89–$119 | AE, DC, D, MC, V.

Holiday Inn Chattanooga Choo-Choo. You'll find gas lights and formal gardens at this downtown hotel, which is housed in a converted turn-of-the-century train station. The main lobby is under the original 85-ft freestanding dome. Restaurant, bars, room service. In-room data ports. Refrigerators. Cable TV. 3 pools (1 indoor). Tennis. Exercise equipment. Shops. Airport shuttle. Free parking. | 1400 Market St. | 423/266–5000 | fax 423/265–4635 | www.choochoo.com | 360 rooms, 8 suites, 48 train-car rooms | $109; $175 suites, $150 train–car rooms | AE, D, DC, MC, V.

Lookout Lake Bed & Breakfast. This B&B 5 mi west of downtown has a 9-acre, private lake for fishing. Guests may also relax in the living room with its TV and video library, in the solarium, in the well-stocked library, or while playing the inn's grand piano. Complimentary breakfast. Some in-room hot tubs, cable TV. Lake. Fishing. Nonsmoking property. Pets allowed. | 3408 Elder Mountain Rd. | 423/821–8088 | 8 | $110–$160 | MC, V.

Marriott–Chattanooga. This popular 16-story Marriott is downtown near local attractions and restaurants. Restaurant, bar, Refrigerators, cable TV. 2 pools (1 indoor). Exercise equipment. Parking (fee). Business services. | 2 Carter Plaza, | 423/756–0002 | fax 423/266–2254 | www.marriott.com | 342 rooms, 2 suites | $119; $450 suites | AE, D, DC, MC, V.

Pettit House Bed & Breakfast. This brick home built in 1900 is 2 mi south of downtown at the foot of Lookout Mountain. The two guest suites have hardwood floors, a king and two twin beds, a private bath with tub and shower, a sitting room, and a private breakfast room. Complimentary breakfast. In-room data ports, cable TV, in-room VCRs. | 109 Ochs Hwy. | 423/821–4740 | www.pettithouse.com | 2 rooms | $145–$175 | AE, MC, V.

★ **Radisson Read House.** This 1926 downtown hotel was originally built to accommodate travelers on the Nashville/Chattanooga Railroad. Restaurants, bar. Cable TV. Pool. Exercise equipment. | 827 Broad St. | 423/266–4121 or 800/333–3333 | fax 423/267–6447 | www.radisson.com | 100 suites, 138 rooms | $108–$118; $118–$128 suites | AE, D, DC, MC, V.

CLARKSVILLE

MAP 12, D1

(Nearby towns also listed: Dickson, Hendersonville, Nashville, Paris)

Founded in 1780, Clarksville, with over 100,000 residents, is the fifth-largest city in the state, located near the Kentucky state line at the confluence of the Red and Cumberland Rivers. Barges still stop to do business at "the Queen City." Contemporary downtown development, the River District and Riverwalk, testify to Clarksville's rediscovery of its waterfront. Downtown also boasts a remarkable number of well-preserved historic buildings in a variety of architectural styles.

Information: **Clarksville/Montgomery County Convention and Visitor Bureau** | 312 Madison St., Clarksville 37040 | 931/648–0001.

Attractions

Beachhaven Vineyard and Winery. A repeat winner at the International Wine Competition, this winery, 15 mi west of downtown, offers free tours and wine samples. | 1100 Dunlop La. | 931/645–8867 | Free | Summer Mon.–Sat. 9–7, Sun. 12–7; winter Mon.–Sat. 9–5, Sun. 12–5.

Clarksville-Montgomery County Museum. Permanent exhibits in history, science, and art include an original 1846 log cabin, a turn-of-the-century toy store, a fire station, a print shop, and a model train display. One floor is dedicated entirely to hands-on learning activities. The museum's eclectic architecture makes this one of the most photographed buildings in Tennessee. | 200 S. 2nd St. | 931/648–5780 | $3 | Tues.–Sat. 10–5, Sun. 1–5.

Dunbar Cave State Natural Area. Excavations show that this 8.1-mi deep cave, 10 mi south of downtown, has been used by human beings for thousands of years, due to its constant water flow and natural air-conditioning. Square dances, radio shows, and Big Band–era concerts were once held in the cavernous mouth of the cave. Guided hikes are available. | 401 Old Dunbar Cave Rd. | 931/648–5526 | www.state.tn.us/environment/parks/dunbar | $4 | Sept.–May, daily 8–4:30; June–Aug., weekends by appointment.

Fort Donelson National Battlefield and Cemetery In 1862, Fort Donelson was the site of the first major Union victory of the Civil War. The battle was significant because Union commander Ulysses S. Grant captured the fort and 13,000 Confederate soldiers, and for its unconventional use of iron-clad gunboats on inland rivers, which marked the beginning of Union control of the north-to-south rivers in the region. Visit the park, 30 mi northwest of Clarksville, to see the fort, river batteries, outer defense earthworks, Surrender House (now Dover Hotel), and a national cemetery. There is also a visitor's center and museum. | 120 Fort Donelson Park Rd., Dover | 931/232–5706 | Free | Daily 8–4:30.

Land Between the Lakes. This 40-mi stretch of land between Kentucky Lake and Lake Barkley, 30 mi west of Clarksville, includes "the Homeplace," an 1850s working farm; a nature center; elk herds and bison ranges; a planetarium; campgrounds; and lots of undeveloped land to explore. | 100 Van Morgan Dr. | 270/924–2000 or 800/LBL–7077 | Free | Daily.

Port Royal State Historic Area. The site of one of Tennessee's earliest communities and trading centers, Port Royal, features a replica of the original 1904 covered bridge over the Red River. The area also includes a museum, hiking trails, picnic areas, and canoeing. | 3300 Old Clarksville Hwy., Adams | 931/358–9696 | Free | Daily.

Queen of Clarksville. The 150-passenger paddleboat offers 90-minute excursions on the Cumberland River. The captain and his crew regale passengers with tales of the river. Saturday night features a dinner dance cruise with food and live music. | 630 N. Riverside Dr. | 931/647–5500 | $8 | Apr.–Nov. daily.

Smith-Trahern Mansion. Built in 1858 by Christopher Smith, a wealthy tobacco grower, the New Orleans–style mansion overlooking the Cumberland River has been fully restored. It features a widow's walk, wrought-iron scrollwork, and columns topped by classical carvings. The house (which is supposedly haunted by Mrs. Smith) also features an art gallery with rotating exhibits. | 101 McClure St. | 931/648–9998 | $1 | Weekdays 9:30–2:30.

ON THE CALENDAR

MAR.: *Old Time Fiddlers Championship.* Musicians compete in 14 categories, including Bluegrass Banjo, Guitar, Fiddle (various levels), Mandolin, and Harmonica. Call for location and schedule. | 931/648–1601.
AUG.: *Clarksville Rodeo.* Cowboys and cowgirls compete in bareback, bull riding, and calf roping at the Clarksville Fairgrounds off U.S.48-13. | 931/648–3071. **SEPT.: *Riverfest.*** The celebration, which takes place along the Riverwalk downtown, includes concerts, arts and crafts, country dancing, a 5K run, and more. | 931/645–7476.

Dining

Hickory Stick Grill. Steak. Steaks, ribs, and burgers anchor the menu at this bar and restaurant. The blue-cheese hamburger is particularly revered, and the fresh salads are an alternative to meat. | 1979 Madison St. | 931/503–8270 | $8–$12 | MC, V | No lunch.

Jackie's Country Kitchen. American. Locals gather here to sip coffee or talk business over lunch, but the restaurant is considerably less busy for dinner. Salads, burgers, and sandwiches make up the menu. | 83 Dover Rd. | 931/645–9111 | $5–$8 | AE, D, MC, V.

Looking Glass Café. Café. This gourmet sandwich shop opens onto a patio of wrought-iron tables enclosed by a 2,000-square-ft yard. Choose from a variety of freshly baked breads such as sundried tomato, Romano swiss, or parsley. All chicken and pasta salads are homemade, and you can order from a hot dinner menu by reservation. | 329-H Warfield Blvd. | 931/552–6344 | $6–$10 | AE, MC, V | Closed Sun.

Red's Smokehouse. Barbecue. Locals have flocked to this rustic River District hangout for more than 30 years to eat barbecued ribs, chicken and pork. | 601 Riverside Dr. | 931/645–4113 | $8–$14 | No credit cards | Closed Sun.

Tipper's Pub. American. Popular with the Fort Campbell crowd, you can get deep-fried appetizers, as well as sandwiches, salads, and 18-ounce steaks at this restaurant 3 mi southeast of downtown. Oysters on the half shell are also popular. | 2150 Fort Campbell Blvd. | 931/920–8011 | $6–$18 | AE, D, MC, V | No lunch weekends.

Lodging

Best Western Executive Inn & Suites. This well-equipped, two-story hotel off I–24 is a half-mile from the Governor's Square Mall, 10 mi south of downtown. Jacuzzi suites are available. Complimentary Continental breakfast. In-room data ports, some in-room hot tubs, cable TV. Pool. Laundry facilities, laundry service. | 250 Holiday Rd. | 931/552–3330 or 800/528–1234 | www.bestwestern.com | 20 rooms, 40 suites | $58.50–$65, $69–$85 suites | AE, D, DC, MC, V.

Days Inn. This standard two-floor chain motel is remarkably quiet despite its location on Route 76, approximately 7 mi south of downtown. Complimentary Continental breakfast. Cable TV. Pool. Business services. Some pets allowed. | 1100 Connector Rd. | 931/358–3194 | fax 931/358–9869 | 81 rooms | $450 | AE, D, DC, MC, V.

Econo Lodge–Clarksville. A shopping mall, restaurants, and a putt-putt golf course are within a short drive of this no-frills chain motel, 20 minutes north of downtown Clarksville. Complimentary Continental breakfast. In-room data ports, some microwaves, some refrigerators, cable TV. Pool. Hot tubs. Laundry facilities. Business services. | 201 Holiday Dr. | 931/645–6300 | fax 931/645–5054 | 42 rooms | $59 | AE, D, DC, MC, V.

Hachland Hill Inn. This downtown brick bed-and-breakfast, built in 1795, is furnished with antiques and handmade quilts. Rooms have private baths and fireplaces. There are also cedar cottages tucked away in nearby woods on the inn's 3-acre grounds. Restaurant. No TV in some rooms. Library. Some pets allowed. | 1601 Madison St. | 931/647–4084 | 7 rooms, 3 cottages | $95 | AE.

Hampton Inn. This reliable chain hotel, 15 minutes north of town off U.S. 79, is located about a quarter of a mi from restaurants and a shopping mall. Movie theaters and horseback riding are also available nearby. Complimentary Continental breakfast. Some microwaves, refrigerators, cable TV. Pool. Exercise equipment. Laundry facilities. | 190 Holiday Rd. | 931/552–2255 | fax 931/552–4871 | 77 rooms | $59 | AE, D, DC, MC, V.

Heritage. This basic motel is conveniently located on U.S. 79, 5 mi north of downtown. Some rooms have views of the countryside. Complimentary breakfast. Cable TV. Pool. Video games. Business services. Some pets allowed. | 3075 Wilma Rudolph Blvd. | 931/645–1400 | fax 931/551–3917 | Travel@knightwave.com | 127 rooms | $50–$70 | AE, D, DC, MC, V.

Quality Inn. Predictable accommodations in downtown Clarksville, near restaurants and antiques shops. Bar, complimentary Continental breakfast. Some microwaves, cable TV. Indoor pool. Hot tub, sauna. Laundry facilities. Business services. Some pets allowed. | 803 N. 2nd St. | 931/645–9084 | fax 931/645–9084, ext. 340 | 129 rooms; 9 suites | $56; $89 suites | AE, D, DC, MC, V.

Red Roof Inn. These well-serviced accommodations are about 7 mi north of town, near several restaurants off I–24. There are honeymoon suites and business king suites with in-room data ports. There is also a dry-cleaning pickup service. Complimentary Continental breakfast. Some microwaves, some refrigerators, cable TV, some in-room VCRs. Pool. Laundry facilities. Some pets allowed. | 197 Holiday Dr. | 931/905–1555 | www.redroof.com | 61 rooms | $45–$100 | AE, D, DC, MC, V.

Riverview Inn. This riverfront lodging, convenient to Clarksville's River District, is also near a shopping mall and within walking distance of restaurants and pubs. Restaurant, bar. In-room data ports, some microwaves, cable TV. Indoor pool. Some pets allowed. Free parking. | 50 College St. | 931/552–3331 | fax 931/647–5005 | 154 rooms, 11 suites | $54–$85 | AE, D, DC, MC, V.

Wingate Inn. This four-story hotel is 10 minutes north of town off I–24, near Governor's Square Mall and more than 20 restaurants. Complimentary Continental breakfast. In-room data ports, some in-room safes, cable TV. Pool. Sauna. Exercise equipment. Video games. Laundry service. | 251 Holiday Dr. | 931/906–0606 or 800/993–7232 | www.wingateinns.com | 82 rooms | $79–$150 | AE, D, DC, MC, V.

CLEVELAND

MAP 12, G4

(Nearby towns also listed: Athens, Chattanooga, Dayton)

Cleveland was the last capital of the Cherokee before they were forceably evacuated in 1838, an event commemorated at nearby Red Clay Historic Park. Incorporated in 1842 with a population of just 400 white settlers, this town near the Ocoee River grew to be the most prosperous along the railroad between Chattanooga and Knoxville, and made it through the Civil War relatively untouched. The town's Victorian homes, built during the industrial boom of the 1870s and 1880s, are a source of local pride.

Information: **Cleveland/Bradley County Chamber of Commerce** | 2145 Keith St., Cleveland 37311 | 423/472–6587 or 800/472–6588 | www.clevelandchamber.com.

Attractions

Ocoee River. Boasting Class II, IV, and V rapids, this river is the premier whitewater river in the Southeast. It runs through the southern portion of the Cherokee National Forest, 30 mi east of Cleveland. | Ocoee Ranger District, Hwy. 64, Parksville | 423/338–5201 | Free | Daily.

Primitive Settlement. The collection of restored log cabins, primarily from the mid-19th century, were relocated to this 13-acre site, 6½ mi east of Cleveland, then furnished with household and farm items used by the area's early settlers. | 693 Kinser Rd. SE | 423/476–5096 | $5 | Daily.

Red Clay State Historic Park. The 263-acre park was the site of the Cherokee Nation's last council ground until 1838, when U.S. troops evacuated these Native Americans and others to a reservation in present-day Oklahoma. Dedicated to the preservation and interpretation of Cherokee history, the park, 12 mi south of Cleveland, includes a museum and replicas of a Cherokee farmstead and council house. | 1140 Red Clay Park Rd. SW | 423/478–0339 | www.state.tn.us/environment/parks/redclay/index.html | Free | Mar.–Nov., daily 8–sunset; Dec.–Feb., daily 8–4:30.

ON THE CALENDAR

AUG.: *Cherokee Days of Recognition.* Red Clay State Historical Park hosts this annual, week-long festival honoring the Cherokee people. Includes authentic arts, food, music, storytelling, dance, and a blowgun competition. | 423/478–0339.

Dining

Gardners Market. Delicatessen. This downtown favorite features homemade baked goods. Imported cookies, coffees, and soaps are for sale. | 262 Broad St. NW | 423/478–3906 | Reservations not accepted | $2–$5 | MC, V | Breakfast also available. Closed Sun.

Gondolier Pizza. Italian. This casual, family-friendly restaurant 2 mi north of downtown offers classics such as spaghetti and manicotti, as well as Greek favorites like gyros platters. Kids' menu. | 3300 Keith St. NW | 423/472–4998 | $5–$10 | D, MC, V.

Lodging

Baymont Inn. Fifteen minutes southeast of downtown Cleveland, this stucco motel is also conveniently within a mile of several restaurants. Complimentary Continental breakfast. Cable TV. Pool. Laundry facilities. Business services. Some pets allowed. | 107 Interstate Dr. NW | 423/339–1000 | fax 423/339–2760 | www.baymontinn.com | 102 rooms, 14 suites | $63, $70 suites | AE, D, DC, MC, V.

Holiday Inn–North. Enjoy mountain views from this two-story motel, just 2½ mi north of downtown Cleveland. White-water rafting and Red Clay State Historic Park are also easily accessible from this convenient location off I–75. Restaurant, room service. Cable TV. Pool. Business services. Some pets allowed. | 2400 Executive Park Dr. | 423/472–1504 | fax 423/479–5962 | 145 rooms | $75 | AE, D, DC, MC, V.

Lincoln Swiss House. This standard motel 3 mi north of town is near several restaurants. Some kitchenettes, cable TV. Some pets allowed. | 2597 Georgetown Rd. | 423/479–3720 | 25 rooms | $29.95–$39.95 | AE, D, MC, V.

Ocoee Mist Farm. This outdoorsy B&B, shadowed by the Chilhowee Mountain, is in Benton, 13 mi east of Cleveland. There are water sports at nearby Lake Ocoee, and the hosts lead llama hikes in the neighboring Cherokee National Forest. Animal lovers will enjoy the many permanent residents of the farm. Complimentary breakfast. Refrigerators, cable TV, in-

THE TRAIL OF TEARS

A particularly tragic example of the U.S. government's mistreatment of Native Americans was played out in part on Tennessee soil.

In 1830 during President Andrew Jackson's term, Congress passed the Indian Removal Act, which declared that all American Indians living east of the Mississippi must move west of the river. This included members of the Cherokee, Chickasaw, Choctaw, Creek, and Seminole tribes in the Southeast.

Although the Cherokee of Georgia successfully challenged the removal policy in the U.S. Supreme Court, in 1838 some 15,000 Cherokee were forcibly removed from their land and homes in North Carolina, Georgia, Alabama, and Tennessee. Many were driven out at gunpoint, after being given only a few minutes to gather up their belongings. They were interned in stockades near Chattanooga before embarking on their forced march to Oklahoma. Their journey became known as the "Trail of Tears."

There were four major routes that made up the the Trail of Tears. Two of these, the Northern Route and the Water Route, have been partially preserved; in 1987 they were designated the Trail of Tears National Historic Trail. All four routes passed through Tennessee, and parts of the trail are preserved throughout the state. An interpretive program and information about trail sites are available at the Red Clay State Historical Area near Cleveland, which was the site of the last Cherokee councils before the large-scale evacuation took place.

room VCRs. Hot tub. Pets allowed. | 377 Parksville Rd., Benton | 423/338–6818 | fax 423/338–6710 | http://ivillage.bbchannel.com/bbc/p614485.asp | 4 rooms | $75–$89 | AE, D, MC, V.

Quality Inn Chalet. You can walk to area restaurants from this conveniently located chain motel, or drive less than 3 mi west to reach downtown Cleveland. Restaurant. Some refrigerators, cable TV. Pool, wading pool. Laundry facilities. Some pets allowed. | 2595 Georgetown Rd. | 423/476–8511 | 97 rooms | $59 | AE, D, DC, MC, V.

COLUMBIA

MAP 12, E3

(Nearby towns also listed: Franklin, Hohenwald, Lewisburg, Shelbyville)

This middle Tennessee town, founded in 1807, is famous for its large number of well-preserved antebellum mansions. From the 1820s until the Civil War broke out, Columbia, today with 32,000 residents, was the second most populous town in the state, and one of the wealthiest. President James K. Polk grew up here; his Federal-style ancestral home is one of the historic residences you can visit here. Columbia's primary crop? Mules, which have long been raised and traded at the town's annual Mule Day.

Information: **Maury County Convention and Visitors Bureau** | 8 Public Sq., Columbia 38401–1076 | 931/381–7176 | www.antebellum.com.

Attractions

Ancestral Home of James K. Polk. Built in 1816 by Polk's father, a wealthy farmer and surveyor, this Federal-style brick house is the only surviving residence of the 11th U.S. president (other than the White House). The landscaped grounds feature three gardens: formal boxwood, white azalea, and wildflower. | 301 W. 7th St. | 931/388–2354 | www.jameskpolk.com | $5 | Apr.–Oct., Mon.–Sat. 9–5, Sun. 1–5; Nov.–Mar., Mon.–Sat. 9–4, Sun. 1–5.

The Athenaeum. A blend of Gothic Revival, Greek Revival, Italianate, and Moorish architecture, this mansion was built in 1835 as a rectory for a nephew of President Polk. | 808 Athenaeum St. | 931/381–4822 | $1 | Feb.–Dec., Tues.–Sat. 10–4, Sun. 1–4.

Rattle and Snap Plantation. One of the finest examples of Greek Revival architecture in the nation, this plantation home, featuring an imposing 10-column facade, was built on the outskirts of town from 1842 to 1845 by George Washington Polk, distant cousin to James K. Polk, and his wife. In addition to the fully restored and furnished antebellum mansion, the plantation includes a carriage house and stables, gardens, an ice house, a gift shop, an interpretive farm, and five dining rooms, which serve for lunch and dinner fare typical of the mid-19th century. Polk acquired the land for the plantation by winning at rattle and snap, a popular Colonial American game that rattled and rolled dried beans like dice. | 1522 N. Main St. | 931/379–5861 | www.rattleandsnap.com | $9.50 | Mon.–Sat. 10–4, Sun. 1–4.

ON THE CALENDAR

APR.: *Mule Day.* This celebration of Columbia's role as the world's largest mule market is attended by as many as 250,000 people each year. Highlights include a mule sale and parade, fiddler's competition, and liar's contest. | 931/381–9557.

SEPT., DEC.: *Home Pilgrimages.* The antebellum homes and churches of Maury County, including Columbia's, are open for self-guided tours during the last weekend of September and the first weekend of December. Call the Maury County Visitors Bureau for exact dates, brochures, tour maps, and ticket information. | 888/852–1860.

Dining

The Ole Lamplighter. American. The log-frame family-run restaurant overlooking the Delk River five minutes north of downtown has two adjoining dining rooms illuminated by an open fireplace. Specialties include rib-eye and New York strip steaks. Other dishes include grilled chicken, seafood, and a 45-item salad bar. Kids' menu. | 1000 Riverside Dr. | 931/381–3837 | $11–$30 | AE, D, DC, MC, V | Closed 1st week in July. No lunch.

Henri's On The Square. American. The menu at this restaurant changes daily, but staples are boneless fried chicken breasts, smoked pork chops, pepper steak, and three side items. Small gift items are for sale. | 34 Public Sq. | 931/381–5566 | Reservations not accepted | $4–$6 | No credit cards | No dinner.

Lodging

Days Inn–Columbia. This member of the popular motel chain is located 1 mi north of the downtown area near historic homes, restaurants, and shopping. Complimentary Continental breakfast. Cable TV. Pool. Business services. | 1504 Nashville Hwy. | 931/381–3297 | fax 931/381–8692 | 53 rooms, 1 suite | $42.50; $95 suite | AE, D, DC, MC, V.

Holiday Inn Express. This hotel is 13 mi north of downtown on U.S. 412. Suites are available, and there is a meeting room next to the lobby. Complimentary breakfast. In-room data ports, refrigerators, cable TV. Pool. Business services. | 1554 Bear Creek Pike | 931/380–1227 | www.holidayinnexpress.com | 52 rooms, 4 suites | $55–$75, $80–$125 suites | AE, D, DC, MC, V.

James K. Polk Motel. The lobby of this locally-owned motel 2 mi north of town features historical pictures and literature about the area, once the president's home. Rooms with three beds are available. Some refrigerators, cable TV. Pool. Pets allowed for a fee. | 1111 Nashville Hwy. | 931/388–4913 | 50 rooms | $32.85–$42.95 | AE, D, MC, V.

Ramada Inn. Sitting on a major thoroughfare, this two-story brick motel, 4 mi north of downtown and its restaurants and shops, is surprisingly quiet. Restaurant, bar, room service. Cable TV. Pool. Some pets allowed. | 1208 Nashville Hwy. | 931/388–2720 | fax 931/388–2360 | 155 rooms | $59; $80 suite | AE, D, DC, MC, V.

COOKEVILLE

MAP 12, G2

(Nearby towns also listed: Celina, Crossville, Jamestown, Lebanon, Wartburg)

This middle Tennessee town of 26,000, the Putnam County seat, has two downtowns—one that developed around the original town square, laid out in the 1850s, and another created around the railroad station, which quickly became the center of town life in the early years of the 20th century. Cookeville is also the home of Tennessee Technological University, a major employer in the area.

Information: **Cookeville/Putnam County Chamber of Commerce** | 302 S. Jefferson Ave., Cookeville 38501 | 931/526–2211.

Attractions

Burgess Falls State Natural Area. A striking 3/4-mile nature trail follows the Falling Water River, passing numerous waterfalls, including one 130-ft wonder. There's also fishing, hiking, and picnicking at this preserve, just 8 mi west of Cookeville. | 4000 Burgess Falls Dr. | 931/432–5312 | Free | 8–sunset.

Center Hill Dam and Lake. The man-made lake is 65 mi long and covers 18,000 acres, approximately 20 mi southwest of Cookeville. Swimming is allowed anywhere on the lake and there are two beaches. You can access several different look-out points along the dam from I-40. | 158 Resource La., Silver Point | 931/858–3125 | Free | Daily.

Edgar Evins State Park. This 6,280-acre park comprises the steep forested hillsides on the shores of Center Hill Lake approximately 20 mi southwest of Cookeville. You can enjoy water sports, camping, and hiking here. | Edgar Evins Park Rd., Silver Point | 931/858–2446 | Free | Daily.

Joe L. Evins Appalachian Center for Crafts. The professional crafts school is set on 600 acres overlooking Center Lake, 15 mi west of Cookeville. Students and teachers exhibit and sell traditional Appalachian and contemporary crafts. | 1560 Craft Center Dr. | 931/597–6801 | Free | Daily.

Cookeville Depot Museum. A railroad museum set in the 1909 train depot is the town's most significant attraction. Exhibits include two vintage cabooses with original interiors. | 116 W. Broad St. | 931/528–8570 | Free | Tue.–Sat. 10–4.

ON THE CALENDAR

NOV.: *Annual Christmas Parade.* An annual Christmas parade, held the weekend after Thanksgiving, kicks off the holiday season downtown. There are generally more than 300 participants in the parade. Enjoy the decorated storefronts and holiday refreshments. | 931/526–2211.

Dining

Bobby Q's. Southern. *Ladies' Home Journal* magazine has featured this restaurant. It offers authentic barbecue, and fried catfish is a specialty at this down-home spot 1 mi from the town square. | 1070 N. Washington Ave. | 931/526–1024 | $6–$12 | No credit cards.

Louie's. American. This restaurant in the Holiday Inn serves steak, pasta, and chicken. Breakfast is available all day, and there are all-you-can-eat lunch buffets on weekdays and brunch on Sunday. Friday nights boast a special seafood buffet. | 970 S. Jefferson Ave. | 931/526–7125 | Breakfast also available | $8–$13 | AE, DC, D, MC, V.

Nick's. American. This spacious hilltop facility has two banquet rooms and a bar/lounge. Picture windows overlook downtown Cookeville. Known for its char-broiled steak, seafood, and ice cream pie. Other dishes include roast round of beef and teriyaki chicken. | 895 S. Jefferson Ave. | 931/528–1434 | $7–$15 | AE, D, DC, MC, V | No lunch Sun.

Odie's Drive-In. Southern. For more than 50 years, this has been the place to go for country home-style cooking in Cookeville. Breakfast includes grits and biscuits and gravy, and lunch features plate specials as well as hamburgers and steaks. | 2240 W. Broad St. | 931/526–3404 | $5–$10 | No credit cards | Breakfast also available. No dinner.

Wavebreak Restaurant. American/Casual. In the Edgar Evins Marina, 15 mi west of Cookeville, this place offers views of Center Hill Lake. Known for its creative burgers, it also has steaks, pasta, and catfish. | 2100 Edgar Evins State Park Rd., Silver Point | 931/858–6176 | $8–$18 | AE, MC, V | Closed Oct.–Apr.

Lodging

Alpine Lodge and Suites. This quiet, secluded property is off Highway 70 N 4 mi east of town. Restaurant, picnic area, complimentary Continental breakfast. In-room data ports, refrigerators, some in-room hot tubs, cable TV, some in-room VCRs. Pool, wading pool. Hot tub. Laundry facilities. Business services. Some pets allowed (fee). | 2021 E. Spring St. | 931/526–3333 | fax 931/528–9036 | 88 rooms, 26 suites | $50 rooms, $60–$70 suites | AE, D, DC, MC, V.

Best Western Thunderbird. This motel, three blocks from I-40, sits 2 mi south of downtown. Its two buildings have outside entrances. Complimentary Continental breakfast. Cable TV. Pool. Business services. Some pets allowed. | 900 S. Jefferson Ave. | 931/526–7115 | 276 rooms, 15 suites | $49; $75 suites | AE, D, DC, MC, V.

Comfort Suites Cookeville. This motel 2 mi south of town is right off I-40 at Exit 287. In-room data ports, some in-room hot tubs, cable TV. Pool. Sauna. Exercise equipment. | 1035 Interstate Dr. | 931/372–1881 | www.comfortsuites.com | 48 suites | $54–$89 | AE, DC, D, MC, V.

Cookeville Super 8 Motel. This two-story chain motel is 2 mi south of downtown just off I-40. Complimentary Continental breakfast. Some microwaves, some refrigerators, cable TV. Outdoor pool. | 1292 Bunker Hill Rd., Exit 287 | 931/528–2020 or 800/800–8000 | fax 931/528–4234 | www.super8.com | 52 rooms | $50–$75 | AE, D, DC, MC, V.

Econo Lodge. These standardized accommodations are 2 mi south of downtown, near area restaurants and shopping. Complimentary Continental breakfast. Some refrigerators, cable TV. Pool. Business services. Some pets allowed (fee). | 1100 S. Jefferson Ave. | 931/528–1040 | fax 931/528–5227 | 70 rooms | $56 | AE, D, DC, MC, V.

Executive Inn. Shopping malls and movie theaters are less than 1 mi away from this two-story motel just off I-40. Restaurant, complimentary Continental breakfast. Cable TV. Pool, wading pool. Laundry facilities. Business services. | 897 S. Jefferson Ave. | 931/526–9521 or 800/826–2791 | 81 rooms | $45 | AE, D, DC, MC, V.

Garden Inn. Perched on a 90-ft solid rock bluff 15 mi east of town, this three-story bed-and-breakfast overlooks virgin timber, landscaped lawns, flower and butterfly gardens, and a stream full of water lilies. In the evenings choose from homemade desserts such as carrot cake, pumpkin crunch, berry pie, and chocolate cake. Two of the guest rooms have fireplaces, and three have hot tubs; all have antiques. Complimentary breakfast. In-room data ports, some in-room hot tubs, cable TV. Hiking. No pets. No kids under 12. No smoking. | 1400 Bee Rock, Monterey | 931/839–1400 | www.thegardenbandb.com | 11 rooms | $135–$145 | AE, D, MC, V.

Hampton Inn. Area shopping and restaurants are not far from this representative of the popular hotel chain, 2 mi south of downtown. Tennessee Tech, city parks, and golf courses are also nearby. Cable TV. Pool. Hot tub. Gym. Some pets allowed. | 1025 Interstate Dr. | 931/520–1117 or 800/426–7866 | 65 rooms | $75 | AE, D, DC, MC, V.

Holiday Inn. A movie theater, shopping mall, and plenty of restaurants are within walking distance of this chain hotel 2 mi south of the downtown area. Restaurant, bar, room service. In-room data ports, cable TV. Indoor/outdoor pool. Hot tub. Exercise equipment. Video games. Business services. Some pets allowed. | 970 S. Jefferson Ave. | 931/526–7125 | fax 931/372–8508 | www.basshotels.com | 200 rooms, 3 suites | $75 | AE, D, DC, MC, V.

Ramada Limited Suites. Two miles south of downtown Cookeville, this well-serviced hotel is near more than 80 restaurants, a mall, and a movie theater. Complimentary Continental breakfast. In-room data ports, minibars, refrigerators, cable TV. Indoor pool. Hot tub. Exercise equipment. Laundry facilities. Business services. | 1045 Interstate Dr. | 931/372–0086 | fax 931/372–0030 | 60 rooms, 53 suites | $64; $70 suites | AE, D, DC, MC, V.

COVINGTON

MAP 12, B3

(Nearby towns also listed: Bolivar, Dyersburg, Henning, Jackson, Memphis)

Covington, the seat of Tipton County, which is the third-largest county in the state's western quarter, owes its size and significance to the coming of the railroad in 1873. Its buildings show how the townspeople spent the railroad money that poured into the town in the latter part of the 19th century—the town's South Main Historic District, a residential area, is now on the National Register of Historic Places, as is the town's Ruffin Theater.

Information: **Covington/Tipton County Chamber of Commerce** | 106 W. Liberty, Covington 38019 | 901/476–9727.

Attractions
Fort Pillow State Historic Area. *(See* Henning.*)* In 1861 the Confederate Army built extensive fortifications here set strategically on the Chickasaw Bluffs overlooking the Mississippi

River. The fort was soon taken over by the Union Army, however, which controlled it throughout most of the Civil War. The park, 10 mi west of Covington, is now a sanctuary for deer and turkey and has been designated a Wildlife Observation Area by the Tennessee Wildlife Resources Agency. It also offers camping, hiking, and excellent bird-watching. | 3122 Park Rd. | 901/738–5581 | www.state.tn.us/environment/parks/pillow/index.html | Free | Daily.

The Ruffin Theater. The Art Deco theater, built in 1937, is on the National Register of Historic Places. It hosts community plays and other performing arts productions. | 113 W. Pleasant Ave. | 901/476–3439 | Prices vary | Call for schedule.

South Main Historic District. The district features 52 private residences on the national historic register, built from before the Civil War to approximately 1918. | S. Main St. between Sherade and South Maple Sts. | 901/476–1619 | Free | Daily.

ON THE CALENDAR
JULY: *World's Oldest Barbeque Cooking Contest.* The public is invited to enjoy live music, arts and craft exhibits, and an antique car show at this annual event, held in conjunction with the Memphis-in-May barbeque cooking contest. The contest takes place the third weekend of the month, Thurs. through Sun. in Cobb-Parr Park, off U.S. 51. | 901/476–9727.

Dining
Little Porky's Pit Barbecue. Barbecue. For more than 30 years this rustic family-run establishment has been serving spare ribs (a specialty), as well as chicken, beef brisket, and pork, all smoked on site. Five minutes north of downtown. | 524 U.S. 51 N | 901/476–7165 | $6–$14 | Breakfast also available | AE, D, MC, V.

Lodging
Days Inn. This two-story motel is a half-mile north of town square on U.S. 51. Complimentary Continental breakfast. Microwaves, refrigerators, cable TV. Outdoor pool. Laundry facilities. | 80 Deena Cove | 901/475–1177 | www.daysinn.com | 35 rooms | $65–$109 | AE, D, DC, MC, V.

Comfort Inn. This two-story motel less than a mile north of town offers standard chain accommodations near local shopping and restaurants. There's also a movie theater nearby. Complimentary Continental breakfast. Refrigerators, microwaves, cable TV. Pool. Hot tub. | 901 U.S. 51 N | 901/475–0380 or 800/228–5150 | 37 rooms | $68 | AE, D, DC, MC, V.

CROSSVILLE

MAP 12, H2

(Nearby towns also listed: Cookeville, Lenoir City, Oak Ridge, Wartburg)

Officially founded in 1901, this town of 9,000 on the Cumberland Plateau in the eastern part of the state was an important crossroads for travelers during the 19th century. Crossville's location at the intersection of U.S. 70, which runs east and west, and U.S. 127, which runs north and south, still makes it an excellent jumping-off spot for exploring the surrounding area. Once known as the hometown of World War I hero Sgt. Alvin C. York, today its golf courses and resort communities are the major draw.

Information: **Greater Cumberland County Chamber of Commerce** | 34 S. Main St., Crossville 38555 | 931/484–8444.

Attractions
Cumberland County Playhouse. Professional and community theater productions are performed on two full-time indoor stages and a seasonal outdoor performance space. | 221 Tennessee Ave. | 931/484–5000 | Prices vary | Call for schedule.

Cumberland General Store. This old-fashioned general merchandise store sells everything from sassafras tea and homestead ham to galvanized bathtubs. | 1 Rte. 68 | 931/484–8481 | fax 931/456–1211 | www.cumberlandgeneral.com | Free | Mon.–Sat. 8–5, Sun. 1–5.

Cumberland Mountain State Park. This 1,720-acre-park, 5 mi south of town off U.S. 127, is on the Cumberland Plateau, the largest forested plateau in America, and features a 35-acre lake. Activities include water sports, hiking, and golf. There are campgrounds and cabins. | 24 Office Dr. | 931/484–6138 | www.state.tn.us/environment/parks/cumbmtn/ | Free | Daily 7 AM–10 PM.

Pioneer Hall Museum. This history museum features exhibits of spinning, weaving, tools, and other artifacts that tell stories about the area's past. It is housed in an 1884 building that was once Pleasant Hill Academy's dormitory, 8 mi west of Crossville. | Main St., Pleasant Hill | 931/277–3872 | Free | Wed. 10–4, Sun. 2–5.

ON THE CALENDAR
JULY: TennFest. This celebration of all things Tennessee is held one weekend during the month. Enjoy music, dance, theater, arts and crafts, and food, all at the Cumberland County Playhouse. | 931/484–5000.
OCT.: Oktoberfest. This celebration of authentic German cuisine and beverage also features live entertainment. It's held annually at the Knights of Columbus Activities Grounds; take I-40 south to exit 322 and follow U.S. 70 east ⅓ mi to reach the grounds. Admission is charged. | 931/484–8444.

Dining
Chesapeat's. American. The buffet brunch packs 'em in every Sunday, and you can order from the dinner menu the rest of the week. Chicken, seafood, steak, and pasta dishes are available at this family-friendly restaurant 2 mi east of town. | 78 Chestnut Hill Rd. | 931/707–9827 | Reservations essential | $9–$15 | MC, V | Closed Mon., Tue. No lunch Wed.–Sat. No dinner Sun.

Halcyon Days. Continental. This formal spot 5 mi east of the town center offers a mix of French and Cajun dishes. The sliced veal sautéed in a lemon-butter sauce is a local favorite. Lobster is served on Wednesdays. There are a wide variety of homemade desserts, including ice creams and sorbets made on the premises, tiramisu, and crème brûlée. | 2444 Genesis Rd., Suite 101 | 931/456–3663 | Reservations essential | $16–$20 | AE, MC, V | Closed Sun. No lunch.

Jake's Sports Grill. American/Casual. This locals joint 1 mi west of town is the place to go for drinking, eating, and watching NASCAR racing on Sunday afternoons. Burgers, sandwiches, and fried appetizers are available for lunch and dinner. | 1112 West Ave. | 931/456–5002 | $5–$10 | MC, V.

Lodging
Days Inn. This stucco standard, 3 mi north of downtown, sits near shopping and restaurants. An outlet mall is 1½ mi to the north, just off I-40. Complimentary Continental breakfast. Cable TV. Pool. Business services. Some pets allowed. | 105 Executive Dr. | 931/484–9691 or 800/626–9432 | 61 rooms | $70 | AE, D, DC, MC, V.

Fairfield Glade. Eleven lakes are in the immediate vicinity of this golf-lovers hotel, which has its own private course and driving range. The property is 15 minutes north of downtown and within walking distance of area restaurants and shopping. 3 restaurants, picnic area, snack bar. Cable TV. Indoor/outdoor pool, wading pool. Driving range, 18-hole golf course, miniature golf, putting green, tennis. Exercise equipment, horseback riding. Dock, boating. Video games. Playground. Business services. | 109 Fairfield Blvd., Fairfield Glade | 931/484–7521 or 931/484–3723 | fax 931/484–3788 | www.fairfield.net | 100 rooms, 6 villas | $100; $130 villas | AE, D, DC, MC, V.

Hampton Inn Crossville. The Cumberland Playhouse, restaurants and an outlet shopping mall are easily accessible from this three-story stucco-and-brick motel in downtown Crossville. There's also a golf course 1 mi to the south. Complimentary Continental breakfast. Cable TV. Pool. Hot tub. Gym. | 3198 N. Main St. | 931/456–9338 or 800/HAMPTON | 60 rooms | $85 | AE, D, DC, MC, V.

Heritage Inn. This motor lodge sits 1 mi north of downtown, off I–40, on what locals call Restaurant Row. The newly renovated rooms are a good bet at budget prices. Cable TV. Pool. Some pets allowed. | 2900 N. Main St. | 931/484–9505 or 800/762–7065 | 64 rooms | $47.50 | AE, D, DC, MC, V.

Homestead Bed & Breakfast. Four miles southeast of downtown on 14 acres bordered by the Appalachians, this farmhouse turned B&B was built in 1934 and is on the National Register of Historic Places. It has a veranda and porch swing, a stocked fishing pond, and a den with a satellite TV; all rooms feature antiques, quilts, and private baths. Complimentary breakfast. Some kitchenettes, some refrigerators, some in-room hot tubs, some in-room VCRs, TV in common area. Pond. Fishing. Library. Laundry facilities. No pets. No kids under 13. No smoking. | 1165 Rte. 68 | 931/456–6355 or 888/782–9987 | fax 931/456–8881 | www.homesteadbb.com | 4 rooms, 2 suites | $70–$115, $115–$125 suites | AE, D, MC, V.

Inn of the Cumberlands. This three-story motel is 3 mi south of downtown, and 1 mi of a golf course. Balconies on every level face a pond behind the inn that feeds off the Obed River. Complimentary Continental breakfast, some microwaves, some refrigerators, cable TV. | 2023 Sparta Hwy. | 931/484–9566 or 800/465–3069 | 4 rooms, 2 suites | $55, $125 suites | AE, D, MC, V.

Ramada Inn. This old-fashioned motor inn, atop a mountain, near the Obed River, sits about 4½ mi north of Crossville center and 8 mi north of the entrance to Cumberland Mountain State Park. Antique and gift shops are within walking distance. Restaurant, room service. Cable TV. Pool. Some pets allowed. | 4083 U.S. 127 | 931/484–7581 or 800/228–2828 | 130 rooms | $84 | AE, D, DC, MC, V.

DAYTON

MAP 12, G3

(Nearby towns also listed: Athens, Chattanooga, Cleveland, Sweetwater)

This eastern Tennessee town of 7,000 is best known as the site of the 1925 Scopes Trial, which pitted evolutionists against fundamentalists and drew national attention. The state legislature had passed a law forbidding the teaching of evolution in the public schools, and John Scopes, a biology teacher, agreed to violate the law and stand trial as a test case. With popular orator and fundamentalist William Jennings Bryan as prosecutor, and famous defense lawyer Clarence Darrow speaking for Scopes, the trial turned into a media event. The national press descended on the little town, Chicago radio station WGN set up the first nationwide radio hookup, and Tennessee unfortunately reinforced its then-reputation for stubborn ignorance.

Information: Rhea Economic and Tourism Council | 107 Main St., Dayton 37321 | 423/775–0361.

Attractions

Scopes Trial Museum. The museum is set within the Rhea County Courthouse, the site of the famous 1925 Scopes Trial, often called the Monkey Trial because it challenged the concept that man is a descendant of the apes. Exhibits provide an overview of the trial, in which William Jennings Bryan and Clarence Darrow battled over the question of teaching evolution in public schools. | 1475 Market St. | 423/775–7801 | www.bryan.edu | Free | Weekdays 8–4:30.

MAY: *Strawberry Festival.* All manner of strawberry-based foods are served up, along with rides, crafts, a parade, and a beauty pageant. | 423/775–0361.

Dining

Country Folks Restaurants. American. This spot 2 mi south of downtown is filled with rustic quilts and knick-knacks. It has a hot food bar and cooked-to-order entrées like steak, fried chicken, and burgers. Kids' menu. Open 24 hours. | 9125 Rhea County Hwy. | 423/775–0414 | $4.95–$7.50 | No credit cards.

Lodging

Days Inn. This dependable chain motel is 1 mi south of town on U.S. 27. It is within walking distance of several restaurants and Wal-Mart. Complimentary Continental breakfast. Hot tub. | 3914 Rhea County Hwy. | 423/775–9718 | www.daysinn.com | 25 | $45–$85 | AE, D, MC, V.

DICKSON

MAP 12, D2

(Nearby towns also listed: Clarksville, Franklin, Hurricane Mills, Nashville)

Dickson, in the center of the state, was founded in 1805 but grew because of a railroad built through the area by Union soldiers during the Civil War. Today it is best known as the home of the Grand Old Hatchery, a live country music show that takes place on Saturday nights.

Information: Dickson Chamber of Commerce | 119 U.S. 70E, Dickson 37055 | 615/446–2349.

Attractions

The Grand Old Hatchery. Live country music is performed each Saturday night at this family-oriented venue downtown. | 113 S. Main St. | 615/797–3204 | $4 | Daily.

Montgomery Bell State Resort Park. The 3,782-acre park, primarily composed of hardwood forest, home to foxes, raccoons, opossums, deer, and a wide variety of birds and wildflowers. Accommodations include campgrounds, cabins, and a resort inn. Fishing, water sports, hiking, and golf are all found at the park, which is 10 mi south of Dickson. | Hwy. 70, Burns 37229 | 615/797–3101 | www.state.tn.us/environment/parks/montbell/index.html | Free | Daily.

MAY: *Old Timer's Day.* The celebration in Dickson central features a parade, arts and crafts, a flea market, and contests. | 615/446–2349.

NOV: *Christmas in the Country.* Get a head start on your holiday shopping at this annual craft fair held downtown the first weekend of November. Local and regional artisans sell pottery, wood crafts, clothing and more. | 615/446–2349.

Dining

Miss Mabel's Tea Room. You can don any of 400 hats and enjoy high tea at this Victorian-style restaurant. You'll be served homemade soup, a chicken salad croissant, and a selection of finger sandwiches, scones with devonshire cream, fruit, and tea breads with your tea. If you prefer, chicken and tuna salads and quiche are also available à la carte daily. | 301 W. College St. | 615/441–6658 | $7–$16 | AE, D, DC, MC, V | Closed Mon. and Sun. No dinner.

DICKSON

INTRO
ATTRACTIONS
DINING
LODGING

Wang's China. Chinese. The specialty at this restaurant 7 mi south of town is shrimp with lobster sauce, and there's a lunch buffet on weekdays. | 107 W. Christi Rd. | 615/441–3398 | $6–$10 | MC, V.

Lodging

Comfort Inn. This recently remodeled motel provides standard chain accommodations. It's 5 mi south of downtown, off I–40. Cable TV. Pool. Hot tub. Some pets allowed. | 2325 Rte. 46 S | 615/446–2423 or 800/228–5150 | 50 rooms | $66 | AE, D, DC, MC, V.

Econo Lodge. This basic motor lodge is on Rte. 46, 5 mi south of downtown. Cable TV. Pool. | 2338 Rte. 46 S | 615/446–0541 or 800/228–5160 | 65 rooms | $50 | AE, D, DC, MC, V.

East Hills Bed and Breakfast Inn. This brick bed-and-breakfast, known for its home-style cooking and Southern hospitality, is on 4½ quiet acres at the edge of town, near Luther Lake. A veranda overlooks the front yard, and a den with fireplaces is a great place to read. The rooms all have private baths and fireplaces, and the cottages have kitchenettes; all are furnished with antiques. Complimentary breakfast. Cable TV. | 100 E. Hills Terr. | 615/441–9428 | www.bbonline.com/tn/easthills/ | 5 rooms, 2 cottages | $65–$85 rooms, $95 cottage | AE, D, DC, MC, V.

Hampton Inn Dickson. This three-story hotel, just north of I–40, is in a business district 4 mi south of downtown and is frequented by corporate travelers. The rooms have king-size beds, and there are Jacuzzi suites. Complimentary Continental breakfast. In-room data ports, some refrigerators, some in-room hot tubs, cable TV. Indoor pool. Hot tub, sauna. Gym. Laundry facilities. Business services. | 1080 E. Christi Rd. | 615/446–1088 | www.hamptoninn.com | 62 rooms | $65–$120 | AE, DC, D, MC, V.

The Inn on Main Street. Enjoy the nostalgic atmosphere of this 1903 bed-and-breakfast, far from the bustle of highways and fast-food joints, on old Main Street next to the town hall. Antiques, crafts, and specialty stores are within walking distance. Complimentary breakfast. Cable TV. Some pets allowed. | 112 S. Main St. | 615/441–5821 | www.bbonline.com/tn/inn-main/ | 4 rooms | $95 | AE, D, MC, V.

Quality Inn–Dickson. Comfortable rooms at affordable prices are the draw at this chain motel located just off I–40, 4 mi south of downtown. The indoor heated pool is open 24 hours. Complimentary Continental breakfast. Cable TV. Pool. Some pets allowed. | 1025 E. Christi Dr. | 615/441–5252 or 888/375–5522 | 46 rooms | $44 | AE, D, DC, MC, V.

Super 8 Dickson. Location and price are this motel's best features—it is 4 mi south of downtown off I–40. Complimentary Continental breakfast. Some microwaves, some refrigerators, some in-room hot tubs, cable TV. Indoor pool. Laundry facilities, no pets. | 150 Suzanne Dr. | 615/446–1923 or 800/800–8000 | www.super8.com | 57 rooms | $45–$60 | AE, D, DC, MC, V.

DYERSBURG

MAP 12, B2

(Nearby towns also listed: Covington, Henning, Tiptonville, Union City)

Dyersburg is the second largest town in the state's western quarter (only Memphis is larger). Founded in 1825 the town grew because of its position on the navigable North Forked Deer River, which gave it access to the Mississippi. It became an important trading center, and when the railroad came through it became even more prosperous.

Information: Dyersburg/Dyer County Chamber of Commerce | 2000 Commerce Ave., Dyersburg 38024 | 901/285–3433.

Attractions

Lenox Bridge. Originally north of town over the Obion River this 1917 turntable bridge is now in the Lakewood Subdivision, approximately 2 mi north of Dyersburg. The only surviving example of its type, it required four people to operate the bridge's handcrank, which rotated its 150-ft span to allow by steamboats. To reach the bridge travel north on Route 78 for approximately 2 mi, then turn onto Route 182, from which you should turn left into the Lakewood Subdivision. | Lakewood Subdivision | Free | Daily.

ON THE CALENDAR

APR.: *Dogwood Festival.* View the dogwood trees in full bloom throughout town and enjoy events like a chili cook-off and the "Dogwood Dash" (a 5K race) at this festival held every second weekend in April. | 901/285–8188.

Dining

Neil's Barbecue and Grill. Barbecue. In addition to ribs and southern-fried catfish flavored with a spicy sauce, this restaurant has steaks and pasta. It's less than 5 mi west of town. | 470 Mall Blvd. #A | 901/285–2628 | Reservations not accepted | $8–$12 | AE, DC, D, MC, V.

Lodging

Aunt Ginny's Bed & Breakfast. This small B&B furnished with antiques is a Victorian farmhouse built in 1886. It is 2½ blocks northeast of downtown. Complimentary Continental breakfast. TV in common area. | 520 Sampson Ave. | 901/285–2028 | 3 rooms | $80–$100 | MC, V.

Comfort Inn. This motel on the outskirts of Dyersburg is directly on U.S. 51, across from a mall and surrounded by restaurants. Some rooms have countryside views. Complimentary Continental breakfast. Some refrigerators, cable TV. Pool. Exercise equipment. Laundry facilities. | 815 Reelfoot Dr. | 901/285–6951 | fax 901/285–6956 | 82 rooms | $65 | AE, D, DC, MC, V.

Holiday Inn. If you are driving through Dyersburg, you can't miss this hotel, located in the commercial district, near "eating alley," the restaurant strip. It's also within walking distance of a nine-theater cinema. Restaurant. Room service, cable TV. Pool. | 770 Hwy. 51 | 901/285–8601 | fax 901/286–0494 | 106 rooms | $59–$65 | AE, D, DC, MC, V.

ELIZABETHTON

MAP 12, H5

(Nearby towns also listed: Bristol, Kingsport, Johnson City, Jonesborough, Tusculum)

Elizabethton, in the northwestern part of the state, was one of the first colonial settlements in the area. The town was incorporated in 1799 just three years after Tennessee was recognized as a state. Visits to the the replica of Fort Watauga and the John and Landon Carter Mansion, the oldest frame house in the state, offer a taste of what frontier life was like.

Information: Elizabethton/Carter County Tourism Council | 500 U.S. 19E Bypass, Elizabethton 37643 | 423/547–3850 or 800/347–0208 | www.tourelizabethton.com.

Attractions

Doe River Covered Bridge. Built in 1882 and listed on the National Register of Historic Sites, this white-clapboard covered bridge, off U.S. 19, is believed to be the oldest of its kind still in use in Tennessee. | 3rd St. | 423/547–3852 or 800/547–3852 | www.tourelizabethton.com | Daily.

The John and Landon Carter Mansion. Recognized as the first frame house in Tennessee, this private residence was built between 1775 and 1780 on land bought from the Cherokee. A mansion by 1780s standards, it still features a finely detailed interior with overmantel paintings plus original wall finishes in three rooms. The owners John Carter and his son, Landon, were prominent in colonial government and military affairs; they took part in the Revolutionary War and in various conflicts with Native Americans. | 1013 Broad St. | 423/543–5808 | Free | May–Sept., daily 8–4:30.

Roan Mountain State Park. The 250-acre park, 20 mi southeast of town, is named for nearby 6,285-ft Roan Mountain, one of the highest peaks in the eastern United States. In early summer, the deep purple flowers of Catawba rhododendron blanket the mountain tops. The park offers camping, cabins, fishing, and hiking. | 427 Rte. 143 | 423/772–3303 or 423/772–3314 | www.state.tn.us/environment/parks | Free | Daily.

Sycamore Shoals State Historic Area. A museum, reconstruction of Fort Watauga, and theater interpret the role this area played in America's westward expansion. It was here, 2 mi east of downtown, around 1770 that Watauga, the first permanent American settlement outside of the original 13 colonies was established. | 1651 W. Elk Ave. | 423/543–5808 | Free | Mon.–Sat. 8–4:30, Sun. 1–4:30.

Watauga Dam and Lake. This Tennessee Valley Authority dam helps create a 6,430-acre impoundment 8 mi east of town. Water sports, camping, and cabins are available around the lake. | Rte. 91 N | 423/547–3100 | Free | Daily.

ON THE CALENDAR

MAY: *Muster at Fort Watauga.* Actors at the Sycamore Shoals State Historic Area bring scenes from colonial days to life. | 423/543–5808.
JUNE: *Covered Bridge Celebration.* The festival, which takes place along Elk Avenue near the landmark Doe River Covered Bridge, features antique cars, kids' activities, nightly entertainment, and more. | 423/547–3852.
JUNE: *Rhododendron Festival.* The event in Roan Mountain State Park features music, food, and of course, an abundance of purple rhododendrons. | 423/772–0190.
JULY–AUG.: *Elizabethton Twins Home Games.* The E-Twins, as they're affectionately known, are a rookie level minor league affiliate of the Minnesota Twins. They play at the Joe O'Brien Field in downtown Elizabethton. | 423/547–6440.
SEPT.: *Overmountain Victory Trail Celebration.* Watch marchers in period costumes depart from Sycamore Shoals Historic Area, beginning the 14-day trek to Kings Mountain, South Carolina. | 423/543–5808.

Dining

Merry Mary's. Café. This spacious café used to be a drugstore. Marble floors, wrought-iron tables and chairs, and antiques for sale contribute to the old-fashioned feel. Mary's is known for its chicken salad and serves sandwiches, ice cream, and homemade soups and desserts. | 547 E. Elk Ave. | 423/543–1444 | $5–$8 | No credit cards | Mon.–Sat. 10–5.

Lodging

Doe River Inn. You can sit in the sunroom or on the patio of this Victorian B&B, enjoying the view of the Doe River and watching the ducks walk right up to the door. Both guest rooms have private bathrooms with old-fashioned claw-foot tubs. It's two blocks from the town's famous covered bridge and antique stores and cafés. Complimentary Continental breakfast. Cable TV, in-room VCRs. Fishing. Laundry facilities, Pets allowed. No smoking. | 217 Academy St. | 423/543–1444 | mary@doeriverinn.com | 2 rooms | $85 | MC, V.

FAYETTEVILLE

(Nearby towns also listed: Lawrenceburg, Lewisburg, Lynchburg, Pulaski, Shelbyville)

Established as the county seat in 1809, Fayetteville, in the central southern part of the state, has one of the most well-preserved town squares of any small town in the area. Some of the buildings and private homes downtown were built during Reconstruction or earlier.

Information: **Fayetteville/Lincoln County Chamber of Commerce** | 208 S. Elk Ave., Fayetteville 37334 | 931/433–1234 | www.vallnet.com/chamberofcommerce.

Attractions

Historic Downtown Fayetteville. Visit the downtown area for antiques shops, a restaurant in an old jailhouse, seasonal festivals, and numerous antebellum homes. | Mulberry Ave. | 931/433–1234 | Daily.

Lincoln County Museum. In the old Borden Milk Plant, the museum houses exhibits on regional history, culture, and industry. | 521 Main Ave. S | 931/438–0339 | Free | Tues.–Sat. 10–4, Sun. 1–4.

ON THE CALENDAR

NOV.: *Host of Christmas Past.* On the second weekend of the month, these events in downtown Fayetteville can get you into the holiday spirit—go on a walking tour of the town's historic homes, experience old-fashioned high tea, take trolley rides, and listen to strolling musicians. | 931/433–1234.

Dining

Cahoot's Restaurant. . Popular for its homemade chicken fingers and fried cheese, this steak and comfort food haven is housed in an old jailhouse and fire station; you can make a group reservation to dine in one of the original cells. | 114 W. Market St. | 931/433–1173 | $5–$16 | AE, MC, V | Closed Sun.

Lodging

Bagley House Bed and Breakfast. This two-story 1830s Colonial was a haven for Union troops during the Civil War. It's still surrounded by an original 3-ft-thick rock wall and 35 acres of woods 3 mi east of Fayetteville, where you can sometimes see wild turkey, deer, and bobcats. Fireplaces grace two guest rooms, the dining room, the kitchen and two parlors, and all rooms have antique furnishings and glassware. In addition to hiking on the property and walking through the hedge garden, you can browse the antique shops in downtown Fayetteville. Complimentary breakfast. TV in common area. Hiking. No pets. No kids under 18. No smoking. | 1801 Winchester Hwy. | 931/433–3799 | 3 rooms | $80 | AE, MC, V.

FRANKLIN

(Nearby towns also listed: Columbia, Murfreesboro, Nashville)

Founded in 1799 and named for Benjamin Franklin, this county seat was one of the wealthiest towns in the state by the time the Civil War broke out, thanks to its location in ideal agricultural territory. During the war, Franklin was the site of a bloody and significant 1864 battle, part of an ill-advised Confederate attempt to re-take Nashville from the Union Army. Many of the town's historic buildings have been preserved or restored, and the entire 15-block downtown area is listed in the National Register of Historic Places. Today, Franklin has become almost engulfed by Nashville's suburbs.

Information: Williamson County–Franklin Chamber of Commerce | City Hall Building, 109 2nd Ave. S, Suite 107, Franklin 37064 | 615/794–1225.

Attractions

Carter House. This 1830 antebellum mansion was caught in the middle of the Battle of Franklin. The house now serves as the interpretation center for the battle. There's a video presentation, a museum, and a guided tour of the mansion and grounds. | 1140 Columbia Ave. | 615/791–1861 | www.carter-house.org | $7 | Mon.–Sat. 9–5, Sun. 1–5.

Franklin Historic District. Centered around a town square, which displays a Confederate monument, Franklin's downtown district features historic structures as well as numerous shops and restaurants. In 1995 Franklin received a "Great American Main Street" award from the National Trust for Historic Preservation. | Main St. | Free | Daily.

Historic Carnton Plantation and McGavock Confederate Cemetery. This mansion, built in 1826 by Randall McGavock, a former mayor of Nashville, served as a Civil War field hospital during the Battle of Franklin. Hundreds of dead and wounded soldiers were brought into the house from the fighting; they eventually covered the plantation grounds as well. After the war, the McGavocks designated nearly 2 acres of their land for the re-interment of close to 1,500 soldiers, making this site the largest private Confederate cemetery. | 1345 Carnton La. | 615/794–0903 | www.carnton.org | $7 | Mon.–Sat. 9–5, Sun. 1–5.

Natchez Trace Parkway. Constructed by the National Park Service in the 1930s on what had long been a trading route, the parkway offers a leisurely scenic drive from Natchez, in southwestern Mississippi, to a point just south of Nashville and west of Franklin—a 450-mile drive in all. There are no billboards or restaurants along the road, and only one service station. Speed limits are low and strictly enforced. Sites of interest along the Tennessee portion of the road include walkable portions of the original trace, on Highway 96 just west of Franklin; an early tobacco farm; and the Meriwether Lewis Park, Grave, and Monument, where the explorer (of Lewis and Clark fame) is buried. | Free | Daily.

THE NATCHEZ TRACE PARKWAY

The Natchez Trace, a road that runs from Natchez, Mississippi, to the outskirts of Nashville, most likely began as a series of paths beaten out by the Natchez, Choctaw, and Chickasaws. Over the years, the paths became a trail that led from the Mississippi River over the low hills of eastern Mississippi and Middle Tennessee into the valley of the Tennessee River. By 1733, French explorers had mapped the trace; by 1810, it was the most heavily traveled road in the Old South. However, when passenger steamboats became the preferred means of travel in the region, the trace reverted to a narrow, peaceful forest-lined lane.

In the late 1930s, the National Park Service began construction of a parkway that closely follows the route of the original trace. The Natchez Trace Parkway offers a leisurely, scenic route from Natchez to Nashville. The narrow strip of land on either side of the road is protected park land; there are no billboards or restaurants along the road, and only one service station. Speed limits are low and strictly enforced. Sites of interest along the Tennessee portion of the road include walkable portions of the original trace, an early tobacco farm, and the Meriwether Lewis Park, Grave, and Monument, where the explorer is buried.

MAY: *Heritage Foundation Town and Country Tour of Homes.* This tour gives you access to houses in downtown Franklin that are on the National Historic Register; some of these are not otherwise open to the public. | 615/591–8500.

AUG.: *Franklin Jazz Festival.* This celebration of traditional jazz on Main St. was named one of the "Top 20 Events in the Southeast" by the Southeast Tourism Society. | 615/791–9924.

DEC.: *Carnton House Christmas Candlight Tour.* The annual carol-singing tour of the neighborhood that features the Historic Carnton Plantation. | 615/791–1861.

Dining

Antonio's Ristorante Italiano. Italian. Food is prepared in an open kitchen at this cozy restaurant in downtown Franklin. Menu options include such favorites as salmon *con calabria* (cheese-stuffed salmon topped with lemon butter, white wine, and sundried tomatoes). | 119 5th Ave. N | 615/790–1733 | $11–$23 | AE, D, MC, V | Closed Sun. No lunch.

Bravo Cesar!. Italian. Across the street from Franklin's cinema, this cozy place off Main Street sports checkered table cloths and serves up a variety of pizzas, calzones, sandwiches, lasagnas, chicken parmigiana, and fettuccine. For lunch, check out the pizza, pasta, and salad buffet. | 414 Main St. | 615/791–7999 | $6–$11 | No credit cards.

The Bunganut Pig. English. Franklin's oldest pub serves classic English dishes such as fish-and-chips and shepherd's pie, in addition to a menu of sandwiches (rib-eye, roast beef, club), burgers, and steaks. Live music nightly; the spotlight is on soloists at the beginning of the week and harder-edge music toward the end of the week. | Carter's Court, 1143 Columbia Ave. | 615/794–4777 | $5–$15 | AE, D, MC, V | Closed Sun.

Fourth and Main. American. Antiques and original art add distinction to this restaurant one block south of the town square in the city's historic district. The menu includes dishes such as fillet of beef, porterhouse, and salmon. Try the Cajun trout, pan-seared with mushrooms, tomatoes, and served with rice. Soloists and duets perform Wednesday through Saturday nights. | 108 4th Ave. S | 615/791–0001 | $7–$20 | AE, D, DC, MC, V.

Franklin Chop House. American. Pastas, sandwiches, and a selection of vegetarian dishes complement the meaty entrées of pork ribs, steaks, seafood, and meatloaf at this casual restaurant, 1 mi east of downtown. The dining area is large and can accommodate crowds. | 1101 Murfreesboro Rd. | 615/591–7666 | $6–$14 | AE, MC, V.

Magnolia's. Contemporary. Windows make up an entire wall of this restaurant, which overlooks the historic factory next door. Fresh flowers and white linens, together with light jazz performed on the patio (Wednesday through Saturday), set the stage for tempting dishes such as crab cakes in a beurre blanc and the 21-day aged New York strip steak with blackpepper crust and brandy cream sauce. | 230 Franklin Rd. | 615/791–9992 | $15–$32 | AE, D, MC, V | No lunch Sat., closed Sun.

Lodging

Amerisuites–Cool Springs. This all-suites property is across from a large mall and not far from I–65, 5 minutes north of downtown. Complimentary breakfast. Kitchenettes, cable TV. Pool. Gym. Some pets allowed. | 650 Bakers Bridge Ave. | 615/771–8900 or 800/834–1516 | 128 suites | $87 | AE, D, DC, MC, V.

Best Western Franklin Inn. At Exit 65, off I–65, this two-story hotel sits on Franklin's eastern edge, on a commercial strip, within walking distance from many restaurants. Restaurant, complimentary Continental breakfast. In-room data ports, cable TV. Pool. Business services. Some pets allowed. | 1308 Murfreesboro Rd. | 615/790–0570 | fax 615/790–0512 | www.bestwestern.com | 142 rooms | $65–$75 | AE, DC, MC, V.

Comfort Inn Franklin. This motel is on I–65 at Exit 65, 3 mi east of Franklin. No fuss, just stop, sleep, and pick up a quick breakfast on your way out. Complimentary Continental breakfast. Cable TV. Pool. | 4206 Franklin Commons | 615/791–6675 or 800/228–5150 | 60 rooms | $70–$85 | AE, D, DC, MC, V.

Country Inn and Suites–Cool Springs. Just west of I–65 at Exit 68B, this four-story chain hotel is in the Cool Springs Galleria Mall, 5 minutes north of downtown. Complimentary Continental breakfast. In-room data ports, some refrigerators, some in-room hot tubs, cable TV. Pool. Laundry facilities. | 7120 S. Springs Dr. | 615/778–0321 | fax 615/778–0322 | 64 rooms, 13 suites | $89 | AE, D, DC, MC, V.

Hampton Inn and Suites. Near the Cool Springs Galleria Mall, not far from I–65 at Exit 68B, the king-sized suites available at this hotel easily accommodate four people. Five minutes north of downtown. Some kitchenettes, cable TV. Pool. Gym. | 7141 S. Springs Dr. | 615/771–7225 or 800/426–7866 | 127 rooms, 50 suites | $82; $106 suites | AE, D, DC, MC, V.

Inn at Walking Horse Farm. Situated on a hilltop overlooking a working farm that encompasses 40 acres on the southern edge of town, this B&B has the look of a country mansion, complete with brick walls and a white-columned entrance. Rooms are appointed with antiques; large fireplaces dominate the common areas. You can tour the large horse barns. Complimentary breakfast. No room phones, no TV. Hiking. No kids under 18. No smoking. | 1490 Lewisburg Pike | 615/790–2076 | 4 rooms | $80–$100 | D, MC, V.

Magnolia House Bed and Breakfast. Built in 1905, this craftsman-style home sits on the site of the Battle of Franklin, ¾ mi south of downtown. The heirloom-filled living room has gleaming wood floors, and guestrooms are furnished with antiques. Complimentary breakfast. In-room data ports, some in-room hot tubs, TV in common area. No smoking. | 1317 Columbia Ave. | 615/794–8178 | magtenn@cs.com | www.bbonline.com/tn/magnolia | 4 rooms | $80–$100 | AE, D, DC, MC, V.

Namaste Acres Barn Bed and Breakfast. Eleven miles west of Franklin, this B&B sports a western theme, right down to the log and rope beds, the rough-sawn walls and beams, and the private fireplaces in each suite. The property offers direct access to the Natchez Trace Parkway and the miles of hiking and horseback riding trails that follow in its path. Complimentary breakfast, picnic area. Cable TV, in-room VCRs. Pool. Hot tub. Hiking, fishing. Laundry facilities. Business services. No kids under 12. No smoking. | 5436 Leipers Creek Rd. | 615/791–0333 | fax 615/591–0665 | namastebb@aol.com | 3 suites | $75–$85 | AE, D, DC, MC, V.

Peacock Hill Country Inn. Small B&B in a rural setting, 15 mi south of Franklin. The 150-year-old building has rooms with private baths and some suites with kitchenettes. There's a cozy fireplace in the common area, and children are welcome. Lunch and dinner are available with a 48-hour advance notice. Complimentary breakfast In-room hot tubs, some kitchenettes, cable TV, in-room VCRs. | 6994 Giles Hill Rd., College Grove | 615/368–7727 or 800/327–6663 | 10 rooms, 3 suites | $125, $225 suites | AE, D, DC, MC, V.

Super 8. Standard motor inn located on a main commercial strip sits just off I–65 on Franklin's eastern side. No frills, just rooms. Two floors. Complimentary Continental breakfast. Cable TV. Exercise equipment. Pool. | 1307 Murfreesboro Rd. | 615/794–7591 | fax 615/794–1042 | 100 rooms | $59 | AE, D, DC, MC, V.

GALLATIN

MAP 12, F2

(Nearby towns also listed: Hendersonville, Lebanon, Nashville)

Gallatin, 35 mi north of Nashville, is known as the original home of Dot Records, a record label founded by Randy Wood, who once ran the country's largest mail-order record shop from this town. Randy introduced Chuck Berry to a nationwide audience, and his Dot label, active from 1946 to 1991, recorded Pat Boone and Billy Vaughn. Many historic buildings are preserved in Gallatin, which was founded in 1802, including Wynnewood, the largest log structure ever built in Tennessee.

Information: Gallatin Chamber of Commerce, | 118 W. Main St., Gallatin 37066 | 615/452–4000.

Attractions

Bledsoe Creek State Park. Popular with fishers and boaters, the park 5 mi east of town also offers campsites and 6 mi of hiking trails. | 400 Zieglers Fort Rd. | 615/452–3706 | www.state.tn.us/environment/parks/bledsoe/index.html | Free | Daily.

Cragfont. The Georgian-style home 7 mi east of Gallatin was built in 1798 by Revolutionary War hero Gen. James Winchester, one of the founders of Memphis. The mansion is called Cragfront because it stands on a rocky bluff above a large spring. You can tour its restored rooms and gardens. | 200 Cragfont Rd. | 615/452–7070 | $4 | Apr.–Nov., Tues.–Sat. 10–4:30, Sun. 1–4:30.

Sumner County Museum. Million-year-old fossils, Native American and African American artifacts, as well as pioneer tools fill this museum's three floors. | 183 W. Main St. | 615/451–3738 | $2 | Apr.–Oct., Wed.–Sat. 9–4:30, Sun. 1–4:30.

Trousdale Place. The home of William Trousdale, who was the governor of Tennessee from 1849 to 1851, is situated in the center of Gallatin. Built around 1813 and listed on the National Register of Historic Places, the house contains its original furniture and a small Confederate library. | 183 W. Main St. | 615/452–5648 | Free | Apr.–Nov., Wed.–Sat. 9–4:30, Sun. 1–5.

Wynnewood. Two stories tall and 142 ft long, this building is considered the largest log structure ever built in Tennessee. Erected in 1828 7 mi east of Gallatin, it first served as a stagecoach inn and later as a mineral springs resort visited regularly by Andrew Jackson. | 210 Old Hwy. 25 | 615/452–5463 | $4 | Apr.–Oct., Mon.–Sat. 10–4, Sun. 1–5; Nov.–Mar., Mon.–Sat. 10–4.

ON THE CALENDAR

APR.: *Sumner County Pilgrimage.* The county's historic homes, many of them private residences, are open to the public during this event. | 615/452–7070.

OCT.: *Festival on Main Street.* Main Street is closed off for this local festival that fills downtown Gallatin with arts and crafts, food, and more. For added color, you can take a tour of a nearby cemetery. | 615/452–4000.

Dining

The Hancock House. American/Casual. The formal dining room of this Colonial Revival log house serves breakfast, brunch, lunch, and dinner, all by reservation only. The fare includes such dishes as grilled chicken breast, filet mignon, and grilled salmon. | 2144 Nashville Pike | 615/452–8431 | Reservations essential | $13–$26 | No credit cards | Breakfast also available.

Lodging

Shoney's Inn. This two-story motel sits just two blocks from Gallatin's town square, across the street from a parking lot. Cable TV. Pool. Business services. | 221 W. Main St. | 615/452–5433 | fax 615/452–1665 | 86 rooms | $61 | AE, D, DC, MC, V.

GATLINBURG

MAP 12, G6

(Nearby towns listed: Great Smoky Mountains National Park, Maryville, Pigeon Forge, Sevierville, Townsend, Walland)

The mountain town of Gatlinburg is Tennessee's gateway to the Great Smoky Mountains National Park. It's mainly a tourist town, full of souvenir and T-shirt shops, and traffic is heavy. However, it offers a great variety of lodging options, and many of its restaurants are more upscale than those in neighboring towns. It's popular with families, honeymooners, hikers, and skiers, and it offers entry to one of America's most visited national parks.

Information: **Gatlinburg Department of Tourism** | 234 Airport Rd., Gatlinburg 37738 | 865/436–2392 or 800/267–7088 | www.gatlinburg.com.

Attractions

Christus Gardens. After surviving a life-threatening bout of tuberculosis in 1957, Ronald S. Ligon expressed his gratitude to Divine Providence by creating this extensive exhibition of life-size dioramas depicting the story of Christ. Wax figures made in London and costumed by the company responsible for the movies *Ben Hur* and *Quo Vadis* are set in tableaux complete with lighting, music, and narration. There are also landscaped gardens and a face of Jesus carved in a 6-ton block of Carrara marble. | 510 River Rd. | 865/436–5155 | www.christusgardens.com | $8.50 | Daily 8 AM–9 PM.

Craft Shops. The 8-mi loop of the Great Smoky Arts and Crafts Community combined with the shops of more than 70 artisans create a shopper's dream, including almost every craft known to man. | Hwy. 321 on Glades Rd. | Daily.

Gatlinburg Fun Mountain. This amusement park boasts Gatlinburg's longest chair lift, and is a popular destination for miniature golf, go-carts, a video arcade, kids' entertainment, and numerous exhilarating rides. | 130 E. Parkway | 865/436–4132 | Free; fees for individual rides and attractions | Daily, noon–10 PM.

Gatlinburg Space Needle. A glass elevator will take you to the top of a 342-ft observation tower, which offers an amusement center and a commanding view of the Smoky Mountains from the center of town. | 115 Airport Rd. | 865/436–4629 | $6 | Daily 9–midnight.

Great Smoky Mountains National Park. *(See Great Smoky Mountains National Park.)* Gatlinburg is the main gateway into this hugely popular national park. | 107 Park Headquarters Rd. | 865/436–1200 | www.nps.gov/grsm | Free | Daily.

Guinness World of Records Museum. Items from noteworthy record-holders like Elvis and Houdini are displayed at this small museum. | 631 Parkway | 865/436–9100 | $8.95 | Daily 9 AM–11 PM.

Ober Gatlinburg Ski Resort. Skiers and snowboarders have their choice of eight trails on 32 acres on Mt. Harrison. There are three chairlifts, two quad and one double, and when temperatures drop, snowmaking equipment blankets all the trails. The on-site Smoky Mountain Snow Sport School offers instruction at all levels. Off-the-slope activities include indoor ice-skating, a bungee tower, and an alpine slide. | 1001 Parkway | 865/436–5423 or 800/251–9202 | www.obergatlinburg.com/ski.htm | Dec.–mid-Mar., daily.

Aerial Tramway. One of America's largest aerial tramways departs every 20 minutes from downtown Gatlinburg and takes riders directly to the Ober Gatlinburg Ski Resort and Amusement Park atop Mt. Harrison. The 15-minute trip offers an impressive panorama of Gatlinburg and the Smokies. Each tram car can carry 120 passengers. | 1001 Parkway | 865/436–5423 | www.obergatlinburg.com | $6 | Dec.–mid-Mar., Mon.–Sat. 9:30 AM–11 PM.

Sightseeing Chairlift. Once you've reached the top of Mount Harrion—take either the Aerial Tramway or a drive up Ski Mountain Road—consider a ride on this two-seater chairlift. The views of the Great Smoky Mountains are breathtaking. | 1001 Parkway | 865/436–5423 | www.obergatlinburg.com | $4 | Dec.–mid-Mar., Mon.–Sat. 9:30 AM–11 PM.

Sky Lift. For more than 40 years people have been riding this double chairlift to the top of Crockett Mountain for impressive views of the Smokies. There's an observation deck at the top. | 765 Parkway | 865/436–4307 | $8.50 | Daily 9:30 AM–11 PM.

ON THE CALENDAR

APR.–NOV.: *Sweet Fanny Adams Theater.* The seasonal theater offers old-style vaudeville entertainment. | 865/436–4039.

MAY: *Gatlinburg Scottish Festival.* Pipe and drum bands, professional athletes, Highland dancing, and sheepdog demonstrations are featured, along with games and contests. | 865/457–2986.

JUNE: *Dulcimer and Harp Festival.* This celebration of old-fashioned music and dancing takes place in nearby Crosby 15 mi from Gatlinburg. | 865/487–5543.

JULY AND OCT.: *Gatlinburg Craftsmen's Fair.* The summer and fall events draw craftspeople from all over the country to the Gatlinburg Convention Center where it takes place. | 865/436–7479 | $4.

NOV.: *Gatlinburg Winter Fest.* Magicians, clowns, live music, and a chili cook-off make this event fun for the entire family. The stage is set by the simultaneous illumination of millions of sparkling lights throughout the city. | 865/436–2392.

Dining

MODERATE

Blaine's Grill and Bar. American. This restaurant, specializing in prime rib, steaks, and hamburgers, doubles as a dance club. Each night at 10 the dining room morphs into a lively dance hall. Outdoor seating is available on a veranda overlooking the city and the surrounding mountains. | 812 Parkway | 865/430–1978 | $6–$17 | AE, D, MC, V.

Brass Lantern. American. The family-friendly restaurant has a casual and cozy atmosphere, featuring exposed brick and brass fixtures. Known for their vegetable soup, the menu ranges from hot dogs to steak. Kids' menu. | 710 Parkway | 865/436–4168 | $8–$16 | AE, D, DC, MC, V.

Legends by Max. Barbecue. The dining room evokes the Tennessee flavor of its cuisine with a hand-crafted bar and old photographs of Gatlinburg hanging from the walls. Specialties include smoked prime rib, smoked pork loin, barbecue rotisserie chicken, plus fish, salad, and sandwich options. | 650 Parkway | 865/436–7343 | $7–$18 | AE, D, MC, V.

Alamo Steakhouse. Steaks. Serving what it calls "steaks with an attitude," the restaurant's focus is on rib-eyes, T-bones, porterhouses, and fillets. The menu also includes a wide variety of hamburgers and seafood entrées. Wood chairs, a wood bar, and a peaked ceiling give the dining room a saloon-like appearance. | 705 E. Parkway | 865/436–9998 | $12–$40 | AE, D, MC, V.

Atrium. American. With more than 25 pancake and waffle options, there's something for everyone at this accommodating restaurant, which serves a selection of sandwiches, soups, and salads. The dining room windows overlook town, and there's a waterfall next to the patio. | 432 Parkway | 865/430–3684 | $5–$7.25 | D, MC, V | Breakfast also available. No dinner.

Buckhorn Inn. Contemporary. The dining room in this 1938 inn, 5 mi east of Gatlinburg, has one much-sought-after 7 PM seating for dinner each night. The windows look out on an expansive view of Mt. Le Conte and the surrounding forests. When the weather's good you can sit on the terrace and enjoy complimentary lemonade or soft drinks before your meal. The menu, which changes daily, might include items such as pan-seared pork loin with apple cranberry compote and panfried Smoky Mountain trout with sundried tomatoes and toasted almond butter. | 2140 Tudor Mountain Rd. | 865/436–4668 | Reservations essential | No lunch | $25 prix–fixe | D, MC, V.

Burning Bush Restaurant. American/Casual. Antique knicknacks and furnishings lend a Colonial air to this local eatery, famous for its broiled Tennessee quail and its 8-ounce beef Rossini—a fillet served over an open English muffin. Other popular menu items include the Smoky Mountain trout, pecan-crusted salmon, and grouper sandwich. | 1151 Parkway | 865/436–4669 | $14–$30 | AE, D, MC, V.

Greenbrier Restaurant. American. Originally a hunter's lodge, this restaurant with its glass-enclosed porch sits atop a mountain with spectacular views of the surrounding Smok-

ies. The original fireplaces only add to the rustic style. Try the chicken Vera Cruz (stuffed with crabmeat and provolone cheese and covered with a white wine sauce), or the pork tenderloin stuffed with walnuts and apples covered with a honey glaze. The steaks are all hand cut here. | 370 Newman Rd. | 865/436–6318 | Reservations not accepted | $14–$22 | AE, D, DC, MC, V | No lunch.

Lineberger's. Seafood. Across the street from the Gatlinburg Convention Center, this long-time favorite (opened in 1948) serves numerous seafood dishes including rainbow trout, salmon, grouper, flounder, and swordfish. It's also known for its generous 2-pound crab leg dinner. Large USDA Angus beef steaks are also available. | 930 Parkway | 865/436–9284 | $8–$22 | AE, D, DC, MC, V | No lunch weekdays.

Maxwell's Beef and Seafood. American. A large fieldstone fireplace stands at the center of the dining room at this local favorite. Pastas, seafood, and steak fill the menu. Try the sautéed rainbow trout with aioli and toasted almonds or the charbroiled salmon. For dessert, don't miss the cheesecake. | 1103 Parkway | 865/436–3738 | $10–$20 | AE, D, MC, V.

Mountain View Dining Room. Contemporary. At Christopher Place Country Inn, 15 mi northeast of Gatlinburg, the dining room is as opulently decorated as the rest of the inn, with red velvet carpet and a grand piano. Dinner is served each night at 7 and reservations are required at least 24 hours in advance. The four-course menu changes daily but might include such dishes as veal scalloppini with gorgonzola sauce, served with sugar-snap peas, or pan-seared salmon with sweet-and-sour chutney. | 1500 Pinnacles Way, Newport | 423/623–6555 | Reservations essential | No lunch | $25 prix–fixe | AE, D, MC, V.

Old Heidelberg Restaurant. German. The Bavarian theme doesn't stop at the traditional Wiener schnitzel, sauerbraten, and knockwurst, but is carried on with the beer steins, the staff in lederhosen, and the nightly Bavarian folk music—yodeling, alpine horns, accordians, and tubas. Menu options include Smoky Mountain trout, grilled chicken, and rack of lamb. | 148 Parkway | 865/430–3094 or 800/726–3094 | $10–$21 | D, MC, V | No lunch.

Open Hearth. American. This festive restaurant (the decor has been described as "Christmas, even in springtime") is situated above a creek, with mountain views. The fireplace and candlelight create a warm, romantic mood. Representative dishes include steak, seafood, prime rib, and flounder. There's live music nightly in season, and entertainment year-round on Friday and Saturday. Kids' menu. | 1654 E. Parkway | 865/436–5648 | No lunch | $12–$29 | AE, D, DC, MC, V.

Pancake Pantry. American. Morning sunlight streams through the spacious windows and bounces off the rustic copper accessories and polished oak paneling at this family favorite. The Austrian apple-walnut pancakes covered with apple cider compote, black walnuts, sweet spices, powdered sugar, and whipped cream are something to come back for. Waffles, omelets, sandwiches, soups, and salads round out the menu. | 628 Parkway | 865/436–4724 | Reservations not accepted | $4.50–$7 | No credit cards | Breakfast also available. No dinner.

Park Grill. Regional. This majestic mountain restaurant has spectacular views of Great Smoky Mountains National Park. Known for tender ribs, panfried flounder, and hickory-grilled moonshine chicken. The in-house pastry chef will take care of your sweet tooth. Kids' menu. | 1100 Parkway | 865/436–2300 | Reservation not accepted | No lunch | $12–$30 | AE, D, DC, MC, V.

The Peddler. Regional. There's a hickery/charcoal grill and mammoth salad bar at this regional restaurant in a converted log cabin overlooking the river. Known for its steak, the menu also includes homemade soups, desserts, and a salad bar with a huge range of ingredients. Kids' menu. | 820 River Rd. | 865/436–5794 | Reservations not accepted | No lunch | $19–$37 | AE, D, DC, MC, V.

Smoky Mountain Brewery. American/Casual. Built in an old barn, the dining room has huge windows, cathedral ceilings, wood floors, tables, and booths. Pizzas and calzones are baked fresh every day. Ribs, trout, and steak are prepared in a stone oven and served sizzling on a skillet. Nightly entertainment includes karaoke Sunday through Tuesday, and live music Wednesday through Saturday nights. | 1004 Parkway | 865/436–4200 | $10–$17 | AE, D, DC, MC, V.

Smoky Mountain Trout House. Seafood. Cooks prepare trout in at least 15 different ways here. Popular favorites include trout Eisenhower (panfried with cornmeal breading and bacon), grilled trout, and brook trout baked with homemade stuffing. Prime rib, country ham, and grilled chicken are also menu options. | 410 Parkway | 865/436–5416 | $12–$17 | AE, D, MC, V | No lunch.

Lodging

Alto. Floor-to-ceiling sliding glass doors with views of the mountains distinguish this motor lodge from others in the area. Discerning budget travelers appreciate the accommodations for the price. Picnic area. Refrigerators, cable TV. Pool, wading pool. Playground. Some pets allowed. | 404 Airport Rd. | 865/436–5175 or 800/456–4336 | fax 865/430–7342 | 21 rooms | $40 | AE, D, MC, V.

Best Western Chalet Inn. This downtown property has two buildings on the edge of Great Smoky Mountain National Park in lovely wooded surroundings. One building is Swiss-chalet style, the other offers views of Little Pigeon River. Complimentary Continental breakfast. Some kitchenettes, refrigerators, cable TV. 2 Pools, wading pool. Business services. | 310 Cottage Dr. | 865/436–5151 | fax 423/523–8363 | 75 rooms | $89.50 | AE, D, DC, MC, V.

Bent Creek Resort. This property rents two-bedroom condos to golf enthusiasts, who come for its private course. It's 11 mi west of Gatlinburg on U.S. 321. Kitchenettes, refrigerators, cable TV. 2 outdoor pools, 1 indoor pool, wading pool. Driving range, 18-hole golf course, putting green, tennis. Gym. Playground. | 3919 E. Parkway | 865/436–2875 or 800/251–9336 | fax 865/436–3257 | 89 condos | $95–$165 | AE, D, MC, V.

Best Western Crossroads. Guests will find standard accommodations, plus some rooms with fireplaces at this chain hotel in the downtown area. Cable TV. Pool, wading pool. Laundry facilities. | 440 Parkway | 865/436–5661 | fax 865/436–6208 | 78 rooms, 10 suites | $50–$100; $139–$150 suites | AE, D, DC, MC, V.

Best Western Twin Islands Motel. This contemporary motel in the town's center sits beside the surging Little Pigeon River. Some rooms have balconies overlooking the water, plus fireplaces and hot tubs. Some kitchenettes, refrigerators, some in-room hot tubs, cable TV. Pool. Fishing. Playground. | 539 Parkway | 865/436–5121 or 800/223–9299 | fax 865/436–6208 | 108 rooms | $80–$140 | AE, D, MC, V.

Bon Air Mountain Inn. Three buildings and a chalet are part of this property in downtown Gatlinburg, near movie theaters and plenty of restaurants. Refrigerators, some in-room hot tubs, cable TV. Pool. Business services. Some pets allowed. | 950 Parkway | 865/436–4857 or 800/848–4857 | fax 865/436–8942 | www.smokeymountainresort.com | 75 rooms; 1 chalet | $89.65; $169.65 chalet | AE, D, MC, V.

Brookside Resort. This cozy resort is nestled in a valley and surrounded by trees. All rooms have hillside views and some have fireplaces. It's just a 10 minute walk west to downtown Gatlinburg. Six brick and wood buildings ranging from two to four floors. Picnic area. In-room data ports, some kitchenettes, refrigerators, cable TV. 2 outdoor pools, wading pool. Hot tub. Playground. Laundry facilities. Business services. | 463 E. Parkway | 865/436–5611 or 800/251–9597 | www.brooksideresort.com | 240 rooms, 60 suites, 8 cottages | $55; $110 suites; $175 cottages | AE, D, DC, MC, V.

★ **Buckhorn.** Hiking trails and a duck pond are highlights of this property set on 25 acres of quiet woods and meadows, 6 mi northeast of Gatlinburg. The country inn, built in 1938, is part of a historic Arts and Crafts community that includes one-bedroom cottages and two-bedroom houses scattered throughout the grounds. Restaurant, complimentary breakfast. Some kitchenettes, some microwaves, some refrigerators, some in-room hot tubs, cable TV. Hiking. | 2140 Tudor Mountain Rd. | 865/436–4668 | fax 865/436–5009 | www.buckhorninn.com | 6 rooms; 7 cottages; 2 houses | $115–$130; $130–$150 cottages; $200–$250 houses | D, MC, V.

Christopher Place Country Inn Bed and Breakfast. Approximately 15 mi northeast of Gatlinburg, this romantic Colonial-style mansion is surrounded by 200 acres of forest. Marble floors, crystal chandeliers, and hand-carved furniture give this resort a luxurious profile. Rooms, all individually appointed, are consistent in their lavish decorations. Restaurant, complimentary breakfast. Some refrigerators, some in-room hot tubs, cable TV, in-room VCRs. Pool. Sauna. Tennis. Gym, hiking. Library. No kids under 13. No smoking. | 1500 Pinnacles Way, Newport | 423/623–6555 or 800/595–9441 | www.christopherplace.com | 8 rooms | $150–$300 | AE, D, MC, V.

Creekside Inn. This hotel is in a quiet neighborhood, a few blocks off U.S. 321 and a 10 minute walk east from downtown. All rooms overlook the Roaring Fork Creek; some have porches. Half of the rooms have fireplaces, hot tubs, and Thomasville furnishings. Four floors. Some kitchenettes, refrigerators, some in-room hot tubs, cable TV. Pool, wading pool. Hot tub. | 239 Sycamore La. | 865/436–5977 | www.creeksideinngatlinburg.com | 43 rooms; 20 suites | $69; $89 suites | AE, D, DC, MC, V.

Days Inn Glenstone Lodge. This hotel, in operation since the mid-'70s, is one of the upscale accommodation choices in the area. It's set in a very wooded area just 1/3 mi south of downtown. Restaurant, picnic area. In-room data ports, some minibars, cable TV. 2 pools (1 indoor), wading pool. Hot tub, sauna. Playground. Business services. Free Parking. | 504 Airport Rd. | 865/436–9361 | fax 865/436–6951 | www.glenstonelodge.com | 206 rooms, 8 suites | $100; $125–150 suites | AE, D, DC, MC, V.

Econo Lodge. This brick, '50s, two-story structure is one of the many motels off U.S. 321 on Airport Road, 2 blocks from downtown. Refrigerators, cable TV. Pool. | 405 Airport Rd. | 865/436–5836 | fax 865/523–8363 | 33 rooms | $77.50; $134.50 suites | AE, D, DC, MC, V.

Edgewater. This downtown high-rise features a lounge with live music on the weekends. Rooms either have views of the Little Pigeon River or the woods; rooms with fireplaces are by request and do not cost extra. Restaurant, bar with entertainment. Cable TV. Indoor/outdoor pool. Hot tub. Business services. Free Parking. | 402 River Rd. | 865/436–4151, 800/423–9582 (outside TN), or 800/423–4532 (in TN) | fax 865/436–6947 | www.edgewaterhotel.com | 202 rooms, 3 suites | $129; $175 suites | AE, D, DC, MC, V.

Gillette Motel. Across the street from the Convention Center, this three-story motel has views of the surrounding mountains. Some kitchenettes, refrigerators, some in-room hot tubs, cable TV. Pool. | 235 Airport Rd. | 865/436–5601 or 800/437–0815 | www.gillettemotel.com | 81 rooms | $85 | AE, D, DC, MC, V.

Greystone Lodge. Most standard rooms have views of the Little Pigeon River and some have fireplaces at this stone lodge–style hotel in the center of Gatlinburg. Complimentary Continental breakfast. Some in-room hot tubs, cable TV. Pool, wading pool. Laundry facilities. Business services. | 559 Parkway | 865/436–5621 | fax 865/430–4471 | www.greystone.com | 251 rooms, 6 suites | $89–$119; $170 suites | AE, D, DC, MC, V.

Hampton Inn. This chain hotel is located directly on U.S. 441, just 200 yards from the main entrance to Great Smoky Mountain National Park. All rooms have mountain views. Complimentary Continental breakfast. Some refrigerators, cable TV, in-room VCRs (and movies). Pool. | 967 Parkway | 865/436–4878 | fax 423/436–4088 | 96 rooms | $77–$129 | AE, D, DC, MC, V.

★ **Holiday Inn Sunspree.** This family-friendly hotel has a Holidome that houses electronic space games, Ping-Pong, and other amusements. There's a general store and a pizza place on-site. The hotel is two blocks from downtown and within walking distance of the ski tramway. Restaurant, bar, picnic area, room service. In-room data ports, refrigerators, cable TV. 3 pools (2 indoor), wading pool. Hot tubs. Exercise equipment. Children's programs. Laundry facilities. Business services. Some pets allowed. | 520 Airport Rd. | 865/436–9201 | fax 865/436–7974 | 400 rooms | $130 | AE, D, DC, MC, V.

Hippensteal's Mountain View Inn. Secluded on more than 20 acres, 7 mi southwest of Gatlinburg, this three-story New England–style B&B looks out on Greenbriar Pinnacle, Mt. Le Conte, and Mt. Harrison. It was built in 1990 by one of the region's leading watercolorists whose works fill two local galleries. A central fireplace in the great room is surrounded by white wicker furniture and English chintz. Each bedroom has its own fireplace. Complimentary breakfast. In-room hot tubs, cable TV, in-room VCRs, no room phones. No smoking. | Grassy Branch Rd. | 865/436–5761 or 800/527–8110 | fax 865/436–8917 | www.hippensteal.com | 11 rooms | $149 | AE, D, MC, V.

Jack Huff's Motor Lodge. This modest lodge is just off U.S. 441, in the center of town. Groups do well at this hotel, as you can sleep up to six people for $85. Some in-room hot tubs, cable TV. Pool, wading pool. Hot tub. | 204 Cherokee Orchard Rd. | 865/436–5171 or 800/322–1817 | www.gatlinburg.com/jackhuffs | 60 rooms | $61 | D, MC, V.

Johnson's Inn. Walk to the Pancake Pantry for breakfast or the mall for a little shopping from this downtown hotel one block off U.S. 441. Some rooms have fireplaces and hot tubs. Some kitchenettes, refrigerators, cable TV, in-room VCRs (and movies). 2 pools, wading pool. Laundry facilities. Business services. | 242 Bishop La. | 865/436–4881 or 800/842–1930 | fax 865/436–2582 | www.johnsonsinn.com | 80 rooms; 1 suite | $85; $135 suite | D, MC, V.

Le Conte View. Right across from the convention center in the center of town, this hotel is an easy walk to shopping and restaurants. Rooms with fireplaces and hot tubs are available. Refrigerators, cable TV. Indoor/outdoor pool, wading pool. Business services. | 929 Parkway | 865/436–5032 or 800/842–5767 | fax 865/436–7973 | www.leconteview.com | 104 rooms; 3 suites | $126; $140 suites | AE, D, DC, MC, V | Closed Dec. 21–25.

McKay's Inn Downtown. Across the street from the convention center in the heart of town, this hotel has a large gabled roof that gives it the appearance of a mountain chalet. Some rooms have private balconies with views of the Smokies; suites have fireplaces and hot tubs. Complimentary Continental breakfast, picnic area. In-room data ports, refrigerators, some in-room hot tubs, cable TV. Pool, wading pool. | 903 Parkway | 865/436–5102 or 877/625–2976 | fax 865/436–3603 | www.mckaysinn.com | 67 rooms, 7 suites | $67–$110 rooms, $119–$139 | AE, D, DC, MC, V.

Oak Square. Close to the conveniences of downtown, this four-story condo complex, just off U.S. 441, has one and two-bedroom units. Some have fireplaces. Kitchenettes, cable TV. 2 pools (1 indoor). Hot tub. | 685 River Rd. | 865/436–7582 or 800/423–5182 | 60 suites | $99–$155 | MC, V.

Olde English Tudor Inn Bed and Breakfast. Perched on a hilltop, less than two blocks from the city's restaurants and shops, this quaint B&B is surrounded by trees. The seven rooms, individually decorated, are appointed with a mixture of Victorian antiques and comfortable contemporary furnishings. Complimentary Continental breakfast. Cable TV, no room phones. No smoking. | 135 W. Holly Ridge Rd. | 865/436–7760 or 800/541–3798 | www.oldeenglishtudorinn.com | 8 rooms, 1 cottage | $85–$120 | AE, D, MC, V.

Park Vista. All rooms in this cylindrical tower have mountain views. Complimentary shuttle service to downtown, 1 mi south is offered. There are two indoor children's play areas. Restaurant, bar with entertainment, room service. Cable TV. Indoor pool, wading pool. Hot tub. Gym. Video games. Playground. Laundry facilities. Business services. | 705 Cherokee Orchard | 865/436–9211 or 800/421–7275 (outside TN) | fax 865/436–5141 | www.parkvista.com | 310 rooms, 2 suites | $59–$129; $170–$400 suites | AE, D, DC, MC, V.

Quality Inn Convention Center. Although this downtown property caters to business people, the convenient location of this hotel—on U.S. 441—makes it a favorite of all travelers. Refrigerators, cable TV. Pool, wading pool. Business services. | 938 Parkway | 865/436–5607 | fax 865/430–3029 | www.reaganresorts.com | 63 rooms | $89.50 | AE, D, DC, MC, V.

Rainbow Motel and Rentals. The well-maintained rooms of this motel are within walking distance of downtown Gatlinburg. Cabins have hot tubs, fireplaces, full kitchens,

decks, swings, and TV/VCRs. Some kitchenettes, some microwaves, refrigerators, some in-room hot tubs, cable TV, in-room VCRs. Pool. | 390 E. Parkway | 865/436–5887 or 800/422–8922 | www.rainbowmotellogcabin.com | 40 rooms, 10 cabins | $30–$65; $75–$125 cabins | D, MC, V.

Ramada Inn. Some rooms have hot tubs and fireplaces at this reliable chain hotel on U.S. 321, just three blocks from downtown. Restaurant. Cable TV. Pool, wading pool. Hot tub. Laundry facilities. Business services. | 200 E. Parkway | 865/436–5043 | 103 rooms | $89 | AE, D, DC, MC, V.

River Edge Motor Lodge. This three-story hotel is on the frontage road through Gatlinburg. It is within walking distance to the Aerial Tramway. Rooms are decorated in green and dark woods, and some have fireplaces. Guests enjoy fresh Krispy Kreme donuts and coffee every morning. Refrigerators, cable TV. Pool, wading pool. | 665 River Rd. | 865/436–9292 or 800/544–2764 | 43 rooms | $99 | AE, D, DC, MC, V.

River Terrace Creekside. This property on U.S. 441 comprises three stone buildings directly across the street from the tram to the Ober Gatlinburg Ski Resort. One building overlooks LeConte creek. All are situated in a wooded area. Some rooms have fireplaces. Complimentary Continental breakfast. Some in-room hot tubs, cable TV. Pool, wading pool. Business services. | 125 LeConte Creek Rd. | 865/436–4865 or 800/473–8319 | fax 865/436–4089 | www.riverterrace.com | 67 rooms, 10 suites | $79; $139 suites | AE, D, DC, MC, V.

Rocky Top Village Inn. Keep your expectations low and you won't be disappointed at this motel four blocks from the Aerial Tramway, just a block from downtown. Three buildings with one, two, and three floors. Picnic tables. Refrigerators, cable TV. Pool, wading pool. | 311 Airport Rd. | 865/436–7826 or 800/553–7738 | fax 865/436–7826 | 84 rooms, 3 suites, 2 cottages | $45; $91 suites; $125 cottages | AE, D, DC, MC, V.

Rocky Waters Motor Inn. Rooms with fireplaces are available at this inn along the river Little Pigeon River, three blocks from downtown. The place was built in 1938 of redwood shingles and stucco. Picnic area. Refrigerators, some in-room hot tubs, cable TV, in-room VCRs (and movies). 2 pools, wading pool. Hot tub. Laundry facilities. Business services. | 333 Parkway | 865/436–7861 or 800/824–1111 | www.rockywaters.com | 100 rooms; 2 suites | $78; $140 suites | AE, D, DC, MC, V.

Rodeway Inn–Skyland. On a hill overlooking Gatlinburg, this motel offers great views of both the mountains and town, which is in the downtown area. Rooms with fireplaces are available. Picnic area, complimentary Continental breakfast. Kitchenettes, refrigerators, some in-room hot tubs, cable TV. Pool. | 223 E. Parkway | 865/436–5821 or 800/756–9669 | 56 rooms | $80–$107 | AE, D, DC, MC, V.

Royal Townhouse. Rooms with fireplaces are available at this no-frills, three-story motel across from the convention center and the Aerial Tramway downtown. Some refrigerators, cable TV. Pool, wading pool. | 937 Parkway | 865/436–5818 or 800/433–8792 | fax 865/436–0411 | 81 rooms | $80 | D, DC, MC, V.

Smokyland. This hotel, in a well-maintained older building, is across the street from a mall in the center of Gatlinburg. Some rooms have fireplaces and hot tubs. Refrigerators, cable TV. Pool, wading pool. | 727 Parkway | 865/436–5191 | 40 rooms | $80–$90 | AE, D, DC, MC, V.

Tennessee Ridge Inn. This modern chalet on top of Crockett Mountain has walls of windows that provide spectacular views of Mt. Le Conte. Two common areas have fireplaces and balconies. All guest rooms have hot tubs, balconies, and king-size beds; four rooms have wood-burning fireplaces. Decorated primarily with Asian-influenced modern furniture. Complimentary breakfast. No room phones, no TV in some rooms. Pool. No kids under 12. No smoking. | 507 Campbell Lead | 865/436–4068 | www.tn-ridge.com | 6 rooms, 1 suite | $125–$159 | D, MC, V.

Travelodge. There's an indoor pool in a faux tropical setting—complete with waterfall and cave—at this chain hotel. Some rooms have views of LeConte Creek. The hotel is close to the Aerial Tramway, ⅓ mi from downtown. Restaurant, picnic tables. Refrigerators, cable TV. 2 pools (1 indoor), wading pool. Hot tub, sauna. Laundry facilities. Business services. | 610 Airport Rd. | 865/436–7851 | fax 865/430–3580 | 136 rooms, 25 suites | $87; $138 suites | AE, D, DC, MC, V.

GREAT SMOKY MOUNTAINS NATIONAL PARK

MAP 12, I3

(Nearby towns also listed: Gatlinburg, Pigeon Forge, Sevierville, Townsend, Walland)

The southern Appalachians are at their most imposing within this rugged national park, named for the smokelike haze among the mountaintops. Divided between Tennessee and North Carolina, this most-visited of all national parks was once the unapproachable realm of the Cherokee Nation; today the Cherokee Reservation lies within its North Carolina section. More than 16 peaks here are higher than 6,000 ft—the highest, in Tennessee, is Clingman's Dome at 6,643 ft. The park is almost entirely wooded, and as you climb the mountains, you will see a change in the vegetation that is as great as if you were traveling from Tennessee to Canada. At lower altitudes are hardwood woodlands and near the tops of the mountains are spruce-fir forests. Perhaps the most intriguing phenomenon of the Smokies is the balds—heathlands high up in the mountains that open up to wide vistas.

Founded in 1934 as a wildlands sanctuary, the park has extensive camping facilities and interpretive programs within its some 500,000 acres, but few recreational services. The park does offer more than 800 mi of maintained trails, from gentle walkways to challenging climbs; 70 mi of the Appalachian Trail pass through it. Cade's Cove includes an outdoor museum featuring buildings typical of those used by the early settlers. Five stables offer horseback trail rides.

Information: Superintendent's Office | 107 Park Headquarters Rd., Gatlinburg 37738 | 865/436–1200 | www.nps.gov/grsm.

Attractions

Sugarlands Visitor Center. Located 2 mi south of Gatlinburg along the northern border of the park, this visitor center has exhibits that illustrate the park's natural history. Displays focus on plant and animal life found in the park. | U.S. 411 | 865/436–1200 | Free | Daily 8–4:30.

ON THE CALENDAR

SEPT.: *Mountain Lights Festival.* Held on the third Saturday of September, this festival centers on rural arts such as making apple-butter, apple-cider, sorghum-molasses, and soap. Demonstrations are held throughout the day at the Oconalustee Visitor Center, on U.S. 441, approximately 10 mi southeast of the Sugarlands Visitor Center. | 865/436–1200.

Lodging

Le Conte Lodge. The park's only lodging, atop Mt. Le Conte approximately 3 mi east of the Sugarlands Visitor Center, is accessible only by trail. It's open mid-March to mid-November and reservations fill up a year in advance, so you need to call early. Some rooms have dormitory-style accommodations, others sleep two to four people. The price of a bed includes breakfast and dinner. You must phone ahead for directions. Complimentary dinner and breakfast. No air-conditioning, no room phones, no TV. No smoking. | 250 Apple Valley Rd., Sevierville | 865/429–5704 | fax 865/774–0045 | reservations@leconte-lodge.com | 50 beds | $76.50 per night, per adult | No credit cards.

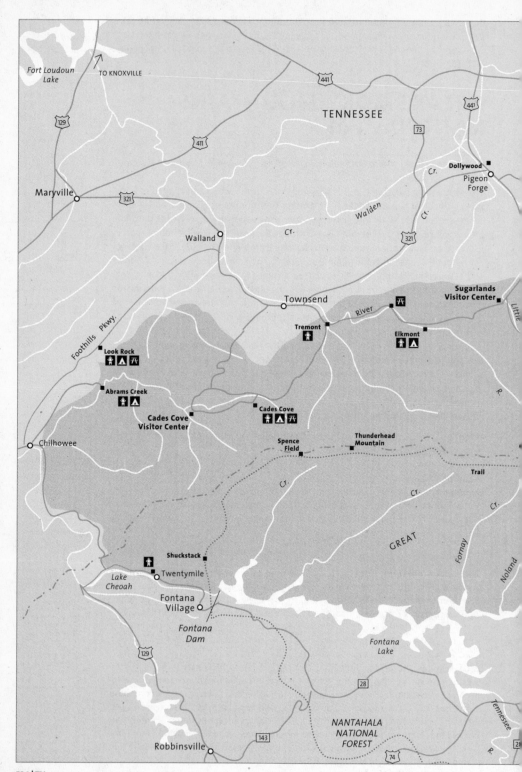

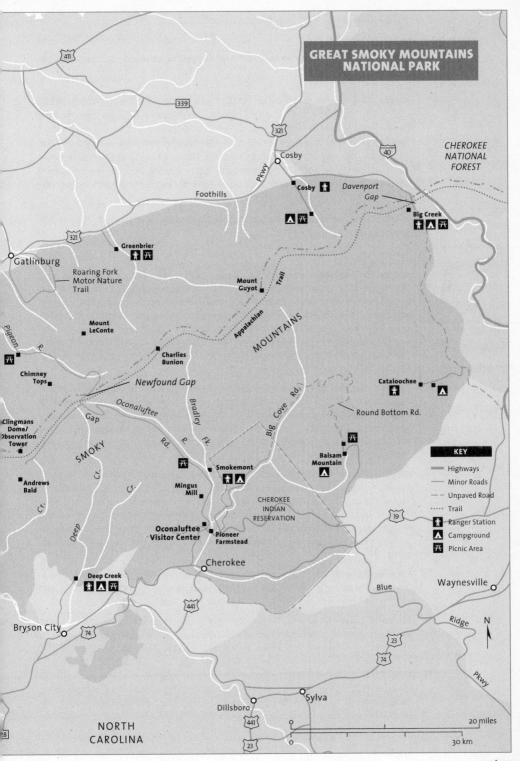

GREAT SMOKY MOUNTAINS NATIONAL PARK

CHEROKEE NATIONAL FOREST

Cosby

Cosby

Davenport Gap

Big Creek

Foothills

Greenbrier

Gatlinburg

Roaring Fork
Motor Nature
Trail

Mount Guyot

Appalachian Trail

MOUNTAINS

Mount
LeConte

Charlies
Bunion

Newfound Gap

Chimney
Tops

Cataloochee

Round Bottom Rd.

Oconaluftee

Gap

Bradley Fk.

Big Cove Rd.

Clingmans
Dome/
Observation
Tower

SMOKY

Rd.

R.

Balsam
Mountain

Smokemont

Andrews
Bald

Ct.

Mingus
Mill

CHEROKEE
INDIAN
RESERVATION

Deep Cr.

Oconaluftee
Visitor Center

Pioneer
Farmstead

Cherokee

Blue

Waynesville

Deep Creek

Ridge

Bryson City

Pkwy

Sylva

Dillsboro

NORTH
CAROLINA

N

KEY

	Highways
	Minor Roads
	Unpaved Road
	Trail
	Ranger Station
	Campground
	Picnic Area

20 miles

30 km

GREENEVILLE

MAP 12, G5

(Nearby towns also listed: Johnson City, Jonesborough, Morristown, Rogersville, Tusculum)

This East Tennessee town, founded in 1783, has a long history. It was once the capital of the "lost state of Franklin," a 1785 attempt to achieve statehood separate from North Carolina. Andrew Johnson, who succeeded to Abraham Lincoln's unfinished term, lived in Greeneville; you can visit two of his homes and his tailor shop. The town's Civil War history can be further explored through several well-preserved homes from the era, each open to the public. Other attractions are the Dickson-Williams Mansion, which served as headquarters for both Union and Confederate troops during the Civil War, and the Doak House Museum, built in 1818.

Information: **Greeneville/Green County Tourism Council** | 115 Academy St., Greeneville 37743 | 423/638–4111.

Attractions

Andrew Johnson National Historic Site. Two homes, the tailor shop, and the gravesite of the 17th president of the United States (and the first to be impeached) are preserved here. In 1826 Johnson migrated to the town of Greeneville from North Carolina. There he met and married his wife, Eliza, who taught him to read and write, and opened the tailor shop preserved here. He became president following Abraham Lincoln's assassination and lead the nation during the troubled years of Reconstruction. Stop at the visitor center for information before exploring the grounds. | College and Depot Sts. | Visitor center 423/638–3551, site headquarters 423/639–3711 | Free | Daily, 9–5.

Cherokee National Forest. (*See* Johnson City.) Greeneville is one of the gateways to this 630,000-acre forest, which stretches across 10 counties in southeastern Tennessee. It offers extensive hiking trails, camping, fishing, and wildlife watching, and is known for its mountain rivers and waterfalls. Float trips, white-water rafting, horseback riding, and self-guided scenic car tours are available. | USDA Forest Svc., 250 Ranger Station Rd. | 423/253–2520 | Free | Daily.

Dickson-Williams Mansion. This historic 1815 home, called the "Showplace of East Tennessee," was occupied in turn by Confederate and Union armies during the Civil War. Confederate General John Hunt Morgan spent his last night here; he was mortally wounded in a surprise cavalry ambush in the mansion's garden the following day. The room in which Morgan stayed still has its original furnishings. Davy Crockett, James K. Polk, and Andrew Jackson were all also guests in this home. | 108 N. Irish St. | 423/638–4111 | $5 | By appointment.

Kinser Park. The 285-acre park, 6 mi southwest of Greeneville, offers more than 100 RV camping sites overlooking the Nolichucky River. Visitors enjoy swimming, fishing, boating, picnicking, golf, tennis, and go-carts. | 423/639–5912 | Free | Apr.–Oct. daily.

Nathaniel Greene Museum. This downtown museum of state history focuses on the accomplishments of local figures such as John Sevier, Samuel Doak, Davy Crockett, and President Andrew Johnson. | 101 W. McKee St. | 423/636–1558 | $2 | Tues.–Sat. 10–4.

ON THE CALENDAR

MAY: *Iris Fest*. Held on the third weekend in May, this festival draws local and out-of-state craft artists to Greeneville's downtown area (along Depot and College Streets). The celebration includes live entertainment and plenty of events for the kids. | 423/638–4111.

Dining

Augustino's. Italian. This busy, family-friendly restaurant, is decorated in a Mediterranean style, with stucco walls and candlelight. Specialties include the veal Parmigiana and the steaks. Sun. brunch. Kids' menu. | 3465 E. Andrew Johnson Hwy. | 423/639–1231 | $9–$18 | AE, D, MC, V | No lunch Sat.

Deidra's Café. Contemporary. The trees that overhang the tables and the stars painted on the ceiling give the feeling of dining in a garden. The selection of items on the chalkboard menu reveals the country French and Italian influences of chef Deidra who studied in both countries. Dishes such as beef tenderloin stuffed with sundried tomato, feta, and Italian parsley and pork chops braised in red wine typify the cuisine. | 140 W. Depot St. | 423/636–8806 | Closed Sun. No dinner Mon. | $15–$20 | AE, D, MC, V.

Olde Tusculum Eatery. American/Casual. Five mi northwest of downtown and across from Tusculum College, this full-service cafeteria, served as a grocery store in the 1800s. Fresh daily quiches, chicken pot pie made with puff pastry, homemade soups, organic salad greens, and sandwiches are all on the menu. | 905 Erwin Hwy., Greeneville | 423/638–9210 | Closed weekends. No dinner | D, MC, V.

Lodging

Big Spring Inn. Built in 1905, this Greek revival B&B is surrounded by gardens and trees. English and American antiques and reproductions fit in with the oak floors, leaded-glass windows, and original chandeliers of the interior. Each room has its individual charms; the Hassie Hacker Doughty room, for instance, has a king-size brass bed, fireplace, bay windows, and a large bath. Complimentary breakfast. Cable TV. No kids under 4. No smoking. | 315 N. Main St. | 423/638–2917 | 4 rooms, 1 suite | Closed Nov.–Mar. | $70–$86 | AE, MC, V.

Charray Inn. On the outskirts of Greeneville in the commercial district, 5 mi east of downtown, this two-story motel offers comfortable, over-sized rooms. Restaurant. In-room data ports, refrigerators, cable TV. Business services. Airport shuttle. | 121 Serral Dr. | 423/638–1331 or 800/852–4682 | fax 423/639–5289 | www.charrayinn.com | 36 rooms | $50 | AE, D, DC, MC, V.

Days Inn. This chain hotel, 10 blocks north of downtown on U.S. 11E, is a bit out of the way if you want to explore Greeneville, but perfect if you're just passing through. Complimentary Continental breakfast. Cable TV. Business services. | 935 E. Andrew Johnson Hwy. | 423/639–2156 | 60 rooms | $54 | AE, D, DC, MC, V.

Hilltop House Bed and Breakfast. This 1920s manor, encircled by gardens and landscaped lawns and shaded by large trees, is 7 mi south of town overlooking the Nolichuckey River. Accented with English antiques and reproductions, the rooms are very large with views of the idyllic surroundings. Complimentary breakfast. Some in-room VCRs, no TV in some rooms. Library. No smoking. | 6 Sanford Cir. | 423/639–8202 | ashworth@greene.xtn.net | www.imagebyte.com/hilltop | 3 rooms | $75–$80 | AE, MC, V.

Holiday Inn. This hotel on U.S. 11E, just 1½ mi east of downtown, is a good place for the hungry traveler. It's surrounded by restaurants and has one of its own. Restaurant, bar. Cable TV. Pool. Business services. | 1790 E. Andrew Johnson Hwy. | 423/639–4185 | fax 423/639–7280 | 90 rooms | $65 | AE, D, DC, MC, V.

Jameson Inn. Rooms in this hotel are hunter green, cream, and shades of amber. They have dark cherry furniture. In the evening you'll be served freshly baked cookies and coffee in the lobby, which has a fireplace and marble tables. Complimentary Continental breakfast. Some microwaves, some refrigerators, TV in common area. Outdoor pool. Exercise equipment. No pets. | 3160 E. Andrew Johnson Hwy., Greeneville | 423/638–7511 | www.jamesoninn.com | 55 rooms | $64 | AE, D, MC, V.

HARROGATE

(Nearby towns also listed: Caryville, Jellico)

Just south of the Cumberland Gap, you'll come to Harrogate, a small town founded in the late 19th century. It is best known for its Abraham Lincoln Museum, one of the largest collections of Lincoln and Civil War memorabilia in the country. The collection is part of the Lincoln Memorial University, chartered in 1897 and dedicated to Abraham Lincoln at the suggestion of one of his Union Army generals, who remembered East Tennessee's support for the Union cause during the Civil War.

Information: Claiborne County Chamber of Commerce | 3222 U.S. 25E, Suite 1, Tazewell 37879 | 423/626–4149.

Attractions

Abraham Lincoln Museum. This is one of the nation's largest collections of Lincoln and Civil War artifacts, featuring more than 20,000 books, manuscripts, photographs, paintings, sculptures, and memorabilia relating to Abraham Lincoln and America's Civil War. Exhibits include the silver-topped cane Lincoln carried to the Ford's Theater in Washington, D.C., the night of his assassination, two life masks of the president, a lock of his hair clipped at his deathbed, and numerous personal belongings. | Cumberland Gap Pkwy. | 423/869–6235 | www.lmunet.edu/museum/index.html | $3 | Weekdays 9–4, Sat. 11–4, Sun. 1–4.

Cumberland Gap National Historical Park. The Cumberland Gap is a natural passageway through the mountains, a famous route traveled by thousands of early American settlers on the move west. Today this famous passageway and the surrounding area (20,100 acres in all) are preserved as a national park, with a visitor center and museum, an overlook of the gap, the remains of an early pioneer settlement, and 55 mi of hiking trails. To reach the main entrance and visitor center from Harrogate, take U.S. 25E 2 mi north of town. | U.S. 25E, ¼ mile south of Middlesboro, KY | 606/248–2817 | Free | Daily.

Lincoln Memorial University. Established in 1897 as the fulfillment of a promise made by General O. O. Howard to President Lincoln, this university offers a curriculum centered on the principles of the 16th U.S. president. The rural campus, featuring many buildings from the early 20th century, is on approximately 1,000 acres surrounded by woods. | U.S. 25E | 423/869–6432 | www.lmunet.edu | Free | Daily.

ON THE CALENDAR

JUNE: *Tunnel Run Car Show.* Held in June of each year, this festival brings over 100 antique cars to Harrogate City Park, located at the intersection of U.S. 25E and U.S. 63, and as many as 3,000 visitors. | 423/869–0211.

SEPT.: *Labor Day Pig Roast.* A big family picnic open to the public, the pig roast is held downtown at Harrogate City Park. Festivities include live bluegrass music, dunking booths, and games for the kids. It is free to residents, $7.50 for guests. | 423/869–0211.

Lodging

Ramada. At the crossroads of two U.S. highways and three states, this standard hotel offers an exceptional mountain view from its elevated location. Within walking distance of town, the hotel is also just 3 mi south of Cumberland Gap National Historic Park. Restaurant, bar, room service. Cable TV. Pool. Laundry facilities. Some pets allowed (fee). | U.S. 25E and U.S. 58, Cumberland Gap | 423/869–3631 | fax 423/869–5953 | ramadainn@wwgap.net | 150 rooms | $71 | AE, D, DC, MC, V.

HENDERSONVILLE

(Nearby towns also listed: Clarksville, Gallatin, Lebanon, Nashville)

Once a small quiet town, 200-year-old Hendersonville is now a populous bedroom community of Nashville. It's on the north shore of Old Hickory Lake, a popular recreation spot. It's also home to several historic houses worth visiting, and Trinity Music City, which offers a variety of entertainments for country music lovers.

Information: **Hendersonville Chamber of Commerce** | 101 Wessington Pl., Hendersonville 37075 | 615/824–2818.

Attractions

Monthaven. This Greek Revival house was used as a hospital during the Civil War. Today it is home to Hendersonville's Arts Council Galleries. Art exhibits, which rotate monthly, are free and open to the public. A gift shop on-site sells local crafts. | 109 Monthaven Blvd. | 615/822–0789 | Free | Weekdays 9–3.

Old Hickory Lake. This 22,500-acre lake is extremely popular with fisherfolk. In 1999, *Field and Stream* magazine named it one of the 50 best places to fish for bass. A 25-pound walleye caught here in 1960 set a world record. | 5 Power Plant Rd. | 615/822–4846 or 615/847–2395 | Free | Daily.

Rock Castle. This seven-story limestone house is considered the prime example of "glorified pioneer-style architecture." The home was built in 1797 by General Daniel Smith. | 139 Rock Castle La. Pike | 615/824–0502 | $5 | Tues.–Sat. 10–4, Sun. noon–4.

Trinity Music City U.S.A. This country music complex owned by Trinity Broadcasting is built around the former home of the late singer Conway Twitty; tours of his home and garden are offered three times a day. Also on-site are a virtual reality theater and an auditorium where the "Praise the Lord" television show is taped. The tapings generally take place on Friday evenings and are free and open to the public; call ahead for an exact schedule. | 1 Music Village Blvd. | 615/822–8333 | Free | Mon.–Sat. 10–6, Sun. 1–6.

ON THE CALENDAR
MAY: *Twittyworth Softball Tournament.* Professional, nationally ranked teams come from all over the eastern half of the United States to play ball at Drakes Creek Park (off U.S. 31E) on Mother's Day weekend. | 615/824–2818.

Lodging
Hendersonville Inn. Family-owned, this is the city's oldest motel. All rooms in this two-story brick structure have double beds. It stands less than a mile west of Trinity Music City USA. Complimentary Continental breakfast. Refrigerators, cable TV. Pool. No pets. | 179 W. Main St. | 615/822–4240 | fax 615/824–7645 | www.hvilleinn.citysearch.com | 27 rooms | $46 | AE, D, MC, V.

HENNING

(Nearby towns also listed: Covington, Dyersburg, Jackson, Memphis)

This tiny town, founded in 1889, not far from the banks of the Mississippi, was the boyhood home of Alex Haley, author of *Roots*. Although the accuracy of Haley's account of American slavery has been questioned by historians, it has passed into American folklore, and Haley can be credited with waking up the country to the horrors of the slave trade and its long-lasting effects.

Information: **Lauderdale County Chamber of Commerce** | 123 So. Jefferson St., Ripley 38063 | 901/635–9541.

Attractions

Alex Haley House Museum. The childhood home of the Pulitzer Prize–winning author of *Roots*, published in 1976, contains family memorabilia and artifacts. Built in 1919 by Haley's maternal grandfather, who ran a mill and lumberyard, the house was erected on the site of the first building used as a school for the education of African-American children. Haley is buried on the grounds. | 200 S. Church St. | 901/738–2240 | $2.50 | Tue.–Sat. 10–5, Sun. 1–5.

Fort Pillow State Historic Area. (*See* Covington.) Henning offers access to this historic park overlooking the Mississippi River, where an 1864 Civil War battle was fought. Today this 1,600 acre historic park is a wildlife sanctuary. | 3122 Park Rd. | 901/738–5581 | www.state.tn.us/environment/parks/pillow/index.html | Free | Daily.

ON THE CALENDAR

SEPT.: *Labor Day Parade.* Floats, bands, food vendors, arts and crafts, and musical performances mark this holiday celebration in downtown Henning (along Graves Avenue and Main Street). | 901/738–5055.

HOHENWALD

MAP 12, E3

(Nearby towns also listed: Columbia, Lawrenceburg, Lewisburg)

Hohenwald, in middle Tennessee, was established by German immigrants in 1897; later they were joined by a group of Swiss settlers. The town's name is German for "high forest," once an apt characterization of the area where the town grew up. Hohenwald is also known as the site of the mysterious death of explorer Meriwether Lewis, who was on his way to Washington, D.C., when he died.

Information: **Hohenwald Chamber of Commerce** | 112 E. Main St., Hohenwald 38462 | 931/796–4084.

Attractions

Historic Blackburn Farmstead and Pioneer Museum. Constructed around 1806 before Hohenwald was founded, the house is considered one of the best-preserved log structures in the area. The home of the only Revolutionary War veteran known to have settled in Lewis County, it also served as the county's first courthouse. The farmstead, corncrib, and other out-buildings have remained intact, with few changes over the years. Open for tours. | 121 John Sharp Rd., Gordonsburg | 931/796–7264 | Free | By appointment only.

Meriwether Lewis Park, Grave, and Monument. One of the leaders of the famed Lewis and Clark expedition was shot here under mysterious circumstance in 1809. Historians disagree as to whether or not he committed suicide. The park, which is 7 mi east of town and surrounds Lewis's gravesite, offers displays on the explorer, bike and hiking trails, a picnic area, and campground. | 189 Meriwether Lewis Park | 931/796–2675 | Free | Daily.

ON THE CALENDAR

OCT.: *Oktoberfest.* Held on the second weekend of October, this festival celebrates German culture with traditional food and music. The celebrations take over the downtown area surrounding Park Ave. and spill along Hwy. 20E in the form of roadside arts and crafts booths as far as Meriwether Lewis Park 7 miles east of town. | 931/796–4084.

Dining

Fish Camp Restaurant. American/Casual. Just south of Centerville and 15 mi north of Hohenwald, this homey spot serves a variety of hearty dishes including shrimp, oysters, chicken, and steak, but is known for its catfish and hushpuppies. | 406 Rte. 100, Centerville | 931/729–4401 | $7–$15 | MC, V.

Lodging

Avaleen Springs Bed and Breakfast. Located 12 mi west of Hohenwald and 10 mi east of Linden, this cedar-walled B&B sits on 30 acres of lush forest. Nature seems to flow in and out of this rustic home. In fact, it does, as the creek is visible under a glass coffee table in the library. Rooms open onto decks with views of a nearby waterfall. Complimentary breakfast. Some refrigerators, some in-room hot tubs, in-room VCRs. Pond. Hiking, fishing. Library. No pets. No smoking. | Rte. 3 and U.S. 412, Linden | 931/589–AVLS or 877/474–3055 | www.bbonline.com/tn/avaleen | 3 rooms | $85–$109 | AE, D, MC, V.

HURRICANE MILLS

MAP 12, D2

(Nearby towns also listed: Dickson, Paris, Wildersville)

The entire village of Hurricane Mills is a part of Loretta Lynn's Ranch, which covers 3,500 acres. Visitors can tour the country superstar's home, a museum, and a re-creation of her childhood house. Other activities include concerts, dances, trail rides, camping, miniature golf, and canoeing.

Information: Humphreys County Area Chamber of Commerce | 124 E. Main St., Waverly 37185 | 931/296–4865.

Attractions

Loretta Lynn's Ranch. When Lynn found the house of her dreams, it came with a small town and an old mill. The property is now a campground and recreation center with a museum chronicling Lynn's life and career, a re-creation of her girlhood home in the hills of Kentucky, a play play house–sized log cabin, and a gift store. Activities include a tour of the property, plus concerts, dances, trail rides, miniature golf, and canoeing. You can even tour the ground floor of the singer's antebellum plantation home. When Loretta is around, she sometimes comes out to talk with her fans. | 44 Hurricane Mills Rd. | 931/296–7700 | www.lorettalynn.com/campground.html | Free | Apr.–Oct., daily 9–5.

Old Mill. This mill, which dates from the early 1900s, now houses a gift shop and Loretta's museum with its collection of memorabilia and pictures chronicling the singer's life. Notes, handwritten by Loretta Lynn, explain the items. | 44 Hurricane Mills Rd. | 931/296–7700.

ON THE CALENDAR

AUG.: *National Motorcross Championships.* Held at the Loretta Lynn Ranch, this cross-country motorcycle race determines the national champion and draws as many as 20,000 visitors. | 931/296–7700.

Dining

Log Cabin Restaurant. Southern. This casual place has been serving Southern country fare like catfish, fried chicken, chicken livers, and barbecue to locals and travelers since it opened in 1966. Constructed as a log home at the turn-of-the-century, the building still has its original hickory logs. It's just north of I–40. | 15530 Rte. 13 | 931/296–5311 | Breakfast also available | $5.25–$13 | AE, D, DC, MC, V.

Lodging

Best Western. For those who don't want to lose time getting on and off the interstate, this hotel is ideally situated, right I–40, 7 mi south of the center of Loretta Lynn's Ranch. The property is landscaped with trees and flowers. Some refrigerators, cable TV. Pool. Hot tub. Playground. Laundry facilities. Some pets allowed. | 15542 Rte. 13 S | 931/296–4251 | fax 931/296–9104 | www.bestwestern.com | 89 rooms | $50–$70 | AE, D, DC, MC, V.

Days Inn Hurricane Mills. This two-story motor lodge is just off I–40 at Exit 143, near a selection of restaurants and a 24-hour gas station, within city limits. Restaurant. Cable TV. Pool. | 15415 Rte. 13 S. | 931/296–7647 | fax 931/296–5488 | www.daysinn.com | 74 rooms | $50–$65 | AE, D, DC, MC, V.

Holiday Inn Express–Hurricane Mills-Waverly. This two-story hotel is conveniently located 6 mi south of the Loretta Lynn's Ranch and less than a mile north of I–40. In-room data ports, some microwaves, some refrigerators, some in-room hot tubs, cable TV. Pool. Laundry facilities. Pets allowed (fee). | 15368 Rte. 13 S | 931/296–2999 | fax 931/296–2999 | 50 rooms | $62–$73 | AE, D, DC, MC, V.

JACKSON

(Nearby towns also listed: Bolivar, Covington, Henning, Wildersville)

Jackson, founded in 1821, was named for president-to-be Andrew Jackson, and became one of the largest cities of West Tennessee. It owes its prominence to the railroad, which made it strategically important during the Civil War. After the war, the railroads were further developed to connect the Deep South with the Midwest. Jackson prospered, and the homes in the historic district reflect that prosperity.

Many freed slaves came to Jackson to work on the railroad; Lane College, established here in 1882, was one of the first colleges established by African-Americans for African-Americans. Jackson was also the home of John Luther "Casey" Jones, the famed train engineer immortalized in the "Ballad of Casey Jones."

Information: Jackson/Madison County Convention and Visitors Bureau | 314 E. Main St., Jackson 38301 | 901/425–8333.

Attractions

Britton Lane Battlefield. Thousands of soldiers fought and died during the heated, four-hour Civil War battle that took place here on Sept. 1, 1862. The site now features a restored Civil War–era cabin used by both sides as a hospital. Monuments mark the site of a Confederate mass grave and the site where more than 200 Union prisoners were captured. | 199 Carriage House Dr. | 901/935–2209 | www.brittonlane1862.madison.tn.us | Free | Daily.

Casey Jones Village. This popular tourist village is dedicated to a figure of American folklore. Legend has it that Jones, an engineer on "Old 382," stayed in the cab when the train was declared a runaway on April 30, 1900, thus sacrificing his own life to save his passengers. Here you'll find the Casey Jones Home and Railroad Museum, a steam locomotive, two 25-ft-long model railroads, and miniature golf. | 56 Casey Jones La. | 901/668–1223 or 800/748–9588 | www.caseyjones.com | Free | Daily.

Casey Jones Home and Railroad Museum. The turn-of-the-century home of the fabled engineer is now a museum of railroad artifacts and Jones memorabilia. These include two 25-ft model-train displays in a restored 1890s mail car. | 56 Casey Jones La. | 901/668–1222 | www.caseyjones.com | $4 | Daily 9–8.

Chickasaw State Rustic Park. Situated on some of the highest terrain in Tennessee, 22 mi southwest of Jackson, this land was part of the Chickasaw Nation prior to 1818. Of the area's 14,384 acres of timberland, 1,280 acres are used for recreation. The balance is state forest, overseen by both the State Forestry Division and the Tennessee Wildlife Resources Agency. The park offers cabins, camping, hiking, boating, swimming, fishing, biking, horseback-riding, and golf. | 20 Cabin La., Henderson | 901/989–5141 | Free | Daily.

Cypress Grove Nature Park. The park 4 mi south of Jackson in the river lowlands. There are boardwalks, two lakes, an observation tower, a picnic pavilion, and the Aerie Trail Raptor Center, which features six large enclosures displaying birds of prey. A 2-mi self-guided walking tour on an elevated boardwalk takes you through virgin cypress forest. | U.S. 70W (Airways Blvd.) and U.S. 45 | 901/425–8364 | Free | Daily.

Pinson Mounds State Archaeological Area. The 1,200-acre area 10 mi south of Jackson is the site of numerous prehistoric Indian structures, including at least 15 earthen ceremonial or burial mounds, habitation areas, and related earthworks. The site features the second-highest mound built by Native Americans in the United States. Because the park is an area of ongoing archeological research and a designated sanctuary, all plants, animals (living and dead), rocks, artifacts, and fossils are protected by state law. | 460 Ozier Rd., Pinson | 901/988–5614 | www.state.tn.us/environment/parks/pinson/index.html | Free | Mar.–Nov., daily; Dec.–Feb., weekdays.

ON THE CALENDAR

JUNE: *Shannon Street Blues Festival.* This event held over the first weekend of the month honors John Lee "Sonny Boy" Williamson, who is known for popularizing the use of the harmonica in the early blues music of the 1920s and 1930s. It takes place at the West Tennessee Farmers Market at 91 Market St. between Lafayette St. and Shannon St. | 901/425–8333 or 901/427–7573.

SEPT.: *Casey Jones Old Time Music Festival.* This annual musical celebration takes place at Casey Jones Village. | 901/686–7342.

Dining

Baudo's. Italian. At this comfortable family spot, a mural gives the impression you're overlooking an Italian countryside. The large menu includes Italian favorites like lasagnas, raviolis, plus more innovative dishes like char-grilled shrimp wrapped in ham and brushed with Dijon mustard and Jack Daniels. | 559 Wiley Parker Rd. | 901/668–1447 | $6–$18 | AE, D, DC, MC, V | Closed Sun. No lunch Sat.

Brook Shaw and Sons Old Country Store and Restaurant. American casual. This 1890s-style general store, decorated with 15,000 antiques, is part of Casey Jones Village. The 500-seat restaurant features three daily buffets as well as an ice cream and confectionery shop. Specialties include Tennessee farm-fed catfish and country ham. Salad bar. Entertainment Fri., Sat. | 56 Casey Jones La. | 901/668–1223 | www.caseyjones.com | $8–$12 | AE, D, DC, MC, V.

Ezra's. American. This casual restaurant in the Garden Plaza Hotel boasts of its hickory-grilled meats (beef, chicken, and seafood), though other options are available, as well as salads, sandwiches, and soups. | 1770 U.S. 45 S Bypass | 901/664–6900 | Breakfast also available | $9–$16 | AE, D, DC, MC, V.

Madison's Restaurant. American. Candles and flowers adorn the tables at this local favorite, one of the nicest in town. The menu offers a little bit of everything: prime rib, steaks, chicken, seafood, pastas, veal, duck, and lamb. | 541 Wiley Parker Rd. | 901/664–5949 | $12–$29 | AE, MC, V | Closed Sun. No lunch.

Lodging

AmeriHost Inn of Jackson. This two-story chain hotel is less than 2 mi east of Casey Jones Village. Complimentary Continental breakfast. In-room data ports, some in-room hot tubs, cable TV. Pool. Hot tub, sauna. | 465 Vann Dr. | 901/661–9995 | fax 901/661–0404 | 61 rooms | $59–$64 | AE, D, DC, MC, V.

Best Western Old Hickory Inn. Across from Casey Jones Village's shops and museum, this hotel offers easy on and off access to I–40, 2 mi north of town. Also nearby are a bowling

alley, go-karting, and a mall. Restaurant, bar with entertainment, room service, complimentary Continental breakfast. Cable TV. Pool, wading pool. Business services. Some pets allowed. | 1849 U.S. 45 S Bypass | 901/668–4222 | fax 901/664–8536 | www.bestwestern.com | 141 rooms | $49–$60 | AE, D, DC, MC, V.

Baymont. Three miles north of downtown Jackson, near several southern chain restaurants, this is a secure inside-access hotel. Complimentary Continental breakfast. Cable TV. Pool. Business services. | 2370 N. Highland Ave. | 901/664–1800 | fax 901/664–5456 | www.budgethotel.com | 102 rooms | $49–$59 | AE, D, DC, MC, V.

Casey Jones Station Inn. This railroad-themed motel 4 mi north of downtown and within a block of the Casey Jones Museum in Casey Jones Village includes authentic cabooses and railroad cars converted to sleeping rooms. Cable TV. Pool. | 1943 U.S. 45 S Bypass (off U.S. 45 Exit 80A) | 901/668–3636 or 800/628–2812 | 53 rooms | $50–$$99.99 | AE, D, DC, MC, V.

Comfort Inn. This hotel is the first you'll come to when you take Exit 80A off I–40. It's 4 mi north of downtown and within walking distance of Casey Jones Village. Complimentary Continental breakfast. Microwaves, cable TV. Pool, wading pool. Exercise equipment. Laundry facilities. Business services. | 1963 U.S. 45 S Bypass | 901/668–4100 | fax 901/664–6940 | 205 rooms | $64–$69 | AE, D, DC, MC, V.

Country Inn and Suites–Jackson. This three-story chain hotel is less than 1 mi north of Casey Jones Village, off I–40. Complimentary snacks—such as cookies, apples, and candy—are provided in the lobby. Complimentary Continental breakfast. Some microwaves, some refrigerators, cable TV. Pool. No pets. | 1935 Emporium Dr. | 901/660–0077 | fax 901/660–2029 | 79 rooms, 17 suites | $79–$99 | AE, D, DC, MC, V.

Days Inn. This no-frills budget motel is centrally located, close to I–40, restaurants, and the Casey Jones Home and Railroad Museum. Cable TV. Pool. Business services. | 1919 U.S. 45 S Bypass | 901/668–3444 | fax 901/668–7778 | www.daysinn.com | 120 rooms | $37–$44 | AE, D, DC, MC, V.

Four Points Sheraton This two-story hotel with English Tudor–style decor boasts antiques, paintings, and some fireplaces. Just ½ mile east of Casey Jones Village and 2 miles north of downtown. Restaurant, bar with entertainment. Some refrigerators, cable TV. Pool. Free parking. | 2267 N. Highland Ave. | 901/668–1571 | fax 901/664–8070 | 103 rooms, 33 suites | $79–$98, $105–$125 suites | AE, D, DC, MC, V.

Garden Plaza Hotel. This five-story chain hotel provides convenient accommodations, just 4 mi north of downtown and within walking distance of Casey Jones Village. Restaurant, bar, room service. Cable TV. Pool. Hot tub. Gym. Some pets allowed. | 1775 U.S. 45 S Bypass | 901/664–6900 or 800/3–GARDEN | 168 rooms | $69–$89 | AE, D, DC, MC, V.

Hampton Inn. This newly renovated hotel offers the comfort and predictability of the chain, and it's just 10 minutes north of downtown, across from the Casey Jones Home and Railroad Museum. Complimentary Continental breakfast. Cable TV. Pool. Business services. | 1890 U.S. 45 S Bypass | 901/664–4312 | fax 901/664–7844 | 120 rooms | $61–$65 | AE, D, DC, MC, V.

Highland Place Bed and Breakfast. This early 1900s house sits behind an iron-gated fence in the North Highland Historic District, 7 blocks north of downtown. Ten-ft-high ceilings, solid cherry paneling, and plantation shutters are just some of the features that give this lodging its distinctive, stately aura. Furnished throughout with antiques, the B&B also has modern amenities like a TV/VCR with plenty of movies in the living room. Complimentary breakfast. Some room phones, no TV in some rooms, TV in common area. Library. No pets. No kids under 12. No smoking. | 519 N. Highland Ave. | 901/427–1472 | www.highland-place.com | 1 room, 3 suites | $80 rooms, $135 suites | MC, V.

Holiday Inn. Only two blocks off I–40, 8 mi north of downtown Jackson, this hotel is near convenience stores and restaurants. Rooms overlook an inside atrium with a pool and lounge.

Restaurant, bar, room service. In-room data ports, refrigerators, cable TV. Indoor pool. Beauty salon. Video games. Free parking. | 541 Carriage House Dr. | 901/668–6000 | fax 901/668–9516 | www.holiday-inn.com | 135 rooms, 54 suites | $75–$125 | AE, D, DC, MC, V.

Howard Johnson Express. This two-story hotel, built in 1998, sits halfway between Nashville and Memphis, just off I-40 at Exit 85. Complimentary Continental breakfast. In-room data ports, some microwaves, some refrigerators, cable TV. Pool. No pets. | 40 Howard Johnson Cove | 901/421–2711 | fax 901/421–2663 | 43 rooms | $41–$61 | AE, D, MC, V.

Ramada. This two-story motel has been completely renovated. It's 10 mi from downtown, conveniently located on a commercial strip, Jackson Bypass. Complimentary Continental breakfast. In-room data ports, cable TV. Pool. Gym. Laundry facilities. Business services. | 2212 N. Highland Ave. | 901/668–1066 | fax 901/660–6597 | www.ramada.com | 88 rooms | $45–$55 | AE, D, DC, MC, V.

JAMESTOWN

(Nearby towns also listed: Celina, Cookeville, Wartburg)

This small 1827 town has a connection with Mark Twain—though not born in Jamestown, he probably was conceived here. His father owned a large tract of land in the area, and Mark Twain may have used the East Tennessee town as a setting in some of his stories. It also has a connection to World War I hero Sgt. Alvin York, a native son who was awarded with a farm in the area after he returned from the war in 1918.

Jamestown also offers access to the natural beauty of the Cumberland Plateau: Big South Fork National River and Recreation Area, Pickett State Rustic Park, and Sergeant Alvin C. York State Historic Park are all nearby. Here you can camp, hike, and horseback ride, swim, fish, canoe, and white-water raft to your heart's content.

Information: **Jamestown/Fentress County Chamber of Commerce** | 114 Central Ave. W, Jamestown 38556 | 931/879–9948.

Attractions

Big South Fork National River and Recreation Area. The Big South Fork of the Cumberland River and its tributaries pass through 90 mi of scenic gorges and valleys containing a wide range of natural and historic features. The huge area offers opportunities for many outdoor sports, from hiking and mountain-biking on the Cumberland Plateau to white-water rafting on the river. It's 24 mi northeast of Jamestown to the visitors center. | 4564 Leatherwood Rd. | 423/569–9778 | www.nps.gov/biso | Free | Daily.

Highland Manor Winery. Situated atop the scenic Cumberland Plateau ½ mile south of Jamestown, this is Tennessee's oldest licensed winery. Free tours and tastings are available. | 2965 U.S. 127 | 931/879–9519 | fax 931/879–2907 | Free | May–Dec., Mon–Sat. 10–5, Sun. 1–5.

Pickett State Rustic Park. This remote 17,372-acre park lies in the Cumberland Mountains 15 miles north of Jamestown. It is known for its uncommon rock formations, natural bridges, numerous caves, and remains of ancient Native American structures. The park claims to be second only to Great Smoky Mountains Park for botanical diversity. It offers cabins and campsites; activities include boating, fishing, and swimming. | 4605 Pickett Park Hwy. | 931/879–5821 | www.state.tn.us/environment/parks/pickett/index.html | Free | Daily.

Sergeant Alvin C. York State Historic Park. This 85-acre park 10 mi north of Jamestown preserves the farmhouse of a World War I hero, where he raised a family of 10 after returning with honors from the war. Most visits begin at the country store, where the welcome center is housed. | 2700 N. York Hwy., Pallmall | 931/879–6456 | Free | Daily 8:30–4:30.

ON THE CALENDAR

MAY: *Spring Music and Crafts Festival.* Traditonal British and Appalachian music and crafts are featured at this Historic Rubgy gala. | 423/628–2430.

OCT.: *Rugby Pilgrimage.* Private Victorian-style homes in the restored British colony are opened to the public. | 423/628–2441.

Dining

Bacaras Family Restaurant. Austrian. Traditional Alpine meals are the specialty here, including hearty dishes such as spaetzle, roesti, Wiener schnitzel, and saurbraten. The restaurant is in what was originally a school house; its large windows, parquet floors, and high ceilings give it a distinctive charm. | 329 Wheeler La. | 931/879–7121 | Closed Sun.–Tues. No lunch | $9–$16 | No credit cards.

Lodging

Wildwood Lodge. Next to the Big South Fork National River and Recreation Area with its 110,000 acres of forest, this B&B is a nature lover's paradise. Just 12 mi northeast of Jamestown, the inn sits on 27 acres of land, crisscrossed with wild-flower walking trails. You don't have to leave the inn to see nature, though; bobcats, deer, and flying squirrels are visible from the spacious woodland deck (3,000 square ft). Natural pine wainscoting gives the rooms a rustic flavor. In the cottage there are no restrictions with regard to pets or kids. Complimentary breakfast. TV in common area. Pond. Hiking, horseback riding, water sports. No pets. No kids under 13. No smoking. | 3636 Pickett Park Hwy. | 931/879–9454 | www.wildwoodlodge.ws | 10 rooms, 1 suite, 1 cottage | $65–$70 | No credit cards.

© Artville

A TENNESSEE UTOPIA

In 1880, after writing the best-selling *Tom Brown's Schooldays,* British author and social reformer Thomas Hughes founded a new, innovative community in northwestern Tennessee on the edge of the Cumberland Plateau. At that time in England, the rule of primogeniture meant that the eldest sons of the British aristocracy inherited the family money and property, leaving younger brothers with greatly diminished prospects. Hughes envisioned Rugby, as the Tennessee town was called, as a place where the second (and subsequent) sons of British aristocrats could start a new life in America. It was to be a cooperative, agricultural community, free of class distinctions, a place where the young aristocrats would go to farm and practice trades—to "work like peasants and live like gentlemen."

For a while, the utopia flourished. At its zenith, the community had more than 350 members, 70 Victorian buildings, and 75,000 acres of farmland. The aristocratic residents built a library and an Episcopal church and attempted to live like British gentlemen, dressing for tea every afternoon and spending their free time playing tennis and croquet. Unfortunately, they knew little about farming and did not care much for physical labor. That, combined with financial woes, land deed problems, and unusually fierce winters, brought about the village's demise within 10 years of its founding.

Today, the town is on the National Historic Register, and has been restored and is a open to the public. Historic Rugby Inc. features 20 of the original Victorian-style buildings, including the library (which remains almost unchanged), Hughes' home, the church, the print works, and the schoolhouse, which now contains the visitor center. The National Trust has called Rugby "one of the most authentically preserved historic villages in America."

JELLICO

MAP 12, I1

(Nearby towns also listed: Caryville, Harrogate)

Founded in the late 1800s, Jellico is near the Kentucky border in a coal-mining region of the Cumberland Mountains. It was the home of opera singer Grace Moore, "the Tennessee Nightingale," who sang in a Jellico church choir before she went on to perform in New York City's Metropolitan Opera in the 1930s and 1940s and to make many Hollywood films.

Information: **Jellico Tourism** | Suite 1, 104 N. Main St., Jellico 37762 | 423/784–3275.

Attractions

Indian Mountain State Park. The 200-acre park at the base of the Cumberland Mountains contains two small fishing lakes and two walking trails; one is paved. While not a large park, it draws campers for its dramatic scenery. It is 3 miles west of I–75, Exit 160 within the city limits of Jellico. | Indian Mountain State Rd. | 423/784–7958 | www.state.tn.us/environment/parks/indian/index.html | Free | Daily.

ON THE CALENDAR
SEPT.: *Swift Silver Mine Lost Treasure Weekend.* Held downtown on the third weekend of September, this festival celebrates the memory of 19th-century silver-seeker John Swift, who is rumored to have hidden vast amounts of silver in the surrounding mountains. The focus of the celebration is a metal detector contest. | 423/784–3275.

Dining

Gregory's Family Tree Restaurant. American. In the Days Inn, adjacent to the lobby, this restaurant serves traditional family-style meals. Chicken salad here is tasty and the rocky top brownies are winners for dessert or snacks. | 1417 5th St.(U.S. 25W) | 423/784–4176 | Breakfast also available | $7–$13 | AE, D, DC, MC, V.

Lodging

Best Western Holiday Plaza Motel. This two-story chain motel sits at the base of the Cumberland Mountains, just off I–75, 2 miles west of Indian State Park. Cable TV. Pool. Pets allowed. | 5th St.(U.S.25W) off I–75 (Exit 160) | 423/784–7241 | fax 423/784–5657 | 50 rooms | $47–$57 | AE, D, DC, MC, V.

Days Inn. Guests enjoy mountain views from this standard, no-frills motor lodge. One mile south of town, the location is convenient to I–75 and fast-food restaurants. Restaurant, complimentary Continental breakfast. Cable TV. Pool. | U.S.25W, 1/2 mile west of I–75 (Exit 160) | 423/784–7281 | fax 423/784–4529 | 126 rooms | $44–$55 | AE, D, DC, MC, V.

JOHNSON CITY

MAP 12, H5

(Nearby towns also listed: Bristol, Elizabethton, Jonesborough, Kingsport, Tusculum)

In the far eastern reaches of the state, Johnson City is the youngest of the Tri-Cities, which include Kingsport and Bristol. It has the reputation of being the fun city of the three, probably because of its two universities: East Tennessee State University and East Tennessee State Normal School, which, along with tourism and manufacturing, are the city's major employers. Gateway to Cherokee National Forest, the city is also a center for lake recreation.

Information: **Johnson City Convention and Visitors Bureau** | Drawer 180, Johnson City 37605 | 423/461–8000.

Attractions

Cherokee Adventures. The Nolichucky River offers some of the best white-water rafting in upper East Tennessee, and this operation, 16½ mi south of Johnson City, offers the greatest variety of rafting options around. | 2000 Jonesborough Rd., Erwin | 423/743–7733 or 800/445–7238 | www.cherokeeadventures.com | $10–$175 | Mar.–Oct.

Cherokee National Forest. (*See* Greeneville.) The 630,000-acre forest, which shares its eastern border with North Carolina, is split into a northern and southern section, with Great Smoky Mountains National Park between them. The forest's 650 mi of footpaths include a 150-mi section of the Appalachian Trail. Other attractions include the Conasauga Fish Viewing Trail, a relatively silt-free stretch of the Conasauga State Scenic River (bring a mask and snorkel), and the Tellico Auto Loop, which passes through a black bear sanctuary. Johnson City abutts the park's western border. Unlike most national parks the forest has no controlled entry, but U.S.23/19W and Hwy.321 provides convenient access along many points to the forest's northern half. | 2800 N. Ocoee, Cleveland | 423/476–9700 | Free | Daily.

East Tennessee State University. There are eight colleges and schools at ETSU that enroll nearly 12,000 students. Among the more than 100 degree programs, an M.D. degree is offered through the James H. Quillen College of Medicine. | 807 University Pkwy. | 423/929–4112 or 423/439–1000 | www.etsu.edu | Free | Daily.

Erwin National Fish Hatchery. Established in the 1890s, this 12-acre site is one of the oldest fish hatcheries run by the U.S. Fish and Wildlife Service. The hatchery, about 15 mi south of Johnson City, ships some 15 million rainbow-trout eggs all over the nation. There are nature trails, picnic areas, and a visitor center. | 520 Federal Hatchery Rd., Erwin | 423/743–4712 | Free | Weekdays 7–3:30.

Hands On! Regional Museum. The interactive exhibits, programs, and classes here are geared toward children under 12. Among the more than 20 permanent hands-on exhibits are re-creations of a TV station, a TVA dam, an airplane cockpit, and a coal mine. | 315 E. Main St. | 423/434–4263 | www.handsonmuseum.org | $5 | Tues.–Fri. 9–5, Sat. 10–5, Sun. 1–5.

Carroll Reece Museum. On the East Tennessee State University campus, this museum focuses on regional art and history. Three of the six galleries are reserved for traveling exhibits; the others display the permanent collection, which includes antique toys, musical instruments, and artifacts related to early settlers. | 807 University Pkwy. | 423/929–4392 or 423/929–6340 | http://cass.etsu.edu/museum cass.etsu.edu/museum | Free | Weekdays 9–4, weekends 1–4.

Rocky Mount Museum. From 1790 to 1791 the two-story log house known as Rocky Mount was the capital of the short-lived Southwest Territory. It is now a living-history museum in which costumed guides act out the roles and do the chores of a family in pioneer times. The adjacent Overmountain Museum is a modern structure with exhibits about life in the region in the late 18th century. Both are 4 mi east of Johnson City. | 200 Hyderhill Rd., Piney Flats | 423/538–7396 | $4 | Memorial Day–Labor Day, daily 9–5; other times call for hours.

Tipton-Hayes Historic Site. This 1798 complex was the estate of one of the founders of Tennessee. The historic site now features 10 original and restored buildings, including a horse barn, granary, smokehouse, and law office. You may also stroll through an herb garden and explore a nearby cave. | 2620 S. Roan St. | 423/926–3631 | www.tipton-hayes.org | Free | Apr.–Oct., daily; Nov.–Mar., weekdays.

Unicoi County Heritage Museum. Originally built as the residence for the superintendent of the Erwin National Fish Hatchery (and located on its grounds), this turn-of-the-century frame house now preserves the history of this small mountain community. The museum collection includes Blue Ridge Pottery from a defunct area factory, early railroad memorabilia, Native American artifacts, antique wedding dresses, and a photograph of the hanging of a circus elephant that killed its trainer in 1916. | 1715 Johnson City Hwy., Erwin | 423/743–9449 | $1 | May–Dec., daily 1–5.

ON THE CALENDAR

NOV.: *Christmas Parade.* Held on the Saturday before Thanksgiving, this parade starts at East Tennessee State University on State of Franklin St.; area marching bands and numerous floats march 2 miles to downtown Johnson City. The parade route changes annually. | 423/461–8000.

Dining

Fifi's. Middle Eastern. The city's only genuine Middle Eastern fare is served here. The many vegetarian dishes such as tabouli, hummus, and baba ganoush are complemented by meaty entrées like beef shawarma and lamb kabob. Belly dancers entertain patrons twice a month. | 803 W. Walnut St. 37604 | 423/232–1818 | $4–$7 | No credit cards | Closed Sun.

Firehouse. Barbecue. Appropriately located in an authentic 1930 firehouse, this restaurant offers a casual atmosphere warmed by an open fireplace and decorated with plenty of firefighter memorabilia. The pulled-pork sandwich and baby back ribs are recommended. Private rooms are available for parties. Kids' menu. | 627 W. Walnut St. | 423/929–7377 | $9–$20 | AE, MC, V.

Galloways Restaurant. American/Casual. The two-story brick house from the early 1900s was known as the Williamsburg Tea Room in the middle part of the 20th century. Today Galloways occupies the same space, serving dishes like beef Wellington, veal Marsala, filet mignon, and a variety of fresh fish entrées. Outdoor dining is available on the porch, which wraps around the entire house. The desserts are all homemade. | 807 N. Roan St. 37604 | 423/926–1166 | $12–$25 | AE, D, MC, V | Closed Sun. No lunch Sat.

Makato. Japanese. Makato is a spacious facility with five distinct dining areas, decorated in a Japanese motif. Murals depict Japanese themes. Visit the sushi bar or try the grilled tuna or filet mignon. Private room are available. Kids' menu. | 3021 Oakland Ave. | 423/282–4441 | $9–$40 | AE, D, DC, MC, V.

Peerless. Seafood. This casual family restaurant has been family owned and operated for 60 years. Specialties include filet mignon, grilled salmon, and Grecian salads. The dining room is spacious and decorated with pictures of famous people who have dined there; banquet halls and private rooms are available. Kids' menu. | 2531 N. Roan St. | 423/282–2351 | $12–$21 | AE, D, DC, MC, V | Closed Sun. No lunch.

Lodging

Comfort Inn. Just off I–181 at Exit 31, this two-story hotel is 2 mi east of Cherokee National Forest and next door to a golf course. Complimentary Continental breakfast. Microwaves, refrigerators, some in-room hot tubs, cable TV. Laundry service. Pets allowed (fee). | 1900 S. Roan St. | 423/928–9600 | fax 423/928–0046 | 143 rooms | $56–$109 | AE, D, DC, MC, V.

Days Inn. These are the largest hotel rooms in the city, and they're conveniently located on I–181, a five-minute walk to malls, and a five-minute drive south to downtown. The grounds include gardens, a courtyard, and an outdoor pool. Restaurant, bar, room service. Refrigerators, cable TV. Pool. Laundry facilities. Business services. Some pets allowed. | 2312 Brown's Mill Rd. | 423/282–2211 | fax 423/282–6111 | 102 rooms | $45–$50 | AE, D, DC, MC, V.

Fairfield Inn by Marriott. This is a good budget motel in the center of town, across from a mall. Complimentary Continental breakfast. In-room data ports, cable TV. Pool. Business services. | 207 E. Mountcastle Dr. | 423/282–3335 | 132 rooms | $40–$57 | AE, D, DC, MC, V.

Garden Plaza. This five-story hotel is 1 mi off I–181 and 2 mi north of downtown. For those fitness-minded travelers, a complimentary shuttle is offered to a local health club. Restaurant, bar, complimentary Continental breakfast, room service. Cable TV. Indoor/outdoor pool.

Business services, airport shuttle. Some pets allowed. | 211 Mockingbird La. | 423/929–2000 or 800/342–7336 | 186 rooms | $85–$100 | AE, D, DC, MC, V.

Hampton Inn. A typical, newly renovated representative of the popular chain, this hotel offers biscuits and gravy in the morning. It's located on the west side of Johnson City, near East Tennessee University and a short drive to restaurants and shopping. Complimentary Continental breakfast. Some minibars, refrigerators, cable TV. Pool. Business services. | 508 State of Franklin Rd. | 423/929–8000 | fax 423/929–3336 | www.hamptoninn.com/hi/johnsoncity | 77 rooms | $66–$71 | AE, D, DC, MC, V.

Holiday Inn. Near the convention center and only two blocks off I–181, this six-story hotel is also within walking distance of malls and restaurants. Restaurant, bar. In-room data ports, cable TV. Pool. Beauty salon. Exercise equipment. Business services, airport shuttle. | 101 W. Springbrook Dr. | 423/282–4611 | fax 423/283–4869 | 205 rooms | $71–$85 | AE, D, DC, MC, V.

Howard Johnson Plaza. Off I–181, this hotel appeals to those who are just passing through. Restaurant, bar with entertainment. Cable TV. Pool. Laundry facilities. Business services. Airport shuttle. | 2406 N. Roan St. | 423/282–2161 | fax 423/282–2488 | 197 rooms | $59–$64 | AE, D, DC, MC, V.

Red Roof Inn Johnson City. About 3 mi north of downtown, just off I–181 at Exit 35, this three-story motel is adjacent to the Johnson City Mall. In-room data ports, cable TV. Business services. Pets allowed. | 210 Broyles St. | 423/282–3040 | fax 423/283–0673 | 115 rooms | $57–$75 | AE, D, MC, V.

Sleep Inn of Johnson City. Just off I–181 at Exit 36, this three-story hotel sits on the northern edge of town. You have complimentary access to a nearby gym. Complimentary Continental breakfast. In-room data ports, some microwaves, some refrigerators, cable TV. Business services. | 925 W. Oakland Ave. | 423/915–0081 | fax 423/915–0029 | 76 rooms | $70–$78 | AE, D, DC, MC, V.

Super 8. For the travelers who wait until late night to find a place to sleep, this motel has a 24-hour desk and snack shop. You can't miss it—even in the dark—it's right on I–181, near plenty of restaurants and a racetrack. Cable TV. Laundry facilities. Business services. | 108 Wesley St. | 423/282–8818 | 63 rooms | $36–$75 | AE, D, DC, MC, V.

JONESBOROUGH

MAP 12, H5

(Nearby towns also listed: Elizabethton, Greeneville, Johnson City, Tusculum)

Laid out in 1780 and rich in history, Jonesborough is the oldest incorporated town in the state. It was the capital of "The Lost State of Franklin," a 1784 attempt to create a new state in Tennessee territory, and future U.S. President Andrew Jackson was admitted to the bar here in 1788. In 1819, *Manumission Intelligence,* the first U.S. newspaper devoted exclusively to the abolition of slavery was published in Jonesborough. Today the town's primary occupation is tourism. Visitors flock to its beautifully restored historic district and its annual story-telling festival.

Information: **Jonesborough Visitors Center** | 117 Boone St., Jonesborough 37659 | 423/753–1010.

Attractions

Historic District. One of the state's top attractions, downtown Jonesborough boasts about 40 18th- and 19th-century buildings, most of which are still in use. A walk down the brick sidewalks and along the wrought-iron fences will lead you past the Chester Inn (*see below*), the Christopher Taylor House (one of the oldest log structures in the state), the May-Ledbetter House (built in 1905 and the first house in town with indoor plumbing), and the Griffith-Lyle House (former home of an early photographer). Tours are available through the Jonesborough Visitors Center. | Main St. and adjacent streets | 423/753–5961 | Free | Daily.

Chester Inn. The oldest frame structure in Jonesborough, built in 1797, once hosted Andrew Jackson and Charles Dickens. It is now the site of the National Storytelling Festival. | 116 W. Main St. | 423/753–5961 | Free | Daily.

Jonesborough Visitors Center and History Museum. Stop here to get a map of the historic district or to sign up for a guided tour. The museum's permanent exhibits offer a glimpse of life on the early frontier. Behind the visitor center is Duncan's Meadow, site of a duel fought by Andrew Jackson. | 117 Boone St. | 423/753–1015 | $2 | Weekdays 8–5, weekends 10–5.

ON THE CALENDAR
JULY: *Jonesborough Days.* The old-fashioned Fourth of July celebration features crafts, food, and fireworks. | 423/753–5281.

AUG.: *Quilt Fest.* Since 1991 quilters have gathered the first weekend of August to display their creations, attend classes, and listen to a keynote speaker. About 40 classes are held around town, and as many as 75 quilts are displayed. | 423/753–6644.

OCT.: *National Storytelling Festival.* It's a three-day celebration of stories, oral traditions, and tall tales from around the world. Register for performances far in advance—it's a very popular event. | 423/753–2171 or 800/525–4514.

DEC.: *Christmas in Jonesborough.* A 12-day event culminating in a Christmas parade down Main Street.

Dining
Dillworth Dining. Southern. Old-time photographs and an exposed kitchen in the center of the dining room set the stage for pintos and relish, cornbread, and a variety of specialty steaks. | 105 E. Main St. | 423/753–9009 | $4–$11 | AE, D, MC, V.

Parson's Table. Continental. Decorated in a Victorian, floral style, this restaurant is known for its rack of lamb and shellfish medley. The name reflects the building's former life as a 19th-century place of worship. Sun. buffet. Kids' menu. | 102 Woodrow Ave. | 423/753–8002 | $20–$32 | AE, D, MC, V | Closed Mon. and Jan. No dinner Sun.

Lodging
Eureka Hotel. This hotel first opened in 1900, and a three-year renovation was completed in 1999. Now it has the original floors, antiques from the early 1900s, and wallpaper modeled after the original patterns. Complimentary breakfast. In-room data ports, cable TV. No pets. No smoking. | 127 W. Main St. | 423/913–6100 | fax 423/913–0429 | www.eureka-jonesborough.com | 16 rooms | $89–$199 | AE, D, MC, V.

KINGSPORT

MAP 12, H5

(Nearby towns also listed: Bristol, Elizabethton, Johnson City, Rogersville)

Kingsport, a model industrial city, was developed by planners in the early 20th century. It began as a port town along the Holston River in the 1760s, but Long Island, in the river near town, was an important spot long before Kingsport was settled. Traditionally it was the sacred place of the Cherokee, and became a gathering place for white settlers in the area. Ultimately the last all-out battle between the Cherokee and new residents was fought here.

With the arrival of the railroad in 1909, the city fathers brought in consultants from Massachusetts and New York City to help them create the perfect industrial city. The plan was simple—factories would line the river, houses would be built on the hills. It worked beyond their wildest dreams, most notably when in 1920 George Eastman of

KINGSPORT

INTRO
ATTRACTIONS
DINING
LODGING

Kodak opened the Eastman Chemical Company here, to this day a major employer. The negative side of the plan was pollution—Kingsport cleaned up in the 1970s, but the problem remains.

Information: **Kingsport Convention and Visitors Bureau** | 151 E. Main St., Kingsport 37662 | 423/392–8820 or 800/743–5282.

Attractions

Bays Mountain Park. Some claim that the 3,000 acres nestled between the Holston River Mountain and Bays Ridge constitute the nation's largest municipal park. One of the purposes of this site 15 miles from downtown is environmental education; there is a natural history museum, planetarium, and farmstead museum in addition to a nature preserve. You also may take nature tours of Bays Mountain Park Lake via barge and annual guided hikes by moonlight. | 853 Bays Mountain Park Rd. | 423/229–9447 | www.baysmountain.com | $3 per car | Daily.

Boone Dam and Lake. The 33-mi-long lake created by the Tennessee Valley Authority dam offers swimming, fishing, and boating. It's about 10 mi east of Kingsport. | 301 Boone Dam Rd. | 423/279–3500 | Free | Daily.

Exchange Place. This 1820s pioneer farmstead and stagecoach stop was once a place where travelers could exchange the different state currencies that existed in early America. Today you can tour the restored Main House, which offers a look at the lifestyle of a well-to-do family of the era, along with a handful of log structures that made up what was once a self-supporting plantation of over 1,400 acres. Period crafts, household chores, and farming methods are demonstrated in the summer. | 4812 Orebank Rd. | 423/288–6071 | Free | May–Oct., Thurs.–Fri. 10–2, Sat. 2–4:30, and by appointment.

Fort Patrick Henry Dam and Lake. The Tennessee Valley Authority dam impounds a 10-mi-long lake 5 miles south of downtown. There's swimming, fishing, and boating. | 3657 Fort Henry Dr. | 423/247–7891 | Free | Daily.

Warriors' Path State Park. On the shores of Fort Patrick Henry Lake, 2 mi southeast of Kingsport, the park offers water sports that include boating and waterskiing. Because the lake water is a little chilly for swimming, one of the area's largest outdoor pools was built, complete with a waterslide. Other activities include camping, hiking, horseback riding, picnicking, and golf. | 490 Hemlock Rd. | 423/239–8531 | Free | Daily.

Netherland Inn House Museum. Built along the Holston River by William King beginning in 1802 for the sole purpose of developing a boatyard from which to ship his salt, the building was sold to Richard Netherland at a sheriff's sale in 1818. Netherland immediately procured a stage contract and established the three-story building as an inn and tavern on the Great Old Stage Road, the main route to western Kentucky and middle Tennessee. It hosted presidents Andrew Jackson, Andrew Johnson, and James Polk. Today the inn is a museum, restored and furnished in period style. | 2144 Netherland Inn Rd. | 423/246–6262 | www.kingsport.com/netherlandinn | $3 | May–Oct., weekends 2–4.

ON THE CALENDAR

JULY: *Kingsport Fun Fest.* One of the state's most lively festivals offers concerts of all types, balloon races, puppet theater, a 5K run, and other activities. Most events are free. | 423/392–8809.

SEPT.: *Fall Folk Arts Festival.* The regional arts and crafts fair is held on the grounds of the early 19th-century stagecoach stop Exchange Place. | 423/288–6071.

Dining

Pratt's Barbecue Express. Barbecue. Barnwood and stone cover the walls, and the booths where you eat also are made from barnwood. The menu includes an all-you-can-eat barbecue buffet, as well as fried chicken and a choice of vegetables. | 1225 E. Stone Dr. | 423/246–2500 | $5 | AE, D, MC | No dinner.

Skoby's. American. Skoby's has dining areas with varied themes—there's one room with an East Orient theme, one decorated like a 1950s diner, one with an equestrian theme, and another offering a historical overview of the Eastman Chemical Company, which is nearby. Notable dishes include pasta Franscesca and broiled orange roughy filets. Kids' menu. | 1001 Konnarock Rd. | 423/245–2761 | $10–$30 | AE, D, DC, MC, V | No lunch.

Lodging
Comfort Inn. Mountain views are plentiful at this chain hotel located 5 mi east of downtown. There's a health spa on-site. Complimentary Continental breakfast. Some in-room hot tubs, cable TV. Pool. Hot tub, steam room. Laundry facilities. Business services. | 100 Indian Center Court | 423/378–4418 | fax 423/246–5249 | 121 rooms | $50–$75 | AE, D, DC, MC, V.

Cleek's Motel. If you don't mind spartan rooms, you can save a buck at this tiny cinderblock property, 6 mi northeast of town. Cable TV. Pets allowed ($10). | 2760 E. Stone Dr. | 423/288–9996 | none | 15 rooms | $34 | No credit cards.

Econo Lodge. Extra-large rooms (some with hot tubs) and coffee available 24 hours a day are some of the perks at this affordable motel, approximately 6 miles northeast of downtown. Complimentary Continental breakfast. Cable TV. Business services. | 1704 E. Stone Dr. | 423/245–0286 | fax 423/245–2985 | 52 rooms | $37–$55 | AE, D, DC, MC, V.

Ramada Inn. On U.S. 11E, south of I–181 and 6 mi east of downtown, this chain hotel is on a commercial strip with shopping and many restaurants. Restaurant, bar, room service. Cable TV. Pool. Tennis. Business services, airport shuttle. | 2005 La Masa Dr. | 423/245–0271 | fax 423/245–7992 | 193 rooms | $66–$150 | AE, D, DC, MC, V.

KNOXVILLE

INTRO
ATTRACTIONS
DINING
LODGING

KNOXVILLE

MAP 12, I2

(Nearby towns also listed: Caryville, Lenoir City, Maryville, Morristown, Norris, Oak Ridge, Walland)

A hilly East Tennessee town with a view of the Great Smoky Mountains, Knoxville is the third-largest city in the state and the home of the main campus of the University of Tennessee. The city began its existence in 1786 as a fort and territorial outpost. It was the state's first capital from 1796 to 1817 and later became a railroad and manufacturing center. Today, Knoxville's name is synonymous with energy—it's the headquarters of the Tennessee Valley Authority (TVA), which built and operates a vast complex of hydroelectric dams. From riverfront shops and restaurants to historic buildings and museums, this city can keep visitors quite busy.

Information: **Knoxville Area Convention and Visitors Bureau** | 601 West Summit Hill Dr., Suite 200B 37902 | 865/523–7263 or 800/727–8045 | www.knoxville.org.

Attractions

ART AND ARCHITECTURE
Sunsphere. This 26-story, golden-ball-topped tower is a remnant of the 1982 World's Fair—and the best place to get a birds-eye view of Knoxville. It's downtown. | 810 Clinch Ave. | 865/523–4228 | Free.

Tennessee Theater. The grand restored 1928 movie palace in the heart of downtown occasionally hosts plays and concerts but it is still primarily a movie theater. Films are preceded by a brief concert on "the mighty Wurlitzer." | 604 Gay St. | 865/522–1174 | Ticket prices vary | Call for schedule.

CULTURE, EDUCATION, AND HISTORY

Bleak House (Confederate Memorial Hall). This 15-room home in West Knoxville served as headquarters to Confederate General James Longstreet during the siege of Knoxville in 1863. The period-furnished 1858 house and Mediterranean-style gardens are owned and operated by the local chapter of the United Daughters of the Confederacy. | 3148 Kingston Pike SW | 865/522–2371 | $5 | Tues., Wed., Fri. 1–4.

Governor William Blount Mansion. The first frame house west of the Appalachians, this is one of the most historically significant buildings this side of the state. Built in 1792 overlooking the Tennessee River, it was the home of William Blount, the first and only governor (1790–1796) of the Southwest Territory and a signer of the U.S. Constitution. Unlike the log structures around it, the "mansion" had many glass windows; Indians living in the area at the time called it the "house with many eyes." Guided tours are offered of the restored house, which is furnished with pieces from the 1790s. | 200 W. Hill Ave. | 865/525–2375 | www.korrnet.org/blount96 | $5 | Mon.–Sat. 9:30–5.

Crescent Bend (Armstrong-Lockett House) and W. Perry Toms Memorial Gardens. Built in 1834, the house is furnished with the Toms Collection of 18th- and 19th-century English furniture. Terraced formal gardens stretch from the house to the banks of the Tennessee River. | 2728 Kingston Pike | 865/637–3163 | $4.50 | Mar.–Dec., Tues.–Sat. 10–4, Sun. 1–4.

Mabry-Hazen House. The 1858 house served as headquarters to both Confederate and Union forces during the Civil War. Today the stately restored building, listed on the National Historic Register, is home to hundreds of antiques and artifacts. Exhibits chronicle the dramatic story of the family that lived here in the Civil War era. | 1711 Dandridge Ave. | 865/522–8661 | $5 | Tues.–Fri. 10–5, Sat. 10–2.

McClung Historical Collection/East Tennessee Historical Center. This repository, open to the public, contains more than 38,000 volumes of history and genealogy about Tennessee and the Southeastern United States. | 314 W. Clinch Ave. | 865/215–8801 | Free | Daily.

Ramsey House (Swan Pond). This stately 1795 Georgian stone house (the county's first such structure) in East Knoxville was a center of social and political life in early East Tennessee. | 2614 Thorngrove Pike | 865/546–0745 | $4 | Apr.–Dec., Tues.–Sat. 10–4, Sun. 1–4; Dec.–Apr., by appointment.

University of Tennessee, Knoxville. Founded in 1794, this public school adds cultural and intellectual energy to this vital city. More than 26,000 undergraduate and graduate students attend for degrees in more than 40 subjects. Located in downtown Knoxville on 290 acres. | W. Cumberland Ave., | 865/974–2184 | fax 865/974–6341 | www.utk.edu | Free to visitors.

MUSEUMS

AKIMA East Tennessee Discovery Center and AKIMA Planetarium. This hands-on family science museum in East Knoxville includes an aquarium, an apiary, and a planetarium. | 516 N. Beaman St., Chilhowee Park | 865/594–1494 | www.korrnet.org/etdc | $3 | Weekdays 9–5, Sat. 10–5.

Beck Cultural Exchange Center—Museum of Black History and Culture. Exhibits at this East Knoxville museum chronicle the history of African-Americans in Knoxville, from slavery to the present. | 1927 Dandridge Ave. | 865/524–8461 | Free | Tues.–Sat. 10–6.

Ewing Gallery of Art and Architecture. The University of Tennessee's gallery presents the works of avant-garde artists and architects of international stature, as well as emerging artists. | 1715 Volunteer Blvd. | 865/974–3200 | Free | Mon.–Sat. 9–5, Sun. 1–5.

Knoxville Museum of Art. The state's newest and largest art museum, located in downtown Knoxville, is an attractive contemporary structure faced in pink Tennessee marble.

In addition to its permanent collection which consists of contemporary paintings, sculpture, prints, and mixed media works by such artists as Bessie Harvey and Robert Rauschenberg, the museum's four galleries host about 15 exhibits each year. | 1050 World's Fair Park Dr. | 865/525–6101 | www.knoxart.org | $4 | Tues.–Sun. 10–5.

Frank H. McClung Museum. The University of Tennessee's museum is known for its local natural history collection and its collection of American Indian artifacts, one of the best in the Southeast. It also has exhibitions on anthropology, archaeology, and ancient Egypt. | 1327 Circle Park Dr. | 865/974–2144 | www.mcclungmuseum.utk.edu | Free | Mon.–Sat. 9–5, Sun. 1–5.

PARKS, NATURAL AREAS, AND OUTDOOR RECREATION

Ijams Nature Center. The nonprofit environmental education center in South Knoxville has 80 acres of woods, meadows, and gardens. | 2915 Island Home Ave. | 865/577–4717 | www.ijams.org | Free | Daily, 8–dusk.

James White Fort. Located on a bluff overlooking the Tennessee River, this complex is at the site of the first settlement in Knoxville. The restored buildings, dating from 1786, include a loom house, a smokehouse, and a blacksmith's shop. Tours are given by well-versed guides in period clothing. | 205 E. Hill Ave. | 865/525–6514 | $5 | Mar.–mid-Dec., Mon.–Sat.; Jan.–Feb., weekdays 9:30–4:30.

SHOPPING

Knox County Regional Farmers' Market. Locally grown fruits, vegetables, fish, and meat are sold. You'll also find everything from regional honey, jams, and jellies to handmade quilts, pottery, and rocking chairs. | 4700 New Harvest La. | 865/524–3276 | Free | Daily.

Old City. A complex of 19th-century brick warehouses has been renovated to house one-of-a-kind stores, restaurants, and bars, and a variety of music clubs. You'll find no chains or national franchises in this East Knoxville neighborhood, 3 blocks from the banks of the Tennessee River. | Parallel to Jackson Ave. and Central St. | Free | Daily.

OTHER POINTS OF INTEREST

Knoxville Zoo. One of the best zoos in the South covers more than 80 acres of East Knoxville and is home to more than 1,000 animals. Most are housed in natural habitat environments. The zoo is known for breeding large cat species and African elephants. The petting zoo and Chimp Ridge are favorite attractions. | 3500 Knoxville Zoo Dr. | 865/637–5331 | www.knoxville-zoo.com | $8 | Daily.

ON THE CALENDAR

APR.: *Dogwood Arts Festival.* The blooming of the city's many dogwood trees is celebrated during this three-week long citywide festival with live entertainment arts, crafts and antique shows in Market Square Mall, at Market St. and Union St. In conjuction, the Tennessee Valley Authority across Market St. in TVA Tower hosts its annual TVA Art, Quilt and Photography Exhibits. Seven trails throughout the city showcase the dogwoods in full bloom. | 865/637–4561.

SEPT.: *Boomsday.* A fireworks display on the riverfront marks Labor Day. | 865/693–1020.

SEPT.: *Tennessee Valley Fair.* It's an old-fashioned country fair transplanted to an urban environment with music, rides, and agricultural and livestock contests. The fair takes place in East Knoxville's Chilhowee Park on Magnolia Ave. | 865/637–5840.

NOV.: *Foothills Craft Guild Fall Show and Sale.* There are more than 125 exhibitors of traditional and contemporary regional crafts at this event, which takes place at the Exhibition Center in downtown Knoxville's World's Fair Park on Henley St. | 865/483–6400.

Dining

INEXPENSIVE

Pete's Café. Southern. The owners and patrons are big Tennessee Vols fans here, so you'll see lots of University of Tennessee mementos at this hangout, which is a 10 to 15 minute walk from campus. The blue-plate special might include fried chicken or turkey and dressing with okra or green beans. | 603 Main Ave. | 865/525–8816 | $5–$7 | No credit cards | Closed weekends. No dinner.

MODERATE

Alex's Havana Café. Cuban. You can't go wrong with traditional fare like arroz con pollo and Cuban sandwiches. Bright Caribbean colors and pictures of Cuba enliven the room. There is also a patio for outdoor dining at this West Knoxville spot. | 5123 Homberg Dr., | 865/588–8681 | Closed Sun.–Mon. | $5–$15 | D, DC, MC, V.

Calhouns. Barbecue. Antiques and farm implements decorate the dining room of this rustic restaurant in West Knoxville. Enjoy prime ribs or pork sandwiches to the manager's musical selections. Kids' menu. | 10020 Kingston Pike | 865/673–3444 | www.calhouns.com | $8–$19 | AE, D, DC, MC, V.

Charlie Pepper's. Southwestern. Images of jalapeños abound at this West Knoxville restaurant, and there are witty touches like stuffed "jackalopes" as well. You should consider one of the innovatively prepared steaks, such as the Cajun-style with bleu cheese, or try the spinach-portabello mushroom quesadillas. | 242 Morrell Rd. | 865/291–9453 | $8–$15 | AE, D, DC, MC, V.

China Inn. Chinese. This West Knoxville restaurant offers a typical Chinese menu, including Peking duck and seafood. The familiar Chinese decor is dressed up with candlelight. | 6450 Kingston Pike | 865/588–7815 | $7–$22 | AE, D, MC, V.

Darryl's 1879. American. Antiques and chandeliers give this West Knoxville spot a sense of elegance, but there are no surprises on the menu, just solid standards like spare ribs and chicken parmesan. Contrary to what the name suggests, the restaurant was founded in 1979; its moniker pays homage to the University of Tennessee's founding in 1879. | 6604 Kingston Pike | 865/584–1879 | $6–$18 | AE, D, DC, MC, V.

Naples. Italian. The dining room of this medium-sized restaurant in East Knoxville is decorated with red-and-white checked tablecloths, candlelight, and walls covered salon-style with framed artwork. The rustic menu includes seafood fettuccine and lasagna, as well as a special kids' menu. | 5500 Kingston Pike | 865/584–5033 | No lunch Sat., Sun. | $7–21 | AE, D, DC, MC, V.

Sullivan's Fine Foods. American. This casual place in West Knoxville offers down-home country cooking and blue-plate specials, including meat loaf and pork loin. You can eat on the patio, shaded by a large maple tree. | 7545 N. Shore Drive | 865/694–9696 | $10–$17 | AE, DC, MC, V.

The Tomato Head. Italian. The paintings on the walls, all by local artists, change monthly, giving this downtown Knoxville place an ever-changing look. The sundried tomato pizza is dynamite, and the calzone really stick to your ribs, too. | 12 Market Sq. | 865/637–4067 | $6–$20 | AE, MC, V | Closed Sun.

EXPENSIVE

Butcher Shop. Steak. The Butcher Shop is housed in a former depot for the L&N Railroad in downtown Knoxville. It's an old brick building, with exposed ceilings, two large banquet rooms decorated with paintings and railroad memorabilia, and four large open charcoal barbecue pits, where customers can grill their own steaks, from prime rib to filet mignon. Kids' menu. | 806 World Fair Park Dr. | 865/637–0204 | $15–25 | AE, D, DC, MC, V | No lunch.

The Chef Bistro. French. Diners enjoy an intimate, casual bistro atmosphere at this restaurant in West Knoxville. Dine on scallops in saffron sauce or filet mignon, while French music and candles set the mood. | 5003 Kingston Pike | 865/584–1300 | Closed Sun. No dinner Mon. | $15–$23 | No credit cards.

Michael's. Continental. This is a dual-purpose facility in West Knoxville that includes a separate nightclub/lounge featuring live DJs on the weekends. The restaurant is an intimate spot for casual candlelit dinners, featuring brass, oak, beveled glass, a fireplace, and an atrium in the lobby. Steak Onassis and peppercorn strip steak are specialties. Kids' menu. | 7049 Kingston Pike | 865/588–2455 | Reservations required on football weekends | No lunch | $12–$30 | AE, D, DC, MC, V.

VERY EXPENSIVE

Chesapeake's. Seafood. This cavernous restaurant in downtown Knoxville sports a nautical theme—from the lobster pots, model ships, large aquarium, and stuffed fish mounted on the walls, it evokes the Maryland coast. Its fresh seafood includes Maine lobster and Maryland crab cakes. Two private rooms and an open-air dining area overlooking a garden are available. Kids' menu. | 500 N. Henley St. | 865/673–3433 | www.coppercellar.com | $15–$30 | AE, D, DC, MC, V.

The Orangery. Continental. This old-world restaurant in West Knoxville is decorated with elegant European antiques and crystal chandeliers. Dine on beef Wellington or rack of lamb to a background of live piano music and soft lighting. | 5412 Kingston Pike | 865/588–2964 | Closed Sun. No lunch Sat. | $17–35 | AE, DC, MC, V.

Lodging

INEXPENSIVE

Days Inn. This typical chain motel (with external entrances) is 12 mi east of downtown restaurants and shopping. Complimentary breakfast. Cable TV. Pool. Some pets allowed (fee). | 200 Lovell Rd. | 865/966–5801 | fax 865/966–1755 | www.daysinn.com | 120 rooms | $43–$75 | AE, D, DC, MC, V.

Executive Inn. These rooms aren't fancy, but there are lots of chain restaurants and stores within a block or two. It's 1½ miles north of downtown. Cable TV. Outdoor pool. | 3400 Chapman Hwy. | 865/577–4451 | 63 rooms | $30–$70 | AE, D, DC, MC, V.

Microtel of Knoxville. This no-frills three-story motel 15–20 minutes east of downtown has an elevator. In-room data ports, cable TV. Pets allowed ($10 deposit). | 309 N. Peters Rd. | 865/531–8041 | fax 865/539–1792 | 105 rooms | $44 | AE, D, DC, MC, V.

Red Roof Inn. These chain accommodations are in a commercial area, about 5 mi north of downtown and 10 mi northwest of the zoo. In-room data ports, cable TV. Business services. Some pets allowed. | 5640 Merchants Center Blvd. | 865/689–7100 | fax 865/689–7974 | www.redroof.com | 84 rooms | $36–$64 | AE, D, DC, MC, V.

Red Roof Inn–West. Standard accommodations off I-40, 12 mi west of downtown. Convenient to restaurants and malls. In-room data ports, cable TV. Business services. Some pets allowed. | 209 Advantage Pl. | 865/691–1664 | fax 865/691–7210 | www.redroof.com | 115 rooms | $34–$70 | AE, D, DC, MC, V.

MODERATE

Best Western Highway Host. This member of the popular lodging chain is 15 minutes north of downtown and less than 20 mi from two major shopping malls and the airport. Several restaurants are within walking distance. Restaurant, bar. Cable TV. Indoor pool. Hot tub. Video games. Laundry facilities. Business services. Free parking. Some pets allowed. | 118 Merchants Dr. | 865/688–3141 | fax 865/687–4645 | 213 rooms | $59–$92 | AE, D, DC, MC, V.

Baymont. Conveniently located hotel, 20 minutes west of downtown, is near restaurants, a movie theater, an antiques mall, and other shopping. Complimentary Continental breakfast. Some refrigerators, cable TV. Pool. Exercise equipment. Laundry facilities. Business services. Some pets allowed. | Campbell Lakes Dr. | 865/671–1010 | fax 865/675–5039 | 98 rooms | $61–$85 | AE, D, DC, MC, V.

Best Western—Luxbury. More than 50 restaurants are within 2 mi of this conveniently located West Knoxville hotel—some within walking distance. Shopping, movie theaters, and a sports bar are also nearby. Complimentary Continental breakfast. In-room data ports, minibars, some refrigerators, cable TV. Pool. Business services. Free parking. | 420 N. Peters Rd. | 865/539–0058 | fax 865/539–4887 | www.bestwestern.com | 97 rooms, 23 suites | $66–$72 | AE, D, DC, MC, V.

Budget Inn. There's a park one block away and restaurants within walking distance from this chain hotel, which is 15 mi west of downtown. Restaurant, bar. Room service, cable TV. Indoor pool. Business services. Some pets allowed. | 323 Cedar Bluff Rd. | 865/693–7330 | fax 865/693–7383 | 178 rooms | $52–$68 | AE, D, DC, MC, V.

Comfort Inn. This standard chain motel with exterior entrances is within walking distance of restaurants, 5 mi north of downtown. Complimentary Continental breakfast. Cable TV. Pool. Business services. | 5334 Central Ave. Pike | 865/688–1010 | fax 865/687–8655 | www.comfortinn.com | 100 rooms | $55–$80 | AE, D, DC, MC, V.

Days Inn. This no-frills hotel is conveniently located in downtown Knoxville. Cable TV. Business services. Some pets allowed (fee). | 1706 W. Cumberland Ave. | 865/521–5000 | www.daysinn.com | 119 rooms | $55–$65 | AE, D, DC, MC, V.

Hampton Inn. Restaurants, the zoo, and shopping malls are all easily accessed from this South Knoxville hotel. Complimentary Continental breakfast. In-room data ports, cable TV. Pool. Exercise equipment. Business services. | 117 Cedar La. | 865/689–1011 | fax 865/689–7917 | www.hamptoninn.com | 130 rooms | $65–70 | AE, D, DC, MC, V.

Howard Johnson Plaza. This four-story standby is on I-75, across from a mall in West Knoxville. Guests enjoy live music in the lobby on weekend evenings. Restaurant, bar with entertainment, room service. In-room data ports, cable TV. Pool. Business services. Some pets allowed (fee). | 7621 Kingston Pike | 865/693–8111 | fax 865/690–1031 | www.hojo.com | 162 rooms | $59–$79 | AE, D, DC, MC, V.

La Quinta Motor Inn. Guests can enjoy area attractions, restaurants, and shopping from this West Knoxville base camp less than 2 mi from almost everything. Complimentary Continental breakfast. In-room data ports, cable TV. Pool. Laundry facilities. Business services. Some pets allowed. | 258 Peters Rd. N | 865/690–9777 | fax 865/531–8304 | www.laquinta.com | 130 rooms | $58–$78 | AE, D, DC, MC, V.

La Quinta Inn. Surrounded by restaurants and other hotels, this five-story La Quinta, off I-75, is also about 8 mi from a shopping mall and movie theater. Just 15 minutes north of downtown. Complimentary Continental breakfast. In-room data ports, cable TV. Pool. Some pets allowed. | 5634 Merchants Center Blvd. | 865/687–8989 | fax 865/687–9351 | www.laquinta.com | 123 rooms | $49–$75 | AE, D, DC, MC, V.

Super 8. Area attractions, restaurants, and a large shopping mall are not far from this two-story chain motel in West Knoxville. Cable TV. Pool, wading pool. Hot tub. Exercise equipment. Business services. Some pets allowed. | 6200 Paper Mill Rd. | 865/584–8511 | www.super8.com | 139 rooms | $54–$95 | AE, D, DC, MC, V.

EXPENSIVE

Candlewood Suites. It's the extras like recliners, oversized desks, plants, and cheery pictures, that make these rooms as close to home as you can find in a chain. Another nice touch is the shop where you can buy what you need to prepare your own meals. The hotel is 10 mi west of downtown Knoxville, off I-40. In-room data ports, kitchenettes, microwaves, refrigerators. Cable TV. Exercise equipment. No pets. | 10206 Parkside Dr. | 865/777–0400 | fax 865/777–0401 | www.candlewoodsuites.com | 75 rooms, 23 suites | $85–$130 | AE, D, DC, MC, V.

Comfort Suites. An antiques mall, zoo, and shopping mall are all within 10 blocks of this well-equipped hotel, which is 15 mi west of downtown. Complimentary Continental breakfast. Microwaves, refrigerators, ome in-room hot tubs, cable TV. Indoor pool. Hot tub. Exercise equipment. Laundry facilities. Business services. | 811 N. Campbell Station Rd. | 865/675–7585 | www.comfortinn.com | 59 suites | $69–$109 | AE, D, DC, MC, V.

Courtyard by Marriott. Restaurants, stores, and movie theaters are within walking distance of this hotel, 15 mi west of downtown. As the name suggests, some rooms have balconies with views of the courtyard. Restaurant. Air conditioning, microwaves, some refrigerators, some in-room hot tubs, cable TV. Indoor pool. Exercise equipment. Laundry facilities. Business services. | 216 Langley Pl. | 865/539–0600 | www.marriott.com | 78 rooms | $84–$104 | AE, D, DC, MC, V.

Holiday Inn West. In a residential neighborhood 4 mi west of downtown but east of Knoxville's suburban commercial center, this Holiday Inn offers a cozy family atmosphere and rooms overlooking a courtyard. The restaurant is cafeteria-style, but there are numerous eateries within 3 mi. The hotel is only minutes from the biggest mall in town and two movie theaters. Restaurant, bar with entertainment, picnic area, room service. Cable TV. Pool. Hot tub. Laundry facilities. Business services. Some pets allowed. | 1315 Kirby Rd. | 865/584–3911 | fax 865/588–0920 | www.holiday-inn.com | 240 rooms | $80–$119 | AE, D, DC, MC, V.

Signature Inn–Cedar Bluff. This early '90s property offers clean, well-kept rooms. It's in West Knoxville, 7 mi west of downtown and 15 minutes from the airport. | 12++X: ++4 rooms. Complimentary Continental breakfast. In-room data ports, cable TV. Pool. Exercise equipment. Business services. | 209 Market Place La. | 865/531–7444 or 800/526–3766 | $77–$80 | AE, D, DC, MC, V.

Wyndham Garden Hotel. This simple but elegant property 7 miles from downtown is the only full-service hotel in West Knoxville. It's within walking distance of restaurants and across the street from a couple of shopping centers. Restaurant, bar, room service. In-room data ports, some kitchenettes, some minibars, refrigerators, cable TV. Pool. Hot tub. Exercise equipment. Laundry facilities. Business services. | 208 Market Place La. | 865/531–1900 | fax 865/531–8807 | www.wyndham.com | 120 rooms, 17 suites | $75–$92; $117–$127 suites | AE, D, DC, MC, V.

VERY EXPENSIVE

Hilton. Full-service hotel with typical amenities and services. This 18-story property is downtown. Restaurant, bar, room service. In-room data ports, some refrigerators, cable TV. Pool. Sauna. Exercise equipment. Business services, parking (fee). | 501 Church Ave. SW | 865/523–2300 | fax 865/525–6532 | www.hilton.com | 318 rooms, 8 suites | $99–$139; $230–$375 suites | AE, D, DC, MC, V.

Holiday Inn Select–Downtown. Downtown in Knoxville's business disctrict, this property is highly accessible to the convention center. Restaurant, bar. In-room data ports, some refrigerators, cable TV. Indoor pool. Hot tub. Exercise equipment. Laundry facilities. Business services, free parking. | 525 Henley St. | 865/522–2800 | fax 865/523–0738 | www.holiday-inn.com | 288 rooms, 5 suites | $90–$180; $250–$400 suites | AE, D, DC, MC, V.

★ **Hyatt Regency.** The eight-story atrium lobby adds to the sleek, modern feel of this full-service hotel. It's situated on a hill overlooking the Tennessee River. Restaurants, bar. Cable TV. Pool. Beauty salon. Exercise equipment. Playground. Business services, airport shuttle. Some pets allowed (fee). | 500 Hill Ave. SE | 865/637–1234 | fax 865/637–1193 | 385 rooms, 20 suites | $130–$160; $175–$425 suites | AE, D, DC, MC, V.

Maple Grove Inn. When you stay at this 1799 Georgian mansion in West Knoxville, you'll be surrounded by 16 wooded acres that are full of dogwoods and magnolias. Four-poster beds are in every room, and one is furnished with wicker pieces. Complimentary break-

fast. Cable TV, some in-room VCRs. Outdoor pool. Tennis. No pets. No kids under 12. No smoking. | 8800 Westland Dr. | 865/690–9565 or 800/645–0713 | fax 865/690–9385 | www.maplegroveinn.com | 6 rooms, 2 suites | $125–$200 | AE, MC, V.

Maplehurst Inn. From the outside, this house built in 1917 doesn't look like much, but it's regal inside. Floral quilts cover handcarved walnut and cherry beds, and there is a pre–World War I Baldwin piano. It's in downtown Knoxville within a ten block walk of museums, restaurants, and the Tennessee River Boat. Complimentary breakfast. Some in-room hot tubs, cable TV. Some pets allowed. | 800 W. Hill Ave. | 865/523–7773 or 800/451–1562 | www.maplehurstinn.com | 11 rooms | $89–$149 | MC, V.

Masters Manor Inn. The first thing you'll see upon entering this 1894 manor, now a B&B, is an ornate staircase with a sturdy bannister. Rooms have huge windows and four-poster beds. The sprawling front porch is a great place to sit and gaze at the magnolia tree on the property. Complimentary breakfast. Cable TV. Laundry facilities. Pets allowed. No smoking. | 1909 Cedar La. | 865/219–9888 or 877/866–2667 | fax 865/219–9811 | www.mastersmanor.com | 6 rooms | $100–$150 | AE, MC, V.

Radisson. This downtown property is seven blocks from the University of Tennessee and also close to the convention center. The zoo is 1 mi away; the Old City is 2 minutes. Restaurant, bars. Cable TV. Indoor pool. Hot tub. Exercise equipment. Business services, free parking. | 401 W. Summit Hill Dr. | 865/522–2600 | fax 865/523–7200 | www.radisson.com | 195 rooms, 2 suites | $119–$129; $175–$350 suites | AE, D, DC, MC, V.

LAWRENCEBURG

MAP 12, D3

(Nearby towns also listed: Fayetteville, Hohenwald, Pulaski, Savannah, GA)

Davy Crockett lived near Lawrenceburg during its early years (it was founded in 1817), and the town has claimed him as their own. His home is now a museum, and a state park in the vicinity bears his name. The willingness of Tennesseans to volunteer during the Mexican War is honored by a noteworthy memorial in the Lawrenceburg town square. The response of the state's residents was so strong, in fact, that the state earned the nickname "Volunteer State," which it still preserves as its motto.

Information: Lawrence County Chamber of Commerce | 1609 N. Locust Ave., Lawrenceburg 38464 | 931/762–4911.

Attractions

David Crockett Cabin and Museum. A replica of the log cabin where the legendary frontiersman once lived is filled with period artifacts, including Crockett's personal papers and clothing. | S. Military Ave. | 931/762–4911 | Free | Weekdays 10–3.

David Crockett State Park. (*See* Tusculum.) The 1,100-acre park 1 mi W of town celebrates the pioneer, who moved his family to the area around 1817. There's an interpretive center with exhibits and a replica of Crockett's gristmill that is staffed in the summer. Visitors enjoy camping, swimming, fishing, hiking, boating, and tennis. | 1400 W. Gaines St. | 931/762–9408 | www.tnstateparks.com | Free | Daily.

Mexican War Monument. A monument on Courthouse Square honors the many Tennesseans who volounteered to fight in the Mexican War. | Public Sq. | 931/762–4911 | Free | Daily.

Old Jail Museum. The jail, built in 1872, is now a museum of local history. | Waterloo St. | 931/762–4911 | Free | By appointment only.

Tennessee Valley Jamboree. Bluegrass and gospel music is performed weekends during the summer at David Crockett State Park. Other shows are at the Lawerence administration building, downtown across from the courthouse. | 1709 Deer Hollow Dr. | 931/762–6249 | Free.

JUNE, SEPT.: *Summertown Bluegrass Reunion*. Although no big-name acts perform, the quality of local bluegrass and gospel musicians at this event is so good you may think the performers are pros. It takes place on the third weekend in June and again on Labor Day weekend, and is held in a lovely country area near Summerton, on Route 240, 13 mi north of Lawrenceburg, off U.S. 43. | 931/964–2100.

Dining
ShowRing Grill. Steak. The trophies, plaques, and pictures that decorate this locally renowned restaurant celebrate the owner's exceptional Chiangus cattle. You can dig into a New York strip or prime rib, or try the more modest steak and roast sandwich served on a homemade yeast roll. Much of the meat is from the restaurant's own herd of grain-fed cattle, and the remainder is prime Omaha steak. | 1202 N. Locust Ave. | 931/766–2882 | $7–$30 | AE, D, MC, V | Closed Sun.–Mon.

Lodging
The Granville House. Large columns and a porch punctuated with wicker furniture front this Victorian B&B built as a private home in 1886; there are period antiques and gas-log fireplaces inside. A gazebo decorates the courtyard out back. Some baths are shared. Located in the heart of town. Complimentary Continental breakfast. Cable TV. No pets. No smoking. | 229 Pulaski St. | 931/762–3129 or 800/366–9813 | 5 rooms | $70–$85 | AE, D, MC, V.

LEBANON

MAP 12, F2

(Nearby towns also listed: Cookeville, Gallatin, Hendersonville, Murfreesboro, Nashville)

This middle Tennessee town, founded in 1802, got its name from its large cedar trees, which reminded settlers of the cedars of Lebanon referred to in the Bible. Famous people that lived here include Andrew Jackson, Sam Houston, and Deford Bailey, who was the first African-American entertainer at the Grand Ole Opry. Today the town's ecomomy is based on light industry.

Information: **Lebanon/Wilson County Chamber of Commerce** | 149 Public Sq., Lebanon 37087 | 615/444–5503.

Attractions
Cedars of Lebanon State Park. The town of Lebanon is the gateway into this 831-acre park, which is within an 8,000-acre state forest and natural area. Unique flora abounds. Activities include swimming, hiking, and horseback riding. There are cabins and campsites. | 328 Cedar Forest Rd. | 615/443–2769 | fax 615/443–2793 | www.stateparks.com | Free | Daily.

Fiddler's Grove Historical Village. The village has 25 historic buildings, some dating from the early 1800s, some reproductions from that era. Among the structures are a general store and a print shop. | 945 Baddour Pkwy. | 615/443–2626 | Free | Daily.

Ju-Ro Stables. The stables run horseback riding excursions around Old Hickory Lake, 10 mi west of Lebanon. | 7149 Cairo Bend Rd., Mt. Julius | 615/449–6621 | www.jurostables.com | $20 per hour | Daily, call for appointment.

OCT. or NOV.: *Cedar Grove Cemetery Tour.* This annual event doesn't conform to a rigid agenda; in some years it takes place at the end of October, in others in the beginning of November, some years it's been held at night by candlelight, and in others during the day. The one constant is the guided tour of this hoary downtown cemetery, filled with moving portrayals of the lives of Civil War veterans, settlers, and prominent families. | 609 S. Maple St. 37087 | 615/444–5503.

Dining

Cherokee Steak House. Steaks. Mounted fish give this place a sporty look. Baby-back ribs are the house specialty, but everything from catfish to pork chops is available. | 450 Cherokee Dock Rd. | 615/444–9002 | $9–$18 | AE, D, DC, MC, V | Closed Mon. No lunch.

Sunset Restaurant. Southern. The look of this place is modest, but you'll be too busy digging in to your home-style meal to notice. You can get a variety of side dishes, from turnip greens to pinto beans, with your catfish or fried chicken. | 640 S. Cumberland St. | 615/444–9530 | $7–$12 | No credit cards | Closed Wed.

Uncle Pete's. Southern. Don't let the fact that this restaurant is in a 24-hour truck stop deter you: the food is delicious. The rolls, the size of your palm, are fresh and the meats come with three sides, which may include pinto beans and macaroni and cheese. Autographed photos of country-music stars line the walls. | 1210 Sparta Pike | 615/449–0030 | $5–$8 | AE, D, DC, MC, V | Breakfast also available.

Lodging

Best Western Executive Inn. Just a mile off the interstate, this chain hotel in downtown Lebanon sports country-inn decor. The property is close to convenience stores. Picnic area. Cable TV. 2 pools (1 indoor). Sauna. Business services. | 631 S. Cumberland St. | 615/444–0505 | fax 615/449–8516 | www.bestwestern.com | 125 rooms, 45 suites | $51–$69; $55–$89 suites | AE, D, DC, MC, V.

Comfort Inn. The rooms here are basic, but six restaurants are within walking distance and hotel amenties are plentiful. Located in South Lebanon. Complimentary Continental breakfast. Some microwaves, some refrigerators, cable TV. Outdoor pool. Hot tub, sauna. Health club. Business services. Pets allowed ($5). | 829 S. Cumberland St. | 615/444–1001 | fax 615/444–1002 | 76 rooms | $69–$89 | AE, D, DC, MC, V.

Days Inn. Right off I–40 and only five blocks south of downtown, this no-frills motor lodge is in a good location for those passing through Lebanon. Complimentary Continental breakfast. Some refrigerators, cable TV. Pool. Laundry facilities. Business services. Some pets allowed. | 914 Murfreesboro Rd. | 615/444–5635 | 52 rooms | $42–$60 | www.daysinn.com | AE, D, DC, MC, V.

Hampton Inn. This property is just off I–40, near gas stations and convience stores. It's a short drive to downtown Lebanon. Guests especially enjoy relaxing in the sauna and hot tub. Complimentary Continental breakfast. Cable TV. Pool. Exercise equipment. Business services. Some pets allowed. | 704 S. Cumberland St. | 615/444–7400 | fax 615/449–7969 | www.hampton-inn.com | 80 rooms, 6 suites | $55–$90; $105–$125 suites | AE, D, DC, MC, V.

Holiday Inn Express. The draw here is the convenient location, with numerous shops and an outlet mall within 3 blocks south of the hotel. Complimentary Continental breakfast. Some kitchenettes, some in-room hot tubs, cable TV. Outdoor pool. Hot tub. Health club. Laundry facilities. Business services. No pets. | 641 S. Cumberland St. | 615/444–7020 | fax 615/443–4185 | 50 rooms, 8 suites | $55–$80 | AE, D, DC, MC, V.

Shoney's Inn. On the commercial strip off I–40, this motel is near many restaurants and a mile from an outlet mall. Refrigerators, cable TV. Indoor pool. Business services. | 822 S. Cumberland St. | 615/449–5781 or 800/222–2222 | fax 615/449–8201 | www.shoneysinn.com | 111 rooms | $42–$62 | AE, D, DC, MC, V.

LENOIR CITY

(Nearby towns also listed: Athens, Crossville, Knoxville, Maryville, Oak Ridge, Sweetwater)

At the confluence of the Tennessee and the Little Tennessee Rivers, Lenoir City is near several of the large dams of the Tennessee Valley Authority system: Fort Loudoun Dam and Lake, Melton Hill Dam and Lake, and the Tellico Dam and Lake. Free tours of the hydropower dam and lock system are available at Fort Loudon Dam. The town was founded in 1907.

Information: Loudoun County Visitors Bureau | 318 Angel Row, Loudoun 37774 | 865/458–2067.

Attractions

Fort Loudoun Dam and Lake. The 14,600-acre lake 1 mi south of town is a good spot for fishing and boating. Free tours of the Tennessee Valley Authority dam and power plant are available by prior arrangement. | 1280 City Park Dr. | 865/986–7027 | Free | Daily.

Fort Loudoun State Historic Area. About 15 mi south of Lenoir City, this park's centerpiece is the reconstructed 18th-century British fort built when the land was still Cherokee country. You can hike and picnic on land or fish and boat on the lake. The visitor's center shows a 15-minute film. | 338 Fort Loudon Rd., Vonore | 423/884–6217 | Free | Daily.

Tellico Dam and Lake. Construction of this Tennessee Valley Authority dam was temporarily halted when it was thought that a newly discovered fish, known commonly as the snail-darter, only existed in the soon-to-be-devastated Little Tennessee River. Eventually the species was found elsewhere, and the project was completed in 1943. There's fishing and boating on the 15,680-acre lake east of downtown, and picnicking along its shores. | 1280 City Park Dr. | 865/986–3737 | Free | Daily.

ON THE CALENDAR

AUG.: *Smoky Mountain Fiddlers' Convention.* Two hundred or more bluegrass musicians compete in approximately 10 instrumental categories during the last weekend before Labor Day. Nearly 7,000 people attend the event, which is held at Legion Field in Loudon, 6 mi south of Lenoir City. The Loudon Merchants' Association sponsors an antique show at the same time, same place. | 865/458–9380.

Dining

Calhoun's. Barbecue. The restaurant sits beside Fort Loudon Lake, seats a whopping 500, and is full of mounted animals that stare down at you while you eat. The cooks make their own barbecue sauce here, and you can taste the difference. Most folks cry out for the baby back ribs, but prime rib is also a favorite. | 4550 City Park Dr. | 865/673–3366 | $10–$15 | AE, D, DC, MC, V | No lunch Mon.–Tues., Thurs., weekends.

Gerald's Smokehouse. Barbecue. Barbecue is big in Lenoir City, and this restaurant does you right. Three kinds of sauce are available, from mild to hot. The baby back ribs are the crowd pleaser, but prime rib is a good option, too. Prints by winners of the Dogwood Arts Festival hang on the walls. | 501 U.S. 321 N | 865/986–6159 | $6–$16 | AE, D, DC, MC, V | Closed Sun.

Lodging

The Captain's Retreat. This 1942 house, now a B&B, sits right beside Fort Lodoun Lake; you can loaf on the dock and watch the birds. The rooms are filled with antiques, and the central room has a cathedral ceiling. Meals are available on request. Complimentary Continental breakfast. Some in-room hot tubs, no room phones, TV in a common area. Lake. Dock.

No pets. No kids under 10. No smoking. | 3534 Lakeside Dr. | 865/986–4229 | fax 865/986–7421. | www.bbonline.com/tn/captains | 4 rooms | $95 | D, MC, V.

Days Inn. A nice, clean motel conveniently located off I–75, just 2 mi north of downtown. In-room data ports, some refrigerators, cable TV. Pool, wading pool. Business services. | 1110 U.S. 321 N | 865/986–2011 or 800/526–4658 | www.daysinn.com | 90 rooms | $40–$60 | D, DC, AE, MC, V.

The Mason Place. This restored 1865 plantation house 6 mi southwest of Lenoir is furnished with period antiques. Lovely fireplaces are scattered throughout; a honeymoon suite, called the smokehouse guest room, is available. Outdoors there's a swimming pool, gazebo, and porches overlooking 3 acres of forest. Complimentary candlelight breakfast. In-room VCRs, no room phones, cable TV in common area. Pool. No kids under 14. | 600 Commerce St., Loudon | 865/458–3921 | www.themasonplace.com | 5 rooms (shower only) | $96–$135 | No credit cards.

Ramada Inn. Conveniences like in-room coffee makes your stay more comfortable at this property 1 mi from downtown. Complimentary Continental breakfast. In-room data ports, some microwaves, some refrigerators, some in-room hot tubs, cable TV. Outdoor pool. Hot tub. Health club. Laundry facilities. Business services. No pets. | 400 Interchange Park Dr. | 865/986–9000 | fax 865/986–9000 | 34 rooms, 6 suites | $60–$95 | AE, D, DC, MC, V.

© Corbis

THE TENNESSEE WALKING HORSE

Tennessee is the only state in the union that's known for its very own breed of horse. The Tennessee walking horse is the product of a century of selective breeding of trotters and pacers in Middle Tennessee, resulting in a horse that has the smoothest ride of any in the world. The breed was developed by plantation owners and supervisors, who needed horses that could be ridden all day without exhausting either the horse or the rider. The walking horse has a natural "running walk," a smooth, four-beat gait that makes it exceptionally easy to ride. Because of its strength and endurance, it could also be used as a utility horse for plowing fields and pulling buggies. The breed's friendly and docile temperament was another plus; Roy Rogers' Trigger Jr. was a Tennessee walking horse.

Although horses are no longer an indispensable part of daily life, the handsome, gentle, intelligent Tennessee walking horse remains a popular riding and show horse; it is, in fact, the fastest growing breed in the nation. The headquarters of the Tennessee Walking Horse Breeders and Exhibitors Association in Lewisburg, Tennessee, features the Walking Horse Hall of Fame. The association sponsors the Tennessee Walking Horse Celebration in Shelbyville each August. The very best show horses of the breed are exhibited during the 10-day event, which attracts more than 200,000 people and offers more than $600,000 in prizes. Shelbyville is also the site of the Tennessee Walking Horse Museum. Another major walking horse event, the International Grand Championship Walking Horse Show, is held in Murfreesboro each August.

LEWISBURG

MAP 12, E3

(Nearby towns also listed: Columbia, Fayetteville, Hohenwald, Pulaski, Shelbyville)

Lewisburg was named for Meriwether Lewis of the Lewis and Clark expedition who founded the city in 1807. It is in the heart of middle Tennessee, which features rolling hills and bluegrass meadows that make perfect Tennessee walking horse territory. The headquarters of the Tennessee Walking Horse Breeders and Exhibitors Association is here.

Information: Marshall County Chamber of Commerce | 227 2nd Ave. N, Lewisburg 37091 | 931/359–3863.

Attractions

Henry Horton State Resort Park. 13 mi north of Lewisburg, the 1,135-acre park on the old estate of a former governor is popular with golfers. There's also swimming and tennis. Cabins and campsites are available. | 4201 Nashville Hwy., Chapel Hill | 931/364–2222 | Free | Daily.

Ladies' Rest Room. This is probably the most functional tourist attraction you'll ever see! The freestanding rest room was constructed in 1924 for the convenience of folks who could travel into town only seldom, and, when they did, had to spend long hours conducting business or shopping. The rest room structure is the only one of its kind left in the state. | Lewisburg town square | 931/359–3863 | Free | Daily dawn–dusk.

Tennessee Walking Horse Breeders and Exhibitors Association. The association's headquarters is the site of the Walking Horse Hall of Fame, featuring an exhibit on the Tennessee Walking Horse Celebration from 1939–to the present. | 250 N. Ellington Pkwy. | 931/359–1574 | www.twhbea.com | Free | Weekdays.

ON THE CALENDAR
JULY: *Miss Marshall County Pageant.* About 20 young women compete for this crown, amid many other events around town, including country music concerts, car shows, and golf and tennis tournaments. | 931/359–3863.

Dining
Cody's Fountain Square. American. Large church windows with stained glass compliment three ample dining rooms that seat 350 in all. Roast beef, fried chicken, and steak with shrimp are the crowd pleasers. | 105 N. 1st St. | 931/359–7488 | Breakfast also available weekends. No dinner Sun.–Thurs., no lunch Sat. | $10–$18 | AE, D, MC, V.

Lodging
Henry Horton Inn. Located on the grounds of the Henry Horton State Resort Park. this brick hotel has rooms with floral spreads and curtains. Some of the wood-frame cabins have working fireplaces. The property is 12 mi north of Lewisburg, on Rte. 31A. Some kitchenettes, some microwaves, some refrigerators, cable TV. Outdoor pool. No pets. No smoking. | 4201 Nashville Hwy., Chapel Hill | 931/364–2222 | www.tnstateparks.com | 65 rooms, 4 suites, 7 cabins | $64 rooms, $85 suites, $100 cabins | AE, D, DC, MC, V.

LYNCHBURG

MAP 12, F3

(Nearby towns also listed: Fayetteville, Shelbyville)

A tiny town with a population of 461 residents, Lynchburg is the home of the Jack Daniels Distillery, the nation's oldest registered distillery. This business is the only game

LYNCHBURG

INTRO
ATTRACTIONS
DINING
LODGING

in town, although there is a pleasant town square with a historic courthouse and a museum.

Information: **Lynchburg Chamber of Commerce** | 10 Mechanic St., Lynchburg 37352 | 931/759–4111.

Attractions

Jack Daniels Distillery. Each year more than 250,000 people take the free 80-minute tour of the nation's oldest (1866) registered distillery. You will see the charcoal brickyard, the fermentation vats, and the safe that killed Mr. Daniels. (He kicked it, got an infection, and died.) Don't expect samples of the famed Tennessee sourmash whiskey—this is a "dry" county. | 280 Lynchburg Hwy. | 615/320–5477 | www.jackdaniels.com | Free | Daily 9–4:30.

Moore County Courthouse. The bricks used in this 1873 courthouse were made right in Lynchburg. Memorials honoring those who died in war accent the grounds. | Public Sq. | 931/759–7346 | Free | weekdays 8–4:30, Sat. 8–noon.

ON THE CALENDAR

JUNE OR JULY: *Frontier Days and Rodeo.* Aside from the rodeo, you can clap along to traditional mountain music and tap your toes as cloggers and square dancers perform in the public square the weekend before July 4. There is a motorless parade of horses and buggies, a carnival, and craft booths. | 931/759–4111.

Dining

Mary Bobo's Boarding House. Southern. A hostess sits at each long communal table, rings a bell announcing the meal at 11 and 1 sharp, and leads discussions about the town's history and trivia. Eat all you can as you pass plates and bowls heaped with food. Two meats such as fried chicken or catfish are served along with six vegetables, bread, and dessert. | 925 Main St. | 931/759–7394 | Reservations essential | Closed Sun. No dinner | $13 | No credit cards.

Lodging

Lynchburg Bed and Breakfast. This 1877 home is painted a cream color and has a red tin roof. The rooms have crisp white linens and ruffled curtains, and are full of antiques such as a matching oak bedroom furniture. The home is one block from the Jack Daniels Distillery. Complimentary Continental breakfast. Cable TV. No pets. No smoking. | 107 Mechanic St. | 931/759–7158 | www.bbonline.com/tn/lynchburg | 3 rooms | $73 | MC, V.

MANCHESTER

MAP 12, F3

(Nearby towns also listed: McMinnville, Monteagle, Murfreesboro, Shelbyville)

Manchester, on the edge of the Cumberland Plateau on the banks of Duck River, was named for Manchester, England in hopes that it also would become an industrial center. Although that didn't come about, the town did become a center for regional arts and crafts.

Information: **Manchester Chamber of Commerce** | 110 E. Main St., Manchester 37355 | 931/728–7635.

Attractions

Foothills Crafts. A nonprofit association of 600 artisans displays and sells works in wood, clay, metal, glass, and fiber at this shop. | 418 Woodbury Hwy. | 931/728–9236 | Free | Daily.

Manchester Arts Center. In addition to its permanent art collection, the center exhibits works by local artists. A resident theater company stages performances here. | 909 Hillsboro Blvd. | 931/728–3434 | Free | Daily.

Normandy Lake. There's fishing, camping, and picnicking on and around the 3,160-acre lake 10 mi west of Manchester. | 158 Barton Springs Rd., Normandy | 256/386–2006 | Free | Daily.

Old Stone Fort State Archaeological Park. The 600-acre downtown park features structures built by Woodland Indians almost 2,000 years ago. There's also camping, fishing, and picnicking. | 732 Stonefront Dr. | 931/723–5073 | Free | Daily.

ON THE CALENDAR

OCT.: *Old Timer's Day.* Music, clogging, and a parade are the highlights of this downtown event. | 931/728–7635.

NOV.: *International Food Fair.* Don't let the name trick you: only area businesses are represented at this annual event. You can sample the specialties of numerous restaurants and coffee shops. The fair is held on the grounds of Central High School. | 931/728–7635.

Dining

Crockett's Roadhouse. American. You'll think you're in a rough-and-tumble roadhouse; inside and out, rough-cut lumber is used. Pork chops and the Roadhouse rib-eye marinated in Jack Daniels sauce are favorites. | 1165 Woodbury Hwy. | 931/728–2845 | $8–$22 | AE, D, MC, V.

Oak Family Restaurant. American. This dining room seats 200 and is decorated with local art. It's known for its prime rib, steak, and lasagna. Salad bar. Sun. buffet. Kids' menu. | 947 Interstate Dr. | 931/728–5777 | Reservations not accepted Sun. | $6–$15 | AE, D, MC, V.

Porky's Pit Barbecue. Barbecue. It's unnecessary to speak of style here, as it's take-out only. But you can leave this place with barbecue meat plus baked beans and potato salad. | 402 McMinnville Hwy. | 931/728–9648 | $2–$12 | No credit cards.

Lodging

Ambassador Inn and Luxury Suites. Comfortable rooms and newly remodeled corporate suites characterize this convenient hotel, 5 minutes from downtown near parks and restaurants. Complimentary Continental breakfast. Refrigerators, cable TV. Pool. Exercise equipment. | 925 Interstate Dr. | 931/728–2200 or 800/237–9228 | fax 931/728–8376 | www.ambassadorinn.com | 60 rooms, 45 suites | $52 rooms; $77 suites | AE, D, DC, MC, V.

Cumberland Motel. This place, built in 1952 less than a mile from downtown, still seems like a 1950s travel lodge. The rooms are decorated with vintage-style pine tongue-and-groove paneling, and nothing about them is fancy. Some microwaves, some refrigerators, cable TV. No pets. | 1203 Hillsboro Blvd. | 931/728–3561 | fax 931/723–4482 | 50 rooms | $25–$35 | MC, V.

Hampton Inn. The rooms here have sturdy hardwood furniture and cheery floral borders on the walls. Only ½ mi from downtown. Complimentary Continental breakfast. In-room data ports, some microwaves, some refrigerators, some in-room hot tubs, cable TV. Outdoor pool. Laundry services. Business services. Pets allowed (fee). | 33 Paradise St. | 931/728–3300 | fax 931/728–0159 | www.hampton-inn.com | 64 rooms, 8 suites | $75, $95 suites | AE, D, DC, MC, V.

Lord's Landing Bed and Breakfast. Children are welcome at this rural B&B set on 50 acres, 15 mi southeast of downtown Manchester. Rooms have private baths and fireplaces. There is also a barn with farm animals and a private air strip for pilots who fly in. Complimentary breakfast. No room phones. Pool. Jacuzzi rooms (4 rooms only). | 375 Lord's Landing La., Hillsboro | 931/467–3830 | www.lordslanding.com | 6 rooms, 1 suite | $95–$120, $150 suite | AE, D, DC, MC, V.

Super 8. Blues and greens are accented with floral patterns in the decor of this standard chain motel, 1½ mi of downtown. Complimentary Continental breakfast. Cable TV. Pool. Some pets allowed. | 2430 Hillsboro Hwy. | 931/728–9720 | www.super8.com | 50 rooms | $31–$45 | AE, D, DC, MC, V.

MARYVILLE

MAP 12, I3

(Nearby towns also listed: Gatlinburg, Knoxville, Lenoir City, Townsend, Walland)

The small mountain town of Maryville is steeped in the story of frontiersman and politican Sam Houston, who moved here from Virginia with his family in 1810 when he was 14 years old. He soon ran away to live with the Cherokee, and later taught for a year at what is now preserved as the Sam Houston Schoolhouse. Houston became an advocate for the Indians and, along with David Crockett, an opponent of Jackson's Indian Removal Act. Sent to Texas in 1832 to negotiate with the Mexicans, he decided to stay. He became president of the Republic of Texas and later governor when the territory became part of the United States.

Information: **Townsend Visitors Center** | 7906 E. Lamar Alexander Pkwy., Townsend 37882 | 865/448–6134.

Attractions

Maryville College. Maryville College, a school of liberal arts founded here in 1819, became one of the first colleges to admit women and one of the few to admit Indians and African-Americans. | 502 E. Lamar Alexander Pkwy. | 865/981–8000 | Free to visitors | Daily.

Sam Houston Schoolhouse. The future president of the Republic of Texas taught here in 1812. The small log structure features teaching artifacts, including a pair of lead knuckles with Houston's name carved in them. Built in 1794, this is considered the oldest schoolhouse in Tennessee. | 3650 Sam Houston School Rd. | 865/983–1550 | 50| Tues.–Sat. 10–5, Sun. 1–5.

ON THE CALENDAR

OCT.: *Foothills Fall Festival.* You can expect to hear all kinds of music at this event, from local jazz bands and national country groups to funk favorites like the Atlanta Rhythm Section. There are also arts and crafts, food booths, and games for the kids. The festival takes place on an early weekend in October at Greenbelt Park in downtown Maryville. | 865/983–2241.

Dining

Texas Roadhouse. Steak. Country-western music cranks out at this spot 5 miles north of Maryville, which features Native American murals and wood-paneled walls. The steaks are hand-cut and the meat of the Roadhouse ribs falls right off the bone. You'll also get sides like sweet potatoes or green beans. | 334 Fountainview Cir., Alcoa | 865/984–4140 | $12–$18 | AE, MC, V.

Lodging

Princess Motel. This motel is across the highway from several restaurants, 4–5 miles south of Maryville, and a walk to the golf course. Cable TV. Pool. | 2614 U.S. 411 S | 865/982–2490 | 30 rooms | $50–$60 | AE, D, DC, MC, V.

The Shamrock. Just 3 mi from downtown, this place is popular with folks who need affordable rooms for extended periods, such as traveling workers. The rooms are plain but they have views of the Smoky Mountains. Cable TV, no room phones. | 204 Courtyard Cir. | 865/984–6281 | 7 rooms | $38–$49 | No credit cards.

MCMINNVILLE

(Nearby towns also listed: Manchester, Murfreesboro)

McMinnville sits on the edge of the Cumberland Plateau, near the enormous and beautiful Cumberland Caverns, which are a National Landmark. Today the area is known as "the Nursery Capital of the World" for its many plant nurseries; young trees, bushes, and ornamental plants of all kinds are shipped from here. The town was founded in 1807 and is home to a number of pre–Civil War mansions.

Information: **McMinnville/Warren County Chamber of Commerce** | 110 South Court Square, McMinnville 37110 | 931/473–6611.

Attractions

Black House. Built before the Civil War in 1825, this attractive Federal-style building served as the home and office of a respected physician. Visitors can tour the residence and the office, which have period furnishings and equipment. | 301 E. Main St. | 931/668–5050 | Free | By appointment.

Cumberland Caverns Park. The second-largest cave system in the nation has been designated a National Landmark by the U.S. Department of the Interior. The caverns feature the usual stalagmites and stalactites, along with numerous pools and waterfalls. The Hall of the Mountain King, the largest cavern room in the eastern United States (600 ft long, 150 ft wide, 140 ft tall), is the site of an elaborate light and sound show. Tours range from 90 minutes to 14 hours. The caverns are a 15-minute drive east town. | 1437 Cumberland Caverns Rd. | 931/668–4396 | www.cumberlandcaverns.com | $9.75 | May–Oct., daily.

Fall Creek Falls State Park and Natural Area. One of the largest of the state parks (16,000 acres) is the site of three major waterfalls. Activities include fishing, hiking, swimming, horseback riding, and golf. There are campsites, cabins, and an inn. It's 40 mi southeast of town. | Rte. 3, Pikesville | 423/881–3241 | Free | Daily.

Rock Island State Rustic Park. This park 10 mi northeast of town has spectacular waterfalls. On its 883 acres are a 19th-century textile mill (still in operation) and an early hydroelectric plant. Activities include camping, swimming, fishing, and boating. | 82 Beach Rd., Rock Island | 615/686–2471 | Free | Daily.

ON THE CALENDAR

SEPT.: *Warren County Agricultural and Livestock Fair.* Sure, you get the expected events like tractor pulls and livestock shows, but this annual downtown fair is so much more. Everything takes place at Fairfield Village, 194 Fairground Road, which includes old and reproduction buildings, such as homes, a hospital, phone company, blacksmith shop, and even an ancient funeral home with all the embalming gear. Policemen patrol on horseback, and if you get out of line they'll toss you in a vintage jail cell. Held the second weekend in September. | 931/473–6611.

Dining

Pish-La-Ki Village. American. The name may be Indian (meaning pale-faced treasure hunter), but the meals here are American. Deep-fried catfish and lamb chops are your best bets. | 208 Pish La Ki Cir. | 931/668–2010 | Closed Mon. | $4–$15 | AE, D, DC, MC, V.

Lodging

Best Western–McMinnville Inn. Many of the rooms in this downtown motel–decorated in burgundy and hunter green—have views of the Smoky Mountains. The Race Car Café is next door. Complimentary Continental breakfast. Some kitchenettes, some microwaves, some in-room hot tubs, cable TV. Outdoor pool. Laundry services. Pets allowed (fee). | 2545

Sparta St. | 931/473–7338 | fax 931/473–1052 | www.bestwestern.com | 49 rooms | $50–$65 | AE, D, DC, MC, V.

Comfort Inn. This budget-oriented motel is central to shopping, a 10-minute drive from Cumberland Caverns, and 3 mi east of downtown. Complimentary Continental breakfast. In-room data ports, some microwaves, some refrigerators, cable TV. Pool. Business services. No pets. | 508 Sunnyside Heights | 931/473–4446 | www.comfortinn.com | 61 rooms | $45–$65 | AE, D, DC, MC, V.

Falcon Manor. Experience old-fashioned Southern chivalry and a relaxed country atmosphere at this 1896 manor, which is set on sprawling groomed grounds in McMinnville. Complimentary breakfast. No room phones, no TV in rooms, TV in common area. Business services. No kids under 11. No smoking. | 2645 Faulkner Springs Rd. | 931/668–4444 | fax 931/815–4444 | www.falconmanor.com | 6 rooms (4 with shared bath, 1 with shower only) | $95–120 | AE, MC, D, V.

MEMPHIS

MAP 12, A3

(Nearby towns also listed: Bolivar, Covington, Henning)

Memphis is Tennessee's largest city, and its economic influence reaches across West Tennessee, down into Mississippi, and across the river into Arkansas. The city was founded in 1819 as a Mississippi River port. However, the site was occupied as early as 3,000 years ago; when the explorer DeSoto passed through here around 1540, he described powerful and populous Native American towns on the bluffs. Memphis became a boomtown in the 19th century, shipping huge quantities of cotton from the Delta plantations. But the city is best known for its music, past and present, which draws hundreds of thousands to Elvis's Graceland and to Beale Street, the birthplace of the blues.

Memphis is also remembered as the place where civil rights leader Dr. Martin Luther King, Jr., was assassinated in 1968. This was a low point for Memphis, but in the 1970s the city began a comeback. Federal Express was founded here in 1972 (the city remains Fed Ex's headquarters) and gradually the downtown was renovated. The famous Peabody Hotel reopened in 1981, and tourists streaming in to Graceland reminded Memphis of its musical heritage. The site of Martin Luther King, Jr.'s death, the Lorraine Motel, was transformed into a civil rights museum, the first of its kind and one of the city's most important attractions.

Information: **Memphis Convention and Visitors Bureau** | 47 Union Ave., Memphis 38103 | 901/543–5300 | fax 901/543–5350 | www.memphistravel.com.

TRANSPORTATION INFORMATION

Airports: Memphis International Airport (2491 Winchester Rd. | 901/922–8000 | www.mscaa.com), 9 mi southeast of downtown, is served by most major airlines and is a hub for Northwest Airlines. Driving time to downtown is about 15 minutes via I–240 northwest. Cab fare (**Yellow Cab** | 901/577–7700.) runs about $20 plus tip.

Amtrak: Amtrak provides limited services to Memphis. | 545 S. Main St. | 800/872–7245 | www.amtrak.com.

Bus Lines: Greyhound (203 Union Ave. | 800/231–2222 | www.greyhound.com) provides service into and out of the Memphis area.

Intra-city Transit: The Memphis Area Transit Authority (1370 Levee Rd. | 901/274–6282 | www.matatransit.com) operates buses ($1.10) throughout downtown and the suburbs (additional fare for zones outside the city limits); a trolley (50) runs a 5-mi route linking the north and south ends of downtown via a riverfront loop.

Car Travel: You can access Memphis via the north–south I–55 and the east–west I–40. I–240 loops around the city.

Driving around Town: Memphis streets are well marked and there is plenty of parking to be found. Poplar Avenue, North Parkway, and Sam Cooper Boulevard are the main east–west thoroughfares. Most of the narrow east–west avenues are crowded during the morning and evening rush hours, with traffic heading west in the morning and east in the evening. If you can, avoid driving through the center of the city at all times. Instead, use I–40, which skirts Memphis on the northern side, and I–240, which goes along the south side. Parking lots are plentiful in downtown, especially around Beale Street, and parking costs no more than $6 for an entire day. Metered street parking is also readily available; be sure to read the signs because there are blackout times and make sure to put enough money in the meter, as cars at expired meters are quickly ticketed and towed.

NEIGHBORHOODS

Beale Street. Music is synonymous with Beale Street. Once the thriving center of Memphis's African-American community, this area has one-of-a-kind nightclubs, restaurants, and shops and is, for many travelers, one of the city's main draws. Statues of Elvis and W. C. Handy preside over things and live music thrives; check out B.B. King's Blues Club, on Second and Beale. Some of Memphis's biggest annual events also take place on Beale Street, including the Zydeco Festival in February and the Music Festival in May.

Midtown. This area is bounded by East Parkway on the east, Cleveland Street on the west, and I–40 on the north. Although it is largely residential, with many imperial homes, there is still a lot to see. The Overton Square entertainment district, an old-timey area that grew up in the 1970s, is the liveliest part of midtown, filled with restaurants, nightclubs, and antiques shops. Midtown is also home to many of Memphis' other major attractions, including the Memphis Brooks Museum of Art and the Memphis Zoo and Aquarium.

WALKING TOUR

Memphis begins at the Mississippi River, so it's only fitting that you begin your walk at **Mud Island,** a 52-acre river park. You can access the island from a footbridge and monorail that you can catch at 125 Front Street. The highlight of the park is the River Walk. After getting back to the mainland, walk down Front Street to the **Pyramid Arena,** an impressive 32-story stainless steel arena. From here, walk six blocks south to Adams Avenue, where you will find the **Magevney House,** an 1830s dwelling built by a pioneer schoolteacher and just one of the many historic homes along Adams Avenue that comprise the **Victorian Village Historic District.** The district includes some 25 blocks on Adams between Front and Manassas streets; houses range from neoclassical to Gothic Revival in style. The **Mallory-Nealy House,** an enormous Italianate Victorian mansion farther east on Adams, is especially noteworthy. Back at the Magevney House, walk west on Adams over to Main Street and catch the trolley south to Union Avenue. It's only a five-minute walk east to 2nd Street, where you'll find the **Memphis Music Hall of Fame,** which is filled with rare photographs and film footage. Then go back to Union Avenue and walk over to see the beautifully restored **Peabody Hotel,** which is between 2nd and 3rd streets. When you've explored the area around the Peabody Hotel, you are off to **Beale Street.** From the Peabody, follow Union Avenue west until you hit Main Street Walk south until you come to the intersection of Main and Beale streets. Here you will find the **Orpheum Theater.** Be sure to step inside to admire its crystal chandeliers and ornate tapestries. Continuing east on Beale Street, you will come upon the **W. C. Handy Memphis Home and Museum,** which recalls the influential composer and musician through an extensive collection of memorabilia.

Walk two more blocks on Beale and you'll come to the **Hunt-Phelan Home,** where costumed docents transport you to the Memphis of the mid-1800s. To cap off your tour, turn around on Beale and walk west until you come to Main Street. Jump on the trolley and go south to Huling Avenue, then get off and make a left on Huling. You will soon find yourself in front of the former Lorraine Motel, where Dr. Martin Luther King, Jr., was murdered. Today it houses the **National Civil Rights Museum.**

Attractions

CULTURE, EDUCATION, AND HISTORY

Beale Street Historic District. Once the main street of a thriving black neighborhood, where musicians B. B. King and W. C. Handy first made a name for themselves, the gradually restored Beale Street district has four blocks of nightclubs, shops, and restaurants. There's live music every night of all kinds, but with an emphasis on jazz and blues, and frequent outdoor music festivals spring through fall. | Beale St. between 2nd St. and 4th St. | 901/526–0110 | Free | Daily.

The Center for Southern Folklore. This funky folk-art gallery also features a performance stage where blues, jazz, and gospel music are presented nightly. | 119 S. Main St. | 901/525–3655 | www.southernfolklore.com | Free; $5 for music performances | Sun.–Wed. 11–7, Thurs.–Sat. 11–11.

Circuit Playhouse. This active community theater in Midtown Memphis, 3 blocks south of Overton Park, often features local actors, directors, designers, and playwrights. | 1705 Poplar Ave. | 901/726–4656 | Prices vary | Call for schedule.

★ **Graceland.** The mansion home of Elvis Presley draws an astounding 650,000 visitors a year. It features the famous Jungle Room, the Meditation Garden, and the King of Rock 'n' Roll's gravesite. The Graceland complex also includes exhibits of Elvis's cars and jets; a museum displaying his personal artifacts, including snapshots and stage outfits; three restaurants; and various gift shops. It's in south Memphis, near the Mississippi state line. | 3764 Elvis Presley Blvd. | 901/332–3322 or 800/238–2000 | www.elvis-presley.com/graceland | $22 for full tour of complex, $12 for mansion only | Mon.–Sat. 9–5, Sun. 10–4. Mansion tour's available Nov.–Feb., Wed.–Mon. 9–5 (reservation recommended).

Historic Elmwood Cemetery. Founded in 1852, Elmwood is the oldest active cemetery in the country and the final resting place for 19 Confederate generals and more than 1,000 Southern soldiers. This South Memphis site, off E. H. Crump Blvd. 3 mi southeast of downtown, has an outstanding collection of Victorian statues and monuments. | 824 S. Dudley St. | 901/774–3212 | www.elmwoodcemetery.org | Free | Daily.

Hunt-Phelan Home. Occupied by the Hunt-Phelan family until 1995, this 1840s white-columned brick mansion is filled with original furnishings. The house served as headquarters for General Ulysses S. Grant in the Civil War; it was the site of the Freedman's Bureau, one of the first schools for newly freed slaves founded in 1828. | 533 Beale St. | 901/525–8225 or 800/350–9009 | $10 | Apr.–Aug., daily 10–4; Sept.–Mar., Thurs.–Mon. 10–4.

Orpheum Theatre. Originally the Grand Opera House, and then a vaudeville palace, this 1888 downtown theater (rebuilt in 1928 after a fire) now hosts concerts and traveling shows—everything from Counting Crows to Lord of the Dance. | 203 S. Main St. | 901/525–7800 | www.orpheum-memphis.org | $12.50–$77.50 | Call for schedule.

Playhouse on the Square. The professional theater company has been performing downtown at Overton Square since the early 1970s. | 51 S. Cooper St. | 901/726–4656 or 901/725–0776 | Prices vary | Call for schedule.

Rhodes College. Founded in 1848, this small Midtown liberal arts college has a lovely wooded campus and distinctive collegiate Gothic architecture. A gallery mounts changing art exhibits. | 2000 N. Parkway | 901/843–3000 | www.rhodes.edu | Free for visitors | Weekdays.

Slavehaven/Burkle Estate. This home, built in 1849 by a German immigrant, was a stop on the Underground Railroad. Visitors can see the secret room, trap door, and tunnel in the basement. | 826 N. 2nd St. | 901/527–3427 | $5 | Memorial Day–Labor Day, Sat. 10–4; Labor Day–Memorial Day, Mon., Thur.–Sat. 10–4.

Sun Studio. This tiny downtown recording studio launched the careers of Elvis Presley, Roy Orbison, Jerry Lee Lewis, Johnny Cash, and others. By day, you can get a 30-minute guided tour of the place; by night it's still an active recording studio. There's a gift shop and a café. | 706 Union Ave. | 901/521–0664 | www.sunstudio.com | $8.70 | Daily 10–6.

Victorian Village. This "village" downtown comprises three preserved or refurbished homes built between 1830 and 1870. | Adams St. between High and Orleans Sts. | No phone | Free | Hours of houses vary.

Magevney House. A small white clapboard built in the 1830s, it is one of the oldest houses in Memphis. The city's first Irish immigrant lived here, and the house was the site of the first Catholic Mass said in Memphis. It's next to St. Peter's Catholic Church in Victorian Village. | 198 Adams Ave | 901/526–4464 | Free | Tues.–Fri. 10–2, Sat. 10–4.

Mallory-Neely House. Built in 1852, the enormous Italianate Victorian mansion features stenciled walls, hand-painted ceilings, parquet flooring, and stained-glass windows bought at the 1893 Chicago World's Fair. It is the only historic property in the city that has retained most of its original furnishings. | 652 Adams Ave., 38105 | 901/523–1484 | www.memphis-museums.org | Free | Tues.–Fri. 10–2, Sat. 10–4, Sun. 1–3:30.

Woodruff-Fontaine House. The three-story, fully furnished 1870 French Victorian house features significant collections of antiques and 19th-century clothing, which are displayed in the 18 rooms. The formal garden has preserved its gingerbread-style playhouse, which is now the museum shop. One of the three houses that makes up Victorian Village. | 680 Adams Ave. | 901/526–1469 | Free | Mon., Wed.–Fri. 10–3:30; Sat. 10–4; Sun. 1–3:30.

MUSEUMS

The Children's Museum of Memphis. A hands-on museum for children with interactive exhibits that allow little ones to try grown-up activities like driving a car, shopping for groceries, cashing a check—even climbing a skyscraper. | 2525 Central Ave. | 901/458–2678 | www.cmom.com | $5 | Tues.–Sat. 9–5, Sun. noon–5.

Dixon Gallery and Gardens. This art museum focuses primarily on American and French Impressionism, 18th-century German porcelain, and antique pewter. It is housed in a Georgian-style home, 2 mi east of the University of Tennessee in East Memphis, where it is situated on a 17-acre estate that features a formal English garden, wild woodlands, and a cutting garden. The Dixon family made their fortune growing cotton. | 4339 Park Ave. | 901/761–5250 | www.dixon.org | $5 | Tues.–Sat. 10–5, Sun. 1–5.

Fire Museum of Memphis. In Memphis' first fire house, this downtown museum features fire-fighting artifacts dating back to the early 1900s. | 118 Adams Ave. | 901/320–5650 | www.firemuseum.com | $5 | Tues.–Sat. 9–5, Sun. 1–5.

W.C. Handy's Museum. This classic Southern shotgun house was the home of William Christopher "W. C." Handy (known as the "Father of the Blues") during his middle years, from 1905–1918. The residence was moved downtown to Beale Street from its original location and is now a museum of Handy history and memorabilia. | 352 Beale St. | 901/527–2583 | Free | Daily.

Memphis Brooks Museum of Art. Made possible by the generosity of the Memphis Brooks family, this 1916 fine art museum in Midtown's Overton Park is Tennessee's oldest and one of the largest in the South. A permanent collection of more than 7,000 pieces from the Renaissance to the present includes paintings, sculpture, decorative arts, and a significant collection of works on paper, including drawings, watercolors, prints, and photographs. The original Beaux Arts–style building and modern additions house art by Renoir, Gains-

borough, Homer, O'Keeffe, Rodin, Goya, Whistler, Bellows, Pollock, and Warhol, among others. | 1934 Poplar Ave. | 901/544–6200 | www.brooksmuseum.org | $5; free Wed. | Tues.–Fri. 10–4, Sat. 10–5, Sun. 11:30–5.

Memphis Pink Palace Museum and Planetarium. Originally built in 1923 as the home of the founder of the Piggly Wiggly chain of grocery stores, this Georgian Revival pink marble mansion now houses permanent and temporary exhibits on the cultural and natural history of the mid-South. There's also an IMAX theater. You can learn about everything from dinosaur fossils to the Civil War, and catch a laser light show, too. | 3050 Central Ave. | 901/320–6320 | www.memphismuseum.org | $7 | Mon.–Thurs. 9–4, Fri. 9–9. Sun. noon–6.

Memphis Rock 'n Soul Museum. The history and legacy of Memphis's music is on display at this first Smithsonian partnership outside of Washington D.C., which opened in April 2000. Six galleries occupying 20,000 square feet are home to the Smithsonian Institution's "Rock 'n Soul: Social Crossroads" exhibition, a collection of artifacts, pictures, words, and music that illuminate the influence of America's cultural and musical past on the Memphis sound. A 2,000-square-foot gallery houses special exhibits. Free with every admission, an audio gallery guide delivers 300 minutes of information, music, and never-heard-before interviews with dozens of famous figures in rock and soul history. The museum is on the second floor of the Gibson Guitar Factory, just a half block south of Beale St. and Hwy. 61 in the Beale St. Entertainment District. | 145 Lt. George W. Lee Ave. | 901/453–0800 | $8.50 | Daily 10–6.

National Civil Rights Museum. In the Lorraine Motel, site of the 1968 assassination of Dr. Martin Luther King Jr., this downtown museum brings to life the American Civil Rights movement through interpretive exhibits. | 450 Mulberry St. | 901/521–9699 | www.midsouth.rr.com/civilrights | $6 | Mon., Wed–Sat. 9–5; Thurs. 9–8; Sun. 1–5.

National Ornamental Metal Museum. The nation's only museum of fine metalwork exhibits jewelry, sculpture, architectural pieces (gates, doors, windows, etc.), and other creative works crafted in metal. On weekends you can watch visiting artists or artisans at work. The gazebo on the grounds offers a wonderful view of the Mississippi River. | 374 Metal Museum Dr. | 901/774–6380 | www.metalmuseum.org | $4 | Tues.–Sat. 10–5, Sun. noon–5.

Peabody Place Museum and Gallery. An extensive and rare private collection of Chinese art is displayed in 7,500 square ft of galleries downtown. The collection includes jade, ivory, porcelain, and cloisonné art along with furnishings, fabrics, scrolls, and other objects, all from China's Manchu Dynasty, which lasted from 1644 until the revolution in 1911. The main entrance is guarded by two 6-ft cloisonné Temple Shizi Guardian Lions, or ìFoo Dogs,î which once stood watch over the Forbidden City in Beijing. | 119 S. Main St. | 901/523–ARTS | $5 | Tues.–Fri. 10–5:30, weekends noon–5.

PARKS, NATURAL AREAS, AND OUTDOOR RECREATION

Crystal Shrine Grotto. The cave exterior and tree-trunk entrance are carved out of concrete; inside, various rocks, quartz, and crystal have been fashioned into the backgrounds for nine scenes from the life of Christ. Built in the 1930s by artist Dionicio Rodriguez, the grotto is hidden inside Memorial Park Cemetery, down a quiet tree-lined drive in East Memphis. | 5668 Poplar Ave. | 901/767–8930 | Free | Daily.

Lichterman Nature Center. The 65-acre educational facility and wildlife sanctuary includes a lake and nature trails. | 1680 Lynnfield Ave. | 901/767–7322 | www.memphismuseum.org | $2 | Tues.–Sat. 9:30–5, Sun. 1:30–5.

Meeman-Shelby Forest State Park. The 13,467-acre park bordering the Mississippi River has two lakes and several hiking trails. It is named after Edward J. Meeman, the conservation editor of the Scripps-Howard newspapers who helped establish this park and Great Smoky Mountains National Park. There are cabins and campsites; activities include boating, fishing, biking, and swimming. The park is 17 mi north of downtown Memphis, off I–40 at Exit 2A. | 910 Riddick Rd. | 901/876–5215 | Free | Daily.

Memphis Botanic Garden. The 96-acre garden in East Memphis's Audubon Park offers 20 different gardens, including the Garden of Tranquility, the Sensory Garden, the Rose Garden (with 1,500 bushes), and the Wildflower Garden. There's also a plant information library. To get there, take I–240, Exit 20B, drive 2.5 mi to Park Ave. The park is bordered by Southern Ave. on the north, Park Ave. on the south, Goodlett Rd. on the west, and Perkins Rd. on the east. | 750 Cherry Rd. | 901/685–1566 | www.memphisbotanicgarden.com | $4, free on Tues. | Mon.–Sat. 9–6, Sun. 11–6.

Mud Island. This 52-acre park on an island in the Mississippi is a tribute to the legendary river. The highlight is River Walk, a five-block long contour map of the Lower Mississippi, complete with city plots, scale-model bridges and levees, and 800,000 gallons of water flowing every minute. At one end of the model river is a simulated Gulf of Mexico—a one-acre pool complete with a 20,000-square-foot sand beach. Also on Mud Island, which is easily accessible from downtown Memphis by a monorail that crosses Woll Harbor, is a museum that chronicles the 10,000-year history of the Mississippi River. You can see 35 scale models of riverboats as well as full-size replicas of portions of steamboats and Civil War ironclads. You can catch the monorail at 125 No. Front St., between Adams St. and Poplar St., behind City Hall. | 125 N. Front St. | 901/576–7241 | www.mudisland.com | $8 | Mon. 10–5, Tues.–Sun. 10–8.

Memphis Belle. Visit World War II's most famous bomber, downtown along the riverfront. It was the first B-17 to successfully complete 25 missions against Nazi targets without losing a single crew member. | 125 N. Front St. | 901/576–7241 | Free | Daily 10–4.

T.O. Fuller State Park. The only state park within Memphis city limits, it's near the Mississippi River, just 11 mi south of downtown. The 384 acres offer opportunities for camping, hiking, swimming, golf, and picnicking. The park was named for a turn-of-the-century African-American activist. | 1500 Mitchell Rd. | 901/543–7581 | www.state.tn.us/environment/parks/tofuller/index.html | Free | Daily.

Chucalissa Archaeological Museum. The reconstructed 15th-century Chickasaw village includes ceremonial or burial mounds, thatched houses, temples, a museum, and a theater. | 1987 Indian Village Dr. | 901/785–3160 | www.people.memphis.edu/chucalissa | $5 | Tue.–Sat. 9–4:30, Sun. 1–4:30.

MEMPHIS

INTRO
ATTRACTIONS
DINING
LODGING

RELIGION AND SPIRITUALITY

Full Gospel Tabernacle. The 1970s soul crooner Al Green is now the pastor of this church. His preaching and singing have made it one of the most popular off-the-beaten-path destinations in Memphis. Services at this South Memphis church are on Wednesday night and Sunday morning; call ahead to see if Green is in town. | 787 Hale Rd. | 901/396–9192 | www.algreen.com | Free | Daily.

Mason Temple. This site in South Memphis is the Church of God in Christ where Dr. Martin Luther King, Jr. delivered his famous "Mountain Top" speech. | 930 Mason St. | 901/947–9300 | www.cogic.org | Free | Weekdays 9–5.

SHOPPING

A. Schwab's Dry Goods Store. A family-owned store since 1876, you will find everything from voodoo potions to 99¢ neckties on the shelves. There are also a few exhibits commemorating the role this downtown store played in the integration movement of the 1950s and 1960s. | 163 Beale St. | 901/523–9782 | Free | Mon.–Sat. 9–5.

SPORTS AND RECREATION

Libertyland. Opened on July 4, 1976, this small family amusement park just 5 minutes south of Midtown has 24 rides, including Elvis Presley's favorite roller coaster, the Zippin Pippin. There's also a 1909 hand-carved wooden horse carousel that is listed in the National Register of Historic Places. | 940 Maxwell Blvd. | 901/274–1776 | www.libertyland.com | $10–$20 | Jun.–Sept., weekdays noon–9, Sat. 10–9, Sun. 1–9.

Memphis International Motorsports Park. The National Hot Rod Association–sanctioned complex includes an 1.8-mi road course, a drag strip, and a dirt oval that is the site of drag racing, tractor pulls, and motorcycle contests. In northwestern Memphis. | 5500 Taylor Forge Dr. | 901/358–7223 or 901/353–6118 | www.memphismotorsports.com | Prices vary | Jan.–Nov., daily.

Pyramid Arena. This 32-story stainless steel pyramid is quite an anomaly on the Memphis skyline, and it's a first-rate facility for concerts and sports events. | 1 Auction Ave. | 901/521–9675 | Free | Daily.

SIGHTSEEING TOURS/TOUR COMPANIES

Delta Queen Steamboat Company. Board one of three paddle-wheelers, the *Delta Queen, Mississippi Queen,* or *American Queen,* for a 3- to 14-night cruise on the Cumberland, Mississippi, Ohio, or Tennessee rivers. All staterooms on the *Delta Queen* and many on the other two boats feature period furnishings, both reproductions and actual antiques. In Memphis, boats dock on the riverfront, at the foot of Beale Street. | 1380 Port of New Orleans Pl., New Orleans, LA | 800/543–1949 | www.deltaqueen.com | Cruise packages start at $350/night per person | Call for cruise times.

Memphis Queen. Enjoy a short sightseeing trip or a daylong cruise on the Mississippi aboard this paddle-wheeler. It hosts sunset dinner cruises and special events as well. | 45 Riverside Dr. | 901/527–5694 | www.memphisqueen.com | $12.50; $28 for dinner cruise | Daily (weather permitting); call for schedule.

OTHER POINTS OF INTEREST

Main Street Trolley. Restored antique trolley cars travel a loop through downtown Memphis, from the South Main Historic District, past Beale Street, to the Pyramid and the Historic Pinch District, and along the river bluffs. At 50¢ for a one-way ticket, it's a bargain. | Along Main Street | 901/577–2648 | 50¢ | Daily.

Memphis Zoo and Aquarium. More than 2,800 animals representing some 400 species live here at this Midtown location. The zoo includes many large natural habitats, including Cat Country, the Primate Canyon, and Animals of the Night. | 2000 Galloway Ave. | 901/276–WILD | www.memphiszoo.org | $8.50 | Daily 9–5.

ON THE CALENDAR

JAN.: *Elvis Presley's Birthday Celebration.* A variety of events to honor the King's birthday are held at Graceland. | 800/238–2000.
FEB.: *Beale Street Zydeco Festival.* Lots and lots of Cajun music in all the Beale St. clubs. Call for admission fee. | 901/529–0999.
FEB.: *Kroger St. Jude Tennis Championships.* An annual men's tournament. | 901/765–4400.
MAY: *Memphis in May International Festival.* The month-long celebration includes a barbecue contest, a Sunset Symphony, and the Beale Street Music Festival. | 901/525–4611.
MAY: *Beale Street Music Festival.* The three-day festival features performances by national and local musicians. Here, there and everywhere on Beale St. | 901/525–4611.
JUNE: *Ducks Unlimited Great Outdoors Sporting and Wildlife Festival.* The three-day event is sponsored by one of the country's largest organizations devoted to the conservation of wetlands and waterfowl. Activities include shooting, archery, wall climbing, biking, paddling, fishing, and golf. It takes place at the Agri-Center International, 7777 Walnut Grove Rd., in southest Memphis. | 901/758–3711.
AUG.: *Elvis Presley International Tribute Week.* Numerous events mark the anniversary of the singer's death. | 800/238–2000.
SEPT.: *Labor Day Fest.* This annual music festival takes place on Beale Street. | 901/526–0110.

SEPT., OCT.: *Mid-South Fair.* This country-style fair offers concerts, rides, and rodeo events, along with agricultural and commercial exhibits at the Mid-South Fairgrounds. | 940 Early Maxwell Blvd. | 901/274–8800.

DEC.: *The Liberty Bowl Football Classic.* Top college teams compete in this annual post-season game at Liberty Bowl Memorial Stadium in Midtown. Call for ticket prices. | 335 South Hollywood St. | 901/795–7700.

Dining

INEXPENSIVE

Bozo's. American/Casual. Established in 1923, this small-town diner, decorated with 1950s nostalgia, is most famous for barbecue, but the menu includes steaks, shrimp, sandwiches, and salads. The restaurant is 25 mi east of Memphis, and the parking lot fills on weekend nights with cars from neighboring counties—so expect a wait. | 342 U.S. 70, Mason | 901/294–3400 | Closed Sun., Mon. | $6–$10 | AE, D, MC, V.

Buntyn. American. This meat-and-three regularly offers 10 or more vegetables with its entrées, which include fried chicken and chicken with dressing. Its immense yeast rolls and crisp corn bread are legendary as are the fruit cobblers and coconut cream pies. Located in the eastern part of the city. Kids' menu. | 4972 Park Ave. | 901/458–8776 | Closed weekends | $7–$12 | MC, V.

India Palace. Indian. A casual Midtown restaurant where the kitchen provides all the flavor. Dishes include Tandoori chicken, lamb vindaloo, *palak paneer,* and 10 grilled or fried breads. The value-priced buffet makes it easy to sample several dishes. | 1720 Poplar Ave. | 901/278–1199 | $6–$14 | AE, D, DC, MC, V.

Gus's Fried Chicken. Southern. In a humble small-town setting 30 minutes northeast of Memphis, this family-owned joint serves up some of the region's best crisp fried chicken with cole slaw and baked beans. Note: It's not for the timid—the seasoning includes spicy red pepper. Guests sit in booths with blues playing in the background. | 520 U.S. 70, Mason | 901/294–2028 | $4–$8 | No credit cards.

Rendezvous. Barbecue. They sell plenty of dry-style barbecued ribs in this downtown restaurant in an 1890 building. Many antiques and collectibles fill the dining room and the service is some of the most efficient in town. The menu also lists shoulder sandwiches, pork loin, chicken, and skillet of shrimp. | 52 S. 2nd St. | 901/523–2746 | $6–$15 | AE, D, DC, MC, V | Closed Sun.–Mon., No lunch Tues.–Thurs.

MODERATE

Alfred's. American/Casual. Not surprisingly music is the theme at this busy restaurant on Beale Street, the city's bluesy entertainment district. Up to 500 people can be accommodated inside and out on the two-storied patio. Southern plate lunches, burgers, pork chops, pasta, catfish, and barbecue ribs make up the comforting menu. The kitchen is open until 3 AM; the bar 'til 5 AM. On the big dance floor and stage there's rock'n'roll Wed.–Sat., jazz on Sun. | 197 Beale St. | 901/525–3711 | www.alfreds.com | $8–$20 | AE, D, DC, MC, V.

Automatic Slim's Tonga Club. Eclectic. Hip and funky in food as well as atmosphere. Fans of this downtown restaurant go for spicy offerings such as Caribbean voodoo stew and coconut mango shrimp. Lunch leans to hearty sandwiches such as Cubano dagwood, beastie boy, and big loaf vegetarian. Don't miss the topless Elvis photos upstairs and the famous tonga martinis. Kids' menu. | 83 S. 2nd St. | 901/525–7948 | No lunch Sat. Closed Sun. | $18–$25 | AE, MC, V.

Boscos Brewing Co. American/Casual. The first brewpub in Tennessee since Prohibition, Boscos offers sample-size servings of beer so you can try a variety of brews, from Flaming Stone beer to Ilse of Skye Scottish Ale to Tennessee Cream Ale. The menu features 16 varieties of pizzas cooked in wood-fired ovens as well as pasta, seafood, steaks, and crab and crawfish cakes, served with beer or wine. Take a brewery tour to see the brewing process.

MEMPHIS

INTRO
ATTRACTIONS
DINING
LODGING

Open-air dining available. It's 10 minutes east of Memphis. | 7615 W. Farmington, Germantown | 901/756–7310 | $8–$20 | AE, D, DC, MC, V.

Cooker Bar and Grille. American. Family chain restaurant in east Memphis known for American regional specialties and home-style cooking, including roast beef, meat loaf, and the popular platter of barbecued ribs and grilled shrimp. Black-and-white photos of the restaurant in the 1920s and 1930s hang on the walls. Kids' menu. | 6120 Poplar Ave. | 901/685–2800 | $6–$20 | AE, D, DC, MC, V.

★ **Corky's.** Barbecue. This is by far the most popular barbecue in Memphis. Be warned: the parking lot is often full and the waiting list long. When you get inside, try the pork ribs, pork shoulder sandwich with slaw, and beef brisket and baked beans. Corky's ribs and pulled-pork shoulder can be shipped anywhere in the country. There are two locations. | 1740 N. Germantown Rd., Cordova | 901/737–1988 | 5259 Poplar Ave. | 901/685–9744 | www.corkys-bbq.com | $5–$22 | AE, D, DC, MC, V.

MEMPHIS BARBECUE

To many folks, Memphis means barbecue, and in Memphis, barbecue means pork. It can be sandwiches of "pulled" pork loin drenched in sweet, tomato-based sauce and topped with coleslaw, or pork ribs coated in spices. (The latter are called "dry ribs," not because the meat isn't succulent and juicy, but because they are sauceless.) Either way, the meat is slow-cooked over hardwood coals in a barrel cooker.

There are dozens of barbecue restaurants in Memphis, peddling subtly different versions of the classic product. Corky's is the powerhouse. The line of people waiting for a table often extends out the door of this restaurant on Poplar Avenue in East Memphis. Corky's also has branches at Memphis International, in Nashville, in Tunica, Mississippi, and in New Orleans. Corky's and the Rendezvous, a downtown restaurant known for dry ribs, also operate thriving mail order businesses. They're happy to Fedex a slab of ribs to barbecue lovers anywhere in the country.

The serious connoisseur of barbecue will also want to seek out some of the smaller, family-run operations. The choices are many—in this city, you can find a good plate of barbecue almost anywhere, including at one combination laundromat and barbecue shop. Some of the best spots are The Bar-B-Q Shop, The Cozy Corner, Gridley's, Interstate, Neeley's, and Payne's. Nearby Tipton County is known for a slightly more vinegary style of barbecue. Bozo's, in the minuscule town of Mason northeast of Memphis, is the most popular restaurant for this variation of the grilled meat theme.

Not surprisingly, this city of barbecue aficionados is the site of the World Championship Barbecue Cooking Contest. Each May, more than 225 cooking teams compete for $40,000 in prizes—and the highly coveted "World Champion" title.

The best barbecue in Memphis, however, might very well be what's prepared in backyards and on front porches across the city. On holiday weekends in the summer, the whole town smells of barbecue smoke.

Erika's. German. A downtown institution where German-food lovers can feast on bratwurst, Wiener schnitzels, potato pancakes, and sauerbraten with red caggage. At lunch the menu includes additional American-style fare. On weekend night's there's liver dumplings, too. Only beer is served, but you can bring your own spirits. | 52 S. 2nd St. | 901/526–5522 | $8–$16 | AE, D, DC, MC, V | No supper Mon.–Thurs. Closed Sun.

Paulette's. Continental. Modeled after a European inn, this charming restaurant in Overton Square features filet Paulette, grilled chicken, salmon, shrimp, crab cakes, and crepe specialties. Kahlua mocha pie is the most popular dessert. At night, the place becomes lively; candlelight and flowers set the stage. Pianist Fri.–Sun. Weekend brunch. | 2110 Madison Ave. | 901/726–5128 | $10–$27 | AE, D, DC, MC, V.

Saigon Le. Chinese, Vietnamese. This unpretentious Midtown restaurant with a casual dining room and friendly service offers some of the best Vietnamese and Chinese cuisine in Memphis. Be sure to try the lacy bird's nest egg rolls wrapped in fresh herbs and lettuce leaves and dipped in a sweet sauce. Other outstanding items are the spring rolls, numerous Vietnamese soups, and crispy shrimp. There are plenty of vegetarian dishes here. | 51 N. Cleveland St. | 901/276–5326 | Closed Sun. | $10–$13 | AE, D, DC, MC, V.

Willinghams. Barbecue. One of the winningest barbecue chefs in the country, John Willinghams serves up his uniquely spiced rubbed ribs, pork shoulder, beef brisket, and Dixie chicken that has been smoked for 4½ hours. You can't go wrong with any of the entrées but be sure to have some chocolate pecan pie, too. This roadhouse grill in the heart of East Memphis is housed in a rustic building filled with celebrity photos (the chef with Mohammed Ali, etc.) and a lot of trophies. | 680 W. Brookhaven Cir. | 901/767–7727 | www.willinghams.com | $6–$28 | AE, MC, V.

EXPENSIVE

Anderton's. American. This Midtown restaurant is popular for seafood, especially lobster sautéed in butter and oysters but it also serves prime rib, tenderloin, and homemade rolls. During the week moderately priced and promptly served plate lunches draw a crowd of business people to this hot-spot, which is outfitted like a schooner. Private dining rooms are available for groups. Kids' menu. | 1901 N. Madison St. | 901/726–4010 | Closed Sun. No lunch Sat. | $11–$32 | AE, D, DC, MC, V.

Buckley's Fine Filet Grill. American. The reasonably priced but limited menu features its famous filet mignon, grilled chicken, salmon, pasta, and Granny Buckley's apple pie. The downtown location has banquet facilities for up to 50; both are decked with antiques and paintings. | 5355 Poplar Ave. | 901/683–4538 | 117 Union Ave. | 901/578–9001 | No lunch Sat., no dinner Sun. | $8–$22 | AE, D, DC, MC, V.

Folk's Folly. Steak. Although it serves salads and seafood, folks flock to Folk's Folly for its USDA prime steaks served with sizzle and a pat of herb butter. The busy restaurant in the heart of East Memphis has live piano music Monday—Saturday in the Cellar Lounge. Save room for bread pudding. Five separate dining rooms, plus eight private rooms for small parties. Meats and other items can be purchased in its retail store. Pianist Mon.–Sat. | 551 S. Mendenhall Rd. | 901/762–8200 | No lunch | $20–$43 | AE, DC, MC, V.

Interstate Barbecue. Barbecue. Often described as the best place to eat barbecue in Memphis, this casual spot serves shoulder sandwiches, pork ribs, beef ribs, chicken, and beef brisket. It also serves two Memphis specialties: barbecue spaghetti with barbecued pork and sauce on top and barbecued bologna, which is a thick slice of bologna, smoked and slathered with sauce and slaw. | 2265 S. 3rd St. | 901/775–2304 | $11–$23 | AE, D, DC MC, V.

Jarrett's Restaurant. Contemporary. A popular bistro in an East Memphis shopping center, Jarrett's offers a spectrum of fish, meats, and pasta. Standouts are the smoked trout ravioli with Arkansas caviar and grouper encrusted in horseradish. Try mocha crème caramel for dessert. The lunch buffet is a gourmet feast. Dine surrounded by flowers and works by local artists on consignment; outdoor dining on a patio is available when weather

permits. The restaurant also hosts wine tastings. | 5689 Quince Rd. | 901/763–2264 | www.jarrets.com | Closed Sun. | $15–$25 | AE, MC, V.

Lulu Grille. Contemporary. Tucked into a corner of an East Memphis shopping center, Lulu Grille is known for fresh seafood such as grilled ruby red trout, steaks, veal wild game, Dijon-crusted rack of lamb, and pasta. Carrot and coconut cakes are sweet endings. In moderate weather, the patio is a popular gathering place. | 565 Erin Dr. | 901/763–3677 | Closed Sun. | $12–$27 | AE, D, DC, MC, V.

McEwen's on Monroe. Contemporary. The narrow high-ceilinged downtown restaurant was recently expanded to include a tapas bar. House-smoked trout with potato pancake and pepper-seared lamb carpaccio are good dinner choices. Try chunky chicken salad and Granny Smith apple salad at lunch. Don't miss the jalapeño corn bread at either time. Chocolate mocha cake is a sweet ending. The eclectic menu is updated regularly. | 122 Monroe St. | 901/527–7085 | Closed Sun. No lunch Sat. No dinner Mon. | $18–$23 | AE, MC, V.

The Pier. Seafood. In an old downtown warehouse overlooking the Mississippi River, this restaurant is known for its clam chowder, fresh fish, and prime rib. The nautical decor and riverview add to the dining experience, which is by candlelight after sunset. | 100 Wagner Pl. | 901/526–7381 | No lunch | $15–$29 | AE, D, DC, MC, V.

Ronnie Grisanti and Sons. Italian. This classy Midtown spot serves us upscale Tuscan fare in a busy dining room decorated with paintings of Italy and tiny white lights. Creative offerings are the specials of the day. Steaks and veal dishes are daily standouts. | 2855 Poplar Ave. | 901/323–0007 | Closed Sun. and 1st week in July. No lunch | $13–$30 | AE, MC, V.

VERY EXPENSIVE

Aubergine. French. If classic French cuisine in an intimate setting is what you want, this is the place. The menu changes frequently at this highly regarded restaurant, but look for lobster salad with cannellini beans, mango, and passion fruit; and 24-hour-braised veal shoulder. | 5007 Black Rd. | 901/767–7840 | Closed Sun., Mon. No lunch Sat. | $23–$30 | AE, DC, MC, V.

Benihana of Tokyo. Japanese. Deft knife-juggling chefs prepare steaks, shrimp, scallops, and lobsters on a steel cooking table surrounded by diners. Known for the Benihana special (grilled lobster with house dressing of mustard and ginger sauce), this lively place, complete with karaoke, also has a sushi bar. The restaurant is housed in a stunning Japanese-style building near the Adams Mark Hotel in East Memphis. Kids' menu and early-bird supper. | 912 Ridge Lake Blvd. | 901/683–7390 | www.benihana.com | $15–$30 | AE, D, DC, MC, V.

Butcher Shop. Steak. Diners can grill their own steaks over a couple of open pits or pay extra for the staff to do it. Beef is big here. The smallest steak is a 14-ounce filet and the largest a 32-ounce T-bone. Other menu choices are seafood, chicken, pasta, and pork. The downtown location is in a turn-of-the-century building on Front Street in the heart of what was once the center of Memphis' cotton trading industry. A second location in the Cordova suburb features a large dining room, heated and covered patio and several private party rooms. Salad bar. Kids' menu. | 101 S. Front St. | 901/521–0856 | 107 S. Germantown Pkwy., Cordova | 901/757–4244 | $20–$28 | AE, D, DC, MC, V.

★ **Chez Philippe.** Continental. High ceilings, silk drapes, large murals, and some of the most professional servers in the city make this a good choice for a special occasion. Classically trained in France, chef Jose Gutierrez adds creative twists to regional ingredients. Try fillet of salmon with orange-potato doughnuts, roast pheasant, and sumptuous desserts like poached pears in chocolate sauce and the soufflé of the day. Candlelight and roses add to the romance of the dining experience. | 149 Union Ave. | 901/529–4188 | www.peabodymemphis.com | Jacket required | Closed Sun. No lunch | $25–$30 | AE, D, DC, MC, V.

Cielo. Contemporary. This restaurant is housed in the Molly Fontaine-Taylor house, a turn-of-the century former residence found in the city's Victorian Village, but the cuisine is a contemporary mix of international flavors. Try the tapas platter, roasted duck breast with orange-cinnamon sauce, and roasted sea bass with black mushrooms and chili sauce. | 679 Adams Ave. | 901/524–1886 | Closed Sun., Mon. No lunch Sat. | $18–$26 | AE, MC, V.

Erling Jensen. French. Danish chef Erling Jensen is one of the most creative cooks in Memphis. In the elegant, but understated East Memphis restaurant, guests may dine on roast rack of lamb with lobster glaze, pheasant with sweet-and-sour cabbage; lobster risotto with orange, papaya, and caviar; and whatever else interests the chef at the time. The service is great and the wine list outstanding. Sun. brunch. | 1044 S. Yates Rd. | 901/763–3700 | No lunch | $28–$48 | AE, DC, MC, V.

KoTo. Contemporary. A small restaurant in Overton Square with a purposely spare decor, KoTo fuses the flavors of Japan, Europe, and America. Try rack of lamb with walnut-coriander crust, filet of beef with shiitake-mushroom bourbon butter, or crab cakes with sesame, caramelized shallots, and shiitake mushrooms. Finish with a creative dessert such as chocolate green tea crème brûlée. Small photos by local artists are on display and jazzy music can be heard sometimes. | 22 S. Cooper St. | 901/722–2244 | No lunch weekends | $22–$28 | AE, D, MC, V.

La Tourelle. French. In a 1910 bungalow in the Overton Square area, this lace-curtained, wood-floored spot has served its customers contemporary French cuisine since the late 1980s. Try lobster salad, rack of lamb crusted with pommery mustard and horseradish, plum-glazed loin pork chops, roasted sea bass, Grand Marnier crème brûlée and cappuccino terrine. Sun. brunch. | 2146 Monroe Ave. | 901/726–5771 | No lunch Mon.–Sat. | $28–$40 | MC, V.

Raji. Eclectic. Chef-owner Raji Jallepalli presides over the kitchen at this gracious restaurant in East Memphis. The ever-changing menu features a four-course prix-fixe meal that fuses Indian seasonings with classic French preparations, such as tenderloin with chutney. | 712 W. Brookhaven Cir. | 901/685–8723 | Reservations essential | Closed Sun., Mon. No lunch | $50–$54 prix–fixe | AE, MC, V.

Tsunami. Pan Asian. An informal but artsy bistro in the eclectic Cooper-Young neighborhood in Midtown, Tsunami fuses the cuisines of the Pacific Rim. Don't miss the rack of lamb, crisp duck breast and, if it's on the menu, the sublime seared sea bass with soy beurre blanc on black Thai rice. The casual atmosphere is enlivened with local art. | 928 S. Cooper St. | 901/274–2556 | No lunch. Closed Sun. | $15–$23 | AE, D, DC, MC, V.

Lodging

INEXPENSIVE

Studio 6–Memphis. This extended-stay property offers suites near restaurants and the mall. It's 15 minutes east of the airport and 20 minutes east of downtown. Kitchenettes, microwaves, refrigerators, cable TV. Pool. Hot tub. Laundry facilities. Business services. Some pets allowed (fee). | 4300 American Way | 901/366–9333 or 800/456–4000 | fax 901/366–7835 | 51 rooms, 67 suites | $55, $59 suites | AE, D, DC, MC, V.

Red Roof Inn–South. Cozy rooms with burgundy accents are close to shopping and the airport. The hotel is a 10-minute drive south from the Overton Park area. In-room data ports, cable TV. Some pets allowed. | 3875 American Way | 901/363–2335 | fax 901/363–2822 | www.redroofinn.com | 109 rooms | $39–$50 | AE, D, DC, MC, V.

MODERATE

Comfort Inn–Poplar East. This Comfort Inn is on I-240 at Exit 24E. It's near a mall and several restaurants, 15 minutes east of downtown. The neighborhood is predominantly a business area. Complimentary Continental breakfast, room service, cable TV. Pool. Exercise equipment. Airport shuttle. Some pets allowed (fee). | 5877 Poplar Ave. | 901/767–6300 | fax 901/767–0098 | www.comfortinn.com | 126 rooms | $59–$79 | AE, D, DC, MC, V.

Hampton Inn. This member of the well-known chain is decorated with reproduction antiques and about 2 mi from Beale Street downtown. Complimentary Continental breakfast. In-room data ports, cable TV. Pool. Business services. | 1180 Union Ave. | 901/276–1175 | fax 901/276–4261 | www.hampton-inn.com | 126 rooms | $66–$81 | AE, D, DC, MC, V.

Holiday Inn Midtown Medical Center. This recently renovated hotel near Overton Park offers predictable accommodations. Restaurant, bar. In-room data ports, cable TV. Pool. Business services, airport shuttle. | 1837 Union Ave. | 901/278–4100 | fax 901/272–3810 | www.holiday-inn.com | 173 rooms | $65–$85 | AE, D, DC, MC, V.

La Quinta Inn. This is the first representative of the chain built around 1980, just 2 mi east of downtown. The rooms have abstract Mexican motifs. Complimentary breakfast. Cable

KODAK'S TIPS FOR PHOTOGRAPHING THE CITY

Streets
- Take a bus or walking tour to get acclimated
- Explore markets, streets, and parks
- Travel light so you can shoot quickly

City Vistas
- Find high vantage points to reveal city views
- Shoot early or late in the day, for best light
- At twilight, use fast films and bracket exposures

Formal Gardens
- Exploit high angles to show garden design
- Use wide-angle lenses to exaggerate depth and distance
- Arrive early to beat crowds

Landmarks and Monuments
- Review postcard racks for traditional views
- Seek out distant or unusual views
- Look for interesting vignettes or details

Museums
- Call in advance regarding photo restrictions
- Match film to light source when color is critical
- Bring several lenses or a zoom

Houses of Worship
- Shoot exteriors from nearby with a wide-angle lens
- Move away and include surroundings
- Switch to a very fast film indoors

Stained-Glass Windows
- Bright indirect sunlight yields saturated colors
- Expose for the glass not the surroundings
- Switch off flash to avoid glare

Architectural Details
- Move close to isolate details
- For distant vignettes, use a telephoto lens
- Use side light to accent form and texture

In the Marketplace
- Get up early to catch peak activity
- Search out colorful displays and colorful characters
- Don't scrimp on film

Stage Shows and Events
- Never use flash
- Shoot with fast (ISO 400 to 1000) film
- Use telephoto lenses
- Focus manually if necessary

From *Kodak Guide to Shooting Great Travel Pictures* © 2000 by Fodor's Travel Publications

TV. Outdoor pool. Business services. Some pets allowed. | 42 S. Camilla St. | 901/526–1050 | fax 901/525–3219 | www.laquinta.com | 128 rooms, 2 suites | $55–$60 | AE, D, DC, MC, V.

EXPENSIVE

Best Western Benchmark Hotel. The view of the Mississippi River and the two-block stroll to Beale Street compensate for the spartan rooms. There is a restaurant on the property. Restaurant. Some refrigerators, cable TV. Business services. No pets. | 164 Union Ave. | 901/527–4100 | fax 901/525–1747 | www.bestwestern.com | 124 rooms | $85 | AE, D, DC, MC, V.

Comfort Inn. This five-story brick and stucco motel is 15 minutes north of Graceland and 6 mi northeast of downtown. Complimentary Continental breakfast. Some kitchenettes, cable TV. Indoor pool. Hot tub. Business services. | 2889 Austin Peay Hwy. | 901/386–0033 | fax 901/386–0036 | 60 rooms, 20 suites | $75, $110–$130 suites | AE, D, DC, MC, V.

Comfort Inn Downtown. The location is great, just five blocks from Beale Street, and the cherry wood and burgundy accents of the rooms create a personal touch. The Mississippi River is in sight, and there is a restaurant next door. Complimentary Continental breakfast. In-room data ports, cable TV. Outdoor pool. Exercise equipment. Free parking. No pets. | 100 N. Front St. | 901/526–0583 | fax 901/525–7512 | www.comfortinn.com | 60 rooms | $90–$94 | AE, D, DC, MC, V.

Courtyard by Marriott. They pride themselves on keeping rooms and spaces fresh and up-to-date. The hotel is near shopping, restaurants, and movie theaters, 25 minutes east of downtown. Restaurant, bar. In-room data ports, microwaves, cable TV. Pool. Hot tub. Exercise equipment. Laundry facilities. Business services. Free parking. | 6015 Park Ave. | 901/761–0330 | fax 901/682–8422 | www.marriott.com | 146 rooms | $69–$99 | AE, D, DC, MC, V.

East Memphis Hilton. This eight-story hotel has a plant-filled lobby and a courtyard with a patio. It's 2 mi off I-240 and is near several restaurants. Downtown is 20 minutes to the west. Restaurant, bar, room service. In-room data ports, cable TV. Pool. Gym. | 5069 Sanderlin Ave. | 901/767–6666 | fax 901/767–5428 | www.hilton.com | 265 rooms | $79–$119 | AE, D, DC, MC, V.

French Quarter Suites. With its mellow rose-brick exterior and classic architectural lines, this pleasant Overton Square hostelry is reminiscent of an older, New Orleans–style inn. All the suites have living rooms and whirlpool baths that accommodate two. Restaurant, bar with entertainment, complimentary Continental breakfast. Microwaves, refrigerators, in-room hot tubs, cable TV. Pool. Exercise equipment. Business services, airport shuttle. | 2144 Madison Ave. | 901/728–4000 or 800/843–0353 (outside TN) | fax 901/278–1262 | www.memphisfrenchquarter.com | 105 suites | $89–$119 suites | AE, D, DC, MC, V.

Marriott. This reliable 13-story hotel is in East Memphis's business district, near a mall and several restaurants. It's a half-hour drive west to downtown. Restaurant, bar. In-room data ports, some refrigerators, cable TV. 2 pools (1 indoor). Hot tub. Exercise equipment. Business services. Airport shuttle. | 2625 Thousand Oaks Blvd. | 901/362–6200 | fax 901/360–8836 | www.marriott.com | 320 rooms | $79–$161 | AE, D, DC, MC, V.

The Ridgeway Inn. Enjoy cappuccino in the elegantly decorated French country lobby of this inn in the business district minutes from the airport and 13 mi east of downtown. Restaurant, bar, room service. Cable TV. Pool. Exercise equipment. Business services, airport shuttle. | 5679 Poplar Ave. | 901/766–4000 or 800/822–3360 | fax 901/763–1857 | 155 rooms | $94–$129 | AE, D, DC, MC, V.

Sleep Inn at Court Square. One side of the hotel has a view of the Mississippi River, and the other has a view of Court Square park. You can easily walk over to Beale Street. The wallpaper is a cheery combination of pink and blue, and each room has a desk. Complimentary Continental breakfast. Cable TV, in-room VCRs. Exercise equipment. Business services. No pets. | 40 N. Front St. | 901/522–9700 | fax 901/522–9710 | www.sleepinn.com | 124 rooms | $90–$110 | AE, D, DC, MC, V.

VERY EXPENSIVE

★ **Adam's Mark.** This unique building, a 27-story glass tower 27 mi east of downtown in the business district, has rooms with panoramic views of Memphis and surrounding areas. Restaurant, bar with entertainment. In-room data ports, some minibars, cable TV. Pool. Exercise equipment. Business services. Airport shuttle. | 939 Ridge Lake Blvd. | 901/684–6664 | fax 901/762–7411 | www.adamsmark.com | 408 rooms, 5 suites | $110–$175, $250–$600 suites | AE, D, DC, MC, V.

Bridgewater House Bed and Breakfast. Leaded-glass windows and Oriental rugs add to the stateliness of this brick Greek Revival B&B. The rooms include silk wall coverings. The owners are chefs, so the chance that you'll have a superb breakfast is excellent. The home is 15 mi east of Memphis, off Exit 14 of I–40. Complimentary breakfast. Cable TV, no room phones. No pets. No kids under 12. No smoking. | 7015 Raleigh La Grange Rd., Cordova | 901/384–0080 or 800/466–1001 | www.bbonline.com/tn/bridgewater | 2 rooms | $110 | D, MC, V.

Embassy Suites. Guests are wowed by the unusual atrium lobby, featuring palm trees, a pond, and live ducks. This five-story hotel is in a commercial and residential area, 25 mi east of downtown. Restaurant, bar, complimentary breakfast. In-room data ports, refrigerators, cable TV. Indoor pool. Hot tub. Exercise equipment. Video games. Laundry facilities. Business services, airport shuttle. | 1022 S. Shady Grove Rd. | 901/684–1777 | fax 901/685–8185 | www.embassysuites.com | 220 suites | $129–$185 suites | AE, D, DC, MC, V.

Holiday Inn Select Memphis Airport. This five-story hotel is 2 mi from Graceland. It's near various restaurants and a 10-minute drive north to downtown. Restaurant, bars. In-room data ports, cable TV. Pool. 2 tennis courts. Exercise equipment. Business services. Airport shuttle. | 2240 Democrat Rd. | 901/332–1130 | fax 901/398–5206 | www.holiday-inn.com | 374 rooms | $99–$124 | AE, D, DC, MC, V.

Hampton Inn and Suites at Peabody Place. Rooms in this seven-floor downtown hotel are decorated with designer bedspreads and floral wall borders. Many of the rooms have views of Beale Street in the downtown area. Complimentary Continental breakfast. Some microwaves, some refrigerators, cable TV. Indoor pool. Hot tub. Exercise equipment. Shops. Laundry services. Business services. No pets. | 175 Peabody Pl. | 901/260–4000 | fax 901/260–4050 | www.hampton-inn.com | 114 rooms, 30 suites | $125–$165 | AE, D, DC, MC, V.

Holiday Inn Select. This 15-story property is across from the Peabody Hotel and two blocks from Beale Street. Restaurant, bar, room service. In-room data ports, some minibars, refrigerators, cable TV. Pool. Exercise equipment. Business services. Airport shuttle. Parking (fee). | 160 Union Ave. | 901/525–5491 | fax 901/529–8950 | www.holiday-inn.com | 192 rooms | $109–$129 | AE, D, DC, MC, V.

The King's Cottage Bed and Breakfast Inn. The owners are explicitly proud of their Christianity, and calligraphy of Bible scriptures can be found in each room. The 1910 stucco-and-brick inn is comfortably cluttered, and the rooms have silk drapes and white bedding accented with roses. It's in the Evergreen District. Complimentary Continental breakfast. Cable TV, in-room VCRs. Pets allowed (fee). No smoking. | 87–89 Clark Pl. | 901/722–8686 | www.thekingscottage.com | 2 rooms | $128 | AE, D, MC, V.

Marriott Memphis–Downtown. Relax and listen to the grand piano that's played in the greenery-filled lobby of this sophisticated high-rise. The nineteen-story hotel is next to the downtown Convention Center. Restaurant, bar. In-room data ports, some refrigerators, cable TV. Indoor pool. Hot tub, sauna. Exercise equipment. Shops. Business services. Parking (fee). Some pets allowed. | 250 N. Main St. | 901/527–7300 | fax 901/526–1561 | www.marriott.com | 402 rooms | $139–$144 | AE, D, DC, MC, V.

★ **Peabody Hotel.** This 14-story Italian Renaissance Revival hostelry, a downtown landmark since 1924, has been impeccably restored. The lobby preserves original stained-glass skylights and a centerpiece fountain, where you'll find the famous Peabody ducks. Each day, the main event is watching the dutiful ducks make their way to the lobby and back up to their rooftop home, all to the stirring sounds of Sousa's "King Cotton March." 4 restaurants, bar with entertainment, room service. In-room data ports, cable TV. Pool. Hot tub. Beauty salon, massage. Gym. Business services, parking (fee). | 149 Union Ave. | 901/529–4000 or 800/732–2639 | fax 901/529–3600 | www.peabodymemphis.com | 468 rooms | $160–$320 | AE, D, DC, MC, V.

Radisson. Expect the usual chain amenities at this hotel in downtown Memphis. Restaurant, bar. In-room data ports, cable TV. Pool. Hot tub. Exercise equipment. Business services. | 185 Union Ave. | 901/528–1800 | fax 901/526–3226 | www.radisson.com | 280 rooms | $109–$119 | AE, D, DC, MC, V.

Radisson Inn Memphis Airport. It's a 15-minute drive east to downtown from this airport hotel. Area restaurants are nearby. The peach-toned rooms are well appointed. Restaurant, bar, room service. Cable TV. Pool. Tennis. Exercise equipment. Business services, airport shuttle. | 2411 Winchester Rd. | 901/332–2370 | fax 901/398–4085 | 211 rooms | $99–$125 | AE, D, DC, MC, V.

Residence Inn by Marriott. These small apartment-style lodgings in the business district, catering chiefly to business people, are near several restaurants, 20 mi east of downtown. Complimentary Continental breakfast. Kitchenettes, microwaves, refrigerators, cable TV. Pool. Hot tub. Laundry facilities. Business services. Some pets allowed (fee). | 6141 Poplar Pike | 901/685–9595 | fax 901/685–1636 | www.marriott.com | 105 suites | $109–$154 | AE, D, DC, MC, V.

MONTEAGLE

MAP 12, G3

(Nearby towns also listed: Chattanooga, Manchester)

Monteagle has a fascinating history, having been developed and promoted by a founder of the temperance movement starting soon after the Civil War ended. The Monteagle Sunday School Assembly, a still active summer colony, was an offshoot of the Chautauqua movement, which began in New York state on the shores of Lake Chatauqua.

The Monteagle Sunday School Assembly began as a kind of Christian summer camp that offered lectures, concerts, and other entertainment and learning experiences to Sunday school teachers, families, and individuals. The religious aspects of the gatherings have become less emphasized, and anyone—with references—can rent the cottages and take part in the programs today. Monteagle is also the gateway to the huge South Cumberland State Recreation Area.

Information: Grundy County Chamber of Commerce | HCR 76, Box 578, Grueth-Laager 37339 | 931/779–4050.

Attractions

Monteagle Wine Cellars. Nineteen wines are produced at this 20-acre vineyard. Martha Stewart touted the Sauvignon Blanc on her TV show. You can tour and taste every day. | U.S. 41, Exit 64 | 931/924–2120 or 800/556–9463 | Free | Mon.–Sat. 8–6, Sun. noon–5.

South Cumberland State Recreation Area. This 19,000-acre complex of parks and caves and other natural wonders is on the Cumberland Plateau. The entrance is just 4 mi north of Monteagle. | Rte. 1, Box 2196 | 931/924–2980 | fax 931/924–2956 | www.state.tn.us/environment/parks/socumb/index.html | Free | Daily dawn–dusk.

★ **Carter State Natural Area.** The 140-acre area features the impressive Lost Cove Caves; to reach them, take a 2-mile hike northeast along the Buggytop Trail. It starts 3 mi south of U.S. 64, on Route 56 in the South Cumberland Recreation Area. | Rte 1, Box 2196 | 931/924–2980 | fax 931/924–2956 | www.state.tn.us/environment/parks/socumb/index.html | Free | Daily dawn–dusk.

Foster Falls Small Wild Area. A highlight is a 60-ft waterfall. Visitors enjoy camping and hiking in this wilderness area, part of the South Cumberland State Recreation Area. | Rte 1, Box 2196 | 931/924–2980 | fax 931/924–2956 | www.state.tn.us/environment/parks/socumb/index.html | Free | Year-round (hiking); Apr.–Oct. (camping).

Great Stone Door. The unusual 150-ft-tall rock formation offers incredible views of the southern portion of Cumberland Plateau. To reach it drive 10 mi north of Monteagle on Rte. 56. | 931/692–3887 | www.state.tn.us/environment/parks/socumb/index.html | Free | Daily.

Grundy Forest State Natural Area. The 212-acre forested area, within the South Cumberland State Recreation Area, features the picturesque Fiery Gizzard Hiking Trail. The entrance is on U.S. 41, 3½ mi south of Monteagle. | Rte 1, Box 2196 | 931/924–2980 | fax 931/924–2956 | Free | Daily.

Grundy Lakes State Park. The park is the site of the Lone Rock Coke Ovens, where locally mined coal was converted to coke using convict labor until 1896. The ovens still remain. Activities include hiking and swimming in the 4 lakes. The entrance is 2 mi west of Monteagle on U.S. 41. | Rte 1, Box 2196 | 931/924–2980 | fax 931/924–2956 | www.state.tn.us/environment/parks/socumb/index.html | Free | Daily.

Savage Gulf State Natural Area. Forests, caves, and waterfalls are among the attractions of this 11,500-acre area within the larger South Cumberland State Recreation Area. There's camping and hiking. To reach entrance, drive 10 mi north of Monteagle on Route 399. | 931/779–3532 | www.state.tn.us/environment/parks/socumb/index.html | Free | Daily.

Sewanee Natural Bridge. Mother Nature created this amazing 27-ft-high, 5-ft-long sandstone bridge. Within the South Cumberland State Recreation Area. To visit drive 5 mi southwest of Monteagle on Route 56, 2 mi south of the U.S. 41 turn-off. | www.state.tn.us/enviroment/parks/socumb/index.html | Free | Daily.

University of the South. The small liberal arts university 4 mi from downtown has a beautiful mountain setting. | 735 University Ave. | 931/598–1000 | www.sewanee.edu | Free to visitors | Mon.–Sat.

ON THE CALENDAR

JUNE: *Sewanee Music Festival.* The festival features symphony orchestra and chamber music concerts, recitals, and special events. Held at the University of the South. Some concerts are free; tickets for others are $10. | 931/598–1225.

JULY, AUG.: *Monteagle Chatauqua Assembly.* This annual summer gathering of Sunday School teachers and a family retreat takes place at the Assembly Grounds, 1 Assemble Ave. You can take part in the programs and make reservations to stay in the inn or one of the cottages on-site. | 931/924–2272.

AUG.: *Monteagle Mountain Market.* You can peruse about 100 arts, crafts, and food booths, and hear some bluegrass picking at this large event. It's held the first full weekend of August at Monteagle Community Center, and has been going on since 1959. | 931/924–5353.

Dining

Jim Oliver's Smoke House Restaurant. Southern. Smoked turkey and barbecue with pintos and fried apples are some of the down-home treats here. The restaurant is crowded with handmade crafts and antique farm implements. | 850 W. Main St. | 931/924–2268 | Breakfast also available | $10–$13 | AE, D, DC, MC, V.

Lodging

Adams Edgeworth Inn. This inn, built in 1896, houses a collection of art and antiques and is on the grounds of Monteagle Chatauqua Assembly. Verandas—with rocking chairs and hammocks—abound. Many bedrooms have details like clawfoot tubs, white wainscoting, and canopy beds. Complimentary breakfast. Cable TV in common area. | Monteagle Assembly Grounds | 931/924–4000 | fax 931/924–3236 | www.1896-edgeworth-mountain-inn.com | 14 rooms | $125–$175 | AE, MC, V.

Best Western Smoke House. Enjoy home-smoked meats at this small resort, on top of Monteagle Mountain. The lodging is set on 25 acres and offers access to 200 mi of local hiking trails. The Hideaway Cabins have hot tubs, and also rockers on a long porch. There are laundry facilities across the street. Located 4 mi from the University of the South campus. Restaurant, room service. Some in-room hot tubs. Cable TV. Pool. Tennis. Playground. Business services. Some pets allowed. | 850 Main St. | 931/924–2091 or 800/489–2091 | www.bestwestern.com | 99 rooms; 12 cabins | $68–$85, $141 cabins | AE, D, MC, V.

Monteagle Inn. Formal gardens and a large front porch are two of the special touches at this 1940s bed-and-breakfast. There is even a courtyard with tables for outdoor dining. The rooms mix antiques, such as sleigh or four-poster beds, and modern pieces like overstuffed recliners. Complimentary breakfast. In-room data ports. TV in common areas. No pets. No smoking. | 204 W. Main St. | 931/924–3869 | fax 931/924–3867 | www.monteagleinn.com | 13 rooms | $120–$135 | AE, MC, V.

MORRISTOWN

MAP 12, G5

(Nearby towns also listed: Greeneville, Knoxville, Rogersville)

Morristown chose a unique solution when it restored its downtown. Instead of removing the fabrications that had been installed to "modernize" the ground floors of its 19th-century storefronts, the town raised the sidewalks along Main Street and cut new doors into the facades of its buildings, installing crosswalks 20 ft above the ground to enable shoppers to cross the street. Morristown also has the distinction of being the boyhood home of pioneer David Crockett, whose father kept a tavern here.

Information: **Morristown Area Chamber of Commerce** | 825 West First North St., Morristown 37815 | 423/586–6382 | www.morristownchamber.com.

Attractions

Cherokee Dam and Lake. There's fishing and boating on this lake created by the Tennessee Valley Authority dam on the Holston River. It's 35 mi west of Morristown. | 1015 TVA Pkwy. | 865/475–3136 | Free | Daily.

Crockett Tavern and Pioneer Museum. Davy Crockett, born in 1786, grew up in Morristown. This is a reconstruction of the original John Crockett Tavern owned and run by his father, now a museum. The original building was burned down after smallpox victims stayed there. | 2002 E. Morningside Dr. | 423/587–9900 | Free | May–Nov., Tues.–Sat. 10–5.

Panther Creek State Park. Located on Cherokee Reservoir 3 mi west of Morristown off Hwy. 11E, the 1,435-acre park offers spectacular views. Activities include camping, fishing, boating, swimming, and horseback riding. | 210 Panther Creek Park Rd. | 423/587–7046 | www.state.tn.us/environment/parks/panther/index.html | Free | Daily.

Rose Center. This 1892 school building downtown is now a community cultural center. There's a regional art gallery and a historical museum. | 442 W. 2nd North St. | 423/581–4330 | www.rosecenter.org | Free | Weekdays 9–5.

ON THE CALENDAR

NOV.: *Christmas Parade.* As many as 300 people take part in this parade along East and West Main streets, held the first Thursday after Thanksgiving. There are marching bands, floats, and a tree-lighting ceremony. | 423/586–6382.

Dining

Angelo's. American. All the woodwork in this restaurant, from the panelling to the tables, dates from the 1940s. Tilapia stuffed with crabmeat and the sirloin and lobster are your best bets. | 3614 W. Andrew Johnson Hwy. | 423/581–4882 | Closed Sun. No lunch | $10–$26 | AE, MC, V.

Lodging

Comfort Suites Morristown. In terms of decor or views, there's not a lot to distinguish this hotel. But if you need the space that suites provide, this is your ticket. Angelo's and several other restaurants are in the immediate vicinity. Complimentary Continental breakfast. In-room data ports, some microwaves, some refrigerators, some in-room hot tubs, cable TV. Indoor pool. Sauna. Exercise equipment. Laundry services. Business services. No pets. | 3660 W. Andrew Johnson Hwy. | 423/585–4000 | fax 423/585–4002 | www.comfortinn.com | 82 suites | $60–$130 | AE, D, DC, MC, V.

Holiday Inn. This member of the popular hotel chain is in the center of Morristown near numerous restaurants. It's within 15 minutes of four golf courses. Restaurant, room service. Cable TV. Pool. Business services. | 3304 W. Andrew Johnson Hwy. | 423/581–8700 | fax 423/581–7128 | www.basshotels.com | 118 rooms | $58–$84 | AE, D, DC, MC, V.

Holiday Inn of Morristown Conference Center. You can enjoy a relaxed atmosphere and friendly southern hospitality at this chain hotel near I–81 in the south part of town. The rooms are pleasantly decorated in hues of burgundy and green. Restaurant. Cable TV. 2 pools, wading pool. Exercise equipment. Business services. Some pets allowed. | 5435 S. Davy Crockett Pkwy. | 423/587–2400 | fax 423/581–7344 | www.basshotels.com | 112 rooms | $62–$105 | AE, D, DC, MC, V.

MURFREESBORO

MAP 12, F2

(Nearby towns also listed: Franklin, Lebanon, Manchester, McMinnville, Nashville, Shelbyville)

Murfreesboro was briefly the capital of Tennessee, from 1819 to 1825, and it has a rich Civil War history. The town is the home of Middle Tennessee State University, the second-largest university in the state and a major employer. The geographic center of state is just off Old Lascassas Pike, a mile from downtown, which places Murfreesboro very near the exact center of Tennessee.

Information: Rutherford County Chamber of Commerce | 501 Memorial Blvd., 37129 | 615/893–6565 | www.rutherfordcounty.org.

Attractions

Cannonsburgh Village. This living-history museum, an expanse of 22 buildings primarily constructed of log, re-creates an 1800s settlement. There is a working blacksmith shop, displays of farm equipment, a schoolhouse, and a museum. | 312 S. Front St. | 615/890–0355 | Free | Property open daily; buildings open Apr.–Oct., Tues.–Sat. 10–5, Sun. 1–5.

Oaklands Historic House Museum. A modest two-room structure when it was built in 1815, the house grew as the Maney family prospered until it was five times its original size and adorned with an Italianate facade. During the Civil War, the mansion played host to both Northern and Southern officers, including Confederate President Jefferson Davis. It was here that Murfreesboro was surrendered to the Confederate army. The rooms and gardens have been restored to look as they did at the time of the Civil War; about 30% of the furniture is original. | 900 N. Maney Ave. | 615/893–0022 | www.merchantfind.com/oaklandsmuseum.htm | $5 | Tues.–Sat. 10–4, Sun. 1–4.

Stones River National Battlefield. The battle of Stones River took place in the cedar forests near the northwest corner of Murfreesboro, not even 1 mi from downtown, as 1862 turned into 1863. A bloody conflict in miserable weather, it had no clear victor. Union forces sustained more casualties, but the Confederates retreated first. The battlefield contains a national cemetery and the oldest intact Civil War monument. | 3501 Old Nashville Hwy. | 615/893–9501 or 615/893–9501 | www.merchantfind.com/stonesriverbattlefield.htm | Daily.

ON THE CALENDAR

APR.: *Charlie Daniels' Rodeo.* Hundreds of cowboys and cowgirls from across the country compete in bareback bronco riding, steer wrestling, and barrel racing. The rodeo takes place the last Friday and Saturday in April at Middle Tennessee State University's Tennessee Livestock Center. | 615/890–0850.

JULY: *Uncle Dave Macon Days.* The popular festival includes old-time country music, arts, crafts, food, and children's activities. Takes place at Cannonsburgh Village. | 615/893–6565 or 800/716–7650 | www.merhcantfind.com/davemacondays.htm.

AUG.: *International Grand Championship Walking Horse Show.* The show is a major Tennessee walking horse event, which takes place annually at Middle Tennessee University's Livestock Center. | 615/890–9120.

Dining

Be Bop's Café. American. The half-pound "Be Bop Burger" rules here. You should order onion rings on the side. This restaurant replicates a 1950s–style diner; it's full of shiny chrome. | 2601 E. Main St. | 615/867–3201 | Closed Sun. | $3–$5 | MC, V.

Demos' Steak and Spaghetti House. Italian. There's an eclectic menu, traditional ambience, and a casual-dining atmosphere at this family-owned and operated restaurant. Blackened-chicken pasta with Cajun alfredo sauce and cheesy lasagna are best-sellers. In the last several years the restaurant has received numerous awards from readers of area newspapers. Kids' menu. | 1115 N.W. Broad St. | 615/895–3701 | $10–$23 | AE, D, DC, MC, V.

Luby's Cafeteria. American. This may be a cafeteria, but folks line up for mildly spicy Cajun-style catfish or pan-grilled cod. Displays include photographs of old Murfreesboro. | 1720 Old Fort Pkwy. | 615/890–4188 | $4–$10 | AE, D, DC, MC, V.

Parthenon Mediterranean. Mediterranean. This casual and romantic restaurant has a fireplace and piano music that add to the warm, inviting atmosphere. Try the fillet Oscar topped with crab, asparagus, and Bearnaise sauce, and the homemade baklava. Kids' menu. | 1935 S. Church St. | 615/895–2665 | $9–$36 | AE, DC, MC, V.

Santa Fe Steak Co. American. Earth tones and white-wash create a southwestern atmosphere at this popular eatery. Don't be shocked at the peanut shells scattered over the stone floors. Locals often order the sizzling skillet fajitas. Kids' menu. | 127 S.E. Broad St. | 615/890–3030 | $7–$20 | AE, D, DC, MC, V.

Slick Pig Bar-B-Que. Barbecue. Pig figurines add a touch of whimsy to this restaurant. Try the hickory-smoked wings or pork barbecue with their own sauce. Typical sides are potato salad or white beans. | 1920 E. Main St. | 615/890–3583 | Closed Sun.–Mon. | $5–$7 | MC, V.

Lodging

Byrn-Roberts Inn. Twelve-ft-tall ceilings and chandeliers grace the only brick Queen Anne home in the town. Rooms have overstuffed chairs in front of working fireplaces. The yard is full of flower beds. Complimentary breakfast. In-room data ports, in-room hot tubs, cable TV. Exercise equipment. No pets. No kids under 14. No smoking. | 346 E. Main St. | 615/867–0308 | fax 615/867–0280 | www.byrn-roberts-inn.com | 4 rooms | $100–$160 | AE, D, MC, V.

Comfort Inn. Numerous restaurants and stores are within a mile of this chain motel, though there isn't much of a view. Located right off I-24. Complimentary Continental breakfast. In-room data ports, some microwaves, some refrigerators, some in-room hot tubs. Cable TV. Outdoor pool. No pets. | 110 N. Thompson La. | 615/890–2811 | fax 615/890–3487 | www.comfortinn.com | 52 rooms | $45–$60 | AE, D, DC, MC, V.

Garden Plaza. There's a large atrium lobby and garden at this hotel, directly off I–24. Rooms are tastefully decorated in deep reds and greens. It's within walking distance of shopping and restaurants. Restaurant, bar, room service. Some minibars, refrigerators, cable TV. Indoor-outdoor pool. Hot tub. Some pets allowed. | 1850 Old Fort Pkwy. | 615/895–5555 or 800/342–7336 | fax 615/895–5555, ext. 165 | 170 rooms | $55–$89, $139 suites | AE, D, DC, MC, V.

Hampton Inn. This hotel within the Mursfreeboro city limits is near shopping, restaurants, and Middle Tennessee State University. There's a casual lobby filled with couches and TV. Complimentary Continental breakfast. Cable TV, in-room VCRs. Pool. Business services. Some pets allowed. | 2230 Armory Dr. | 615/896–1172 | fax 615/895–4277 | www.hamptoninn.com | 119 rooms | $54–$70 | AE, D, DC, MC, V.

Holiday Inn. Appealing to families, this hotel features video games in the rooms. There's lots of shopping and dining nearby, and it's close to Civil War attractions, such as the Stone River Battle Ground. Restaurant, bar, room service. Cable TV. Indoor-outdoor pool. Hot tub. Exercise equipment. Video games. Laundry facilities. Business service, free parking. | 2227 Old Fort Pkwy. | 615/896–2420 | fax 615/896–8738 | www.basshotels.com | 180 rooms | $63–$75 | AE, D, DC, MC, V.

Howard Johnson. This comfortable motel with large rooms is directly off I–40 in Murfreesboro. Restaurant, complimentary Continental breakfast. Some refrigerators, some microwaves, some in-room hot tubs. Cable TV. Pool. Laundry facilities, laundry service. Business services. Some pets allowed (fee). | 2424 S. Church St. | 615/896–5522 or 800/406–1411 | fax 615/890–0024 | www.hojo.com | 80 rooms | $30–$89 | AE, D, DC, MC, V.

Quality Inn Murfreesboro. The rooms are modest and generic, but you can walk to shops and restaurants, including Demo's and Shooney's, just 3 blocks away. The hotel was built in 1996 and is in a residential neighborhood. Complimentary Continental breakfast. Some microwaves, some refrigerators, some in-room hot tubs, Cable TV. Outdoor pool. Tennis. Pets allowed (fee). | 118 Westgate Blvd. | 615/848–9030 | fax 615/896–3470 | www.qualityinn.com | 78 rooms | $40–$100 | AE, D, DC, MC, V.

Ramada Limited. Lush greenery welcomes guests to the lobby of this Ramada. It's near restaurants and shopping, and the hotel offers a discount to neighboring Ponderosa restaurant. Complimentary Continental breakfast. Cable TV. Pool, wading pool. Business services. Some pets allowed. | 1855 S. Church St. | 615/896–5080 | www.ramada.com | 81 rooms | $30–$85 | AE, D, DC, MC, V.

Shoney's Inn. This motel is on the edge of town near several restaurants. It's medium-sized rooms are decorated in a contemporary style. It's 4 mi northwest of Stones River National Battlefield and 1 mi northwest of Cannonsburgh. Complimentary Continental breakfast. Some refrigerators, cable TV. Pool. | 1954 S. Church St. | 615/896–6030 or 800/222–2222 | fax 615/896–6037 | www.shoneysinn.com | 125 rooms | $51–$75 | AE, D, DC, MC, V.

Simply Southern. This bed-and-breakfast is practically on the Middle Tennessee State University campus and within walking distance of restaurants and shops. Rooms have private baths, and there's a fireplace, pool table, piano, and large front porch with wicker rockers. Complimentary breakfast. In room TV/VCR. Refrigerators. | 211 N. Tennessee Blvd. | 615/896–4988 or 888/723–1199 | info@simplysouthern.net | www.simplysouthern.net | 4 rooms, 1 suite | $85–$95, $145 suite | AE, D, DC, MC, V.

Wingate Inn. This classy hotel is situated between two malls, 10 mi east The rooms feature dark-wood furniture and four-poster beds. Complimentary Continental breakfast. In-room data ports, in-room hot tubs, some minibars, cable TV. Pool. Hot tub. Exercise equipment. Business services. Laundry facilities. Some pets allowed. | 165 Chaffin Pl. | 615/849–9000 or 800/228–1000 | fax 615/849–9066 | www.wingateinns.com | 86 rooms; 2 suites | $89–$12, $125–$250 suites | AE, D, DC, MC, V.

NASHVILLE

(Nearby towns also listed: Clarksville, Dickson, Franklin, Gallatin, Hendersonville, Lebanon, Murfreesboro)

Home of the Grand Ole Opry, Tennessee's fast-growing capital city (with a population of 542,600) prides itself on its cultural, historic, and educational heritage, which has earned it a reputation as the "Athens of the South." The sprawling city occupies 538 square miles, bisected from east to west by the Cumberland River. In addition to entertainment, other leading local industries include computer manufacturing, health care management, hospitality, and automobile technology. Much of Nashville's role as a cultural leader is derived from the presence of 16 colleges and universities, two medical schools, two law schools, and six graduate business schools. Several schools, including Vanderbilt University, have national or international reputations, and many have private art galleries.

Bolstering Nashville's reputation as a cultural hub are dozens of clubs, performance venues, and the Tennessee Performing Arts Center, opened in 1985. The District, the 16-square-block area of downtown between Church St. and Broadway, has emerged as a destination for tourists and locals alike, with restaurants, specialty shopping, and numerous entertainment options. Many restored historic buildings are found downtown, arguably the most famous of which is the Ryman Auditorium, home to the Grand Ole Opry from 1943 to 1974. Adjacent to downtown, Music Row is home to the Country Music Hall of Fame, as well as to major recording studios and music publishing and licensing companies. Farther afield, Greater Nashville offers a variety of cultural attractions including historic plantations and homes (such as that of President Andrew Jackson), museums, and parks.

Information: Nashville Convention and Visitors Bureau | 161 4th Ave. N, Nashville, TN 37219 | 615/259–4700 | or www.nashvillecvb.com.

TRANSPORTATION INFORMATION

Airports: Nashville International Airport (615/275–1675) is about 8 mi east of downtown, and is served by most major airlines. To reach downtown by car, take I–40 west.
Airport Transportation: Cab fare from the airport to downtown runs about $20 plus tip. **Downtown Airport Express** (615/275–1180) has service to downtown hotels for $9.
Bus Lines: Greyhound (200 8th Ave. S | 800/231–2222 | www.greyhound.com) runs service in and out of Nashville.
Intra-city Transit: Metropolitan Transit Authority (MTA) buses (615/862–5950) serve the county; fare is $1.35 in exact change. **Nashville Trolley Company** (615/862–5969) trolleys cover downtown and Music Row in summer months; the fare is 90¢.
Other: from the north and south, I–65 leads into Nashville; take I–24 from the northwest and southeast; I–40 from the east and west, and I–440 to loop around the city.
Driving around Town: The Cumberland River bisects the center of Nashville north–south. Numbered avenues run parallel to the river to its west, while numbered streets are east of and parallel to it. I–40 divides the city as well, running east and west through town. I–24 and I–65 also cut through Nashville. All these highways lead into downtown, which is west of the river. Try to stay off the roads during rush hours, between 7:30 and 8:30 in the morning and again between 4:30 and 5:30 in the evening; traffic is especially bad around Opryland and downtown, where there are one-way streets. If you want to avoid the congested city center, take Briley Parkway, which loops around the edge of Nashville toward the northeast section of the area. Downtown, meter parking is hard to find during business hours but after 6, meters are free if you're lucky

enough to grab a spot. Otherwise, look for a parking garage; there are plenty of them and the cost is $5 or $6 per day.

NEIGHBORHOODS

Belle Meade. Besides upscale shopping, this affluent suburb southwest of Vanderbilt University has the Belle Meade Mansion, a Greek Revival house that was once the center-piece of one of the nation's first and finest thoroughbred breeding farms.

Downtown Nashville. The heart of Nashville has seen a renaissance in the last decade, with new skyscrapers rising over the honky-tonks of lower Broadway and a new stadium for the city's recently acquired NFL team, the Tennessee Titans. In the Historic Second Avenue Business District, restored 19th-century warehouses and storefronts now house restaurants, specialty shops, and tourist attractions like the Hard Rock Café and Planet Hollywood. The old Ryman Auditorium, the original home of the Grand Ole Opry, is a country music shrine; it still hosts a variety of performances and concerts.

Green Hills. This prosperous, well-groomed neighborhood adjoining Belle Meade is home to Cheekwood, a 1923 Georgian Revival mansion with botanical gardens and a collection of art and antiques.

West End. Prestigious Vanderbilt University dominates this neighborhood southwest of downtown. Centennial Park, home of the city's replica of the Parthenon, is across West End Avenue from Vanderbilt. This college neighborhood is filled with restaurants, shops, bars, and clubs. Music Row, on 16th and 17th avenues and Demonbreun Street, is at the eastern edge of the West End. This is where you'll find the Country Music Hall of Fame as well as recording studios and record industry offices.

Attractions

ART AND ARCHITECTURE

The Parthenon. This full-size reproduction of the Parthenon in Athens was built for Tennessee's 1897 centennial exposition. Inside is a 42-ft statue of the Greek goddess Athena—the tallest indoor sculpture in the Western world. In the basement is the Cowan Collection, with 63 works of art by 19th- and early 20th-century American artists. | Centennial Park, West End Ave. and 25th Ave. N | 615/862–8431 | fax 615/880–2265 | www.parthenon.org | $2.50 | Apr.–Sept., Tues. 9–7:30, Weds.–Sat. 9–4:30, Sun. noon–4:30.

CULTURE, EDUCATION, AND HISTORY

Belle Meade Plantation. Called the "queen of the Tennessee plantations," this 1853 mansion is a stunning example of the Greek Revival tradition. It was the Confederate head-quarters during the Battle of Nashville—you can still find bullet holes riddling the front columns. At the turn of the century, Belle Meade was considered the nation's finest thor-oughbreed breeding farm. Tours of the restored house and grounds are conducted by guides in period dress. | 5025 Harding Rd. 37205 | 615/356–0501 or 800/270–3991 | www.belle-meadeplantation.com | $10 | Daily 9–5.

Belmont Mansion. Built in 1850, the Italianate villa was considered one of the finest res-idences of its time. It was originally the home of Adelicia Acklen, one of the city's more colorful characters. When her first husband died during the Civil War, she was left with thousand of bales of cotton threatened by Confederate troops. More concerned about her fortune than her safety, Adelicia traveled to Louisiana and "negotiated" the sale of her cot-ton to England, netting her almost $1 million in gold. At one point, Belmont contained 36 rooms with 10,900 square ft of living space and 9,400 square ft of service area in the base-ment. The house and grounds also featured a 200-ft-long greenhouse, an art gallery, sev-eral gazebos, a bowling alley, a bear house, a zoo, and a water tower (still standing) that provided irrigation for the gardens and water to run the fountains. Today 15 of the rooms, with their original marble statues, Venetian glass, and art, are open to the public. | 1900

Belmont Blvd. | 615/460–5459 | fax 615/460–5688 | www.belmontmansion.com | $6 | June–Aug., Mon.–Sat. 10–4, Sun. 1–5; Sept.–May, Tues.–Sat. 10–4.

Fisk University. The historically black university, one of the first in the nation, was founded in 1867. Money for the school was raised by the famed Jubilee Singers, a student gospel group that performed around the world. Fisk boasts such distinguished alumni as W. E. B. DuBois and Booker T. Washington. The university sits directly west of downtown, off 18th Avenue North, in the middle of a historic district that features several architectural landmarks, including Jubilee Hall, built in 1876 with funds raised by the Fisk Jubilee Singers. | 1000 17th Ave. N | 615/329–8500 | www.fisk.edu | Free to visitors | Daily.

Fort Nashborough. This is a re-creation (on a smaller scale) of Nashville's first settlement, which was named after General Francis Nash, a North Carolina general killed during the Revolutionary War. The one-quarter-size reconstruction has stockaded walls and exhibits of pioneer implements. | 170 1st Ave. N 37201 | 615/255–8192 | Free | Tues.–Sun. 9–5 (weather permitting).

The Hermitage. President Andrew Jackson built this Greek Revival mansion for his wife, Rachel. Today the house, on 600 acres, is a museum devoted to the Jackson family. Almost all of the furnishings, including furniture, silver, porcelain, and portraits, belonged to the Jacksons. Many of the former president's personal possessions are also on display here, including a sword, hundreds of books, eyeglasses, and Bible. Jackson and his wife are buried in the garden. Also on the premises is Tulip Grove. This was home also to Jackson's nephew, who was his private secretary in Washington, and his wife, who served as White House hostess. | 4580 Rachel's La. | 615/889–2941 | www.thehermitage.com | $9.50 | Daily 9–5.

Sam Davis Home. This is the family home and farm of a young man who refused to give up the name of his informer when he was caught behind Union lines with intelligence on Union troop movements. He was condemned as a spy and chose to die on the gallows rather than betray the Confederacy. You can tour the restored house, smokehouse, slave cabins, and family cemetery where Davis is buried. | 1399 Sam Davis Rd. 37167 | 615/459–2341 | $5 | Mon.–Sat. 10–4, Sun. 1–4.

State Capitol. The Greek Ionic building was constructed between 1845 and 1859. President James K. Polk and the building's architect, are both buried on the premises. Visitors can take guided or self-guided tours. | 505 Deaderick St. | 615/741–1621 | Free | Tours weekdays 9–11, 1–3.

Travellers Rest Historic House. This Federal-style, 16-room house is situated on the site of an Indian village. It was built in 1799 by John Overton, one of the founders of Memphis, who was also Andrew Jackson's law partner and presidential campaign manager. The house is now a museum with period furniture and exhibits on the Civil War. | 636 Farrell Pkwy. | 615/832–8197 | $7 | Tues.–Sat. 10–4, Sun. 1–4.

Vanderbilt University. Vanderbilt University was founded in 1873 on a million-dollar endowment from Commodore Cornelius Vanderbilt, who hoped it would "contribute to strengthening the ties which should exist between all sections of our common country." Vanderbilt University is a comprehensive research university, the largest private employer in middle Tennessee, and the second largest private employer in the state. The campus is set on 316 acres, was designated a registered National Historic Landmark in 1966, and a national arboretum in 1988. | 2201 West End Ave. 37201 | 615/322–7771 | www.vanderbilt.edu | Free | Daily 9–5.

MUSEUMS

Aaron Douglas Gallery. This Fisk University Gallery houses an impressive collection of African Art. | Jackson St. between 17th and D.B. Tod | 615/329–8720 | donations appreciated | Tue.–Fri. 10–5 PM; Sat. 1–4 PM.

Carl Van Vechten Gallery. The highlight of this Fisk University Gallery is the Stieglitz Collection of modern art, a gift to the school from Georgia O'Keeffe. | Intersection of D.B.Todd and Jackson St. | 615/329–8685 | www.dubois.fisk.edu/~gallery | Free | Tue.–Fri. 10–5 PM; Sat 1–5 PM.

★ **Cheekwood–Nashville's Home of Art and Gardens.** The Georgian-style mansion, built in 1932, is now a museum with a permanent collection of 19th- and 20th-century American art, Worcester porcelains, antique silver, Oriental snuff bottles, and period furniture. The 55-acre hilltop site features the original gardens with pools, fountains, statuary, extensive boxwood plantings, and views of the Tennessee hills. A number of gardens have been added since the estate was opened to the public, including a Japanese garden, an herb garden, two perennial gardens, a color garden, a water garden, a seasons garden, and an award-winning wildflower garden. | 1200 Forrest Park Dr. 37205 | 615/356–8000 | www.cheekwood.org | $8 | Mon.–Sat. 9–5, Sun. 11–5.

Country Music Hall of Fame and Museum. Costumes, song manuscripts, instruments, films, and photos celebrate the lives and stories of well-loved country music stars from Roy Acuff to Patsy Cline to Vince Gill. Elvis, Roy Orbison, Dolly Parton, and countless others recorded their music here at RCA Studio B. Now the studio is a hands-on exhibit area that demonstrates how records are produced. | 4 Music Square E | 615/416–2001 | www.country.com/hof/hof-f.html | $10.75 | Daily 9–5.

Cumberland Science Museum. There are 150 interactive exhibits, along with animal shows, science demonstrations, and a planetarium. | 800 Fort Negley Blvd. | 615/862–5160 | www.csmisfun.com | $7.95 | Tues.–Sat. 10–5, Sun. 12:30–5:30.

Farris Agricultural Museum. There are exhibits of farm and home artifacts from the 19th and early 20th centuries. The Tennessee Agriculture Hall of Fame is here, too. | Ellington Center, 440 Hogan Rd. | 615/360–0197 | www.state.tn.us/agriculture/market/agmuseum.html | Free | Weekdays 9–4.

Museum of Beverage Containers and Advertising. It purports to be the largest collection of its kind, with more than 36,000 vintage soda and beer cans and more than 5,000 vintage bottles. The gift shop sells bottles, cans, signs, and bottlecaps. Located 10 mi north of Nashville. | 1055 Ridgecrest Dr., Millersville | 615/859–5236 | www.gono.com/cc/museum.htm | $4 | Mon.–Sat. 9–5, Sun. 1–5.

Music Valley Wax Museum of the Stars. Fifty country music stars are immortalized in wax. Also here is a "Sidewalk of the Stars," with more than 250 hand- and footprints and autographs of famous folk. | 2515 McGavock Pike | 615/883–3612 | $3.50 | May–Sept., daily 9–9; Oct.–Apr., daily 9–5.

Nashville Toy Museum. This museum has one of the nation's most prestigious model train collections, with trains operating on mammoth layouts. The entire collection, which spans 150 years, also features toy soldiers from around the world, a trove of vintage German teddy bears, giant ship models, and dolls. | 2613-B McGavock Pike | 615/883–8870 | fax 615/ 391–0556 | $3.50 | May–Sept., daily 9–9; Oct.–Apr., daily 9–5.

Ryman Auditorium and Museum. Built in 1891 as a revival hall, this was the original home of the Grand Ole Opry, hosting the popular country music show from 1943 to 1974. The 2,000-seat renovated auditorium now is the venue for a variety of performances and concerts. The museum houses country music memorabilia. | 116 5th Ave. N | 615/254–1445 | www.ryman.com | $6.50 | Daily 8:30–4.

Tennessee State Museum. The museum traces the state's history from the time of Native American settlement to the present with its collection of more than 6,000 artifacts and photographs. There are also temporary art and history exhibits. | 505 Deaderick St. | 615/741–2692 | www.tnmuseum.org | Free | Tues.–Sat. 10–5, Sun. 1–5.

Willie Nelson's Museum and Gift Emporium. The museum and gift emporium features the memorabilia of country favorites like Patsy Cline, Elvis Presley, Willie Nelson, and Audie

Murphy. | 2613-A McGavock Pike | 615/885–1515 | $3.25 | Memorial Day–Labor Day, daily, 8 AM–10 PM; Labor Day–Memorial Day, daily, 9–5.

PARKS, NATURAL AREAS, AND OUTDOOR RECREATION

Cheatham Lake, Lock, and Dam. There's camping, fishing, swimming, and boating on and along the lake. | 1798 Cheatham Dam Rd. | 615/792–5697 or 615/254–3734 | Call for camping and launch fees | Daily.

J. Percy Priest Lake. The lake is a good place for camping, waterskiing, fishing, boating, and picnicking. | 3737 Bell Rd. | 615/889–1975 | fax 615/391–0005 | www.orn.usace.army.mil | Free | Weekdays.

Radnor Lake State Natural Area. The 1,100-acre wildlife preserve and lake are only 6 mi from downtown. The area features a large wildlife population and some of the highest hills in the Nashville Basin. | 1160 Otter Creek Rd. | 615/373–3467 | www.state.tn.us/environment/parks/radnor | Free | Daily.

RELIGION AND SPIRITUALITY

The Upper Room Chapel and Museum. The chapel features an 8-ft by 17-ft wood carving based on Leonardo da Vinci's *The Last Supper,* along with other religious art. | 1908 Grand Ave. | 615/340–7207 | www.upperroom.org/chapel | Free | Weekdays 8–4:30.

SHOPPING

Ernest Tubb Record Shop. Opry stars used to make impromptu appearances at this downtown record store. | 417 Broadway | 615/255–7503 | Free | Sun.–Thurs. 9–6, Mon. 9–9, Fri.–Sat. 9AM–midnight.

SPORTS AND RECREATION

Nashville Shores. This sprawling outdoor recreation complex features a water park and a manmade beach on Percy Priest Lake. There are twin water slides, a pool area with a waterfall and giant artificial lily pads, and a beachfront with volleyball courts, miniature golf, jet skis, and paddle boats. Cabins and camping sites are available. | 4001 Bell Rd. | 615/889–7050 | www.nashvilleshores.com | Call for rates | Sat. 10–8, Sun. 10–7.

Tennessee Titans Football Stadium. Nashville's NFL team, the Tennessee Titans, play in this new, state-of-the-art stadium, which opened in August 1999. | 534 Chestnut St. | 615/565–4200 | www.titansonline.com.

THE TENNESSEE FOX TROT CAROUSEL

There's not a single steed in sight on this merry-go-round, which is situated along Nashville's riverfront downtown. The figures that go 'round and 'round on the "sculpto-pictorama" created by noted artist Red Grooms include Davy Crockett wrestling a bear, President Andrew Jackson, Olympic medalist Wilma Rudolph, and other characters, real and imagined, from Tennessee's history. The wildly colorful carnival ride/public art work spins to tunes like Turkey in the Straw and the Tennessee Waltz.

Grooms, a New York-based artist who grew up in Nashville, conceived of the Tennessee Fox Trot Carousel as a tribute to his hometown. It opened in November of 1998. It costs $1.50 a spin, and the proceeds go to Nashville arts projects and scholarships.

© Corbis

SIGHTSEEING TOURS/TOUR COMPANIES

Grand Ole Opry Tours. The company offers tours of varying lengths that include homes of country music stars, Music Row, recording studios, and backstage at the Grand Ole Opry. | 1 Gaylord Dr. | 615/889–9490 | fax 615/231–9615 | www.country.com | $22–$24 | Daily 8–3:30.

Gray Line Bus Tours. The company offers tours of the city, the Grand Ole Opry area, historic sites, and a "homes of the stars" tour, which highlights 14 dwellings of famous entertainers. | 2416 Music Valley Dr., #102, 37214 | 615/883–5555 or 800/251–1864 | fax 615/883–6710 | $18–$63 | Daily 7 AM–9 PM.

OTHER POINTS OF INTEREST

Opryland USA. One of Nashville's top attractions, this complex includes a huge hotel/convention center with 9 acres of indoor gardens, a 1.2-million-square-ft mall, dozens of shops and restaurants, the Wildhorse Saloon, a golf course, and riverboat rides. The Grand Ole Opry is still performed and broadcast from its Opryland home each weekend. The Opryland complex is on Briley Parkway, about 20 minutes northeast of downtown. Take I–40 to Exit 215, then I–24 to Exit 54, and Briley Parkway (I–155) to Exit 11. | 615/889–6611 | fax 615/871–6166 | www.grandoleopry.com | Mon.–Thurs. 10–5, Fri. 10–8, Sat. 10–9.

General Jackson. The world's largest showboat features cruises on the Cumberland River with dinner and live entertainment. | Opryland complex | 615/889–6611 | fax 615/871–6166 | www.grandoleopry.com | $21–$60 | Call for schedule and rates.

★ **Grand Ole Opry.** This is now the home of the popular country music show featuring some of the biggest names in the business, both old-timers and newcomers. There are performances every weekend; the Saturday-night show is broadcast live, as it has every weekend since 1925. | Opryland complex | 615/889–6611 | fax 615/871–6166 | www.grandoleopry.com | $20–$22 | Fri. 7:30, Sat. 6:30, 9:30.

Opryland Hotel and Convention Center. The property includes 2,883 guest rooms, a meeting and entertainment center, numerous shops and restaurants, and 9 acres of interior tropical gardens complete with rivers and waterfalls. The gardens are a tourist attraction in themselves. | 2800 Opryland Dr. 37214 | 615/889–1000 | fax 615/871–5728 | www.opryhotel.com | Free | 24 hrs.

Opryland Museums. The Grand Ole Opry Museum celebrates Hall of Fame members with audio-visual and interactive exhibits. The Roy Acuff Museum features musical instruments, photos, and Roy memorabilia. The Minnie Pearl Museum pays tribute to the beloved country comedienne and features the star's personal items, costumes, and photos. | Opryland complex | 615/889–6611 | fax 615/871–6166 | www.grandoleopry.com | Free | Mon.–Thurs. 10–5, Fri. 10–8, Sat. 10–9.

Opry Mills. The 1.2-million-square-ft mall opened on the site of the now-defunct Opryland theme park. Features theme restaurants, including a rain-forest restaurant, and live entertainment throughout the mall. | Opryland complex 37214 | 615/889–6611 | fax 615/871–6166 | www.grandoleopry.com | Free | Hours are still to be determined.

Tennessee Fox Trot Carousel. Internationally renowned artist and Nashville native Red Grooms created this carousel in his signature playful style. Instead of horses, there are 37 figures of important people in Nashville history. Hop on Andrew Jackson, Davy Crockett, Kitty Wells, Chet Atkins, or one of the other colorful characters and enjoy the ride. | Riverfront Park, 1st Ave. and Broadway, 37201 | 615/254–7020 | $2 | Mon.–Thurs. noon–5, Fri. noon–8, Sat. 11–8, Sun. noon–6.

ON THE CALENDAR

MAY: *Iroquois Steeplechase.* The horse race, at Percy Warner Park on Old Hickory Blvd., is a Nashville tradition. | 615/322–7284.

MAY: *Tennessee Crafts Fair.* It's the largest market of Tennessee crafts. Takes place at Centennial Park in western Nashville. | 615/665–0502.

JUNE: *International Country Music Fan Fair.* Country stars perform and meet their fans at this popular annual event at the Tennessee State Fairgrounds 4 mi south of downtown. | 615/889–7503.

SEPT.: *Tennessee State Fair.* It's a traditional state fair with all the trimmings: concerts, crafts, rides, and exhibits at the Tennessee State Fairgrounds. | 615/862–8980.

SEPT.: *Longhorn World Championship Rodeo.* Rodeo events and fair with food and entertainment in Whitescreek, 10 mi northwest of Nashville. | 615/876–1016 or 800/357–6336.

OCT.: *Southern Festival of Books.* Southern and national writers discuss their work and meet their readers. | 615/320–7001.

NOV., DEC.: *A Country Christmas at Opryland.* The holiday celebration in the Ryman area of the Opryland Hotel features spectacular decorations and special events. | 615/872–0600.

Dining

NASHVILLE

INTRO
ATTRACTIONS
DINING
LODGING

INEXPENSIVE

Bluebird Café. Eclectic. This restaurant in the western part of Nashville always draws a crowd with its nightly entertainment. Open mikes and country music are popular. Sandwiches are big here—Cajun catfish and pork barbecue are favorites. | 4104 Hillsboro Rd. | 615/383–1461 | $7–$9 | AE, D, DC, MC, V | No lunch.

Elliston Place Soda Shop. American. This West End hangout is the oldest restaurant in Nashville (the building dates back to 1939). Classic diner decor—lots of neon, a working soda fountain, lunch counter, and high-backed booths with individual jukeboxes—is the backdrop for the classic diner menu. Known for burgers and fries, plus homemade milkshakes and other soda-fountain favorites. | 2111 Elliston Pl. | 615/327–1090 | $6–$11 | MC, V | Breakfast also available. Closed Sun.

Golden Dragon. Chinese. Typical Chinese fare is served in an Asian-themed dining room at this western Nashville spot. Known for Hunan, Szechwan, and Shanghai dishes. Try the sweet-hot seafood plate. Buffet lunch, dinner. Kids' menu. | 94 White Bridge Rd. 37205 | 615/356–4558 | $6.95–$14.95 | AE, D, DC, MC, V.

Hog Heaven. Barbecue. Casual barbecue restaurant. There are two locations—27th Avenue and Davidson Drive. The Davidson Drive location does take-out only. Known for barbecued pork, chicken, and ribs. | 115 27th Ave. N | 615/329–1234 | 998 Davidson Dr. | 615/353–3885 | $6–$11 | AE, MC, V | Closed Sun., Mon.

La Hacienda Taqueria. Mexican. La Hacienda serves authentic Mexican food in an unpretentious atmosphere in south Nashville. Locals come for the chicken enchiladas and California-style cheese-topped burritos. | 2615 Nolensville Rd. | 615/256–6142 | $8–$13 | AE, D, MC, V.

Sitar. Indian. The friendly staff and relaxed atmosphere make this comfortable Indian eatery in downtown Nashville a standout. The dining room is decorated with traditional Indian artwork, and there's a very affordable hot buffet lunch with favorites like chicken tikka masala and sag paneer. | 116 21st Ave. N | 615/321–8889 | $6.95–$9.95 | AE, D, DC, MC, V.

Towne House Tea Room and Restaurant. American. This luncheon spot is in a historic 24-room downtown mansion, built in the 1840s, and it retains much of the home's original decor, including fireplaces, oak floors, antiques, and paintings. Specialties include homemade baked goods, soups, and sandwiches, plus salads and selected hot-lunch items. | 165 8th Ave. N | 615/254–1277 | Breakfast also available. Closed Sun. No dinner Mon.–Thurs. No lunch Sat. | $7–$14 | AE, D, DC, MC, V.

MODERATE

Green Hills Grille. American. Cactii adorn this West Nashville space decorated in light earth tones—tans, red rock, exposed brick. Large bay windows provide lots of natural light. Known for smoked chicken enchiladas and adobo barbecue chicken salad. Kids' menu. | 2122 Hillsboro Dr. | 615/383–6444 | $9–$20 | AE, D, DC, MC, V.

J. Alexander's. American. This West Nashville restaurant is open and airy, with four distinct dining areas, including a solarium. Decor includes dark-wood paneling, some exposed brick, and framed artwork by local artists. Known for hardwood-grilled beef, chicken and pork, fresh seafood. Kids' menu. | 73 White Bridge Rd. | 615/352–0981 | $8–$24 | AE, D, DC, MC, V.

Loveless Café. Southern. Family-owned and run since opening in the early '70s, Loveless is in a 1920s country house, 20 mi southwest of downtown, which has been operated as a restaurant for more than a half-century. The atmosphere here is rustic, with red-and-white checked tablecloths, hardwood floors, and walls decorated with pictures of country music stars who have eaten there. The cuisine is real down-home Southern cooking: fried chicken, biscuits and gravy, chicken-fried steak, plus home-made jams and jellies. There's deck dining out back, overlooking the lawn. Kids' menu. | 8400 Rte. 100 | 615/646–9700 | Breakfast also available | $8–$20 | AE, MC, V.

Old Spaghetti Factory. American. Brick walls, hardwood floors, and booths made out of converted antique beds create a comfortable, rustic ambience in this converted tobacco warehouse in downtown Nashville, capable of seating 500. There are stained-glass windows, antique light fixtures, and an authentic Nashville trolley car parked right in the middle of the dining room, plus an extensive collection of original photographs and prints of Historic Nashville. Guests pass through the doorway arch of the old Bank of London on their way from the vestibule into the main room. The mostly spaghetti menu is perfect for kids. Chicken parmigiana and spaghetti with meatballs are popular. Kids' menu. | 160 2nd Ave. N | 615/254–9010 | No lunch Sun. | $8–$15 | AE, D, DC, MC, V.

Royal Thai. Thai. Top-notch Thai cooking in an elegant atmosphere is what you'll find at this downtown place. Expect all your favorites, such as the seafood red curry. | 204 Commerce St. | 615/255–0821 | No lunch Sun. | $8–$25 | AE, D, DC, MC, V.

Sunset Grill. Contemporary. The decor is low-key at this Midtown grill—the food is the real attraction. The chef uses locally grown produce and meats, and offers diverse fare such as vegan soups, hearty salads, and lots of creative seafood dishes. Expect at least two fresh fish specials every lunch, and three at dinner. Homemade chocolate bomb and chocolate sushi are dessert favorites. Kids' menu. | 2001-A Belcourt Ave. | 615/386–3663 | No lunch weekends | $8–$29 | AE, D, DC, MC, V.

EXPENSIVE

Bound'ry. Eclectic. Bound'ry is a large, lavishly appointed space in downtown, decorated in a Mediterranean theme with stucco walls and murals depicting classical Greek scenes. Curved booths are nestled in gleaming polished-wood settings and two fireplaces warm the dining room. Assorted statuary, columns, and copper railing accent the spaces. When you're finished eating you can adjourn to the balcony for cigars and martinis. Open-air dining in front, with a tree in the center of the patio. | 911 20th Ave. S | 615/321–3043 | No lunch | $15–$31 | AE, D, DC, MC, V.

Capitol Grille. Contemporary. The Capitol Grille occupies the ground floor of the stately Hermitage Hotel, built in 1908, and retains much of the original decor. The room is swathed in the original polished-oak paneling; marble columns stretch up toward the domed ceiling, where a chandelier hangs from each of the six domes; the original marble bathrooms remain intact, and there's an open fireplace in the dining room. The Napoléon-style seared grouper is a favorite, as is the crème brûlée for dessert. Serves smoked pork chops, grilled chicken breast, lamb chops and salmon. Sun. brunch. | 231 6th Ave. N | 615/345–7116 | $22–$32 | AE, D, DC, MC, V.

★ **Mario's.** Northern Italian. Founded in 1965, Mario's is super high-end fine dining—the restaurant claims to have won "every fine dining award in the United States." The split-level dining room is decorated with Mario's extensive personal wine collection, plus antique credenzas, and wood-burning fireplace. Known for veal, both saltimbocca and osso bucco. Extensive wine list. Specializes in veal and pasta. | 2005 Broadway | 615/327–3232 | Closed Sun. No lunch | $18–$27 | AE, D, DC, MC, V.

The Merchants. Contemporary. This restaurant is housed in the former Merchants Hotel, built in 1892. The first-floor dining room offers a casual bar/grill atmosphere and menu, while the second floor features formal dining in a room with hardwood floors, brick walls, and ceiling fans. Many of the old hotel's original elements have been incorporated into the decor, including original fireplaces, wainscoting, and custom sconces. Live piano music is performed nightly. Chef's specialties include roasted pork tenderloin and grilled Lexington lamb chops. Dine on the open-air patio overlooking Broadway. | 401 Broadway | 615/254–1892 | $15–$31 | AE, D, DC, MC, V.

Mere Bulles. Continental. Mere Bulles offers fine Continental-style dining in a convenient location on Second Avenue. Live jazz, blues, and swing is heard nightly. The interior is spacious, there's an open fireplace in dining room, and archways and windows overlook the Cumberland River. Try the striped Norwegian salmon or the grouper. Sun. brunch. | 152 2nd Ave. N | 615/256–1946 | $23–$40 | AE, D, DC, MC, V.

101st Airborne. American. World War II army tanks, old Red Cross vans, and cannons line the approach to this restaurant, 10 mi from downtown. The interior is decorated with vintage war memorabilia, pictures, and uniforms. House special prime rib is a dinner favorite. Also try the homemade upside-down apple-walnut pie with cinnamon ice cream for dessert. Kids' menu. Entertainment Fri. Sun. brunch. | 1362-A Murfreesboro Rd. | 615/361–4212 | No lunch Sat. | $15–$21.95 | AE, D, DC, MC, V.

Prime Cut Steakhouse. Steak. This popular steak house is housed in a converted 1892 warehouse with stone walls and exposed vents along the ceiling. There are two dining areas, plus a separate bar/lounge. The spacious outdoor courtyard seats 60. Filet mignon and Porterhouse are popular cuts. Open-air dining patio with umbrella tables that seats 40 people, with views of the stadium. Entertainment Fri., Sat. Kids' menu. | 170 2nd Ave. N | 615/242–3083 | No lunch | $21–$30 | AE, D, DC, MC, V.

Sperry's. Seafood. A reconstructed English Tudor–style building in West Nashville is home to this elegant steak house, which also is known for fresh seafood. This is steeplechase country, and the framed paintings that hang among the lush draperies in the dining room reflect equestrian themes. A double fireplace separates the bar/lounge area from the columns, wood paneling, and wall hangings in the banquet room. Choose from no fewer than seven fresh fish entrées nightly, plus Alaskan king crab, lobster tail, steaks, and chops galore. | 5109 Harding Rd. | 615/353–0809 | No lunch | $12.95–$38.95 | AE, DC, MC, V.

The Stockyard. Steak. Housed in an authentic former stockyard (that's an auction house for livestock), The Stockyard restaurant is something of a Nashville institution. An antique building situated in the heart of the historic district, the restaurant boasts three complete floors of authentic Old Nashville ambience—antique furniture and wallpaper, plus top-drawer eats. It's ranked among the top 10 steak houses in the nation by the American Hospitality Association. There's live country music nightly at this celebrity favorite, and you can admire the largest lobster tank east of the Mississippi. Entertainment. Kids' menu. | 901 2nd Ave. N | 615/255–6464 | No lunch | $20–$50 | AE, D, DC, MC, V.

Valentino's. Northern Italian. Valentino's is set in an old West End house converted into an old world–style restaurant. Secluded and intimate, the dimly lit brick interior has a romantic Tuscan quality, which is complemented by the open fireplace. Try the veal, it's the best in town. | 1907 West End Ave. | 615/327–0148 | No lunch Sat. or Sun. | $16–$34 | AE, D, DC, MC, V.

Zola. Mediterranean. This West Nashville restaurant's three dining areas are festooned with antiques, curios, statuary, found objects, and framed artwork, as well as a banana tree. The cuisine is just as eclectic, offering adventurous Mediterranean fare including Moroccan and Turkish dishes, and an entire vegetarian menu. The chef uses all fresh organically grown produce. Paella, Tuscan rib-eye steak, and Spanish pork tenderloin are popular. No smoking. | 3001 West End Ave. | 615/320–7778 | Closed Sun. | $14–$24 | AE, D, MC, V.

VERY EXPENSIVE

Arthur's. Continental. Arthur's Restaurant is situated off the lobby of the Union Station Hotel. The restaurant is done up in wood, fabric, and stone, and features 20-ft ceilings, columns, and stained-glass windows. Famous for rack of lamb. Fillet of blue marlin and halibut are also popular. Homemade soufflés—in a variety of flavors—and Bananas Foster flamed at the table are favorite desserts. | 1001 Broadway | 615/255–1494 | www.arthursrestaurant.com | Jacket required | No lunch | $32–$68 | AE, D, DC, MC, V.

Café One Two Three. Southern. Enjoy Southern classics with a twist at this West Nashville restaurant created in the style of a '20s speakeasy, with hardwood floors, brick walls, and an open fireplace. It's decorated with prohibition-era artifacts and pictures. Try chef's specialties like fried grit cakes or Southern Spinach Salad. | 123 12th Ave. N | 615/255–2233 | Closed Sun. No lunch | $19–$32 | AE, MC, V.

★ **F. Scott's.** Contemporary. Three separate dining areas are elegant and understated, with champagne/mustard-color walls, black lacquer enameled chairs and fixtures, pewter table lamps, and antique wall sconces. Rib-eye and porterhouse steaks are popular at this West Nashville place—also try the homemade desserts like chocolate almond torte. There's live jazz nightly. Kids' menu. | 2210 Crestmoor Rd. | 615/269–5861 | No lunch | $18–$32 | AE, D, DC, MC, V.

The Mad Platter. Eclectic. Housed in the brick storefront of a 120-year-old building in the historic Germantown section of the city, The Mad Platter is casual and inviting, with exposed-brick walls, wood-stove, and ceiling fans. The extensive wine list changes regularly. The kitchen turns out traditional dishes one better—like crab cakes with passion-fruit-honey-mustard sauce or grilled pork loin with basil, strawberries, and brie. | 1239 6th Ave. N | 615/242–2563 | www.madplatter.com | Reservations suggested | No supper Mon. Closed Sun. | $20–$50 | AE, D, MC, V.

New Orleans Manor. Seafood. Old-fashioned gaslamps illuminate the driveway as you approach this restaurant in a classic house with white columns. Inside, buffets are displayed in the front hallway of the former home; dining areas occupy the smaller rooms off the main hall. Try the all-you-can-eat seafood buffet, plus salad bar and dessert buffet. Kids' menu. | 1400 Murfreesboro Rd. | 615/367–2777 | No lunch. Closed Sun. and Mon. | $31–$55 | AE, D, DC, MC, V.

The Wild Boar. French. Enjoy some of the finest dining in the nation amid wood walls decorated with stuffed boar's heads, paintings in a hunting theme, and a more modern touch: an indoor waterfall. This West Nashville restaurant is known for its lobster Thermidor and original French-style crème brûlée with Tahitian vanilla bean. Pianist Fri., Sat. | 2014 Broadway | 615/329–1313 | www.wboar.com | No lunch Sat. Closed Sun. | $22–$34 | AE, D, DC, MC, V.

Lodging

INEXPENSIVE

La Quinta Inn. This is the first La Quinta in Nashville, built around 1980. This facility is surrounded by hospitals, but downtown is just 2 mi away. The rooms have abstract Mexican motifs. Complimentary Continental breakfast. Cable TV. Outdoor pool. Business services. Some pets allowed. | 42 S. Camilla St. | 901/526–1050 | fax 901/525–3219 | www.laquinta.com | 128 rooms, 2 suites | $55–$60 | AE, D, DC, MC, V.

Ramada Limited. Newly renovated rooms in mauve hues are open to the outside. Directly off I–40 in a suburb of Nashville, this hotel is 10 mi from downtown and Music Row. Complimentary Continental breakfast. Cable TV. Pool. Business services. Some pets allowed (fee). | 5770 Old Hickory Blvd., Hermitage | 615/889–8940 | fax 615/871–4444 | www.ramada.com | 100 rooms | $35–$70 | AE, D, DC, MC, V.

Red Roof Inn. This casual motor inn is near a few restaurants, groceries, and convience stores, 6½ mi from the Grand Ole Opry. Cable TV. Airport shuttle. Some pets allowed. | 510 Claridge St. | 615/872–0735 | fax 615/871–4647 | www.redroof.com | 120 rooms | $40–$56 | AE, D, DC, MC, V.

Red Roof Inn–South. This hotel is off I–65 at Exit 69, 5 mi from downtown, 9 mi from the Country Music Hall of Fame, 13 mi from Opryland, and near restaurants. Cable TV. Some pets allowed. | 4271 Sidco Dr. | 615/832–0093 | fax 615/832–0097 | www.redroof.com | 85 rooms | $45–$70 | AE, D, DC, MC, V.

MODERATE

Baymont Inn. Located 10 minutes from Music Row off busy Whitebridge Rd., this hotel offers comfortable rooms and a homey atmosphere. Complimentary Continental breakfast. Cable TV. Pool. Business services. | 5612 Lenox Ave. | 615/353–0700 | fax 615/352–0361 | 120 rooms, 4 suites | $73, $75–$120 suites | AE, D, DC, MC, V.

Baymont Inn. This Baymont is near a mall and countless restaurants, and is 14 mi north of Nashville. Complimentary Continental breakfast. Cable TV. Pool. Business services, free parking. Some pets allowed. | 120 Cartwright Ct., Goodlettsville | 615/851–1891 | fax 615/851–4513 | 100 rooms, 30 suites | $55–$70, $79–$120 suites | AE, D, DC, MC, V.

Days Inn Rivergate. This member of the popular chain is across from Rivergate mall, surrounded by shopping and dining. It is 12 mi north of Nashville. Complimentary Continental breakfast. Microwaves, refrigerators, some in-room hot tubs, cable TV. Business services. Laundry facilities. | 809 Wren Rd., Goodlettsville | 615/859–1771 | fax 615/859–7512 | www.daysinn.com | 47 rooms | $50–$96 | AE, D, DC, MC, V.

Fiddlers Inn. Fiddlers is directly across from the Grand Ole Opry. Cable TV. Pool. Business services. | 2410 Music Valley Dr. | 615/885–1440 | fax 615/883–6477 | 202 rooms | $54–$70 | AE, D, MC, V.

Guesthouse Inn and Suites Medcenter. Rooms here have all the basic amenities and come in various sizes. The hotel is off I–40, 2 mi from downtown, and two blocks from Vanderbilt University and several restaurants. Complimentary Continental breakfast. Minibars, microwaves, refrigerators, cable TV. Laundry facilities. Business services. | 1909 Hayes St. | 615/329–1000 or 800/777–4904 | www.guesthouse.net | 108 rooms | $64–$91 | AE, D, DC, MC, V.

Hampton Inn Nashville–Briley Parkway. This hotel has standard chain accommodations near the airport and 5½ mi from downtown Nashville. Complimentary Continental breakfast. In-room data ports, cable TV. Pool. Business services. Airport shuttle. | 2350 Elm Hill Pike | 615/871–0222 | fax 615/885–5325 | www.hampton-inn.com | 120 rooms | $73–$93 | AE, D, DC, MC, V.

Hampton Inn Nashville/Goodlettsville. Clean and basic accommodations are offered at this hotel by the Rivergate Mall and neighboring shopping centers; it's 14 mi north of downtown. Complimentary Continental breakfast. In-room data ports, minibars, microwaves, refrigerators, some in-room hot tubs, cable TV. Pool. Business services. | 202 Northgate Circle, Goodlettsville | 615/851–2828 | fax 615/851–2830 | www.hampton-inn.com | 63 rooms, 2 suites | $70–$80, $89 suites | AE, D, DC, MC, V.

Hampton Inn–Nashville I–65 North. This Hampton Inn is off I–65 and is 3 mi from downtown. The hotel offers tour services into Nashville. Complimentary Continental breakfast. Cable TV. Pool. Exercise equipment. Video games. Business services. | 2407 Brick Church Pike

| 615/226–3300 | fax 615/226–0170 | www.hampton-inn.com | 125 rooms | $64–$79 | AE, D, DC, MC, V.

Holiday Inn Express. This Holiday Inn is directly off I–24, 10 minutes from local attractions, and 7 mi from the Grand Ole Opry. Dining room, complimentary Continental breakfast. Cable TV. Pool. Hot tub. Laundry facilities. Business services. Airport shuttle. | 981 Murfreesboro Rd. | 615/367–9150 | fax 615/361–4865 | www.basshotels.com | 210 rooms | $59–$85 | AE, D, DC, MC, V.

Holiday Inn Express. Directly behind Rivergate Mall, this motor hotel 13 mi north of Nashville offers standard accommodations for short-stay visitors. Complimentary Continental breakfast. Some in-room hot tubs, cable TV. Pool. | 909 Conference Dr., Goodlettsville | 615/851–6600 | fax 615/851–4723 | www.basshotels.com | 66 rooms | $56–$120 | AE, D, DC, MC, V.

Holiday Inn Express. This hotel is 10 mi east of downtown and 1 mi north of the airport. Three local restaurants are nearby. The cozy great room with a fireplace creates a ski-lodge atmosphere. Some of the rooms, which are accessed from an interior corridor, have balconies. Complimentary Continental breakfast. Cable TV. Pool. Business services. Airport shuttle. | 1111 Airport Center Dr. | 615/883–1366 | fax 615/889–6867 | www.basshotels.com | 206 rooms | $59–$99 | AE, D, DC, MC, V.

Quality Inn and Suites. This hotel is off I–65, 3 mi from downtown and 10 mi from the Opry Mills Mall. Complimentary Continental breakfast. In-room data ports, cable TV. Pool. Exercise equipment. Laundry facilities. Business services. | 2401 Brick Church Pike | 615/226–4600 | fax 615/228–6412 | 142 rooms, 30 suites | $59–$69, $129 suites | AE, D, DC, MC, V.

La Quinta. This newly renovated hotel is centrally located—4 mi north of downtown and 10 minutes from the airport. It's close to the Country Music Hall of Fame and Opryland, and a perfect place for spotting the stars who stay across the street in the Regal Maxwell Hotel. Complimentary Continental breakfast. Microwaves, cable TV. Pool. Laundry facilities. Business services. Some pets allowed. | 2001 Metrocenter Blvd. | 615/259–2130 | fax 615/242–2650 | www.laquinta.com | 120 rooms | $67–$89 | AE, D, DC, MC, V.

Ramada Inn Airport. Centrally located—off I–40 and I–24—between the airport and downtown. It's close to Opryland, and 10 minutes from Music Row. In the evenings, there's live music in the lounge. Restaurant, bar with entertainment, room service. In-room data ports, cable TV. Pool. Laundry facilities, laundry services. Business services, airport shuttle. | 709 Spence La. | 615/361–0102 | fax 615/361–4765 | www.ramada.com | 228 rooms | $64–$71 | AE, D, DC, MC, V.

Red Roof Inn. This newly remodeled hotel is within walking distance of 12 different restaurants, 1 mi from the Grand Ole Opry, the Opry Mills Mall, and the Factory Outlet Mall. The lobby is furnished with comfortable wing-back chairs. Cable TV. Pool. Some pets allowed. | 2460 Music Valley Dr. | 615/889–0090 | fax 615/889–0086 | www.redroof.com | 86 rooms | $70–$85 | AE, D, DC, MC, V.

Shoney's Inn. On the Trolley Line and a stone's throw from Music Row and the Country Music Hall of Fame, this Shoney's Inn offers guests a discount for an all-you-can-eat breakfast at the namesake restaurant. Some microwaves, some refrigerators, some in-room hot tubs. Cable TV. Pool. Business services. | 1521 Demonbreun St. | 615/255–9977 or 800/222–2222 | fax 615/242–6127 | www.shoneysinn.com | 147 rooms | $62–$81, $106 suites | AE, D, DC, MC, V.

Shoney's Inn North. Big, clean, airy rooms are featured at this recently renovated hotel 15 minutes from the Grand Ole Opry, 1 mi from the Antique Mall, and 2 mi from the Rivergate Mall. Guests receive a discount at neighboring Shoney's Restaurant. Complimentary Continental breakfast. Some refrigerators, some microwaves, cable TV. Pool. Business services. | 100 Northcreek Blvd., Goodlettsville | 615/851–1067 or 800/222–2222 | fax 615/851–6069 | www.shoneysinn.com | 111 rooms | $61–$71, $106 suites | AE, D, DC, MC, V.

Super 8. This no-frills hotel is off I–65 and near various restaurants. It's 5 mi west of downtown, 10 mi from Opryland, and 3 mi from Vanderbilt University. Complimentary Continental breakfast. Cable TV. Business services. Some pets allowed. | 412 Robertson Ave. | 615/356–0888 or 800/800–8000 | fax 615/356–0888, ext. 118 | www.super8.com | 73 rooms | $42–$62, $52–$77 suites | AE, D, DC, MC, V.

Wilson Inn. Atop a small hill off Briley Parkway, this hotel is 3 mi north of the airport and 7 mi south of downtown. Complimentary Continental breakfast. Some minibars, refrigerators, cable TV. Business services. Airport shuttle. Some pets allowed. | 600 Ermac Dr. | 615/889–4466 or 800/945–7667 | fax 615/889–0464 | 94 rooms, 16 suites | $65, $89 suites | AE, D, DC, MC, V.

EXPENSIVE

Amerisuites. This hotel offers contemporary, clean suites, and is near suburban Brentwood, a mall, and Restaurant Row. It's also 5 mi south of downtown Nashville, and within 5 mi of both the 100 Oaks Mall and the Galleria Mall. Complimentary Continental breakfast. Kitchenettes, refrigerators, cable TV, in-room VCRs and movies. Pool. Exercise equipment. Laundry facilities. Business services, free parking. Some pets allowed (fee). | 202 Summit View Dr., Brentwood | 615/661–9477 | fax 615/661–9936 | www.amerisuites.com | 126 suites | $74–$150 suites | AE, D, DC, MC, V.

Carole's Yellow Cottage. This 1902 Victorian house, in the Edgefield community, is on the National Register of Historic Places and within walking distance of the Nashville Convention Center, Adelphia Football Coliseum, and Gaylord Entertainment Center. Rooms have 12-ft ceilings with ceiling fans, original pine floors, and European furnishings. Old maps, original paintings, and other artwork hang on the walls. Complimentary breakfast. Cable TV, in-room VCRs. No pets. No smoking. | 801 Fatherland St. | 615/226–2952. | www.bbonline.com/tn/yellowcottage | 2 rooms | $100–$125 | AE, D.

Clarion. This hotel is 6 mi east of downtown, 4 mi south of Opryland. Restaurant, bar with entertainment. Cable TV. Pool. Gym. Playground. Business services, airport shuttle. | 733 Briley Pkwy. | 615/361–5900 | fax 615/367–0339 | 200 rooms | $79–$89 | AE, D, DC, MC, V.

Clubhouse Inn and Suites. The best thing about this modest hotel is its proximity to the airport, which is 2 mi away. Standard rooms are done in floral patterns. Complimentary breakfast. Refrigerators, cable TV. Pool. Hot tub. Laundry facilities. Business services, free Parking, airport shuttle. | 2435 Atrium Way | 615/883–0500 | fax 615/889–4827 | www.clubhouseinn.com | 152 rooms | $79–$104 | AE, D, DC, MC, V.

Clubhouse Inn Conference Center. This hotel is in the thick of downtown Nashville. It's only blocks from the Convention Center, restaurants, and clubs. Across the street from Union Station. Restaurant, bar, complimentary breakfast. Cable TV. Pool. Exercise equipment. Business services. | 920 Broadway | 615/244–0150 | fax 615/244–0445 | www.clubhouseinn.com | 285 rooms | $94–$124 | AE, D, DC, MC, V.

Courtyard by Marriott. Just outside downtown in a quiet neighborhood, this Courtyard is far enough away from the action to provide an escape from the noise yet close enough to access the nightlife if you're interested. It's a half-mile from Music Row and Vanderbilt University. Restaurant, bar. Refrigerators, some microwaves, cable TV. Exercise equipment. Laundry facilities. Business services. | 1901 West End Ave. | 615/327–9900 | fax 615/327–8127 | www.marriott.com | 218 rooms, 5 suites | $85–$105, $125–$145 suites | AE, D, DC, MC, V.

★ **Courtyard by Marriott–Airport.** Rooms are surprisingly spacious at this low-rise hotel 7 mi east of downtown, 2 mi north of the airport. Guests enjoy the sunny, gardenlike courtyard. Restaurant, bar, room service. Refrigerators, cable TV. Pool. Hot tub. Exercise equipment. Laundry facilities. Business services, free parking, airport shuttle. | 2508 Elm Hill Pike | 615/883–9500 | fax 615/883–0172 | www.marriott.com | 145 rooms | $90–$125 | AE, D, DC, MC, V.

Fairfield Inn–Nashville Opryland. This hotel is near two malls and several restaurants and is 20 minutes from downtown and a half-mile from the Grand Ole Opry. Complimentary Continental breakfast. Cable TV. Indoor pool. Exercise equipment. Laundry facilities. Business services, airport shuttle. | 211 Music City Cir. | 615/872–8939 | fax 615/872–7230 | www.fairfieldinn.com | 109 rooms, 4 suites | $59–$93 | AE, D, DC, MC, V.

1501 Lincoln House. Windows in the rooms here reach almost to the top of the 12-ft ceilings, bathing the rooms in light. Floral bedding accents the solid colored walls. The 1893 Victorian home is just a few blocks from Vanderbilt University. Complimentary breakfast. Cable TV, some room phones. No pets. No smoking. | 1501 Linden Ave. | 615/298–2701 or 800/226–0317 | www.bbonline.com/tn/linden | 3 rooms | $95–$135 | AE, MC, V.

Hampton Inn–Brentwood. Rooms have been completely renovated at this hotel located in Brentwood's business district, 9 mi south of Nashville. Complimentary Continental breakfast. Exercise equipment. Laundry services. Pool. Some refrigerators, cable TV. Business services. | 5630 Franklin Pike Cir., Brentwood | 615/373–2212 | fax 615/370–9832 | www.hampton-inn.com | 114 rooms | $79–$91 | AE, D, DC, MC, V.

Hampton Inn and Suites–Nashville Airport. This is one of the more upscale properties within this popular chain. It's 1½ mi from the airport, near outlet stores and 8 mi east of downtown. Complimentary Continental breakfast. Some kitchenettes, some refrigerators, cable TV, in-room VCRs. Pool. Exercise equipment. Laundry facilities, laundry services. Business services, airport shuttle. | 583 Donelson Pike | 615/885–4242 or 800/426–7866 | fax 615/885–6726 | www.hampton-inn.com | 142 rooms | $94–$129 | AE, D, DC, MC, V.

Holiday Inn Brentwood. This member of the noted chain is off I–65 in residential Brentwood, which is 13 mi south of downtown. It's 10 minutes from the Nashville Speedway. Restaurant, bar, room service. In-room data ports, cable TV. Pool. Hot tub. Exercise equipment. Laundry facilities. | 760 Old Hickory Blvd., Brentwood | 615/373–2600 | fax 615/377–3893 | www.basshotels.com | 248 rooms | $79–$145 | AE, D, DC, MC, V.

Ramada Inn Suites–South. In between the airport and Opryland, this quiet hotel features a sparkling atrium lobby with live plants native to the south. The hotel was renovated in 1998. Complimentary Continental breakfast. Kitchenettes, refrigerators, microwaves, cable TV. Pool. Exercise equipment. Laundry facilities. Business services, airport shuttle. Laundry services. Free parking. Some pets allowed. | 2425 Atrium Way | 615/883–5201 or 888/298–2054 | fax 615/883–5594 | www.ramada.com | 120 suites | $83–$137 suites | AE, D, DC, MC, V.

Residence Inn by Marriott. This hotel is underwent renovations in 2000. Many rooms have fireplaces, and the large suites include second-story lofts. It's 15 mi east of downtown and 4 mi south of Opryland Spring House golf course. Complimentary Continental breakfast. Kitchenettes, refrigerators, microwaves, cable TV. Pool. Hot tub. Laundry facilities, laundry services. Business services. Pets allowed. | 2300 Elm Hill Pike | 615/889–8600 | fax 615/871–4970 | www.residenceinn.com | 168 suites | $72–$159 | AE, D, DC, MC, V.

Shoney's Inn. This Shoney's offers a complimentary shuttle to the Opryland hotel, and it's near all the conveniences of the Opryland area. It's right across the street from the Grand Ole Opry and 10 mi from downtown. Bar, complimentary Continental breakfast. Cable TV, indoor pool. Hot tub. Business services, airport shuttle, free parking. | 2420 Music Valley Dr. | 615/885–4030 or 800/222–2222 | fax 615/391–0632 | www.shoneysinn.com | 185 rooms | $100–$135 | AE, D, DC, MC, V.

VERY EXPENSIVE

Amerisuites. Amerisuites offers shuttle services to Opryland, the convention center, and to the Hard Rock Café downtown. It's a half-mile from the Factory Outlet Stores of America, and 1½ mi from the Grand Ole Opry. Complimentary Continental breakfast. Refrigerators, cable TV. Pool. Exercise equipment. Laundry facilities. Business services, airport shuttle, free parking. | 220 Rudy's Cir. | 615/872–0422 | fax 615/872–9283 | www.amerisuites.com | 125 suites | $80–$130 suites | AE, D, DC, MC, V.

Crocker Springs Bed and Breakfast. When you stay at this 1880s farmhouse, 4 mi off I–24 and 14 mi from downtown Nashville, you'll have a delightful view of the owners' 58-acre spread. The rooms have pine floors and pitched pine ceilings. Stefanie's Quilt Room has a full-size feather bed, Todd's Paisley Room has a decorative queen-size iron bed, and the Rose Room includes an antique iron day bed, a queen-size bed, and a claw foot bathtub with shower. The Blue Sitting Room has a fireplace and TV. Complimentary breakfast. No room phones, TV in common area. Pond. Hiking, fishing. Some pets allowed. No smoking. | 2382 Crocker Springs Rd. | 615/876–8502 or 800/373–4911 | fax 615/876–4083 | www.bbonline.com/tn/crockersprings | 3 rooms | $100–$200 | AE, D.

Daisy Hill Bed and Breakfast. It's cozy here when you sit out on the brick patio and survey the owners' gardens. This 1925 Tudor Revival home is on the National Register of Historic Places. Each room design is on a national theme: French country, Scottish Highlands, and Norwegian. Complimentary breakfast. No room phones, TV in common area. Pets allowed. No kids under 12. No smoking. | 2816 Blair Blvd. | 615/297–9795 | www.bbonline.com/tn/daisyhill | 3 rooms | $95–$130 | AE, MC, V.

Doubletree. This nine-story contemporary hotel is in the heart of downtown. The welcoming lobby is decorated with flowers and a grand piano. Nightlife is just two blocks away. Free shuttle to anywhere within 5 mi. Restaurant, bar, room service. In-room data ports, some minibars, cable TV. Indoor pool. Exercise equipment. Business services. | 315 4th Ave. N | 615/244–8200 | fax 615/747–4894 | www.doubletree.com | 336 rooms | $89–$189 | AE, D, DC, MC, V.

Doubletree Guest Suites. This hotel, 9 mi east of downtown, has a spacious, contemporary lobby and a lounge with live music in the evenings. Free shuttle service to anywhere within 5 mi of the hotel is provided. Restaurant, bar. In-room data ports, refrigerators, cable TV. Indoor-outdoor pool. Exercise equipment. Video games. Business services, airport shuttle. | 2424 Atrium Way | 615/889–8889 | fax 615/883–7779 | www.doubletree.com | 138 suites | $170–$210 suites | AE, D, DC, MC, V.

East Park Inn. The chandelier in the dining room and the Dalí prints are just a few of the nice touches in this Queen Anne home dating from the 1880s. The rooms include exposed-hardwood floors, a sleigh bed, and wicker furniture. The inn is in Edgefield. Complimentary breakfast. Some in-room hot tubs, TV in common area. No smoking. | 822 Boscobel St., Edgefield | 615/226–8691 or 800/484–1195 | www.bbonline.com/tn/eastpark | 2 rooms | $150 | AE, D, DC, MC, V.

Embassy Suites. This hotel is among office buildings in a business district 8 mi east of downtown and 2 mi south of the airport. The interior atrium has waterfalls, plants, and flowers. Restaurant, bar, complimentary breakfast, room service. Minibars, refrigerators, microwaves, cable TV. Indoor pool. Hot tub. Exercise equipment. Video games. Laundry services. Business services, airport shuttle. Some pets allowed (fee). | 10 Century Blvd. | 615/871–0033 or 800/362–2779 | fax 615/883–9245 | www.embassysuites.com | 296 suites | $129–$169 suites | AE, D, DC, MC, V.

The Hermitage. Near the State Capitol, the state museum, and Music Row, the Hermitage is Nashville's only Beaux-Arts building. Opened originally in 1910, it was the headquarters of the 1920 suffragette movement. The lobby and exterior have Italian Sienna, Grecian, and Tennessee marble. A restoration was completed in 1995, revealing the lobby's three-story ceiling and skylight. Restaurant, bars. Refrigerators, microwaves, minibars, cable TV. Business services. | 231 6th Ave. N | 615/244–3121 | fax 615/254–6909 | www.thehermitagehotel.com | 120 suites | $129–$209 | AE, D, DC, MC, V.

Hillsboro House Bed and Breakfast. Built in 1904, this Victorian home is just four blocks from Vanderbilt University in the Belmont–Hilsboro area. The rooms combine English country touches like gingham, with contemporary furniture. You can stroll through the herb garden. Complimentary breakfast. Cable TV. Some pets allowed. No smoking. | 1933 20th Ave. S | 615/292–5501 or 800/228–7851 | www.bbonline.com/tn/hillsboro | 3 rooms | $110 | AE, D, MC, V.

Hilton Suites–Brentwood. Conveniently located accommodations 20 minutes from downtown Nashville. There's a complimentary shuttle to Brentwood-area restaurants, and a two-hour beverage reception each evening. Restaurant, bar, complimentary breakfast, room service. Minibars, refrigerators, cable TV, in-room VCRs. Indoor pool. Hot tub. Exercise equipment. Laundry service. Business services. Some pets allowed. | 9000 Overlook Blvd., Brentwood | 615/370–0111 or 800/774–1500 | fax 615/370–0272 | www.hilton.com | 203 suites | $125–$165 | AE, D, DC, MC, V.

Loews Vanderbilt Plaza. A pristine, white lobby and top-notch service are the first things guests encounter at this quiet, European-style luxury hotel, across the street from Vanderbilt University and 1 mi from Music Row. Guest rooms are elegant with dark-cherry furniture and skyline views. Musicians play nightly in the piano bar. 2 restaurants, bar with entertainment, room service. In-room data ports, minibars, microwaves, cable TV. Beauty salon. Exercise equipment. Shops. Business services. Some pets allowed. | 2100 West End Ave. | 615/320–1700 | fax 615/320–5019 | www.loewsvanderbilt.com | 327 rooms, 13 suites | $184–$249, $450–$975 suites | AE, D, DC, MC, V.

Marriott. This member of the popular Marriott chain is on 17 acres, near a lake, surrounding parks, and Nashville Shores Waterpark. Poolside rooms are particularly nice. The hotel is 5 minutes from the airport. Restaurant, bar, picnic area. In-room data ports, cable TV. Indoor-outdoor pool. Hot tub. Tennis. Exercise equipment. Laundry services, laundry facilities. Business services, airport shuttle. | 600 Marriott Dr. | 615/889–9300 | fax 615/889–9315 | www.marriott.com | 399 rooms | $98–$175 | AE, D, DC, MC, V.

★ **Opryland Hotel.** This is one of the 25 largest hotels in the world. There's an indoor river and 110-foot-wide waterfall; harp music is played nightly at the Cascades, an interior tropical garden that has a second indoor space with streams, waterfalls, and a lake. The Victorian-style rooms, some of which overlook the gardens, are decorated in beige and rose tones. 5 restaurants, bar with entertainment, room service. In-room data ports, some refrigerators, cable TV. 2 outdoor pools, wading pool. Beauty salon, massage. 18-hole golf course. Health club, exercise equipment. Video games. Laundry services. Business services, airport shuttle. No pets. | 2800 Opryland Dr. | 615/889–1000 | fax 615/871–5728 | www.opryhotel.com | 2,648 rooms; 236 suites | $194–$314, $279–$1,225 suites | AE, D, DC, MC, V.

Radisson Hotel Opryland. This is a contemporary-style, well-maintained hotel. Across the street from the Opryland Hotel. Rooms overlook an atrium. Restaurant, bar, room service. Cable TV. Pool, wading pool. Hot tub. Exercise equipment. Video games. Laundry services. Business services, airport shuttle, free parking. | 2401 Music Valley Dr. | 615/889–0800 or 877/OPRYINN | fax 615/883–1230 | www.radisson.com | 306 rooms | $129 | AE, D, DC, MC, V.

Regal Maxwell House. Expect Southern hospitality in a contemporary environment at this large, contemporary hotel just off I–265. It's just 2 minutes from downtown, 15 minutes from the Opry, and 1⅕ mi from a golf course. Rooms are spacious, and are decorated in rose or beige floral prints. Restaurant, bar. Cable TV. Pool. Hot tub. Tennis. Exercise equipment. Business services. Pets allowed. | 2025 Metrocenter Blvd. | 615/259–4343 | www.maxwellhotel.com | 285 rooms, 4 suites | $119–$148, $175–$350 suites | AE, D, DC, MC, V.

Renaissance Nashville. Spacious rooms are furnished with period reproductions at this slick, contemporary high-rise, which connects to the Convention Center, the Nashville Arena, and the Ryman Auditorium. Close to the Country Music Hall of Fame and Opryland. Restaurant, bar with entertainment, room service. Some refrigerators, cable TV. Indoor pool. Hot tub. Exercise equipment. Business services. Airport shuttle. | 611 Commerce St. | 615/255–8400 | fax 615/255–8163 | www.renaissancehotels.com | 649 rooms, 24 suites | $124–$235, $275–$1,200 suites | AE, D, DC, MC, V.

The Rose Garden Bed and Breakfast. You can see the hosts' hybrid tea rose gardens from the patio or from the all-season, five-person hot tub. The gardens have more than 80 hybrid tea rose varieties, 30 hosta selections, a perennial garden, and a shade garden. Located near the junction of Rte. 70 and Rte. 100 at the northern tip of the Natchez Trace, and close to

Percy Warner Park (home of the Iroquois steeplechase), Belle Meade Mansion, Bellevue Mall, and Vanderbilt University. The rooms have modern furnishings, and a collection of antique copper pots adds a little flavor. Complimentary breakfast. In-room data ports, kitchenette, microwave, refrigerator, cable TV, in-room VCRs. Hot tub. Business services. No pets. No kids. No smoking. | 6213 Harding Rd. | 615/356–8003 | fax 615/352–7661 | www.bbonline.com/tn/rosegarden | 2 rooms | $125 | No credit cards.

Sheraton–Music City. This Georgian-style member of the popular Sheraton chain is set on 23 landscaped acres atop a hill. The semiformal decor makes for a casual, comfortable atmosphere. It's 2 mi north of the airport and 10 mi east of downtown. Restaurant, bar with entertainment. Some refrigerators, cable TV. Indoor-outdoor pool, wading pool. Beauty salon, hot tub. Tennis. Gym. Business services, airport shuttle. Some pets allowed. | 777 McGavock Pike | 615/885–2200 | fax 615/231–1134 | www.sheraton.com | 392 rooms, 20 suites | $139–$179, $150–$550 suites | AE, D, DC, MC, V.

Sheraton Nashville Downtown. Enjoy skyline views from the guest rooms or from Pinnacle, Nashville's only revolving rooftop restaurant, which is on the top floor. Glass elevators overlook a greenery-filled atrium lobby. The State Capitol building is right across the street. Restaurant, bars. Cable TV. Indoor pool. Exercise equipment. Business services, airport shuttle. | 623 Union St. | 615/259–2000 | fax 615/742–6056 | www.sheraton.com | 473 rooms | $189–$209 | AE, D, DC, MC, V.

Union Station. This hotel is in a renovated historic train station (1897) and has an amazing 128-panel stained-glass roof in the lobby. The building is a Romanesque landmark, with limestone walls that are 4 ft thick in some spots. During World War II the dining room served as a USO canteen. Two blocks from Music Row. Restaurant, bar. Cable TV. Tennis. Business services. Airport shuttle. Some pets allowed. | 1001 Broadway | 615/726–1001 or 800/331–2123 | fax 615/248–3554 | www.grandheritage.com | 124 rooms, 12 suites | $125–$275, $205–$305 suites | AE, D, DC, MC, V.

NORRIS

MAP 12, I2

(Nearby towns also listed: Caryville, Knoxville, Oak Ridge)

Norris began as housing for the workers who built Norris Dam, the first hydroelectric dam created by the Tennessee Valley Authority in the mid-1930s. The town was planned as a model community—houses were all-electric (electricity was the TVA's main product) and there were several styles to choose from. Roads were adapted to the existing contours of the land and advertising billboards were banned. The town stands today as an example of good planning and adherence to high standards.

Information: **Anderson County Tourism Council** | 115 Welcome Ln., Clinton 37716 | 865/457–4542 or 800/524–3602 | www.yallcome.org.

Attractions

Appalachian Artisans Craft Shop. It's the oldest crafts cooperative in Tennessee, located across from the Museum of Appalachia. | Rte. 61 | 865/494–9854 | Free | Mon.–Sat. 10–6.

Lenoir Museum. The museum features early Americana. There are exhibits on dairy farming and woodworking, and an 18th-century grist mill. | 221 Norris Freeway | 865/494–9688 | Free | Daily 9–5.

Museum of Appalachia. The 65-acre complex of 30 log cabins displays Cherokee baskets, and even old jail cells. There's also an Appalachia Hall of Fame. | 2819 Rte. 61, Clinton | 865/494–0514 | www.korrnet.org/accc/musapp.html | $7 | Daily 8–5.

Norris Dam State Park. This park, 2 mi north of downtown Norris, is home to the first hydro-electric dam, built in 1936 by the Tennessee Valley Authority. | 125 Village Green Cir | 865/494–0720 | www.tva.gov | Free | Daily.

ON THE CALENDAR
OCT.: *Tennessee Fall Homecoming.* Hundreds of musicians and craftsmen participate in this yearly festival at the Museum of Appalachia. Visitors enjoy live music on three stages and countless demonstrations from craftspeople, including lessons in making molasses, applebutter and quilting. | 865/494–7680.

Dining

Golden Girls. Southern. The Golden sisters were home-cooking long before those interloping "Golden Girls" aired on TV. Catfish and tenderloin are some of the main courses that make the Girls beloved around town. The restaurant is in a modern log cabin, and University of Tennessee mementos hang everywhere in sight. | 2211 Rte. 61, Clinton | 865/457–3302 | Breakfast also available | $4–$5 | AE, D, DC, MC, V.

Lodging

Holiday Inn Express. Burgundy and hunter green are the color scheme in these rooms, which come with conveniences like in-room coffeemakers. Several restaurants are in the neighborhood, directly off I–75 at the Route 61 exit. Complimentary Continental breakfast. In-room data ports, some minibars, some microwaves, some refrigerators, some in-room hot tubs. Cable TV. Outdoor pool. Laundry facilities. Business services. Pets allowed (fee). | 141 Buffalo Rd. | 865/457–2233 | fax 865/457–2233 | www.hiexpress.com | 29 rooms, 22 suites | $70–$100 | AE, D, DC, MC, V.

OAK RIDGE

MAP 12, H2

(Nearby towns also listed: Crossville, Knoxville, Lenoir City, Norris)

Oak Ridge, the atomic city, is the site of the world's oldest nuclear reactor. It was built in the early 1940s by the Manhattan Project, the federal program that buillt the first atomic bomb. Today many of the tourist attractions focus on this period of the town's history.

Information: **Oak Ridge Convention and Visitors Bureau** | 302 S. Tulane Ave., Oak Ridge 37803–6726 | 865/482–7821 or 800/887–3429 | www.visit-or.org.

Attractions

American Museum of Science and Energy. Originally named the American Museum of Atomic Energy when it was founded in 1949, the museum eventually changed its name and broadened its mission. Today it's the largest museum of its kind, offering hands-on exhibits about all kinds of energy forms and their uses. | 300 S. Tulane Ave. | 865/576–3200 | www.amse.org | Free | Daily 9–5.

Bull Run Steam Plant. This TVA-built facility has an impressive 800-ft-high chimney. It utilizes coal to power the steam turbines that produce electricity. You can visit the roadside overlook and power exhibits in the lobby. | 1265 Edge Moor Rd. | 865/945–7200 | Weekdays 9–5.

Children's Museum of Oak Ridge. The hands-on museum provides kids with a look at world cultures. There are 12 exhibition areas, including a log cabin and a coal mine. | 461 W. Outer Dr. | 865/482–1074 | www.visit-or.org/brochure/children-museum2.jpg | $4 | Weekdays 9–5, Weekends 1:30–4:30.

The Department of Energy's Graphite Reactor. The federal government created the world's first nuclear reactor here as part of the Manhattan Project, a secret program designed to develop the first atomic bomb. Decommissioned in 1963, the site now features interpretive exhibits on the reactor's history and related topics. | 1 Bethel Valley Rd. | 865/574–4160 | Free | Mon.–Sat. 9–4.

Frozen Head State Park. (*See* Wartburg.) One of Tennessee's most scenic parks, it has 11,876 acres of relatively undisturbed forest with some of the richest wildflower areas in the state. It's 14 different mountains range from 1,340 ft to over 3,000 ft tall. Activities include camping, hiking, fishing, and horseback riding. The main entrance is 15 mi northwest of Oak Ridge. | 964 Flat Fork Rd., Wartburg | 865/346–3318 | www.state.tn.us/environment/parks/frzhead/index.html | Free | Daily 8–dusk.

Jackson Square Historic Park. Gardens, brick walkways, and history markers commemorate the original town built in the early 1940s during the Manhattan Project years. The park runs along Tennessee Avenue, which is now a business district, between Kentucky and Towne Streets. | Tennessee Ave. | 865/425–3450 | Free | Daily.

Melton Hill Dam and Lake. There's camping, swimming, fishing, and boating on and along the 44-mi-long lake created by the Tennessee Valley Authority dam, 6 mi southeast of downtown. | 2009 Grubb Rd. | 865/988–2440 | fax 865/988–2450 | www.tva.gov | Free | Daily.

Oak Ridge Art Center. These galleries display a permanent collection of works by contemporary regional, national, and international artists. The center also mounts changing exhibits. | 201 Badger Ave. | 865/482–1441 | Free | Tues.–Fri. 9–5, Sat.–Mon. 1–4.

Secret City Scenic Excursion Train. This World War II–era diesel covers 13 mi of track, and runs through the Manhattan Project's K25 complex. The train rides take place during select weekends and runs are most frequent in October when the leaves are at their peak, around holidays like Halloween and Christmas, and during Mayfest. | Rte. 58, in front of the East Tennessee Technology Park | 865/241–2140 | $10 | Apr.–Dec., select weekends, Sat. 10–4, Sun. noon–4.

PACKING IDEAS FOR COLD WEATHER

- ❏ Driving gloves
- ❏ Earmuffs
- ❏ Fanny pack
- ❏ Fleece neck gaiter
- ❏ Fleece parka
- ❏ Hats
- ❏ Lip balm
- ❏ Long underwear
- ❏ Scarf
- ❏ Shoes to wear indoors
- ❏ Ski gloves or mittens
- ❏ Ski hat
- ❏ Ski parka
- ❏ Snow boots
- ❏ Snow goggles
- ❏ Snow pants
- ❏ Sweaters
- ❏ Thermal socks
- ❏ Tissues, handkerchief
- ❏ Turtlenecks
- ❏ Wool or corduroy pants

*Excerpted from *Fodor's: How to Pack: Experts Share Their Secrets*
© 1997, by Fodor's Travel Publications

University of Tennessee Arboretum. The 250-acre research facility, 1 mi south of downtown, has 1,500 species of plants and trees. You can walk along short trails through various plant habitats. | 901 Kerr Hollow Rd. | 865/483–3571 | fax 865/483–3572 | www.korrnet.org/utas | Free | Weekdays.

ON THE CALENDAR

MAY: *Mayfest.* Held throughout May, this event showcases home-grown talent and includes performances by local bands, folk and popular dancers, martial artists, and mimes. | 865/425–3610.

Dining

Magnolia Tree Restaurant. Eclectic. Moussaka and lasagna are the crowd pleasers here. Stained glass and Tiffany lamps splash the room with color. | 1938 Oak Ridge Tpke. | 865/482–5853 | Closed Sun. | $8–$11 | AE, D, MC, V.

Burchfield's. American. Modern paintings, halogen lighting, and an atrium give this spot a fresh, contemporary look. Favorite dishes include the loaded pasta, which contains penne, ham, bacon and red potato, or the Jack Daniels sirloin. | 215 S. Illinois Ave. | 865/481–2468 | Breakfast also available | $8–$18 | AE, D, DC, MC, V.

Lodging

Comfort Inn. Guest rooms with dark cherry furniture are near restaurants and the Oak Ridge Mall. The hotel is near the Tinseltown 14-screen movie theater, and 1 mi from Oak Ridge central. Complimentary Continental breakfast. Refrigerators (in suites), cable TV. Pool. Laundry facilities. Business services. Some pets allowed. | 433 S. Rutgers Ave. | 865/481–8200 | fax 865/483–6142 | www.comfortinn.com | 102 rooms, 20 suites | $71–$81, $71–$91 suites | AE, D, DC, MC, V.

Days Inn. This member of the popular chain is located in downtown Oak Ridge, just blocks from a variety of restaurants. Complimentary Continental breakfast. Refrigerators, cable TV. Pool. Playground. Business services. Some pets allowed. Free parking. | 206 S. Illinois Ave. | 865/483–5615 | fax 865/483–5615 | www.daysinn.com | 80 rooms | $35–$57 | AE, D, DC, MC, V.

Garden Plaza Hotel. Rooms are larger than the average hotel room, and business people are the most frequent guests. The hotel is in the heart of downtown, five minutes from anywhere in Oak Ridge, and within walking distance to the Civic Center. Restaurant, bar, room service. Some minibars, some refrigerators, cable TV. Indoor-outdoor pool. Hot tub. Business services. Some pets allowed. | 215 S. Illinois Ave. | 865/481–2468 or 800/342–7336 | fax 865/481–2474 | 168 rooms | $79–$109 | AE, D, DC, MC, V.

Hampton Inn. Guests are greeted by a friendly atmosphere and complimentary cookies and fruit in the cozy lobby. The hotel is downtown, near restaurants and shops, and within walking distance of the American Museum of Science and Energy. Complimentary Continental breakfast. In-room data ports, some refrigerators, cable TV. Indoor Pool. Hot tub, sauna. Exercise equipment. Laundry facilities. Business services. | 208 S. Illinois Ave. | 865/482–7889 | fax 865/482–7493 | www.hamptoninn.com | 60 rooms | $63–$89 | AE, D, DC, MC, V.

Oak Ridge Inn and Suites. The rooms aren't fancy, but restaurants and shops are within a block. In-room data ports, microwaves, refrigerators. Outdoor pool. Exercise equipment. Laundry facilities, laundry services. Business services. No pets. | 420 S. Illinois Ave. | 865/483–4371 | fax 865/483–5972 | 142 rooms, 3 suites | $49–$79 | AE, D, DC, MC, V.

Ridge Inn Plaza. This inexpensive motel is located within a half mile of shops. A Mexican restaurant shares the same lot. Microwaves, refrigerators. Cable TV. Outdoor pool. Business services. Pets allowed (fee). | 1590 Oak Ridge Tpke. | 865/482–9968 | fax 865/482–9834 | 49 rooms | $37 | AE, D, DC, MC, V.

PARIS

(Nearby towns also listed: Clarksville, Hurricane Mills, Union City)

This Paris, founded 1823, also has an Eiffel Tower–a 65-ft reproduction of the one in France. Paris is near the Kentucky line and offers access to Kentucky Lake, one of the largest man-made lakes in the world, and a range of other natural areas, including the Tennessee National Wildlife Refuge.

Information: **Paris/Henry County Chamber of Commerce** | Box 8, Paris, 38242 | 901/642–3431 or 800/345–1103.

Attractions

Eiffel Tower. At 65 ft, this is the world's largest replica of France's Eiffel Tower. | 1000 Maurice Fields Dr. | No phone | Free | Daily.

Historic Walking Tour. Pick up a cassette and tape player at the chamber of commerce or Paris-Henry County Heritage Center then explore downtown Paris, the North Poplar Street Historic District and the old City Cemetery using an audio-taped walking tour called "Paris Revisited." | 2508 E. Wood St. | 901/642–3431 or 800/345–1103 | Free | Weekdays, 8–4:30.

Nathan Bedford Forrest State Park. The 800-acre park was the site of a Civil War Battle in which Confederate General Forrest, undetected by Union forces, attacked and destroyed a federal supply and munitions depot. There's camping, hiking, boating, and fishing. | 16055 U.S. 79N | 901/584–6356 | www.state.tn.us/environment/parks/forrest/index.html | Free | Wed.–Sun.

Tennessee River Folklife Museum. The museum is on the grounds of the Nathan Bedford Forrest State Park and explores culture and life on the Tennessee River, which includes musseling, crafts, and commercial fishing. | 16055 U.S. 79N | 901/584–6356 | Free | Mar.–Nov., Wed.–Sun. 9–4.

Paris-Henry County Heritage Center. Now a museum, research, and education center, this Italianate mansion, built in 1916, includes the original marble floors and staircase, stained-glass windows, and mahogany woodwork. | 614 N. Poplar St. | 901/642–1030 | fax 901/642–1096 | Free | Weekdays 9–5, weekends by appointment.

Paris Landing State Park. Paris Landing served as a steamboat and freight landing in the 19th century. The 841-acre park is situated on the western shore of Kentucky Lake, 18 mi east of Paris. There are cabins, camp sites, and a resort. Activities include hiking, boating, fishing, swimming, camping, and golf. | 1825 Pilot Knob Rd., Buchanan | 901/644–7359 | www.state.tn.us/environment/parks/paris/index.html | Free | Daily 7–dusk.

Tennessee National Wildlife Refuge. Situated on the shores of Kentucky Lake in west central Tennessee, 18 mi east of Paris, this refuge is a wintering place for Canada geese and several species of duck. The diverse habitats—from reservoir water and freshwater marsh to oak-hickory forests—supports more than 200 species of birds, 47 species of mammals, 90 species of reptiles and amphibians and more than 100 species of fish. | 810 E. Wood St. | 901/642–2091 | fax 901/644–3351 | www.southeast.fws.gov/tennessee/index/html | Free | Daily dawn–dusk.

ON THE CALENDAR

APR.: *The World's Biggest Fish Fry.* Besides all the fish that you can eat, there's a rodeo, music, a catfish race, and a parade. The events take place at the Paris Fairgrounds. | 901/642–3431 or 800/345–1103.

SEPT.: *Eiffel Tower Kid Fest and Balloon Festival.* Held annually on the Friday and Saturday after Labor Day, this celebration includes a kids' festival and ends on Saturday evening with tethered hot air balloon rides. This is one of four quarterly held events in the Eiffel Tower Series. It's held in Memorial Park. | 901/642–3431.

Dining

Ace's Pizza. American/Casual. Hand-painted murals of Chicago's skyline adorn the walls of this Chicago native's restaurant in the heart of Paris. Locals come for Ace's special pizza, with sausage, green peppers, mushrooms, onions and pepperoni, or for Chicago-style hotdogs. You can also get lasagna, spaghetti, chicken parmiagiana, and Italian beef sandwiches. | 1047 Mineral Wells Ave. | 901/644–0558 | $3–$10 | MC, V | Closed Sun.

Hong Kong Restaurant. Chinese. Buffet specials are the draw at this downtown place, including moo goo gai pan, sesame chicken, and Mongolian beef. | 1021 Mineral Wells Ave. | 901/644–1810 | $5–$7 | AE, MC, V.

Paulettes. American/Casual. A favorite lunch spot in downtown Paris, this restaurant is known for homemade breads and rolls, soups, pies, cheesecakes, and cakes, especially strawberry cake. Kids' menu. | 200 S. Market St. | 901/644–3777 | $5–$12 | MC, V | Closed Sun.

Lodging

Best Western Traveler's Inn. This motor inn is 1 mi east of downtown, on U.S. 79. It's near several restaurants, and Kentucky Lake and Paris Landing State Park are 17 mi to the east. Bar, complimentary Continental breakfast. Cable TV. Pool. | 1297 E. Wood St. | 901/642–8881 | fax 901/644–2881 | www.bestwestern.com | 98 rooms | $40–$57 | AE, D, DC, MC, V.

Hampton Inn. This motor inn is located in Paris' business district. Kentucky Lake is just 15 mi to the east. It's just 6 mi from the Henry County Airport. Complimentary breakfast. Cable TV. Pool. Hot tub. Gym. Laundry services. | 1510 E. Wood St. | 901/642–2838 | www.hampton-inn.com | 100 rooms | $45–$69 | AE, D, DC, MC, V.

Mansard Island Resort and Marina. This property is on the shores of Kentucky Lake adjacent to the Tennessee National Wildlife Refuge. You can enjoy wildlife, fishing and boating during your stay. Just 12 mi north of Paris. Microwaves, refrigerators, cable TV. Pool. Volleyball. Dock, water sports, boating, fishing. Playground. Laundry facilities. Pets allowed (fee). | 60 Mansard Island Dr., Springville | 901/642–5590 | fax 901/642–3120 | www.mansardisland.com | 40 rooms in 6 cottages, 8 apartments, 7 town houses, and 4 mobile homes | $63 1–bedroom town houses, $88 2–bedroom town houses, $78 apartments, $70 cottages | AE, D, MC, V.

Swiss Villa Inn. Boaters and anglers who come to enjoy nearby Kentucky Lake, about 12 mi to the east, take note of the space around this single-story motel—there is plenty of parking for boats in front of each unit. It's just 2½ mi west of downtown. Microwaves, refrigerators. Cable TV. No pets. | 1315 E. Wood St. | 901/642–4121 | 35 rooms | $35 | AE, D, MC, V.

Terrace Woods Lodge. This typical motor-inn is 1 mi north of downtown on Rotue 641. It's 15 mi. west of Kentucky Lake, and there are four golf courses within a 15-mi radius. Microwaves, refrigerators, cable TV. | 1190 N. Market St. | 901/642–2642 | 19 rooms | $29–$35 | AE, D, DC, MC, V.

PIGEON FORGE

MAP 12, G6

(Nearby towns also listed: Gatlinburg, Great Smoky Mountains National Park, Sevierville)

Pigeon Forge is a tourist town near Great Smoky Mountains National Park. It's a kind of small-scale Branson, Missouri—a number of music halls give concerts nightly, and more are on the way. It all began when Dolly Parton opened the theme park Dollywood here. There are also abundant theme restaurants and dinner-theater venues, like the Alabama Grill, named for the country group Alabama; country music dinner-theater venues such as the Country Tonite Theatre and the Dixie Stampede Dinner and Show.

Information: Pigeon Forge Department of Tourism | 2450 Parkway, Pigeon Forge 37868–1390 | 865/453–8574 or 800/251–9100 | www.pigeon-forge.tn.us.

Attractions

The Comedy Barn. The shows here are billed as "clean, family comedy." There are also music, magic, and animal acts. | 2775 Parkway | 865/428–5222 or 800/295–2844 | fax 865/429–4368 | www.comedybarn.com | $16.95 | Shows at 3:15 PM and 8:15 PM.

Country Tonite Theatre. It's a country variety show with music, comedy, and dance. | 129 Showplace Blvd. | 865/453–2003 or 888/544–7469 | www.countrytonite.com/music.htm | $20.95 | Mar.–Dec., Fri.–Wed., shows at 3 PM and 8 PM.

Dixie Stampede and Dinner Show. An entertainment extravaganza while you dine. A pre-show includes comedy and live bluegrass music. The dinner show is a spectacular performance of 32 horses and riders, singers, and dancers who involve the audience. Dinner is typical Southern fare, featuring rotisserie chicken and corn on the cob. | 3849 Parkway | 865/453–4400 or 800/356–1676 | www.dixiestampede.com | $33 | Shows at 6 PM, 8:30 PM.

Dollywood. Superstar Dolly Parton's 100-acre entertainment park features music, crafts shows, rides, and restaurants. | 1020 Dollywood Ln | 865/428–9488 | www.dollywood.com | $34.25 | Mid-Apr.–Oct., daily 9–9.

Flyaway. The 21-ft-tall wind tunnel produces up to 115 mph winds. It allows you to experience the sensation of skydiving—without jumping out of a plane. | 3106 Parkway | 865/453–7777 | www.smokymtnmall.com/mall/flyaway.html | $22.59 | Mar.–Nov., weekdays 4–6:30, Sat. 9:45–7, Sun. 9:45–5; Dec.–Feb. 10–5.

Louise Mandrell Theater. Louise Mandrell performs in family-oriented performances accompanied by singers, dancers, and her nine-piece orchestra in this 1,400-seat state-of-the-art theater. Show music ranges from big band and gospel to country, blues and rock 'n' roll. | 2046 Parkway | 800/768–1170 | www.louisemandrell.com | $26 | Apr.–Dec. daily 7:30.

The Old Mill. Built in 1830, but never restored, this is the oldest-operating mill in the country. Tours are available. | 2944 Middle Creek Rd. | 865/453–4628 | fax 865/429–2191 | www.old-mill.com | $3 | Apr.–Nov., Mon.–Sat. 9:30–4, tours every half hour.

Ogle's Water Park. The 8-acre water park, 1½ mi north of the city center, has 10 water slides, wave pools, a "Lazy River" ride, and a large play area. | 2530 Parkway | 865/453–8741 |

WHAT TO PACK IN THE TOY TOTE FOR KIDS

- ❏ Audiotapes
- ❏ Books
- ❏ Clipboard
- ❏ Coloring/activity books
- ❏ Doll with outfits
- ❏ Hand-held games
- ❏ Magnet games
- ❏ Notepad
- ❏ One-piece toys
- ❏ Pencils, colored pencils
- ❏ Portable stereo with earphones
- ❏ Sliding puzzles
- ❏ Travel toys

*Excerpted from *Fodor's: How to Pack: Experts Share Their Secrets*
© 1997, by Fodor's Travel Publications

www.pigeon-forge.tn.us | $20 | Labor Day–Memorial Day, daily 10–7, Memorial Day–Labor Day, weekends 10–7.

Smoky Mountain Car Museum. Check out the cars of the stars, including James Bond's 007 Aston Martin, Al Capone's bulletproof Cadillac, Elvis Presley's Mercedes, and Billy Carter's service truck. | 2970 Parkway | 865/453–3433 | $5 | May–Oct., daily 10–5.

Theaters. There are several famous theaters in the Pigeon Forge area. Among them: **Memories Theatre** (2141 Parkway | 865/428–7852), where some of the best Elvis impersonators around perform here. If you're not into Elvis try **Music Mansion Theatre** (100 Music Rd. | 865/428–7469 | Apr.–Dec.) the most popular show in the Smokies starring songwriter and performer James Rogers. The **Tennessee Music Theatre** (2135 Parkway | 865/428–5600) offers a variety of music, including country, bluegrass, gospel, and rock 'n' roll oldies, is performed here. The **Smoky Mountain Jubilee** (2115 Parkway | 865/428–1836) hosts country and gospel music, clogging, and comedy shows. Price and show times vary, so call ahead for schedules and reservations.

ON THE CALENDAR

NOV.: *Pigeon Forge Winterfest.* More than 16 special events held over 3½ months follow an official lighting ceremony in Patriot Park during the second week of November. Events include Celebrate Freedom (believed to be the largest salute to veterans in U.S. history), Wilderness Wildlife Week, and the Fine Art and Photography Show and Sale. | 800/WINTERFEST.

Dining

Alabama Grill. American/Casual. Next door to the Louise Mandrell Theater, this theme restaurant has country music memorabilia and plays a lot of the music of its namesake, the band Alabama. On the menu are barbecued St. Louis ribs, soup, salad, steaks, and seafood. | 2050 Parkway | 865/908–8777 | $6–$18 | AE, D, MC, V.

Apple Tree Inn. American. Apples are the theme here at this casual family restaurant, where they serve up Southern specialties like chicken and dumplings and spoon bread, which is pretty much what it sounds like, with honey on it. Soup, salad bar. Kids' menu. Even decorations are apple-themed, like apple lighting and apple design-inset tables. | 3215 Parkway | 865/453–4961 | Breakfast also available. Closed Jan.–mid-Mar. | $5–$13.50 | AE, MC, V.

Beach House Grill. American. The inside of this restaurant reminds you of a beach with palm trees and an aquarium. It specializes in fresh seafood, including crab legs, lobster, catfish, shrimp, and oysters Rockefeller on the half shell. If seafood doesn't appeal, you can also get salads, pastas, steaks, and ribs. | 2586 Parkway | 865/428–4643 | $4–$25 | AE, DC, MC, V.

Chef Jacques' Tastebuds Café. Eclectic. Wine bottles line the walls of this tiny gourmet paradise, where the staff are as unique as the food—don't be surprised if the maitre d' bursts into song. Chef Giacomo Jacques Lijoi serves up an amazingly varied and adventurous menu which includes daily specials like wild boar, fresh Tennessee ostrich, kangaroo, and stuffed pan-sautéed rattlesnake, as well as more traditional Continental dishes. | 1198 Weirs Valley Rd. | 865/428–9781 | Closed Sun., Mon. | $17–$26 | AE, D, DC, MC, V.

Corky's Ribs and BBQ. Barbecue. Blues music, old trumpets, album covers, and New Orleans memorabilia are on the walls in this casual place. You can get practically anything barbecued here, but the ribs are the big draw. | 3584 Parkway | 865/453–7427 | $5–$17 | AE, D, MC, V.

Heartlander's Showcar Café. American/Casual. In addition to the restaurant, which serves everything from salads and sandwiches to prime rib and seafood, there's a full retail shop that sells NASCAR collectibles and a room with video games. It all sits 2 mi north of downtown. | 2301 Parkway | 865/908–9007 | $6–$13 | AE, MC, V.

Lucy's Fireside Restaurant. Southern. You can order breakfast anytime at this small restaurant that has been open for 30 years. The owner serves tomatoes and cucumbers grown in her garden, as well as pinto beans, fried corn bread, homemade biscuits, country salt-cured ham and gravy, and sandwiches. | 2616 Parkway | 865/453–9646 | Closed Jan.–Mar. No dinner | $8–$18 | No credit cards.

Old Mill. American. This is a working mill that still grinds fresh corn and wheat for market and overlooks the Little Pigeon River, near traffic light number 7. There's an old general store on the premises, where they sell the mill's produce and other goods, and the freshly-ground cornmeal is used in the corn chowder and corn fritters that are the restaurant's signature dishes. Enjoy Southern standbys like catfish or chicken and dumplings, in a restaurant built from the timbers of an old barn. Kids' menu. No smoking. | 2940 Middle Creek | 865/429–3463 | Breakfast also available | $8–$23 | AE, D, MC, V.

Peso Peso's Fine Mexican Food. Mexican. The walls here are weathered blues, yellows and fuschia, and flower pots sit at every green-checkered table. You can choose from a number of dishes prepared by chefs from Guadelajara, including chile rellenos, handmade tamales, and salsa made fresh every day. Top everything off with a chocolate chimichanga or a *bunuela* (deep-fried flour tortilla with chocolate syrup, honey and ice cream). | 3152 Parkway, Suite 1 | 865/453–6526 | fax 865/908–5182 | Closed Sun. No lunch | $6–$15 | D, MC, V.

Ponderosa Steakhouse. American. This standard family chain restaurant has a daily buffet featuring steak, chicken, and seafood. | 4074 Parkway | 865/453–4500 | $8–15 | D, DC, MC, V.

Pop's Catfish & Seafood. American. Local residents and tourists come to this family restaurant for the all-you-can-eat fried catfish and chicken tenders served with hushpuppies and green onions. | 3516 Parkway | 856/428–8627 | $6–$15 | D, MC, V.

Sagebrush Steakhouse. American. You can get anything from hamburgers to 22 oz. porterhouse steaks here. Oreo brownies and apple and blackberry cobblers are homemade. | 3909 Parkway | 865/429–3428 | $8–$18 | AE, D, DC, MC, V.

Santo's Italian Restaurant. Italian. There is a large mural on the wall of *The Last Supper,* a fireplace, and live piano music by request at this family restaurant. In addition to classic pasta dishes like fettucine alfredo and pasta carbonara, you can get fillet and seafood combinations. Top everything off with a slice of Oreo cheesecake or Italian cream cake. | 3270 Parkway | 865/428–5840 | $9–$23 | AE, D, DC, MC, V.

Star Buffet Chinese Restaurant. Chinese. The only Chinese restaurant in town, Star Buffet has both a buffet and a sit-down menu with many options. | 2528 McGall St. | 865/453–5587 | $5–$7 | MC, V.

Lodging

Americana Inn. Familiar, dark-wood-paneled motel. Some rooms offer mountain views at this hotel, conveniently located on U.S. 441, 1 mi north of downtown. Shopping is across the street. Restaurant. Cable TV. Pool. Hot tub. | 2825 Parkway | 865/428–0172 | www.pigeon-forge.tn.us/hot-mot.html | 170 rooms | $55–$75 | D, MC, V.

Baymont Inn and Suites. This hotel is located 2 mi north of the city center, approximately 10 mi south of I–40's Exit 407. There are restaurants nearby. The Smoky Mountain Jubilee and Memory Theater is within a half-mile of Dollywood, the Dixie Stampede and the Super Track are 3 mi away. Restaurant, complimentary Continental breakfast. Some refrigerators, cable TV. Pool. Laundry facilities. Business services. | 2179 Parkway | 865/428–7305 | fax 865/428–8977 | www.baymontinns.com | 126 rooms, 13 suites | $59–$79, $69–$124 suites | AE, D, DC, MC, V.

Best Western Plaza Inn. This hotel offers standard chain accommodations. It's 5 mi north of the Great Smoky Mountains and 1 mi west of Dollywood. Outlet malls and music theaters are also nearby. Refrigerators and coffeemakers are in all rooms, which are decorated in bright whites. Complimentary Continental breakfast. Refrigerators, Microwaves, some in-room hot tubs, cable TV. Indoor-outdoor pool. Hot tub, sauna. Video games. Business

services. | 3755 Parkway | 865/453–5538 | fax 865/453–2619 | www.bwplazainn.com | 200 rooms | $49–$129 | AE, D, DC, MC, V.

Bilmar Motor Inn. The entrance to Dollywood is 1 mi east of this three-story family owned and operated motel. Complimentary Continental breakfast. Some microwaves, some refrigerators, some in-room hot tubs, cable TV, no room phones. 2 pools. Hot tub. No pets. | 3786 Parkway | 865/453–5593 or 800/343–5610 | 76 rooms | Jan.–Feb. | $69–$79 | AE, MC, V.

Briarstone Inn. Conveniently located on the Parkway, this motel is notably quiet, however, because the rooms, some with fireplaces, face away from the main road. It's near restaurants and 3 mi north of hiking trailheads. Refrigerators, some in-room hot tubs, cable TV. Pool. Hot tubs. Business services. | 3626 Parkway | 865/453–3050 or 800/523–3919 | www.tn-traveler.com/smr | 57 rooms | $32–$120 | AE, D, DC, MC, V.

Capri. The trolley that stops in front of this motel, half a mile south of the city center, will take you anywhere in Pigeon Forge. On U.S. 441, the property offers quick access to neighboring skiing and hiking areas. Family suites sleep up to six. Complimentary Continental breakfast. Some refrigerators, cable TV, some in-room VCRs. Pool. Hot tub. Business services. | 4061 Parkway | 865/453–7147 or 800/528–4555 | fax 865/453–7157 | 106 rooms, 2 suites | $50–$84, $80–$124 suites | AE, D, MC, V.

Country Inn and Suites. Some rooms in this hotel have mountain views and fireplaces. It's set on a quiet block off the Parkway, about a mile north of downtown. Complimentary Continental breakfast, picnic area. Refrigerators, room service, some in-room hot tubs, cable TV. 2 pools (1 indoor). Hot tub. Exercise equipment. Laundry facilities. Business services. | 204 Sharon Dr. | 865/428–1194 | fax 865/453–2564 | www.smokymountainresort.com/countryinn.html | 138 rooms, 27 suites | $63–$95, $105–$119 suites | AE, D, DC, MC, V.

Creekstone Inn. All rooms have balconies overlooking Little Pigeon River at this hotel, which is 1 block from the Parkway in a quiet neighborhood, approximately 1 mi south of the city center. There are restaurants nearby. Refrigerators, cable TV. Pool. | 4034 River Rd. | 865/453–3557 or 800/523–3919 | www.smokymountainresort.com | 153 rooms, 20 suites | $63–$80, $80–$90 suites | AE, D, MC, V.

Days Inn. Located on the Parkway in the heart of Pigeon Forge, sandwiched between two restaurants, this modest motel is just 15 minutes from Gatlinburg, and 5 mi from the Gatlinburg airport. Restaurant. Refrigerators, some in-room hot tubs, cable TV. Pool. Tennis. Laundry services. Business services. | 2760 Parkway | 865/453–4707 | fax 865/428–7928 | www.daysinn.com | 143 rooms | $38–$98, $74–$120 suites | AE, D, DC, MC, V.

Econo Lodge. Standard accommodations near restaurants provide easy access to U.S. 441. Half-mile from the Beltz Outlet Mall and the Dixie Stampede. Complimentary Continental breakfast. Some in-room hot tubs, cable TV. Pool, wading pool. Business services. | 114 Pickle St. | 865/453–2999 | fax 865/453–6580 | www.econolodge.com | 65 rooms | $69–$89 | AE, D, DC, MC, V.

Grand Resort Hotel and Convention Center. This is the largest, and one of the more upscale, hotels in Pigeon Forge. It sits at the foot of the Smoky Mountains. Fireplaces warm some rooms. Floral patterns ornament some rooms, others are done in light colors or pastels. Restaurant, complimentary Continental breakfast. Room service, cable TV. Pool. Hot tub. Business services. Some pets allowed. | 3171 Parkway | 865/453–1000 or 800/362–1188 | fax 865/428–3944 | www.lodging4u.com/pf/grand/default.html | 425 rooms | $70–$100 | AE, D, DC, MC, V.

Hampton Inn and Suites. This six-story hotel has a lobby that resembles a ski lodge, including fireplaces on each side of the room. It is just ¼ mi from the Tanger Five Oaks Mall, which has upscale retail clothing stores, and 3 mi north of Dollywood. You can have a cookout on the property using a hibachi grill and picnic tables. Complimentary breakfast. In-room data ports, some kitchenettes, cable TV, some in-room VCRs. Outdoor pool. Exercise equipment. Shops. Laundry facilities. No pets. | 2025 Parkway | 865/310–8082 or 800/310–8082 | www.hampton-inn.com | 101 rooms | $99 | AE, D, DC, MC, V.

Heartlander Country Resort. Rooms at this hotel located at the northern tip of Pigeon Forge have inside access and some mountain views. All rooms have private balconies. Complimentary Continental breakfast. Cable TV. 2 pools (1 indoor). Hot tub. Video games. Business services. Some pets allowed. | 2385 Parkway | 865/453–4106 | fax 865/429–0159 | 160 rooms | $59–$119 | AE, D, DC, MC, V.

Hidden Mountain Resorts. Accommodations at this large resort range from single-room to seven-bedroom villas. The west location, 3 mi northwest of town, is more secluded and has a fishing lake stocked with catfish and bluegill. The east location, only 1 mi west of Pigeon Forge, has villas with indoor whirlpools. Kitchenettes, microwaves, cable TV, in-room VCR. Pool. Exercise equipment. Laundry facilities. No pets. | Hidden Mountain East: 475 Apple Valley Rd. Hidden Mountain West: 1650 Walt Price Rd. | 865/453–9850 or 800/541–6837 | www.hidden-mountain.com | 250 cabins; 71 villas | $85–$145 cabins; $125–$165 villas | AE, MC, V.

Hilton's Bluff. This two-story country inn, ½ mi west of the Parkway, is surrounded by dogwood and honeysuckle. The emphasis is on honeymoon suites—this B&B has three of them—each with heart-shaped hot tubs. All rooms have private balconies or decks. The dining room has large glass French doors looking out onto the countryside. Complimentary breakfast. No room phones, cable TV. | 2654 Valley Heights Dr. | 865/428–9765 or 800/441–4188 | www.bbonline.com/tn/hiltonsbluff/index.html | 10 rooms | $79–$129 | AE, MC, V.

Holiday Inn. Nearby trolley service makes the entire town accessible from this Holiday Inn in the heart of Pigeon Forge. There's a lovely indoor pool with a waterfall. Just 1 mi north of Dollywood. Restaurant. In-room data ports, some refrigerators, some in-room hot tubs, cable TV. Indoor pool. Exercise equipment. Hot tub. Video games. Laundry facilities. Business services. | 3230 Parkway | 865/428–2700 | www.4lodging.com/chambers/pigeon_forge. html | 210 rooms | $49–$129 | AE, D, DC, MC, V.

Howard Johnson. The Pigeon Forge trolley stops right in front of the hotel, conveniently on the Parkway next to a mall. Restaurant. Some in-room hot tubs, cable TV. Pool, wading pool. Laundry services. Business services. | 2826 Parkway | 865/453–9151 | fax 865/453–4141 | www.hojo.com | 145 rooms | $29–$85 | AE, D, DC, MC, V.

Knights Inn. Accommodations at this hotel in the northern section of Pigeon Forge are a cut above the chain-hotel norm. Rooms are overized and some have mountain views. It's next door to the town's music theaters. Refrigerators, cable TV. Pool. | 2162 Parkway | 865/428–3824 or 800/523–3919 | fax 865/453–2564 | www.smokymountainresort.com/knights.html | 65 rooms | $47–$57 | AE, D, MC, V.

Mountain Breeze. Decidedly typical, this motor lodge is located on U.S. 441 next door to the Factory Merchants Mall. It's 2 mi from Dollywood. Refrigerators, cable TV. Pool. | 2926 Parkway (U.S. 441) | 865/453–2659 | 71 rooms | $60–$95 | D, MC, V.

Music Road Hotel. If you like water activities, this hotel is the place to stay with its 24-hour water-park pool, with separate pool areas for kids and adults. All rooms have private balconies, some of which are oversized. The hotel is two or 3 blocks from music theaters. Complimentary Continental breakfast. Microwaves, refrigerators, cable TV. 3 pools. Water sports. Video games. Laundry facilities. Business services. No pets. | 303 Henderson Chapel Rd. | 865/429–7700 or 800/429–7700 | www.musicroadhotel.com | 163 rooms | $149 | AE, MC, V.

Norma Dan. Some rooms have scenic wooded views while others have balconies overlooking the pool at this hotel located at the southern end of Pigeon Forge, near Gatlinburg and Dollywood. There's a fireplace in the cozy lobby. Picnic area. Some refrigerators, cable TV. Pool, wading pool. Hot tub. Laundry facilities. Business services. | 3864 Parkway | 865/453–2403 or 800/582–7866 | fax 865/428–1948 | 85 rooms | $28–$88 | AE, D, DC, MC, V.

Park Tower Inn. Just half a block from Parkway and 3 mi north of Dollywood, this six-story hotel has kitchenettes on each floor. Some microwaves, refrigerators, some in-room hot tubs. Cable TV. Indoor/outdoor pool. Exercise equipment. Laundry facilities. No pets. | 201 Sharon Dr. | 865/453–8605 or 800/453–8605 | 154 rooms | $100 | AE, D, DC, MC, V.

Quality Inn of Pigeon Forge. This is your standard motel with exterior corridors, 2 mi west of Dollywood and near area restaurants. Some rooms have fireplaces. Complimentary Continental breakfast, picnic area. Some in-room hot tubs, minibars, refrigerators, cable TV. Pool, wading pool. Hot tub. Business services. | 3756 Parkway | 865/453–3490 or 800/925–4443 | 127 rooms | $79–$129 | AE, D, DC, MC, V.

Radisson Inn and Suites. The Belz Factory Outlet Mall and restaurants are only a half-mile east of this seven-story hotel on a quiet block, just off the Parkway. Complimentary Continental breakfast. Microwaves, refrigerators, some in-room hot tubs, cable TV. Indoor-outdoor pool. Exercise equipment. Video games. Laundry facilities. No pets. | 2423 Teaster La. | 865/429–3700 or 800/333–3333 | www.radisson.com | 77 rooms, 3 suites | $109 rooms, $199 suites | AE, D, DC, MC, V.

Ramada. Standard chain accommodations located half mile from Dollywood, five minutes from Gatlinburg. It's next door to the Smoky Mountain Convention Center, in the center of Pigeon Forge. Restaurant. Refrigerators, some in-room hot tubs, cable TV, some in-room VCRs. Pool. Hot tub. Business services. | 4010 Parkway | 865/453–1823 or 800/523–3919 | fax 865/453–2564 | www.ramada.com | 123 rooms | $51–$70 | AE, D, DC, MC, V.

Riverchase. Exterior access rooms face the parking lot away from the highway. Kids will love the water slide at the pool. In the heart of Pigeon Forge, it's 2 mi from Dollywood and 5 mi to Gatlinburg. Some rooms have fireplaces. Some in-room hot tubs, cable TV. Indoor-outdoor pool. | 3709 Parkway | 865/428–1299 | fax 865/453–1678 | 109 rooms | $60–$110 | AE, D, MC, V.

Rivergate Inn. All rooms at this three-story hotel, in the center of town, overlook the Pigeon River. Refrigerators. Cable TV. No pets. No smoking. | 3307 N. River Rd. | 865/428–0872 | fax 865/453–6364 | rgitravel@aol.com | 14 rooms | $99 | AE, D, MC, V | Jan.–Mar.

Riverside Motor Lodge. Some rooms have fireplaces and mountain views and the suites are spacious at this motor lodge. There's a grocery store next door. Guests have access to the outdoor pool at a neighboring hotel. All rooms have private balconies. Some have river views. Kitchenettes, some in-room hot tubs, cable TV. Indoor pool. Hot tub. | 3575 Parkway | 865/453–5555 or 800/242–8366 | 56 suites | $99–$150 suites | AE, D, MC, V.

Rodeway Inn/Mountain Skys. This Pigeon Forge lodge is 5 mi north of the Great Smoky Mountain National Park. Guests receive free pancakes and coffee at the adjacent Smoky Mountain Pancake House. The trolley to Dollywood stops in front of motel. Refrigerators, cable TV. Complimentary breakfast. Pool. | 4236 Parkway | 865/453–3530 | fax 865/423–2564 | www.smokymountainresorts.com | 116 rooms | $26–$108 | AE, D, DC, MC, V.

Schular Inn. There's a sundeck on the top of this five-story hotel, 1½ mi west of Dollywood, an indoor sauna and both indoor and outdoor hot tubs. Complimentary breakfast. Some kitchenettes, microwaves, refrigerators, cable TV. 2 pools. Wading pool. Laundry facilities. No pets. | 2708 Parkway | 865/453–2700 or 800/451–2376 | www.schularinn.com | 199 rooms | $89.95 | AE, D, DC, MC, V.

Tennessee Mountain Lodge. This standard motor lodge offers some rooms with river views. It's on the Parkway, several blocks west of Dollywood. Many restaurants are nearby. Refrigerators, cable TV. Pool, wading pool. Business services. | 3571 Parkway | 865/453–4784 or 800/446–1674 | 50 rooms | $28–$60 | AE, D, MC, V.

Travelodge. This motel, at the southern end of Pigeon Forge, ¾ mi from Dollywood, is close to a trolley stop and restaurants. There are exterior corridors and some poolside rooms. Cable TV. Indoor and outdoor pools, wading pool. Hot tub. Playground. Laundry service, laundry facilities. Free parking. | 4025 Parkway | 865/453–9081 | fax 865/428–3240 | www.travelodge.com | 120 rooms, 11 suites | $49–$79 | AE, D, DC, MC, V.

Valley Forge Inn. Some rooms have river views and fireplaces at this downtown hotel located at the northern end of Pigeon Forge, near restaurants. Complimentary Continental breakfast. Some in-room hot tubs, refrigerators, cable TV. 2 pools (1 indoor), wading pool. Hot tub. Laundry facilities. | 2795 Parkway | 865/453–7770 or 800/544–8740 | 172 rooms | $63–$93 | AE, D, MC, V.

PULASKI

(Nearby towns also listed: Fayetteville, Lawrenceburg, Lewisburg)

Pulaski was the site of the trial and execution of Sam Davis, a young spy known as the "Boy Hero of the Confederacy." A museum and a historic trail focus on the capture and hanging of Davis. Pulaski is also notorious as the birthplace of the Ku Klux Klan. The Klan began as a social club: A group of idle young men invented costumes and initiation ceremonies, and as they rode around town in their ghostly garb they noticed how their appearance frightened the ex-slaves. It did not take long for all this to turn into violence, and the fun became a terrorist movement that spread throughout the South, and later into the Midwest.

Information: Giles County Chamber of Commerce | 100 S. 2nd St., Pulaski 38478–3219 | 931/363–3789 | www.public.usit.net/gilecofo.:

Attractions

Brown-Daly-Horne House (Colonial Bank of Tennessee). Built in 1855, by the turn of the century this structure had become a prime example of Queen Anne architecture. Now a bank, the building is listed on the National Register of Historic Places. | 307 W. Madison St. | 931/363–1582 | Free | Daily 9–3.

Giles County Courthouse. The grand neoclassical building, built in 1909, dominated the town square. Its 1858 bell still strikes every hour. The exterior features Corinthian columns that support a cupola. Inside, a balcony encircles the third floor while 16 statues hold up the arched vault of the rotunda, which has stained-glass skylights. | Pulaski Public Sq | 931/363–5300 | Free | Weekdays.

Sam Davis Museum. Sam Davis was a young man who refused to give up the name of his informer when he was caught behind Union lines with intelligence on Union troop movements during the Civil War. He was condemned as a spy and chose to die on the gallows rather than betray the Confederacy. The museum stands on the spot where the "Boy Hero of the Confederacy" was executed in 1863. The museum contains Civil War memorabilia including the leg irons worn by Davis. *(See also* Sam Davis House in Nashville.) | Sam Davis Ave., near Rte. 64 | 931/363–3789 | Free | By appointment only; call chamber of commerce.

ON THE CALENDAR
SEPT.: *Bluegrass Moonlight Jam.* Bring your own instrument or just come and tap your toes to the music in Giles Agri Park. Admission proceeds benefit local Giles County youth projects. Held in conjunction with the annual Giles County Chamber of Commerce chili cookoff. Admission to the musical performances is $3. | 931/363–3789.

Dining
Hickory House. Barbecue. Two blocks off the town square and next to the football stadium, this restaurant and caterer serves barbecue pork, ribs, and chicken cooked over a hickory wood fire. Famous patrons include Tanya Tucker, Michael Jackson, and Quincy Jones. | 330 So. Patterson St. | 931/363–0231 | $7–$17 | AE, D, MC, V.

Lodging
Milky Way Farms. Purchased in 1932 by the founder of Mars Candy Company, this property consisted of 2,800 acres including the existing mansion and 38 barns. Today the fully

restored mansion serves as a bed and breakfast and can handle both corporate retreats and individuals, by reservation only. You can fish from the banks of a 20-acre lake, or just sit on the Adirondack chairs out front and enjoy the scenery. It is 8½ mi north of Pulaski off I–65. Complimentary Continental breakfast. No room phones, TV in common area. | 1864 Milky Way Rd. | 931/363–9769 | 8 rooms; 12 suites | $89 rooms, $185 suites | AE, MC, V.

ROGERSVILLE

MAP 12, G5

(Nearby towns also listed: Greeneville, Kingsport, Morristown)

Rogersville is near some of the world's unusual springs. The Ebbing and Flowing Spring is one of only two springs in the world known to flow at regular intervals. David Crockett's grandparents lived in this town shortly before it was founded in 1789. The town was also the site of the first newspaper printed in Tennessee.

Information: **Rogersville/Hawkins County Chamber of Commerce** | 107 E. Main St., Rogersville 38757 | 423/272–2186.

Attractions

Crockett Spring Park. The park is on the property where Davy Crockett's grandparents lived; they were killed by marauders here in 1777. There's a natural spring and a stone-walled cemetery. | 200 Crockett St. | 423/272–1961 | Free | Daily.

Ebbing and Flowing Spring. This is one of only two springs in the world known to flow at regular intervals—that's every two hours and 40 minutes. The property also includes a natural dam, a stone gristmill, a 19th-century Methodist church, and a one-room schoolhouse. | Ebbing and Flowing Spring Rds | 423/272–2186 | Free | Daily.

Rogersville Depot Museum. This restored Southern Railway depot now serves as a visitor center and museum focused on the printing industry of Rogersville where Tennessee's first newspaper, the *Knoxville Gazette,* was printed. | 415 S. Depot St. | 423/272–1961 | Free | Weekdays 9–5.

ON THE CALENDAR

OCT.: *Heritage Days.* This art fair held along downtown Main St. includes 150 juried craft booths, Appalachian music and dance, antique cars, quilts, farm equipment, and a children's yard. Held on the second full weekend of the month. | 423/272–1961.

Dining

El Puebito. Mexican. You can order fajitas, taquitos mexicanos, chile dishes, fried ice cream and flans. Wash everything down with a selection of domestic and Mexican beers. | 120 E. Main St. | 423/921–0057 | $6–$9 | AE, D, MC, V.

Lodging

Holiday Inn Express. You'll be served late-afternoon seasonal refreshments which include iced-tea and cookies in the summer, and soup, crackers, hot cider, and cocoa in the winter. Board games and checkers are available at the front desk. The hotel is in the commercial area of town just 2 mi south of downtown. View the Appalachian Mountains from all rooms. Ten second-story rooms allow smoking. Complimentary Continental breakfast. Microwaves, refrigerators, some in-room hot tubs, cable TV. Outdoor pool. Laundry service. Some pets allowed (fee). | 7139 Rte. 11W | 423/272–1842 or 800/HOLIDAY | fax 423/272–1634 | www.hiexpress.com | 43 rooms | $70 | AE, D, DC, MC, V.

SAVANNAH

(Nearby towns also listed: Bolivar, Lawrenceburg)

Savannah is near the enormous Pickwick Lake and the Mississippi/Alabama border. Also the largest town along the Tennessee River, it has recently established the Savannah Historic Trail, with markers, reader boards, and scenic overlooks of the Tennessee River that guide visitors through the history of the town, which was founded in 1821. The Cherokee passed through here on the Trail of Tears and writer Alex Haley's grandparents Queen and Alex Haley Sr. lived on a small farm outside Savannah. The town is also near the site of the Battle of Shiloh, a famous Civil War battle.

Information: Hardin County Tourism Board | 507 Main St., Savannah 38372 | 901/925–2364 or 800/552–3866 | www.hardincountytn.com.

Attractions

Pickwick Landing State Resort Park. Once the living area for the Tennessee Valley Authority construction crews and their families, this 1,400-acre park on the shores of Pickwick Lake, 13 mi south of town, is one of the most visited parks in the state. You can stay in cabins, camp sites, or a resort. Activities include hiking, fishing, boating, swimming, and golf. | 1 Park Rd. | 901/689–3129 | www.state.tn.us/environment/parks/pickwick/index.html | Free | Daily.

Savannah Historic Trail. You can get a map for the self-guided tour at the Hardin County Tourism Board. The trail, which includes markers, reader boards, scenic overlooks of the Tennessee River, walkways, and seating areas, will guide you through the town's Civil War history, the experiences of Native Americans who passed through the area on the Trail of Tears, and the history of Alex Haley's family in the town (his grandparents lived and are buried here). The 2-mi stretch off Main Street also features impressive residences built between 1860 and 1930. | Contact the Hardin County Tourism Board: 507 Main St. | 901/925–2364 or 800/552–3866 | Free | Daily 8 AM–10 PM.

Shiloh National Military Park. In 1862 Shiloh was the site of one of the bloodiest battles of the Civil War. Combined casualties in the eight-day fight reached a total of 23,746. Self-guided tour information and guided driving tours of the battlefield are available. The park sits 9 mi south of Savannah. More than 3,000 Union troups are buried at the **National Cemetery,** a 10-acre site on a bluff overlooking Pittsburg Landing and the Tennessee River. **The Visitor Center** (1055 Pittsburg Landing Rd. | 901/689–5696) has regular showings of a film about the Battle of Shiloh. Self-guided tour information and guides for driving tours are available here. | 1055 Pittsburg Landing Rd. | 901/689–5275 | www.americanparks.com/park-list/tnshiloh.htm | Daily 8–5 | $2.

Tennessee River Museum. Exhibits cover the Tennessee Valley's archaeology and palentology, riverboats, and the role the river played in the Civil War. | 507 Main St. | 901/925–2364 | fax 901/925–6987 | $3 | Mon.–Sat. 9–5, Sun. 1–5.

ON THE CALENDAR

APR.: *Living History Demonstration.* This event is held annually in an open field at Shiloh National Military Park to coincide with the anniversary of the Battle of Shiloh. Volunteer reenactors dressed in Confederate uniforms demonstrate Civil War encampments of infantry, artillery, and cavalry. There also are demonstrations of some of the medical practices of the time. | 901/689–5696.

Dining

Jon's Pier. American. Located near Pickwick Lake, a resort area, this restaurant is 15 mi south of Savannah. Though it specializes in prime rib, you can also get a variety of seafood dishes, the most popular of which are fried, blackened, and charbroiled shrimp and cat-fish. | Rte. 57 S., Pickwick | 901/689–3575 | $7–$17 | AE, D, MC, V.

Savannah Cooks. Contemporary. This is the place for fresh, healthy, unprocessed food—and nothing fried. The menu has specialty coffee drinks (espresso, cappuccino, mochas), homemade muffins and scones for breakfast, and soups, sandwiches, and salads served with homemade beer bread for lunch. There are daily specials. | 804 Main St. | 901/925–8046 | Breakfast also available. Closed weekends. No dinner | $3–$7 | No credit cards.

Woodys. American Casual. This downtown eatery draws a big lunch crowd for grilled or fried shrimp, chicken, burgers, steaks, and hush puppies. Historic photos of Savannah and its people decorate the walls. Known for steak, burgers, fried shrimp, hush puppies. | 705 Main St. | 901/925–0104 | No dinner Sun. | $6–$13 | AE, MC, V.

Lodging

Pickwick Landing. All facilities within the park are available to guests at this state-owned complex. Lodge rooms overlook Pickwick Lake, and have a tree-house feel. Dining room. Some kitchenettes, cable TV. Pool, wading pool. 18-hole golf course. Tennis. Boating. | Rte. 57 S, Pickwick Dam | 901/689–3135 or 800/250–8615 | fax 901/689–3606 | www.state.tn.us/environment/parks/pickwick/inn.htm | 78 rooms, 3 suites, 10 cabins | $46–$150, $175 suites, $430 cabins | AE, MC, V.

Comfort Inn Savannah. Just 10 mi north of Pickwick Lake, 3 mi south of downtown, and right off Route 128, this facility provides free boat and RV parking. Second-floor rooms have exterior hallways accessible only by stairs. Complimentary Continental breakfast. In-room data ports, some refrigerators, cable TV. Pool. Laundry facilities. No pets. | 1314 Pickwick Rd. | 901/925–4141 | www.comfortinn.com | 42 rooms | $45–$80 | AE, D, DC, MC, V.

Savannah Lodge. This standard, no-frills motor lodge is located downtown, near fast-food and other restaurants. Drive 20 minutes southwest to reach Shiloh National Park, and 10 mi south to Pickwick Landing State Resort Park. Cable TV. Pool. | 420 S. Pickwick Rd. | 901/925–8586 | 41 rooms | $29–$39 | AE, D, DC, MC, V.

Savannah Motel. This downtown property is within 2 blocks of restaurants and shops. Some microwaves, some refrigerators, cable TV. Pets allowed (fee). | 105 Main St. | 901/925–3392 | 20 rooms | $30–$40 | AE, D, MC, V.

Shaws Komfort Motel. Personalized service and newly furnished rooms are the draws at this motel located on U.S. 64. Its highway location makes it especially convenient to Shiloh National Park and Pickwick Landing State Resort Park. Restaurant. Cable TV. Some pets allowed. | 2302 Wayne Rd. | 901/925–3977 | 31 rooms | $29–$36 | AE, D, DC, MC, V.

White Elephant Bed and Breakfast. This Queen Anne–style house, now a B&B, is furnished with many antiques. The front parlors have curved glass bay windows, as does one of the guest rooms. Rooms have private baths, some with claw-foot tubs. Just a block from Main Street. Complimentary breakfast. No room phones. | 304 Church St. | 901/925–6410 | www.bbonline.com/tn/elephant/index.html | 41 rooms | $90–$120 | AE, D, DC, MC, V.

SEVIERVILLE

MAP 12, G6

(Nearby towns also listed: Gatlinburg, Great Smoky Mountains National Park, Pigeon Forge)

Founded in 1795, Sevierville was named after John Sevier, the first governor of Tennessee. Today it is the seat of Sevier County and a marketing center for surrounding farmlands. The beauty of the Smoky Mountains is less than 16 mi to the south, and several stables in Sevierville offer horseback riding in the mountains.

Information: **Sevierville Chamber of Commerce** | 866 Winfield Dunn Pkwy., Sevierville 37876 | 865/453–6411 or 800/255–6411.

Attractions

Douglas Dam and Lake. The TVA dam has created a lake that is 43-mi-long. There's swimming, fishing, and boating. The Douglas Lake Marina is off Route 66, 9 mi north of Sevierville. | Douglas Dam Rd. | 865/453–3889 | www.tva.gov | Free | Daily.

Forbidden Caverns. The large cave, 13 mi east of town, features special lighting effects and a stereo presentation. It's always 58° inside. | 455 Blowing Cave Rd. | 865/453–5972 | $8 | Apr.–Nov., daily 10–6.

Smoky Mountain Deer Farm. The petting zoo is home to deer, zebras, camels, kangaroos, wallabies, miniature horses, reindeer, and prairie dogs. | 478 Happy Hollow La. | 865/428–3337 | www.deerfarmzoo.com | $6 | Daily 10–5:30.

Tennessee Smokies. An affiliate of the Toronto Bluejays, this AA minor league team plays half of its 140 seasonal games at Sevierville/Sevier County Stadium in Smokies Park, off I–40, just north of town. | 3540 Line Dr., Kodak | 865/286–2300 or 888/978–2288 | $4–$9 | Closed Oct.–Mar.

ON THE CALENDAR

MAY: *Bassmaster Megabucks Tournament*. Each Mother's Day weekend fishermen compete to catch the heaviest bass in Douglas Lake from a 10-hole bass course designed by tournament officials. The weigh-in is held at Sevierville/Sevier County Stadium at Exit 407 of I–40. | 334/272–9530.

Dining

Applewood Farmhouse. Southern. There's much more than a restaurant here—there's a vinyard and home winery, a working apple mill where homemade cider is pressed, a fudge and candy shop, and, of course, the restaurant, which is inside a 1921 farmhouse, full of polished oak and antique furniture. Sit by an open fireplace with an orchard view, order country ham with redeye gravy or fried chicken, then take a stroll amongst the apple trees by the banks of the Little Pigeon River, 3 mi south of U.S. 411. Kids' menu. | 240 Apple Valley Rd. | 865/428–1222 | Breakfast also available | $12.95–$16.95 | AE, D, DC, MC, V.

Buddy's Bar-B-Q. Barbecue. For nearly 30 years, the owners have been serving hickory-smoked pork, beef, chicken, and ribs at this casual spot, located about 1 mi north of downtown, off I–40. | 705 Winfield Dunn Pkwy. | 865/428–5001 | $2–$9 | D, MC, V.

Chef Jacques' Roasted Pepper Café. Mediterranean. Tennessee's foremost chef, Jacques Lijoi, brings his anything-goes-gourmet approach to town with an eclectic variety of Mediterranean-inspired dishes: Greek, Italian, and Spanish recipes get the Chef Jacques treatment—bold, unusual flavor combinations that somehow work out brilliantly. Meats marinated in Balsamic vinegar and honey, lots of fresh herbs and garlic, locally-grown meat and produce, and a top-notch wine list make this one of the most sophisticated dining experiences in town. | 964 Dolly Parton Pkwy. | 865/908–0033 | Breakfast also available. Closed Sun., Mon. | $19–$27 | AE, D, DC, MC, V.

Lodging

Comfort Inn—Mountain View Suites. This hotel stands alone on Route 66, off I–40 on the way to Sevierville. It is 3 mi from restaurants and shopping, nearly 2 mi northwest of town. Some rooms have views of the countryside and mountains in the distance. All suites, with partitioned living/sleeping areas and a sofa. Complimentary Continental breakfast. Mini-bars, refrigerators, cable TV. Indoor-outdoor pool, wading pool. Hot tub. Business services. | 860 Winfield Dunn Pkwy. | 865/428–5519 | fax 865/428–6700 | www.comfortinn.com | 95 suites | $54–$159 suites | AE, D, DC, MC, V.

Days Inn. Centrally located on U.S. 441, this standard chain lodging offers easy access to shopping and restaurants. Rooms are accessed from the outside. Trolley service available right outside. Restaurant. Complimentary Continental breakfast. Some refrigerators, cable TV. Pool. Business services. | 1841 Parkway | 865/428–3353 | fax 865/428–7613 | www.daysinn.com | 100 rooms | $74–$140 | AE, D, DC, MC, V.

Little Greenbrier Lodge. This two-story lodge—built in 1939—is on the border of Great Smoky Mountains National Park, 150 yards from the Little Greenbrier Trailhead. Rooms have Victorian period decor, and many have private balconies overlooking the mountains and valley. Complimentary breakfast. No room phones, no TV in rooms, TV in common area. No kids under 12. No smoking. | 3685 Lyon Springs Rd. | 865/429–2500 or 800/277–8100 | www.littlegreenbrierlodge.com | 10 rooms (8 with shower only, 2 with shared bath) | $100–$110 | MC, V.

Oak Tree Lodge. This standard motel-style lodging on U.S. 441, 2 mi south of town, is next to a mall and restaurants. The hotel offers discounted horseback riding at a neighboring stable. Picnic area, complimentary Continental breakfast. Refrigerators, cable TV. Indoor-outdoor pool. Business services. | 1620 Parkway | 865/428–7500 or 800/637–7002 | fax 865/429–8603 | www.oaktreelodge-tn.com | 80 rooms | $60–$90 | AE, D, DC, MC, V.

Quality Inn. Just off I–40 at Exit 407, this three-story, white hotel is 10 mi north of Sevierville. Horses graze near the property. Fast-food restaurants are nearby. The hotel offers free breakfast at a neighboring restaurant. Breakfast. Some in-room hot tubs, cable TV. Indoor pool. Business services. | 3385 Winfield Dunn Pkwy. | 865/933–7378 | fax 865/933–9145 | 78 rooms | $58–$98 | AE, D, DC, MC, V.

Sleep Inn. This three-story motel is on U.S. 441 a half-mile south of downtown and within a mile of Five Oaks Shopping Center. Complimentary Continental breakfast. Some refrigerators, cable TV. Outdoor pool. No pets. | 1020 Parkway | 888/429–0484 | www.sleepinn.com | 70 rooms | $99 | AE, D, DC, MC, V.

SHELBYVILLE

MAP 12, F3

(Nearby towns also listed: Columbia, Fayetteville, Lewisburg, Lynchburg, Manchester, Murfreesboro)

Located on the edge of the once-vast cedar forests of Middle Tennessee, Shelbyville has been manufacturing pencils since the early 20th century. Today it's the home of the Tennessee Walking Horse Celebration, the largest show of the breed, and the Tennessee Walking Horse Museum. On the Tennessee Walking Horse and Eastern Railroad, visitors can travel to nearby Wartrace on a restored 1940s diesel passenger train.

Information: Shelby/Bedford County Chamber of Commerce | 100 Cannon Blvd., Shelbyville 37160 | 931/684–3482 or 888/662–2525 | www.shelbyvilletn.com/index.htm.

Attractions

Walking Horse and Eastern Railroad. The railroad offers diesel train excursions from Shelbyville to Wartrace, 8 mi to the east. Coaches date from the 1940s. | 112 East Side Sq | 931/684–7376 | $18 | June–Oct., Sat. 10 AM.

Tennessee Walking Horse Museum. The museum showcases the history of the Tennessee Walking Horse, a celebrated breed known for its mild temperament, stately manners, and smooth gait. | 721 Whitthorne St. | 931/684–5915 | fax 931/684–5949 | www.twhnc.com | $4 | Weekdays 9–5.

MAY: *Spring Fun Show.* This walking horse show is a warmup for the national Tennesse walking horse celebration in August.Both take place in the Calfonic Arena on Evans Street downtown. | 931/684–5915.

JULY: *Great Celebration Mule and Donkey Show.* The competition features 1,000 mules and donkeys from all over the nation. The animals compete in some 150 classes in indoor and outdoor arenas, held on the National Celebration Grounds downtown. | 931/684–5915, ext. 106.

AUG. AND SEPT.: *Tennessee Walking Horse National Celebration.* This is the largest show of the breed. Festivities include a barn-decorating contest, dog show, trade fair, and food booths. The events take place at Calfonic Arena in the National Celebration Center the 10 days leading up to Labor Day. | 931/684–5915.

Dining

Legends. Steak. Families head here after Sunday church when the daily special is chicken and dressing. The restaurant specializes in hand-cut steaks served with owner Johnny Fleeman's line of gourmet marinades and sauces. You can also get pastas, salads, sandwiches, and soups. Top everything off with the signature dessert, "Hershey's Cake Extreme." Located 2 mi north of downtown off Route 231. | 1609 Main St. | 931/680–7473 | $8–$10 | AE, D, DC, MC, V.

Lodging

Best Western Celebration Inn. This typical chain motel is located on Route 41 in downtown Shelbyville, 500 ft from the Tennessee Walking Horse Museum. Complimentary Continental breakfast. Some in-room hot tubs, cable TV. Indoor pool. Exercise equipment. Laundry facilities. Microwaves. Refrigerators. | 724 Madison St. | 931/684–2378 | fax 931/685–4936 | www.bestwestern.com | 58 rooms, 12 suites | $58–$125, $145 suites | AE, D, DC, MC, V.

Olde Gore House Bed and Breakfast and Tea Room. Off Madison Street, Shelbyville's main thoroughfare, this two-story 1880s colonial has a balcony that's accessible from your room. By reservation only, you'll be served English tea with small sandwiches and sweets on a glassed-in sun porch. Rooms are upstairs and each has a private bathroom. Complimentary breakfast. Cable TV, TV in common area. No pets. No smoking. | 410 Belmont Ave. | 931/685–0636 | www.bbchannel.com/bbc/p603935.asp | 2 rooms | $85 | AE, MC, V.

Super 8 Shelbyville. This conveniently located motor lodge is in downtown Shelbyville, directly on U.S. 231. It's just 2 mi west of the Calsonic Arena. There are restaurants nearby. Restaurant. Cable TV. Pool. Some pets allowed (fee). | 317 N. Cannon Blvd. | 931/684–6050 or 800/684–0466 | fax 931/684–2714 | 72 rooms | $55 | AE, D, DC, MC, V.

SWEETWATER

MAP 12, H3

SWEETWATER

INTRO
ATTRACTIONS
DINING
LODGING

(Nearby towns also listed: Athens, Dayton, Lenoir City)

The Lost Sea, a 4.5-acre underground lake, is Sweetwater's main attraction, as many billboards will remind you. The largest underground body of water in the world and a U.S. Registered Natural Landmark, it is in a section of the Craighead Cavern System, where the South mined saltpeter during the Civil War.

Information: Madisonville/Monroe County Chamber of Commerce | Box 37, Madisonville 37354 | 423/442–9147.

Attractions

Fleas Unlimited. For over a decade, 550 vendors from Tennessee, Georgia, and Alabama have been making a pilgrimage to this year-round market to sell everything from tires to antique furniture and jewelry in 150,000 feet of air-conditioned space. | 121 County Rd. | 423/337–3532 | Free | Weekends 8–5.

Lost Sea. You can take a guided cruise in a glass-bottom boat on the world's largest underground lake (4½ acres), which is a Registered U.S. Natural Landmark. Note the rare crystalline formations on the cavern walls. The lake is accessible via the Craighead Cavern System, 4½ mi south of town. For a time, the cave was designated a nuclear fallout shelter and outfitted with supplies to accommodate 30,000 people. | 140 Lost Sea Rd. | 423/337–6616 | fax 423/337–0803 | $10 | Daily, 6AM–10PM.

ON THE CALENDAR

SEPT.: *Sequoya Birthplace Festival.* This arts and crafts fair is held annually on the second weekend of the month at the Sequoya Museum, dedicated to Sequoya, a Cherokee Indian who created the Cherokee alphabet. Events are Native American dancing, flute playing, crafts, demonstrations of eighteenth century Cherokee life, and pottery making. The museum is located at 576 Route 360, in Vonore, about 15 mi north of Sweetwater. | 423/884–6246.

Dining

Dinner Bell. American. This restaurant means casual country dining, family-style. There's a whole menu of hearty country staples to choose from—steaks, chicken, seafood, etc.—but most people just belly up to the buffet, which is loaded with five meats, fried chicken, homemade cobblers, and banana pudding. Salad bar. Buffet. Kids' menu. | 576 Oakland Rd. and I–75 | 423/337–5825 | Breakfast also available | $6–$14 | AE, D, MC, V.

Gondolier Pizza and Steak House. Mediterranean. Located at the 68 Plaza Shopping center, 1 mi south of the city center, the Italian and Greek menu has a variety of specialties including pizza, lasagna, fettuccine alfredo, veal parmiagiana, baklava, and gyros. | 789 Rte. 68 | 423/337–5200 | $3–$12 | AE, D, MC, V.

Lodging

Budget Host. Located off I–75, 6 mi northwest of the Lost Sea, this hotel offers clean, comfortable rooms facing the interstate. Some refrigerators, cable TV. Laundry facilities. Some pets allowed (fee). | 207 Rte. 68 | 423/337–9357 | fax 423/337–7436 | www.budgetinn.com | 61 rooms | $34–$44 | AE, D, DC, MC, V.

Comfort Inn. This member of the popular lodging chain enjoys a peaceful setting 2½ mi from I–75, and 4 mi east of the Lost Sea. There's a pond and picnic area on the grounds. Downtown Sweetwater and local restaurants are nearby. Some rooms have balconies overlooking the duck pond. Complimentary Continental breakfast, picnic area. Microwaves, refrigerators, cable TV. Pool, wading pool. Business services. Some pets allowed. | 731 S. Main St. | 423/337–6646 | fax 423/337–5409 | www.comfortinn.com | 60 rooms | $32–$65 | AE, D, DC, MC, V.

Magnolia House Bed-and-Breakfast. Named for the 35-ft magnolia tree in the front yard, this clapboard turn-of-the-century, two-story farmhouse was once the home of Walter Hunt, former Sheriff of Monroe County. It is a few blocks to downtown galleries and antique shops and a half-mile south of the Tellico River, which has trout fishing. Restored in 1996, it sits on 8 acres of landscaped pasture, which you can see from rocking chairs on the porch. Rooms have reproduction farm furniture, antique family photos, and original art by owner Michael Hannan. Rooms have private half-bathrooms and share a full bathroom. Complimentary breakfast. Refrigerators, cable TV. No pets. No smoking. | 305 Rte. 165, Tellico Plains | 423/253–3446 or 800/323–4750 | www.tellico.net/~hannans | 3 rooms | $55 | AE, MC, V.

TIPTONVILLE

(Nearby towns also listed: Dyersburg, Union City)

Tiptonville is the gateway to Reelfoot Lake, in the northwest corner of the state. This shallow lake was created by an earthquake in 1811. It covers some 15,000 acres and averages 5.2 feet in depth. Growing in the lake are thousands of cypress trees whose tangled roots interwine under the water. Some of the best fishing in the country is found here, home to approximately 57 species of fish. The lake is also the winter home of ducks, geese, and American bald eagles.

Information: Reelfoot Lake Chamber of Commerce | Rte. 1, Box 140B, Tiptonville 38079 | 901/253–8144.

Attractions

Marijac Memorial River Park. Along the banks of the Mississippi River half-mile west of town, this acre-wide park has picnic tables and outdoor grills. Formerly the property of Mary and Jack Fields, a prominent couple in town who owned a lot of farmland, the land was donated to the town in 1999. | Rte. 21 | 901/253–8144 | Free | Daily.

Reelfoot Lake. This shallow lake was created by a series of earthquakes in 1811. It features vast expanses of lily pads and towering cypress trees that grow out of the water. An important hunting and fishing destination, it's also the winter home of ducks, geese, and eagles. | Rtes. 21, 21, and 78 | 901/538–2666 | www.state.tn.us/environment/parks/reelfoot/index.html | Free | Daily.

Reelfoot Lake State Resort Park. This 25,000-acre park is considered one of the greatest hunting and fishing preserves in the nation. There is a 3-mi boardwalk that winds over cypress wetlands and through a stand of large cypress trees. In winter guided tours to view bald eagles are offered by park naturalists. The park has a resort and camp sites and offers hiking, biking, and fishing. | Rtes. 21, 22, and 78 | 901/253–7756 | www.state.tn.us/environment/parks/reelfoot/index.html | Free | Jan.–Oct., daily.

Reelfoot National Wildlife Refuge. The 10,428-acre refuge sits on the north shore of Reelfoot Lake. Winter waterfowl peak at 100,000 geese and 250,000 ducks, and this protected area is excellent bald eagle watching territory as well. From Tiptonville, drive 15 mi north on Route 22 to reach the refuge entrance. | Rte. 157, Walnut Log | 901/538–2481 | Free | Daily sunrise–sunset.

ON THE CALENDAR

OCT.: *Arts and Crafts Festival.* Sponsored by Reelfoot Arts and Crafts Inc., this annual craft fair has nearly a mile-long strip along Reelfoot Lake of exhibits of hand-made crafts, ceramics, clothing, and furniture. Vendors come from over 16 states. Exhibits of paintings, jewelry and photographs are housed in the National Guard Armory, the American Legion Building and the Tennessee Visitors Center. Held annually on the first weekend of the month, Friday–Sunday 9–5. | 901/253–7276.

Dining

Boyette's Dining Room. American/Casual. Boyette's and Reelfoot Lake go together like fried catfish and hushpuppies, which happen to be mainstays on the menu of this bustling restaurant. Conveniently located across from the visitor's center of the park, eating at this restaurant is a 75-year-old local tradition. Kids' menu. | Lake Rd. | 901/253–7307 | $6–$16 | No credit cards.

Lakeview Dining Room. Southern. Exactly 1 mi south of the Reelfoot Lake State Resort Park visitor's center, this restaurant has three dining areas—including a rose-colored dining

room, a main room with a large mural of the lake painted on the back wall, and a third room that's blue with a duck and geese motif. The specialty here is jumbo frog legs, which are batter dipped and fried, and fried crappie. For dessert you can choose from nine different kinds of cheesecake. | Rte. 22 | 901/253–7516 | $5–$13 | D, MC, V.

Reelfoot Lake State Park Restaurant. American/Casual. Near Reelfoot Lake State Resort Park, this is a buffet and sit-down restaurant in the Air Park Inn, specializing in catfish caught from the lake. | Rte. 1 | 901/253–7756 | Breakfast also available | $4–$8 | AE, D, MC, V.

Lodging

Air Park Inn. Guests at this hotel enjoy access to all the facilities at Reelfoot Lake State Resort Park. The lodging overlooks Reelfoot Lake, and is surrounded by cypress trees. Restaurant. Cable TV. Pool. Tennis. Business services. | Rte. 1 | 901/253–7756 or 800/250–8617 | fax 901/253–8940 | www.state.tn.us/environment/parks/reelfoot/inn.htm | 12 rooms, 8 suites | Closed early Oct.–Dec. | $56–$65 | AE, MC, V.

Bluebank Resort. This small resort located on the shores of Reelfoot Lake offers fishing and hunting packages. The lodge houses a common room with pool tables and a lakeside deck with tables. Some rooms have fireplaces and balconies overlooking the lake. Cabins house from 2 to 16 people. Choose from between three types of lodgings: the Hunter's Lodge is located on the lake, with kitchen, picnic area, and private fishing; the Marina Lodge is surrounded by a boardwalk deck; the Resort Lodging is the main inn, with restaurant and golfing nearby. Restaurant. Kitchenettes, cable TV. Pool. Hot tub. Some pets allowed. | 813 Lake Dr. | 901/253–6878 or 901/253–8976 | www.bluebankresort.com | 18 rooms, 2 suites, 13 cabins | $85–$95, $135 suites, $60–$365 cabins | AE, D, DC, MC, V.

Blue Basin Cove Bed and Breakfast. Couples and families come to this B&B on Reelfoot Lake, 5 mi east of Tiptonville, to go fishing for crappie March through June; there's a boat and bait shop on the property. Bald eagles are the main attraction in winter. Two buildings have units that sleep up to six people. Complimentary breakfast. Some kitchenettes, refrigerators. Cable TV, no room phones. Dock, fishing. Pets allowed. | Off Rte. 213, R.D. 1 | 901/253–9064 | www.bluebasin.com | 5 rooms | $65 | AE, MC, V.

Boyette's Resort. Across the street from the Reelfoot Lake visitor's center, this complex has cottages that are rustic with cyprus walls and knotty pine cabinets; all have screened in porches. Restaurants are less than a mile away. Some kitchenettes. Cable TV. Outdoor pool. Pets allowed. | Rte. 213, R.D. 1, Box 1230 | 901/253–6523 | www.lakereelfoot.net | 16 rooms, 3 1-bedroom cottages, 10 2-bedroom cottages, 4 family houses | $40 rooms | AE, D, MC, V.

Cypress Point Resort. This resort is on the shores of Reelfoot Lake, just 3 mi east of Tiptonville, and offers four-day fishing packages. The two buildings are surrounded by cypress trees. Cabins have screened-in porches. Restaurant. Kitchenettes, cable TV. Pool. Some pets allowed. | Rte. 1 | 901/253–6654 or 901/253–6659 | www.cypresspointresort.com | 25 rooms | $69–$89 | AE, D, DC, MC, V.

TOWNSEND

MAP 12, 13

(Nearby towns also listed: Gatlinburg, Great Smoky Mountains National Park, Maryville, Walland)

Townsend, in the Great Smoky Mountains, offers access to Cades Cove, a beautiful, remote wildlife area, and Tuckaleeche Caverns, noted for its onyx formations and underground waterfalls. The town, founded in 1910, is also a haven for artists.

Information: Townsend Visitors Center | 7906 E. Lamar Alexander Pkwy., Townsend 37882 | 865/448–6134 | www.townsendtennessee.com.

Attractions

Cades Cove. Wildlife has the right-of-way in this beautiful and remote area of the Great Smoky Mountains National Park, accessible via Townsend. (*See* Great Smoky Mountains Park.) | Cades Cove Rd. | 865/436–1200 | fax 865/436–1313 | www.nps.gov | Free | Daily dawn–dusk.

Tuckaleechee Caverns. Every half-hour you can take a guided tour of these caverns under the Smoky Mountains which maintain a constant 58°. Trails are paved with wooden steps and limestone and you can hear calcite dripping from the stalactites as you walk past rock formations. Entrance is 1 mi southwest off Route 321. | 825 Cavern Rd. | 865/448–2274 | www.smokymountains.org | $9 | Mar.–Nov., daily 10–6.

ON THE CALENDAR

SEPT.: *Heritage Festival.* Held annually on the last Friday and Saturday of the month, this music and crafts festival has all-day demonstrations of 18th-century Woodland Indian campfire, Appalachian crafts, antique engine and tractor shows, and bluegrass and mountain music. It takes place at the Townsend Visitor's Center. | 865/448–6134 or 800/525–6834.

Dining

Back Porch Restaurant. Southern. Dine on a porch overlooking Short Creek, just 2½ mi east of downtown Tiptonville, off Route 321. The inside resembles a country store with antique memorabilia displayed throughout including a gasoline-powered washing machine, a Tennessee moonshine still that sits on the hearth of the fireplace, and a honey separator. The owner's wife cooks daily homemade specials, such as chicken pot pie, fried chicken with gravy, meatloaf, and grits. | 7016 E. Lamar Alexander Pkwy. | 865/448–6333 | Reservations not accepted | No dinner | D, MC, V.

Carriage House. American. Two miles west of downtown, this casual place serves steaks, fish, sandwiches, seafood, fried chicken, and homemade cobblers and pies. | 8310 Rte. 73 | 865/448–2263 | $8–$13 | AE, MC, V.

Deadbeat Pete's. Southwestern. You come here for the Santa Fe chicken, fajitas, homemade salsa, and live bluegrass and country music. The restaurant is full of antiques and collectibles, and dollar bills line the walls. | 7613 Old Hwy. 73 | 865/448–0900 | No lunch Mon.–Thurs. | $6–$15 | AE, MC, V.

Smokin' Joe's BBQ. Barbecue. Next door to Cades Cove and Smoky Mountain National Park off Route 321, this restaurant has a pig motif and draws a large out-of-state following for its open-pit barbecued meats. Pork, Boston butt roast, chicken, and beef barbecues come with five side dishes. | 8215 Rte. 73 | 865/448–3212 | $3–$20 | D, MC, V.

Timbers. American. Live country western music every night and Timber's famous fried chicken are the big draws here. Steak and seafood, including scampi, blackened trout, and fresh rainbow trout, are also on the regular menu. Top everything off with a slice of Jack Daniels bourbon pecan pie. A full Southern breakfast is served daily. | 8123 E. Lamar Alexander Pkwy. | 865/448–6838 | Breakfast also available | $6–$16 | AE, DC, MC, V.

Lodging

Abode and Beyond Bed and Breakfast. Atop Little Mountain and surrounded by wildlife, this B&B sits on five acres against the backdrop of the Smoky Mountains. Upon request owners Jean and David "Buffalo Bill" Nelson, a cowboy poet who has opened for Billy Ray Cyrus, entertain you around a campfire with old-time western songs and stories. Rooms are on the ground floor: the Rawhide Room has western memorabilia including a cowboy bathtub; the Blue Room is entirely in hues of blue. The upstairs loft has a headdress from the film *Dances With Wolves* and games to play. Complimentary breakfast. Microwave, refrigerator. Cable TV, in-room VCRs, no room phones. Laundry facilities. No pets. No kids under 10. | 275 Little Mountain Way | 865/448–9097 | www.tnabode.com | 2 rooms | $90–$105 | No credit cards.

"Bear"ly Rustic Cabin Rentals. These cabins range in size from one to five bedrooms and sleep from 2 to 25 people. They are spread out around Townsend in the woods, countryside, or along the Little River, which runs along the north edge of town. Prices vary for cabins with more than one bedroom. Microwaves, refrigerators, some in-room hot tubs, cable TV. No pets. | 3751 E. Lamar Alexander Pkwy. | 888/448–6036 | www.townsendcabin.com | 40 rooms | $79–$139 | AE, MC, V.

Best Western Valley View Lodge. These standard chain accommodations are set on 17 lawn-like acres enclosed by white fences. Great Smoky Mountains National Park is just 3 mi to the south. Rooms with fireplaces are available. Picnic area, complimentary Continental breakfast. Some minibars, refrigerators, cable TV. 3 pools (1 indoor). Hot tubs. Business services. Some pets allowed. | 7726 Lamar Alexander Pkwy. | 865/448–2237 | fax 865/448–9957 | www.valleyviewlodge.com | 138 rooms, 12 cabins, 4 guesthouses | $46–$89, $119–$131 cabins, $95–$110 guesthouses | AE, D, DC, MC, V.

Family Inns. This motor lodge is on U.S. 321, 3 mi north of the entrance to Great Smoky Mountains National Park. There's a picnic area on Little River, behind the motel. There are benches and tables along the riverfront. Picnic area, complimentary Continental breakfast. Some kitchenettes, some refrigerators, cable TV. Pool. Business services. | 7239 E. Lamar Alexander Pkwy. | 865/448–9100 or 800/332–8282 | fax 865/448–6140 | 54 rooms | $46–$85 | AE, D, DC, MC, V.

Headrick's River Breeze Motel. This two-building motel is just 1½ mi from the west entrance to the Great Smoky Mountain National Park and 9 mi from Cades Cove. Some rooms have balconies. Some kitchenettes, some microwaves, some refrigerators. Cable TV, no room phones. Outdoor pool. No pets. | 8242 Rte. 73 | 865/448–2389 or 800/879–0047 | www.headricksriverbreeze.com | 23 rooms | $49–$85 | AE, D, MC, V.

Hampton Inn–Townsend. Located in the center of town, 8 mi north of the Smoky Mountains and 5 mi north of Cades Cove, this motel serves a deluxe breakfast buffet featuring biscuits and gravy. Suites have fireplaces and microwaves. Complimentary Continental breakfast. Refrigerators, some microwaves, cable TV. Pool. Business services. | 7824 E. Lamar Alexander Pkwy. | 865/448–9000 | fax 865/448–9524 | www.hamptoninn.com | 54 rooms, 2 suites | $49–$74, $150 suites | AE, D, DC, MC, V.

Highland Manor. Enjoy the country-inn atmosphere at this motor lodge located on U.S. 321, on a hilltop in downtown Townsend. The Smoky Mountains are just 2 mi away. Some rooms have fireplaces and private balconies. Picnic area, complimentary Continental breakfast. Some refrigerators, some in-room hot tubs, cable TV. Pool, wading pool. Exercise equipment. Business services. | 7766 E. Lamar Alexander Pkwy. | 865/448–2211 or 800/213–9462 | www.thesmokies.com/highland-manor/index.html | 58 rooms | $50–$105 | AE, D, DC, MC, V.

Pioneer Cabins and Guest Farm. Guests enjoy lounging on the porches of these cabins set on 43 private acres, 1 mi west of town. Fishermen will enjoy the fishing pond while kids ooh and aah at the petting farm. Hiking trails, a pony ride, and a small animal petting farm are all on the property. A you-pick vegetable garden is available for guest use. Cabins are all different sizes, accomodating 2–14 people. All have hot tubs, fireplaces, and kitchens stocked with coffee, filters, and hot chocolate. Picnic area. Kitchenettes, cable TV, in-room VCRs. Pond. Hiking. Fishing. Laundry facilities. | 253 Boat Gunnel Rd. | 865/448–6100 or 800/621–9751 | fax 865/448–9652 | 7 cabins | $98–$147.50 | No credit cards.

Richmont Inn. This bed-and-breakfast—built in the style of the Appalachian cantilever barn—is filled with many 18th-century antiques and offers lovely views of Laurel Valley and Rich Mountain. Rooms vary in style—from folk art–inspired to Pioneer log furnishing, to 1940s country. The inn sits 3 mi to the west of town. Complimentary breakfast. No room phones, no smoking. No kids under 12. | 220 Winterberry La. | 865/448–6751 | www.richmontinn.com | 9 rooms, 3 suites | $115–$165, $165–$220 suites | No credit cards.

Talley-Ho Inn. Some rooms have fireplaces and mountain views at this lodging located 1 mi west of the west entrance to Great Smoky Mountains National Park. Private balconies and terraces. Restaurant. Some refrigerators, some in-room hot tubs, cable TV. Pool, wading pool. Tennis. Business services. | 8314 Rte. 73 | 865/448–2465 or 800/448–2465 | fax 865/448–3913 | www.talleyhoinn.com | 46 rooms | $42–$85 | AE, D, DC, MC, V.

TUSCULUM

(Nearby towns also listed: Elizabethon, Greeneville, Johnson City, Jonesborough)

This little town, founded in 1959 along the Nolichucky River, is well worth a stop. Andrew Johnson was a trustee of Tusculum College, where his official presidential library is now located. The town is also near the birthplace of frontiersman Davy Crockett.

Information: Greeneville/Green County Tourism Council | 115 Academy St., Greeneville 37743 | 423/638–4111.

Attractions
Andrew Johnson Library. The 17th president's papers and manuscripts, as well as a good collection of Civil War–era newspapers are housed here in an 1841 building on the campus of Tusculum College. | 60 Shiloh Rd. | 423/636–7348 | fax 423/638–7166 | www.tusculum.edu | Free | Weekdays 9–5.

Davy Crockett Birthplace State Park. (*See* Lawrenceburg.) The birthplace of the legendary frontiersman (and congressman), 10 mi east of Tusculum, has been preserved by the Tennessee Department of Environment and Conservation. The park consists of 105 partially wooded acres of land along the Nolichuckey River, with a museum, and a replica of the log cabin in which Crockett was born. There's camping, fishing, and picnicking. | 1245 Davy Crockett Park Rd.,Limestone | 423/257–2167 or 423/257–2168 | www.state.tn.us/environment/parks/davyshp/index.html | Free | Daily 8–dusk.

ON THE CALENDAR
OCT.: *Food Lion South Atlantic Conference Fall Sports Festival.* This celebration held on the last weekend of the month includes eight teams of the South Atlantic Conference in tournament play: men's and women's cross country, soccer, and golf, and women's volleyball. Greene Valley Developmental Center hosts the cross country tournament; River Trace Golf Course and Link Hills Country Club host the golf tournament. The other events are on the Tusculum College campus. | 423/638–4111.

UNION CITY

(Nearby towns also listed: Dyersburg, Paris, Tiptonville)

The Emerson E. Parks Covered Bridge, one of only three covered bridges in the state, is located near Union City, a West Tennessee town founded in 1824. Also here are the Obion County Museum, which features historic displays that change seasonally, and the Dixie Gun Works Old Car Museum.

Information: Obion County Chamber of Commerce | Box 70, Union City 38261 | 901/885–0211 | www.obioncounty.com/chamber.

Attractions
Davy Crockett Cabin. This is a reproduction of the last home Crockett lived in before setting off for Texas, where he died in the siege at the Alamo in 1836. The cabin was deconstructed in 1934 and wasn't put back together until the 1955 TV show about the frontiersman

raised public interest. It was completed in 1956; materials included some of the logs from the original cabin. The cabin, approximately 20 mi south of Union City in Rutherford, is now a museum with period furnishing; Crockett's mother is buried on the property. | 219 N. Trenton St., Rutherford | 901/665–6195 | $1 | Memorial Day–Labor Day, Mon.–Sat. 9–5, Sun. 1–5.

Dixie Gun Works Old Car Museum. The collection includes 36 antique cars, all in running condition, plus farm and steam engines, all displayed inside the museum, which is located on the southern edge of town. | Reelfoot Ave. | 901/885–0700 | Free | Mon.–Fri., 8–5, Sat., 8–12.

Emerson E. Parks Covered Bridge. One of only three covered bridges left in Tennessee, this bridge, built in 1910, is located on Main Street. You can walk but not drive across it. | Main St. | 901/297–3177 (City Hall) | Free | Daily.

Obion County Museum. The museum mounts new displays about the history of the area each season. There's a furnished log cabin on the grounds. | 1004 Edwards St. | 901/885–6774 | www.obioncounty.com/edu/museum.html | Free | Weekends 1–4.

ON THE CALENDAR

SEPT.: *Fall Festival.* Held annually on the second full weekend of the month, this festival includes a parade, chalk art, and the "Pride of Obion County" luncheon downtown. The fairgrounds, 1 mi north of downtown, have hot air balloon rides, a rodeo, barbecue cookoff, and a lip-synching contest. Fairgrounds admission is $5, hot air balloon rides are $1 per ride. | 901/885–0211.

Dining

PV's Hut. American/Casual. Folks come to PV's for its famous cheeseburger dressed with slaw, pickles, and onions. This family-run restaurant, only 1 block from downtown, also serves homemade spaghetti on Thursdays, plus homemade soups, chili, chocolate pecan and coconut pies, and banana pudding. | 209 E. Florida Ave. | 901/885–5737 | Reservations not accepted | Closed Sun. and Mon. | $5–$6 | No credit cards.

Lodging

Union City Hampton Inn. This business travelers' mainstay is in a commercial area near a shopping mall, just 5 mi north of town center. Some kitchenettes. Cable TV. Pool, exercise equipment. No pets. No smoking. | 2201 W. Reelfoot Ave. | 901/885–8850 | www.hamptoninn.com | 84 rooms | $64 | AE, D, DC, MC, V.

WALLAND

MAP 12, 13

(Nearby towns also listed: Gatlinburg, Great Smoky Mountains National Park, Knoxville, Maryville, Townsend)

This tiny, peaceful town, which dates back to 1902, offers access to the Smoky Mountains without the touristy glitz of Pigeon Forge or Gatlinburg. You can rent a cabin or stay in a bed-and-breakfast and simply enjoy the beauty of the mountains.

Information: Townsend Visitors Center | 7906 E. Lamar Alexander Pkwy., Townsend 37882 | 865/448–6134.

Attractions

Great Smoky Mountains National Park. (*See* Great Smoky Mountains National Park.) The park's Cades Cove entrance and visitor's center is 12 mi south of Townsend. | 7906 E. Lamar Alexander Pkwy. | 865/436–1200 | fax 865/436–1313 | www.nps.gov/grsm | Free | Daily.

YEAR-ROUND: *Blue Grass Night.* Every Friday night, you can hear professional and amateur musicians play blue grass at the Rocky Branch Community Center, on Rocky Branch Road off Route 321. | 865/448–6134.

Dining

The Mill House Restaurant. Continental. This restaurant is just off U.S. 321, across from the site of a pre–Civil War grist mill. It is always a welcome destination after a Sunday afternoon drive in Great Smoky Mountains National Park. There are white tablecloths but the look is casual country. A sprawling porch allows you to have an after-dinner drink while looking out at the mountains. Chef/owner Richard Estes makes dishes such as pork masala, rainbow trout stuffed with crabmeat dressing, and his signature dessert, "Little River Mud Pie." | 4537 Old Walland Hwy. | 865/982–5726 | $15–$26 | AE, D, DC, V, MC.

Lodging

Inn at Blackberry Farm. This beautiful property sits on 1,100 acres at the foothills of the Smoky Mountains, 4 mi southwest of Walland. Eight miles of hiking trails, two ponds for fly fishing, and a covered boathouse are on-site. Bikes and golf carts are available for touring the property. There are a range of buildings— a main building, a guest house, 8 cottages, a 12-bedroom gatehouse, and a 3-bedroom home. Rooms are individually decorated but the main building is English Country style, with antiques and hardwood floors. Cottages all have porches, hot tubs and fireplaces. Some rooms offer mountain views, others face the meadows or woods. Dining room, picnic area, complimentary breakfast. Cable TV in common area, no room phones. Pool, ponds. Tennis courts. Hiking, boating. Fishing. Bicycles. Video Games. No kids under 10. Business services. | 1471 W. Millers Cove Rd. | 865/984–8166 or 800/862–7610 | fax 865/983–5708 | www.blackberryfarm.com | 44 rooms | $445–$695 rooms, $845–$895 cottages, $945 gatehouse, $1,595–$1,895 3–bedroom house | AE, MC, V.

Twin Valley Bed and Breakfast Horse Ranch. By day you can catch bass and catfish in the nearby ½ acre pond, and the owners will clean them for you to grill at the outdoor pavilion. Horses are available for riding lessons. Evening cookouts serve ribeye steak, barbecue chicken, hot dogs, and hamburgers. In addition to two rooms in the main house, this horse ranch has five cabins that sleep up to 17 people. Two back country shelters are available for camping. The property is off Route 321, 3 mi from mile marker 20. Complimentary breakfast. Some kitchenettes, some in-room hot tubs, some in-room VCRs, no TV in some rooms, no room phones, TV in common area. Exercise equipment. Dock. No pets. No smoking. | 2848 Old Chilhowee Rd. | 800/872–2235 | www.bbonline.com/tn/twinvalley | 2 rooms, 5 cabins | $95 (for rooms or cabins) | MC, V.

WARTBURG

MAP 12, G2

(Nearby towns also listed: Cookeville, Crossville, Jamestown)

The town of Wartburg was founded in 1968 on the edge of the Cumberland Mountains. Today it offers access to Frozen Head State Park, popular with hikers, and Obed National Wild and Scenic River, a favorite of white-water enthusiasts and rock climbers.

Information: **County Executive Office** | Box 387, Wartburg 37887 | 423/346–6288.

Attractions

Frozen Head State Park and Natural Area. (*See* Oak Ridge.) Wartburg offers access to this 12,000-acre park, which contains 50 mi of hiking trails, rivers for trout fishing, camping, and picnic sites. It sits 2 mi east of town. | 964 Flat Fork Rd. | 423/346–3318 | www.state.tn.us/environment/parks/frzhead/index.html | Free | 8–dusk.

Obed National Wild and Scenic River. You can enjoy hiking trails, and view the river from several bridges 2 mi north of Wartburg. White-water rafting and rock climbing are also popular here, and there is a campground on-site. | 208 Maiden St. | 423/346–6295 | fax 423/346–3362 | www.nps.gov/rivers/obed.html | Free | Daily.

ON THE CALENDAR
APR.: *Annual Wildflower Pilgrimage.* During the second and third weekends of the month, botanists give guided hikes of the Cumberland Mountains. All tours meet at the Townsend Visitor's Center, 2 mi east of downtown Wartburg. Saturdays at 10 and 2, Sundays at 2. | 423/346–3318.

Dining
Angie's. American/Casual. In a commercial area off Route 27, this buffet and sit-down restaurant runs specials every night, such as steak and chicken dinners. | 721 Main St. | 423/346–2504 | $5–$7 | No credit cards.

Lodging
Yesterday's Inn Bed and Breakfast. This three-story 1930s country farmhouse has two porches with sitting areas. Back Home, the restaurant, is open to the public for lunch and dinner. On 4 acres looking out on the Frozen Head Mountains, the B&B is just 1 mi south of Wartburg on U.S. 27. Restaurant. Complimentary breakfast. Cable TV, no room phones. No pets. No smoking. | 3579 Morgan County Hwy. | 423/346–5188 | 3 rooms | $50 | No credit cards.

WILDERSVILLE

MAP 12, D3

(Nearby towns also listed: Hurricane Mills, Jackson)

In the central part of the state near the Tennessee River, Wildersville is a small town near Natchez Trace State Resort Park. The park is on the Western Trace, an alternative route that was sometimes taken by 19th-century travelers. The park sits amid the Natchez Trace State Forest, which offers a variety of wilderness and recreational experiences. Wildersville is also known as the site of the Battle of Parker's Cross Roads, fought between Gen. Nathan Bedford Forrest's Confederate troops and Union soldiers led by Col. Cyrus L. Dunham and Col. John W. Fuller on fought December 31, 1862.

Information: **Henderson County Chamber of Commerce** | Box 737, Lexington TN 38351 | 901/968–2126.

Attractions
Natchez Trace State Resort Park. This park consists of more than 14,000 acres within the 48,000-acre Natchez Trace State Forest. It has four lakes, but Pin Oak and Cub Creek are the best-developed areas. Picnic facilities, a camp store and gas station, an archery range, tennis courts, cabins, an 18-room inn and a restaurant are among the numerous amenities. The main entrance is 8 mi east of Wilderville | 567 Pin Oak Ln. | 901/968–8176 | www.state.tn.us/environment/parks | Free | Daily dawn–dusk.

ON THE CALENDAR
JUNE: *Battle of Parker's Cross Roads Reenactment and Living History.* Held the second weekend in June on even-numbered years, Civil War history buffs reenact the famous 1862 battle on the original site—the Parker's Cross Roads Battlefield. It's at the intersection of Route 22N and I-40, 2 mi northwest of town. | 901/968–2126.

Dining

Cotton Patch Restaurant. Southern. Surrounded by authentic and reproduction Civil War memorabilia, you can order fresh farm-raised catfish, country hams, barbecued pork, and homemade onion rings. Top everything off with a slice of chocolate chess pie. Breakfasts include homemade biscuits, eggs, pancakes, and grits. The restaurant is on the site of the Battle of Parker's Cross Road. | 20630 Rte. 22N | 901/968–5533 | Breakfast also available. | $5–$12 | AE, MC, V.

Lodging

Best Western Crossroads Inn. This standard chain hotel in Wildersville's small town center, offers easy access to the state park. Fishing spots are found all around, in the Natchez Trace Forest, along the Big Sandy River, and in Beech Lake. Complimentary Continental breakfast. Cable TV. Pool. | 21045 Rte. 22N | 901/968–2532 | fax 901/968–2082 | www.bestwestern.com | 40 rooms | $42–$67 | AE, D, DC, MC, V.

Pin Oak Lodge. This lovely modern, state-owned complex, done in blonde wood, is about halfway between Nashville and Memphis, and is composed of numerous buildings scattered along Pin Oak Lake. Natchez State Park facilities are available to guests. Restaurant, picnic areas. Kitchenettes (in cottages), cable TV (in motel rooms). Pool, wading pool. Tennis. Dock. Playground. | 567 Pin Oak Lodge Ln., | 901/968–8176 | fax 901/968–6515 | 47 rooms, 18 cabins, 10 villas | $62–$67, $55–$65 cabins, $115–$125 villas | AE, D, MC, V.

Index

Notes

Notes

Notes

Notes

Notes

Notes

Notes

TALK TO US

Fill out this quick survey and receive a free *Fodor's How to Pack* (while supplies last)

---

1 Which Road Guide did you purchase?
(Check all that apply.)
- ❏ AL/AR/LA/MS/TN
- ❏ AZ/CO/NM
- ❏ CA
- ❏ CT/MA/RI
- ❏ DE/DC/MD/PA/VA
- ❏ FL
- ❏ GA/NC/SC
- ❏ ID/MT/NV/UT/WY
- ❏ IL/IA/MO/WI
- ❏ IN/KY/MI/OH/WV
- ❏ KS/OK/TX
- ❏ ME/NH/VT
- ❏ MN/NE/ND/SD
- ❏ NJ/NY
- ❏ OR/WA

2 How did you learn about the Road Guides?
- ❏ TV ad
- ❏ Radio ad
- ❏ Newspaper or magazine ad
- ❏ Newspaper or magazine article
- ❏ TV or radio feature
- ❏ Bookstore display/clerk recommendation
- ❏ Recommended by family/friend
- ❏ Other:_____

3 Did you use other guides for your trip?
- ❏ AAA
- ❏ Compass American Guide
- ❏ Fodor's
- ❏ Frommer's
- ❏ Insiders' Guide
- ❏ Mobil
- ❏ Moon Handbook
- ❏ Other:_____

4 Did you use any of the following for planning?
❏ Tourism offices ❏ Internet ❏ Travel agent

5 Did you buy a Road Guide for (check one):
- ❏ Leisure trip
- ❏ Business trip
- ❏ Mix of business and leisure

6 Where did you buy your Road Guide?
- ❏ Bookstore
- ❏ Other store
- ❏ On-line
- ❏ Borrowed from a friend
- ❏ Borrowed from a library
- ❏ Other:_____

7 Why did you buy a Road Guide? (Check all that apply.)
- ❏ Number of cities/towns listed
- ❏ Comprehensive coverage
- ❏ Number of lodgings ❏ Driving tours
- ❏ Number of restaurants ❏ Maps
- ❏ Number of attractions ❏ Fodor's brand name
- ❏ Other:_____

8 Did you use this guide primarily:
- ❏ For pretrip planning ❏ While traveling
- ❏ For planning and while traveling

9 What was the duration of your trip?
- ❏ 2-3 days ❏ 11 or more days
- ❏ 4-6 days ❏ Taking more than 1 trip
- ❏ 7-10 days

10 Did you use the guide to select
❏ Hotels ❏ Restaurants

11 Did you stay primarily in a
- ❏ Hotel ❏ Hostel
- ❏ Motel ❏ Campground
- ❏ Resort ❏ Dude ranch
- ❏ Bed-and-breakfast ❏ With family or friends
- ❏ RV/camper ❏ Other:_____

12 What sights and activities did you most enjoy?
- ❏ Historical sights ❏ Shopping
- ❏ Sports ❏ Theaters
- ❏ National parks ❏ Museums
- ❏ State parks ❏ Major cities
- ❏ Attractions off the beaten path

13 How much did you spend per adult for this trip?
- ❏ Less than $500 ❏ $751-$1,000
- ❏ $501-$750 ❏ More than $1,000

14 How many traveled in your party?
___ Adults ___ Children ___ Pets

15 Did you
- ❏ Fly to destination ❏ Rent a van or RV
- ❏ Drive your own vehicle ❏ Take a train
- ❏ Rent a car ❏ Take a bus

16 How many miles did you travel round-trip?
- ❏ Less than 100 ❏ 501-750
- ❏ 101-300 ❏ 751-1,000
- ❏ 301-500 ❏ More than 1,000

17 What items did you take on your vacation?
- ❏ Traveler's checks ❏ Digital camera
- ❏ Credit card ❏ Cell phone
- ❏ Gasoline card ❏ Computer
- ❏ Phone card ❏ PDA
- ❏ Camera ❏ Other

18 Would you use Fodor's Road Guides again?
❏ Yes ❏ No

19 How would you like to see Road Guides changed?

❏ More ❏ Less Dining
❏ More ❏ Less Lodging
❏ More ❏ Less Sports
❏ More ❏ Less Activities
❏ More ❏ Less Attractions
❏ More ❏ Less Shopping
❏ More ❏ Less Driving tours
❏ More ❏ Less Maps
❏ More ❏ Less Historical information
❏ Other:_____

20 Tell us about yourself.

❏ Male ❏ Female

Age:
❏ 18-24 ❏ 35-44 ❏ 55-64
❏ 25-34 ❏ 45-54 ❏ Over 65

Income:
❏ Less than $25,000 ❏ $50,001-$75,000
❏ $25,001-$50,000 ❏ More than $75,000

Name:_____ E-mail: _____

Address:_____ City: _____ State: _____ Zip: _____

Fodor's Travel Publications
Attn: Road Guide Survey
280 Park Avenue
New York, NY 10017

Atlas

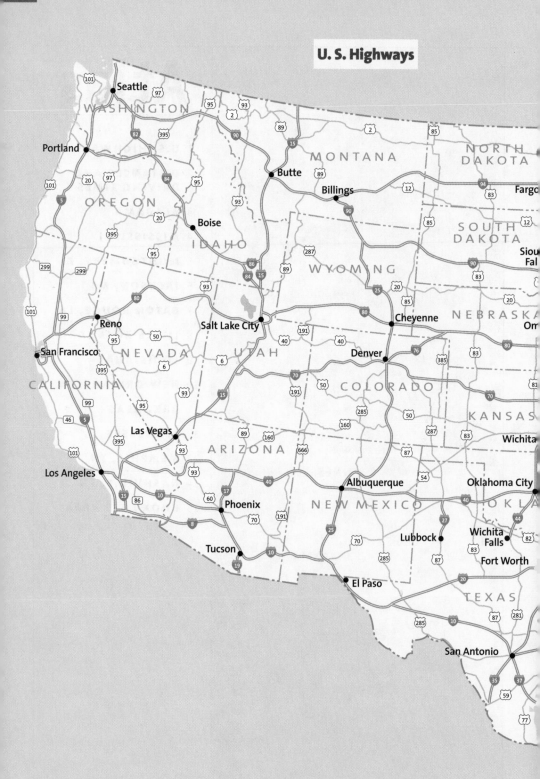

U. S. Highways

Distances and Driving Times

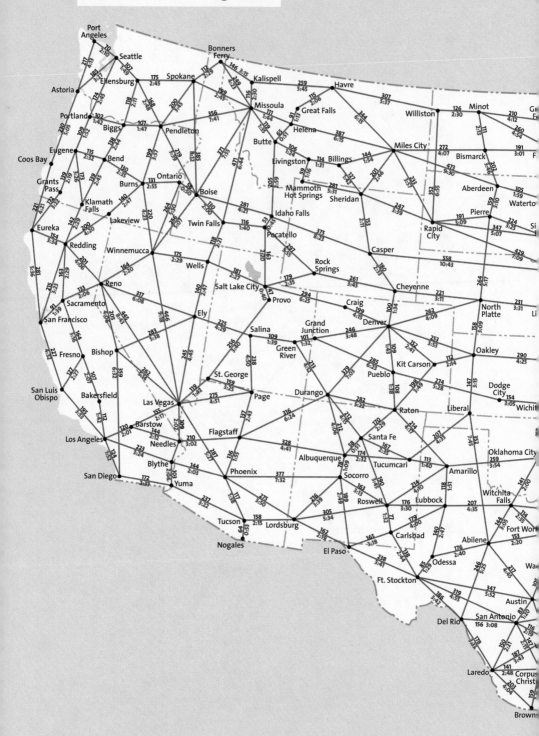

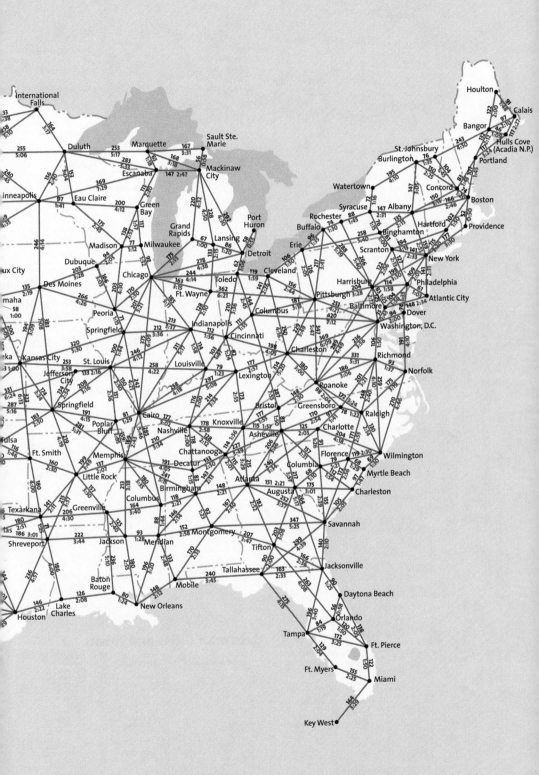

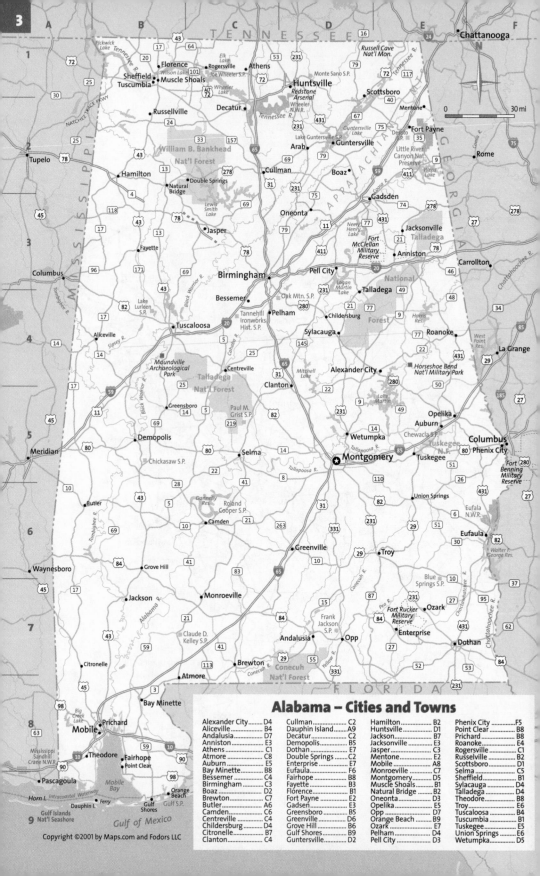

Alabama – Cities and Towns

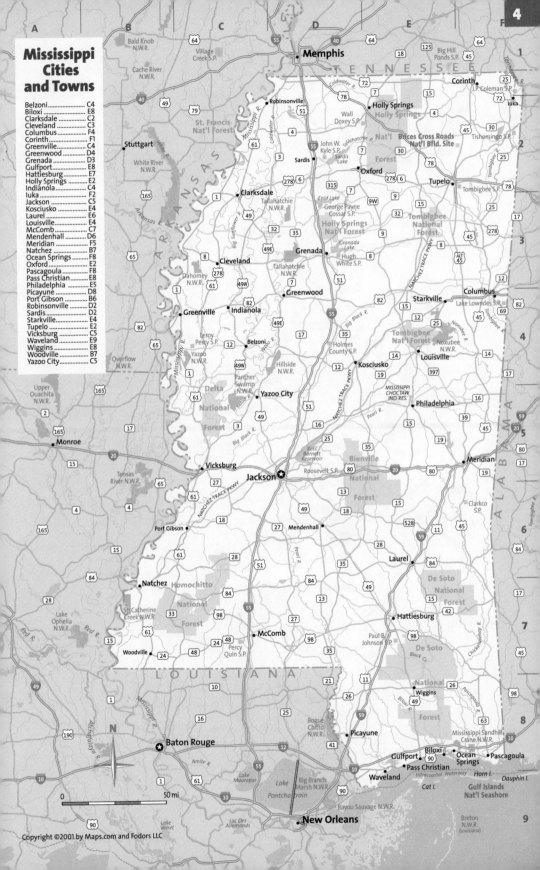

Mississippi Cities and Towns

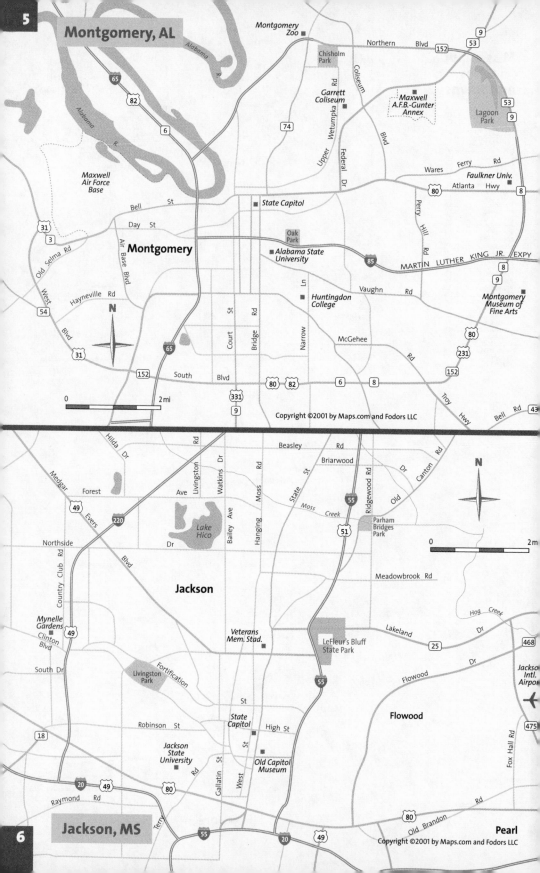

Montgomery, AL

5

Montgomery
Zoo

Chisholm
Park

Northern Blvd

Garrett
Coliseum

Coliseum Blvd

Maxwell
A.F.B.-Gunter
Annex

Lagoon
Park

Upper Wetumpka Rd

Federal Dr

Wares Ferry Rd

Faulkner Univ.

Atlanta Hwy

Maxwell
Air Force
Base

Bell St

Day St

Air Base Blvd

State Capitol

Montgomery

Oak
Park

Alabama State
University

Perry Hill Rd

MARTIN LUTHER KING JR. EXPY

Old Selma Rd

Hayneville Rd

West Blvd

Huntingdon
College

Ln

Vaughn Rd

Montgomery
Museum of
Fine Arts

Court St

Bridge Rd

Narrow

McGehee Rd

N

South Blvd

Troy Hwy

Bell Rd

0   2 mi

Copyright ©2001 by Maps.com and Fodors LLC

Jackson, MS

6

Hilda Dr

Livingston Rd

Watkins Dr

Beasley Rd

State St

Briarwood Dr

Canton Rd

Medgar Evers Blvd

Forest

Moss Rd

Hanging Moss Creek

Ridgewood Rd

Old Canton Rd

N

Northside Dr

Lake
Hico

Bailey Ave

Livingston
Ave

Parham
Bridges
Park

Jackson

Country Club Rd

Meadowbrook Rd

Hog Creek Dr

Mynelle
Gardens

Clinton
Blvd

Veterans
Mem. Stad.

LeFleur's Bluff
State Park

Lakeland Dr

South Dr

Livingston
Park

Fortification St

Flowood Dr

Jackson
Intl.
Airport

Flowood

Robinson St

State
Capitol

High St

Jackson
State
University

Gallatin St

West St

Old Capitol
Museum

Fox Hall Rd

Raymond Rd

Terry Rd

Old Brandon Rd

Pearl

Copyright ©2001 by Maps.com and Fodors LLC

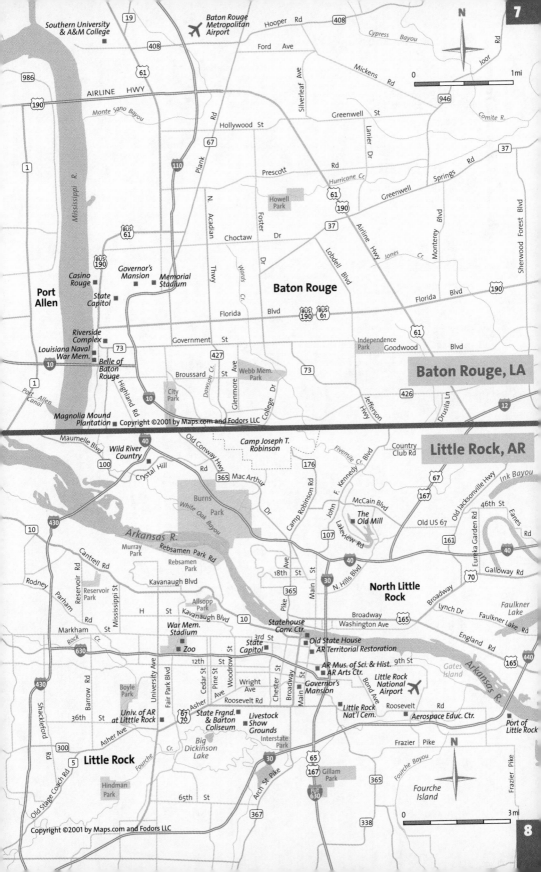

N

Southern University & A&M College

19

Baton Rouge Metropolitan Airport

Hooper Rd

408

Cypress Bayou

Joor Rd

Ford Ave

408

61

0   1mi

946

AIRLINE HWY

190

Monte Sano Bayou

1

Mickens Rd

Silverleaf Ave

Greenwell St

Comite R.

986

61

Hollywood St

Rd

110

Prescott Rd

Lanier Dr

37

67

Howell Park

Hurricane Cr.

Greenwell Springs Rd

Plank Rd

61

Monterey Blvd

Sherwood Forest Blvd

N. Acadian Thwy

Foster Dr

190

37

Airline Hwy

Jones Cr.

BUS 61

Choctaw Dr

Wards Cr.

Lobdell Blvd

BUS 190

Casino Rouge

Governor's Mansion

Memorial Stadium

Baton Rouge

Florida Blvd

190

Port Allen

State Capitol

Florida Blvd

BUS 190 BUS 61

61

Riverside Complex

Mississippi R.

73

Government St

Independence Park

Goodwood Blvd

Louisiana Naval War Mem.

10

Belle of Baton Rouge

427

Glenmore Ave

Webb Mem. Park

73

Baton Rouge, LA

1

Port Allen Canal

Highland Rd

10

Broussard St

City Park

Dawson Cr.

College Dr

Jefferson Hwy

426

12

Magnolia Mound Plantation   Copyright ©2001 by Maps.com and Fodors LLC

Little Rock, AR

Maumelle Blvd

40

Old Conway Hwy

Camp Joseph T. Robinson

Fivemile Cr.

Country Club Rd

67

Wild River Country

100

Crystal Hill

Rd

365

Mac Arthur Dr

176

John F. Kennedy Blvd

167

Burns Park

Camp Robinson Rd

McCain Blvd

Old Jacksonville Hwy

46th St

Eanes Rd

White Oak Bayou

The Old Mill

Old US 67

10

430

Arkansas R.

Murray Park

Rebsamen Park Rd

107

Lakeview Rd

161

Eureka Garden Rd

40

Cantrell Rd

Rebsamen Park

40

Galloway Rd

Rodney

Reservoir Rd

Parham

Reservoir Park

Kavanaugh Blvd

18th St

Main St

30

N. Hills Blvd

North Little Rock

Broadway

70

165

Faulkner Lake

Mississippi St

H St

Allsopp Park

365

Pike Ave

Lynch Dr

Faulkner Lake Rd

Markham St

Kavanaugh Blvd

10

Broadway

England Rd

630

War Mem. Stadium

Statehouse Conv. Ctr.

Washington Ave

165

Barrow Rd

Rock Cr.

3rd St

Old State House

440

430

Zoo

State Capitol

AR Territorial Restoration

Gates Island

9th St

Arkansas R.

Univ. of AR at Littlle Rock

12th St

Cedar St

Pine St

Woodrow St

Chester St

Broadway

Main St

Bond Ave

AR Mus. of Sci. & Hist.

AR Arts Ctr.

Governor's Mansion

Little Rock National Airport

165

36th St

University Ave

Fair Park Blvd

Asher Ave

67 70

Wright Ave

Roosevelt Rd

Little Rock Nat'l Cem.

Roosevelt Rd

Aerospace Educ. Ctr.

Port of Little Rock

Shackleford Rd

Boyle Park

State Frgnd. & Barton Coliseum

Livestock Show Grounds

Frazier Pike

N

300

Asher Ave

Big Dickinson Lake

Interstate Park

Frazier Pike

5

Little Rock

Fourche Cr.

30

65

167

Gillam Park

365

Fourche Bayou

Fourche Island

Hindman Park

65th St

367

FUT 630

338

Copyright ©2001 by Maps.com and Fodors LLC

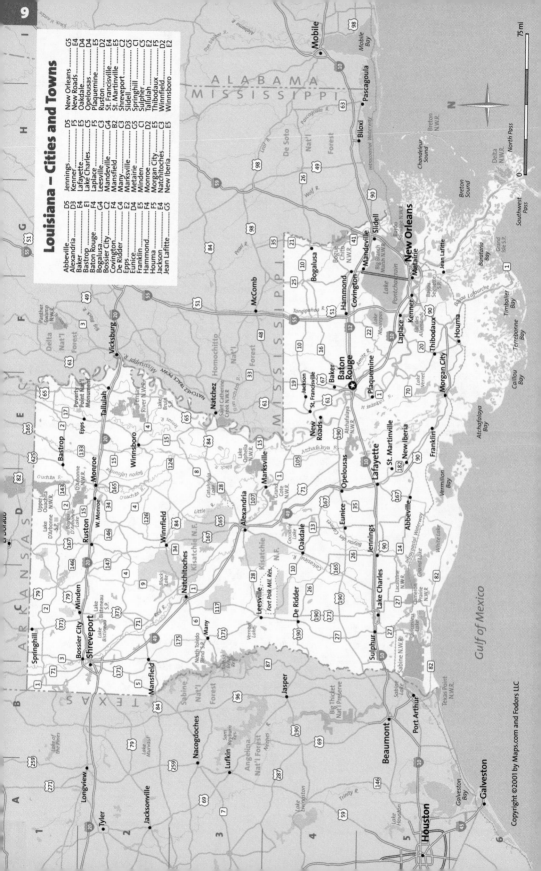

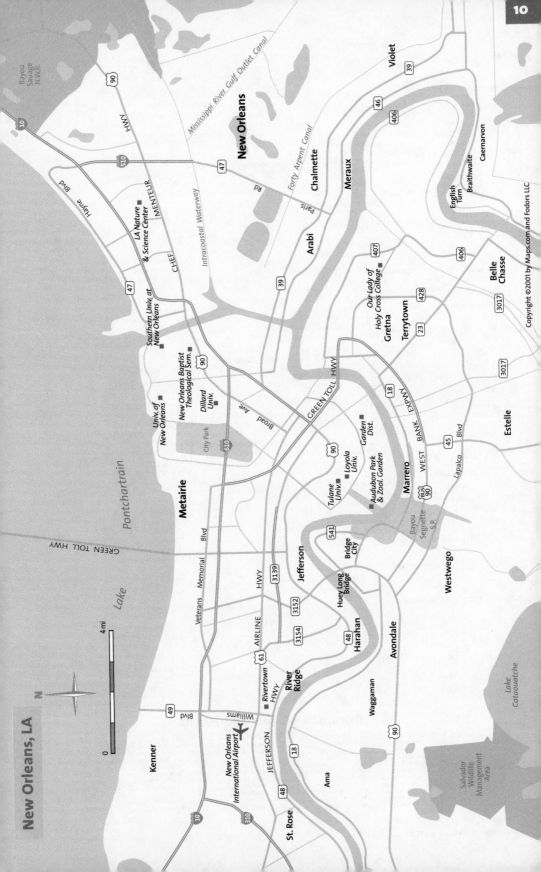

Arkansas – Cities and Towns

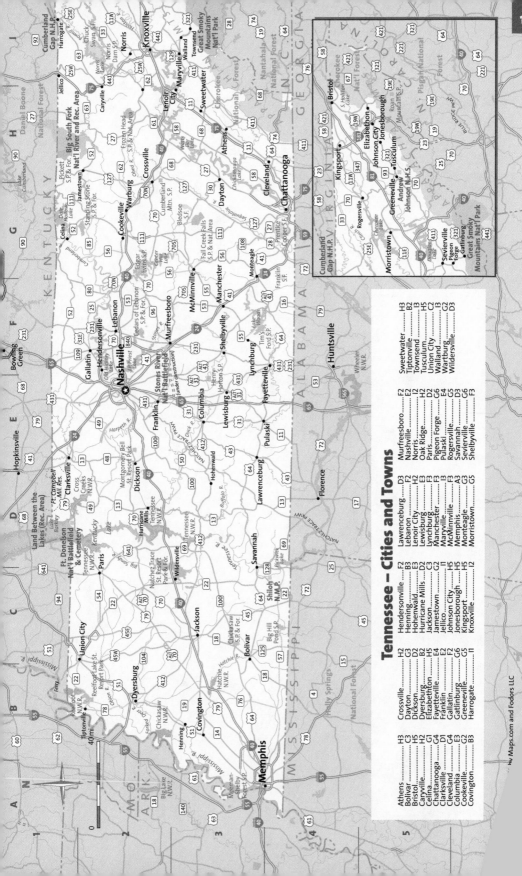

Tennessee – Cities and Towns

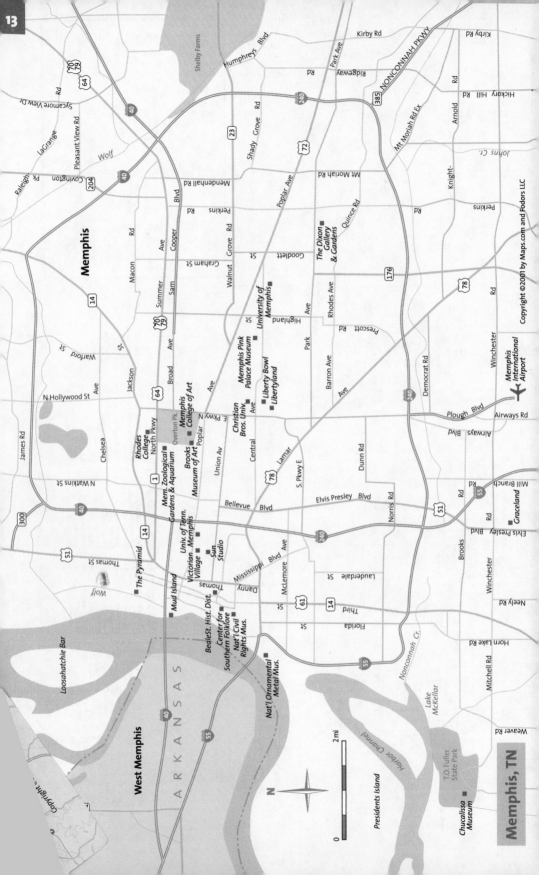

Memphis

West Memphis

ARKANSAS

Copyright ©2001 by Maps.com and Fodors LLC

Shelby Farms

Kirby Rd

Kirby Rd

Humphreys Blvd

Park Ave

Ridgeway

NONCONNAH PKWY

385

Mt Moriah Rd Ex

Hickory Hill Rd

Arnold

64
70
79

Sycamore View Dr

Pleasant View Rd

Covington

Raleigh Pk

LaGrange Rd

204

40

Wolf

40

Humphreys Rd

240

23

72

Shady Grove Rd

Mt Moriah Rd

Poplar Ave

Quince Rd

176

78

Perkins

Johns Cr

Knight-

Mendenhall Rd

Perkins Rd

Cooper Ave

Sam Cooper Blvd

Graham St

Walnut Grove Rd

Goodlett St

The Dixon Gallery & Gardens

Memphis

14

Macon Rd

Summer Ave

University of Memphis

Rhodes Ave

Highland

Prescott Rd

Winchester Rd

Warford St

Jackson Ave

Broad Ave

Memphis Pink Palace Museum

Liberty Bowl Libertyland

Park Ave

Barron Ave

Ave

Democrat Rd

Memphis International Airport

240

N Hollywood St

64

70
79

Christian Bros. Univ.

E Pkwy N

Poplar Ave

Ave

Memphis College of Art

Rhodes College

Overton Pk

North Pkwy

Dunn Rd

Plough Blvd

Airways Rd

Chelsea

N Watkins St

1

Mem. Zoological Gardens & Aquarium

Brooks Museum of Art

Union Av

Central

Lamar

S. Pkwy E

78

Airways Blvd

James Rd

300

40

14

51

Thomas St

The Pyramid

Univ. of Tenn. Memphis

Victorian Village

Sun Studio

Bellevue Blvd

Mississippi Blvd

Elvis Presley Blvd

Norris Rd

240

51

Mill Branch Rd

55

Graceland

Elvis Presley Blvd

Brooks Rd

Wolf

Mud Island

Thomas St

Danny Thomas Blvd

McLemore St

Lauderdale St

Winchester Rd

Neely Rd

Loosahatchie Bar

Beale St. Hist. Dist.

Center for Southern Folklore

Nat'l Civil Rights Mus.

Florida St

Third St

61

14

Horn Lake Rd

Mitchell Rd

40

55

Nat'l Ornamental Metal Mus.

Noncennah Cr.

55

Lake McKellar

Weaver Rd

N

Harbor Channel

Presidents Island

2 mi

0

T.O. Fuller State Park

Chucalissa Museum

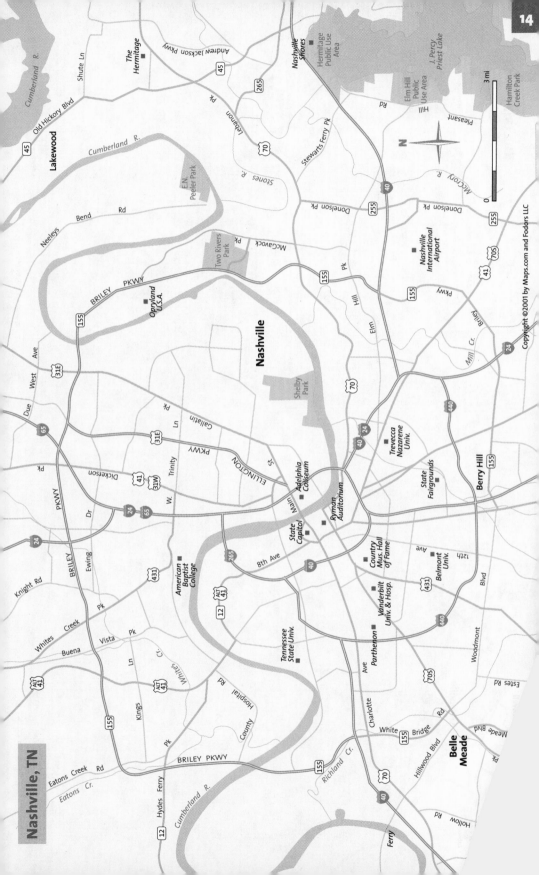

Nashville, TN

Lakewood

Nashville

Berry Hill

Belle Meade

Opryland U.S.A.

The Hermitage

Nashville Shores

Hermitage Public Use Area

Elm Hill Public Use Area

Hamilton Creek Park

J. Percy Priest Lake

Nashville International Airport

Two Rivers Park

E.N. Peeler Park

Shelby Park

State Capitol

Ryman Auditorium

Adelphia Coliseum

Country Mus. Hall of Fame

State Fairgrounds

Trevecca Nazarene Univ.

Belmont Univ.

Vanderbilt Univ. & Hosp.

Parthenon

Tennessee State Univ.

American Baptist College

Cumberland R.

Stones R.

Richland Cr.

McCrory R.

Mill Cr.

Whites Cr.

Eatons Cr.

BRILEY PKWY

ELLINGTON PKWY

Copyright ©2001 by Maps.com and Fodors LLC

3 mi

0

N

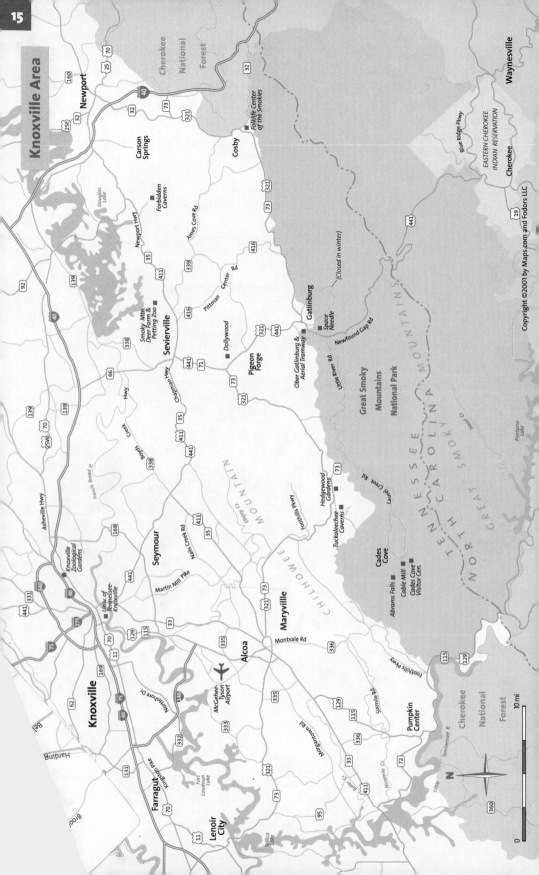

Knoxville Area

Cherokee National Forest

Newport

Waynesville

Carson Springs

Cosby

Folklife Center of the Smokies

Blue Ridge Pkwy

EASTERN CHEROKEE INDIAN RESERVATION

Cherokee

Douglas Lake

Forbidden Caverns

Jones Cove Rd

Newport Hwy

Smoky Mtn. Deer Farm & Petting Zoo

Sevierville

Pittman Center Rd

Dollywood

Gatlinburg

Space Needle

Ober Gatlinburg & Aerial Tramway

(Closed in winter)

Newfound Gap Rd

Little River Rd

Great Smoky Mountains National Park

GREAT SMOKY MOUNTAINS

Pigeon Forge

Chapman Hwy

French Broad R.

Boyds Creek Hwy

Hedgewood Gardens

Foothills Pkwy

Tuckaleechee Caverns

Laurel Creek Rd

Hazel Cr.

Fontana Lake

Seymour

Nails Creek Rd

Martin Mill Pike

Knoxville Zoological Gardens

Univ. of Tennessee-Knoxville

Maryville

Cades Cove

Cable Mill

Cades Cove Visitor Cen.

Abrams Falls

TENNESSEE

NORTH CAROLINA

Asheville Hwy

Alcoa

Montvale Rd

McGhee-Tyson Airport

Northshore Dr

Knoxville

Foothills Pkwy

Pumpkin Center

Cherokee National Forest

Sixmile Rd

Morgantown Rd

Little Tennessee R.

Nantahala Cr.

Abrams Cr.

Fort Loudoun Lake

Kingston Pike

Farragut

Harding

Bell

Lenoir City

Tellico Lake

N

10 mi

0

Copyright ©2001 by Maps.com and Fodors LLC